Psychological Science

7TH EDITION

7TH EDITION

Psychological Science

ELIZABETH A. PHELPS
Harvard University

ELLIOT T. BERKMAN
University of Oregon

MICHAEL S. GAZZANIGA
University of California, Santa Barbara

W. W. NORTON & COMPANY
Independent Publishers Since 1923

W. W. NORTON & COMPANY has been independent since its founding in 1923, when William Warder Norton and Mary D. Herter Norton first published lectures delivered at the People's Institute, the adult education division of New York City's Cooper Union. The Nortons soon expanded their program beyond the Institute, publishing books by celebrated academics from America and abroad. By mid-century, the two major pillars of Norton's publishing program—trade books and college texts—were firmly established. In the 1950s, the Norton family transferred control of the company to its employees, and today—with a staff of four hundred and a comparable number of trade, college, and professional titles published each year—W. W. Norton & Company stands as the largest and oldest publishing house owned wholly by its employees.

Printed in Canada

Editor: Sheri L. Snavely
Developmental Editor: Beth Ammerman
Project Editor: Linda Feldman
Assistant Editor: Chloe Weiss
Media Editor: Kaitlin Coats
Associate Media Editor: Christina Fuery
Media Project Editor: Danielle Belfiore
Assistant Media Editor: Emilia Pesantes
Ebook Production Manager: Emily Schwoyer
Marketing Manager: Casey Johnson
Production Managers: Eric Pier Hocking, Sean Mintus, and Richard Bretan
Design Director: Rubina Yeh
Designer: FaceOut Studio/Lissi Sigillo
Photo Editor: Ted Szczepanski
Director of College Permissions: Megan Schindel
Permissions Manager: Bethany Salminen
Permissions Specialist: Elizabeth Trammell
Composition: Graphic World
Manufacturing: Transcontinental
Managing Editor, College: Marian Johnson
Managing Editor, College Digital Media: Kim Yi

Library of Congress Cataloging-in-Publication Data

Names: Gazzaniga, Michael S., author.
Title: Psychological science / Michael S. Gazzaniga, University of California, Santa Barbara, Elizabeth Phelps, Harvard University, Elliot Berkman, University of Oregon.
Description: Seventh edition. | New York, NY : W. W. Norton & Company, [2022] | Includes bibliographical references and index.
Identifiers: LCCN 2021032552 | ISBN 9780393884586 (hardcover) | ISBN 9780393428186 (paperback) | ISBN 9780393884722 (epub)
Subjects: LCSH: Psychology.
Classification: LCC BF121 .G393 2022 | DDC 150—dc23
LC record available at https://lccn.loc.gov/2021032552

For Tyler, Alexandra, Connor, Samantha, and Evangeline—*LP*

For my wife, Natalie—*ET*

With gratitude, Lilly, Emmy, Garth, Dante, Rebecca, Leonardo, Fiala, and Carmen—*MG*

Brief Contents

Meet the Authors

ELIZABETH (LIZ) A. PHELPS is the Pershing Square professor of human neuroscience at Harvard University. Her career is characterized by distinguished scholarship and cutting-edge research in cognitive neuroscience, along with her passion to communicate the excitement of psychology to students by teaching introductory psychology nearly every year of her career. The primary inspiration behind her research is the observation that emotions color our lives, and even subtle, everyday variations in our emotional experience can alter our thoughts and actions. Liz received her PhD from Princeton University and served on the faculty of Yale University and New York University. Professor Phelps is the recipient of the 21st Century Scientist Award from the James S. McDonnell Foundation, the George A. Miller Prize in Cognitive Neuroscience, the Distinguished Scholar Award from the Social and Affective Neuroscience Society, and the William James Award from the Association for Psychological Science. She is a Fellow of the American Association for the Advancement of Science, the Society for Experimental Psychology, and the American Academy of Arts and Sciences. She has served on several distinguished boards and has served as the president of three societies, including Society for Neuroeconomics, the Association for Psychological Science, and the Social and Affective Neuroscience Society

ELLIOT T. BERKMAN is a professor of psychology at the University of Oregon. He teaches social psychology, introductory psychology, and graduate courses in statistics and neuroimaging. His research is about the motivational and cognitive factors that contribute to success and failure in real-world goals such as cigarette smoking cessation and dieting. His teaching, research, and mentorship have been recognized with the APS Janet Taylor Spence Transformative Early Career Award, the Excellence in Graduate Mentorship Award from the University of Oregon, the Social-Personality Health Network Early Career Award, the Joseph A. Gengerelli Distinguished Dissertation Award, the UCLA Social Psychology Dissertation Award, the Arthur J. Woodward Peer Mentoring Award, and the UCLA Distinguished Teaching Award. He received his PhD in 2010 from the University of California, Los Angeles. His blog, The Motivated Brain, is located at Psychology Today, and he tweets as @Psychologician.

MICHAEL S. GAZZANIGA is distinguished professor and director of the Sage Center for the Study of the Mind at the University of California, Santa Barbara. He received a PhD from the California Institute of Technology, where he worked with Roger Sperry and had primary responsibility for initiating human split-brain research. He has carried out extensive studies on both subhuman primate and human behavior and cognition. He is the founding editor of the *Journal of Cognitive Neuroscience* and also a founder of the Cognitive Neuroscience Society. For 20 years he directed the Summer Institute in Cognitive Neuroscience, and he serves as editor in chief of the major reference text *The Cognitive Neurosciences*. He is a member of the American Academy of Arts and Sciences, the National Academy of Medicine, and the National Academy of Sciences. He has written many notable books, including, most recently, *Psychological Science*, 6e; *Cognitive Neuroscience*, 5e; and *The Consciousness Instinct: Unraveling the Mystery of How the Brain Makes the Mind*.

Preface

Welcome to the seventh edition of *Psychological Science*! A lot has happened in the world in the past few years: social upheaval, contentious elections, and a global pandemic. The field of psychological science grew and changed because of these developments. At the same time, psychological scientists continued to make headways on methodological reforms stemming from the replication crisis. When we set out to revise this edition as new coauthors, our goal was to update *Psychological Science* to reflect the latest developments in the field while also strengthening the parts that we loved about the previous editions. This book retains the soul of *Psychological Science*—a science-forward, comprehensive text with a focus on the intersection of neuroscience and psychology—while bringing new style and content that will resonate with the introductory psychology students of the post-pandemic era.

The Soul of *Psychological Science*

Longtime users of this book will be familiar with the seventh edition's nuanced, accurate presentation of robust and innovative findings in psychological science, as well as its strong focus on critical thinking. A distinguishing characteristic of *Psychological Science* is the integration of neuroscience data and methods to inform psychological questions. Over the past few decades, neuroscience has become increasingly integrated with psychological research, and this book remains at the frontier of teaching students the ways that neuroscience is increasingly woven throughout psychology. As in most introductory textbooks, one chapter focuses on the brain and neuroscience methods, but we do not stop there. Throughout the book, we introduce level-appropriate neuroscience data along with psychological findings when considering a broad range of psychological questions. Our goal when discussing neuroscience is not just to show that a behavioral or mental function has a brain basis. Instead, we specifically identify how neuroscience findings have advanced our understanding of psychological questions. Many introductory students question why they need to learn about neurons and the brain. By emphasizing how brain data has enhanced psychological science throughout the text, we aim to help students understand the value of this approach.

As every introductory psychology instructor knows, the most important lessons from an introductory psychology course are not about the content, but rather the process of critical and scientific thinking. The content of psychological science is an outstanding vehicle to teach students this kind of thinking because people are "intuitive scientists" when it comes to psychology. We naturally hypothesize about the causes of our own and other people's thoughts and behaviors. The "You Be the Psychologist" feature in this textbook leverages this inherent curiosity to scaffold the scientific thinking process for our readers. In these sections, students are encouraged to hypothesize about the factors contributing to some psychological phenomenon, consider alternative explanations for it, weigh the strengths and limitations of methodological tools to study it, and ponder the conditions under which the phenomenon does and does not hold. Asking questions and critically thinking about interesting questions that are relevant to their lives is highly engaging for students, and practicing this kind of thinking is an evidence-based way to improve learning. Indeed, we designed several features around the best practices for learning outlined in APA's Introductory Psychology Initiative, including a focus on basic concepts and integrative themes, application of psychological principles to students' lives, and scientific thinking.

Understanding the thought process that drives psychological research can also help students appreciate the methodological issues around scientific replication. Like all sciences, psychology is "self-correcting" only when its knowledge base is updated by teachers and researchers to reflect the current state of the evidence. We are proud that the seventh edition upholds that essential scientific activity by showcasing the psychological principles that are supported by current, replicable evidence. The first two chapters feature thoughtful discussions of open science and replication. Mentions of open science and reproducibility follow throughout the text, building on the foundation laid in the first two chapters.

Updates for the Post-Pandemic World

We are passionate teachers who are dedicated to understanding the perspectives of our undergraduate students. We witnessed the many ways that the social and political turmoil of the past few years and the massive disruption caused by the global pandemic upended our students' lives and understanding of the world. And, though we've been in the field for decades, we keenly remember (and are reminded by our students) what it was like to be new to the science of psychology. Knowing that the challenges of learning are compounded by the changes in course delivery brought on by the pandemic, we made many revisions in this edition that consider the learning process from the student perspective.

CONNECTING PSYCHOLOGY TO STUDENTS' LIVES Psychology is perhaps the academic discipline that is most inherently relevant to people's everyday lives. Students become motivated to learn about the field of psychology when they understand the connection between the concepts they learn about in class and what they see around themselves from day to day. A side effect of psychology's embrace of the rigors of experimental research is that a great proportion of studies are conducted in laboratory settings. Nonetheless, the idea that psychology is *the science of us*, the science of human minds and behavior, is always at the forefront in this text. It is critical for students to learn that laboratory studies are not an end unto themselves, but rather a means to model and understand human behavior in the wild. The "Psychology Outside the Lab" feature highlights ways that features of human psychology and methods from psychological science play out in the world beyond academia. This feature makes an explicit case for the relevance of the material to students' lives and includes concrete and relatable examples, including the racial justice movement and the COVID-19 pandemic.

OUR FOCUS ON STUDENT LEARNING Our commitment to empathic and active pedagogy also emerges in the text's research-based emphasis on students' conceptual understanding. Along with the Learning Objectives and "Red Q" questions from previous editions, we've also created new "Learning Tips" in each chapter to help make tricky concepts accessible to all students. We drew from our decades of collective teaching experience to compile a list of topics that are often confusing to introductory psychology students. The Learning Tips target one or two areas in each chapter that are particularly challenging for students to understand. Each Learning Tip zooms in on one tricky concept, definition, or distinction and presents students with our advice for thinking about and understanding it. This feature is emblematic of the ways the seventh edition is particularly student focused. Revisiting a concept, at a different time and from a different perspective, will enhance students' understanding and retention of it.

OUR FOCUS ON DIVERSITY, EQUITY, AND INCLUSIVITY Promoting the values of diversity, equity, and inclusion was a primary goal of ours for the seventh edition. Too often, diversity in psychology texts is limited only to racial/ethnic diversity and, even then, is inadequately addressed under the label of "culture." This revision adopts a broad conceptualization of diversity and inclusivity to encompass not only race/ethnicity but also gender identity, sexuality, immigration status, socioeconomic class, body type, neurodiversity, disability, and age, among others. We do not mince words about the race- and gender-based social hierarchies that systematically advantage some groups of people and disadvantage others. Throughout the text, we address the many ways structural racism manifests across the field of psychology, including in the chapters on health, social psychology, and clinical psychology.

Psychological science observes the human world, but it is also a product of that world. The insidious effects of structural racism and other forms of systemic discrimination also harm and distort the field of psychological science itself. Despite some recent progress, the fact remains that scholars from many groups have been excluded from the field. Women; queer and nonbinary people; people with disabilities; non-Americans and immigrants; people living in poverty; and Black, Indigenous, and other people of color, among many others, are underrepresented as psychological scientists. Even when such scholars enter the field, their work is underappreciated and undercited. The lack of representation and acknowledgment of people in these groups harms the field by narrowing its scope and limiting its reach. The seventh edition does not sugarcoat these realities, but it does take steps to increase the visibility of the scholarship and personhood of psychological scientists from groups that have been excluded from the field. Recent research and classic discoveries by scientists who have historically been undervalued by the field are featured throughout the text.

Another benefit of the equity focus in the seventh edition is to increase the sense of belonging of all readers in the field. Students who do not see people who look and live like them featured as scientists, used as examples, shown in photos, and included in quiz questions receive the implicit messages that psychological science is not for them and that they do not belong in the field. We took particular care throughout the book, not only in the studies featured in the narrative but also in the examples, figures and illustrations, chapter-opening vignettes, and quiz questions, to be broadly inclusive of people of all genders, sexualities, abilities, nationalities, bodies, incomes, races, and ethnicities. The implicit message for readers is simple: Psychological science is for all people.

Major Changes in the Seventh Edition

We revised the style of the narrative to go along with our student-centered approach in the seventh edition. This edition maintains the focus on high-quality science that has always been a hallmark of *Psychological Science* while providing a clear and digestible experience for the reader. Our aim was to provide comprehensive and accurate coverage of the major ideas under each topic while keeping the text concise and easy to read. We wanted to convey the nuances of the most important findings in psychological science without the complex and sometimes confusing language that often accompanies scientific writing. Much of the narrative has been recast into a livelier, more relaxed style that allows the voices of the authors to come through. The length of the text has also been reduced compared with previous editions. These stylistic changes were accompanied by increased use of tables, figures, and other visual features to break up lengthy blocks of text. On the following page is a table with the major changes made to each chapter.

Wrapping It Up

We hope you enjoy the seventh edition of *Psychological Science* as much as we enjoyed writing it. We know many students taking introductory psychology will not major in psychology, and only a small fraction will go on to be researchers in psychology. As such, our goal as authors is to encourage students to *think like* psychological scientists without assuming they will all *become* psychological scientists. Learning about and developing a passion for critical thinking about psychological questions foster life skills that benefit students across the natural sciences, social sciences, and humanities. More than anything, we hope we will encourage introductory students to use these critical-thinking skills as they evaluate information and understand the behavior of those around them in their everyday lives.

Major Changes in the 7th Edition

CHAPTER 1

- Increased emphasis on critical thinking as a key learning outcome
- New section on diversity and inclusion in psychological science
- New section on the science of learning
- New sections on computational modeling, big data, and data science

CHAPTER 2

- New running example through the chapter on using e-cigarettes, a highly relevant topic
- Expanded coverage of replication and open science practices
- New coverage of A/B testing in marketing and on social media
- New coverage of the Bem ESP study as an example of questionable research practices

CHAPTER 3

- Streamlined discussion of neurotransmitters and the action of drugs
- Reorganized discussion of brain anatomy, highlighting regions most relevant to psychological science
- New discussion of the insular cortex
- Increased emphasis on the value of brain methods in informing psychological questions
- Additional online teaching tools for brain anatomy and neurons

CHAPTER 4

- Increased discussion of attention as a gateway to consciousness
- New critical-thinking exercise on meditation and brain changes
- Revised discussion on the impact of brain injury on consciousness
- Updated coverage of drugs and consciousness

CHAPTER 5

- Revised and streamlined discussion of principles of perception, including Gestalt principles
- Updated and expanded section on depth and motion perception
- New critical-thinking discussion on the special status of face processing in the brain

CHAPTER 6

- Expanded coverage of social learning, including its contribution to attitudes about race
- Increased emphasis on principles of learning common to classical and operant conditioning
- Streamlined and reorganized discussion of principles of classical conditioning
- Added coverage of instructed learning

CHAPTER 7

- Reorganized coverage of memory principles based on stages of memory processing
- Streamlined discussion of types of memory
- Updated discussion of memory replay and reconsolidation
- Integrated tips for enhancing memory into neuroscience of memory
- Eliminated discussion of molecular basis of memory

CHAPTER 8

- New and revised coverage of emotion and decision making
- New discussion of the value of big data in psychological research on decision making
- Expanded discussion of critical periods and communication in language learning
- Reduced coverage of group differences in intelligence

CHAPTER 9

- Updated section on the lifelong effects of early experiences
- New coverage on the effects of neonatal opioid exposure
- Updated coverage on identity development, including sexual and gender identity
- New critical-thinking section on the effects of screen time on development
- Refocused discussion of the factors that promote thriving in older adulthood

CHAPTER 10

- New critical-thinking component to the learning unit on lie detectors
- New section on cultural differences in emotional display rules
- New coverage on the relation between motivation and meaning in life
- New section on SMART goals
- New coverage on the needs for consistency and coherence

CHAPTER 11

- New, more extensive coverage of social and cultural effects on health
- Substantially expanded coverage of health disparities between groups
- Updated sections on healthy eating and smoking, incorporating the latest research
- New critical-thinking component in the section on everyday health behaviors

CHAPTER 12

- Removal of discussion of the Stanford Prison Study, elements of which had been fabricated
- Enhanced critical-thinking elements in the coverage of social norms marketing
- Updated coverage of the IAT to reflect the current scientific consensus
- New coverage of stereotype threat and the shooter bias to the section on prejudice

CHAPTER 13

- Added coverage of gene-environment correlations in shaping behavior and personality
- Removal of outdated Freudian theories of personality
- Added coverage of cultural variation in the structure of personality
- Substantially revised section on personality psychology in the workplace and I/O psychology context
- Added coverage of cognitive-affective system theory in advancing the person-situation debate in the personality literature

CHAPTER 14

- Reorganization of the chapter into sections about disorders of emotion, thought, and behavior
- New section on disorders linked to trauma
- Emphasis on the socially defined nature of psychological disorders
- Added coverage of addictions as disorders of behavior

CHAPTER 15

- Expanded and updated discussion of stigma and cultural differences in the treatment of psychopathology
- Added discussion of internet-based treatments
- New coverage on the treatment of addiction
- New critical-thinking exercise on the efficacy of antidepressants

Acknowledgments

As new authors of *Psychological Science,* we've benefited from the advice and responses of many reviewers, both well-known researchers and star instructors. Thanks go out to the many colleagues who reviewed specific revisions; read chapters for inclusivity, accuracy, and consistency; and shared their experience with our book. We would like to thank our students at New York University, Harvard University, and the University of Oregon over the years for informing our approach to this revision. We wrote the seventh edition with you in mind. We particularly would like to acknowledge Jagdeep Bala and Jordan Pennefather at the University of Oregon for their guidance and student-mindedness in helping us craft this revision. In addition to the excellent reviews supplied by Ines Segert (University of Missouri) and Becky Gazzaniga over six editions, we'd like to thank Adriana Uruena-Agnes at the University of South Florida for thoughtfully accuracy checking every word and figure in each chapter of the book and providing valuable insight and advice.

***PSYCHOLOGICAL SCIENCE, 7E,* TEXT AND MEDIA REVIEWERS** We thank the reviewers who have worked to further strengthen *Psychological Science.* Your excellent revisions, inspired ideas, and insightful guidance have shaped an inclusive book and resources that greatly benefit instructors and students alike. Your students are lucky to have you in their classroom.

Julie A. Alvarez, *Tulane University*
Clarissa J. Arms-Chavez, *Auburn University Montgomery*
Laurie Bayet, *American University*
Kristen T. Begosh, *University of Delaware*
Leslie Berntsen, *University of Southern California*
Sara K. Blaine, *Auburn University*
Mary M. Boggiano, *The University of Alabama at Birmingham*
Katherine A. Boss-Williams, *Augusta University*
Peter Chen, *Auburn University*
Alyson J. Chroust, *East Tennessee State University*
Marc Coutanche, *University of Pittsburgh*
Craig W. Cummings, *The University of Alabama*
Annie S. Ditta, *University of California, Riverside*
Renee Engeln, *Northwestern University*
Patrick J. Ewell, *Kenyon College*
Elena K. Festa, *Brown University*
Patricia Ann George, *University of Southern California*
Seth A Gitter, *Auburn University*
Oliver Hardt, *McGill University*
Alison Harris, *Claremont McKenna College*
Tasha R. Howe, *Humboldt State University*
Mary Hughes-Stone, *San Francisco State University*
Jesse Husk, *St. Francis Xavier University*
Tina Kao, *New York City College of Technology* and *City University of New York*
Natalie Kerr, *James Madison University*
Nate Kornell, *Williams College*
Shannon Layman, *University of Texas at Arlington*
Diane Leader, *Georgia Institute of Technology*
Christine Lomore, *St. Francis Xavier University*
Agnes Ly, *University of Delaware*
Kate MacDuffie, *University of Washington*
Amanda M. Marín-Chollom, *Central Connecticut State University*
Jillian Marshall, *Connecticut College*
Martha Mendez-Baldwin, *Manhattan College*
Jeong Min Lee, *Georgia State University*
Tamara Nelson, *Rutgers University*
Kristin Pauker, *University of Hawai'i at Manoa*
Evava Pietri, *Indiana University-Purdue University, Indianapolis*
Dylan Selterman, *University of Maryland*
Melissa Paquette Smith, *University of California, Los Angeles*
Samuel D. Spencer, *University of Hawaii at Manoa*
Christopher Stanzione, *Georgia Institute of Technology*
Clayton L. Stephenson, *University of Southern California*
Ekeoma Uzogara, *West Chester University of Pennsylvania*
Gretchen Van de Walle, *Rutgers University*
Andreas Wilke, *Clarkson University*
Manda Williamson, *The University of Nebraska-Lincoln*
Rachel Wu, *University of California, Riverside*
Dasa Zelthamova-Demircan, *University of Oregon*

PSYCHOLOGICAL SCIENCE INTERNATIONAL REVIEWERS

George Alder, *Simon Fraser University*
Ron Apland, *Vancouver Island University*
Sunaina Assanand, *University of British Columbia, Vancouver*
Alan Baddelay, *University of York*
Lisa Best, *University of New Brunswick*
David Bilkey, *University of Otago*
Colin Blakemore, *Oxford University*
Karen Brebner, *St. Francis Xavier University*
Joseph L. Brooks, *University of Kent*
Natasha Buist, *Victoria University of Wellington*
Tara Callaghan, *St. Francis Xavier University*
Jennifer Campbell, *University of British Columbia*
Dennis Cogan, *Touro College, Israel*
Martin Conway, *City University London*
Michael Corballis, *University of Auckland*
Ian Deary, *University of Edinburgh*
James Enns, *University of British Columbia*
Raymond Fancher, *York University*
Margaret Forgie, *University of Lethbridge*
Laura Gonnerman, *McGill University*
Peter Graf, *University of British Columbia*
Pascal Haazebroek, *Leiden University*
John Hallonquist, *Thompson Rivers University*
Linda Hatt, *University of British Columbia Okanagan*
Steven Heine, *University of British Columbia*
Mark Holder, *University of British Columbia Okanagan*
Jacob Jolij, *University of Groningen*
Steve Joordens, *University of Toronto–Scarborough*
Gert Kruger, *University of Johannesburg*
Celia Lie, *University of Otago*
Christine Lomore, *St. Francis Xavier University*
Monicque M. Lorist, *University of Groningen*
Neil Macrae, *University of Aberdeen*
Karl Maier, *Salisbury University*
Doug McCann, *York University*
Peter McCormick, *St. Francis Xavier University*
John McDowall, *Victoria University of Wellington*
Patricia McMullen, *Dalhousie University*
Martijn Meeter, *VU University Amsterdam*
Heather Schellink, *Dalhousie University*
Enid Schutte, *University of the Witwatersrand*
Allison Sekuler, *McMaster University*
Andra Smith, *University of Ottawa*
Ashley Smyth, *South African College of Applied Psychology*
Rhiannon Turner, *Queen's University Belfast*
Judith ter Vrugte, *University of Twente*
Maxine Gallander Wintre, *York University*
Heather Cleland Woods, *University of Glasgow*

PSYCHOLOGICAL SCIENCE, PREVIOUS EDITIONS, TEXT AND MEDIA REVIEWERS

Stephanie Afful, *Fontbonne University*
Rahan Ali, *Pennsylvania State University*
Gordon A. Allen, *Miami University of Ohio*
Mary J. Allen, *California State University, Bakersfield*
Julie A. Alvarez, *Tulane University*
Cheryl Armstrong, *Fitchburg State University*
Christopher Arra, *Northern Virginia Community College*
Lori Badura, *State University of New York, Buffalo*
Mahzarin Banaji, *Harvard University*
David H. Barlow, *Boston University*
Carolyn Barry, *Loyola University Maryland*
Scott Bates, *Utah State University*
Holly B. Beard, *Midlands Technical College*
Bernard C. Beins, *Ithaca College*
Matthew C. Bell, *Santa Clara University*
Joan Therese Bihun, *University of Colorado, Denver*
David Bilkey, *University of Otago*
Joe Bilotta, *Western Kentucky University*
Andrew Blair, *Palm Beach State College*
Kathleen H. Briggs, *University of Minnesota*
John P. Broida, *University of Southern Maine*
Joseph L. Brooks, *University of Kent*
Tom Brothen, *University of Minnesota*
Michele R. Brumley, *Idaho State University*
Dave Bucci, *Dartmouth College*
Joshua W. Buckholtz, *Harvard University*
Randy Buckner, *Harvard University*
Natasha Buist, *Victoria University of Wellington*
William Buskist, *Auburn University*
Elisabeth Leslie Cameron, *Carthage College*
Katherine Cameron, *Coppin State University*
Timothy Cannon, *University of Scranton*
Tom Capo, *University of Maryland*
Stephanie Cardoos, *University of California, Berkeley*
Crystal Carlson, *Saint Mary's University of Minnesota*
Charles Carver, *University of Miami*
Michelle Caya, *Trident Technical College*
Sarah P. Cerny, *Rutgers University, Camden*
Christopher F. Chabris, *Union College*
Clarissa Chavez, *Auburn University*
Jonathan Cheek, *Wellesley College*
Stephen Clark, *Keene State College*
Caroline Connolly, *University of Pennsylvania*
Brent F. Costleigh, *Brookdale Community College*
Graham Cousens, *Drew University*
Marc Coutanche, *University of Pittsburgh*
Craig Cummings, *University of Alabama*
Eric Currence, *The Ohio State University*
Dale Dagenbach, *Wake Forest University*
Haydn Davis, *Palomar College*
Suzanne Delaney, *University of Arizona*
Heidi L. Dempsey, *Jacksonville State University*
Joseph Dien, *Johns Hopkins University*
Michael Domjan, *University of Texas at Austin*

Wendy Domjan, *University of Texas at Austin*
Jack Dovidio, *Colgate University*
Dana S. Dunn, *Moravian College*
Howard Eichenbaum, *Boston University*
Naomi Eisenberger, *University of California, Los Angeles*
Sadie Leder Elder, *High Point University*
Clifford D. Evans, *Loyola University Maryland*
Patrick Ewell, *Kenyon College*
Valerie Farmer-Dougan, *Illinois State University*
Greg Feist, *San Jose State University*
Kimberly M. Fenn, *Michigan State University*
Fernanda Ferreira, *University of South Carolina*
Vic Ferreira, *University of California, San Diego*
Holly Filcheck, *Louisiana State University*
Sara Finley, *Pacific Lutheran University*
Joseph Fitzgerald, *Wayne State University*
Trisha Folds-Bennett, *College of Charleston*
Adam E. Fox, *St. Lawrence University*
Howard Friedman, *University of California, Riverside*
David C. Funder, *University of California, Riverside*
Christopher J. Gade, *University of California, Berkeley*
Christine Gancarz, *Southern Methodist University*
Wendi Gardner, *Northwestern University*
Preston E. Garraghty, *Indiana University*
Margaret Gatz, *University of Southern California*
Caroline Gee, *Saddleback College*
Peter Gerhardstein, *Binghamton University*
Katherine Gibbs, *University of California, Davis*
Bryan Gibson, *Central Michigan University*
Rick O. Gilmore, *Pennsylvania State University*
Jamie Goldenberg, *University of South Florida*
Jon Grahe, *Pacific Lutheran University*
Leonard Green, *Washington University in St. Louis*
Raymond Green, *Texas A&M–Commerce*
Sarah Grison, *Parkland College*
James Gross, *Stanford University*
Tom Guilmette, *Providence College*
Meara Habashi, *University of Iowa*
Jane S. Halonen, *University of West Florida*
Thomas Wayne Hancock, *University of Central Oklahoma*
Erin E. Hardin, *University of Tennessee, Knoxville*
Brad M. Hastings, *Mount Ida College*
Mikki Hebl, *Rice University*
Nicholas Heck, *Marquette University*
John Henderson, *University of South Carolina*
Norman Henderson, *Oberlin College*
Mark Henn, *University of New Hampshire*
Justin Hepler, *University of Illinois at Urbana-Champaign*
Terence Hines, *Pace University*
Sara Hodges, *University of Oregon*
Cynthia Hoffman, *Indiana University*
Don Hoffman, *University of California, Irvine*
James Hoffman, *University of Delaware*
Kurt Hoffman, *Virginia Polytechnic Institute and State University*
Tasha R. Howe, *Humboldt State University*
Howard C. Hughes, *Dartmouth College*
Mary Hughes-Stone, San Francisco State University
Jay Hull, *Dartmouth College*
Malgorzata Ilkowska, *Georgia Institute of Technology*
Jake Jacobs, *University of Arizona*
Alisha Janowsky, *University of Central Florida*
Jennifer Johnson, *Bloomsburg University of Pennsylvania*
Thomas Joiner, *Florida State University*
Linda Juang, *San Francisco State University*
William Kelley, *Dartmouth College*
Dacher Keltner, *University of California, Berkeley*
Lindsay A. Kennedy, *University of North Carolina at Chapel Hill*
Sheila M. Kennison, *Oklahoma State University–Stillwater*
Mike Kerchner, *Washington College*
Rondall Khoo, *Western Connecticut State University*
Stephen Kilianski, *Rutgers University*
Brian Kinghorn, *Brigham Young University, Hawaii*
Erica Kleinknecht O'Shea, *Pacific University*
Christopher Koch, *George Fox University*
Lisa Kolbuss, *Lane Community College*
William Knapp, *Eastern Oregon University*
Gabriel Kreiman, *Harvard University*
Caleb Lack, *University of Central Oklahoma*
Gerard A. Lamorte III, *Rutgers University*
Lori Lange, *University of North Florida*
Mark Laumakis, *San Diego State University*
Natalie Kerr Lawrence, *James Madison University*
Steven R. Lawyer, *Idaho State University*
Benjamin Le, *Haverford College*
Dianne Leader, *Georgia Institute of Technology*
Mark Leary, *Duke University*
Ting Lei, *Borough of Manhattan Community College*
Charles Leith, *Northern Michigan University*
Catherine Craver Lemley, *Elizabethtown College*
Emily Leskinen, *Carthage College*
Gary W. Lewandowski Jr., *Monmouth University*
Celia Lie, *University of Otago*
Stephanie Little, *Wittenberg University*
Christine Lofgren, *University of California, Irvine*
Christine Lomore, *St. Francis Xavier University*
Liang Lou, *Grand Valley State University*
Jeff Love, *Pennsylvania State University*
Monica Luciana, *University of Minnesota*
Agnes Ly, *University of Delaware*
Margaret F. Lynch, *San Francisco State University*
Kate MacDuffie, *Duke University*
Karl Maier, *Salisbury University*
Mike Mangan, *University of New Hampshire*
Gary Marcus, *New York University*
Leonard Mark, *Miami University (Ohio)*
Howard Markowitz, *Hawaii Pacific University*
Debra Mashek, *Harvey Mudd College*
Tim Maxwell, *Hendrix College*
Ashley Maynard, *University of Hawaii*
Dan McAdams, *Northwestern University*
David McDonald, *University of Missouri*
John McDowall, *Victoria University of Wellington*
Bill McKeachie, *University of Michigan*
Corrine L. McNamara, *Kennesaw State University*

Mary E. McNaughton-Cassill, *University of Texas at San Antonio*
Matthias Mehl, *University of Arizona*
Paul Merritt, *Clemson University*
Peter Metzner, *Vance-Granville Community College*
Dennis Miller, *University of Missouri*
Hal Miller, *Brigham Young University*
Judi Miller, *Oberlin College*
Michele M. Miller, *University of Illinois, Springfield*
Ronald Miller, *Saint Michael's College*
Vanessa Miller, *Texas Christian University*
Cindy Miller-Perrin, *Pepperdine University*
Douglas G. Mook, *University of Virginia*
Kevin E. Moore, *DePauw University*
Elizabeth Morgan, *Springfield College*
Beth Morling, *University of Delaware*
Heather Morris, *Trident Technical College*
Joe Morrisey, *State University of New York, Binghamton*
Todd Nelson, *California State University–Stanislaus*
Julie Norem, *Wellesley College*
Erica Kleinknecht O'Shea, *Pacific University*
Maria Minda Oriña, *St. Olaf College*
Dominic J. Parrott, *Georgia State University*
Lois C. Pasapane, *Palm Beach State College*
Kristin Pauker, *University of Hawaii*
David Payne, *Wallace Community College*
James Pennebaker, *University of Texas at Austin*
Zehra Peynircioglu, *American University*
Brady Phelps, *South Dakota State University*
Jackie Pope-Tarrance, *Western Kentucky University*
Steve Prentice-Dunn, *University of Alabama*
Gabriel Radvansky, *Notre Dame University*
Patty Randolph, *Western Kentucky University*
Catherine Reed, *Claremont McKenna College*
Lauretta Reeves, *University of Texas at Austin*
Ann Renken, *University of Southern California*
Heather Rice, *Washington University in St. Louis*
Jennifer Richeson, *Yale University*
Alan C. Roberts, *Indiana University*
Brent W. Roberts, *University of Illinois at Urbana-Champaign*
Caton Roberts, *University of Wisconsin–Madison*
William Rogers, *Grand Valley State University*
Alex Rothman, *University of Minnesota*
Wade C. Rowatt, *Baylor University*
Paul Rozin, *University of Pennsylvania*
Sharleen Sakai, *Michigan State University*
Samuel Sakhai, *University of California, Berkeley*
Juan Salinas, *University of Texas at Austin*
Laura Saslow, *University of California, San Francisco*
Richard Schiffman, *Rutgers University*
Lynne Schmelter-Davis, *Brookdale Community College*
David A. Schroeder, *University of Arkansas*
Shannon Scott, *Texas Woman's University*
Constantine Sedikedes, *University of Southampton*
Ines Segert, *University of Missouri*
Margaret Sereno, *University of Oregon*
Andrew Shatté, *University of Arizona*
J. Nicole Shelton, *Princeton University*
Arthur Shimamura, *University of California, Berkeley*
Rebecca Shiner, *Colgate University*
Jennifer Siciliani-Pride, *University of Missouri–St. Louis*
Nancy Simpson, *Trident Technical College*
Scott Sinnett, *University of Hawaii*
Reid Skeel, *Central Michigan University*
John J. Skowronski, *Northern Illinois University*
Rachel Smallman, *Texas A&M University*
Dennison Smith, *Oberlin College*
Kyle Smith, *Ohio Wesleyan University*
Mark Snyder, *University of Minnesota*
Sheldon Solomon, *Skidmore College*
Sue Spaulding, *University of North Carolina, Charlotte*
Jason Spiegelman, *Community College of Baltimore County*
Christopher Stanzione, *Georgia Institute of Technology*
Faye Steuer, *College of Charleston*
Courtney Stevens, *Willamette University*
Benjamin C. Storm, *University of California, Santa Cruz*
Dawn L. Strongin, *California State University–Stanislaus*
James R. Sullivan, *Florida State University*
Lorey Takahashi, *University of Hawaii*
George Taylor, *University of Missouri–St. Louis*
Lee Thompson, *Case Western Reserve University*
Dianne Tice, *Florida State University*
Rob Tigner, *Truman State College*
Boyd Timothy, *Brigham Young University, Hawaii*
Peter Tse, *Dartmouth College*
Lauren Usher, *University of Miami*
David Uttal, *Northwestern University*
Robin R. Vallacher, *Florida Atlantic University*
Kristy L. vanMarle, *University of Missouri*
Simine Vazire, *University of California, Davis*
Shaun Vecera, *University of Iowa*
Anré Venter, *University of Notre Dame*
Angela Vieth, *Duke University*
Athena Vouloumanos, *New York University*
Judith ter Vrugte, *University of Twente*
Angela Walker, *Quinnipiac University*
Benjamin Walker, *Georgetown University*
Elaine Walker, *Emory University*
Brian Wandell, *Stanford University*
Kenneth A. Weaver, *Emporia State University*
Kevin Weinfurt, *Duke University*
Rajkumari Wesley, *Brookdale Community College*
Fred Whitford, *Montana State University*
Doug Whitman, *Wayne State University*
Gordon Whitman, *Old Dominion University*
Karen Wilson, *St. Francis College*
Nicole L. Wilson, *University of California, Santa Cruz*
Clare Wiseman, *Yale University*
Al Witkofsky, *Salisbury University*
Heather Cleland Woods, *University of Glasgow*
Vanessa Woods, *University of California, Santa Barbara*
John W. Wright, *Washington State University*
Jill A. Yamashita, *California State University, Monterey Bay*
Dahlia Zaidel, *University of California, Los Angeles*
Dasa Zeithamova-Demircan, *University of Oregon*

THE NORTON EDITORIAL TEAM In the modern publishing world, where most books are produced by large multinational corporations that focus primarily on the bottom line, W. W. Norton stands out as a beacon to academics and authors, both for remaining committed to the best-quality publications and for providing outstanding team members to help ensure that quality. Norton's employees own the company, and therefore every individual who worked on this book has a vested interest in its success; that personal connection shows in the great enthusiasm the team members brought to their work.

The past five editions of *Psychological Science* would simply not exist without Sheri Snavely. Sheri has reinvented the book over and over again by inspiring authors to bring their own vision to the text. We are grateful to Sheri for inviting us into the Norton family for this edition and encouraging us at each step in the process to let our voices and perspectives shine through. We deeply valued Sheri's guidance and her attention to both the student and instructor experience of the text.

We are forever indebted to senior developmental editor Beth Ammerman for her seamless and collaborative editing. A great editor is most often invisible to the reader, so we wish to inform readers: When the prose in this revision sings, it is because of Beth.

We are grateful to media editor Kaitlin Coats and her team, assistant media editor Emilia Pesantes and associate media editor Christina Fuery, for creating and producing first-rate digital tools to support both students and instructors. They worked on the ebook and InQuizitive online assessment; a myriad of top-quality instructor resources, test questions, and video; and the exciting new 3D brain and neuron animations. We appreciate all their efforts to ensure these tools give instructors the highest-quality materials they need to teach the course and to give students every opportunity to learn challenging topics interactively and effectively.

Many others also provided crucial support. Assistant editor Chloe Weiss kept the project running smoothly and managed our rigorous editorial review program, allowing us to revise chapters based on high-quality extensive feedback from professors in the field. She also worked tirelessly to ensure that the book's content and illustration program is inclusive, reflecting today's psychologists and psychology students in all their variety. Project editor Linda Feldman patiently saw this project through from start to finish. We are grateful for her sharp eyes and attention to detail, making sure every change in the pages was made and finding ways to include all our material while still having clean and spacious pages. Photo editor Ted Szczepanski did a wonderful job of researching and editing all the photos in the book and finding excellent photos that reflect real people from a wide array of identities. Production managers Eric Pier Hocking, Sean Mintus, and Richard Bretan made sure all the trains ran on time so the book and resources were ready for instructors to consider for their courses. Art director Lissi Sigillo worked her magic in creating a design that was both beautiful and accessible to a variety of learners. Head of design at W. W. Norton, Debra Morton Hoyt, worked to give us a beautiful cover that mirrors the energy and fresh perspective of the new edition.

THE NORTON SALES AND MARKETING TEAM Thanks to the book's marketing manager, Casey Johnson, for analyzing the market and using her substantial sales experience as the basis for putting together a cutting-edge and informative marketing campaign. She understands what instructors and students need to be successful and is doing a marvelous job of making sure the book's message reaches travelers and professors. A big thank-you to psychology sales specialist Dorothy Laymon, our boots on the ground for rallying the troops, doing countless presentations, and understanding so intuitively the challenges that instructors and students face today. In fact, we are grateful to the whole psychological science sales team—travelers, managers, science specialists, media specialists, and institutional sales group. Indeed, the entire sales force, led by Erik Fahlgren and Dennis Fernandes, has supported this book and is distinguished by their knowledge of psychology and consultative partnerships with instructors.

Digital Tools for Instructors and Students

The *Psychological Science* teaching and learning resources give you all the tools you need to increase student retention, understanding, and engagement.

InQuizitive

Created by a cognitive psychologist, InQuizitive adaptive assessment is built on evidence-based principles of learning, including retrieval practice, learning by doing, and metacognitive monitoring. Personalized question sets target students' individual areas for improvement, and formative answer-specific feedback helps them understand core concepts. Game-like elements and a variety of interactive question types maximize engagement.

Norton Teaching Tools

Norton Teaching Tools are your first stop when looking for creative resources to design or refresh your course. The Norton Teaching Tools site is a searchable, sortable database of resources for engaging students in active and applied learning, in the classroom or online. Norton Teaching Tools for *Psychological Science* include Active Learning + Lecture PowerPoints, Activities and Demonstrations, Class Discussion Topics, Suggested Video Links, and much more.

Testmaker

New Norton Testmaker makes it easy to build customized, outcome-driven assessments from more than 3,800 questions in the *Psychological Science* test bank. Search and filter test bank questions by question types, difficulty levels, new APA Introductory Psychology Initiative Student Learning Outcomes, and more. You can customize questions to fit your course, or simply "grab and go" with our ready-to-use quizzes. Easily export your tests and quizzes to Microsoft Word or Common Cartridge files for your learning management system.

3D Brain and Neuron Animations

A **new** interactive 3D brain and **new** interactive neuron animations give students the opportunity to visualize and interact with difficult concepts in the Biology and Behavior chapter. The interactive 3D brain gives students a hands-on way to explore brain structure and function by rotating, zooming, and adding/removing structures. The interactive neuron animations help students comprehend challenging processes by moving beyond traditional video animations, pausing at key points to allow students to interact with them.

ZAPS 3.0

New ZAPS 3.0 Interactive Labs are brief, easy-to-use activities that invite students to actively participate in the process of psychological research and discovery. **New** in ZAPS Version 3.0: streamlined content, embedded videos, added formative assessment and feedback, enhanced data literacy content, a **brand-new** suite of instructor support tools, and four **new** lab activities on developmental, clinical, and social psychology.

HIP Guide

New *High-Impact Practices: A Teaching Guide for Psychology* (the HIP Guide) recommends practical methods for applying the latest psychological research on teaching and learning in order to design and teach introductory courses that respond to current challenges. The HIP Guide includes advice on teaching in online and hybrid environments, creating an inclusive learning environment, incorporating active learning into the course, and more.

Resources for your LMS

Easily add high-quality, integrated Norton digital resources to your online, hybrid, or lecture courses. All activities can be accessed right within your existing learning management system.

Videos

A robust library of videos brings psychology to life. Concept Videos are brief (1 to 2 minutes), friendly animated illustrations of the most important concepts in introductory psychology. Demonstration Videos show a real instructor and students participating in classroom demonstrations.

Contents

WORLD
MEMORY
CHAMPIONSHIP
DECEMBER 1st - 3rd, 2017
JAKARTA, INDONESIA

8 Thinking, Decisions, Intelligence, and Language 282

9 Human Development 328

HEY WILLIAMSBURG,
WEAR A MASK!

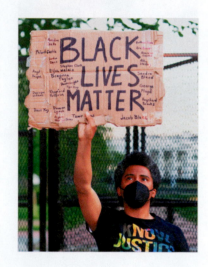

13 Personality 494

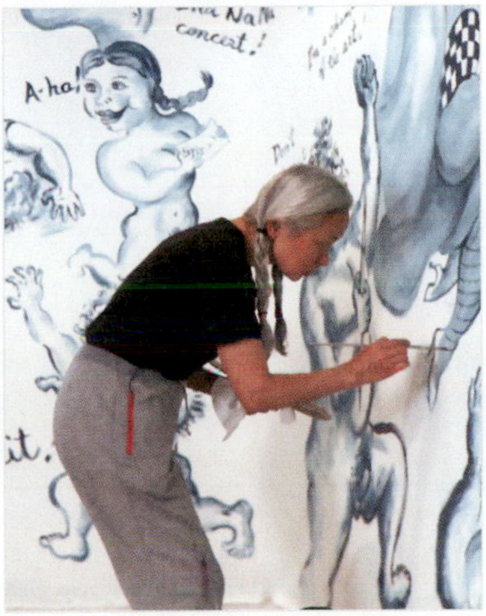

14 Psychological Disorders 538

7TH EDITION

Psychological Science

1

The Science of Psychology

Big Questions

- What Is Psychological Science? 4
- What Is the Scientific Scope of Psychology? 9
- What Are the Latest Developments in Psychology? 15

WHY IS PSYCHOLOGY ONE OF THE MOST POPULAR MAJORS at many colleges? The simple answer is that people want to understand the minds and actions of themselves and others. Knowing how humans think, feel, and behave can be incredibly useful. The science of psychology can help you understand your motives, your personality, even why you remember some things and forget others. In addition, psychology will prepare you for many professions, and much of the research you will read about in this book can be used to make people's lives better. It will benefit you whether you're studying environmental science (how do you encourage people to recycle?), anthropology (how does culture shape behavior?), biology (how do animals learn?), or philosophy (do people have free will?). Whatever your major, this class will help you succeed in your academic work and your broader life beyond it, now and in the future.

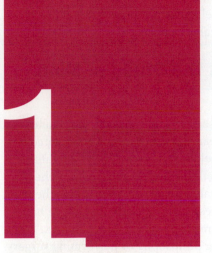

What Is Psychological Science?

Learning Objectives

- Define psychological science.
- Define critical thinking, and describe what it means to be a critical thinker.
- Identify major biases in thinking, and explain why these biases result in faulty thinking.

Psychology involves the study of thoughts, feelings, and behavior. The term *psychologist* is used broadly to describe someone whose career involves understanding people's minds or predicting their behavior. We humans are intuitive psychologists. We could not function very well in our world without natural ways to understand and predict others' behavior. For example, we quite rapidly get a sense of whether we can trust a stranger before we interact with them. But we cannot simply use our own common sense or gut feelings as a guide to know whether many of the claims related to psychology are fact or fiction. Will playing music to newborns make them more intelligent? Do birds of a feather flock together, or do opposites attract? Psychological science uses data to find answers.

1.1 Psychological Science Is the Study of Mind, Brain, and Behavior

psychological science The study, through research, of mind, brain, and behavior.

Psychological science is the study, through research, of mind, brain, and behavior. But what exactly does each of these terms mean, and how are they all related?

Mind refers to mental activity. The mind includes the memories, thoughts, feelings, and perceptual experiences (sights, smells, tastes, sounds, and touches) we have while interacting with the world. Mental activity results from biochemical processes within the *brain*. *Behavior* describes the totality of observable human (or animal) actions. These actions range from the subtle to the complex. Some occur exclusively in humans, such as debating philosophy or performing surgery. Others occur in all animals, such as eating and drinking.

For many years, psychologists focused on behavior rather than on mental states. They did so largely because they had few objective techniques for assessing the mind. The advent of technology to observe the working brain in action has enabled psychologists to study mental states and has led to a fuller understanding of human behavior. Although psychological science is most often associated with its important contributions to understanding and treating mental disorders, much of the field seeks to understand mental activity (both typical and atypical), the biological basis of that activity, how people change as they develop through life, how people differ from one another, how people vary in their responses to social situations, and how people acquire healthy and unhealthy behaviors.

Q How do the mind and the brain relate?

ANSWER: The mind (mental activity) is produced by biochemical processes in the brain.

1.2 Psychological Science Teaches Critical Thinking

One of this textbook's most important goals is to provide a basic, state-of-the-art education about the methods of psychological science. Even if your only exposure to psychology is through the introductory course and this textbook, you will become psychologically literate. That means you will learn not only how to critically evaluate psychological claims you hear about in social and traditional media but also how to use data to answer your own questions about people's minds and behavior. With a good understanding of the field's major

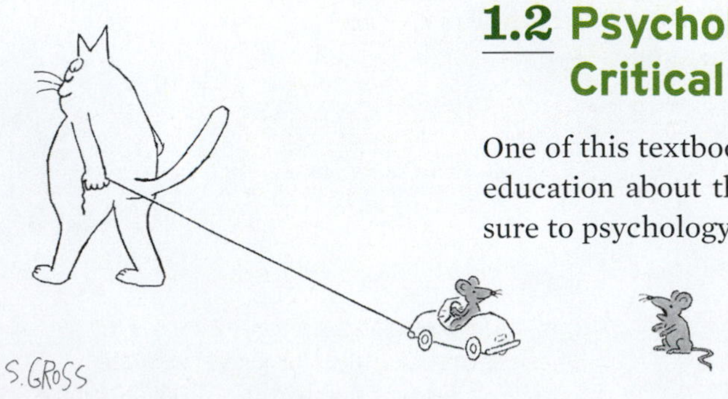

"For God's sake, think! Why is he being so nice to you?"

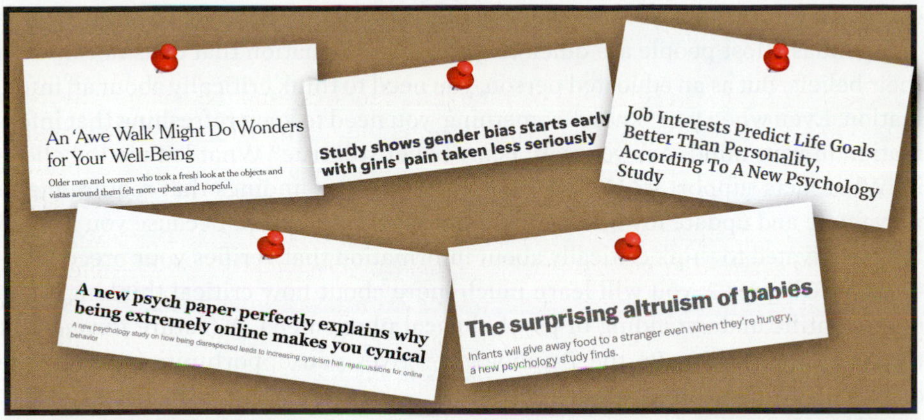

FIGURE 1.1
Psychology in the News
Psychological research is often in the news because the findings are intriguing and relevant to people's lives.

issues, theories, and controversies, you will also avoid common misunderstandings about psychology.

The media love a good story, and findings from psychological research are often provocative (**FIGURE 1.1**). Unfortunately, media reports can be distorted or even flat-out wrong. Throughout your life, as a consumer of psychological science, you will need to be skeptical of overblown media reports of "brand-new" findings obtained by "groundbreaking" research. With the rapid expansion of online information sharing and thousands of searchable research findings on just about any topic, you need to be able to sort through and evaluate the information you find in order to gain a correct understanding of the phenomenon (observable thing) you are trying to investigate.

One of the hallmarks of a good scientist—or a savvy consumer of scientific research—is *amiable skepticism*. This trait combines openness and wariness. An amiable skeptic remains open to new ideas but is wary of new "scientific findings" when good evidence and sound reasoning do not seem to support them. An amiable skeptic develops the habit of carefully weighing the facts when deciding what to believe. Thinking in this way—systematically questioning and evaluating information using well-supported evidence—is called **critical thinking**.

critical thinking Systematically questioning and evaluating information using well-supported evidence.

Critical thinking is useful in every aspect of your life. It is also important in all fields of study throughout the humanities and the sciences. In fact, psychological science itself sheds light on the way people typically think when they encounter information. Many decades of psychological research have shown that people's intuitions are often wrong, and they tend to be wrong in predictable ways that make critical thinking very difficult. Through scientific study, psychologists have discovered types of situations in which common sense fails and biases influence people's judgments.

Being aware of your own biases in thinking will also help you do better in your classes, including this one. Many students have misconceptions about psychological phenomena before they have taken a psychology course. The psychologists Patricia Kowalski and Annette Kujawski Taylor (2004) found that students who employ critical thinking skills complete an introductory course with a more accurate understanding of psychology than students who complete the same course but do not employ critical thinking skills. As you read this book, you will benefit from the critical thinking skills that you will learn about and get to practice. These skills are the most valuable lessons from this course, and you will bring them to your other classes, your workplace, and your everyday life.

Being a critical thinker involves looking for holes in evidence, using logic and reasoning to see whether the information makes sense, and considering alternative explanations (**FIGURE 1.2**). It also requires

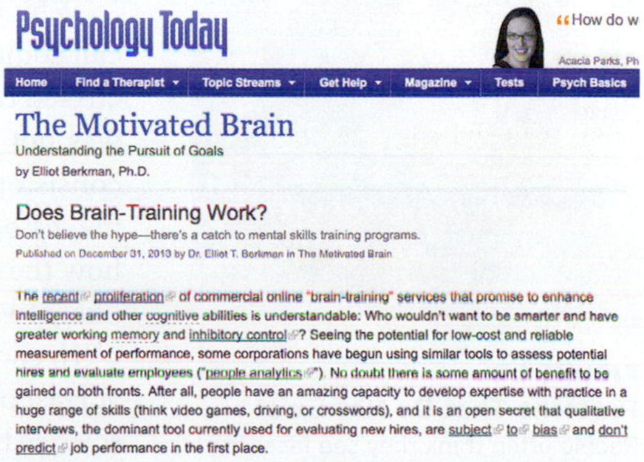
Psychology Today

"How do w

Acacia Parks, Ph

Home | Find a Therapist | Topic Streams | Get Help | Magazine | Tests | Psych Basics

The Motivated Brain
Understanding the Pursuit of Goals
by Elliot Berkman, Ph.D.

Does Brain-Training Work?
Don't believe the hype—there's a catch to mental skills training programs.
Published on December 31, 2013 by Dr. Elliot T. Berkman in The Motivated Brain

The recent proliferation of commercial online "brain-training" services that promise to enhance intelligence and other cognitive abilities is understandable: Who wouldn't want to be smarter and have greater working memory and inhibitory control? Seeing the potential for low-cost and reliable measurement of performance, some corporations have begun using similar tools to assess potential hires and evaluate employees ("people analytics"). No doubt there is some amount of benefit to be gained on both fronts. After all, people have an amazing capacity to develop expertise with practice in a huge range of skills (think video games, driving, or crosswords), and it is an open secret that qualitative interviews, the dominant tool currently used for evaluating new hires, are subject to bias and don't predict job performance in the first place.

FIGURE 1.2
Critically Evaluating Research
Psychologists use critical thinking to evaluate provocative research questions. Here, Elliot Berkman cautions against believing the hype about brain training.

considering whether the information might be biased, such as by personal or political agendas. Most people are quick to question information that does not fit with their beliefs. But as an educated person, you need to think critically about all information. Even when you "know" something, you need to keep refreshing that information in your mind. Ask yourself: Is my belief still true? What led me to believe it? What facts support it? Has science produced new findings that require me to reevaluate and update my beliefs? This exercise is important because you may be least motivated to think critically about information that verifies your preconceptions. In Chapter 2, you will learn much more about how critical thinking helps our scientific understanding of psychological phenomena. A feature throughout the book called "You Be the Psychologist" gives you opportunities to practice critical thinking about psychology.

Q **What is amiable skepticism?**

ANSWER: being open to new ideas but carefully considering the evidence

1.3 Psychological Science Helps Us Understand Biased or Inaccurate Thinking

Psychologists have cataloged some ways that intuitive thinking can lead to errors (Gilovich, 1991; Hines, 2003; Kida, 2006; Stanovich, 2013). These errors and biases do not occur because we lack intelligence or motivation. Just the opposite is true. Most of these biases occur *because* we are motivated to use our intelligence. We want to make sense of events that involve us or happen around us. Our minds are constantly analyzing all the information we receive and trying to make sense of that information. These attempts generally result in relevant and correct conclusions.

Indeed, the human brain is highly efficient at finding patterns and noting connections between things. By using these abilities, we make new discoveries and advance society. But sometimes we see patterns that do not really exist (**FIGURE 1.3**). We see images of famous people in toast. We play recorded music backward and hear satanic messages. We believe that events, such as the deaths of celebrities, happen in threes. Often, we see what we expect to see and fail to notice things that do not fit with our expectations. For instance, as you will learn in Chapter 12, our stereotypes about people shape our expectations about them, and we interpret their behavior in ways that confirm these stereotypes.

FIGURE 1.3
Patterns That Do Not Exist
People often think they see faces in objects. When someone claimed to see the face of the Virgin Mary on this grilled cheese sandwich, the sandwich sold to a casino for $28,000 on eBay.

Why is it important to care about errors and biases in thinking? False beliefs can sometimes lead to dangerous actions. During the coronavirus pandemic that circled the globe in 2020, many people were motivated to believe that the disease was not as deadly as reported. Sometimes people reject information that is not consistent with their political beliefs or that threatens their self-image (for example, as being invulnerable to illness). People who dismissed the evidence about how the virus was spread were less likely to engage in social distancing and more likely to contract the disease (Hamel et al., 2020; Owens, 2020).

In each chapter, the feature "You Be the Psychologist" draws your attention to at least one major example of biased or erroneous thinking and how psychological science has provided insights into it. The following are a few of the common biases you will encounter.

- *Ignoring evidence (confirmation bias).* People are inclined to overweigh evidence that supports their beliefs and tend to downplay evidence that does not match what they believe. When people hear about a study that is consistent with their beliefs, they generally believe the study has merit. When they hear about a study that contradicts those beliefs, they look for flaws or other problems. One factor that contributes to confirmation bias is the selective sampling of information. For instance, people with certain political beliefs may visit only websites that are consistent with those beliefs. However, if we restrict ourselves to evidence that supports our views, then of course we will believe we are right. Similarly, people show selective memory, tending to better remember information that supports their existing beliefs.

- *Seeing causal relationships that do not exist.* An extremely common reasoning error is the misperception that two events that happen at the same time must somehow be related. In our desire to find predictability in the world, we sometimes see order that does not exist. For instance, over the past 200 years, the mean global temperature has increased, and during that same period the number of pirates on the high seas has decreased. Would you argue that the demise of pirates has led to increased global warming?
- *Accepting after-the-fact explanations.* Another reasoning bias is known as *hindsight bias*. We are wonderful at explaining why things happened in the past, but we are much less successful at predicting future events. Think about the shooting in 2016 at the Pulse nightclub in Orlando, Florida. In hindsight, we know that there were warning signs that the shooter might become violent, such as a history of violence against women (**FIGURE 1.4**). Yet none of these warning signs prompted anyone to take action. People saw the signs but failed to predict the tragic outcome. More generally, once we know the outcome, we interpret and reinterpret old evidence to make sense of that outcome. We need to be wary of after-the-fact explanations because they give a false sense of certainty about our ability to make predictions about future behavior.
- *Taking mental shortcuts.* People often follow simple rules, called *heuristics*, to make decisions. These mental shortcuts are valuable because they often produce reasonably good decisions without too much effort (Kahneman, 2011). But at times heuristics can lead to inaccurate judgments and biased outcomes. One example of this problem occurs when things that come most easily to mind guide our thinking. This shortcut is known as the *availability heuristic*. For example, child abductions are much more likely to be reported in the news than more common dangers are, and the vivid nature of the reports makes them easy to remember. After hearing a series of news reports about child abductions, parents may overestimate their frequency and become overly concerned that their children might be abducted. As a result, they may underestimate other dangers facing their children, such as bicycle accidents, food poisoning, or drowning. Similar processes lead people to drive rather than fly even though the chances of injury or death from passenger vehicles are much greater than the chances of dying in a plane crash. In Chapter 8, we will consider a number of heuristic biases.

FIGURE 1.4
Orlando Pulse Shootings
In hindsight, there were warning signs that the shooter, Omar Mateen, was troubled. But it is very difficult to predict violent behavior in advance.

Q Why should you be suspicious of after-the-fact explanations?

ANSWER: Once people know an outcome, they interpret and reinterpret old evidence to make sense of that outcome, giving a false sense of predictability.

YOU BE THE PSYCHOLOGIST

1.4 Why Are People Unaware of Their Weaknesses?

FIGURE 1.5
Judging a Performance
Judges react to an audition.

Another bias in thinking is that people are motivated to feel good about themselves, and this motivation affects how they interpret information (Cai et al., 2016). For example, many people believe they are better than average on any number of dimensions. Ask your friends, for example, if they think they are better-than-average drivers. More than 90 percent of drivers hold this belief despite the statistical reality that only 50 percent can be above average. People use various strategies to support their positive views, such as choosing a definition of what it means to be good at something in a self-serving way. The flip side of this is that people are resistant to recognizing their own weaknesses. Consider the following.

You are judging an audition for a musical, and the singer, while passionate, is just awful (**FIGURE 1.5**). Everyone in the room is laughing or holding back laughter out of politeness. When the judges react unenthusiastically and worse, the performer is crushed and cannot believe the verdict. "But everyone says I am a great singer," he argues. "Singing is my life!" You sit there thinking, *How does he not know how bad he is?*

How is it that people who are tone-deaf can believe their singing talents merit participating in singing competitions? The social psychologists David Dunning and Justin Kruger have an explanation: People are often blissfully unaware of their weaknesses because they cannot judge those weaknesses at all (Dunning et al., 2003; Kruger & Dunning, 1999). How does this limitation come about?

Take a moment to consider some possibilities. This kind of thinking is known as *hypothesis generation*, and it occurs near the beginning of the scientific process. Hypothesis generation is also one of the most fun parts of thinking like a psychologist. You get to explore the idea space of explanations. Are people unaware of their weaknesses because they have never bothered to think carefully about them? Or is it that they have never received honest feedback? Try to come up with three explanations for the effect. And keep in mind that there is rarely only one explanation for something in psychology, so combinations of explanations count, too!

In studies of college students, Dunning and Kruger found that people with the lowest grades rate their mastery of academic skills much higher than is warranted by their performance (**FIGURE 1.6**). A student who receives a grade of C may protest to the instructor, "My work is as good as my roommate's, but she got an A." This result hints that one explanation might be that people lack the ability to evaluate their own performance in areas where they have little expertise—a phenomenon known as the *Dunning-Kruger effect*.

Of course, additional explanations might also be at play. Think like a psychologist and ask yourself: Why do people hold overly rosy estimations of their own abilities to begin with? How does it benefit us, and when might it be harmful? What function does it serve for us in social situations? In Chapter 12, you will learn

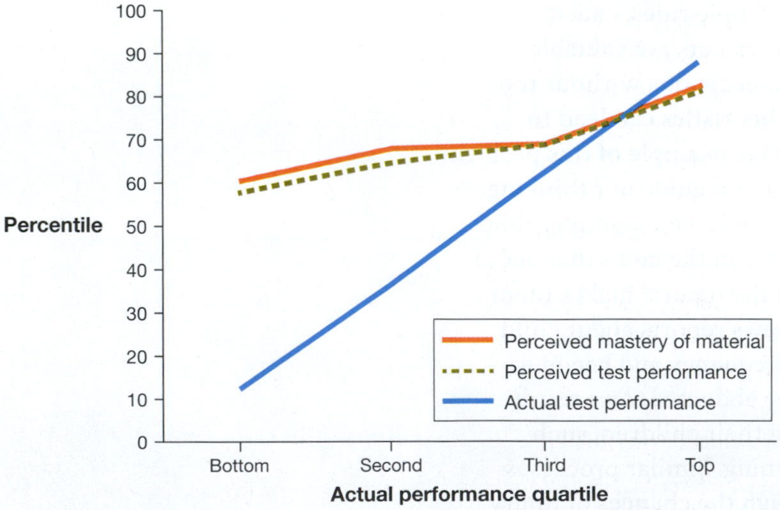

FIGURE 1.6
Personal Ratings Versus Actual Performance
Students rated their mastery of course material and test performance. Points on the *y*-axis reflect how the students perceived their percentile rankings (value on a scale of 100). Points on the *x*-axis reflect these students' actual performance rank (*quartile* here means that people are divided into four groups). The top students' predictions were close to their actual results. By contrast, the bottom students' predictions were far off.

why most people believe they are better than average in many things. As is often the case in psychology research, the answer to one question leads us to the next. Thinking like a psychologist begins, and ends, by asking questions and considering multiple possible answers. ■

Q **Why should you be skeptical of people's descriptions of their personal strengths?**

ANSWER: because people often lack the expertise to accurately evaluate and compare their abilities.

What Is the Scientific Scope of Psychology?

Learning Objectives

- Trace the history of the mind/body problem and the nature/nurture debate.
- Define the concept of functionalism and understand how it fits into an evolutionary framework.
- Identify the major areas of research within psychology and the focus of their work.

Psychology originated with the ancient philosophers, who explored questions about human nature. For example, the Chinese philosopher Confucius emphasized human development, education, and interpersonal relations, all of which remain contemporary topics in psychology around the world (Higgins & Zheng, 2002; **FIGURE 1.7**). But it was not until the 1800s that psychologists began to use scientific methods to investigate mind, brain, and behavior. Now, psychologists study a wide range of topics, from brain and other biological mechanisms to life span development to cultural and social issues.

1.5 Many Psychological Questions Have a Long History

Since at least the times of ancient Greece, people have wondered why humans think and act in certain ways. The **mind/body problem** was perhaps the quintessential psychological issue: Are the mind and body separate and distinct, or is the mind simply the subjective experience of ongoing brain activity? Throughout history, the mind has been viewed as residing in many organs of the body, including the liver and the heart. The ancient Egyptians, for example, elaborately embalmed each dead person's heart, which was to be weighed in the afterlife to determine the person's fate. They simply threw away the brain. In the following centuries, scholars continued to believe that the mind was separate from the body, as though thoughts and behaviors were directed by something other than the squishy ball of tissue between our ears. Around 1500, the artist Leonardo da Vinci challenged this doctrine when he dissected human bodies to make his anatomical drawings more accurate. His dissections led him to many conclusions about the brain's workings. Some of da Vinci's specific conclusions about brain functions were not accurate, but his work represents an early and important attempt to link the brain's anatomy to psychological functions (**FIGURE 1.8**).

mind/body problem A fundamental psychological issue: Are mind and body separate and distinct, or is the mind simply the physical brain's subjective experience?

FIGURE 1.7
Confucius
Confucius studied topics that remain important in contemporary psychology.

In the 1600s, the philosopher René Descartes promoted the influential theory of *dualism*. This term refers to the idea that the mind and the body are separate yet intertwined. In earlier views of dualism, mental functions had been considered the mind's sovereign domain, separate from body functions. Descartes proposed a somewhat different view. The body, he argued, was nothing more than an organic machine governed by "reflex." Many mental functions—such as memory and imagination—resulted from body functions. Deliberate action, however, was controlled by the rational mind. And in keeping with the prevailing religious beliefs, Descartes concluded that the rational mind was divine and separate from the body. Nowadays, psychologists reject dualism. In their

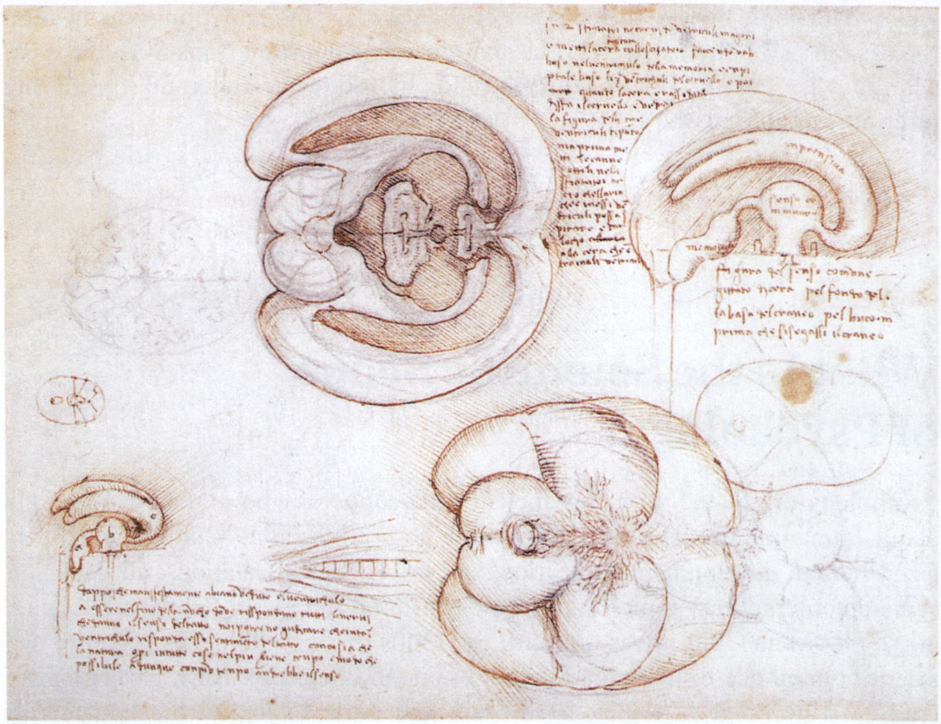

FIGURE 1.8

Da Vinci and the Brain

This drawing by Leonardo da Vinci dates from around 1506. Da Vinci used a wax cast to study the brain. He believed that sensory images arrived in the middle region of the brain. He called this region the *sensus communis*.

view, the mind arises from brain activity, and the activities of the mind change the brain. The mind and brain do not exist separately.

Other questions considered by the ancients are still explored by psychologists today. Greek philosophers such as Aristotle and Plato debated whether an individual's psychology is attributable more to *nature* or to *nurture*. That is, are psychological characteristics biologically innate? Or are they acquired through education, experience, and **culture**—the beliefs, values, rules, norms, and customs existing within a group of people who share a common language and environment? The **nature/nurture debate** has taken one form or another throughout psychology's history. Psychologists now widely recognize that nature and nurture dynamically interact in human psychological development. For example, consider a college basketball player who is very tall (nature) and has an excellent coach (nurture). That player has a better chance of excelling enough to become a professional player than does an equally talented player who has only the height or the coach. In many of the psychological phenomena you will read about in this book, nature and nurture are so enmeshed that they cannot be separated.

Learning Tip

Students often confuse the mind/body problem and the nature/nurture debate. This is understandable because they are similar in some ways. Remember, however, that the mind/body problem speaks to the *separation of mental life and the body*. For instance, is an emotion separate from the brain that produces it? In contrast, the nature/nurture debate is about the *origin of mental life*. Is an emotion caused by genetics or culture (regardless of whether the emotion "lives" in the mind or brain)?

culture The beliefs, values, rules, norms, and customs that exist within a group of people who share a common language and environment.

nature/nurture debate The arguments concerning whether psychological characteristics are biologically innate or acquired through education, experience, and culture.

Q **Why is it important for psychologists to pay attention to both nature and nurture?**

ANSWER: They both contribute to our mental activity and behavior, individually and in interaction with each other.

1.6 Mental Processes and Behaviors Serve Functions for Individuals and Groups

In the mid-1800s in Europe, psychology arose as a field of study built on the experimental method. In *A System of Logic* (1843), the philosopher John Stuart Mill declared that psychology should leave the realms of philosophy and speculation and become a science of observation and experiment. Indeed, he defined psychology as "the science of the elementary laws of the mind" and argued that only through the methods of science would the processes of the mind be understood. Throughout the 1800s, early psychologists increasingly studied mental activity through careful scientific observation.

If one person could be credited for laying the intellectual foundation for modern psychology, it would be William James, a brilliant scholar whose wide-ranging work has had an enormous, enduring impact on psychology (**FIGURE 1.9**). In 1873, James abandoned a career in medicine to teach physiology at Harvard University. In 1875, he gave his first lecture on psychology. (He later quipped that it was also the first lecture on psychology he had ever heard.) He was among the first professors at Harvard to openly welcome questions from students rather than have them listen silently to lectures. James also was an early supporter of women trying to break into the male-dominated sciences. He trained Mary Whiton Calkins, who was the first woman to set up a psychological laboratory and was the first woman president of the American Psychological Association (**FIGURE 1.10**).

James's personal interests were more philosophical than physiological. He was captivated by the nature of conscious experience. To this day, psychologists find rich delight in reading James's penetrating analysis of the human mind, *Principles of Psychology* (1890). It was the most influential book in the early history of psychology, and many of its central ideas have held up over time.

A core idea James had that remains a central pillar of psychology today is that the mind is much more complex than its elements and therefore cannot be broken down. For instance, he noted that the mind consists of an ever-changing, continuous series of thoughts. This **stream of consciousness** is the product of interacting and dynamic stimuli coming from both inside our heads, such as the decision of what to have for lunch, and outside in the world, such as the smell of pie wafting from downstairs. Because of this complexity, James argued, the mind is too complex to understand merely as a sum of separate parts, such as a decision-making unit, a smelling unit, and so forth. Trying to understand psychology like that, he said, would be like people trying to understand a house by studying each of its bricks individually. More important to James was that the bricks together form a house and that a house has a particular function (i.e., as a place where you can live). The mind's elements matter less than the mind's usefulness to people.

James argued that psychologists ought to examine the functions served by the mind—how the mind operates. According to his approach, which became known as **functionalism**, the mind came into existence over the course of human evolution. It works as it does because it is useful for preserving life and passing along genes to future generations. In other words, it helps humans *adapt* to environmental demands.

Nowadays, psychologists take for granted that any given feature of human psychology serves some kind of purpose. Some features, particularly those

FIGURE 1.9
William James
In 1890, James published the first major overview of psychology. Many of his ideas have passed the test of time. In theorizing about how the mind works, he moved psychology beyond considering minds as sums of individual units (e.g., a sensory part, an emotional part, and so forth) and into functionalism.

FIGURE 1.10
Mary Whiton Calkins
Calkins was an important early contributor to psychological science. In 1905, she became the first woman president of the American Psychological Association.

stream of consciousness A phrase coined by William James to describe each person's continuous series of ever-changing thoughts.

functionalism An approach to psychology concerned with the adaptive purpose, or function, of mind and behavior.

natural selection In evolutionary theory, the idea that those who inherit characteristics that help them adapt to their particular environments have a selective advantage over those who do not.

diversity and inclusion The value and practice of ensuring that psychological science represents the experiences of all humans.

ANSWER: The mind is too complex to understand as a sum of separate parts.

that are common to all humans (e.g., sensation and perception), are likely to have evolved through the evolutionary process of **natural selection**, by which features that are adaptive (that facilitate survival and reproduction) are passed along and those that are not adaptive (that hinder survival and reproduction) are not passed along. Language is a good example, as it is easy to see how the ability to represent and communicate ideas in social groups would be beneficial for human survival: just try communicating to your brother without using words that the third tree on the left about a quarter of a mile down the road has the best apples. Other features, particularly those that are specific to a culture or an individual, probably did not evolve through natural selection but might still be functional. Cultural traditions, such as religious rules against eating certain types of foods, or personal quirks, such as nail biting, are viewed within psychology as "functional" in the sense that they arose to solve a problem: Food prohibitions can protect against illness, and nervous habits can be ways people learn to reduce their anxiety.

Q According to William James's functionalism, why should psychologists focus on the operations of the mind?

1.7 The Field of Psychology Spans the Range of Human Experience

Psychologists are interested in mental phenomena ranging from basic sensory and brain processes to abstract thoughts and complex social interactions (**FIGURE 1.11**). Those topics are universal to humans, but the way we experience sensations, thoughts, feelings, and so forth can vary dramatically within an individual person and across people. Consider, for example, your own emotional range within a day when you were a toddler compared to now, or what a refugee of the Syrian civil war would consider to be a stressful event compared with a typical North American undergraduate student.

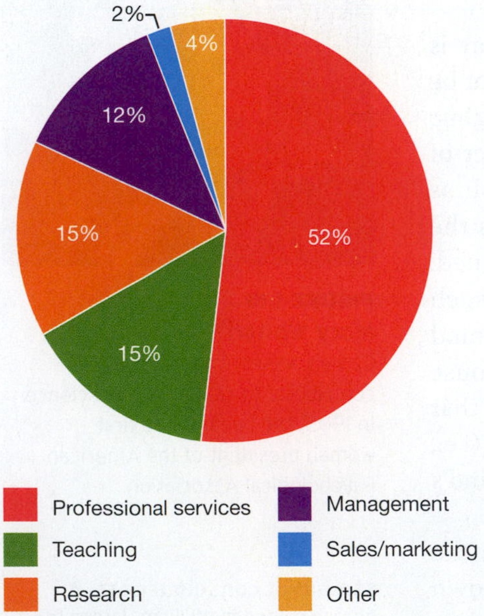

FIGURE 1.11
Employment Settings for Psychologists
This chart shows the types of settings where psychologists work, based on a survey of those obtaining a doctorate or professional degree in psychology in 2017 (American Psychological Association, 2018).

After decades of focusing on a relatively narrow slice of the world population, the field of psychology is finally beginning to increase its **diversity and inclusion**. The field views as critical to its mission not only racial, ethnic, and cultural diversity but also diversity in terms of age, ability, gender identity, sexual orientation, socioeconomic status, and immigration status, among other features. As part of this shift toward a broader and more central view of diversity and inclusion, the field is moving away from viewing cultural psychology as an area unto itself. Culture and many other forms of diversity are becoming integral to all areas of psychology as researchers learn that key developmental, social, personality, cognitive, and clinical phenomena can vary considerably as a function of culture and personal experiences. The internet allows researchers to gather data from across the globe, and it is becoming more and more common for research projects to feature samples from several and even dozens of countries. Many psychology departments now ask applicants to professor positions to include as part of the application package a statement about how their research considers diversity and inclusion. The field still lacks diversity in many ways, but this progress shows that there is motivation to change.

Psychologists began to specialize in specific areas of research as the kinds of human experiences under investigation by psychological science broadened over the years. **TABLE 1.1** describes some of the most popular areas of specialization in psychology. The psychology departments at most universities have clusters of professors in several of these areas. Some departments offer master's and doctorate degrees with these specializations.

Q Which area of psychology specializes in understanding the thoughts, feelings, and behaviors of daily life?

ANSWER: social-personality psychology

Table 1.1 Areas of Specialization in Psychology

AREA	FOCUS	SAMPLE QUESTIONS	CHAPTER
Clinical	The area of psychology that seeks to understand, characterize, and treat mental illness is called **clinical psychology**. Clinical psychology is one of the most common specializations in the field. Advanced degrees in clinical psychology focus on research, clinical work/therapy, or a blend of the two.	Are there underlying psychological or biological causes across different mental disorders? What are the most effective ways to treat personality disorders? Can mindfulness meditation reduce psychological distress in anxiety disorders?	14 15
Cognitive	Laboratory research in **cognitive psychology** aims to understand the basic skills and processes that are the foundation of mental life and behavior. Topics such as attention, memory, sensation, and perception are within the scope of cognitive psychology.	Why is multitasking harder than working on tasks one after the other? How does damage in particular areas of the brain alter color perception but not motion perception? Do some people learn more quickly than others to associate cause and effect?	3 4 5 6 7 8
Cultural	**Cultural psychology** studies how cultural factors such as geographical regions, national beliefs, and religious values can have profound effects on mental life and behavior. A major contribution of cultural psychology is to highlight the profound ways that the samples used in psychological studies can influence the results and their implications. Cultural psychology is the area most closely linked to the adjacent fields of sociology and anthropology.	Why does the southern United States have the highest rate of per capita gun violence in the country? Do people think of themselves in fundamentally different ways depending on where they were raised? Does thinking about a forgiving versus vengeful deity influence moral behavior such as lying?	1 2
Developmental	**Developmental psychology** studies how humans grow and develop from the prenatal period through infancy and early childhood, through adolescence and early adulthood, and into old age. Developmental psychology encompasses the full range of topics covered by other areas in psychology, focusing on how experiences change across the life span and the periods in life when they are particularly important.	How does stress experienced by the mother alter the developing immune system of a fetus in utero? Why do children learn languages more easily than adults? In what ways is risk-taking functional for adolescents as they seek to establish themselves in new social groups?	9

continued

Table 1.1 Areas of Specialization in Psychology (continued)

AREA	FOCUS	SAMPLE QUESTIONS	CHAPTER
Health	**Health psychology** is concerned with how psychological processes influence physical health and vice versa. Psychological factors such as stress, loneliness, and impulsivity can powerfully influence a range of health disorders and even mortality. In contrast, optimism, social support, and conscientiousness can promote healthy behaviors.	How can strong friendships protect or "buffer" us from the harmful effects of stress? Does memory training help people resist temptations such as excessive alcohol or tobacco use? When does experiencing discrimination increase the likelihood of heart disease?	11
Industrial/ Organizational	**Industrial/organizational** (I/O) psychology explores how psychological processes play out in the workplace. This field is one of the more pragmatic specializations in psychology because it speaks to real-world problems such as dealing with interpersonal conflicts at work and organizational change. I/O psychology blends social-personality psychology approaches with principles from management, communication, and marketing. Research on I/O psychology happens in organizational settings as well as in psychology departments and business schools.	What are ways that organizations can increase employee motivation in stressful times? How can critical feedback be provided to managers so that it is gentle yet results in behavior change? What types of people should organizations hire into specialized versus more general roles?	
Relationships	The quality of our close relationships, including romantic partnerships and intimate friendships, is the most consistent predictor of overall happiness and well-being, and relationship issues are the most common reason people seek psychotherapy. **Close relationships psychologists** research our intimate relationships, properties that make them succeed or fail, and the two-way effects between intimate relationships and other aspects of our lives.	What differentiates long-lasting marriages from those that end in early divorce? In what ways do romantic partners influence each other's goal pursuit? Is it important for relationship satisfaction that partners "match" on certain personality traits? If so, which ones?	12
Social-Personality	**Social-personality psychology** is the study of everyday thoughts, feelings, and behaviors—and the factors that give rise to them. Social-personality psychology focuses on the situational and dispositional causes of behavior and the interactions between them. Social and personality psychology were once separate fields, but scholars from both sides now recognize that mental life and behavior cannot be fully understood without both pieces and their interaction.	How do people understand and explain other people's behaviors? What are the causes of stereotyping and prejudice and what are their effects on victims? Does personality remain stable across the life span? If not, in what ways does personality change as people age and why?	10 12 13

What Are the Latest Developments in Psychology?

Learning Objectives

- Identify recent developments in psychological science.
- Explain how the science of learning can help your performance in class.

In the many decades since psychology was founded, researchers have made significant progress in understanding mind, brain, and behavior. As in all sciences, this wisdom progresses incrementally: As psychologists ask more questions about what is already known, new knowledge springs forth. During various periods in the history of the field, new approaches have transformed psychology, such as when William James prompted psychologists to collect data to study minds. We do not know what approaches the future of psychology will bring, but this section outlines some of the developments that contemporary psychologists are most excited about.

1.8 Biology Is Increasingly Emphasized in Explaining Psychological Phenomena

Recent decades have seen remarkable growth in the understanding of the biological bases of mental activities. This section outlines three major advances that have helped further the scientific understanding of psychological phenomena: developments in neuroscience, progress in genetics and epigenetics, and advances in immunology and other peripheral systems.

BRAIN IMAGING There is a very long history of brain science in psychology. Since ancient times, people have recognized that alterations to the soft mass of tissue between our ears can cause profound changes in mind and behavior. Pioneers such as Pierre Paul Broca discovered that damage to specific regions can correspond to specific changes in parts of our psychology, such as speech and language. But technology such as electroencephalography (EEG), which measures changes in electrical activity, and now devices that measure subtle changes in the magnetic field caused by changes in blood flow have significantly accelerated progress in brain science.

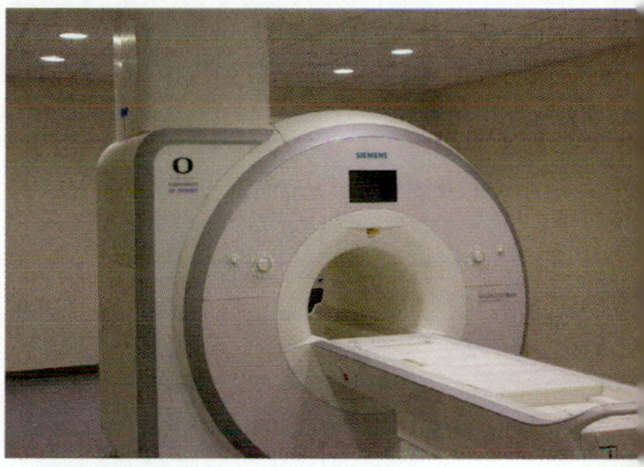

FIGURE 1.12
fMRI
Functional magnetic resonance imaging (fMRI) can reveal changes in brain activation in response to different mental processes.

One method, functional magnetic resonance imaging (fMRI), enables researchers to study the working brain as it performs its psychological functions in close to real time (**FIGURE 1.12**). Since its development, the progress in understanding the neural basis of mental life has been rapid and dramatic. Knowing where in the brain something happens does not by itself reveal much. However, when consistent patterns of brain activation are associated with specific mental tasks, the activation appears to be connected with the tasks. Earlier scientists disagreed about whether psychological processes are located in specific parts of the brain or are distributed throughout the brain. Research has made clear that there is some *localization* of function. That is, different areas of the brain are specialized for different functions, such as language, control over behavior, and abstract thinking.

However, many brain regions have to work together to produce complex behaviors and mental activity. One of the greatest contemporary scientific challenges is mapping out how various brain regions are connected and how they work together to produce mental activity. To achieve this mapping, the *Human Connectome Project* was launched in 2010 as a major international research effort involving collaborators at a number of universities. A greater understanding of brain connectivity may be especially useful for understanding how brain circuitry changes in psychological disorders (**FIGURE 1.13**).

FIGURE 1.13
Brain Connectivity
Psychologist Damien Fair received a MacArthur "Genius" Fellowship for his research on the ways parts of the brain are connected to each other and how those patterns of connectivity relate to disorders in children and adolescents.

Neuroscience approaches, such as fMRI, were originally used to study basic psychological processes, such as how people see or remember information. Today, such techniques are used to understand a wide range of phenomena, from how emotions change during adolescence (Silvers et al., 2017), to how people process information regarding social groups (Freeman & Johnson, 2016), to how thinking patterns contribute to depression (Hamilton et al., 2015).

GENETICS AND EPIGENETICS The *human genome* is the basic *genetic code*, or blueprint, for the human body. For psychologists, this map represents the foundational knowledge for studying how specific genes—the basic units of hereditary transmission—affect thoughts, actions, feelings, and disorders. By identifying the genes involved in memory, for example, researchers might eventually be able to develop treatments, based on genetic manipulation, that will assist people who have memory problems.

Meanwhile, the scientific study of genetic influences has made clear that though nearly all aspects of human psychology and behavior have at least a small genetic component, very few single genes cause specific behaviors. Combinations of genes can predict certain psychological characteristics, but the pathways of these effects are mostly unknown. Adding to the complexity of this picture, a number of biological and environmental processes can influence how genes are expressed (for example, which genes get "turned on" and when) without changing the genetic code itself. **Epigenetics** is the study of the ways these environmental mechanisms can get "under the skin," particularly in early life, to influence our mind and behavior.

epigenetics The study of biological or environmental influences on gene expression that are not part of inherited genes.

IMMUNOLOGY AND OTHER PERIPHERAL SYSTEMS Scientists have made enormous progress in understanding how the immune system protects our bodies and interacts with other systems that respond to stress, regulate our digestion, and metabolize energy. And all of these systems interact with brain function, structure, and development in fascinating ways. For psychologists, this knowledge reveals the deep and multilayered connections between our minds and other systems previously thought to be relatively independent. Some recent discoveries have transformed how psychologists conceive of stress, pain, and even depression (Alfven et al., 2019; Peirce & Alviña, 2019).

One particularly active area of research in psychology explores the two-way relation between the *gut microbiome*, the billions of microorganisms that live in our digestive tract, and our mind and behavior. Rapidly emerging science on the *gut-brain axis* reveals that the composition and diversity of these microorganisms can alter, and be altered by, the way our bodies respond to stress, mount an immune response, and direct attention (Foster et al., 2017; **FIGURE 1.14**). Through its complex interactions with the immune and metabolic systems, hormones, and neurotransmitters, the gut microbiome has a role in a variety of health conditions including irritable bowel syndrome, autism spectrum disorders, and anxiety.

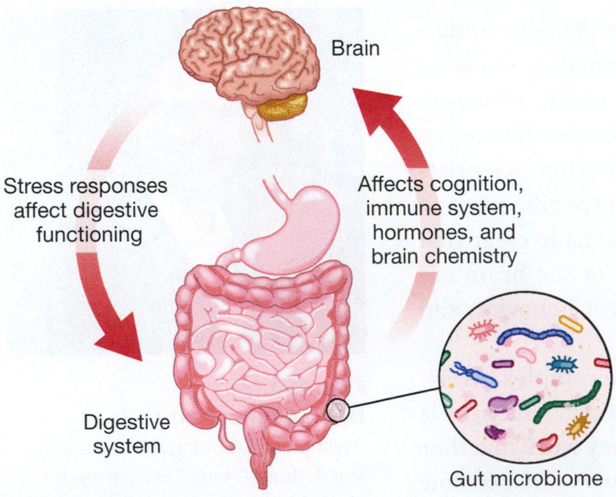

FIGURE 1.14
Gut-Brain Axis
Peripheral systems in the body, including the digestive system shown here, have two-way communication with the brain.

Biological data can provide a unique window into understanding human psychology. But keep in mind that human psychology is the product of many factors beyond just biological ones. Our early experiences, our genes, our close relationships, our brains, and our cultures all contribute to who we are and what we do.

Q **What does brain imaging help psychologists study?**

ANSWER: localization of mental activity

1.9 Psychology Is a Computational and Data Science

The widespread availability of very fast computers, low storage costs, and the internet connecting it all has transformed the way psychologists do their jobs. What began as a handy technological tool is now an integral part of the way psychologists gather, share, and analyze their data. Psychology is part of the "data science" revolution in at least three ways.

behaviorism A psychological approach that emphasizes environmental influences on observable behaviors.

COMPUTATIONAL MODELING During the first half of the twentieth century, psychology was largely focused on studying observable behavior to the exclusion of mental events such as thoughts and feelings, an approach known as **behaviorism.** Evidence slowly emerged, however, that learning is not as simple as the behaviorists believed it to be. Research across psychology in memory, language, and development showed that the simple laws of behaviorism could not explain, for example, why culture influences how people remember a story, why grammar develops systematically, and why children interpret the world in different ways during different stages of development. All of these findings suggested that psychologists would need to study people's mental functions and not just their overt actions to understand behavior.

To address this need, the psychologist George A. Miller and his colleagues launched the *cognitive revolution* in psychology (FIGURE 1.15) in the 1950s. In 1967, Ulric Neisser integrated a wide range of cognitive phenomena in his book *Cognitive Psychology*. This classic work named and defined the field and fully embraced the mind, which the behaviorist B. F. Skinner had argued was "fictional" (Skinner, 1974). (Radical behaviorism held that unobservable mental events are part of behavior, not its cause.)

FIGURE 1.15
George A. Miller
In 1957, Miller launched the cognitive revolution by establishing the Center for Cognitive Science at Harvard University.

The cognitive revolution was accelerated by the computer age. Psychologists learned how to use simple computerized tasks to indirectly measure some components of cognition, including attention, working memory, inhibitory control, and reward learning. At first, the data extracted from these tasks were relatively simple measures such as reaction times and error rates. Now psychologists use computers to help build and test mathematical models of behavior that capture some of the important but invisible factors that underlie it. Just as mathematical models help physicists estimate the force of gravity using equations that describe the motion of the planets (FIGURE 1.16), computational models help psychologists understand processes such as a person's ability to learn about rewards. As these tools continue to develop, they will sharpen psychologists' ability to look inside the black box of the mind with increasing precision.

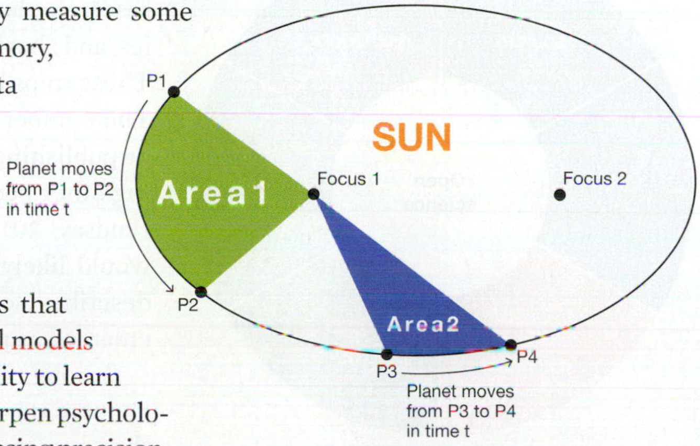

FIGURE 1.16
Computational Modeling
Computers can solve mathematical models that describe the motion of the planets and the invisible properties of thought.

BIG DATA The computer that guided the *Apollo 11* flight to the moon in 1969 had about 72 kilobytes of memory, which is about enough memory for 0.2 seconds of a typical YouTube video. Zoom forward to today, when about 300 hours of video are uploaded to YouTube every minute. The world is awash in data, and much of them are directly relevant to psychological questions. Psychologists are partnering with computer scientists to answer some of those questions using data available online from sources such as social media platforms, electronic medical records, and—yes—even YouTube.

big data Science that uses very large data sets and advanced computational methods to discover patterns that would be difficult to detect with smaller data sets.

The **big data** approach uses tools from the computer science world, such as data mining and machine learning, to identify complex patterns in large data sets. These new methods have allowed psychologists to study topics such as ethnic discrimination in geographical regions based on Google searches, risk of alcoholism using specific combinations of genes or gene expressions, and personality profiles gleaned from activity on Twitter. The availability of very large data sets has also increased the diversity of the samples used in psychology research. At the same time, these methods are not without controversy. For instance, critics have questioned the ethics of using data that were originally collected for one purpose to answer different research questions. As big data moves forward, it is clear that the technology is advancing faster than our capacity to understand its implications. The related and equally important field of **data ethics** grapples with issues of privacy, equal access to information, and how much we can control information about ourselves.

data ethics The branch of philosophy that addresses ethical issues in data sciences, including data accessibility, identifiability, and autonomy.

replicability The likelihood that the results of a study would be very similar if it were run again.

open science movement A social movement among scientists to improve methods, increase research transparency, and promote data sharing.

REPLICABILITY, OPEN SCIENCE, AND DATA SHARING One of the features of a good scientific study is **replicability**, meaning that the results would be more or less the same if someone ran the study again. There is an unavoidable element of chance in psychological science because studies use small groups of people, or samples, to make inferences about larger groups of individuals. So, it is always possible that something about the particular sample or the details of how a study was run might cause a study not to replicate in a new sample. Psychologists have known about this possibility for a very long time and have taken measures to prevent it. Even so, a large-scale study by the Open Science Collaboration surprised the field in revealing that less than half of a sample of experiments in prominent psychology journals replicated (Open Science Collaboration, 2015). This and similar disturbing results prompted a movement to adopt reforms to increase the reliability of the results in the field.

In the ensuing years, the field coalesced around an **open science movement** to improve the methods used in psychological science by making research plans and designs more transparent, documenting failed studies, and sharing data among researchers, among other steps (**FIGURE 1.17**). These steps have been adopted with enthusiasm by scientists in the field. The number of psychologists using best practices, such as writing down or publishing their research plans at the beginning of a study and allowing other people access to their data, has increased each year (Nosek & Lindsay, 2018). This textbook features studies that have replicated or would likely replicate based on the rigor of their methods. Chapter 2 describes some of the best practices for psychological research that emerged as part of the open science movement.

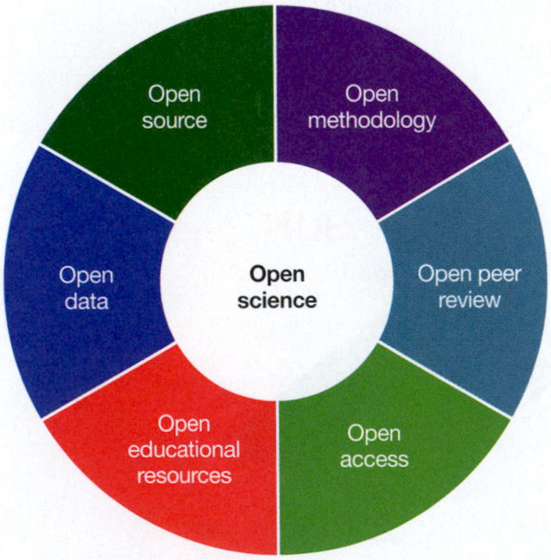

FIGURE 1.17
Open Science
Open science emphasizes research transparency and data accessibility. Psychologists have developed tools to help promote open science at all phases of the research process.

Among the benefits of the open science movement is a shift in norms about data sharing in psychology. It is now increasingly expected that researchers share original, anonymous data from experiments, and numerous internet platforms have sprung up to facilitate this access. These platforms host data from all areas of psychology, from lab experiments to developmental psychology studies to neuroimaging repositories. With some help from colleagues in computer science, psychological scientists are learning to combine data from these growing databases to conduct some of the most powerful and inclusive studies in the history of psychology.

Q What is data ethics?

ANSWER: the branch of philosophy examining ethical questions around the collection, use, and sharing of human data

1.10 Culture Provides Adaptive Solutions

Through evolution, specialized mechanisms and adaptive behaviors have been built into our bodies and brains. For instance, a mechanism that produces calluses has evolved, protecting the skin from the abuses of physical labor.

Likewise, specialized circuits have evolved in the brain to address the most demanding adaptive challenges we face, many of which involve dealing with other people (Mills et al., 2014). These challenges include selecting mates, cooperating in hunting and in gathering, forming alliances, competing for scarce resources, and even warring with neighboring groups. This dependency on group living is not unique to humans, but the nature of interactions within and between groups is especially complex in human societies. The complexity of living in groups gives rise to culture, and culture's various aspects are transmitted from one generation to the next through learning. For instance, musical preferences, some food preferences, subtle ways of expressing emotion, and tolerance of body odors are affected by the culture one is raised in. Many of a culture's "rules" reflect adaptive solutions worked out by previous generations.

Human cultural evolution has occurred much faster than human biological evolution, and the most dramatic cultural changes have come in the past few thousand years. Although humans have changed only modestly in physical terms in that time, they have changed profoundly in regard to how they live together. Even within the past century, dramatic changes have occurred in how human societies interact. The flow of people, commodities, and financial instruments among all regions of the world, often referred to as *globalization*, has increased in velocity and scale in ways that were previously unimaginable. Even more recently, the internet has created a worldwide network of humans, essentially a new form of culture with its own rules, values, and customs.

Over the past two decades, recognition has grown that culture plays a foundational role in shaping how people view and reason about the world around them—and that people from different cultures possess strikingly different minds (Heine, 2015). For example, the social psychologist Richard Nisbett and his colleagues (2001) have demonstrated that people from most European and North American countries are much more analytical than people from most Asian countries. Westerners break complex ideas into simpler components, categorize information, and use logic and rules to explain behavior. Easterners tend to be more holistic in their thinking, seeing everything in front of them as an inherently complicated whole, with all elements affecting all other elements (**FIGURE 1.18**).

(a)

(b)

FIGURE 1.18
Cultural Differences
(a) Westerners tend to be "independent" and autonomous, stressing their individuality.
(b) Easterners—such as this Cambodian family—tend to be more "interdependent," stressing their sense of being part of a collective.

The culture in which people live shapes many aspects of their daily lives. Pause for a moment and think about the following questions: How do people decide what is most important in their lives? How do people relate to family members? to friends? to colleagues at work? How should people spend their leisure time? How do they define themselves in relation to their own culture—or across cultures?

Culture shapes beliefs and values, such as the extent to which people should emphasize their own interests versus the interests of the group. This effect is more apparent when we compare phenomena across cultures. Culture instills certain rules, called *norms*, which specify how people ought to behave in different contexts. For example, norms tell us not to laugh uproariously at funerals and to keep quiet in libraries. Culture can influence our biology by altering our behavior. For instance, diet is partly determined by culture, and some diets have epigenetic effects. Culture also has material aspects, such as media, technology, health care, and transportation. Many people find it hard to imagine life without computers, televisions, cell phones, and cars. We also recognize that each of these inventions has changed the fundamental ways in which people interact. Historical and social changes can have similar effects. For instance, the increased participation of women in the workforce has changed the nature of contemporary Western culture in numerous ways, from a fundamental change in how women are viewed to more practical changes, such as people marrying and having children later in life, a greater number of children in day care, and a greater reliance on convenient, fast foods.

Q What are cultural norms?

ANSWER: socially upheld rules regarding how people ought to behave in certain situations

1.11 Psychological Science Crosses Levels of Analysis

Four broadly defined levels of analysis reflect the most common research methods for studying mind and behavior (**FIGURE 1.19**). The *biological level of analysis* deals with how the physical body contributes to mind and behavior (such as through the chemical and genetic processes that occur in the body). The *individual level of analysis* focuses on individual differences in personality and in the mental processes that affect how people perceive and know the world. The *social level of analysis* involves how group contexts affect the ways in which people interact and influence each other. The first three together are sometimes

FIGURE 1.19
Levels of Analysis

	LEVEL	FOCUS	WHAT IS STUDIED?
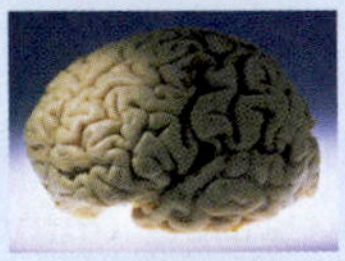	Biological	Brain systems	Neuroanatomy, animal research, brain imaging
		Neurochemistry	Neurotransmitters and hormones, animal studies, drug studies
		Genetics	Gene mechanisms, heritability, twin and adoption studies
	Individual	Individual differences	Personality, gender, developmental age groups, self-concept
		Perception and cognition	Thinking, decision making, language, memory, seeing, hearing
		Behavior	Observable actions, responses, physical movements
	Social	Interpersonal behavior	Groups, relationships, persuasion, influence, workplace
		Social cognition	Attitudes, stereotypes, perceptions
	Cultural	Thoughts, actions, behaviors—in different societies and cultural groups	Norms, beliefs, values, symbols, ethnicity

referred to as the **biopsychosocial model**. On top of that is the *cultural level of analysis*, which explores how people's thoughts, feelings, and actions are similar or different across cultures. Differences between cultures highlight the role that cultural experiences play in shaping psychological processes, whereas similarities between cultures reveal evidence for universal phenomena that emerge regardless of cultural experiences.

biopsychosocial model An approach to psychological science that integrates biological factors, psychological processes, and social-contextual influences in shaping human mental life and behavior.

Studying a psychological phenomenon at one level of analysis (e.g., behavioral or neural data alone) has traditionally been the favored approach, but these days researchers have started to explain behavior at several levels of analysis. By crossing levels in this way, psychologists are able to provide a more complete picture of mental and behavioral processes.

To understand how research is conducted at the different levels, consider the many ways psychologists have studied listening to music (Hallam et al., 2016). Why do you like some kinds of music and not others? Do you prefer some types of music when you are in a good mood and other types when you are in a bad mood? If you listen to music while you study, how does it affect how you learn?

At the biological level of analysis, for instance, researchers have studied the effects of musical training. They have shown that training can change not only how the brain functions but also its anatomy, such as by changing brain structures associated with learning and memory (Herdener et al., 2010). Interestingly, music does not affect the brain exactly the way other types of sounds, such as the spoken word, do. Instead, music recruits brain regions involved in a number of mental processes, such as those involved in mood and memory (Levitin & Menon, 2003; Peretz & Zatorre, 2005). Music appears to be treated by the brain as a special category of auditory information. For this reason, patients with certain types of brain injury become unable to perceive tones and melody but can understand speech and environmental sounds perfectly well.

Working at the individual level of analysis, researchers have used laboratory experiments to study music's effects on mood, memory, decision making, and various other mental states that exist within an individual person (Levitin, 2006). In one study, music from participants' childhoods evoked specific memories from that period (Janata, 2009; **FIGURE 1.20**). Moreover, music affects emotions and thoughts. Listening to sad background music leads young children to interpret a story negatively, whereas listening to happy background music leads them to interpret the story much more positively (Ziv & Goshen, 2006). Our cognitive expectations also shape how we experience music (Collins et al., 2014).

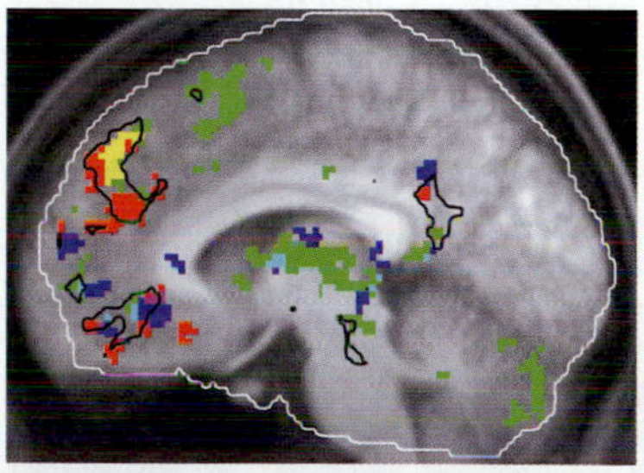

FIGURE 1.20
Your Brain on Music
The researcher Petr Janata played familiar and unfamiliar music to study participants. Activity in green indicates familiarity with the music, activity in blue indicates emotional reactions to the music, and activity in red indicates memories from the past. The yellow section in the frontal lobe links together familiar music, emotions, and memories.

A study of music at the social level of analysis might investigate how the effect of music changes or the types of music people prefer change when they are in groups compared with when they are alone. For example, music reduces stress regardless of context but especially when enjoyed in the presence of others (Linnemann et al., 2016). Romantic partners can also influence the way we experience music. For example, in heterosexual couples, men experience more stress reduction from listening to music than their partners do, particularly when the two individuals have shared music preferences (Wuttke-Linnemann et al., 2019).

The cross-cultural study of music preferences has developed into a separate field, *ethnomusicology*. One finding from this field is that African music has rhythmic structures different from those in Western music (Agawu, 1995), possibly because of the important role of dancing and drumming in many African cultures. Because musical preferences differ across cultures, some psychologists have noted that attitudes about outgroup members can color perceptions of their musical styles. For example, researchers from the United States and the United Kingdom found that societal attitudes toward rap and hip-hop music revealed subtle prejudicial attitudes against Black people and a greater willingness to discriminate against them (Reyna et al., 2009).

Combining the levels of analysis usually provides more insights than working within only one level. Psychologists may also collaborate with researchers from other scientific fields, such as biology, computer science, physics, anthropology, and sociology. Such collaborations are called *interdisciplinary*. For example, psychologists interested in understanding the hormonal basis of obesity might work with geneticists exploring the heritability of obesity as well as with social psychologists studying human beliefs about eating. Throughout this book, you will see how this multilevel, multidisciplinary approach has led to breakthroughs in understanding psychological activity.

Q **Suppose a research study explores people's memory for song lyrics. At what level of analysis are the researchers working?**

ANSWER: the individual level

1.12 Psychological Education Embraces the Science of Learning

The study of how people learn and retain new information is one of the oldest and most robust areas of research in psychology. It is only appropriate, then, that psychologists would apply this knowledge when teaching students about their field. Throughout this book, we highlight some of the tips and tricks that psychologists have discovered to improve how people study and learn. The learning-science principles identified in psychology research can be effective in many contexts in and out of the classroom, so you should put them to good use in all of your courses and in whatever career you ultimately choose. These topics and the science behind them are covered in depth in Chapter 6.

Despite a long history of studying learning in the lab, psychologists have only recently found ways to translate those results into the world of education (Roediger, 2013). However, some of the most effective learning strategies are easy to deploy and have been put to use in classrooms, benefiting students of all ages (Dunlosky et al., 2013). The following are among the most effective strategies, and they are put into practice in this text where possible.

distributed practice Learning material in several bursts over a prolonged time frame.

retrieval-based learning Learning new information by repeatedly recalling it from long-term memory.

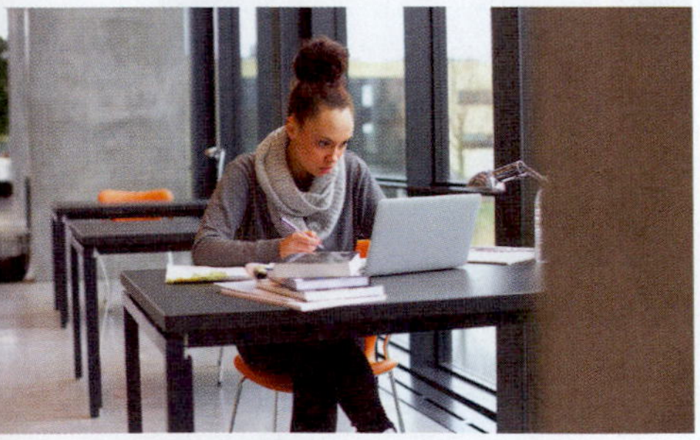

FIGURE 1.21
Distributed Practice
Distributing practice sessions across time is one of the proven ways to increase memory. The student shown cramming in this photo is missing an opportunity to benefit from distributed practice.

DISTRIBUTED PRACTICE At some point in their college career, most students learn by experience that cramming for an exam is an ineffective way to study (FIGURE 1.21). **Distributed practice**—learning material in bursts over a prolonged time frame—is the opposite of cramming and is one of the best ways to learn (Benjamin & Tullis, 2010). Why does distributed practice work? It might be that the extra work it takes to remember material you learned before switching to something else is beneficial. It might also be the case that after the initial study period, each time you study the material you are reminded of that first time. Distributed practice might also promote better learning because every time you pull up a memory and then remember it again, it gets stronger.

RETRIEVAL, OR TESTING It turns out that tests are not only good for figuring out whether you know something. Being tested on material can actually help you learn that material better, an effect known as **retrieval-based learning**. Repeatedly recalling content from memory makes that content stick in your mind better and longer (Karpicke, 2012). Part of the reason is that getting information into your head is only the first part of learning. You then need to *retrieve* that information to be able to make use of it. Testing and other forms of retrieval-based learning are ways to practice that second part, thereby teaching yourself how to call up the information stored in memory. The questions and practice tests throughout this book and online are there to help you practice retrieval.

ELABORATIVE INTERROGATION Asking "Why?" can help you learn, especially when the material to be learned is factual knowledge, such as many of the psychological phenomena described in this book. **Elaborative interrogation**—thinking through why a fact is true, or why it is true in some cases but not others—helps you link the new fact to existing knowledge in your mind and integrate it into your understanding of the world. In this book, we frequently describe why something is true of human psychology or behavior, but elaborative interrogation is even more effective when the learner (you!) reasons through why something might be true. This process is the inspiration for the "You Be the Psychologist" feature in each chapter.

elaborative interrogation Learning by asking yourself why a fact is true or a process operates the way it does.

The features in this book have been shown to facilitate learning in other ways. For instance, the "You Be the Psychologist" feature will also engage you in **self-explanation**—reflecting on your learning process and trying to make sense of new material in your own terms. Another beneficial technique is **interleaved practice**, or switching between topics during studying instead of completing one topic before moving on to the next. Interleaving is one way to distribute study time, and it is additionally helpful because it forces you to compare and contrast different topics. This textbook is organized into chapters by topic, but research on interleaved practice suggests that you might consider jumping between topics in a couple of chapters as you go.

self-explanation Reflecting on your learning process and trying to make sense of new material in your own words.

interleaved practice Switching between topics during studying.

You might be surprised that some common techniques—including summarizing, rereading, and highlighting—do not usually improve learning (Dunlosky et al., 2013). If you find yourself reading this passage for a second time, we recommend taking a practice test instead or, better yet, taking a break for a day or two and coming back to test your knowledge then.

Q What learning technique would explain why teachers give quizzes that are not worth many points?

ANSWER: retrieval- or testing-based learning

1.13 How Will Psychology Benefit You in Your Career?

PSYCHOLOGY OUTSIDE THE LAB

Some students take introductory psychology courses because of a long-standing interest in people and the desire to learn more about what makes people, including themselves, tick. Others enroll because they wish to fulfill a general education requirement or because the class is a prerequisite for another course they are eager to take. Whatever *your* reason for being in this class, the things you will learn in this book will be highly relevant to multiple aspects of your life, including your chosen career.

Many careers involve interacting with coworkers, customers, clients, or patients (FIGURE 1.22). In these cases, understanding what motivates people, how to influence them, and how to support them is essential. For instance, a medical professional with interpersonal skills will create rapport with patients. Good rapport in turn encourages patients to be honest about their health behaviors, and

(a)

(b)

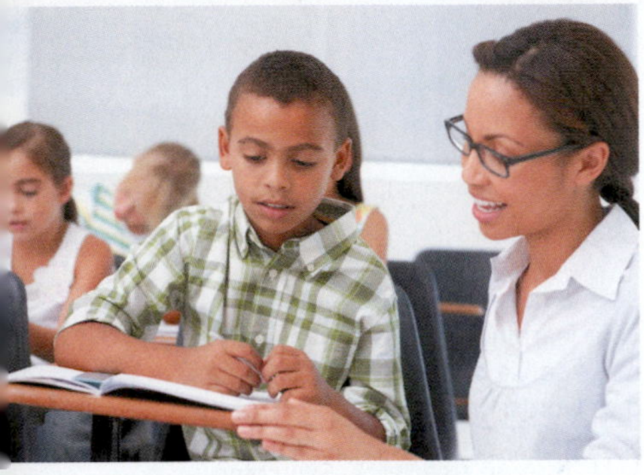

FIGURE 1.22
Studying Psychology Develops Interpersonal Skills
Dealing with other people is an important part of most careers. **(a)** Medical professionals need to gauge people's moods and their motivations to recover. **(b)** Teachers need to understand people's behavior and how people learn.

the resulting disclosures may improve the practitioner's ability to accurately diagnose the patients' medical conditions. A rehabilitation nurse who understands the psychological challenges of complying with medical advice is better equipped to help patients respond to those challenges and thus improve. Given the many ways psychology is relevant to the medical field, it is not surprising that the Medical College Admission Test (MCAT), the standardized test required for admission to medical school, now includes an extensive 95-minute section on the psychological, social, and biological foundations of behavior.

Indeed, having a career that involves working with people (which is most careers!) means using psychology every day. Teachers manage their students' behavior and foster their motivation to learn. Police officers gather eyewitness reports, elicit confessions, and monitor the behavior of both individuals and crowds. People in sales, marketing, and branding craft messages, create campaigns, and help manufacturers increase the appeal of their products. Anyone who works on a team benefits from knowing how to play nice, engage in effective problem solving, and focus on the task at hand.

Other workers shape information or technology that will be used by consumers or the public. For the information or technology to be accessible and effective, these workers need to understand how people make sense of information and the psychological barriers to modifying existing beliefs or adopting new technologies. For example, an engineer who designs cockpits for airplanes benefits from knowing how human attention shifts during an emergency. A statistician who understands how people process visual cues is well equipped to create graphs that will help consumers make accurate impressions of the data.

What about someone who works with animals? A solid grasp of psychological topics, such as the biological basis of behavior, can help in the training and retraining of nonhuman creatures. For example, an animal trainer could use reinforcement techniques (discussed in Chapter 6) to motivate an injured animal to engage in physical therapy.

Psychology is even relevant to traditionally solo enterprises. Fiction writers create compelling characters, convey personalities, indicate psychological depth, depict interpersonal struggles, and evoke emotions in readers.

Though you do not need to be a psychology major for the lessons in this book to benefit your career, majoring in psychology is a good career move. The majority of graduating psychology majors go directly into the workforce, with a median starting salary in 2018 of $57,750 (National Association of Colleges and Employers, 2019). According to 2014 data by the U.S. Census Bureau, undergraduate psychology majors are employed in a wide variety of settings and fields. The largest concentrations are in social services, management, education, and health care. Other fields include computer technology, statistics, finance, arts and entertainment, and sales.

Whatever your chosen field, understanding psychology will help you understand yourself and thus help you do your job. And if you are thinking about a career in psychology or a related field, there is good news. According to the U.S. Department of Labor (U.S. Bureau of Labor Statistics, 2015), opportunities for people with graduate degrees in psychology are expected to grow approximately 19 percent by 2024. This outlook is equally positive around the globe. ■

Q **Why would it be useful for a police detective to study psychology?**

ANSWER: Possibilities include understanding people's motives for crime and knowing the limits of human memory

Your Chapter Review

It's time to complete your study experience! Go to **INQUIZITIVE** to practice actively with this chapter's concepts and get personalized feedback along the way.

Chapter Summary

What Is Psychological Science?

1.1 Psychological Science Is the Study of Mind, Brain, and Behavior *Mind* refers to mental activity, which results from biological processes within the *brain*. *Behavior* describes the totality of observable human (or animal) actions. The term *psychologist* is used broadly to describe someone whose career involves understanding mental life or predicting behavior.

1.2 Psychological Science Teaches Critical Thinking Learning to think critically improves how people process information. Amiable skepticism requires a careful examination of how well evidence supports a conclusion. Using critical thinking skills and understanding the methods of psychological science are important for evaluating research reported in the popular media.

1.3 Psychological Science Helps Us Understand Biased or Inaccurate Thinking People engage in common biases in thinking. These biases probably evolved along with the ability to quickly categorize information and make decisions, but they often result in faulty conclusions. Some common biases in thinking include ignoring evidence (confirmation bias), seeing relationships that do not exist, accepting after-the-fact explanations, and taking mental shortcuts.

1.4 You Be the Psychologist: Why Are People Unaware of Their Weaknesses? People often fail to see their own inadequacies. People sometimes lack the expertise in a domain to know the difference between good and bad performance. Humans are also motivated to think well of themselves, so they might not internalize valid criticism. Thinking like a psychologist involves asking "why" about all aspects of human mental life and behavior.

What Is the Scientific Scope of Psychology?

1.5 Many Psychological Questions Have a Long History The nature/nurture debate questioned whether psychological characteristics are biologically innate or are acquired through education, experience, and culture. Today we know nature and nurture interact and their influences often cannot be separated. The mind/body problem questioned whether the mind and body are separate and distinct or whether the mind is simply the subjective experience of ongoing brain activity. Dualist notions about the separation of the brain and mind have been replaced with the idea that the (physical) brain enables the mind.

1.6 Mental Processes and Behaviors Serve Functions for Individuals and Groups Psychologists study mental activity and behavior using scientific methods. Following initial attempts to understand individual components of the mind, the field coalesced around the idea that the mind is too complex to understand as a collection of individual parts. Functionalism is the idea that the mind evolved to solve specific problems in the environment. Human mental activity, behavior, and even culture are guided by evolution and environmental challenges.

1.7 The Field of Psychology Spans the Range of Human Experience Psychological science now encompasses the breadth of human experience. Developmental psychologists focus on changes in mental activity and behavior across the life span. Cognitive psychologists and cognitive neuroscientists seek to understand the building blocks of thinking using tools that measure specific psychological, behavioral, and neural processes. Clinical psychologists study disorders of the mind, and health psychology examines the bidirectional relationship between mental life and physical health.

What Are the Latest Developments in Psychology?

1.8 Biology Is Increasingly Emphasized in Explaining Psychological Phenomena Tremendous advances in neuroscience have revealed the working brain. New insights into the immune, stress, and metabolic systems have revealed the complex ways that the rest of the body influences the brain and vice versa. These advances are increasing our knowledge of mind, brain, and behavior.

1.9 Psychology Is a Computational and Data Science Advances in computation have dramatically changed how psychological science is conducted. Computational modeling to identify hidden features of cognition is now common in many fields. Big data approaches use very large data sets to identify patterns and predict behavior. The open science reform movement has increased the transparency and accessibility of psychological science using data and information sharing.

1.10 Culture Provides Adaptive Solutions Cultural norms specify how people should behave in different contexts. They reflect solutions to adaptive problems that have been worked out by a group of individuals, and they are transmitted through learning.

1.11 Psychological Science Crosses Levels of Analysis Psychologists examine behavior from various analytical levels: biological (brain systems, neurochemistry, genetics), individual (personality, perception, cognition), social (interpersonal behavior), and cultural (within a single culture, across several cultures).

1.12 Psychological Education Embraces the Science of Learning Research on learning and memory has generated insights into how to improve study habits. Techniques such as distributed practice, retrieval-based learning, and elaborative interrogation have been shown to increase memory for new topics and are used throughout this book to help students learn.

1.13 Psychology Outside the Lab: How Will Psychology Benefit You in Your Career? The study of psychological science is highly relevant to multiple aspects of life, including a chosen career. There are growing opportunities for those with degrees in psychology.

Key Terms

behaviorism, p. 17
big data, p. 18
biopsychosocial model, p. 21
critical thinking, p. 5
culture, p. 10
data ethics, p. 18
distributed practice, p. 22
diversity and inclusion, p. 12
elaborative interrogation, p. 23
epigenetics, p. 16
functionalism, p. 11
interleaved practice, p. 23
mind/body problem, p. 9
natural selection, p. 12
nature/nurture debate, p. 10
open science movement, p. 18
psychological science, p. 4
replicability, p. 18
retrieval-based learning, p. 22
self-explanation, p. 23
stream of consciousness, p. 11

Practice Exercises

1. When you mention to your family that you enrolled in a psychology course, your family members share their perceptions of the field. Which of their comments demonstrates the most accurate understanding of psychological science?
   a. "You're going to learn how to get in touch with your feelings."
   b. "The concept of 'psychological science' is such an oxymoron. It is impossible to measure and study what goes on in people's heads."
   c. "You may be surprised by the range of questions psychologists ask about the mind, the brain, and behavior, and the scientific methods they use to answer those questions."
   d. "By the end of the class, you'll be able to tell me why I am the way I am."

2. Match each definition with one or more of the following biological methods of psychology: epigenetics, immunology, electroencephalography.
   a. a technique that measures changes in electrical activity near the scalp to infer neural activity
   b. the study of factors that influence gene expression without being part of the inherited genetic code
   c. the study of the bidirectional interactions between the immune system and mental life and behavior

3. Titles of recent research articles appear below. Indicate which of the four levels of analysis—cultural, social, individual, or biological—each article likely addresses.
   a. "Pals, Problems, and Personality: The Moderating Role of Personality in the Longitudinal Association Between Adolescents' and Best Friends' Delinquency" (Yu et al., 2013)

b. "The Role of Dynamic Microglial Alterations in Stress-Induced Depression and Suppressed Neurogenesis" (Kreisel et al., 2013)
c. "Culture, Gender, and School Leadership: School Leaders' Self-Perceptions in China" (Law, 2013)
d. "Anchoring Bullying and Victimization in Children Within a Five-Factor Model-Based Person-Centered Framework" (De Bolle & Tackett, 2013)

4. Match each definition below with the study technique that evidence indicates is effective in supporting learning: distributed practice, retrieval-based learning, elaborative interrogation.
   a. taking tests such as this quiz
   b. asking yourself why a fact is true or why it is true only in certain conditions
   c. learning material in several intervals that are spread over a prolonged period of time

5. Ivy and Nikole are having an argument about the nature of the mind. Ivy claims that the essence of the mind is a continuous series of thoughts that are influenced in complex ways by physical sensations in the body and stimuli in the outside world, whereas Nikole argues that the mind is distinct from the body. In this conversation, Ivy is espousing a theory that the mind is a(n) ______, and Nikole is arguing for ______.
   a. introspection; dualism
   b. stream of consciousness; the nature/nurture distinction
   c. flow state; the nature/nurture distinction
   d. stream of consciousness; dualism

6. Imagine you have decided to seek mental health counseling. You mention this to a few of your friends. Each friend shares an opinion with you. Based on your understanding of psychological science, which friend offers the strongest advice?
   a. "I wouldn't bother if I were you. All therapy is a bunch of psychobabble."
   b. "I know a therapist who uses this really cool method that can fix any problem. Seriously, she knows the secret!"
   c. "That's great! Psychologists do research to figure out which interventions are most helpful for people with different concerns."
   d. "Well, I guess if you like relaxing on couches and talking, you might get a lot out of therapy."

7. Which of the following practices are hallmarks of critical thinking? Check all that apply.
   a. asking questions
   b. considering alternative explanations
   c. considering the possibility that biases are coloring the evidence
   d. keeping an open mind
   e. looking for holes in evidence
   f. skepticism
   g. reasoning logically to see whether information makes sense
   h. accepting statements from an authority

8. Psychologists work in a wide variety of research-related subfields. Match each sample research question with one of the following subfields: industrial/organizational psychology, cognitive psychology, personality psychology, developmental psychology.
   a. How do people make decisions and solve problems?
   b. Do people who are outgoing report being happier?
   c. When do children start to form mental representations of the world?
   d. How does office design influence worker productivity?

9. You attend your friend's piano audition for a position in the student musical and you notice that he frequently misses notes and is off tempo. He does not get the spot. According to research on common biases in how people evaluate their own abilities, which of the following statements is he likely to make?
   a. "I'm not surprised, since I didn't play well."
   b. "I played as well as the person who got the spot, and so I should have gotten it."
   c. "I thought I was good, but now I see that others may have been better."
   d. "The judges must be poor interpreters of musical ability."

10. Your brother reads that research shows eating ice cream makes people more intelligent. He starts downing a pint of ice cream every day to increase his intelligence. To help your brother better understand this claim (and avoid a stomachache), which of the following questions would help you evaluate whether to believe the study? Check all that apply.
   a. "Does the article mention how much ice cream people had to eat to become more intelligent?"
   b. "Does the article say how the researchers measured intelligence?"
   c. "Does the article mention whether the person who conducted the research is a famous scholar?"
   d. "How did the researchers design the study? Were they doing good science?"
   e. "Who sponsored the study? Was it paid for and conducted by researchers at the world's largest ice cream company?"

B2B SALES STRATEGY & BRAND COMMUNICATION
SALES STATS
UNDERSTANDING
PEOPLE IN THE
WORK PLACE
HOW TO
SUCCEED
29%
23%
12%
11%
35%
22%
15%
15%
22%
INVESTMENT PLAN

2 Research Methodology

Big Questions

IN 2003, A CHINESE PHARMACIST named Hon Lik patented a device that used ultrasonic waves to vaporize liquid containing nicotine (**FIGURE 2.1**). Few people had heard of e-cigarettes when Hon's invention hit the U.S. market in 2007. But the use of e-cigarettes increased exponentially in the years since, and by 2019 more than a quarter of U.S. high school students and more than 10 percent of middle school students reported having used them (Cullen et al., 2019). Despite beliefs about their safety, e-cigarettes contain many toxic and cancer-causing substances and are particularly harmful to young people.

What factors lead people to start using e-cigarettes? What are effective ways to help them stop? Indeed, can scientists be confident in any claim about human psychology and behavior? This chapter will describe how evidence is gathered and verified in psychology. By understanding how psychologists study human behavior and mental processes, you will learn how to interpret information that is being presented to you. And by understanding how to interpret information, you will become an educated consumer and presenter of information.

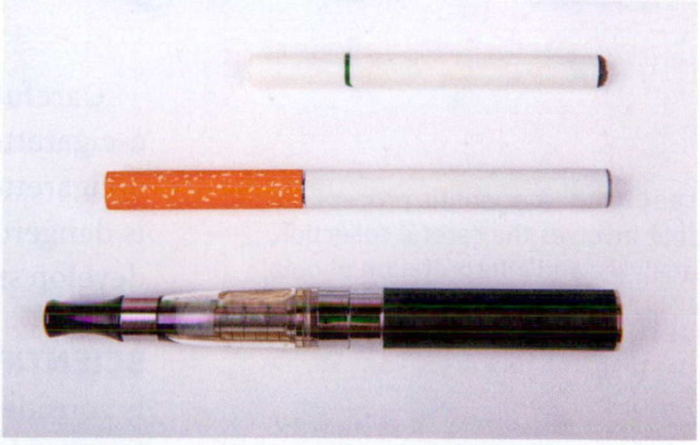

FIGURE 2.1
E-cigarettes
E-cigarettes have been marketed as an alternative to combustible tobacco cigarettes. But they contain many harmful chemicals and remain largely unregulated.

How Is the Scientific Method Used in Psychological Research?

Learning Objectives

- Identify the three primary goals of science.
- Describe the scientific method.
- Differentiate among theories, hypotheses, and research.

Psychology is a science. As scientists, psychologists gain accurate knowledge about behavior and mental processes only by observing the world and measuring aspects of it. This approach is called *empiricism*. Empirical research involves data collection and analysis and requires carefully planned, systematic steps. Using the methods of science allows psychologists to be confident that empirical results provide a true understanding of mental activity and behavior.

2.1 Science Has Three Primary Goals

There are three primary goals of science: *description*, *prediction*, and *explanation*. Psychological science uses research to describe *what* a phenomenon is, predict *when and where* it will occur, and explain the mechanisms behind *why* it occurs. For example, consider the observation that people vape even though they know it can be harmful. To understand how this behavior happens, we need to address each of the three goals.

We begin by asking: How many people really use e-cigarettes, and are they aware of the harms? Answering this question can help us describe the phenomenon of vaping tobacco products, specifically measuring the *prevalence* of this unsafe behavior. Related descriptive questions are: What are people's beliefs about vaping? How did they start? Answering these questions can help us predict who is more likely to vape and what causes them to begin in the first place.

Next, what psychological processes give rise to the decision to start vaping? Answering this question can help us understand the causal factors that explain why people vape. Ultimately, knowing about the causes of vaping can help inform prevention and treatment programs that will benefit public health. Psychological questions relevant to treatment include: What are the psychological aspects of quitting that such programs can target? Which people at risk to begin vaping would benefit most from prevention programs?

Careful scientific study also enables us to understand other aspects of e-cigarette use, such as why people do it in the first place. Understanding how e-cigarette use is harmful and why people continue do it, even when they know it is dangerous, will enable scientists, the medical community, and policymakers to develop strategies to reduce the behavior.

research A scientific process that involves the careful collection, analysis, and interpretation of data.

data Measurements gathered during the research process.

scientific method A systematic and dynamic procedure of observing and measuring phenomena, used to achieve the goals of description, prediction, control, and explanation; it involves an interaction among research, theories, and hypotheses.

SCIENTIFIC METHOD Scientific evidence obtained through empirical research is considered the best possible evidence for supporting a claim. **Research** involves the careful collection, analysis, and interpretation of **data**, which are measurements gathered during the research process. In conducting research, scientists follow a systematic procedure called the **scientific method**. This procedure begins with the observation of a phenomenon and the question of why that phenomenon occurred.

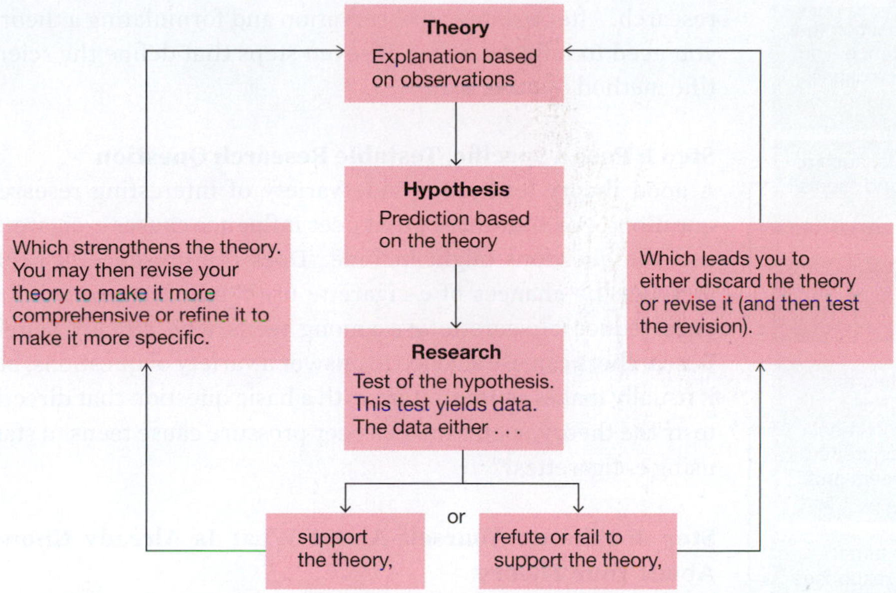

FIGURE 2.2
The Scientific Method
The scientific method is a cyclical process: A theory is generated based on evidence from many observations and refined based on hypothesis tests (scientific studies). The theory guides scientists in casting one or more testable hypotheses. Scientists then conduct research to test the hypotheses. Sound research produces findings that will prompt scientists to reevaluate and adjust the theory. A good theory evolves over time, and the result is an increasingly accurate model of some phenomenon.

THE ROLE OF THEORY The scientific method is an interaction among research, theories, and hypotheses (**FIGURE 2.2**). A **theory** is an explanation or model of how a phenomenon works. Consisting of interconnected ideas or concepts, a theory is used to explain prior observations and to make predictions about future events. A **hypothesis** is a specific, testable prediction, narrower than the theory it is based on.

theory A model of interconnected ideas or concepts that explains what is observed and makes predictions about future events. Theories are based on empirical evidence.

hypothesis A specific, testable prediction, narrower than the theory it is based on.

How can we know whether a theory is good? The best theories are those that produce a wide variety of testable hypotheses. An especially important feature of good theories is that they should be *falsifiable*. That is, it should be possible to test hypotheses that show the theory is wrong. For example, a theory of cognitive development might predict that basic numerical skills such as counting must develop before more advanced skills such as subtraction. Evidence that children can subtract before they can count would falsify the claim, calling the theory into question. Falsifiable theories help advance science because our understanding of a phenomenon is enhanced both when evidence supports a theory and when it does not.

Good theories also tend toward simplicity. This idea has historical roots in the writings of the fourteenth-century English philosopher William of Occam. Occam proposed that when two competing theories exist to explain the same phenomenon, the simpler of the two theories is generally preferred. This principle is known as *Occam's razor* or the *law of parsimony*. There is little need for more-complex theories if a simple one captures the data.

Q Which scientific goal is fulfilled by a project seeking to understand the causes of teen vaping?

ANSWER: explanation

2.2 The Scientific Method Is a Systematic Way to Test Hypotheses

The opening of this chapter considered teen vaping. Let's say that, based on what you have read online, you develop the theory that peer influence causes teen e-cigarette use. To determine whether this theory is accurate, you need to conduct

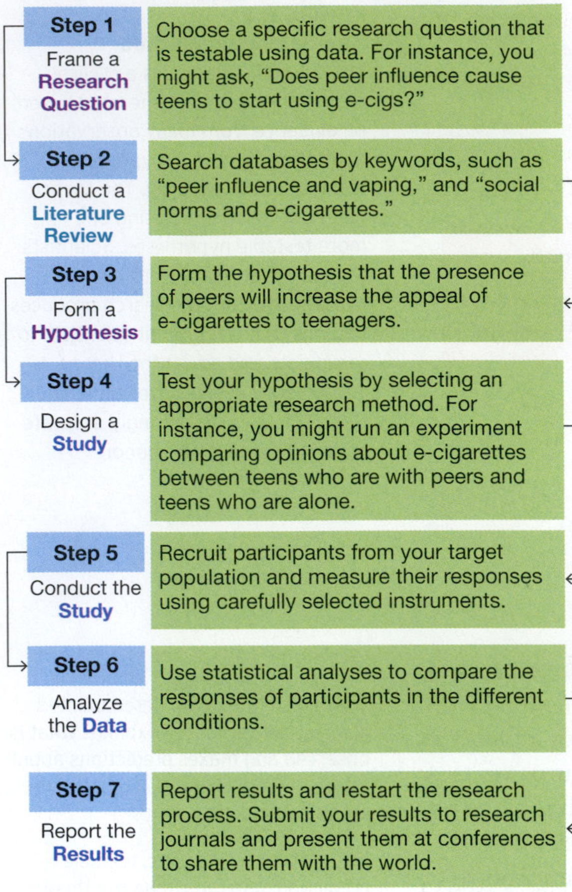

Step 1
Frame a Research Question
Choose a specific research question that is testable using data. For instance, you might ask, "Does peer influence cause teens to start using e-cigs?"
Step 2
Conduct a Literature Review
Search databases by keywords, such as "peer influence and vaping," and "social norms and e-cigarettes."
Step 3
Form a Hypothesis
Form the hypothesis that the presence of peers will increase the appeal of e-cigarettes to teenagers.
Step 4
Design a Study
Test your hypothesis by selecting an appropriate research method. For instance, you might run an experiment comparing opinions about e-cigarettes between teens who are with peers and teens who are alone.
Step 5
Conduct the Study
Recruit participants from your target population and measure their responses using carefully selected instruments.
Step 6
Analyze the Data
Use statistical analyses to compare the responses of participants in the different conditions.
Step 7
Report the Results
Report results and restart the research process. Submit your results to research journals and present them at conferences to share them with the world.

FIGURE 2.3
The Scientific Method in Action

research. After making an observation and formulating a theory, you need to follow a series of seven steps that define the scientific method (**FIGURE 2.3**):

Step 1: Pose a Specific, Testable Research Question

A good theory leads to a wide variety of interesting research questions. For your theory that peer influence causes e-cigarette use, the questions might include "Does the presence of peers increase the chances of e-cigarette use?" and "Can peer influence reduce e-cigarette use among teens who already vape?" Researchers can use science to answer a variety of questions, but it usually makes sense to start with a basic question that directly tests the theory, such as "Does peer pressure cause teens to start using e-cigarettes?"

Step 2: Educate Yourself About What Is Already Known About Your Theory

Once you have a research question, you want to search the literature to see what scientists have already discovered that is relevant to your theory. A literature review is a review of the scientific literature related to your theory. There are many resources available to assist with literature reviews, including scientific research databases such as PsycINFO, Google Scholar, and PubMed. You can search these databases by keywords, such as "peer pressure and vaping" or "social norms and e-cigarettes." The results of your searches will reveal whether and how other scientists have tested the same idea or similar ones. Their approaches and findings will help guide the direction of your research.

Step 3: Form a Hypothesis That Will Guide Your Studies

Based on what you learn in your literature review, you design tests—that is, specific research studies—aimed at examining the theory's predictions. These specific, testable research predictions are your *hypotheses*. Results from a test that are consistent with a good hypothesis can provide support for your theory. And, equally important, results that are inconsistent with your hypothesis should be taken as evidence against it.

Step 4: Design a Study

Designing a study refers to deciding which research method (and thus, level of analysis) you want to use to test your hypothesis. To test whether peer influence is related to e-cigarette use, you could conduct a survey: Give people a questionnaire that asks how many of their friends use e-cigarettes and whether and how often they themselves vape. A survey like this is a good way to get some initial insight into your hypothesis. In a large survey of high school students, about 50 percent of teens who had three or four friends who used e-cigarettes also used them, whereas 80 percent of teens with no e-cigarette-smoking friends also did not use them (Barrington-Trimis et al., 2015).

Instead of a survey, you could conduct a naturalistic observation: Watch a group of teens over time and record whether they use e-cigarettes. You could strengthen the design by including a control group. For example, you might follow for a year two groups of teenagers who do not use e-cigarettes at the beginning of your study: one group of teens that has close friends who use e-cigarettes and another group of teens that does not. You would track whether teens in both groups start using e-cigarettes.

Alternatively, you could perform an actual experiment, assigning one group of people to experience peer pressure to use e-cigarettes and a second group not to experience it. Obviously, this experiment would be risky and unethical. For research like this, scientists use simulated peer pressure or pretend scenarios in the lab that mimic what teens might experience in real life. As you will learn later in this chapter, there are advantages and disadvantages to each of these methods.

Step 5: Conduct the Study

Once you choose your research method, you conduct the study: Recruit participants and measure their responses. Many people call this step collecting data or gathering data. If you conduct a survey to see whether people whose friends use e-cigarettes are more likely to start using themselves, your data will provide information about your participants' and their friends' e-cigarette use. You must be careful in determining the appropriate number and type of participants and how you determine who has and has not yet started using e-cigarettes.

All research involves variables. A **variable** is something in the world that can vary and that the researcher can manipulate (change), measure (evaluate), or both. In a study of social influences on e-cigarette use, some of the variables could be the age at which someone started using e-cigarettes, the number of times they use e-cigarettes in a given period of time, and the probability that a friend is around when they use e-cigarettes. Researchers must define these variables precisely and in ways that reflect the methods used to assess them. You will do so by developing an **operational definition** for each of your variables. Operational definitions are important for research. They *qualify* (describe) and *quantify* (measure) variables so the variables can be understood objectively. Using good operational definitions lets other researchers know precisely what variables you used, how you manipulated them, and how you measured them. These concrete details make it possible for other researchers to use identical methods in their attempts to replicate your findings.

variable Something in the world that can vary and that a researcher can manipulate (change), measure (evaluate), or both.

operational definition A definition that *qualifies* (describes) and *quantifies* (measures) a variable so the variable can be understood objectively.

For example, you will need to decide exactly how to qualify "friend," "e-cigarette use," and "start using e-cigarettes" and how to ask participants about them. In describing "friend," what happens if Person A says she is friends with Person B, but Person B does not report being friends with Person A? What if one teen uses e-cigarettes but his friends are unaware that he uses? Then, you will need to operationalize the initiation of e-cigarette use. Does a person need to use e-cigarettes a certain number of times, or does any use count as starting to use?

Step 6: Analyze the Data

The next step is to analyze your data. There are two main ways to analyze data. First, you want to describe the data. What was the average amount of peer influence? How "typical" is that average? Second, you will want to know what conclusions you can draw from your data. You need to know whether your results are meaningful or whether they happened by chance. Answering this question using statistical methods enables you to make inferences about your data—to infer whether your findings might be true for the general population. You accomplish data analyses by using statistics, which are described later in the chapter.

Step 7: Report the Results

Unreported results have no value, because no one can use any of the information. Instead, scientists make their findings public to benefit society, to support the scientific culture, and to permit other scientists to build on their work. Various forums are available for distributing the results of scientific research.

Brief or initial reports can be presented at scientific conferences, where scientists present work in short talks or on printed posters. During poster sessions, researchers stand by their posters and answer questions for those who stop by to read the poster (**FIGURE 2.4**). Conference presentations are especially good for reporting preliminary data or for presenting exciting or cutting-edge results.

Full reports can be published in a peer-reviewed scientific journal or on a preprint server, where other scientists can evaluate and comment on the work. *Peer review* is a process by which other scientists with similar expertise evaluate and critique research reports. Peer review provides a check to ensure the quality of the methods and the validity of the conclusions. Preprints are increasingly popular because they enable scientists to present results to the field and the general public far more quickly than they would otherwise be able to in scientific journals. Preprints also can be reviewed by many people. Preprints can be peer reviewed, but only after they are made public. Whether published in a journal or made available as a preprint, full reports consist of the background and significance of the research, the full methodology for how the question was studied, the complete results of the statistical analyses, and a discussion of what the results mean in relation to the accumulated body of scientific evidence.

Ideally, the results of research are relevant to the general public because they speak to important or interesting topics. People in the media attend scientific conferences and read scientific journals so they can report on exciting findings.

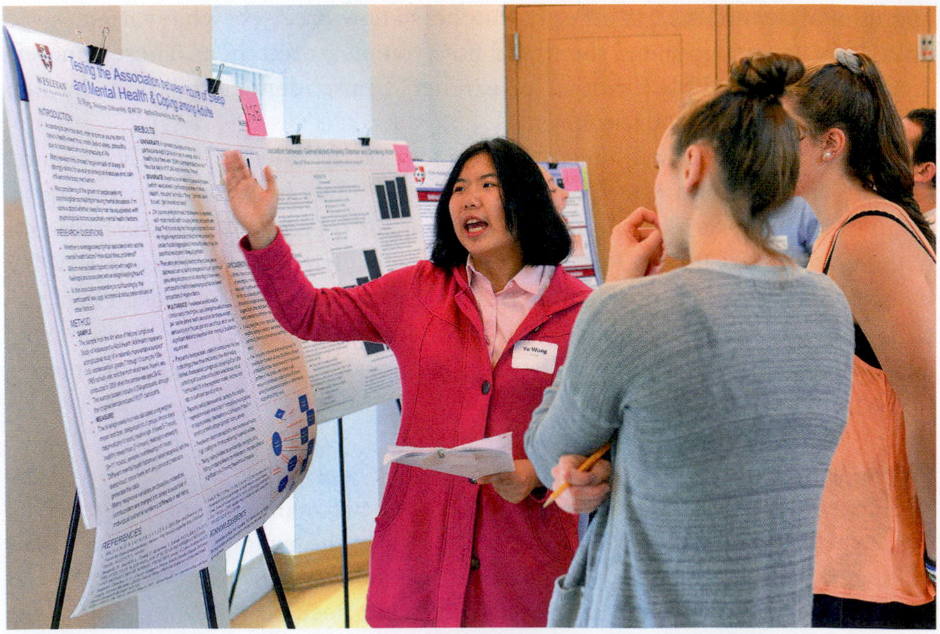

FIGURE 2.4
Poster Sessions
A scientific poster presents information about the hypotheses, methods, results, and conclusions of a research study. During a poster session, the researchers discuss their findings with interested observers.

Scientists are increasingly communicating directly to general audiences through blogs, social media, and video presentations of their work.

Q **In the scientific method, what do you call a specific, testable prediction?**

ANSWER: hypothesis

2.3 The Scientific Method Is Cyclical

Good research reflects the cyclical process shown in Figure 2.2. Once the results of a research study are in, the researchers return to the original theory to evaluate the implications of the data. If the study used appropriate methods and data analysis to test the hypothesis, the data either support and strengthen the theory or suggest that the theory be modified or discarded. Then the process starts all over again. This is important because no single study can provide a definitive answer about any phenomenon. Instead, we have more confidence in scientific findings when research outcomes are replicated.

REPLICATION Replication involves repeating a study to see if the results are the same (or similar). When the results from two or more studies are the same, or at least support the same conclusion, confidence increases in the findings. Ideally, researchers not affiliated with those who produced the original finding conduct replication studies. These independent replications provide more powerful support because they rule out the possibility that some feature of the original setting, such as the personality of the experimenter, may have contributed to the findings.

replication Repetition of a research study to confirm or contradict the results.

The past few decades have seen an explosion of research findings, particularly in medicine. Unfortunately, it seems that one week we hear about some finding and then the next week we hear about a conflicting finding. For example, is a diet heavy in protein and light in carbohydrates healthy or not? It is hard for nonexperts to know what to believe about such phenomena. Recently, numerous scientists have called for new efforts to increase the likelihood that published studies are accurate (Ioannidis, 2014). Replication is an important method for increasing our confidence in scientific outcomes (Goodman et al., 2016).

The growing emphasis on replication has also affected psychological science (Klein et al., 2014). In an initiative called the Reproducibility Project, a large group of psychologists sought to replicate findings that had been published during the year 2008 in three selected journals. Of the 100 studies they repeated, only 39 percent replicated (Open Science Collaboration, 2015). Their findings, published in the prestigious journal *Science*, provoked strong reactions from many psychologists.

WHY MIGHT A STUDY NOT REPLICATE? Studies do not always replicate. A challenge for scientists in psychology and all other fields is to understand why. Sometimes studies fail to replicate because the theory itself is wrong and the

false positive A result that occurs when there is no real effect but a study produces a statistically significant result by chance.

original study was a **false positive**. A false positive occurs when the hypothesis under investigation is false but the study produces a seemingly trustworthy result by chance. False positives are inevitable in science, but it is possible to keep their frequency low.

It is also possible that a study does not replicate because factors that are not hypothesized to be important turn out to make a difference. For example, most psychologists would expect research participants to complete a survey the same way whether it is administered in person or online, but the format can sometimes make a difference in their responses (Luttrell et al., 2017). Studies about aspects of human psychology and behavior that are less sensitive to minor factors like these are more likely to replicate (Van Bavel et al., 2016).

questionable research practices Practices that unintentionally make the research less replicable.

However, for many years, scientists engaged in a number of **questionable research practices** that unintentionally made their studies less likely to replicate. The open science movement has educated researchers about the effects of these practices, but they continue to appear in some studies.

- *Small samples.* Psychology researchers estimate how larger populations of people would respond by testing smaller, representative samples of people. It is intuitive that larger samples would produce more accurate estimates of how the entire population would respond. Consider, for example, a study of attitudes about wearing face masks among incoming first-year students at your college or university. A study that includes half of all incoming students is likely to provide a far better approximation of what the entire population feels than a study that includes only 10 incoming students. The issue is how strongly random chance influences the smaller sample. What if 8 out of the 10 students in the smaller sample happened to come from the same town? Or if 9 of them identified as women? A larger sample is less prone to be skewed toward one particular town, gender, or any other factor that might distort the results. Scientists might assume that a small sample is sufficient, when a larger one is actually required to achieve an accurate estimation of the population effects (Bakker et al., 2016).

HARKing "Hypothesizing after the results are known" instead of generating a theory before running the study and analyzing the results.

- *HARKing.* The morning after every surprising election, political pundits take to the airwaves and explain why they saw the result coming (**FIGURE 2.5**). These predictions are not credible because pundits can selectively focus on data that supported the outcome and ignore the data that did not. In the scientific setting, this kind of after-the-fact prediction is a questionable research practice called "hypothesizing after the results are known," or **HARKing** (Kerr, 1998). HARKing is problematic because it can leave readers thinking that the study was designed to test the one and only hypothesis that was supported, when in fact random chance could have led to support for any number of hypotheses. Researchers are allowed to offer post hoc ("after the fact") guesses about why they obtained their results, but they must also be explicit about what the predicted results were a priori (before the study was conducted).
- p-*hacking.* In a simpler world, a study would have one hypothesis that could be tested with one statistical test. That test would yield a *p* value, from which, if it were less than 0.05, the researchers could infer that the data

FIGURE 2.5

Hypothesizing After the Results Are Known (HARKing)

It is problematic to generate a hypothesis only *after* the results are known. Results cannot be used to support a hypothesis if the results themselves helped form that hypothesis. Surprising findings need to be replicated in a new, independent study. The practice of preregistration aims to prevent HARKing because it forces researchers to lock in their hypothesis before starting a study.

supported their hypothesis. Instead, researchers make many choices about which data to include or exclude, which statistical tests to run, and which variables to use in the analysis. Running statistical tests over and over with different variations until one of them yields a statistically significant (trustworthy) result is called **p-hacking** (Simmons et al., 2011). (The concept of statistical significance is discussed further in Section 2.14.) Researchers often engage in this practice unintentionally, believing that selecting the optimal subset of their data or analysis will improve the quality of their research. Nonetheless, reporting only an analysis that produced the desired result and omitting others that did not overestimates the strength of the results.

- *Underreporting null effects.* A null effect means finding no difference between conditions or no relationship between variables. In the same way that *p*-hacking is misleading because analyses are omitted from a paper, underreporting null effects can cause readers to draw invalid inferences because entire studies or hypothesis tests are missing from the story. Researchers sometimes run several studies or include redundant measures within a study that all test the same hypothesis. This can become a questionable research practice if the researcher reports only the studies or measures that support the hypothesis. Omitting any inconsistent results amounts to running replications without reporting the failures to replicate. As a result, underreporting null effects can mislead readers about the strength of the evidence for a hypothesis.

***p*-hacking** Testing the same hypothesis using statistical tests in different variations until one produces a statistically significant result.

BEST PRACTICES FOR PSYCHOLOGICAL SCIENCE As discussed in Chapter 1, psychology researchers have embraced a set of reforms that are leading to higher-quality science (Nosek & Bar-Anan, 2012). The animating principle behind the open science movement is transparency about all aspects of the research process. The open science movement is making it the norm in psychological science to document hypotheses in advance; articulate a specific analysis plan; and share research materials, data, and reports freely with other researchers. Together, this set of open practices allows readers to be fully informed consumers of research who can draw valid inferences on their own (Vazire, 2018).

Open science is a set of tools and strategies that systematically protect the field against questionable research practices, including those described above. For example, **preregistration** is when researchers lay out their hypotheses, methods, and analysis plan ahead of time and publish it on a time-stamped website (Chambers, 2017). When a study is preregistered, readers can know whether the results were predicted a priori, the analyses presented were planned in advance, and all the tests and studies were reported. Preregistrations can also include a special analysis called a *power analysis* that helps researchers determine whether their sample size is sufficiently large to detect an effect that would be meaningful.

preregistration Documenting a study's hypotheses, methods, and analysis plan ahead of time and publishing it on a time-stamped website.

META-ANALYSIS **Meta-analysis** is a type of study that, as its name implies, is an analysis of multiple analyses. In other words, it is a study of studies that have already been conducted. With meta-analysis, many studies that have addressed the same issue are combined and summarized in one "study of studies."

meta-analysis A "study of studies" that combines the findings of multiple studies to arrive at a conclusion.

Suppose that 10 studies have been conducted on men's and women's effectiveness as leaders. Among these 10 studies, five found no differences, two favored women, and three favored men. Researchers conducting a meta-analysis would not just count up the numbers of different findings from the research literature. Instead, they would weight more heavily those studies that had larger samples,

FIGURE 2.6
Larger Samples
Suppose researchers want to compare how many women go to the beach versus how many men do. Why might the results be more accurate if the researchers use a large sample (such as the big picture here) rather than a small sample (such as the detail)?

which are more likely to provide more-accurate reflections of what is true in a population (**FIGURE 2.6**). The researchers would also consider the size of each effect. That is, they would factor in whether each study found a large difference, a small difference, or no difference between the groups being compared—in this case, between women and men. (The researchers who conducted this meta-analysis on men's and women's effectiveness found no overall differences; Eagly et al., 1995.)

Because meta-analysis combines the results of separate studies, many researchers believe that meta-analysis provides stronger evidence than the results of any single study. Meta-analysis has the concept of replication built into it.

Q How does preregistration prevent HARKing?

ANSWER: It forces researchers to publicly document their hypothesis before conducting a study.

2.4 Critical Thinking Is Essential to Evaluating Scientific Findings

As you learned in Chapter 1, one paramount goal of your education is to become a critical thinker. Critical thinking was defined in Chapter 1 as systematically questioning and evaluating information using well-supported evidence. Critical thinking is a skill: It is not something you can just memorize and learn, but something that improves over time with practice. Many of your courses should provide opportunities for you to use your critical thinking abilities. Critical thinking is not just for scientists. It is essential for becoming an educated consumer of information.

To develop the skeptical mindset you need for critical thinking, you should question every kind of information. For any claim you see or hear, ask yourself: What is the evidence in support of that claim? For example, the opening vignette of this chapter made the claim that vaping is particularly harmful to young people. What kind of evidence was presented in support of this claim? Was the evidence based on direct, unbiased observation, or did it seem to be the result of rumor, hearsay, or intuition? Now consider your own beliefs and behavior. Do you believe that vaping is dangerous? If you do, what evidence led you to this belief? What is the quality of the evidence? If you do not believe vaping is dangerous, why? Are you aware of the evidence on both sides, or have you only seen evidence in favor of one side?

Another aspect of thinking critically is to ask for the definition of each part of a claim. For example, imagine you hear the claim that using a cell phone while driving is more dangerous than driving while intoxicated. Upon hearing this claim, a critical thinker will ask for definitions. For example, what do they mean by "using a cell phone"? Do they mean talking or texting? Do they mean a handheld or a hands-free device? And what do they mean by "intoxicated"? Would achieving this state require only a little alcohol or a lot of alcohol? Could the person have used another drug?

Answering questions of this kind is the second step in critical thinking: the systematic evaluation of information. To answer these questions, we need to go to the source of the claim.

To get to the source of any claim, you need to think about where you first saw or heard it. Did you hear the claim on TV or the radio? Did you read about it in a newspaper? Did you see it on the internet? Was it from a website known for *fake news*, which is not news at all but stories without supporting evidence that are made up for personal reasons, advertising, or political purposes? Next, you need to think about the evidence offered by the source to support the claim.

Here is where the "well-supported evidence" comes in. Was the evidence behind the claim derived from the scientific method? If so, were the methods sound? Or does the evidence appeal to intuition or stand simply on the authority of the person making the claim? Did the source retrieve this information from a newswire? Did it come from an interview with a scientist? Was it summarized from a scientific journal?

In science, well-supported evidence typically means research reports based on empirical data that are published in peer-reviewed journals or preprint servers (**FIGURE 2.7**). Peer review usually happens before publication, but it can happen after studies are made public in online forums. Peer review ensures that reports describe research studies that are well designed (using appropriate research and analysis methods, considering all factors that could explain the findings), that are conducted in an ethical manner, and that address an important question.

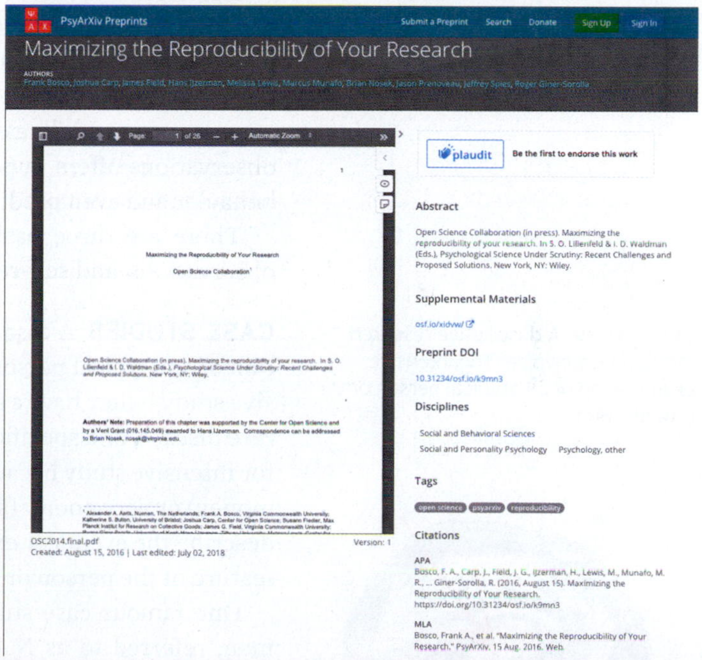

FIGURE 2.7
Preprint Servers
Scientific manuscripts can be shared on preprint servers, where other scientists can evaluate them and the general public can access the methods and results.

However, peer review does not mean that flawed studies are never published. Scientists regularly identify issues with published papers and only rarely do the authors publish a correction or retract the paper. Thus, critical thinkers must *always* stay vigilant—always be on the lookout for unreasonable claims and conclusions that may not be valid interpretations of the data. Hone your critical thinking skills by practicing them as often as possible.

Q Why would a critical thinker place more trust in a publication that has been peer-reviewed?

ANSWER: The peer review helps ensure that the study was well designed, conducted in an ethical manner, and addresses an important question.

Learning Objectives

- Distinguish among descriptive studies, correlational studies, and experiments.
- List the advantages and disadvantages of different research methods.
- Explain the difference between random sampling and random assignment, and explain when each might be important.

What Types of Studies Are Used in Psychological Research?

Once a researcher has defined a hypothesis, the next issue to be addressed is the type of research method to be used. There are three main types of research methods: *descriptive*, *correlational*, and *experimental*. These methods differ in the extent to which the researcher has control over the variables in the study. The amount of control over the variables in turn determines the type of conclusions the researcher can draw from the data.

2.5 Descriptive Research Consists of Case Studies, Observation, and Self-Report Methods

descriptive research Research methods that involve observing behavior to describe that behavior objectively and systematically.

Descriptive research involves observing behavior to *describe* that behavior objectively and systematically. Descriptive research helps psychologists achieve the scientific goals of describing human mental life and behavior and (sometimes) predicting when or how behaviors might occur. However, by nature, descriptive research cannot achieve the goal of explanation. Only the experimental method, described later in this chapter, can do that.

Descriptive methods are widely used to assess many types of behavior. For example, an observer performing descriptive research might record the types of foods that people eat in cafeterias, count the number and types of behaviors that penguins engage in during their mating season, or tally the number of times poverty or mental illness is mentioned during a presidential debate. Each of these observations offers important information that can be used to describe current behavior and even predict future behavior.

There are three basic types of descriptive research methods: case studies, observations, and self-report methods and interviews.

case study A descriptive research method that involves the intensive examination of an atypical person or organization.

CASE STUDIES A **case study** is the intensive observation, recording, and description of an atypical person or organization. Individuals might be selected for intensive study if they have a special or unique aspect, such as an exceptional memory, a rare disease, or a specific type of brain damage. An organization might be selected for intensive study because it is doing something very well (such as making a lot of money) or very poorly (such as losing a lot of money). The goal of a case study is to describe the events or experiences that led up to or resulted from the exceptional feature of the person or organization.

One famous case study in psychological science involves a young American man, referred to as N.A., whose unusual injury impaired his memory (Squire, 1987). After a brief stint in college, N.A. joined the Air Force and was stationed in the Azores. One night, he was assembling a model airplane in his room. His roommate was joking around with a miniature fencing foil, pretending to jab at the back of N.A.'s head. When N.A. turned around suddenly, his roommate accidentally stabbed him through the nose and up into his brain (**FIGURE 2.8**). Although N.A. seemed to recover from his injury in most ways, he developed extreme problems remembering events that occurred after the injury. He could remember events before his accident, but he simply could not remember new information. He had trouble watching television because he would forget the story lines, and he had difficulty having conversations because he would forget what others had just said. The case study of N.A. spurred researchers to generate new hypotheses about how the brain supports memory.

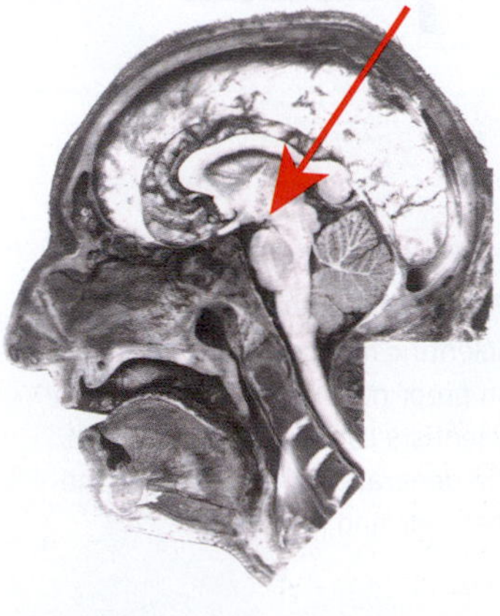

FIGURE 2.8
Case Study Data
The damage in this region to Patient N.A. provided new insights into how the brain creates memories.

Not all people with brain injuries suffer the same types of challenges as N.A. Such differences highlight the major limitation with case studies. Because only one person or organization is the focus of a case study, scientists cannot tell from that study if the same thing would happen to other people or organizations who have the same experiences. The findings from case studies do not necessarily *generalize*, or apply to the general population.

OBSERVATIONAL STUDIES Two main types of observational techniques are used in research: participant observation and naturalistic observation. In **participant observation** (**FIGURE 2.9**), the researcher is involved in the situation. In **naturalistic observation** (**FIGURE 2.10**), the observer is passive, remains separated from the situation, and makes no attempt to change or alter ongoing behavior.

FIGURE 2.9
Participant Observation
Researchers can study human behavior by observing it in the world. Scientists have learned which factors contribute to youth smoking by observing children and teenagers at tobacco points of sale.

Observation in the scientific sense involves systematically assessing and *coding* overt behavior. Suppose you hear that one popular student in a middle school dissuaded her entire class from using e-cigarettes. You develop the hypothesis that people with high status within a social network can be exceptionally influential on the behavior of others. How would you operationally define "high status"? How would you measure someone's being "exceptionally influential"? Once you have defined your terms, you collect data by observing the behavior of students in a middle school. Then you need to code the behaviors you observe. This coding might involve narrative summaries of patterns of behavior. Alternatively, you could count the number of times students mimic the behavior of high-status individuals after interacting with them. You might then compare how often students mimic after interacting with more versus less popular peers. Indeed, research has shown that the behavior of an entire school class can be altered by changing the behavior of just a few high-status people (Paluck et al., 2016).

FIGURE 2.10
Naturalistic Observation
Using naturalistic observation, the primatologist Jane Goodall observes a family of chimpanzees. Animals are more likely to act naturally in their native habitats than in captivity.

SELF-REPORTS AND INTERVIEWS Ideally, observation is an unobtrusive approach to studying behavior. By contrast, asking people about themselves, their thoughts, their actions, and their feelings is a much more interactive way of collecting data. Methods of posing questions to participants include surveys, interviews, and questionnaires. The type of information sought can range from demographic facts (e.g., ethnicity, age, religious affiliation) to past behaviors, personal attitudes, beliefs, and so on: "Have you ever used an illegal drug?" "Should people who drink and drive be jailed for a first offense?" "Are you comfortable sending food back to the kitchen in a restaurant when there is a problem?" Questions such as these require people to recall certain events from their lives or reflect on their mental or emotional states.

Self-report methods, such as surveys or questionnaires, can be used to gather data from a large number of people in a short time. Responses can be invited in person or via the internet, phone, or mail from a sample drawn from the population of interest. Self-report surveys are easy to administer and cost-efficient. Responses on surveys are usually numeric, for instance on a 1-to-5 scale of liking, or short answer.

Interviews, another type of interactive method, can be used successfully with groups that cannot be studied through surveys or questionnaires, such as young children. Responses to interviews are typically spoken or written in sentences or paragraphs. Interviews are also helpful in gaining a more in-depth view of a respondent's opinions, experiences, and attitudes. Thus, the answers from interviewees sometimes inspire avenues of inquiry that the researchers had not planned. Detailed interviews are a method that psychologists have

participant observation A type of descriptive study in which the researcher is involved in the situation.

naturalistic observation A type of descriptive study in which the researcher is a passive observer, separated from the situation and making no attempt to change or alter ongoing behavior.

self-report methods Methods of data collection in which people are asked to provide information about themselves, such as in surveys or questionnaires.

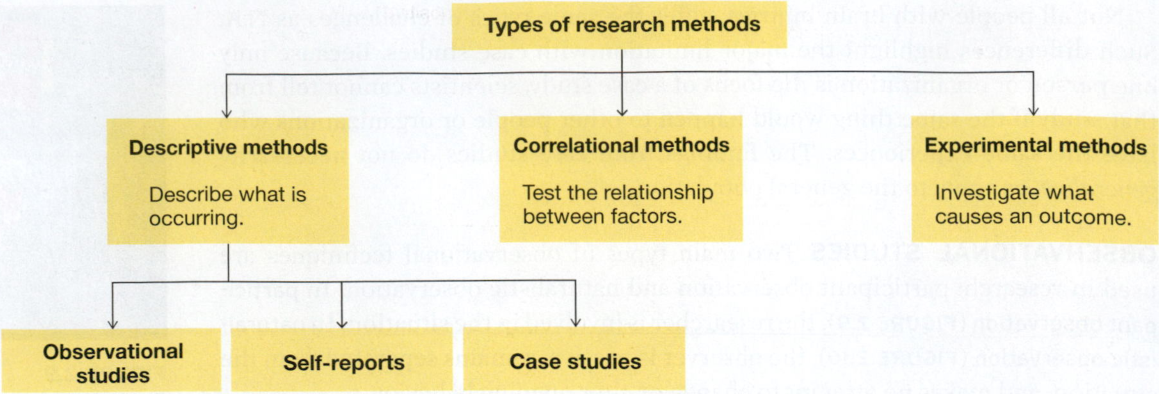

FIGURE 2.11
Types of Research Methods

in common with sociologists, who also use interviews to learn about a given culture or group of people. (For a recap of the types of research methods, see FIGURE 2.11.)

Q What is a major limitation of case studies?

ANSWER: Their findings might not generalize, or apply, to people beyond the particular case.

2.6 Correlational Studies Describe and Predict How Variables Are Related

correlational studies A research method that describes and predicts how variables are naturally related in the real world, without any attempt by the researcher to alter them or assign causation between them.

scatterplot A graphical depiction of the relationship between two variables.

Correlational studies examine how variables are naturally related in the real world, without any attempt by the researcher to alter them or conclude that one variable causes the other. Correlational studies are used to describe some types of relationships between variables, but they cannot be used to determine causal relationships between variables.

DIRECTION OF CORRELATION The first step in examining the correlation between two variables is to create a **scatterplot**. This type of graph provides a convenient picture of the data. Some sample scatterplots and their corresponding correlation coefficients can be seen in FIGURE 2.12.

When higher values on one variable predict higher values on a second variable (and lower predict lower), we say there is a *positive correlation* between them. A positive correlation describes a situation where both variables either increase or decrease together—they "move" in the same direction. For example, people with higher ACT scores generally have higher college GPAs. People with lower ACT scores generally have lower college GPAs. However, remember that correlation does not equal "cause and effect." Scoring higher or lower on the ACT will not *cause* you to earn a higher or lower GPA.

Remember, too, that *positive* in this case does not mean "good." For example, there is a strong positive correlation between smoking and cancer. There is nothing good about this relationship. The correlation simply describes how the two variables are related: In general, people who smoke experience higher rates of cancer. The more they smoke, the higher their risk of getting cancer.

In a *negative correlation*, the variables move in opposite directions. An increase in one variable predicts a decrease in the other variable. A decrease in one variable predicts an increase in the other variable. Here, *negative* does not mean "bad."

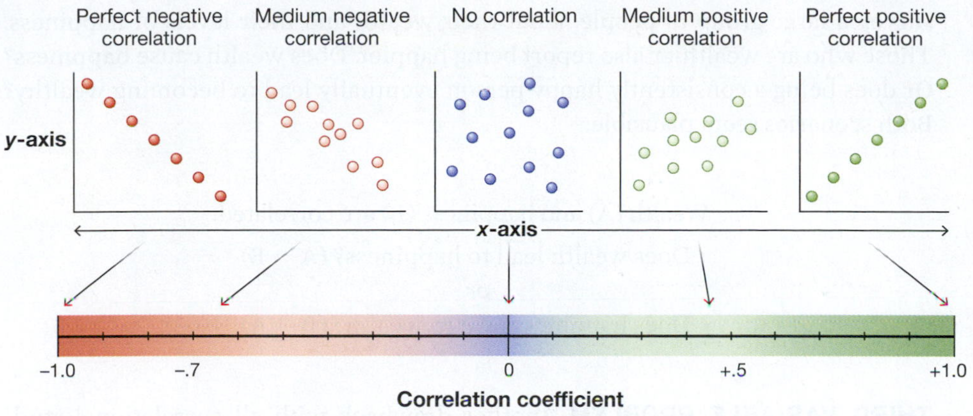

FIGURE 2.12
Strength and Direction of Correlations
Correlations can have values between -1.0 and +1.0. These values reveal the strength and direction of relationships between two variables. The greater the scatter of values, the lower the correlation. A perfect correlation occurs when all the values fall on a straight line.

Consider exercise and heart disease. In general, the more regularly people exercise, the less likely they are to develop heart disease.

Some variables are not related at all. In the case of a *zero correlation*, a change in one variable does not predict a change in the second variable. For example, there is a zero correlation between height and likability. Tall people are neither more nor less likable than those who are shorter.

In analyzing the relationship between two variables, researchers can compute a **correlation coefficient**. This descriptive statistic provides a numerical value (between –1.0 and +1.0) that indicates the strength of the relationship (indicated by the magnitude of the correlation coefficient) and direction (indicated by the positive or negative sign) of the relationship between the two variables.

correlation coefficient A descriptive statistic that indicates the strength and direction of the relationship between two variables.

THINKING CRITICALLY ABOUT CORRELATIONS You can practice your critical thinking skills by interpreting what different types of correlations mean. Recall that there is generally a negative correlation between regular exercise and heart disease. For some people, however, there is a *positive* correlation between these variables: More exercise is related to more or worse heart disease. Why? Because being diagnosed with heart disease can spur people to become more physically active. Sometimes, the same phenomenon can exhibit a negative correlation or a positive correlation, depending on the specific circumstances.

Credit: xkcd.com

Consider an example. Some medical studies have found that people who take aspirin every day are less likely to have a heart attack than people who do not take the drug daily. The data reveal a negative correlation between taking aspirin and risk of a heart attack. But does this mean that taking aspirin *causes* a reduction in heart attacks? Not necessarily. Perhaps people who are at increased risk for heart attacks tend not to take aspirin. Or there might be a third variable, such as financial resources that enable people to take aspirin daily and reduce their risk for heart disease. Complications of this kind prevent researchers from drawing causal conclusions from correlational studies. Two such complications are the directionality problem and the third variable problem.

DIRECTIONALITY PROBLEM One problem with correlational studies is in knowing the direction of the relationship between variables. This sort of ambiguity is known as the **directionality problem**. For example, the more illness or pain a person experiences, the less likely they might be to exercise, in part because exertion becomes more unpleasant. Consider another example. Suppose you

directionality problem A problem encountered in correlational studies; the researchers find a relationship between two variables, but they cannot determine which variable may have caused changes in the other variable.

survey a large group of people about their wealth and their levels of happiness. Those who are wealthier also report being happier. Does wealth cause happiness? Or does being a consistently happy person eventually lead to becoming wealthy? Both scenarios seem plausible:

Wealth (A) and happiness (B) are correlated.

- Does wealth lead to happiness? (A → B)

or

- Does happiness lead to wealth? (B → A)

THIRD VARIABLE PROBLEM Another drawback with all correlational studies is the **third variable problem**. Instead of variable A producing variable B, as a researcher might assume, it is possible that a third variable, C, is responsible for both A and B. Consider the relationship between peer influence and vaping. It is possible that people who are highly sensitive to rewards in their daily lives are more likely to seek the approval of their peers. It is also possible that these people are likely to use e-cigarettes. Thus, the factor that leads to both heightened susceptibility to peer influence and vaping is the third variable, reward sensitivity:

third variable problem A problem that occurs when the researcher cannot directly manipulate variables; as a result, the researcher cannot be confident that another, unmeasured variable is not the actual cause of differences in the variables of interest.

Peer influence (A) is correlated with vaping (B).

- Reward sensitivity (C) is strongly associated with peer influence. (C → A)

and

- Reward sensitivity (C) is associated with the use of e-cigarettes. (C → B)

Sometimes the third variable is obvious. Suppose you were told that the more churches there are in a town, the greater the rate of crime. Would you conclude that churches cause crime? In looking for a third variable, you would realize that the population size of the town affects the number of churches and the frequency of crime. But sometimes third variables are not so obvious and may not even be identifiable. This is often the case where there are genetic influences on both a behavior and a disease. Researchers will observe a correlation between the two and assume that the behavior causes the disease. But the genetic predisposition actually is responsible for the correlation. Thus, it is impossible to conclude on the basis of correlational research that one of the variables *causes* the other.

ETHICAL REASONS FOR USING CORRELATIONAL DESIGNS Despite their limitations, correlational studies are widely used in psychological science. Some research questions require correlational research designs for ethical reasons. For example, as mentioned earlier, it would be unethical to experimentally assign teens to experience peer pressure to see if they started using e-cigarettes. Doing so would put the teens at risk.

There are many important real-world experiences that we want to know about but would never expose people to as part of an experiment. Suppose you want to know whether experiencing depression causes disruptions in attentional control. Even if you have a strong causal hypothesis, it would be unethical to induce depression in a random selection of your participants to test its effects on attention. To answer this research question, you would need to study the correlation between depression and attention. You could correlate the severity or frequency of depression people have experienced with their performance on attentional control measures, or even track people's depression severity and attention capacity across time to see if they are related.

MAKING PREDICTIONS By providing important information about the natural relationships between variables, researchers can make valuable predictions. If you found the association you expected between depression and attentional control, you could predict that people who experience depression will—on average—have more difficulty with tasks that involve attentional control than will otherwise similar people who do not experience depression. Because your study drew on but did not control the participants' level of depression, however, you have not established a causal connection (FIGURE 2.13).

In a related example, correlational research has identified a strong relationship between depression and suicide. For this reason, clinical psychologists often assess symptoms of depression to determine suicide risk. Typically, researchers who use the correlational method use other statistical procedures to rule out potential third variables and problems with the direction of the effect. Once they have shown that a relationship between two variables holds even when potential third variables are considered, researchers can be more confident that the relationship is meaningful.

FIGURE 2.13
Correlation or Causation?
According to the players on the 2013 Boston Red Sox baseball team, facial hair causes a person to play better baseball. After two newly bearded players made some game-saving plays, the rest of the team stopped shaving (Al-Khatib, 2013). Did their beards cause the Red Sox to win the World Series that year? The facial hair may have been correlated with winning, but it did not cause an increase in talent. The team won through ability, practice, and luck.

Q Suppose a study finds that hair length has a negative correlation with body weight: People with shorter hair weigh more. Why should you avoid acting on these results by growing your hair to lose weight?

ANSWER: Because correlation does not imply causation. A third variable, such as sex, could cause this relationship.

2.7 The Experimental Method Controls and Explains

Scientists ideally want to explain what causes a phenomenon. For this reason, researchers rely on the experimental method. In experimental research, the researcher has maximal control over the situation. Only the experimental method enables the researcher to control the conditions under which a phenomenon occurs and therefore to understand the cause of the phenomenon. In an **experiment**, the researcher manipulates one variable to measure the effect on a second variable.

experiment A research method that tests causal hypotheses by manipulating and measuring variables.

TYPES OF VARIABLES Scientists try to be as specific and as objective as possible when describing variables. Different terms are used to specify whether a variable is being manipulated or measured. An **independent variable** is the variable that is manipulated. Researchers manipulate the variable by assigning different participants to different levels of the variable. In a study, for example, one group of participants might be with several friends while reporting their opinions about e-cigarettes. Another group would be alone. Here, the independent variable is being with friends or not, which varies between the two groups.

independent variable The variable that is manipulated in a research study.

A **dependent variable** is the variable that is measured, which is why it is sometimes called the *dependent measure*. The dependent variable is the outcome that gets measured after a manipulation occurs. That is, the value of the dependent variable *depends* on the changes produced by the independent variable. Thus, in a study you could measure how often people expressed favorable opinions about e-cigarettes. Here, the dependent variable is opinions about e-cigarettes.

dependent variable The variable that is measured in a research study.

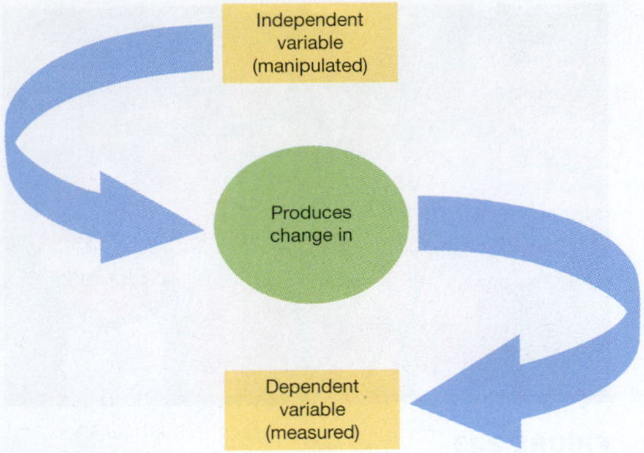

FIGURE 2.14
Independent and Dependent Variables
The independent variable is manipulated by the experimenter. In a good experiment, only changes in the level of the independent variable produce changes in the dependent variable, which is measured.

experimental group The participants in an experiment who receive the treatment.

control group The participants in an experiment who receive no intervention or who receive an intervention that is unrelated to the independent variable being investigated.

MANIPULATING VARIABLES In an experiment, to manipulate the independent variable (IV), the researchers systematically vary the task the participants are assigned or the stimuli they are exposed to (see **FIGURE 2.14**). It is critical that this assignment or exposure happens in a fair and unbiased way. This is best achieved with random assignment, which is described in Section 2.8. In a study on the effects of peer influence on vaping, the IV would be the presence or type of peer influence. All participants would provide opinions about e-cigarettes. Some participants might do so in the presence of friends, some might do so with similar-aged strangers, and still others might be alone as they complete their ratings.

An IV has "levels," meaning the different values that are manipulated by the researcher. All IVs must have at least two levels: a "treatment" level and a "comparison" level. In the study of peer influence and vaping, the teens who experience peer influence would be receiving the "treatment." The group of study participants who receive the treatment is the **experimental group**. In this hypothetical study some participants would be influenced by friends and others by same-aged strangers, so there would be two experimental groups.

In an experiment, you should always compare your experimental group with at least one **control group**. A control group consists of similar (or identical) participants who experience everything the experimental group receives except for the treatment. In this example, participants in the control group would answer all the same questions about e-cigarettes, but they would do so when alone. This use of a control group allows for the possibility that simply asking questions about e-cigarettes causes people's opinions about them to change.

So far, we have described research where different people are in the control and experimental groups. This is called a *between-groups* design because different people receive different treatments. However, sometimes study participants serve as their own control group. In a *repeated-measures* design (sometimes called within-subject design), the same people receive both treatments. For example, teens would report their opinions about e-cigarettes at least twice, once in the presence of peers and once alone. Differences in responses would be attributable to the different treatments. A disadvantage of this method is that repeating the test means people have experience with the task the second time, and this prior knowledge could influence performance. One thing scientists do to address that disadvantage is to randomly vary the order of the experiences. In this case, some teens would complete the measures with peers first, and others would complete them alone first.

In either type of experiment, the dependent variable (DV) is whatever behavioral effect is—or behavioral effects are—measured. The benefit of an experiment is that the researcher can study the causal relationship between the variables. If the IV consistently influences the DV, then the IV is assumed to cause the change in the DV.

Learning Tip

The distinction between the IV and the DV can be confusing because the IV is not "independent" at all—it depends on choices made by the experimenter! But from the perspective of causal inference, scientists are interested in knowing how a manipulation of the IV affects the DV. In that sense, the DV is *dependent* on the value of the IV. To help you remember that the DV depends on the IV, keep in mind that in diagrams of causal theories, the arrow is always *pointed toward* the DV (see Figure 2.16).

ESTABLISHING CAUSALITY The ability to draw causal conclusions from an experiment depends on rigorous control. Here, *control* means the steps taken by the researcher to ensure that the manipulation of the IV is the only difference between the experimental and control groups.

A **confound** is anything that affects a dependent variable and that might unintentionally vary between the study's different experimental conditions. The logic of experiments is that the only reason responses on the dependent measure would be different between the groups is because of the different levels of the independent measure. Confounds are a problem because they introduce another, uncontrolled difference between the groups. Confounds act as undetected third variables that could account for the observed relationship. Controlling for confounds is the foundation of the experimental approach because it allows the researcher to eliminate alternative explanations for the group differences.

confound Anything that affects a dependent variable and that may unintentionally vary between the experimental conditions of a study.

random assignment Placing research participants into the conditions of an experiment in such a way that each participant has an equal chance of being assigned to any level of the independent variable.

In the study of peer influence and opinions about vaping, what if participants in the peer influence condition completed the opinion survey in a large room with windows, but the participants in the alone condition completed the survey in a small, windowless room? Given that different environments can influence people's moods, which in turn might alter their opinions, any observed difference in opinions between the peer and alone conditions might instead be caused by the room where the study took place. In this example, the peer influence independent variable is *confounded* with study location, making it impossible to tell which influenced opinions about vaping.

The more confounds and thus alternative explanations that can be eliminated, the more confident a researcher can be that the change in the independent variable is causing the change (or effect) in the dependent variable. For this reason, researchers have to watch vigilantly for potential confounds. As consumers of research, we all need to think critically about confounds that could be causing particular results.

Q In an experiment, which variable is manipulated, and which is measured?

ANSWER: The independent variable is manipulated, and the dependent variable is measured.

2.8 Participants Need to Be Randomly Assigned to Conditions and Carefully Selected

RANDOM ASSIGNMENT In an experiment, once researchers obtain a representative sample of the population, they use **random assignment** to assign participants to the experimental and control groups (**FIGURE 2.15**). Random assignment gives each potential research participant an equal chance of being assigned to any level of the independent variable.

FIGURE 2.15
Random Assignment
In random assignment, participants are assigned at random to the control group or the experimental group. Random assignment is used when the experimenter wants to test a causal hypothesis.

For your vaping study, there might be three levels of the independent variable: completing surveys with friends, completing surveys with strangers, and completing them alone. First, you would gather participants by taking a sample from the population. Then, to randomly assign those participants, you might have them draw numbers from a hat to determine who is assigned to the control group (surveys alone) and to each experimental group (surveys with friends and with strangers).

Of course, the groups might be a little different just by chance. For example, any of your groups might include some people with less experience with e-cigarettes and some people who use e-cigarettes a great deal, some people with many friends who vape and some who do not know anyone who vapes. But these differences will

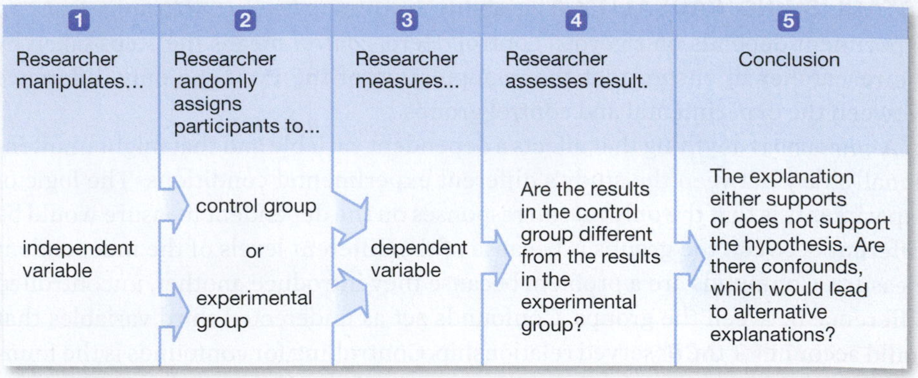

1
Researcher manipulates...
2
Researcher randomly assigns participants to...
3
Researcher measures...
4
Researcher assesses result.
5
Conclusion
independent variable
control group
or
experimental group
dependent variable
Are the results in the control group different from the results in the experimental group?
The explanation either supports or does not support the hypothesis. Are there confounds, which would lead to alternative explanations?

FIGURE 2.16
The Experimental Method in Action
An experiment examines how one variable changes as another is manipulated by the researcher. The results can demonstrate causal relationships between the variables.

population Everyone in the group the experimenter is interested in.

sample A subset of a population.

FIGURE 2.17
Population
The population is the group researchers want to know about (e.g., U.S. college students). For the results of an experiment to be considered useful, the participants should be representative of the population.

tend to average out when participants are assigned to either the control or experimental groups randomly, so that the groups are equivalent *on average*. This is the central logic of random assignment: Any known and unknown factors will tend to balance out across the groups if the sample size is large enough. In contrast, not using random assignment can create confounds that limit causal claims. Without random assignment, you are uncertain whether there is some difference between your groups caused by the way participants were selected into them. (For a recap of the experimental method, see **FIGURE 2.16**.)

POPULATION AND SAMPLING The group you ultimately want to know about is the **population** (**FIGURE 2.17**). To learn about the population, you study a subset from it. That subset, the people you actually study, is the **sample**. *Sampling* is the process by which you select people from the population to be in the sample. In a case study, the sample size is one. The sample should represent the population, and the best method for ensuring that it does is *random sampling* (**FIGURE 2.18**). This method gives each member of the population an equal chance of being chosen to participate in the study. In addition, larger samples yield more-accurate results (see Figure 2.6). However, sample size is often limited by resource constraints, such as time, money, and work space.

Most of the time, a researcher will use a *convenience sample* (**FIGURE 2.19**). As the term implies, this sample consists of people who are conveniently available for the study. However, because a convenience sample is not a random sample of the population, the sample is almost certainly biased. For instance, a sample of students at a small religious school may differ from a sample of students at a large state university. Researchers acknowledge the limitations of their samples when they present their findings.

An important decision for any study is how to select participants. Psychologists typically want to know that their findings generalize to people beyond the individuals in the study. In studying the effects of peer influence on vaping, you ultimately would not focus on the behavior of the specific participants. Instead, you would seek to discover general laws about human behavior. If your results generalized to all people, that would enable you, other psychologists, and the rest of humanity to predict, in general, how peer influence affects vaping. Other results, depending on the nature of the study, might generalize to all college students, to students who belong to sororities and fraternities, to women, to men over the age of 45, and so on.

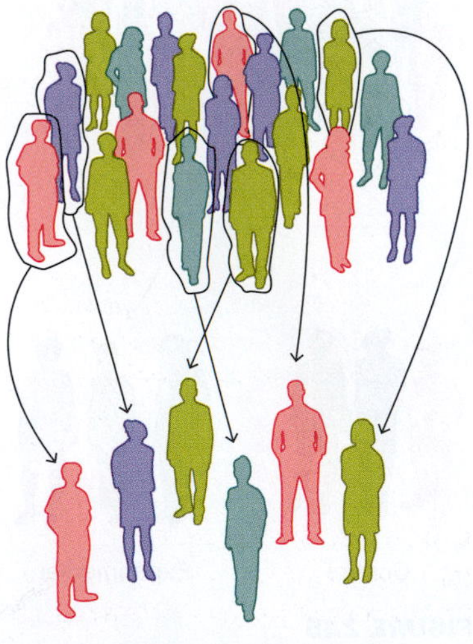

FIGURE 2.18
Random Sample
A random sample is one where every member of the population of interest (e.g., students from schools throughout the United States) is equally likely to be included.

Learning Tip

If you find yourself confused about random sampling and random assignment and forgetting which term is which, focus for a moment on the words *sampling* and *assignment*. The purpose of random *sampling* is to select a group of people from the target population into a study. The purpose of random *assignment* is to divide the people already in a study into the study conditions. In both cases, researchers use a random selection process to ensure fairness: of selection into the study in the case of random sampling, and of selection into the study groups in the case of random assignment.

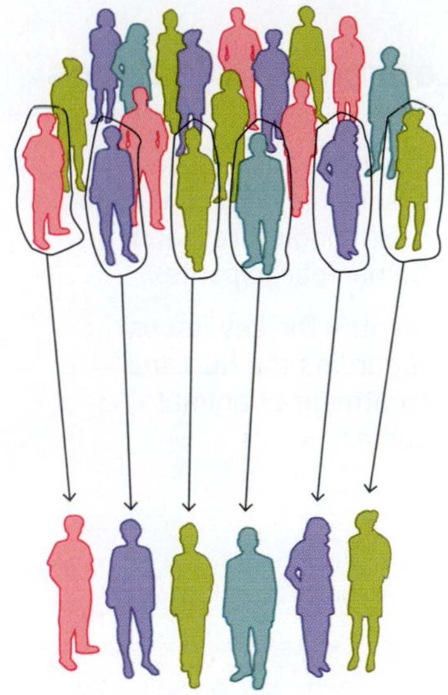

FIGURE 2.19
Convenience Sample
A convenience sample is taken from a subgroup of the full population that happens to be available (e.g., students at a particular school). Researchers often use a convenience sample when they do not have enough resources for a true random sample.

GENERALIZING ACROSS CULTURES Psychology studies seek to understand human mental processes and behavior. To make valid inferences about humans in general, studies would need to sample randomly from all of humanity. However, few if any studies meet the criterion that all humans on the planet are equally likely to be selected as participants. A truly random sample of humanity would be incredibly difficult to obtain. Also, many ideas and practices do not translate easily across cultures, just as some words do not translate easily across languages. For these reasons, most psychology research uses samples drawn from a very narrow slice of the human population (Henrich et al., 2010).

Many aspects of our mental life and behavior vary from culture to culture. The goals of cross-cultural research are to identify which aspects of human psychology are universal (e.g., caring for the young) and which vary across cultures (e.g., roles for adolescents) and to understand why (**FIGURE 2.20**). **Culturally sensitive research** considers the significant role that culture plays in how people think, feel, and act (Adair & Kagitcibasi, 1995; Zebian et al., 2007). Scientists use culturally sensitive practices so that their research respects—and perhaps reflects—the "shared system of meaning" that each culture transmits from one generation to the next (Betancourt & López, 1993, p. 630).

culturally sensitive research
Studies that take into account the role that culture plays in determining thoughts, feelings, and actions.

In cities with diverse populations, such as Toronto, London, and Los Angeles, cultural differences exist among various groups of people living in the same neighborhoods and having close daily contact. Researchers therefore need to be sensitive to cultural differences even when they are studying people in the same neighborhood or the same school. Researchers must also guard against applying a psychological concept from one culture to another without considering whether the concept is the same in both cultures. For example, treatments that are effective for treating depression in European Americans are not as effective for Asian Americans because of differences in cultural values around expressing strong emotions (Huang & Zane, 2016).

Q **How does random assignment help eliminate confounds in experiments?**

ANSWER: Any differences between the participants in the conditions, both known and unknown, tend to average out.

(a) (b)

FIGURE 2.20
Cross-Cultural Studies
(a) The living space and treasured possessions of a family in Malaysia, for example, differ from **(b)** those of a family in India. Cross-cultural researchers might study how either family would react to crowding or to the loss of its possessions.

Learning Objectives

- Identify ethical issues associated with conducting psychological research on human participants.
- Identify the key issues regarding the humane treatment of animal subjects.

What Are the Ethics Governing Psychological Research?

Psychologists have a responsibility to carefully consider the ethics of the research they conduct. Will the study contribute to the betterment of humanity? Do participants understand what exactly they are agreeing to do? Are the requests reasonable, or will they put the participants in danger of physical or emotional harm over the short or long term? If animals are involved, will they be treated humanely? Is their use justified?

2.9 There Are Ethical Issues to Consider in Research with Human Participants

Psychological science could not happen without human participants. However, there are limits to how researchers can manipulate what people do in studies. As noted in the section on correlations, there are ethical reasons why researchers cannot always use the experimental method. And there are some aspects of human experience that are unethical to study in the lab, with or without experimental designs. For example, it would be unethical to randomly assign people to drink and drive to study the effect of intoxication on driving ability. In studying severe psychopathology, it would be unethical to conduct even an observational study on self-injurious behavior because any observer would have the obligation to intervene.

In 1979, the National Commission for the Protection of Human Subjects of Biomedical and Behavioral Research issued the Belmont Report, describing three fundamental ethical principles that all human subjects research should uphold: respect for persons, beneficence, and justice (**FIGURE 2.21**).

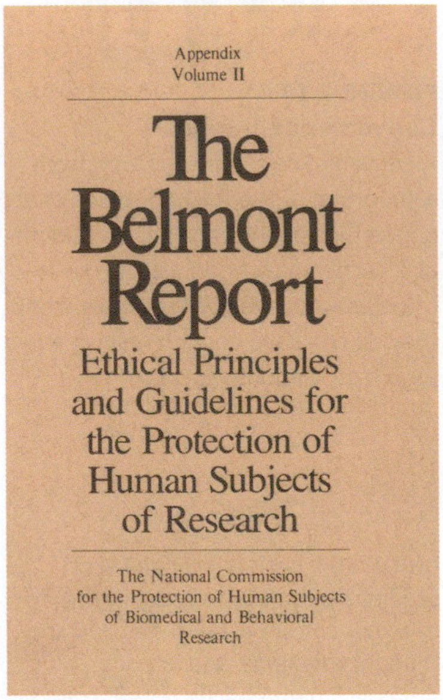

FIGURE 2.21
Belmont Report
Following horrific examples of abuses of human subjects by researchers, the National Commission for the Protection of Human Subjects of Biomedical and Behavioral Research issued the Belmont Report, which described the key ethical principles that should guide all research using human participants.

RESPECT FOR PERSONS People who participate in research must retain their autonomy when deciding to participate and throughout the duration of the psychological study. Respecting the autonomy of research participants means ensuring that they know what will happen to them during the study and that they have control over their personal information. Informed consent is the ongoing process of ensuring that participants understand what they are asked to do and actively agree to it. Compensating people with either money or course credit for their participation in research does not alter this fundamental right. Ethical standards require giving people all relevant information that might affect their willingness to participate (**FIGURE 2.22**).

It is not always possible to inform participants fully about a study's details. If knowing the study's specific goals may alter the participants' behavior, thereby rendering the results meaningless, researchers may need to use *deception*. That is, they might mislead the participants about the study's goals or not fully reveal what will take place. Researchers use deception only when other methods are not appropriate and when the deception does not involve situations that would strongly affect people's willingness to participate. If deception is used, a careful *debriefing* must take place after the study's completion, in which the researchers inform the participants of the study's goals. They also explain the need for deception to eliminate or counteract any negative effects it produces.

Another aspect of respecting autonomy is providing participants with an assurance of privacy. Two main aspects of privacy must be considered. One

institutional review boards (IRBs) Groups of people responsible for reviewing proposed research to ensure that it meets the accepted standards of science and provides for the physical and emotional well-being of research participants.

aspect is *confidentiality*. This term means that personal, identifying information about participants cannot be shared with others. In some studies, *anonymity* is maintained. Although this term is often confused with confidentiality, anonymity means that the researchers do not collect personal, identifying information in the first place. Without such information, responses can never be traced to any individual. Anonymity helps make participants comfortable enough to respond honestly.

BENEFICENCE Researchers have an ethical obligation to weigh the potential benefits of a study against its risks and to minimize risks as much as possible. Risks to a participant's health or well-being might be acceptable in a study that has a potentially large benefit, such as a cure for a fatal disease. In contrast, studies that have limited potential benefits to participants or society need to pose very low risk.

The vast majority of psychology studies are low risk. However, even though risk may be low, researchers still have to think carefully about whether the benefit of the study outweighs the risk. Part of informed consent is making sure participants are fully aware of any risks of a study before they decide to participate.

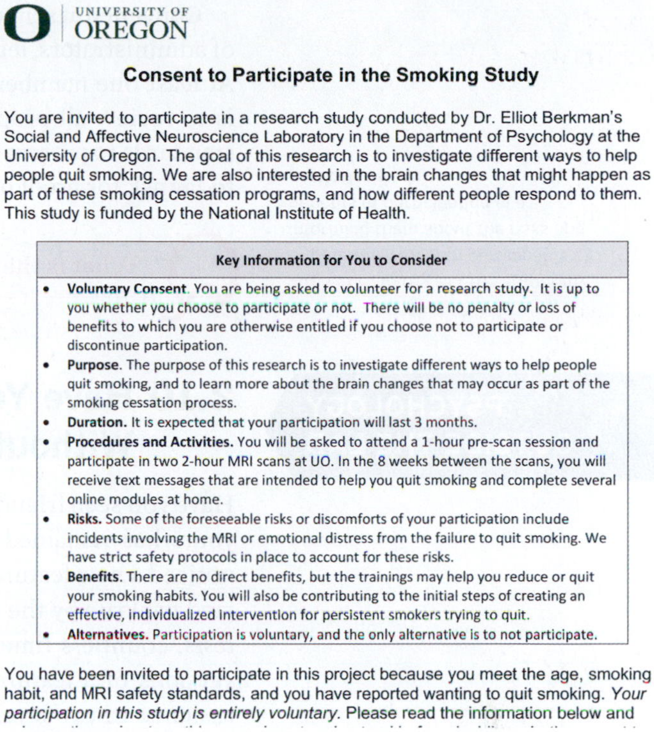
UNIVERSITY OF OREGON

Consent to Participate in the Smoking Study

You are invited to participate in a research study conducted by Dr. Elliot Berkman's Social and Affective Neuroscience Laboratory in the Department of Psychology at the University of Oregon. The goal of this research is to investigate different ways to help people quit smoking. We are also interested in the brain changes that might happen as part of these smoking cessation programs, and how different people respond to them. This study is funded by the National Institute of Health.

Key Information for You to Consider

- **Voluntary Consent**. You are being asked to volunteer for a research study. It is up to you whether you choose to participate or not. There will be no penalty or loss of benefits to which you are otherwise entitled if you choose not to participate or discontinue participation.
- **Purpose**. The purpose of this research is to investigate different ways to help people quit smoking, and to learn more about the brain changes that may occur as part of the smoking cessation process.
- **Duration.** It is expected that your participation will last 3 months.
- **Procedures and Activities.** You will be asked to attend a 1-hour pre-scan session and participate in two 2-hour MRI scans at UO. In the 8 weeks between the scans, you will receive text messages that are intended to help you quit smoking and complete several online modules at home.
- **Risks.** Some of the foreseeable risks or discomforts of your participation include incidents involving the MRI or emotional distress from the failure to quit smoking. We have strict safety protocols in place to account for these risks.
- **Benefits.** There are no direct benefits, but the trainings may help you reduce or quit your smoking habits. You will also be contributing to the initial steps of creating an effective, individualized intervention for persistent smokers trying to quit.
- **Alternatives.** Participation is voluntary, and the only alternative is to not participate.

You have been invited to participate in this project because you meet the age, smoking habit, and MRI safety standards, and you have reported wanting to quit smoking. *Your participation in this study is entirely voluntary.* Please read the information below and

FIGURE 2.22
Informed Consent Form
This portion of an approved form gives you a sense of how researchers typically obtain informed consent in writing.

JUSTICE This principle refers to fairness in the distribution of the costs and benefits of research across a population. Everyone should have an equal chance to participate in and benefit from research. It would be unethical for the risks of participating in a research study to be borne by one group of people while its benefits went to another group. Unfortunately, medical research has a history of violating this principle. The Tuskegee Study referenced in **FIGURE 2.23** violated the principle of justice because only African American men were included as participants even though everyone vulnerable to syphilis benefited from the results. That study also violated respect for persons because participants were not informed of their diagnosis. The outrage that followed when a whistleblower informed the public about the Tuskegee Study contributed to the creation of the Belmont Report and the formalization of the fundamental research ethics principles.

FIGURE 2.23
Justice
Between 1932 and 1972, the U.S. Public Health Service and the Tuskegee Institute, in Alabama, studied the progression of untreated syphilis in African American men. Without their knowledge, 400 men with syphilis were randomly assigned to receive treatment or not. In 1997, the U.S. government officially apologized to the participants and their families. Here, President Bill Clinton and Vice President Al Gore appear at a news conference with participant Herman Shaw.

INSTITUTIONAL REVIEW BOARDS (IRBs) Most countries now have formal guidelines based on the Belmont Report or similar sets of principles to ensure the health and well-being of all study participants. These guidelines are in effect in all places where research is conducted, including colleges, universities, and research institutes. **Institutional review boards (IRBs)** are responsible for monitoring research and enforcing the guidelines.

Convened at schools and other institutions where research is done, IRBs consist of administrators, legal advisers, trained scholars, and members of the community. At least one member of the IRB must not be a scientist. The purpose of the IRB is to review all proposed research to ensure that it meets scientific and ethical standards to protect the safety and welfare of participants. Most scientific journals today ask for proof of IRB approval before publishing research results.

Q What is the purpose of informed consent?

ANSWER: to respect the autonomy of potential research participants by informing them about the risks and benefits of participating in a particular study

PSYCHOLOGY OUTSIDE THE LAB

2.10 Have You Participated in Research Without Knowing It?

Have you seen friends on social media post about changes to their newsfeed when yours has remained the same? Or have you ever visited a favorite website and noticed a new feature or layout? If so, you probably have participated in a randomized trial run by the company. Internet companies run these experiments, or *A/B tests,* countless times each year to see how their users will respond to different versions of a feature. A/B tests are simple experiments where participants are assigned to two levels of the IV, "A" and "B," that correspond to the two versions of the site (FIGURE 2.24).

Most of the time, A/B tests are innocuous examples of how the scientific method can be applied to answer marketing questions, such as whether users click more often on a button when it is on the left or right, whether they spend more time on a site with a lighter or darker background image, or whether they are more likely to share an article whose first line is in boldface or italics. Advocates of A/B testing claim that using the scientific method to inform product design is better than having designers simply choose to implement A or B.

experimentation aversion A tendency for people to prefer to receive an untested treatment than to participate in a randomized study to evaluate the effectiveness of the treatment.

Would you rather unwittingly be part of an A/B test or simply be assigned to an untested condition? Interestingly, people seem to be **experimentation averse:** We generally think that implementing either A or B, even if both are untested, is more acceptable than randomized A/B testing to determine the better option (Meyer et al., 2019). Consider your own response to learning that you have been part of experiments without your knowledge. Do you feel experimentation aversion? If so, why do you think taking part in a controlled experiment, where A and B are systematically compared, is worse than an uncontrolled one, where one or the other option is simply imposed on you?

There are times when corporations run A/B trials examining more than just people's engagement with a website, such as their psychological responses to features of a page. In 2012, the social media platform Facebook ran an experiment with more than 689,000 people to test whether increasing or decreasing the amount of content with positive emotion in a user's feed would alter the emotional content of the user's posts (Kramer et al., 2014). They found evidence of *emotional contagion,* in that people who saw slightly more positive content in their feed generated more positive posts, whereas people who saw less positive content generated fewer positive posts.

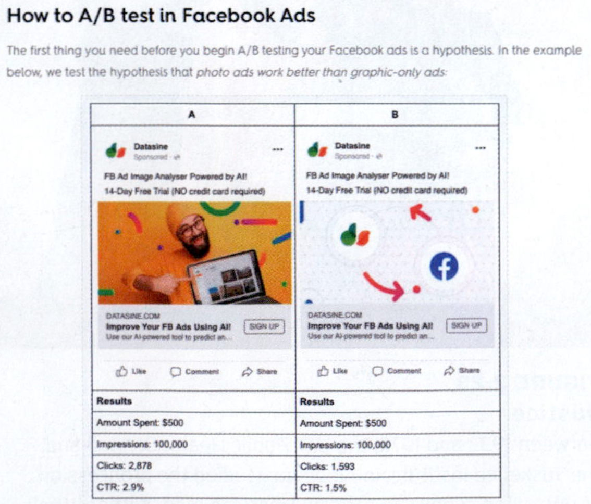

FIGURE 2.24
A/B Testing Online
Internet companies such as Facebook routinely use A/B testing to improve their platform. Here, they offer their advertisers the ability to conduct A/B tests for improving their ads.

This result was controversial for several reasons. It was the first time many users of Facebook realized that the site frequently conducted A/B tests and did so without telling its users about the random assignment. Some users were surprised by the amount of information that Facebook knew and stored about their behavior on the site. The researchers also published their study in a prominent peer-reviewed journal, *Proceedings of the National Academy of Sciences*, which was an apparent violation of the journal's policy that participants in reports published in the journal give informed consent to participate (Verma, 2014). The researchers argued that Facebook users gave their consent to participate in research by agreeing to the company's explicit data-use policy.

Randomized testing is not unique to internet companies. Retail stores, fast food companies, and even banks use A/B testing all the time. But the quantity and richness of the data that internet companies have about their users is far greater than what other corporations have and is expanding rapidly. The Facebook study revealed that many people are unaware that they are participating in research as they use social media platforms. Researchers will need to adapt their practices to the complex online environment to uphold the ethical principles of respect for persons, beneficence, and justice described in the Belmont Report. ■

Q What is experimentation aversion?

ANSWER: the tendency to prefer untested treatments or conditions over random assignment to one of the other treatment or condition

2.11 There Are Ethical Issues to Consider in Research with Animals

Many people have ethical concerns about research with nonhuman animals. These concerns involve two questions: Does research threaten the health and well-being of the animals? And is it fair to the animals to study them to improve the human condition?

HEALTH AND WELL-BEING Research with animals must always consider the health and well-being of the animals. Federal mandates govern the care and use of animals in research, and these mandates are strictly enforced. An accounting and reporting system is in place for all institutions conducting animal research. Violators of the mandates are prevented from conducting further research.

All colleges, universities, and research institutions conducting research with vertebrate animals must have an Institutional Animal Care and Use Committee (IACUC). This committee is like an IRB, but it evaluates animal research proposals. In addition to scientists and nonscientists, every IACUC includes a certified doctor of veterinary medicine, who must review each proposal to ensure that the research animals will be treated properly before, during, and after the study.

BENEFICENCE Animals share similarities with humans that make them good "models" for particular human behaviors or conditions. For example, as you will learn more about in Chapters 3 and 7, the human brain has a region called the hippocampus, and people with damage to this region suffer from memory loss. It would be unethical for researchers to create hippocampal damage in people in an effort to find treatments for their memory loss. However, many animals also have a hippocampus, and they display similar types of memory

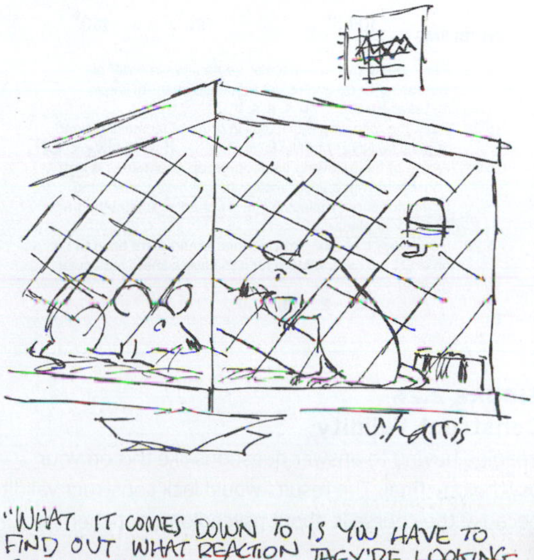

"WHAT IT COMES DOWN TO IS YOU HAVE TO FIND OUT WHAT REACTION THEY'RE LOOKING FOR, AND YOU GIVE THEM THAT REACTION."

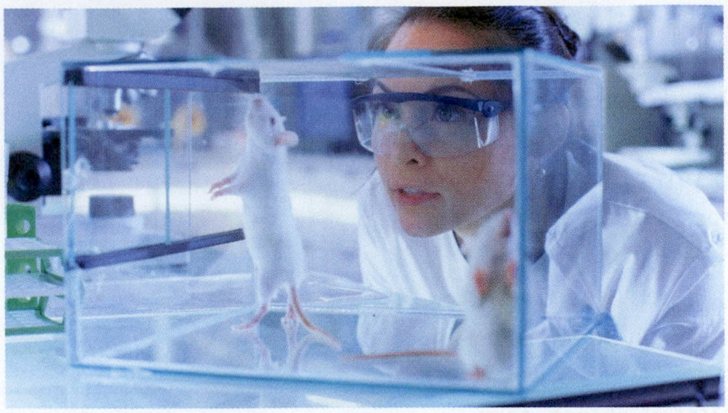

FIGURE 2.25
Animal Research
Researchers observe the behaviors of transgenic mice to understand how certain genes affect behavior.

loss when this region is damaged. As a way to help humans, researchers thus may find it necessary to conduct animal research. For example, scientists can damage or temporarily "turn off" the hippocampus in rats or mice to test treatments that may help reverse the resulting memory loss. Following the principle of beneficence, researchers balance the harm to the animals against the potential benefits to society in conducting studies like this. This balancing involves making sure that the research methods are sound and that the inclusion of animals is justified by the relative importance of the information that will be obtained by their use.

Another valuable animal model is the transgenic mouse. Transgenic mice have been produced by manipulating genes in developing mouse embryos—for example, by inserting strands of foreign DNA into the genes. Studying the behavior of mice with specific genetic changes enables scientists to discover the role that genes play in behavior and disease (**FIGURE 2.25**).

Q **Why are animals used in research?**

ANSWER: They may provide valuable information that cannot be ethically obtained by studying humans.

How Are Data Analyzed and Evaluated?

Learning Objectives

- Identify three characteristics that reflect the quality of data.
- Describe measures of central tendency and variability.
- Discuss the rationale for inferential statistics.

After a researcher has conducted a study and collected data, the next step is to analyze the data to reveal the results. This section examines the characteristics that make for good data and the statistical procedures that researchers use to analyze data.

2.12 Good Research Requires Valid, Reliable, and Accurate Data

If you collect data to answer a research question, the data must be *valid*. Valid data should accurately measure the constructs (or concepts) that you think they measure, reflect the way the phenomenon of interest occurs outside of the laboratory, and reveal effects due specifically and only to manipulation of the independent variable.

Construct validity is the extent to which variables measure what they are supposed to measure. For example, suppose that at the end of the semester your psychology professor gives you a final examination that consists of chemistry problems. This kind of final examination would lack construct validity—it would not accurately measure your knowledge of psychology (**FIGURE 2.26**).

Now imagine you are a psychological researcher. You hypothesize that "A students" spend more time studying than "C students." To test your hypothesis, you ask students to self-report the amount of time they spend studying. However, what if C students tended to do other things—such as sleeping, playing video games, or scrolling on Instagram—while they claimed to be studying? If this were the case,

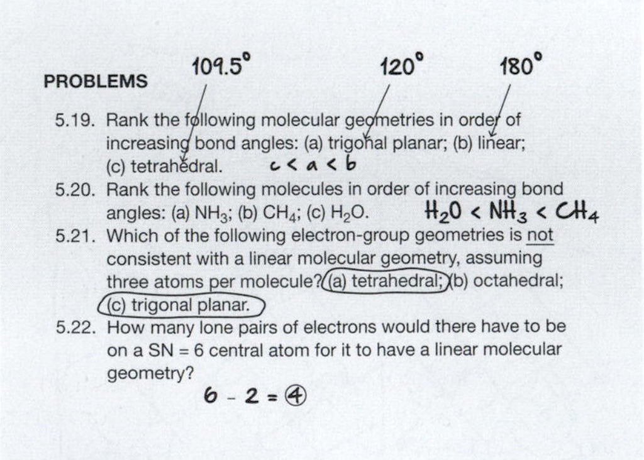
PROBLEMS

5.19. Rank the following molecular geometries in order of increasing bond angles: (a) trigonal planar; (b) linear; (c) tetrahedral.

5.20. Rank the following molecules in order of increasing bond angles: (a) NH_3; (b) CH_4; (c) H_2O.

5.21. Which of the following electron-group geometries is not consistent with a linear molecular geometry, assuming three atoms per molecule? (a) tetrahedral; (b) octahedral; (c) trigonal planar.

5.22. How many lone pairs of electrons would there have to be on a SN = 6 central atom for it to have a linear molecular geometry?

FIGURE 2.26
Construct Validity
Imagine having to answer questions like this on your psychology final. The results would lack construct validity because the course is about psychology, not chemistry.

the data would not accurately reflect studying and would therefore lack construct validity.

External validity is the degree to which the findings of a study can be generalized to other people, settings, or situations. A study is externally valid if (1) the participants adequately represent the intended population, and (2) the variables were manipulated and measured in ways similar to how they occur in the "real world."

Internal validity is the degree to which the effects observed in an experiment are due to the independent variable and not to confounds. For data to be internally valid, the experiment must be well designed and well controlled (**FIGURE 2.27**). That is, the participants across all groups must be as similar as possible, and there must be a control group (**FIGURE 2.28**). Only by comparing experimental groups to control groups can you determine that any changes observed in the experimental groups are caused by the independent variable and not something else (for example, practice or the passage of time). Internal validity follows from the principles of the experimental method described in Sections 2.7 and 2.8, such as random assignment to conditions, adequately large sample sizes, and control over known and unknown confounds.

Another important aspect of data is **reliability**, the stability and consistency of a measure over time. If the measurement is reliable, the data collected will not vary substantially over time. For instance, one option for measuring the duration of studying would be to have an observer use a stopwatch. However, there will probably be some variability in when the observer starts and stops the watch relative to when the student actually starts studying. Consequently, the data in this scenario would be less reliable than data collected by an automated feature in an online study system that measured how much time students spent working on assignments.

The third and final characteristic of good data is **accuracy**, the degree to which the measure is error free. A measure may be reliable but still not accurate. Psychologists think about this problem by turning it on its head and asking: How do errors seep into a measure?

Suppose you use a stopwatch to measure the duration of studying. The problem with this method is that each measurement will tend to overestimate or underestimate the duration (because of human error or variability in recording times). This type of problem is known as a *random error* or *unsystematic error*. Although an error is introduced into each measurement, the value of the error differs each time. But suppose the stopwatch has a glitch, so that it always overstates the time measured by 1 minute. This type of problem is known as a *systematic error* or *bias*, because the amount of error introduced into each measurement is constant. Generally, systematic error is more problematic than random error because the latter tends to average out over time and therefore is less likely to produce inaccurate results.

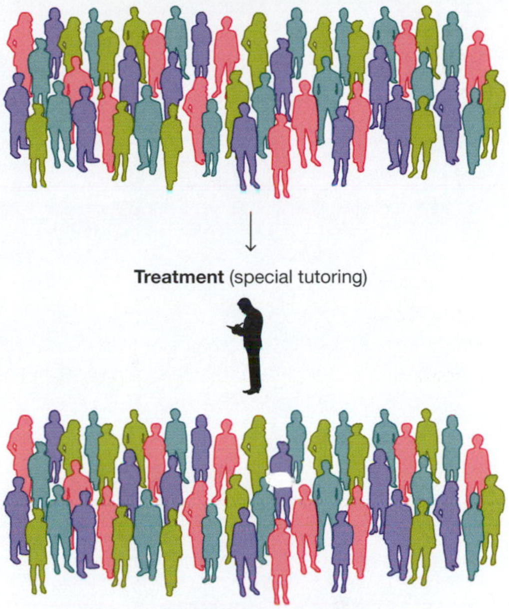

FIGURE 2.27
A Study Lacking Internal Validity
In this study, your entire sample is one experimental group that receives the treatment of special tutoring. You determine the group's average score on the final exam, but you cannot compare that result with the result from a control group.

construct validity The extent to which variables measure what they are supposed to measure.

external validity The degree to which the findings of a study can be generalized to other people, settings, or situations.

internal validity The degree to which the effects observed in an experiment are due to the independent variable and not to confounds.

reliability The degree to which a measure is stable and consistent over time.

accuracy The degree to which an experimental measure is free from error.

Q You want to know whether the results of your study generalize to other groups. What kind of validity are you most concerned about?

ANSWER: external validity

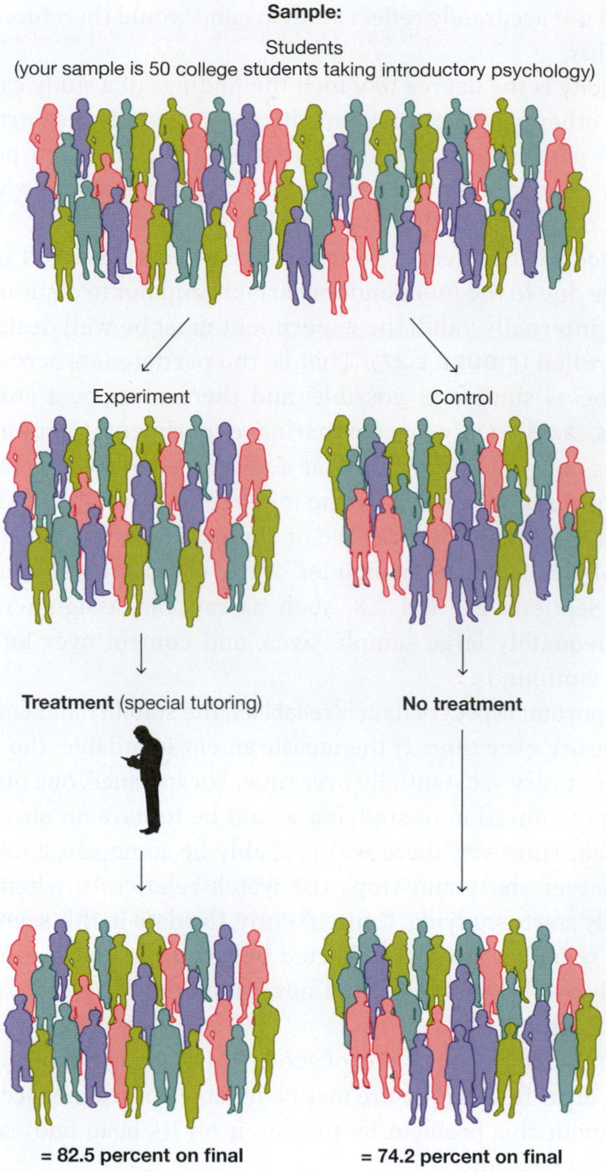

FIGURE 2.28

A Study with Internal Validity

In this better study, you divide the sample into an experimental group and a control group. Only the experimental group receives the treatment. You can then compare that group's results with the results from the control group.

descriptive statistics Statistics that summarize the data collected in a study.

central tendency A measure that represents the typical response or the behavior of a group as a whole.

mean A measure of central tendency that is the arithmetic average of a set of numbers.

median A measure of central tendency that is the value in a set of numbers that falls exactly halfway between the lowest and highest values.

2.13 Descriptive Statistics Provide a Summary of the Data

Researchers summarize the basic patterns in their data using **descriptive statistics**, which provide an overall summary of the study's results (see **FIGURE 2.29**). The simplest descriptive statistics are measures of **central tendency**, which describe a typical response or the behavior of the group as a whole. The most intuitive measure of central tendency is the **mean**, the arithmetic average of a set of numbers. The class average on an exam is an example of a mean score. In the hypothetical study of the effect of peer influence on opinions about e-cigarettes, a basic way to

You measure the number of seconds that 11 participants take to drive around a simulated racetrack:

- One takes 55 seconds.
- One takes 69 seconds.
- One takes 56 seconds.
- One takes 65 seconds.
- One takes 60 seconds.
- Two take 45 seconds.
- One takes 48 seconds.
- One takes 38 seconds.
- One takes 34 seconds.
- One takes 25 seconds.

Written in ascending order, the number of seconds per participant looks like this:

25 34 38 45 45 48 55 56 60 65 69

Mean
The arithmetic average of a set of numbers

$$\frac{\text{total \# of seconds}}{\text{total \# of participants}} = \frac{25+34+38+45+45+48+55+56+60+65+69}{11} = \frac{540}{11} = 49$$

Median
The value that falls exactly halfway between the lowest and highest values

25 34 38 45 45 48 55 56 60 65 69 = **48**

Mode
The most frequent score or value in a set of numbers

25 34 38 **45 45** 48 55 56 60 65 69 = **45**

Range
The distance between the largest and smallest values

25 34 38 45 45 48 55 56 60 65 **69** = **69 – 25 = 44**

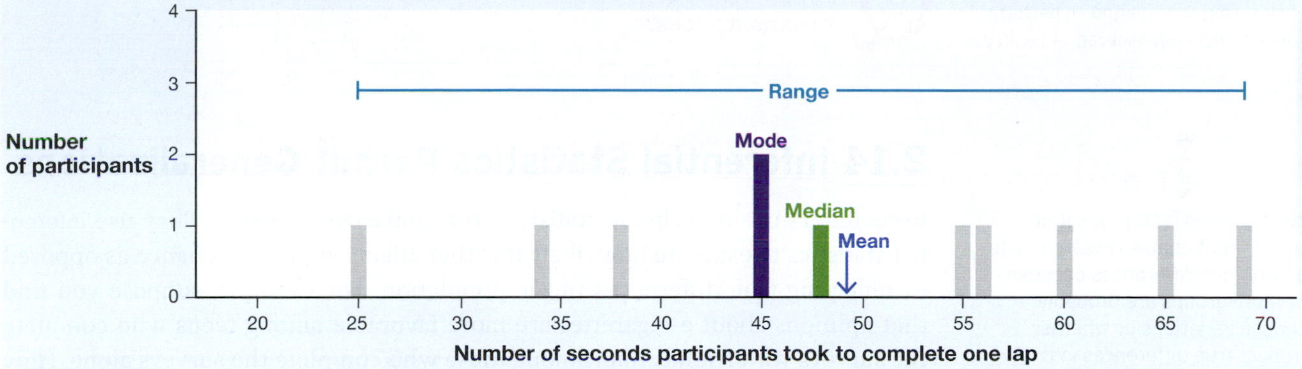

FIGURE 2.29
Descriptive Statistics
Descriptive statistics are used to summarize a data set and to measure the central tendency and variability in a set of numbers. The mean, median, and mode are all measures of central tendency.

summarize the results would be to look at the mean opinion rating in each of the three groups.

A second measure of central tendency is the **median**, the value in a set of numbers that falls exactly halfway between the lowest and highest values. If you received the median score on a test, half the people who took the test scored lower than you and half the people scored higher.

Sometimes researchers will summarize data using a median instead of a mean because if one or two numbers in the set are dramatically larger or smaller than all the others (known as *outliers*), the mean will give either an inflated or a deflated summary of the average. This effect occurs in studies of average incomes. Approximately 50 percent of Americans make more than \$52,000 per year, but a small percentage of people make so much more (multiple millions or billions for the richest) that the mean income is much higher (around \$70,000) than the median and is not an accurate measure of what most people earn. The median provides a better estimate of how much money the average person makes.

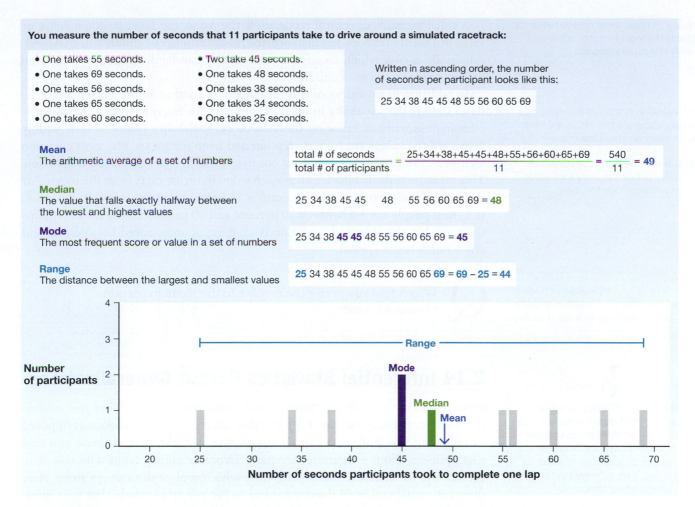

"I think you should be more explicit here in step two."

mode A measure of central tendency that is the most frequent score or value in a set of numbers.

A third measure of central tendency is the **mode**, the most frequent score or value in a set of numbers. For instance, the modal number of children in an American family is two, which means that more American families have two children than any other number of children.

variability In a set of numbers, how widely dispersed the values are from each other and from the mean.

standard deviation A statistical measure of how far away each value is, on average, from the mean.

In addition to measures of central tendency, another important characteristic of data is the **variability** in a set of numbers. In many respects, the mean is meaningless without knowing the variability. Variability refers to how widely dispersed the values are from each other and from the mean. The most common measure of variability—how spread out the scores are—is the **standard deviation.** This measure reflects how far away each value is, on average, from the mean. For instance, if the mean score for an exam is 75 percent and the standard deviation is 5, most people scored between 70 percent and 80 percent. If the mean remains the same but the standard deviation is 15, most people scored between 60 and 90—a much larger spread.

Q **Why might you prefer the median to the mean in certain circumstances?**

ANSWER: Because the mean can be distorted by outliers, but the median is simply the middle value.

2.14 Inferential Statistics Permit Generalizations

inferential statistics A set of procedures that enable researchers to decide whether differences between two or more groups are probably just chance variations or whether they reflect true differences in the populations being compared.

Researchers use descriptive statistics to summarize data sets. They use **inferential statistics** to estimate how likely it is that effects are due to chance as opposed to reflecting true differences in the population. For example, suppose you find that opinions about e-cigarettes are more favorable among teens who complete the surveys with friends than among those who complete the surveys alone. How different would you need those means to be for you to conclude that peer influence changes opinions about vaping?

The key problem is that there is always some variability from sample to sample, whether or not there is a true difference between groups. If you were to run your experiment again, do you think the means of your groups would be exactly the same as they were the first time? Probably not. How much would they change? Statistical techniques combine features of the data, such as means and standard deviations, along with some assumptions about the amount of error to help researchers quantify how much the observed data might change if the experiment were run again.

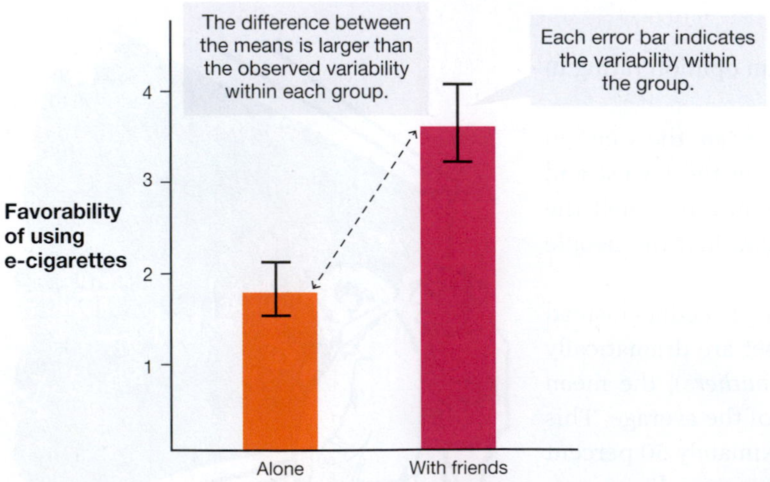

FIGURE 2.30
Evaluating Differences in Research Results
In this hypothetical experiment comparing two groups of teens' opinions of e-cigarettes, the group assigned to the "with friends" condition expressed more positive views about vaping. That result is reflected in the difference between the means for the groups. Error bars have been added to show the variability of data within each condition.

The bar graph in **FIGURE 2.30** shows the means for a hypothetical study that compared favorability ratings of e-cigarettes measured either alone or with friends. The mean favorability is visibly higher for the friend group, but is this difference larger than would be expected by chance? The error bars show the variability that was observed within each group during the study. The difference between the means is much larger than the observed variability within each group. Thus, this difference between the groups does not appear to have happened by chance. It appears to be a real difference.

When the results obtained from a study would be very unlikely to occur if there really were no differences between the groups of participants, the researchers conclude that the results are *statistically significant*. According to accepted standards, researchers typically conclude there is a significant effect only if the obtained results are unlikely (occurring 5 percent of the time or less) compared with what would be expected if the hypothesized effect were not real—in other words, if the significance level was 0.05 or less.

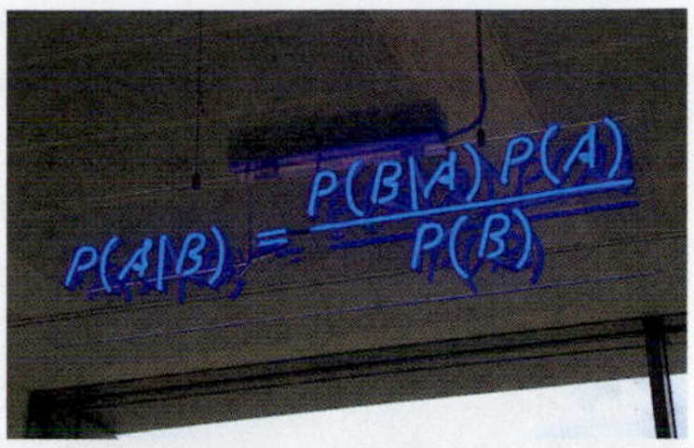

FIGURE 2.31
Bayes' Theorem
The statistician Thomas Bayes derived this equation for calculating the probability of an event, A, knowing that a separate event, B, has occurred. Bayes' theorem has many applications in science and engineering. Here, Bayes' theorem is honored in neon in the offices of the artificial intelligence company HP Autonomy.

BAYESIAN STATISTICS More and more, researchers embrace the view that their conclusions are not black and white but rather occur in shades of gray—what statisticians call *probabilistic*. Significance testing renders a yes/no answer to a question that inherently has some chance in it. Would it be fair or accurate to conclude that peer influence has no effect on opinions about e-cigarettes if the study yielded a significance level of 0.06, but to reach the opposite conclusion if the significance level were 0.049? The psychologists Ralph Rosnow and Robert Rosenthal (1989) expressed this point when they quipped, "Surely God loves the 0.06 as much as the 0.05."

Probabilistic statistics represent an alternative approach to significance testing. These statistics give an estimate of the likelihood of a hypothesis that combines beliefs about a hypothesis with observed data. For example, consider the relative health risks of tobacco cigarettes versus e-cigarettes. The risks of smoking cigarettes are severe and supported by decades of good studies. The risks of e-cigarettes might be just as bad, but the evidence is only beginning to emerge. A single study that showed that smoking cigarettes is dangerous *would not* change scientists' beliefs about the risks of smoking because those beliefs are already strongly supported by evidence. However, a comparable study that showed that vaping nicotine in an e-cigarette is harmful *would* change beliefs because there was more uncertainty about the hypothesis to begin with. New results are most informative when there is not much existing knowledge.

These kinds of probabilistic techniques are called **Bayesian statistics** after the minister, philosopher, and statistician Thomas Bayes, who derived an equation for updating existing beliefs based on new information that became known as *Bayes' theorem* (**FIGURE 2.31**). Bayes' theorem is a formula that enables researchers to know how much a set of data should change their beliefs about whether a hypothesis is true.

Bayesian statistics A class of statistics that combines existing beliefs ("priors") with new data to update the estimated likelihood that a belief is true ("posterior").

Q **What does it mean if an observed difference between groups is described as statistically significant?**

ANSWER: The observed difference is unlikely if there is no true difference between the populations sampled in the study.

2.15 Should You Believe in Extrasensory Perception?

YOU BE THE PSYCHOLOGIST

In the opening scene of the classic 1984 movie *Ghostbusters*, the audience meets Dr. Peter Venkman (played by Bill Murray) in his psychology research laboratory (**FIGURE 2.32**). He is studying *extrasensory perception* by asking participants to accurately guess which symbol appears on the back of a playing card, delivering an electric shock to participants when they give the incorrect answer.

FIGURE 2.32
Psi Research
In *Ghostbusters*, Bill Murray plays Dr. Peter Venkman, a psychologist studying extrasensory perception. Daryl Bem's paper claiming to demonstrate the existence of extrasensory perception and other unusual abilities, or psi, spurred psychologists to adopt a range of methodological improvements.

In *Ghostbusters*, Venkman is portrayed as a fraud, delivering shocks to a male participant who is answering correctly but not to a female participant who is answering incorrectly. But suppose you earnestly wanted to find out whether people can read minds, envision parts of the world that their eyes cannot see, or change events that have already happened. How would you go about testing the hypothesis that people have extrasensory perception?

Psychologists have used the experimental method to study paranormal topics such as these, collectively referred to as *psi*. In an infamous example, social psychologist Daryl Bem published a set of nine studies purporting to give empirical support for psi in the most prominent journal in social and personality psychology (Bem, 2011). The paper claimed to find evidence that people could know things before they happened. For example, one study showed that people preferred locations on a screen where positive (erotic) images would later appear, and another found that participants had a stronger preference for pictures that they would only later be trained to like than for pictures they would not later be trained to like.

The results of the Bem paper shocked the field, and some readers questioned their long-held disbelief of psi. How would you react if you read this paper? What kinds of information would you look for based on what you have learned in this chapter? From a Bayesian perspective, how strong would the evidence need to be to compel you to update your beliefs about the existence of these kinds of effects, assuming that you did not believe in them in the first place? Take a few moments to apply your critical thinking skills to an unexpected result such as this one.

When Bem's paper was published, many researchers scrutinized his scientific approach and found deep problems. In fact, the publication of this paper is one of the sparks that launched the reproducibility movement in psychology. The psychologist Eric-Jan Wagenmakers led a group of scholars in writing a rebuttal titled "Why Psychologists Must Change the Way They Analyze Their Data" (Wagenmakers et al., 2011) that pointed out several methodological flaws, including selective reporting of results, omission of null results, and a confusion between exploratory and confirmatory inferential statistics. Others characterized the procedure that Bem followed as wandering through a "garden of forking paths," selectively making decisions at each intersection that favored the hypothesis to eventually arrive at the desired location (Gelman & Loken, 2014).

What the Bem study really discovered was not evidence for psi at all. Instead, the paper showed how easily practices that had become the norm could lead psychologists to absurd conclusions. Psychologists would routinely exercise "experimenter degrees of freedom" (Simmons et al., 2011) in making choices about when to stop collecting data from new participants, how many individual studies to include in a single paper, and which measures to report and which to exclude. Few researchers intended to publish misleading results. Most of the research was conducted in good faith following what researchers had learned was the standard for scientific practice, and they were shocked to learn how flawed that standard was. Open scientific practices are now the norm, for good reason.

In the end, psychologists used their newfound best practices to put psi to the test in a more rigorous way. Several groups, including one led by Bem himself, failed to replicate the effects (Galak et al., 2012; Schlitz et al., 2018). These failures to replicate are convincing because the researchers spelled out their full methods in advance and all the studies they conducted were reported. In a way, the debacle itself shows that psi probably is not real. If it were, someone with the ability to foresee the future would have told Bem not to publish the study! ■

Q **Why are psi studies unlikely to replicate?**

ANSWER: Because the psi effects found in the original studies are unlikely to be real. Some results will be statistically significant by chance. But when studies are preregistered, carefully conducted, and fully reported, chance results will not replicate.

Your Chapter Review

It's time to complete your study experience! Go to **INQUIZITIVE** to practice actively with this chapter's concepts and get personalized feedback along the way.

Chapter Summary

How Is the Scientific Method Used in Psychological Research?

2.1 Science Has Three Primary Goals The three primary goals of science are *description* (describing what a phenomenon is), *prediction* (predicting when a phenomenon might occur), and *explanation* (explaining what causes a phenomenon to occur).

2.2 The Scientific Method Is a Systematic Way to Test Hypotheses Scientific inquiry relies on objective methods and empirical evidence to answer testable questions. The scientific method is based on the use of theories to generate hypotheses that can be tested by collecting objective data through research. After a theory has been formulated based on observing a phenomenon, the seven steps of the scientific method are framing research questions, reviewing the scientific literature to see if and/or how people are testing the theory, forming a hypothesis based on the theory, choosing a research method to test the hypothesis, conducting the research study, analyzing the data, and disseminating the results.

2.3 The Scientific Method Is Cyclical The data from scientific studies either support and strengthen a theory or require reconsidering or revising the theory. Replication involves repeating a study to see if the same results occur. Replication is increasingly important in psychology. New best practices address the main reasons why a study might not replicate. Meta-analysis is a powerful tool to look across studies to help determine whether a finding is replicable.

2.4 Critical Thinking Is Essential to Evaluating Scientific Findings Critical thinking is a skill that helps people become educated consumers of information. Critical thinkers question claims, seek definitions for the parts of the claims, and evaluate the claims by looking for well-supported evidence.

What Types of Studies Are Used in Psychological Research?

2.5 Descriptive Research Consists of Case Studies, Observation, and Self-Report Methods A case study, one kind of descriptive study, examines an atypical individual or organization. However, the findings of a case study may not generalize. Researchers observe and describe naturally occurring behaviors to provide a systematic and objective analysis. Data collected by observation must be defined clearly and collected systematically. Surveys, questionnaires, and interviews can be used to directly ask people about their thoughts and behaviors.

2.6 Correlational Studies Describe and Predict How Variables Are Related Correlational studies are used to examine how variables are naturally related in the real world. These studies cannot be used to establish causality or the direction of a relationship (i.e., which variable caused changes in the other variable).

2.7 The Experimental Method Controls and Explains An experiment can demonstrate a causal relationship between variables. Experimenters manipulate one variable, the independent variable, to determine its effect on another, the dependent variable. Research participants are divided into experimental groups and control groups. People in the experimental group experience one level of the independent variable, and those in the control group experience another for comparison. In evaluating the data, researchers must look for confounds—elements other than the variables that may have affected the results. Inferences about how the independent variable influences the dependent variable are valid only when all confounds are addressed.

2.8 Participants Need to Be Randomly Assigned to Conditions and Carefully Selected Researchers use random assignment to levels of the independent variable (conditions) to establish causality between an intervention and an outcome. Random assignment means that all participants have an equal chance of being assigned to any level of the independent variable, thereby controlling for preexisting differences when the sample size is large enough. Researchers sample participants from the population they want to study (e.g., teenagers). They use random sampling when everyone in the population is equally likely to participate in the study, a condition that rarely occurs. Culturally sensitive research recognizes the differences among people from different cultural groups and from different language backgrounds.

What Are the Ethics Governing Psychological Research?

2.9 There Are Ethical Issues to Consider in Research with Human Participants Ethical research is governed by principles that ensure fair, safe, and informed treatment of participants. The Belmont Report described three fundamental ethical principles for research using human participants: respect for persons, beneficence, and justice. Institutional review boards (IRBs) judge study proposals to make sure the studies will be ethically sound.

2.10 Psychology Outside the Lab: Have You Participated in Research Without Knowing It? Companies use simple experiments called A/B tests to improve their products. Internet companies can run thousands of such tests in a day. Many people do not realize that they are participants in studies when they log on to social media platforms. Researchers need to adapt the ethical principles for research, given the amount and personal nature of the information available to companies.

2.11 There Are Ethical Issues to Consider in Research with Animals Research involving nonhuman animals provides useful, although simpler, models of behavior and of genetics. The purpose of such research may be to learn about animals' behavior or to make inferences about human behavior. Judges from Institutional Animal Care and Use Committees (IACUCs) study proposals to make sure the animals will be treated properly. Researchers must weigh their concerns for individual animals against their concerns for humanity's future.

How Are Data Analyzed and Evaluated?

2.12 Good Research Requires Valid, Reliable, and Accurate Data Data must be meaningful (valid) and their measurement reliable (i.e., consistent and stable) and accurate. Construct validity requires that variables reflect what they are intended to measure. External validity requires that the procedures accurately capture an experience in the real world. Internal validity is established when the experiment's results can be used for causal inference.

2.13 Descriptive Statistics Provide a Summary of the Data Measures of central tendency (mean, median, and mode) and variability are used to describe data. The mean is the arithmetic average. The median is the middle value. The mode is the most common value.

2.14 Inferential Statistics Permit Generalizations Inferential statistics enable psychologists to decide whether the observed data are unlikely if there was no true difference in the underlying populations being compared. Bayesian statistics help researchers know how much to update their beliefs about a hypothesis based on the new data.

2.15 You Be the Psychologist: Should You Believe in Extrasensory Perception? An infamous study claimed to show evidence for extrasensory perception and other unusual abilities. A closer look at the experimental method revealed how common practices could lead to misleading results. The paper prompted psychologists to change how they conduct, analyze, and report their research.

Key Terms

accuracy, p. 55
Bayesian statistics, p. 59
case study, p. 40
central tendency, p. 56
confound, p. 47
construct validity, p. 55
control group, p. 46
correlation coefficient, p. 43
correlational studies, p. 42
culturally sensitive research, p. 49
data, p. 30
dependent variable, p. 45
descriptive research, p. 40
descriptive statistics, p. 56
directionality problem, p. 43
experiment, p. 45
experimental group, p. 46
experimentation aversion, p. 52
external validity, p. 55
false positive, p. 36
HARKing, p. 36
hypothesis, p. 31
independent variable, p. 45
inferential statistics, p. 58
institutional review boards (IRBs), p. 50
internal validity, p. 55
mean, p. 56
median, p. 56
meta-analysis, p. 37
mode, p. 58
naturalistic observation, p. 41
operational definition, p. 33
participant observation, p. 41
p-hacking, p. 37
population, p. 48
preregistration, p. 37
questionable research practices, p. 36
random assignment, p. 47
reliability, p. 55
replication, p. 35
research, p. 30
sample, p. 48
scatterplot, p. 42
scientific method, p. 30
self-report methods, p. 41
standard deviation, p. 58
theory, p. 31
third variable problem, p. 44
variability, p. 58
variable, p. 33

Practice Exercises

1. Which of the following is a good research practice that increases scientists' confidence in the findings from a given research study?
   a. meta-analysis
   b. operationalization of variables
   c. replication
   d. parsimony

For the following four questions, imagine you are designing a study to investigate whether deep breathing causes reductions in student stress levels. Because you are investigating a causal question, you will need to employ experimental research. For each step in the design process, determine the best scientific decision.

2. Which hypothesis is stronger? Why?
   a. Stress levels will differ between students who engage in deep breathing and those who do not.
   b. Students who engage in deep breathing will report less stress than those who do not engage in deep breathing.

3. Which sampling method is strongest? Why?
   a. Obtain an alphabetical list of all students enrolled at the college. Invite every fifth person on the list to participate in the study.
   b. Post a note to your Facebook to recruit your friends and ask them to spread the word.
   c. Post flyers around local gyms and yoga studios inviting people to participate in your study.

4. Which set of conditions should be included in the study? Why?
   a. All participants should be given written directions for a deep-breathing exercise and complete it at assigned times.
   b. Some participants should be given written directions for a deep-breathing exercise. Other participants should be given a DVD with demonstrations of deep-breathing exercises.
   c. Some participants should be given written directions for a deep-breathing exercise and complete it at assigned times. Other participants should be given written information about student stress in general (but without any information about reducing stress).

5. How should participants be chosen for each condition? Why?
   a. Once people agree to participate in the study, flip a coin to assign each participant to the experimental condition or the control condition.
   b. Let participants select which condition they would like to be in.

6. Which operational definition of the dependent variable, stress, is stronger? Why?

   a. Stress is a pattern of behavioral and physiological responses that match or exceed a person's abilities to respond in a healthy way.

   b. Stress will be measured using five questions asking participants to rate aspects of their stress level on a scale from 1 to 10, where 1 equals *not at all stressed* and 10 equals *as stressed as I've ever been.*

For the following three questions, imagine you want to know whether students at your college talk about politics in their day-to-day lives. To investigate this issue, you would like to conduct an observational study and need to make three design decisions. For each decision, recommend the best practice.

7. Should you conduct the study in a lab or in a natural setting (e.g., in the campus dining hall)? Why?

8. Should you write down everything you hear or keep a running tally of prespecified categories of behavior? Why?

9. Should participants know you are observing them? Why?

10. Indicate which quality of good data is violated by each description. Response options are "accuracy," "reliability," and "validity."

   a. A booth at the local carnival announces the discovery of a new way to assess intelligence. The assessment method involves interpreting the pattern of creases on one's left palm.

   b. At the end of a long night of grading, a professor reads what he believes to be the last essay in the pile. He assigns it a grade of 80 percent. When he goes to write the grade on the back of the paper, he realizes he already graded this paper earlier in the evening—and gave it only a 70 percent the first time around.

   c. A 5-year-old counts the jelly beans in a jar, often skipping over numbers ending in 8 (e.g., 8, 18, 28).

3 Biology and Behavior

Big Questions

SINCE 2007 THE AMERICAN PSYCHOLOGICAL Association has conducted an annual *Stress in America* survey to assess what factors cause people to feel stress and how much stress we experience in our everyday lives (American Psychological Association, 2020). If there is one take-home message from these surveys, it is that Americans are stressed—a lot. And the levels are increasing. In 2020 the COVID-19 pandemic added more stress to our already stressed lives. How does stress affect us? Psychologists know that it has physiological consequences that impact the brain in uneven but predictable ways. In fact, even relatively mild stress can diminish the function of brain regions that help us think flexibly, execute long-term goals, and control emotions. Everyday events—such as running late for work or fighting with a friend—not only make us feel bad but can also affect higher brain functions. This is why if you have a bad day you might find it harder to stick to a diet, focus on studying for an exam, or avoid overreacting when upset.

To understand what makes us who we are, how we behave, and why, we need to know how the nervous system works. Physiological processes—such as the activities of cells—are the basis of psychological processes. By studying the nervous system, we not only can understand how behaviors and mental states are generated but also can gain novel insights into psychological phenomena. However, biology alone does not explain our behavior. Aspects of our biology interact with our environments, so we also need to consider how nature and nurture influence each other in shaping us. In this chapter, we explore how the brain enables the mind and behavior and how it interacts with our genes and bodies. In other words, how does the brain make us who we are?

Learning Objectives

- Distinguish between the two basic divisions of the nervous system.
- Distinguish between the functions of distinct types of neurons.
- Describe the structure of the neuron.
- Describe the electrical and chemical changes that occur when neurons communicate.
- Describe how agonists and antagonists can influence the action of neurotransmitters.

How Does the Nervous System Operate?

The nervous system's response to the world around us is responsible for everything we think, feel, or do. Essentially, each of us *is* a nervous system. The entire nervous system is divided into two basic units: the central nervous system and the peripheral nervous system. The **central nervous system (CNS)** consists of the brain and the spinal cord (**FIGURE 3.1**). The **peripheral nervous system (PNS)** consists of all the other nerve cells in the rest of the body and includes the somatic and autonomic nervous systems. The somatic component is involved in voluntary behavior, such as when you reach for an object. The autonomic component is responsible for the less voluntary actions of your body, such as controlling your heart rate and other bodily functions. The CNS and PNS are anatomically separate, but their functions are highly interdependent. The PNS sends a variety of information to the CNS. The CNS organizes and evaluates that information and then directs the PNS to perform specific behaviors or make bodily adjustments.

central nervous system (CNS) The brain and the spinal cord.

peripheral nervous system (PNS) All nerve cells in the body that are not part of the central nervous system. The peripheral nervous system includes the somatic and autonomic nervous systems.

neurons The basic units of the nervous system; cells that receive, integrate, and transmit information. They operate through electrical impulses, communicate with other neurons through chemical signals, and form neural networks.

3.1 Neurons Are the Basic Units of the Nervous System

The basic units of the nervous system are the nerve cells, called **neurons** (**FIGURE 3.2**), which receive, integrate, and transmit information. Complex networks of neurons sending and receiving signals are the functional basis of all psychological activity. Although the actions of single neurons are simple to describe, human complexity results from billions of neurons. Each neuron communicates with tens of thousands of other neurons. Neurons do not communicate randomly or arbitrarily, however. They communicate selectively with other neurons to form circuits, or *neural networks*. These networks develop through genetic influence, maturation and experience, and repeated firing.

FUNCTIONS OF NEURONS Neurons are specialized for communication with each other. Unlike other cells in the body, nerve cells are excitable: They are

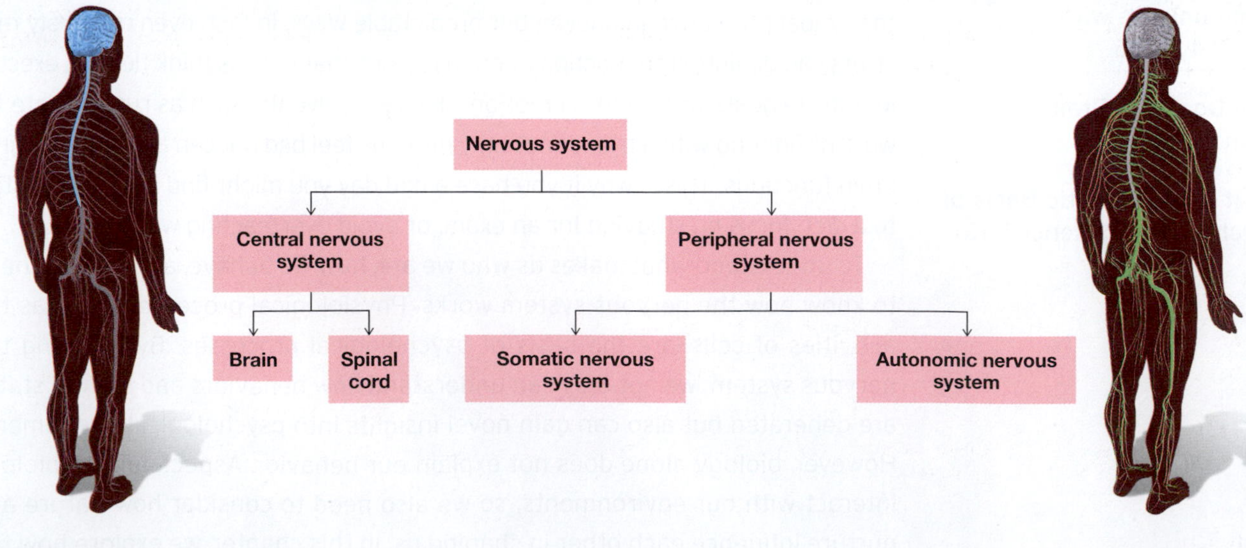

FIGURE 3.1
The Basic Divisions of the Nervous System

powered by electrical impulses and communicate with other nerve cells through chemical signals. During the reception phase, neurons take in chemical signals from neighboring neurons. During integration, incoming signals are assessed. During transmission, neurons pass their own signals to yet other receiving neurons.

There are many types of neurons. *Sensory neurons* detect information from the physical world and pass that information along to the brain. To get a sense of how fast that process can work, think of the last time you touched something hot or accidentally pricked yourself with a sharp object, such as a tack. Those signals triggered your body's nearly instantaneous response and sensory experience of the impact. The sensory nerves that provide information from the skin and muscles are called *somatosensory nerves*. (This term comes from the Greek for "body sense." It means sensations experienced from within the body.) *Motor neurons* direct muscles to contract or relax, thereby producing movement. *Interneurons* act as relay stations facilitating communication between sensory and motor neurons.

Sensory and motor neurons work together to control movement. For instance, if you are using a pen to take notes as you read these words, you are contracting and relaxing your hand muscles and finger muscles to adjust your fingers' pressure on the pen. When you want to use the pen, your brain sends a message via motor neurons to your finger muscles so they move in specific ways. Receptors in both your skin and your muscles send back messages through sensory neurons to help determine how much pressure is needed to hold the pen. This symphony of neural communication for a task as simple as using a pen is remarkable, yet most of us employ motor control so easily that we rarely think about it. In fact, our *reflexes*, automatic motor responses, occur before we even think about those responses. For each reflex action, a handful of neurons simply convert sensation into action.

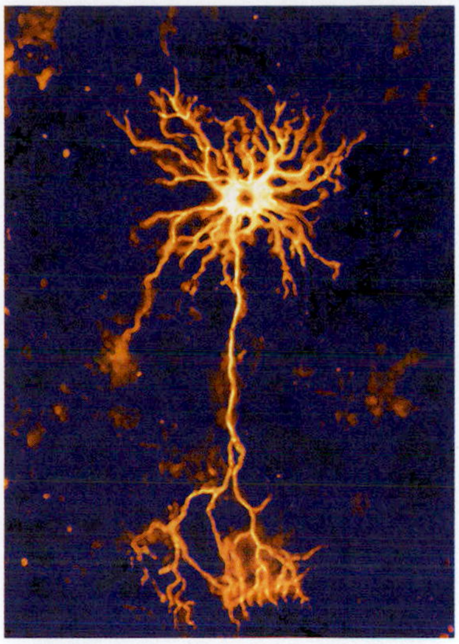

FIGURE 3.2
Human Neuron
Neurons like this one are the basic units of the human nervous system.

NEURON STRUCTURE In addition to performing different functions, neurons have a wide assortment of shapes and sizes. A typical neuron has four structural regions that participate in communication functions: the dendrites, the cell body, the axon, and the terminal buttons (**FIGURE 3.3**). The **dendrites** are short, branchlike appendages that detect chemical signals from neighboring neurons. In the **cell body**, also known as the *soma* (Greek for "body"), the information received via the dendrites from thousands of other neurons is collected and integrated.

Once the incoming information from many other neurons has been integrated in the cell body, electrical impulses are transmitted along a long, narrow outgrowth known as the **axon**. Axons vary tremendously in length, from a few millimeters

dendrites Branchlike extensions of the neuron that detect information from other neurons.

cell body The site in the neuron where information from thousands of other neurons is collected and integrated.

axon A long, narrow outgrowth of a neuron by which information is conducted from the cell body to the terminal buttons.

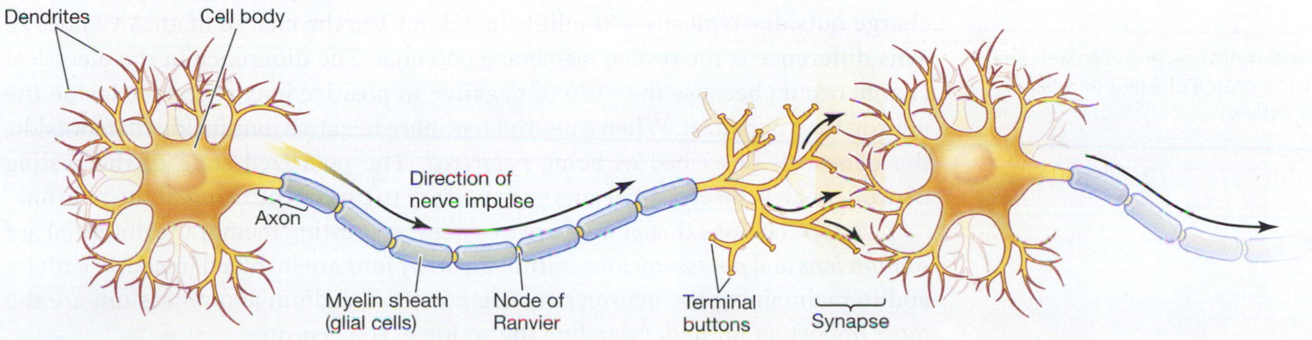

FIGURE 3.3
Neuron Structure
Messages are received by the dendrites, processed in the cell body, transmitted along the axon, and sent to other neurons via chemical substances released from the terminal buttons across the synapse. (The myelin sheath and the nodes of Ranvier are discussed on p. 73.)

to more than a meter. The longest axons stretch from the spinal cord to the big toe. You may have heard the term *nerve* in reference to a "pinched nerve." In this context, a nerve is a bundle of axons that carry information between the brain and other specific locations in the body. At the end of each axon are knoblike structures called **terminal buttons**.

terminal buttons At the ends of axons, small nodules that release chemical signals from the neuron into the synapse.

synapse The gap between the terminal buttons of a "sending" neuron and the dendrites of a "receiving" neuron, where chemical communication occurs between the neurons.

The site where chemical communication occurs between neurons is called the **synapse**. Since neurons do not touch one another, they communicate by sending chemicals into the synapse, a tiny gap between the terminal buttons of the "sending" neuron and the dendrites of the "receiving" neurons. Chemicals leave the terminal buttons of one neuron, cross the synapse, and pass signals along to the dendrites of other neurons.

The outer surface of a neuron is a *membrane*, a fatty barrier that does not dissolve in the watery environment inside and outside the neuron. The membrane is selectively permeable. In other words, some substances move in or out of the membrane, and some do not. Located on the membrane are *ion channels*. These specialized pores allow *ions* to pass in and out of the cell when the neuron transmits signals down the axon. Ions are electrically charged molecules, some charged negatively and some charged positively. By controlling the movement of ions, the membrane plays an important role in communication between neurons: It regulates the concentration of electrically charged molecules that are the basis of the neuron's electrical activity.

Q **What is the positional order of neuronal cell structures (cell body, dendrites, terminal buttons, and axon), from receiving component to sending component?**

ANSWER: Between the synapses, the positional order is dendrites, cell body, axon, and terminal buttons.

3.2 Action Potentials Produce Neural Communication

Neural communication depends on a neuron's ability to respond to incoming stimulation. The neuron responds by changing electrically and then passing along chemical signals to other neurons. An **action potential**, also called *neural firing*, is the electrical signal that passes along the axon. This signal causes the terminal buttons to release chemicals that transmit signals to other neurons. The following sections examine some factors that contribute to the firing of an action potential.

action potential The electrical signal that passes along the axon and subsequently causes the release of chemicals from the terminal buttons.

RESTING MEMBRANE POTENTIAL When a neuron is resting, not active, the electrical charge inside the neuron is slightly more negative than the electrical charge outside—typically –70 millivolts (about 1⁄20 the charge of an AA battery). This difference is the **resting membrane potential**. The difference in the electrical charge occurs because the ratio of negative to positive ions is greater inside the neuron than outside it. When a neuron has more negative ions inside than outside, the neuron is described as being *polarized*. The polarized state of the resting neuron creates the electrical energy necessary to power the firing of the neuron.

resting membrane potential The electrical charge of a neuron when it is not active.

Two types of ions that contribute to a neuron's resting membrane potential are *sodium ions* and *potassium ions*. Although other ions are involved in neural activity and in maintaining the neuron's resting potential, sodium and potassium are the most important for understanding the action of the neuron.

Ions pass through the neuron membrane at the ion channels (**FIGURE 3.4**). Each channel matches a specific type of ion: Sodium channels allow sodium ions but not potassium ions to pass through the membrane, and potassium channels allow

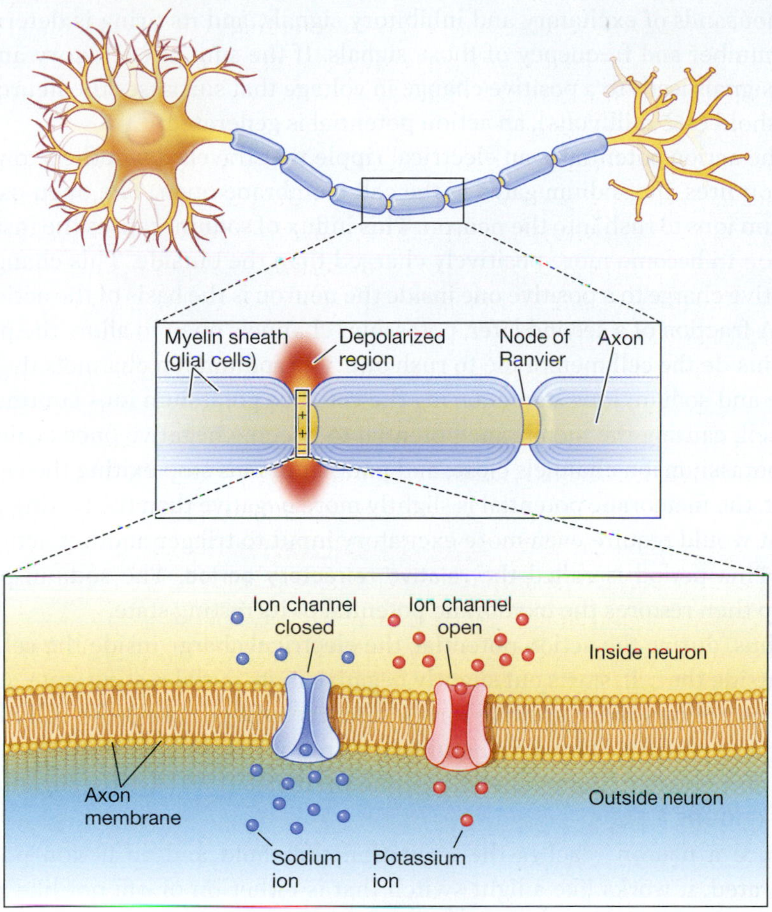

FIGURE 3.4
Resting Membrane Potential
A neuron at rest is polarized: It has a more negative electrical charge inside than outside. The passage of negative and positive ions inside and outside the neuron is regulated by ion channels in the membrane, such as those located at the nodes of Ranvier.

passage of potassium ions but not sodium ions. The flow of ions through each channel is controlled by a gating mechanism. When a gate is open, ions flow in and out of the neuron through the cell membrane. A closed gate prevents their passage. Ion flow is also affected by the cell membrane's selective permeability. That is, much like a bouncer at an exclusive nightclub, the membrane allows some types of ions to cross more easily than others.

Another mechanism in the membrane that contributes to polarization is the *sodium-potassium pump*. This pump increases potassium and decreases sodium inside the neuron, thus helping maintain the resting membrane potential.

CHANGES IN ELECTRICAL POTENTIAL LEAD TO AN ACTION POTENTIAL

A neuron receives chemical signals from nearby neurons through its dendrites. These chemical signals impact local ion channels, thus influencing the polarization of the neuron. By affecting polarization, these chemical signals tell the neuron whether to fire. The signals arrive at the dendrites by the thousands and are of two types: excitatory and inhibitory. *Excitatory signals* depolarize the cell membrane (i.e., decrease polarization by decreasing the negative charge inside the cell relative to outside the cell). Through depolarization, these signals increase the likelihood that the neuron will fire. *Inhibitory signals* hyperpolarize the cell (i.e., increase polarization by increasing the negative charge inside the cell relative to outside the cell). Through hyperpolarization, these signals decrease the likelihood that the neuron will fire. Excitatory and inhibitory signals received by the dendrites are combined within the neuron. Any one signal received by the neuron has little influence on whether the neuron fires. Normally, a neuron is barraged by thousands of excitatory and inhibitory signals, and its firing is determined by the number and frequency of those signals. If the sum of excitatory and inhibitory signals leads to a positive change in voltage that surpasses the neuron's firing threshold (–55 millivolts), an action potential is generated.

The action potential is an electrical ripple that travels down the axon. When a neuron fires, the sodium gates in the cell membrane open. The open gates allow sodium ions to rush into the neuron. This influx of sodium causes the inside of the neuron to become more positively charged than the outside. This change from a negative charge to a positive one inside the neuron is the basis of the action potential. A fraction of a second later, potassium channels open to allow the potassium ions inside the cell membrane to rush out. The sodium ion channels then start to close and sodium ions stop entering the cell, but potassium ions continue to exit the cell, causing the membrane potential to become negative once again. Finally, the potassium ion channels close, and potassium ions stop exiting the cell. At this point, the membrane potential is slightly more negative than the resting potential, and it would require even more excitatory input to trigger another action potential. This period is called the **relative refractory period**. The sodium-potassium pump then restores the membrane potential to its resting state.

relative refractory period The brief period of time following action potential when a neuron's membrane potential is more negative, or hyperpolarized, making it harder to fire again.

Thus, during the action potential, the electrical charge inside the cell, relative to outside the cell, starts out slightly negative in its initial resting state. As the cell fires and allows more positive ions inside, the charge across the cell membrane becomes positive. Through natural restoration, including the activity of the sodium-potassium pump, the charge then returns to its slightly negative resting state (**FIGURE 3.5**).

Once a neuron reaches the excitation threshold and an action potential is generated, it works like a light switch that is either on or off, not like a dimmer switch. The **all-or-none principle** dictates that a neuron fires with the same potency each time. In other words, it does not fire in a way that can be described as weak or strong; it either fires or it does not. What is affected by the strength of the

all-or-none principle The principle that when a neuron fires, it fires with the same potency each time; a neuron either fires or not, although the frequency of firing can vary.

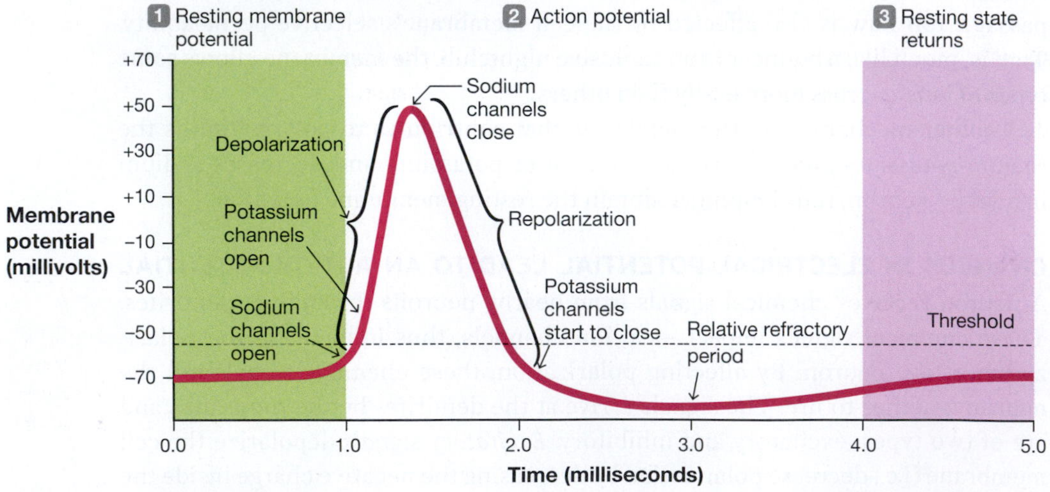

FIGURE 3.5
Action Potential
The electrical charge inside the neuron relative to outside the neuron starts out negative (resting membrane potential, -70 millivolts). As the neuron fires, it allows more positive ions inside the cell (depolarization), resulting in a reversal of polarity such that the charge inside the neuron is more positive than outside. It then returns to its slightly negative resting state. This happens at each portion of the exposed axon as the action potential travels down the axon.

stimulation is how often the neuron fires: the stronger the stimulation, the more frequently action potentials are generated. For the sake of comparison, suppose you are playing a video game in which you fire missiles by pressing a button. Every time you press the button, a missile is launched at the same velocity as the previous one. It makes no difference how hard you press the button. If you keep your finger on the button, additional missiles fire in rapid succession. Likewise, if a neuron in the visual system, for example, receives information that a light is bright, it might respond by firing more rapidly and more often than when it receives information that the light is dim. But regardless of whether the light is bright or dim, the strength of the firing will be the same every time.

ACTION POTENTIALS TRAVEL DOWN THE AXON When the neuron fires, the cell membrane's depolarization moves along the axon like a wave. Sodium ions rush through their channels, causing adjacent sodium channels to open. Thus, like toppling dominoes, sodium ion channels open in a series. Once an ion channel opens and closes, there is a short **absolute refractory period** in which it cannot open again. This is followed by the relative refractory period, described earlier, in which it takes greater excitation to fire the neuron again. Because the absolute and relative refractory periods prevent ion channels from responding again after they were just active, the action potential always moves in one direction: down the axon away from the cell body to the terminal buttons.

absolute refractory period The brief period of time following an action potential when the ion channel is unable to respond again.

The action potential travels down the entire length of the axon. The axons of many types of neurons are covered by a **myelin sheath**. A myelin sheath encases and insulates many axons like the plastic tubing around wires in an electrical cord. The myelin sheath is made up of *glial cells*, commonly called *glia* (Greek for "glue"), and grows along an axon in short segments. Between these segments are small gaps of exposed axon called the **nodes of Ranvier** (after the researcher who first described them). Because of the insulation provided by the myelin sheath, the action potential does not have to traverse the entire length of the axon. Instead it skips quickly along the gaps of the myelin sheath, impacting the ion channels located at the nodes of Ranvier. The presence of the myelin greatly increases the speed with which an action potential travels down the axon (**FIGURE 3.6**).

myelin sheath A fatty material, made up of glial cells, that insulates some axons to allow for faster movement of electrical impulses along the axon.

nodes of Ranvier Small gaps of exposed axon between the segments of myelin sheath, where action potentials take place.

To understand the importance of the neural insulation provided by the myelin sheath, consider the disease multiple sclerosis (MS), which affects more than 250,000 Americans (Goldenberg, 2012) and is characterized by deterioration of the myelin sheath. Since the myelin insulation helps messages move quickly along

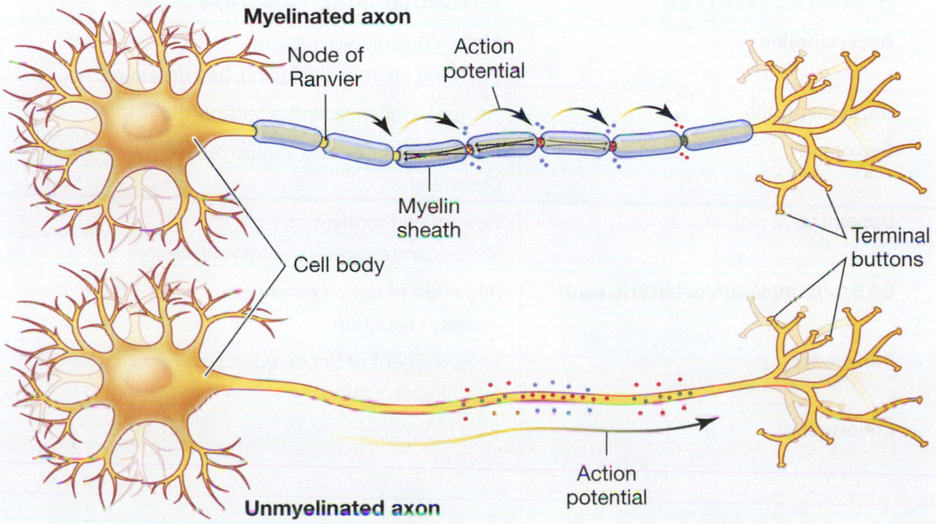

FIGURE 3.6
Myelin Sheath
The action potential travels down each part of an unmyelinated axon. On axons covered by a myelin sheath, the action potential jumps between breaks in the myelin (called nodes of Ranvier), resulting in faster neural transmission.

axons, demyelination slows down neural impulses and interrupts normal neural communication. The earliest symptoms of MS can begin in young adulthood and often include numbness in the limbs and blurry vision. Over time, movement, sensation, and coordination can become impaired, and many people who have MS need help walking. As the myelin sheath disintegrates, axons are exposed and may start to break down. The life expectancy of people with MS is five to 10 years less than that of people who are not afflicted.

Q **What happens when a neuron is depolarized past its firing threshold?**

ANSWER: An action potential occurs—that is, the neuron fires an electrical signal along the axon.

3.3 Neurotransmitters Influence Mental Activity and Behavior

As noted earlier in this chapter, neurons do not touch one another. They are separated by a small space known as the synapse, the site of chemical communication between neurons. The neuron that sends the signal is called the *presynaptic neuron*, and the one that receives the signal is called the *postsynaptic neuron*. Inside each terminal button of the presynaptic neuron are **neurotransmitters**, chemicals that are made in the axon or cell body and stored in vesicles (small, fluid-filled sacs). More than 60 chemicals convey information in the nervous system. Different neurotransmitters influence emotion, thought, or behavior, depending on the type of receptor and the location within the brain. **TABLE 3.1** summarizes seven neurotransmitters that are particularly important in understanding how we think, feel, and behave.

neurotransmitters Chemical substances that transmit signals from one neuron to another.

NEUROTRANSMITTERS BIND WITH SPECIFIC RECEPTORS After an action potential travels to the terminal button, it causes the vesicles to attach to the presynaptic membrane and release their neurotransmitters into the synapse

Table 3.1 Common Neurotransmitters and Their Major Functions

NEUROTRANSMITTER	PSYCHOLOGICAL FUNCTIONS
Acetylcholine	Motor control over muscles Learning, memory, sleeping, and dreaming
Norepinephrine	Arousal, vigilance, and attention
Serotonin	Emotional states and impulsiveness Dreaming
Dopamine	Reward and motivation Motor control over voluntary movement
GABA (gamma-aminobutyric acid)	Inhibition of action potentials Anxiety reduction
Glutamate	Enhancement of action potentials Learning and memory
Endorphins	Pain reduction Reward

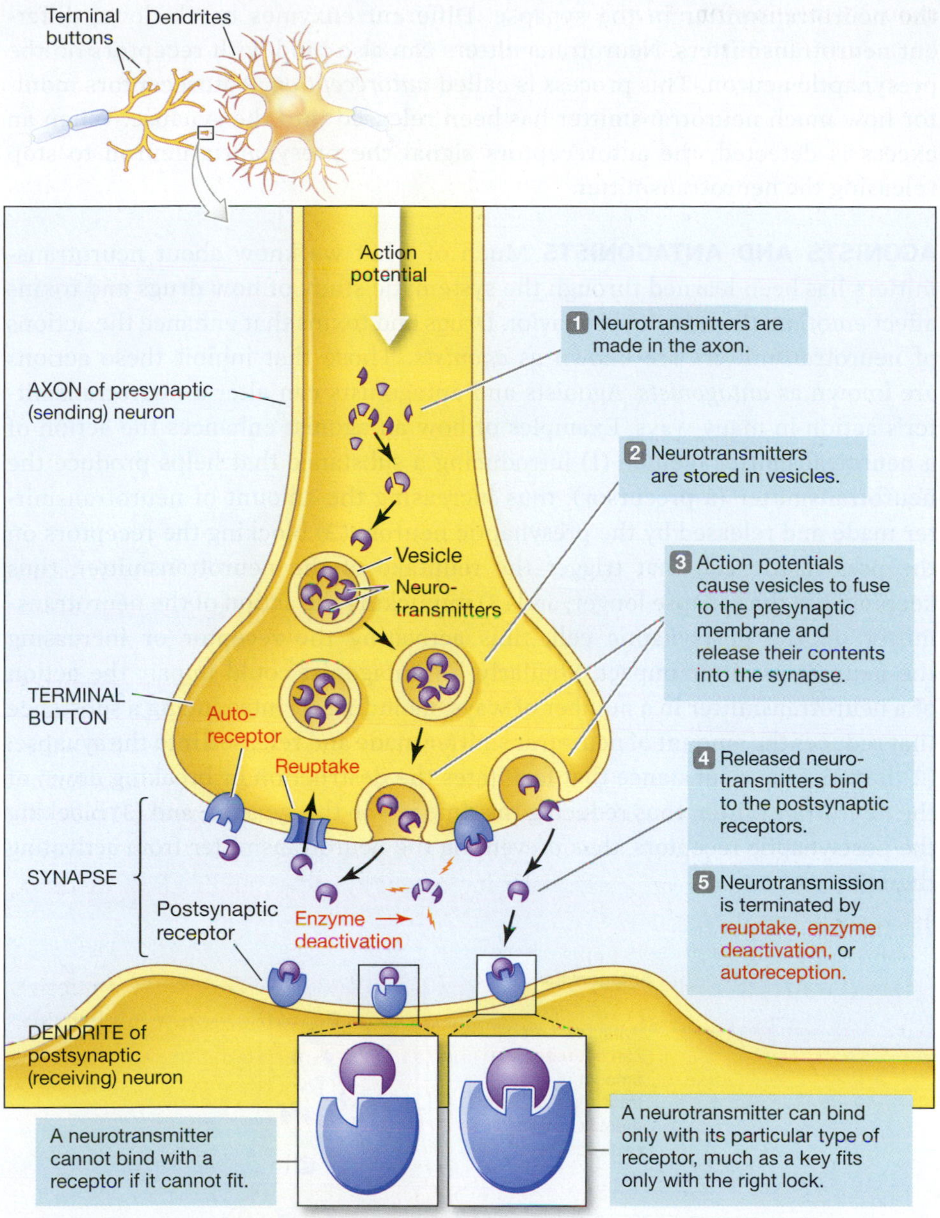

Terminal buttons
Dendrites
Action potential
1 Neurotransmitters are made in the axon.
AXON of presynaptic (sending) neuron
2 Neurotransmitters are stored in vesicles.
Vesicle
Neuro-transmitters
3 Action potentials cause vesicles to fuse to the presynaptic membrane and release their contents into the synapse.
TERMINAL BUTTON
Auto-receptor
Reuptake
4 Released neuro-transmitters bind to the postsynaptic receptors.
SYNAPSE
5 Neurotransmission is terminated by reuptake, enzyme deactivation, or autoreception.
Postsynaptic receptor
Enzyme deactivation
DENDRITE of postsynaptic (receiving) neuron
A neurotransmitter cannot bind with a receptor if it cannot fit.
A neurotransmitter can bind only with its particular type of receptor, much as a key fits only with the right lock.

FIGURE 3.7
How Neurotransmitters Work

(**FIGURE 3.7**). These neurotransmitters then travel across the synapse and attach themselves, or *bind*, to receptors on the dendrites of the postsynaptic neuron. **Receptors** are specialized protein molecules located on the postsynaptic membrane that specifically respond to the chemical structure of the neurotransmitter available in the synapse. Much the same way a lock opens only with the correct key, each receptor on the postsynaptic neuron can be influenced by only one type of neurotransmitter. The binding of a neurotransmitter with a receptor can cause ion channels to open or to close more tightly, producing an excitatory or an inhibitory signal in the postsynaptic neuron.

receptors In neurons, specialized protein molecules on the postsynaptic membrane; neurotransmitters bind to these molecules after passing across the synapse.

Once a neurotransmitter is released into the synapse, it exerts an effect until its influence is terminated. The three major events that terminate the neurotransmitter's influence in the synapse are reuptake, enzyme deactivation, and autoreception. **Reuptake** occurs when the neurotransmitter is taken back into the presynaptic terminal buttons. An action potential prompts terminal buttons to release the neurotransmitter into the synapse and then take it back for recycling. *Enzyme deactivation* occurs when an enzyme destroys

reuptake The process whereby a neurotransmitter is taken back into the presynaptic terminal buttons, thereby stopping its activity.

the neurotransmitter in the synapse. Different enzymes break down different neurotransmitters. Neurotransmitters can also bind with receptors on the presynaptic neuron. This process is called *autoreception*. Autoreceptors monitor how much neurotransmitter has been released into the synapse. When an excess is detected, the autoreceptors signal the presynaptic neuron to stop releasing the neurotransmitter.

AGONISTS AND ANTAGONISTS Much of what we know about neurotransmitters has been learned through the systematic study of how drugs and toxins affect emotion, thought, and behavior. Drugs and toxins that enhance the actions of neurotransmitters are known as *agonists*. Those that inhibit these actions are known as *antagonists*. Agonists and antagonists can alter a neurotransmitter's action in many ways. Examples of how an agonist enhances the action of a neurotransmitter include (1) introducing a substance that helps produce the neurotransmitter (a precursor), thus increasing the amount of neurotransmitter made and released by the presynaptic neuron; (2) blocking the receptors on the presynaptic cell that trigger the reuptake of the neurotransmitter, thus keeping it in the synapse longer; and (3) mimicking the action of the neurotransmitter on the postsynaptic cell, thus activating the receptor or increasing the neurotransmitter impact. Similarly, an antagonist could impair the action of a neurotransmitter in a number of ways, including (1) introducing a substance that reduces the amount of neurotransmitter made and released into the synapse; (2) introducing a substance that facilitates the destruction or breaking down of the neurotransmitter, thus reducing the time it is in the synapse; and (3) blocking the postsynaptic receptors, thus preventing the neurotransmitter from activating them (**FIGURE 3.8**).

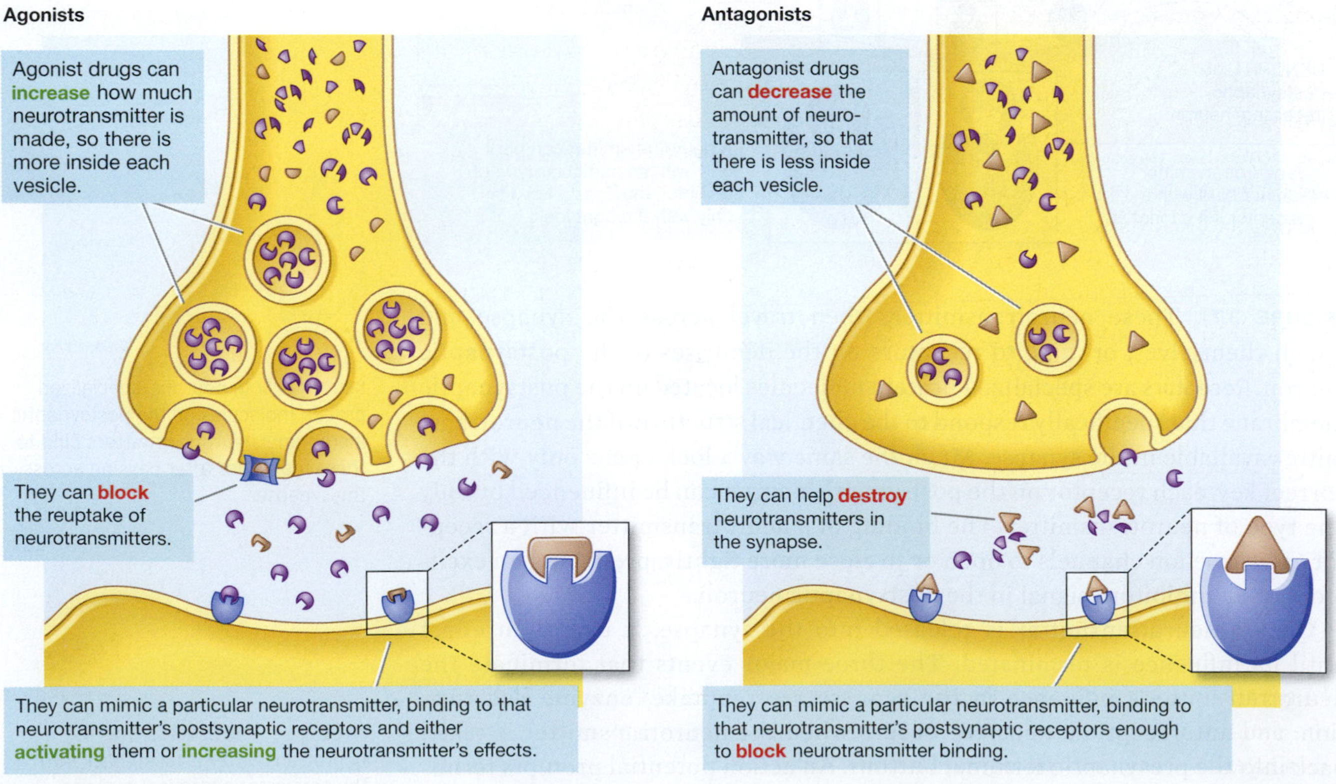

Agonists
Agonist drugs can increase how much neurotransmitter is made, so there is more inside each vesicle.
They can block the reuptake of neurotransmitters.
They can mimic a particular neurotransmitter, binding to that neurotransmitter's postsynaptic receptors and either activating them or increasing the neurotransmitter's effects.
Antagonists
Antagonist drugs can decrease the amount of neurotransmitter, so that there is less inside each vesicle.
They can help destroy neurotransmitters in the synapse.
They can mimic a particular neurotransmitter, binding to that neurotransmitter's postsynaptic receptors enough to block neurotransmitter binding.

FIGURE 3.8
How Drugs Work

Learning Tip

To help remember the difference between agonist and antagonist, remember that an AGonist helps the postsynaptic neuron respond AGain and AGain by increasing the action of the neurotransmitter. An ANTAgonist is ANTI, or against the neurotransmitter working, and reduces the action of the neurotransmitter.

Addictive drugs such as heroin have their effects because they are chemically similar to endorphins, which are naturally occurring neurotransmitters. The receptors on the postsynaptic neuron cannot differentiate between the ingested drug and the real neurotransmitter released from a presynaptic neuron. That is, although a neurotransmitter fits a receptor the way a key fits a lock, the receptor/lock cannot tell a real neurotransmitter/key from a forgery, so either will open it. Another agonist is the class of antidepressant drugs called selective serotonin reuptake inhibitors (SSRIs). As their name implies, SSRIs bind with receptors on the presynaptic cell that trigger the reuptake of serotonin, thus inhibiting its reuptake and increasing its availability in the synapse.

An agonist that acts by introducing a substance that increases production of the neurotransmitter dopamine is levodopa (L-DOPA), which is used to treat Parkinson's disease. Parkinson's is a degenerative and fatal neurological disorder marked by muscular rigidity, tremors, and difficulty initiating voluntary action. It affects about 1 in every 200 older adults. The actor Michael J. Fox is one of the many famous people who have developed this disease (**FIGURE 3.9**). With Parkinson's disease, the dopamine-producing neurons slowly die off. In the later stages of the disorder, people suffer from cognitive and mood disturbances. Administering L-DOPA helps the surviving neurons produce more dopamine. When used to treat Parkinson's disease, L-DOPA often produces a remarkable, though temporary, recovery.

FIGURE 3.9
A Public Figure with Parkinson's
Michael J. Fox was diagnosed with Parkinson's disease in 1991, at age 30. He has since created the Michael J. Fox Foundation, which advocates for research toward finding a cure for Parkinson's.

Interestingly, many drugs that are used to treat schizophrenia have the opposite effect of L-DOPA. They are dopamine antagonists and block dopamine from binding to receptors on the postsynaptic neuron. Because Parkinson's patients take dopamine agonists, thus increasing the function of dopamine, at times they may start to experience some of the psychotic symptoms typical of schizophrenia, such as hallucinations. On the flip side, schizophrenic patients taking dopamine antagonists may eventually start to experience involuntary muscle movements. In treating neurological and psychological disorders, it can be a delicate task to discover the right balance of enhancing or inhibiting neurotransmitters' function through different types of agonist or antagonist drugs.

Q How do agonists differ from antagonists?

ANSWER: Agonists enhance the effects of neurotransmitters, whereas antagonists inhibit their effects.

What Are the Basic Brain Structures and Their Functions?

Learning Objectives

- Describe different methods for assessing brain function and activity.
- Identify the basic structures of the brain and their primary functions.
- Explain how the study of split brains contributes to understanding the functions of the cerebral hemispheres.

The brain is best viewed as a collection of interacting neural circuits. These circuits have accumulated and developed throughout human evolution. Just as our ancestors adapted to their environments, the brain has evolved specialized mechanisms to regulate breathing, food intake, body fluids, and sexual and social behavior. It has also developed sensory systems to aid in navigation and assist in recognizing friends and foes. Everything we are and do is orchestrated by the brain and, for more rudimentary actions, by the spinal cord (**FIGURE 3.10**).

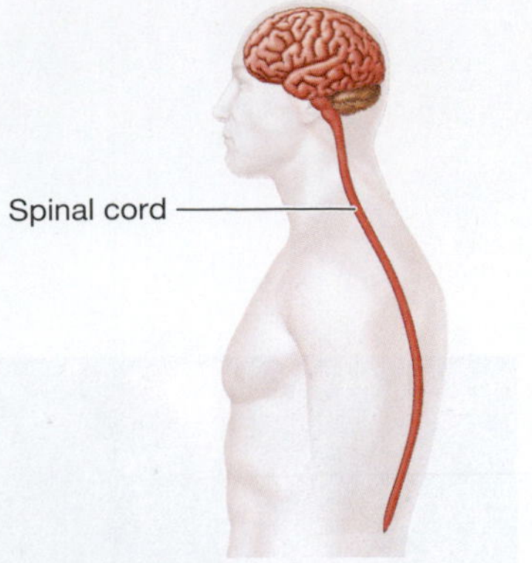

FIGURE 3.10
The Brain and the Spinal Cord
This drawing illustrates the brain's exterior and its connection with the spinal cord. The view is from the left side of the body.

3.4 The Ability to Study Brain Function Has Improved Dramatically

For most of human history, theorists and researchers have tried to understand how the brain works. By the beginning of the nineteenth century, anatomists understood the brain's basic structure reasonably well. But debates over how the brain produces mental activity continue. One early debate concerned the function of different parts of the brain. Did different parts do different things? Or were all areas of the brain equally important in cognitive functions such as problem solving and memory?

BRAIN REGIONS HAVE SPECIALIZED FUNCTIONS In the early nineteenth century, the neuroanatomist Franz Gall and his assistant, the physician Johann Spurzheim, hypothesized about the effects of mental activity on brain anatomy. Gall and Spurzheim proposed that if a person used a particular mental function more than other mental functions, the part of the brain where the emphasized function was performed would grow. This growth would produce a bump in the overlying skull. By carefully feeling the skull, one could describe the personality of the individual. This practice came to be known as *phrenology* (**FIGURE 3.11**).

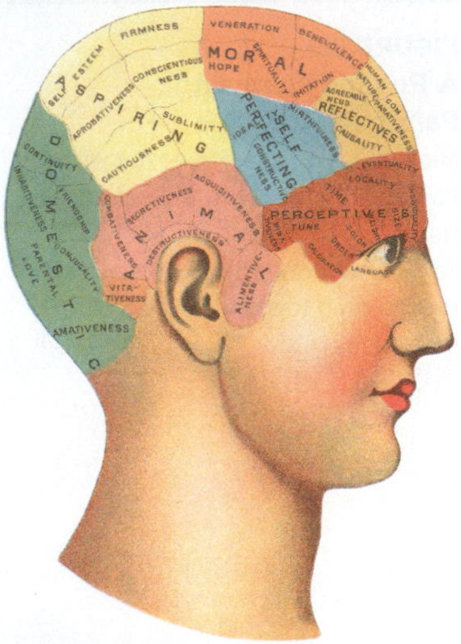

FIGURE 3.11
Phrenology
In a phrenological map, each region of the skull is associated with a mental function. Each association is meant to reflect a process occurring in the brain under the skull.

Gall was a physician, not a scientist. He noted correlations, but he did not practice the scientific method and sought only to confirm, not disprove, his ideas. In any case, at the time, the technology was not available to test this theory scientifically. The pseudoscience of phrenology soon fell into the hands of frauds and quacks, but it helped spread the notion that brain functions were localized.

The first strong scientific evidence that brain regions perform specialized functions came from the work of the nineteenth-century physician and anatomist Pierre Paul Broca (Finger, 1994). One of Broca's patients had lost the ability to say anything other than the word *tan*, though he could still understand language. After the patient died, in 1861, Broca performed an autopsy, which was the only way to link brain structure and function at the time. When he examined the patient's brain, Broca found a large area of damage in a section of the front left side. This observation led him to conclude that this particular region was important for speech. Broca's theory has survived the test of time. This left frontal region, crucial for the production of language, became known as **Broca's area** (**FIGURE 3.12**). In Chapter 8, you will learn about other brain regions involved in language.

Broca's area A small portion of the left frontal region of the brain, crucial for the production of language.

TECHNIQUES TO STUDY BRAIN FUNCTION As Broca demonstrated in the mid-1800s, studying the behavioral deficits of patients with brain injuries allowed scientists a window into the function of the brain. This technique of studying the psychological consequences of discrete brain lesions informed most of what we knew about the function of the human brain until the latter part of the twentieth century. Demonstrating that a brain injury results in a deficit in a specific psychological process, but not others, is a powerful means to discover the function of regions of the brain, and this *brain lesion methodology* is still widely used today. Although Broca had to wait until his patient died to determine where in the brain the lesion was, the advent of brain imaging technologies enabled a view of the brain anatomy of living patients, thus enhancing our ability to localize specific regions of the brain whose damage caused the psychological deficit.

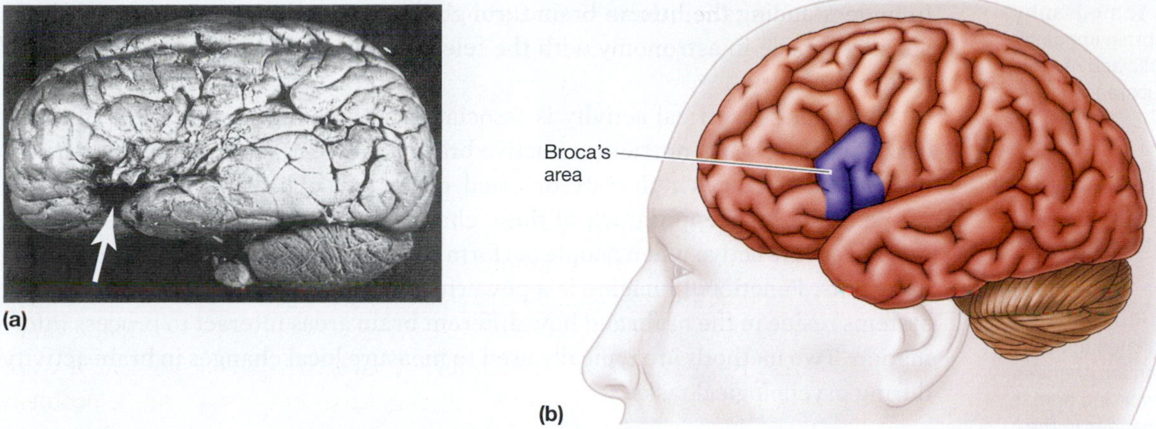

FIGURE 3.12
Broca's Area
(a) Pierre Paul Broca studied a patient's brain and identified the damaged area as crucial for speech production. **(b)** This illustration shows the location of Broca's area.

Of course, there are some downsides to relying on studies with brain-injured patients to understand the function of the human brain. Most notably, these studies can be done only on people who have naturally occurring brain lesions, have suffered injuries, or have undergone surgical interventions to treat a disease. To overcome this and other limitations, psychologists are increasingly using techniques that allow a glimpse into the function of the brains of healthy individuals in action. For instance, one method that measures electrical activity in the brain is **electroencephalography (EEG)**. Small electrodes on the scalp act like microphones that pick up the brain's electrical activity instead of sounds (**FIGURE 3.13**). This measurement is useful because different behavioral states produce different and predictable EEG patterns. As a measure of specific cognitive states, however, the EEG is limited. Because the recordings (*electroencephalograms*) reflect all brain activity, they are too "noisy" or imprecise to isolate specific responses to particular stimuli. A more powerful way of examining how brain activity changes in response to a specific stimulus involves conducting many trials with a single individual and averaging across the trials. Because this method enables researchers to observe patterns associated with specific events, it is called *event-related potential* (*ERP*). ERPs provide information about the speed at which the brain processes events and their timing, but because they measure electrical activity at the scalp that is the sum of all activity of the neural tissue underneath, it is difficult to pinpoint where in the brain those processes take place.

electroencephalography (EEG)
A technique for measuring electrical activity in the brain.

Until the 1980s, researchers did not have methods for localizing ongoing mental activity to specific brain regions in the working brain. The invention of *functional brain imaging* methods changed that situation swiftly and dramatically. Advances

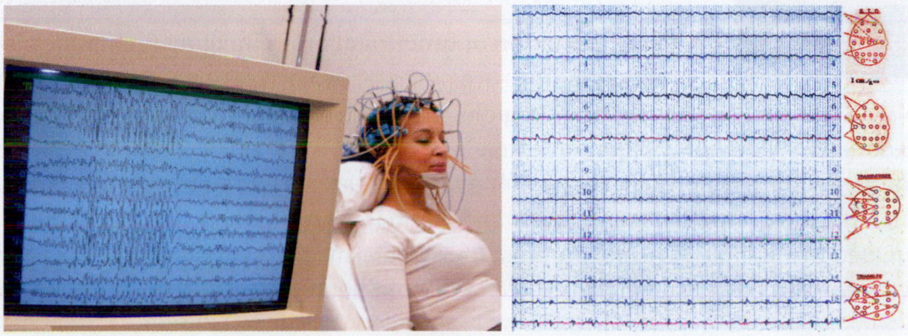

FIGURE 3.13
Electroencephalograph
Electroencephalography (EEG) measures the brain's electrical activity.

positron emission tomography (PET) A method of brain imaging that assesses metabolic activity by using a radioactive substance injected into the bloodstream.

magnetic resonance imaging (MRI) A method of brain imaging that uses a powerful magnetic field to produce high-quality images of the brain.

functional magnetic resonance imaging (fMRI) An imaging technique used to examine changes in the activity of the working human brain by measuring changes in the blood's oxygen levels.

transcranial magnetic stimulation (TMS) The use of strong magnets to briefly interrupt normal brain activity as a way to study brain regions.

in understanding the human brain through imaging techniques is comparable to advances made in astronomy with the telescope—both have revealed realities of wild complexity.

The brain's electrical activity is associated with changes in the flow of blood carrying oxygen and nutrients to active brain regions. Most brain imaging methods measure changes in the rate, or speed, of the flow of blood to different regions of the brain. By keeping track of these changes, researchers can monitor which brain areas are active when people perform particular tasks or experience particular events. Functional imaging is a powerful tool for uncovering where different systems reside in the brain and how different brain areas interact to process information. Two methods are typically used to measure local changes in brain activity during psychological tasks.

- *Positron emission tomography (PET)*. After the injection of a relatively harmless radioactive substance into the bloodstream, a **positron emission tomography (PET)** scan enables researchers to find the most active brain areas by tagging different brain chemicals with a radioactive tracer. The increased radioactive material in active brain regions leads these regions to emit more radiation that can be detected outside the body. One downside of PET is the need to inject a radioactive substance into the body. For safety reasons, researchers limit the use of this technology.
- *Functional magnetic resonance imaging (fMRI)*. With **magnetic resonance imaging (MRI)**, a powerful magnetic field is used to momentarily disrupt the magnetic forces around the body, shifting the orientation of polarized ions. During this process, energy is released from tissues inside the body in a form that can be measured by detectors on the MRI scanner. Because different types of tissues release energy differently, the researchers can adjust the MRI scanner to measure specific tissues or substances in the body. For example, the MRI scanner can be programmed to measure the anatomy of the brain because myelinated axons and cell bodies have different magnetic properties, which is extremely valuable for providing information about brain structure. It can be used to determine the location of brain damage or of a brain tumor. **Functional magnetic resonance imaging (fMRI)** makes use of the brain's blood flow to map the working brain (**FIGURE 3.14**). Whereas PET can measure blood flow directly by tracking a radioactive substance, with fMRI the scanner is programmed to detect blood flow indirectly by assessing changes in the blood's oxygen level within the brain. As with all functional imaging methods, the participant performs an experimental task that differs from a control task in only one way, which reflects the particular mental function of interest. The researchers then compare experimental and control images to examine differences in blood flow and therefore brain activity.

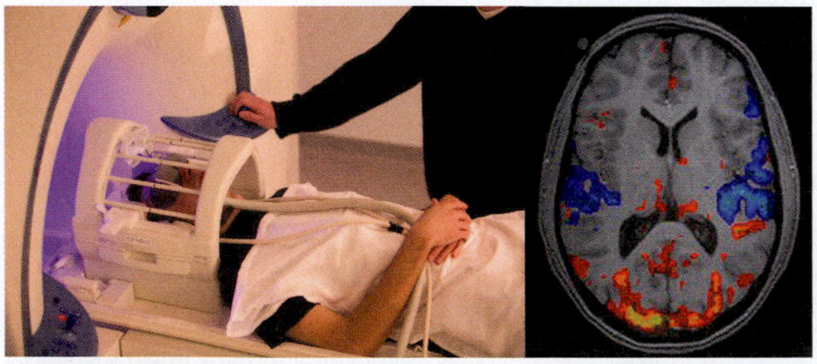

FIGURE 3.14
Functional Magnetic Resonance Imaging
Functional magnetic resonance imaging (fMRI) maps mental activity by assessing the blood's oxygen level in the brain.

One limitation of functional brain imaging techniques is that the findings are necessarily correlational. We know that certain brain regions are active while a task is performed. We do not know whether each brain region is necessary for that particular task. To see whether a brain region is necessary for a task, researchers compare performance when that area is working effectively and when it is not. And ideally, this would be assessed in a sample of healthy brains. **Transcranial magnetic stimulation (TMS)** uses a very fast but powerful magnetic field to disrupt neural activity momentarily in a specific brain region (**FIGURE 3.15**). This technique has its limitations, particularly that it can be used only for short durations to examine brain areas close to the scalp. When used along with functional imaging, however, it is a powerful method for examining which brain regions are necessary for specific psychological functions.

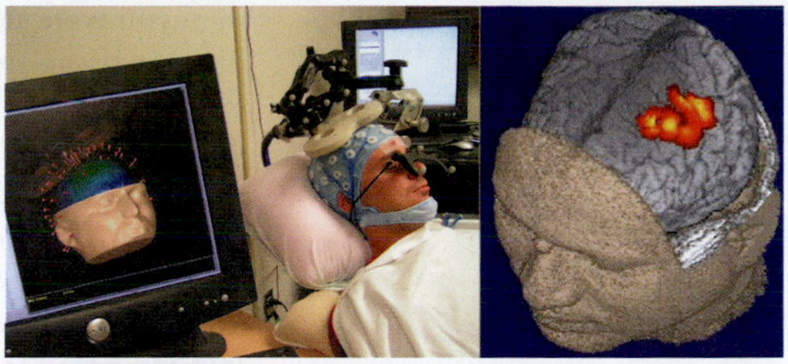

FIGURE 3.15
Transcranial Magnetic Stimulation
Transcranial magnetic stimulation (TMS) momentarily disrupts brain activity in a specific brain region.

Q How do PET and fMRI differ from EEG in terms of the brain activity they measure?

ANSWER: EEG provides information on when a brain response occurs. By contrast, fMRI and PET provide information about where a response occurs.

3.5 The Cerebral Cortex Underlies Complex Mental Activity

The largest part of the human brain is the *forebrain*. The forebrain is made up of the cerebral cortex and underlying subcortical areas and consists of two hemispheres. The **cerebral cortex** is the outer layer of the cerebral hemispheres and gives the brain its distinctive wrinkled appearance (**FIGURE 3.16**). (*Cortex* is Latin for "bark"—the kind on trees. The cerebral cortex does not feel like bark, however. It has the consistency of a soft-boiled egg.) Each hemisphere has its own cortex. In humans, the cortex is relatively enormous—the size of a large sheet of newspaper—and folded in against itself many times so as to fit within the skull. Two of these folds on the surface of the cerebral cortex form large grooves, called the *lateral fissure* and *central fissure*, which divide the brain into "lobes." Each cerebral hemisphere has four lobes: the occipital, parietal, temporal, and frontal lobes.

cerebral cortex The outer layer of brain tissue, which forms the convoluted surface of the brain; the site of all thoughts, perceptions, and complex behaviors.

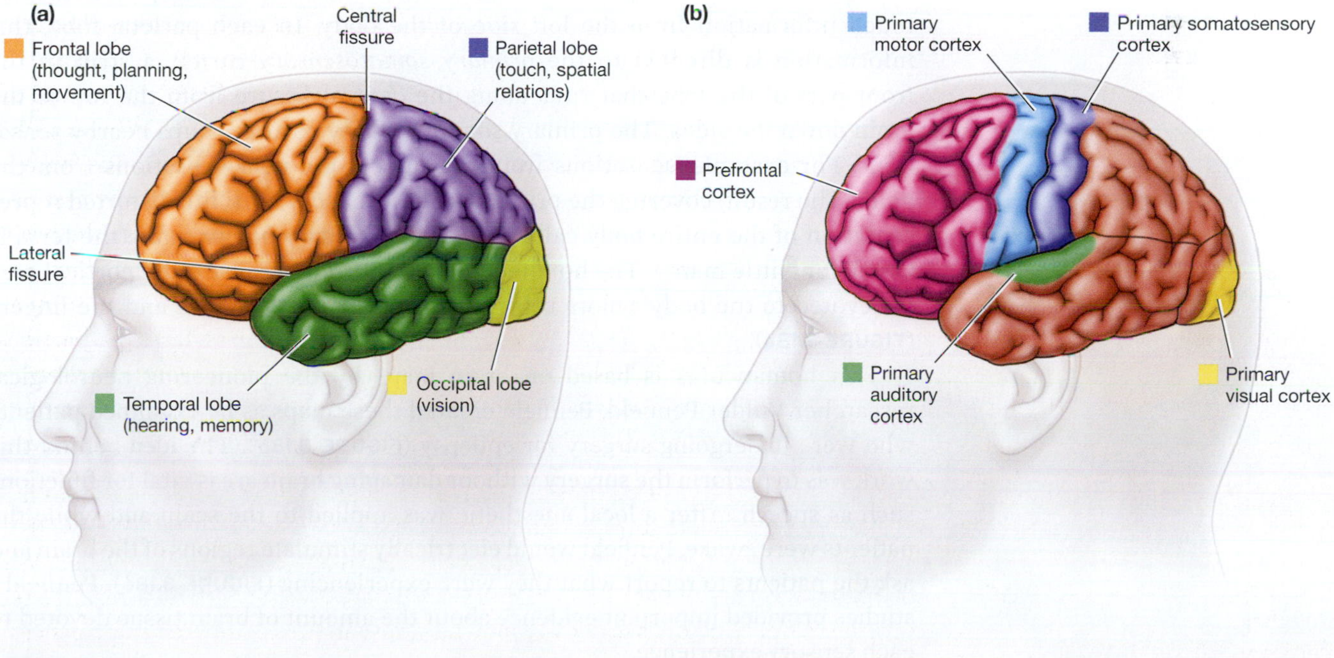

FIGURE 3.16
The Cerebral Cortex
(a) This diagram identifies the lobes of the cerebral cortex. **(b)** The colored areas mark important regions within those lobes.

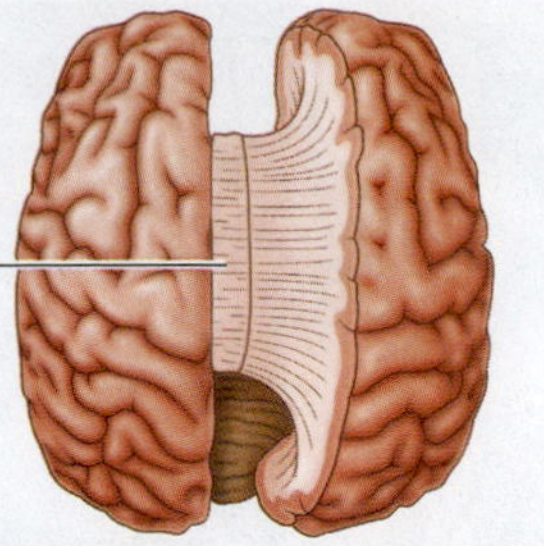

FIGURE 3.17
The Corpus Callosum
In this top view of the brain, the right cerebral hemisphere has been pulled away to expose the corpus callosum. This fibrous structure connects the two hemispheres of the cerebral cortex.

corpus callosum A massive bridge of millions of axons that connects the hemispheres of the brain and allows information to flow between them.

occipital lobes Regions of the cerebral cortex—at the back of the brain—important for vision.

parietal lobes Regions of the cerebral cortex—in front of the occipital lobes and behind the frontal lobes—important for the sense of touch and for attention to the environment.

If you were to take a cross-section of the cerebral cortex, you would see two distinct tissue types. The outer layer of the cerebral cortex (the bark) consists of *gray matter*, which is dominated by neurons' cell bodies, dendrites, and nonmyelinated axons that communicate only with nearby neurons. Underneath, you would see the *white matter*, which consists mostly of axons and the fatty myelin sheaths that surround them. These myelinated axons travel between brain regions. The **corpus callosum**, a massive bridge of millions of myelinated axons (white matter), connects the hemispheres and allows information to flow between them (**FIGURE 3.17**). Gray matter and white matter are clearly distinguishable throughout the rest of the brain and spinal cord as well.

The four lobes of the cerebral cortex are the site of all thoughts, detailed perceptions, and complex behaviors. They enable us to comprehend ourselves, other people, and the outside world. By extending our inner selves into the world, the cerebral cortex is also the source of culture and communication. Each of the four lobes of the cerebral cortex has specialized functions.

OCCIPITAL LOBES The **occipital lobes** are at the back portion of the head. Devoted almost exclusively to vision, they include many visual areas. By far, the largest of these areas is the *primary visual cortex*, the major destination for visual information. Visual information is typically organized for the cerebral cortex in a way that preserves spatial relationships. That is, the image relayed from the eye is "projected" more or less faithfully onto the primary visual cortex. As a result, two objects near one another in a visual image will activate neurons near one another in the primary visual cortex. Surrounding the primary visual cortex is a patchwork of secondary visual areas that process various attributes of the visual image, such as its colors, forms, and motions.

PARIETAL LOBES The **parietal lobes** are devoted partially to touch. Their labor is divided between the cerebral hemispheres. The left hemisphere receives touch information from the right side of the body, and the right hemisphere receives touch information from the left side of the body. In each parietal lobe, this information is directed to the *primary somatosensory cortex*, a strip in the front part of the lobe that runs along the central fissure from the top of the brain down the sides. The primary somatosensory cortex groups nearby sensations. For example, sensations from the fingers are near sensations from the palm. The result, covering the primary somatosensory area, is a distorted representation of the entire body called the *somatosensory homunculus* (the term is Greek for "little man"). The homunculus is distorted because more cortical area is devoted to the body's more sensitive areas, such as the face and the fingers (**FIGURE 3.18a**).

This homunculus is based on brain maps by the pioneering neurological researcher Wilder Penfield. Penfield created these maps as he examined patients who were undergoing surgery for epilepsy (**FIGURE 3.18b**). The idea behind this work was to perform the surgery without damaging brain areas vital for functions such as speech. After a local anesthetic was applied to the scalp and while the patients were awake, Penfield would electrically stimulate regions of the brain and ask the patients to report what they were experiencing (**FIGURE 3.18c**). Penfield's studies provided important evidence about the amount of brain tissue devoted to each sensory experience.

Other parts of the parietal lobe are involved in attention. A stroke or other damage to the right parietal region can result in the neurological disorder

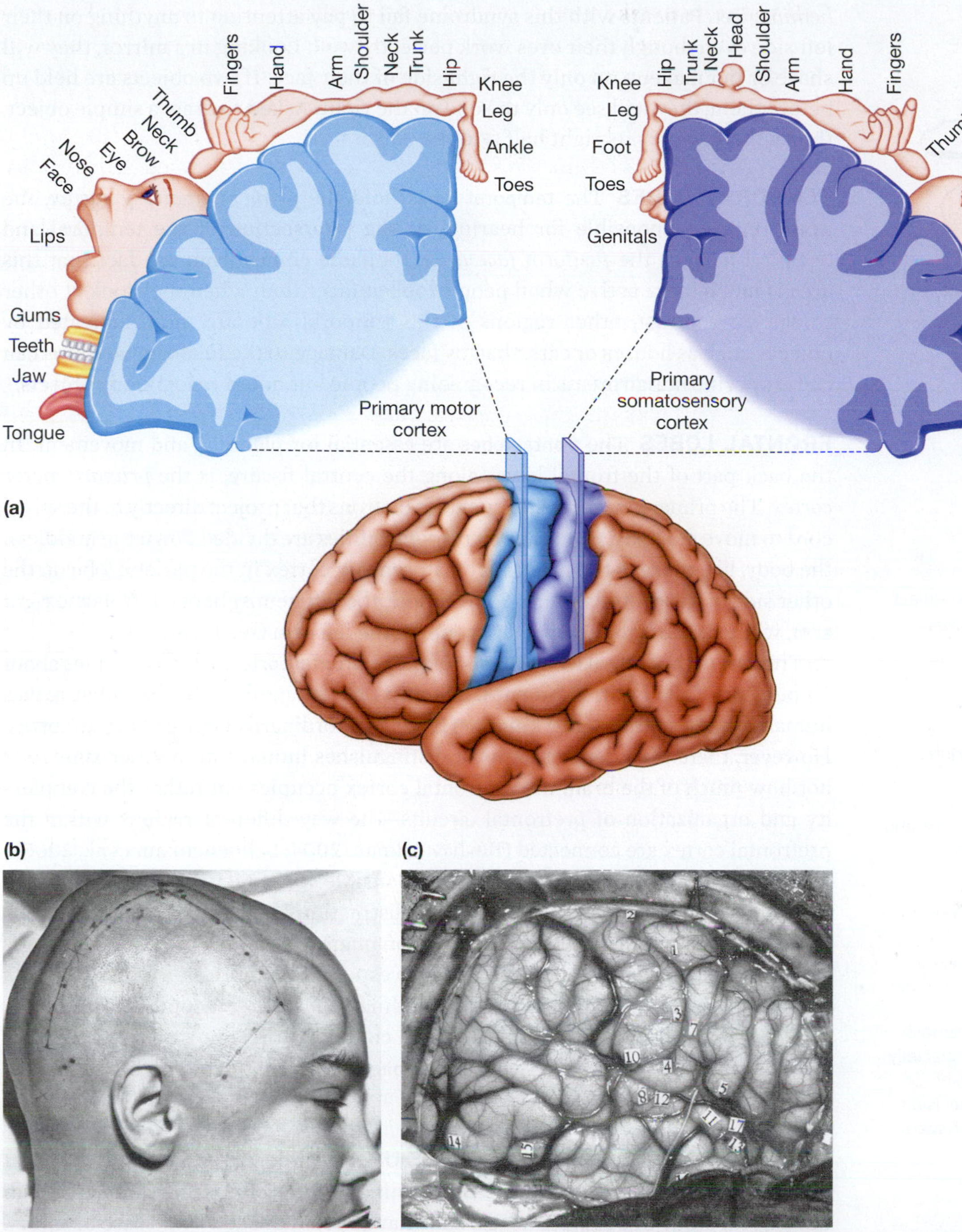

FIGURE 3.18

The Primary Somatosensory and Motor Homunculus

(a) The cortical representation of the body surface is organized in strips that run down the both the right and left sides of the brain. Connected areas of the body tend to be represented next to each other in the cortex, and more sensitive skin regions have more cortical area devoted to them. **(b)** Wilder Penfield's mappings of the brain provided the basis for our knowledge of the homunculus. This photograph shows one of Penfield's patients immediately before direct stimulation of the brain. **(c)** Here, you can see the exposed surface of the patient's cortex. The numbered tags denote locations that were electrically stimulated.

hemineglect. Patients with this syndrome fail to pay attention to anything on their left side even though their eyes work perfectly well. Looking in a mirror, they will shave or put makeup on only the right side of their face. If two objects are held up before them, they will see only the one on the right. Asked to draw a simple object, they will draw only its right half (**FIGURE 3.19**).

FIGURE 3.19
Hemineglect
This drawing, made by a hemineglect patient, omits much of the flower's left side.

temporal lobes Regions of the cerebral cortex—below the parietal lobes and in front of the occipital lobes—important for processing auditory information, for memory, and for object and face perception.

frontal lobes Regions of the cerebral cortex—at the front of the brain—important for movement and higher-level psychological processes associated with the prefrontal cortex.

prefrontal cortex The frontmost portion of the frontal lobes, especially prominent in humans; important for attention, working memory, decision making, appropriate social behavior, and personality.

TEMPORAL LOBES The **temporal lobes** hold the *primary auditory cortex*, the brain region responsible for hearing. At the intersection of the temporal and occipital lobes is the *fusiform face area*. Its name comes from the fact that this area is much more active when people look at faces than when they look at other things. In contrast, other regions of the temporal lobe are more activated by objects, such as houses or cars, than by faces. Damage to the fusiform face area can cause specific impairments in recognizing people but not in recognizing objects.

FRONTAL LOBES The **frontal lobes** are essential for planning and movement. In the back part of the frontal lobes, along the central fissure, is the *primary motor cortex*. The primary motor cortex includes neurons that project directly to the spinal cord to move the body's muscles. Its responsibilities are divided down the middle of the body, like those of the primary somatosensory cortex in the parietal lobe on the other side of the central fissure. For example, the left hemisphere controls the right arm, whereas the right hemisphere controls the left arm (see Figure 3.18a).

The rest of the frontal lobes consist of the **prefrontal cortex**, which occupies about 30 percent of the brain in humans. Scientists have long thought that what makes humans unique in the animal kingdom is our extraordinarily large prefrontal cortex. However, there is evidence that what distinguishes humans from other animals is not how much of the brain the prefrontal cortex occupies but rather the complexity and organization of prefrontal circuits—the way different regions within the prefrontal cortex are connected (Bush & Allman, 2004; Schoenemann et al., 2005).

Parts of the prefrontal cortex are responsible for directing and maintaining attention, keeping ideas in mind while distractions bombard people from the outside world, and developing and acting on plans. The entire prefrontal cortex is indispensable for rational activity. It is also especially important for many aspects of human social life, such as understanding what other people are thinking, behaving according to cultural norms, and contemplating one's own existence. It provides both the sense of self and the capacity to empathize with others or feel guilty about harming them.

THE PREFRONTAL CORTEX IN CLOSE-UP Psychologists have learned a great deal of what they know about the functioning of different brain regions through the careful study of people whose brains have been damaged by disease or injury. Perhaps the most famous historical example of brain damage is the case of Phineas Gage. Gage's case provided the basis for the first modern theories of the prefrontal cortex's role in both personality and self-control.

In 1848, Gage was a 25-year-old foreman on the construction of Vermont's Rutland and Burlington Railroad. One day, he dropped a tool called a tamping iron, which was over a yard long and an inch in diameter. The iron rod hit a rock, igniting some blasting powder. The resulting explosion drove the rod into his cheek, through his frontal lobes, and clear out through the top of his head (**FIGURE 3.20**). Gage was still conscious as he was hurried back to town on a cart, and he was able to walk, with assistance, upstairs to his hotel bed. He

Learning Tip

To remember the four lobes of the cerebral cortex, you can use the silly mnemonic of Freud Taking Off his Pants, or FTOP, for frontal, temporal, occipital, and parietal (their relative positions from the side view, moving counterclockwise).

(a) (b) (c)

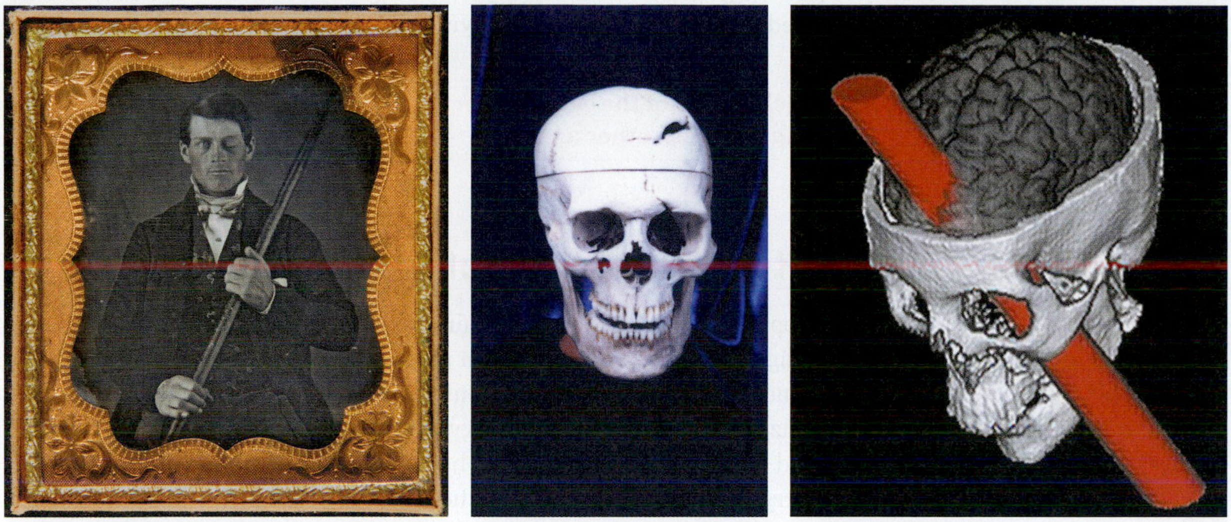

FIGURE 3.20

Phineas Gage

Analysis of Gage's damaged skull provided the basis for the first modern theories about the role of the prefrontal cortex in both personality and self-control. **(a)** This photo shows Gage holding the rod that passed through his skull. **(b)** Here, you can see the hole in the top of Gage's skull. **(c)** This computer-generated image reconstructs the rod's probable path through the skull.

wryly remarked to the awaiting physician, "Doctor, here is business enough for you." He said he expected to return to work in a few days. In fact, Gage lapsed into unconsciousness and remained unconscious for two weeks. Afterward, his condition steadily improved. Physically, he recovered remarkably well.

Unfortunately, Gage's accident led to major personality changes. Whereas the old Gage had been regarded by his employers as "the most efficient and capable" of workers, the new Gage was not. As one of his doctors later wrote, "The equilibrium or balance, so to speak, between his intellectual faculties and animal propensities seems to have been destroyed. He is fitful, irreverent, indulging at times in the grossest profanity . . . impatient of restraint or advice when it conflicts with his desires. . . . A child in his intellectual capacity and manifestations, he has the animal passions of a strong man" (Harlow, 1868, p. 340). In summary, Gage was "no longer Gage."

Unable to get his foreman's job back, Gage exhibited himself in various New England towns and at the New York Museum (owned by the circus showman P. T. Barnum). He worked at the stables of the Hanover Inn at Dartmouth College. He moved around, drove coaches and tended horses. After a decade, his health began to decline, and in 1860 he started having epileptic seizures and died within a few months. Gage's recovery was initially used to argue that the entire brain works uniformly and that the healthy parts of Gage's brain had taken over the work of the damaged parts. However, the medical community eventually recognized that the psychological impairments caused by the injury had been severe, and his case strengthened the evidence that some areas of the brain in fact have specific functions.

Reconstruction of Gage's injury through examination of his skull has made it clear that the prefrontal cortex was the area most damaged by the tamping rod (Damasio et al., 1994). Recent studies of patients with injuries to this brain region reveal that it is particularly concerned with social functions—such as following social norms, understanding what other people are thinking, and feeling emotionally connected to others—as well as with long-term planning and controlling impulses. People with damage to this region do not typically have problems with memory or general knowledge, but they often have profound disturbances in their

ANSWER: The human prefrontal cortex is exceptional in its complexity and organization; it supports unique human abilities, such as complex social understanding and self-awareness.

ability to get along with others and follow through with commitments, including those required to maintain steady employment.

Q Which region of the cerebral cortex is most exceptional in humans, compared with other animals?

3.6 Splitting the Brain Splits the Mind

Studying people who have undergone brain surgery has given researchers a better understanding of the conscious mind. On rare occasions, when epilepsy does not respond to modern medications, surgeons may remove the part of the brain in which the seizures begin. Another strategy, pioneered in the 1940s and sometimes still practiced when other interventions have failed, is to cut connections within the brain to try to isolate the site where the seizures begin. After the procedure, a seizure that begins at that site is less likely to spread throughout the cortex.

The major connection between the hemispheres that may readily be cut without damaging the gray matter is the corpus callosum (see Figure 3.17). When this massive fiber bundle is severed, the brain's halves are almost completely isolated from each other. The resulting condition is called **split brain**. This surgical procedure has provided many important insights into the basic organization and specialized functions of each brain hemisphere (**FIGURE 3.21**).

split brain A condition that occurs when the corpus callosum is surgically cut and the two hemispheres of the brain do not receive information directly from each other.

What is it like to have your brain split in half? Perhaps the most surprising thing about split-brain patients after their operations is how normal they are. Unlike patients after other types of brain surgery, split-brain patients have no immediately apparent problems. In fact, some early investigations suggested the surgery had not affected the patients in any discernible way. They could walk normally, talk normally, think clearly, and interact socially. In the 1960s, this book's coauthor Michael Gazzaniga, working with the Nobel laureate Roger Sperry, conducted a series of tests on split-brain patients (Gazzaniga, 2015). The results were stunning: Just as the brain had been split in two, so had the mind!

The hemispheres normally work together. Images from the visual field's left side (the left half of what you are looking at) go to the right hemisphere. Images from the visual field's right side go to the left hemisphere (**FIGURE 3.22**). The left hemisphere also controls the right hand, and the right hemisphere controls the left hand. In a healthy person, the corpus callosum allows the hemispheres to

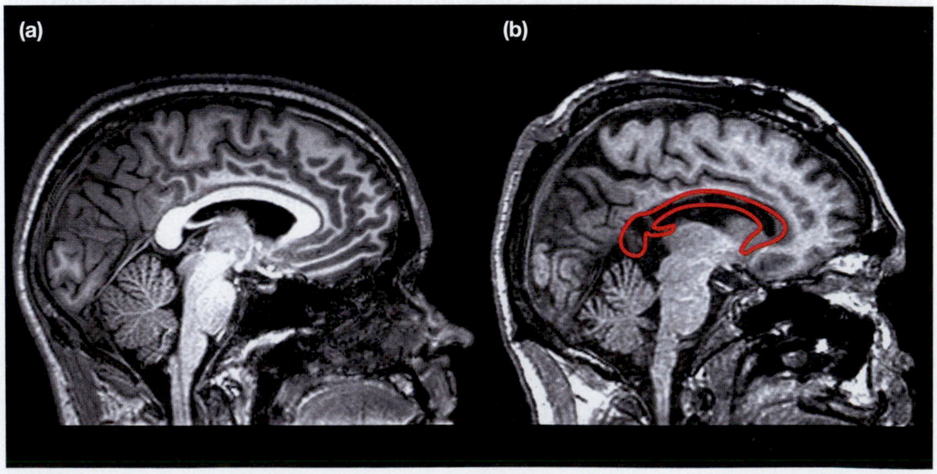

FIGURE 3.21
Split Brain
(a) This image shows the brain of a normal person whose corpus callosum is intact. **(b)** This image shows the brain of a patient whose corpus callosum has been cut (area indicated by the red outline). With the corpus callosum severed, the two hemispheres of the brain are almost completely separated.

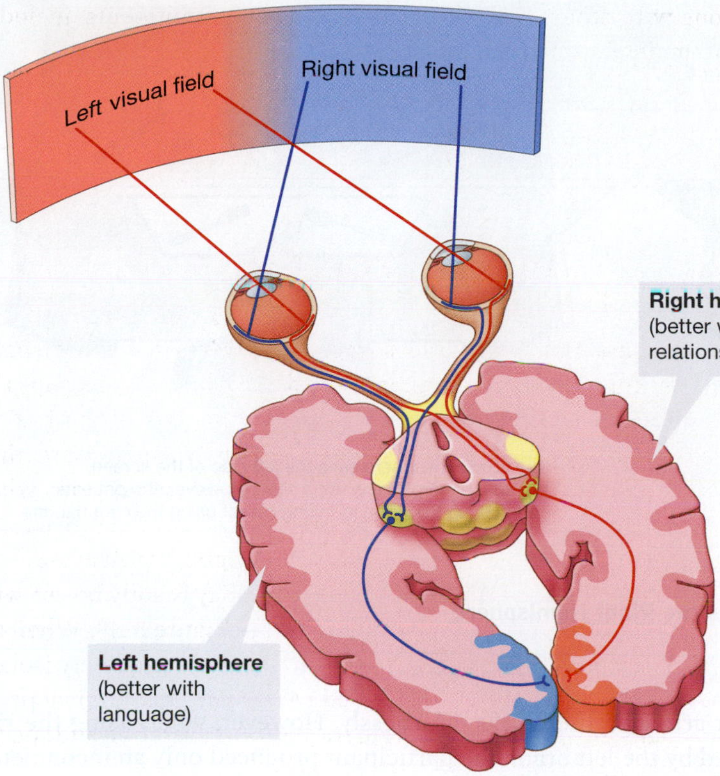

FIGURE 3.22
Visual Input
Images from the left side go to the brain's right hemisphere. Images from the right side go to the left hemisphere.

communicate so that the right brain knows what the left is doing. By contrast, in split-brain patients, the hemispheres are separated, so this communication cannot take place—the hemispheres function as completely independent entities. This division allows researchers to independently examine the function of each hemisphere without the influence of the other. The researchers can provide information to, and receive information from, a single hemisphere at a time. Splitting the brain, then, produces two half brains. Each half has its own perceptions, thoughts, and consciousness.

Psychologists have long known that in most people the left hemisphere is dominant for language. If a split-brain patient sees two pictures flashed on a screen briefly and simultaneously—one to the visual field's right side and one to the left side—the patient will report that only the picture on the right was shown. Why is this? The left hemisphere (or "left brain"), with its control over speech, sees only the picture on the right side. It is the only picture a person with a split brain can talk about.

In many split-brain patients, the right hemisphere has no discernible language capacity. The mute right hemisphere (or "right brain"), having seen the picture on the left, is unable to articulate a response. However, the right brain can act on its perception: If the picture on the left was of a spoon, the right hemisphere can easily pick out an actual spoon from a selection of objects. It uses the left hand, which is controlled by the right hemisphere. Still, the left hemisphere does not know what the right one saw (**FIGURE 3.23**).

Normally, the competencies of each hemisphere complement each other. The left brain is generally hopeless at spatial relationships, whereas the right hemisphere is much more proficient. In one experiment (Bogen & Gazzaniga, 1965), a split-brain participant was given a pile of blocks and a drawing of a simple arrangement in which to put them. For example, the participant was asked to produce a square. When using the left hand, controlled by the right hemisphere,

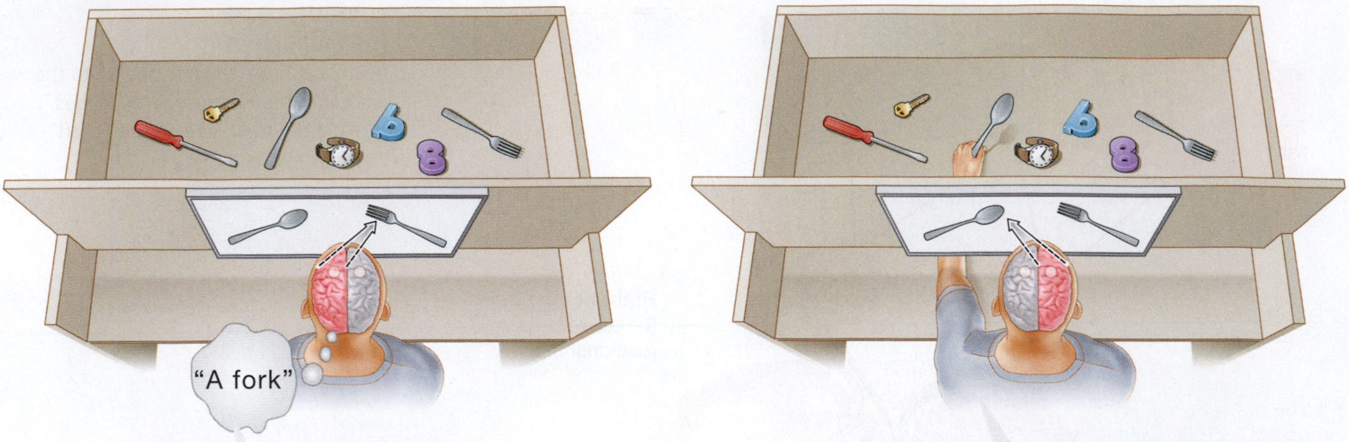

"A fork"
When split-brain patients are asked what they see, the left hemisphere sees the fork on the right side of the screen and can verbalize that.
The right hemisphere sees the left side of the screen, but cannot verbalize what is seen. However, the patients can pick up the corresponding object using their left hands.

FIGURE 3.23
Split-Brain Experiment: The Left Hemisphere Versus the Right Hemisphere

the participant arranged the blocks effortlessly. However, when using the right hand, controlled by the left brain, the participant produced only an incompetent, meandering attempt. During this dismal performance, the right brain presumably grew frustrated, because it made the left hand try to slip in and help!

INTERPRETER Studies of split-brain patients have revealed an interesting relationship between the brain's hemispheres, which work together to construct coherent conscious experiences. This collaboration can be demonstrated by asking split-brain patients to use their disconnected left hemisphere to explain behavior produced by the right hemisphere. Keep in mind that the left hemisphere does not know why the behavior was produced.

In one such experiment (Gazzaniga & LeDoux, 1978), the split-brain patient saw different images flash simultaneously on the left and right sides of a screen. Below those images was a row of other images. The patient was asked to point with each hand to a bottom image that was most related to the image flashed above on that side of the screen. In a particular trial, a picture of a chicken claw was flashed to the left hemisphere. A picture of a snow scene was flashed to the right hemisphere. In response, the left hemisphere pointed the right hand at a picture of a chicken head. The right hemisphere pointed the left hand at a picture of a snow shovel. The (speaking) left hemisphere could have no idea what the right hemisphere had seen or why the left hand pointed to the snow shovel. When the participant was asked why he pointed to those pictures, he (or, rather, his left hemisphere) calmly replied, "Oh, that's simple. The chicken claw goes with the chicken, and you need a shovel to clean out the chicken shed." The left hemisphere evidently had interpreted the left hand's response in a manner consistent with the left brain's knowledge, which was a chicken claw (**FIGURE 3.24**).

The left hemisphere's propensity to construct a world that makes sense is called the *interpreter*. This term means that the left hemisphere is interpreting what the right hemisphere has done with only the information that is available to it (Gazzaniga, 2000). In this last example, the left hemisphere interpreter

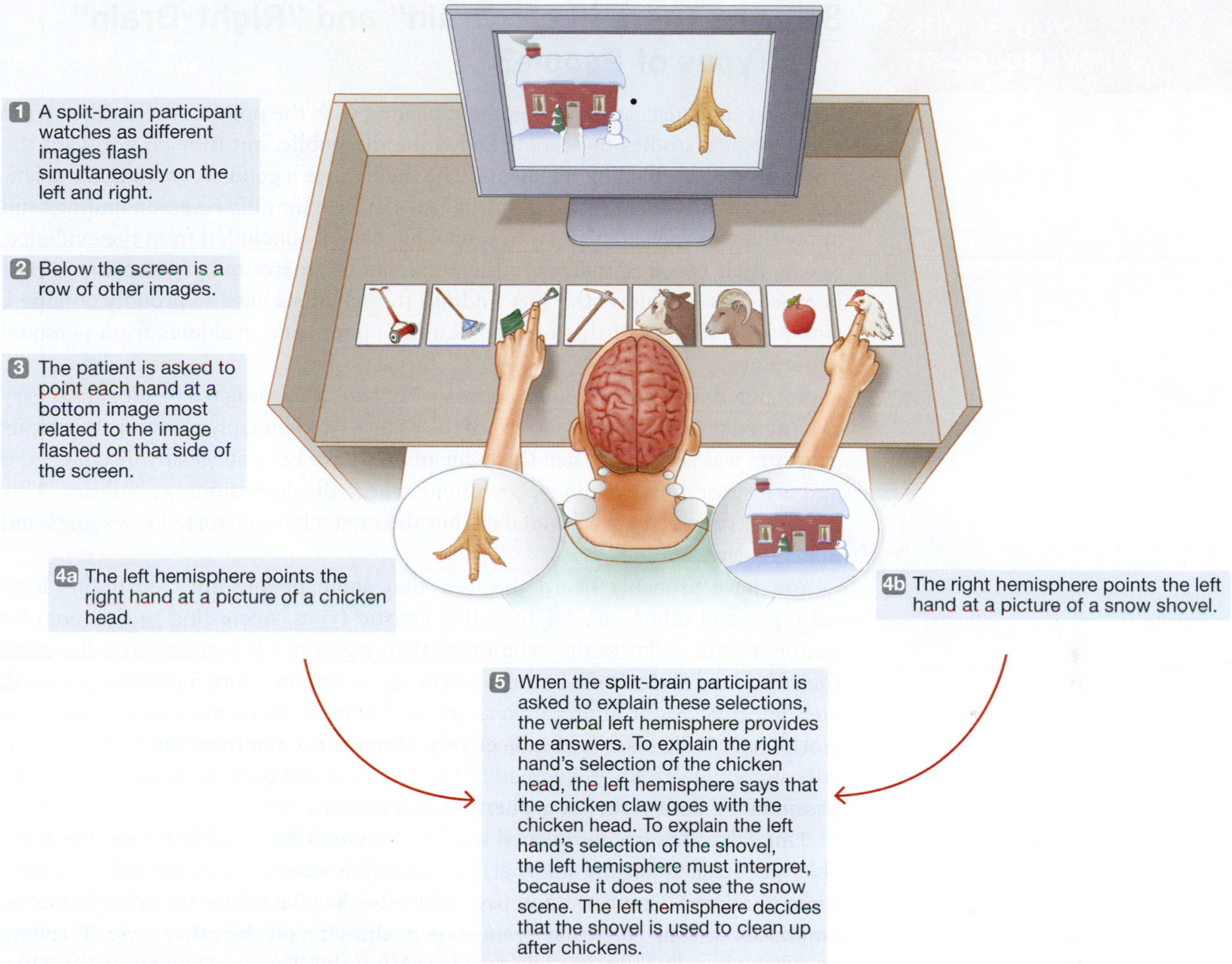

1 A split-brain participant watches as different images flash simultaneously on the left and right.
2 Below the screen is a row of other images.
3 The patient is asked to point each hand at a bottom image most related to the image flashed on that side of the screen.
4a The left hemisphere points the right hand at a picture of a chicken head.
4b The right hemisphere points the left hand at a picture of a snow shovel.
5 When the split-brain participant is asked to explain these selections, the verbal left hemisphere provides the answers. To explain the right hand's selection of the chicken head, the left hemisphere says that the chicken claw goes with the chicken head. To explain the left hand's selection of the shovel, the left hemisphere must interpret, because it does not see the snow scene. The left hemisphere decides that the shovel is used to clean up after chickens.

FIGURE 3.24
The Left Hemisphere Interprets Outcomes
On the basis of limited information, the left hemisphere attempts to explain behavior produced by the right hemisphere.

created a ready way to explain the left hand's action. Although the disconnected right hemisphere controlled the left hand, the left hemisphere's explanation was unrelated to the right hemisphere's real reason for commanding that action. Yet to the patient, the movement seemed perfectly plausible once the action had been interpreted.

To give another example: If the command *stand up* is flashed to split-brain patients' right hemisphere, the patients will stand up. But when asked why they have stood up, they will not reply, "You just told me to," because the command is not available to the (speaking) left hemisphere. Instead, unaware of the command, the patients will say something like, "I just felt like getting a soda." The left hemisphere is compelled to concoct a sensible story that explains, or interprets, the patients' actions after they have occurred.

Q What surgery creates the split brain?

ANSWER: cutting the corpus callosum so that the two hemispheres are separated

YOU BE THE PSYCHOLOGIST

3.7 Are There "Left-Brain" and "Right-Brain" Types of People?

Some psychologists are cautious about dealing with the popular press. They want psychological studies to become known by the public, but they do not want the findings to be garbled by the media. The media love a good story. To make scientific studies attention grabbing, journalists may oversimplify research findings and apply them in ways that go far beyond what can be concluded from the evidence. Seeing their research twisted in the press can be frustrating to scientists in part because it overshadows the very findings the scientists have so proudly obtained. One of the authors of this textbook knows about such problems from personal experience.

As noted in the previous section, Michael Gazzaniga and Roger Sperry conducted research on the activity of the brain's two hemispheres after the corpus callosum was severed. When the hemispheres have been surgically disconnected and are separately examined, each hemisphere displays different abilities. This discovery provided a wealth of data, but the media have distorted Gazzaniga and Sperry's early findings.

You have probably heard the idea that some people are "left-brain" logical types and others are "right-brain" artistic types. According to this popular notion, people differ to the extent that their right or left hemispheres dominate their thinking styles. Left-brain thinkers are said to be more analytical, rational, and objective. Right-brain thinkers are said to be more creative and to view the world more holistically and subjectively. Moreover, a dominant left brain supposedly suppresses right-brain creativity, so people could become more creative and passionate if their right hemisphere were released.

This false idea has permeated society (**FIGURE 3.25**). Multiple tests are available, particularly on the internet, to determine whether you are left- or right-brain dominant. Countless pop psychology books give advice on living better by emphasizing your particular brain style or drawing on the other style. Teachers have been heavily influenced by the idea (Alferink & Farmer-Dougan, 2010). They have been urged to develop different classroom plans for left-brain thinkers and for right-brain thinkers, and they have been encouraged to liberate the "more creative" right brain. According to one study, nearly 90 percent of teachers in the United Kingdom and the Netherlands believe in the idea of left-brain versus right-brain thinking (Dekker et al., 2012).

However, the scientific evidence is overwhelming: People are not either left-brain or right-brain dominant (Hines, 1987). The hemispheres *are* specialized for certain functions, such as language or spatial relationships. However, each hemisphere is capable of carrying out most cognitive processes, though sometimes in different ways. Most cognitive processes involve the coordinated efforts of both hemispheres. In addition, a recent study that examined brain activity in more than 1,000 individuals ages 7 to 29 found no differences between people in the extent to which their right or left hemisphere was active (Nielsen et al., 2013).

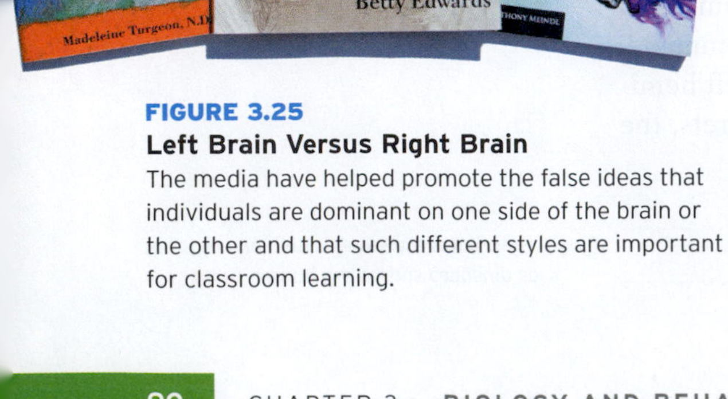

FIGURE 3.25

Left Brain Versus Right Brain

The media have helped promote the false ideas that individuals are dominant on one side of the brain or the other and that such different styles are important for classroom learning.

Most psychological researchers do not want to spend their time trying to disprove a hypothesis that was introduced by the popular press, but the notion that analytical and creative processing are opposed and are related to which hemisphere is "dominant" is a brain myth that many believe. Could you use your critical thinking skills (see Chapter 1) to evaluate these claims? If you wanted to study this, how would you? Imagine you had access to a functional brain imaging method, such as fMRI or PET, that allowed you to measure the relative amount of activity in the right and left hemispheres, or a population of split-brain patients, along with validated tasks that tap into "creative" versus "analytical" processing. How would you use some combination of these experimental tools, or others, to assess the hypothesis that creative processing engages the right hemisphere and analytical processing engages the left hemisphere? How about the hypothesis that these two types of mental processes are opposed such that engaging in one inhibits the other? ■

Q Do people differ in the extent to which their hemispheres are dominant?

ANSWER: No. Although each hemisphere has specialized functions, and people vary in their creative and analytical abilities, there are not significant differences in how much one hemisphere is used over the other.

3.8 The Insula and Subcortical Structures Contribute to Taste, Emotions, Memory, and Reward

Below the outside surface of the cerebral cortex lie the *insula* and *subcortical* regions, which are so named because they lie under the cortex. The insula, or insular cortex, is a part of the cerebral cortex that lies deep within folds of the lateral fissure. Subcortical structures that are important for understanding psychological functions include the thalamus, the hypothalamus, the hippocampus, the amygdala, and the basal ganglia (**FIGURE 3.26**).

INSULA The **insula**, or insular cortex, is a relatively large structure that has a number of functions. It houses the primary *gustatory cortex*, which is necessary for the sense of taste (Pritchard et al., 1999) and is important for perceiving disgust (Wicker et al., 2003). Other parts of the insula play a role in your ability to be aware of bodily states related to emotion, such as when you are nervous and feel your heart racing (Critchley et al., 2004), along with the experience of pain (Ogino et al., 2007). The insula has also been shown to be more active when you experience empathy for someone else's pain (Singer, 2006).

insula The part of the cerebral cortex lying inside the lateral fissure; important for taste, pain, perception of bodily states, and empathy.

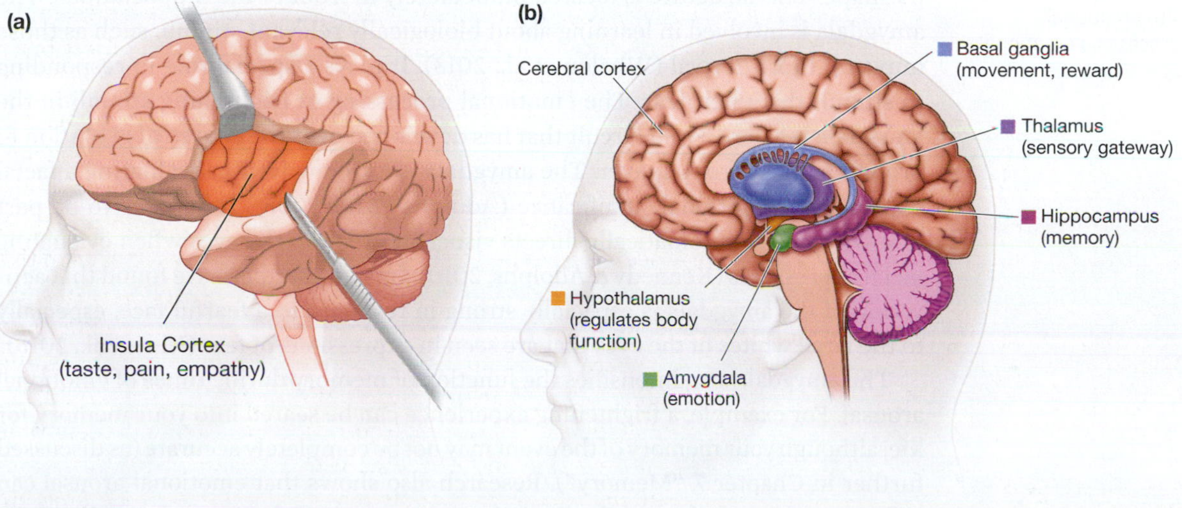

FIGURE 3.26
The Insula and the Subcortical Regions
(a) The insula, or insular cortex, lies within the lateral fissure (pulled back). **(b)** The subcortical regions are responsible for many aspects of emotion and motivation.

thalamus The gateway to the brain; it receives almost all incoming sensory information before that information reaches the cortex.

THALAMUS The **thalamus** is the gateway to the cortex: It receives almost all incoming sensory information, organizes it, and relays it to the cortex. The only exception to this rule is the sense of smell. The oldest and most fundamental sense, smell has a direct route to the cortex. During sleep, the thalamus partially shuts the gate on incoming sensations while the brain rests. (The thalamus is discussed further in Chapter 5, "Sensation and Perception.")

hypothalamus A brain structure that is involved in the regulation of bodily functions, including body temperature, body rhythms, blood pressure, and blood glucose levels; it also influences our basic motivated behaviors.

HYPOTHALAMUS The **hypothalamus** is the brain's main regulatory structure. It is indispensable to an organism's survival. Located just below the thalamus, it receives input from and projects its influence to almost everywhere in the body and brain. It affects the functions of many internal organs, regulating body temperature, body rhythms, blood pressure, and blood glucose levels. It is also involved in many motivated behaviors, including thirst, hunger, aggression, and sexual desire.

hippocampus A brain structure that is associated with the formation of memories.

HIPPOCAMPUS The **hippocampus** takes its name from the Greek for "sea horse" because of its shape. This structure plays an important role in the formation of new memories. It seems to do so by creating new interconnections within the cerebral cortex with each new experience.

The hippocampus and surrounding regions are involved in how we remember the arrangements of places and objects in space, such as how streets are laid out in a city or how furniture is positioned in a room. An interesting study that supported this theory focused on London taxi drivers. Eleanor Maguire and colleagues (2003) found that one hippocampal region was much larger in taxi drivers' brains than in most other London drivers' brains. Moreover, the volume of gray matter in this hippocampal region was highly correlated with the number of years of experience as a taxi driver. Is a person with a larger volume in this hippocampal region more likely to drive a taxi? Or does this hippocampal region grow as the result of navigational experience? Recall from Chapter 2 that correlation does not prove causation. The Maguire study did not *conclude* that parts of the hippocampus change with experience. However, there is evidence that the hippocampus is important for navigating in our environments (Nadel et al., 2013).

amygdala A brain structure that serves a vital role in learning to associate things with emotional responses and in processing emotional information.

AMYGDALA The **amygdala** takes its name from the Latin for "almond" because of its shape. This structure is located immediately in front of the hippocampus. The amygdala is involved in learning about biologically relevant stimuli, such as those important for survival (Whalen et al., 2013). It plays a special role in responding to stimuli that elicit fear. The emotional processing of frightening stimuli in the amygdala is a hardwired circuit that has developed over the course of evolution to protect animals from danger. The amygdala is also involved in evaluating a facial expression's emotional significance (Adolphs et al., 2005). It appears to be part of a system that automatically directs visual attention to the eyes when evaluating facial expressions (Kennedy & Adolphs, 2010). Imaging studies have found that activation of the amygdala is especially strong in response to a fearful face, especially to the large whites of the eyes that are seen in expressions of fear (Kim et al., 2016).

The amygdala also intensifies the function of memory during times of emotional arousal. For example, a frightening experience can be seared into your memory for life, although your memory of the event may not be completely accurate (as discussed further in Chapter 7, "Memory"). Research also shows that emotional arousal can influence what people attend to in their environments (Schmitz et al., 2009).

basal ganglia A system of subcortical structures that are important for the planning and production of movement.

BASAL GANGLIA The **basal ganglia** are a system of subcortical structures crucial for planning and producing movement. These structures receive input from the entire cerebral cortex. They send that input to the motor centers of the brain stem. Via the thalamus, they also send the input back to the motor planning area of the cerebral cortex. Damage to the basal ganglia can produce symptoms that range from the tremors and rigidity of Parkinson's disease to the involuntary writhing movements of Huntington's disease. In addition, damage to the basal ganglia can impair the learning of movements and habits, such as automatically looking for cars before you cross the street.

Within the basal ganglia, the *nucleus accumbens* is important for experiencing reward and motivating behavior. As discussed in Chapter 6, nearly every pleasurable experience—from eating food you like to looking at a person you find attractive—involves dopamine activity in the nucleus accumbens that makes you want the thing or person you are experiencing. The more desirable objects are, the more they activate basic reward circuitry in our brains.

Q Which brain region structure is considered the sensory gateway to the cortex?

ANSWER: the thalamus, because almost all sensory information goes first to the thalamus before being sent to relevant regions of the cortex

3.9 The Brain Stem and Cerebellum House Basic Programs for Survival and Movement

Below the cerebral cortex and subcortical structures lie the spinal cord and brain stem. The spinal cord is a rope of neural tissue. As shown in Figure 3.10, the cord runs inside the hollows of the vertebrae from the base of the skull to just above the pelvis. One of its functions is the coordination of reflexes, such as the reflexive movement of your leg when a doctor taps your knee or the reflexive movement of your arm when you jerk your hand away from a flame. The cord's most important function is to carry sensory information up to the brain and carry motor signals from the brain to the body parts below to initiate action.

brain stem An extension of the spinal cord; it houses structures that control functions associated with survival, such as heart rate, breathing, swallowing, vomiting, urination, and orgasm.

cerebellum A large, convoluted protuberance at the back of the brain stem; it is essential for coordinated movement and balance.

In the base of the skull, the spinal cord thickens and becomes more complex as it transforms into the **brain stem** (**FIGURE 3.27**). The brain stem consists of the *medulla oblongata*, the *pons*, and the *midbrain*. It houses the nerves that control the most basic functions of survival, such as heart rate, breathing, swallowing, vomiting, urination, and orgasm. A significant blow to this region can cause death. As a continuous extension of the spinal cord, the brain stem also performs functions for the head similar to those that the spinal cord performs for the rest of the body. Many reflexes emerge from here, analogous to the spinal reflexes; gagging is one example.

The brain stem also contains a network of neurons known collectively as the *reticular formation*. The reticular formation projects up into the cerebral cortex and affects general alertness. It is also involved in inducing and terminating the different stages of sleep (as discussed in Chapter 4, "Consciousness").

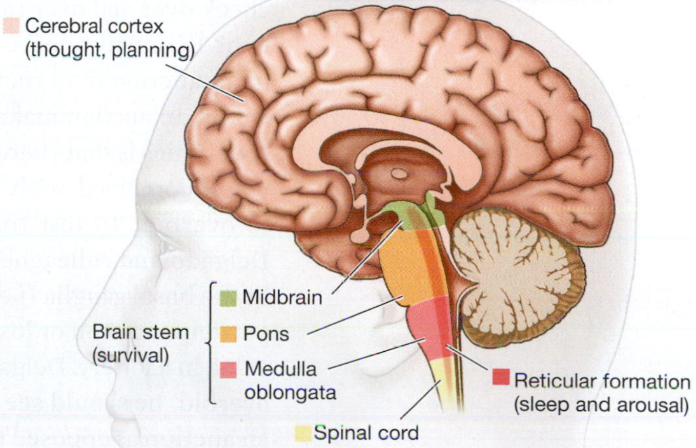

FIGURE 3.27
The Brain Stem
This drawing shows the brain stem and its parts, in relation to the cerebral cortex.

CEREBELLUM The **cerebellum** (Latin, "little brain") is a large protuberance connected to the back of the brain stem (**FIGURE 3.28**). Its size and convoluted surface make it look like an extra brain. The cerebellum is extremely important for proper motor function, and damage to its different parts produces very different effects. For example, damage to the little nodes at the very bottom causes head tilt, balance problems, and a loss of smooth compensation of eye position for head movement. Try turning your head while looking at this book. Notice that your eyes remain focused on the material. Your eyes would not be able to do that if an injury affected the bottom of your cerebellum. Damage to the ridge that runs up the back of the cerebellum would affect your walking. Damage to the bulging lobes on either side would cause a loss of limb coordination, so you would not be able to perform tasks such as reaching smoothly to pick up a pen.

The cerebellum's most obvious role is in motor learning and motor memory, and it operates unconsciously. For example, the cerebellum allows you to ride a bicycle effortlessly while planning your next meal. The cerebellum may also be involved in cognitive processes such as making plans, remembering events, using language, and experiencing emotion.

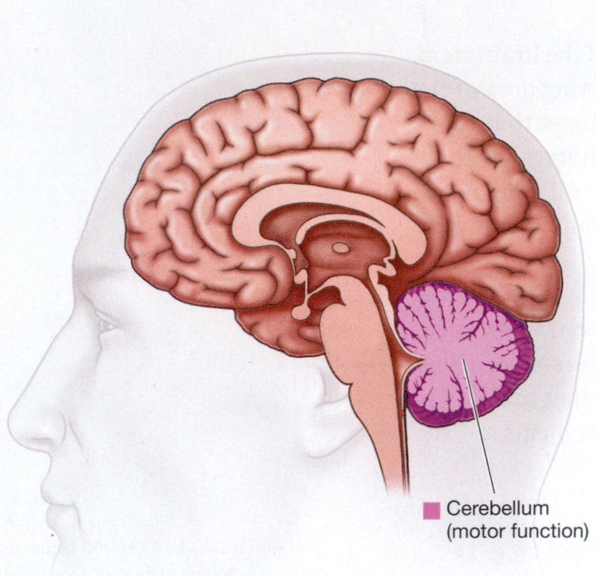

FIGURE 3.28
The Cerebellum
The cerebellum is located at the back of the brain: It is below the cerebral cortex and behind the brain stem.

Q **What functions are most associated with the cerebellum?**

ANSWER: motor learning, coordination of movements, and motor memory

PSYCHOLOGY OUTSIDE THE LAB

3.10 Auction Overbidding

Have you ever been to an auction or have you bid on an item on eBay? If so, did you check over and over to see if someone else bid higher so you could bid more and win? Economists have long known that people often pay more for an item won in an auction than they would if they bought the same item in a store. But why would an auction make someone pay too much, or *overbid*? One hypothesis from economics is that there is a "joy of winning" an auction (see **FIGURE 3.29**), which, when combined with the value of the item won in the auction, causes people to overbid. To test this hypothesis, psychologist and neuroscientist Mauricio Delgado and colleagues (2005) used fMRI to track the brain's reward responses in the basal ganglia (i.e., in the nucleus accumbens and surrounding areas) when participants won or lost an auction, as compared with winning or losing the same value in a lottery. Delgado hypothesized that if the joy of winning causes people to overbid, he should see greater fMRI activity in reward regions when people win an auction as opposed to a lottery. However, this is not what he found. Instead, he found that when people lose an auction, the brain responds as if something tangible were lost, even though nothing was lost other than the social competition of the auction. Furthermore, the magnitude of this auction-loss signal predicted how much people overbid. In other words, the brain's response suggested that overpaying in auctions is related to the anticipated *fear of losing* the auction, not the joy of winning. Of course, fMRI data can tell us only whether brain regions are more or less active during different tasks; they do not indicate fear or joy or show what caused the overbidding.

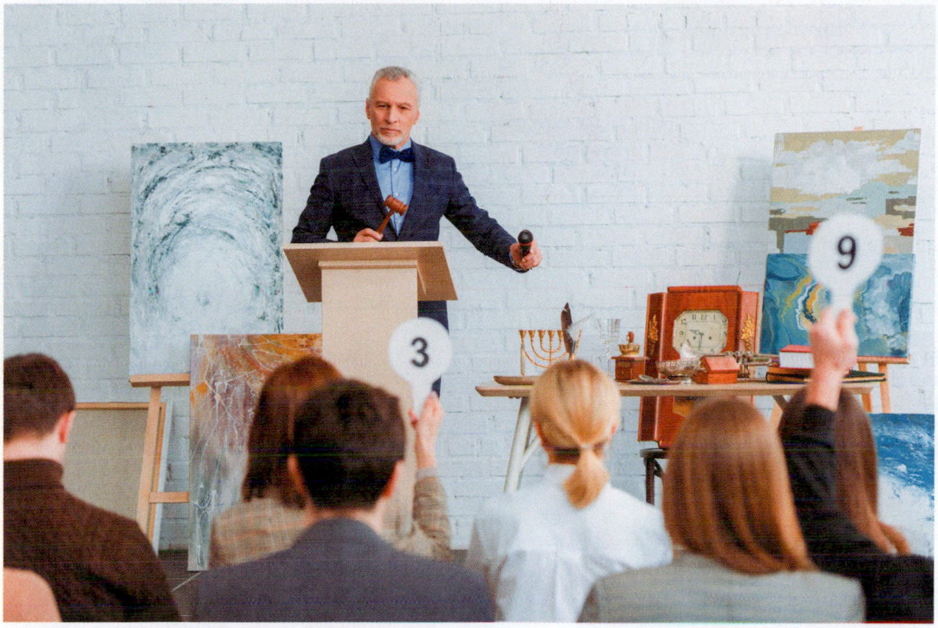

FIGURE 3.29
Auction Overbidding
People tend to overpay in auctions, and brain research, combined with psychological studies, helps show why.

To confirm that avoiding loss drives overbidding in auctions, Delgado and his colleagues followed up with a psychological study in which they told participants they would either get a $15 bonus if they won the auction (gain condition), or have a $15 bonus taken away if they lost the auction (loss condition). By emphasizing the potential loss, Delgado and colleagues found that participants overbid even more. The researchers also observed that their "loss" framing generated more profit for a hypothetical auctioneer. Thus, the unexpected take-home message from this brain imaging study (combined with the psychological study): If you want people to pay more in an auction, emphasize the potential loss. ■

somatic nervous system (SNS) A component of the peripheral nervous system; it transmits sensory signals and motor signals between the central nervous system and the skin, muscles, and joints.

Q **Can fMRI provide causal evidence that anticipation of loss leads to overbidding in an auction?**

ANSWER: No; fMRI provides correlational evidence showing the relation between changes in brain activity and a behavior or mental state.

How Does the Brain Communicate with the Body?

Learning Objectives

- Differentiate between the subdivisions of the peripheral nervous system.
- Identify the primary structures of the endocrine system.
- Explain how the nervous system and the endocrine system communicate to control thought, feeling, and behavior.

As discussed earlier in this chapter, the peripheral nervous system (PNS) transmits a variety of information to the central nervous system (CNS). It also responds to messages from the CNS to perform specific behaviors or make bodily adjustments. In the production of psychological activity, however, both of these systems interact with a different mode of communication within the body: the endocrine system.

3.11 The Peripheral Nervous System Includes the Somatic and Autonomic Systems

Recall that the PNS has two primary components: the somatic nervous system and the autonomic nervous system. The **somatic nervous system (SNS)** transmits sensory signals to the CNS via nerves. Specialized receptors in the skin, muscles, and joints send sensory information to the spinal cord, which relays it to the brain.

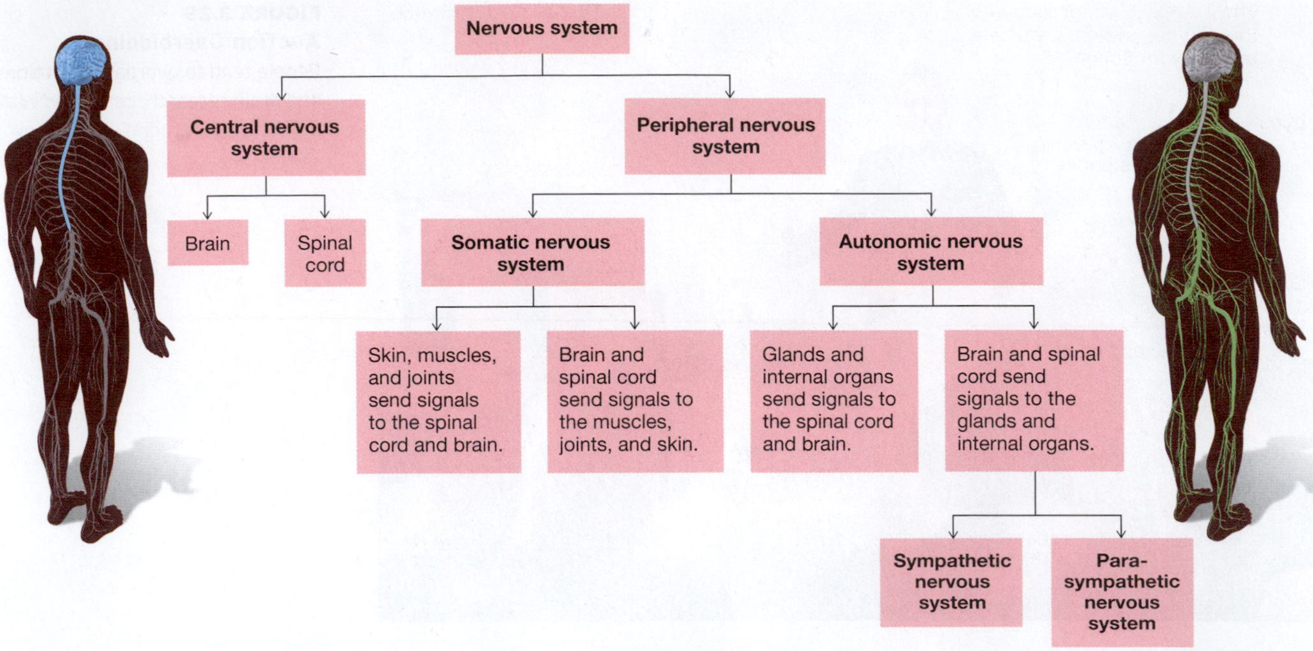

FIGURE 3.30
The Divisions of the Nervous System
This flowchart builds on Figure 3.1 by adding further information about the somatic and autonomic nervous systems.

autonomic nervous system (ANS) A component of the peripheral nervous system; it transmits sensory signals and motor signals between the central nervous system and the body's glands and internal organs.

sympathetic division A division of the autonomic nervous system; it prepares the body for action.

parasympathetic division A division of the autonomic nervous system; it returns the body to its resting state.

In addition, the CNS sends signals through the SNS to muscles, joints, and skin to initiate, modulate, or inhibit movement (FIGURE 3.30).

The second major component of the PNS, the **autonomic nervous system** (ANS), regulates the body's internal environment by stimulating glands (such as sweat glands) and by maintaining internal organs (such as the heart). Nerves in the ANS also carry somatosensory signals from the glands and internal organs to the CNS. These signals provide information about, for example, the fullness of your stomach or how anxious you feel.

SYMPATHETIC AND PARASYMPATHETIC DIVISIONS Two types of signals, sympathetic and parasympathetic, travel from the central nervous system to organs and glands, controlling their activity (FIGURE 3.31). To understand these signals, imagine you hear a fire alarm. In the second after you hear the alarm, signals go out to parts of your body telling them to prepare for action. As a result, blood flows to skeletal muscles; epinephrine is released, increasing your heart rate and blood sugar; your lungs take in more oxygen; your digestive system suspends activity as a way of conserving energy; your pupils dilate to maximize visual sensitivity; and you perspire to keep cool.

These preparatory actions are prompted by the autonomic nervous system's **sympathetic division**. Should there be a fire, you will be physically prepared to flee. If the alarm turns out to be false, your heart will return to its normal steady beat, your breathing will slow, you will resume digesting food, and you will stop perspiring. This return to a normal state will be prompted by the ANS's **parasympathetic division**. Most of your internal organs are controlled by inputs from sympathetic and parasympathetic systems. The more aroused you are, the greater the sympathetic system's dominance.

It does not take a fire alarm to activate your sympathetic nervous system. For example, when you meet someone you find attractive, your heart beats quickly, you perspire, you might start breathing heavily, and your pupils widen. Such signs of sexual arousal provide nonverbal cues during social interaction. These signs

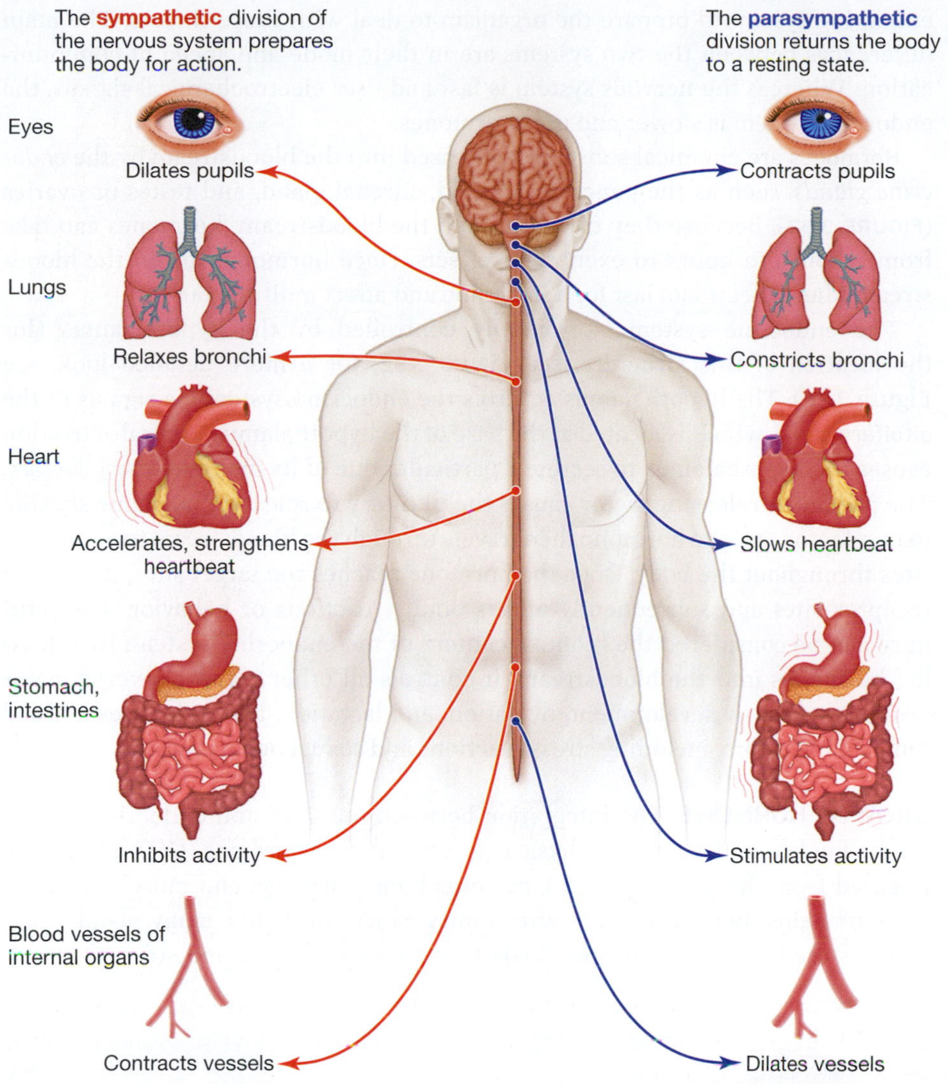

FIGURE 3.31
The Sympathetic and Parasympathetic Divisions of the Autonomic Nervous System

occur because sexual arousal has activated the ANS's sympathetic division. The sympathetic division is also activated by psychological states such as anxiety or unhappiness. Some people worry a great deal or do not cope well with stress. Their bodies are in a constant state of arousal. Important research in the 1930s and 1940s by Hans Selye demonstrated that chronic activation of the sympathetic division is associated with medical problems that include heart disease and asthma. Selye's work is discussed further in Chapter 11, "Health and Well-Being."

Q Which division of the autonomic nervous system helps you calm down after taking a stressful exam?

ANSWER: the parasympathetic division

3.12 The Endocrine System Communicates Through Hormones

Like the nervous system, the **endocrine system** is a communication network that influences thoughts, behaviors, and actions. The two systems work together to regulate psychological activity. The brain receives information from the nervous system about potential threats to the organism and then communicates with the

endocrine system A communication system that uses hormones to influence thoughts, behaviors, and actions.

endocrine system to prepare the organism to deal with those threats. The main differences between the two systems are in their mode and speed of communication: Whereas the nervous system is fast and uses electrochemical signals, the endocrine system is slower and uses hormones.

hormones Chemical substances, released from endocrine glands, that travel through the bloodstream to targeted tissues; the tissues are subsequently influenced by the hormones.

Hormones are chemical substances released into the bloodstream by the *endocrine glands*, such as the pancreas, thyroid, adrenal gland, and testes or ovaries (**FIGURE 3.32**). Because they travel through the bloodstream, hormones can take from seconds to hours to exert their effects. Once hormones are in the bloodstream, their effects can last for a long time and affect multiple targets.

pituitary gland A gland located at the base of the hypothalamus; it sends hormonal signals to other endocrine glands, controlling their release of hormones.

The endocrine system is primarily controlled by the hypothalamus (for the location of this structure, see Figure 3.32; for a more detailed look, see Figure 3.26). The hypothalamus controls the endocrine system via signals to the **pituitary gland**, which is located at the base of the hypothalamus. Neural activation causes the hypothalamus to secrete a particular one of its many *releasing factors*. The particular releasing factor causes the pituitary to release a hormone specific to that factor, and the hormone then travels through the bloodstream to endocrine sites throughout the body. Once the hormone reaches the target sites, it binds to receptor sites and subsequently affects bodily reactions or behavior. The pituitary can be considered the "control center" of the endocrine system: By releasing hormones into the bloodstream, it controls all other glands; governs major processes such as development, ovulation, and lactation; and influences a broad range of behaviors, including stress reactions and sexual behaviors.

GROWTH HORMONE The integration between the CNS and endocrine system can be finely tuned. Consider physical growth. *Growth hormone (GH)*, a hormone released from the pituitary gland, prompts bone, cartilage, and muscle tissue to grow or helps them regenerate after injury. Since the 1930s, many people have administered or self-administered GH to increase body size and strength. Many

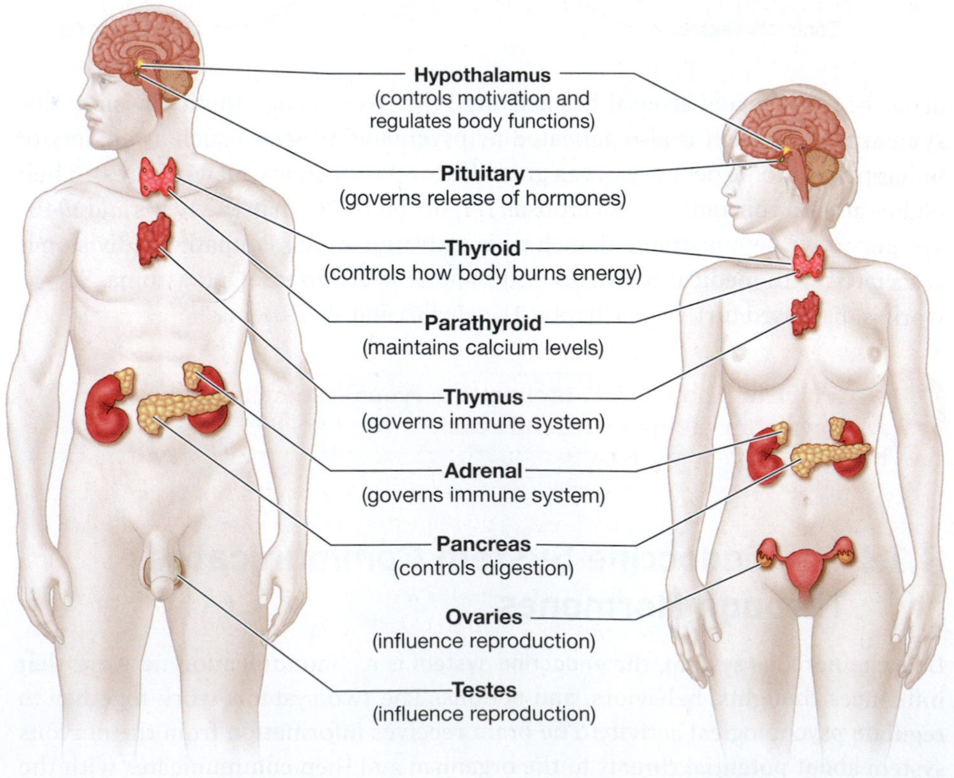

FIGURE 3.32
The Hypothalamus and the Major Endocrine Glands

athletes have sought a competitive advantage by using GH. For example, in early 2013, the legendary cyclist Lance Armstrong admitted to using GH and other hormones, including testosterone, to boost his performance. In an interview with Oprah Winfrey, Armstrong claimed that because doping was so pervasive in the sport, it was impossible for any cyclist to win a major championship without doping (**FIGURE 3.33**).

The releasing factor for GH stimulates the eating of protein by making it especially enjoyable (Dickson & Vaccarino, 1994). The area of the hypothalamus that stimulates release of GH is also involved in sleep/wake cycles. Thus, the bursts of GH, the need for protein, and the consumption of protein are controlled by the body's internal clock. All these connections illustrate how the CNS, the PNS, and the endocrine system work together to ensure the organism's survival: These systems prompt the behaviors that provide the body with the substances it needs when it needs them.

FIGURE 3.33
Growth Hormone and Cycling
In January 2013, Lance Armstrong appeared on *The Oprah Winfrey Show* to admit using doping techniques to enhance his cycling performance.

Q Which gland is the "control center" of the endocrine system and why?

ANSWER: the pituitary gland, because it receives signals directly from the hypothalamus and then directs activation of the other endocrine glands

How Does the Brain Change?

Learning Objectives

- Explain how environmental factors, including experiences, influence brain organization.
- Discuss how the brain recovers after injury.

In terms of brain development, every experience is a learning experience. Throughout our lives, our brains change. That is, the circuitry is reworked and updated. And as we mature, the brain normally develops according to a fairly predictable pattern. At specific points in life, particular brain structures progress and cognitive abilities increase.

Indeed, the brain is extremely adaptable, especially during childhood. This ability to change in response to experience or injury is known as **plasticity**. In general, plasticity has *critical periods*. During these times, particular experiences must occur for development to proceed normally.

plasticity A property of the brain that allows it to change as a result of experience or injury.

3.13 The Brain Rewires Itself Throughout Life

Connections form between brain structures when growing axons are directed by certain chemicals that tell them where to go and where not to go. The major connections are established by chemical messengers, but the detailed connections are governed by experience. Consider an extreme example, which was discovered through research on brain development. If a cat's eyes are sewn shut at birth, depriving the animal of visual input, the visual cortex fails to develop properly. If the sutures are removed weeks later, the cat will never see normally, even though its eyes function just fine. Adult cats that are similarly deprived do not lose their sight (Wiesel & Hubel, 1963). Thus, during brain development, ongoing activity in the visual pathways is necessary to refine the visual cortex enough for it to function.

To study the effects of experience on brain development, researchers reared rats in a number of different laboratory environments. One group was raised in relatively deprived circumstances, with minimal comfort and no opportunities for social interaction. Another group was raised in an enriched environment, with many companions, interesting things to look at, puzzles, obstacles, toys, running wheels, and even balance beams. The "luxury" items might simply have approximated rat life in the wild, but they enabled the luxury group to develop bigger, heavier brains than the deprived group (Rosenzweig et al., 1972). Not only is experience important for normal development, but it may be even

(a)

(b)

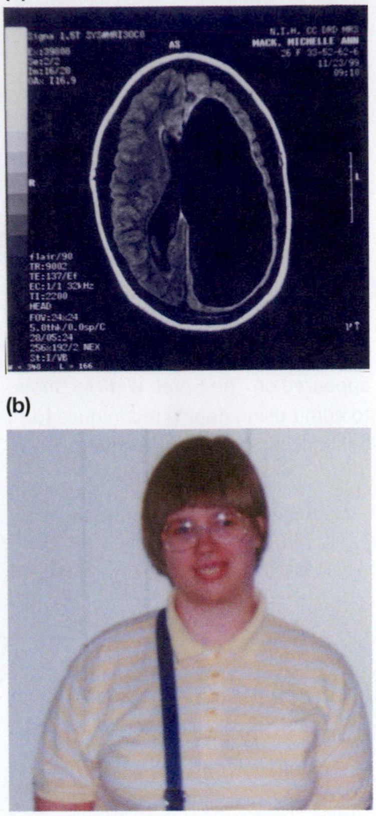

FIGURE 3.34

Michelle Mack and a Case of Extreme Plasticity

(a) Michelle Mack suffered a stroke before birth that obliterated her left hemisphere (black areas shown here, in a scan taken when she was an adult; note that hemispheres are reversed on this scan). **(b)** Over time, Mack's right hemisphere took over the duties of the left hemisphere to a surprising extent.

more so for superior development. Nowadays, as a result of these findings, most laboratory animals are kept in environments that provide enrichment (Simpson & Kelly, 2011). Some evidence suggests that the opportunity for physical exercise might have the most beneficial effects on brain development and learning (Mustroph et al., 2012).

The extent to which the brain can be reorganized is revealed in dramatic cases where an infant is born with only one hemisphere. Michelle Mack is one such person. When Mack was a youngster, her parents noticed that she had difficulty performing certain simple tasks. When Mack was 27 years old, doctors discovered that she was missing the left hemisphere of her brain (**FIGURE 3.34**). This condition may have resulted from a stroke she experienced in the womb.

Without a left hemisphere, Mack should have shown severe deficits in skills processed in that half of the brain, including language and motor actions for the right side of the body. Losing a hemisphere as an adult would result in devastating loss of function. But Mack's speech is only minimally affected, and she can move the right side of her body with some difficulty. Mack is able to lead a surprisingly independent life. She graduated from high school, has a job, pays her bills, and does chores. Somehow, her right hemisphere developed language-processing capabilities as well as functions that ordinarily occur across both hemispheres.

Michelle Mack's case shows that nurture can influence nature. As she interacted with the world over time, her experiences enabled her brain to reorganize itself. Her right hemisphere took over processing for the missing left hemisphere.

Brain plasticity decreases with age. Even into very old age, however, the brain can grow new connections among neurons and even grow new neurons. The rewiring and growth within the brain represents the biological basis of learning. Until about 30 years ago, scientists believed that adult brains produced no new brain cells, although they could rewire to support new learning. There is now evidence that new neurons are produced in some brain regions (Eriksson et al., 1998). The production of new neurons is called *neurogenesis*.

Elizabeth Gould and her colleagues have demonstrated that environmental conditions can play an important role in neurogenesis. For example, they have found that for rats, shrews, and marmosets (a species of monkey), stressful experiences—such as being confronted by strange males in their home cages—interfere with neurogenesis during development and adulthood (Gould & Tanapat, 1999). In addition, when animals are housed together, they typically form dominance hierarchies that reflect social status. Dominant animals, those who possess the highest social status, show greater increases in new neurons than subordinate animals do (Kozorovitskiy & Gould, 2004). Thus, social environment and stress can strongly affect brain plasticity, a dynamic process we are only beginning to understand (Opendak et al., 2016).

Q **What is neurogenesis?**

ANSWER: a type of brain plasticity that involves production of new neurons

3.14 The Brain Can Recover from Injury

Just as the brain reorganizes in response to amount of use, it also reorganizes in response to brain damage. Following an injury in the cortex, the surrounding gray matter may assume the function of the damaged area, like a local business scrambling to pick up the customers of a newly closed competitor. This remapping seems to begin immediately, and it continues for years. Such plasticity involves all levels of the central nervous system, from the cortex down to the spinal cord.

Reorganization can occur in children in accord with the sensitive periods of normal development. Young children who have severe and uncontrollable epilepsy that has paralyzed one or more limbs sometimes undergo a *radical hemispherectomy*. This surgical procedure removes an entire cerebral hemisphere. Just as in the case of Michelle Mack, the remaining hemisphere eventually takes on most of the lost hemisphere's functions. The children regain almost complete use of their limbs. However, adults cannot undergo radical hemispherectomy. If the procedure were performed on adults, it would cause permanent paralysis and loss of function due to reduced capacity for neural reorganization with age.

However, even though adults do not have the same degree of plasticity as children, cortical reorganization can lead to recovery from more limited brain injuries. For instance, if a stroke were to damage the part of your motor cortex controlling your hand, with extensive practice and rehabilitation it might be possible for some of this motor function to be taken over by adjoining cortical areas, thus partially restoring your ability to control that hand. At the same time, this cortical reorganization can lead to some bizarre results. The neurologist V. S. Ramachandran has discovered that an amputee who has lost a hand may, when their eyes are closed, perceive a touch on the cheek as if it were on the missing hand (Ramachandran & Hirstein, 1998). On the somatosensory homunculus, the hand is represented next to the face. The unused part of the amputee's cortex (the part that would have responded to the now-missing hand) to some degree assumes the function of the closest group and is now activated by a touch on the amputee's face. Somehow, the rest of the brain has not kept pace with the somatosensory area enough to figure out these neurons' new job, so the brain still codes the input as coming from the hand, and thus the amputee experiences a "phantom hand" (**FIGURE 3.35**).

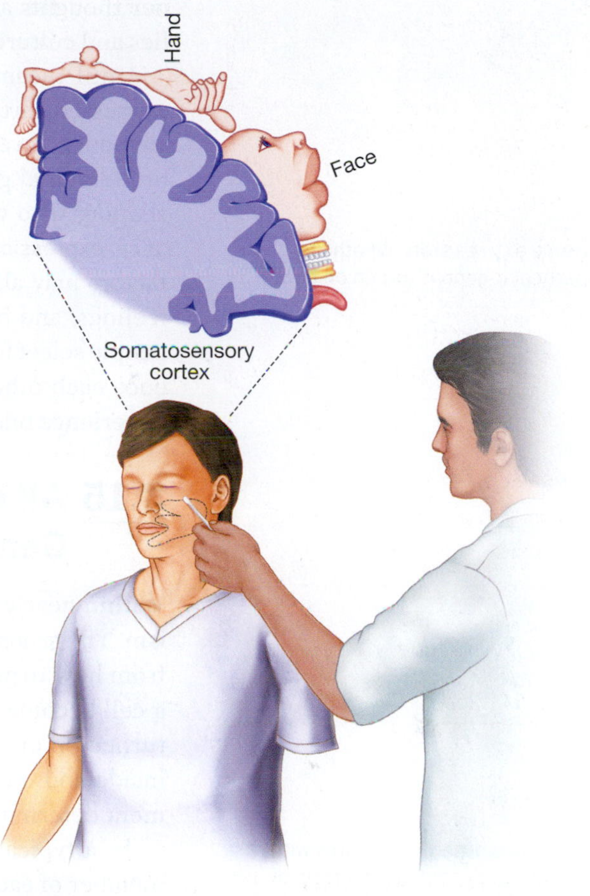

FIGURE 3.35
Cortical Remapping Following Amputation
The participant felt a cotton swab touching his cheek as touching his missing hand.

Q **Why would a physical therapist instruct a patient to use their impaired hand as much as possible following an injury to the hand-controlling region of the motor cortex?**

ANSWER: Increased effort and use of the hand could promote cortical reorganization, which might improve functional control of the hand.

What Is the Genetic Basis of Psychological Science?

Learning Objectives

- Explain how genes are transmitted from parents to offspring.
- Discuss the goals and methods of behavioral genetics.
- Explain how environmental factors, including experience, influence genetic expression.

So far, this chapter has presented the basic biological processes underlying psychological functions. This section considers how genes and environment affect psychological functions. From the moment of conception, we receive the genes we will possess for the remainder of our lives, but to what extent do those genes determine our thoughts and behaviors? How do environmental influences, such as the families and cultures in which we are raised, alter how our brains develop and change?

Until recently, genetic research focused almost entirely on whether people possessed certain types of genes, such as genes for psychological disorders or for particular levels of intelligence. Although it is important to discover the effects of individual genes, this approach misses the critical role of our environment in shaping who we are. Research has shown that environmental factors can affect **gene expression**—whether a particular gene is turned on or off. Environmental factors may also influence how a gene, once turned on, influences our thoughts, feelings, and behavior. Genetic predispositions also influence the environments people select for themselves. Once again, biology and environment mutually influence each other. All the while, biology and environment—one's genes and every experience one ever has—influence the development of the brain.

gene expression Whether a particular gene is turned on or off.

3.15 All of Human Development Has a Genetic Basis

Within nearly every cell in the body is the genome for making the entire organism. The *genome* is the blueprint that provides detailed instructions for everything from how to grow a gallbladder to where the nose gets placed on a face. Whether a cell becomes part of a gallbladder or a nose is determined by which genes are turned on or off within that cell, which in turn is determined by cues from both inside and outside the cell. The genome provides the options, and the environment determines which option is taken (Marcus, 2004).

In a typical human, nearly every cell contains 23 pairs of **chromosomes**. One member of each pair comes from the mother, the other from the father. The chromosomes are made of *deoxyribonucleic acid (DNA)*, a substance that consists of two intertwined strands of molecules in a double helix shape. Segments of those strands are **genes** (**FIGURE 3.36**). Each gene—a particular sequence of molecules along a DNA strand—specifies an exact instruction to manufacture a distinct *polypeptide*. Polypeptides are the building blocks of proteins, the basic chemicals that make up the structure of cells and direct their activities. There are thousands of types of proteins, and each type carries out a specific task. The environment determines which proteins are produced and when they are produced.

chromosomes Structures within the cell body that are made up of DNA, segments of which comprise individual genes.

genes The units of heredity that help determine an organism's characteristics.

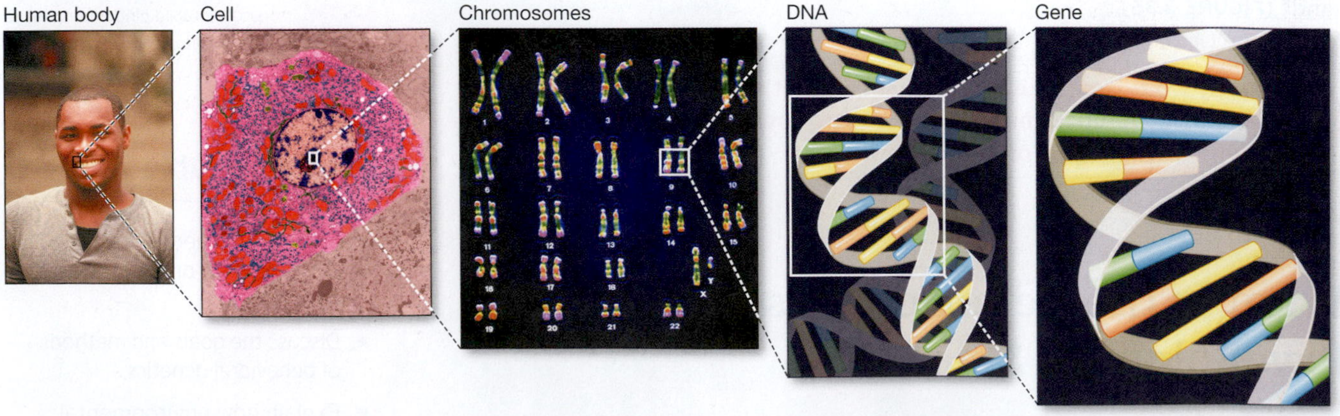

FIGURE 3.36
The Human Body Down to Its Genes
Each cell in the human body includes pairs of chromosomes, which consist of DNA strands. DNA has a double helix shape, and segments of it consist of individual genes.

FIGURE 3.37
Gene Expression and Environment
The North American buckeye butterfly has seasonal forms that differ in terms of the color patterns on their wings. **(a)** Generations that develop to adulthood in the summer—when temperatures are higher—take the "linea" form, with pale beige wings. **(b)** Generations that develop to adulthood in the autumn—when the days are shorter—take the "rosa" form, with dark reddish-brown wings.

For example, a certain species of butterfly becomes colorful or drab, depending on the season in which the individual butterfly is born (Brakefield & French, 1999). The environment causes a gene to be expressed during the butterfly's development that is sensitive to temperature or day length (**FIGURE 3.37**). In humans as well, gene expression not only determines the body's basic physical makeup but also determines specific developments throughout life. It is involved in all psychological activity. Gene expression allows us to sense, to learn, to fall in love, and so on.

In February 2001, two groups of scientists published separate articles that detailed the results of the first phase of the *Human Genome Project*, an international research effort. This achievement represents the coordinated work of hundreds of scientists around the world to map the entire structure of human genetic material. The first step of the Human Genome Project was to map the entire sequence of DNA. In other words, the researchers set out to identify the precise order of molecules that make up each of the thousands of genes on each of the 23 pairs of human chromosomes (**FIGURE 3.38**). Since it was first launched, the Human Genome Project has led to many discoveries and encouraged scientists to work together to achieve grand goals (Green et al., 2015).

One of the most striking findings from the Human Genome Project is that people have fewer than 30,000 genes. That number means humans have only about twice as many genes as a fly (13,000) or a worm (18,000), not much more than the number in some plants (26,000), and fewer than the number estimated

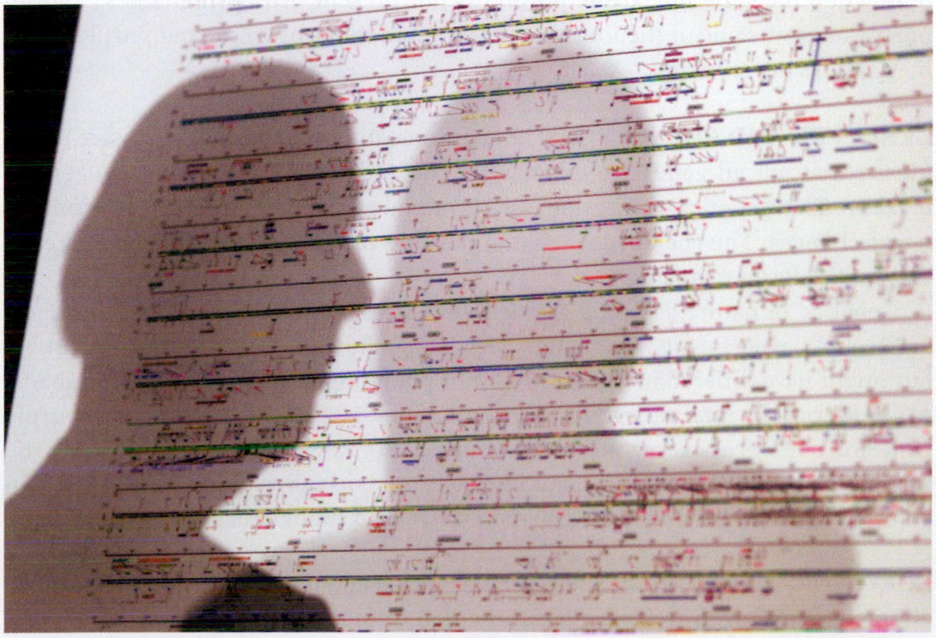

FIGURE 3.38
Human Genome Project
A map of human genes is presented by J. Craig Venter, president of the research company Celera Genomics, at a news conference in Washington, D.C., on February 12, 2001. This map is one part of the international effort by hundreds of scientists to map the entire structure of human genetic material.

ANSWER: a particular sequence of DNA that provides instructions for building polypeptides and subsequently proteins

to be in an ear of corn (50,000). Why are we so complex if we have so few genes? The number of genes might be less important than subtleties in how those genes are expressed and regulated (Baltimore, 2001).

Q **What is a gene?**

3.16 Heredity Involves Passing Along Genes Through Reproduction

The first clues to the mechanisms responsible for heredity were discovered by the monk Gregor Mendel around 1866. The monastery where Mendel lived had a long history of studying plants. For studying inheritance, Mendel developed an experimental technique, *selective breeding*, that strictly controlled which plants bred with which other plants.

In one simple study, Mendel selected pea plants that had either only purple flowers or only white flowers (**FIGURE 3.39**). He then cross-pollinated the two types to see which color of flowers the plants would produce. Mendel found that the first generation of pea offspring tended to be completely white or completely purple. If he had stopped there, he would never have discovered the basis of heredity. However, he then allowed each plant to self-pollinate into a second generation. This second generation revealed a different pattern: Of the hundreds of pea plants, about 75 percent had purple flowers and 25 percent had white flowers. This 3:1 ratio repeated itself in additional studies. It also held true for other characteristics, such as pod shape.

(a)

(b)

FIGURE 3.39
Parent Plants Display Genetic Differences
Mendel studied pea plants. To observe the effects of cross-breeding, he started with **(a)** pea plants with purple flowers, and **(b)** pea plants with white flowers.

From this pattern, Mendel deduced that the plants contained separate units, now referred to as genes, that existed in different versions (e.g., white and purple). In determining an offspring's features, some of these versions would be dominant and others would be recessive. We now know that a **dominant gene** from either parent is expressed (becomes apparent or physically visible) whenever it is present. A **recessive gene** is expressed only when it is matched with a similar gene from the other parent. In pea plants, white flowers are recessive, so white flowers occur only when the gene for purple flowers is not present. All "white genes" and no purple ones was one of the four possible combinations of white and purple genes in Mendel's experiments.

dominant gene A gene that is expressed in the offspring whenever it is present.

recessive gene A gene that is expressed only when it is matched with a similar gene from the other parent.

genotype The genetic constitution of an organism, determined at the moment of conception.

phenotype Observable physical characteristics, which result from both genetic and environmental influences.

GENOTYPE AND PHENOTYPE The existence of dominant and recessive genes means that not all genes are expressed. The **genotype** is an organism's genetic makeup. That genetic constitution is determined at the moment of conception and never changes. The **phenotype** is that organism's observable physical characteristics and is always changing.

Genetics, or nature, is one of the two influences on phenotype. So, for instance, in Mendel's experiments, two plants with purple flowers had the same phenotype but might have differed in genotype. Either plant might have had two (dominant) genes for purple. Alternatively, either plant might have had one (dominant) purple gene and one (recessive) white gene (**FIGURE 3.40**). Environment, or nurture, is the second influence on phenotype. For instance, humans inherit their height and skin color. But good nutrition leads to increased size, and sunlight can change skin color.

POLYGENIC EFFECTS Mendel's flower experiments dealt with single-gene characteristics. Such traits appear to be determined by one gene each. When a

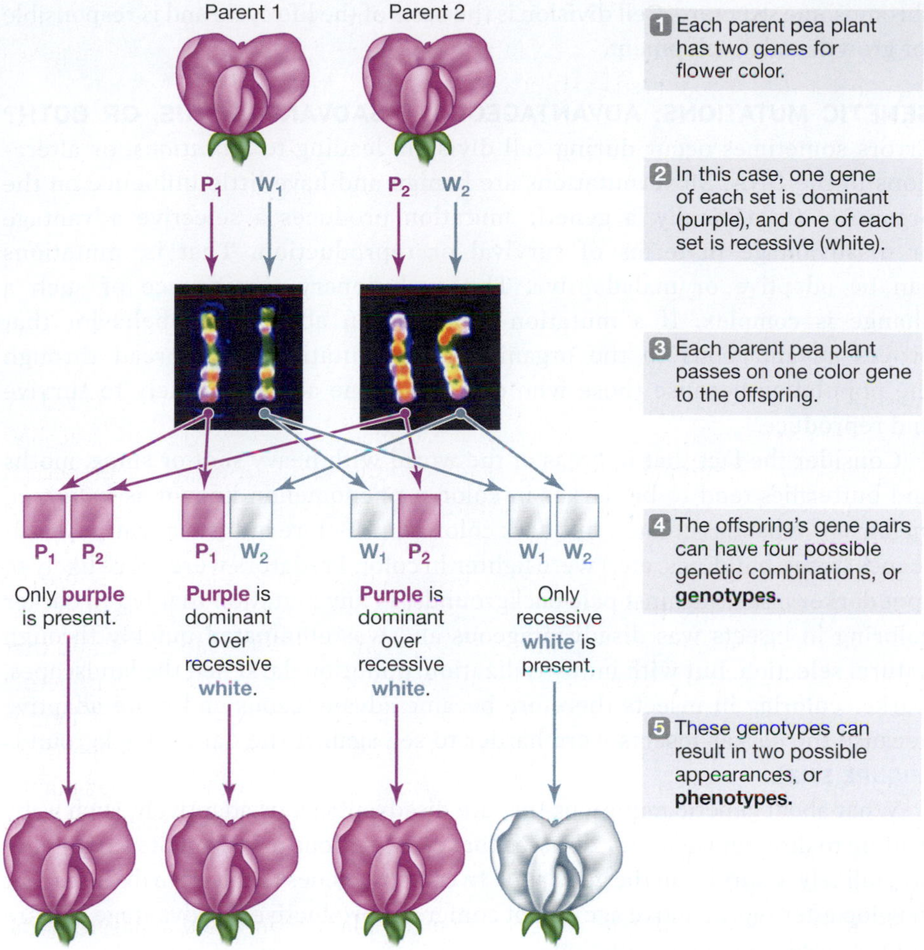

Parent 1
Parent 2
1 Each parent pea plant has two genes for flower color.
P_1 W_1
P_2 W_2
2 In this case, one gene of each set is dominant (purple), and one of each set is recessive (white).
3 Each parent pea plant passes on one color gene to the offspring.
P_1 P_2
P_1 W_2
W_1 P_2
W_1 W_2
4 The offspring's gene pairs can have four possible genetic combinations, or **genotypes.**
Only **purple** is present.
Purple is dominant over recessive **white**.
Purple is dominant over recessive **white**.
Only recessive **white** is present.
5 These genotypes can result in two possible appearances, or **phenotypes.**

FIGURE 3.40

Genotypes and Phenotypes

Mendel's experiments with cross-breeding pea plants resulted in purple flowers 75 percent of the time and white flowers 25 percent of the time.

population displays a range of variability for a certain characteristic, such as height or intelligence, the characteristic is *polygenic*. In other words, the trait is influenced by many genes (as well as by environment).

Consider human skin color. There are not just three or four separate skin colors. There is a spectrum of colors. The huge range of skin tones among Americans alone (phenotype) shows that human skin color is not the end product of a single dominant/recessive gene pairing (genotype). Instead, the variety shows the effects of multiple genes.

SEXUAL REPRODUCTION Although they have the same parents, siblings may differ from each other in terms of eye color, height, personality and many other traits. These differences occur because each person has a specific combination of genes. Most cells in the human body contain 23 pairs of chromosomes. These pairs include the sex chromosomes, which are denoted X and Y because of their shapes. Females have two X chromosomes. Males have one X chromosome and one Y (**FIGURE 3.41**).

After one sperm and one egg combine during fertilization, the resulting fertilized cell, known as a *zygote*, contains 23 pairs of chromosomes. Half of each pair of chromosomes comes from the mother, and the other half comes from the father. From any two parents, 8 million combinations of the 23 chromosomes are possible. The net outcome is that a unique genotype is created at conception, accounting for the *genetic variation* of the human species.

The zygote grows through *cell division*. This process has two stages: First the chromosomes duplicate. Then the cell divides into two new cells with an identical

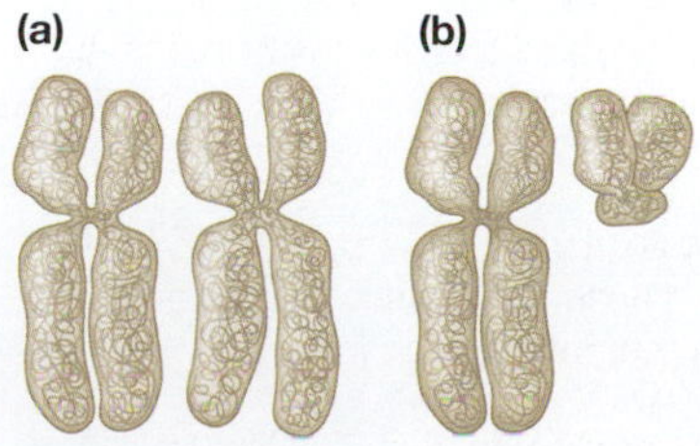

(a)
(b)

FIGURE 3.41

Sex Chromosomes

(a) In females, the 23rd pair of chromosomes consists of two X chromosomes. **(b)** In males, the 23rd pair consists of one X and one Y chromosome. The Y chromosome is much smaller than the X chromosome.

chromosome structure. Cell division is the basis of the life cycle and is responsible for growth and development.

GENETIC MUTATIONS: ADVANTAGEOUS, DISADVANTAGEOUS, OR BOTH?

Errors sometimes occur during cell division, leading to *mutations*, or alterations in the DNA. Most mutations are benign and have little influence on the organism. Occasionally, a genetic mutation produces a selective advantage or disadvantage in terms of survival or reproduction. That is, mutations can be adaptive or maladaptive. The evolutionary significance of such a change is complex. If a mutation produces an ability or a behavior that proves advantageous to the organism, that mutation may spread through the population because those who carry the gene are more likely to survive and reproduce.

Consider the fact that in areas of the world with heavy soot or smog, moths and butterflies tend to be darker in color, a phenomenon known as *industrial melanism*. What has created this dark coloration? Before industrialization, landscapes (trees, buildings, etc.) were lighter in color. Predators were more likely to spot darker insects against pale backgrounds, so any mutation that led to darker coloring in insects was disadvantageous and was eliminated quickly through natural selection. But with industrialization, pollution darkened the landscapes. Darker coloring in insects therefore became advantageous and more adaptive because the darker insects were harder to see against the darker backgrounds (**FIGURE 3.42**).

FIGURE 3.42
Industrial Melanism
Because predators have an easier time catching insects they can spot, darker moths and darker butterflies are better able to survive in more-polluted areas. As a result, the lighter moths and lighter butterflies in those areas tend to die off, leaving more of the moths and butterflies with the selective advantage of darkness.

What about genetic mutations that are disadvantageous adaptively, such as by leading to disease? Genes for diseases that cause serious impairments early in life are unlikely to survive in the gene pool. In contrast, genes that lead to diseases that develop after reproductive age do not confer a reproductive disadvantage and are not removed from the population.

The dominance or recessiveness of a gene also helps determine whether it remains in the gene pool. For instance, *sickle-cell disease* is a genetic disorder that alters the bloodstream's processing of oxygen. It can lead to pain, organ and bone damage, and anemia. The disease occurs mainly in people of certain racial or ethnic groups, including those of African descent: Approximately 8 percent of African Americans are estimated to have the (recessive) gene for it (Centers for Disease Control and Prevention, 2011b). Because the sickle-cell gene is recessive, only people who receive it from both parents will develop the disease. Those who receive a recessive gene from only one parent have what is called *sickle-cell trait*. They may exhibit symptoms under certain conditions (such as during exercise), but they will have a generally healthy phenotype in spite of a genotype that includes the trait (**FIGURE 3.43**).

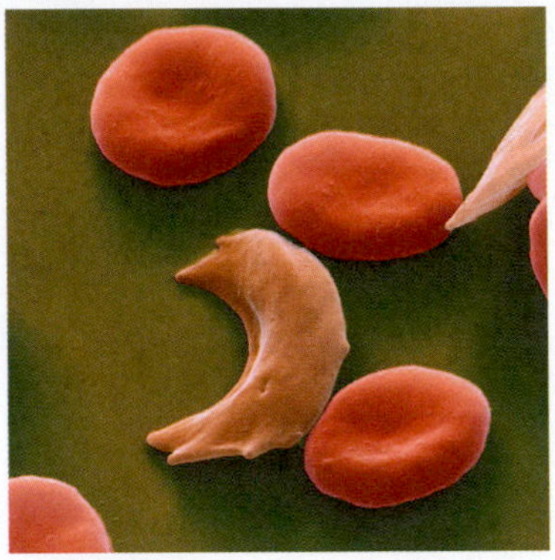

FIGURE 3.43
Sickle-Cell Disease
Sickle-cell disease occurs when people receive recessive genes for the trait from both parents. It causes red blood cells to assume the distinctive "sickle" shape seen here in the left cell. Sickle-cell disease is most common among African Americans.

Recessive genes do not interfere with most people's health. For this reason, the recessive genes for diseases such as sickle-cell anemia can survive in the gene pool. This particular gene also has some benefit in that it increases resistance to malaria, a parasitic disease prevalent in certain parts of Africa. People with only one sickle-cell gene enjoy this resistance without suffering from sickle-cell disease. In contrast to recessive gene disorders like this one, most dominant gene disorders are lethal for most of their carriers and therefore do not last in the gene pool.

Q **Can human variation in skin color be understood as a single-gene dominant/recessive trait?**

ANSWER: No, human skin color is a polygenic characteristic and influenced by the environment.

3.17 Genes Affect Behavior

What determines the kind of person you are? What factors make you more or less bold, intelligent, or able to read a map? Your abilities and your psychological traits are influenced by the interaction of your genes and the environments in which you were raised and to which you are now exposed. The study of how genes and environment interact to influence psychological activity is known as *behavioral genetics*. Behavioral genetics has provided important information about the extent to which biology influences mind, brain, and behavior.

Any research suggesting that abilities to perform certain behaviors are biologically based is controversial. Most people do not want to be told that what they can achieve is limited or promoted by something beyond their control, such as their genes. It is easy to accept that genes control physical characteristics such as sex, eye color, and predisposition to diseases such as cancer and alcoholism. But can genes determine whether people will get divorced, how happy they are, or what careers they choose?

Increasingly, science indicates that genes lay the groundwork for many human traits. From this perspective, it is as if people are born with the ingredients for a recipe: The basic materials are there, but how the dish turns out can vary depending on how it is prepared and cooked. Psychologists study the ways in which traits and characteristics are influenced by nature, nurture, and their combination. In other words, who we are is determined by how our genes are expressed in distinct environments.

BEHAVIORAL GENETICS METHODS Most of us, at one time or another, have marveled at how different siblings can be, even those raised around the same time and in the same household. The differences are to be expected, because most siblings do not share identical genes or identical life experiences. Within the household and outside it, environments differ subtly and not so subtly. Siblings have different birth orders. Their mother may have consumed different foods and other substances during her pregnancies. The siblings may have different friends and teachers. Their parents may treat them differently. Their parents are at different points in their own lives.

It is difficult to know what causes the similarities and differences between siblings, who always share some genes and often share much of their environments. Therefore, behavioral geneticists use two methods to assess the degree to which traits are inherited: twin studies and adoption studies.

Twin studies compare similarities between different types of twins to determine the genetic basis of specific traits. **Monozygotic twins**, or *identical twins*, result from one zygote (fertilized egg) dividing in two. Each new zygote, and therefore each twin, has the same chromosomes and the same genes on each chromosome (**FIGURE 3.44a**). However, monozygotic twins' DNA might not be as identical as long thought, because of subtle differences in how the mother's and father's genes are combined (Bruder et al., 2008). **Dizygotic twins**, sometimes called *fraternal* or *nonidentical twins*, result when two separately fertilized eggs develop in the mother's womb simultaneously. The resulting twins are no more similar genetically than any other pair of siblings (**FIGURE 3.44b**). To the extent that monozygotic twins are more similar than dizygotic twins, the increased similarity is most likely due to genetic influence.

monozygotic twins Also called *identical twins*; twin siblings that result from one zygote splitting in two and that therefore share the same genes.

dizygotic twins Also called *fraternal twins*; twin siblings that result from two separately fertilized eggs and therefore are no more similar genetically than nontwin siblings.

Adoption studies compare the similarities between biological relatives and adoptive relatives. Nonbiological adopted siblings may share similar home environments, but they have different genes. Therefore, the assumption is that

FIGURE 3.44
The Two Kinds of Twins
(a) Monozygotic (identical) twins result when one fertilized egg splits in two. **(b)** Dizygotic (fraternal) twins result when two separate eggs are fertilized at the same time.

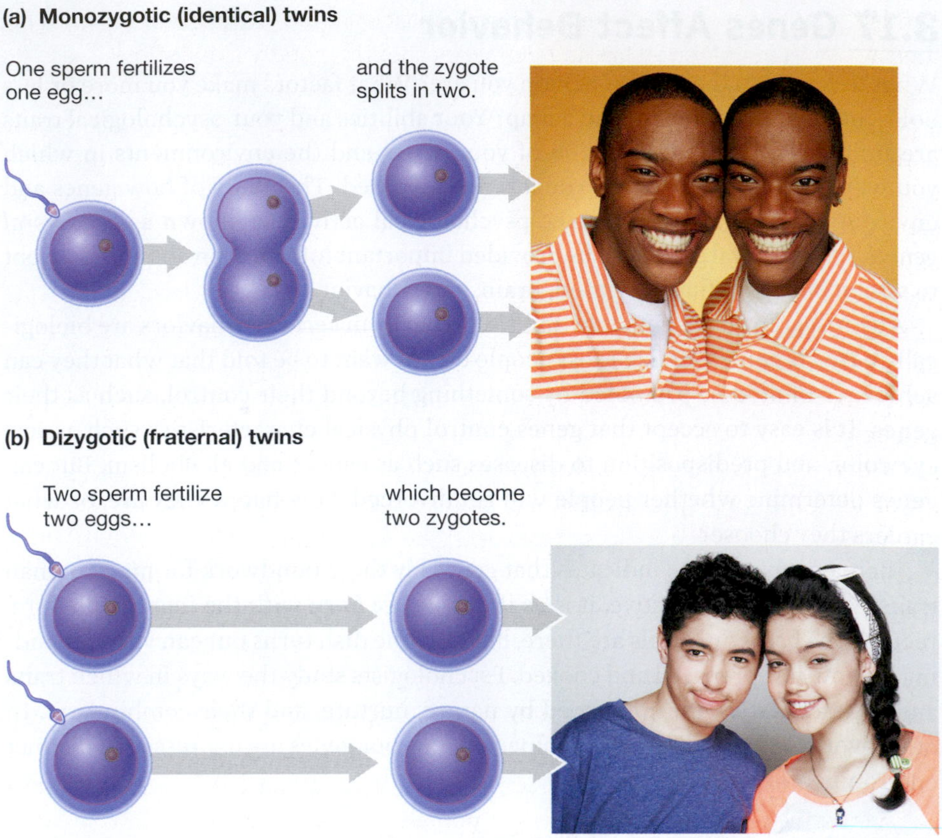
(a) Monozygotic (identical) twins
One sperm fertilizes one egg...
and the zygote splits in two.
(b) Dizygotic (fraternal) twins
Two sperm fertilize two eggs...
which become two zygotes.

similarities among nonbiological adopted siblings have more to do with environment than with genes.

How much influence would you say your home life has had on you? It turns out that growing up in the same home has relatively little influence on many traits, including personality traits. Indeed, after genetic similarity is controlled for, even biological siblings raised in the same home are no more similar than two strangers plucked at random off the street.

One way to conduct a behavioral genetic study is to compare monozygotic twins who have been *raised together* with ones who were *raised apart*. Thomas Bouchard and his colleagues (1990) at the University of Minnesota identified more than 100 pairs of identical and nonidentical twins, some raised together and some raised apart. The researchers examined a variety of these twins' characteristics, including intelligence, personality, well-being, achievement, alienation, and aggression. The general finding from the Minnesota Twin Project was that identical twins, whether they were raised together or not, were likely to be similar.

Some critics have argued that most of the adopted twins in the Minnesota study were raised in relatively similar environments. This similarity came about, in part, because adoption agencies try to match each child to an appropriate adoptive home. However, this argument does not explain the identical twins Oskar Stohr and Jack Yufe, who were born in Trinidad in 1933 (Bouchard et al., 1990). Oskar was raised Catholic in Germany and eventually joined the Nazi Party. Jack was raised Jewish in Trinidad and lived for a while in Israel. Few twins have such different backgrounds. Yet when they met at an interview for the study, they were wearing similar clothes, exhibited similar mannerisms, and shared odd habits, such as flushing the toilet before using it, dipping toast in coffee, storing rubber bands on their wrists, and enjoying startling people by sneezing loudly in elevators.

Another striking example of the influence of genetics on seemingly idiosyncratic behaviors was portrayed in the 2018 documentary *Three Identical Strangers*, which tells the tale of rare monozygotic triplets who were adopted into families with different parenting styles and found each other in their early 20s (see **FIGURE 3.45**). Like Oskar Stohr and Jack Yufe, when they met in early adulthood the triplets seemed to have striking similarities. As they got older, however, some differences became apparent. If you have not seen the movie and find questions of nature versus nurture interesting, it would be worthwhile to take a look. It provides a thought-provoking exploration of the ways genes and environment might interact in determining psychological traits and behavior.

FIGURE 3.45
Three Identical Strangers
Rare monozygotic triplets who were adopted and raised apart found each other in their early 20s and discovered they had some striking similarities.

Of course, it is hard to know how much to conclude from a few case studies of identical twins or triplets raised apart, and some critics feel that nothing more than coincidence is at work in these case studies. They argue that if a researcher randomly selected any two people of the same age, many surprising similarities would exist in those people and their lives, just by coincidence, even if they differed in most other ways. But twins and other relatives share similarities beyond coincidental attributes and behavior quirks. For instance, intelligence and personality traits such as shyness tend to run in families because of strong genetic components.

Moreover, there is some evidence that twins raised apart may be more similar than twins raised together. This phenomenon might occur if parents encourage individuality in twins raised together by emphasizing different strengths and interests in each twin. In effect, the parents would actively create a different environment for each twin.

UNDERSTANDING HERITABILITY **Heredity** is the transmission of characteristics from parents to offspring by means of genes. A term that is often confused with *heredity* is **heritability**. This term refers to the proportion of the variation in some specific trait in a population that is due to genetics. Heritability is a statistic relevant to understanding the population as a whole, not an individual. Knowing the heritability of a trait does not indicate whether an individual's expression of that trait is due to genes or environment.

heredity Transmission of characteristics from parents to offspring through genes.

heritability A statistical estimate of the extent to which variation in a trait within a population is due to genetics.

Consider a specific trait, in a particular population: for instance, height in American women. The heritability for a trait depends on the *variation*: the measure of the overall difference among a group of people for that particular trait. To know the heritability of height, we need to know how much individual American women vary in that trait. Once we know the typical amount of variation within the population, we can see whether people who are related—sisters or a mother and daughter—show less variation than women chosen at random.

Say that within the population of American women, height has a heritability of .60. This figure means that 60 percent of the variation in height among American women is genetic. It does not mean that any individual necessarily gets 60 percent of her height from genetics and 40 percent from environment. Heritability estimates aid in identifying the causes of differences between individuals in a population.

Q When studying trait similarity and genes, why do researchers compare monozygotic twins with dizygotic twins?

ANSWER: Unlike dizygotic twins, monozygotic twins have the same genes. Therefore, if each pair of twins grew up together, then greater trait similarity in monozygotic twins than in dizygotic twins is likely due to genes.

3.18 Genetic Expression Can Be Modified

As noted at the beginning of this section, researchers focus more on how particular genes are expressed than on whether they are possessed. Several exciting advances have enhanced our understanding of how environments influence gene expression as well as how researchers can manipulate that expression.

Consider how social and environmental contexts might shape gene expression during development. In a longitudinal study of criminality, Avshalom Caspi and his colleagues (2002) followed a group of more than 1,000 New Zealanders from their births in 1972–73 until adulthood. The group was made up of all the babies that were born in the town of Dunedin over the course of a year. Every few years, the researchers collected enormous amounts of information about the participants and their lives. When the participants were 26 years old, the investigators examined which factors predicted who became a violent criminal.

Prior research had demonstrated that children who are mistreated by their parents are more likely to become violent offenders. But not all mistreated children become violent, and these researchers wanted to know why not. They hypothesized that the enzyme monoamine oxidase (MAO) is important in determining susceptibility to the effects of mistreatment, because low levels of MAO have been implicated in aggressive behaviors (this connection is discussed further in Chapter 12, "Social Psychology").

The gene that controls MAO is called MAOA and comes in two forms, one of which leads to higher levels of MAO and the other to lower levels. The MAO enzyme is involved in the degradation of a class of neurotransmitters called monoamines, which includes dopamine, serotonin, and norepinephrine. By influencing the level of MAO enzyme, the MAOA gene regulates the impact of these neurotransmitters in the brain. Caspi and colleagues found that boys with the low-MAOA gene appeared to be especially susceptible to the effects of early-childhood mistreatment. Those boys were also much more likely to be convicted of a violent crime than those with the high-MAOA gene. Only 1 in 8 boys was mistreated *and* had the low-MAOA gene. That minority, however, were responsible for nearly half of the violent crimes committed by the group (**FIGURE 3.46**).

The New Zealand study is a good example of how nature and nurture together affect behavior—in this case, unfortunately, violent behavior. The Dunedin study has been crucial for providing evidence regarding gene effects. One of the impressive aspects of the study is that more than 95 percent of the participants still alive continue to participate (Poulton et al., 2015).

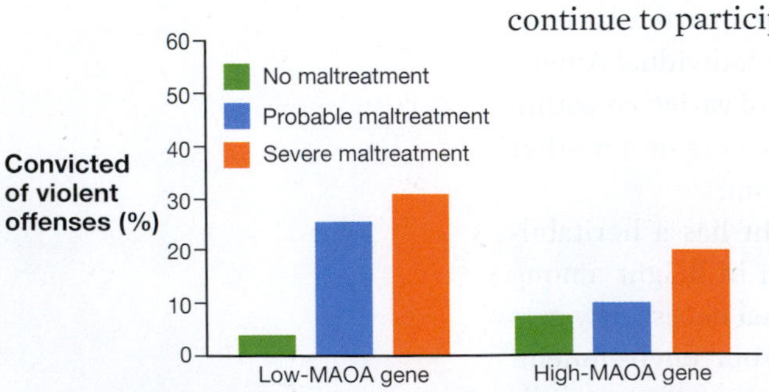

FIGURE 3.46
MAOA, Maltreatment, and Violence
Males who had the low-MAOA gene were much more likely to have been convicted of violent crimes than others if they had been maltreated as children. The effects of maltreatment had less of an effect for those with the high-MAOA gene.

EPIGENETICS An exciting new field of genetic study is *epigenetics* (Berger et al., 2009; Holliday, 1987). This term literally means "on top of genetics." Epigenetics researchers look at the processes by which environment affects genetic expression. They have found that various environmental exposures do not alter DNA, but they do alter gene expression. For example, living under stress or consuming a poor diet makes some genes more active and some less active.

According to recent research, these changes in how DNA is expressed can be passed along to future generations (Daxinger & Whitelaw, 2012). For example, rats raised by stressed mothers are more likely to be stressed themselves

(Zucchi et al., 2013). The biological mechanisms are too complex to consider here, but a simple way to think about epigenetic processes is that a parent's experiences create tags on DNA that tell it when to express. These tags may then be passed along with the DNA to future generations.

The potential implications of epigenetics for understanding health problems and health benefits are enormous. It is possible that smoking cigarettes or drinking alcohol, like chronic stress or bad nutrition, can create epigenetic tags (Pembrey et al., 2006). Further research will reveal how individuals' life circumstances might change how their genes operate and how such processes may affect future generations (Grossniklaus et al., 2013).

GENETIC MODIFICATIONS Researchers can employ various gene manipulation techniques to enhance or reduce the expression of a particular gene or even to insert a gene from one animal species into the embryo of another. The researchers can then compare the genetically modified animal with an unmodified one to test theories about the affected gene's function (**FIGURE 3.47**). Such techniques have dramatically increased our understanding of how gene expression influences thought, feeling, and behavior.

One technique is to create transgenic mice in which particular genes have been "knocked out," or rendered inactive by being removed from the genome or disrupted within the genome. If a gene is important for a specific function, knocking out that gene should interfere with the function. This experimental technique has revolutionized genetics, and in recognition the 2007 Nobel Prize was awarded to the three scientists who developed it: Mario Capecchi, Oliver Smithies, and Sir Martin Evans.

One remarkable finding from genetic manipulation is that changing even a single gene can dramatically change behavior. Through various gene manipulations, researchers have created anxious mice, hyperactive mice, mice that cannot learn or remember, mice that groom themselves to the point of baldness, mice that fail to take care of their offspring, and even mice that progressively increase alcohol intake when stressed (Marcus, 2004; Ridley, 2003).

In one study, a gene from the highly social prairie vole was inserted into the developing embryos of normally antisocial mice. The resulting transgenic mice exhibited social behavior more typical of prairie voles than of mice (Insel & Young, 2001). Another study found that knocking out specific genes led mice to forget other mice they had previously encountered. These "knockouts" also failed to investigate new mice placed in their cages, though normal mice would do so readily. In essence, knocking out one gene led to multiple impairments in social recognition (Choleris et al., 2003).

These findings do not indicate that mice have a specific gene for being social. They indicate that—in mice and in humans—changing one gene's expression leads to the expression or nonexpression of a series of other genes. This effect ultimately influences even complex behaviors. In other words, genes seldom work in isolation to influence mind and behavior. Rather, interaction among thousands of genes gives rise to the complexity of human experience.

OPTOGENETICS One problem with most studies of brain function is that they use correlational methods. Recall from Chapter 2 that correlational techniques do not support causal conclusions. For example, fMRI studies show which areas of the brain are most active while a person performs a task, but these findings do not mean there is a causal relationship between the brain activity and the task.

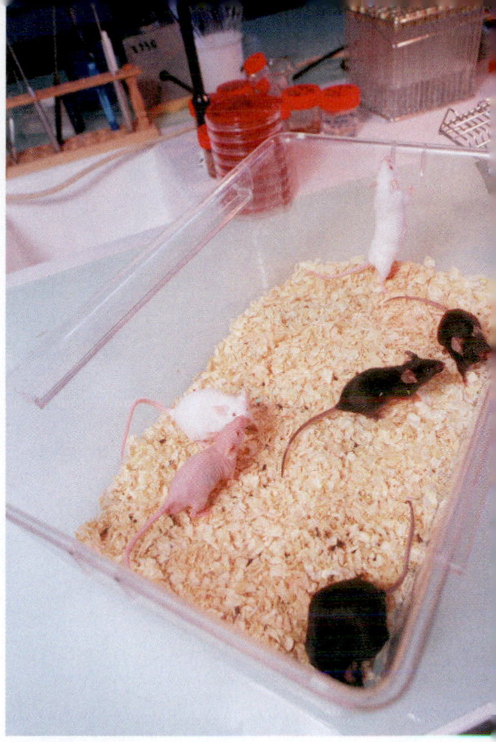

FIGURE 3.47
Genetic Modifications
The two white mice and three brown mice in this photo are genetically normal. The sixth mouse is hairless because it has been genetically modified. Specifically, this mouse has received two *nu* genes, which cause the "nude" mutation. These genes also affect the immune system, so the mouse is a good laboratory subject for studies related to immune function.

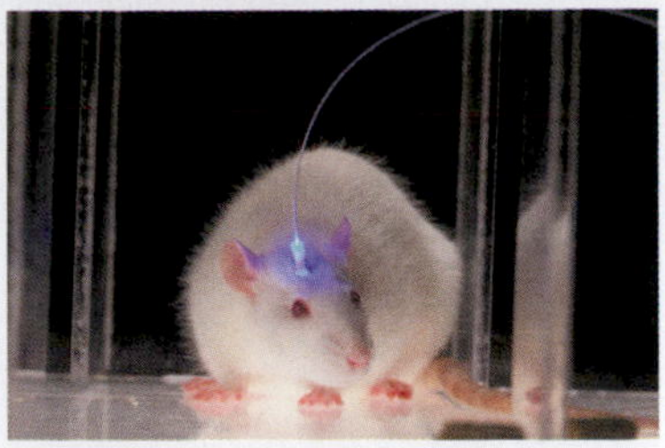

FIGURE 3.48
Optogenetics
This mouse has been implanted with an optogenetic device.

To address this limitation, scientists have developed *optogenetics*. This research technique provides precise control over when a neuron fires. That control enables researchers to better understand the causal relationship between neural firing and behavior. Optogenetics combines the use of light (optics) with gene alterations (Boyden et al., 2005; **FIGURE 3.48**). The genes are experimentally altered to change a particular subpopulation of neurons in the brain. Specifically, the membrane ion channels are changed within the neurons. (Recall that ion channels allow ions to enter the neuron and trigger action potentials.) The changes to the membrane ion channels make these specific neurons sensitive to different types of light (e.g., red, green, blue). By inserting fiber optics into that region of the brain and shining a particular type of light, researchers are able to trigger action potentials in the neurons of interest (Williams & Deisseroth, 2013). Using similar techniques, researchers can modify neurons so that firing is inhibited when light is presented (Berndt et al., 2014).

These techniques enable researchers to show that activating or deactivating specific neurons causes changes in brain activity or behavior. For instance, turning on one set of neurons led animals to act more anxiously (Tye et al., 2011). Turning off another set of neurons reduced cocaine use in animals addicted to that drug (Stefanik et al., 2013). The development of optogenetics is an excellent example of how cutting-edge methods enable researchers to ask increasingly direct questions about biology and behavior.

Q What is epigenetics?

ANSWER: the study of how the environment changes genetic expression in a way that might be passed along to offspring

Your Chapter Review

It's time to complete your study experience! Go to **INQUIZITIVE** to practice actively with this chapter's concepts and get personalized feedback along the way.

Chapter Summary

How Does the Nervous System Operate?

3.1 Neurons Are the Basic Units of the Nervous System The human nervous system is divided into two basic units: the central nervous system (the brain and the spinal cord) and the peripheral nervous system (all the other nerve cells in the rest of the body). Nerve cells, or neurons, are the basic units of the nervous system. Neurons are linked as neural networks, and neural networks are linked together. Neurons receive and send electrical and chemical messages. All neurons have the same basic structure, but they vary by function and by location in the nervous system.

3.2 Action Potentials Produce Neural Communication Changes in a neuron's electrical charge are the basis of an action potential, or neural firing. Firing is the means of communication within networks of neurons. A neuron at rest is polarized; that is, it has a greater negative electrical charge inside than outside. The passage of negative and positive ions inside and outside the neuron is regulated by ion channels, such as those located at the nodes of Ranvier.

3.3 Neurotransmitters Influence Mental Activity and Behavior Neurons do not touch. They release chemicals (neurotransmitters) into the small gaps between neurons called synapses. Neurotransmitters bind with the receptors of postsynaptic neurons, thus changing the charge in those neurons. Neurotransmitters' effects are halted by reuptake of the neurotransmitters into the presynaptic neurons, by enzyme deactivation, or by autoreception. Neurotransmitters have been identified that influence aspects of the mind and behavior in humans. Drugs and toxins can enhance or inhibit the activity of neurotransmitters by affecting their synthesis, their release, their breakdown, their reuptake, and their action on the postsynaptic neuron.

What Are the Basic Brain Structures and Their Functions?

3.4 The Ability to Study Brain Function Has Improved Dramatically Using various technologies, psychologists collect data about the ways people's bodies respond to particular tasks or events. For example, electroencephalography (EEG) measures the brain's electrical activity. Brain imaging is done using positron emission tomography (PET), magnetic resonance imaging (MRI), and functional magnetic resonance imaging (fMRI). Transcranial magnetic stimulation (TMS) disrupts normal brain activity, allowing researchers to infer the brain processing involved in particular thoughts, feelings, and behaviors.

3.5 The Cerebral Cortex Underlies Complex Mental Activity The lobes of the cortex play specific roles in vision (occipital); touch (parietal); hearing (temporal); and movement, rational activity, social behavior, and personality (frontal).

3.6 Splitting the Brain Splits the Mind Cutting the corpus callosum separates the brain's two hemispheres. Splitting the hemispheres from each other reveals their primary functions. The left hemisphere's propensity to construct a world that makes sense is called the interpreter.

3.7 You Be the Psychologist: Are There "Left-Brain" and "Right-Brain" Types of People? The idea of "left-brain" and "right-brain" people is a myth. The hemispheres are specialized for certain functions, such as language or spatial relationships. However, each hemisphere is capable of carrying out most cognitive processes, though sometimes in different ways.

3.8 The Insula and Subcortical Structures Contribute to Taste, Emotions, Memory, and Reward The insula and subcortical structures play a key part in psychological processes because they control taste, pain, and empathy (insula); relay of sensory information (the thalamus); vital functions (the hypothalamus); memories (the hippocampus); threat and fear (the amygdala); and the planning and production of movement and reward circuitry (the basal ganglia).

3.9 The Brain Stem and Cerebellum House Basic Programs for Survival and Movement The top of the spinal cord forms the brain stem, which includes the medulla, a structure that controls heart rate, breathing, and other autonomic functions; the pons; and the midbrain. The reticular formation is a network of neurons in the brain stem that extends into the cortex and influences general alertness and sleep. The cerebellum ("little brain") is the bulging structure connected to the back of the brain stem. This structure is essential for coordination of movement and balance.

3.10 Psychology Outside the Lab: Auction Overbidding Brain imaging can be used to inform our understanding of a range of psychological behaviors, including why we might pay too much at an auction.

How Does the Brain Communicate with the Body?

3.11 The Peripheral Nervous System Includes the Somatic and Autonomic Systems The somatic system transmits sensory signals and motor signals between the central nervous system and the skin, muscles, and joints. The autonomic system regulates the body's internal environment through the sympathetic division, which responds to alarm, and the parasympathetic division, which returns the body to its resting state.

3.12 The Endocrine System Communicates Through Hormones Endocrine glands produce and release chemical substances. These substances travel to body tissues through the bloodstream and influence a variety of processes, including the stress response and sexual behavior. The endocrine system is largely controlled through the actions of the hypothalamus and the pituitary gland. The hypothalamus controls the release of hormones from the pituitary gland. The pituitary controls the release of hormones from other endocrine glands in the body.

How Does the Brain Change?

3.13 The Brain Rewires Itself Throughout Life Plasticity is the brain's capacity to continually change in response to a person's environment. Although brain plasticity decreases with age, the brain retains the ability to rewire itself throughout life. This ability is the biological basis of learning.

3.14 The Brain Can Recover from Injury The brain can reorganize its functions in response to brain damage. However, this capacity decreases with age. Perceptual irregularities are attributed to the cross-wiring of connections in the brain during cortical reorganization.

What Is the Genetic Basis of Psychological Science?

3.15 All of Human Development Has a Genetic Basis Human behavior is influenced by genes. Through genes, people inherit both physical attributes and personality traits from their parents. Chromosomes are made of genes, and the Human Genome Project has mapped the genes that make up humans' 23 pairs of chromosomes.

3.16 Heredity Involves Passing Along Genes Through Reproduction Genes may be dominant or recessive. An organism's genetic constitution is referred to as its genotype. The organism's observable characteristics are referred to as its phenotype. Many characteristics are polygenic. An offspring receives half of its chromosomes from its mother and half of its chromosomes from its father. Because so many combinations of the 23 pairs of chromosomes are possible, there is tremendous genetic variation in the human species. Mutations resulting from errors in cell division also give rise to genetic variation.

3.17 Genes Affect Behavior Behavioral geneticists examine how genes and environment interact to influence psychological activity. Twin studies and adoption studies provide insight into heritability.

3.18 Genetic Expression Can Be Modified Genes and environmental contexts interact in ways that influence observable characteristics. Epigenetics is the study of how genetic expression may change due to experience. Genetic manipulation has been achieved in mammals such as mice. Animal studies using gene knockouts, which allow genes to be turned on and off, are valuable tools for understanding genetic influences on behavior and on health. Through optogenetics, researchers modify genes to trigger action potentials in neurons.

Key Terms

absolute refractory period, p. 73
action potential, p. 70
all-or-none principle, p. 72
amygdala, p. 92
autonomic nervous system (ANS), p. 96
axon, p. 69
basal ganglia, p. 92
brain stem, p. 93
Broca's area, p. 78
cell body, p. 69
central nervous system (CNS), p. 68
cerebellum, p. 93
cerebral cortex, p. 81
chromosomes, p. 102
corpus callosum, p. 82
dendrites, p. 69
dizygotic twins, p. 107
dominant gene, p. 104
electroencephalography (EEG), p. 79
endocrine system, p. 97
frontal lobes, p. 84
functional magnetic resonance imaging (fMRI), p. 80
gene expression, p. 102
genes, p. 102
genotype, p. 104
heredity, p. 109
heritability, p. 109
hippocampus, p. 92
hormones, p. 98
hypothalamus, p. 92
insula, p. 91
magnetic resonance imaging (MRI), p. 80
monozygotic twins, p. 107
myelin sheath, p. 73
neurons, p. 68
neurotransmitters, p. 74
nodes of Ranvier, p. 73
occipital lobes, p. 82
parasympathetic division, p. 96
parietal lobes, p. 82
peripheral nervous system (PNS), p. 68
phenotype, p. 104
pituitary gland, p. 98
plasticity, p. 99
positron emission tomography (PET), p. 80
prefrontal cortex, p. 84
receptors, p. 74
recessive gene, p. 104
relative refractory period, p. 72
resting membrane potential, p. 70
reuptake, p. 74
somatic nervous system (SNS), p. 95
split brain, p. 86
sympathetic division, p. 96
synapse, p. 70
temporal lobes, p. 84
terminal buttons, p. 70
thalamus, p. 92
transcranial magnetic stimulation (TMS), p. 80

Practice Exercises

1. Which label accurately describes neurons that detect information from the physical world and communicate that information along to the central nervous system?
   a. motor neuron
   b. sensory neuron
   c. interneuron
   d. glia

2. Parkinson's disease is associated with the loss of neurons that produce which of the following neurotransmitters?
   a. acetylcholine
   b. norepinephrine
   c. dopamine
   d. serotonin

3. Drugs can produce the following actions on neurotransmitter activity. Label each example as either an agonist or antagonist effect.
   a. mimic the neurotransmitter and activate the postsynaptic receptor
   b. block the reuptake of the neurotransmitter
   c. decrease neurotransmitter release from the presynaptic neuron
   d. clear the neurotransmitter from the synapse

4. Which of the following statements about behavioral genetics is false?
   a. Heritability refers to traits passed from parent to offspring.
   b. Similarities among nonbiological adopted siblings are inferred to reflect environmental influences.
   c. Identical twins raised apart are often more similar than identical twins raised together.
   d. Greater similarities between monozygotic twins compared with dizygotic twins are inferred to reflect genetic influences.

5. What is the role of a neuron's membrane in an action potential?
   a. It is a fatty layer that insulates the axon.
   b. It secretes neurotransmitters to communicate with surrounding neurons.
   c. It absorbs nutrients.
   d. It contains ion channels that regulate electrical potential and firing.

6. Which of the following techniques can provide information about whether a particular brain region is necessary for a task?
   a. electroencephalography (EEG)
   b. functional magnetic resonance imaging (fMRI)
   c. positron emission tomography (PET)
   d. transcranial magnetic stimulation (TMS)

7. Which statement about split-brain patients is true?
   a. They have had surgery to therapeutically remove one hemisphere of the brain.
   b. The left hemisphere can perceive stimuli, but the right hemisphere cannot.
   c. The left hemisphere can verbally report its perception. The right hemisphere cannot articulate what it saw but can act on its perception.
   d. The left hemisphere is analytical, and the right hemisphere is creative.

8. When a neuron is at rest, how does the electrical charge inside the cell compare with the charge outside?
   a. The outside and the inside are equivalent in charge.
   b. The outside is more negatively charged than the inside.
   c. The inside is more negatively charged than the outside.
   d. It varies depending on whether it is a presynaptic or postsynaptic neuron.

9. Someone suffers a stroke that causes damage to the left motor cortex. Which of the following impairments will the person most likely exhibit?
   a. an inability to comprehend spoken language
   b. an inability to recognize faces
   c. paralysis of the left side of the body
   d. paralysis of the right side of the body

10. What pair of words best matches genotype and phenotype, respectively?
   a. underlying and observed
   b. observed and underlying
   c. dominant and recessive
   d. recessive and dominant

4 Consciousness

Big Questions

ALTHOUGH THERE ARE MANY GOOD REASONS TO FLOSS, a Brazilian ad campaign for Colgate showed how distracting it can be when someone has food on their teeth. The ads displayed smiling men with food stuck on their front teeth next to smiling women. If you look closely, however, there is something a little off. For instance, in one ad, the woman has her hands at her sides, but there is also a hand on the man's shoulder (**FIGURE 4.1**). The cleverness of these ads is that they play on the limits of your *consciousness*. We can be fully aware of only a few things at a time. If the food on someone's teeth is distracting you and grabbing your attention, you may be less likely to notice something else, such as a phantom hand.

As this example illustrates, attention is the gateway to consciousness, which is limited in its capacity. We also experience variations in our conscious experience. Every day our consciousness shifts when we sleep. People manipulate consciousness, through meditation or drugs, for instance. Changes to the brain through injury can also affect consciousness. Because of the very nature of consciousness, conscious experiences differ from person to person.

FIGURE 4.1
Brazilian Ad for Dental Floss with a Phantom Hand

Learning Objectives

- Define consciousness.
- Discuss the role of attention in consciousness.
- Discuss how unconscious processes influence thought and behavior.
- Define automatic and controlled processing in relation to consciousness.

What Is Consciousness?

Consciousness consists of one's moment-by-moment personal, subjective experiences. You know you are conscious—that you have consciousness—because you are experiencing the outside world through your senses and because you know that you are thinking. Conscious experiences exist, but their subjective nature makes them difficult to study empirically. For a moment, reflect on the color of the walls in the room you are in. What is it like to see that color (**FIGURE 4.2**)? Now think about the taste of an apple. Do you think your experiences of these sensations are the same as someone else's? Your subjective experiences of sensation are sometimes called *qualia*, meaning the qualitative experiences of your conscious state. Because each of us experiences consciousness personally, we cannot know if any two people's experiences, or qualia, are the same. Consciousness involves not just your sensations and thoughts but also your memories and anything else you are experiencing in the moment.

Your mind and body do many things you are not consciously aware of. For instance, you have many highly active biological systems, such as your immune system, but you are not conscious of their functioning. At every moment, your brain is regulating your body temperature and controlling your breathing without your awareness. When you retrieve a memory or look at a scenic view, you may become aware of the content of that memory or scene but not the mental and neural processes that generated it. You are not conscious of most of the operations of the brain and mind that do these things. What gives rise to your consciousness, and why are you conscious of only certain experiences?

consciousness One's moment-to-moment subjective experience of the world.

change blindness A failure to notice large changes in one's environment.

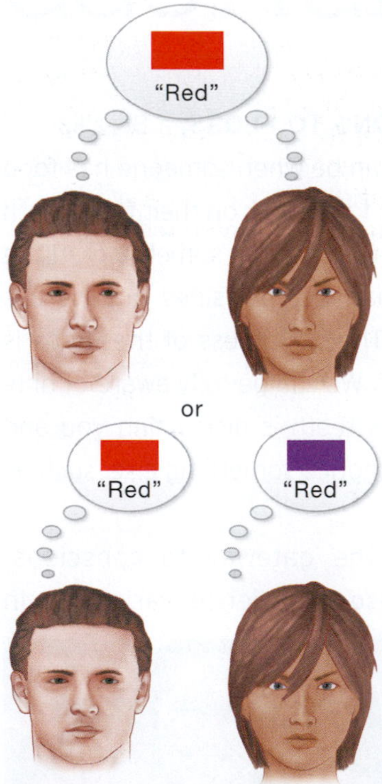

FIGURE 4.2
Seeing Red
One difficult question related to consciousness is whether people's subjective experiences of the world are similar. For instance, does red look the same to everyone who has normal color vision?

4.1 Consciousness Is Limited

Most of the time, conscious experience is unified and coherent. In other words, in your subjective experience, the world makes sense and one thought or perception flows from another. Consciousness is often described as a continuous stream, and thoughts float on that stream. There is a limit, however, to how many things the mind can be conscious of at the same time. As you read this chapter, are you focused intently on the material? Is your mind wandering, occasionally or often? You cannot pay attention to reading while doing several other things, such as watching television or talking to a friend. As you focus on what is going on in the TV show, you might realize that you have no idea what you just read or what your friend just said. Likewise, you can think about what you will do tomorrow, what kind of car you would like to own, and where you most recently went on vacation—but you cannot think about them all at the same time. You are able to fully process only a limited amount of the information available to you at any given time.

CHANGE BLINDNESS The limited nature of consciousness means that we often miss things, even big things, because we are focusing on something else. Consider the phenomenon known as **change blindness**. Because we cannot attend to everything in the vast array of visual information available, we are often "blind" to large changes in our environments. For example, would you notice if the person you were talking to suddenly changed into another person? In two studies, a stranger approached participants on a college campus and asked for directions (**FIGURE 4.3**). Then the stranger was momentarily blocked by a large object and, while out of view, was replaced with another person of the same sex and race. Fifty percent of the people giving directions never noticed that they were talking to a different person. When giving directions to a stranger, we normally do not attend to the distinctive features of the stranger's face or clothing. If we are unable to recall those features later, it is not because we forgot them. More likely, it is because we never processed those features very much in the first place. After all, how often do we need to remember such information (Simons & Levin, 1998)?

In Simons and Levin's first study, older people were less likely to notice a change in the person asking them for directions, whereas younger people did better. Are older people especially inattentive, or do they have extremely limited consciousness? Or do they tend to process a situation's broad outlines rather than its details? Perhaps the older people encoded the young stranger as simply "a college student" and did not look for individual characteristics. To test this idea, Simons and Levin (1998) conducted an additional study. This time, the stranger was easily categorized as being from a specific and different social group. That is, the same experimenters dressed as construction workers and asked college students for directions. Sure enough, the college students failed to notice the replacement of one construction worker with another. This finding supports the idea that the students encoded the strangers as belonging to a broad category of "construction workers" without looking more closely at them. For these students, construction workers seemed pretty much all alike and interchangeable.

As change blindness illustrates, we can consciously perceive only a limited amount of information. Large discrepancies exist between what most of us believe we see and what we actually see. Thus, our perceptions of the world are often inaccurate, and we have little conscious awareness of our perceptual failures. We simply do not know how much information we miss in the world around us. This is why using cell phones while driving—or even while walking—can be dangerous. We fail to notice important objects in our environment that might indicate threats to our safety. In one study (Hyman et al., 2010), students using cell phones while walking across campus failed to notice a brightly colored clown riding a unicycle who was heading toward their walking path. Students who were listening to music were much more likely to notice the clown.

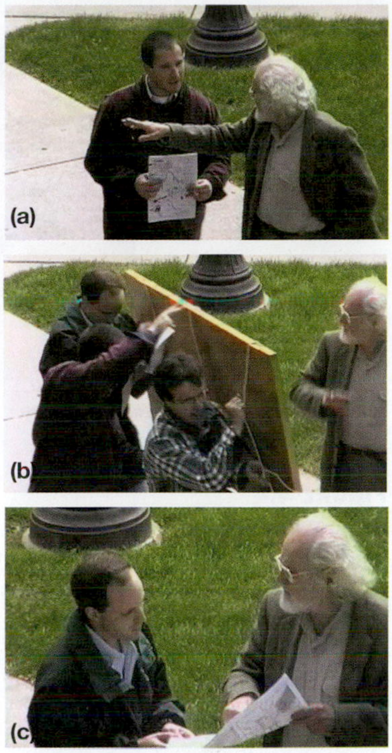

FIGURE 4.3
Change Blindness
In change blindness studies, people fail to notice a change in the identity of the person asking directions. **(a)** A participant is approached by a stranger asking for directions. **(b)** The stranger is momentarily blocked by a large object. **(c)** While being blocked, the stranger is replaced by another person.

Q How do the limits on consciousness contribute to change blindness?

ANSWER: Major changes to the environment may go unnoticed when conscious awareness is focused elsewhere.

4.2 Attention Is the Gateway to Conscious Awareness

Attention involves being able to focus selectively on some things and not others. Although they are not the same thing, attention and consciousness often go hand in hand. For instance, imagine you are at a party and people are engaged in conversations all around you. Despite all this noise, you are able to zero in on what your friends are telling you about their recent vacation. Attention selects what enters your limited consciousness. By selecting your friend's voice to focus on and ignoring other voices and sounds, you become consciously aware of the selected information, which allows you to fully perceive and process it.

In 1953, the psychologist E. C. Cherry described attention this way: You can focus on a single conversation in the midst of a chaotic party. However, a particularly pertinent stimulus—such as hearing your name or a juicy piece of gossip mentioned in another conversation—can capture your attention. Because your

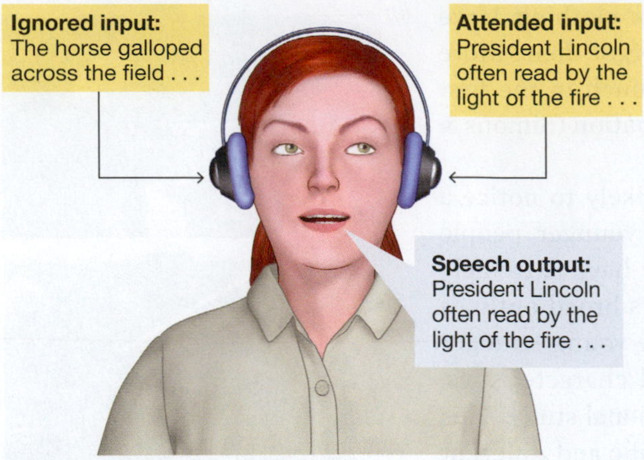
Ignored input:
The horse galloped across the field . . .
Attended input:
President Lincoln often read by the light of the fire . . .
Speech output:
President Lincoln often read by the light of the fire . . .

FIGURE 4.4
Shadowing
In this procedure, the participant receives a different auditory message in each ear. The participant is required to repeat, or "shadow," only one of the messages.

attention is now divided, you can understand less about the new stimulus than you would if you gave it your full attention. If you really want to hear the other conversation or piece of gossip, you need to focus your attention on it. Of course, when you redirect your attention in this way, you probably will not be able to follow what the closer (and therefore probably louder) partygoer is saying, so you will lose the thread of your original conversation.

Cherry developed selective-listening studies to examine what the mind does with unattended information when a person pays attention to one task. He used a technique called *shadowing*. In this procedure, the participant wears headphones that deliver one message to one ear and a different message to the other. The participant is asked to attend to one of the two messages and "shadow" it by repeating it aloud. As a result, the participant usually notices the unattended sound (the message given to the other ear) but will have little knowledge about the content of the unattended sound (**FIGURE 4.4**).

Imagine you are participating in one of these experiments. You are repeating whatever is spoken into one ear (shadowing) and ignoring the message spoken into the other ear. If your own name was spoken into the unattended ear, you would probably hear your name but know nothing about the rest of the message. Some important information gets through. It has to be personally relevant information, such as your name or the name of someone close to you, or it has to be particularly loud, meaningful, or different in some obvious physical way.

In 1958, the psychologist Donald Broadbent developed filter theory to explain the selective nature of attention. He assumed that people have a limited capacity for sensory information. They screen incoming information to let in only the most important material. In this model, attention is like a gate that opens for important information and closes for irrelevant information. But when and how do we open and close the gate? What happens when we close the gate to ignore some information? More recent models of attention have revised the nature of the attentional filter, but they all propose some type of gateway to prioritize processing and awareness of relevant information.

endogenous attention Attention that is directed voluntarily.

exogenous attention Attention that is directed involuntarily by a stimulus.

ENDOGENOUS VERSUS EXOGENOUS ATTENTION Sometimes you decide what to attend to. For example, you have decided to attend to what you are reading right now. Intentionally directing the focus of your attention in this way is called **endogenous attention**. However, some stimuli demand attention and virtually shut off the ability to attend to anything else. Say you are focusing all your attention on reading this book, and suddenly you develop a muscle cramp. What will happen to your attention? The sharp jab of the cramp will grab your attention, and whatever you are reading will leave your consciousness until you attend to the pain. Similarly, some stimuli, such as emotional stimuli that signal potential danger, may readily capture attention because they provide important information (Phelps et al., 2006). An object may also draw your attention because it is socially relevant to you (Tipper et al., 2008). When the focus of your attention is driven by a stimulus or event, it is called **exogenous attention**.

Learning Tip

To remember the difference between endogenous and exogenous attention, think of the first two letters of each word. ENdogenous attention is driven from withIN you—you decide where to allocate your attention. EXogenous attention is driven by EXternal stimuli or events—something outside of you demands the focus of your attention.

ATTENTION AS A WINDOW TO CONSCIOUSNESS IN THE BRAIN

The impact of attention on how the brain processes stimuli happens early in the perceptual process. The brain does respond to some unattended stimuli, suggesting they are perceived at some level, but attending to and becoming consciously aware of a stimulus enhances and expands the brain's response to that stimulus. For example, in an early fMRI study, Frank Tong and colleagues (1998) examined the relationship between conscious awareness and responses in the brain. Images in which houses were superimposed on faces were shown to participants, who were instructed to attend to either the face or the house (**FIGURE 4.5**). By directing their attention, participants could switch between seeing the face or the house, but they could be consciously aware of only one at a time. The researchers used fMRI to measure responses in the participants' brains (imaging methods are discussed in Chapter 3). When participants reported seeing a face, activity increased in brain regions associated with face recognition. When participants reported seeing a house, activity increased in brain regions associated with scene recognition. In other words, brain activity in these regions followed the conscious perception of the face or house, which varied depending on how the participants allocated their attention.

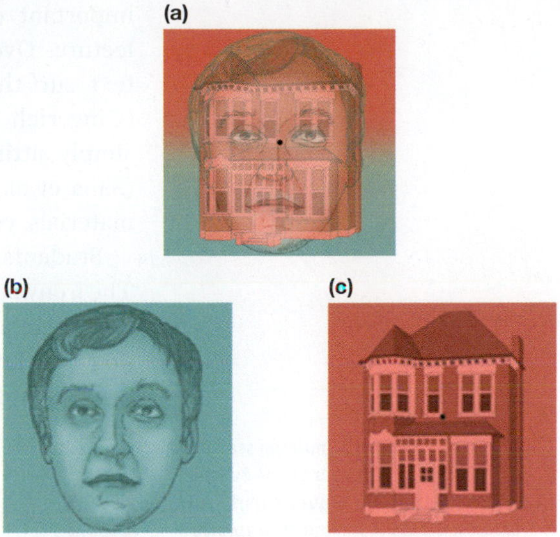

FIGURE 4.5
Consciousness and Neural Responses
(a) Research participants were shown images with houses superimposed on faces. Then the participants were asked to attend to **(b)** the face or **(c)** the house. When they reported seeing a face, activity increased in face-recognition areas of the brain. When they reported seeing a house, activity increased in scene-recognition areas.

By showing patterns of brain activity that track conscious perception of different types of stimuli, this early fMRI study suggested it might be possible to observe conscious experience by looking at brain activity. In similar studies, researchers have identified several aspects of conscious experience by examining patterns of brain activity while asking participants to attend to different things. For example, brain activity patterns can show whether you are attending to faces or bodies (Norman et al., 2006; O'Toole et al., 2014), which emotions you are experiencing (Kragel & LaBar, 2016), or whether you are thinking of yourself or a close friend (Chavez et al., 2017). Some people have referred to these techniques as "mind reading," although that term implies a level of sophistication and reliability that is not supported by current techniques. Nonetheless, people share common patterns of brain activity that provide insights into their conscious experiences (Haxby et al., 2014).

ANSWER: Exogenous attention occurs when attention is unintentionally shifted to an emotional stimulus.

Q **You see an accident on the side of the road and cannot help but slow down to look at the traumatic scene. Why?**

4.3 Laptops in the Classroom

It can be hard to pay complete attention for an entire class period, even with the most engaging lecturers. For this reason, many of your instructors try to engage students in active participation during class. The rise of laptop computers and smartphones in the classroom over the past decade has made it even more difficult for instructors to hold students' attention (**FIGURE 4.6**). Ideally, such technology enables students to take notes, access supplementary materials, or participate in classroom exercises. Unfortunately, students can also tune out lectures by checking social media or email, texting, or watching TikTok.

FIGURE 4.6
Technology in the Classroom
Today's students use electronic devices in the classroom productively (as in taking notes) and nonproductively (as in texting).

After reading the earlier sections of this chapter, you might not be surprised that attending to your computer or smartphone might lead you to miss important details going on around you, such as crucial information in the lecture. Overwhelming evidence shows that students who use social media, text, surf the internet, and so on during class do more poorly in college courses (Gingerich & Lineweaver, 2014; Junco & Cotten, 2012). Even those who are simply sitting near someone playing around on the internet score lower grades (Sana et al., 2013). If you use your laptop or smartphone to look at irrelevant materials, you are hurting yourself and others.

Students often do not feel like they are missing anything when they multitask. The irony is that it takes attention to know what you are missing. If your attention is elsewhere and you miss something vital mentioned by your instructor, you might not even know that you missed anything. You might have the illusion that you were paying attention because you have no awareness of events that happened when your attention was otherwise occupied.

Q Why should you avoid using a laptop during lectures?

ANSWER: Laptop use in the classroom may shift attention away from the lecture, leading you to miss or superficially process information.

4.4 Unconscious Processing Can Influence Behavior

Just because people fail to attend to or consciously perceive something in their environment does not mean that they are unaffected by it. Sir Francis Galton (1879) first proposed that mental activity below the level of conscious awareness can influence behavior. The influence of unconscious thoughts was also at the center of Freud's theories of human behavior. For example, the classic mistake called a *Freudian slip* occurs when an unconscious thought is suddenly expressed at an inappropriate time or in an inappropriate social context. Freud compared consciousness to the tip of the iceberg that can be seen above water, whereas the unconscious, below the water, was the driving force influencing behavior. Many of Freud's ideas about how the unconscious works are difficult to test using scientific methods (for further discussion of Freud's theory, see Chapter 13, "Personality"), and few psychologists today believe his interpretation of the unconscious is correct. However, psychologists today agree that unconscious processes influence people's thoughts and actions as they go through their daily lives.

THE WORLD OF FREUDIAN SLIPS
THANKS FOR FORCING ME TO COME HERE.
YES, THIS IS SURELY THE BEST AND MOST BORING SHOW ON TV.
I'M VERY UNHAPPY TO SEE YOU BOTH.

Studies of selective listening show that unattended information is processed at least to some extent. These studies found that even when participants could not repeat an unattended message, they still had processed its contents. In one experiment, participants were told to attend to the message coming in one ear: "They threw stones at the bank yesterday." At the same time, the unattended ear was presented with one of two words: *river* or *money*. Afterward, participants could not report the unattended words. However, those presented with *river* interpreted the sentence to mean someone had thrown stones at a riverbank. Those presented with *money* interpreted the sentence to mean someone had thrown stones at a financial institution (MacKay, 1973). Thus, the participants extracted meaning from the word even though they did not process the word consciously.

The processing of irrelevant details of attended stimuli can also unconsciously influence behavior. Consider the change blindness studies discussed earlier. When college students focused on giving directions to a stranger, they were less likely to notice the change in the stranger's identity if the stranger was clearly identified as a member of another social group, such as a construction worker. The group membership of the stranger was irrelevant to giving directions, but this irrelevant factor had a subtle, unconscious influence on how the students processed the stranger's identity. In this case, the stranger's irrelevant social group membership influenced perception, but similar unconscious processes come into play when social group stereotypes unconsciously influence attitudes and behaviors, such as with implicit bias (see Chapter 12).

PRIMING **Priming** occurs when the response to a stimulus is influenced or facilitated by recent experience with that stimulus or a related stimulus. Priming can influence how you perceive an object, the speed or ease with which you respond, and the choices you make. For example, if I were to ask you to say the first word that comes to mind that begins with the letters *cha*, there are several possibilities—*chat*, *chase*, *charm*, *character*, *change*, and so on. However, if you had just read the sentence "The family was having dinner at the table" in another task, you would be more likely to later come up with *chair*. Reading the word *table* activates the related concept of *chair*, so it more easily comes to mind (Roediger et al., 1992). Although it is possible people remember reading the related sentence earlier, the facilitation that occurs with priming is apparent even when they cannot remember the earlier event or stimulus, demonstrating that it is implicit, or unconscious (Levy et al., 2004).

priming A facilitation in the response to a stimulus due to recent experience with that stimulus or a related stimulus.

SUBLIMINAL PERCEPTION Priming can also occur when people are unaware of the stimulus that influences behavior. **Subliminal perception** occurs when stimuli are processed by sensory systems but, because of their short durations or subtlety, do not reach consciousness. Urban legends concerning subliminal perception have long been a part of popular culture. According to these legends, movie theaters flash brief statements on-screen suggesting that we buy a drink or some popcorn, musicians embed satanic messages in their songs to encourage their listeners' malevolent impulses, and advertisers embed suggestive words in images (**FIGURE 4.7**). More than 8 out of 10 first-year college students believe that they can be influenced to purchase something through subliminal perception (Taylor & Kowalski, 2012). But can our behavior really be manipulated without our knowledge or awareness? The evidence suggests otherwise—that subliminal messages, if they work at all, have minimal effects on most behavior (Greenwald, 1992).

subliminal perception The processing of information by sensory systems without conscious awareness.

During the 1980s, programs using subliminal messages for self-improvement were developed and promoted. For example, hearing subliminal messages while sleeping was supposed to make you more confident or improve your memory. In a classic study, students were given a subliminal program that was meant to improve their confidence or their memory (Pratkanis et al., 1994). The researchers intentionally mislabeled some of the subliminal tapes, however. Half of the tapes labeled "memory" were actually about self-confidence and vice versa. This research indicated that people's beliefs about which tapes they listened to influenced the effects of the messages. People who thought they were hearing subliminal messages about memory reported improved memory, even if they heard the self-confidence tape. People who thought they were hearing subliminal messages about self-confidence reported improved self-confidence, even if they heard the memory tape.

FIGURE 4.7
Subliminal Perception in Print
Do you see subliminal messages in this advertisement? If you look closely at the lettuce you should see a dollar bill.

Even if material presented subliminally has little or no effect on complex actions, such as buying something you did not intend to buy, there is evidence that it can subtly influence behavior (Kihlstrom, 2016a). In one study, participants exerted greater physical effort when large images of money were flashed at them, even though the flashes were so brief the participants did not report seeing the money (Pessiglione et al., 2007). Other studies have shown that the subliminal presentation of frightening stimuli can evoke arousal (Morris et al., 1998). These studies found that the subliminal images of money and of frightening stimuli produce activity in brain regions involved in emotion and motivation. Subliminal cues may be most powerful when they work on people's motivational states. For example, flashing the word *thirst* may prove more effective than flashing the explicit directive *Buy Coke*. Indeed, researchers found that subliminal presentation of the word *thirst* led participants to drink more, especially when they were actually thirsty (Strahan et al., 2002). Thus, many stimuli in our environment nudge us in one direction or another, but such a modest effect is not enough to improve our self-image or persuade us to buy things we do not want.

Q **Which type of subliminal messages are most likely to affect behavior?**

ANSWER: Messages that invoke emotion or motivation may subtly shift behavior, but such messages do not affect complex behaviors like buying or self-confidence.

4.5 Automatic Processing Reduces Demands on Consciousness

Do you remember when you first learned to read? Have you ever tried to help a new reader make their way through a children's book? It is a slow process of sounding out and identifying each word and requires a lot of concentration and conscious effort. However, as you read this textbook, the words jump out automatically, and you can devote your conscious efforts to fully understanding the content and its significance to psychological science. This is because, for you, reading has become automatic. Now that you are highly practiced at reading, it is impossible for you to see a letter string that makes up a word and not immediately identify the meaning of the word. *Automatic processing* occurs when a task is so well learned that we can do it without much attention.

All of us can execute routine or automatic tasks, such as driving, walking, or understanding the meanings of the words on this page, without much conscious effort. By contrast, difficult or unfamiliar tasks require people to pay attention. Such *controlled processing* is slower than automatic processing, but it helps people perform in complex or novel situations. If a rainstorm starts while you are driving, you will need to pay more attention to your driving and be very conscious of the road conditions (FIGURE 4.8).

FIGURE 4.8
Automatic Processing Versus Controlled Processing
Driving can become automatic after extensive practice, but during a rainstorm even an experienced driver must revert to controlled processing.

In general, automatic processing is beneficial in that it allows us to devote our limited consciousness to other tasks. In fact, paying too much attention can interfere with automatic behaviors. Thinking of each step you take as you walk makes walking much more awkward. However, in some circumstances automatic processing has costs. For instance, imagine you learned to drive in the United States and are used to driving on the right side of the road. If you were to visit South Africa, where they drive on the left side of the road, you might find it especially difficult. Many of your learned tendencies, such as where to look for oncoming traffic, would be wrong. To drive safely in South Africa, you would need to engage in effortful controlled processing to overcome the overlearned, automatic responses you learned when driving in the United States.

The cost of automaticity is demonstrated in the Stroop task (Stroop, 1935). In this task participants are asked to identify as quickly as possible the color in which letter strings are printed. Try it yourself. If you read down the list on the left side of **FIGURE 4.9**, in which the color of each word matches the meaning of the printed text, you will find this easy. Chances are you will also be able to name the color of the letter strings without much difficulty as you make your way down the middle list, in which the letter strings are not words. However, most people slow down significantly when trying to name the colors of the letter strings on the list to the right. In this list, the letter strings spell out color names, but the words are printed in colors that do not match the color names. Because people cannot turn off the automatic ability to read the meaning of the word, when they try to say the incongruous name of the ink in which the word is printed, there is significant interference. Even without using a timer to verify that your responses are slower, you will likely find it much more difficult to name the colors of the ink of the letter strings on the right side of Figure 4.9.

RED	GROSH	GREEN
GREEN	THORT	BLUE
RED	FLERG	RED
BLUE	BLASH	BLUE
BLUE	LARMP	GREEN
GREEN	STERP	RED
BLUE	PLARK	GREEN

FIGURE 4.9
The Stroop Task
Go down each list and say the color each word is printed in as quickly as possible. Most people find it harder to do this when the word color and color name do not match.

Q **When Tara was learning to knit, she had to pay attention to every stitch. Now she can knit while watching television. Why can she knit now without giving it full attention?**

ANSWER: Learning a complex task like knitting requires controlled processing. Once you learn the task, it becomes automatic and no longer requires full attention.

What Is Altered Consciousness?

Learning Objectives

- Discuss the effects of meditation on consciousness.
- Define the concept of "flow."
- Compare and contrast theories of hypnosis.

When we are awake, we often assume our experience of consciousness from moment to moment is consistent, even though the content of our conscious thoughts varies. However, if you think about it, you can probably identify times when you felt particularly attentive or focused, or zoned out and inattentive, or caught up in the moment. A person's subjective sense of consciousness varies naturally over the course of the day. This variation is usually due to the person's actions or how they choose to engage their attention. Watching television might encourage zoning out, whereas learning to play a piece on the piano might focus attention. Being in a state that changes your subjective perception of consciousness from how you typically experience it is referred to as altered consciousness. At times, when you are awake and not under the influence of any drugs, you can experience states of altered consciousness. The following sections discuss three ways of naturally altering waking consciousness: meditation, immersion in an action, and hypnosis.

4.6 Meditation Produces Relaxation by Guiding Attention

As discussed earlier, attention is the gateway to consciousness. Typically, we endogenously shift our attention to focus on the task at hand, or our attention is driven exogenously by stimuli in an environment. During **meditation**, a person focuses attention on an external object, an internal event, or a sense of awareness to create a state of altered consciousness. Through intense contemplation, the meditator develops a deep sense of tranquility. There are two general forms of meditation. In *concentrative meditation*, you focus attention on one thing, such as your breathing pattern, a mental image, or a specific phrase (sometimes called a *mantra*). In *mindfulness meditation*, you let your thoughts flow freely, paying attention to them but trying not to react to them. You hear

meditation A mental procedure that focuses attention on an external object, an internal event, or a sense of awareness.

the contents of your inner voice, but you allow them to flow from one topic to the next without examining their meaning or reacting to them in any way (**FIGURE 4.10**).

FIGURE 4.10
Meditation
To practice concentrative meditation, focus your attention on your breathing pattern, in and out. To practice mindfulness meditation, let your thoughts flow freely without reacting to them.

Different forms of meditation are popular in many Eastern religions, including Hinduism, Buddhism, and Sikhism. Religious forms of meditation are meant to bring enlightenment. Most forms of meditation popular in the West are meant to expand the mind, bring about feelings of inner peace, and help people deal with the tensions and stresses in their lives. In fact, using meditation techniques to reduce stress has become so popular that many people have apps on their phones or watches reminding them to take short meditation intervals throughout the day, for instance by focusing on their breathing for a minute.

Take a moment to try this exercise and see if you notice an effect from this type of concentrative meditation. Focus your awareness on one specific aspect of your current experience: breathing. Breathe in and out slowly. Pay close attention to your breathing and nothing else. After a few minutes return to your reading. Ready? Begin.

Did you notice a change in the quality of your awareness or experience a sense of calm? Or did you find it hard to focus on breathing and nothing else? Although brief meditation exercises like this can be effective, most meditators practice for longer periods and report added benefits with extensive practice or intensive, prolonged periods of meditation.

Psychologists have examined the impact of both concentrative and mindfulness meditation techniques on health. Many early studies found a number of health benefits from meditation, including lower blood pressure, fewer reports of stress, and changes in the hormonal responses underlying stress. These studies have been criticized, however, because they had small samples and lacked appropriate control groups. In a more rigorous study, a large number of heart patients were randomly assigned to a meditation program or an educational program. After 16 weeks, the patients performing meditation improved more than the control group on a number of health measures, including blood pressure and cholesterol level (Paul-Labrador et al., 2006). Unfortunately, this study does not show which aspects of meditation produced the health benefits. Was it simply relaxing and reducing stress, which would have health benefits regardless of how it was achieved (see Chapter 11, "Health and Well-Being," for a discussion of the relation between health and stress)? Or is it something else about the altered consciousness achieved with meditation that is beneficial?

Psychologists have also studied how meditation affects cognitive processing, brain function, and even the immune system (Cahn & Polich, 2006). In one study, participants were assigned randomly to five days of either intensive meditation training or relaxation training. Those who underwent the meditation training showed greater stress reduction and more significant improvement in attention than did the group that underwent relaxation training (Tang et al., 2007). In another study, participants who underwent an eight-week meditation course not only reported less anxiety but also exhibited patterns of brain electrical activity that had previously been shown to correlate with positive emotional states. Furthermore, this pattern of brain activity was correlated with measures of enhanced immune function (Davidson et al., 2003).

Q Suppose a person meditating focuses on thoughts of waves rolling onto a beautiful beach. Is the person practicing concentrative meditation or mindfulness meditation?

ANSWER: concentrative, because the person is focusing on a specific image

4.7 Does Meditation Change the Structure of the Brain?

YOU BE THE PSYCHOLOGIST

It should not be too surprising that brain activity patterns change with meditation practice. Given that there are documented changes in psychological states with meditation, one would expect a corresponding change in the brain activity patterns that underlie these psychological states. However, some researchers have suggested that long-term meditation not only changes brain activity patterns but also affects brain anatomy or structure and helps maintain brain function over the life span. For instance, the volume of gray matter in the brain typically diminishes with age. One study found that gray matter volume did not diminish in older adults who practiced meditation (Pagnoni & Cekic, 2007). This finding suggests that meditation might help preserve brain integrity and associated cognitive functioning as people age.

As you know from reading Chapter 2, however, correlation is not causation. This was a small study that used a cross-sectional approach. That is, the researchers scanned highly practiced meditators (who had practiced meditating for at least three years) of different ages and compared them with a control group that did not meditate. They found a negative correlation between gray matter volume and age in the control participants but not the meditators. What could be the problem with this approach? Could it be that people who choose to meditate differ substantially from people who do not, especially in terms of lifestyle choices such as diet and a willingness to take care of their health? How might you design a study to determine that it is meditation and not some other factor that slows the reduction in gray matter volume with age?

One way to get around some of these issues would be to use a longitudinal design, in which participants are randomly assigned to one of two groups and you study them over time. For instance, you might assign the experimental group to meditation training and ask them to practice for 16 weeks. The control group might receive some other kind of educational instruction that requires a similar time commitment. Then you could compare the brains of participants before and after meditation practice or the control condition.

Imagine you did a study like this and failed to find a difference in the rate of decline in gray matter volume between the experimental and control groups. Would you believe that the first study was a false-positive result or that the results of the earlier study were valid and the difference between the cross-sectional and longitudinal studies was due to factors other than meditation? If so, are there other factors that may have made it difficult to see any difference between the groups with this longitudinal design? For instance, maybe 16 weeks is not long enough to see age-related decline in gray matter in the control participants. Or maybe 16 weeks of meditation practice is not enough to see a benefit in brain structure (even though, as the studies described above indicate, there should be a behavioral benefit). You could extend the study length and amount of meditation practice, but that might increase the potential that participants do not complete the study. What factors related to participant dropout might influence your results?

These are the types of concerns that those who study meditation and its effect on the brain must address. Think about it for a second: What type of evidence would you like to see before you are convinced that meditation not only changes brain function but also helps diminish the impact of aging on brain structure? ■

Q Does showing that long-term meditators have less age-related change in brain structure prove meditation reduces neural aging and decline?

ANSWER: No. Correlation does not equal causation. Those who practice meditation may also have other lifestyle differences that affect brain aging.

FIGURE 4.11
Religious Ecstasy
During a service at an evangelical church in Toronto, a man is overcome with religious ecstasy. According to the photographer, the man was speaking in tongues (a form of prayer that involves uttering unintelligible sounds).

4.8 People Can Lose Themselves in Activities

The activities we choose to engage in can sometimes change our conscious experience in such a way that we are less aware of other things. For instance, zoning out in front of the TV might distract you from studying. Or listening to music can change your mood and focus and also prompt you to dance. Several types of activities and behaviors change how we are aware of the world around us.

EXERCISE, RELIGIOUS PRAYER, AND FLOW Why do many people listen to music while exercising? In offering a distraction from physical exertion, music can bring about an energizing shift in consciousness that can both motivate and energize us during exercise. But sometimes exercise alone can create a more extreme change in subjective conscious experience. One minute a person might feel pain and fatigue, and the next minute euphoria and a glorious release of energy. Commonly known as *runner's high*, this state, which is partially mediated by physiological processes, results in a shift in consciousness.

Shifts in consciousness that are similar to runner's high occur at other moments in our lives. Religious ceremonies often decrease awareness of the external world and create feelings of euphoria, or *religious ecstasy*. Like meditation, religious ecstasy directs attention away from the self by means of chanting, dancing, and/or other behaviors. In this way, it allows a person to focus on the religious experience (**FIGURE 4.11**).

One psychological theory about such peak experiences is based on the concept of *flow*. Flow is "a particular kind of experience that is so engrossing and enjoyable [that it is] worth doing for its own sake even though it may have no consequence outside itself" (Csikszentmihalyi, 1999, p. 824). That is, a person might perform a particular task out of fascination with it rather than out of a desire for an external reward. Flow is an optimal experience in that the activity is completely absorbing and satisfying and seems to happen automatically. People experiencing flow lose track of time, forget about their problems, and fail to notice other things going on (Csikszentmihalyi, 1990). When athletes talk about being "in the zone," they are referring to a state of flow (Jackson et al., 2001). Flow experiences have been reported during many activities, including playing music (O'Neil, 1999), playing a moderately challenging version of the computer game Tetris (Keller & Bless, 2008), and simply doing satisfying jobs (Demerouti, 2006). In the view of the psychologist Mihaly Csikszentmihalyi (1999), flow experiences bring personal fulfillment.

FIGURE 4.12
Escapist Entertainment
Simple entertainment, such as playing video games, may have benefits. When such activity veers toward obsession, it may have negative effects.

ESCAPING THE SELF At times, conscious thoughts can be dominated by worries, frustrations, and feelings of personal failure. Sometimes people get tired of dealing with life's problems and try to make themselves feel better through escapist pursuits. Potential flow activities such as sports or music may help people escape thinking about their problems. In these cases, people escape by immersing themselves in a personally fulfilling activity. But sometimes people choose to escape the self solely to avoid engaging with life: To forget their troubles, they play video games, watch television, surf the web, text, and so on. The selective appeal of escapist entertainment is that it distracts people from reflecting on their problems or their failures, thereby helping them avoid feeling bad about themselves.

Many escapist activities tend to be relatively harmless distractions in moderation, but when engaged in too frequently they come at great personal expense. For example, some people who obsessively play online games such as World of Warcraft have lost their jobs and their marriages (**FIGURE 4.12**). In an extreme case, one couple took the life of their child: In South Korea in 2010, Kim Jae-beom and his common-law wife, Kim Yun-jeong, neglected their 3-month-old daughter to the point that she died of starvation. The couple reportedly spent every night raising a virtual daughter as part of a role-playing game they engaged in at an internet café.

Some ways of escaping the self are self-destructive, such as binge eating or unsafe sex. According to the social psychologist Roy Baumeister (1991), people engage in such behaviors to escape their problems by seeking to reduce self-awareness. This state of lowered self-awareness may reduce long-term planning, reduce meaningful thinking, and help bring about uninhibited actions. Later in this chapter, we will look at another common way people try to escape their problems—namely, using drugs or alcohol to alter consciousness.

Q What is flow?

ANSWER: the state of being deeply immersed in a completely enjoyable and satisfying experience that may have no consequences beyond itself

4.9 Hypnosis Is Induced Through Suggestion

"You are getting sleeeeeeepy. Your eyelids are drooping. . . . Your arms and legs feel very heavy." Your eyelids really are drooping. You are fully relaxed. You hear, "You want to bark like a dog," and the next thing you know, you are bow-wowing at the moon. In this way, stage performers or magicians sometimes hypnotize audience members and instruct them to perform silly behaviors. Has the hypnotist presented a real change in mental state or just good theater? Would you really sit up on stage and start barking on command?

Hypnosis is a social interaction during which a person, responding to suggestions, experiences changes in memory, perception, and/or voluntary action (Kihlstrom, 2016b; Kihlstrom & Eich, 1994). Psychologists generally agree that hypnosis affects some people, but they do not agree on whether it produces a genuinely altered state of consciousness (Jamieson, 2007).

hypnosis A social interaction during which a person, responding to suggestions, experiences changes in memory, perception, and/or voluntary action.

During a hypnotic induction, the hypnotist makes a series of suggestions to at least one person (**FIGURE 4.13**). As the listener falls more deeply into the hypnotic state, the hypnotist makes more suggestions. If everything goes according to plan, the listener follows all the suggestions without hesitation.

Sometimes the hypnotist suggests that, after the hypnosis session, the listener will experience a change in memory, perception, or voluntary action. Such a *posthypnotic suggestion* is usually accompanied by the instruction to not remember the suggestion. For example, a hypnotist might suggest, much to the delight of the audience, "When I say the word *dog*, you will stand up and bark like a dog. You will not remember this suggestion." Therapists sometimes hypnotize patients and give them posthypnotic suggestions to help them diet or quit smoking, but evidence suggests that hypnosis has only modest effects on these behaviors (Barnes et al., 2010; Wadden & Anderton, 1982). Evidence clearly indicates, however, that posthypnotic suggestions can at least subtly influence some types of behaviors.

FIGURE 4.13
Hypnosis
Are hypnotized people merely playing a part suggested to them by the hypnotist?

Consider a study of moral judgment conducted by Thalia Wheatley and Jonathan Haidt (2005). Participants in this study received a posthypnotic suggestion to feel a pang of disgust whenever they read a certain word. The word itself was neutral: the word *often*. Subsequently, participants made more severe moral judgments when reading stories that included the word, even when the stories were innocuous. Because the participants were unaware of the hypnotic suggestions, they were often surprised by their reactions. To explain their reactions, they sometimes made up justifications for their harsh ratings, such as a feeling that the lead character seemed "up to something."

Many people cannot be hypnotized, and standardized tests are available to assess people's hypnotic suggestibility (Kallio & Revonsuo, 2003). Suggestibility seems related less to obvious traits such as intelligence and gullibility than to the tendencies to get absorbed in activities easily, to not be distracted easily, and to have a rich imagination (Balthazard & Woody, 1992; Crawford et al., 1996; Silva & Kirsch, 1992). Even with these tendencies, a person who dislikes the idea of being hypnotized or finds it frightening probably would not be hypnotized easily. To be hypnotized, a person must willingly go along with the hypnotist's suggestions. No evidence indicates that people will do things under hypnosis that they find immoral or otherwise objectionable.

THEORIES OF HYPNOSIS Some psychologists believe that people under hypnosis essentially play the role of a hypnotized person. They are not faking hypnosis. Rather, they act the part as if in a play, willing to perform actions called for by the "director," the hypnotist. According to this *sociocognitive theory of hypnosis*, hypnotized people behave as they expect hypnotized people to behave, even if those expectations are faulty (Kirsch & Lynn, 1995; Spanos & Coe, 1992). Alternatively, the *neodissociation theory of hypnosis* acknowledges the importance of social context to hypnosis, but it views the hypnotic state as an altered state (Hilgard, 1973). According to this theory, hypnosis is a trancelike state in which conscious awareness is separated, or dissociated, from other aspects of consciousness (Gruzelier, 2000).

Numerous brain imaging studies have supported the neodissociation theory of hypnosis (Rainville et al., 2002). In one of the earliest such studies, Stephen Kosslyn and colleagues (2000) demonstrated that when hypnotized participants were asked to imagine black-and-white objects as having color, they showed activity in visual cortex regions involved in color perception. Hypnotized participants asked to drain color from colored images showed diminished activity in those same brain regions. This activity pattern did not occur when participants were not hypnotized. These results suggest the brain activity pattern followed the hypnotic suggestions. It seems unlikely that a person could alter brain activity to please a hypnotist, even if that hypnotist is a psychological researcher.

FIGURE 4.14
Self-Hypnosis
This advertisement promotes one way that patients can learn self-hypnosis.

HYPNOSIS FOR PAIN One of the most powerful uses of hypnosis is *hypnotic analgesia*, a form of pain reduction. Laboratory research has demonstrated that this technique works reliably (Hilgard & Hilgard, 1975; Nash & Barnier, 2008). For instance, plunging an arm into extremely cold water causes pain, and the pain will intensify over time. On average, people can leave their arm in the water for only about 30 seconds, but after receiving hypnotic analgesia they can hold out longer. As you might expect, people high in suggestibility who are given hypnotic analgesia can tolerate the cold water the longest (Montgomery et al., 2000).

There is overwhelming evidence that in clinical settings, hypnosis is effective in dealing with immediate pain (e.g., while having surgery, undergoing dental work, or recovering from burns) and chronic pain (e.g., from arthritis, cancer, or diabetes; Patterson & Jensen, 2003). A patient can also be taught self-hypnosis to feel more comfortable while recovering from surgery (**FIGURE 4.14**). Hypnosis may work more by changing the patient's interpretation of pain than by diminishing pain. That is, the patient feels the sensations associated with pain but feels detached from those sensations (Price et al., 1987). An imaging study confirmed this pattern by showing that while hypnosis does not affect the sensory processing of pain, it reduces brain activity in regions that process the emotional aspects of pain (Rainville et al., 1997). Findings such as these provide considerable support for the dissociation theory of hypnosis. It seems implausible that either expectations about hypnosis or social pressure could result in the changes in brain activity seen during hypnotic analgesia or explain how people given hypnotic analgesia are able to undergo painful surgery and not feel it.

Q Can everyone be hypnotized?

ANSWER: Hypnotic suggestibility varies between individuals and is related to personal qualities such as being focused, imaginative, easily absorbed, and willing to participate.

What Is Sleep?

Learning Objectives

- Describe the stages of sleep.
- Discuss the functions of sleeping and dreaming.
- Identify common sleep disorders.

At regular intervals, the brain does a strange thing: It goes to sleep. A common misconception is that the brain shuts itself down during sleep. Nothing could be further from the truth. Many brain regions are more active during sleep than during wakefulness. It is even possible that some complex thinking, such as working on difficult problems, occurs in the sleeping brain (Monaghan et al., 2015).

Sleep is part of the normal rhythm of life. Brain activity and other physiological processes are regulated into patterns known as **circadian rhythms**. (*Circadian* means "about a day.") For example, body temperature, hormone levels, and sleep/wake cycles operate according to circadian rhythms. Regulated by a biological clock, circadian rhythms are influenced by the cycles of light and dark. Humans and nonhuman animals continue to show these rhythms, however, even when removed from light cues.

circadian rhythms Biological patterns that occur at regular intervals as a function of time of day.

4.10 Sleep Is an Altered State of Consciousness

The average person sleeps around 8 hours per night, but individuals differ tremendously in the number of hours they sleep. Infants sleep much of the day. People tend to sleep less as they age. Some adults report needing 9 or 10 hours of sleep a night to feel rested, whereas others report needing only a few hours a night. There may be a genetic basis for the amount of sleep you need, as researchers have identified a gene that influences sleep (Koh et al., 2008). Called *sleepless*, this gene regulates a protein that, like many anesthetics, reduces action potentials in the brain (see Chapter 3 if you need a refresher on action potentials). Loss of this protein leads to an 80 percent reduction in sleep.

People's sleep habits can be quite extreme. When a 70-year-old retired nurse, Miss M., reported sleeping only an hour a night, researchers were skeptical. On her first two nights in a research laboratory, Miss M. was unable to sleep, apparently because of the excitement. But on her third night, she slept for only 99 minutes, then awoke refreshed, cheerful, and full of energy (Meddis, 1977). You might like the idea of sleeping so little and having all those extra hours of spare time, but most of us do not function well with a lack of sleep. And as discussed in later chapters, sufficient sleep is important for memory and good health and is often affected by psychological disorders, such as depression.

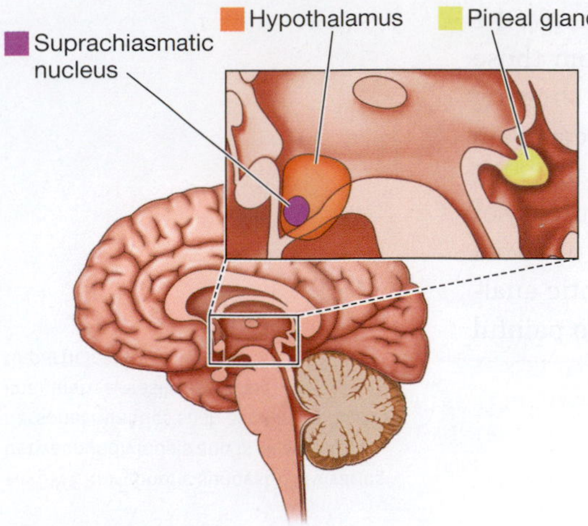

FIGURE 4.15
The Pineal Gland and the Sleep/Wake Cycle
Changes in light register in the suprachiasmatic nucleus of the hypothalamus. In response, this region signals the pineal gland when the time for sleep or the time for wakefulness has come.

SLEEPING BRAIN Multiple brain regions are involved in producing and maintaining circadian rhythms and sleep. Information about light detected by the eyes is sent to a small region of the hypothalamus called the *suprachiasmatic nucleus*. This region then sends signals to a tiny structure called the *pineal gland* (**FIGURE 4.15**). The pineal gland then secretes *melatonin*, a hormone that travels through the bloodstream and affects various receptors in the body, including the brain. Bright light suppresses the production of melatonin, whereas darkness triggers its release. Melatonin is necessary for circadian cycles that regulate sleep (Gandhi et al., 2015). Researchers have noted that taking melatonin can help people cope with jet lag and shift work, both of which interfere with circadian rhythms (Crowley & Eastman, 2015). Taking melatonin also appears to help people fall asleep (Ferracioli-Oda et al., 2013), although it is unclear why this happens.

The difference between being awake and being asleep has as much to do with conscious experience as with biological processes. When you sleep, your conscious experience of the outside world is largely turned off. To some extent, however, you remain aware of your surroundings and your brain still processes information. Your mind is analyzing potential dangers, controlling body movements, and shifting body parts to maximize comfort. For this reason, people who sleep next to children or pets tend not to roll over onto them. Nor do most people fall out of bed while sleeping—the brain is aware of at least the edges of the bed. (Because the ability to not fall out of bed when asleep is learned or perhaps develops with age, infant cribs have side rails and young children may need bed rails when they transition from crib to bed.)

Before the development of objective methods to assess brain activity, most people believed the brain went to sleep along with the rest of the body. In the 1920s, researchers invented the electroencephalograph, or EEG. As discussed in Chapter 3, this machine measures the brain's electrical activity. When people are awake, they have many sources of sensory activity. As a result, the neurons in their brains are extremely active. The EEG shows this activity as short, frequent, irregular brain signals known as *beta waves*. When people focus their attention on something or when they close their eyes and relax, brain activity slows and becomes more regular. This pattern produces *alpha waves*.

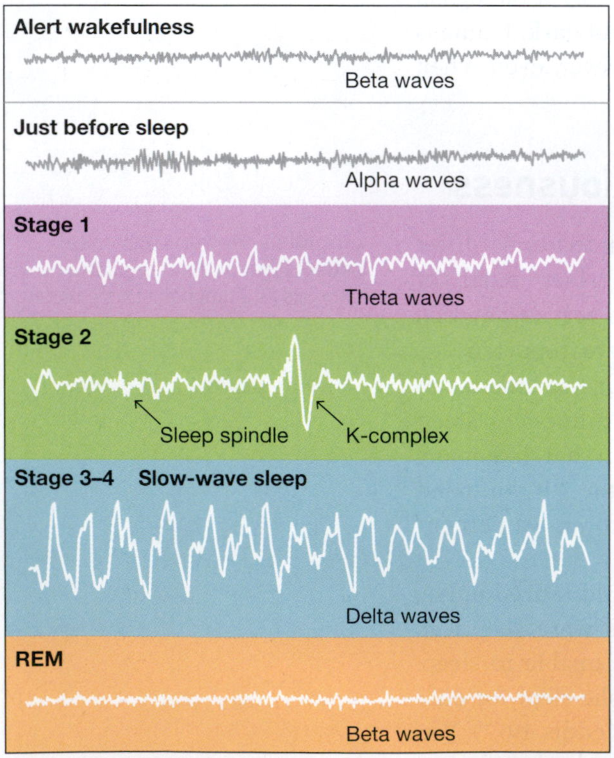

FIGURE 4.16
Brain Activity During Sleep
Using an EEG, researchers can measure the patterns of electrical brain activity during different stages of normal sleep.

STAGES OF SLEEP As evidenced by changes in EEG readings, sleep occurs in stages (see **FIGURE 4.16**). When you drift off to sleep, you enter stage 1. Here, the EEG shows short bursts of irregular waves called *theta waves*. You can easily be aroused from stage 1, and if awakened, you will probably deny that you were sleeping. In this light sleep, you might see fantastical images or geometric shapes. You might have the sensation of falling or that your limbs are jerking. As you progress to stage 2, your breathing becomes more regular, and you become less sensitive to external stimulation. You are now really asleep. Although the EEG continues to show theta waves, it also shows occasional bursts of activity called *sleep spindles* and large waves called *K-complexes*. Some researchers believe that sleep spindles and K-complexes are signals from brain mechanisms involved with shutting out the external world and keeping people asleep (Halász, 2016). Two findings indicate that the brain must work to maintain sleep. First, abrupt noises can trigger K-complexes. Second, as people age and sleep more lightly, their EEGs show fewer sleep spindles.

The progression to deep sleep occurs through stages 3 and 4, which nowadays are typically seen as one stage because their brain activity is nearly identical (Silber et al., 2007). This period is marked by large, regular brain patterns called *delta waves*, and it is often referred to as *slow-wave sleep*. People in slow-wave sleep are hard to wake and are often disoriented when they do wake up. People still process some information in slow-wave sleep, however, because the mind continues to evaluate the surroundings for potential danger. For example, parents in slow-wave sleep can be aroused by their children's cries. Yet they can blissfully ignore sounds, such as sirens or traffic noise, that are louder than crying children but are not necessarily relevant.

REM SLEEP After about 90 minutes of sleep, the sleep cycle reverses, returning to stage 1. At this point, the EEG suddenly shows a flurry of beta wave activity that usually represents an awake, alert mind. The eyes dart back and forth rapidly beneath closed eyelids. Because of these *rapid eye movements*, this stage is called **REM sleep**. It is sometimes called *paradoxical sleep* because of the paradox of a sleeping body with an active brain. Indeed, some neurons in the brain, especially in the occipital cortex and brain stem regions, are more active during REM sleep than during waking hours. But while the brain is active during REM episodes, most of the body's muscles are paralyzed. At the same time, the body shows signs of genital arousal: Most males of all ages develop erections, and most females of all ages experience clitoral engorgement.

REM sleep The stage of sleep marked by rapid eye movements, paralysis of motor systems, and dreaming.

REM sleep is psychologically significant because of its relation to dreaming. About 80 percent of the time when people are awakened during REM sleep, they report dreaming, compared with less than half of the time during non-REM sleep (Solms, 2000). As discussed in the next section, dreams differ between these two types of sleep.

Over the course of a typical night's sleep, the cycle repeats about five times. The sleeper progresses from slow-wave sleep to REM sleep, then back to slow-wave sleep and to REM sleep (**FIGURE 4.17**). As morning approaches, the sleep

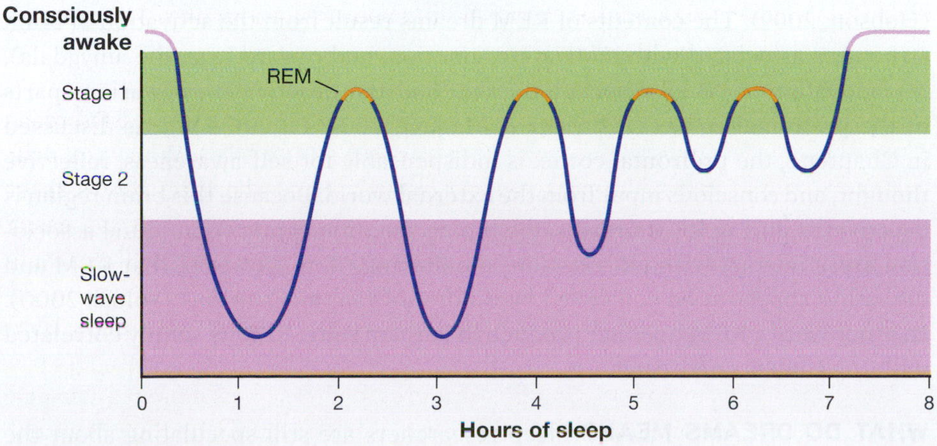

FIGURE 4.17
Stages of Sleep
This chart illustrates the normal stages of sleep over the course of the night.

cycle becomes shorter, and the sleeper spends relatively more time in REM sleep. People briefly awaken many times during the night, but they do not remember these awakenings in the morning. As people age, they sometimes have more difficulty going back to sleep after awakening.

Q **What hormone, released by the pineal gland, promotes sleep?**

ANSWER: melatonin

4.11 People Dream While Sleeping

dreams Products of an altered state of consciousness in which images and fantasies are confused with reality.

Because **dreams** are the products of an altered state of consciousness, dreaming is one of life's great mysteries. Indeed, no one knows whether dreaming serves any biological function. Why does the sleeper's mind conjure up images, fantasies, stories that make little sense, and scenes that ignore physical laws and the rules of both time and space? Why does the mind then confuse these conjurings with reality? Why does it sometimes allow them to scare the dreamer awake? Usually, only when people wake up do they realize they have been dreaming. Of course, dreams sometimes incorporate external sounds or other sensory experiences, but they do so without the type of consciousness experienced during wakefulness.

Although some people report that they do not remember their dreams, everyone dreams unless a particular kind of brain injury or a particular kind of medication interferes. In fact, on average people spend six years of their lives dreaming. If you want to remember your dreams better, you can teach yourself to do so: Keep a pen and paper or a voice recorder next to your bed so you can record your dreams as soon as you wake up. If you wait, you are likely to forget most of them.

REM DREAMS AND NON-REM DREAMS Dreams occur in REM and non-REM sleep, but the dreams' contents differ in the two types of sleep. REM dreams are more likely to be bizarre. They may involve intense emotions, visual and auditory hallucinations (but rarely taste, smell, or pain), and an uncritical acceptance of illogical events. Non-REM dreams are often very dull. They may concern mundane activities such as deciding what clothes to wear or taking notes in class.

The activation and deactivation of different brain regions during REM and non-REM sleep may be responsible for the different types of dreams. During non-REM sleep, there is general deactivation of many brain regions; during REM sleep, some areas of the brain show increased activity, whereas others show decreased activity (Hobson, 2009). The contents of REM dreams result from the activation of brain structures associated with motivation, emotion, and reward (e.g., the amygdala); the activation of visual association areas; and the deactivation of various parts of the prefrontal cortex (Schwartz & Maquet, 2002; **FIGURE 4.18**). As discussed in Chapter 3, the prefrontal cortex is indispensable for self-awareness, reflective thought, and conscious input from the external world. Because this brain region is deactivated during REM dreams, the brain's emotion centers and visual association areas interact without conscious monitoring. Note, however, that REM and dreaming appear to be controlled by different brain mechanisms (Solms, 2000). In other words, REM does not produce the dream state. REM is simply correlated with the contents of dreams.

WHAT DO DREAMS MEAN? Sleep researchers are still speculating about the meaning of dreams. Sigmund Freud published one of the first theories of dreaming in his book *The Interpretation of Dreams* (1900). Freud speculated that dreams contain hidden content that represents unconscious conflicts within the mind of

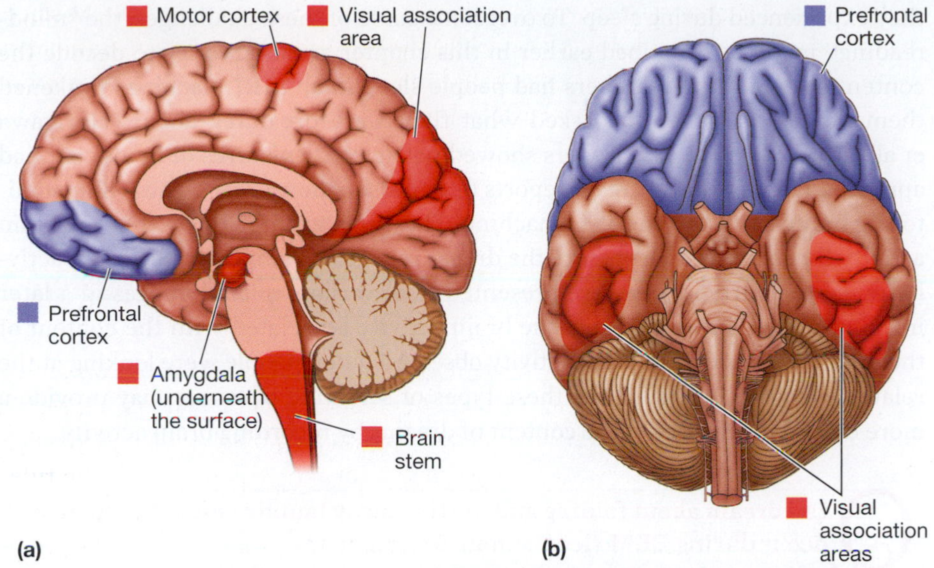

FIGURE 4.18
Brain Regions and REM Dreams
These two views of the brain show the regions that are activated (shown in red) and deactivated (shown in blue) during REM sleep. **(a)** As seen here from the side, the motor cortex, brain stem, and visual association areas are activated, as are brain regions involved in motivation, emotion, and reward (e.g., the amygdala). A region of the prefrontal cortex is deactivated. **(b)** As shown here from below, other visual association areas are activated as well. (This view also reveals the full size of the prefrontal cortex.)

the dreamer. The *manifest content* is the dream the way the dreamer remembers it. The *latent content* is what the dream symbolizes; it is the material that has been disguised to protect the dreamer from confronting a conflict directly. Virtually no support exists for Freud's ideas that dreams represent hidden conflicts and that objects in dreams have special symbolic meanings. However, there is evidence that daily life experiences influence the content of dreams. The content of your dreams is more likely to reflect aspects of your conscious thoughts while awake. For example, you may be especially likely to have dreams that make you feel anxious while studying for exams.

Although most people think their dreams are uniquely their own, many common themes occur in dreams. Have you ever dreamed about showing up unprepared for an exam or finding that you are taking the wrong test? Many people in college have dreams like these. Even after you graduate and no longer take exams routinely, you probably will have similar dreams about being unprepared. Retired instructors sometimes dream about being unprepared to teach classes!

ACTIVATION-SYNTHESIS HYPOTHESIS Sleep researchers John Alan Hobson and Robert McCarley (1977) proposed the **activation-synthesis hypothesis**, which has dominated scientific thinking about dreaming. Hobson and McCarley theorized that random brain activity occurs during sleep and that this neural firing can activate mechanisms that normally interpret sensory input. The sleeping mind tries to make sense of the resulting sensory activity by synthesizing it with stored memories. From this perspective, dreams are the side effects of mental processes produced by random neural firing.

activation-synthesis hypothesis
A hypothesis of dreaming proposing that the brain tries to make sense of random brain activity that occurs during sleep by synthesizing the activity with stored memories.

Critics of Hobson and McCarley's hypothesis argue that dreams are seldom as chaotic as might be expected if they were based on random brain activity (Domhoff, 2003). Indeed, the conscious experience of most dreams is fairly similar to waking life, with some intriguing differences. The differences include a lack of self-awareness, reduced attention and voluntary control, increased emotionality, and poor memory (Nir & Tononi, 2010).

There are many alternative theories about the significance of dreams, but research in this area has been difficult in part because people often do not remember their dreams. When they do remember, it is unclear whether what they report reflects the actual content of the dream or an elaborated interpretation of what they experienced during sleep. To overcome some of these challenges, the "mind-reading" methods described earlier in this chapter are used to try to decode the content of dreams. Researchers had people sleep in an MRI machine, awakened them numerous times, and asked what they were dreaming about (Horikawa et al., 2013). Next the researchers showed participants pictures of items that had appeared in many of the dream reports (e.g., person, house, car), also while monitoring brain activity in the MRI machine. They then examined whether the brain activity that occurred just before the dream report was similar to the brain activity when the participants were presented with various related images in a later imaging study. They found that the brain activity associated with the content of the dream was similar to brain activity observed when people were looking at the related pictures. In the future, these types of scientific advances may provide a more objective measure of the content of dreams by recording brain activity.

Q **Is a dream about folding and putting away laundry more likely to occur during REM sleep or non-REM sleep?**

ANSWER: Non-REM sleep, when dreams are often dull and lack the bizarre qualities typical of REM dreams.

4.12 Sleep Is an Adaptive Behavior

In terms of adaptiveness, sleep might seem illogical. Tuning out the external world during sleep can be dangerous and thus a threat to survival. Beyond that, humans might have advanced themselves in countless ways if they had used all their time productively rather than wasting it by sleeping. But we cannot override indefinitely our need for sleep. Eventually, our bodies shut down whether we want them to or not.

Why do we sleep? Some animals, such as some frogs, never exhibit a state that can be considered sleep (Siegel, 2008). Most animals sleep, however, even if they have peculiar sleeping styles. For example, some dolphin species have *unihemispherical sleep*, in which the cerebral hemispheres take turns sleeping. Sleep must serve an important biological purpose. Research suggests sleep is adaptive for three functions: restoration, avoiding danger at certain times of the day, and facilitation of learning.

RESTORATION AND SLEEP DEPRIVATION According to the *restorative theory*, sleep allows the body, including the brain, to rest and repair itself. Various kinds of evidence support this theory: After people engage in vigorous physical activity, such as running a marathon, they generally sleep longer than usual. Growth hormone, released primarily during deep sleep, facilitates the repair of damaged tissue. Sleep apparently enables the brain to replenish energy stores and also strengthens the immune system (Hobson, 1999). More recently, researchers have demonstrated that sleep may help the brain clear out metabolic by-products of neural activity, which can be toxic if they build up, just as a janitor takes out the trash (Xie et al., 2013). These by-products are cleared away through the interstitial space—fluid-filled space between the cells of the brain. During sleep, a 60 percent increase in this space permits efficient removal of the debris that has accumulated while the person is awake.

Numerous laboratory studies have examined sleep deprivation's effects on physical and cognitive performance. Surprisingly, most studies find that two or three days of sleep deprivation have little effect on strength, athletic ability, or the performance of complex tasks. When deprived of sleep, however, people find it difficult to perform quiet tasks, such as reading. They find it nearly impossible to perform boring or mundane tasks.

A long period of sleep deprivation causes mood problems and decreases cognitive performance. People who suffer from chronic sleep deprivation may experience attention lapses and reduced short-term memory, perhaps in part because of the accumulation of metabolic by-products of neural activity (Kuchibhotla et al., 2008). Studies using rats have found that extended sleep deprivation compromises the immune system and leads to death. Sleep deprivation is also dangerous because it makes people prone to *microsleeps*, in which they fall asleep during the day for periods ranging from a few seconds to a minute (Coren, 1996).

Sleep deprivation might serve one very useful purpose: When people are suffering from depression, depriving them of sleep sometimes alleviates their depression. This effect appears to occur because sleep deprivation leads to increased activation of serotonin receptors, as do drugs used to treat depression (Wolf et al., 2016; the treatment of depression is discussed in Chapter 15, "Treatment of Psychological Disorders"). For people who are not suffering from depression, however, sleep deprivation is more likely to produce negative moods than positive ones.

CIRCADIAN RHYTHM AND SLEEP The *circadian rhythm theory* proposes that sleep has evolved to keep animals quiet and inactive during times of the day when there is the greatest danger, usually when it is dark. According to this theory, animals need only a limited amount of time each day to accomplish the necessities of survival, and it is adaptive for them to spend the remainder of the time inactive, preferably hidden. Thus, an animal's typical amount of sleep depends on how much time that animal needs to obtain food, how easily it can hide, and how vulnerable it is to attack. Small animals tend to sleep a lot. Large animals vulnerable to attack, such as cows and deer, sleep little. Large predatory animals that are not vulnerable sleep a lot. We humans depend greatly on vision for survival. We are adapted to sleeping at night because our early ancestors were more at risk in the dark. That is, early humans who slept at night (and out of harm's way) were the ones who survived long enough to reproduce and thus became our ancestors.

FACILITATION OF LEARNING Scientists have found that neural connections made during the day, which serve as the basis of learning, are strengthened during sleep (Wilson & McNaughton, 1994). When research participants sleep after learning, their recall is better than that of participants in control conditions where they must remain awake (Mazza et al., 2016). Robert Stickgold and colleagues (2000) conducted a study in which participants had to learn a complex task. After finding that participants improved at the task only if they had slept for at least 6 hours following training, the researchers argued that learning the task required neural changes that normally occur only during sleep. Both slow-wave sleep and REM sleep appear to be important for learning to take place. People who dream about the task while sleeping may be especially likely to perform better. In one study, participants learned how to run a complex maze. Those who then slept for 90 minutes performed better on the maze afterward than the sleepless competitors did. Those who dreamed about the maze, however, performed the best (Wamsley et al., 2010).

Indeed, there is some evidence that when students study more, such as during exam periods, they experience more REM sleep, and during this sleep, a greater

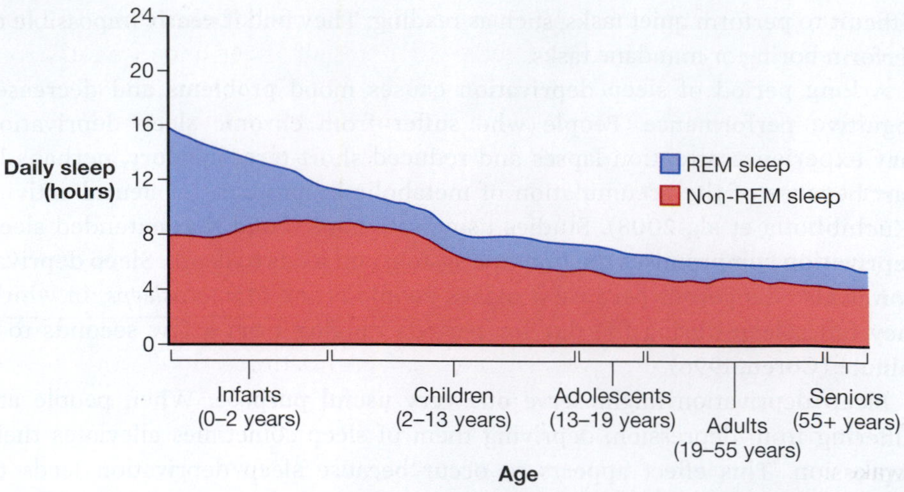

FIGURE 4.19
Sleep Patterns Across the Life Span
As we age, the amount of sleep required decreases and less time is spent in REM sleep.

mental consolidation of information might be expected to take place (Smith & Lapp, 1991). The argument that sleep, especially REM sleep, promotes the development of brain circuits for learning is also supported by the changes in sleep patterns that occur over the life course. Infants and the very young, who learn an enormous amount in a few years, sleep the most and also spend the most time in REM sleep (**FIGURE 4.19**).

Findings linking sleep to learning should give caution to students whose main style of studying is the all-nighter. In one study, students who were sleep deprived for one night showed reduced activity the next day in the hippocampus, a brain area essential for memory (Yoo et al., 2007). These sleep-deprived students also showed poorer memory at subsequent testing. According to the investigators, there is substantial evidence that sleep not only consolidates memories but also seems to prepare the brain for its memory needs for the next day (Oudiette & Paller, 2013). The best advice for preparing for exams is to study, sleep, and then study again (Mazza et al., 2016).

Q **After an exhausting day helping your friend move into a new apartment, you sleep a great deal that night. Which theory of sleep does this behavior support?**

ANSWER: the restorative theory

4.13 Sleep Disorders Interfere with Daily Life

insomnia A disorder characterized by an inability to sleep that causes significant problems in daily living.

Sleep problems are relatively common throughout life. Nearly everyone has trouble falling asleep occasionally, but for some people the inability to sleep causes significant problems in their daily lives. **Insomnia** is a sleep disorder in which people's mental health and ability to function in daily life are compromised by difficulty both falling asleep and staying asleep. Insomnia is associated with diminished psychological well-being, including feelings of depression (American Psychiatric Association, 2013; Bootzin & Epstein, 2011).

An estimated 12 percent to 20 percent of adults have insomnia. It is more common in women than in men and in older adults than in younger adults (Espie, 2002; Ram et al., 2010). One factor that complicates the estimation of how many people have insomnia is that many people who believe they are poor sleepers overestimate how long it takes them to fall asleep and often underestimate how much sleep they get on a typical night. For instance, some people experience *pseudoinsomnia*, in which they dream they are not sleeping. Their EEGs would indicate sleep, but if you roused them they would claim to have been awake.

Ironically, a major cause of insomnia is worrying about sleep. When people experience this kind of insomnia, they may be tired enough to sleep. As they try to fall asleep, however, they worry about whether they will get to sleep and may even panic about how a lack of sleep will affect them. This anxiety leads to heightened arousal, which interferes with normal sleep patterns. To overcome these effects, many people take sleeping pills, which may work in the short run but lead to dependency down the road. Then if they try to stop taking the pills, they may lie awake wondering whether they can get to sleep on their own.

According to research, the most successful treatment for insomnia combines drug therapy with cognitive-behavioral therapy (CBT, discussed in Chapter 15). CBT helps people overcome their worries about sleep and relieves the need for drugs, which should be discontinued before the end of therapy (Morin et al., 2009). Other factors that contribute to insomnia include poor sleeping habits (see the next section for ways to improve your sleeping habits).

Another fairly common sleeping problem is **obstructive sleep apnea**. People with this disorder stop breathing for short periods during sleep because their throat closes. In struggling to breathe, the person briefly awakens and gasps for air. Obstructive sleep apnea is most common among middle-aged men and is often associated with obesity, although it is unclear if obesity is a cause or a consequence of apnea (Pack & Pien, 2011; Spurr et al., 2008). People with apnea are often unaware of their condition, since the main symptom is loud snoring and they do not remember their frequent awakenings during the night. Yet chronic apnea causes people to have poor sleep, which is associated with daytime fatigue and problems such as an inability to concentrate while driving. Moreover, apnea is associated with cardiovascular problems and stroke. For serious cases, physicians often prescribe a continuous positive airway pressure (CPAP) device. During sleep, this device blows air into the person's nose or nose and mouth (**FIGURE 4.20**).

obstructive sleep apnea A disorder in which people, while asleep, stop breathing because their throat closes; the condition results in frequent awakenings during the night.

A student who falls asleep during a lecture is likely sleep deprived, but a professor who falls asleep while lecturing is probably experiencing an episode of **narcolepsy**. In this rare disorder, excessive sleepiness that lasts from several seconds to minutes occurs during normal waking hours. During episodes of narcolepsy, people may experience the muscle paralysis that accompanies REM sleep, perhaps causing them to go limp and collapse. Obviously, those with narcolepsy have to be very careful about the activities they engage in during the day, as unexpectedly falling asleep can be dangerous or fatal, depending on the situation. Evidence suggests that people with narcolepsy have low levels of a neurochemical that regulates wakefulness and REM sleep and that genetics may play a role in the development of narcolepsy (Chabas et al., 2003; Nishino, 2007). The most widely used treatments for this condition are drugs that act as stimulants. Some researchers have found evidence, however, that narcolepsy may be an autoimmune disorder and that treating it as such (using appropriate medication) produces excellent results (Cvetkovic-Lopes et al., 2010; Mahlios et al., 2013).

narcolepsy A sleep disorder in which people experience excessive sleepiness during normal waking hours, sometimes going limp and collapsing.

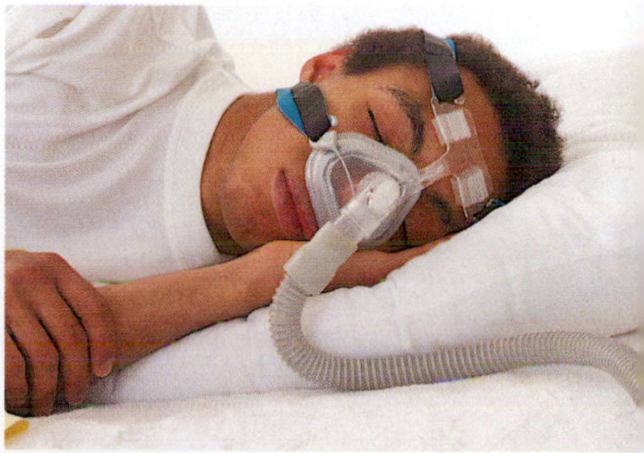

FIGURE 4.20
Obstructive Sleep Apnea
This man suffers from obstructive sleep apnea. Throughout the night, a continuous positive airway pressure (CPAP) device blows air into his nose to keep his throat open.

REM behavior disorder is roughly the opposite of narcolepsy. In this condition, the normal paralysis that accompanies REM sleep is disabled. People with this disorder act out their dreams while sleeping, often striking their sleeping partners. No treatment exists for this rare condition, which is caused by a neurological deficit and is most often seen in elderly males.

By contrast, sleepwalking is most common among young children. Technically called *somnambulism,* this relatively common behavior occurs during slow-wave sleep, typically within the first hour or two after falling asleep. During an episode, the person is glassy-eyed and seems disconnected from other people and the surroundings. No harm is done if the sleepwalker wakes up during the episode. Gently walking a sleepwalker back to bed is safer than leaving the person to wander around and potentially get hurt.

Q Suppose a person frequently has trouble falling asleep but is unbothered and functions well enough in daily life. Does the person have insomnia?

ANSWER: No. Insomnia is a sleep disorder that affects mental health and causes functional impairments in a person's daily life.

PSYCHOLOGY OUTSIDE THE LAB

4.14 How Can You Get a Good Night's Sleep?

College students are incredibly busy. They juggle their academic work with extracurricular activities, jobs, volunteer positions, social calendars, and family commitments. Obligations seemingly expand beyond the available hours in a day. Not surprisingly, when it comes time to go to bed, racing thoughts can make it difficult to fall asleep. Over time, however, sleep deprivation poses risks for both physical and mental well-being. Thankfully, four simple "sleep hygiene" strategies can set you up for sleep success:

1. **Plan.** Create a weekly calendar. Use it to schedule your classes, study time, social time, exercise, down time, and so on. Honestly estimate the amount of time it will take you to complete tasks. Schedule sufficient time for each task in your calendar.
2. **Know your priorities.** There will be occasions when your schedule simply cannot accommodate all the things you have to do. When you are so pressed for time, you will need to make decisions about what to cut. Knowing your priorities can help you make those decisions. If doing well on your biology exam is a top priority, consider skipping the party that weekend. Yes, your decision will have consequences (you might miss your friend's crazy antics), but knowing your priorities will make it easier to accept those consequences.
3. **Stick to the plan.** Procrastination can wreak havoc on your sleep. If you find yourself procrastinating on important tasks, consider working with a mental health practitioner to figure out why you procrastinate and how you might overcome this tendency.
4. **Practice saying no.** College is a great time to explore the activities available on your campus or in your community, but exploring all those options simultaneously is a recipe for disaster. Be selective.

Of course, sometimes sleep may elude you. Even when you are dog-tired as you lie in bed, you may find yourself unable to doze off. In such cases, the strategies described below might help you develop better sleep:

1. **Establish a regular routine.** Every day (including weekends), go to bed at the same time and wake up at the same time. Changing the time you go to bed or wake up each day alters your regular nightly sleep cycle and can disrupt other physiological systems.

2. **Avoid alcohol and caffeine just before going to bed.** Alcohol might help you get to sleep more quickly, but it will interfere with your sleep cycle and may cause you to wake up early the next day. Caffeine is a stimulant: It interferes with a chemical (adenosine) that helps you sleep, so it will prevent you from falling asleep.
3. **Exercise regularly.** Regular exercise will help maintain your sleep cycle. Exercising creates arousal that interferes with sleep, however, so do not exercise right before going to bed. But a little stretching before bedtime can help your mind and body relax.
4. **Remember, your bed is for sleeping.** Most of us do not sleep in our kitchens, nor should we eat in our beds. Or watch TV. Or study. Your mind needs to associate your bed with sleeping. The best way to make that association is to use your bed exclusively for sleeping. And maybe a little cuddling.
5. **Relax.** Do not worry about the future (easier said than done, right?). Have a warm bath or listen to soothing music. Download a couple of meditation and relaxation podcasts. Use the techniques presented in them to help you deal with chronic stress and guide you to restfulness.
6. **Get up.** When you cannot fall asleep, get up and do something else. Do not lie there trying to force sleep (we all know how well that works, or rather does not work; **FIGURE 4.21**). If you start feeling sleepy a bit later, crawl back into bed and give sleep another try.
7. **Do not try to catch up on sleep.** When you have trouble falling asleep on a particular night, do not try to make up for the lost sleep by sleeping late the next morning or napping during the day. Those zzzz's are gone. You want to be sleepy when you go to bed the next night. Sleeping late, napping, or both will make the next night's sleep more difficult.
8. **Avoid electronic devices late at night.** Most electronic devices emit blue light, which can signal the brain to remain awake, making it more difficult to fall asleep. If possible, you should put your phone, tablet, or both away early. You can also install programs on most devices that will cause the device to emit a red frequency rather than blue. Red light has the opposite effect of blue light and can signal the body to begin winding down.

The sleep attitudes and habits you establish during college will be with you for the rest of your life. Be good to yourself. Set yourself up for academic success, as well as physical and mental health, by prioritizing good sleep and taking charge of your sleep.

For additional resources, visit the National Sleep Foundation's website: https://www.sleepfoundation.org/ ■

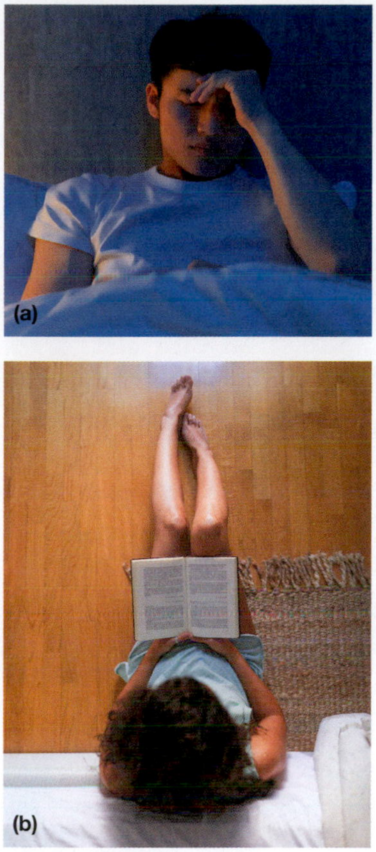

FIGURE 4.21
One Strategy for Better Sleep
(a) When you cannot fall asleep, do not stay in bed. **(b)** Instead, get up and do something else, especially something relaxing, such as reading and drinking a cup of warm milk or (uncaffeinated) herbal tea.

Q **What time should you go to bed if you want to establish good sleeping habits?**

ANSWER: The specific time depends on you, but it should be the same time every night.

How Do Brain Injury and Drugs Affect Consciousness?

Learning Objectives

- Describe how different conditions resulting from brain injury affect consciousness.
- Describe the neurochemical and psychological effects of stimulants, depressants, opioids/narcotics, hallucinogens/psychedelics, and other commonly used drugs.

As discussed in Chapter 3, the brain enables all the functions of the body and mind, including the experience of consciousness. Although changes in our attention and environment while awake can naturally alter our conscious state, and everyone's consciousness shifts every day from sleep to waking, external factors that impact brain function also alter consciousness. Changes in brain structure through injury and changes in brain chemistry through drugs can profoundly change conscious experience.

4.15 Brain Injury Can Diminish Consciousness

At least since the time of the ancient Roman gladiators, people have understood that a head injury can produce disturbances in mental activity, such as unconsciousness or loss of speech. In Chapter 3, we discussed how brain injuries can influence specific functions related to conscious awareness. For example, patients with hemineglect will show problems with attention, and split-brain patients report awareness only of stimuli processed by the left hemisphere. However, some types of brain injuries result in more global changes in consciousness, from mild confusion to no evidence of consciousness at all.

traumatic brain injury (TBI)
Impairments in mental functioning caused by a blow to or very sharp movement of the head.

TRAUMATIC BRAIN INJURY Traumatic brain injury (TBI) is impairment in mental functioning caused by a blow to or very sharp movement of the head, commonly caused by an accident or a sports injury. TBIs are responsible for about 30 percent of all injury deaths (Faul et al., 2010) and are also a substantial cause of disabilities that can last from days to decades. TBIs can impair thinking, memory, emotions, and personality. Recall the case of Phineas Gage, described in Chapter 3, who underwent substantial psychological changes after his brain injury.

TBIs can range from mild to severe. The greater the severity of the injury, the more likely the TBI is to be permanent. A *concussion* is formally known as mild TBI. Despite the term *mild*, concussion is far from trivial, as the brain swelling and resulting brain damage can have long-lasting effects. Signs of concussion include mental confusion, dizziness, a dazed look, memory problems, and sometimes the temporary loss of consciousness. Most people will recover from concussion within one to two weeks (Baldwin et al., 2016). However, concussions may have a cumulative effect with each new injury. That is, each concussion can lead to more serious, longer-lasting symptoms (Baugh et al., 2012; Zetterberg et al., 2013).

There has been increased interest in the long-term effects of concussion, particularly as they affect professional athletes. In the 2015 movie *Concussion*, Will Smith plays the pathologist Bennet Omalu, who conducted an autopsy on the former NFL player Mike Webster (**FIGURE 4.22**). Webster had a history of homelessness and self-injury. Omalu found evidence of severe TBI, the type that results from repeated blows to the head. In the ensuing years, Omalu and his colleagues examined other NFL players and found that many had similar symptoms and evidence of TBIs (Omalu et al., 2005; Small et al., 2013). Numerous studies have since documented the long-term effects of sports concussions (Bailes et al., 2013). A recent study found evidence of brain damage in 99 percent of deceased former NFL players (Mez et al., 2017). Although this number seems shockingly high, it is important to remember that the investigators in this study examined the brains that were available to them, which did not represent a random sample of NFL players. In other words, it is hard to know how much these findings generalize to the population of NFL players. Nevertheless, a large number of players seem to be affected, and these findings have led to guidelines for reducing the occurrence of such injuries (Harmon et al., 2013).

FIGURE 4.22
Concussion
In *Concussion* (2015), Will Smith plays Dr. Bennet Omalu. Omalu's pathology work was instrumental in revealing the relationship between concussions suffered by NFL players and severe TBIs.

Concussions are a special concern for the developing brains of teen and college athletes. According to the University of Pittsburgh Medical Center Sports Medicine Concussion Program (2020), between 1.7 and 3 million sports-related concussions occur annually among student athletes in the United States. The American

Academy of Neurology (2013) advises that an athlete should not return to action until all symptoms of concussion have cleared up, which often takes several weeks.

COMA Medical advances are enabling a greater number of people to survive traumatic brain injuries. Doctors now save the lives of many people who previously would have died from injuries sustained in car accidents or on battlefields. A good example is the remarkable survival of Congresswoman Gabrielle Giffords, who was shot in the head by an assailant in 2011. Immediately after the shooting, Giffords could only respond to simple commands. Today, although Giffords remains partially paralyzed, her accomplishments include hiking the Grand Canyon, skydiving, and continuing her governmental and political work (**FIGURE 4.23**).

FIGURE 4.23
Gabrielle Giffords
Representative Gabrielle Giffords made a remarkable recovery from the traumatic brain injury she suffered after being shot in the head. Among her many accomplishments since then is the energetic speech she delivered at the 2016 Democratic National Convention.

Surviving is just the first step toward recovery, however, and many of those who sustain serious brain injuries fall into comas or, like Giffords, are induced into coma as part of medical treatment. The coma allows the brain to rest. Most people who regain consciousness after such injuries do so within a few days, but some people do not regain consciousness for weeks. In this state, they have sleep/wake cycles—they open their eyes and appear to be awake, close their eyes and appear to be asleep—but they do not seem to respond to their surroundings.

People in a coma do not respond to external stimuli, so it is hard to know whether they have consciousness. However, brain imaging may be used to identify those who are conscious but unable to respond. A 23-year-old woman in an apparent coma was asked to imagine playing tennis or walking through her house (Owen et al., 2006). This woman's pattern of brain activity became quite similar to the patterns of control subjects who also imagined playing tennis or walking through a house (**FIGURE 4.24**). The woman could not give outward signs of awareness, but researchers believe she was able to understand language and respond to the experimenters' requests.

The implications of this finding are extraordinary. Could the researchers' method be used to reach other people who are in coma, aware of their surroundings but unable to communicate? Indeed, this research team has now evaluated 54 coma patients and found 5 who could willfully control brain activity to communicate (Monti et al., 2010). One 29-year-old man was able to answer five of six yes/no questions correctly by thinking of one type of image to answer yes and another type to answer no. These advances add up to one astonishing fact: Some people in comas are conscious of what is happening around them. The ability to communicate from a coma might ultimately allow some patients to express thoughts, ask for more medication, and increase the quality of their lives (Fernández-Espejo & Owen, 2013).

When people appear to have emerged from coma (their eyes are open, and they have sleep/wake cycles) yet do not respond to external stimuli for more than a month, they are in a condition called

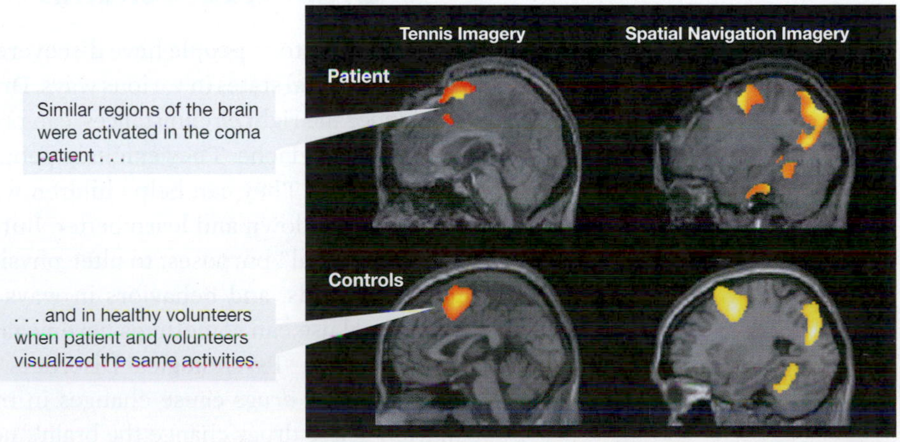

Tennis Imagery
Spatial Navigation Imagery
Patient
Controls
Similar regions of the brain were activated in the coma patient . . .
. . . and in healthy volunteers when patient and volunteers visualized the same activities.

FIGURE 4.24
In a Coma but Aware
The brain images on the top are from the patient, a young woman in a coma who showed no outward signs of awareness. The images on the bottom are a composite from the control group, which consisted of healthy volunteers. Both the patient and the control group were told to visualize, first, playing tennis, and second, walking around a house. Right after the directions were given, the neural activity in the patient's brain appeared similar to the neural activity in the control group's brains.

unresponsive wakefulness syndrome (Laureys et al., 2010). This unresponsive state is not associated with consciousness. Normal brain activity does not occur when a person is in this state, in part because much of the person's brain may be damaged beyond recovery. The longer the unresponsive wakefulness state lasts, the less likely it is that the person will ever recover consciousness or show normal brain activity.

Some people who emerge from a coma are able to make deliberate movements, such as following an object with their eyes. They may even try to communicate. This situation is referred to as a *minimally conscious state*. The prognosis for those in an unresponsive wakefulness state is much worse than for those in a minimally conscious state. Differentiating between states of consciousness by behavior alone is difficult, but brain imaging may prove useful for identifying the extent of a patient's injury and likelihood of recovery. Researchers have found that measuring brain metabolism via positron emission tomography imaging can identify which patients in unresponsive states are likely to regain consciousness (Stender et al., 2016).

BRAIN DEATH The imaging of brain activity can also be used to tell whether a person is brain dead. *Brain death* is the irreversible loss of brain function. Unlike patients suffering from unresponsive wakefulness syndrome, who still show activity in regions of the brain stem, with brain death no activity is found in any region of the brain. As discussed in Chapter 3, the brain is essential for integrating brain activity that keeps the bodily organs, such as the heart and lungs, alive. When the brain no longer functions, the rest of the body quickly stops functioning unless it is supported by mechanical interventions.

Q How does unresponsive wakefulness syndrome differ from brain death?

ANSWER: Those in a state of unresponsive wakefulness show some abnormal brain function, while those who are brain dead show no brain function.

4.16 Drugs Alter Consciousness by Changing Brain Neurochemistry

Throughout history, people have discovered that ingesting certain substances can alter their mental states in various ways. Drugs are a mixed blessing. The right ones, taken under the right circumstances, can provide soothing relief from severe pain or a moderate headache. They can help people suffering from depression lead more satisfying lives. They can help children who have attention-deficit/hyperactivity disorder settle down and learn better. But many of these same drugs can be used for "recreational" purposes: to alter physical sensations, levels of consciousness, thoughts, moods, and behaviors in ways that users believe are desirable. This recreational use can sometimes have negative consequences, including addiction (see Chapter 14, "Psychological Disorders," for a discussion of addiction).

Psychoactive drugs cause changes in mood, awareness, thoughts, feelings, or behavior. These drugs change the brain's neurochemistry by activating neurotransmitter systems: either by imitating the brain's natural neurotransmitters (e.g., marijuana, opiates) or changing the activity of particular neurotransmitter receptors (e.g., cocaine). The effects of a particular drug depend on which neurotransmitter systems it imitates or activates (**TABLE 4.1**).

Stimulants, for example, are drugs that increase behavioral and mental activity. They stimulate, or heighten, activity of the central nervous system. Stimulants also activate the sympathetic nervous system, increasing heart rate and blood

Table 4.1 Psychoactive Drugs

TYPE	PSYCHOLOGICAL EFFECT(S)	EXAMPLES	NEUROTRANSMITTER SYSTEM(S)
Stimulants	Increase behavioral and mental activity	Amphetamines, methamphetamine, cocaine, nicotine, caffeine	Dopamine, norepinephrine, acetylcholine (nicotine)
Depressants	Decrease behavioral and mental activity	Antianxiety drugs (barbiturates, benzodiazepines), alcohol	GABA
Opioids	Reduce the experience of pain, bring pleasure	Heroin, morphine, codeine	Endorphins
Hallucinogens/ psychedelics	Alter thoughts or perceptions	LSD, PCP, peyote, psilocybin mushrooms	Serotonin (LSD, peyote, psilocybin), glutamate (PCP)
Combination	Mixed effects	Marijuana, MDMA	Cannabinoid (marijuana), serotonin, dopamine, norepinephrine (MDMA)

pressure. They improve mood, but they also cause people to become restless, and they disrupt sleep. Amphetamines, methamphetamine, and cocaine are potent stimulants. Nicotine and caffeine are mild stimulants.

Some stimulants work by interfering with the normal reuptake of dopamine by the releasing neuron—allowing dopamine to remain in the synapse and thus prolonging its effects—whereas other stimulants also increase the release of dopamine (Fibiger, 1993). Activation of dopamine receptors is associated with greater reward or increased liking (Volkow et al., 2011).

Depressants have the opposite effect of stimulants. They reduce behavioral and mental activity by depressing the central nervous system. Alcohol is the most widely used depressant—in fact, it is the most widely used and abused drug (**FIGURE 4.25**). Antianxiety drugs, such as benzodiazepines, commonly given to calm people and reduce worry, are also depressants. In sufficiently high doses, depressants can induce sleep, which is why they are sometimes referred to as sedatives. Chapter 15 discusses the clinical use of depressants.

FIGURE 4.25
Alcohol
The open display and easy availability of alcohol make us forget that it is a widely abused depressant.

Opioids, sometimes called narcotics, include heroin, morphine, and codeine. These drugs, derived from the opium poppy, bind with a special type of receptor in the brain (called the mu opioid receptor) and, in doing so, mimic the action of the neurotransmitter endorphins that help relieve pain. Opioids also provide intense feelings of pleasure, relaxation, and euphoria. Activation of opioid receptors is involved in the experience of reward (Berridge & Kringelbach, 2013; Smith et al., 2011).

Hallucinogens, sometimes called psychedelics, produce alterations in cognition, mood, and perception. These drugs change how users experience the world around them. The most common hallucinogen is *lysergic acid diethylamide* (*LSD*). LSD was discovered in 1938 and is made from a chemical found in certain types of fungus, called ergot, that grow on rye and other wheats. It is usually taken orally, and the drug experience, informally referred to as a "trip," lasts for about 12 hours. LSD changes sensory experiences and can produce extreme hallucinations, pleasurable or unpleasurable. People using LSD have a distorted sense of time.

A naturally occurring form of LSD might have been responsible for the bizarre behavior that led to accusations of witchcraft in Salem, Massachusetts, in 1692. Some residents of Salem, especially teenagers and children, suffered from seizures, convulsions, hallucinations, blindness, prickling sensations, nausea, and other symptoms. Their behavior was taken as signaling demonic possession and witchery, and as punishment they were put to death by burning at the stake. It is possible, however, that ergot caused these symptoms. The "witches" of Salem may have inadvertently eaten LSD-tainted bread.

Many other substances, such as certain plants and fungi, have psychedelic properties. For example, eating the top part of the peyote cactus or certain types of mushrooms, such as *psilocybin mushrooms*, produces hallucinogenic effects. These psychedelic substances have been used in various religious rites throughout history.

Many commonly used drugs do not fit neatly into these major categories because they produce a range of psychological effects. For instance, marijuana acts as a depressant but also has a slight hallucinogenic effect, as you will see later in the chapter.

Q Which type of drug heightens behavioral and mental activity?

ANSWER: stimulants, such as caffeine, nicotine, amphetamines, and cocaine

4.17 People Use—and Abuse—Many Psychoactive Drugs

This section considers a few common psychoactive drugs in more detail. Some of these drugs have legitimate medical uses, but all of them are frequently abused outside of medical use.

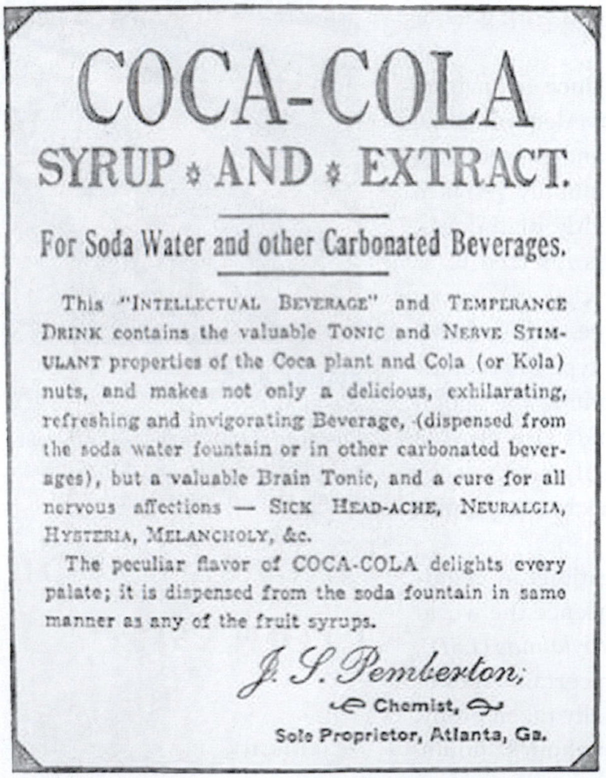

COCA-COLA
SYRUP AND EXTRACT.
For Soda Water and other Carbonated Beverages.
This "INTELLECTUAL BEVERAGE" and TEMPERANCE DRINK contains the valuable TONIC and NERVE STIMULANT properties of the Coca plant and Cola (or Kola) nuts, and makes not only a delicious, exhilarating, refreshing and invigorating Beverage, (dispensed from the soda water fountain or in other carbonated beverages), but a valuable Brain Tonic, and a cure for all nervous affections — SICK HEAD-ACHE, NEURALGIA, HYSTERIA, MELANCHOLY, &c.
The peculiar flavor of COCA-COLA delights every palate; it is dispensed from the soda fountain in same manner as any of the fruit syrups.
J. S. Pemberton;
Chemist,
Sole Proprietor, Atlanta, Ga.

FIGURE 4.26
Early Coke Ad
This advertisement's claim that Coca-Cola is "a valuable Brain Tonic" may have been inspired by the incorporation of cocaine into the drink before 1906.

COCAINE Cocaine is a stimulant derived from the leaves of the coca bush, which grows primarily in South America. After inhaling (snorting) cocaine as a powder or smoking it in the form of crack cocaine, users experience a wave of confidence. They feel good, alert, energetic, sociable, and wide-awake. Cocaine produces its stimulating effects by increasing the concentration of dopamine in the synapse. These short-term effects are especially intense for crack cocaine users. However, habitual use of cocaine in large quantities can lead to paranoia, psychotic behavior, and violence (Ottieger et al., 1992).

Cocaine has a long history of use in America. John Pemberton, a pharmacist from Georgia, was so impressed with cocaine's effects that in 1886 he added the drug to soda water for easy ingestion, thus creating Coca-Cola. In 1906, the U.S. government outlawed cocaine, so it was removed from the drink. To this day, however, coca leaves from which the cocaine has been removed are used in the making of Coke (**FIGURE 4.26**).

AMPHETAMINES AND METHAMPHETAMINE Amphetamines are stimulants that increase dopamine in the synapse. Their primary effect is to reduce fatigue. Amphetamines have a long history of use for weight loss and for staying awake. However, their numerous negative side effects include insomnia, anxiety, and potential for addiction. Legitimate medical purposes include the treatment of narcolepsy and of attention-deficit/hyperactivity disorder (ADHD, discussed in greater detail in Chapter 15). The drug Adderall contains amphetamine and is prescribed to treat ADHD. It is also widely abused as a study aid on college campuses. Self-reports of nonmedical stimulant use by college students increased from 5 percent in 2003 to just under 20 percent in 2018 (Kennedy, 2018; McCabe et al., 2014).

Another widely used stimulant is methamphetamine, which breaks down into amphetamine in the body. Methamphetamine was first developed in the early twentieth century for use as a nasal decongestant, but its recreational use became popular in the 1980s. The National Survey on Drug Use and Health estimates that more than 5 percent of Americans ages 12 and over have tried methamphetamine at some point in their lives, although its use has declined in recent years (National Institute on Drug Abuse, 2020). One factor that encourages the use of this drug and may explain its popularity is that it is easy to make from common over-the-counter drugs, as depicted in the critically acclaimed television show *Breaking Bad*.

By blocking the reuptake of dopamine and increasing its release, methamphetamine produces high levels of dopamine in the synapse. In addition, methamphetamine stays in the body and brain much longer than, say, cocaine, so its effects are prolonged. Over time, methamphetamine depletes dopamine levels and damages various brain structures, including the frontal lobes, temporal lobes, and reward regions (**FIGURE 4.27**). The drug's effects on these brain regions may explain the harm done to memory and emotion in long-term users (Kim et al., 2006; Thompson et al., 2004).

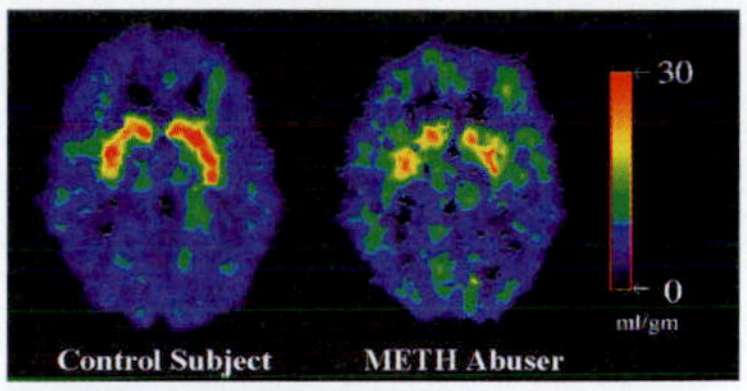

FIGURE 4.27
Methamphetamine's Effects on the Brain
The brain on the left is a healthy control subject who had not taken drugs, while the brain at right is that of a methamphetamine abuser. The red areas shown in the control subject's brain indicate healthy activity of dopamine neurons in rewards regions of the basal ganglia. This dopamine activity is diminished after extensive drug use in the methamphetamine abuser.

OPIOIDS Opioids include prescription medications such as oxycodone and morphine as well as the illegal drug heroin. Opioids have been used to relieve pain and suffering for hundreds of years. Indeed, before the twentieth century, heroin was widely available without a prescription and was marketed by Bayer, the aspirin company (**FIGURE 4.28**). Opioids not only block pain but are experienced as extremely enjoyable if taken in larger doses. For instance, heroin provides a rush of intense pleasure that is often described as similar to orgasm. This rush evolves into a pleasant, relaxed stupor. Opioids, however, may be highly addictive because they have dual physical effects: They increase pleasure by binding with mu opioid receptors and increase wanting of the drug by indirectly activating dopamine receptors (Kuhn et al., 2003).

During the past decade there has been an epidemic of opioid abuse. Most experts view the current epidemic as resulting from the greater use of prescription opiates for chronic pain (Compton et al., 2016). Physicians were encouraged by pharmaceutical companies to increase their prescription of opiates due to concerns that pain was not being treated aggressively enough. The greater availability of prescription drugs led to more recreational use as well as subsequent abuse and addiction.

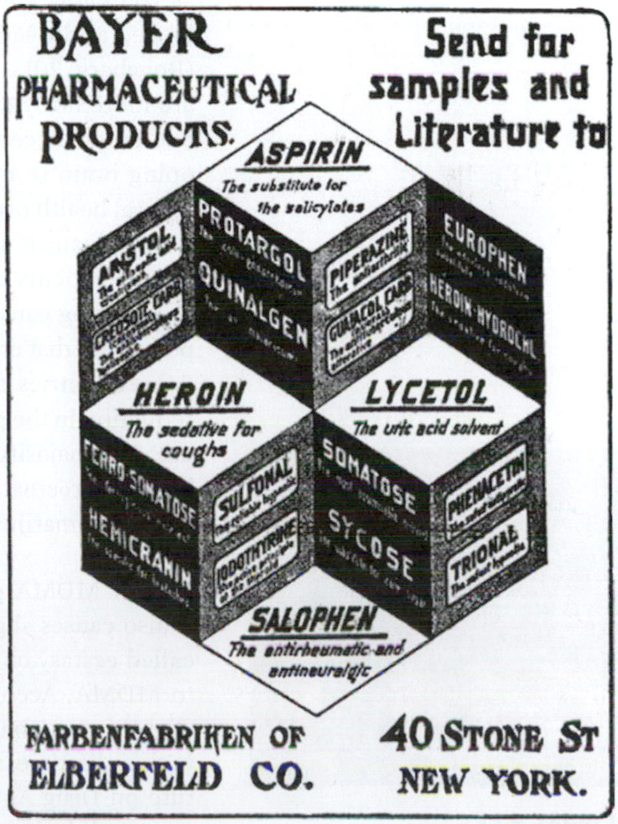

FIGURE 4.28
Early Heroin Ad
Before 1904, Bayer advertised heroin as "the sedative for coughs."

MARIJUANA The most widely used illicit drug in the world is marijuana, the dried leaves and flower buds of the cannabis plant. Many drugs can easily be categorized as stimulants, depressants, or hallucinogens, but marijuana can have the effects of all three types. The psychoactive ingredient in marijuana is *THC*, or tetrahydrocannabinol. This chemical produces a relaxed mental state, an uplifted or contented mood, and some perceptual and cognitive distortions. For some users, it impairs perception, whereas for others it makes perceptions more vivid, especially taste perceptions.

Like depressants, marijuana decreases reaction times and impairs motor coordination, memory formation, and the recall of recently learned information. As opposed to alcohol, which is metabolized and cleared in a few hours, THC and the by-products of its metabolism remain in the body for up to a month. With THC still in their system, frequent users of marijuana may get high with a lower dose than infrequent users. Most first-time users do not experience the "high" obtained by more experienced users. In this way, marijuana differs from most other drugs. Generally, the first time someone uses a drug, the effects are very strong, and over time the person has to use more of the drug to get the same effect. The opposite is true for marijuana.

Although the brain mechanisms that marijuana affects remain somewhat mysterious, researchers have discovered a class of receptors that are activated by naturally occurring THC-like substances. Activation of these *cannabinoid receptors* appears to adjust mental activity and perhaps alter pain perception. The large concentration of these receptors in the hippocampus may partly explain why marijuana impairs memory (Ilan et al., 2004).

Heavy long-term use of marijuana is associated with a smaller hippocampus and amygdala, brain regions involved in processing memory and emotion (Yücel et al., 2008). Whether smoking marijuana causes long-term deficits in cognitive processes is more controversial. One study found that frequent marijuana use in childhood predicted cognitive problems in adulthood (Meier et al., 2012). But as you know, correlation does not prove causation. Other researchers who have looked at the same data argue that socioeconomic status is a confounding factor (Rogeberg, 2013). That is, children who grow up in impoverished circumstances are more likely to smoke marijuana *and* more likely to show cognitive deficits in adulthood. Recent evidence suggests, though, that marijuana may affect the developing brain to make adolescent heavy users more likely to develop significant mental health problems (Bechtold et al., 2016; Ryan et al., 2017).

Marijuana is also used for its medicinal properties (**FIGURE 4.29**). For instance, cancer patients undergoing chemotherapy report that marijuana is effective for overcoming nausea. The medical use of marijuana is controversial because of the possibility that chronic use can cause health problems or lead to abuse of the drug. Some countries and American states have concluded that such risks are offset by a reduction in the problems created by criminal activity associated with illegal drug use. The majority of states allow medical use of marijuana, and several states have legalized recreational use, including the populous state of California. However, the use of marijuana remains a federal crime in the United States.

FIGURE 4.29
Medicinal Use of Marijuana
Employees assist customers at the River Rock Medical Marijuana Center in Denver, Colorado.

MDMA MDMA produces an energizing effect similar to that of stimulants, but it also causes slight hallucinations. The street version of MDMA is sold as pills called ecstasy or Molly, but these pills often contain other stimulants in addition to MDMA. According to the National Survey on Drug Use and Health, in 2018 slightly more than 7 percent of the people surveyed reported having tried ecstasy in their lifetime, and close to 1 percent had used it in the past year (National Institute on Drug Abuse, 2020). The drug first became popular in the 1990s among young adults in nightclubs and at all-night parties known as raves.

Compared with amphetamines, MDMA is associated with less dopamine activity and more serotonin activity. The serotonin release may explain ecstasy's hallucinogenic properties. Research on animals has shown that MDMA can cause damage to a number of brain regions, particularly the prefrontal cortex and the hippocampus (Halpin et al., 2014). Studies with humans show evidence of a range of impairments from long-term ecstasy use, especially memory problems and a diminished ability to perform complex tasks (Parrott, 2013). Of course, any drug can be toxic in large doses or when taken for long periods. Currently, controversy exists over whether occasional recreational use of ecstasy by itself causes long-term damage. Some ecstasy users take very high doses or regularly use other drugs, such as methamphetamine, that are known to be neurotoxic (Gallagher et al., 2014). In addition, many pills sold as ecstasy or Molly contain other dangerous chemicals, such as drugs used to anesthetize animals. Even when they contain only MDMA, the doses vary widely, increasing the likelihood of overdose (Morefield et al., 2011; Wood et al., 2011). Several college students in the northeast attending concerts during the summer of 2013 died after consuming what they believed to be Molly (**FIGURE 4.30**).

FIGURE 4.30
Deaths from MDMA
Concertgoers are shown at Electric Zoo 2013, a Labor Day weekend of electronic dance music in New York City. Two attendees died after taking MDMA sold as Molly, and the festival was ended a day early.

Growing evidence suggests that MDMA may have potential benefits for use in the treatment of posttraumatic stress disorder (Doblin et al., 2014; you will learn more about this disorder in Chapter 14). The drug promotes feelings of compassion and trust and reduces the negative emotions that people have about their traumatic experiences even after the drug wears off (Mithoefer et al., 2013). Recent evidence also suggests that MDMA may help those with autism cope with social anxiety (Mithoefer et al., 2016). When used as part of treatment, MDMA does not have negative effects on health or cognition (White, 2014).

Q **What type of drug is in Adderall, used to treat ADHD?**

ANSWER: an amphetamine (a stimulant)

4.18 Alcohol Abuse Is Responsible for Many Societal Problems

Alcohol, the second-most commonly used psychoactive drug throughout the world after caffeine, is a depressant that inhibits neural activity by activating GABA receptors. These effects may explain why alcohol is typically experienced as relaxing. GABA reception may also be the primary mechanism by which alcohol interferes with motor coordination and results in slowed reaction time and slurred speech. Drugs that block the effects of alcohol on GABA receptors also prevent alcohol intoxication. However, these drugs are not used to treat alcoholics, because reducing the symptoms of being drunk could easily lead to even greater alcohol abuse.

Many societies have a love/hate relationship with alcohol. On the one hand, moderate drinking is an accepted aspect of social interaction and may even be good for one's health, although there is some controversy about its purported benefits (Stockwell et al., 2016). On the other hand, alcohol is a major contributor to many societal problems, such as spousal abuse and other forms of violence. Although the percentage of traffic fatalities due to alcohol is dropping, alcohol was still a factor in close to 30 percent of fatal accidents in the United States in 2018 (United States Department of Transportation, 2020). From 2011 to 2015, about 95,000 deaths each year in the United States were caused by alcohol. The overall cost of problem drinking—from lost productivity due to employee absence, health care expenses, and so on—was estimated to be close to a quarter of a trillion dollars in 2010 alone (Centers for Disease Control and Prevention, 2020a).

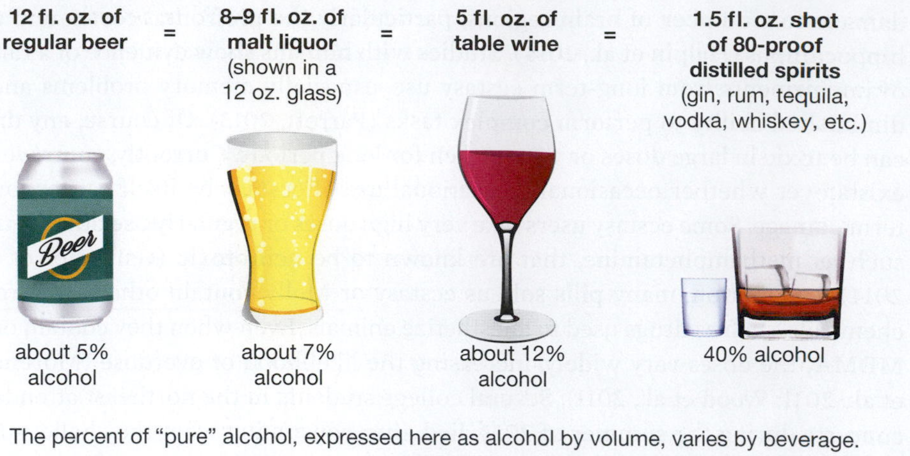

FIGURE 4.31
One Standard Drink
It is important to remember that having more than five drinks in one sitting counts as binge drinking. But a drink of one kind may be much more powerful than a drink of another kind. How can you know just how much alcohol is in any one drink? These depictions show the alcohol content by volume and equivalent serving sizes for different types of alcoholic drinks.

Source: Based on https://www.niaaa.nih.gov/alcohols-effects-health/overview-alcohol-consumption/what-standard-drink

Alcohol is prevalent on college campuses, and "binge drinking"—for women, having 4 or more drinks, and for men, having 5 or more drinks within 2 hours—is especially common (**FIGURE 4.31**). The 2019 National Survey on Drug Use and Health reports that 52.5 percent of college students reported drinking in the past month, and 33 percent reported binge drinking. Although the legal age for drinking in the United States is 21, among people 12–20 years old, 39.7 percent had used alcohol and 11.1 percent reported binge drinking in the past month (National Institute on Drug Abuse, 2020). Every year, more than 1,800 college students die as a result of excessive alcohol use (Hingson et al., 2009; Thompson & Huynh, 2017). About one third of college students reported having had sex during a drinking binge, and the heaviest drinkers were likely to have had sex with a new or casual partner (Leigh & Schafer, 1993), thus increasing their risk for exposure to sexually transmitted diseases. Date rape also often involves alcohol (White & Hingson, 2014).

In every region of the world, across a wide variety of measures—drinking versus abstinence, heavy drinking versus occasional drinking, alcohol-related disorders, and so on—men drink more than women (**FIGURE 4.32**). Men are twice as likely to report binge drinking, chronic drinking, and recent alcohol intoxication. Although gender differences in alcohol use are smaller for university students and adolescents (Swendsen et al., 2012), young males are much more likely to be binge drinkers (Patrick et al., 2013).

One possible explanation is that women do not metabolize alcohol as quickly as men do and generally have smaller body volumes, so they consume less alcohol than men to achieve the same effects. Another possible explanation is that women's drinking may be more hidden because it is less socially accepted than men's drinking. According to this view, women's alcohol consumption may be underreported, especially in cultures where it is frowned on or forbidden. In some cultures, "real men" are expected to drink a lot and prove they can "hold" their liquor, whereas women who do the same are seen as abnormal.

FIGURE 4.32
Male Drinking
Across the globe, men drink the most alcohol.

Alan Marlatt (1999), a leading researcher on substance abuse, has noted that people view alcohol as the "magic elixir," capable of increasing social skills, sexual pleasure, confidence, and power. They anticipate that alcohol will have positive effects on their emotions and behavior. For example, people tend to think that alcohol reduces anxiety, so both light and heavy drinkers turn to alcohol after a difficult day. Alcohol can interfere with the cognitive processing of threat cues, so anxiety-provoking events seem less troubling when people are intoxicated. This effect occurs, however, only if people drink *before* the anxiety-provoking events. In fact, according to the research, drinking after a hard day can increase people's focus on and obsession with their problems (Sayette, 1993). In addition, while moderate doses of alcohol are associated with better moods, larger doses are associated with worse moods.

Expectations about alcohol's effects are learned very early in life through observation. Children may see that people who drink have a lot of fun and that drinking is an important aspect of many celebrations. Teenagers may view drinkers as sociable and grown-up, two things they desperately want to be. Studies have shown that children who have very positive expectations about alcohol are more likely to start drinking and become heavy drinkers than children who do not share those expectations (Leigh & Stacy, 2004).

According to the social psychologists Jay Hull and Charles Bond (1986), expectations about alcohol can also influence the way people are affected by drinking. They based this conclusion on studies in which researchers gave participants tonic water with or without alcohol. Regardless of the drinks' actual contents, some participants were told they were drinking just tonic water and some were told they were drinking tonic water with alcohol. This design allowed for a comparison of those who thought they were drinking tonic water but were actually drinking alcohol with those who thought they were drinking alcohol but were actually drinking tonic water. This research demonstrated that consuming alcohol impairs motor processes, information processing, and mood, whether or not people think they have consumed it. However, just thinking that one has consumed alcohol—regardless of whether one has actually consumed it—leads to less inhibition about various social behaviors, such as aggression and sexual arousal. Thus, some behaviors generally associated with drunkenness are accounted for by learned beliefs about intoxication rather than by alcohol's effects on the brain. Sometimes the learned expectations and the physiological effects work in opposite ways. For instance, alcohol tends to increase sexual arousal, but it interferes with sexual performance.

Q What is the definition of binge drinking?

ANSWER: drinking five or more drinks in one sitting

Your Chapter Review

It's time to complete your study experience! Go to **INQUIZITIVE** to practice actively with this chapter's concepts and get personalized feedback along the way.

Chapter Summary

What Is Consciousness?

4.1 Consciousness Is Limited Consciousness is our moment-by-moment subjective experiences. At any one time, a person can be conscious of a limited number of things. Change blindness illustrates how selective an individual's attention can be: We often do not notice large changes in an environment because we fail to pay attention.

4.2 Attention Is the Gateway to Conscious Awareness Attention involves selecting some stimuli for conscious processing while ignoring other stimuli. Attention and consciousness go hand in hand. By filtering out some information, attention helps determine what enters conscious awareness.

4.3 Laptops in the Classroom Because consciousness is limited, attending to a laptop during class may make a student more likely to miss the content of a lecture.

4.4 Unconscious Processing Can Influence Behavior Thought and behavior can be influenced by stimuli that are not experienced at a conscious level, as demonstrated by implicit biases and priming. Subliminal perception occurs when people are influenced by hidden messages. Although stimuli can have some effects on people without their awareness, there is currently no evidence that subliminal messages can compel people to perform complex actions against their will.

4.5 Automatic Processing Reduces Demands on Consciousness Although learning a task may require a great deal of concentration and controlled processing, highly practiced tasks can become automatic and require less conscious effort. Reducing the demand for conscious awareness can be a benefit in that it frees up consciousness for other tasks, but automaticity can also have costs depending on the situation.

What Is Altered Consciousness?

4.6 Meditation Produces Relaxation by Guiding Attention By guiding attention, meditation can produce an altered state of consciousness. The goal of meditation, particularly as it is practiced in the West, is to bring about a state of deep relaxation. Studies suggest that meditation can have multiple benefits for people's physical and mental health.

4.7 You Be the Psychologist: Does Meditation Change the Structure of the Brain? There are many challenges in designing studies that can conclusively demonstrate that meditation reduces brain changes associated with aging.

4.8 People Can Lose Themselves in Activities Exercise, religious practices, and other engaging activities can produce a state of altered consciousness called flow. In this state, people become completely absorbed in what they are doing. Flow is experienced as a positive state. In contrast to activities that generate flow, activities used to escape the self or reduce self-awareness can have harmful consequences.

4.9 Hypnosis Is Induced Through Suggestion Scientists debate whether hypnotized people merely play the role they are expected to play or truly experience an altered state of consciousness. Consistent with the latter view, brain imaging research has shown changes in brain activity among hypnotized participants.

What Is Sleep?

4.10 Sleep Is an Altered State of Consciousness Sleep is characterized by four stages in which brain activity varies. These stages range from short bursts of irregular waves (stages 1–2) to large, slow brain waves during deep, restful sleep (stages 3–4). REM sleep is marked by a return to short, fast brain waves and is accompanied by rapid eye movements, body paralysis, and dreaming.

4.11 People Dream While Sleeping REM dreams and non-REM dreams activate and deactivate distinct brain regions. Sigmund Freud believed that dreams reveal unconscious conflicts, but evidence does not support this view. Activation-synthesis hypothesis posits that dreams are the product of the mind's efforts to make sense of random brain activity during sleep.

4.12 Sleep Is an Adaptive Behavior Three theories account for sleep: Sleep allows the body, including the brain, to rest and restore itself. Sleep protects animals from harm at times of the day when they are most susceptible to danger. And sleep facilitates learning through the strengthening of neural connections.

4.13 Sleep Disorders Interfere with Daily Life Insomnia is an inability to sleep that causes significant problems in daily living. Other sleep disorders include obstructive sleep apnea, narcolepsy, REM behavior disorder, and somnambulism (sleepwalking).

4.14 Psychology Outside the Lab: How Can You Get a Good Night's Sleep? Good sleep hygiene involves planning, setting priorities, sticking to the plan, and saying no to behaviors that might interfere with sleep. To sleep well, people should have a routine, avoid stimulants or alcohol before trying to sleep, exercise during the day, reserve the bed for sleep, relax at bedtime, get up for a while if they have trouble falling asleep, avoid electronic devices late at night, and not try to catch up on lost sleep.

How Do Brain Injury and Drugs Affect Consciousness?

4.15 Brain Injury Can Diminish Consciousness Concussions can temporarily alter consciousness. A person in a minimally conscious state shows some awareness of external stimuli. A person with unresponsive wakefulness syndrome does not show consciousness. A person who is brain dead has no brain activity and is not alive; the person's body is being kept alive artificially.

4.16 Drugs Alter Consciousness by Changing Brain Neurochemistry Psychoactive drugs are mind-altering substances. Each drug affects one or more specific neurotransmitters, leading to psychological effects. They can be divided into categories (stimulants, depressants, opioids, hallucinogens) based on these effects, but some psychoactive drugs do not fit neatly into categories because they have various effects.

4.17 People Use—and Abuse—Many Psychoactive Drugs Stimulants, including cocaine and amphetamines, increase behavioral and mental activity. Opioids, including morphine and heroin, produce a relaxed state, insensitivity to pain, and euphoria. During the past decade, there has been an epidemic of opioid abuse, especially of heroin addiction. THC (the active ingredient in marijuana) produces a relaxed state, an uplifted mood, and perceptual and cognitive distortions. MDMA, or ecstasy, produces energizing and hallucinogenic effects.

4.18 Alcohol Abuse Is Responsible for Many Societal Problems Alcohol has its effects by activating GABA receptors. As a depressant, it decreases behavioral and mental activity. Throughout the world, men drink more than women. Alcohol's effects are influenced by the drinker's expectations.

Key Terms

activation-synthesis hypothesis, p. 137
change blindness, p. 120
circadian rhythms, p. 133
consciousness, p. 120
dreams, p. 136
endogenous attention, p. 122
exogenous attention, p. 122
hypnosis, p. 131
insomnia, p. 140
meditation, p. 127
narcolepsy, p. 141
obstructive sleep apnea, p. 141
priming, p. 125
REM sleep, p. 135
subliminal perception, p. 125
traumatic brain injury (TBI), p. 144

Practice Exercises

1. What is a key distinction between a person in an unresponsive wakefulness state and a person in a minimally conscious state?
   a. The person in the minimally conscious state is less responsive to their surroundings.
   b. The person in the unresponsive wakefulness state is less likely to regain full consciousness at some point in the future.
   c. The person in the minimally conscious state is dreaming, whereas the person in the unresponsive wakefulness state is in a coma.

2. A researcher subliminally flashes the word *thirst* to participants in Condition A, and nothing to participants in Condition B. Both groups of participants are then given the opportunity to drink some water. What do you predict about the participants' behavior?
   a. Participants in Conditions A and B will behave nearly identically.
   b. Participants in Condition A will drink more water than participants in Condition B, especially if they are thirsty.
   c. Participants in Condition B will drink more water than participants in Condition A, especially if they are thirsty.

3. Match each definition with one of the following attention terms: change blindness, automatic processing, controlled processing, shadowing.
   a. well-practiced tasks that can be done quickly, with little conscious effort
   b. repeating the auditory input to one ear while different input is transmitted to the other ear
   c. failure to notice large changes in one's environment
   d. difficult or challenging tasks that require conscious effort

4. For each description below, name the sleep disorder: insomnia, apnea, narcolepsy, somnambulism.
   a. Marcus falls asleep suddenly while practicing piano.
   b. Emma walks through the living room in the middle of the night, seemingly oblivious to those around her.
   c. Sophia spends most of the night trying to fall asleep and is anxious and has a hard time functioning during the day.
   d. Ivan snores loudly and stops breathing for short periods while sleeping.

5. Which of the following pieces of evidence does *not* support the idea that sleep is an adaptive behavior?
   a. Sleep allows the body and brain to restore themselves.
   b. Some animals, such as some frogs, do not sleep.
   c. Humans sleep at night because our ancestors were more at risk in the dark.
   d. Students who study more tend to have more REM sleep.

6. Which of the following instruction sets would a yoga teacher trained in concentrative meditation be most likely to give?
   a. "Close your eyes while sitting in a comfortable position. Let your thoughts move freely through your mind, like clouds passing through the sky. Acknowledge them, but do not react to them."
   b. "Lying on your back, rest your hands gently on your abdomen. As you breathe in and out, focus attention on your breath. Notice the rhythmic rise and fall of your abdomen and the slow, deep movement of your chest."
   c. "Standing in place, bend one knee and lift that leg. Grasp the foot and bring it back as far as possible. Then lower the foot and repeat this action with the other knee, leg, and foot."

7. Which of the following drugs is classified as a stimulant?
   a. marijuana
   b. cocaine
   c. heroin
   d. alcohol
   e. LSD

8. Which of the following is an example of exogenous attention?
   a. You focus your attention on reading the textbook.
   b. You attend to the road while driving.
   c. You attend to an unexpected, sudden loud noise.

9. Match each of the following drugs with the appropriate description of a user's typical response: alcohol, marijuana, MDMA, opiates, stimulants.

a. increased heart rate, elevated mood, restlessness
b. relaxation, contentment, vivid perceptual experiences
c. impaired motor skills, decreased sexual performance
d. energy, slight hallucinations
e. lack of pain, euphoria, intense pleasure

10. Which statement is false in regard to REM sleep?

a. You are more likely to report dreaming if woken from REM sleep.
b. You are more likely to sleepwalk during REM sleep.
c. As morning approaches, the sleep cycle becomes shorter and the sleeper spends relatively more time in REM sleep.
d. Most of the body's muscles are paralyzed during REM sleep.

5 Sensation and Perception

Big Questions

WHAT COLOR IS THE DRESS IN FIGURE 5.1? Did you answer white and gold or blue and black? This viral image was posted to the internet by a mother looking for a dress to wear to her daughter's upcoming wedding. People viewing the image could not agree on the color. How could two people seeing the same image perceive such different colors? How we see the world is a combination of incoming signals from our environment and our expectations of what these signals mean based on our experience. We expect objects to be constant and their colors consistent, even though the color signals that our eyes receive actually change as the object moves into the light or darkness. Your mind unconsciously adjusts your perception of color depending on whether it interprets an object as illuminated by a bright light or in a shadow. In this small image, the source of the light is ambiguous. If you perceive the dress as in shadow, the colors appear lighter and you will see white and gold. But if you perceive the dress as brightly lit, the colors appear darker and you will (correctly) see blue and black.

A number of brain regions work together to convert physical information from our environment into meaningful forms. Sensation and perception transform light and sound waves, chemicals, air temperature, physical pressure, and so on into phenomena such as the sight of a person you love, the smell of a spring day, the feeling of holding hands. Research on sensation and perception asks: How are we able to see, hear, taste, smell, and feel touch and pain?

FIGURE 5.1
The Dress

Learning Objectives

- Distinguish between sensation and perception.
- Describe how sensory information is translated into meaningful signals.
- Explain the concept of threshold. Distinguish between absolute threshold and difference threshold.
- Explain how thresholds are related to signal detection and sensory adaptation.

How Do We Sense and Perceive the World Around Us?

This chapter will discuss how various types of stimuli are detected, how the brain constructs useful information about the world on the basis of what has been detected, and how we use this constructed information to guide ourselves. An important lesson in this chapter is that our sensation and perception of the world do not work like cameras or digital recorders, faithfully and passively capturing the physical properties of stimuli we encounter. Rather, what we see, hear, taste, smell, or feel from touch results from brain processes that actively construct perceptual experiences from sensory information. This constant conversion of sensation to perception allows us to adapt to the details of our physical environments.

5.1 Sensory Information Is Translated into Meaningful Signals

Imagine that before you take a drink of root beer, you accidentally splash some of the soda on your face. What do your senses tell you? You smell a fragrance, you feel cool and tingly moisture on your skin, and you experience a sharp taste on your tongue. Your sensory systems have detected these features of the soda. This process is sensation.

Sensation is the detection of physical stimuli and transmission of that information to the brain. Physical stimuli can be light or sound waves, molecules of food or odor, or temperature and pressure changes. Sensation is the basic experience of those stimuli. It involves no interpretation of what we are experiencing.

Perception is the brain's further processing, organization, and interpretation of sensory information. Perception results in our conscious experience of the world. Whereas the essence of sensation is detection, the essence of perception is the construction of useful and meaningful information about a particular sensation. For example, when you are splashed on the face while taking a sip of your drink, you associate the sensations (smell, moist and tingly feeling, and sharp taste) with the perception of root beer.

Say that you drive up to a traffic signal as the light turns green. The light is detected by specialized neurons in your eyes, and those neurons transmit signals to your brain. As a result of these steps, you have sensed a stimulus: light. When your brain processes the resulting neural signals, you experience the green light and register the meaning of that signal: Go! As a result of these additional steps, you have perceived the light and the signal. (The basic movement from sensation to perception is depicted in FIGURE 5.2.)

Sensation and perception are integrated into experience. At the same time, experience guides sensation and perception. In other words, the processing of sensory information is a two-way street. **Bottom-up processing** is based on the physical features of the stimulus. As each sensory aspect of a stimulus is processed, the aspects build up into perception of that stimulus. You recognize a splash of root beer based on your experience of the scent, moisture, and taste. **Top-down processing** is how knowledge, expectations, or past experiences shape the interpretation of sensory information. That is, context affects perception: What we expect to see (higher level) influences what we perceive (lower level). We are unlikely to see a blue, apple-shaped object as a real apple because we know from past experience that apples are not blue.

sensation The detection of physical stimuli and the transmission of this information to the brain.

perception The processing, organization, and interpretation of sensory signals in the brain.

bottom-up processing Perception based on the physical features of the stimulus.

top-down processing The interpretation of sensory information based on knowledge, expectations, and past experiences.

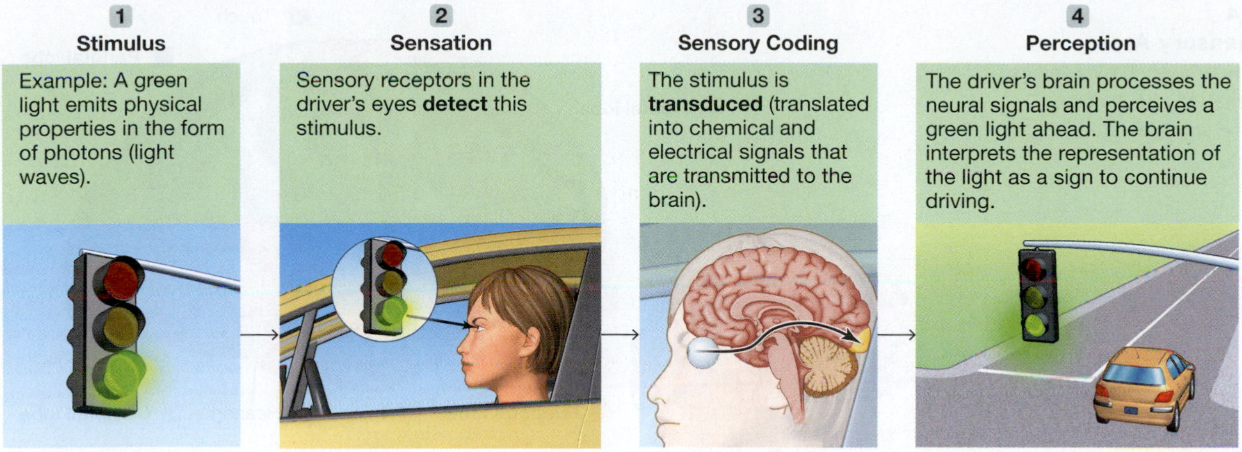

1
Stimulus
Example: A green light emits physical properties in the form of photons (light waves).
2
Sensation
Sensory receptors in the driver's eyes **detect** this stimulus.
3
Sensory Coding
The stimulus is **transduced** (translated into chemical and electrical signals that are transmitted to the brain).
4
Perception
The driver's brain processes the neural signals and perceives a green light ahead. The brain interprets the representation of the light as a sign to continue driving.

FIGURE 5.2
From Sensation to Perception

Consider the incomplete letters in **FIGURE 5.3**. The same shape appears in the center of each word, but you perceive (lower level) the shape first as *H* and then as *A*. Your perception depends on which interpretation makes sense in the context of the particular word (higher level). Likewise, Y0U C4N R3AD TH15 PR377Y W3LL even though it is nonsensical. The ability to make sense of "incorrect" stimuli through top-down processing is why proofreading our own writing can be so difficult.

FIGURE 5.3
Context
Context plays an important role in object recognition.

TRANSDUCTION Our sensory systems translate the physical properties of stimuli into patterns of neural impulses. The different features of the physical environment are coded by activity in different neurons. For example, a green stoplight will be coded by a particular neural response pattern in part of the eye before being processed by areas of the brain involved in perceiving visual information.

When a hand touches a hot skillet, that information must be sent to the brain. The brain cannot process the physical stimuli directly, so the stimuli must be translated into signals the brain can interpret. The translation of stimuli is called **transduction**. This process involves specialized cells in the sense organs called *sensory receptors*. The sensory receptors receive stimulation—physical stimulation in the case of vision, hearing, and touch and chemical stimulation in the case of taste and smell. The sensory receptors then pass the resulting impulses to the brain in the form of neural impulses. With the exception of smell, most sensory information first goes to the thalamus, a structure in the middle of the brain (see Figure 3.26). This information is projected from the thalamus to a specific region of the cerebral cortex for each sense. With smell, sensory information bypasses the thalamus and goes directly to the cortex. In these primary sensory areas, the perceptual process begins in earnest (**FIGURE 5.4**).

transduction The process by which sensory stimuli are converted to neural signals the brain can interpret.

Each sense organ contains receptors designed to detect specific types of stimuli. For example, receptors in the visual system respond only to light waves and can signal only visual information. (**TABLE 5.1** lists the stimuli, receptors, and pathways to the brain for each major sensory system.)

QUALITY VERSUS QUANTITY To function effectively, the brain needs *qualitative* and *quantitative* information about a stimulus. Qualitative information consists of the most basic qualities of a stimulus. For example, it is the difference between a tuba's honk and a flute's toot. It is the difference between a salty taste

FIGURE 5.4
Primary Sensory Areas
These are the primary brain regions where information about vision, hearing, taste, smell, and touch are projected.

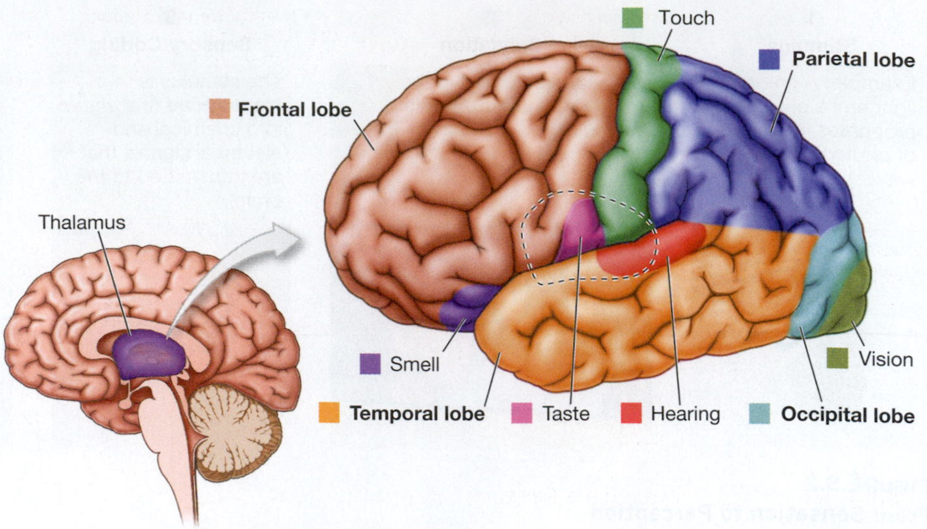

and a sweet one. Quantitative information consists of the degree, or magnitude, of those qualities: the loudness of the honk, the softness of the toot, the relative saltiness or sweetness. If you were approaching a traffic light, qualitative information might include whether the light was red or green. Regardless of the color, quantitative information would include the brightness of the light.

We can identify qualitative information because different sensory receptors respond to qualitatively different stimuli. In contrast, quantitative differences in stimuli are coded by the rate of a particular neuron's firing or the number of neurons firing. A more rapidly firing neuron is responding at a higher frequency to a more intense stimulus, such as a brighter light, a louder sound, or a heavier weight (FIGURE 5.5).

Table 5.1 The Stimuli, Receptors, and Pathways for Each Sense

SENSE	STIMULI	RECEPTORS	PATHWAYS TO THE BRAIN
Vision	Light waves	Light-sensitive rods and cones in retina of eye	Optic nerve
Hearing	Sound waves	Pressure-sensitive hair cells in cochlea of inner ear	Auditory nerve
Taste	Molecules dissolved in fluid on the tongue	Cells in taste buds on the tongue	Portions of facial, glossopharyngeal, and vagus nerves
Smell	Molecules dissolved in fluid on membranes in the nose	Sensitive ends of olfactory mucous neurons in the mucous membranes	Olfactory nerve
Touch	Pressure on the skin	Sensitive ends of touch neurons in skin	Cranial nerves for touch above the neck, spinal nerves for touch elsewhere

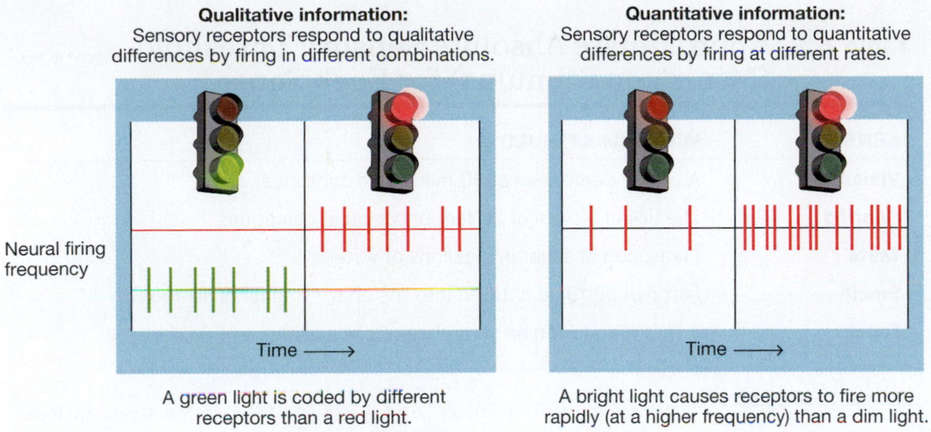

Qualitative information:
Sensory receptors respond to qualitative differences by firing in different combinations.
Quantitative information:
Sensory receptors respond to quantitative differences by firing at different rates.
Neural firing frequency
Time
Time
A green light is coded by different receptors than a red light.
A bright light causes receptors to fire more rapidly (at a higher frequency) than a dim light.

FIGURE 5.5
Qualitative Versus Quantitative Sensory Information

Sensation and perception result from a symphony of sensory receptors and the neurons those receptors communicate with. The receptors and neurons fire in different combinations and at different rates. The sum of this activity is the huge range of perceptions that make up our experience of the world.

Q What is transduction?

ANSWER: the translation of physical stimuli received by sensory receptors into neural signals that the brain can interpret

5.2 Detection Requires a Certain Amount of the Stimulus

For more than a century, psychologists have tried to understand the relationship between the world's physical properties and how we sense and perceive them. *Psychophysics*, a subfield developed during the nineteenth century by the researchers Ernst Weber and Gustav Fechner, examines our psychological experiences of physical stimuli. For example, how much physical energy is required for our sense organs to detect a stimulus? How much change is required before we notice that change? To study the limits of humans' sensory systems, researchers present very subtle changes in stimuli and observe how participants respond.

absolute threshold The minimum intensity of stimulation necessary to detect a sensation half the time.

difference threshold The minimum amount of change required to detect a difference between two stimuli.

SENSORY THRESHOLDS Your sensory organs constantly acquire information from your environment. You do not notice much of this information. It has to surpass some level before you can detect it. The **absolute threshold** is the minimum intensity of stimulation that must occur before you experience a sensation. In other words, it is the stimulus intensity you would detect 50 percent of the time (FIGURE 5.6). For instance, how loudly must someone in the next room whisper for you to hear it? In this case, the absolute threshold for auditory stimuli would be the quietest whisper you could hear half the time. (TABLE 5.2 lists some approximate minimum stimuli for each sense.)

A **difference threshold**, sometimes called a *just noticeable difference*, is the smallest difference between two stimuli that you can notice. If your friend is watching a television show while

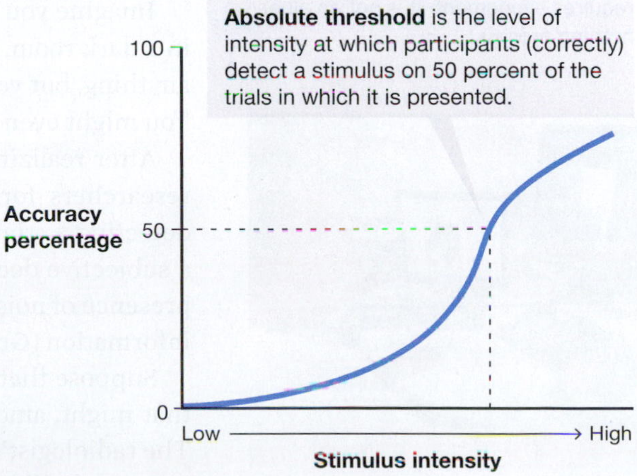

FIGURE 5.6
Absolute Threshold
This graph shows the relation between the intensity of stimulus input and a person's ability to correctly detect the input.

Table 5.2 Approximate Absolute Sensory Threshold (Minimum Stimulus) for Each Sense

SENSE	MINIMUM STIMULUS
Vision	A candle flame seen at 30 miles on a dark, clear night
Hearing	The tick of a clock at 20 feet under quiet conditions
Taste	1 teaspoon of sugar in 2 gallons of water
Smell	1 drop of perfume diffused into the entire volume of six rooms
Touch	A fly's wing falling on your cheek from a distance of 0.04 inch

SOURCE: Galanter (1962).

FIGURE 5.7
Difference Threshold
How much does the television volume need to change for you to notice? That amount of change is the difference threshold.

you are reading and a commercial comes on that is louder than the show, you might look up, noticing that something has changed (FIGURE 5.7). The difference threshold is the minimum change in volume required for you to detect a difference.

The difference threshold increases as the stimulus becomes more intense. Pick up a 1-ounce letter and a 2-ounce letter, and you will easily detect the difference. But pick up a 5-pound package and a package that weighs 1 ounce more, and the difference will be harder, maybe impossible, to tell. The principle at work here is called *Weber's law*. This law states that the just noticeable difference between two stimuli is based on a proportion of the original stimulus rather than on a fixed amount of difference. That is, the more intense the stimulus, the bigger the change needed for you to notice.

SIGNAL DETECTION THEORY According to classical psychophysics, sensory thresholds were unambiguous. Either you detected something or you did not, depending on whether the intensity of the stimulus was above or below a particular level. As research progressed, it became clear that early psychophysicists had ignored the fact that people are bombarded by competing stimuli, including the "noise" produced by both internal stimuli (moods, emotions, memory, physical states such as arousal or nausea) and other external stimuli (such as an air conditioner's sound, a cold wind, a cluttered room). The competing internal and external sources affect judgment and attention.

signal detection theory (SDT)
A theory of perception based on the idea that the detection of a stimulus requires a judgment—it is not an all-or-nothing process.

Imagine you are a participant in a study of sensory thresholds. You are sitting in a dark room, and an experimenter asks if you heard a sound. You did not hear anything, but you might second-guess yourself since someone has asked about it. You might even convince yourself that you sensed a weak stimulus.

After realizing that their methods of testing absolute thresholds were flawed, researchers formulated **signal detection theory (SDT)**. This theory states that detecting a stimulus is not an objective process. Detecting a stimulus is instead a subjective decision with two components: (1) sensitivity to the stimulus in the presence of noise and (2) the criteria used to make the judgment from ambiguous information (Green & Swets, 1966).

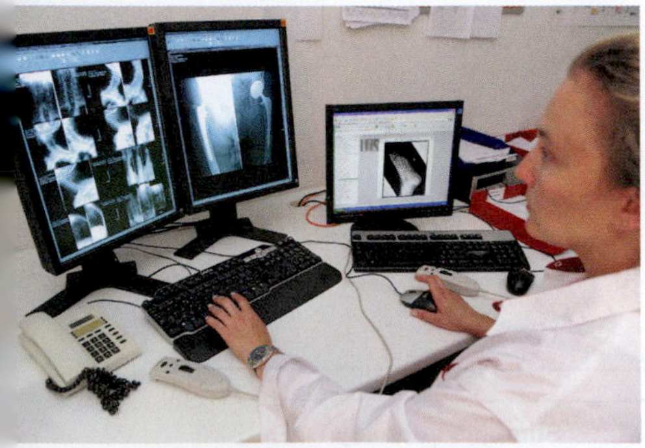

FIGURE 5.8
Signal Detection Theory
Radiology illustrates the subjective nature of detecting a stimulus.

Suppose that a radiologist is looking for the kind of faint shadow on an X-ray that might, among other possibilities, signal an early-stage cancer (FIGURE 5.8). The radiologist's judgment can be influenced by knowledge about the patient (e.g., age, sex, family medical history), medical training, experience with similar X-rays, motivation, and attention. The radiologist's judgment can also be influenced by awareness of the consequences: Being wrong could mean missing a fatal cancer or, conversely, could cause unnecessary and potentially dangerous treatment.

Any research study on signal detection involves a series of trials in which a stimulus is presented in only some trials. In each trial, participants must state whether they sensed the stimulus. A trial of this kind, in which a participant judges whether an event occurs, can have one of four outcomes. If the signal is presented and the participant detects it, the outcome is a *hit*. If the participant fails to detect the signal, the outcome is a *miss*. If the participant reports there was a signal that was not presented, the outcome is a *false alarm*. If the signal is not presented and the participant does not detect it, the outcome is a *correct rejection* (**FIGURE 5.9**). The participant's sensitivity to the signal is usually computed by a formula comparing the hit rate with the false-alarm rate. This comparison corrects for any bias the participant might bring to the testing situation.

Response bias is a participant's tendency to report or not report detecting the signal in an ambiguous trial. The participant might be strongly biased against responding and need a great deal of evidence that the signal is present. Under other conditions, that same participant might need only a small amount of evidence. In the example of the radiologist, the possibility of causing unnecessary and painful treatment for a slow-growing cancer that is not life-threatening might cause the radiologist to suggest a cancer diagnosis only with clear X-ray evidence—that is, it might create a bias to say, "No, stimulus absent." On the flip side, the possibility of missing a potentially deadly, fast-growing cancer might cause the radiologist to diagnose possible cancer with relatively weak X-ray evidence—that is, it might create a bias to say, "Yes, stimulus present."

Learning Tip

Signal detection theory is important because it distinguishes sensitivity from response bias. To remember the difference, think of *sen*sitivity as determined by what your *senses* can detect, and response bias as a tendency that can be *biased* or pushed around depending on the consequences of the decision.

SENSORY ADAPTATION Our sensory systems are tuned to detect changes in our surroundings. It is important for us to be able to detect such changes because they might require responses. It is less important to keep responding to unchanging stimuli. **Sensory adaptation** is a decrease in sensitivity to a constant level of stimulation.

Imagine you visit a friend's house, and your friend has a cat. When entering the house, you notice a faint smell of the litter box, but when you mention this your friend cannot smell it. A little while into your visit, you no longer notice the smell yourself. Researchers have found that if a stimulus is presented continuously, the responses of the sensory systems that detect it tend to diminish over time. Similarly, when a continuous stimulus stops, the sensory systems usually respond strongly as well.

Q **While waiting for a friend, you mistakenly wave to someone who looks like your friend but is not. In signal detection terms, what type of outcome is this?**

ANSWER: It is a false alarm because you detected a signal that was not really present.

5.3 The Brain Constructs a Stable Representation of the World from Five Senses

In general, we think of the five senses as operating independently because they detect different environmental signals and engage different sense organs and brain circuits (see Table 5.1 for a summary). However, perception results from a

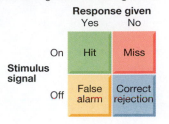

There are four possible outcomes when a participant is asked whether something occurred during a trial:

Stimulus signal	Response given: Yes	Response given: No
On	Hit	Miss
Off	False alarm	Correct rejection

Those who are biased toward reporting a signal tend to be "yea-sayers." They have many false alarms:

Stimulus signal	Response given: Yes	Response given: No
On	89%	11%
Off	41%	59%

Those who are biased toward denying that a signal occurred tend to be "nay-sayers." They have many misses:

Stimulus signal	Response given: Yes	Response given: No
On	45%	55%
Off	26%	74%

FIGURE 5.9
Payoff Matrices for Signal Detection Theory
The percentages in this figure were invented to show representative numbers. Actual percentages vary from question to question.

sensory adaptation A decrease in sensitivity to a constant level of stimulation.

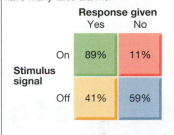

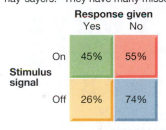

construction of these signals into a stable, unified representation of the world, and most of the things we perceive involve more than one sensation. For instance, an orange engages your sense of vision, touch, smell, and taste, and maybe even hearing as you peel off the skin. The expectation of the taste you will experience when biting into an orange is based on visual and odor cues and your past experiences that lead you to anticipate the taste you associate with an orange. If, instead, you taste a lime, you might have an especially strong reaction because your expectations were violated. At times, our perception of one sense is influenced by input from another sense.

An example of how two senses interact in perception is illustrated in the McGurk effect, an auditory illusion in which auditory and visual cues provide conflicting information (McGurk & MacDonald, 1976). In a typical version of this illusion, participants listen to the sound "BA" repeatedly. This is presented along with seeing a person's mouth pronouncing "BA" on some trials. On other trials, it is paired with a person mouthing "DA," and on still other trials, the person's mouth is pronouncing "VA." Although the auditory signal is consistently *BA*, what the participant hears will vary depending on whether the visual cues suggest the person is saying *BA*, *DA*, or *VA*.

SYNESTHESIA Even though perception can be influenced by signals from multiple senses, most of us can still distinguish the input from the different senses. That is, we are able to differentiate the color and shape of an orange from its smell and its taste. However, some people experience unusual combinations of sensations. Consider the case of Bill, who hates driving because the sight of road signs tastes like a mixture of pistachio ice cream and earwax (McNeil, 2006). This sort of experience—such as when a visual image has a taste—is called *synesthesia*. For another person with synesthesia, M.M., any personal name has a specific taste; for example, the name *John* tastes like cornbread (Simner et al., 2006). For others with synesthesia, colors evoke smells, sights evoke sounds, and numbers come in colors (e.g., 5 is always green, 2 is always orange; **FIGURE 5.10**). For each person, the associations do not vary—if road signs have a taste, for example, they always taste the same. Reports of people with synesthesia date as far back as ancient Greece (Ferry, 2002). Estimates of the percentage of the population that report these cross-sensory experiences range from 1 in 2,000 to 1 in 200. How can we understand such bizarre sensations?

FIGURE 5.10
Synesthesia
This figure is an artistic rendering of the color/letter and color/number associations for one person with synesthesia.

The neurologist V. S. Ramachandran conducted a series of experiments to better understand what is happening when someone reports, for example, that a sound is lime green or that chicken tastes pointy (Ramachandran & Hubbard, 2001). Because the brain area involved in seeing colors is near the brain area involved in understanding numbers, he theorized that in people with color/number synesthesia, these two brain areas are somehow connected. In this situation, one area of the brain might have adopted another area's role. To test his hypothesis, Ramachandran examined brain scans taken of people with synesthesia when they looked at black numbers on a white background. He found evidence of neural activity in the brain area responsible for color vision. Control participants without synesthesia show evidence for activity in this brain area when they looked at the same numbers. Although synesthesia is a rare condition, it shows that there is not a perfect correspondence between the physical world and our experience of it. Yes, our brains create stable representations based on the information our senses provide. Our senses often provide imperfect information, however, and at times our brains may interpret this information imperfectly.

Q If a person hears the taste of food, what would this form of perception be called?

ANSWER: synesthesia

How Do We See?

If we acquire knowledge through our senses, then vision is by far our most important source of knowledge. Vision allows us to perceive information at a distance. Does a place look safe or dangerous? Does a person look friendly or hostile? Even our metaphors for knowledge and for understanding are often visual: "I see," "The answer is clear," "I'm fuzzy on that point." It is not surprising, then, that most of the scientific study of sensation and perception is concerned with vision. Indeed, much of the brain is involved in seeing. Some estimates suggest that up to half of the cerebral cortex may participate in visual perception in some way.

Learning Objectives

- Explain how light is processed by the eyes and the brain.
- Compare and contrast trichromatic and opponent-process theories of color vision.
- Identify the Gestalt principles of perceptual organization and describe object constancy.
- Distinguish between binocular and monocular depth cues.
- Describe depth perception, size perception, and motion perception.

5.4 Sensory Receptors in the Eye Transmit Visual Information to the Brain

Sight seems so effortless, so automatic, that most of us take it for granted. Every time we open our eyes, our brain springs into action to make sense of the energy arriving through it. Of course, the brain can do so only based on sensory signals from the eyes. If the eyes are damaged, the sensory system fails to process new information.

This section focuses on how energy is transduced in the visual system and then perceived, but what we commonly call *seeing* is much more than transducing energy. As the psychologist James Enns notes in his book *The Thinking Eye, the Seeing Brain* (2005), very little of what we call seeing takes place in the eyes. Rather, what we see results from constructive processes that occur throughout much of the brain to produce our visual experiences. In fact, even if one's eyes are completely functional, damage to the visual cortex will impair vision.

Some people describe the human eye as working like a crude camera, in that it focuses light to form an image. This analogy does not do justice to the intricate processes that take place in the eye, however. Light first passes through the *cornea*, the eye's thick, transparent outer layer. The cornea focuses the incoming light, which then enters the *lens*. There, the light is bent further inward and focused to form an image on the **retina**, the thin inner surface of the back of the eyeball. The retina contains the sensory receptors that transduce light into neural signals. If you shine a light in someone's eyes so that you can see the person's retina, you are in fact looking at the only part of the central nervous system that is visible from outside the body.

retina The thin inner surface of the back of the eyeball, which contains the sensory receptors that transduce light into neural signals.

More light is focused at the cornea than at the lens. But the lens is adjustable, whereas the cornea is not. The *pupil*, the dark circle at the center of the eye, is a small opening in the front of the lens. By contracting (closing) or dilating (opening), the pupil determines how much light enters the eye. The *iris*, a circular muscle, determines the eye's color and controls the pupil's size. The pupil dilates not only in dim light but also when we see something we like, such as a beautiful painting or a cute baby (Lick et al., 2016).

Behind the iris, muscles change the shape of the lens. They flatten it to focus on distant objects and thicken it to focus on closer objects. This process is called *accommodation*. The lens and cornea work together to collect and focus light rays reflected from an object. As people get older, the lens hardens and it becomes more difficult to focus on close images, a condition known as *presbyopia*. After age 40, many people require reading glasses when trying to focus on nearby objects.

rods Retinal cells that respond to low levels of light and result in black-and-white perception.

cones Retinal cells that respond to higher levels of light and result in color perception.

RODS AND CONES The retina has two types of receptor cells: **rods** and **cones**. The name of each type comes from its distinctive shape. Rods respond at extremely low

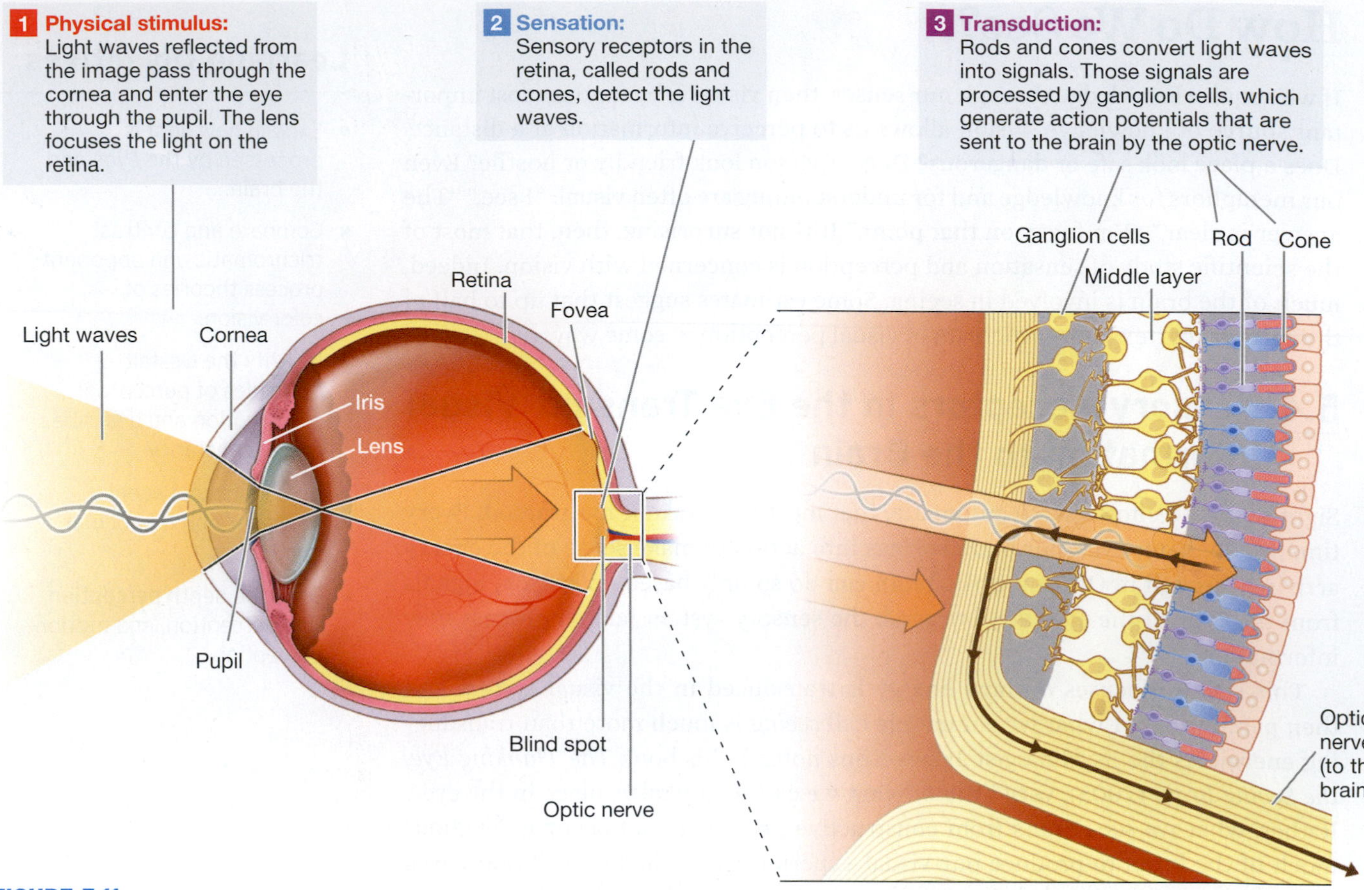

1 Physical stimulus:
Light waves reflected from the image pass through the cornea and enter the eye through the pupil. The lens focuses the light on the retina.
2 Sensation:
Sensory receptors in the retina, called rods and cones, detect the light waves.
3 Transduction:
Rods and cones convert light waves into signals. Those signals are processed by ganglion cells, which generate action potentials that are sent to the brain by the optic nerve.
Light waves
Cornea
Retina
Fovea
Iris
Lens
Pupil
Blind spot
Optic nerve
Ganglion cells
Middle layer
Rod
Cone
Optic nerve (to the brain)

FIGURE 5.11
How We Are Able to See

levels of light and are responsible primarily for night vision. They do not support color vision, and they are poor at fine detail. This is why, on a moonless night, objects appear in shades of gray. It is also why it is difficult to read without sufficient light, since reading involves decoding the fine details of different letters. In contrast to rods, cones are less sensitive to low levels of light. They are responsible primarily for vision under brighter conditions and for seeing both color and detail.

fovea The center of the retina, where cones are densely packed.

Each retina holds approximately 120 million rods and 6 million cones. Near the retina's center, cones are densely packed in a small region called the **fovea** (FIGURE 5.11). Although cones are spread throughout the remainder of the retina (except in the blind spot, as you will see shortly), they become increasingly scarce near the outside edge. Conversely, rods are concentrated at the retina's edges. None are in the fovea. If you look directly at a very dim star on a moonless night, the star will appear to vanish. Its light will fall on the fovea, where there are no rods. If you look just to the side of the star, however, the star will be visible. Its light will fall just outside the fovea, where there are rods.

TRANSMISSION FROM THE EYE TO THE BRAIN The visual process begins with the generation of electrical signals by the sensory receptors in the retina. These receptors contain *photopigments*, protein molecules that become unstable and split apart when exposed to light. Rods and cones do not fire action potentials like other neurons. Instead, decomposition of the photopigments alters the membrane potential of the photoreceptors and triggers action potentials in downstream neurons. Immediately after light is transduced by the rods and cones, other

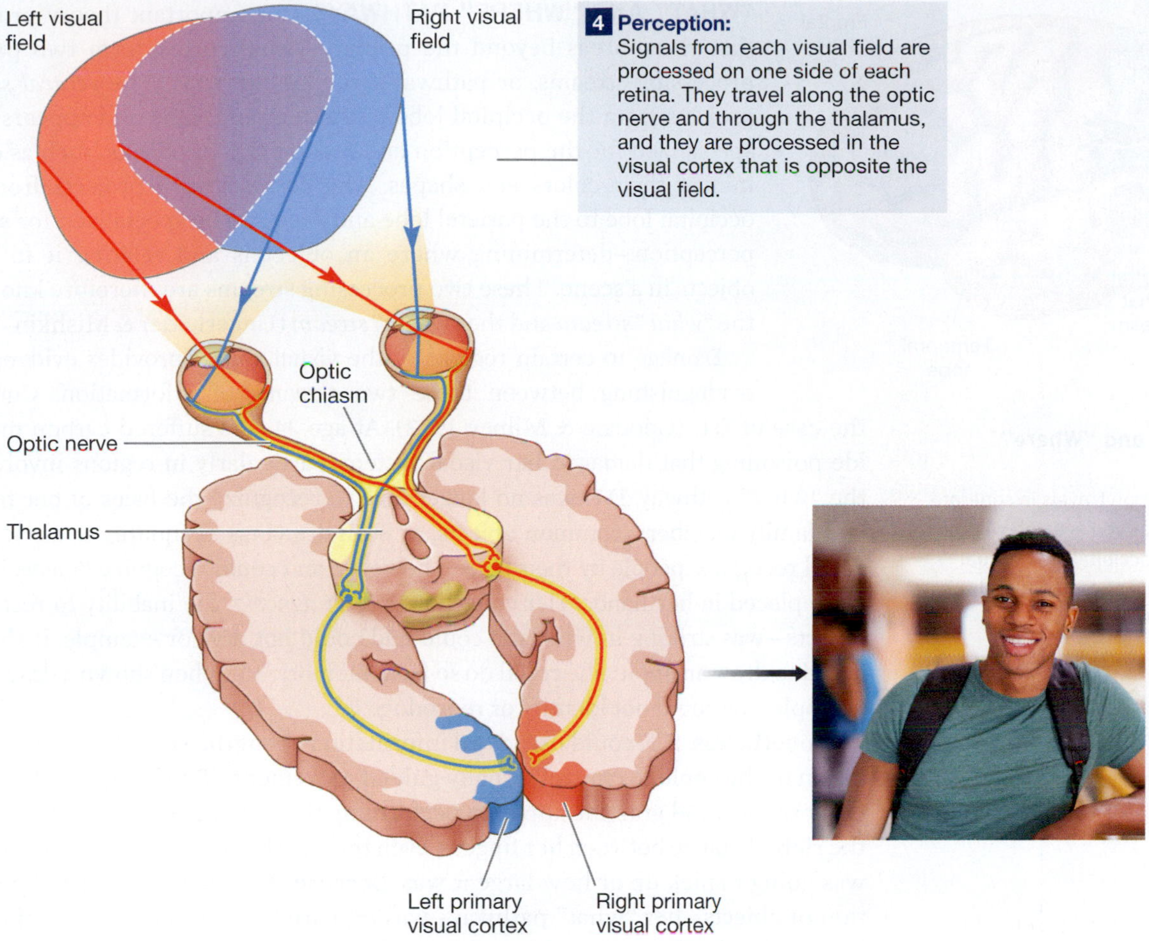

Left visual field
Right visual field
4 Perception:
Signals from each visual field are processed on one side of each retina. They travel along the optic nerve and through the thalamus, and they are processed in the visual cortex that is opposite the visual field.
Optic chiasm
Optic nerve
Thalamus
Left primary visual cortex
Right primary visual cortex

cells in the middle layer of the retina perform a series of sophisticated computations. The outputs from these cells converge on the retinal *ganglion cells*. Ganglion cells are the first neurons in the visual pathway with axons. During the process of seeing, they are the first neurons to generate action potentials.

The ganglion cells send their signals along their axons from inside the eye to the thalamus. These axons are gathered into a bundle, the *optic nerve*, which exits the eye at the back of the retina. The point at which the optic nerve exits the retina has no rods or cones, producing a blind spot in each eye. If you stretch out one of your arms, make a fist, and look at your fist, the size that your fist appears to you is about the size of your blind spot. Because your two eyes are separated by a few inches, the blind spot for each eye covers a slightly different region of the visual space in front of you. The brain normally fills in this gap automatically, so you are not aware of it. However, you can find your blind spot by using the exercise in **FIGURE 5.12**.

At the *optic chiasm*, half of the axons in the optic nerves cross. (The axons that cross are the ones that start from the portion of the retina nearest the nose.) This arrangement causes all information from the left side of visual space (i.e., everything visible to the left of the point of gaze) to be projected to the right hemisphere of the brain, and vice versa. In each case, the information reaches the visual areas of the thalamus and then travels to the *primary visual cortex*, cortical areas in the occipital lobes at the back of the head. The pathway from the retina to this region carries all the information that we consciously experience as seeing.

FIGURE 5.12
Find Your Blind Spot
To find your blind spot using your right eye, hold this book in front of you and look at the dot. Close your left eye. Move the book toward and away from your face until the rabbit's head disappears. You can repeat this exercise for your left eye by turning the book upside down.

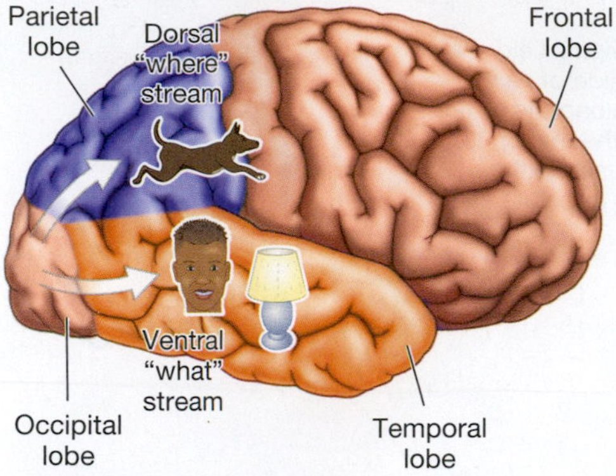

FIGURE 5.13
The "What" and "Where" Pathways
Visual information travels in separate "streams"—what you see and where it is—from the occipital lobe (visual cortex) to different parts of the brain for further processing.

"WHAT" AND "WHERE" PATHWAYS One important theory proposes that visual areas beyond the primary visual cortex form two parallel processing streams, or pathways (see FIGURE 5.13). The *ventral stream* projects from the occipital lobe to the temporal lobe and appears to be specialized for the perception and recognition of objects, such as determining their colors and shapes. The *dorsal stream* projects from the occipital lobe to the parietal lobe and seems to be specialized for spatial perception—determining where an object is and relating it to other objects in a scene. These two processing streams are therefore known as the *"what" stream* and the *"where" stream* (Ungerleider & Mishkin, 1982).

Damage to certain regions of the visual cortex provides evidence for distinguishing between these two streams of information. Consider the case of D.F. (Goodale & Milner, 1992). At age 34, she suffered carbon monoxide poisoning that damaged her visual system, particularly in regions involved in the "what" pathway. D.F. was no longer able to recognize the faces of her friends and family members, common objects, or even drawings of squares or circles. She could recognize people by their voices, however, and could recognize objects if they were placed in her hands. Her condition—*object agnosia*, the inability to recognize objects—was striking in what she could and could not do. For example, if she was asked to draw an apple, she could do so from memory, but when shown a drawing of an apple, she could not identify or reproduce it.

Nonetheless, D.F. could use visual information about the size, shape, and orientation of the apple to control visually guided movements. She could reach around other objects and grab the apple. In performing this action, D.F. would put exactly the right distance between her fingers, even though she could not tell you what she was going to pick up or how large it was. Because D.F.'s conscious visual perception of objects—her "what" pathway—was impaired, she was not aware of taking in any visual information about objects she saw. Because her "where" pathway appeared to be intact, these regions of her visual cortex allowed her to use information about the size and location of objects despite her lack of awareness about those objects. As illustrated by D.F.'s case, different neurological systems operate independently to help us understand the world around us.

Q **Does the fovea have more rods or cones?**

ANSWER: The fovea has only cones, no rods.

5.5 The Color of Light Is Determined by Its Wavelength

We can distinguish among millions of shades of color. Color is not a property of an object, however. The object appears to be a particular color because of the wavelengths of light it reflects. It is a weird but true fact: Color does not exist in the physical world. It is always a product of our visual system.

Visible light consists of electromagnetic waves ranging in length from about 400 to 700 nanometers (abbreviated *nm*; this length is one billionth of a meter). In simplest terms, the color of light is determined by the wavelengths of the electromagnetic waves that reach the eye. In the center of the retina, the cone cells transduce light into neural impulses in downstream neurons. Different theories account for this transduction.

TRICHROMATIC THEORY According to the *trichromatic theory*, color vision results from activity in three types of cones that are sensitive to different wavelengths. One type of cone is most sensitive to short wavelengths (blue–violet light), another type is most sensitive to medium wavelengths (yellow–green light), and the third type is most sensitive to long wavelengths (red–orange light; **FIGURE 5.14**). The three types of cones in the retina are therefore called "S," "M," and "L" cones because they respond maximally to short, medium, and long wavelengths, respectively. For example, yellow light looks yellow because it stimulates the L and M cones about equally and hardly stimulates the S cones. In fact, we can create yellow light by combining red light and green light because each type of light stimulates the corresponding cone population. As far as the brain can tell, there is no difference between yellow light and a combination of red light and green light!

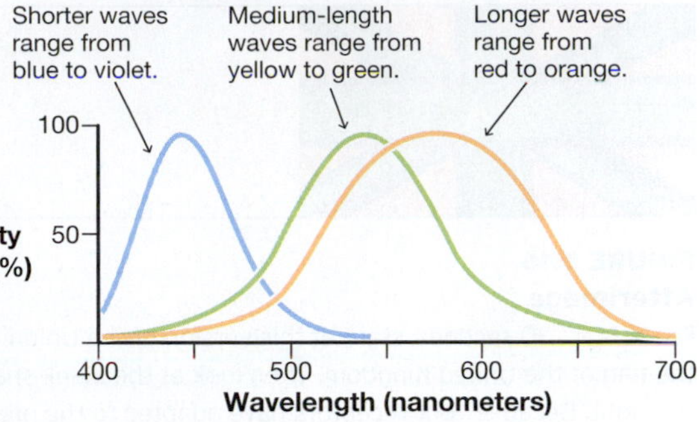

FIGURE 5.14
The Experience of Color
The color of light is determined by the wavelength of the electromagnetic wave that reaches the eye. This graph shows the percentage of light at different wavelengths that is absorbed by each kind of cone.

There are two main types of color blindness, determined by the relative activity among the three types of cone receptors. The term *blindness* is somewhat misleading, because people with this condition do see color. They just have partial blindness for certain colors. People may be missing the photopigment sensitive to either medium or long wavelengths, resulting in red–green color blindness (**FIGURE 5.15**). Alternatively, they may be missing the short-wavelength photopigment, resulting in blue–yellow color blindness. These genetic disorders occur in about 8 percent of males but less than 1 percent of females.

OPPONENT-PROCESS THEORY Some aspects of color vision cannot be explained by the responses of three types of cones in the retina. For example, why can some people with red–green color blindness see yellow? In addition, most people have trouble visualizing certain color mixtures. It is easier to imagine reddish yellow or bluish green, say, than reddish green or bluish yellow. In addition, some colors seem to be "opposites."

A complement to the trichromatic theory is the *opponent-process theory* (Hering, 1878/1964). According to this theory, red and green are opponent colors, as are blue and yellow. When we stare at a red image for some time, we see a green afterimage when we look away; when we stare at a green image, we see a red afterimage. In the former case, the receptors for red become fatigued when you stare at red. The green receptors are not fatigued and therefore the afterimage appears green (**FIGURE 5.16**).

Since colors are themselves optical effects, how do we account for what appear to be opponent colors? While the trichromatic theory characterizes the properties of different types of cones, the opponent-process theory describes the second stage in visual processing. This stage occurs in the ganglion cells—the cells that make up the optic nerve, which carries information to the brain. Different combinations of cones converge on the ganglion cells in the retina. One type of ganglion cell receives excitatory input from L cones (the ones that respond to long wavelengths, which are seen as red) but is inhibited by M cones (medium wavelengths, which are seen as green). Cells of this type create the perception that red and green are opponents. Another type of ganglion cell is excited by input from S cones (short wavelengths, which are seen as blue) but is inhibited by both L- and M-cone activity (long and medium wavelengths, which when combined are perceived as yellow). These different types of ganglion cells, working in opposing pairs, create the perception that blue and yellow are opponents.

(a)

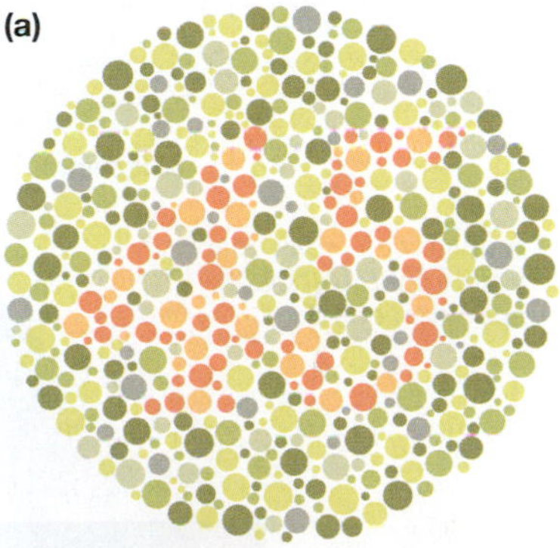

(b)

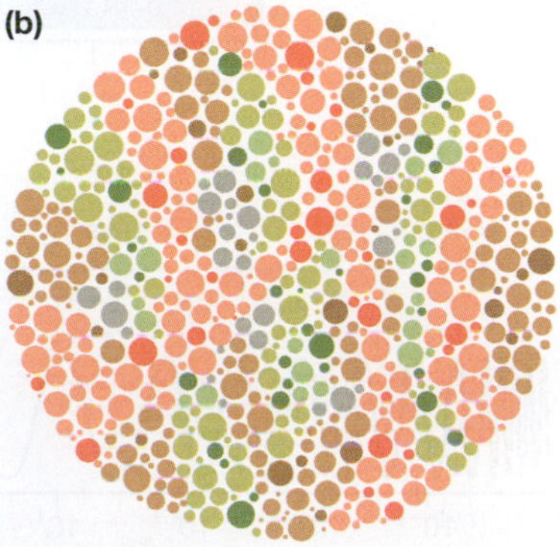

FIGURE 5.15
Red-Green Color Blindness
You should be able to see the number 45 in one of these circles. **(a)** If you are not red-green color-blind, you will see 45 here. **(b)** If you are red-green color-blind, you will see 45 here.

FIGURE 5.16
Afterimage
For at least 30 seconds, stare at this version of the Union Jack, the flag of the United Kingdom. Then look at the blank space to the right. Because your receptors have adapted to the green and orange in the first image, the afterimage appears in the opponent colors red and blue.

HUE, SATURATION, AND LIGHTNESS Ultimately, how the brain converts physical energy to the experience of color is quite complex and can be understood only by considering the response of the visual system to different wavelengths at the same time. In fact, when we see white light, our eyes are receiving the entire range of wavelengths in the visible spectrum (**FIGURE 5.17**).

Color is categorized along three dimensions: hue, saturation, and lightness. *Hue* consists of the distinctive characteristics that place a particular color in the spectrum—the color's greenness or orangeness, for example. These characteristics depend primarily on the light's dominant wavelength when it reaches the eye. *Saturation* is the purity of the color. Saturation varies according to the mixture of wavelengths in a stimulus. Basic colors of the spectrum (e.g., blue, green, red) have only one wavelength, whereas pastels (e.g., baby blue, emerald green, and pink) have a mixture of many wavelengths, so they are less pure. *Lightness* is the color's perceived intensity. This characteristic is determined chiefly by the total amount of light reaching the eye. How light something seems also depends on the background, however, since the same color may be perceived differently depending on whether you are looking at it against a bright or dark background (**FIGURE 5.18**).

Q **Are afterimages best explained by trichromatic theory or opponent-process theory? How so?**

ANSWER: Opponent-process theory best explains afterimages. According to this theory, staring at one color causes receptor fatigue. Looking elsewhere then leads unfatigued receptors for the "opposing," color to produce an afterimage.

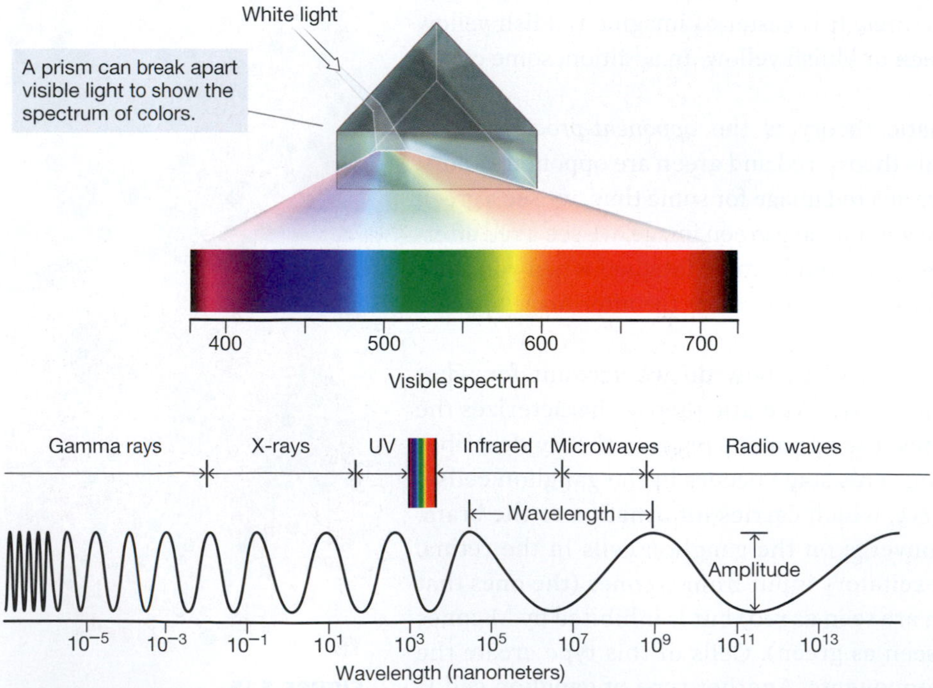

FIGURE 5.17
The Color Spectrum
When white light shines through a prism, the spectrum of color that is visible to humans is revealed. As shown here, the visible color spectrum is only a small part of the electromagnetic spectrum: It consists of electromagnetic wavelengths from just under 400 nm (the color violet) to just over 700 nm (the color red).

FIGURE 5.18
Lightness
For each pair, which central square is lighter? In fact, the central squares in each pair are identical. Most people see the gray square that is surrounded with red, for example, as lighter than the gray square surrounded with green.

5.6 Perceiving Objects Requires Organization of Visual Information

The information the retina projects to the brain results in a two-dimensional representation of edges and colors that the brain automatically transforms into a three-dimensional world of objects and background. Within the brain, what exactly happens to the information the senses take in? How does that information get organized? The visual system uses a number of organizing principles to help determine the meaning of visual input—or the most likely interpretation based on experience with the world. Perceptual psychologists attempt to characterize these basic principles of visual perception.

Optical illusions are among the tools psychologists have for understanding how the brain organizes and interprets such information. Many perceptual psychologists believe that illusions reveal the mechanisms that help visual systems determine the identity of objects, their sizes, and their distances in the environment. In doing so, illusions illustrate how we form accurate representations of the three-dimensional world. Researchers rely on these tricks to discover automatic perceptual systems that, in most circumstances, result in accurate perception.

FIGURE 5.19
Figure or Ground?
Distinguishing the figure from the background is a basic organizing principle of vision. Here, you see either two faces against a yellow background or a yellow vase against a black background, but you cannot see both at the same time.

FIGURE AND GROUND One of the visual system's most basic organizing principles is distinguishing between figure and ground. In order to simplify the visual world, we automatically divide visual scenes into objects and background. Determining that a collection of lines, shapes, and colors composes one figure or object in turn changes how we perceive those visual cues moving forward.

A classic illustration distinguishing figure from ground is the *reversible figure illusion*. In **FIGURE 5.19**, you can see either a full vase or two faces looking at each other—but not both at the same time. In identifying either figure—indeed, *any* figure—the brain assigns the rest of the scene to the background. In this illusion, the "correct" assignment of figure and ground is ambiguous. The figures periodically reverse (switch back and forth) as the visual system strives to make sense of the stimulation. In ways like this, visual perception is dynamic and ongoing.

At times, there is not enough information to distinguish the figure from the background and we have to rely on experience to make this judgment. In **FIGURE 5.20**, it is hard to see the Dalmatian standing among the many black spots scattered on the white background. This effect occurs because the part of the image corresponding to the dog lacks contours that define the dog's edges and because the dog's spotted coat resembles the background. Many observers find that they first recognize one part of the dog—say, the head. From that detail, they are able to discern the dog's shape. Once you perceive the dog, it becomes difficult to *not* see it the next time you look at the figure. Thus, experience can inform how we identify figures and distinguish them from the background.

FIGURE 5.20
What Do You See?
These fragments make up a picture of a dog sniffing the ground. Once a part of the dog is detected, the mind organizes the picture's elements automatically to produce the perception of a dog. Once you perceive the dog, you cannot choose not to see it.

GESTALT PRINCIPLES OF PERCEPTUAL ORGANIZATION *Gestalt* is a German word that means "shape" or "form." Gestalt psychologists theorized that perception is more than the result of a collection of sensory data; in other words, the whole of perceptual experience is more than the sum of its parts. They postulated that the brain uses innate principles to group sensory information into organized wholes.

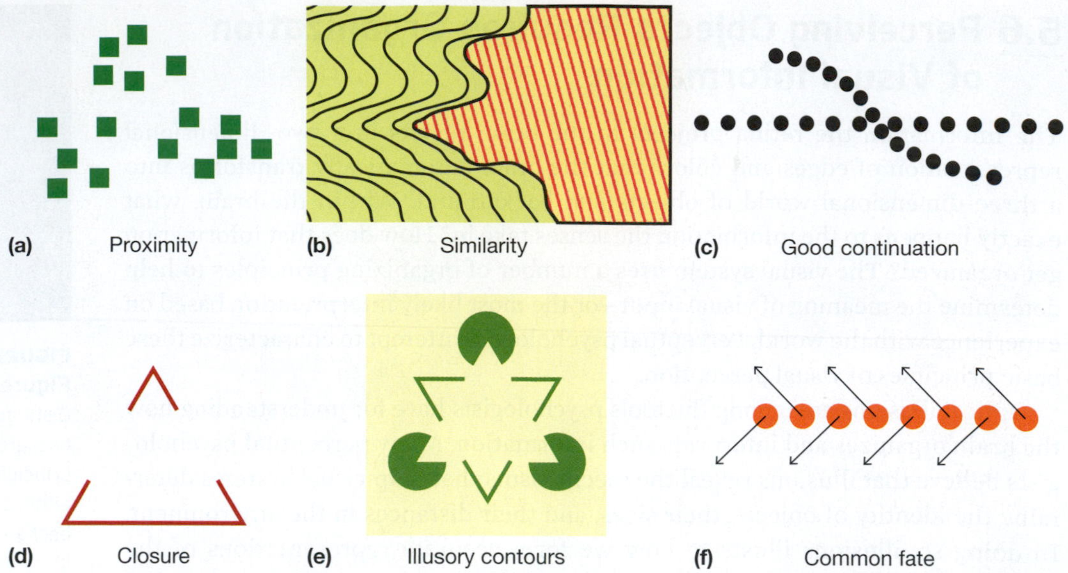

FIGURE 5.21

Gestalt Principles

(a) Proximity: These 16 squares appear to be grouped as three objects. **(b) Similarity:** This rectangle appears to consist of two locked pieces. **(c) Good Continuation:** We interpret two continuous lines that intersect. **(d) Closure:** We see these forms as parts of a triangle. **(e) Illusory Contours:** The two triangles are illusions, and implied depth cues make one triangle appear brighter than the surrounding area. **(f) Common Fate:** Parts of the visual scene that move together are grouped together.

One of these principles is that we automatically differentiate figure from ground. But how do we determine what gets grouped together as a figure or object in order to distinguish it from the background? How do we perceive, say, "a car" as opposed to "metal, tires, glass, door handles, hubcaps, fenders," and so on? For us, an object exists as a unit, not as a collection of features. Gestalt perceptual grouping laws help explain how we group together some visual cues to perceive objects (**FIGURE 5.21**). These Gestalt grouping laws include:

- *Proximity:* The closer two figures are to each other, the more likely we are to group them and see them as part of the same object.
- *Similarity:* We tend to group figures according to how closely they resemble each other, whether in shape, color, or orientation.

In accordance with the principles of similarity and proximity, we tend to cluster elements of the visual scene into distinct groups. For example, we might perceive a flock of birds as a single entity because all the elements, the birds, are similar and in close proximity.

- *Good continuation:* We tend to group together edges or contours that are smooth and continuous as opposed to those having abrupt or sharp edges.
- *Closure:* We tend to complete figures that have gaps. The principles of good continuation and closure sometimes can result in seeing contours, shapes, and cues to depth when they do not exist, as is the case with illusory contours.
- *Common fate:* We tend to see things that move together as belonging to the same group. For example, you would have no difficulty seeing the Dalmatian in the scene presented in Figure 5.20 if the subset of black dots that represent the Dalmatian all began moving in the same direction.

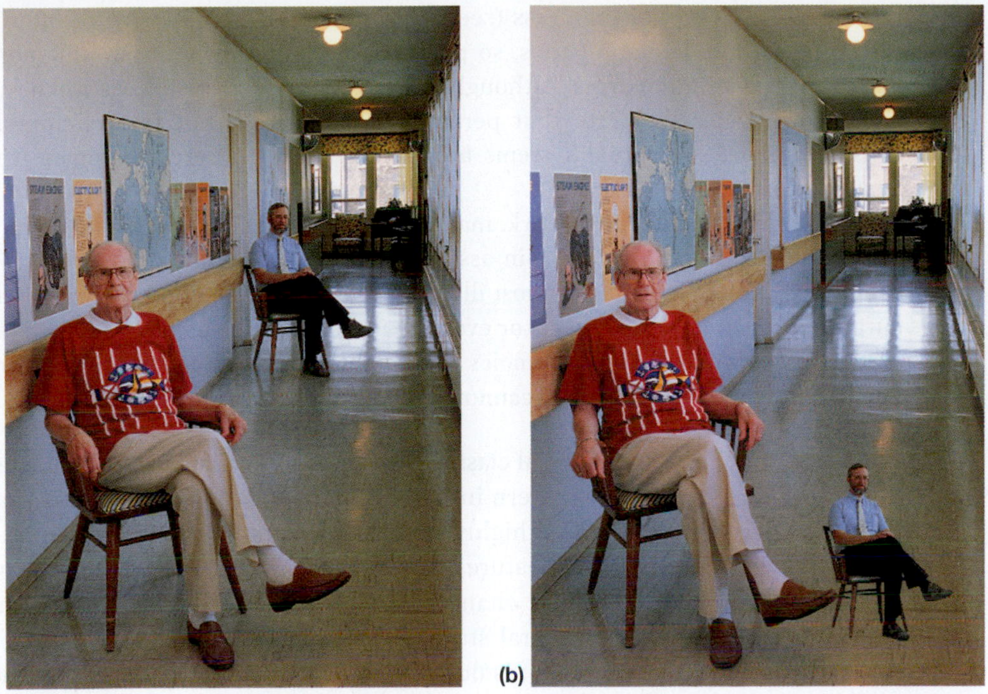

(a) (b)

FIGURE 5.22
Size Constancy
When you look at each of these photos, your retinal image of the man in the blue shirt is the same. Why, then, does he appear larger in **(a)** than in **(b)**?

OBJECT CONSTANCY Once we perceive a collection of sensory information as belonging to the same object, **object constancy** leads us to perceive the object as unchanging despite changes in sensory data that compose the object. Consider your image in the mirror. What you see in the mirror might look like it is your actual size, but the image is much smaller than the parts of you being reflected. (If you doubt this claim, try tracing around the image of your face in a steamy bathroom mirror.) Similarly, how does the brain know that a person is 6 feet tall when the retinal image of that person changes size according to how near or far away the person is? How does the brain know that snow is white and a tire is black, even though snow at night or a tire in bright light might send the same cues to the retina?

For the most part, changing an object's angle, distance, or illumination does not change our perception of that object's size, shape, color, or lightness. But to perceive any of these four constancies, we need to understand the relationship between the object and at least one other factor. For *size constancy*, we need to know how far away the object is from us (**FIGURE 5.22**). For *shape constancy*, we need to know what angle or angles we are seeing the object from. For *color constancy*, we need to compare the wavelengths of light reflected from the object with those reflected from its background. Likewise, for *lightness constancy*, we need to know how much light is being reflected from the object and from its background (**FIGURE 5.23**). In order to see objects as constant despite changes in size, shape, color, or lightness, the brain computes the relative magnitude of the sensory signals it receives rather than relying on each sensation's absolute magnitude. The perceptual system's ability to make relative judgments allows it to maintain constancy across various perceptual contexts. Think back to the opening vignette for this chapter: The reason people see different

FIGURE 5.23
Object Constancy
The image on the retina is vastly different for each of these four drawings of a car. Since we know how large a car normally is, knowing how far away the car is from us enables us to maintain size constancy. Knowing the angles we are seeing the car from enables us to maintain shape constancy. The shadows help maintain color and lightness constancy because they suggest the angle of lighting and we know that light makes colors brighter.

object constancy Correctly perceiving objects as constant in their shape, size, color, and lightness, despite raw sensory data that could mislead perception.

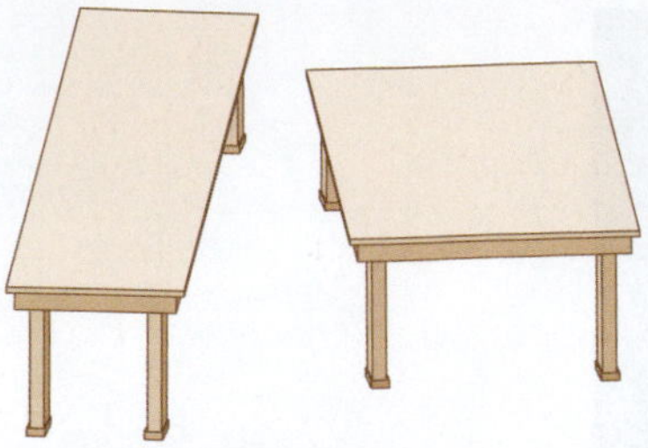

FIGURE 5.24
The Tabletop Illusion
Created by the psychologist Roger Shepard, this illusion demonstrates the brain's automatic perceptual processes. Even when we know the two tabletops are the same size and shape—even if we have traced one image and placed it on top of the other—perspective cues make us see them as different.

colors in the picture of the dress (see Figure 5.1) is that the source of lighting in the background is ambiguous, so people make different relative judgments about the colors in the dress. Although their precise mechanisms are unknown, these constancies illustrate that perceptual systems do not just respond to sensory inputs. Perceptual systems are in fact tuned to detect changes from baseline conditions.

By studying how illusions work, many perceptual psychologists have come to believe that the brain has built-in assumptions that influence perceptions. We cannot make ourselves *not* see most illusions, even when we know they are inaccurate representations of objects or events (**FIGURE 5.24**). Thus, the visual system is a complex interplay of constancies that enable us to see both a stable world and perceptual illusions that we cannot control.

FACE PERCEPTION One special class of objects that the visual system is sensitive to is faces. Indeed, any pattern in the world that has facelike qualities will look like a face (**FIGURE 5.25**). As highly social animals, humans are able to notice the subtle differences in facial features that differentiate unique individuals and to perceive and interpret slight changes in the configuration of features that convey facial expressions. Several studies support the idea that human faces reveal "special" information that is not available from other stimuli. For example, we can more readily discern information about a person's mood, attentiveness, sex, race, age, and so on by looking at that person's face than we can by listening to the person talk, watching the person walk, or studying their clothing (Bruce & Young, 1986).

Some people have particular deficits in the ability to recognize faces—a condition known as *prosopagnosia*—but not in the ability to recognize other objects (Susilo & Duchaine, 2013). People with prosopagnosia cannot tell one face from another, but they are able to judge whether something is a face or not and whether that face is upside down or not. This specific impairment in recognizing faces implies that facial recognition differs from nonfacial object recognition (Steeves et al., 2006).

Prosopagnosia can be present from birth (Behrmann & Avidan, 2005). Developmental prosopagnosia is thought to affect up to 2.5 percent of the population and to be related to genetic factors (Grüter et al., 2008). Individuals with developmental prosopagnosia report difficulties identifying unique individuals and learn to rely on other cues, such as voice, but they often do not realize they have a specific deficit recognizing faces, relative to most others, until adulthood. Prosopagnosia can also be acquired following a brain injury. Certain brain regions appear to be dedicated solely to perceiving faces (Haxby et al., 2000), and damage to these regions results in prosopagnosia. As part of the "what" stream discussed earlier, a region of the *fusiform gyrus* in the temporal lobe is critical for perceiving faces (Grill-Spector et al., 2004; McCarthy et al., 1997). This brain area responds most strongly to upright faces, as we would perceive them in the normal environment (Kanwisher et al., 1998).

FIGURE 5.25
Face Perception
A face that appears to be crying can be seen in this dramatic photo of a Norwegian glacier.

Additional evidence suggesting that we process faces differently from other objects comes from research showing that people have a surprisingly hard time recognizing faces, especially unknown faces, that are upside down. We are much worse at this than we are at recognizing other inverted objects. The inversion interferes with the way people perceive the relationships among facial features (Hayward et al., 2016). For instance, if the eyebrows are bushier than usual, this facial characteristic is obvious if the face is upright but not detectable when the face is inverted.

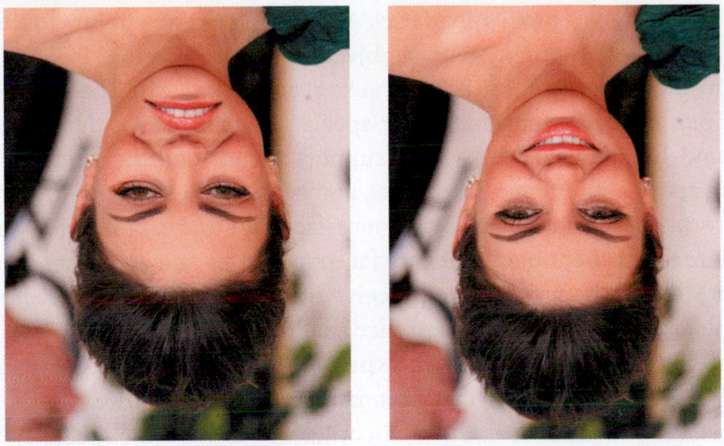

FIGURE 5.26
The Thatcher Illusion
Here, the two inverted pictures of Mila Kunis look normal. Turn your book upside down to reveal a different perspective. Our tendency to process upright faces holistically makes small distortions in any feature obvious. When faces are inverted, this holistic processing is disrupted, and we are less likely to notice changes in the relative orientation of specific features.

One interesting example of the perceptual difficulties associated with inverted faces is evident in the Thatcher illusion (Thompson, 1980; **FIGURE 5.26**). The Thatcher illusion got its name because it was first demonstrated using a picture of former British prime minister Margaret Thatcher (Thompson, 1980). This illusion showed that if the picture is altered so that the eyes and mouth of the face are upside down, the picture looks quite disturbing when it is upright. But if the distorted picture is upside down, most people will not notice anything is wrong (Thompson, 1980). At first it was thought that this effect emerged only with pictures of Margaret Thatcher, but since then it has been demonstrated with most human faces, and the effect has even been demonstrated with monkeys observing monkey faces. It has been suggested that we process the features in upright faces holistically, encoding all the features as a configuration so we easily detect when any feature is changed (Dahl et al., 2010). In contrast, when faces are upside down, the features of the face are processed separately and we are less sensitive to the relations among them, so changing a single one does not have the same impact. The Thatcher illusion supports the idea that when it comes to perceiving objects, faces are special.

Q **How do the Gestalt principles of proximity and similarity help explain our visual perceptions of crowds?**

ANSWER: When we see people (similar objects) gathered closely together (organized proximally) we perceive them as a "crowd" rather than as individuals.

5.7 Are Faces Special?

YOU BE THE PSYCHOLOGIST

Research on the perception of faces has shown that, in many ways, the processing of faces differs from the processing of other objects. For instance, most people can detect relatively small differences in the facial features of upright faces, whereas similarly subtle differences would be difficult to detect with other object categories. In contrast, turning faces upside down impairs the perception of faces more than turning any other object upside down impairs the brain's perception of it. Also, there is a region of the brain, the fusiform face area (or fusiform gyrex), that seems to be devoted to processing faces. All of this evidence points to the conclusion that when it comes to perceiving objects, faces are special.

But why are faces special? Is it because recognizing other people from facial cues was particularly important as our species evolved, so we developed unique abilities and brain mechanisms that support facial identification? Or is there something special about faces as objects, and our experience with them? In other words, are faces special because they are faces, and the faces of other people matter more than other objects? Or, are faces special because they are objects with specific properties that cause us to perceive them differently than other objects?

Psychologist Isabel Gauthier has argued that faces are special as a class of objects only because, through our extensive experiences with them, we have developed significant expertise in identifying the small variations in features that distinguish individual faces (Gauthier et al., 2000). In other words, faces are special not because they are faces, but because they are objects with special properties. Gauthier proposes that by becoming experts in identifying faces, we process them differently from other object categories where features may vary more widely, or with which we have less experience. The *expertise hypothesis* suggests that faces are special only because they are objects with certain properties that we interact with extensively.

How might you go about testing the expertise hypothesis concerning faces? One possibility might be to identify other object categories that have the same properties as faces, and test whether these objects also show the psychological and brain response patterns typical of faces, such as inversion effects and activity in the fusiform face area. Can you think of other categories of objects that might have similar properties as faces? That is, are there any other types of object categories where individual examples of the category are distinguished based on variation of a relatively small number of features? Furthermore, among categories of objects with this property, are there any where people are expert at identifying unique or individual examples of that category?

Most categories of objects don't have both of these properties. For instance, many of us have a lot of experience identifying different houses, but houses vary in terms of many more features than faces, so the perceptual challenges are not quite the same. However, it may be possible to find object categories, and people, that meet both of these criteria. It has been suggested that bird or car experts may develop special skills in identifying unique bird species or makes of cars, respectively, from the limited features that distinguish them. If you could find individuals who had years of experience identifying different species of birds or types of cars, how might you alter studies supporting the conclusion that faces are special in order to find evidence for or against the expertise hypothesis? ■

Q **Would proponents of the expertise hypothesis expect the Thatcher illusion to occur with highly familiar objects other than faces?**

ANSWER: Yes, they would expect the brain to perceive other highly familiar objects holistically when oriented typically, but as separate components when oriented upside down.

5.8 Perception of Depth, Size, and Motion Is Guided by Internal and External Cues

binocular depth cues Cues of depth perception that arise from the fact that people have two eyes.

monocular depth cues Cues of depth perception that are available to each eye alone.

Identifying an object based on its specific physical characteristics is the most basic way we extract meaning from visual information, but to perceive a three-dimensional visual world, we also need to infer how far away an object is and its relative size. In addition, while it is possible to extract meaning from a static scene, the visual signals we receive move and change as we move our eyes and our bodies and as things move around us. How we perceive depth, size, and motion depends on a range of cues generated internally, such as the movement of our eyes, combined with cues from the external world and our experience with it.

DEPTH PERCEPTION We are able to perceive depth in the two-dimensional patterns of photographs, movies, videos, and television images. But we are still able to distinguish these two-dimensional images from our three-dimensional world because some depth cues are apparent in two-dimensional images while others are not. There are several types of depth cues. **Binocular depth cues** are available from both eyes together and are present only when viewing the three-dimensional world. They provide internal cues about how far away something is. **Monocular depth cues** are available from each eye alone and provide organizational information that can be used to infer depth. Motion depth cues emerge when we move through space and depend on relative changes to visual input with motion.

One of the most important cues to depth perception is **binocular disparity** (or *retinal disparity*). This cue is caused by the distance between humans' two eyes. Because each eye has a slightly different view of the world, the brain has access to two different but overlapping retinal images. The brain uses the disparity between these two retinal images to compute distances to nearby objects (**FIGURE 5.27**). The ability to determine an object's depth based on that object's projections to each eye is called *stereoscopic vision*.

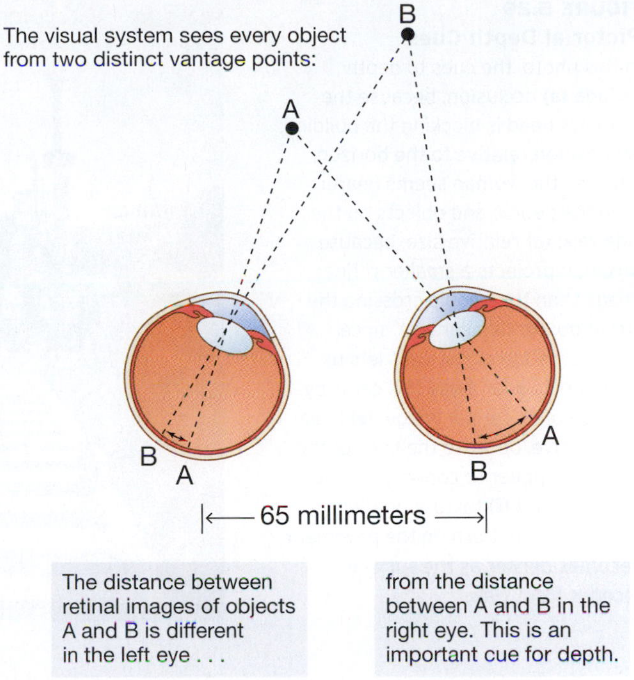
The visual system sees every object from two distinct vantage points:
A
B
B
A
A
B
65 millimeters
The distance between retinal images of objects A and B is different in the left eye . . .
from the distance between A and B in the right eye. This is an important cue for depth.

FIGURE 5.27
Binocular Disparity
To demonstrate your own binocular disparity, hold one of your index fingers out in front of your face and close first one eye and then the other. Your finger appears to move because each eye, due to its position relative to the finger, has a unique retinal image.

A related binocular depth cue is **convergence**. This term refers to the way that the eye muscles turn the eyes inward when we view nearby objects. To focus both eyes on a close object requires the eyes to converge more than if the object is far away. The brain knows how much the eyes are converging through feedback from eye muscles and uses this information to perceive distance (**FIGURE 5.28**).

Although binocular disparity is an important cue for depth perception, it is useful only for relatively close objects. An object that is very far away will create

binocular disparity A depth cue; because of the distance between the two eyes, each eye receives a slightly different retinal image.

convergence A cue of binocular depth perception; when a person views a nearby object, the eye muscles turn the eyes inward.

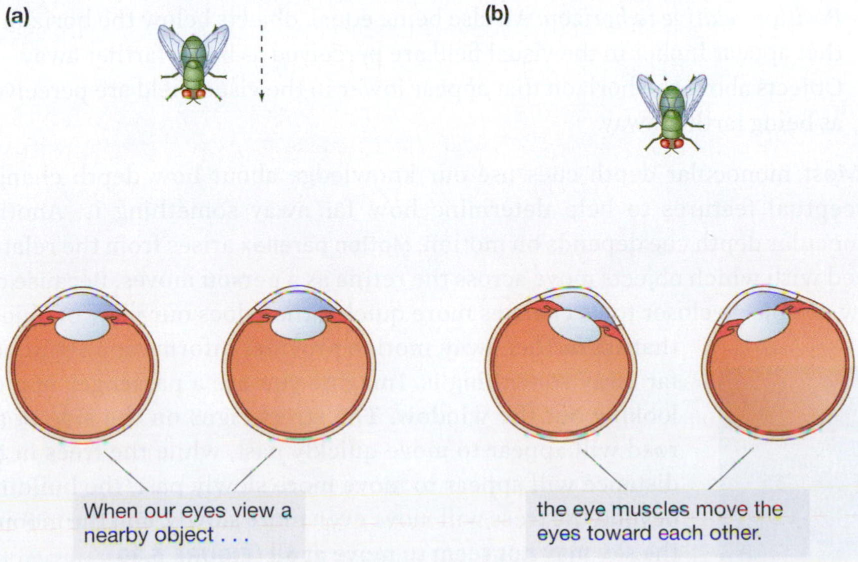
(a)
(b)
When our eyes view a nearby object . . .
the eye muscles move the eyes toward each other.

FIGURE 5.28
Convergence
(a) When viewing things at a distance, the eyes aim out on parallel lines.
(b) As an object approaches, the eyes converge. To demonstrate such convergence, hold one of your index fingers in front of your face, about a foot away. Slowly bring your finger toward your eyes. Do you notice your eyes converging?

FIGURE 5.29
Pictorial Depth Cues
In this photo, the cues to depth include **(a)** occlusion, because the woman's head is blocking the building; **(b)** position relative to the horizon, because the woman seems nearer than the people and objects on the sidewalk; **(c)** relative size, because this man projects a smaller retinal image than the people crossing the street do; **(d)** familiar size, since our knowledge of car sizes lets us estimate how far away this car is by the size of its retinal image; **(e)** linear perspective, because the lines of the sidewalk appear to converge in the distance; and **(f)** texture gradient, because the pattern on the pavement becomes denser as the surface recedes from view.

little binocular disparity and require minimal convergence. Monocular depth cues are effective with only one eye and can distinguish the relative distance of even faraway objects. Artists routinely use these cues to create a sense of depth in two-dimensional images, so monocular depth cues are sometimes called *pictorial depth cues* (**FIGURE 5.29**). The Renaissance painter, sculptor, architect, and engineer Leonardo da Vinci first identified many of these cues, which include:

- *Occlusion:* A near object occludes (blocks) an object that is farther away.
- *Relative size:* Far-off objects project a smaller retinal image than close objects do, if the far-off and close objects are the same physical size.
- *Familiar size:* Because we know how large familiar objects are, we can tell how far away they are by the size of their retinal images.
- *Linear perspective:* Seemingly parallel lines appear to converge in the distance.
- *Texture gradient:* As a uniformly textured surface recedes, its texture continuously becomes denser.
- *Position relative to horizon:* All else being equal, objects below the horizon that appear higher in the visual field are perceived as being farther away. Objects above the horizon that appear lower in the visual field are perceived as being farther away.

motion parallax A monocular depth cue observed when moving relative to objects, in which the objects that are closer appear to move faster than the objects that are farther away.

Most monocular depth cues use our knowledge about how depth changes perceptual features to help determine how far away something is. Another monocular depth cue depends on motion. **Motion parallax** arises from the relative speed with which objects move across the retina as a person moves. Because our view of objects closer to us changes more quickly than does our view of objects that are farther away, motion provides information about how far away something is. Imagine you are a passenger in a car looking out the window. The street signs on the side of the road will appear to move quickly past, while the trees in the distance will appear to move more slowly past, the buildings beyond the trees will move even more slowly, and the moon in the sky may not seem to move at all (**FIGURE 5.30**).

Learning Tip

The prefix *bi-* means "two," so binocular depth cues require two eyes. The prefix *mono-* means "one," so monocular depth cues require only one eye.

SIZE PERCEPTION For size, distance matters. The size of an object's retinal image depends on that object's distance from the observer. The farther away the object is, the smaller its retinal image. To determine an object's size, the visual system needs to know how far away the object is. Most of the time, enough depth information is available for the visual system to work out an object's distance and thus infer how large the object is. Size perception sometimes fails, however, and an object may look bigger or smaller than it really is.

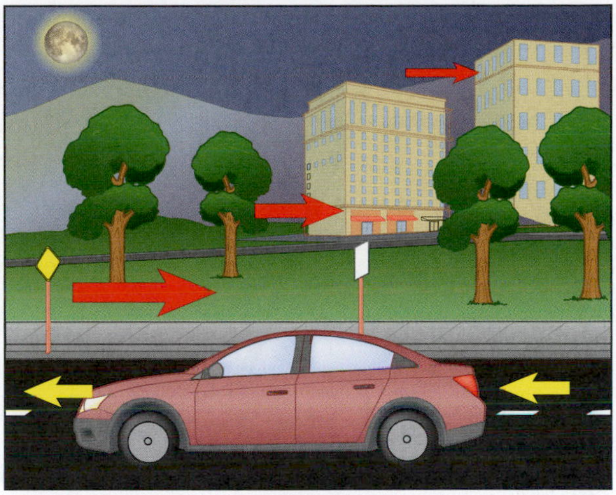

FIGURE 5.30
Motion Parallax
As we move past objects, those closer to us appear to move faster than do those farther away.

Optical illusions that result in errors in size estimates often arise when normal perceptual processes incorrectly represent the distance between the viewer and the stimuli. In other words, depth cues can fool us into seeing depth when it is not there. Alternatively, a lack of depth cues can fool us into *not* seeing depth when it *is* there. This section considers two phenomena related to both depth perception and distance perception: Ames boxes (also called Ames rooms) and the Ponzo illusion.

Ames boxes were crafted in the 1940s by Adelbert Ames, a painter turned scientist. These constructions present powerful depth illusions. Inside the Ames boxes, rooms play with linear perspective and other distance cues. One such room makes a far corner appear the same distance away as a near corner (**FIGURE 5.31**).

In both a normal room and this Ames box, the nearby child projects a larger retinal image than the child farther away does. Normally, however, the nearby child would not appear to be a giant, because the perceptual system would take depth into account when assessing size. Here, the depth cues are wrong, so the nearby child appears farther away than he is, and the disproportionate size of his image on your retina makes him look huge.

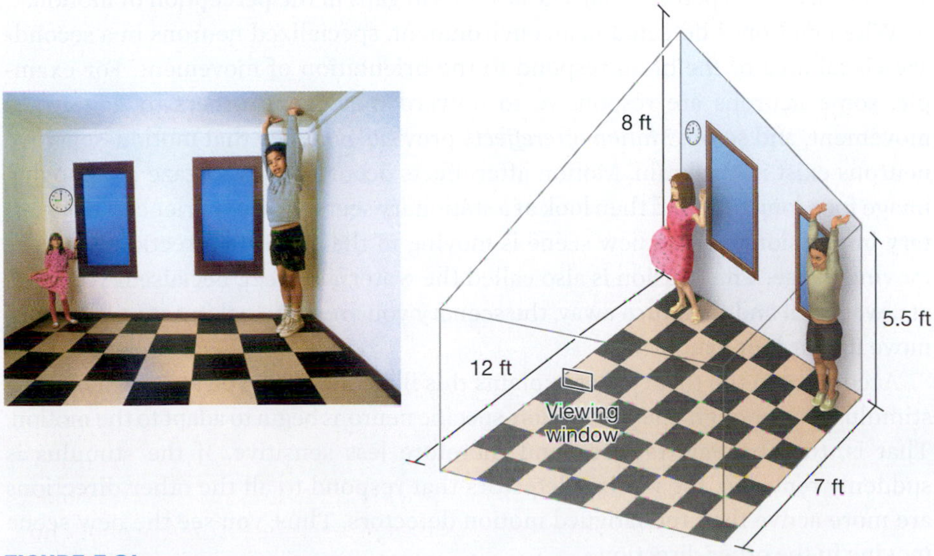

FIGURE 5.31
The Ames Box and Depth Perception
Ames played with depth cues to create size illusions. For example, he made a diagonally cut room appear rectangular by using crooked windows and floor tiles. When one child stands in a near corner and another (of similar height) stands in a far corner, the room creates the illusion that they are the same distance from the viewer. Therefore, the closer child looks like a giant compared with the child farther away.

FIGURE 5.32
The Ponzo Illusion
The two horizontal lines appear to be different sizes but are actually the same length.

The Ponzo illusion, first described by the psychologist Mario Ponzo in 1913, is another classic example of a size/distance illusion (**FIGURE 5.32**). The common explanation for this effect is that monocular depth cues make the two-dimensional figure seem three-dimensional (Rock, 1984). As noted earlier, seemingly parallel lines appear to converge in the distance. Here, the two lines drawn to look like railroad tracks receding in the distance trick your brain into thinking they are parallel. Therefore, you perceive the two parallel lines in the center as if they are at different distances away from you and thus different in size when they actually are the same size.

This illusion shows how much we rely on depth perception to gauge size. The brain defaults to using depth cues even when depth is absent. Once again, the brain responds as efficiently as possible.

MOTION PERCEPTION We know how motion cues play a role in depth perception, but how does the brain perceive motion? We use several cues to detect motion. For instance, when our head is still and our eyes move as we stay focused on an object, that is a cue that the object is moving. In addition, motion is generally detected by the relative movement of visual information. If you view one object, say, a billiard table, as a frame of reference, and a billiard ball changes its position on the table, that is a cue the ball is moving. At times, relative movement can result in the perception of illusory movement. For instance, if you are sitting on a train that is moving so slowly you do not perceive the motion, it may appear that the train station outside the window is slowly moving because you assume your train car is an unmoving frame of reference.

Subtle changes in static visual images that are presented in rapid succession can also give the illusion of movement. Movies are made up of still-frame images, presented one after the other to create the illusion of motion pictures. This phenomenon is based on *stroboscopic movement*, a perceptual illusion that occurs when two or more slightly different images are presented in rapid succession (**FIGURE 5.33**). This apparent motion illusion demonstrates that the brain, much as it fills in gaps to perceive objects, also fills in gaps in the perception of motion.

When motion is detected in an environment, specialized neurons in a secondary visual area of the brain respond to the orientation of movement. For example, some neurons are responsive to upward movement, others to downward movement, and so on. *Motion aftereffects* provide evidence that motion-sensitive neurons exist in the brain. Motion aftereffects occur when you gaze at a moving image for a long time and then look at a stationary scene. You experience a momentary impression that the new scene is moving in the opposite direction from the moving image. This illusion is also called the waterfall effect, because if you stare at a waterfall and then turn away, the scenery you are now looking at will seem to move upward for a moment.

According to the theory that explains this illusion, when you stare at a moving stimulus long enough, these direction-specific neurons begin to adapt to the motion. That is, they become fatigued and therefore less sensitive. If the stimulus is suddenly removed, the motion detectors that respond to all the other directions are more active than the fatigued motion detectors. Thus, you see the new scene moving in the other direction.

Further evidence that the brain has specialized regions for processing motion comes from studies with brain-injured patients. Consider the dramatic case of M.P., a German woman. After receiving damage to secondary visual areas of her brain—areas critical for motion perception—M.P. saw the world as a series of snapshots rather than as a moving image (Zihl et al., 1983). Pouring tea, she would see

FIGURE 5.33
How Moving Pictures Work
This static series would appear transformed if you spun the wheel. With the slightly different images presented in rapid succession, the stroboscopic movement would tell your brain that you were watching a moving horse.

the liquid frozen in air and be surprised when her cup overflowed. Before crossing a street, she might spot a car far away. When she tried to cross, however, that car would be right in front of her. M.P. had a unique deficit: She could perceive objects and colors but not continuous movement.

Q How does the distance of an object affect the size of the retinal image it casts?

ANSWER: The farther the object is from the viewer, the smaller its retinal image becomes.

How Do We Hear?

Learning Objectives

- Describe how sound waves are transduced into neural activity in the ear.
- Discuss the advantages and disadvantages of cochlear implants.
- Explain the significance of temporal and place coding for auditory perception.

For humans, hearing, or **audition**, is second to vision as a source of information about the world. In addition to providing more information about what is happening in an environment, it also provides a medium for some experiences that are unique to humans. Although other animals can communicate through vocal signals, human evolution led to spoken language that can be used to convey complex ideas. The appreciation of music, and the pleasure it provokes, is also unique to humans. But how does the brain derive the meaning of language, music, and other sounds from signals in the air that travel to our ears?

5.9 Audition Results from Changes in Air Pressure

The process of hearing begins with the movements and vibrations of objects that cause the displacement of air molecules. Displaced air molecules produce a change in air pressure, and that change travels through the air. The pattern of the changes in air pressure during a period of time is called a **sound wave** (**FIGURE 5.34**).

audition Hearing; the sense of sound perception.

sound wave A pattern of changes in air pressure during a period of time; it produces the perception of a sound.

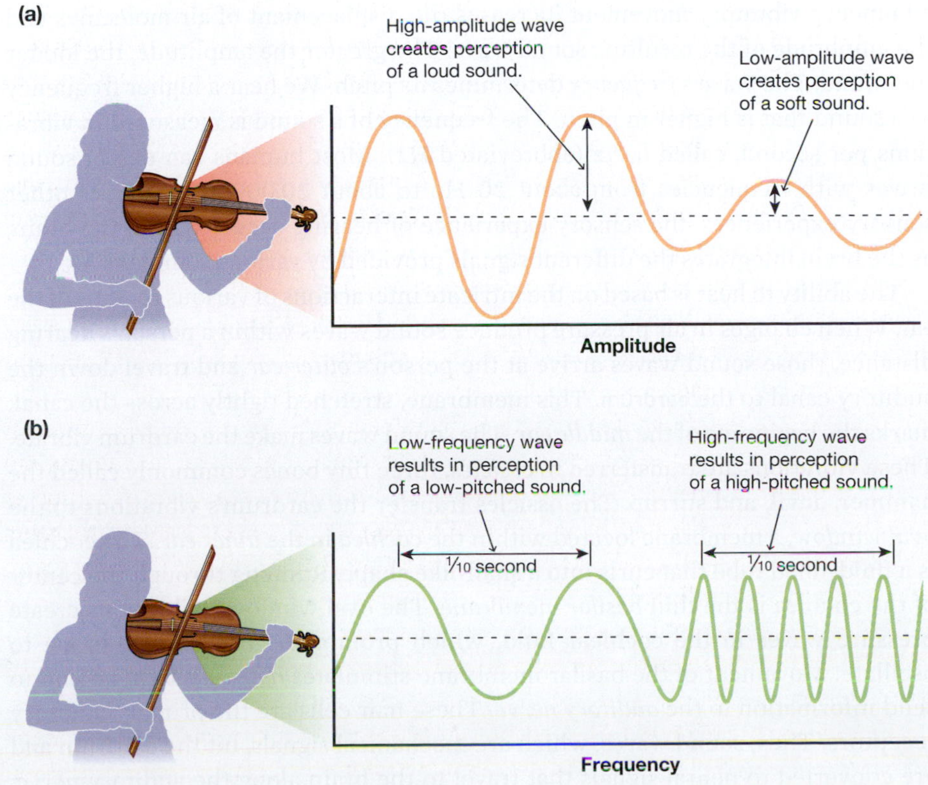
(a)
High-amplitude wave creates perception of a loud sound.
Low-amplitude wave creates perception of a soft sound.
Amplitude
(b)
Low-frequency wave results in perception of a low-pitched sound.
High-frequency wave results in perception of a high-pitched sound.
1/10 second
1/10 second
Frequency

FIGURE 5.34
Sound Waves
The **(a)** amplitude and **(b)** frequency of sound waves are processed into the perceptual experiences of loudness and pitch.

1 Physical stimulus:
Sound waves from the music enter your outer ear, making the eardrum vibrate. Then they pass to the middle ear, making the ossicles and the oval window vibrate. Finally, they pass to the cochlea, in your inner ear.

2 Sensation:
Pressure waves in the cochlea move the basilar membrane, stimulating the sensory receptors, called hair cells, in your inner ear.

Outer ear

Middle ear Inner ear

Semicircular canals

Cochlea

Auditory nerve

Hammer
Ossicles Anvil
Stirrup

Sound

Auditory canal

Eardrum

Oval window

Cochlea, partially uncoiled

Vibrations from the oval window enter the cochlea.

Signals exit the cochlea and enter the auditory nerve (to the brain).

Basilar membrane

3 Transduction:
When the hair cells bend, they convert the pressure waves into signals that are sent to the brain by the auditory nerve.

Hair cells

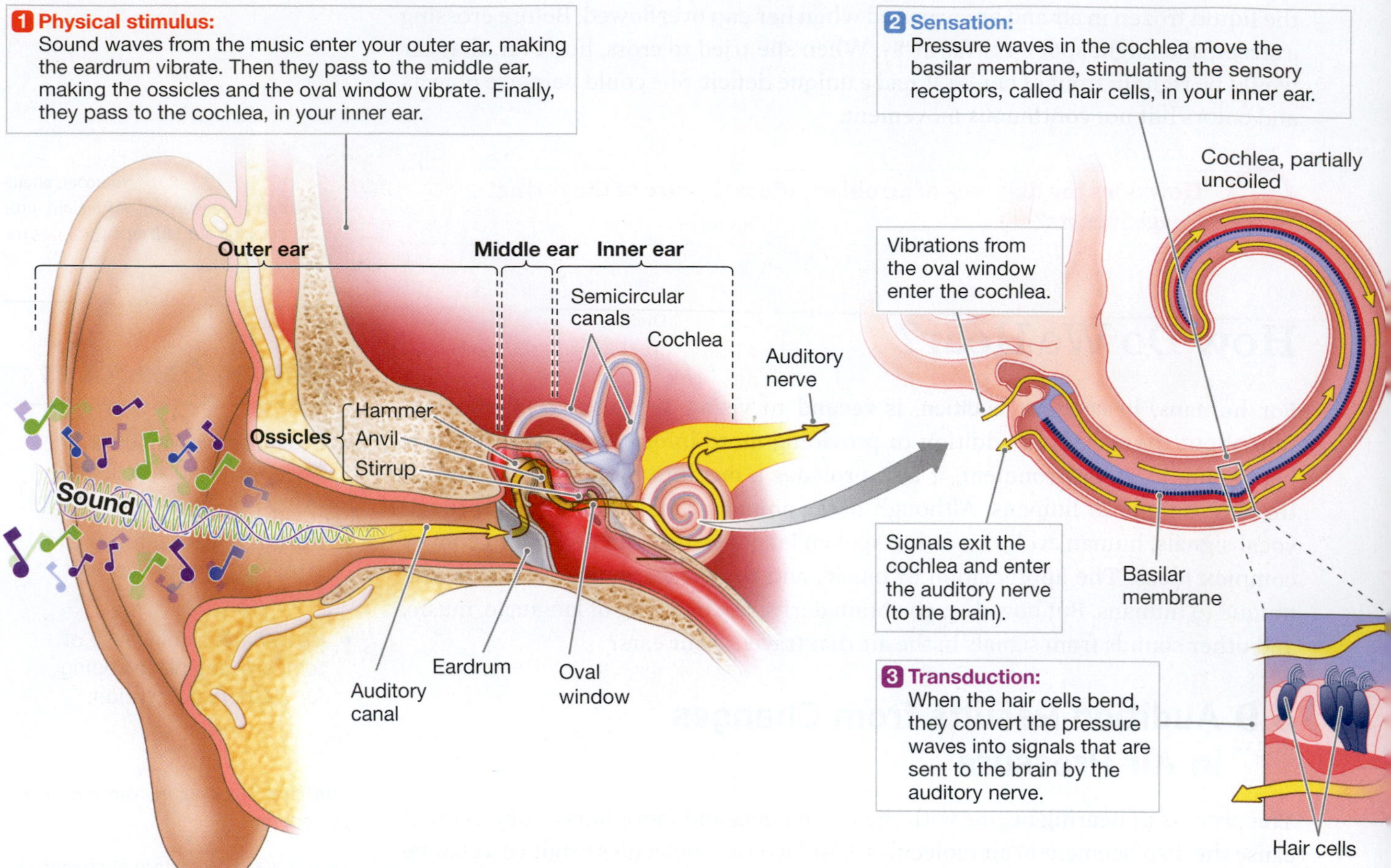

FIGURE 5.35
How We Are Able to Hear

eardrum A thin membrane that marks the beginning of the middle ear; sound waves cause it to vibrate.

A sound wave's *amplitude* determines its loudness. Increasing the intensity of an object's vibratory movement increases the displacement of air molecules and the amplitude of the resulting sound wave. The greater the amplitude, the louder the sound. The wave's *frequency* determines its pitch: We hear a higher frequency as a sound that is higher in pitch. The frequency of a sound is measured in vibrations per second, called *hertz* (abbreviated *Hz*). Most humans can detect sound waves with frequencies from about 20 Hz to about 20,000 Hz. Like all other sensory experiences, the sensory experience of hearing occurs within the brain, as the brain integrates the different signals provided by various sound waves.

The ability to hear is based on the intricate interactions of various regions of the ear. When changes in air pressure produce sound waves within a person's hearing distance, those sound waves arrive at the person's *outer ear* and travel down the auditory canal to the **eardrum**. This membrane, stretched tightly across the canal, marks the beginning of the *middle ear*. The sound waves make the eardrum vibrate. These vibrations are transferred to *ossicles*, three tiny bones commonly called the hammer, anvil, and stirrup. The ossicles transfer the eardrum's vibrations to the *oval window*, a membrane located within the *cochlea* in the *inner ear*. The cochlea is a fluid-filled tube that curls into a snail-like shape. Running through the center of the cochlea is the thin *basilar membrane*. The oval window's vibrations create pressure waves in the cochlear fluid, which prompt the basilar membrane to oscillate. Movement of the basilar membrane stimulates *hair cells* to bend and to send information to the *auditory nerve*. These hair cells are the primary auditory receptors. Thus, sound waves, which are mechanical signals, hit the eardrum and are converted to neural signals that travel to the brain along the auditory nerve.

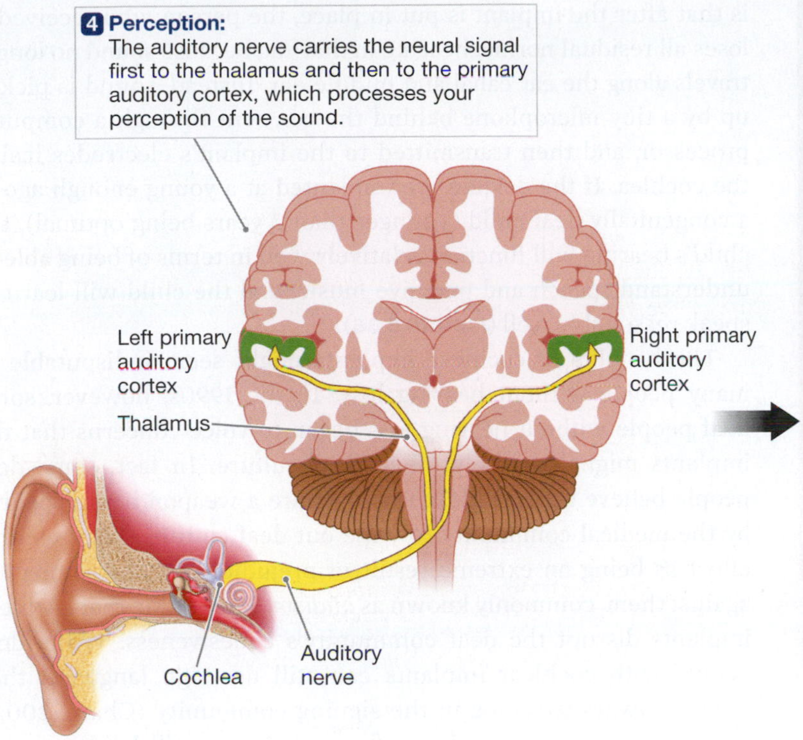

4 Perception:
The auditory nerve carries the neural signal first to the thalamus and then to the primary auditory cortex, which processes your perception of the sound.
Left primary auditory cortex
Right primary auditory cortex
Thalamus
Cochlea
Auditory nerve

This conversion of sound waves to brain activity produces the sensation of sound (**FIGURE 5.35**). Auditory neurons in the thalamus extend their axons to the *primary auditory cortex*, which is located in the temporal lobe.

VESTIBULAR SYSTEM Another sensory system that relies on the ears helps us maintain balance. The **vestibular sense** uses information from receptors in the semicircular canals of the inner ear. These canals contain a liquid that moves when the head moves, bending hair cells at the ends of the canal. The bending generates nerve impulses that inform us of the head's rotation. In this way, the vestibular sense is responsible for our sense of balance. It explains why inner-ear infections or standing up quickly can make us dizzy. The experience of being seasick or carsick results in part from conflicting signals arriving from the visual system and the vestibular system.

vestibular sense Perception of balance determined by receptors in the inner ear.

COCHLEAR IMPLANTS A cochlear implant is a small electronic device that can help provide the sense of sound to a person who has a severe hearing impairment. The implant was the first neural implant used successfully in humans. Over 300,000 of these devices have been implanted worldwide since 1984, when the U.S. Food and Drug Administration (FDA) approved them for adults. In 1990, the FDA approved them for 2-year-olds. It has since approved them for 1-year-olds. Over 38,000 children in the United States have cochlear implants.

The cochlear implant has helped people with severe hearing problems due to the loss of hair cells in the inner ear. Unlike a hearing aid, the implant does not amplify sound. Rather, it directly stimulates the auditory nerve. The downside

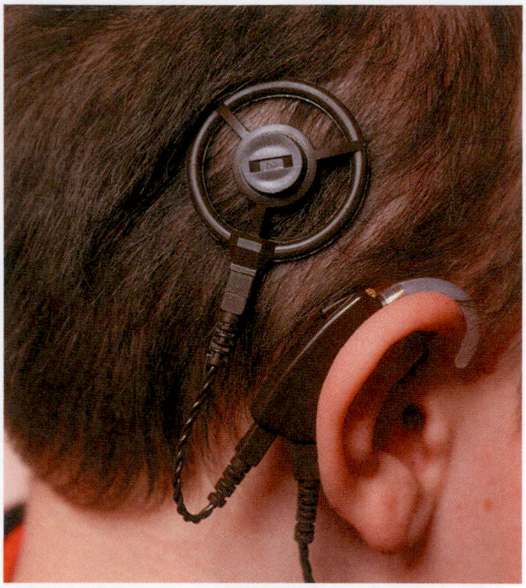

FIGURE 5.36
Cochlear Implants
Cochlear implants consist of a microphone around the ear and a transmitter fitted to the scalp, linked to electrodes that directly stimulate the auditory nerve.

is that after the implant is put in place, the person who received it loses all residual normal hearing in that ear, because sound no longer travels along the ear canal and middle ear. Instead, sound is picked up by a tiny microphone behind the ear, sent through a computer processor, and then transmitted to the implant's electrodes inside the cochlea. If the devices are implanted at a young enough age in a congenitally deaf child (younger than 2 years being optimal), the child's hearing will function relatively well in terms of being able to understand speech and perceive music, and the child will learn to speak reasonably well (**FIGURE 5.36**).

The benefits of cochlear implants might seem indisputable to many people without hearing loss. In the 1990s, however, some deaf people without hearing loss began to voice concerns that the implants might adversely affect deaf culture. In fact, some deaf people believe that cochlear implants are a weapon being wielded by the medical community to wipe out deaf culture. They see this effort as being an extreme result of prejudice and discrimination against them, commonly known as *audism*. They argue that cochlear implants disrupt the deaf community's cohesiveness. While deaf people with cochlear implants can still use sign language, they are not always welcome in the signing community (Chase, 2006). This attitude has slowly been changing but is still held by many deaf signers.

Q **What are the primary auditory receptors?**

ANSWER: the hair cells on the basilar membrane, which bend with auditory vibrations and transduce the mechanical signal into neural impulses

5.10 Pitch Is Encoded by Frequency and Location

temporal coding A mechanism for encoding low-frequency auditory stimuli in which the firing rates of cochlear hair cells match the frequency of the sound wave.

How does the firing of auditory receptors signal different frequencies of sound, such as high notes and low notes? In other words, how is pitch coded by the auditory system? Two mechanisms for encoding the frequency of an auditory stimulus operate in parallel in the basilar membrane: temporal coding and place coding.

Temporal coding is used to encode relatively low frequencies, such as the sound of a tuba. The firing rates of cochlear hair cells match the frequency of the pressure wave, so that a 1,000 Hz tone causes hair cells to fire 1,000 times per second. Think of the boom, boom, boom of a bass drum. Physiological research has shown that this strict matching between the frequency of auditory stimulation and firing rate of the hair cells can occur only for relatively low frequencies—up to about 4,000 Hz. At higher frequencies, temporal coding can be maintained only if hair cells fire in volleys, in which different groups of cells take turns firing, so that the overall temporal pattern matches the sound frequency. Think of one group of soldiers firing their weapons together while another group reloads. Then that second group fires while another group reloads. Then that third group fires . . . and so on.

"Great! O.K., this time I want you to sound taller, and let me hear a little more hair."

The second mechanism for encoding frequency is **place coding**. During the nineteenth century, the physiologist

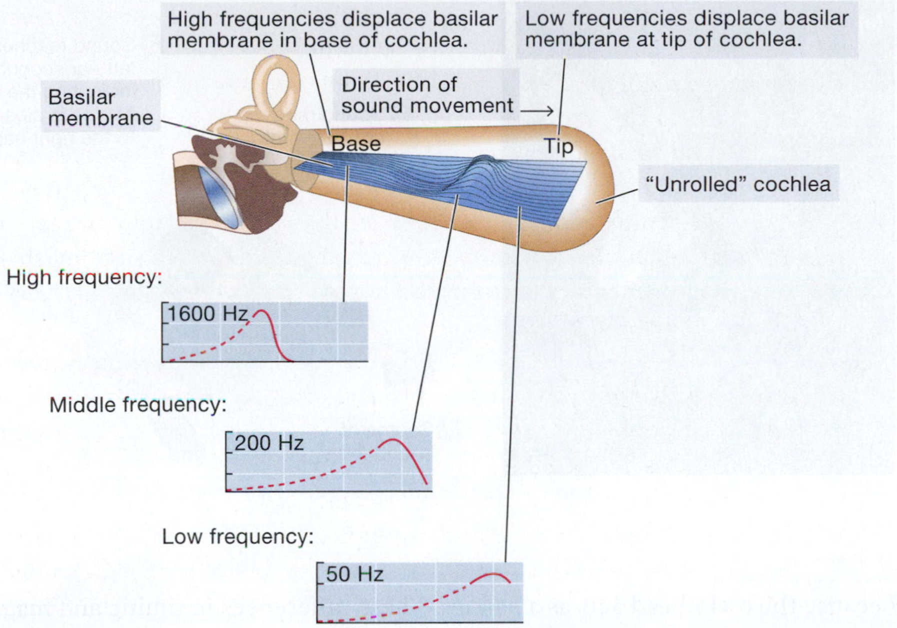

FIGURE 5.37
Place Coding
In this "unrolled" cochlea, high-, medium-, and low-frequency sound waves activate different regions of the basilar membrane.

Hermann von Helmholtz proposed that different receptors in the basilar membrane respond to different frequencies. According to this idea, low frequencies would activate a different type of receptor than high frequencies would. Later, the perceptual psychologist Georg von Békésy discovered that Helmholtz's idea was theoretically correct but wrong in the details. Békésy (1957) discovered that all of the receptors on the basilar membrane are similar, but different frequencies activate receptors at different locations.

place coding A mechanism for encoding the frequency of auditory stimuli in which the frequency of the sound wave is encoded by the location of the hair cells along the basilar membrane.

The basilar membrane responds to sound waves like a clarinet reed, vibrating in resonance with the sound. Because the membrane's stiffness decreases along its length, higher frequencies vibrate better at its base, while lower frequencies vibrate more toward its tip. Thus, hair cells at the base of the cochlea are activated by high-frequency sounds; hair cells at the tip are activated by low-frequency sounds (Culler et al., 1943). The frequency of a sound wave is thus encoded by the receptors on the area of the basilar membrane that vibrates the most (FIGURE 5.37).

Both temporal coding and place coding are involved in the perception of pitch. Most of the sounds we hear—from conversations to concerts—are made up of many frequencies and activate a broad range of hair cells. Our perception of sound relies on the integrated activities of many neurons.

SOUND LOCALIZATION Locating the origin of a sound is an important part of auditory perception, but the sensory receptors cannot code where events occur. Instead, the brain integrates the different sensory information coming from each ear.

Much of our understanding of auditory localization has come from research with barn owls. These nocturnal birds have finely tuned hearing, which helps them locate their prey. In fact, in a dark laboratory, a barn owl can locate a mouse through hearing alone. The owl uses two cues to locate a sound: the time the sound arrives in each ear and the sound's intensity in each ear. Unless the sound comes from exactly in front or in back of the owl, the sound will reach one ear first. Whichever side it comes from, the sound will be softer on the other side

FIGURE 5.38
Auditory Localization
(a) Like barn owls, **(b)** humans draw on the intensity and timing of sounds to locate where the sounds are coming from.

(a)
(b)
3 Sound reaches left ear second, indicating the source is closer to the right ear.
2 Sound reaches right ear first.
1 Source of sound (here, a cell phone)

because the owl's head acts as a barrier. These differences in timing and magnitude are minute, but they are not too small for the owl's brain to detect and act on. Although a human's ears are not as finely tuned to the locations of sounds as an owl's ears, the human brain uses information from the two ears similarly (**FIGURE 5.38**).

Q How is sound localized in space?

ANSWER: Depending on the location a sound is coming from, there will be slight differences in the timing and intensity of the auditory stimulation for the two ears.

PSYCHOLOGY OUTSIDE THE LAB

5.11 Are Your Listening Habits Damaging Your Hearing?

Portable listening devices let us take our music wherever we go (**FIGURE 5.39**). State-of-the-art headphones and earbuds make the listening experience like being in the recording studio with our favorite artists. But blasting music through headphones and earbuds is a known cause of hearing loss. According to the National Institutes of Health (2017), noise-induced hearing loss is caused by exposure to "sounds that are too loud or loud sounds that last a long time." Exposure to music typically occurs over long periods of time and thus falls into the second category of risk.

Loud noises—in headphones or earbuds, in the car, in a room, at a concert—can permanently damage the sensitive hair cells in the inner ear that transmit signals to brain areas involved in sound perception. Once those hair cells are damaged, they cannot be repaired. Eventually, they die. If we do not protect those fragile structures, we will not be able to rely on them to hear music, lectures, the television, or any sounds at all.

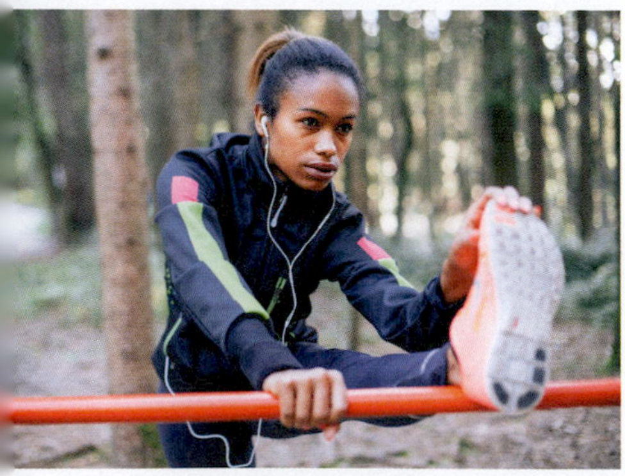

FIGURE 5.39
Listening on the Go
Portable music is now a way of life, but it's important to listen smartly and safely—at a reasonable volume—to protect your hearing.

Researchers based in New York City studied the noise exposure of college students who use personal listening devices, such as phones and iPods (Levey et al., 2011). As students emerged from the subway adjacent to the urban campus, the researchers invited them to complete a short questionnaire to assess their music-listening habits and asked if they would put their headphones or earbuds on a special mannequin. This mannequin was equipped with a sound-level meter that measured the intensity of the noise coming from the headset.

On average, the music was playing at 92.6 decibels (about the intensity of a power mower or a motorcycle roaring by). The research participants reported using their listening devices an average of 18.4 hours per week. The average intensity and duration of noise exposure certainly puts these students at risk for noise-induced hearing loss. To hear examples of other noises that can put your hearing at risk, check out the National Institutes of Health's "noise meter": https://www.nidcd.nih.gov/health/listen-infographic.

But how can we know if the energy waves we are pumping through our headphones need to be taken down a notch or two? According to the Centers for Disease Control and Prevention (2020b), if you or others need to shout to be heard when wearing headphones, the sound is too loud. Or if you cannot understand someone an arm's length away who is talking at a normal volume, you may be damaging your hearing. Also, if you can hear the music, even faintly, when the headphones or earbuds are not in your ears, they are likely too loud.

Music is a part of who we are. But for those of us who have not already suffered hearing loss, so is our hearing. Enjoying music while protecting our hearing will help keep music part of us for the long haul. ■

Q How do loud sounds lead to hearing loss?

ANSWER: by permanently damaging the hair cells in the inner ear

How Do We Taste and Smell?

Learning Objectives

- Discuss the five basic taste sensations.
- Describe how culture influences taste perception.
- Describe the neural pathway for smell.
- Explain the relationship between pheromones and smell.

Taste and smell often go hand in hand, but they are distinct senses that engage different sensory receptors and brain circuits. What they have in common is that the external signals triggering both taste and smell are chemical in nature, either chemicals in foods that reach the tongue or chemicals in the air that reach the nose. Of course, sometimes chemicals from food are also released into the air, such as when eating a fragrant cheese, resulting in the combined sensation of both taste and smell when eating.

Food provides us with the calories and nutrients necessary for survival. However, since we are not all dietitians, how do we know what to eat? Here again, taste and smell can come together to help us decide what to eat. The taste or smell of food might help us detect that it has gone bad. Thus, one of the jobs of **gustation**, our sense of taste, and **olfaction**, our sense of smell, is to keep poisons out of our digestive systems while allowing safe food in.

gustation The sense of taste.

olfaction The sense of smell.

5.12 There Are Five Basic Taste Sensations

The stimuli for taste are chemical substances from food that dissolve in saliva. But the operations of these stimuli are still largely a mystery, and no simple explanation of taste could do justice to the importance of taste in our daily experience. Animals love tasty food, some flavors more than others. Humans in many cultures spend a substantial amount of time planning their meals to bring enjoyment. Beyond the basic chemistry of the sense and its importance for survival, how is the perception of taste determined?

The taste receptors are part of the **taste buds**. These sensory organs are mostly on the tongue (in tiny, mushroom-shaped structures called *papillae*) but are also spread throughout the mouth and throat. Most individuals have approximately 8,000 to 10,000 taste buds. When food, fluid, or some other substance (e.g., dirt) stimulates the taste buds, they send signals to the thalamus. These signals are

taste buds Sensory organs in the mouth that contain the receptors for taste.

then routed to the insula and frontal lobe, which produce the experience of taste (**FIGURE 5.40**).

A near-infinite variety of perceptual experiences can arise from the activation of unique combinations of taste receptors. Scientists once believed that different regions of the tongue were more sensitive to certain tastes, but they now know that the different taste buds are spread relatively uniformly throughout the tongue and mouth (Lindemann, 2001).

Every taste experience is composed of a mixture of five basic qualities: sweet, sour, salty, bitter, and *umami* (Japanese for "savory" or "yummy"). Only within the last decade have scientists recognized umami as the fifth taste sensation (Barretto et al., 2015). This delicious taste was perhaps first created intentionally in the late 1800s, when the French chef Auguste Escoffier invented a veal stock that did not taste primarily sweet, sour, salty, or bitter. Independently of Escoffier, in 1908, the Japanese cook and chemist Kikunae Ikeda identified the taste as arising from the detection of glutamate, a substance that occurs naturally in foods such as meat, some cheese, and mushrooms. Glutamate is the sodium salt in glutamic acid. As *monosodium glutamate*, or *MSG*, this salt can be added to various foods as a flavor enhancer. Soy sauce is full of the umami flavor.

Taste alone does not affect how much you like a certain type of food. As you might know from having had colds, food seems tasteless if your nasal passages are blocked. That is because taste relies heavily on the sense of smell. A food's texture also matters: Whether a food is soft or crunchy, creamy or granular, tender or tough affects the sensory experience. That experience is also affected if the food causes discomfort, as can happen with spicy chilies. The entire taste experience occurs not in your mouth but in your brain, which integrates these various sensory signals.

SUPERTASTERS Some people experience especially intense taste sensations. Linda Bartoshuk, the researcher who first studied these individuals, whom she called supertasters, found that they have more taste buds than most people do (Bartoshuk et al., 1994). Recent evidence, however, suggests that underlying

FIGURE 5.40
How We Are Able to Taste

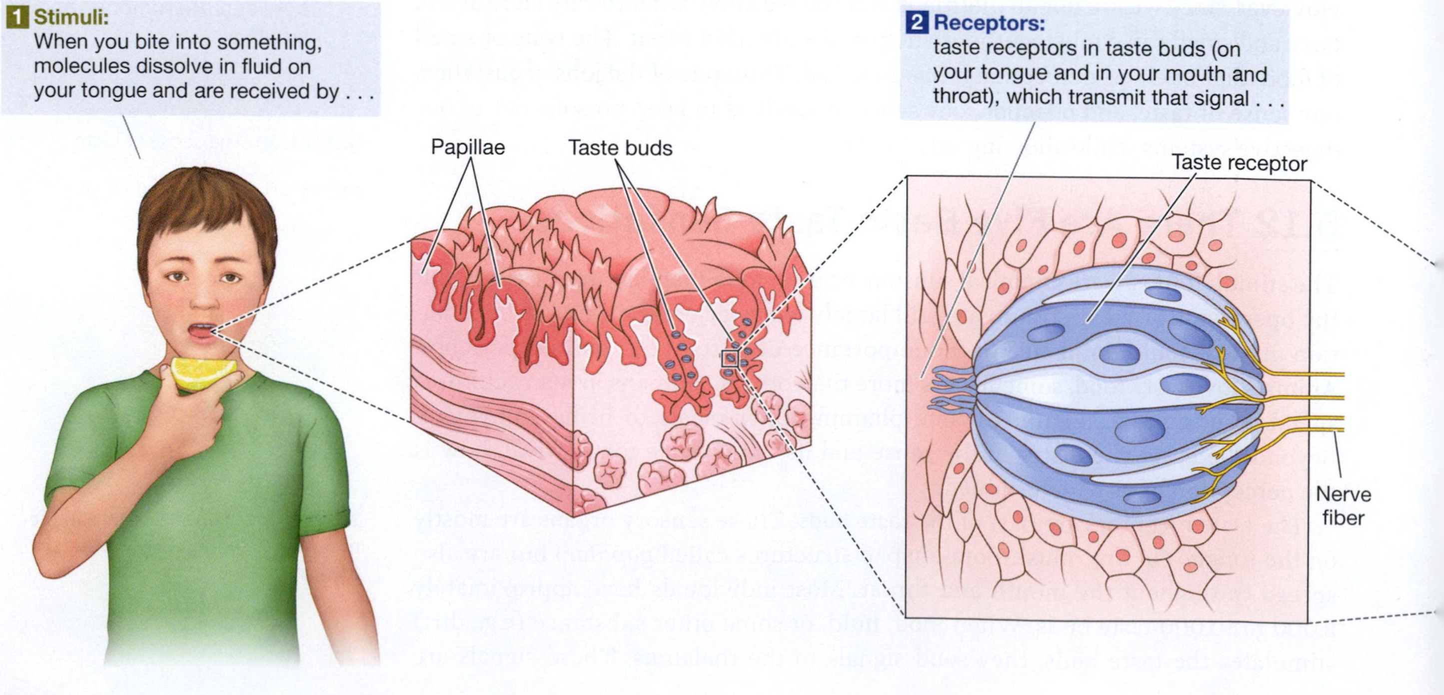

1 Stimuli:
When you bite into something, molecules dissolve in fluid on your tongue and are received by . . .
2 Receptors:
taste receptors in taste buds (on your tongue and in your mouth and throat), which transmit that signal . . .
Papillae
Taste buds
Taste receptor
Nerve fiber

genetics, rather than the number of taste buds, is the major determinant of whether a person is a supertaster (Garneau et al., 2014; **FIGURE 5.41**). First identified by their extreme dislike of bitter substances—such as grapefruit, broccoli, and coffee—supertasters are highly aware of flavors and textures and are more likely than others to feel pain when eating very spicy foods (Bartoshuk, 2000). They tend to be thin. Women are more likely than men to be supertasters. Taster status is also a function of age, because people lose half their taste receptors by age 20. Although it might sound enjoyable to experience intense tastes, many supertasters and young children are especially picky eaters because particular tastes can overwhelm them. When it comes to sensation, more is not necessarily better.

CULTURAL INFLUENCES Everyone has individual taste preferences. For example, some people hate anchovies, while others love them. Some people love sour foods, while others prefer sweet ones. These preferences come partly from differences in the number of taste receptors. The same food can actually taste different to different people, because the sensation associated with that food differs in different people's mouths. But cultural factors influence taste preferences as well. Some cultures like red hot peppers, others like salty fish, others rich sauces, and so on.

Cultural influences on food preferences begin in the womb. In a study of infant food preferences, pregnant women were assigned to four groups: Some drank carrot juice every day during the last two months of pregnancy, then drank carrot juice again every day during the first two months *after* childbirth; some drank a comparable amount of water every day during both of those periods; some drank

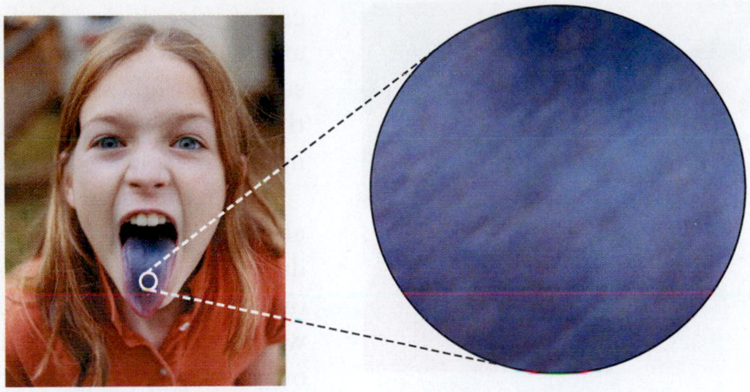

FIGURE 5.41

Are You a Supertaster?

To determine whether you are a supertaster, punch a small hole (about 7 mm) into a small square of wax paper; swab blue food coloring on the front of your tongue, then place the wax paper over it; use a magnifying glass to view the part of your tongue that shows through the hole. The papillae look like pink dots because they do not take up the blue dye. Count the pink dots you can see in the hole. In general, 15 to 35 taste buds is average, and above 35 means you may be a supertaster.

3 **Pathway to the brain:**
along a cranial nerve, through the thalamus, to other areas of your brain.

4 **Resulting perception:**
As a result, you know the taste is good or bad.

Thalamus

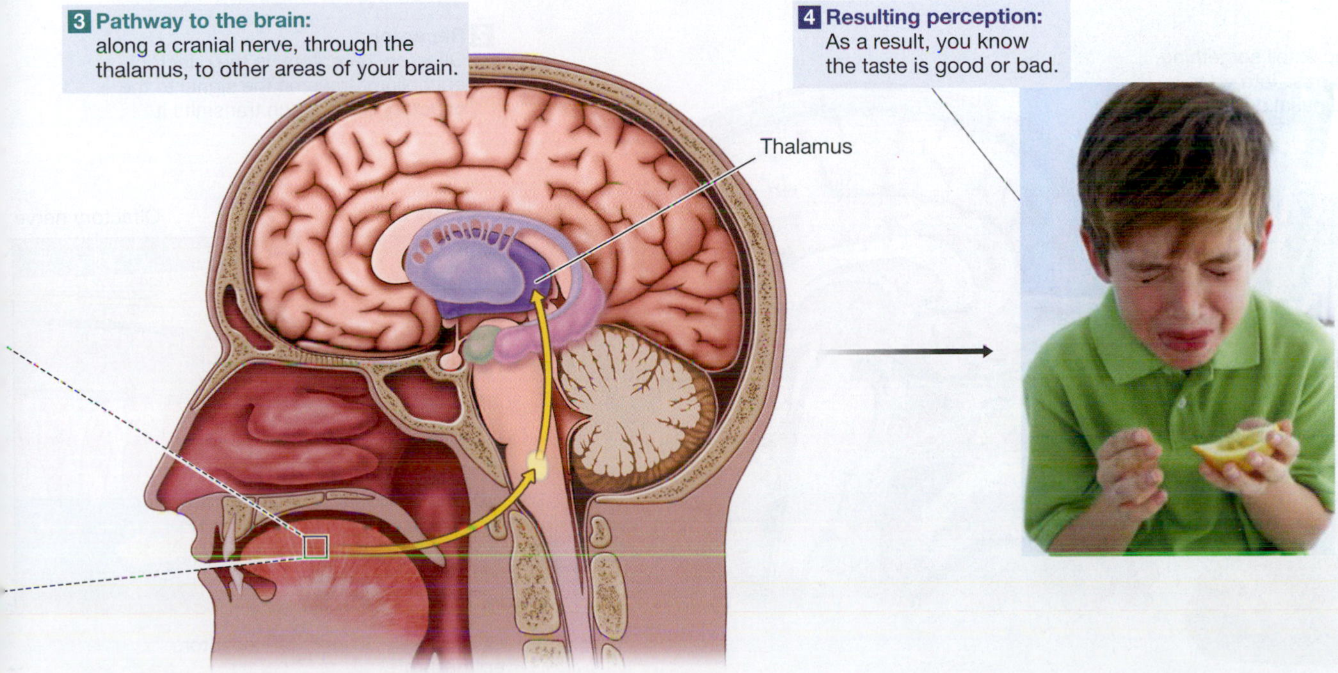

FIGURE 5.42
Taste Preferences Are Affected by the Mother's Diet

carrot juice during the first period, then drank water during the second period; and some drank water during the first period, then drank carrot juice during the second period (Mennella et al., 2001). All the mothers breast-fed their babies, so the taste of what each mother ate was in the breast milk that constituted each newborn's sole food source during the first few months of life (**FIGURE 5.42**).

When the babies were several months old, they were all fed carrot juice (either alone or mixed with their cereal). The infants whose mothers drank carrot juice during the two months before childbirth, the first two months after childbirth, or both periods showed a preference for carrot juice compared with the infants whose mothers drank only water during those same months. Thus, through their own eating behaviors before and immediately following birth, mothers apparently pass their eating preferences on to their offspring. Once again, as noted throughout this book, nature and nurture are inextricably entwined.

Q **What are the five basic taste qualities?**

ANSWER: sweet, sour, salty, bitter, and umami (savory)

5.13 Smell Is the Detection of Odorants

The human sense of smell is vastly inferior to that of many animals. For example, dogs have 40 times more olfactory receptors than humans do and are 100,000 to 1 million times more sensitive to odors. Our less developed sense of smell comes from our ancestors' reliance on vision. Yet smell's importance in our daily lives is made clear, at least in Western cultures, by the vast sums of money spent on fragrances, deodorants, and mouthwash.

Of all the senses, smell, or olfaction, has the most direct route to the brain. It may, however, be the least understood sense. We smell something when chemical particles, or *odorants*, pass into the nose and, when we sniff, into the nasal cavity's upper and back portions.

olfactory epithelium A thin layer of tissue within the nasal cavity that contains the receptors for smell.

In the nose and the nasal cavity, a warm, moist environment helps the odorant molecules come into contact with the **olfactory epithelium**. This thin layer of

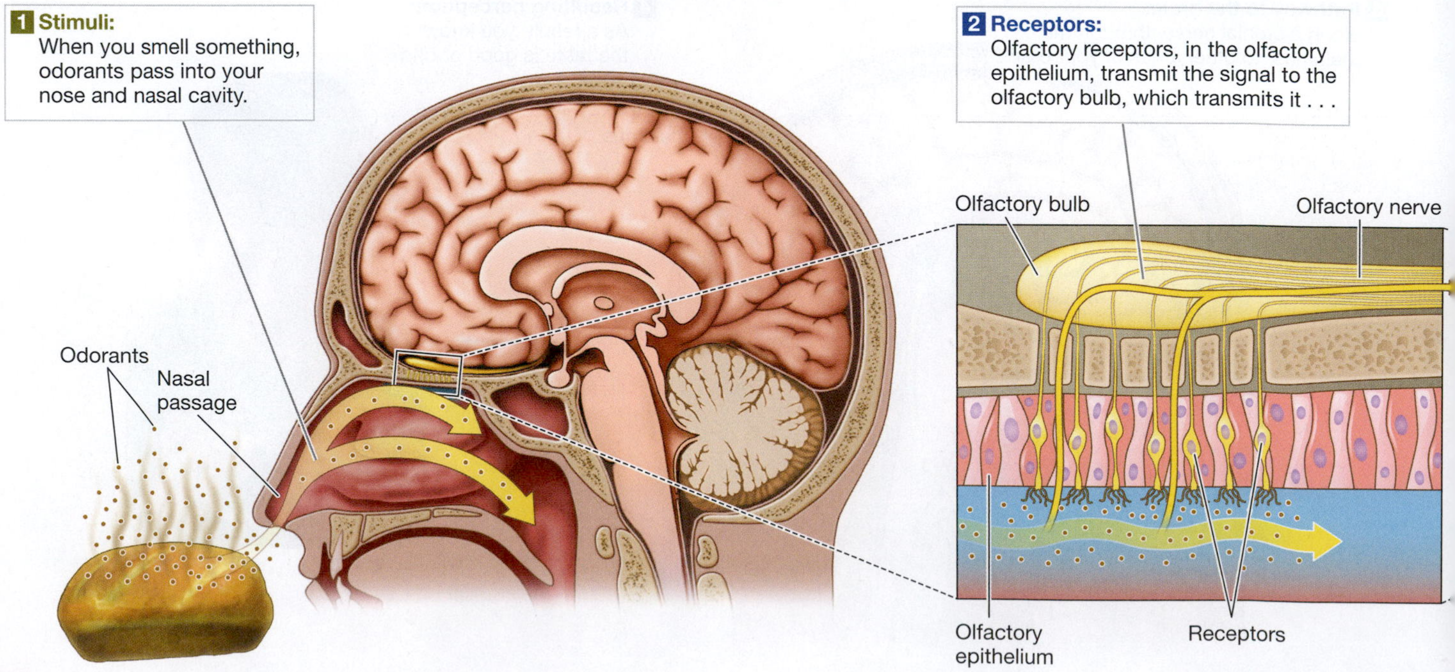
1 Stimuli:
When you smell something, odorants pass into your nose and nasal cavity.
2 Receptors:
Olfactory receptors, in the olfactory epithelium, transmit the signal to the olfactory bulb, which transmits it . . .
Olfactory bulb
Olfactory nerve
Odorants
Nasal passage
Olfactory epithelium
Receptors

tissue is embedded with thousands of smell receptors, each of which is responsive to different odorants. It remains unclear exactly how these receptors encode distinct smells. One possibility is that each type of receptor is uniquely associated with a specific odor. For example, one type would encode only the scent of roses. This explanation is unlikely, however, given the huge number of scents we can detect. Moreover, the scent of a rose actually consists of a mixture of 275 chemical components (Ohloff, 1994). The combination of these odorants produces the smell that we recognize as a rose. A more likely possibility is that each odorant stimulates several types of receptors and the activation pattern across these receptors determines the olfactory perception (Lledo et al., 2005). As in all sensory systems, sensation and perception result from the specificity of receptors and the pattern of receptor responses.

Unlike other sensory information, smell signals bypass the thalamus, the early relay station for all the other senses. Instead, the smell receptors transmit information directly to the **olfactory bulb**. Located just below the frontal lobes, the olfactory bulb is the brain center for smell. From the olfactory bulb, smell information goes to other brain areas.

olfactory bulb The brain center for smell, located below the frontal lobes.

Information about whether a smell is pleasant or unpleasant is processed in the brain's prefrontal cortex, and people can readily make that distinction. However, most people are pretty bad at identifying odors by name (Yeshurun & Sobel, 2010). Think about the smell of newly fallen rain. Even though it is familiar, it is hard to describe. If you test this claim by asking your friends or relatives to close their eyes and sniff familiar food items from the fridge, they will probably not be able to identify the smells at least half the time (de Wijk et al., 1995). Women, though, are generally better than men at identifying odors (Bromley & Doty, 1995; Ohla & Lundström, 2013), perhaps because they have more cells in the olfactory bulb than men do (Oliveira-Pinto et al., 2014).

The intensity of a smell is processed in brain areas that are also involved in emotion and memory (Anderson et al., 2003). As a result, it is not surprising that olfactory stimuli can evoke feelings and memories (**FIGURE 5.43**). Many people find that the aromas of certain holiday foods cooking, the smell of bread baking, and/or the fragrances of particular perfumes generate fond childhood memories.

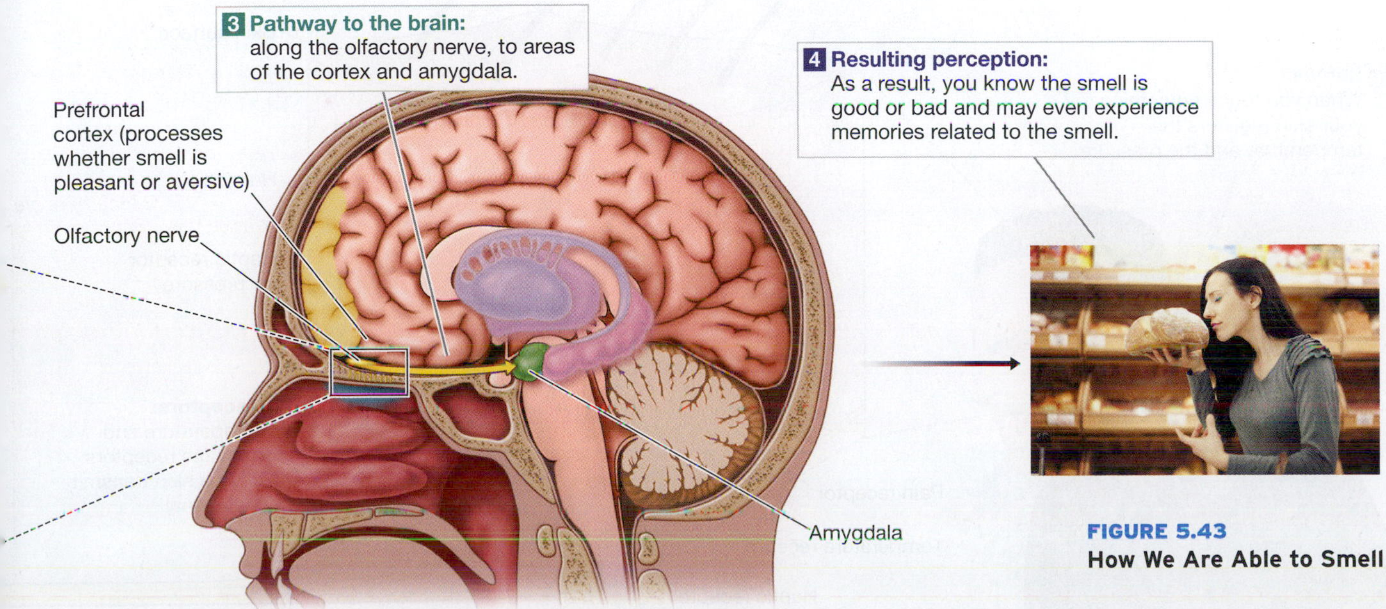

3 Pathway to the brain: along the olfactory nerve, to areas of the cortex and amygdala.
4 Resulting perception: As a result, you know the smell is good or bad and may even experience memories related to the smell.
Prefrontal cortex (processes whether smell is pleasant or aversive)
Olfactory nerve
Amygdala

FIGURE 5.43
How We Are Able to Smell

PHEROMONES The sense of smell is also an important mode of communication and involved in social behavior. *Pheromones* are chemicals released by animals that trigger physiological or behavioral reactions in other animals and insects. These chemicals do not elicit "smells" we are conscious of, but they are processed in a manner similar to the processing of olfactory stimuli. Specialized receptors in the nasal cavity respond to the presence of pheromones. Pheromones play a major role in sexual signaling in many animal species, and they may similarly affect humans.

Q How is the processing of olfactory information different from the other senses?

ANSWER: Information about smell does not go through the thalamus. Instead, it goes directly to the olfactory bulb.

How Do We Feel Touch and Pain?

Learning Objectives

- Describe how the sense of touch is processed by the skin and the brain.
- Distinguish between the two types of pain.
- Discuss gate control theory and the control of pain.

Touch, the **haptic sense**, conveys sensations of temperature, pressure, and pain. Touch is perceived through the skin, which is our largest sense organ. Touch is the first sense to develop in a fetus, and the comfort evoked by touch is thought to play an important role in forming attachments to caregivers (see Chapter 9). Social touch has been linked to the release of endorphins, chemical signals that promote a sense of pleasure or well-being. This is thought to be, in part, why many people enjoy getting a massage. However, touch is also linked to pain, which can be invaluable in avoiding injury.

5.14 The Skin Contains Sensory Receptors for Touch

haptic sense The sense of touch.

Anything that makes contact with our skin provides *tactile stimulation*. This stimulation gives rise to the experience of touch. The haptic receptors for both temperature and pressure are sensory neurons that reach to the skin's outer

FIGURE 5.44
How We Are Able to Experience Touch: The Haptic Sense

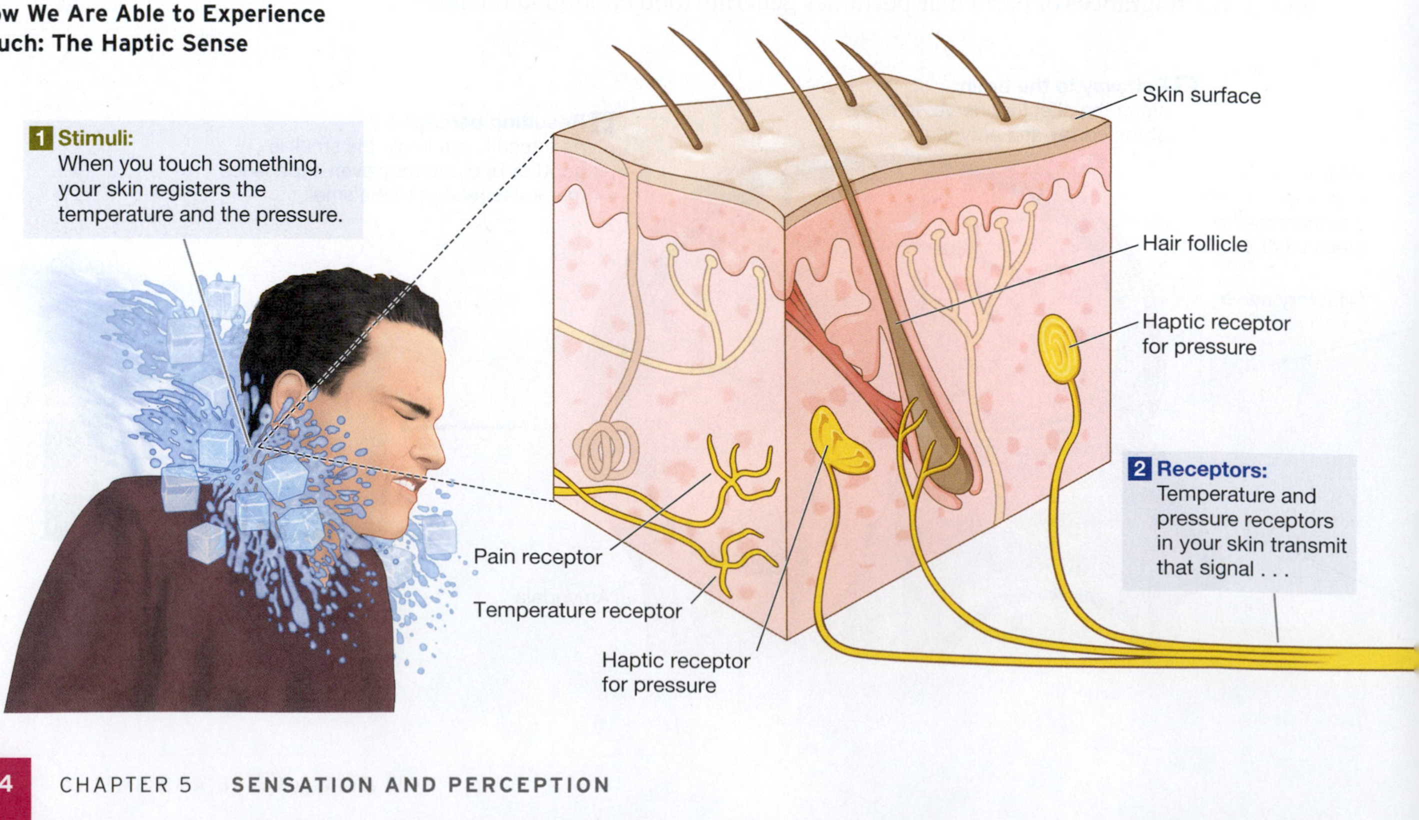

1 Stimuli:
When you touch something, your skin registers the temperature and the pressure.
Skin surface
Hair follicle
Haptic receptor for pressure
Pain receptor
Temperature receptor
Haptic receptor for pressure
2 Receptors:
Temperature and pressure receptors in your skin transmit that signal . . .

layer. Their long axons enter the central nervous system by way of spinal or cranial nerves. (Simply put, spinal nerves travel from the rest of the body into the spinal cord and then to the brain. By contrast, cranial nerves connect directly to the brain.)

For sensing temperature, there appear to be receptors for warmth and receptors for cold. Intense stimuli can trigger both warmth and cold receptors, however. Such simultaneous activation can produce strange sensory experiences, such as a false feeling of wetness. Some receptors for pressure are nerve fibers at the bases of hair follicles that respond to movement of the hair. Four other types of pressure receptors are capsules in the skin. These receptors respond to continued vibration; light, fast pressure; light, slow pressure; or stretching and steady pressure.

The integration of various signals and higher-level mental processes produces haptic experiences (**FIGURE 5.44**). For instance, stroking multiple pressure points can produce a tickling sensation, which can be pleasant or unpleasant, depending on the mental state of the person being tickled. And imaging research has helped explain why we cannot tickle ourselves: The brain areas involved in touch sensation respond less to self-produced tactile stimulation than they do to external tactile stimulation (Blakemore et al., 1998).

Touch information travels to the thalamus. The thalamus sends it to the primary somatosensory cortex in the parietal lobe. As discussed in Chapter 3, electrical stimulation of the primary somatosensory cortex can evoke the sensation of touch in different regions of the body (see Figure 3.18). Large amounts of cortical tissue are devoted to sensitive body parts, such as the fingers and the lips. Very little cortical tissue is devoted to other areas, such as the back and the calves. As a result, you can probably tell what something is if you feel it with your fingers, but you will not have equal sensitivity if the same thing touches your back.

Q **Why can you not tickle yourself?**

ANSWER: The brain responds less to tactile sensations that are self-produced compared to those that are externally generated.

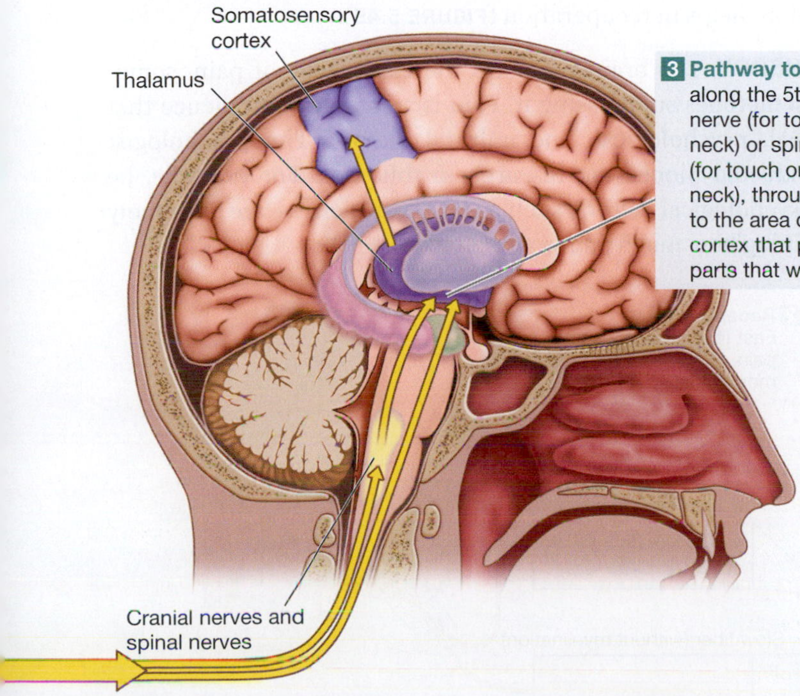

3 Pathway to the brain: along the 5th cranial nerve (for touch above the neck) or spinal nerves (for touch on or below the neck), through the thalamus, to the area of the somatosensory cortex that processes the body parts that were touched.

4 Resulting perception: As a result, you perceive the shock of cold water on your neck and down the rest of your body.

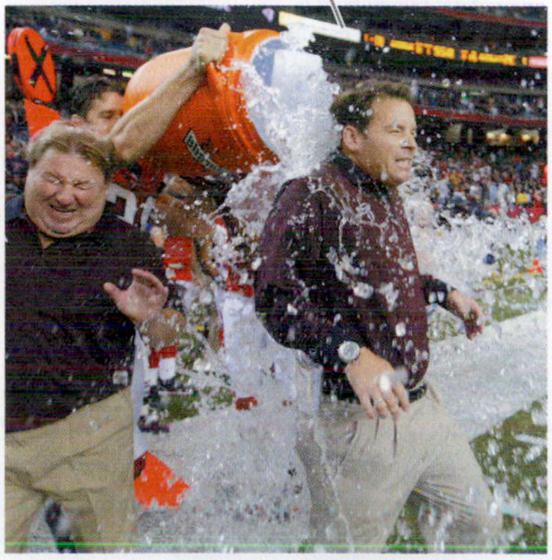

5.15 Pain Receptors Exist Throughout the Body

Pain is part of a warning system that stops you from continuing activities that may harm you. For example, the message may be to remove your hand from a jagged surface or to stop running when you have damaged a tendon. Children born with a rare genetic disorder that leaves them insensitive to pain usually die young, no matter how carefully they are supervised. They simply do not know how to avoid activities that harm them or to report when they are feeling ill (Melzack & Wall, 1982).

Pain receptors can be found in the skin and throughout the body. Like other sensory experiences, the actual experience of pain is created by the brain. For instance, a person whose limb has been amputated may sometimes feel "phantom" pain in the nonexistent limb. The person really feels pain, but the pain occurs because of painful sensations *near* the site of the missing limb or even because of a nonpainful touch on the cheek. The brain simply misinterprets the resulting neural activity.

Most experiences of pain result when damage to the skin activates haptic receptors. The nerve fibers that convey pain information are thinner than those for temperature and pressure and are found in all body tissues that sense pain: skin, muscles, membranes around both bones and joints, organs, and so on. Two kinds of nerve fibers have been identified for pain: *fast fibers* for sharp, immediate pain and *slow fibers* for chronic, dull, steady pain.

An important distinction between these fibers is the myelination or nonmyelination of their axons, which travel from the pain receptors to the spinal cord. As discussed in Chapter 3, myelination speeds up neural communication. Myelinated axons, like heavily insulated wire, can send information quickly. Nonmyelinated axons send information more slowly.

Think of a time when you touched a hot skillet. A sharp, fast, localized pain at the moment your skin touched the pan caused you to jerk your hand away. It was followed by a slow, dull, more diffuse burning pain. The fast-acting receptors are activated by strong physical pressure and temperature extremes, whereas the slow-acting receptors are activated by chemical changes in tissue when skin is damaged. In terms of adaptation, fast pain leads us to recoil from harmful objects and therefore is protective, whereas slow pain keeps us from using the affected body parts and therefore helps in recuperation (**FIGURE 5.45**).

GATE CONTROL THEORY The brain regulates the experience of pain, sometimes producing it, sometimes suppressing it. Pain is a complex experience that depends on biological, psychological, and cultural factors. The psychologist Ronald Melzack conducted pioneering research in this area. For example, he demonstrated that psychological factors, such as past experiences, are extremely important in determining how much pain a person feels.

FIGURE 5.45
How We Experience Touch: The Sense of Pain

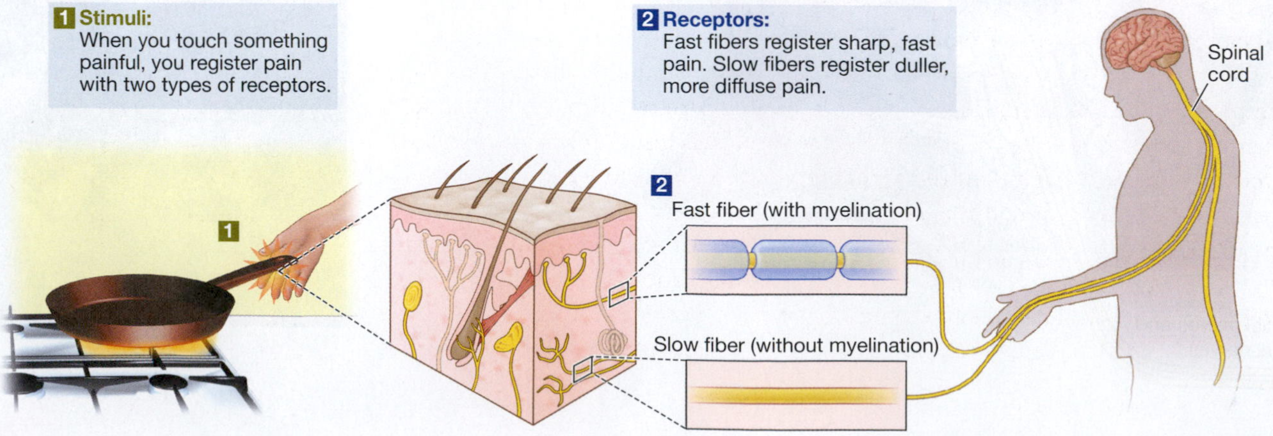

1 Stimuli:
When you touch something painful, you register pain with two types of receptors.
2 Receptors:
Fast fibers register sharp, fast pain. Slow fibers register duller, more diffuse pain.
Spinal cord
1
2
Fast fiber (with myelination)
Slow fiber (without myelination)

With his collaborator Patrick Wall, Melzack formulated the *gate control theory of pain*. According to this theory, we experience pain when pain receptors are activated and a neural "gate" in the spinal cord allows the signals through to the brain (Melzack & Wall, 1965). These ideas were radical in that they conceptualized pain as a perceptual experience within the brain rather than simply a response to nerve stimulation. The theory states that pain signals are transmitted by small-diameter nerve fibers. These fibers can be blocked at the spinal cord (prevented from reaching the brain) by the firing of larger sensory nerve fibers. Thus, sensory nerve fibers can "close a gate" and prevent or reduce the perception of pain. This is why scratching an itch is so satisfying, why rubbing an aching muscle helps reduce the ache, and why vigorously rubbing the skin where an injection is about to be given reduces the needle's sting (**FIGURE 5.46**).

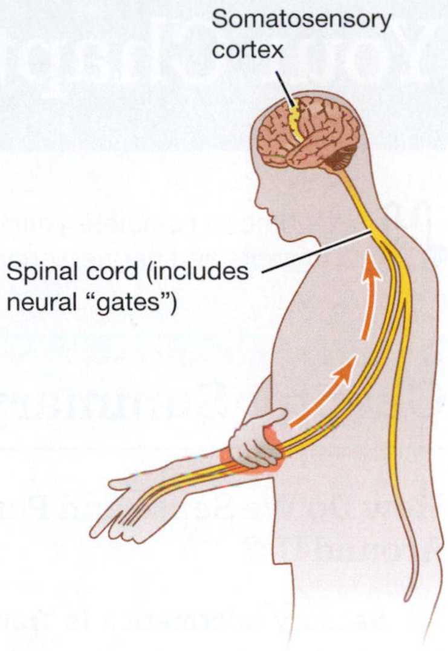

FIGURE 5.46
Gate Control Theory
According to the gate control theory of pain, neural "gates" in the spinal cord allow signals through. Those gates can be closed when information about touch is being transmitted (e.g., by rubbing a sore arm or by distraction).

A number of cognitive states, such as distraction, can also close the gate. Athletes sometimes play through pain because of their intense focus on the game. Wounded soldiers sometimes continue to fight during combat, often failing to perceive a level of pain that would render them inactive at other times. An insect bite bothers us more when we are trying to sleep and have few distractions than when we are wide-awake and active.

Conversely, some mental processes, such as worrying about or focusing on the painful stimulus, seem to open the pain gates wider. Research participants who are well rested rate the same level of a painful stimulus as less painful than do participants who are fearful, anxious, or depressed (Loggia et al., 2008). Likewise, positive moods help people cope with pain. In a systematic review of the literature, Swedish researchers found that listening to music was an extremely effective means of reducing postoperative pain, perhaps because it helps patients relax (Engwall & Duppils, 2009).

Christopher deCharms and colleagues (2005) have pioneered techniques that offer hope for people who suffer from painful conditions. The researchers sought to teach people in pain—many of these people in chronic pain—to visualize their pain more positively. For example, participants were taught to think about a burning sensation as soothing, like the feeling of being in a sauna. As they tried to learn such techniques, they viewed fMRI images that showed which regions of their brains were active as they performed the tasks. Many participants learned techniques that altered their brain activity and reduced their pain.

Of course, there are more traditional ways to control pain. Most of us have taken over-the-counter drugs, usually ibuprofen or acetaminophen, to reduce pain perception. If you have ever suffered from a severe toothache or needed surgery, you have probably experienced the benefits of pain medication. When a dentist administers Novocain to sensory neurons in the mouth, pain messages are not transmitted to the brain, so the mouth feels numb. General anesthesia slows down the firing of neurons throughout the nervous system, and the patient becomes unresponsive to stimulation (Perkins, 2007).

You can use your knowledge of pain perception anytime you need to reduce your own pain or to help others in pain. Distraction is usually the easiest way to reduce pain. If you are preparing for a painful procedure or suffering after one, watching an entertaining movie can help, especially if it is funny enough to elevate your mood. Music may help you relax, making it easier to deal with pain. Rapid rubbing can benefit a stubbed toe, for example, or a finger that was caught in a closing drawer. You will also feel less pain if you are rested, not fearful, and not anxious. Finally, try to visualize your pain as something more pleasant. Of course, severe pain is a warning that something in the body is seriously wrong. If you experience severe pain, you should be treated by a medical professional.

Q **Why do people often rub parts of their bodies that are injured?**

ANSWER: Rubbing activates sensory receptors that can close the pain gate, reducing the experience of pain.

Your Chapter Review

It's time to complete your study experience! Go to **INQUIZITIVE** to practice actively with this chapter's concepts and get personalized feedback along the way.

Chapter Summary

How Do We Sense and Perceive the World Around Us?

5.1 Sensory Information Is Translated into Meaningful Signals Sensation is the detection of physical stimuli in the environment. Perception is our conscious experience of those stimuli. Bottom-up processing is based on features of a stimulus. Top-down processing is based on context and expectations. Transduction is the process of converting sensory stimuli into a pattern of neural activity. Transduction takes place at sensory receptors, specialized cells within each sense organ that send signals from our environment to activate neurons. Most sensory information goes to the thalamus and then specialized brain regions.

5.2 Detection Requires a Certain Amount of the Stimulus Information from our environment needs to surpass some level before we can detect it. An absolute threshold is the minimum amount of stimulus intensity needed to activate a sensory receptor. A difference threshold is the amount of change required for detection by a sensory receptor. Signal detection theory is about the subjective nature of detecting a stimulus. Sensory adaptation occurs when sensory receptors stop responding to an unchanging stimulus.

5.3 The Brain Constructs a Stable Representation of the World from Five Senses In perception, the brain integrates millions of diverse neural inputs to produce stable representations from five independent senses, which can interact at times. This activity produces awareness, a conscious experience of the physical world. In some individuals, the representations of different senses are combined in unusual ways, such as in synesthesia.

How Do We See?

5.4 Sensory Receptors in the Eye Transmit Visual Information to the Brain Light is focused by the lens onto the retina, which is at the back of the eye. The retina houses the photoreceptors: rods and cones. Rods and cones communicate with ganglion cells of the optic nerve. This nerve exits the eye at the blind spot and crosses into the brain at the optic chiasm. There, axons from each eye cross into opposite sides of the brain, so the left hemisphere processes information from the right visual field and vice versa. The information is processed in the thalamus and the primary visual cortex (in the occipital lobe). From the visual cortex, the ventral stream processes "what" information about objects, and the dorsal stream processes "where" information about locations.

5.5 The Color of Light Is Determined by Its Wavelength The human eye detects electromagnetic radiation wavelengths of 400–700 nanometers. The retina contains three types of cones. Each type is responsive to a different wavelength (short, medium, or long), and this responsiveness enables us to perceive colors. Color blindness is caused by a malfunction in one or more of the cone types. Colors are differentiated by their hue, saturation, and lightness.

5.6 Perceiving Objects Requires Organization of Visual Information Gestalt principles—such as proximity, similarity, continuity, closure, and common fate—account for the ways in which perceptual information is organized into wholes and objects. Object constancy refers to the way the brain accurately perceives images even with minimal or changing stimulus cues. The four constancies are size, shape, color, and lightness. Humans are especially good at recognizing faces. The fusiform gyrus is one of the brain regions most responsible for this ability.

5.7 You Be the Psychologist: Are Faces Special? Psychologists debate whether faces are processed in a special way because they are important social signals or because they are objects with unique properties.

5.8 Perception of Depth, Size, and Motion Is Guided by Internal and External Cues Depth perception is critical for locating objects in space. To perceive depth, the brain draws on binocular and monocular cues. Size perception depends on distance: Close objects produce large retinal images, whereas far objects produce small retinal images. Motion is detected by motion-sensitive neurons in the visual cortex.

How Do We Hear?

5.9 Audition Results from Changes in Air Pressure The amplitude and frequency of sound waves cause the perceptual experiences of loudness and pitch, respectively. Sound waves travel from the outer ear through the auditory canal to the eardrum. Vibrations from these waves stimulate the ossicles, bones of the inner ear. The vibrations of these bones stimulate the oval window, a membrane on the cochlea, a fluid-filled chamber in the inner ear. Pressure waves from the cochlear fluid stimulate the basilar membrane. This stimulation causes the ear's sensory receptors, the hair cells, to bend and activate neurons in the auditory nerve. These neurons send messages through the thalamus to the primary auditory cortex (in the temporal lobe). Cochlear implants can help with hearing loss by directly stimulating the auditory nerve, overcoming the lack of hair cells in the inner ear.

5.10 Pitch Is Encoded by Frequency and Location Low-frequency sound waves are sensed through temporal coding, as cochlear hair cells fire at a rate equivalent to the frequency of the waves. For high-frequency sound waves, groups of hair cells must take turns firing. High-frequency sound waves are also sensed through place coding—that is, by hair cells at different locations in the cochlea.

5.11 Psychology Outside the Lab: Are Your Listening Habits Damaging Your Hearing? Loud noises can permanently damage the sensitive hair cells that line the ear canals and transmit signals to the nerves involved in sound perception. Once those hair cells are damaged, they cannot be repaired.

How Do We Taste and Smell?

5.12 There Are Five Basic Taste Sensations Gustation, the sense of taste, is produced by taste buds. The taste buds are located in the papillae, structures on the tongue. The five types of taste buds yield the taste sensations: sweet, sour, salty, bitter, and umami (savory). Cultural factors help determine taste preferences.

5.13 Smell Is the Detection of Odorants Olfaction occurs when odorants stimulate smell receptors, which are located in the olfactory epithelium in the nose and nasal cavity. Smell receptors send messages to neurons in the olfactory bulb, located below the frontal lobes. The signals are sent directly to other brain areas, including those that regulate memory and emotion. Pheromones are chemicals that do not produce odor but are processed by the smell receptors. Pheromones can motivate sexual behavior in nonhuman animals and may function similarly in humans.

How Do We Feel Touch and Pain?

5.14 The Skin Contains Sensory Receptors for Touch Touch is known as the haptic sense. Tactile stimulation activates touch receptors in the skin, which respond to temperature, pressure, and pain. Touch information travels to the thalamus, which sends it to the primary somatosensory cortex (in the parietal lobe).

5.15 Pain Receptors Exist Throughout the Body The perception of pain prompts organisms to protect themselves from damage. Fast, myelinated fibers process sharp, sudden pain. Slow, nonmyelinated fibers process dull, chronic pain. According to the gate control theory, pain perception requires both the activation of pain receptors and spinal cord processing of the signal. The gate can be closed or occupied if other stimuli are processed simultaneously. Activities such as rubbing an area around the painful one, distracting oneself, or thinking happy thoughts can decrease the perception of pain.

Key Terms

absolute threshold, p. 163
audition, p. 183
binocular depth cues, p. 178
binocular disparity, p. 179
bottom-up processing, p. 160
cones, p. 167
convergence, p. 179
difference threshold, p. 163
eardrum, p. 184
fovea, p. 168
gustation, p. 189
haptic sense, p. 194
monocular depth cues, p. 178
motion parallax, p. 180
object constancy, p. 175
olfaction, p. 189
olfactory bulb, p. 193
olfactory epithelium, p. 192
perception, p. 160
place coding, p. 187
retina, p. 167
rods, p. 167
sensation, p. 160
sensory adaptation, p. 165
signal detection theory (SDT), p. 164
sound wave, p. 183
taste buds, p. 189
temporal coding, p. 186
top-down processing, p. 160
transduction, p. 161
vestibular sense, p. 185

Practice Exercises

1. Which answer accurately lists the order in which these structures participate in sensation and perception (except for smell)?
   a. thalamus, specialized receptors, cortex
   b. specialized receptors, cortex, thalamus
   c. cortex, specialized receptors, thalamus
   d. specialized receptors, thalamus, cortex

2. Match each process of detecting and interpreting information—sensation, perception, bottom-up processing, top-down processing-with its definition.
   a. processing based on prior knowledge and expectation
   b. detection of sensory signals by receptors
   c. processing and interpretation of sensory signals
   d. perception based on physical features of sensory stimuli

3. Which sense organ is largest in humans?
   a. eyes, due to the large number of cones densely packed in the fovea
   b. ears, due to the curvature of the cochlea, which increases surface area of the basilar membrane to house an infinite number of hair cells
   c. nose, due to the dense array of cells packed within the olfactory epithelium
   d. tongue, due to the large number of taste buds that can be housed within each papilla
   e. skin, due to the large surface area

4. In audition, detecting the ________ of the sound wavelength results in the perception of loudness. Detecting the ________ of the wavelength results in the perception of pitch.
   a. frequency, amplitude
   b. amplitude, frequency
   c. frequency, hertz
   d. hertz, frequency

5. Identify each of the following visual perceptions as an example of size constancy, shape constancy, color constancy, or lightness constancy.
   a. recognizing a dinner plate as circular, even when viewing it at an angle makes it appear elliptical
   b. labeling grass as green, even in the dark
   c. identifying a building as a skyscraper, even though it appears smaller than other objects in your field of vision
   d. recognizing a door as a door, even when it is fully open so that you see only the edge
   e. knowing that your friend is wearing the same T-shirt when it is illuminated differently by bright fluorescent lights or dull lamp lights

6. Imagine you have a dull, chronic pain across your lower back. No matter how you position yourself, you cannot make the pain go away. Which combination of descriptors is most related to the signaling of this type of pain?
   a. activated by chemical changes in tissue, fast fibers, nonmyelinated axons
   b. activated by strong physical pressure or temperature extremes, fast fibers, myelinated axons
   c. activated by chemical changes in tissue, slow fibers, nonmyelinated axons
   d. activated by strong physical pressure or temperature extremes, slow fibers, myelinated axons

7. After hours of waiting, a bird-watcher hears the call of a rare bird species. The bird-watcher reacts by turning their head about 45 degrees to the left and sees the bird. Which of the following statements best describes how the bird-watcher knew where to turn their head?
   a. The call reached the bird-watcher's left ear before the right ear; the call was less intense in the bird-watcher's right ear than in the left ear.
   b. The call reached the bird-watcher's left ear before the right ear; the call was less intense in the bird-watcher's left ear than in the right ear.
   c. The call reached the bird-watcher's right ear before the left ear; the call was less intense in the bird-watcher's right ear than in the left ear.
   d. The call reached the bird-watcher's right ear before the left ear; the call was less intense in the bird-watcher's left ear than in the right ear.

8. In which lobe of the brain (frontal, occipital, parietal, temporal) does each of the following sensory cortices reside?
   a. primary auditory cortex
   b. primary somatosensory cortex
   c. primary visual cortex

9. Which of the following statements about the gustatory system are true?
   a. Taste is a mixture of five basic kinds of gustatory receptors.
   b. Different regions of the tongue are more sensitive to different tastes.
   c. The texture of a food can affect how its taste is perceived.
   d. People lose half of their taste buds by age 20.
   e. Supertasters tend to be overweight and are more likely to be male.

10. Imagine you are preparing to conduct a brain imaging study of visual processing. Which pathway—dorsal or ventral—do you hypothesize will be activated by each of the following experimental tasks?
   a. deciding which of two objects is farther away
   b. describing an object's color
   c. describing a silhouette's shape
   d. naming an object
   e. selecting which two of three objects are closest together

6 Learning

Big Questions

BY THE 1970S, ALL THE WOLVES IN YELLOWSTONE NATIONAL PARK had been killed as part of a predator control plan. In 1987, the U.S. Fish and Wildlife Service announced a recovery plan to reintroduce wolves to the park. Farmers and ranchers were skeptical, fearing that the wolves would prey on their sheep and cattle. Scientists came up with a solution. Nonlethal doses of poison were added to sheep carcasses, which were placed where wolves would find them. When the wolves ate the meat, they immediately vomited. The wolves soon learned to associate eating sheep with becoming ill, and they avoided preying on sheep. Using this procedure to help wolves learn to not eat sheep is an example of how psychological science can be put to work in "the real world."

The principles behind the wolves' learning are also the basis for how humans learn. This chapter examines how the process of learning takes place. This material represents some of psychology's central contributions to our understanding of behavior. Learning theories have been used to improve quality of life and to train humans as well as nonhuman animals to perform new tasks. To understand behavior, therefore, we need to know what learning is. How do we learn to adjust our response when stimuli are presented over and over? How do we learn associations between stimuli or events in the world? And how do we learn about the consequences of actions?

Learning Objectives

- Define learning.
- Identify three types of learning processes.
- Describe the nonassociative learning processes, habituation and sensitization, and explain the significance of each.

How Do We Learn?

The ability to learn is crucial for all animals. To survive, animals need to learn things such as which types of foods are dangerous, when it is safe to sleep, and which sounds or sights signal potential dangers. Learning is central to almost all aspects of human existence. It makes possible our basic abilities (such as walking and speaking) and our complex ones (such as flying airplanes, performing surgery, or maintaining intimate relationships). Learning also shapes many aspects of daily life: clothing choices; musical tastes; cultural values, such as the value of recycling and protecting the environment; and so on (**FIGURE 6.1**).

6.1 Learning Results from Experience

learning A relatively enduring change in behavior resulting from experience.

nonassociative learning Responding after repeated exposure to a single stimulus or event.

associative learning Linking two stimuli or events that occur together.

Learning is defined as a relatively enduring change in behavior resulting from experience. Learning occurs when an animal benefits from experience so that it is better adapted to its environment and more prepared to deal with it in the future. For example, the animal may be better able to predict when certain events are likely to happen.

Psychologists often distinguish *learning* from *memory* (see Chapter 7), although the two concepts are clearly related. The study of learning examines how we adjust our behavior based on the repetition of stimuli or on predictive associations between stimuli, actions, or consequences. In contrast, the study of memory focuses on how we acquire, store, and retrieve knowledge about facts, events, places, and skills. Psychologists generally differentiate three types of learning (**FIGURE 6.2**): nonassociative, associative, and social.

FIGURE 6.1
Learning in Daily Life
Children whose parents encourage them to recycle may develop a positive attitude toward the environment.

NONASSOCIATIVE LEARNING The simplest form of learning occurs after repeated exposure to a single stimulus or event. For example, if you move to a new house by some train tracks, the rumble of passing trains might disturb your sleep. After you live in the house for a while, you quit waking up to the sound of trains. The change in response to the stimulus is a form of **nonassociative learning**.

ASSOCIATIVE LEARNING The second type of learning is coming to understand, through personal experiences, how stimuli or events are related. For example, your dog runs for the door when you pick up the leash because it has learned this action leads to a walk. You might associate working with getting paid. **Associative learning** is the linking of two events that, in general, take place one right after the other. Associations develop through *conditioning*, a process in which environmental stimuli and behavioral responses become connected.

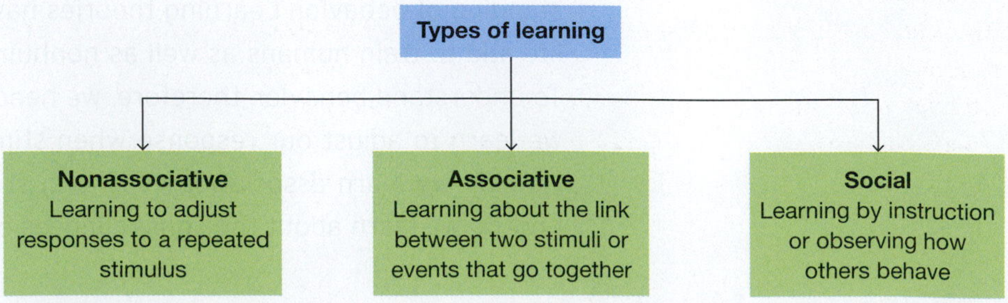

FIGURE 6.2
Types of Learning

SOCIAL LEARNING The third type of learning is also concerned with understanding how stimuli or events are associated, but the learning occurs through social means—either verbal instruction or observation. For example, during the COVID-19 pandemic, you might have learned from media sources about the association between wearing masks and the risk of virus transmission, and you also may have observed examples of others practicing this behavior in an effort to reduce the spread of the virus. **Social learning** involves acquiring behaviors and predictive associations between stimuli or events through interactions with others.

social learning Acquiring or changing a behavior after verbal instruction or exposure to another individual performing that behavior.

Q The sound of a dentist's drill makes you nervous. What type of learning produced your fear?

ANSWER: associative learning

6.2 Nonassociative Learning Involves Habituation and Sensitization

Nonassociative learning, the simplest form of learning, occurs when you gain new information after repeated exposure to a single stimulus or event. The two most common forms of nonassociative learning are habituation and sensitization (**FIGURE 6.3**).

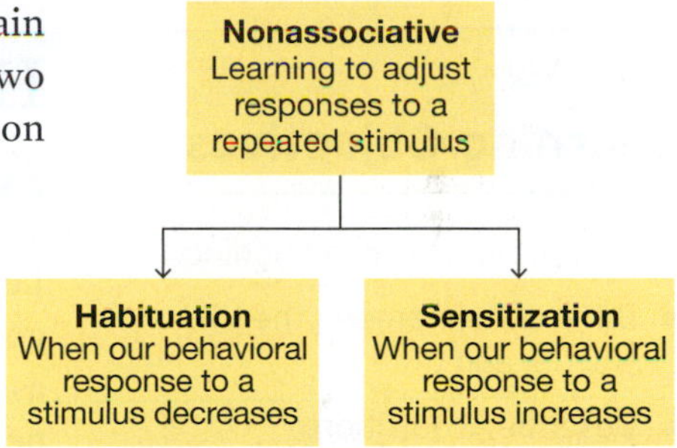

Nonassociative
Learning to adjust responses to a repeated stimulus
Habituation
When our behavioral response to a stimulus decreases
Sensitization
When our behavioral response to a stimulus increases

FIGURE 6.3
Types of Nonassociative Learning

Habituation leads to a decrease in a behavioral response after repeated exposure to a stimulus. We tend to notice new things around us. If something is neither rewarding nor harmful, habituation leads us to ignore it. Recall the discussion of sensory adaptation in Chapter 5. Habituation is unlike sensory adaptation in that you can still perceive the stimuli. You just do not respond to them because you have learned that they are not important.

We constantly habituate to meaningless events around us. If you have lived in or visited a major city, you were probably very attentive to sirens at first. When you heard one, you looked around to see if there was immediate danger. But soon you no longer reacted to sirens. In fact, you barely noticed them. It is not that you do not hear them. You just do not respond because you have habituated to them.

What happens if the sirens suddenly stop? You are likely to immediately notice the change. The increase in a response because of a change in something familiar is *dishabituation*. This process is important in the animal world. For instance, birds might stop singing when they detect a predator, such as a hawk. The absence of birdsong alerts other animals, such as squirrels, to potential danger.

All animals show habituation and dishabituation. Indeed, much of what psychologists have learned about nonassociative learning has come from studying simple invertebrates such as Aplysia, a type of marine snail (**FIGURE 6.4**). Habituation can be demonstrated quite easily by touching the animal repeatedly, which initially causes it to withdraw its gills. After about 10 touches, it stops responding, and this lack of response lasts about 2 to 3 hours. Repeated habituation trials can lead to a state of habituation that lasts several weeks.

Sensitization leads to an increase in a behavioral response after exposure to a stimulus. The stimuli that most often lead to sensitization are those that are meaningful to the animal, such as something threatening or painful. If you are studying and smell something burning, you probably will not habituate to this smell. In fact, you might focus even greater attention on your sense of smell to assess the possible threat of fire, and you will be highly vigilant for any indication of smoke or flames. In general, sensitization leads to heightened responsiveness to other

habituation A decrease in behavioral response after repeated exposure to a stimulus.

sensitization An increase in behavioral response after exposure to a stimulus.

FIGURE 6.4
Simple Model of Learning
Aplysia, a type of marine invertebrate, are used to study the neurochemical basis of learning.

ANSWER: Habituation decreases a behavioral response, whereas sensitization increases a behavioral response.

Learning Objectives

- Define classical conditioning.

- Differentiate among the UR, US, CS, and CR.

- Describe acquisition, extinction, spontaneous recovery, generalization, discrimination, and second-order conditioning.

- Describe the Rescorla-Wagner model of classical conditioning, including the role of prediction errors.

```
┌─────────────────────────┐
│      Associative         │
│ Learning the relationship│
│   between two stimuli    │
│       or events          │
└─────────────────────────┘
      │                │
      ▼                ▼
┌───────────┐    ┌───────────┐
│ Classical │    │  Operant  │
│conditioning│   │conditioning│
│When we learn│  │When we learn│
│that a      │   │that a      │
│stimulus    │   │behavior    │
│predicts    │   │leads to    │
│another     │   │a           │
│stimulus    │   │consequence │
└───────────┘    └───────────┘
```

FIGURE 6.5
Two Types of Associative Learning

stimuli. Giving a strong electric shock to the animal's tail leads to sensitization. Following the shock, a mild touch anywhere on the body will cause it to withdraw its gills.

The neurobiologist Eric Kandel and colleagues (Carew et al., 1972; Kandel et al., 2014) have used Aplysia to study the neural basis of nonassociative learning. Their findings show that alterations in the functioning of the synapses lead to habituation and sensitization. For both types of simple learning, presynaptic neurons alter their neurotransmitter release. A reduction in neurotransmitter release leads to habituation. An increase in neurotransmitter release leads to sensitization. Knowing the neural basis of simple learning gives us the building blocks to understand more complex learning processes in both human and nonhuman animals. For this research, Kandel received the Nobel Prize in 2000.

 What is the primary difference between habituation and sensitization?

How Do We Learn Predictive Associations?

Learning helps us solve adaptive challenges by enabling us to predict when things go together. Consider the need to find water. Over time, each person has learned to associate the sound of flowing liquid with drinking. If you were lost in the wilderness and desperately thirsty, you could listen for the sound of running water, hoping that by locating the sound you could find the source.

6.3 Classical Conditioning Is Learning What Goes Together

In **classical conditioning**, also known as **Pavlovian conditioning**, a neutral stimulus elicits a response because it has become associated with a stimulus that already produces that response (**FIGURE 6.5**). In other words, you learn that one event predicts another. For example, you learn that a needle and syringe at the doctor's office are associated with getting a shot. Now you feel nervous whenever you see a syringe at the doctor's office.

The term *Pavlovian* is derived from the name of Ivan Pavlov, a Russian physiologist who studied the digestive system and won a Nobel Prize for this work in 1904. He was interested in the *salivary reflex*—the automatic, unlearned response that occurs when a food stimulus is presented to a hungry animal, including a human. To study this reflex, Pavlov created an apparatus to collect saliva from dogs and measured the different amounts of saliva that resulted when he placed various types of food into a dog's mouth (**FIGURE 6.6**).

As with so many major scientific advances, Pavlov's contribution to psychology started with a simple observation. One day he was annoyed to realize that the laboratory dogs were salivating before they tasted their food. Indeed, the dogs started salivating the moment a lab technician walked into the room or whenever they saw the bowls that usually contained food. Pavlov's genius was in recognizing that this behavioral response was a window to the working mind. Unlike inborn reflexes, salivation at the sight of a bowl or a person is not automatic. Therefore, that response must have been acquired

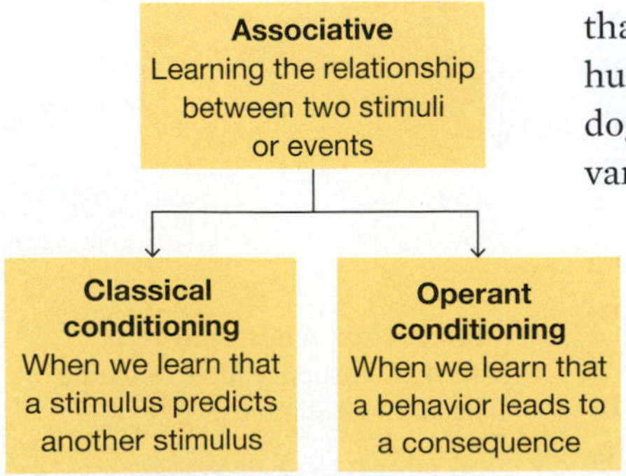

(a)

(b)

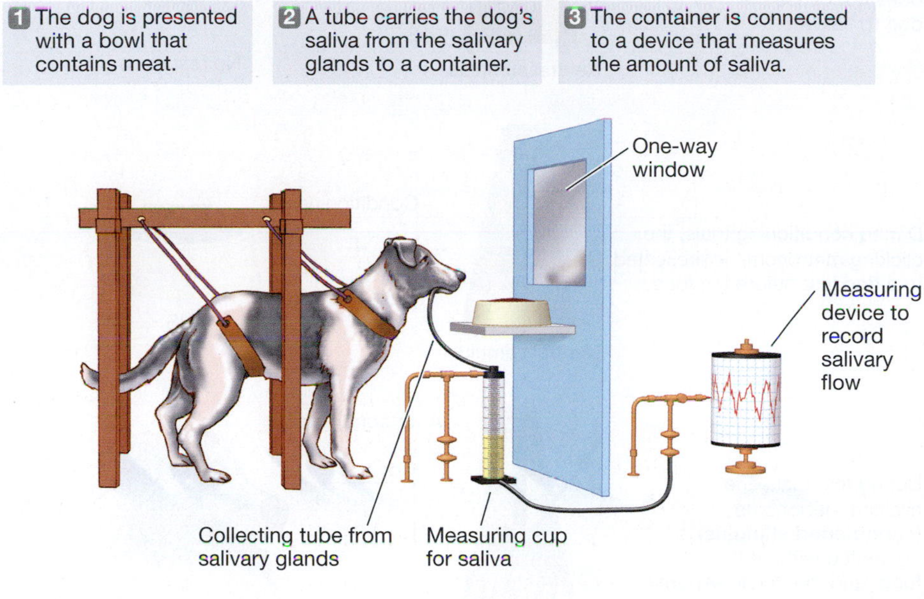
1 The dog is presented with a bowl that contains meat.
2 A tube carries the dog's saliva from the salivary glands to a container.
3 The container is connected to a device that measures the amount of saliva.
One-way window
Measuring device to record salivary flow
Collecting tube from salivary glands
Measuring cup for saliva

FIGURE 6.6
Pavlov's Apparatus and Classical Conditioning
(a) Ivan Pavlov, pictured here with his colleagues and one of his canine subjects, conducted groundbreaking work on classical conditioning. **(b)** Pavlov's apparatus collected and measured a dog's saliva.

through experience. This insight led Pavlov to devote the next 30 years of his life to studying the basic principles of learning.

Pavlov conducted the basic research on conditioning using the salivary reflex. In these studies, a *neutral stimulus* unrelated to the salivary reflex, such as the clicking of a metronome, is presented along with a stimulus that reliably produces the reflex, such as food. The neutral stimulus can be anything that the animal can see or hear as long as it is not something that is usually associated with being fed. This pairing is called a *conditioning trial*. It is repeated a number of times. Then come the *test trials*. Here, the metronome sound is presented alone and the salivary reflex is measured. Pavlov found that under these conditions, the sound of the metronome on its own produced salivation. This type of learning is now referred to as classical conditioning, or Pavlovian conditioning.

Pavlov called the salivation elicited by food the **unconditioned response (UR)**. The response is "unconditioned" because it is unlearned. It occurs without prior training and is an automatic behavior, such as some simple reflexes. Similarly, the food is the **unconditioned stimulus (US)**. Normally, without any training, the food leads to salivation (UR). Thus, before learning takes place, the US produces the UR.

Because the clicking of the metronome produces salivation only after training, it is the **conditioned stimulus (CS)**. That is, before conditioning, the clicking of the metronome is unrelated to salivation. After learning takes place, the clicking serves as a "signal" that food is about to become available. The increased salivation that occurs when only the conditioned stimulus is presented is the **conditioned response (CR)**. It is the response that has been learned. In the case of Pavlov's

classical conditioning (Pavlovian conditioning) A type of associative learning in which a neutral stimulus comes to elicit a response when it is associated with a stimulus that already produces that response.

unconditioned response (UR) A response that does not have to be learned, such as a reflex.

unconditioned stimulus (US) A stimulus that elicits a response, such as a reflex, without any prior learning.

conditioned stimulus (CS) A stimulus that elicits a response only after learning has taken place.

conditioned response (CR) A response to a conditioned stimulus; a response that has been learned.

FIGURE 6.7
Pavlov's Classical Conditioning

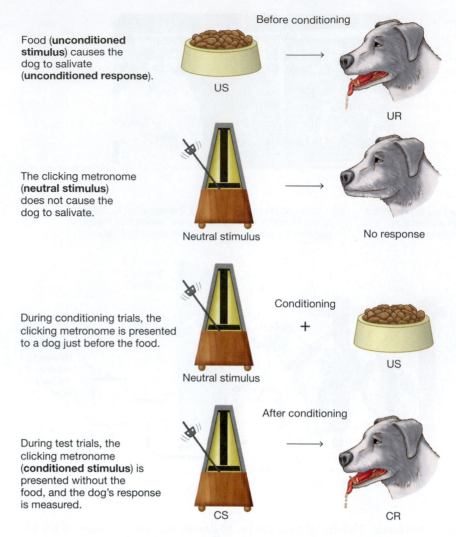

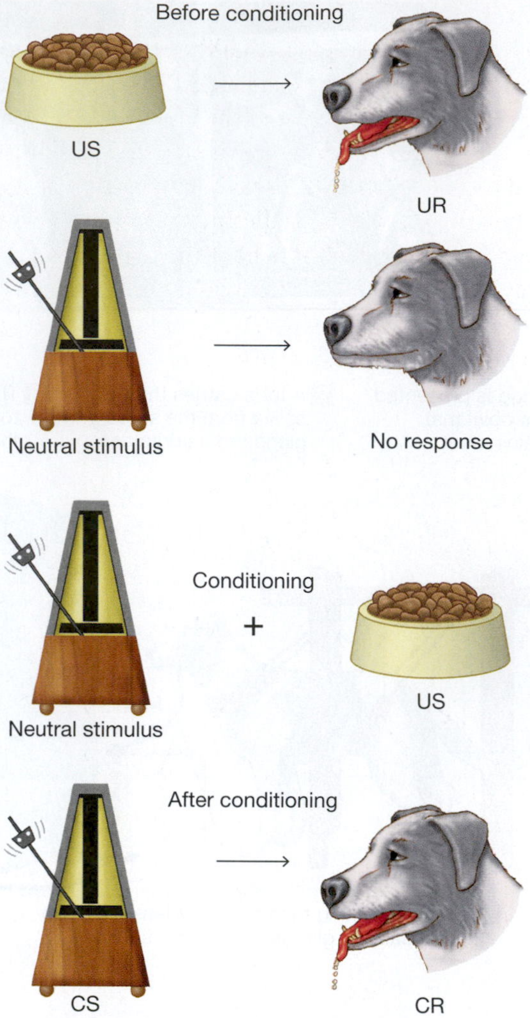
Before conditioning
Food (**unconditioned stimulus**) causes the dog to salivate (**unconditioned response**).
US
UR
The clicking metronome (**neutral stimulus**) does not cause the dog to salivate.
Neutral stimulus
No response
During conditioning trials, the clicking metronome is presented to a dog just before the food.
Conditioning
+
Neutral stimulus
US
After conditioning
During test trials, the clicking metronome (**conditioned stimulus**) is presented without the food, and the dog's response is measured.
CS
CR

dogs, both the CR and the UR were salivation. However, the CR and the UR are not always identical: The CR usually is weaker than the UR. In other words, the metronome sound produces less saliva than the food does (**FIGURE 6.7**).

A key aspect of behaviors that can be classically conditioned is that they are elicited automatically by the US. These behaviors are not voluntary actions but rather are behaviors that occur naturally in response to the US, such as feelings, preferences, or bodily reflexes. For example, suppose you are watching a movie in which a character is attacked. As you watch the attack scene, you feel tense, anxious, and perhaps disgusted. When watching the frightening scene, your feelings occur naturally. That is, the stimulus (the frightening scene) and your response (feeling anxious) are unconditioned. Now imagine a piece of music that does not initially have much effect on you but that you hear in the movie just before each frightening scene. A good example is the musical theme from the 1975 horror movie *Jaws* (**FIGURE 6.8**). Eventually, you will begin to feel tense and anxious as soon as you hear the music. You have learned that the music (the CS) predicts scary scenes (the US). Because of this learning, you feel the tension and anxiety (the CR) when hearing the music. As in Pavlov's studies, the CS (music) produces a somewhat different emotional response than the US (the scary scene). The response may be weaker. It may be more a feeling of apprehension than one of fear or disgust. If you later hear this music in a different context, such as on the radio, you will again feel tense and anxious even though you are not watching the movie. You have been classically conditioned to be anxious when you hear the music.

FIGURE 6.8
Classical Conditioning in a Thriller
Like many suspenseful or scary movies, *Jaws* uses a classical-conditioning technique to make us feel afraid. The "duh-duh, duh-duh" soundtrack music plays just before each shark attack.

From his research, Pavlov concluded that the critical element in the acquisition of a learned association is that the stimuli occur together in time. Subsequent research has shown that the strongest conditioning occurs when there is a very brief delay between the onset of the conditioned stimulus and the unconditioned stimulus. Thus you will develop a stronger conditioned response to a piece of music if it begins just before a scary scene than if it begins during or after the scary scene: The music's role in predicting the frightening scene is an important part of the classical conditioning. The next time you watch a horror movie, pay attention to the way the music gets louder just before a scary part begins. And if you have not seen the classic movie *Jaws* yet, now might be a good time, because you will really understand how that music works.

Learning Tip

In classical conditioning:
Conditioned means learned and *unconditioned* means not learned.
A *stimulus* elicits a reaction and a *response* is the reaction.

Put them together and:
unconditioned stimulus: the stimulus that elicits a reaction without learning
unconditioned response: the unlearned reaction
conditioned stimulus: the stimulus that elicits a learned reaction
conditioned response: the learned reaction

Q What is the difference between a conditioned stimulus and an unconditioned stimulus?

ANSWER: An unconditioned stimulus elicits an involuntary (unconditioned) response without learning. A conditioned stimulus comes to elicit an involuntary (conditioned) response by being associated with the unconditioned stimulus.

6.4 Learning Is Acquired and Persists Until Extinction

Pavlov believed that conditioning is the basis for how animals learn in order to adapt to their environments. By learning to predict which objects signal pleasure or pain, animals acquire new adaptive behaviors. For instance, when an animal learns that a metronome beat predicts the appearance of food, this process of association is called **acquisition**. Acquisition is the formation of an association between a conditioned stimulus (here, a metronome) and an unconditioned stimulus (here, food; **FIGURE 6.9a**).

acquisition The gradual formation of an association between the conditioned and unconditioned stimuli.

Once a behavior is acquired, how long does it persist? What if the animal expects to receive food every time it hears the beat of the metronome, but food stops appearing and the metronome is still beating? Animals sometimes have to learn when associations are no longer meaningful. Normally, after standard Pavlovian conditioning, the metronome (CS) leads to salivation (CR) because the animal learns to associate the metronome with the food (US). If the metronome is presented many times and food does not arrive, the animal eventually learns that the metronome is no longer a good predictor of food. Because of this new learning, the animal's salivary response gradually disappears. This process is known as **extinction**. The conditioned response is *extinguished* when the conditioned stimulus no longer predicts the unconditioned stimulus (**FIGURE 6.9b**).

extinction A process in which the conditioned response is weakened when the conditioned stimulus is repeated without the unconditioned stimulus.

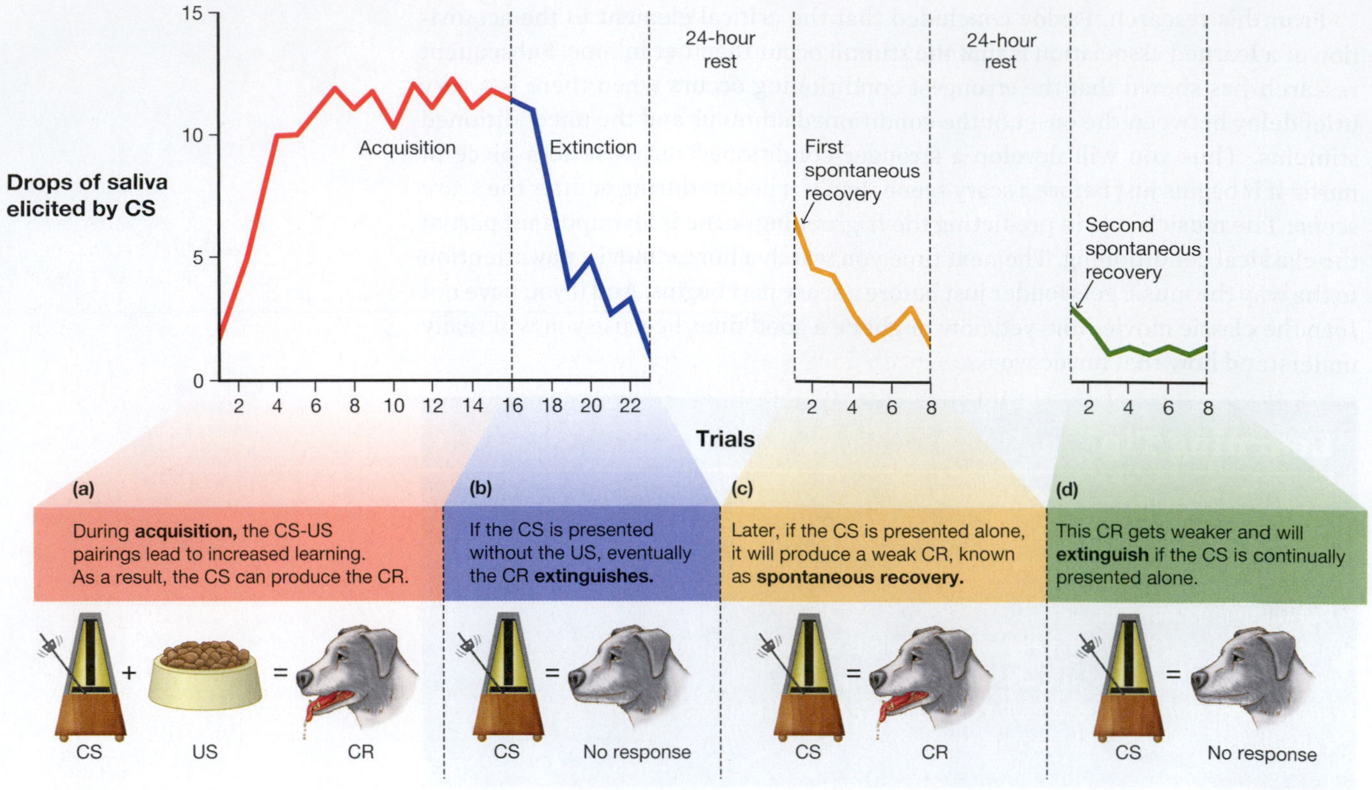

Drops of saliva elicited by CS
15
10
5
0
Acquisition
Extinction
24-hour rest
First spontaneous recovery
24-hour rest
Second spontaneous recovery
2 4 6 8 10 12 14 16 18 20 22
2 4 6 8
2 4 6 8
Trials
(a)
During **acquisition,** the CS-US pairings lead to increased learning. As a result, the CS can produce the CR.
(b)
If the CS is presented without the US, eventually the CR **extinguishes.**
(c)
Later, if the CS is presented alone, it will produce a weak CR, known as **spontaneous recovery.**
(d)
This CR gets weaker and will **extinguish** if the CS is continually presented alone.
CS + US = CR
CS = No response
CS = CR
CS = No response

FIGURE 6.9
Acquisition, Extinction, and Spontaneous Recovery

spontaneous recovery When a previously extinguished conditioned response reemerges after the presentation of the conditioned stimulus.

Now suppose that, sometime after extinction, the metronome is set in motion. Starting the metronome will once again produce the conditioned response of salivation. Through such **spontaneous recovery**, the extinguished CS again produces a CR (**FIGURE 6.9c**). This recovery is temporary, however. It will fade quickly unless the CS is again paired with the US. Even a single pairing of the CS with the US will reestablish the CR, which will then again diminish if CS-US pairings do not continue. The fact that spontaneous recovery occurs tells us that extinction replaces the associative bond but does not eliminate that bond. Extinction is a form of new learning that overwrites the previous association: The animal learns that the original association no longer holds true (e.g., the metronome no longer signals that food will follow; Bouton, 1994; Bouton et al., 2016; **FIGURE 6.9d**).

Q What leads to the extinction of a conditioned response?

ANSWER: repeated presentations of the conditioned stimulus without the unconditioned stimulus

6.5 Learning Involves Expectancies and Prediction

Since Pavlov's time, learning theorists have tried to understand the mental processes that underlie conditioning. Two important principles have emerged from this work: (1) Classical conditioning is a way that animals come to *predict* the occurrence of events, and (2) the strength or likelihood of a CR is determined by how accurately the CS predicts the US. Consider rain—both dark clouds and umbrellas are associated with rain, but which is better at predicting rain? Dark clouds are almost always present when it rains. Umbrellas are often present when it rains but not always. Sometimes there are dark clouds and rain but no umbrellas.

Indeed, sometimes umbrellas are used on sunny days. We eventually learn that dark clouds are better signals of rain than umbrellas are (Schoenbaum et al., 2013).

The psychologist Robert Rescorla (1966) conducted some of the first studies that highlighted the role of expectation and prediction in learning. The cognitive model of classical learning, published by Rescorla and his colleague Allan Wagner, profoundly changed our understanding of learning (Rescorla & Wagner, 1972). The **Rescorla-Wagner model** states that an animal learns to expect that some predictors (potential CSs) are better than others. Again, for learning to take place, the conditioned stimulus should ideally come before the unconditioned stimulus, thereby setting up an expectation for it. In addition, according to the Rescorla-Wagner model, whether a conditioned association is acquired, maintained, strengthened, or extinguished is determined by the extent to which a US, or its absence, is unexpected or surprising. Learning theorists refer to the difference between the expected and actual outcomes as *prediction error*.

Rescorla-Wagner model A cognitive model of classical conditioning; it holds that learning is determined by the extent to which an unconditioned stimulus is unexpected or surprising.

PREDICTION ERRORS Suppose that after a stimulus appears, something surprising happens. It could be either the presence of an unexpected event or a stronger version of the expected stimulus than anticipated. This prediction error is considered a *positive prediction error* and strengthens the association between the CS and the US. Now suppose an expected event does not happen. The absence of the event leads to a *negative prediction error*, which weakens the CS-US association. Note here that *positive* and *negative* do not mean good and bad. Rather, *positive* means the presence of something unexpected, whereas *negative* refers to the absence of something expected. In both cases, the prediction error affects the strength or likelihood of the association between the CS and the US.

Say you always use an electric can opener to open a can of dog food. Your dog associates the sound of the can opener (CS) with the appearance of food (US). That is, the dog has learned that the sound signals the arrival of food. The dog wags its tail and runs around in circles when it hears that sound, expecting to be fed (FIGURE 6.10a). Now say the electric can opener breaks and you replace it with a manual one. Without hearing the sound of the electric can opener, your dog receives food. This change will produce a large positive prediction error. In turn, the error will cause your dog to pay attention to events in its environment that might have produced the unexpected food (FIGURE 6.10b). Over time, your dog will learn to associate being fed with your use of the new can opener (FIGURE 6.10c).

Eventually, learning will reach its maximum. At that point, no prediction errors will be generated because the food is fully predicted by the new can opener and no further updates to the association are needed. But suppose one day you decide to make a

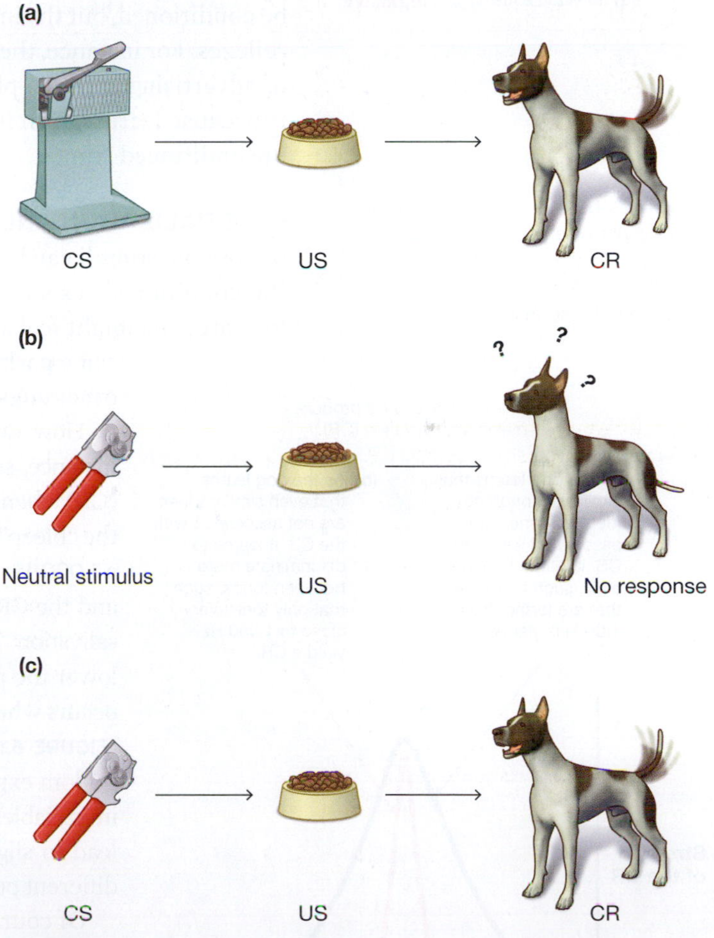

FIGURE 6.10
Rescorla-Wagner Model
The Rescorla-Wagner model of learning emphasizes prediction error. **(a)** Here, a dog associates the sound of an electric can opener with the arrival of food. **(b)** With the substitution of a manual can opener for the electric one, the dog is initially surprised. What happened to the reliable predictor of the dog's food? **(c)** This prediction error causes the dog to check the environment for a new stimulus. When the dog comes to associate the manual can opener with the arrival of food, the new stimulus has become the better predictor of the expected event: time to eat!

tuna fish sandwich and use the new can opener to open the can of tuna. Your dog sees the can opener but does not receive food. This will produce a negative prediction error and your dog learns that the relationship between the can opener and dog food is not so reliable. Of course, if the new can opener breaks, it will stop signaling the arrival of food altogether. The dog will need to learn what new event signals the arrival of food. Prediction errors, whether positive or negative, create a surprising situation that leads to learning about the relationship between the CS and US.

Q **What produces a prediction error?**

ANSWER: a difference between the expected outcome and the actual one, strengthening or weakening the CS-US association

6.6 Learning Shapes Both Conditioned and Unconditioned Stimuli

Pavlov's dogs provided a powerful example of how simple reflexive behaviors can be conditioned, but the impact of classical conditioning extends far beyond simple reflexes. For instance, the principles of classical conditioning underlie many types of advertising and also play a role in the development of anxiety disorders. This is because learning can influence what types of stimuli serve as conditioned and unconditioned stimuli.

stimulus generalization Learning that occurs when stimuli that are similar but not identical to the conditioned stimulus produce the conditioned response.

GENERALIZATION AND DISCRIMINATION In any learning situation, hundreds of possible stimuli can be associated with the unconditioned stimulus to produce the conditioned response. Imagine you were bitten by a dog in the park. Going forward, you might feel a little nervous when you encounter that same dog in the same park, but are you also afraid of that same dog on the street, or other dogs of the same breed, or all dogs?

How does the brain determine which stimuli are relevant? For instance, suppose a dog is classically conditioned so that it salivates (CR) when it hears a 1,000-hertz (Hz) tone (CS). (If you have ever heard the "bleep" tone on television that covers up swearing, you know what a 1,000 Hz tone sounds like.) After the dog is conditioned to the tone and the CR is established, tones similar to 1,000 Hz will also produce salivation. The farther the tones are from 1,000 Hz (i.e., the higher or lower the pitch), the less the dog will salivate. **Stimulus generalization** occurs when stimuli similar but not identical to the CS produce the CR (**FIGURE 6.11a**). Generalization is adaptive because in nature the CS is seldom experienced repeatedly in an identical way. Slight differences in variables—such as background noise, temperature, and lighting—lead to slightly different perceptions of the CS. As a result of these different perceptions, animals learn to respond to variations in the CS.

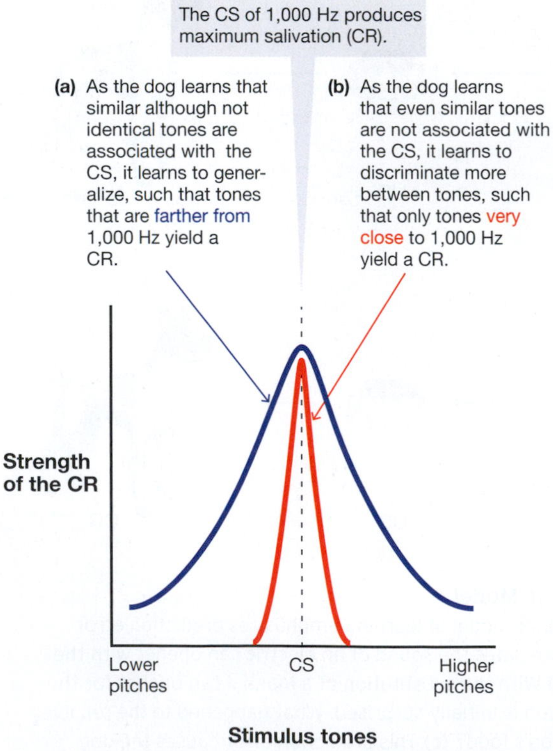

The CS of 1,000 Hz produces maximum salivation (CR).
(a) As the dog learns that similar although not identical tones are associated with the CS, it learns to generalize, such that tones that are farther from 1,000 Hz yield a CR.
(b) As the dog learns that even similar tones are not associated with the CS, it learns to discriminate more between tones, such that only tones very close to 1,000 Hz yield a CR.
Strength of the CR
Lower pitches
CS
Higher pitches
Stimulus tones

FIGURE 6.11
Stimulus Generalization and Stimulus Discrimination

Of course, generalization has limits. The ability to discriminate among stimuli is also important. **Stimulus discrimination** occurs when an animal learns to differentiate between two similar stimuli if one is consistently associated with the US and the other is not. Pavlov and his students demonstrated that dogs can learn to make very fine distinctions between similar stimuli. For example, dogs can learn to detect subtle differences in tones of different frequencies (**FIGURE 6.11b**). For humans and other animals, the ability to generalize and discriminate among stimuli is important for many aspects of daily life, such as being able to distinguish poisonous

FIGURE 6.12

The Adaptive Value of Stimulus Generalization and Stimulus Discrimination

Stimulus generalization and stimulus discrimination are important components of learning. These processes may take place even when a learned response has not been classically conditioned. **(a)** When people touch poison ivy and get an itchy rash, they learn to fear this three-leafed plant, and so they avoid it. **(b)** People may then experience stimulus generalization if they fear and avoid similar three-leafed plants—even nonpoisonous ones, such as fragrant sumac. By teaching people to avoid three-leafed plants, stimulus generalization therefore helps keep people safe. **(c)** People may also experience stimulus discrimination related to poison ivy. They do not fear and avoid dissimilar plants—such as Virginia creeper, which has five leaves and is nonpoisonous. If stimulus discrimination did not occur, fear of poison ivy would cause us to avoid activities near wooded areas, such as hiking and gardening.

(a)

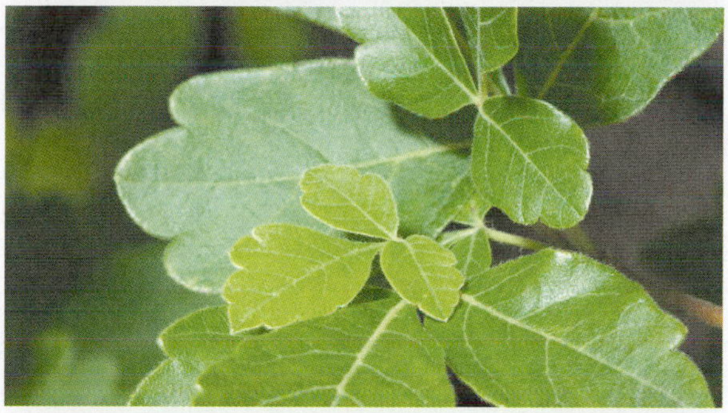
(b)

(c)

plants from edible ones or knowing which pets are safe to play with (**FIGURE 6.12**).

SECOND-ORDER CONDITIONING Sometimes a conditioned stimulus does not become directly associated with an unconditioned stimulus. Instead, the conditioned stimulus becomes associated with other conditioned stimuli that are already associated with the unconditioned stimulus. Once an association between a CS and a US is well learned so that it consistently produces a CR, the CS itself can take on value. For example, we value money because of its associations, not because of its physical characteristics. Once the CS has value, other stimuli may become associated with the CS only and can also produce CRs. The CRs can be learned even without the learner ever associating the CS with the original US. This phenomenon is known as *second-order conditioning*.

In one of Pavlov's early studies, a CS-US bond was formed between a tone (CS) and meat (US) so that the tone (CS) led to salivation (CR). In a second training session, a black square was repeatedly presented just after the tone. There was no US (no presentation of the meat) during this phase of the study. After a few trials, the black square was presented alone. It, too, produced salivation.

stimulus discrimination A differentiation between two similar stimuli when only one of them is consistently associated with the unconditioned stimulus.

Second-order conditioning helps account for the complexity of learned associations, especially in people. For example, Air Jordans are one of the world's most popular sneaker styles. But why do people like them so much? Air Jordans get their name from basketball legend Michael Jordan, who is widely admired for his tremendous athletic achievements. As advertisers know, pairing a sneaker brand with a famous athlete leads people to like the sneaker more. Before he became famous, Michael Jordan most likely did not automatically evoke a feeling of admiration in most people, but at the height of his career he had devoted fans across the world. Through classical conditioning Michael Jordan (the CS) came to evoke positive feelings (the CR) because of his athletic achievements (the US). Once he acquired these qualities, Air Jordans (the new CS) also became popular (the CR) because they were paired with Michael Jordan (the old CS).

Q **Which learning process helps you react differently toward flying insects that sting than toward those that do not sting while hiking in the woods?**

ANSWER: stimulus discrimination

How Do Consequences of an Action Shape Behavior?

Learning Objectives

- Define operant conditioning.
- Distinguish between positive reinforcement, negative reinforcement, positive punishment, and negative punishment.
- Identify factors that influence the acquisition of operant behaviors.
- Distinguish between schedules of reinforcement.

Our behaviors often represent means to particular ends. We buy food to eat it, we study to get good grades, we work to receive money, and so on. We learn that behaving in certain ways leads to rewards, and we learn that not behaving in other ways keeps us from punishment. A particular behavior produces a particular outcome. How do the consequences of our actions shape learning?

6.7 Operant Conditioning Is Learning Actions from Consequences

Classical conditioning is a relatively passive and automatic process. During classical conditioning the animal does not have to do anything to learn what goes together. Learning occurs simply by being in the presence of two stimuli (the CS and US), one of which automatically evokes a response (the UR).

In contrast, operant conditioning depends on the animal taking an action that leads to a consequence. In operant conditioning, behaviors represent a way to attain something (a reward) or avoid something (a punishment). They are *instrumental*—done for a purpose (**FIGURE 6.13**). This type of learning is sometimes called **instrumental conditioning**, but we will refer to it here as **operant conditioning**. B. F. Skinner, the psychologist most closely associated with this process, chose the term *operant* to express the idea that animals *operate* on their environments to produce effects (**FIGURE 6.14**). Through operant conditioning, an animal learns predictive associations between an action and its consequences that determine the likelihood of that action being repeated.

operant conditioning (instrumental conditioning) A learning process in which the consequences of an action determine the likelihood that it will be performed in the future.

LAW OF EFFECT The study of operant conditioning began in the late nineteenth century in Cambridge, Massachusetts, at the home of the Harvard psychologist William James. A young graduate student working with James, Edward Thorndike,

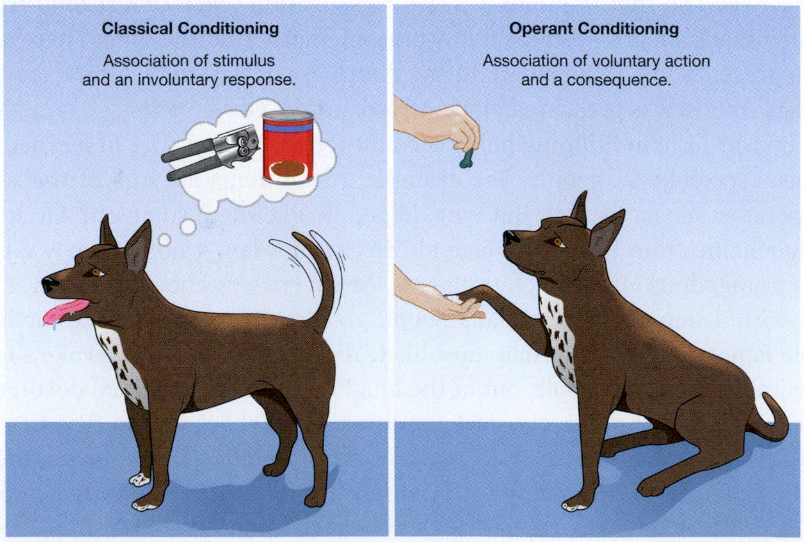

FIGURE 6.13
Classical Versus Operant Conditioning
Classical conditioning involves learning an association between two stimuli, one of which elicits an involuntary response; no voluntary action is required. Operant conditioning requires a voluntary action to be performed and has a consequence.

took inspiration from Charles Darwin's painstakingly precise observations of animal behavior. In James's basement, Thorndike performed carefully controlled experiments in comparative animal psychology. Specifically, he studied whether nonhuman animals showed signs of intelligence. As part of his research, Thorndike built a *puzzle box*, a small cage with a trapdoor (**FIGURE 6.15a**). The trapdoor would open if the animal inside performed a specific action, such as pulling a string. Thorndike placed food-deprived animals, initially chickens, inside the puzzle box to see if they could figure out how to escape.

When Thorndike moved to Columbia University to complete his PhD, he switched from using chickens to using cats in his studies. To motivate the cats, he would place food just outside the box. When a cat was first placed in the box, it usually attempted to escape through numerous behaviors that did not work. After 5 to 10 minutes of struggling, the cat would *accidentally* press a lever that pulled a string, and the door would open. Thorndike would then return the cat to the box and repeat the trial. On each subsequent trial, the cat would press the lever a bit more quickly, gradually getting faster and faster at escaping. Over the course of many trials, it would learn to escape from the puzzle box within seconds (**FIGURE 6.15b**).

From this line of research, Thorndike (1927) developed a general theory of learning. According to this **law of effect**, any behavior that leads to a "satisfying state of affairs" is likely to occur again. Any behavior that leads to an "annoying state of affairs" is less likely to occur again. In other words, the frequency with which a behavior occurs is influenced by its consequences.

WATSON, SKINNER, AND BEHAVIORISM B. F. Skinner developed a formal learning theory based on the law of effect developed by Thorndike. As a young man, Skinner had wanted to be a novelist so that he could explore large questions

FIGURE 6.14
B. F. Skinner
B. F. Skinner studies an animal's operations on its laboratory environment.

law of effect Thorndike's general theory of learning: Any behavior that leads to a "satisfying state of affairs" is likely to occur again, and any behavior that leads to an "annoying state of affairs" is less likely to occur again. Or, the likelihood of the occurrence of a behavior is influenced by its consequences.

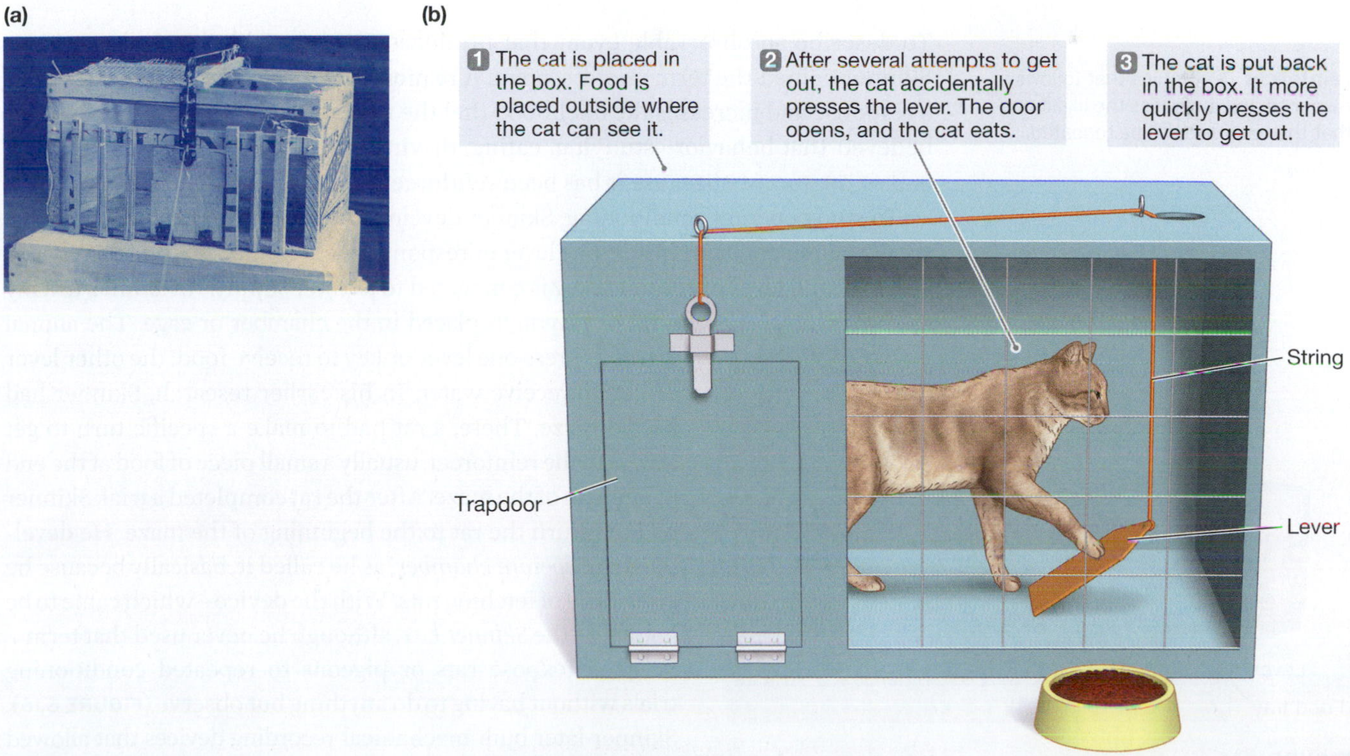
(a)
(b)
1 The cat is placed in the box. Food is placed outside where the cat can see it.
2 After several attempts to get out, the cat accidentally presses the lever. The door opens, and the cat eats.
3 The cat is put back in the box. It more quickly presses the lever to get out.
String
Trapdoor
Lever

FIGURE 6.15
Thorndike's Puzzle Box
(a) Thorndike used puzzle boxes, such as the one depicted here, **(b)** to assess learning in animals.

about the human condition. Then he read two works of nonfiction that changed his life. The first was the 1924 book *Behaviorism* by John B. Watson. In this book, Watson challenged as unscientific psychology's study of conscious and unconscious mental processes. Watson believed that if psychology was to be a science, it had to stop focusing on mental events that could not be observed directly. He developed the school of thought known as **behaviorism**, which emphasized environmental effects on observable behaviors. The second work was a 1927 article in the *New York Times Magazine* in which the novelist H. G. Wells expressed admiration for the work of Ivan Pavlov. Increasingly, the behaviorists' perspective made sense to Skinner. He became convinced that psychology was his calling.

behaviorism A psychological approach that emphasizes environmental influences on observable behaviors.

Inspired by the work of Watson and of Pavlov, Skinner believed that he could dramatically change an animal's behavior by providing incentives to the animal for performing particular acts. For the next half century, he conducted systematic studies of animals, often pigeons or rats, to discover the basic rules of learning. His groundbreaking work led Skinner to form radical ideas about behaviorism, such as how it might be applied to entire communities to create a utopian way of life (Skinner, 1948b). In the process, he outlined many of the most important principles that shape the behavior of animals, including humans. These principles remain as relevant today as they were 80 years ago.

Q **What is the law of effect in Edward Thorndike's general theory of learning?**

ANSWER: The likelihood of the occurrence of a behavior is influenced by its consequences.

6.8 Reinforcement Increases Behavior, Punishment Decreases Behavior

To describe an observable event that produces an observable learned response, Skinner coined the term *reinforcement*. A **reinforcer** is a stimulus that occurs after a response and increases the likelihood that the response will be repeated. Skinner believed that behavior—studying, eating, driving on the proper side of the road, and so on—occurs because it has been reinforced.

reinforcer A stimulus that follows a response and increases the likelihood that the response will be repeated.

To study operant conditioning, Skinner developed a simple device consisting of a small chamber or cage. Inside, one lever or response key is connected to a food supply, and a second lever or response key is connected to a water supply. An animal, usually a rat or pigeon, is placed in the chamber or cage. The animal learns to press one lever or key to receive food, the other lever or key to receive water. In his earlier research, Skinner had used a maze. There, a rat had to make a specific turn to get access to the reinforcer, usually a small piece of food at the end of one arm of the maze. After the rat completed a trial, Skinner had to return the rat to the beginning of the maze. He developed the *operant chamber*, as he called it, basically because he grew tired of fetching rats. With the device—which came to be known as the *Skinner box*, although he never used that term—he could expose rats or pigeons to repeated conditioning trials without having to do anything but observe (**FIGURE 6.16**). Skinner later built mechanical recording devices that allowed the experimenter to conduct trials without being present. Today's operant chambers interface with computers to enable researchers to record behavioral data.

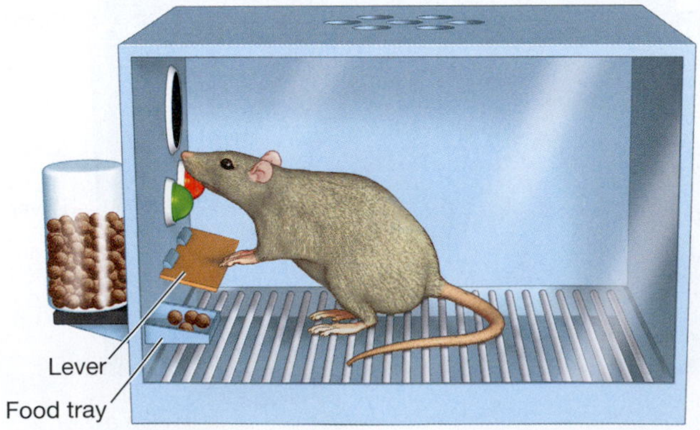

FIGURE 6.16
Operant Chamber
This diagram shows B. F. Skinner's operant chamber. Skinner is pictured with one in Figure 6.14.

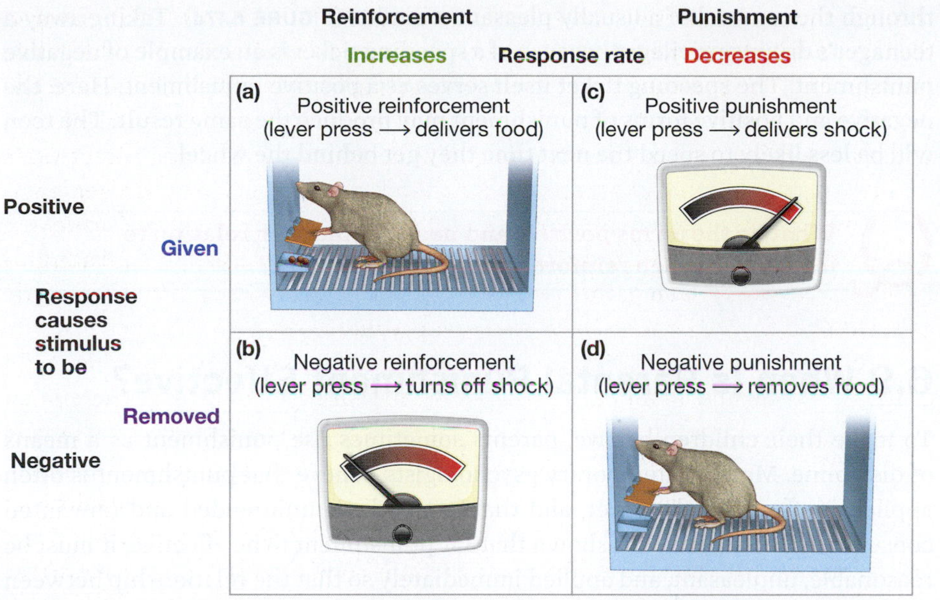

FIGURE 6.17
Positive Reinforcement and Negative Reinforcement, Positive Punishment and Negative Punishment
(a) In positive reinforcement, the response rate increases because responding causes the stimulus to be given. **(b)** In negative reinforcement, the response rate increases because responding causes the stimulus to be removed. **(c)** In positive punishment, the response rate decreases because responding causes the stimulus to be given. **(d)** In negative punishment, the response rate decreases because responding causes the stimulus to be removed.

Reinforcement always increases behavior. Through the administration of a stimulus after a behavior, **positive reinforcement** increases the probability of that behavior's being repeated (FIGURE 6.17a). Positive reinforcement is often called a *reward*. *Positive* simply means that something is being added, not whether the reinforcement is good. Rewarded behaviors increase in frequency, as when people work harder in response to receiving praise or increased pay. In contrast, **negative reinforcement** increases behavior through the *removal* of an unpleasant stimulus (FIGURE 6.17b). For instance, when a rat is required to press a lever to turn off an electric shock, the pressing of the lever has been negatively reinforced. *Negative* simply means that something is being removed.

positive reinforcement The administration of a stimulus to increase the probability of a behavior's recurrence.

negative reinforcement The removal of an unpleasant stimulus to increase the probability of a behavior's recurrence.

Negative reinforcement is quite common in everyday life. You put on a coat to avoid being cold. You pick up a fussy baby to stop the crying. In each case, you are engaging in a behavior to try to avoid or escape an unwanted stimulus. If the action you take successfully reduces the unwanted stimulus, then the next time you feel cold or are with a crying baby, the more likely you are to repeat the behavior that reduced the stimulus. The behavior has been negatively reinforced. Note, however, that while picking up the crying infant is negatively reinforcing for you, it positively reinforces the infant for crying! The infant learns that crying increases the likelihood of being picked up and comforted. Likewise, the parent who gives a child candy to stop a tantrum is negatively reinforced (the tantrum stops), but the child is positively reinforced to have more tantrums in the future.

Punishment reduces the probability that a behavior will recur. Punishment and reinforcement have opposite effects on behavior. Whereas reinforcement increases a behavior's probability, punishment decreases its probability. For example, giving your dog a treat each time it acts a certain way (reinforcement) will increase the likelihood it will act that way. Sternly saying "bad dog" each time it performs an action (punishment) will decrease the likelihood of its performing that action.

punishment A stimulus that follows a behavior and decreases the likelihood that the behavior will be repeated.

Punishment can make a behavior less likely to occur through positive or negative means. Again, *positive* or *negative* here means whether something is added or removed, not whether it is good or bad. **Positive punishment** decreases the behavior's probability through the administration of a stimulus (FIGURE 6.17c). Usually the stimulus in positive punishment is unpleasant. Being reprimanded is a form of positive punishment. **Negative punishment** decreases the behavior's probability

positive punishment The administration of a stimulus to decrease the probability of a behavior's recurrence.

negative punishment The removal of a stimulus to decrease the probability of a behavior's recurrence.

through the removal of a usually pleasant stimulus (FIGURE 6.17d). Taking away a teenager's driving privileges because of a speeding ticket is an example of negative punishment. The speeding ticket itself serves as a positive punishment. Here, the negative and positive forms of punishment may produce the same result: The teen will be less likely to speed the next time they get behind the wheel.

Q What do the terms *positive* and *negative* mean in relation to learning through reinforcement or punishment?

ANSWER: *Positive* means something is added. *Negative* means something is removed.

PSYCHOLOGY OUTSIDE THE LAB

6.9 When Is Parental Punishment Effective?

To make their children behave, parents sometimes use punishment as a means of discipline. Many contemporary psychologists believe that punishment is often applied ineffectively, however, and that it may have unintended and unwanted consequences. Research has shown that for punishment to be effective, it must be reasonable, unpleasant, and applied immediately so that the relationship between the unwanted behavior and the punishment is clear. But considerable potential exists for confusion. For example, if a student is punished after admitting to cheating on an exam, the student may then associate the punishment with being honest rather than with the original offense. As a result, the student learns not to tell the truth. As Skinner once pointed out, one thing people learn from punishment is how to avoid it. Rather than learning how to behave appropriately, they may learn not to get caught.

Punishment can also lead to negative emotions, such as fear and anxiety. Through classical conditioning, these emotions may become associated with the person who administers the punishment. If a child thus learns to fear a parent or teacher, the long-term relationship between child and adult may be damaged (Gershoff, 2002). In addition, punishment often fails to offset the reinforcing aspects of the undesired behavior. In real life, any behavior can be reinforced in multiple ways. For instance, thumb sucking may be reinforced because it makes a child feel good, because it provides relief from negative emotions, and because it alleviates hunger. Punishment may not be sufficient to offset such rewards, but it may reinforce the child's secrecy about thumb sucking. For these and other reasons, most psychologists agree with Skinner's recommendation that reinforcement be used rather than punishment. A child complimented for being a good student is likely to perform better academically than one punished for doing poorly. After all, reinforcing good behavior tells the child what to do. Punishing the child for bad behavior does not tell the child how to improve.

One form of punishment that most psychologists believe is especially ineffective is physical punishment, such as spanking. Spanking is very common in the United States, however (FIGURE 6.18a). Although it has declined somewhat since the mid-1980s, a 2015 Child Trends study found that 65 percent of women and 78 percent of men agreed or strongly agreed that it is sometimes necessary to give a child a "good, hard spanking" (Lamotte, 2008). Beliefs about the appropriateness of spanking involve religious beliefs and cultural views, as well as legal issues. Many countries (e.g., Austria, Denmark, Israel, Sweden, and Italy) have banned corporal punishment in homes, schools, or both (FIGURE 6.18b). Even the United Nations has passed resolutions discouraging it.

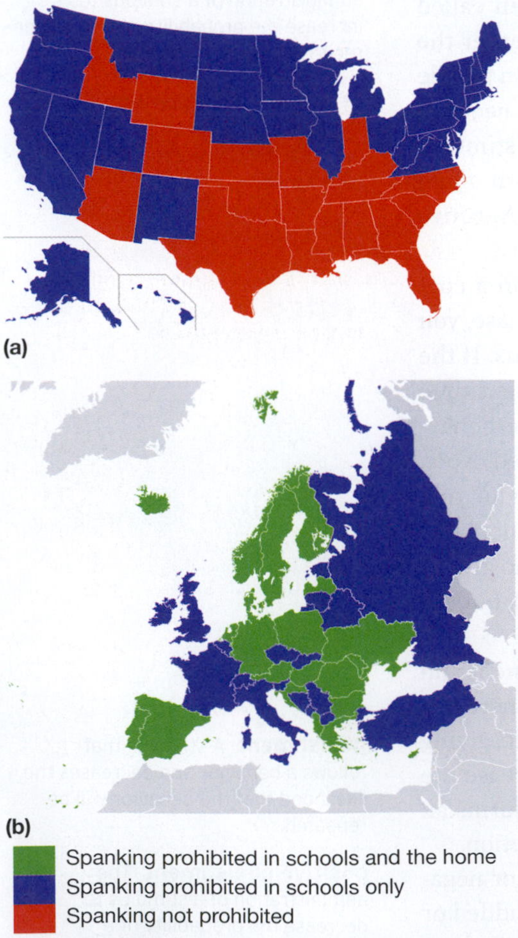

FIGURE 6.18
Legality of Spanking
These maps compare **(a)** the United States and **(b)** Europe in terms of the legality of spanking children.

A recent meta-analysis involving more than 160,000 children found that spanking was not effective in improving children's behavior (Gershoff & Grogan-Kaylor, 2016). Indeed, spanking was associated with many negative outcomes, including more aggression and antisocial behavior, more mental health problems, lower self-esteem, and negative relationships with parents. Importantly, the evidence indicates that other forms of punishment are more effective for decreasing unwanted behaviors (Kazdin & Benjet, 2003). Time-outs, small fines, and removal of privileges can effectively modify behavior. Yet many psychologists believe that any method of punishment is less effective than providing positive reinforcement for "better" behaviors. By rewarding the behaviors they wish to see, parents are able to increase those behaviors while building more positive bonds with their children. ■

Q **If you take away a child's toy because the child is banging it against the wall, what kind of punishment is this?**

ANSWER: negative punishment

6.10 Learning Shapes Actions and Reinforcers

Observing the behaviors of animals inside a Skinner box provided an important means to test the principles of operant conditioning, but the power of these principles is readily apparent in everyday human life. Many of our behaviors have been learned through reinforcement. The reach of operant conditioning in determining our actions is broad because both the behaviors learned and the value of reinforcements and punishments can be modified through learning.

SHAPING As outlined earlier, a key difference between classical and operant conditioning is that in operant conditioning, the animal must perform an action that can then be reinforced. What happens if the animal never accidentally performs the desired action? Suppose you want to teach your dog to fetch your slippers. Your dog would have to "accidentally" fetch your slippers at least once. If the animal does not naturally perform the desired action, you cannot reinforce it. An animal inside a Skinner box has so little to do that it typically presses the lever or key sooner rather than later. One major problem with operant conditioning outside the Skinner box is that the same animal might take a while to perform the action you are looking for.

shaping A process of operant conditioning; it involves reinforcing behaviors that are increasingly similar to the desired behavior.

Rather than wait for the animal to spontaneously perform the action, you can use an operant-conditioning technique to teach the animal to do so. This powerful process, called **shaping**, consists of reinforcing behaviors that are increasingly similar to the desired behavior. For instance, if you want to teach your dog to roll over, you might initially reward any behavior that even slightly resembles rolling over, such as lying down. Once this behavior is established, you reinforce behaviors more selectively—lying down and rolling on its side, then lying down and rolling onto its back, and so forth. Reinforcing *successive approximations* eventually produces the desired behavior. In other words, the animal learns to discriminate which behavior is being reinforced. The notion of successive approximations is familiar to many of us through the children's game of "hot-cold." In this game, an object is hidden and the player is given cues to try to find it, such as "Getting warmer" or "Hot" as the player moves closer and closer to the object, and "Chilly" or "Freezing" when the player moves farther away.

Shaping has been used to condition animals to perform amazing feats: pigeons playing table tennis, dogs playing the piano, pigs doing housework such as picking up clothes and vacuuming, and so on (**FIGURE 6.19**). Shaping has also been used

FIGURE 6.19
Shaping
Shaping, an operant-conditioning technique, consists of reinforcing behaviors that are increasingly similar to the desired behavior. This technique can be used to train animals to perform extraordinary behaviors. Here, a trained dog water-skis for a boat show.

to teach appropriate social skills to people with psychological disorders, to teach language to children with autism, and to teach basic skills such as how to dress themselves to individuals with intellectual disabilities. More generally, parents and educators often use shaping to encourage desired behavior in children. For example, they praise children for their initial—often illegible—attempts at handwriting, whereas later in the learning process only legible handwriting is praised.

SECONDARY REINFORCERS The most obvious stimuli that act as reinforcers are those necessary for survival, such as food or water. Because they satisfy biological needs, these stimuli are called *primary reinforcers*. From an evolutionary standpoint, the learning value of primary reinforcers makes a great deal of sense: Animals that repeatedly perform behaviors reinforced by food or water are more likely to survive and pass along their genes. But many apparent reinforcers, such as a compliment, money, or an A on a paper, do not directly satisfy biological needs.

Stimuli that serve as reinforcers but do not satisfy biological needs are called *secondary reinforcers*. These reinforcers are established through classical conditioning, as described earlier in this chapter: We learn to associate a neutral stimulus, such as money (CS), with rewards such as food, security, and power (US). Money is really only pieces of metal or paper, or electronically represented as numbers in our bank account, but these and other neutral objects become meaningful through their associations with unconditioned stimuli.

Q How would you teach a dog to stand on a skateboard with shaping?

ANSWER: You would reward successive approximations of the behavior, such as first giving a treat if the dog stands near the skateboard, then only if the dog places a paw on the skateboard, then two paws, and finally only rewarding the dog for standing on the skateboard.

YOU BE THE PSYCHOLOGIST

6.11 Can You Challenge Superstitious Behaviors?

Do you have a lucky charm? Do you wear your "good luck" jeans every time you take an exam? The list of people's superstitions is virtually endless (**FIGURE 6.20**). In North America and Europe, people avoid the number 13. In China, Japan, Korea, and Hawaii, they avoid the number 4. Tennis great Serena Williams reportedly wears the same unwashed socks every game as long as she is winning. A recent beer commercial portrayed a hapless fan who wanted to watch the game, but because his team scored each time he went to the basement to get a cold one, he decided to stay in the basement. By missing the game, he was trying to help the team win.

FIGURE 6.20
Superstitions
According to superstition, bad luck will come your way if **(a)** a black cat crosses your path or **(b)** you walk under a ladder.

Even pigeons might be superstitious. In one study, Skinner (1948a) placed hungry pigeons in a cage and delivered food every 15 seconds regardless of what the pigeons were actually doing. He found that pigeons quickly learned to repeat behaviors they had been performing when the food was delivered because those actions had accidentally been reinforced. This repetition meant the pigeons were more likely to be performing those behaviors the next time food arrived. One pigeon was conditioned to turn counterclockwise, another to thrust its head into one corner of the cage. Yet another developed a pendulum motion of the head and body, in which the head was extended forward and swung from right to left with a sharp movement followed by a somewhat slower return.

The tendency to associate events that occur together in time is incredibly strong because the brain is compelled to figure things out. When a chance reinforcer occurs close in time to some behavior, humans and nonhuman animals sometimes associate the reinforcement with the behavior. Whereas pigeons just develop behaviors that look like superstitions, people look for reasons to explain outcomes, and the observed association serves that purpose. These resulting associations, combined with the tendency to notice evidence consistent with the perceived association and discount inconsistent evidence (that is, confirmation bias), can lead people to cling to superstitions.

Most superstitions are harmless, but if they get too extreme they can interfere with daily living. As a critical thinker who understands psychological reasoning, you should be aware of the tendency to associate events with other events that occur at the same time and to favor evidence consistent with one's beliefs. Do you have a behavior you perform because you think it may lead to a good outcome, even though it seems illogical? Could you state your superstition as a hypothesis? If so, what type of evidence could you gather and objectively assess in order to verify or discredit your superstition? How could you apply the scientific method to evaluate other phenomena that have been linked to superstitious behavior, such as astrology? ■

Q **In terms of learning, what is the main cause of superstitious behavior?**

ANSWER: receiving chance reinforcement

6.12 Operant Conditioning Is Influenced by Value and Timing

For a behavior to be acquired or diminished through operant conditioning, the animal must come to expect that the behavior will be reinforced or punished. Furthermore, the reinforcement or punishment must be effective. What factors influence the likelihood that an operant response is learned?

REINFORCER POTENCY Some reinforcers are more powerful than others. In other words, some reinforcers are more valuable to the animal than others, and the effectiveness of a reinforcer in operant conditioning is a function of its value. The psychologist David Premack (1959; Holstein & Premack, 1965) theorized about how a reinforcer's value could be determined. The key is the amount of time a person, when free to do anything, willingly engages in a specific behavior associated with the reinforcer. For instance, most children would choose to spend more time eating ice cream than eating spinach. Ice cream is therefore more reinforcing for children than spinach is. One great advantage of Premack's theory is that it can account for differences in individuals' values. For people who prefer spinach to ice cream, spinach serves as a more potent reinforcer. Also, a reinforcer's value can vary with context. If you are hungry, ice cream will have a high value. If you are very full, its value will drop, and you might find something else—not necessarily a food—more reinforcing.

One logical application of Premack's theory is the *Premack principle*. According to this principle, a more-valued activity can be used to reinforce the performance of a less-valued activity. Parents use the Premack principle all the time. They tell their children, "Eat your spinach and then you'll get dessert," "Finish your homework and then you can go out," and so on.

IMMEDIATE VERSUS DELAYED REINFORCEMENT Another factor that predicts the effectiveness of operant conditioning is the timing between the action and the reinforcement or punishment. The longer the delay between the action and its consequence, the worse the learning. This effect was demonstrated in a study in which rats were taught to press a lever to receive food. Delaying the food even a few seconds after the lever press resulted in a decrease in the number of times the rats pressed the lever going forward. If the delivery of food was delayed for a full minute, the rat never learned to associate the lever press with food (Dickinson et al., 1992). The delay may have made it difficult for the rat to determine exactly which behavior led to the delivery of food. Studies in rats demonstrate that delayed punishment is also less effective (Kamin, 1959).

The diminishing impact of delayed reinforcement and punishment on behavior has important implications for how we apply operant principles. For instance, if you come home from work or school and yell at your new puppy because you discover it had an accident on the rug while you were out, how does your puppy know which of the many things it did during the day caused you to yell? Using operant-conditioning principles to house-train a puppy is much more effective if you can catch the puppy in the act. Similarly, if a child misbehaves in a store but is punished by having a favorite toy taken away several hours later at home, how is the child to know that the removal of the toy is the consequence of misbehaving at the store? Fortunately, with humans, we can use language to conceptually create links between the behavior and consequence, in this case by telling the child immediately in the store that the misbehavior will be punished at home later.

However, even though humans have the ability to anticipate reinforcers that will be delayed, another factor that influences the impact of delayed reinforcement is that rewards in the future are often viewed as less potent, or valuable. **Temporal discounting** is when the value of a reward diminishes over time. For instance, suppose I offered you a choice between $10 now or $20 a year from now. Everyone knows that $20 is more valuable than $10, but most people would prefer having the money in hand. In other words, the value of money is diminished if the reinforcement is delayed. Temporal discounting plays an important role in efforts to achieve long-term goals. A dieter may have to choose between the satisfaction of eating a piece of cake now and the more abstract, delayed goal of achieving a healthy weight in the future. Temporal discounting is thought to underlie a wide range of poor choices that humans make, such as those leading to obesity, drug addiction, and a lack of retirement savings.

temporal discounting The tendency to discount the subjective value of a reward when it is given after a delay.

Q **Why might delaying positive reinforcement be less effective?**

ANSWER: temporal discounting

6.13 Operant Conditioning Is Influenced by Schedules of Reinforcement

Imagine you own a casino. To maximize profits, you want to increase the frequency and persistence of gambling by your patrons while paying out as little as possible. Gambling is a form of operant conditioning in that the patron learns the actions required to obtain a potential reward. Although, it is not realistic to reinforce the gambler's behavior with a "win" every time they play, if their gambling behavior is never reinforced by a win, eventually the gambler will no longer expect reinforcement and may cease gambling altogether. At this point, the behavior would be extinguished. When and how often should a reinforcer be given if your goal is to have patrons consistently gamble without frequent large payouts? In other words, what factors influence the rate and persistence of operant responses?

SCHEDULES OF REINFORCEMENT For fast learning, it is best to reinforce a behavior each time it occurs. This process is known as **continuous reinforcement**. In the real world, behavior is seldom reinforced continuously. People do not receive praise each time they behave acceptably. The intermittent reinforcement of behavior is more common. This process is known as **partial reinforcement**.

Partial reinforcement's effect on conditioning depends on the reinforcement schedule. Reinforcement can be scheduled in numerous ways. Most schedules vary in terms of the basis for providing reinforcement and the regularity with which reinforcement is provided. For instance, partial reinforcement can be administered according to either the number of behavioral responses or the passage of time, such as paying factory workers by the piece (behavioral responses) or by the hours spent working (passage of time).

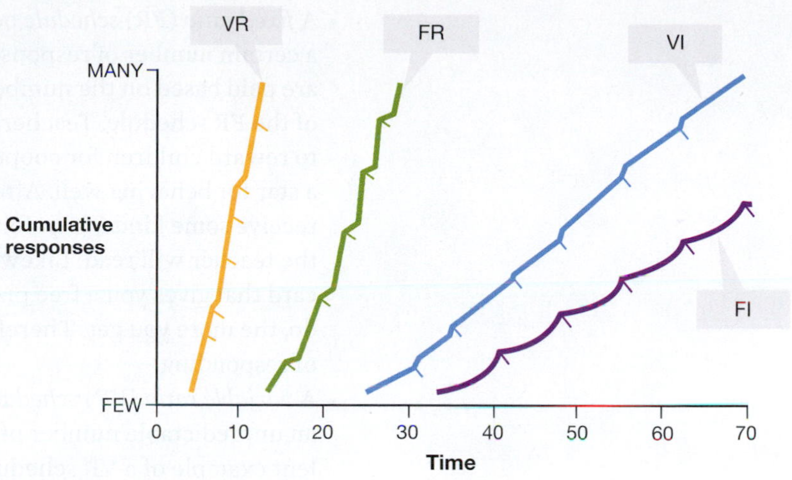

FIGURE 6.21
Partial Reinforcement Schedules Influence the Rate and Pattern of Responding

continuous reinforcement A type of learning in which behavior is reinforced each time it occurs.

partial reinforcement A type of learning in which behavior is reinforced intermittently.

A *ratio schedule* is based on the number of times the behavior occurs, as when a behavior is reinforced on every third or tenth occurrence. An *interval schedule* is based on a specific unit of time, as when a behavior is reinforced when it is performed every minute or hour. Partial reinforcement also can be given on a predictable *fixed schedule* or on a less predictable *variable schedule*. Combining the basis for reinforcement with the regularity of reinforcement yields the four most common reinforcement schedules: fixed interval, variable interval, fixed ratio, and variable ratio (**FIGURE 6.21**).

- A *fixed interval (FI) schedule* occurs when reinforcement is provided after a certain amount of time has passed. Imagine that you feed your cat twice a day. After some number of days, the cat will start to meow and rub against you at about the feeding times, especially if you are in the location where you typically put out the food. Your cat has not learned to read the clock. Rather, the cat has learned that after a certain amount of time has passed, feeding is likely. Once the cat is fed, it will probably go away and sleep. At the next mealtime, it will return and start meowing and rubbing again. Providing meals on this schedule reinforces the "feed me" behavior. Note the scalloping pattern in Figure 6.21, which indicates an increase in the behavior just before the opportunity for reinforcement and then a dropping off after reinforcement. Many students follow this kind of pattern when taking courses with regularly scheduled exams. They work extremely hard on the days before the exam and then slack off a bit immediately after the exam.
- A *variable interval (VI) schedule* occurs when reinforcement is provided after the passage of time, but the time is not regular. Although you know you will eventually be reinforced, you cannot predict when it will happen. For example, getting texts from friends occurs on a variable interval schedule. You might check for messages throughout the day if you find receiving such messages reinforcing. Unlike the cat learning on an FI schedule, you never know when you will receive reinforcement, so you have to check back frequently. Professors give pop quizzes because they encourage more regular studying by students. If you cannot predict when you will be quizzed, you have to keep up with your classwork and always be prepared.

- A *fixed ratio (FR) schedule* occurs when reinforcement is provided after a certain number of responses have been made. Factory workers who are paid based on the number of objects they make are a good example of the FR schedule. Teachers sometimes use this kind of schedule to reward children for cooperative classroom behavior. Students can earn a star for behaving well. After they collect a certain number of stars, they receive some kind of reinforcer, such as getting to select the next book the teacher will read. Likewise, your local pizzeria might give you a punch card that gives you a free pizza after you buy 10. In each case, the more you do, the more you get. Therefore, FR schedules typically produce high rates of responding.
- A *variable ratio (VR) schedule* occurs when reinforcement is provided after an unpredictable number of responses. Games of chance provide an excellent example of a VR schedule. At a casino, you might drop a lot of money into a slot machine that rarely rewards you with a win. Such behavior is not simply the result of an addiction to gambling. Rather, people put money in slot machines because the machines *sometimes* provide monetary rewards. VR schedules lead to high rates of responding that last over time because you know that eventually there will be a payoff for responding. You just do not know when it will happen—or even if you will still be the player on that machine at that time.

partial-reinforcement extinction effect The greater persistence of behavior under partial reinforcement than under continuous reinforcement.

As mentioned earlier, continuous reinforcement leads to fast learning, but the behaviors do not last. The **partial-reinforcement extinction effect** refers to the greater persistence of behavior under partial reinforcement than under continuous reinforcement. During continuous reinforcement, the learner can easily detect when reinforcement has stopped. But when the behavior is reinforced only some of the time, the learner needs to repeat the behavior comparatively more times to detect the absence of reinforcement. This is especially true if the reinforcement ratio is variable, since it is unclear precisely when to expect reinforcement. Thus, the less frequent and more variable the reinforcement during training, the greater the resistance to extinction. To condition a behavior so that it persists, it is best to first reinforce it continuously to promote acquisition of the learned behavior, and then slowly change to partial reinforcement to prevent extinction of the learned behavior. Parents naturally follow this strategy in teaching behaviors to their children, as in toilet training.

Learning Tip

To remember the four schedules of reinforcement:
If the schedule is predictable, it is *fixed*.
If the schedule is not predictable, it is *variable*.
If the schedule depends on the passage of time, it is *interval*.
If the schedule depends on the number of responses, it is *ratio*.

Put them together:
fixed interval: Reinforcement is given after a predictable passage of time.
variable interval: Reinforcement is given after an unpredictable passage of time.
fixed ratio: Reinforcement is given after a predictable number of responses.
variable ratio: Reinforcement is given after an unpredictable number of responses.

Q What type of partial reinforcement produces the most persistent responses?

ANSWER: variable ratio schedule

What Do Different Types of Associative Learning Have in Common?

Learning Objectives

- Describe how biology and evolution constrain learning.
- Describe the role of dopamine in learning.
- Describe how classical and operant conditioning contribute to phobias and drug addiction.

Although classical and operant conditioning are different—classical conditioning involves noticing patterns between stimuli, while operant conditioning requires that the animal perform an action that has a consequence—both types of conditioning involve learning associations. In classical conditioning it is the association between the occurrence of the CS and US. In operant conditioning the association between the action and consequence is learned. This shared reliance on learning associations is reflected in a number of ways. For instance, factors such as timing and intensity are important for both classical and operant conditioning, but both types of learning are also constrained by biological and evolutionary factors. In addition, both types of learning depend on the function of the neurotransmitter dopamine. Classical and operant conditioning also interact in guiding behaviors. Through classical conditioning, stimuli can acquire a value. Money, for instance, has come to acquire its value through its pairing with primary rewards such as food and safety. This acquired value then enables that stimulus to act as a reinforcer or to act as reinforcement or punishment for actions, such as when we work for money. This interplay between classical and operant conditioning underlies a number of complex human behaviors.

6.14 Learning Is Influenced by Biology and Evolution

Both Pavlov and Skinner emphasized that timing and intensity were critical for learning associations, whether it was the association of the CS and US or action and consequence. Timing is important in that learning is better if the stimuli or events to be associated occur close in time. Intensity matters in that associations are learned more easily if the unconditioned stimulus elicits a strong unconditioned response or if the reinforcer is more highly valued.

Beyond timing and intensity, however, few factors were thought to limit learning. This is the principle of **equipotentiality**. This principle suggests that any object or phenomenon could be converted to a conditioned stimulus when associated with any unconditioned stimulus, or any behavior can be learned as long as it is reinforced. In other words, the factors underlying the learning of predictive associations do not vary for different types of stimuli, reinforcers, or behaviors. However, by the mid-1960s, a number of challenges arose suggesting that some conditioned stimuli were more likely than others to produce learning, and some behaviors were more easily learned than others. Timing and intensity alone were not sufficient to learn predictive associations in classical and operant conditioning. Biology and evolution had a hand in influencing what was learned.

equipotentiality The principle that any conditioned stimulus paired with any unconditioned stimulus should result in learning.

CONDITIONED TASTE AVERSIONS Research conducted by the psychologist John Garcia and colleagues showed that certain pairings of stimuli are more likely to become associated than others. For instance, when animals receive nonlethal amounts of poison in their food that make them ill (as the wolves in Yellowstone

Park did), they quickly learn to avoid the tastes or smells associated with the food (Garcia & Koelling, 1966).

Likewise, many people can recall a time when they ate a particular food and later became ill with nausea, stomach upset, and vomiting. Whether or not the food caused the illness, most people respond to this sequence of events by demonstrating a *conditioned taste aversion*. This response occurs even if the illness clearly was caused by a virus or some other condition. Contrary to Pavlov's ideas, the association occurs even though the food and the sickness are not experienced close together in time. Conditioned taste aversions are especially likely to develop if the taste was not part of the person's usual diet (Lin et al., 2017). The association between a novel taste and getting sick, even when the illness occurs hours after eating, is so strong that a taste aversion can be formed in one trial. Some people cannot stand even the smell of a food they associate with a stomach-related illness.

For most species, including humans, conditioned taste aversions are easy to produce with food, but they are very difficult to produce with light or sound. This difference is also contrary to what would be expected by Pavlovian theory. The difference makes sense, however, because smell and taste—not light or sound—are the main cues that guide most animals' eating behavior. From an evolutionary viewpoint, animals that quickly associate a certain taste with illness, and therefore avoid that taste, will be more successful. That is, they will be more likely to survive and pass along their genes.

The adaptive value of a response varies according to the evolutionary history of the particular species, however. For example, although taste aversions are easy to condition in rats and humans, they are difficult to condition in birds. This difference occurs because in selecting food, rats and humans rely more on taste and birds rely more on vision. Accordingly, birds quickly learn to avoid a visual cue they associate with illness. Different types of stimuli cause different reactions even within a species. For instance, rats freeze and startle if a CS is auditory, but they rise on their hind legs if the CS is visual (Holland, 1977).

BIOLOGY CONSTRAINS LEARNING ACTIONS Behaviorists like Skinner believed that any behavior could be shaped through reinforcement. We now know that animals have a hard time learning behaviors that run counter to their evolutionary adaptation. A good example of biological constraints was obtained by Marian and Keller Breland, a husband-and-wife team of psychologists who used operant-conditioning techniques to train animals for commercials (Breland & Breland, 1961). Many of their animals refused to perform certain tasks they had been taught. For instance, a raccoon learned to place coins in a piggy bank, but eventually it stopped doing so and instead stood over the bank and briskly rubbed the coins in its paws. This rubbing behavior was not reinforced. In fact, it delayed reinforcement. One explanation for the raccoon's behavior is that the task was incompatible with innate adaptive behaviors. The raccoon associated the coin with food and treated it the same way: Rubbing food between the paws is hardwired for raccoons (**FIGURE 6.22**).

FIGURE 6.22
Biological Constraints on Learning Actions
Animals have a hard time learning behaviors that run counter to their evolutionary adaptation. For example, raccoons are hardwired to rub food between their paws, as this raccoon is doing. They have trouble learning *not* to rub objects.

Similarly, pigeons can be trained to peck at keys to obtain food or secondary reinforcers, but it is difficult to train them to peck at keys to avoid electric shock. They can learn to avoid shock by flapping their wings, however, because wing flapping is their natural means of escape. The psychologist Robert Bolles (1970) has argued that animals have built-in defensive reactions to

FIGURE 6.23

Biological Preparedness

Animals have evolved to be able to detect threats. Thus, **(a)** we will quickly see the snake in this group of images, and **(b)** we will have a harder time detecting the flowers in this group. In both cases, the snakes grab our attention (Hayakawa et al., 2011).

threatening stimuli. Conditioning is most effective when the association between the response and the reinforcement is similar to the animal's built-in predispositions.

BIOLOGICAL PREPAREDNESS Another situation where biology and evolution influence learned associations is when animals learn about potential dangers associated with stimuli. For example, monkeys can more easily be conditioned to fear snakes than to fear objects such as flowers or rabbits (Cook & Mineka, 1989). The psychologist Martin Seligman (1970) has argued that animals are genetically programmed to fear specific objects. He refers to this programming as *biological preparedness*. Preparedness helps explain why animals tend to fear potentially dangerous things (e.g., snakes, fire, heights) rather than objects that pose little threat (e.g., flowers, shoes, babies; **FIGURE 6.23**).

Perceived threats may also come from within an animal's own species. For example, when people participate in conditioning experiments in which aversive stimuli are paired with members of their own racial group or members of a different racial group, they more easily associate the negative stimuli with outgroup members, and this association is harder to extinguish (Olsson et al., 2005). This pattern of learning mirrors that observed for more typical biologically prepared stimuli, such as snakes. This finding suggests that people may be predisposed to be wary of culturally defined outgroup members. Presumably, this tendency has come about because outgroup members have been more dangerous over the course of human evolution. However, even though there may be a predisposition to associate negative events with outgroup members, who we consider members of our ingroup or outgroup is learned from our culture. This tendency has sometimes been exploited to create or enhance prejudice toward outgroups during wars and other intergroup conflicts.

Q **Your friend was frightened when she was on a tall bridge and found an unusual flower. She is now afraid of heights and tall bridges, but not unusual flowers. Why?**

ANSWER: We are biologically prepared to learn to fear some stimuli, such as heights, more than others, such as flowers.

6.15 Dopamine Activity Underlies Learning from Rewards

FIGURE 6.24
Enjoyment of Music
As music gives this listener pleasurable chills, dopamine activity is occurring in the listener's brain.

DOPAMINE AND REWARD As noted earlier, people often use the term *reward* as a synonym for positive reinforcement. One important component of the neural basis of reward and reinforcement is the neurotransmitter dopamine, as has been shown by research over the past 50 years (Gershman & Daw, 2017; Schultz, 2016). Dopamine release sets the value of a rewarding unconditioned stimulus in classical conditioning or a rewarding reinforcer in operant conditioning. Drugs that block dopamine's effects disrupt conditioning.

When hungry rats are given food, they experience an increased dopamine release in the nucleus accumbens, a structure in the basal ganglia. The greater the hunger, the greater the dopamine release (Rolls et al., 1980). Food tastes better when you are hungry, and water is more rewarding when you are thirsty, because more dopamine is released under deprived conditions than under nondeprived conditions. Drugs that enhance dopamine activation, such as cocaine and amphetamines, increase the reward value of stimuli. Even looking at funny cartoons activates the nucleus accumbens (Mobbs et al., 2003). Have you ever experienced chills while listening to a piece of music? This tingling sense feels like a shiver down the spine and might give you goosebumps (**FIGURE 6.24**). Using PET imaging and fMRI, researchers have shown that when people experience optimal pleasure while listening to music, there is dopamine activity in the nucleus accumbens (Salimpoor et al., 2011).

Until recently, psychologists believed that rewards increase behavior primarily because of the pleasure those rewards produce and that dopamine was responsible for the subjective feelings associated with reward. But researchers have found that the relationship between dopamine and reward is a bit more nuanced. Terry Robinson and Kent Berridge (1993) introduced an important distinction between the wanting and liking aspects of reward. With drugs, for instance, *wanting* refers to the desire or craving a user has to consume the substance. *Liking* refers to the subjective sense of pleasure the user receives from consuming the substance. Although wanting and liking often go together, there are circumstances under which wanting occurs without liking (Berridge et al., 2010; Kringelbach & Berridge, 2009). For example, a smoker may desire a cigarette but then not particularly enjoy smoking it (**FIGURE 6.25**). Dopamine appears to be especially important for the wanting aspect of reward. Other neurotransmitters, such as endogenous opiates, may be more important for the liking aspect of reward (Berridge & Kringelbach, 2013).

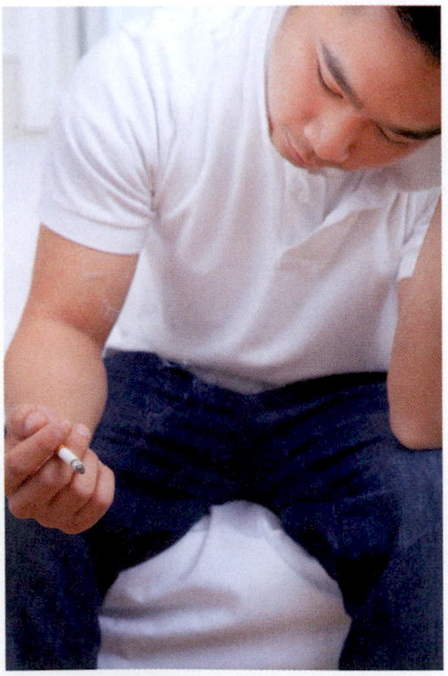

FIGURE 6.25
Wanting Versus Liking
Although this person wants a cigarette because he is addicted, he no longer enjoys the behavior of smoking.

DOPAMINE AND PREDICTION ERROR What links dopamine activity to *learning* about rewards? As reviewed earlier in this chapter, Rescorla and Wagner (1972) coined the term *prediction error* to refer to the difference between the expected and the actual outcome in classical conditioning. For instance, if a dog expected to receive food when it heard a metronome, but no food was delivered, this was a (negative) prediction error. Rescorla and Wagner proposed that prediction errors form the basis for the expectancies and predictions underlying classical conditioning. Later research showed that prediction errors are also important in operant conditioning (Schultz, 1998). For instance, when an action leads to an unexpected reward, it generates a prediction error. If, however, the reward is fully expected following the action, there is no prediction error. Dopamine activity in brain reward regions underlies prediction errors in classical and operant conditioning.

In an effort to determine how the brain might code prediction errors when learning stimuli that predict rewards, Wolfram Schultz and his colleagues (1997) examined

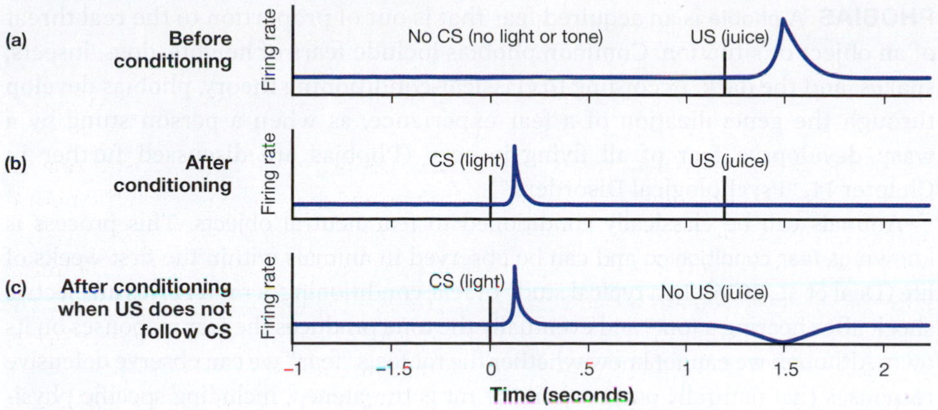

FIGURE 6.26
Prediction Error and Dopamine Activity
Dopamine activity in the brain signals the receipt of a reward. **(a)** The blue line clearly shows a spike in dopamine activity. This activity resulted from a positive prediction error after the unexpected arrival of the US. **(b)** Once the US was associated with the CS, the spike in dopamine activity occurred after the arrival of the CS but not after the arrival of the expected US. **(c)** Dopamine activity continued after the arrival of the CS. However, once the US no longer appeared, negative prediction error resulted in decreased dopamine activity.

how dopamine neurons respond during classical conditioning. In their studies, monkeys were initially left thirsty. When those monkeys unexpectedly received fruit juice (US), they experienced a positive prediction error, and the reward regions in their brains showed a great deal of dopamine activity (**FIGURE 6.26a**). The monkeys were then conditioned to predict the arrival of juice (US) after the presentation of a light or tone (CS). In subsequent trials, after the monkeys had learned the association well, the reward regions of their brains showed a burst of dopamine activity in response to the light or tone (CS) but none for the juice (US) (**FIGURE 6.26b**). Why was the US no longer producing dopamine activity? Because the monkeys had learned that the light or tone fully predicted the juice, and the juice was no longer a surprise. When, on later trials, the juice (US) was no longer given following the light or tone (CS), the monkeys experienced a negative prediction error—the expected result did not happen—and the reward regions showed a reduction in activity of dopamine neurons at the time of the expected juice reward (**FIGURE 6.26c**).

Prediction error signals alert us to important events in our environment (Schultz, 2016). For example, unexpected food alerts us that we need to learn cues to predict the arrival of that food (classical conditioning) or the behaviors that resulted in food (operant conditioning). Thus, it appears that error prediction and its related dopamine activity play an important role in learning associations in classical and operant conditioning (Eshel et al., 2013; Glimcher, 2011; Smith et al., 2011).

The work of Schultz and colleagues demonstrated that during the course of conditioning, as the animal learns that certain cues signal rewards, those cues themselves produce dopamine activity. This shift in dopamine to the cue that predicts reward helps explain the effectiveness of second-order conditioning in classical conditioning and secondary reinforcers in operant conditioning. Through conditioning, seeing a loved one, getting a good grade, or receiving a paycheck may begin to produce dopamine activation. Money is an excellent example of a secondary reinforcer, as mentioned earlier, and anticipated monetary rewards have been found to activate dopamine systems (Knutson et al., 2001). Things become reinforcing because they become associated with positive value, and through dopamine activity, these cues themselves become rewarding (Berridge, 2012).

Q **How does wanting something differ from liking it?**

ANSWER: Wanting refers to the desire to do something, whereas liking refers to the subjective value associated with doing that something.

6.16 Phobias and Addictions Have Learned Components

Classical and operant conditioning help explain many complex behavioral phenomena, including phobias and addiction.

phobia An acquired fear that is out of proportion to the real threat of an object or a situation.

fear conditioning A type of classical conditioning that turns neutral stimuli into threatening stimuli.

PHOBIAS A **phobia** is an acquired fear that is out of proportion to the real threat of an object or situation. Common phobias include fears of heights, dogs, insects, snakes, and the dark. According to classical-conditioning theory, phobias develop through the generalization of a fear experience, as when a person stung by a wasp develops a fear of all flying insects. (Phobias are discussed further in Chapter 14, "Psychological Disorders.")

Animals can be classically conditioned to fear neutral objects. This process is known as **fear conditioning** and can be observed in animals within the first weeks of life (Deal et al., 2016). In a typical study of fear conditioning, a rat receives an electric shock after hearing a tone, and eventually the tone produces the fear responses on its own. Although we cannot know whether the rat feels "fear," we can observe defensive responses that naturally occur when the rat is threatened, including specific physiological and behavioral reactions. One interesting response is *freezing*, or keeping still. Humans are among the many species that respond to threats by freezing. Immediately keeping still might be a hardwired response that helps animals avoid the notice of predators, which often are attracted by movement (LeDoux, 2002; Tovote et al., 2016).

In 1919, John B. Watson became one of the first researchers to demonstrate the role of classical conditioning in the development of phobias. In this case study, Watson taught an infant named Albert B. to fear neutral objects. It is important to note Watson's motives for conditioning "Little Albert." At the time, the prominent theory of phobias was based on ideas proposed by Sigmund Freud about unconscious repressed sexual desires. Believing that Freudian ideas were unscientific and unnecessarily complex, Watson proposed that phobias and their behavioral expression could be explained by simple learning principles, such as classical and operant conditioning.

To test his hypothesis, Watson devised a learning study. He asked a woman to allow her son, Albert B., to participate in the study. Because this child was emotionally stable, Watson believed the experiment would cause him little harm. When Albert was 9 months old, Watson and his lab assistant, Rosalie Rayner, presented him with various neutral objects, including a white rat, a rabbit, a dog, a monkey, costume masks, and a ball of white wool. Albert showed a natural curiosity about these items, but he displayed no overt emotional responses.

When Albert was 11 months old, Watson and Rayner (1920) began the conditioning trials (FIGURE 6.27a). This time, as they presented the white rat and Albert

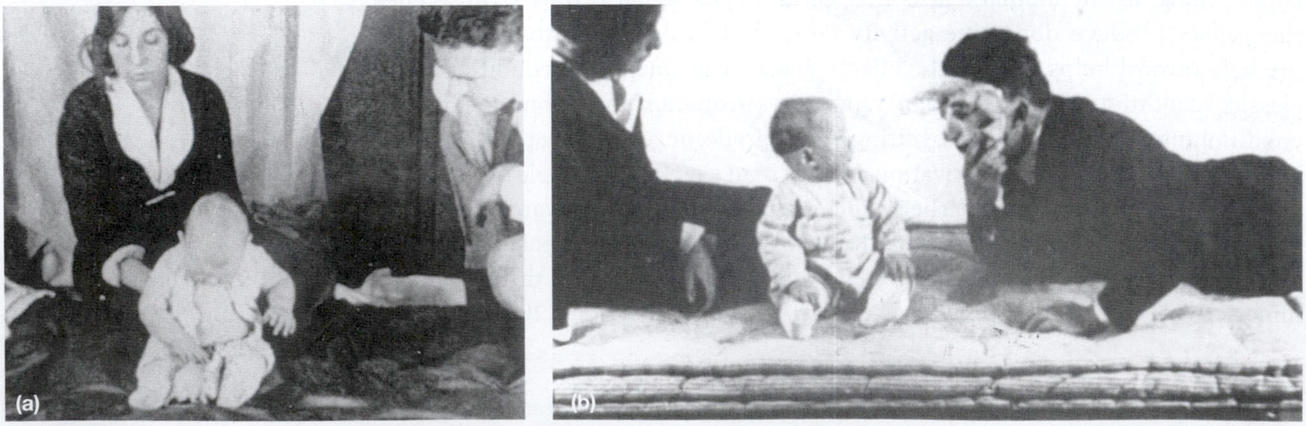

FIGURE 6.27
Case Study of "Little Albert"
(a) In Watson's experiment, Little Albert was presented with a neutral object—a white rat—that provoked a neutral response. Albert learned to associate the rat with a loud clanging sound that scared him. Eventually he showed the conditioned fear response when he saw the previously neutral rat. **(b)** The fear response generalized to other stimuli presented with the rat, such as costume masks.

reached for it, Watson banged a hammer into an iron bar, producing a loud clanging sound. The sound scared the child, who immediately withdrew and hid his face. Watson did this a few more times at intervals of five days until Albert would whimper and cringe when the rat was presented alone. Thus, the pairing of the CS (rat) and US (smashing sound) led to the rat's producing a fear response (CR) on its own. The fear response generalized to other stimuli that Watson had presented along with the rat at the initial meeting (**FIGURE 6.27b**). Over time, Albert became frightened of them all, including the rabbit and the ball of wool. When presented with these stimuli, he would try to crawl away. Even a Santa Claus mask with a white beard produced a fear response. These studies showed that classical conditioning is an effective method of inducing phobias. By crawling away, Albert also demonstrated the role of operant conditioning in phobias. His actions to avoid the stimuli were reinforced by the reduction in fear.

FIGURE 6.28
Little Albert as an Adult
The best evidence indicates that Watson's study participant Little Albert was William Albert Barger, who lived to be 87.

Watson had planned to extinguish Little Albert's learned phobias. However, Albert's mother removed the child from the study before Watson could conduct the extinction trials. For many years, no one seemed to know what had become of Little Albert. His fate was one of psychology's great mysteries. Although Watson did not keep track of Albert, various researchers have sought to identify him over the years (Griggs, 2015). The available evidence suggests that he was William Albert Barger, who died in 2007 at age 87 (Powell et al., 2014). Barger's relatives described him as easygoing, so he does not seem to have suffered long-term problems from being in the study (**FIGURE 6.28**). However, Barger reportedly disliked animals, especially dogs, throughout his life and covered his ears whenever he heard barking.

In his detailed plans for the extinction and reconditioning of phobias, Watson described a method of continually presenting the feared items to Albert paired with more pleasant things, such as candy. A colleague of Watson's, Mary Cover Jones (1924), used this method on a child who was afraid of rabbits and other furry objects. Jones eliminated the fear of rabbits in a 3-year-old named Peter by bringing the rabbit closer as she provided Peter with a favorite food. Such classical-conditioning techniques have since proved valuable for developing very effective behavioral therapies to treat phobias. You will learn more about these kinds of behavioral treatments in Chapter 15.

DRUG ADDICTION Classical and operant conditioning also play important roles in drug addiction. Through operant conditioning, the act of taking a drug becomes associated with the drug's effects, which may lead to increased and repeated consumption. At the same time, other cues that are present when taking the drug can become associated with the drug's effects through classical conditioning. Classically conditioned drug effects are common and demonstrate conditioning's power. For example, the smell of coffee can become a conditioned stimulus (CS). The smell alone can lead coffee drinkers to feel activated and aroused, as though they have actually consumed caffeine (Plassmann & Wager, 2014; **FIGURE 6.29**).

FIGURE 6.29
Experiencing Coffee
For people who regularly drink coffee, just the smell of the beverage can produce some of the effects of caffeine.

Likewise, for heroin addicts, the action of injecting the drug gets reinforced by the high the drug produces, and just the sight of the needle or the feeling when it is inserted into the skin can become a CS. For this reason, addicts sometimes inject themselves with water to reduce their cravings when heroin is unavailable. Even the sight of a straight-edge razor blade, used as part of administering heroin, can briefly increase an addict's cravings (Siegel, 2005).

When former heroin addicts are exposed to environmental cues associated with their drug use, such as people and places, they often experience cravings. This effect occurs partly because the environmental cues have previously signaled ingestion of the drugs. If the resulting cravings are not satisfied, the addict may experience withdrawal—the unpleasant physiological and psychological state of tension and anxiety that occurs when addicts stop using drugs. Addicts who quit using drugs in treatment centers often relapse when they return to their old environments because they experience conditioned craving.

Shepard Siegel and his colleagues have also conducted research into the relationship between drug tolerance and specific situations. Tolerance is a process in which addicts need more and more of a drug to experience the same effects. Siegel's research has shown that tolerance is greatest when the drug is taken in the same physical location where previous drug use occurred. Presumably, the body has learned to expect the drug in that location, so it compensates for the drug by altering neurochemistry or physiology to metabolize it prior to the actual drug delivery. Similarly, college students show greater tolerance to alcohol when it is provided with familiar cues (e.g., a drink that looks and tastes like beer) than when the same amount of alcohol is provided in a novel form (e.g., a blue, peppermint-flavored drink; Siegel et al., 2000). The impact of tolerance can be so great that addicts regularly take drug doses that would be fatal for the inexperienced user. Conversely, Siegel's findings imply that if addicts take their usual large doses in novel settings, they are more likely to overdose. That is, when addicts take drugs in novel settings in which the conditioned drug cues are not present, their bodies may not respond sufficiently to compensate for the drugs (Siegel, 1984; Siegel, 2016; Siegel et al., 1982).

Q Why might it be easier for addicts to abstain in a clinic than in their own neighborhood?

ANSWER: The clinic will most likely present the addicts with fewer learned drug cues that could induce drug craving.

How Do We Learn from Others?

Learning Objectives

- Define social learning.
- Define the observational learning processes of modeling and vicarious learning.
- Define instructed learning.

Suppose you were teaching someone to fly an airplane. Obviously, just rewarding arbitrary correct behaviors would be a disastrous way to train an aspiring pilot. People learn many behaviors not by doing them but by being told how to do them and watching others do them. For example, we learn social etiquette through instruction and observation. We often acquire attitudes about politics, religion, and the habits of celebrities from parents, peers, teachers, and the media. Research on social learning examines how we learn about behaviors and predictive associations from others.

6.17 Social Learning Occurs Through Observation and Instruction

Social learning is a powerful adaptive tool for humans. Humans do not need to personally experience a stimulus or event to learn that it is good or bad or should be approached or avoided. Children can learn basic skills by watching adults perform those skills. They can learn which things are safe to eat by watching what adults eat (Wertz & Wynn, 2014). They can learn to fear dangerous objects and dangerous situations by being told about these dangers or watching adults avoid those objects and situations. Children even acquire beliefs through observation and instruction. Young children are sponges, absorbing everything that goes on around them. They learn by watching and listening as much as by doing.

FIGURE 6.30
Bandura's Bobo Doll Studies
In Bandura's studies, two groups of preschool children were shown a film of an adult playing with a large inflatable doll called Bobo. One group saw the adult play quietly (not shown here), and the other group saw the adult attack the doll (shown in the top row here). When children were allowed to play with the doll later, those who had seen the aggressive display were more than twice as likely to act aggressively toward the doll.

BANDURA'S OBSERVATIONAL STUDIES The most influential work on social learning was conducted in the 1960s by the psychologist Albert Bandura. In a now-classic series of studies, Bandura divided preschool children into two groups. One group watched a film of an adult playing quietly with a large inflatable doll called Bobo. The other group watched a film of the adult attacking Bobo furiously: whacking the doll with a mallet, punching it in the nose, and kicking it around the room. When the children were later allowed to play with a number of toys, including the Bobo doll, those who had seen the more aggressive display were more than twice as likely to act aggressively toward the doll (Bandura et al., 1961). These results suggest that exposing children to violence may encourage them to act aggressively (**FIGURE 6.30**).

Since Bandura's groundbreaking research, several studies have examined whether there is a relationship between watching violence and acting violently. A meta-analysis of studies involving the effects of media violence showed that exposure to violent media increases the likelihood of aggression (Gentile et al., 2007). However, longitudinal studies, which follow participants over time in assessing childhood TV watching and later violent behavior outside the laboratory, suggest that factors other than exposure to violence may underlie some of these findings. Additional variables—such as personality, poverty, or parental negligence—could have affected both TV viewing habits and violent tendencies. Despite the problems with specific studies, however, most research in this area shows a relationship between exposure to violence and aggressive behavior (Bushman & Anderson, 2015).

MODELING (DEMONSTRATION AND IMITATION) Because humans can learn through observation, we can be taught many complex skills through demonstration. For instance, parents use slow and exaggerated motions to show their children how to tie their shoes. Indeed, YouTube is so popular in part because people can learn to do many things by watching instructional videos.

The imitation of observed behavior is called **modeling**. The term indicates that people are reproducing the behaviors of *models*—those being observed. Modeling in humans is influenced by numerous factors. Generally, we are more likely to imitate the actions of models who are attractive, have high status, and are somewhat similar to ourselves. In addition, modeling is effective only if the observer is physically capable of imitating the behavior. Simply watching LeBron James

modeling The imitation of observed behavior.

FIGURE 6.31
Defend Like LeBron?
Simply watching an athlete execute a move does not enable us to perform that move if it exceeds our physical ability.

successfully shut down the NBA's best players does not mean we could do the same (**FIGURE 6.31**).

The influence that models have on behavior sometimes occurs implicitly, without people being aware that their behaviors are being altered. Other times people might not want to admit that they have changed their ways of speaking or dressing to resemble those of people they admire, such as celebrities or the cool kids in the class. Overwhelming evidence says, however, that people do imitate what they see in others.

For example, adolescents whose favorite actors smoke in movies are much more likely to smoke (Tickle et al., 2001). The more smoking that adolescents observe in movies, the more positive their attitudes about smoking become and the more likely they are to begin smoking (Sargent et al., 2005). Surprisingly, these effects are strongest among children whose parents do not smoke. Why would this be so? Perhaps what such children learn about smoking comes completely through the media, which tend to glamorize the habit. For example, movies often present smokers as attractive, healthy, and wealthy, not like the typical smoker. Adolescents do not generally decide to smoke after watching one movie's glamorous depiction of smoking. Rather, images of smokers as mature, cool, sexy—things adolescents want to be—shape adolescents' attitudes about smoking and subsequently lead to imitation. As adolescent viewers learn to associate smoking with people they admire, they incorporate the general message that smoking is desirable.

In light of findings such as these, the movie industry has come under considerable pressure to reduce depictions of smoking. Indeed, since 1995 there has been a reduction in on-screen smoking and a related decline in adolescent smoking rates (Sargent & Heatherton, 2009; **FIGURE 6.32**). Of course, correlation is not proof of causation. Several public health efforts to reduce youth smoking, such as media campaigns and bans on marketing of tobacco products to children, might be responsible for the reduction in smoking as well as its reduced portrayals in the movies.

vicarious learning Learning the consequences of an action by watching others being rewarded or punished for performing the action.

VICARIOUS LEARNING (REINFORCEMENT AND CONDITIONING) Through **vicarious learning**, people learn about an action's consequences by watching others

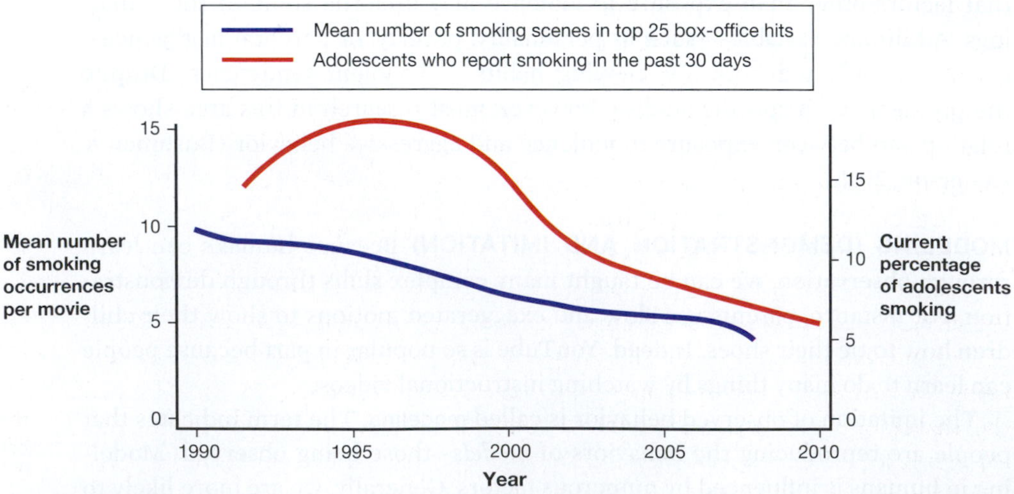

FIGURE 6.32
Movie Smoking and Adolescent Smoking
This double-*y*-axis graph compares the declining rate of smoking in movies with the declining rate of adolescent smoking.

being rewarded or punished for performing the action (**FIGURE 6.33**). For instance, a teacher may make an example of a student who did not do the homework by scolding this student in front of classmates. By observing the consequences of this student's behavior, other students learn vicariously about the importance of completing homework. In one of his studies, Bandura showed children a film of an adult aggressively playing with a Bobo doll, but this time the film ended in one of three different ways (Bandura, 1965). In the first version, a control condition, the adult experienced no consequences for the aggressive behavior. In the second version, the adult was rewarded for the behavior. When subsequently allowed to play with the Bobo doll, the children who saw the model being punished were less likely to be aggressive than the group who saw the model being rewarded or the control group.

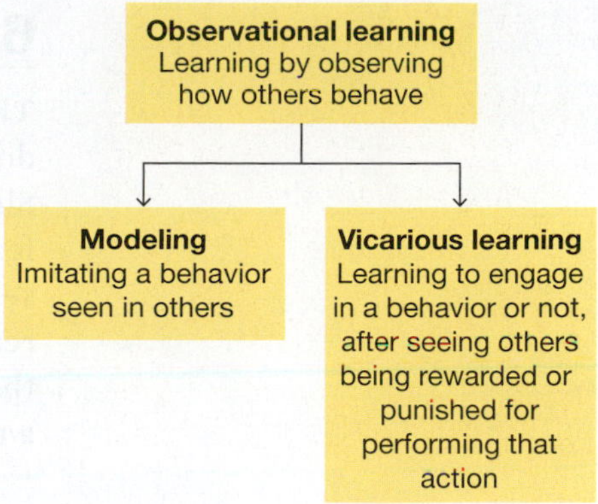

Observational learning
Learning by observing how others behave
Modeling
Imitating a behavior seen in others
Vicarious learning
Learning to engage in a behavior or not, after seeing others being rewarded or punished for performing that action

FIGURE 6.33
Two Types of Observational Learning

These findings do not mean that the children in the punishment group did not remember the behavior they observed. Later, all the children were offered small gifts to perform the model's actions, and all performed the actions reliably. Direct rewards revealed that all the children remembered the model's behavior and could reproduce it. However, without direct rewards, the children in the punishment group were less likely to modify their behavioral response toward the Bobo doll to align with the adult model's behavior.

INSTRUCTED LEARNING Some other species can learn socially through observation, but humans have one advantage in that we are the only species that can be verbally instructed about the associations between stimuli or between actions and consequences. The importance of **instructed learning** in human development was first emphasized by the Russian psychologist Lev Vygotsky (1962), who believed social interaction not only leads to increased levels of knowledge but actually changes a child's thoughts and behaviors. Inspired by Vygotsky's work, Michael Tomasello and colleagues (1993) argued that social learning, including verbal instruction, underlies the uniquely complex nature of human culture (**FIGURE 6.34**).

instructed learning Learning associations and behaviors through verbal communication.

Although instructed learning may play a key role in education, development, and cultural learning, it occurs throughout the lifespan and is not limited to learning about social associations. For instance, the COVID-19 pandemic changed behavior throughout the world as people tried to avoid getting the virus and stop its spread throughout communities. Note that no one could *see* the danger that lurked from the virus. To our perceptual systems, germs are an imaginary concept, unless of course one has a microscope. The only way most of us learn about germs is by being told they exist and are dangerous. Nevertheless, once people have learned the association between germs and sickness, they will take proactive actions (immunizations, handwashing, social distancing) to avoid the potential negative consequences.

FIGURE 6.34
Instructed Learning
Humans have the adaptive advantage of being able to learn about behaviors and associations between stimuli or events through verbal communication.

Q **When you see another student suspended for cheating, you are less likely to cheat. Why?**

ANSWER: Your behavior has been influenced by vicarious learning.

6.18 Fear Can Be Learned Through Social Means

The psychologist Susan Mineka noticed that monkeys raised in laboratories do not fear snakes, whereas monkeys raised in the wild fear snakes intensely. She set out to explore whether monkeys, by observing other monkeys reacting fearfully to snakes, could develop a phobia of snakes. Mineka and colleagues set up an experiment with two groups of rhesus monkeys. One group was reared in the laboratory, and one group was reared in the wild. To obtain food, the monkeys had to reach beyond a clear box that contained either a snake or a neutral object (Cook & Mineka, 1989, 1990).

When a snake was in the box, the wild-reared monkeys did not touch the food. They also showed signs of distress, such as clinging to their cages and making threatening faces. The laboratory-raised monkeys reached past the box even if it contained a snake, and they showed no overt signs of fear. The researchers then showed the laboratory-raised monkeys the wild monkeys' fearful response to see if it would affect the laboratory monkeys' reactions to the snake. The laboratory monkeys quickly developed a fear of the snakes, and this fear was maintained over a three-month period.

Humans, too, can learn to fear particular stimuli by observing others. For example, a person might become afraid of swimming in the open ocean after watching a movie in which a swimmer is attacked by a shark. People can also learn to fear particular things, such as germs, simply by hearing that they are dangerous. In fact, for some people, socially acquired fears result in phobias, as can be seen in those who go to great lengths to avoid all germs. Thus, social forces play an important role in the learning of fear (Olsson & Phelps, 2007).

Are these socially acquired fears different from fears learned through direct experience with something aversive, as in classical conditioning? Brain research suggests they may not be too different. Although observing others and receiving verbal instruction engage different brain circuits than perceiving a neutral stimulus (the CS) paired with an aversive event (the US) does, once these fears are acquired they all depend on similar brain systems for their bodily expression. Research in humans and other species demonstrates that the amygdala, a small almond-shaped structure in the medial temporal lobe, is critical for the acquisition and expression of conditioned defensive responses, such as freezing or autonomic nervous system arousal, in the presence of an aversive CS. These defensive responses are the body's reflexive reactions to threat (LeDoux, 2015a). In a series of studies, Elizabeth Phelps and colleagues either paired a colored square with a mild shock (classical conditioning), asked research participants to watch another person receive a shock when presented with a colored square (observational learning), or told participants that when presented with a colored square they may receive a mild shock (instructed learning) (**FIGURE 6.35**). In all cases, when the colored square was later presented, participants demonstrated a learned defensive response (e.g., sweating indicative of autonomic nervous system arousal). Furthermore, the amygdala played a critical role in the expression of learned defensive responses for both conditioned fears and socially acquired fears (Funayama et al., 2001; LaBar et al., 1995; Olsson et al., 2007; Phelps et al., 2001). These findings suggest that similar brain mechanisms underlie conditioned, observational, and instructed fear learning (Olsson & Phelps, 2007).

(a) (b) (c)

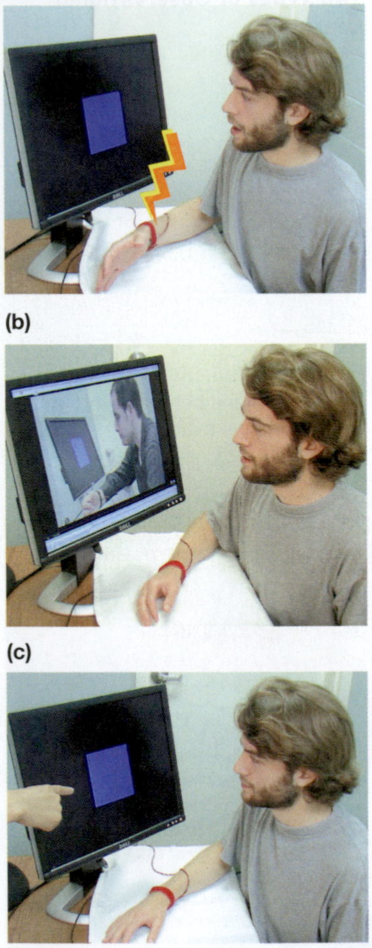

FIGURE 6.35
Social Learning of Fear
Fear can be learned by **(a)** classical conditioning, such as pairing a shape with a mild shock; **(b)** observational learning, watching someone else receive a mild shock paired with a shape; or **(c)** instructed learning, being told a mild shock will be paired with a shape.

Q How do people learn to fear germs they cannot see?

ANSWER: instructed learning

6.19 Social Learning Has Implications for Criminal Justice

PSYCHOLOGY OUTSIDE THE LAB

Social learning plays a role in acquiring all types of predictive associations, but it is uniquely important for cultural learning. Watching others and hearing what they say underlies our understanding of our culture's expectations, norms, and prejudices. In the United States, one place where the impact of social learning is apparent is the criminal justice system. Although most people believe that criminal justice should be blind to race, the data suggest that it is not. In the United States, Black males are 6 times more likely to be incarcerated than White males (Sentencing Project, 2018) and are more likely to receive jail time for equal offenses, and Black males receive longer sentences than White males for equivalent crimes (Schmitt et al., 2017). Researchers have demonstrated that it is not just the race of the defendant that predicts harsher sentences. For both Black and White males, those whose facial features are more stereotypically Black (broad nose, thick lips, dark skin) receive longer sentences than those with more stereotypically White features (Blair et al., 2004), and Black defendants with more stereotypically Black features are more likely to receive the death sentence when the victim is White (Eberhardt et al., 2006).

Stanford psychologist Jennifer Eberhardt (FIGURE 6.36) has devoted her career to trying to understand racial bias in the criminal justice system. She is a MacArthur "Genius" award winner and codirector of Stanford University's SPARQ (Social Psychologists Answer Real-World Questions) Center. Her research derives insights from laboratory studies, collaborations with law enforcement, and examinations of sentencing and other criminal justice data. In her book *Biased: Uncovering the Hidden Prejudice That Shapes What We See, Think, and Do* (Eberhardt, 2019), she argues that the systemic racism apparent in our criminal justice system is due to the fact that cultural learning in the United States results in an association between Black race and criminality that seeps into our perceptions and actions. This learning is expressed implicitly, without our awareness, which makes it especially hard to counteract. Over the past few decades, data from social psychologists on implicit biases (see Chapter 12) have slowly started to influence the conversation about race in the United States. As Eberhardt argues in her book, the challenge for social psychologists now is to figure out how we can diminish the impact of these prejudicial, socially acquired associations in the criminal justice system and beyond. ■

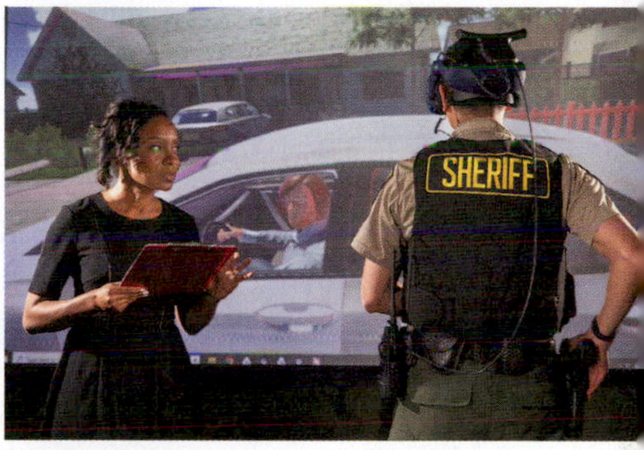

FIGURE 6.36
Jennifer Eberhardt
Psychologist Jennifer Eberhardt proposes that learned cultural associations between Black race and criminality in the United States underlie racial disparities in criminal justice.

Q **What type of learning is proposed to underlie racial bias in the U.S. criminal justice system?**

ANSWER: social learning

Your Chapter Review

It's time to complete your study experience! Go to **INQUIZITIVE** to practice actively with this chapter's concepts and get personalized feedback along the way.

Chapter Summary

How Do We Learn?

6.1 Learning Results from Experience Learning is a relatively enduring change in behavior, resulting from experience. Learning enables animals to better adapt to their environment. The three major types of learning are nonassociative, associative, and social. Nonassociative learning is a change in behavior after repeated exposure to a single stimulus or event. Associative learning is the linking of two stimuli or events. Social learning is acquiring or changing a behavior after being verbally instructed or exposed to another individual performing that behavior.

6.2 Nonassociative Learning Involves Habituation and Sensitization Habituation leads to a decrease in a behavioral response after repeated exposure to a stimulus. Habituation occurs when the stimulus stops providing new information. Sensitization leads to an increase in a behavioral response after exposure to a repeated stimulus. Sensitization occurs in cases where increased attention to a stimulus may prove beneficial, such as in dangerous or exciting situations.

How Do We Learn Predictive Associations?

6.3 Classical Conditioning Is Learning What Goes Together Pavlov established the principles of classical conditioning. Through classical conditioning, associations are made between two stimuli, such as the clicking of a metronome and the presence of food. What is learned is that one stimulus predicts another.

6.4 Learning Is Acquired and Persists Until Extinction Learning the association between two stimuli is called acquisition; learning that the association no longer exists when the stimuli are no longer paired is called extinction. Spontaneous recovery occurs when, after a period of time, a previously extinguished conditioned response is once again expressed.

6.5 Learning Involves Expectancies and Prediction The Rescorla-Wagner theory describes how the strength of association between two stimuli depends on how unexpected or surprising the unconditioned stimulus is. Positive prediction error results when an unexpected stimulus is presented. Positive prediction error strengthens the association between the CS and the US. Negative prediction error results when an expected stimulus is missing. Negative prediction error weakens the CS-US association.

6.6 Learning Shapes Both Conditioned and Unconditioned Stimuli Once an association between a CS and US has become so well-established that the CS acquires value, other stimuli that are associated with the CS alone may also become conditioned through second-order conditioning. Stimuli that are similar to a conditioned stimulus may elicit a conditioned response through generalization, but animals can also learn to discriminate between similar stimuli.

How Do Consequences of an Action Shape Behavior?

6.7 Operant Conditioning Is Learning Actions from Consequences Operant conditioning is the learning process in which an action's consequences determine the likelihood of that action being repeated. Through operant conditioning, an animal learns predictive associations between actions and consequences.

6.8 Reinforcement Increases Behavior, Punishment Decreases Behavior Reinforcement increases the likelihood that a behavior will be repeated. In positive reinforcement, a pleasurable stimulus is delivered after a behavior (e.g., giving a dog a treat for sitting). In negative reinforcement, an aversive stimulus is removed after a behavior (e.g., letting a puppy out of its crate when it acts calmly). Punishment decreases the probability that a behavior will repeat. Positive punishment involves the administration of an aversive stimulus, such as a squirt of water in the face, to decrease behavior. Negative punishment involves the removal of a rewarding stimulus, such as money, to decrease behavior.

6.9 Psychology Outside the Lab: When Is Parental Punishment Effective? Although some forms of parental punishment, such as time-outs, can be effective, spanking is generally ineffective and can lead to a number of negative outcomes. Many psychologists believe that any method of parental punishment is less effective than providing positive reinforcement for "better" behaviors.

6.10 Learning Shapes Actions and Reinforcers Operant conditioning requires an animal to perform an action to be reinforced. When the desired action is not performed spontaneously, shaping can be used to reinforce successive approximations of the desired behavior. Reinforcers may be primary (those that satisfy biological needs) or secondary (those that do not directly satisfy biological needs but acquire their value through conditioning).

6.11 You Be the Psychologist: Can You Challenge Superstitious Behaviors? Accidental reinforcement of behaviors occurring close in time can lead to superstitious behaviors in humans and other animals. Although these are generally harmless, at times superstitions can interfere with daily life. Given the human tendency to see associations and believe that they are true, proving that a behavior is superstitious can be challenging.

6.12 Operant Conditioning Is Influenced by Value and Timing Whether or not an association is learned between an action and consequences can depend on how closely in time they occur. If there is a delay in the consequence of an action, learning can be difficult. Humans can conceptually link an earlier action with a later consequence, but the value of reinforcement may diminish when the consequence occurs in the future. Some reinforcers are more valuable than others, which can influence the likelihood or ease of learning.

6.13 Operant Conditioning Is Influenced by Schedules of Reinforcement Learning occurs in response to continuous reinforcement and partial reinforcement. Partial reinforcement may be delivered on a ratio schedule or an interval schedule. Each type of schedule may be fixed or variable. Partial reinforcement administered on a variable ratio schedule is particularly resistant to extinction.

What Do Different Types of Associative Learning Have in Common?

6.14 Learning Is Influenced by Biology and Evolution An animal's innate biological responses and actions influence what is learned or how easily the animal can learn. For instance, sickness is more likely to be associated with the taste of food eaten hours earlier than another stimulus experienced closer in time. Animals are also predisposed to learn species-typical reward or defensive behaviors from reinforcement or punishment. Stimuli that were natural threats through evolution, such as snakes, are more readily associated with aversive events.

6.15 Dopamine Activity Underlies Learning from Rewards The brain has specialized centers that produce pleasure when stimulated. Behaviors and stimuli that activate these centers are reinforced. The nucleus accumbens has dopamine receptors, which are activated by rewarding stimuli. Through conditioning, secondary reinforcers can also activate dopamine receptors. The neurotransmitter dopamine provides one neurobiological basis for learning from prediction errors. Dopamine release increases after positive prediction error and decreases after negative prediction error.

6.16 Phobias and Addictions Have Learned Components Phobias involve learned fear associations. Addictions involve learned reward associations. Classical and operant conditioning can explain how people learn to associate not only the fearful stimulus or drug itself with the fear or reward but also a host of other "neutral" stimuli. In the case of drug addiction, addicts often inadvertently associate environmental aspects of the purchase and use of the drug with the rewarding consequences and biological changes produced by the drug. These learned associations are major factors in relapse, as seemingly innocuous stimuli can trigger cravings even years after drug use is discontinued.

How Do We Learn from Others?

6.17 Social Learning Occurs Through Observation and Instruction Social learning is a powerful adaptive tool. Humans and other animals learn from being instructed and by watching the behavior of others. The imitation of observed behavior is referred to as modeling. Instructed learning involves acquiring associations and behavior through verbal communication. Vicarious learning occurs when people learn about an action's consequences by observing others being reinforced or punished for their behavior.

6.18 Fear Can Be Learned Through Social Means Monkeys have learned to fear snakes (but not flowers) by watching other monkeys react fearfully. These findings suggest that monkeys can learn by observation if the behavior is biologically adaptive. People also learn fear by observation or by instruction. People being instructed that a stimulus is paired with a shock, or observing other people receive a shock, experience activation in the amygdala—a brain area important for processing threatening stimuli—even though they themselves did not receive any shocks.

6.19 Psychology Outside the Lab: Social Learning Has Implications for Criminal Justice Social learning of cultural associations between Black race and criminality is proposed to contribute to racial bias in the U.S. legal system. The psychologist Jennifer Eberhardt has devoted her career to understanding how race influences policing and legal decisions.

Key Terms

acquisition, p. 209
associative learning, p. 204
behaviorism, p. 216
classical conditioning (Pavlovian conditioning), p. 207
conditioned response (CR), p. 207
conditioned stimulus (CS), p. 207
continuous reinforcement, p. 223
equipotentiality, p. 225
extinction, p. 209
fear conditioning, p. 230
habituation, p. 205
instructed learning, p. 235
law of effect, p. 215
learning, p. 204
modeling, p. 233
negative punishment, p. 217
negative reinforcement, p. 217
nonassociative learning, p. 204
operant conditioning (instrumental conditioning), p. 214
partial reinforcement, p. 223
partial-reinforcement extinction effect, p. 224
phobia, p. 230
positive punishment, p. 217
positive reinforcement, p. 217
punishment, p. 217
reinforcer, p. 216
Rescorla-Wagner model, p. 211
sensitization, p. 205
shaping, p. 219
social learning, p. 205
spontaneous recovery, p. 210
stimulus discrimination, p. 213
stimulus generalization, p. 212
temporal discounting, p. 222
unconditioned response (UR), p. 207
unconditioned stimulus (US), p. 207
vicarious learning, p. 234

Practice Exercises

1. On the first day of summer school, the air conditioner in Matt's history classroom broke down. All the other rooms were unaffected. After several weeks of attending class in the sweltering room, Matt started sweating every time he approached the history room. In this example of classical conditioning, what are the US, UR, CS, and CR?

2. Which of the following statements is true about extinction learning?
   - a. It involves fewer presentations of the CS than during acquisition.
   - b. It permanently eliminates the expression of the conditioned response.
   - c. It is a form of new learning that replaces the associative bond between the CS and US but does not eliminate it.

3. During ____, organisms become less responsive to stimuli; during ____, organisms become more responsive to stimuli.
   - a. tolerance, sensitization
   - b. habituation, sensitization
   - c. sensitization, habituation
   - d. addiction, dependence

4. Jason just moved his dog's food to the cupboard, which creaks noisily when it is opened. In which situation is Jason's dog likely to learn an association between the sound of the cupboard opening and the food?
   - a. The door reliably opens shortly after the food is delivered.
   - b. The door reliably opens shortly before the food is delivered.

c. The door reliably opens just as the food is delivered.
d. The door reliably opens along with the sound of a can opener, which has previously signaled food delivery.

5. Identify each statement as an example of negative punishment, positive punishment, negative reinforcement, or positive reinforcement.
   a. Whenever a puppy barks, it gets its belly rubbed, so it barks more.
   b. A teenager who stays out too late is given extra chores to do.
   c. A person with a clean driving record receives a reduced insurance premium.
   d. Your date arrives an hour late, and you refuse to speak to them for the rest of the evening.

6. Match each scenario with one of the following reinforcement schedules: fixed ratio, variable ratio, fixed interval, variable interval.
   a. Your mail arrives at the same time every day.
   b. Every once in a while, you receive exciting mail.
   c. Every seventh newspaper you receive is loaded with coupons.
   d. You buy a packet of baseball cards each week. Sometimes the packet includes a valuable card, but other times it does not.

7. Match each example with the type of learning it describes: nonassociative, associative, social.
   a. Maya finds that she is speaking up more in class after her professor compliments her on the questions she asks.
   b. Donae no longer responds to a persistent beep from a broken appliance in his apartment.
   c. After watching a YouTube video, Rohan is able to change the air filter in his heater.

8. Which of the following statements are true?
   a. Any behavior can be shaped through reinforcement.
   b. Psychologists believe that punishment is more effective than positive reinforcement for shaping behavior.
   c. Animals can be conditioned to fear flowers as easily as they can be conditioned to fear snakes.
   d. A conditioned taste aversion can be learned in a single trial.

9. Why is it important for addiction treatment to include exposure to conditioned environmental drug cues?

10. Which statement correctly describes the relationship between dopamine and reinforcement?
   a. Dopamine is more important for the "liking" rather than the "wanting" aspect of reward.
   b. Dopamine activity in the brain is increased when a behavior leads to an unexpected reward.
   c. Only primary reinforcers are linked with dopamine activity.

WORLD MEMORY CHAMPIONSHIP
DECEMBER 1st - 3rd, 2017
JAKARTA, INDONESIA

7 Memory

Big Questions

AUSTRALIAN FORENSIC PSYCHOLOGIST DONALD THOMSON was shocked when he was arrested and charged with rape. He had been identified as the culprit by a woman who had been assaulted the day before. Fortunately for Dr. Thomson, when the details of the assault were revealed, he discovered he had a foolproof alibi: At the time of the crime, he was on live television. Ironically, he had been featured on a show about memory and was discussing his research on the potential fallibility of eyewitness identification. The victim confirmed she was watching the program immediately before the assault, and it was determined she had mistakenly identified Dr. Thomson as the culprit. Dr. Thomson was lucky. The Innocence Project reports that faulty eyewitness identification accounts for 69 percent of cases where DNA evidence later exonerated someone who had been convicted of a crime (Innocence Project, n.d.). Although we can generally rely on our memories to guide us, occasionally they can be flawed. Most of the time our memory mistakes are harmless, but in the case of mistaken eyewitness identification they can have life-changing consequences.

Memories reflect our personal history and are crucial to every aspect of our everyday lives. Normally, each of us remembers millions of pieces of information. These memories range from the trivial to the vital. Each person's sense of self, or identity, is made up of what that person knows from memories. Psychologists have identified different types of memory and study how these memories are formed, maintained, and retrieved. They also explore the factors that lead to accurate memories as well as common memory mistakes and their causes.

What Is Memory, and What Are Memory Systems?

Learning Objectives

- Define memory.
- Identify and describe implicit memory systems.
- Differentiate episodic and semantic memory.
- Generate examples of each type of implicit and explicit memory.

memory The ability to store and retrieve information.

Memory is the ability to store and retrieve information. Memory enables organisms to take information from experiences and retain it for later use. Because these basic functions of memory, the storing and retrieving of information, are not unique to living organisms, we also use the term *memory* to describe artificial information-storing devices. However, this analogy is imperfect. For living organisms, memory does not work like computer storage or a digital camera, faithfully recording the information that is inputted. Instead, in much the same way that perception transforms sensory signals to create a stable representation of the world, our memories are influenced by the situation or context and the way we process, interpret, and use information. The memories we retrieve can be incomplete, biased, and distorted. Two people's memories for the same event can differ vastly, because each person stores and retrieves memories of the event distinctively. In other words, memories are personal and unique stories. In addition, not all experiences are equally likely to be remembered. Some life events pass swiftly, leaving no lasting memory. Others are remembered but later forgotten. Still others remain in our memories for a lifetime.

Although the term *memory* is most often used to refer to your ability to consciously recollect information at will, such as remembering what you had for lunch yesterday, memory is expressed whenever you exhibit a response or behavior that is modified by past experience. Psychologists have identified different types of memory that rely on different brain circuits, or systems, for storage and expression.

7.1 There Are Many Types of Memories and Memory Systems

Throughout each day, you express your memories through your thoughts, words, and actions. Your ability to walk, bike, or drive home relies on your memory for those skills. Knowing the address of your home and how to get there represents other types of memories. Remembering a phone call you made just before you drove home is yet another expression of memory. Psychologists have investigated the different forms of memory expression since the early twentieth century, and much of what has been learned about how different types of memory are organized in behavior and the brain was discovered through studies in patients with brain injuries. The most famous of these patients is H.M.

FIGURE 7.1
Henry Molaison (H.M.)
Known to the world only by his initials, Molaison became one of the most famous people in memory research by participating in countless experiments.

THE CASE OF H.M. H.M., or Henry Molaison, was born in 1926 and died at a nursing home in 2008. Until his death, the larger world did not know H.M.'s real name or what he looked like (**FIGURE 7.1**). His privacy was guarded by the researchers who studied his memory. Although H.M. lived until his 80s, in many ways his world stopped in 1953, when he was 27. As a young man, H.M. suffered from severe epilepsy. Every day, he had several grand mal seizures, an affliction that made it impossible for him to lead a normal life. Seizures are uncontrolled random firings of groups of neurons, and they can spread across the brain. H.M.'s seizures originated in the temporal lobes of his brain and would spread from there.

Because the anticonvulsive drugs available at that time could not control H.M.'s seizures, surgery was the only choice for treatment. The reasoning behind this surgery was that if the seizure-causing portion of his brain was removed, he would stop having seizures. In September 1953, H.M.'s doctors removed parts of

FIGURE 7.2

A Drawing of H.M.'s Brain

The portions of the medial temporal lobe that were removed from H.M.'s brain are indicated by the shaded regions.

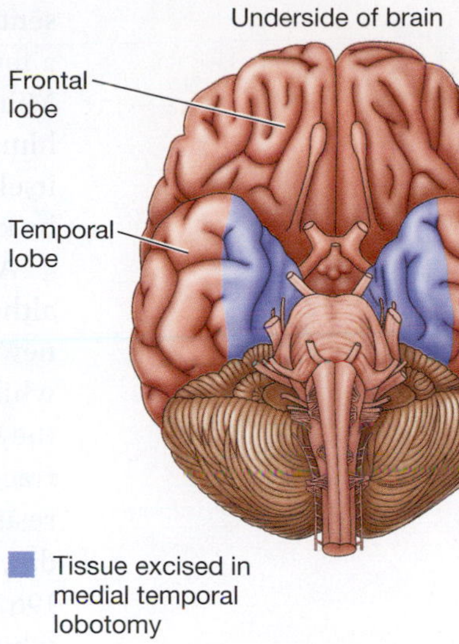

his medial temporal lobes, including the hippocampus (**FIGURE 7.2**). The surgery quieted his seizures, but it had an unexpected and very unfortunate side effect: H.M. seemed to have lost the ability to remember new information for more than a few moments.

H.M. never remembered the day of the week, what year it was, or his own age. Still, he could talk about his childhood, explain the rules of baseball, and describe members of his family, things he knew at the time of the surgery. In other words, his ability to remember details from his life prior to surgery was relatively intact. According to the psychologists who tested him, his IQ was slightly above average.

H.M. suffered from **amnesia**, an inability to retrieve vast quantities of information from memory as a result of brain injury or psychological trauma. There are two basic types of amnesia: retrograde and anterograde. In **retrograde amnesia**, people lose past memories for events, facts, people, or even personal information. Most portrayals of amnesia in the movies and on television are of retrograde amnesia, as when characters in soap operas awaken from comas and do not know who they are. (**FIGURE 7.3a**). By contrast, in **anterograde amnesia**, which is more common in real life, people lose the ability to form new memories (**FIGURE 7.3b**). After his surgery, H.M. suffered from anterograde amnesia. He could remember details of his life prior to 1953 but could not remember anything that happened after that.

Despite this very poor memory, H.M. could hold a normal conversation as long as he was not distracted. This ability showed that he was still able to remember things for short periods. After all, to grasp the meaning of spoken language, a person needs to remember the words recently spoken, such as the beginning and end of a

amnesia A deficit in long-term memory—resulting from disease, brain injury, or psychological trauma—in which the individual loses the ability to retrieve vast quantities of information.

retrograde amnesia A condition in which people lose past memories, such as memories for events, facts, people, or even personal information.

anterograde amnesia A condition in which people lose the ability to form new memories.

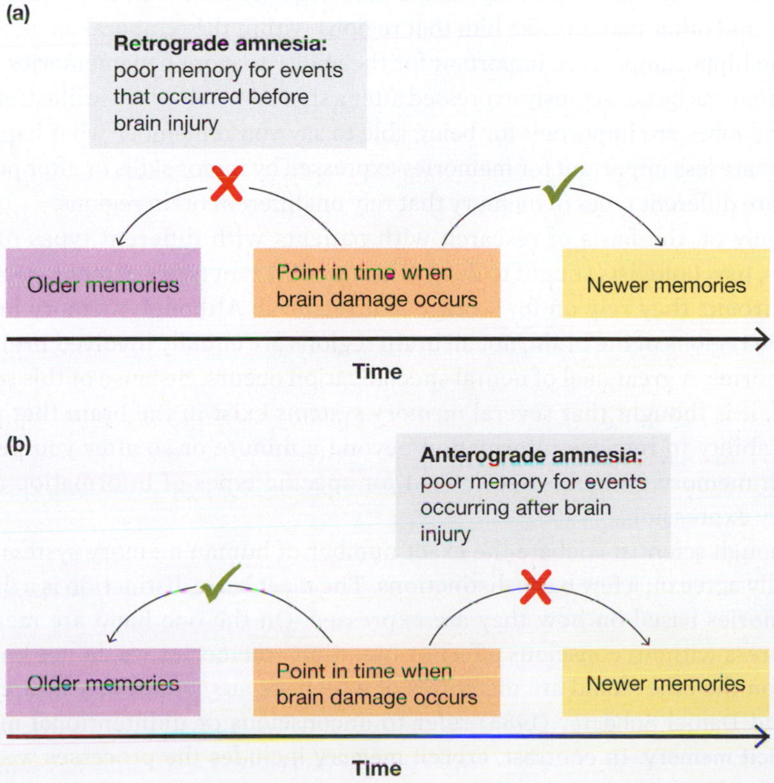

FIGURE 7.3

Retrograde Amnesia Versus Anterograde Amnesia

Amnesia can involve either of two forms of memory loss. **(a)** Retrograde amnesia is an inability to access memories that were created before the brain damage. **(b)** Anterograde amnesia is an inability to create new memories after the brain damage.

sentence. But H.M. would lose the thread of a conversation if it extended beyond a few minutes. People who worked with H.M.—such as the psychologist Brenda Milner, who followed his case for over 40 years—had to introduce themselves to him every time they met (Milner et al., 1968). As H.M. put it, "Every day is alone in itself." Because of his profound memory loss, he remembered little. But somehow, he knew that he remembered nothing. How could this have been the case?

As researchers studied H.M., they discovered he could learn some new things, although he did not seem to know he had learned them. For instance, he learned new motor tasks. In one series of tests, he was asked to trace the outline of a star while watching his hand in a mirror. Most people do poorly the first few times they try this difficult task. On each of three consecutive days, H.M. was asked to trace the star 10 times. His performance improved over the three days, and this result indicated that he had retained some information about the task. On each day, however, H.M. could not recall ever having performed the task before (Milner, 1962). His ability to learn new motor skills enabled him to get a job at a factory, where he mounted cigarette lighters in cardboard cases. But his condition left him unable to describe the job or the workplace.

priming A facilitation in the response to a stimulus due to recent experience with that stimulus or a related stimulus.

Another example of H.M.'s intact memory abilities was demonstrated with priming. As described in Chapter 4, **priming** is the facilitation of a response to a stimulus based on past experience with that stimulus or a related stimulus. In one study H.M. was shown a list of words. Later he could not remember having seen the list. However, when presented with words so quickly that they were hard to read, H.M. was more likely to identify words that had been on the list. Healthy control participants also showed this facilitation in identifying briefly presented words they had recently encountered, but unlike H.M., they were also able to recall having seen the list earlier (Postle & Corkin, 1998).

DIFFERENT BRAIN REGIONS SUPPORT DIFFERENT MEMORY SYSTEMS

Studies of H.M.'s strange condition contributed many clues to how memories are stored—normally and abnormally—in the brain. For instance, we know from studies of H.M. and other patients like him that regions within the temporal lobes, specifically the hippocampus, are important for the ability to store new memories for life events that can be consciously expressed after a short time. As his case illustrates, the temporal lobes are important for being able to say you remember what happened, but they are less important for memories expressed by motor skills or after priming. These are different types of memory that rely on different brain regions.

Largely on the basis of research with patients with different types of brain injuries, psychologists sought to determine the different types of memory and the brain circuits they rely on for storage and retrieval. Although memory involves multiple regions of the brain, not all brain regions are equally involved in all types of memories. A great deal of neural specialization occurs. Because of this specialization, it is thought that several *memory systems* exist in the brain that underlie the ability to retrieve information beyond a minute or so after you perceive it. Each memory system is specialized for specific types of information and/or memory expression.

implicit memory Memory that is expressed through responses, actions, or reactions.

explicit memory Memory that is consciously retrieved.

Although scientists debate the exact number of human memory systems, they generally agree on a few basic distinctions. The most basic distinction is a division of memories based on how they are expressed. On the one hand are memories we express without conscious effort or intention—memories we do not know we know; on the other hand are memories of which we are consciously aware. Peter Graf and Daniel Schacter (1985) refer to unconscious or unintentional memory as **implicit memory**. In contrast, **explicit memory** includes the processes we use to

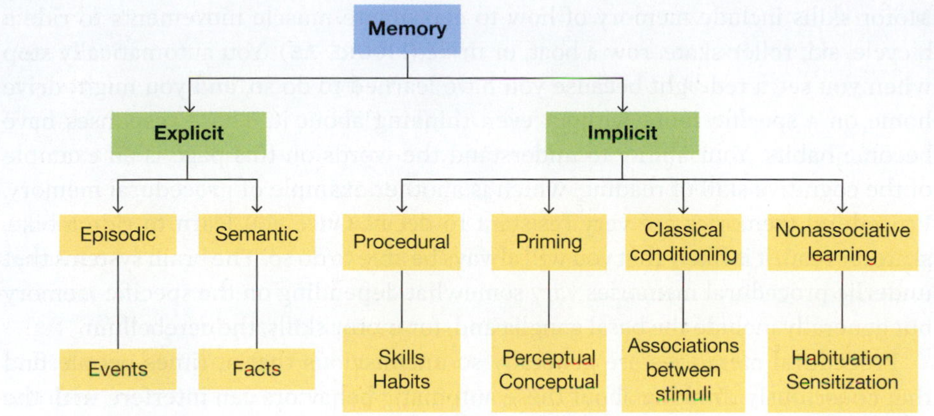

FIGURE 7.4
Memory Systems in the Brain
Among the many memory systems in the brain, a major distinction is whether the memory expression is explicit or implicit. There are two explicit memory systems, episodic and semantic, and several types of implicit memory.

remember information we can say we know. Implicit and explicit memory can be further subdivided into a few different memory systems (**FIGURE 7.4**).

Q What is the difference between retrograde and anterograde amnesia?

ANSWER: Retrograde amnesia is the inability to retrieve old memories, and anterograde amnesia is the inability to form new memories.

7.2 Implicit Memories Are Expressed Through Actions and Reactions

Implicit memories are memories you do not put into words. They are memories for past experiences that are expressed in your responses, actions, or reactions. Implicit memories are often called unconscious or automatic memories. Although you may be aware that you have an implicit memory—for instance, you know that you can ride a bike—your expression of that memory, the motor actions needed to ride a bike, occurs without conscious deliberation. You just do it.

Several memory systems are expressed implicitly. For example, if you always experience joy at hearing holiday music, you might have past associations between the holidays and having fun. As discussed in Chapter 6, classical conditioning results in learned associations that influence your reactions. They represent one type of implicit memory system. The brain systems that mediate these associative, implicit memories vary depending on the nature of the association, but they include the basal ganglia and amygdala as well as the cerebellum. Also discussed in Chapter 6, habituation and sensitization involve changes in the response to a stimulus based on repeated experience with that stimulus. This simple form of nonassociative learning represents another type of implicit memory that depends on changes in the responsiveness of neurons involved in perceiving the repeated stimulus.

PROCEDURAL MEMORY Another implicit memory system involves skills and habits. Suppose that while driving home you realize you have been daydreaming and have no memory of the past few minutes. During that time, you used implicit memories of how to drive and how to get where you were going, so you did not crash the car or go in the wrong direction. This type of implicit memory is called **procedural memory**. Procedural memories include skilled and goal-oriented behaviors that become automatic, such as motor skills, cognitive skills, and habitual behaviors. Procedural memories are reflected in *knowing how* to do something.

procedural memory A type of implicit memory that involves skills and habits.

FIGURE 7.5
Implicit Memory
The motor skill of knowing how to ride a bicycle is a procedural memory, a type of implicit memory. Once you learn how to ride a bike, you can usually remember how to do it again, unconsciously, at any age.

Motor skills include memory of how to coordinate muscle movements to ride a bicycle, ski, roller-skate, row a boat, or drive (**FIGURE 7.5**). You automatically stop when you see a red light because you have learned to do so, and you might drive home on a specific route without even thinking about it. These responses have become habits. Your ability to understand the words on this page is an example of the cognitive skill of reading, which is another example of procedural memory. Procedural memories are very resistant to decay. Once you learn to ride a bike, skate, or read, it is likely that you will always be able to do so. The brain systems that underlie procedural memories vary somewhat depending on the specific memory but generally include the basal ganglia and, for motor skills, the cerebellum.

Procedural memories are generally so unconscious that at times people find that consciously thinking about these automatic behaviors can interfere with the smooth production of those behaviors. The next time you are walking down a hallway try to think about each movement involved in the process. It is hard to verbally describe how to walk, and consciously focusing on what is required for each step will slow you down. Thinking about automatic actions is why athletes sometimes choke under pressure while aiming a free throw, hovering over a short putt, or landing a triple axel.

PRIMING As described earlier, H.M. was able to learn new motor skills, even though he had no knowledge of having learned them, demonstrating an ability to learn some types of procedural memories. He also showed evidence of implicit memory through priming (see Chapter 4). As mentioned earlier, priming is reflected in a facilitation in a response to a stimulus due to recent experience with that stimulus (called repetition priming) or a related stimulus. Priming can be *perceptual*, in which a response to the same stimulus is facilitated, or it can be *conceptual*, where a response to a conceptually related stimulus is facilitated. For instance, the word *table* might facilitate a response to the word *chair*.

Priming is thought to be mediated by the brain circuits involved in processing the relevant aspects of the prime. That is, for perceptual priming, brain regions that underlie perceptual processing come into play, whereas for conceptual priming, brain regions involved in conceptual processing are important. For example, a study by Margaret Keane and colleagues (1995) examined H.M. and another patient, L.H., who suffered from bilateral damage to regions of the occipital lobe. Despite this damage and some visual deficits, L.H. was still able to read complete words. Both patients were presented with lists of words. When the words were then presented so briefly that they were difficult to read, H.M. was more likely to identify the words he had seen earlier, showing evidence of perceptual priming. L.H. failed to show perceptual priming. In contrast, L.H. was able to report that he remembered some of the words presented earlier, whereas H.M. had no explicit memory of seeing the list.

Q **Practicing a dance routine requires what type of implicit memory?**

ANSWER: procedural memory

7.3 Explicit Memories Can Be Declared

Explicit memories are those that are consciously retrieved. They have been called *declarative* memories because you can declare that you know them. They are also sometimes described as *knowing that*. You know that Ottawa is the capital of Canada, or you know that you had a tuna fish sandwich for lunch yesterday. Exams you take in school usually test explicit memory.

(a) (b)

FIGURE 7.6
Explicit Memory
(a) These World War II veterans, assembled aboard the USS *Intrepid* on Memorial Day, drew on episodic memory to recall past experiences. **(b)** Game shows such as *Jeopardy!* test semantic memory.

In 1972, the psychologist Endel Tulving proposed that explicit memory can be divided into episodic memory and semantic memory. **Episodic memory** consists of a person's memory of past experiences that can be identified as occurring at a time and place. In other words, you can remember the episode when the event occurred. If you can remember aspects of your 16th birthday, such as where you were and what you did there, this information is part of your episodic memory. **Semantic memory** is knowledge of concepts, categories, and facts independent of personal experience. You might not remember where or when you learned the information, but you know it (**FIGURE 7.6**). For instance, people know what Jell-O is, they know the capitals of countries they have never visited, and even people who have never played baseball know that three strikes mean the batter is out. Semantic memory is the vast store of knowledge about the world acquired throughout your life.

episodic memory Memory for one's past experiences that are identified by a time and place.

semantic memory Memory for facts independent of personal experience.

As the case of H.M. illustrates, the medial temporal lobes are responsible for the formation of new episodic memories. Within the medial temporal lobes, the hippocampus is the brain region thought to be critical for episodic memories. However, as H.M.'s ability to remember events from his life prior to 1953 illustrates, the hippocampus appears to be necessary for forming new episodic memories but not for retrieving older episodic memories. The long-term storage of episodic memories involves the particular brain regions engaged during the perception, processing, and analysis of the material being learned. For instance, visual information is stored in the cortical areas involved in visual perception. Sound is stored in the areas involved in auditory perception. Thus, remembering something seen and heard involves reactivating the cortical circuits involved in the initial seeing and hearing (**FIGURE 7.7**). The hippocampus forms links, or pointers, between the different storage sites and then directs the gradual strengthening of the connections between these links (Squire et al., 2004). Once the connections are strengthened sufficiently, the hippocampus becomes less important for the retrieval of the episodic memory.

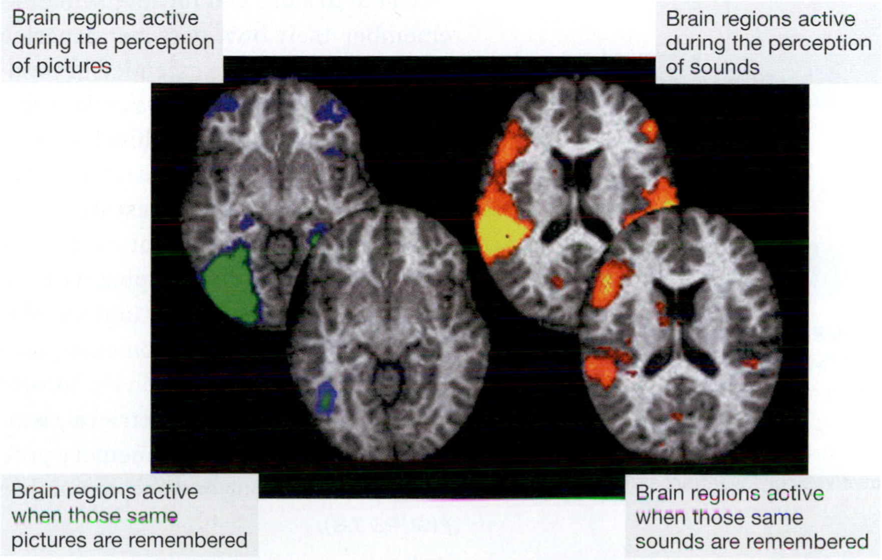

FIGURE 7.7
Brain Activation During Perception and Remembering
These four horizontally sliced brain images were acquired using magnetic resonance imaging. In each pair, the top image shows the brain areas that are activated during a particular sensory-specific perception. The bottom image shows the regions of the sensory cortex that are activated when that sensory-specific information is remembered. Notice that the perceptions and the memories involve similar cortical areas.

Learning Tip

To remember the difference between explicit memories (episodic and semantic) and implicit procedural memories, think of explicit memories as *knowing that* and procedural memories as *knowing how*. You know *that* bicycles have two wheels and *that* you rode yours yesterday. You know *how* to ride a bicycle.

Although the hippocampus is important for acquiring episodic memories, there is evidence that other medial temporal lobe regions play a role in the acquisition of semantic memory. This was discovered in studies of three British children who had experienced brain damage early in life (Vargha-Khadem et al., 1997). One child suffered the injury during a difficult birth. The other two suffered it during early childhood (one had seizures at age 4; the other had an accidental drug overdose at age 9). These injuries resulted in damage to localized parts of the hippocampus and did not extend to other regions of the medial temporal lobe. The three children had trouble reporting what they had for lunch, what they had been watching on television 5 minutes earlier, and what they did during summer vacation. Their parents reported that the children had to be constantly monitored to make sure they remembered things such as going to school. Their episodic memory deficit was not as extensive as H.M.'s, but nevertheless it was significant. Remarkably, these three children attended mainstream schools and did reasonably well. Moreover, when tested as young adults, their IQs fell within the normal range. They learned to speak and read, and they could remember many facts. For instance, when asked "Who is Martin Luther King Jr.?" one of the children, tested at age 19, responded, "An American; fought for black rights, black rights leader in the 1970s [actually 1960s]; got assassinated [in 1968]" (Vargha-Khadem et al., 1997, p. 379). These three, then, were able to store and retrieve semantic information even though they could not remember their own personal experiences. In contrast to H.M., whose medial temporal lobe damage extended beyond the hippocampus, their ability to acquire new semantic knowledge was relatively intact.

As mentioned earlier in this chapter, when we use the word *memory* in our daily lives, we are more often than not referring to explicit memories, both episodic and semantic. Similarly, most research on memory examines explicit memories for events learned in the laboratory. For this reason, most of the research discussed in the remainder of this chapter, with some exceptions, deals with explicit memories. However, all memories undergo three stages of processing. The first is acquisition or encoding, when you experience an event that results in a memory. The second stage is storage, when the memory of this experience is formed and maintained. The final stage is retrieval, when the memory of the past experience is expressed. At each stage of memory processing, various factors influence whether the memory is strong or weak, remembered or forgotten, and accurate or distorted (**FIGURE 7.8**).

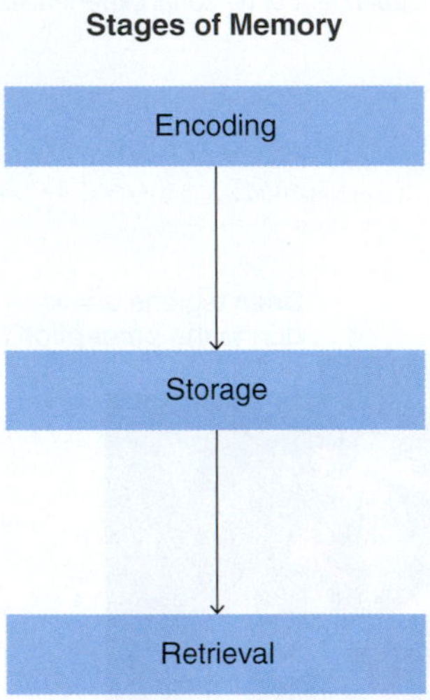

FIGURE 7.8
The Stages of Memory
All memories go through three stages of processing: encoding, in which memories are acquired; storage, which involves consolidation; and retrieval.

Q **Is your memory of what you ate for breakfast yesterday a semantic memory or an episodic memory?**

ANSWER: episodic, because it is a personal memory of an event that occurred at a time and place

Learning Objectives

- Discuss the levels of processing model.
- Explain how schemas influence memory.
- Define mnemonics.

How Are Memories Encoded?

We form lasting memories for only a subset of our experiences. The process by which the perception of a stimulus or event gets transformed into a memory is called **encoding**. Encoding can be automatic, in that we simply remember some things we attend to and not others, or it can be effortful. That is, we can manipulate how we process information in order to enhance the likelihood of encoding and later remembering that information.

FIGURE 7.9
Penny
Which penny is correct? The answer is in the text.

7.4 Encoding Turns Perception into Memory

encoding The process by which the perception of a stimulus or event gets transformed into a memory.

Encoding starts with attention. It goes without saying that you are more likely to remember something you attended to and perceived initially. Although Chapter 4 introduced the idea that some subliminal information can influence behavior, there is little evidence that explicit memories can be formed without attention and conscious perception. Manipulations of attention have been shown to significantly affect the likelihood of memory encoding (Craik et al., 1996). The more attention paid to a stimulus, the more likely it is to be encoded into memory.

To get a sense of the importance of attention for memory encoding, try to answer the following question: Of all the examples of pennies in FIGURE 7.9, which is an accurate representation of a penny? Do you remember whether Lincoln's profile is facing to the right or left? Do you know where the year is printed? Do you remember what, if anything, is written above Lincoln's head? Unless you are a coin collector, it is unlikely you have paid much attention to these details. Even though you may be very familiar with what a penny looks like, you may have failed to encode these details due to a lack of attention. Now if you look at an actual penny, you will realize the correct answer is *a*.

However, even when you are attending, you will remember some stimuli better than others. One factor that influences the success of memory encoding is the extent to which the to-be-remembered information taps into existing knowledge structures in the brain. For instance, if you can read and understand a word, you have a stored representation of that word. Some words, or the concepts they represent, may have more extensive representations than others. According to the *dual-coding hypothesis*, information that can be coded verbally and visually will be remembered more easily than information that can be coded only verbally. Consistent with this hypothesis is evidence showing that under identical encoding conditions, concrete words—those representing concepts that readily evoke visual images, like the word *dog*—are more likely to be remembered than abstract words representing concepts that are not easily visualized, such as the word *keep*. The dual-coding hypothesis is also supported by data showing that pictures that can be verbally labeled are more likely to be remembered than words when given similar levels of attention (Paivio & Csapo, 1969).

Q According to the dual-coding hypothesis, would a presentation of the word *car* or the word *ride* be more likely to encode into memory, and why?

ANSWER: *Car*, because it includes an easily visualized concept, which allows for both visual and verbal encoding

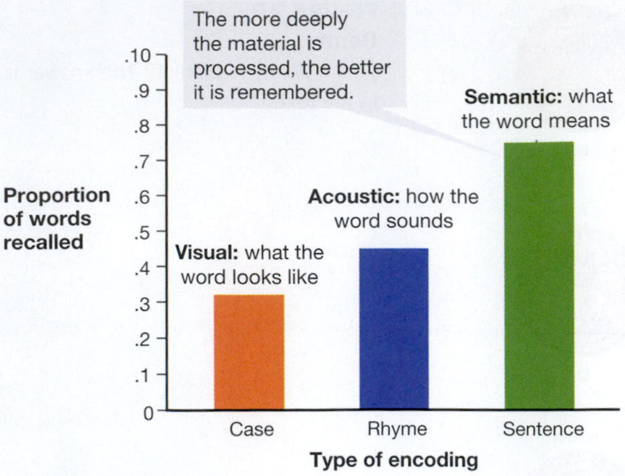

FIGURE 7.10
Levels of Processing
This graph shows the results of a study on the influence of levels of processing on encoding. Participants were asked to consider a list of words according to how the words were printed (uppercase or lowercase), how they sounded (whether they rhymed), or what they meant (whether they fit in a sentence). Later, participants were asked to recall the words.

7.5 Attention to Meaning Improves Encoding

Another factor proposed to influence the likelihood of memory encoding is the depth of mental processing. In their *levels of processing model*, the psychologists Fergus Craik and Robert Lockhart (1972) suggested that the more deeply an item is encoded and the more meaning it has, the better it is remembered. Although rehearsing an item might improve memory for that item, the way the item is rehearsed matters. Craik and Lockhart proposed that different types of rehearsal lead to different levels of encoding. *Maintenance rehearsal* is simply repeating the item over and over. *Elaborative rehearsal* encodes the information in more meaningful ways, such as thinking about the item conceptually or deciding whether it refers to oneself. In other words, in this type of rehearsal, we elaborate on basic information by linking it in meaningful ways to existing knowledge.

Suppose you show research participants a list of words and then ask them to do one of three things. You might ask them to make a *visual* judgment about what each word looks like. For example, "Is it printed in capital or lowercase letters?" You might ask them to make an *acoustic* judgment about the sound of each word. "Does it rhyme with *boat*?" Or you might ask them to make a *semantic* judgment about each word's meaning. "Does it fit in the sentence *They had to cross the ____ to reach the castle*?" Once participants have completed the task, you ask them to recall as many words as possible. You will find that words processed at the deepest level, based on meaning, are remembered the best (Craik & Tulving, 1975; **FIGURE 7.10**). Brain imaging studies have shown that semantic encoding activates more brain regions than shallow encoding and that this greater brain activity is associated with better memory (Cabeza & Moscovitch, 2013; Kapur et al., 1994).

schemas Cognitive structures in long-term memory that help us perceive, organize, and understand information.

SCHEMAS Another example of how meaning influences memory encoding is through the use of schemas. **Schemas** are cognitive structures in semantic memory that help us perceive, organize, understand, and use information. As we sort through incoming information, schemas guide our attention to relevant features. Thanks to schemas, we construct new memories by filling in holes within existing memories, overlooking inconsistent information, and interpreting meaning based on past experiences.

In Chapter 8, you will learn more about schemas and how they represent information. The basic idea is that they provide structures for understanding events in the world. For instance, you might have a schema for grocery shopping at markets in the United States, which you learned from experience. That schema most likely includes shopping carts, abundant choices, and set prices. You may expect to choose your own fruit and vegetables in the produce section. Your schema enables you to easily predict and navigate a trip to the grocery store. However, because schemas are based on your past experiences, their usefulness can vary depending on the circumstance. Your grocery store schema will not be so useful when you go to the market in France, where you may not be allowed to touch the produce, or in Morocco, where you have to bargain for your prices. You may learn these differences the hard way: by making mistakes (**FIGURE 7.11**).

(a)

(b)

FIGURE 7.11
Schemas of Grocery Shopping
Your schema for shopping in **(a)** a grocery store in the United States might not work so well in **(b)** a market in Morocco.

To see how schemas affect your ability to encode information, read the following paragraph carefully:

> The procedure is actually quite simple. First arrange things into different bundles depending on makeup. Don't do too much at once. In the short run this may not seem

important; however, complications easily arise. A mistake can be costly. Next, find facilities. Some people must go elsewhere for them. Manipulation of appropriate mechanisms should be self-explanatory. Remember to include all other necessary supplies. Initially the routine will overwhelm you, but soon it will become just another facet of life. Finally, rearrange everything into their initial groups. Return these to their usual places. Eventually they will be used again. Then the whole cycle will have to be repeated. (Bransford & Johnson, 1972, p. 722)

How easy did you find this paragraph to understand? Can you recall specific sentences from it? It might surprise you to know that in a research setting, college students who read this paragraph found it easy to understand and relatively straightforward to recall. How is that possible? It was easy when the participants knew that the paragraph described washing clothes. Go back and reread the paragraph. Notice how your schema for doing laundry helps you understand what the paragraph means and how the words and sentences are connected to one another. By linking information to existing knowledge, schemas can enhance meaning and influence encoding.

Q According to the levels of processing model of encoding, does maintenance rehearsal or elaborative rehearsal of information encode more deeply, and why?

ANSWER: elaborative rehearsal, because it makes the information more meaningful by attaching it to existing knowledge and beliefs

7.6 Organization Affects Memory Encoding

Schemas can also influence memory encoding by helping organize the incoming information. Not only did the laundry schema help you make sense of the paragraph in the previous section, it also related all the sentences to a single concept. Imagine you are presented with a list of 20 random words and then are asked to remember them about an hour later. Although you would likely remember seeing the word list and be able to recall a handful of items on the list, chances are you would forget most of them. Now imagine you were presented with a list of 20 words, all of which were items you would find in a kitchen. You would likely recall many more items from that list. In this case, the category of kitchen items organizes the list during encoding, thus aiding later recall (Hunt & Einstein, 1981).

Another way organization can aid memory encoding is by chunking information. **Chunking** is the process of breaking down information into meaningful units. For instance, master chess players who glance at a scenario on a chessboard, even for a few seconds, later can reproduce the exact arrangement of pieces (Chase & Simon, 1973). They can do so because they instantly chunk the board into a number of meaningful subunits based on their past experiences with the game (FIGURE 7.12). If the pieces are arranged on the board in ways that make no sense in terms of chess, however, experts are no better than novices at reproducing the board. In general, the greater your expertise with the material, the more efficiently you can chunk information during encoding, and therefore the more you can remember.

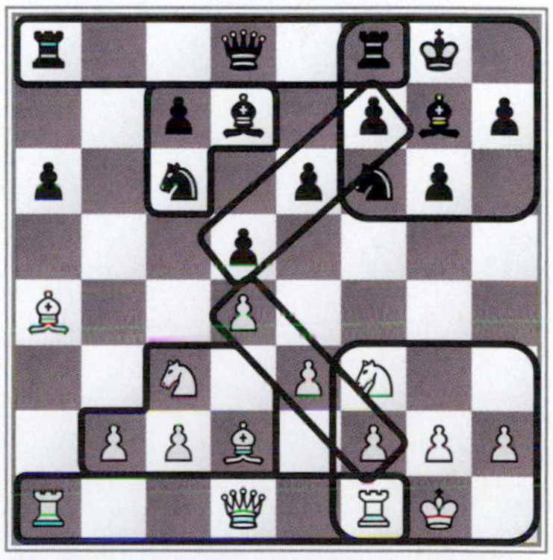

FIGURE 7.12
Chunking
Expert chess players chunk the game pieces into meaningful subunits.

MNEMONICS **Mnemonics** are learning aids or strategies to improve memory. Have you ever been to a restaurant with a large group of people and encountered a server who did not write down a single order but nevertheless delivered all the correct food items to the correct people? Chances are the server was using a mnemonic to remember the order. Next time you find yourself in a situation like this, ask the server how they did it.

chunking Organizing information into meaningful units to make it easier to remember.

mnemonics Learning aids or strategies that improve recall through the use of retrieval cues.

(a)

(b)

FIGURE 7.13

Memory Champions

(a) Nelson Dellis is a 4-time U.S. champion. **(b)** Emma Alam, of Pakistan, won the 2020 World Memory Championship, breaking world records in the process. Memory athletes, like Dellis and Alam, are experts at using mnemonics.

Mnemonic strategies work by focusing attention on organizing incoming information and linking it to existing knowledge structures. Suppose you want to remember the names of classmates you just met. First, you might visualize items from various places on your typical route across campus, or you might visualize parts of the physical layout of some familiar location, such as your bedroom. Then you would associate your classmates' names with the items and places you have visualized. You might picture Justin climbing on your dresser, Malia sitting on a chair, and Anthony hiding under the bed. When you later need to remember the names, you would visualize your room, mentally walk yourself through it, and retrieve the name of the person associated with each piece of furniture.

This mnemonic strategy of associating items you want to remember with physical locations is referred to as the *method of loci*, or memory palace. It is the most widely known mnemonic and dates back to the ancient Greeks, but many other mnemonic strategies can help organize to-be-remembered information and tie it into existing knowledge. Another common strategy is the "peg" method, which establishes a series of mental pegs to "hang" memories on.

Nelson Dellis is a 4-time USA Memory Champion. He is a memory athlete—someone who practices the skill of using mnemonics to achieve amazing memory feats. In order to win this championship, he had to memorize 1,000 digits in an hour, one randomly shuffled deck of cards in 2 minutes, and 10 randomly shuffled decks of cards (520 cards) in 1 hour. In addition to the method of loci and the peg method, Dellis uses strategies such as making up funny or interesting stories that can be visualized and related to the to-be-remembered items (which he calls the story method) or linking number sequences with familiar people.

Memory athletes like Nelson Dellis and Emma Alam, who won the 2020 World Memory Championship (**FIGURE 7.13**), train extensively to use mnemonic strategies optimally, but research suggests there is nothing special about their memory abilities prior to training. In fact, Dellis claims he can teach a mnemonic for memorizing the 46 presidents of the United States, in order, in about 12 minutes (to try it, see https://www.youtube.com/watch?v=LTmh71_jocs). In support of the conclusion that memory athletes' superior memories are due to mnemonic training, as opposed to an innate ability, a recent brain imaging study examined 23 memory athletes and control participants during a memory task. Not surprisingly, the memory athletes were much better at remembering items than the control participants, and they showed different patterns of connections among brain regions during memory encoding. The researchers then trained some of the control participants in the use of common mnemonic strategies for four months. This training not only increased their memory performance but also resulted in brain activity patterns that were more similar to those of the memory athletes (Dresler et al., 2017).

Q How do mnemonics improve memory?

ANSWER: by organizing new information in ways that increase cohesion between the items to remember, deepen their meaning, or link them with existing knowledge

How Are Memories Stored and Maintained?

The second stage of memory is storage. Anytime perception ends and the perceived information is still available for processing, it is in memory storage. Memories can be stored for anywhere between less than a second and forever. In

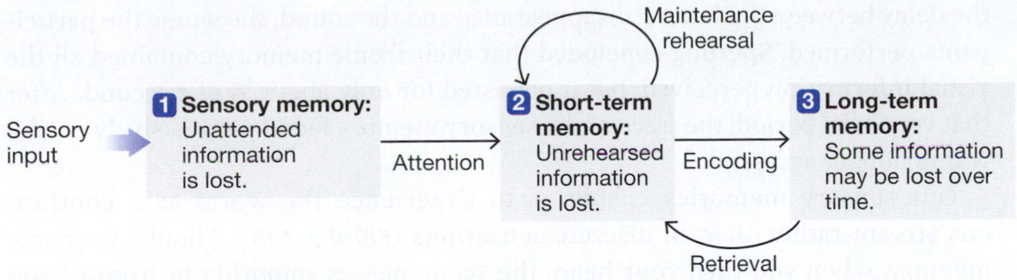

FIGURE 7.14
Three Memory Storage Systems
Atkinson and Shiffrin's model of three systems emphasizes that memory storage varies in duration.

1968, the psychologists Richard Atkinson and Richard Shiffrin proposed a three-part model of memory. Their model consists of sensory memory, short-term or working memory, and long-term memory (**FIGURE 7.14**), which are differentiated by the length of time the information is retained in memory.

7.7 Sensory Memory Is Brief

Learning Objectives

- Distinguish among sensory memory, short-term memory, and long-term memory.
- Describe working memory, including its capacity and duration.
- Review evidence supporting the distinction between working memory and long-term memory.
- Define consolidation and reconsolidation.

Sensory memory is a temporary memory system closely tied to the sensory systems. It is not what we usually think of when we think about memory, because it lasts only a fraction of a second. In fact, normally we are not aware that it is operating.

As discussed in Chapter 5, we obtain all our information about the world through our senses. Our sensory systems transduce, or change, that information into neural impulses. A sensory memory occurs when a light, a sound, an odor, a taste, or a tactile impression leaves a vanishing trace on the nervous system for a fraction of a second after the sensory information is gone. When you look at something and quickly glance away, you can briefly picture the image and recall some of its details. This type of visual sensory memory is called *iconic memory*. When someone protests, "You're not paying attention to me," you might be able to repeat back the last few words the person spoke, even if you were thinking about something else. This type of auditory sensory memory is called *echoic memory*.

sensory memory A memory system that very briefly stores sensory information in close to its original sensory form.

The psychologist George Sperling initially proposed the existence of sensory memory. In a classic experiment (Sperling, 1960), three rows of letters were flashed on a screen for $1/_{20}$ of a second. Participants were asked to recall all the letters. Most people believed they had seen all the letters, but they could recall only three or four. These results might be taken to suggest that sensory memory stores only three or four items. However, participants reported that even though all the letters were briefly available after being flashed, in the time it took them to name the first three or four, they forgot the other letters. These reports suggest that the participants very quickly lost their memories of exactly what they had seen, but their sensory memories initially contained all that was perceived.

Sperling tested this hypothesis by showing all the letters exactly as he had done before, but this time he presented a high-, medium-, or low-pitched sound as soon as the letters disappeared. A high pitch meant the participants should recall the letters in the top row, a medium pitch meant they should recall the letters in the middle row, and a low pitch meant they should recall the letters in the bottom row. When the sound occurred right after the letters disappeared, the participants correctly remembered almost all the letters in the signaled row. But the longer the delay between the letters' disappearance and the sound, the worse the participants performed. Sperling concluded that their iconic memory contained all the visual information perceived, but it persisted for only about $\frac{1}{3}$ of a second. After that very brief period, the trace of the sensory memory faded progressively until it was no longer accessible.

Our sensory memories enable us to experience the world as a continuous stream rather than in discrete sensations (**FIGURE 7.15**). Thanks to iconic memory, when you turn your head, the scene passes smoothly in front of you rather than in jerky bits. Your memory retains information just long enough for you to connect one image with the next in a way that corresponds to the way objects move in the real world. Similarly, a movie projector plays a series of still pictures that follow each other closely enough in time to look like continuous action.

FIGURE 7.15
Sensory Storage
If you stood in front of this sparkler, you could see the word *LOVE* spelled by the sparkler because the visual input would be maintained briefly in sensory storage.

Q **How do iconic and echoic memory differ?**

ANSWER: Iconic memory is sensory memory for visual information. Echoic memory is sensory memory for auditory information.

7.8 Working Memory Is Active

When we pay attention to something, the information passes from sensory stores to *short-term memory*. Researchers initially saw short-term memory as simply a buffer or holding place. There, information was rehearsed until it was stored or forgotten. Subsequently, researchers realized that short-term memory is not just a storage system. Instead, it is an active memory process that deals with multiple types of information. Because of this, contemporary models refer to **working memory**. Working memory actively retains and manipulates multiple pieces of temporary information from different sources (Baddeley, 2002; Baddeley & Hitch, 1974). Working memory represents what we are consciously focusing on at any point in time.

working memory A limited-capacity cognitive system that temporarily stores and manipulates information for current use.

Information remains in working memory for about 20 to 30 seconds. It then disappears unless you actively prevent it from doing so. You retain the information by monitoring it—that is, thinking about or rehearsing it. As an example, try to remember some new information. Memorize a meaningless string of letters, the consonants X C J. As long as you keep repeating the string over and over, you will keep it in working memory. But if you stop rehearsing, you will probably soon forget the letters. After all, you are bombarded with other events that compete for your attention, and you may not be able to stay focused.

Now try to remember K T G. This time, count backward in threes from 309. The counting prevents rehearsal of the letter string, and the longer people spend counting, the less able they are to remember the consonants. After only 18 seconds of counting, most people have a hard time recalling the consonants (Brown, 1958; Peterson & Peterson, 1959). This result indicates that working memory lasts less than half a minute without continuous rehearsal.

MEMORY SPAN New items in working memory interfere with the recall of older items because working memory can hold a limited amount of information. The cognitive psychologist George Miller (1956) noted that the limit is generally seven items (plus or minus two). This figure is referred to as *memory span*. More-recent research suggests that Miller's estimate may be too high and that working memory may be limited to as few as four items (Conway et al., 2005).

The capacity of working memory increases as children develop (Garon et al., 2008) and decreases with advanced age (McCabe et al., 2010). Memory span also varies among individuals. As a result, some intelligence tests use memory span as part of the measure of IQ. Researchers have attempted to increase working memory through training exercises, with the hope that the exercises will boost intelligence (Klingberg, 2010; Morrison & Chein, 2011). Such training has increased working memory, but this learning did not transfer to other cognitive abilities involved in intelligence (Redick et al., 2013; Shipstead et al., 2012). This type of limited learning is generally true of "brain training" apps or programs. That is, people get better at the task they practice, but they do not improve in their general everyday cognition or memory (Simons et al., 2016).

Because working memory is limited, you might expect almost everyone to have great difficulty remembering a string of letters such as BMWPHDIBM-MAUPSBAMAC. These 19 letters would tax even the largest memory span. But what if we organized the information into smaller, meaningful units? For instance, BMW PHD IBM MA UPS BA MAC. Here the letters are separated to produce acronyms for international companies and academic degrees. In other words, the letters have been organized into chunks of meaningful units. As discussed earlier in this chapter, *chunking* helps memory encoding by organizing information. For working memory, this organization expands the amount of information that can be maintained. Although working memory span is limited to as little as four items, these items can be individual letters, words, or any other chunk of information that is meaningful. The more efficiently you chunk information, the more information you can hold in your limited-capacity working memory.

Q How does working memory relate to attention?

ANSWER: Information enters and is held in working memory via attention, actively thinking about it, or rehearsing it.

7.9 Long-Term Memory Can Be Permanent

When people talk about memory, they are usually referring to **long-term memory**. Long-term memory can last from a few minutes to forever, and its capacity is limitless. To think about long-term memory's capacity, try to imagine counting everything you know and everything you are likely to know in your lifetime. No matter how much you already know, you can always learn more. Long-term memory enables you to remember nursery rhymes from childhood, the meanings and spellings of words you rarely use (such as *aardvark*), how to tie your shoes, what you had for lunch yesterday, and so on.

long-term memory The storage of information that lasts from minutes to forever.

DISTINGUISHING LONG-TERM MEMORY FROM WORKING MEMORY Long-term memory is distinct from working memory in two important ways: It has a longer duration, and it has far greater capacity. Controversy exists, however, as to whether long-term memory represents a truly different type of memory storage from working memory.

Evidence supporting the idea that long-term memory and working memory are separate storage systems came from research that required people to recall long lists of words. The ability to recall items from the list depended on the order of presentation. That is, items presented early or late in the list were remembered better than those in the middle. This phenomenon is known as the **serial position effect**. This effect actually consists of two separate effects. The *primacy effect* refers to the better memory that people have for items presented at the beginning

serial position effect The finding that the ability to recall items from a list depends on the order of presentation, such that items presented early or late in the list are remembered better than those in the middle.

FIGURE 7.16
The Serial Position Effect
This graph helps illustrate the primacy effect and the recency effect, which together make up the serial position effect. The serial position effect, in turn, helps illustrate the difference between long-term memory and working memory.

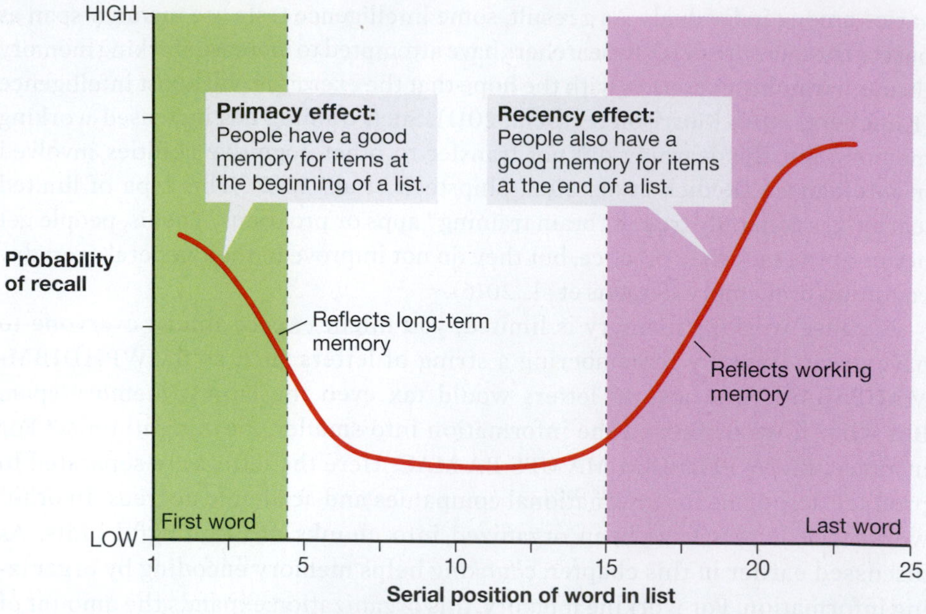

of the list. The *recency effect* refers to the better memory that people have for the most recent items, the ones at the end of the list (**FIGURE 7.16**).

One explanation for the serial position effect relies on a distinction between working memory and long-term memory. When research participants study a long list of words, they rehearse the earliest items the most. As a result, that information is more likely to be stored in long-term memory. By contrast, the last few items are still in working memory when the participants have to recall the words immediately after reading them.

In some studies, researchers introduce a delay between the presentation of the list and the recall task. Such delays do not interfere with the primacy effect, but they do interfere with the recency effect. You would expect this result if the primacy effect involved long-term memory and the recency effect involved working memory. The recency effect might not be entirely related to working memory, however. You probably remember your most recent class better than the classes you had earlier. If you had to recall the past presidents or past prime ministers of your country, you would probably recall the early ones and most recent ones best and have poorer recall for those in between. You most likely do not maintain the information about your classes or about world leaders in working memory.

Perhaps the best support for the distinction between working memory and long-term memory comes from case studies such as that of H.M., the patient described earlier in this chapter. His working memory was perfectly normal, as shown by his ability to keep track of a conversation as long as he stayed actively involved in it. Aspects of H.M.'s long-term memory were intact, since he remembered events that occurred before his surgery. He was unable, however, to transfer new information from working memory into long-term memory.

In another case, a 28-year-old accident victim with damage to the left temporal lobe had extremely poor working memory, with a memory span of only one or two items. However, he had perfectly normal long-term memory: a fine memory for day-to-day happenings and reasonable knowledge of events that occurred before his surgery (Shallice & Warrington, 1970). Somehow, despite the deficits in his working memory, he was relatively good at retrieving information from long-term memory.

These case studies demonstrate that working memory can be separated from long-term memory. Still, the two types of memory are highly interdependent, at least for most of us. For instance, when we think about our memories, information from long-term memory enters working memory to be actively processed. And to chunk information in working memory, we need to form meaningful connections based on information stored in long-term memory.

Q How can the distinction between long-term memory and working memory explain the primacy and recency effects?

ANSWER: The primacy effect occurs because items presented earlier have been encoded into long-term memory, and the recency effect occurs because items presented later are still available in working memory.

7.10 Long-Term Memory Requires Consolidation

In contrast to working memory, in which information is actively, and mostly consciously, maintained and manipulated, long-term memory seems passive. We are not aware of our long-term memories in storage, and it seems as if they are dormant in our minds, just waiting to be retrieved. However, the storage of long-term memory results from active processes in the brain that occur over an extended period of time. This process of forming the lasting connections that represent long-term memory is called **consolidation**. Because consolidation is gradual, it is not uncommon following a concussion or other head injury to forget what happened immediately before. The head injury appears to disrupt the consolidation of memory.

consolidation The gradual process of memory storage in the brain.

In 1949, the psychologist Donald Hebb proposed that memory results from alterations in synaptic connections. In Hebb's model, memories are stored in multiple regions of the brain that are linked through memory circuits. When one neuron excites another, some change takes place that strengthens the connection between the two neurons. Subsequently, the firing of one neuron becomes increasingly likely to cause the firing of the other neuron. In other words, "cells that fire together wire together."

Recall from Chapter 6 the work of Eric Kandel using Aplysia, a type of sea slug. Kandel showed that alterations in the functioning of the synapses lead to habituation and sensitization. His research also demonstrated that long-term storage of information results from the development of new synaptic connections between neurons (Kandel, 2001). This research supports the idea that memory results from physical changes in connections between neurons. In other words, Hebb was right: Long-term memory involves the creation of neural circuits (Tonegawa et al., 2015).

LONG-TERM POTENTIATION In the 1970s, researchers discovered long-term potentiation, a process that is central to the neural changes underlying memory storage (Bliss & Lømo, 1973). The word *potentiate* means to strengthen, to make something more potent. **Long-term potentiation (LTP)** is the strengthening of a synaptic connection, making the postsynaptic neurons more easily activated by presynaptic neurons. LTP serves as a model of how neural plasticity (discussed in Chapter 3) might underlie long-term memory.

long-term potentiation (LTP) Strengthening of a synaptic connection, making the postsynaptic neurons more easily activated by presynaptic neurons.

LTP also supports Hebb's contention that learning results from a strengthening of synaptic connections between neurons that fire together. As the synapse between two neurons strengthens during consolidation, the two neurons become better connected, as though a freeway had been built between them. To demonstrate this process in the lab, researchers first establish that stimulating one neuron with a single electrical pulse leads to a certain amount of firing in a second neuron. (Recall from Chapter 3 that neurons fire when they receive sufficient stimulation.) The researchers then provide intense electrical stimulation to the first neuron. For example, they might give it 100 pulses of electricity in 1 second. Finally, they administer a single electrical pulse to the first neuron and measure the second

FIGURE 7.17

Long-Term Potentiation (LTP)

(a) This diagram depicts the basic process used in testing for LTP between two neurons. **(b)** This graph shows the steps involved in LTP.

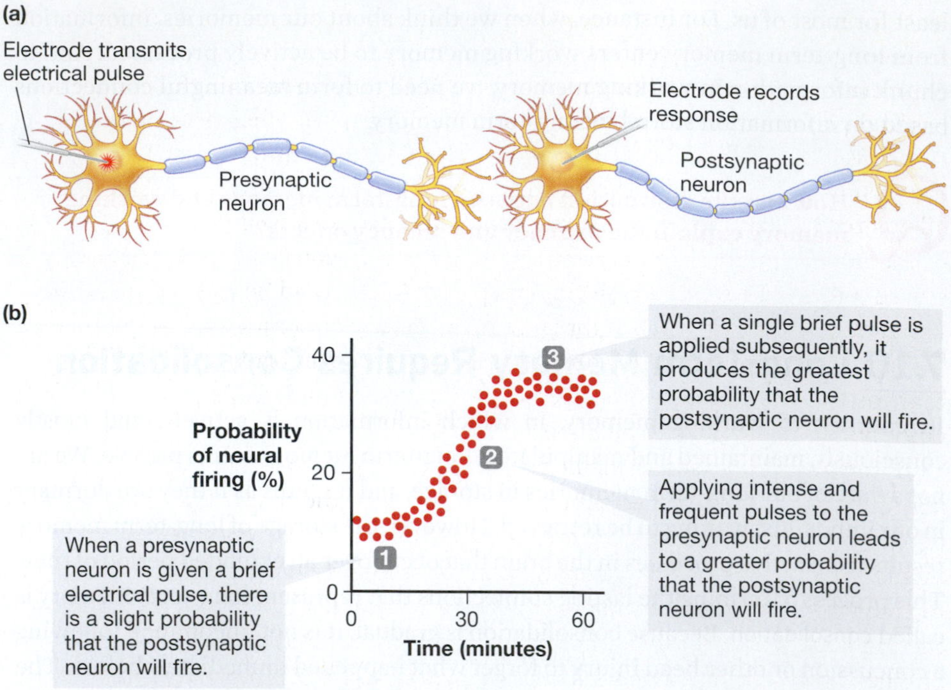

(a)
Electrode transmits electrical pulse
Presynaptic neuron
Electrode records response
Postsynaptic neuron
(b)
Probability of neural firing (%)
40
20
0
0
30
60
Time (minutes)
1
2
3
When a presynaptic neuron is given a brief electrical pulse, there is a slight probability that the postsynaptic neuron will fire.
Applying intense and frequent pulses to the presynaptic neuron leads to a greater probability that the postsynaptic neuron will fire.
When a single brief pulse is applied subsequently, it produces the greatest probability that the postsynaptic neuron will fire.

neuron's firing. If LTP has occurred, the intense electrical stimulation will have increased the likelihood that stimulating the first neuron produces firing in the second neuron (**FIGURE 7.17**).

Learning Tip

To remember how memories are consolidated in the brain through long-term potentiation, use Hebb's mnemonic: Neurons that *fire together wire together*. Additional tip: Also remember this as an example of a mnemonic.

Over the past few decades, researchers have made considerable progress in understanding how LTP works (Herring & Nicoll, 2016). A critical player in LTP is the *NMDA receptor* on the postsynaptic neuron. This type of glutamate receptor responds only when large amounts of glutamate are available in the synapse and when the postsynaptic neuron is sufficiently depolarized. LTP leads to an increase in the number of glutamate receptors on the postsynaptic neuron, which increases its responsivity to glutamate released by the presynaptic neuron. It can also produce more synapses between neurons. Memory results from strengthening synaptic connections among networks of neurons. They fired together, so they wired together.

The finding that the NMDA receptor is involved in LTP led researchers to examine genetic processes that might influence memory. For instance, the neuroscientist Joseph Tsien modified genes in mice to make the genes' NMDA receptors more efficient. When tested in standard memory tasks, these transgenic mice performed amazingly well, learning novel tasks more quickly than normal mice and showing increased memory (Tsien, 2000). The mice were such great learners that Tsien named them "Doogie mice," after the 1990s television character Doogie Howser, a boy doctor (**FIGURE 7.18**).

FIGURE 7.18

Doogie Mice

Doogie mice (such as the one pictured here) and regular mice were given a test of learning and memory. In the first part, both kinds of mice had the chance to familiarize themselves with two objects. In the second part, the researchers replaced one of the objects with a novel object. The Doogie mice quickly recognized the change, but the normal mice did not recognize it.

Q **How does long-term potentiation support Hebb's idea that neurons that fire together wire together?**

ANSWER: LTP demonstrates that the receptivity of a postsynaptic neuron increases after repeated neurotransmission from the presynaptic neuron.

7.11 Slow Consolidation Can Be Beneficial

In some ways, it seems counterintuitive that storing memories would require a gradual process of strengthening. Would it not be more efficient to have memories stored instantly in the brain when we perceive something? It has been argued that a slow consolidation process has several benefits, a primary one being that it allows things that happen after you experience an event to influence the storage of memory for that event. During consolidation, memories for some events are stored and others are not, resulting in forgetting. It would be better if the memories that persisted were those for more important or consequential events, but we do not always know whether something is important while it is happening. Events that you think about more often, those that you are reminded of, or those that elicit emotion are more likely to be important.

If the consolidation of memories involves enhancing connections between neurons that represent the memory, it follows that the more these neurons fire together, the more likely they are to wire together. One way this occurs is by memory *replay* in the brain. Replay occurs when the neural circuit representing the memory fires again. Reminders of the memory when you are awake can replay the memory in your brain. It has also been demonstrated in rodents that neural circuits representing memories replay during sleep. Events that are recently learned or on your mind during the day may be more likely to be replayed during sleep. It has even been shown that reminders of events during sleep, such as a sound or smell associated with an event, can lead to better memory (Hu et al., 2020). As discussed in Chapter 4, sleep is known to be important for memory. One reason is that the replay of memories during sleep enhances memory consolidation.

Emotion is another factor than can influence memory consolidation. If you think about the memories from your life that persist, they are likely to be memories for emotional events, such as your first kiss, birthday celebrations, or an accident. James McGaugh (2000) has shown that the emotional reaction to an event, specifically the stress hormones that are released with autonomic arousal (see Chapter 3), can influence the likelihood that the memory for that event is consolidated. He has found that when an event elicits autonomic arousal, the amygdala influences consolidation in the hippocampus and basal ganglia, thus enhancing the storage of that event in long-term memory. Evidence that arousal is influencing memory consolidation, and not memory encoding, is supported by studies showing that manipulating stress hormones after an event has occurred can influence whether or not the memory is retained.

FLASHBULB MEMORIES Do you remember where you were when you heard the U.S. Capitol had been taken over during the counting of electoral votes for the presidential election of 2020 (**FIGURE 7.19a**)? For most people, this was shocking news. Events like this can cause people to experience what Roger Brown and James Kulik (1977) termed **flashbulb memories**. These are vivid memories of the circumstances in which people first learn of a surprising and consequential or emotionally arousing event. When in 1977 Brown and Kulik interviewed people about their memories of the assassinations of President John F. Kennedy and Martin Luther King Jr., they found that people described these memories from the 1960s in highly vivid terms. The details included whom they were with, what they were doing or thinking, who told them or how they found out, and what their emotional reactions were to the event. Brown and Kulik proposed that, in our minds, memories for these types of events seem like pictures taken with a camera flash.

flashbulb memories Vivid episodic memories for the circumstances in which people first learned of a surprising and consequential or emotionally arousing event.

(a)

(b)

FIGURE 7.19
Flashbulb Memories
Flashbulb memories are vivid, detailed memories for shocking and consequential events, such as **(a)** the attack on the U.S. Capitol in 2021 and **(b)** the terrorist attack on the World Trade Center on 9/11 in 2001.

One reason flashbulb memories are so persistent may be that these shocking events elicit arousal, which enhances their consolidation. People rarely forget these events occurred, and as you would expect, later memory for the consequential event itself is generally very good.

However, since the original findings by Brown and Kulik, several studies have demonstrated that memories for some of the details of these consequential events may not be as accurate as they seem. For example, following the terrorist attacks on September 11, 2001 (FIGURE 7.19b), a study was conducted of more than 3,000 people in various cities across the United States (Hirst et al., 2009). Participants were initially surveyed a few weeks after the attack, and again a year, three years, and 10 years later. When tested after a year, memories for personal details related to 9/11—such as how they learned about the attack, how they felt, and what they were doing beforehand—were different from the initial reports more than 40 percent of the time. This inconsistency in memories for personal details of the attack was similar for people who were living in New York City on 9/11 and others from across the country. Despite the inconsistency in memory for details, people were highly confident that the details of their vivid memories were correct. Three and 10 years later, people recalled the experience pretty much the same way they did after the first year, even though several aspects of those reports were inconsistent with their initial reports (Hirst et al., 2015). This pattern appears to be generally true of flashbulb memories. Although the inconsistent reports suggest that forgetting of some details takes place, people tend to repeat the same story over time, and this repetition bolsters their confidence of their memory (Hirst & Phelps, 2016).

Although flashbulb memories are not perfectly accurate, people generally remember central details of the important, consequential event, and there is some evidence that other select details, such as where you were at the time, are more consistently recalled over time (Rimmele et al., 2012). For other types of personal details, memory accuracy over time is no different from that for ordinary events (Talarico & Rubin, 2003), despite greater confidence that these details of flashbulb memories are accurate.

Q **Why is a slow consolidation of memories beneficial?**

ANSWER: It allows for reminders, replay, and emotions *after* the event to influence the consolidation process, increasing the likelihood that more important and consequential events are remembered.

7.12 Reconsolidation May Follow Retrieval

Until about 20 years ago, it was generally believed that once a memory was consolidated, it was in a stable state in the brain and was unchanging. However, in the past few decades there has been emerging evidence that sometimes when a memory is retrieved (but not always) it is consolidated again. This second consolidation process is called **reconsolidation** (see FIGURE 7.20).

reconsolidation The re-storage of memory after retrieval.

It has been argued that reconsolidation has two functions: memory updating and memory strengthening (Alberini & LeDoux, 2013). Updating occurs when memory for a past event is retrieved and information in the current circumstance is relevant for that memory. Through reconsolidation, this new information is incorporated into the original memory. In this way, reconsolidated memories may differ from their original versions.

To imagine how this would work, think of a filing drawer with memories being the files and the information contained in them. You could think of memory

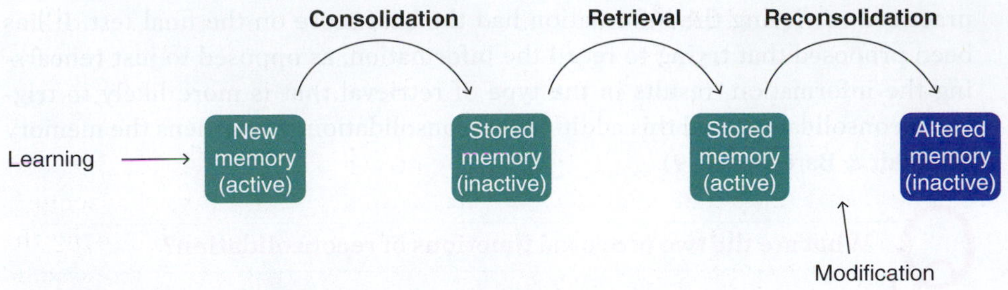

FIGURE 7.20
Reconsolidation
When a memory is first learned it is in an active state and must be consolidated to be stored in long-term memory. Sometimes when a memory is retrieved, it once again enters an active state and is then reconsolidated. During the reconsolidation process, the original memory can be modified or strengthened, resulting in an altered memory.

retrieval as taking out the file and looking at it. Sometimes you might just take out the file, look at the information it contains, and put it back. Other times, you might take out the file and add new information or make corrections. These instances would be similar to reconsolidation updating. Importantly, just as a file is not modified every time it is pulled from the file drawer, reconsolidation updating does not occur every time a memory is retrieved. Reconsolidation is thought to be triggered when aspects of the retrieval context cue that there may be new, relevant information to learn at the time of memory retrieval, which results in something like a prediction error (Sinclair & Barense, 2019; see Chapter 6, "Learning," for a discussion of prediction error).

As you might imagine, the idea of updating memories through reconsolidation has received considerable attention. It has implications not only for what it means to remember something but also for the accuracy of that memory. Reconsolidation updating provides a means for memories to be dynamic and to change over time. It also opens up the intriguing possibility that distressing memories could be changed by retrieving them and interfering with reconsolidation (Kroes et al., 2016). Researchers have shown that fear memories can be altered by using extinction (discussed in Chapter 6) during the period when memories are being reconsolidated (Monfils et al., 2009), but this seems to apply only to some forms of memory expression, and there is not yet sufficient evidence that reconsolidation is a viable method for modifying distressing memories in humans outside the laboratory (Phelps & Hofmann, 2019).

A second proposed function of reconsolidation is to strengthen memories. Through this second storage process, the memory becomes stronger. It has been suggested that strengthening memories through reconsolidation might play a role in the benefits of retrieval practice for learning.

Retrieval practice is a strategy of bringing information to mind by deliberately trying to recall it. Recent research in classrooms has shown that repeated testing that includes retrieval practice strengthens memory better than spending the same amount of time reviewing information you have already read does (Roediger & Karpicke, 2006). In a recent study, one group of students read a 276-word passage on sea otters and then practiced recalling the information, a second group studied the information in four repeated 5-minute study periods, and a third group made concept maps to organize the information by linking together different ideas (Karpicke & Blunt, 2011). The time spent studying was the same for each group. One week later, the students took a final test. Those who practiced retrieving the information had the best score on the final test. It has been proposed that trying to recall the information, as opposed to just rehearsing the information, results in the type of retrieval that is more likely to trigger reconsolidation, and this additional reconsolidation strengthens the memory (Sinclair & Barense, 2019).

Q **What are the two proposed functions of reconsolidation?**

ANSWER: memory modification and strengthening

How Are Memories Retrieved?

Learning Objectives

- Describe the encoding specificity principle.
- Define prospective memory.
- Define retrieval-induced forgetting.

Memory retrieval is the expression of a memory after encoding and storage. Retrieval is also the indication that a memory was encoded and stored, so it goes without saying that what happens at these earlier stages of memory will influence retrieval. The previous two sections highlighted factors that influence encoding and storage. In this section we discuss how the circumstances of retrieval help determine whether or not a memory is expressed.

7.13 Retrieval Cues Bring Back the Past

retrieval cue Any stimulus that promotes memory recall.

As discussed earlier in the chapter, the capacity of long-term memory is limitless—it is made up of a vast array of knowledge and information. What determines which memory is retrieved at any time? A **retrieval cue** can be anything that helps a person (or a nonhuman animal) recall a memory. Encountering stimuli—such as the fragrance of a roasting turkey, a favorite song from years past, a familiar building, and so on—can unintentionally trigger memories. Retrieval cues can also lead us to intentionally search for memories, such as when cued with a question while taking an exam.

encoding specificity principle The idea that any stimulus that is encoded along with an experience can later trigger a memory of the experience.

One factor that has been proposed to influence memory retrieval is whether the retrieval context is similar in some way to the encoding context. For example, when encoding an item into memory, you are storing not just that item but also aspects of the encoding context or situation, such as the room you are in, any smells or sounds, and even your mood at the time. According to the **encoding specificity principle**, any stimulus encoded along with an experience can later trigger a memory of the experience (Tulving & Thomson, 1973).

In a study testing this principle, participants were asked to remember 80 words in either of two rooms. The rooms differed in location, size, scent, and other aspects. The participants were then tested for recall in the room in which they studied or in the other room. When they were tested in the other room, participants recalled an average of 35 words correctly. When they were tested in the room where they studied, participants recalled an average of 49 words correctly (Smith et al., 1978). This kind of memory enhancement, when the recall situation is similar to the encoding situation, is known as *context-dependent memory*.

Context-dependent memory can be based on things such as physical location, odors, and background music, many of which produce a sense of familiarity (Hockley, 2008). In the most dramatic research demonstration of context-dependent memory, scuba divers who learned information underwater later recalled that information better underwater than on land (Godden & Baddeley, 1975; **FIGURE 7.21**).

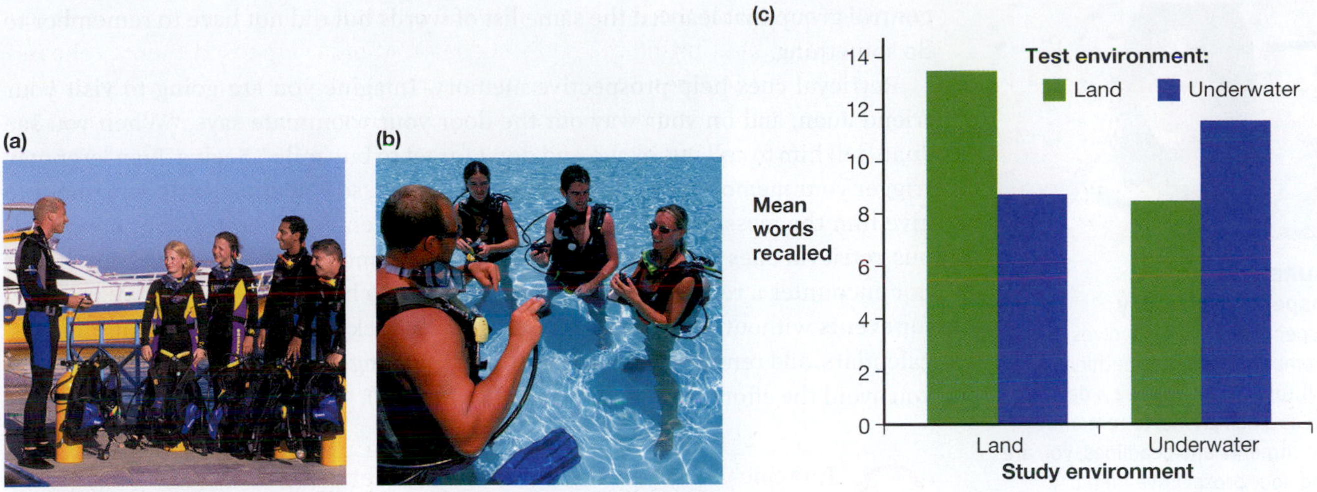

FIGURE 7.21

Context-Dependent Memory

A unique study showed that we encode the physical context of a memory along with the information, and the context can help retrieve the memory. People learned lists of words either **(a)** on land or **(b)** underwater. **(c)** When they had to recall the words later on, they remembered more words if they were tested in the same environment where they had learned the words.

Like physical context, internal cues can affect the recovery of information from long-term memory. Think about mood. When you are in a good mood, do you tend to recall good times? At the end of a bad day, do negative memories tend to surface? Memory can be enhanced when a person's internal states match during encoding and recall. This effect is known as *state-dependent memory.*

State-dependent memory also applies to internal states brought on by drugs or alcohol. You most likely will not remember much of anything you learn while intoxicated. Whatever you do learn, however, may be easier to recall when you are intoxicated than when you are sober—though do not count on it (Goodwin et al., 1969).

Q What are the retrieval cues for context-dependent memory and state-dependent memory?

ANSWER: Physical/situational factors act as retrieval cues in context-dependent memory, and internal conditions act as retrieval cues in state-dependent memory.

7.14 Retrieval Cues Aid Prospective Memory

Have you ever gotten a call, email, or text reminding you of an upcoming appointment? Do you post notes or make lists with items you need to buy at the grocery store? Although retrieval cues can prompt remembering events from the past, an important function of retrieval cues in everyday life is to remind people of upcoming tasks. Unlike the other types of remembering discussed so far in this chapter, **prospective memory** involves remembering to do something at some future time (Graf & Uttl, 2001).

prospective memory
Remembering to do something at some future time.

Remembering to do something in the future can be more challenging than remembering the past. In a study of prospective memory, participants had to learn a list of words (Cook et al., 2007). In one condition, they also had to remember to do something, such as press a key when they saw a certain word. The group that had to remember to do something took longer to learn the list than did the

FIGURE 7.22
Prospective Memory
Prospective memory involves remembering to do something in the future. When you use a device, such as a cell phone, to remember appointments and deadlines, you are cuing your prospective memory.

control group that learned the same list of words but did not have to remember to do something.

Retrieval cues help prospective memory. Imagine you are going to visit your friend Juan, and on your way out the door your roommate says, "When you see Juan, tell him to call me, okay? And don't forget to buy milk." Seeing Juan later may trigger your memory of what your roommate said, so you effortlessly remember to give him the message. But sometimes particular environments do not have obvious retrieval cues for particular prospective memories. For example, you might not encounter a retrieval cue for remembering to buy milk. Prospective memory for events without retrieval cues is one reason sticky notes and cell phone alarms, calendars, and reminders are so popular. By jogging your memory, these cues help you avoid the effort of remembering (**FIGURE 7.22**).

Q **Imagine you set an alarm to serve as a retrieval cue to remember an online appointment. What type of memory is the alarm meant to cue?**

ANSWER: prospective memory

7.15 Retrieval Can Promote Forgetting

retrieval-induced forgetting Impairment of the ability to recall an item in the future after retrieving a related item from long-term memory.

In general, retrieval and rehearsal lead to better memory in the future, but in some circumstances retrieval can actually impair future remembering. **Retrieval-induced forgetting** occurs when retrieving an item from long-term memory impairs the ability to recall a related item in the future.

In a study demonstrating this effect, participants were asked to remember pairs of words consisting of category names and items from that category. Each category name was paired with six items—for example, *fruit-orange*, *fruit-apple*, *fruit-strawberry*, and so on. Some participants then practiced retrieving half of the category items by being cued with the category name and the first two letters, such as *fruit-or*___. At a later test, the participants were asked to remember all the items. Those participants who practiced retrieving some of the category items showed worse memory for the items they did not practice retrieving. This result is not particularly surprising, since practice improves memory. However, memory for the nonpracticed items in this group was also worse than memory for those items in the group that did not practice retrieval at all. In other words, retrieving some of the items from a category impaired memory for other items from the same category (Anderson et al., 2000).

Although retrieval-induced forgetting may seem like a very specific memory phenomenon, it may have some real-world consequences. For instance, having a conversation about shared memories for some details of an event but not others can impair later memory for the nondiscussed details for both the speaker and listener (Cuc et al., 2007). It has also been shown that probing memory for some details of a staged crime scene can impair later memory for other details (MacLeod, 2002; Shaw et al., 1995). These findings and others have implications for interrogation techniques used to probe memories of eyewitnesses to crimes (Camp et al., 2012).

Q **How might repeatedly remembering and discussing the wonderful guacamole served at a party last weekend affect your memory of the other foods provided?**

ANSWER: Retrieval-induced forgetting could impair your memory of the other food items.

7.16 What Is the Best Way to Ace Exams?

PSYCHOLOGY OUTSIDE THE LAB

What tools does psychology offer to help you study more effectively for the exams you will take during college? Many students read the text, highlight what they think is important, and then reread the highlighted material for hours the night before an exam. Despite the popularity of this method, it is not associated with effective learning or good grades (Blasiman et al., 2017). Researchers have identified a number of methods that will help you remember information more easily (Putnam et al., 2016). These methods include:

1. **Prepare for and attend class.** Many professors advise students on what to read before class. Do it! They are trying to maximize the likelihood you will learn the information. Read the material for comprehension, but take your time and try to understand the ideas as you read. Speed-reading does not work, no matter how much you practice it. There is a trade-off between speed and accuracy (Rayner et al., 2017). Once you are prepared, be sure to attend class. You simply cannot get by with reading the text and looking at online lecture notes. Your instructor may tie together ideas across lectures, present new ways of thinking about the material, or mention information not found in the textbook.
2. **Distribute your learning.** Although studying right before an exam can refresh information in your mind, cramming alone does not work. Instead, distribute your study sessions. Six sessions of 1 hour each are much better for learning than one 6-hour marathon. By spreading your studying over multiple sessions, you will retain the information longer (Dempster, 1988). During each session, you should study each subject a little bit. Spacing out your study sessions requires you to begin earlier in the term rather than waiting until the night before exams, but it is perhaps the best way to learn the information and do well on exams.
3. **Elaborate the material.** Imagine you and two friends decide to engage in a little friendly competition in which you each memorize a list of 20 words. Friend A simply reads the words. Friend B, after reading each word, copies the word's definition from a dictionary. You, after reading each word, think about how the word is relevant to you. For example, you see the word *rain* and think, "My car once broke down in the middle of a torrential rainstorm." Who is most likely to remember that list of words later? You are. The deeper your level of processing, the more likely you are to remember material, particularly if you make the material personally relevant.

   When you are learning something new, do not just read the material or copy down textbook descriptions. Think about the meaning of the material and how the concepts are related to other concepts. Organize the material in a way that makes sense to you, putting the concepts in your own words. Making the material relevant to you is an especially good way to process material deeply and therefore to remember it easily.
4. **Practice retrieval.** To make your memories more durable, you need to practice retrieving the information you are trying to learn. In fact, repeated testing is a more effective memory-building strategy than spending the same amount of time reviewing information you have already read. Thus, to prepare for an exam, you should practice recalling the information over and over again. Sometimes the stress of taking an exam can interfere with memory. Practicing retrieval protects memories from the negative effects of stress (Smith et al., 2016).

After reading a section in this or any other book, look back to the main section heading. If that heading is not already a question, rephrase it as a question. Test yourself by trying to answer the heading's question without looking at the text. Make use of in-chapter test questions by answering these questions as you encounter them. Then answer them again a couple of days later. For this book, be sure to take the practice test provided at the end of each chapter. Take advantage of online test questions supplied by the textbook publisher. This book's online testing system is InQuizitive.

You can also develop your own practice materials. Write quiz questions. Make flash cards on pieces of card stock or on the computer (https://quizlet.com is a great website for creating and using flash cards). On one side of the flash card, write a key term. On the other side, write the definition of that term. Then drill using the flash cards in both directions. Can you recall the term when you see the definition? Can you provide the definition when you see the term? A good way to drill is to study with another member of your class and take turns quizzing each other.

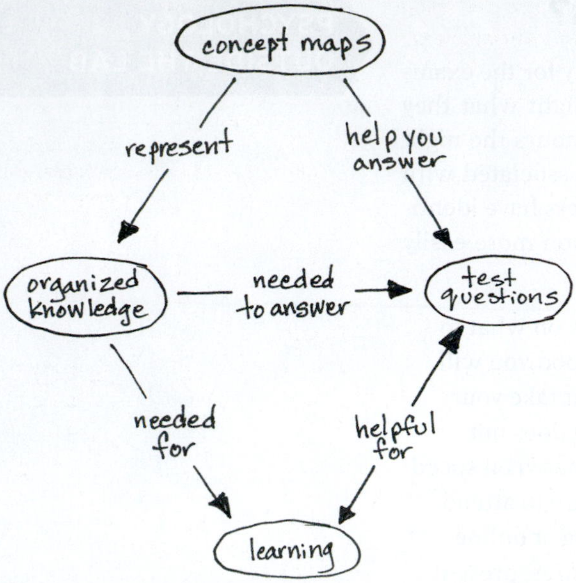

FIGURE 7.23

Concept Map as Memory Aid

This concept map presents some ideas about—you guessed it—concept maps. When you need to visualize the relationships among different ideas about any subject, you can adapt this model. The ovals represent main ideas. The arrows indicate connections between ideas. A concept map can become far more complex. In fact, it can become as complex as you need it to be. For example, you might use many branches to represent an especially complex idea or color-code ideas that originated from different sources.

5. **Overlearn.** With material in front of us, we are often overly confident that we "know" the information and believe we will remember it later. But recognition is easier than recall. Thus, if you want to be able to recall information, you need to put in extra effort when encoding the material. Even after you *think* you have learned it, review it again. Test yourself by trying to recall the material a few hours (and a few days) after studying. Keep rehearsing until you can recall the material easily.
6. **Use verbal mnemonics for rote memory.** Sometimes you may need to learn long lists of items, but understanding the items does not matter. In these cases, verbal mnemonics can help. For example, how many days are there in September? In the Western world, at least, most people can readily answer this question thanks to the old saying that begins *Thirty days hath September*. Children also learn *i before e except after c* and, along with that saying, *"weird" is weird.* By memorizing such phrases, we more easily remember things that are difficult to remember. Advertisers, of course, often create slogans or jingles that rely on verbal mnemonics so that consumers cannot help but remember them. Students have long used acronyms to remember information, such as HOMES to remember the great lakes (Huron, Ontario, Michigan, Erie, and Superior). In studying Chapter 13, the acronym OCEAN will help you remember the five major personality traits: openness to experience, conscientiousness, extraversion, agreeableness, and neuroticism. Even complex ideas can be understood through simple mnemonics. For example, the phrase *cells that fire together wire together* is a way to remember long-term potentiation, the brain mechanism responsible for learning (discussed in Section 7.10). However, mnemonics are not useful for increasing understanding of the material, and ultimately having a greater conceptual understanding is important for learning and memory.
7. **Use visual imagery.** Creating a mental image of material may help you. Visual imagery strategies include doodling a sketch to help you link ideas to images, creating a flowchart to show how a process unfolds over time, or drawing a concept map that shows the relationships between ideas (**FIGURE 7.23**).

To use all of these strategies, you need to remember them. As a first step toward improving your study skills, create a mnemonic to remember these strategies! ■

Q Why might a student remember the information on a test more accurately *after* taking the test?

ANSWER: Taking the test served as practiced recall, an effective process for strengthening memory.

What Are Common Memory Mistakes?

Learning Objectives

- Describe the pattern of forgetting over time.
- Generate examples of source misattribution.
- Discuss susceptibility to false memories.
- Describe contemporary views on repressed memories.

People often assume that their memories are accurate and unchanging over time. Research has shown clearly, however, that human memory is biased, distorted, and prone to a great deal of forgetting. Memory is a constantly active process, involving consolidation and reconsolidation of information manipulated in working memory. For example, 10 minutes after you see a movie, you probably remember plenty of its details, but the next day you might remember mostly the plot and the main characters. Years later, you might remember the gist of the story, or you might not remember having seen the movie at all. We forget far more than we remember. You might also have memories that are false, such as remembering a particular person was in a film when she was not or getting plot details wrong. In this section, you will learn how human long-term memory sometimes provides less-than-accurate portrayals of past events.

7.17 Forgetting Is an Inability to Remember

The study of forgetting has a long history in psychological science. The late-nineteenth-century psychologist Hermann Ebbinghaus (1885/1964) examined how long it took people to relearn lists of nonsense syllables (e.g., vut, bik, kuh) they had learned previously. Ebbinghaus provided compelling evidence that forgetting occurs rapidly at first and levels off after a few days (see **FIGURE 7.24**). Most of us do not need to memorize nonsense syllables, but Ebbinghaus's general findings apply to meaningful material as well. Although the rate of forgetting seems to level off after a while, you are still more likely to remember something that happened

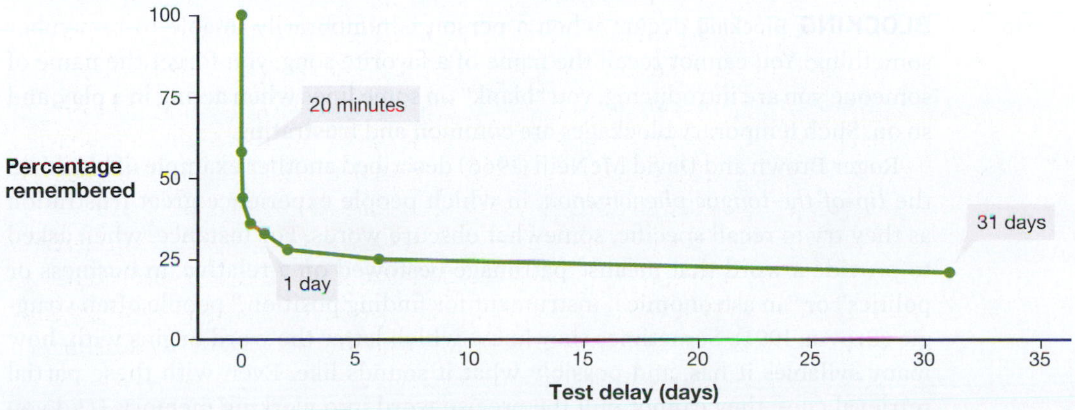

FIGURE 7.24
Forgetting Curve
In the late 1800s, Hermann Ebbinghaus used nonsense syllables (meaningless three-letter strings) to show that most information is forgotten quickly, within a day, and the rate of forgetting slows over time.

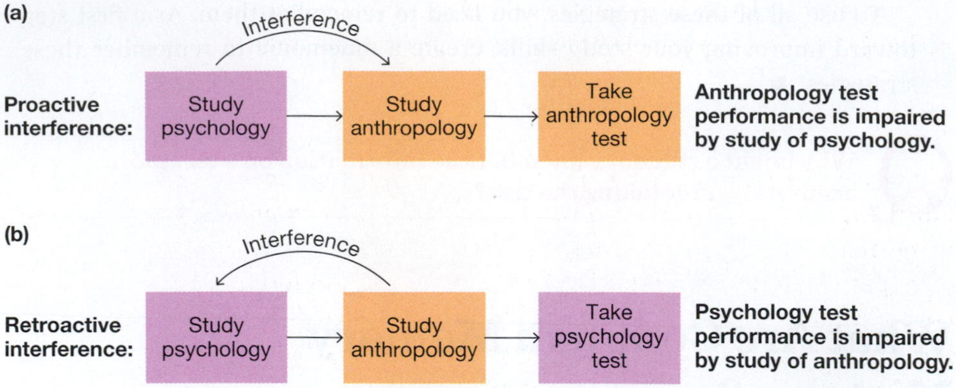

FIGURE 7.25
Proactive Interference Versus Retroactive Interference
(a) Proactive interference occurs when information already known (psychology material) interferes with the ability to remember new information (anthropology material). **(b)** Retroactive interference occurs when new information (anthropology material) interferes with memory for old information (psychology material).

last month as opposed to last year. In fact, forgetting seems to continue until at least about five years after learning. If a memory lasts longer than five years, there is a good chance it will likely last a lifetime (Bahrick, 1984).

However, even if you cannot remember something, traces of the memory might exist. For instance, you may remember very little of the Spanish or calculus you took in high school, but relearning these subjects would take you less time and effort than it took to learn them the first time. The difference between the original learning and relearning is called *savings*.

Many early theorists argued that forgetting results from decay in the representation of the memory in a person's nervous system. Indeed, some evidence indicates that unused memories are forgotten. Research over the past few decades, however, has established that some forgetting occurs because of *interference* from other information. Additional information can lead to forgetting through proactive interference or retroactive interference. In both cases, competing information displaces the information we are trying to retrieve.

proactive interference Interference that occurs when prior information inhibits the ability to remember new information.

retroactive interference Interference that occurs when new information inhibits the ability to remember old information.

In **proactive interference**, old information inhibits the ability to remember new information. For instance, if you study for your psychology test, then switch to studying for your anthropology test, and then take the anthropology test, your performance on the test might be impaired by your knowledge about psychology (**FIGURE 7.25a**). In **retroactive interference**, new information inhibits the ability to remember old information. So when it comes time to take the psychology test, your performance might suffer because you recall the freshly reinforced anthropology material instead (**FIGURE 7.25b**).

blocking The temporary inability to remember something.

BLOCKING **Blocking** occurs when a person is temporarily unable to remember something: You cannot recall the name of a favorite song, you forget the name of someone you are introducing, you "blank" on some lines when acting in a play, and so on. Such temporary blockages are common and frustrating.

Roger Brown and David McNeill (1966) described another example of blocking: the *tip-of-the-tongue phenomenon*, in which people experience great frustration as they try to recall specific, somewhat obscure words. For instance, when asked to provide a word that means "patronage bestowed on a relative, in business or politics" or "an astronomical instrument for finding position," people often struggle (Brown, 1991). Sometimes they know which letter the word begins with, how many syllables it has, and possibly what it sounds like. Even with these partial retrieval cues, they cannot pull the precise word into working memory. (Did you know the words were *nepotism* and *sextant*?) Blocking often occurs because of interference from words that are similar in some way, such as in sound or meaning. For example, you might repeatedly call an acquaintance Margaret although her name is Melanie. The tip-of-the-tongue phenomenon increases with age, perhaps because older people have more memories that might interfere.

ABSENTMINDEDNESS **Absentmindedness** results from the shallow encoding of events. The major cause of absentmindedness is failing to pay attention. For instance, you absentmindedly forget where you left your keys because when you put them down, you were also reaching to answer your phone. You forget the name of a person you are talking with because when you met 5 minutes ago, you were paying attention to their face, not their name. You forget whether you took your vitamins this morning because you were distracted by an interesting question from your roommate (**FIGURE 7.26**). Recall that when prospective memory fails, you fail to remember to do something. Often, this form of absentmindedness occurs because you are caught up in another activity.

FIGURE 7.26
Absentmindedness
The major cause of absentmindedness is failing to pay sufficient attention when encoding memories. The celebrated musician Yo-Yo Ma is pictured here with his $2.5 million eighteenth-century cello, which was returned to him after he absentmindedly left it in a cab.

absentmindedness The inattentive or shallow encoding of events.

This lack of attention can produce serious consequences. For example, in the United States an average of 38 children, mostly infants, die each year because they are left unattended in hot cars (NoHeatStroke.org, 2021). In many cases, the parent forgot to drop the child off at day care on their way to work. It is easy to imagine forgetting your lunch in the car, but your child? Such incidents are rare, but they seem to be especially likely when the parent's typical routine does not include day care drop-off duty. While the parent is driving, their brain shifts to "autopilot" and automatically goes through the process of driving to the workplace instead of stopping at day care first. During most of our daily activities, of course, we are consciously aware of only a small portion of both our thoughts and our behaviors.

Q **Why do people often forget where they left their keys?**

ANSWER: Absentmindedness: They are not paying attention when they put their keys down.

7.18 Persistence Is Unwanted Remembering

Most people are unhappy about forgetting. They wish they could better remember the material for exams, their friends' birthdays, the geologic time periods, and so on. But imagine what life would be like if you could not forget. Imagine, for example, walking up to your locker and recalling not just its combination but all the combinations for all the locks you have ever used.

Consider the case of a Russian newspaper reporter who had nearly perfect memory. If someone read him a tremendously long list of items and he visualized the items for a few moments, he could recite the list, even many years later. But his memory was so cluttered with information that he had great difficulty functioning in society. Tortured by this condition, he was institutionalized (Luria, 1968). Not being able to forget is as maladaptive as not being able to remember. Normal forgetting helps us retain and use the most meaningful and important information.

persistence The continual recurrence of unwanted memories.

Persistence occurs when unwanted memories are remembered despite the desire not to have them. Most people experience persistence at some point. If you ever embarrassed yourself at a party or at school and could not stop reliving the experience in your mind for a few days, then you have experienced persistence.

In some cases, unwanted memories are so persistent and traumatic that they destroy the life of the individual who suffers from them. One prominent example of persistence occurs in posttraumatic stress disorder (PTSD; discussed further in Chapter 14, "Psychological Disorders"). PTSD is a serious mental health problem, with an estimated prevalence of 7 percent in the United States (Kessler et al., 2005b). The most common causes of PTSD include events that threaten people or those close to them. For example, the unexpected death of a loved one, a physical or sexual assault, a car accident, a natural disaster, or the sight of someone badly injured or killed can be a source of PTSD. In PTSD, memories of the traumatic event are habitually retrieved, causing significant distress. Cues and contexts that pose no threat evoke the memory and cause the sufferer to relive the traumatic event. In the case of PTSD, memory persistence leads to prolonged stress reactions that can have significant consequences for physical and mental health.

Q **What psychological disorder is caused by the persistence of unwanted memories?**

ANSWER: posttraumatic stress disorder (PTSD)

7.19 People Reconstruct Events to Be Consistent

memory bias The changing of memories over time so that they become consistent with current beliefs or attitudes.

Memory bias is the changing of memories over time so that they become consistent with current beliefs, knowledge, or attitudes. As one of psychology's greatest thinkers, Leon Festinger (1987), put it: "I prefer to rely on my memory. I have lived with that memory a long time, I am used to it, and if I have rearranged or distorted anything, surely that was done for my own benefit" (p. 1).

Consider students who take courses in study skills. Students often fail to heed the advice they receive in such courses, and there is only modest evidence that the courses are beneficial. Yet most students who take them describe the courses as extremely helpful. How can something that generally produces unimpressive outcomes be endorsed so positively?

To understand this phenomenon, researchers randomly assigned students to either a genuine study skills course or a control group that received no special training. Students who took the real course showed few signs of improvement. In fact, their performance on the final exam was slightly poorer than the control group's. Still, they considered the study skills program helpful. The experiment had one feature that helps explain why. At the beginning of the course, participants were asked to rate their studying skills. At the end of the course, they again rated themselves and were asked to recall how they had originally rated themselves. In describing their earlier ratings, students in the study skills course recalled themselves as having been significantly worse than they had rated themselves at the beginning. In this way, the students were "getting what they want[ed] by revising what they had" (Conway & Ross, 1984).

People tend to recall their past beliefs, knowledge, and attitudes as being consistent with their current ones. Often, they revise their memories when they change attitudes, knowledge, and beliefs. People also tend to remember events as casting them in prominent roles or favorable lights. As discussed further in Chapter 12, people also tend to exaggerate their contributions to group efforts, take credit for successes and blame failures on others, and remember their successes more than their failures. Societies, too, bias their recollections of past events. Groups' collective memories can seriously distort the past. Most societies' official histories tend to downplay their past behaviors that were unsavory, immoral, and even murderous. Perpetrators' memories are generally shorter than victims' memories.

Q **Someone who acted as a bully in middle school now has an anti-bullying attitude in college. How might this attitude change affect their memory?**

ANSWER: They might remember their bullying behaviors in a way that justifies the behaviors or minimizes their negative impact.

7.20 People Make Source Misattributions

Source misattribution occurs when people misremember the time, place, person, or circumstances involved with a memory. A good example of this phenomenon is the false fame effect. Ask yourself: Is Richard Shiffrin famous? Try to think for a second how you know him. If you thought he was famous, you might have recalled that Shiffrin was one of the psychologists who introduced the model of sensory, short-term, and long-term memory (an accomplishment that might make him famous in some scientific circles). Alternatively, you might have remembered reading his name before, even if you could not remember where.

source misattribution Memory distortion that occurs when people misremember the time, place, person, or circumstances involved with a memory.

In a study of the false fame effect, the psychologist Larry Jacoby had research participants read aloud a list of made-up names (Jacoby et al., 1989). The participants were told that the research project was about pronunciation. The next day, Jacoby had the same people participate in an apparently unrelated study. This time, they were asked to read a list of names and decide whether each person was famous or not. The participants misjudged some of the made-up names from the previous day as being those of famous people. Because the participants knew they had heard the names before but probably could not remember where, they assumed the familiar names were those of famous people.

Another example of source misattribution is the sleeper effect. The sleeper effect occurs when an argument that is not very persuasive at first because it comes from a questionable source seems more credible over time as the source is forgotten. Suppose you see an online ad for a way to learn French while you sleep. You probably will not believe the claims in the ad. Yet over time you might remember the promise but fail to remember the source. Because the promise occurs to you without the obvious reason for rejecting it, you might come to believe that people can learn French while sleeping, or you might at least wonder whether it is possible.

SOURCE AMNESIA **Source amnesia** is a form of misattribution that occurs when people have a memory for an event but cannot remember where they encountered the information. Consider your earliest childhood memory. How vivid is it? Are you actually recalling the event or some retelling of the event? How do you know you are not remembering something you saw in a photograph or video or heard about in a story related to you by family members? Most people cannot remember specific episodic memories from before age 3 or 4 because of what is called *infantile amnesia*. The ability to form lasting episodic memories is thought to depend on the early development of the prefrontal cortex and language abilities. If you have a specific memory from around this age or earlier, the memory is likely to have come from another source, such as your parents, siblings, or a picture from your childhood.

source amnesia A type of misattribution that occurs when people have a memory for an event but cannot remember where they encountered the information.

CRYPTOMNESIA An intriguing example of source misattribution is **cryptomnesia**, in which people think they have come up with a new idea. Instead, they have retrieved an old idea from memory and failed to attribute the idea to its proper source (Macrae et al., 1999). For example, students who take verbatim notes while conducting library research sometimes experience the illusion that they have composed the sentences themselves (Ferro & Martins, 2016). This mistake can later lead to an accusation of plagiarism. Be especially vigilant about indicating verbatim notes while you are taking them.

cryptomnesia A type of misattribution that occurs when people think they have come up with a new idea yet have retrieved a stored idea and failed to attribute the idea to its proper source.

George Harrison, the late Beatle, was sued because his 1970 song "My Sweet Lord" is strikingly similar to the song "He's So Fine," recorded in 1962 by the

Chiffons. Harrison acknowledged that he knew "He's So Fine," but he vigorously denied having plagiarized it. He argued that with a limited number of musical notes available to all musicians, and an even smaller number of chord sequences appropriate for rock and roll, some compositional overlap is inevitable. In a controversial verdict, the judge ruled against Harrison.

Q **Why should students doing library research be careful when taking verbatim notes?**

ANSWER: The students might experience cryptomnesia, forgetting that the words belonged to someone else, and therefore inadvertently plagiarize the material.

7.21 Suggestibility Biases Memory

suggestibility The development of biased memories from misleading information.

During the early 1970s, Elizabeth Loftus and her colleagues conducted important research on biased memories. The results demonstrated that people have a tendency, known as **suggestibility**, to develop biased memories when provided with misleading information.

These studies generally involved showing research participants a video of an event and then asking them specific questions about it. The different wordings of the questions altered the participants' memories for the event. In one experiment, a group of participants viewed a video of a car—a red Datsun—approaching a stop sign (Loftus et al., 1978). A second group viewed a video of that same scene but with a yield sign instead of a stop sign. Each group was then asked, "Did another car pass the red Datsun while it was stopped at the stop sign?" Some participants in the second group claimed to have seen the red Datsun stop at the stop sign, even though they had seen it approaching a yield sign (**FIGURE 7.27**).

In another experiment, Loftus and John Palmer (1974) showed participants a video of a car accident. When participants heard the word *smashed* applied to the video, they estimated the cars to be traveling faster than when they heard *contacted*, *hit*, *bumped*, or *collided*. In a related study, participants saw a video of a car accident and then were asked about seeing the cars either *smash into* or *hit* each other. One week later, they were asked if they had seen broken glass on the ground in the video. No glass broke in the video, but nearly one third of those who heard *smashed* falsely recalled having seen broken glass. Very few of those who heard *hit* recalled broken glass.

Are these sorts of laboratory analogues appropriate for studying eyewitness accuracy? After all, the sights and sounds of a traffic accident, for example, impress the event on the witness's awareness. Some evidence supports the idea that such memories are better in the real world than in the laboratory. One study examined the reports of witnesses to a fatal shooting (Yuille & Cutshall, 1986). All the witnesses had been interviewed by the police within two days of the incident. Months afterward, the researchers found the eyewitness reports, including the details, highly stable.

FIGURE 7.27
Loftus's Studies on Suggestibility
When asked whether another car passed the red Datsun when it was at a stop sign, many participants who had seen the car stopped at a yield sign misremembered seeing a stop sign instead.

Given that emotion affects memories, it makes sense for accounts from eyewitnesses to be more vivid than accounts from laboratory research participants. It remains unclear, however, how accurate those stable memories were in the first place, especially the details. And by retelling their stories over and over again—to the police, to friends and relatives, to researchers, and so on—eyewitnesses might inadvertently develop stronger memories for inaccurate details.

FALSE MEMORIES How easily can people develop false memories? To consider this question, read aloud the following list: *sour, candy, sugar, bitter, good, taste, tooth, nice, honey, soda, chocolate, heart, cake, tart, pie.* Now put aside your book and write down as many of the words as you remember.

Researchers have devised tests such as this for investigating whether people can be misled into recalling or recognizing events that did not happen (Roediger & McDermott, 1995). For instance, without looking back at the list, answer this question: Which of the following words did you recall—*candy, honey, tooth, sweet, pie*?

If you recalled *sweet* or think you did, you have experienced a false memory, because *sweet* was not on the original list. All the words on that list are related to sweetness, though. This basic procedure produces false recollections reliably. It occurs because each word makes you think of related words. This semantic knowledge of related words leads to potential confusion about which of the related words you actually read. A brain imaging study showed that related words produce overlapping patterns of brain activity in the frontmost portion of the temporal lobe, where semantic information is processed (Chadwick et al., 2016). As a result, even though the memories are false, people are often extremely confident in saying they have seen or heard the words they recollect falsely.

Now think back to when you were 5. Do you remember getting lost in a mall and being found by a kind old man who returned you to your family? No? Well, what if your family told you about this incident, including how panicked your parents were when they could not find you? According to research by Loftus, you might then remember the incident, even if it did not happen.

In an initial study, a 14-year-old named Chris was told by his older brother Jim, who was part of the study, about the "lost in the mall" incident. The context was a game called "Remember When . . ." All the other incidents narrated by Jim were true. Two days later, when asked if he had ever been lost in a mall, Chris began reporting memories of how he felt during the mall episode. Within two weeks, he reported the following:

> I was with you guys for a second and I think I went over to look at the toy store, the Kay-bee toy and uh, we got lost and I was looking around and I thought, "Uh-oh. I'm in trouble now." You know. And then I . . . I thought I was never going to see my family again. I was really scared you know. And then this old man, I think he was wearing a blue flannel shirt, came up to me. . . . [H]e was kind of old. He was kind of bald on top. . . . [H]e had like a ring of gray hair . . . and he had glasses. (Loftus, 1993, p. 532)

You might wonder whether there was something special about Chris that made him susceptible to developing false memories. In a later study, however, Loftus and her colleagues used the same method to assess whether they could implant false memories in 24 participants. Seven of the participants falsely remembered events that had been implanted by family members who were part of the study. How could this be so?

When people imagine an event happening, they form a mental image of the event, and they might later confuse that mental image with a real memory.

(a)

(b)

FIGURE 7.28
Fallibility of "Repressed Memory"
(a) Eileen Franklin (center) claimed to have recovered a previously repressed memory that her father had murdered a friend of hers two decades earlier. **(b)** George Franklin was found guilty and imprisoned based on his daughter's testimony. Evidence subsequently emerged proving his innocence, and he was released.

Essentially, this is a problem in monitoring the source of the image. To Chris, the memory of being lost in the mall became as real as other events in childhood. Children are particularly susceptible, and false memories—such as of getting fingers caught in mousetraps or having to be hospitalized—can easily be induced in them. It is unlikely, however, that false memories can be created for certain types of unusual events, such as receiving an enema (Pezdek & Hodge, 1999).

REPRESSED MEMORIES Over the past few decades, one of the most heated debates in psychological science has centered on repressed memories. On the one side, some psychotherapists and patients claim that long-repressed memories for traumatic events can resurface during therapy. Recovered memories of sexual abuse are the most commonly reported repressed memories, and in the early 1990s there was a rash of reports about celebrities who claimed to have recovered memories of such abuse. On the other side, memory researchers such as Elizabeth Loftus point out that little credible evidence indicates that recovered memories are genuine or at least sufficiently accurate to be believable. Part of the problem is best summarized by the memory researcher Daniel Schacter: "I am convinced that child abuse is a major problem in our society. I have no reason to question the memories of people who have always remembered their abuse, or who have spontaneously recalled previously forgotten abuse on their own. Yet I am deeply concerned by some of the suggestive techniques that have been recommended to recover repressed memories" (Schacter, 1996, p. 251).

Schacter alludes to the frightening possibility that false memories for traumatic events have been implanted by well-meaning but misguided therapists. Convincing evidence indicates that methods such as hypnosis, age regression, and guided recall can implant false memories. In a few infamous examples, adults have accused their parents of abuse based on memories that the accusers later realized were not reality but the products of therapy (**FIGURE 7.28**).

Consider the dramatic case of Diana Halbrook. Halbrook came to believe that she had been abused. She also believed that she had been involved in satanic ritualistic abuse that involved killing a baby. When she expressed doubts to her therapist and her "support" group about these events' veracity, they told her she was in denial and not listening to "the little girl" within. After all, the other members of the support group had recovered memories of being involved in satanic ritualistic abuse. After Halbrook left her therapy group, she came to believe she had not been abused and had not killed. Tellingly, "though thousands of patients have 'remembered' ritual acts, not a single such case has ever been documented in the United States despite extensive investigative efforts by state and federal law enforcement" (Schacter, 1996, p. 269).

Understandably, people on both sides of the debate about repressed memories hold strong and passionate beliefs. While research shows that some therapeutic techniques seem especially likely to foster false memories, it would be a mistake to dismiss all adult reports of early abuse. Some abuse certainly could have occurred and been forgotten until later, and we cannot ignore the memories of actual victims. In the latter half of the 1990s, the incidence of recovered memories fell dramatically. However, we do not know whether this decline occurred because of less media attention to reports, because fewer people sought therapy to uncover their past memories, or because therapists stopped using these suggestive methods.

Q **Why should witnesses of a crime be asked to write down their complete memory before being asked any specific questions?**

ANSWER: Because of suggestibility, the specific questions asked could influence the witness's memory.

YOU BE THE PSYCHOLOGIST

7.22 How Can Psychologists Inform the Use of Memory in the Courtroom?

At this beginning of this chapter, you learned about the documented problem of mistaken eyewitness identification (**FIGURE 7.29**). In the criminal justice system, one of the most powerful forms of evidence is the eyewitness account. Research has demonstrated that very few jurors are willing to convict an accused individual on the basis of circumstantial evidence alone. But add one person who says, "That's the one!" and conviction becomes much more likely. This effect occurs even if it is shown that the witness had poor eyesight or some other condition that raises questions about the testimony's accuracy. Eyewitness testimony's power is troubling. If eyewitnesses are told that another witness chose the same person, their confidence increases, even when the identifications were false (Luus & Wells, 1994).

One major problem with eyewitness testimony is that people tend to remember evidence that confirms their beliefs. For instance, they may believe that certain types of people are more likely to commit crimes and therefore might be more likely to identify people with those characteristics as the likely criminal. Confirmation biases might even affect what potential eyewitnesses notice in the world around them.

The way police interview eyewitnesses may also be influenced by confirmation bias (Wells & Seelau, 1995). For instance, police often ask witnesses to identify the culprit by showing them a lineup of potential suspects or a photospread of faces. Witnesses may feel compelled to pick someone and choose the person who most resembles the culprit. Once the choice is made, they may become more confident that it is the actual culprit, even if they were unsure initially. The officers can also unintentionally influence the identification, such as by asking more questions about their suspect than about the other potential culprits or confirming that the witness picked the suspected culprit. Ideally, the person who conducts the lineup or presents the photos should not know the suspect's identity. That is, as noted in Chapter 2, the person running the "study" should be blind to the conditions of the study so as not to bias the results.

How good are observers, such as jurors, at judging eyewitnesses' accuracy? The general finding from a number of studies is that people cannot differentiate accurate eyewitnesses from inaccurate ones (Clark & Wells, 2008; Wells, 2008). The problem is that eyewitnesses who are wrong are just as confident as (or *more* confident than) eyewitnesses who are right. Eyewitnesses who vividly report trivial details of a scene are probably less credible than those with poor memories for trivial details. After all, eyewitnesses to real crimes tend to be focused on the weapons or on the action. They fail to pay attention to minor details. Thus, strong confidence for minor details may be a cue that the memory is likely to be inaccurate or even false. Some witnesses are particularly confident, however, and jurors find them convincing.

Because of concerns about the accuracy of eyewitness identification, psychologists are increasingly being asked to testify about memory in the courtroom. Imagine you were asked to serve as a memory expert in a legal proceeding. Given what you have learned, what are the types of situations where you would expect an eyewitness account to be accurate or inaccurate? If the eyewitness knew the culprit before the crime, are they as likely to be mistaken? What aspects of the crime or witness interrogation might influence the memory of the eyewitness? What evidence would you present to convince a jury that an eyewitness confident in their memory could be mistaken? ■

FIGURE 7.29
Eyewitness Accounts Can Be Unreliable
Jennifer Thompson (right) was raped in 1984 and identified Ronald Cotton (left) as the rapist. He was convicted and imprisoned. A decade later, DNA evidence revealed he was innocent. After his release, Thompson, distressed by the injustice her highly confident but mistaken memory had caused, apologized to Cotton. The two became friends and advocates and wrote a book about their experience.

Q Should the memory of a confident eyewitness who recalls minor details of a crime be considered more trustworthy than that of a less confident eyewitness?

ANSWER: No, confidence is unrelated to the accuracy of eyewitness memories.

Your Chapter Review

Want to earn a better grade on your test?

It's time to complete your study experience! Go to **INQUIZITIVE** to practice actively with this chapter's concepts and get personalized feedback along the way.

Chapter Summary

What Is Memory, and What Are Memory Systems?

7.1 There Are Many Types of Memories and Memory Systems Memory is divided into several systems. The study of patients such as H.M. has provided evidence regarding the different types of memory and the brain regions involved. Memory systems can be divided based on whether they are expressed consciously, called explicit memory; or through responses, actions, and reactions, called implicit memory.

7.2 Implicit Memories Are Expressed Through Actions and Reactions Implicit memories are expressed without conscious attention or deliberation. One type of implicit memory is procedural memory for skills and habits. Other types of implicit memories are developed through priming, learned association through classical conditioning, and nonassociative learning (habituation and sensitization).

7.3 Explicit Memories Can Be Declared Explicit memories are often called declarative memories because they require conscious effort to declare them as knowledge. There are two explicit memory systems: episodic memories for personal events and semantic memories for general knowledge of facts and concepts independent of personal experience. Episodic memory and semantic memory are believed to be distinct memory systems, based on evidence from brain-damaged patients who can form semantic but not episodic memories.

How Are Memories Encoded?

7.4 Encoding Turns Perception into Memory Encoding starts with attention. The more attention paid to a stimulus, the more likely it is to be encoded into memory. The *dual-coding hypothesis* suggests that information that can be coded verbally and visually will be remembered more easily than information that can be coded only verbally.

7.5 Attention to Meaning Improves Encoding According to the levels of processing model, deep encoding enhances memory. Maintenance rehearsal—repeating an item over and over—leads to shallow encoding and poor recall. Elaborative rehearsal links new information with existing knowledge, leading to deeper encoding and better recall. Schemas are cognitive structures that help us understand and organize information.

7.6 Organization Affects Memory Encoding Organizing information can help encoding by linking it to existing knowledge. Chunking is the process of breaking down information into meaningful units. Mnemonics are learning aids or strategies to improve memory. The method of loci is a mnemonic that links incoming information to familiar locations.

How Are Memories Stored and Maintained?

7.7 Sensory Memory Is Brief Sensory memory detects environmental information from each of the five senses and holds it for less than 1 second. Sensory memory enables the brain to experience the world as a continuous stream. Iconic memory is visual sensory memory. Echoic memory is auditory sensory memory.

7.8 Working Memory Is Active Many memory researchers today describe short-term memory more accurately as working memory. This active processing system keeps a limited number of items available for use within 20 to 30 seconds. Working memory span can be increased by chunking.

7.9 Long-Term Memory Can Be Permanent Long-term memory is a relatively permanent, virtually limitless storage space. Long-term memory is distinct from working memory, as evidenced by the serial position effect and case studies of individuals with certain types of brain damage.

7.10 Long-Term Memory Requires Consolidation Memory involves the creation or strengthening of neural circuits. Consolidation is a gradual process of memory storage. Long-term potentiation (LTP) identifies how synaptic connections may be strengthened during consolidation.

7.11 Slow Consolidation Can Be Beneficial Gradual consolidation allows memory storage to be modified after encoding. Reminders of memories and sleep can lead to memory replay. Emotion, and specifically stress hormones, enhances consolidation via the amygdala influencing the hippocampus. Flashbulb memories are vivid, persistent memories of shocking and consequential events.

7.12 Reconsolidation May Follow Retrieval Memory retrieval may result in a second consolidation window, called reconsolidation. Reconsolidation is triggered when there is something relevant and new to learn about an older memory. Reconsolidation can update or strengthen a memory.

How Are Memories Retrieved?

7.13 Retrieval Cues Bring Back the Past Anything that helps a person recall a memory is a retrieval cue. The encoding specificity principle states that any stimulus encoded along with an experience can serve as a retrieval cue during recall. Context-dependent memory can occur when aspects of the encoding context match the retrieval context. State-dependent memory can occur when a person's internal states match during encoding and recall.

7.14 Retrieval Cues Aid Prospective Memory Prospective memory is remembering what to do in the future. In daily life, many common retrieval cues, such as sticky notes and calendars, are used to jog prospective memory.

7.15 Retrieval Can Promote Forgetting Retrieval-induced forgetting occurs when retrieving an item from long-term memory impairs the ability to recall a related item in the future. Retrieval-induced forgetting can occur in conversations and in interrogations about memories of a crime.

7.16 Psychology Outside the Lab: What Is the Best Way to Ace Exams? Psychological research has identified several strategies for improving learning and exam performance. Students should distribute learning, elaborate material, practice retrieval, and use strategies such as mnemonics or visual imagery.

What Are Common Memory Mistakes?

7.17 Forgetting Is an Inability to Remember Memories are forgotten over time. The rate of forgetting is rapid at first and slows over time. Forgetting can be caused by proactive and retroactive interference from older and newer memories. Blocking is a common retrieval failure that occurs when well-known information cannot be recalled, as in the tip-of-the-tongue phenomenon. Absentmindedness is forgetting caused by inattention and the shallow encoding of events.

7.18 Persistence Is Unwanted Remembering Persistence is the continued recurrence of unwanted memories. Highly stressful or traumatic events could cause significantly disruptive persistence, as in posttraumatic stress disorder (PTSD).

7.19 People Reconstruct Events to Be Consistent Memory bias is the changing of memories so they become consistent with current beliefs, knowledge, or attitudes. Memory bias tends to cast memories in a favorable light and is common in individuals, groups, and societies.

7.20 People Make Source Misattributions Source misattribution is memory distortion that occurs when people misremember the time, place, person, or circumstances involved with a memory. The false fame effect, the sleeper effect, source amnesia, and cryptomnesia are examples. Source amnesia is memory for an event without memory for the source. Cryptomnesia is the failure to remember the source of an idea, so the idea is remembered as original even though it may not be.

7.21 Suggestibility Biases Memory Suggestibility is the development of biased memories based on misleading information. Suggestibility could play a role in eyewitness testimony, as research shows that eyewitnesses can develop biased memories based on leading questions. False memories are created as a result of the natural tendency to form mental representations of stories. Psychologists continue to debate the validity of repressed memories. Some therapeutic techniques are highly suggestive and may contribute to the occurrence of false repressed memories.

7.22 You Be the Psychologist: How Can Psychologists Inform the Use of Memory in the Courtroom? One major problem with eyewitness testimony is that people tend to remember evidence that confirms their beliefs. The way police interview eyewitnesses may also be influenced by confirmation bias. In general, people cannot differentiate accurate eyewitnesses from inaccurate ones, in part because eyewitnesses are often confident even when they are wrong.

Key Terms

absentmindedness, p. 271
amnesia, p. 245
anterograde amnesia, p. 245
blocking, p. 270
chunking, p. 253
consolidation, p. 259
cryptomnesia, p. 273
encoding, p. 251
encoding specificity principle, p. 264
episodic memory, p. 249
explicit memory, p. 246
flashbulb memories, p. 261
implicit memory, p. 246
long-term memory, p. 257
long-term potentiation (LTP), p. 259
memory, p. 244
memory bias, p. 272
mnemonics, p. 253
persistence, p. 271
priming, p. 246
proactive interference, p. 270
procedural memory, p. 247
prospective memory, p. 265
reconsolidation, p. 262
retrieval cue, p. 264
retrieval-induced forgetting, p. 266
retroactive interference, p. 270
retrograde amnesia, p. 245
schemas, p. 252
semantic memory, p. 249
sensory memory, p. 255
serial position effect, p. 257
source amnesia, p. 273
source misattribution, p. 273
suggestibility, p. 274
working memory, p. 256

Q Practice Exercises

1. What is the sequence of memory stages?
   a. storage (consolidation) → encoding → retrieval
   b. encoding → retrieval → storage (consolidation)
   c. retrieval → storage (consolidation) → encoding
   d. encoding → storage (consolidation) → retrieval

2. Which of the following phenomena increase the likelihood of forgetting? Choose all that apply.
   a. shallow encoding
   b. elaborative encoding
   c. blocking
   d. proactive interference
   e. retroactive interference
   f. chunking

3. All the details of flashbulb memories are always more accurate than those of normal memories. True or false?

4. Which finding(s) supports the conclusion that working memory and long-term memory are distinct memory processes? Choose all that apply.
   a. Patient H.M. retained working memory without being able to form new long-term memories.
   b. The primacy effect requires long-term memory, whereas the recency effect requires working memory.
   c. The primacy effect requires working memory, whereas the recency effect requires long-term memory.
   d. choices a and b
   e. choices a and c

5. How can capacity of working memory be increased?
   a. blocking
   b. maintenance rehearsal
   c. chunking
   d. reconsolidation

6. Imagine you are a manager seeking to hire a new employee. Before leaving work Monday afternoon, you look through a stack of 30 resumes organized alphabetically by last name. When you return to work Tuesday morning, which job applicant are you most likely to remember?
   a. Alvarado, because of the primacy effect
   b. Martonosi, because of persistence
   c. Russo, because of reconsolidation
   d. Zambino, because of the recency effect

7. Which statement is accurate regarding effective study strategies when preparing for an examination?
   a. Maintenance rehearsal is the most effective way to deepen encoding.
   b. Six 1-hour study sessions are more effective than one 6-hour study session.
   c. Elaborative rehearsal is likely to lead to blocking.
   d. Practiced retrieval will increase retroactive interference.

8. You ask a friend to memorize the following list: bed, rest, night, tired, blanket, pillow, relaxed. Later, you ask your friend to tell you as many words from the list as they can remember. In addition to remembering some of the words, your friend lists the word *sleep*, which did not appear on the original list. Which of the following phenomena is most related to your friend's error in recall?
   a. context-dependent encoding
   b. culturally relevant schemas
   c. false memories
   d. state-dependent encoding

9. Which memory flaw is demonstrated in each of the following examples?
   a. A friend introduces you to her brother; 5 minutes later, you find you cannot remember the brother's name.
   b. You see someone on a bus whom you think you recognize from high school. Later you realize he is familiar because he appeared in a TV commercial you have seen.

10. Fill in the blanks. People experiencing ______ amnesia are unable to recall memories from the past, whereas people experiencing ______ amnesia are unable to form new memories.

TABLE
5

8 Thinking, Decisions, Intelligence, and Language

Big Questions

APPROXIMATELY 95 PERCENT OF AMERICANS say they support organ donation, yet only 58 percent are registered organ donors (Donate Life America, 2021). In Europe, some countries report that less than 15 percent of the population participates in organ donor programs, whereas other countries have greater than 90 percent participation (Davidai et al., 2012). As in the United States, the vast majority of Europeans support organ donation, so why do participation rates vary so much? A primary difference between countries is how people are asked if they want to be organ donors. Countries such as Spain, which has the highest organ donation rate in the world, ask citizens if they want to "opt out" of organ donation. This means that all citizens are considered organ donors by default and must explicitly indicate if they do not want to participate in organ donation. Other countries ask citizens to "opt in" to organ donor programs. For example, when you get your driver's license in the United States, you have to check an additional box if you want to be an organ donor. The subtle shift from asking people to opt out instead of opt in can significantly increase the number of organ donors (DeRoos et al., 2019). We often think of our decisions as a reflection of our values or preferences. However, psychologists have shown that subtle and seemingly unimportant details, such as how a question is asked or framed, can influence the choices we make. Because of this psychological factor, both the United Kingdom and the Netherlands changed their policies in 2020 to ask citizens if they want to opt out of national organ donor programs.

This chapter is about thinking. Being able to think enables us to consider information. In Chapter 7, you learned about semantic memory, the vast store of knowledge and information you have learned throughout your life. But how do we use this information? We come up with ideas, represent ideas in our minds, use ideas to make decisions and solve problems, and communicate ideas to others. Thinking is tied to language and intelligence. Complex thinking can occur without language, but language makes it possible to express our thoughts—ideas, problems, solutions, decisions, and so on. In turn, language can shape our thoughts.

Learning Objectives

- Distinguish between analogical and symbolic representations.
- Describe the prototype and exemplar models of concepts.
- Discuss the positive and negative consequences of using schemas and scripts.

What Is Thought?

In exploring the nature of thought, this chapter draws on the findings of cognitive psychology, which seeks to understand how the mind works. As defined in Chapter 1, cognitive psychology is the study of mental functions such as intelligence, thinking, language, memory, and decision making. In short, this branch of psychology studies **cognition**, which can be broadly defined as the mental processes involved in acquiring knowledge and comprehension through thought and experiences.

cognition The mental activity that includes thinking and the understandings that result from thinking.

thinking The mental manipulation of representations of knowledge about the world.

analogical representations Mental representations that have some of the physical characteristics of what they represent.

symbolic representations Abstract mental representations that do not correspond to the physical features of objects or ideas.

8.1 Thinking Involves Two Types of Mental Representations

Cognitive psychology was originally based on two ideas about thinking: (1) Knowledge about the world is stored in the brain in representations, and (2) **thinking** is the mental manipulation of these representations. In other words, we use representations to understand objects we encounter in our environments. Thinking allows us to take information, consider it, and use it to build models of the world, set goals, and plan our actions accordingly.

We use representations in countless ways. For example, a road map represents streets. A menu represents food options. A photograph represents part of the world. The challenge for cognitive psychologists is to understand the nature of our everyday mental representations. Some of these representations are similar to maps or pictures, except that they are purely in our minds. Other representations are more abstract, such as language.

In thinking, we use two basic types of mental representations: analogical and symbolic. Together, these two types of representations form the basis of human thought and intelligence and the ability to solve the complex problems of everyday life. An analogy compares two things that are similar in some way. For instance, "A is to B as C is to D" is an analogy because in the same way that A comes right before B in the alphabet, C comes right before D. Similarly, **analogical representations** have some characteristics of what they represent. These representations are usually images. For example, maps are analogical representations that correspond to geographical layouts. The movements of a clock represent the passage of time. Family trees depict relationships between relatives. A realistic drawing of a violin is an attempt to show the musical instrument from a particular perspective (**FIGURE 8.1a**).

FIGURE 8.1
Analogical Representations and Symbolic Representations
(a) Analogical representations, such as this picture of a violin, have some characteristics of what they represent. **(b)** Symbolic representations, such as the word *violin*, are abstract and do not have relationships to the physical qualities of objects.

By contrast, **symbolic representations** are abstract. These representations are usually words, numbers, or ideas. They do not have relationships to physical qualities of objects in the world. For example, the word *violin* stands for a musical instrument (**FIGURE 8.1b**). There are no correspondences between what a violin looks like, what it sounds like, and the letters or sounds that make up the word *violin*. In Chinese, the word for violin is

小提琴

In Mandarin, it is pronounced *xiǎotíqín*, or *shiaw ti chin*. Like the English word *violin*, it is a symbolic representation because it bears no systematic relationship to the object it names. The individual characters that make up the word stand for different parts of what makes a violin, but they are arbitrary. You cannot "see" any part of a violin in their shapes.

Mental maps rely on both analogical and symbolic representations. For example, most of us can pull up a visual image of Africa's contours even if we have never seen the actual contours with our own eyes. But to understand the difference between these two types of mental representations, consider the following question about two U.S. cities: *Which is farther east: San Diego, California, or Reno, Nevada?*

If you are like most people (at least most Americans), you answered that Reno is farther east than San Diego. In fact, though, San Diego is farther east than Reno. Even if you formed an analogical representation of a map of the southwestern United States, your symbolic knowledge probably told you that a city on the Pacific Coast is always farther west than a city in a state that does not border the Pacific Ocean. You were not taking into account the way that northern Nevada juts west and Southern California juts east (**FIGURE 8.2**).

FIGURE 8.2
Mental Maps and Symbolic Limitations
Your symbolic knowledge probably informed you that California is farther west than Nevada and therefore San Diego must be west of Reno. But as you can see from this map, symbolic knowledge was inadequate in this case.

Q When an architect produces a blueprint for a new house, is this representation analogical or symbolic?

ANSWER: A blueprint is an analogical representation because it is a two-dimensional image that physically and spatially corresponds to a three-dimensional house.

8.2 Concepts Are Symbolic Representations

As the example of Reno and San Diego shows, thinking also reflects a person's general knowledge about the world. Say that you are shown a drawing of a small, yellow, dimpled object and asked to identify it. Your brain forms a mental image (analogical representation) of a lemon and provides you with the word *lemon* (symbolic representation). So far, so good.

However, in the real world your information would be incomplete. Picturing a lemon and knowing its name do not tell you what to do with a lemon. But knowing that parts of a lemon are edible helps you decide how to use the fruit. For example, you could make lemonade. Because you know that the lemon juice will taste strong and sour, you might dilute it with water and add sugar. In short, how you think about a lemon influences what you do with it.

CATEGORIES One question of interest to cognitive psychologists is how we use knowledge about objects efficiently. Think of a violin. You know it makes music, which is something it has in common with many other objects, such as drums and pianos. A violin also has strings, a quality it shares with a subset of those other objects. Because of these overlapping properties, you group these objects together.

Grouping things based on shared properties is called *categorization*. This mental activity reduces the amount of knowledge we must hold in memory and is therefore an efficient way of thinking. We can apply a category such as "musical instruments"—objects that produce music when played—automatically to all members of the category. Applying a category spares us the trouble of storing this same bit of knowledge over and over for each musical instrument. However, we

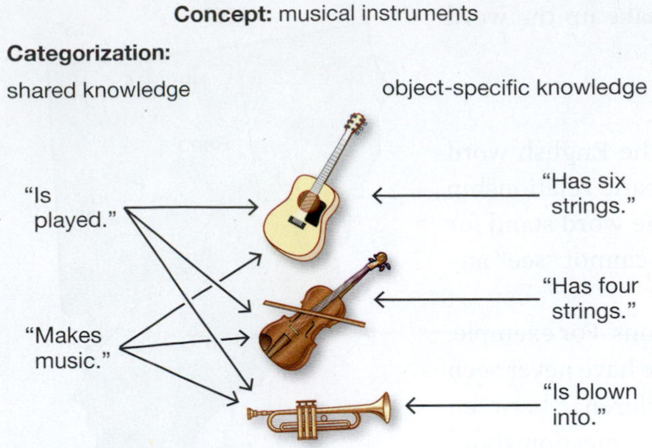

FIGURE 8.3
Categorization
We group objects into categories according to the objects' shared properties.

also have to store unique knowledge for each member of the category. For example, a violin has four strings, whereas a guitar has six strings (**FIGURE 8.3**).

CONCEPTS A **concept** is a category, or class, of related items (such as musical instruments or fruits). A concept consists of mental representations of those items. By enabling us to organize mental representations around a common theme, a concept ensures that we do not have to store every instance of an object individually. Instead, we store an abstract representation based on the properties that particular items or particular ideas share.

Cognitive psychologists have described a number of ways that people form concepts, but there are two leading models. The **prototype model**, developed by Eleanor Rosch (1975), is based on a "best example." That is, when you think about a category, you tend to look for a best example, or prototype, for that category. Once you have the prototype, you categorize new objects based on how similar they are to the prototype. In this model, each member of a category varies in how much it matches the prototype (**FIGURE 8.4**).

By contrast, the **exemplar model** proposes that any concept has no single best representation (Medin & Schaffer, 1978). Instead, all the examples, or exemplars, of category members that you have encountered form the concept. For instance, your representation of dogs is made up of all the dogs you have seen in your life. If you see an animal in your yard, you compare this animal with your memories of other animals you have encountered. If it most closely resembles the dogs you have encountered (as opposed to the cats, squirrels, rats, and other animals), you conclude it is a dog (**FIGURE 8.5**).

How would you explain the difference between a dog and a cat to someone who has never seen either? Most dogs bark, but a dog is still a dog if it does not bark. It is still a dog if it loses its tail or a leg. The exemplar model assumes that, through experience, people form a fuzzy representation of a concept because there is no single representation of any concept. And the exemplar model accounts for the observation that some category members are more prototypical than others: The prototypes are simply category members a person has encountered more often. This model points to one way in which people's thoughts are unique and formed by personal experience.

concept A category, or class, of related items consisting of mental representations of those items.

prototype model A way of thinking about concepts: Within each category, there is a best example—a prototype—for that category.

exemplar model A way of thinking about concepts: All members of a category are examples (exemplars); together they form the concept and determine category membership.

	Oranges	Tomatoes	Olives
Seeds/pits	✓	✓	✓
Edible	✓	✓	✓
Sweet	✓		

FIGURE 8.4
The Prototype Model of Concepts
According to the prototype model, some items within a group or class are more representative than others of that category. For this reason, an orange seems to be the prototype of the category "fruit." By contrast, olives do not seem to be very representative of the category.

FIGURE 8.5
The Exemplar Model of Concepts
Quick—what animal are you looking at? Is it a dog or a sheep or a pig? How does it match your exemplars for these animals? It is actually a Mangalitsa pig.

CONCEPTUAL THINKING IN THE BRAIN Brain imaging methods have enabled researchers to study how different types of knowledge are represented in brain activity (Ghio et al., 2016; Haxby et al., 2014). As mentioned in Chapter 4, patterns of brain activity can be used to identify aspects of conscious experience, such as whether people are looking at faces or objects. Imaging studies have shown that different categories of objects, such as animals or tools, are represented in different regions of the brain based on our perception of those objects (Martin, 2007). Thinking about animals activates visual areas, indicating that simply what they look like allows us to categorize objects appropriately as animals. For tools, however, brain activity occurs in regions of the brain involved in movement as well as visual areas, suggesting that we categorize certain objects as tools by how we use them in addition to what they look like (Martin et al., 1996).

In addition, we categorize some objects in multiple ways. An imaging study found that patterns of brain activity could differentiate thoughts about animals that pose threats to humans from thoughts about those that do not, even across animal classes (Connolly et al., 2016). We most likely have this ability because categorizing animals as dangerous or not dangerous is adaptive, whether those animals are mammals, reptiles, or bugs. These different patterns of brain activity reflect the different properties of categories of objects in our environment.

Q **Imagine you are learning how to identify edible mushrooms. To make your judgment, you compare all fungi in the environment to the portabella mushrooms in the grocery store. Are you using a prototype or exemplar model of concept development?**

ANSWER: You are using a prototype model because you are categorizing fungi as edible or not based on a comparison to your "best example" of portabella mushrooms.

8.3 Schemas Organize Useful Information About Environments

The prototype and exemplar models explain how we classify objects we encounter and how we represent those objects in our minds. But when we think about aspects of the world, our knowledge extends well beyond a simple list of facts about the specific items we encounter. Instead, a different class of knowledge enables us to interact with the complex realities of our environments. As we move through various real-world settings, we act appropriately by drawing on knowledge of which objects, behaviors, and events apply to each setting. Knowledge of how to behave in each setting relies on schemas. As discussed in Chapter 7, schemas help us perceive, organize, understand, and process information. For example, at a casino blackjack table, it is appropriate to squeeze in between the people already sitting down. If a stranger tried to squeeze into a group of people dining together in a restaurant, however, the group's reaction would likely be quite negative. We can use schemas because common situations have consistent rules (e.g., libraries are quiet and contain books) and because people have specific roles within situational contexts (e.g., a librarian behaves differently in a library than a reader does).

One common type of schema helps us understand the sequence of events in certain situations. Roger Schank and Robert Abelson (1977) have referred to these schemas about sequences as scripts. A **script** is a schema that directs behavior over time within a situation. For example, *going to the movies* is a script most of us are familiar with (**FIGURE 8.6**). For example, we expect to buy a ticket or print one if we bought it online. Next, we might buy a snack before selecting a seat.

(a)
(b)
(c)

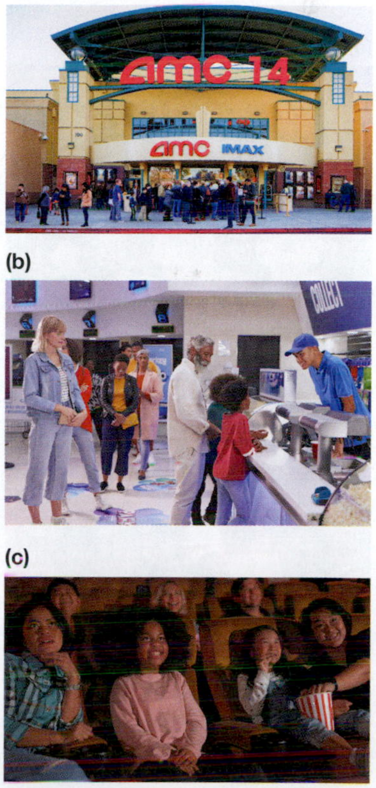

FIGURE 8.6
Script Theory of Schemas
Your script for going to the movies might include **(a)** purchasing a ticket, **(b)** getting a snack, and **(c)** sitting quietly while watching the movie.

script A schema that directs behavior over time within a situation.

FIGURE 8.7
A Teen Draws a Scientist
A special program at the Virginia Institute of Marine Science brings real-life scientists into classrooms at area schools. At the beginning of one semester, a student at Booker T. Washington Middle School drew the scientist on the left. At the end of that semester, after months of interacting with a marine researcher who was a woman, the same student produced the drawing on the right.

Popcorn is a traditional snack at movie theaters. Caviar is not. Although quiet talking might be appropriate before the movie, most of us expect talking to cease once the feature begins.

In general, schemas and scripts allow us to organize information and common scenarios to help us understand and process information more efficiently. However, sometimes schemas, like prototypes, have unintended consequences, such as reinforcing sexist or racist beliefs or other **stereotypes**. For example, when children and teens are asked to draw a scientist, very few draw women as scientists, because they unconsciously associate being a scientist with being male (Chambers, 1983; McCann & Marek, 2016; FIGURE 8.7). Similarly, an analysis of comments on the website Rate My Professors shows that words like *genius* and *smart* are used much more often to describe male professors than female professors (Jaschik, 2015).

stereotypes Cognitive schemas that allow for easy, fast processing of information about people based on their membership in certain groups.

Gender roles are the prescribed behaviors for females and males within a culture. They represent a type of schema that operates at the unconscious level. In other words, we follow gender roles without consciously knowing we are doing so. One reason we need to become aware of the way schemas direct our thinking is that they may unconsciously cause us to think, for example, that women are less qualified to become STEM scientists (O'Brien et al., 2017) or are less likely to be geniuses. Indeed, by age 6, girls are less likely to believe members of their gender are "really, really smart" and by this age also begin avoiding activities that are associated with being that smart (Bian et al., 2017).

Such gender role stereotypes can limit women's opportunities. In the past, orchestra conductors always chose men for principal positions because the conductors believed that women did not play as well as men. The schema of women as inferior musicians interfered with the conductors' ability to rate auditioners objectively when the conductors knew the names and genders of the musicians. After recognizing this bias, the top North American orchestras began holding auditions with the musicians hidden behind screens and their names withheld from the conductors (FIGURE 8.8). Since these methods were instituted, the number of women in orchestras has increased considerably (Goldin & Rouse, 2000).

(a)

(b)

FIGURE 8.8
Gender Roles Revised
(a) As shown in this photo of the New York Philharmonic from 1960, stereotypes about men's and women's abilities to play musical instruments often fueled the formation of all-male orchestras. **(b)** Changes in attitudes and in audition procedures have contributed to the diversification of talent in contemporary orchestras.

If schemas and scripts are potentially problematic, why do they persist? Their adaptive value is that, because they usually work well, these shortcuts minimize the amount of attention required to navigate familiar environments. They also enable us to recognize and avoid unusual or dangerous situations. Mental representations in all forms assist us in using and understanding information about objects and events.

Q **At fast-food restaurants we pay when we order, but at fine-dining restaurants we pay after eating. How do schemas help us behave appropriately in each place?**

ANSWER: One type of schema is a script, which provides information about the sequence of events within a specific situation.

How Do We Make Decisions and Solve Problems?

Learning Objectives

- Describe common heuristics and explain how they influence decision making.
- Discuss the role of emotions in decision making.
- Review strategies that facilitate problem solving and insight.

Throughout each day, we make decisions: what to eat for breakfast, which clothes to wear, which route to take to work or school, and so on. We scarcely notice making many of these decisions. Other decisions—such as which college to attend, whether to buy a house, and whom to marry—are much more consequential and require greater reflection. We also solve problems: how to get home if the car has broken down, how to earn extra money for a vacation, how to break bad news, and so on. Thinking enables us to use information to make decisions and solve problems.

In **decision making**, we select among alternatives. Usually, we identify important criteria and determine how well each alternative satisfies these criteria. For example, if you can go to either Paris or Cancún for spring break, you need to choose between them. What criteria would you use in making this decision (**FIGURE 8.9a**)? In **problem solving**, we overcome obstacles to move from a present state to a desired goal state. For example, if you decide to go to Paris but do not have enough money for a plane ticket, you have a problem that you must solve by finding a way to pay for the trip. In general, you have a problem when a barrier or a gap exists between where you are and where you want to be (**FIGURE 8.9b**).

decision making A cognitive process that results in the selection of a course of action or belief from several options.

problem solving Finding a way around an obstacle to reach a goal.

8.4 Decision Making Often Involves Heuristics

Many decisions are made under some degree of risk—that is, uncertainty about the possible outcomes. For example, when you chose the college you attend now, you could not know for certain that your experience would be a good one. When making this choice you might have weighed all the evidence about the relative advantages of attending your college against the other options you had available and decided that your college was likely the best option. When we think about decision making, we tend to imagine this type of reasoned decision: comparing the options and choosing the one that is likely to be the best given the available information. However, if you think about the choices we make every day, they can vary from this type of reasoned decision quite a bit. For instance, why do some people avoid flying but have no problem driving, when the probability of being hurt or dying in a car crash is much higher than the chances of being involved in a plane crash? Why do people who want to lose weight sometimes choose to eat

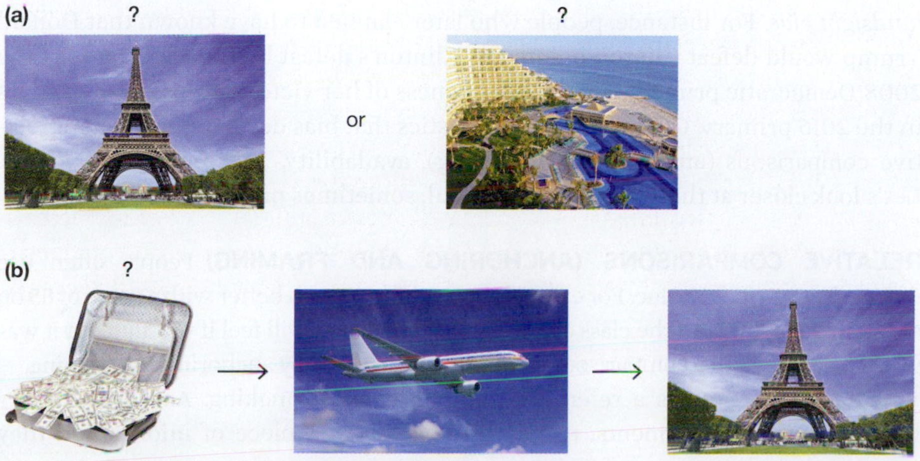

FIGURE 8.9
Decision Making Versus Problem Solving
(a) If you have two options, you need to choose between them by making a decision. Perhaps you find yourself in the rather nice position of having to choose between Paris and Cancún.
(b) If a problem arises once your decision is made, you need to solve it. Perhaps you are wondering how to afford your plane ticket.

high-calorie junk food when they are tired or stressed? Why do you go to a movie with your friend when you should be studying for a midterm?

For most of psychology's history, the prevailing theory was that people are rational—that they make decisions by considering possible alternatives and choosing the best one. This theory, which is common in economics, highlighted how people should make decisions. In the 1970s, the researchers Daniel Kahneman and Amos Tversky (1979) shattered many intuitions and theories about how people make decisions by focusing less on what people *should* do and more on what they *actually* do. Through their research, Kahneman and Tversky helped us understand that people are far from calm and rational thinkers. Rather, decision makers are biased, use irrelevant criteria, and can be unduly influenced by their emotions. These findings have had impacts on many fields, including economics, politics, and finance. In 2002 Kahneman became the first psychologist to win the Nobel Prize, specifically the Nobel Prize in Economic Sciences. (The Nobel Prize is awarded only to living scientists. Tversky died in 1996, but he was mentioned in the announcement.)

heuristics Shortcuts (rules of thumb or informal guidelines) used to reduce the amount of thinking that is needed to make decisions.

In examining how people make everyday decisions, Kahneman and Tversky identified several common mental shortcuts (rules of thumb or informal guidelines). Known as **heuristics**, these shortcuts in thinking are fast and efficient strategies that people typically use to make decisions. Heuristic thinking often occurs unconsciously: We are not aware of taking these mental shortcuts. Indeed, since the processing capacity of the conscious mind is limited, heuristic processing is useful partly because it requires minimal cognitive resources and allows us to focus on other things. Heuristic thinking can be adaptive because under some circumstances it is beneficial to make quick decisions rather than weigh all the evidence before deciding. Why do some people always want to buy the second-cheapest item, no matter what they are buying? They believe that by using this strategy, they save money but avoid purchasing the worst products. Other people want to buy only brand-name items. Such quick rules of thumb often provide reasonably good decisions, with outcomes that are acceptable for the individuals.

As Tversky and Kahneman have demonstrated, however, heuristics can result in biases, and these biases may lead to errors, faulty decisions, erroneous beliefs, and false predictions. In fact, as noted in Chapter 1, heuristic thinking is one of the principal sources of biases in reasoning. Consider the 2016 U.S. presidential election. Right until the results started arriving on election night, forecasters predicted a Hillary Clinton victory. Many of Clinton's supporters were overly optimistic because of *confirmation bias*, focusing only on information that supported their views. In addition, when events turned out contrary to their predictions, many people created after-the-fact explanations. This error in reasoning is known as *hindsight bias*. For instance, people who later claimed to have known that Donald Trump would defeat Clinton pointed to Clinton's defeat by Barack Obama in the 2008 Democratic primary and the narrowness of her victory over Bernie Sanders in the 2016 primary. Other common heuristics that bias decision making are relative comparisons (anchoring and framing), availability, and representativeness. Let's look closer at these sometimes helpful, sometimes problematic strategies.

RELATIVE COMPARISONS (ANCHORING AND FRAMING) People often use comparisons to judge value. For example, you will feel much better with a score of 85 on an exam if you find out the class average was 75 than you will feel if you find out it was 95. In making relative comparisons, people are influenced by anchoring and framing.

anchoring The tendency, in making judgments, to rely on the first piece of information encountered or information that comes most quickly to mind.

An *anchor* serves as a reference point in decision making. **Anchoring** occurs when, in making judgments, people rely on the first piece of information they encounter or on information that comes most quickly to mind (Epley & Gilovich, 2001). For example, a study demonstrating the anchoring effect asked participants to estimate the year the telephone was invented. Before providing this estimate, however, half of the participants were asked if the telephone was invented before or after 1850, and the other half were asked if the telephone was invented before or after 1920. Although the participants' estimates were correctly between 1850 and 1920 (the telephone was invented in 1876), those who were first asked if the telephone was invented before or after 1850 estimated it was invented in 1870, whereas those who were asked about 1920 estimated the telephone was invented in 1900. The initial year participants were asked to consider (1850 or 1920) served as an anchor, or reference point. When asked to generate an estimate of the actual year the telephone was invented, participants adjusted their response from this initial reference point, resulting in different estimations depending on whether this initial number was too long ago or too recent (Jacowitz & Kahneman, 1995).

After making an initial judgment based on an anchor, people compare subsequent information to that anchor and adjust away from the anchor until they reach a point where the information seems reasonable. People often adjust insufficiently, leading to erroneous judgments (Asch, 1946). Suppose you are shopping for a used car. The salesperson describes one vehicle as having high mileage and being slightly rusty, dependable, fuel efficient, and clean. The same salesperson describes a second vehicle as being clean, fuel efficient, dependable, and slightly rusty, with high mileage. Which car would you choose? Even though the descriptions are identical, people are influenced by the order of presentation and adjust their impressions based on the first few attributes listed, which serve as the initial anchors. Anchoring effects can influence many types of decisions.

The way information is presented can alter how people perceive their choices. Would you rather take a course where you have a 70 percent chance of passing or one where you have a 30 percent chance of failing? Even though the chances of passing (or failing) are identical, many students would choose the first course. This decision is influenced by how the choice is framed. **Framing** a choice by emphasizing the potential loss or potential gain can lead to different decisions. Research on framing indicates that when people make choices, they may weigh losses and gains differently. They are generally much more concerned with costs than with benefits, an emphasis known as *loss aversion* (Kahneman, 2007; **FIGURE 8.10**).

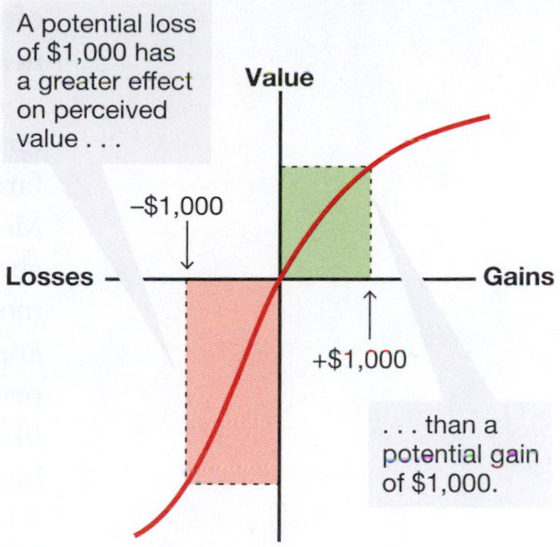

FIGURE 8.10
Loss Aversion
Suppose you bought a stock. How bad would you feel if the value dropped and you sold the stock for a loss of $1,000 (lower left)? By contrast, how good would you feel if the value rose and you sold the stock for a profit of $1,000 (upper right)? For most people, potential losses affect decision making more than potential gains do.

framing In decision making, an emphasis on the potential losses or potential gains from at least one alternative.

AVAILABILITY HEURISTIC The **availability heuristic** is the general tendency to make a decision based on the answer that comes most easily to mind. In other words, when we think about events or make decisions, we tend to rely on information that is easy to retrieve. Recall the study on false fame discussed in Chapter 7. Some participants read aloud a list of made-up names. The next day, those names were available in those participants' memories, even if the participants could not remember where they had heard the names. Based on their familiarity with the names, the participants decided the people were famous.

availability heuristic Making a decision based on the answer that most easily comes to mind.

As an example of the availability heuristic, answer the following question: Is *r* more commonly the first letter in a word or the third letter?

r _ _ _ _ _? or _ _ r _ _?

How did you determine the answer to this question? If you are like most people, you thought of words with *r* as the first letter (such as *right* and *read*). Then you thought of words with *r* as the third letter (such as *care* and *sir*). Because words with *r* at the beginning came most easily to mind, you concluded that *r* is more often the first letter of a word. However, *r* is much more likely to be the third letter in a word.

Now consider this question: In most industrialized countries, are there more farmers or more librarians? If you live in an agricultural area, you probably said farmers. If you do not live in an agricultural area, you probably said librarians. Most people who answer this question think of the librarians they know (or know about) and the farmers they know (or know about). If they can retrieve many more instances in one category, they assume it is the larger category. In fact, there are many more farmers than librarians in most industrialized countries. Because people who live in cities and suburbs tend not to meet many farmers, they are likely to believe there are more librarians. Information that is readily available biases decision making.

representativeness heuristic
Placing a person or an object in a category if that person or object is similar to one's prototype for that category.

REPRESENTATIVENESS HEURISTIC The **representativeness heuristic** is the tendency to place a person or an object in a category if the person or object is similar to our prototype for that category. We use this heuristic when we base a decision on the extent to which each option reflects what we already believe about a situation. For example, say that Helena is intelligent, ambitious, and scientifically minded. She enjoys working on mathematical puzzles, talking with other people, reading, and gardening. Would you guess that she is a cognitive psychologist or a postal worker? Most people would use the representativeness heuristic: Because her characteristics seem more representative of psychologists than of postal workers, they would guess that Helena is a cognitive psychologist.

But the representativeness heuristic can lead to faulty thinking if we fail to take other information into account. One very important bit of information is the *base rate*. This term refers to how frequently an event occurs. People pay insufficient attention to base rates in reasoning. Instead, they focus on whether the information presented is representative of one conclusion or another. For example, there are many more postal workers than cognitive psychologists, so the base rate for postal workers is higher than that for cognitive psychologists. Therefore, any given person, including Helena, is much more likely to be a postal worker. Although Helena's traits may be more representative of cognitive psychologists overall, they also likely apply to a large number of postal workers.

Q Why might someone be more inclined to buy an item with an expensive regular price that is on sale than a similar item at a reasonable and equivalent regular price?

ANSWER: The expensive price serves as an anchor for what a price should be for the item, so the sale price may seem more attractive than the equivalent regular price for an item that was never overpriced.

8.5 Emotions Influence Decision Making

Kahneman and Tversky's work showed that decisions are often biased by heuristics, or shortcuts in reasoning. Another factor that can bias decisions, sometimes in unexpected ways, is emotion. Think about the effects of emotions on your own decision making. For example, would you prefer to go out dancing in a nightclub or to a poetry reading in a quiet café? In considering this question, did you think rationally about all the implications of either choice? Or did you consider how you would feel in either situation?

INTEGRAL EMOTIONS INFORM CHOICE VALUE Emotions influence decision making in several ways (Lerner et al., 2015; Phelps et al., 2014). One way emotion can influence decisions is by providing an internal signal about the value of different choice options. If you are deciding between going to a nightclub or a poetry reading, there are many factors you could consider. You might consider who else will be there or how far you have to travel. These things might make one option more appealing, or valuable, than the other. If you consider how you would feel in both situations, then your anticipated emotion provides a signal about the relative value of the two choice options. Choices you anticipate will elicit a better feeling are more valuable. In this way, the emotion is *integral* to the decision. The real or anticipated emotional reaction that arises naturally from considering the choice provides information about the value of the choice that can help guide the decision.

For example, as mentioned in the previous section, loss aversion is the tendency to weigh potential losses more than gains when making decisions. One factor that has been hypothesized to contribute to loss aversion is the greater emotional impact of a potential loss than a potential gain of the same or greater amount. In other words, it is suggested that people are loss averse because losses hurt more than gains feel good.

In a test of this hypothesis, Peter Sokol-Hessner and colleagues (2009) asked participants to decide whether or not to take a gamble in which they could potentially win money or lose money. To assess the emotional reaction to losses and gains, the researchers assessed autonomic arousal. Participants who showed greater arousal to losses, as opposed to gains, were also more loss averse. That is, if the prospect of losing money was more emotionally arousing than the prospect of winning money, participants were more likely to make choices to avoid losses.

As you learned in Chapter 2, a correlation does not imply causation, so a correlation between arousal and loss aversion does not prove that emotional arousal to losses caused loss aversion. To demonstrate a causal relationship between arousal and loss aversion, the researchers would need to manipulate arousal and show that it changes loss aversion. To do so, Sokol-Hessner and colleagues (2015) conducted two additional studies. They showed that teaching people a strategy to manage their emotional reaction to the choice reduced both arousal and loss aversion, and giving a drug that reduced arousal also made people less loss averse.

For some decisions, such as trading stocks, loss aversion and emotional reactions are associated with worse decisions. A study of stock traders found that the greater a trader's arousal response to market losses, the worse the long-term profits (Lo & Repin, 2002). However, at other times, the emotions integral to decisions provide signals that are important for making a good choice. There are many factors that go into choosing whom to marry. For most people, feeling love for their potential spouse is an essential one.

AFFECTIVE FORECASTING People use their emotional responses to choices in the moment to help guide decisions, but another way people often use emotion to guide decisions is by choosing to do things they believe will make them happy in the future and avoiding doing things they believe they will later regret. Unfortunately, people are poor at **affective forecasting**—predicting how they will feel about things in the future (Gilbert & Wilson, 2007). Even more important, people generally do not realize how poor they are at predicting their future feelings.

affective forecasting The tendency for people to overestimate how events will make them feel in the future.

People overestimate how happy they will be to experience positive events, such as having children or seeing their candidate win an election. Likewise, they overestimate the extent to which negative events—such as breaking up with a romantic partner, losing a job, or being diagnosed with a serious medical illness—will affect them in the future (Gilbert et al., 1998; Wilson & Gilbert, 2003). In one study,

FIGURE 8.11

Faulty Affective Forecasting

When soccer fans were asked to predict their happiness if their team won or lost a championship game, they expected to be much happier if their team won and much less happy if their team lost. One week after the game, however, the winning team's fans were not as happy as they expected to be, whereas the losing team's fans were happier than they expected to be.

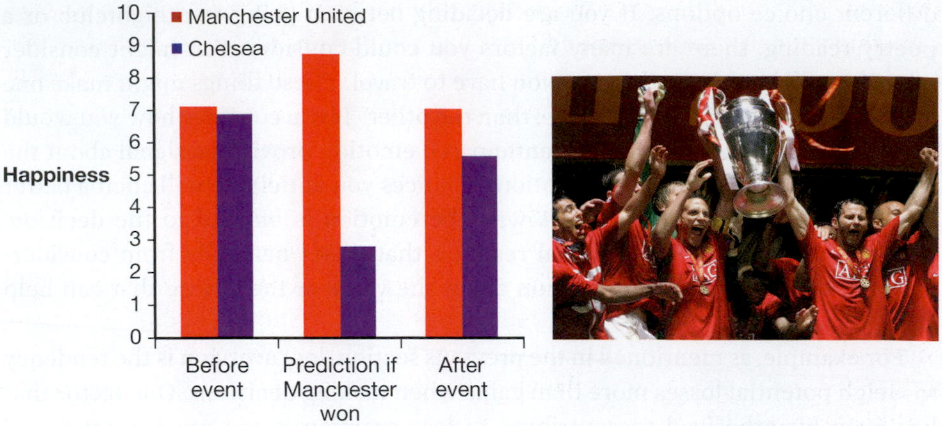

die-hard soccer fans were asked to predict their level of happiness if Manchester won the contest between Manchester United and Chelsea for the 2008 UEFA Champions League soccer final. Before the match, there were no differences in happiness between Manchester United and Chelsea fans. Manchester United fans expected to be much happier than Chelsea fans if Manchester won the game. Seven days after Manchester won, however, the team's fans were less happy than they expected to be, whereas Chelsea fans were much happier than they expected to be (Dolan & Metcalfe, 2010; **FIGURE 8.11**). Likewise, when we think about having children, we tend to focus on the joyful aspects of child rearing and downplay the struggles. When we think about the death of a loved one, we consider only the immediate, intense pain. Over time, however, life continues, with its daily joys and sorrows. The pleasure of the gain or the pain of the loss becomes less prominent against the backdrop of everyday events.

After a negative event, people engage in strategies that help them feel better (Gilbert & Wilson, 2007). For example, they rationalize why the event happened, and they minimize the event's importance. These strategies are generally adaptive in that they protect the sufferers' mental health. After all, making sense of an event helps reduce its negative emotional consequences. Even after suffering anguish because of a negative event, most people will adapt and return to their typical positive outlook.

People have an amazing capacity for manufacturing happiness. One study found that people who had been paralyzed were more optimistic about their futures than were people who had won lotteries (Brickman et al., 1978). Generally, however, people seem unaware that they can find positive outcomes from tragic events. When asked to predict how they will feel following a tragic event, people overestimate their pain and underestimate how well they will cope with the event (Gilbert et al., 2004).

AFFECTIVE STATES INCIDENTALLY BIAS DECISIONS In contrast to emotions that are integral to, and derive from, the choice being made, affective states that are completely unrelated to choices can also bias decisions. In these cases, the affect or emotion is *incidental* to the choice (Lerner et al., 2015; Phelps et al., 2014). For example, have you ever rudely snapped at someone because you were angry about something else? Have you ever made a decision to buy something when you were in a bad mood and regretted it later? In these examples, an affective state, being angry or in a bad mood, influenced unrelated decisions.

An example of the influence of incidental affective states on decision making was found with the *endowment effect*. The endowment effect is the tendency to value things we own more than we would pay to buy them—as if the fact that we own something endows it with some additional value in our minds. A study by Jennifer Lerner and colleagues (2004) found that participants in a neutral or slightly happy mood showed the typical endowment effect: That is, the price participants required to sell an object they owned was more than the price participants were willing to pay to buy the same object. However, participants who were in a sad mood showed a reversal of the endowment effect: They required less to sell an object than they were willing to pay to buy the same object. Why would an unrelated mood change the price required to buy or sell? According to the *appraisal tendency framework*, moods elicit tendencies, such as wanting to move toward something or away from it (Lerner et al., 2015). These mood-related tendencies influence how we appraise unrelated information and choices encountered while in that affective state.

People may rely on their moods to inform decisions and judgments even more if they are unaware of a mood's source. For instance, Norbert Schwarz and Gerald Clore (1983) asked people to rate their overall life satisfaction. To answer this question, people potentially must consider a multitude of factors, including situations, expectations, personal goals, and accomplishments. As the researchers noted, however, in arriving at their answers respondents did not labor through all these elements but instead seemed to rely on their current moods. People in good moods rated their lives as satisfactory, whereas people in bad moods gave lower overall ratings (**FIGURE 8.12**). Likewise, people's evaluations of plays, lectures, politicians, and even strangers were influenced by their moods. If people were made aware of the sources of their moods (as when a researcher suggested that a good mood might be caused by the bright sunshine), their incidental feelings had less influence over their judgments.

(a)

(b)

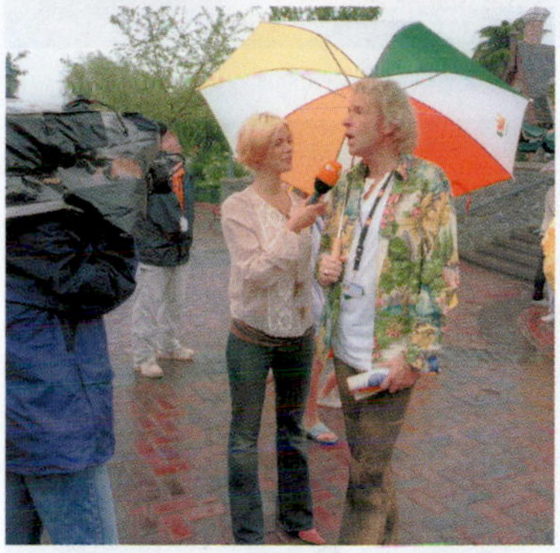

FIGURE 8.12
Moods and Life Satisfaction
Mood affects a person's satisfaction with life, and weather affects mood. As a result, people may report being more satisfied with their lives on **(a)** sunny days than on **(b)** rainy days.

Q **People sell stocks when the stock market goes down even though many finance experts advise investors to retain or increase their holdings at such times. How does loss aversion explain this behavior?**

ANSWER: People may weigh potential losses more than gains, and as a result they are more concerned with losing additional money if the stock market goes down further than with making money if the stock market goes up.

8.6 Big Data, Mood, and Decisions

YOU BE THE PSYCHOLOGIST

Psychological research on decision making typically investigates individuals making decisions in the laboratory or in online studies. However, data concerning our decisions are being gathered daily by stores, banks, online retailers, government agencies, social media companies, cell phone providers, apps, health care providers, and internet search engines. This "big data" on decisions (see Chapter 1) is used by many of these organizations, and others, for a variety of purposes. Marketers and companies with financial interests use big data on consumer decisions to find ways to increase profits. As the opening vignette of this chapter illustrates, governments use big data on decisions to design policies that help meet the goals of their societies. Increasingly, psychological scientists are also turning to big data to characterize the ways humans make decisions and the range of factors that influence choices.

Given the challenges of studying emotions in laboratory settings, the relation between decision making and emotion is a topic that scientists have started to investigate using publicly available big data sets. One such study showed that incidental affective states can have a subtle but broad influence on everyday decisions

(a)

(b)

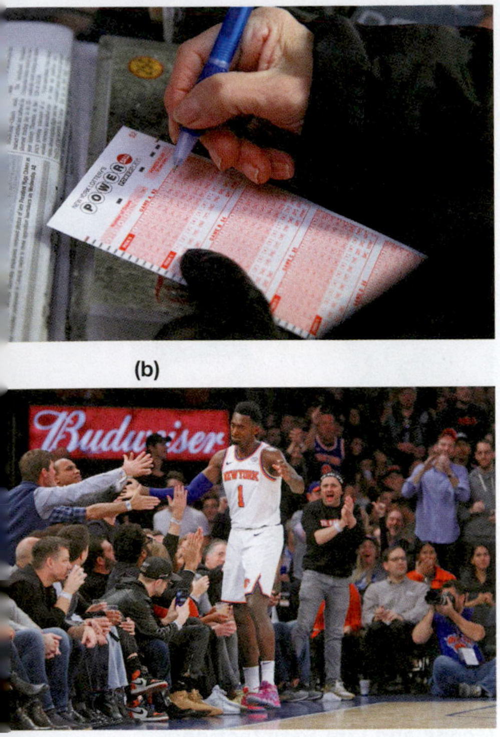

FIGURE 8.13

Lottery Sales and Sports Team Wins

Using big data that was publicly available, psychologists found that lottery sales in New York City went up the day after local sports teams did better than expected. These findings suggest that incidental affective states are related to everyday decisions.

(Otto et al., 2016). This study looked at decisions to play the lottery. Many people play the lottery, even though the odds of winning are astonishingly small and any rational decision analysis would suggest it is a waste of money. However, as research on decision making has shown, people are not always rational when making decisions, and lottery sales are a major source of revenue for local governments.

This study examined the role of incidental affective states on lottery sales in New York City. To estimate the affective state of New Yorkers, the researchers relied on findings showing that people tend to be in a good mood when things turn out better than expected (Rutledge et al., 2014). They hypothesized that having things turn out better than expected would make New Yorkers feel lucky and more optimistic, and as a result they would be more likely to play the lottery. To determine when things were better than expected, they looked at two factors that vary in daily life—the weather and the performance of local sports teams.

The researchers were interested in quantifying when the circumstances of New Yorkers were better than expected, not just good. Consistent sunny weather and teams that always win would lead people to expect good weather and winning, and they might not influence daily fluctuations in mood as much as a sunny, warm day after a string of cloudy, cold days or a mediocre local sports team beating a much better team from another city would. By examining New York City weather patterns and the performance of New York City sports teams, the researchers were able to identify specific days when the weather pattern shifted suddenly to better weather or when the local teams beat the odds and won an improbable game the night before. The researchers found that when either the weather or the performance of local sports teams was better than anticipated, lottery sales went up (**FIGURE 8.13**). To verify that it was specifically local circumstances that were related to increased lottery sales, they also examined weather patterns and sports team performance in other large cities and lottery sales in New York City, and no relationship was found.

By using big, publicly available data, this study found that even small shifts in local circumstances might influence affective states, which in turn may have an unexpected impact on whether people decide to play the lottery. How might you extend this research to discover what other types of decisions are more common when people are in a good mood? Do you think people are more likely to buy cupcakes, sign up for online dating, go out to dinner, or donate to charity if they are in a good mood? How could you use big data to investigate whether these relationships exist? How do you think everyday decisions might differ when public events cause people to be in a bad mood? And how might you use public data to determine more directly what people are feeling? Could social media postings provide insights into the emotional reactions people have to public events and their influence on everyday decisions? These are the types of questions psychologists are beginning to ask using big data. If you had access to large data sets, such as purchase decisions or trends in social media postings, what questions or hypotheses about the relationship between affective states and decisions would you want to answer? ■

Q **Why might someone in a good mood be more likely to gamble on the lottery?**

ANSWER: Incidental affective states can influence the appraisal or evaluation of unrelated decisions, such that positive moods make people more optimistic about their chances of winning the lottery.

8.7 Problem Solving Achieves Goals

Problem solving involves using available information to help achieve goals. Problems come in two forms. Some are easily defined, such as: How do you get into your car (goal) when you have locked the keys inside (problem)? How can you make enough money (problem) to spend your spring break somewhere nice (goal)? Other problems are less easily defined: What type of job are you likely to find satisfying and rewarding?

This section examines some of the best ways to solve problems. For the purposes of this discussion, people have problems when they have no simple and direct means of attaining a particular goal. To solve the problem, they must make a plan to reach an attainable goal, devise strategies to overcome obstacles to carrying out the plan, monitor progress to keep on track, and evaluate the results to see if the goal has been attained. How a person thinks about a problem can help or hinder the person's ability to find solutions.

ORGANIZATION OF SUBGOALS One approach to the study of problem solving is to identify people's steps in solving particular problems. Researchers examine how people proceed from one step to the next, the typical errors people make in negotiating tricky or unintuitive steps, and how people decide on more efficient (or, in some cases, less efficient) solutions. For example, in the classic Tower of Hanoi problem, participants are given a board that has a row of three pegs on it. The peg on one end has three disks stacked on it in order of size: small on top, medium in the middle, large on the bottom. The task is to move the disks, one at a time, to the peg on the other end without putting a larger disk on a smaller disc. Solving the problem requires breaking the task into *subgoals*, which are shown in **FIGURE 8.14**.

Using subgoals is important for many problems. Suppose that as a high school junior you decided you would like to become a doctor. To achieve this goal, you first needed to attain the more immediate subgoal of getting your bachelor's degree. Some might get their degree four years after graduating high school, while others might attend a community college part-time while working to support their families and transfer to a four-year university later. No matter the path, to get your bachelor's degree, you first need to graduate high school or receive your GED. Either of these subgoals would require developing good study skills and paying attention in class. When you are facing a complex problem and the next step is not obvious, identifying the appropriate steps or subgoals and their order can be challenging.

CHANGING REPRESENTATIONS TO OVERCOME OBSTACLES *Have you heard about the new restaurant that opened on the moon? It has great food but no atmosphere!* The premise of this joke is that *atmosphere* means one thing when interpreted in light of the restaurant schema but something else in the context of the moon. Humor often violates an expectation, so "getting" the joke means rethinking some common representation. In problem solving, too, we often need to revise a mental representation to overcome an obstacle.

One strategy that problem solvers commonly use to overcome obstacles is **restructuring** the problem. This technique consists of representing the problem in a novel way. Ideally, the new view reveals a solution that was not visible under the old problem structure. In one now-famous study, Martin Scheerer (1963) gave participants a sheet of paper that had a square of nine dots on it. The task was to connect all nine dots using at most four straight lines, without lifting the pencil off the page. See if you can solve this problem yourself in **FIGURE 8.15**.

In trying to solve a problem, we commonly think back to how we have solved similar problems. We tend to persist with previous strategies, or **mental sets**. These established ways of thinking are often useful, but sometimes they make it difficult to find the best solution.

The task is to move the disks to the peg on the other end. You can move only one disk at a time. You cannot place a larger disk on top of a smaller disk.

The solution is presented below. Before you look at it, simulate the task by stacking three coins of unequal size. For example, if you have U.S. coins, use a penny, a nickel, and a quarter:

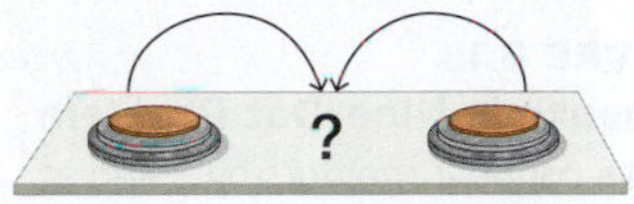

?

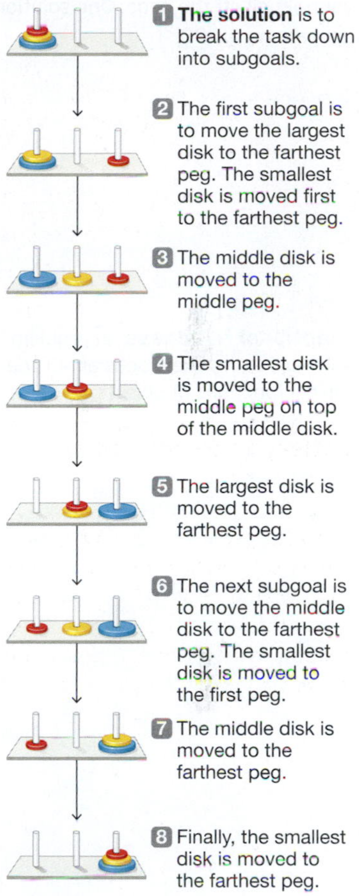

1 The solution is to break the task down into subgoals.
2 The first subgoal is to move the largest disk to the farthest peg. The smallest disk is moved first to the farthest peg.
3 The middle disk is moved to the middle peg.
4 The smallest disk is moved to the middle peg on top of the middle disk.
5 The largest disk is moved to the farthest peg.
6 The next subgoal is to move the middle disk to the farthest peg. The smallest disk is moved to the first peg.
7 The middle disk is moved to the farthest peg.
8 Finally, the smallest disk is moved to the farthest peg.

FIGURE 8.14
The Tower of Hanoi Problem

restructuring A new way of thinking about a problem that aids its solution.

mental sets Problem-solving strategies that have worked in the past.

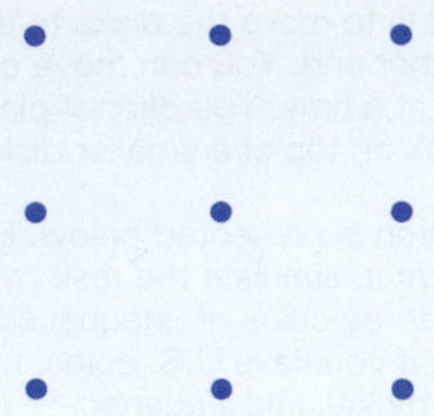

FIGURE 8.15
Scheerer's Nine-Dot Problem
Try to connect the dots by using at most four straight lines, without lifting your pencil off the page. One solution appears on p. 300.

In 1942, the psychologist Abraham Luchins demonstrated a classic example of a mental set. He asked participants to measure out specified amounts of water, such as 100 cups, using three jars of different sizes. Say that jar A held 21 cups, jar B held 127 cups, and jar C held 3 cups. The solution to this problem was to fill jar B, use jar A to remove 21 cups from jar B's 127 cups, then use jar C to remove 3 cups of water twice, leaving 100 cups in jar B. The structure to the solution is (B – A) – 2(C). Participants were given many of these problems. In each problem, the jar sizes and goal measurements differed, but the same formula applied.

Then participants were given another problem: They were given jar A, which held 23 cups; jar B, which held 49 cups; and jar C, which held 3 cups. They were asked to measure out 20 cups. Even though the simplest solution was to fill jar A and use jar C to remove 3 cups from jar A's 23, participants usually came up with a much more complicated solution that involved all three jars. Having developed a mental set of using three jars in combination to solve this type of problem, they had trouble settling on the simpler solution of using only two jars. Surprisingly, when given a problem with a simple solution for which the original formula did not work, many participants failed to solve the problem most efficiently (**FIGURE 8.16**).

functional fixedness In problem solving, having fixed ideas about the typical functions of objects.

One type of mental set results from having fixed ideas about the typical functions of objects. Such **functional fixedness** can also create difficulties in problem solving. To overcome functional fixedness, the problem solver needs to reinterpret an object's potential function (**FIGURE 8.17**). One research example involves the candle problem, developed by Karl Duncker (1945). Participants are in a room with a bulletin board on the wall. They are given a candle, a book of matches, a box of tacks, and the following challenge: *Using only these objects, attach the candle to*

	Desired water	Jar A	Jar B	Jar C
Trial 1	100	21	127	3
Trial 2	8	18	48	11
Trial 3	62	10	80	4
Trial 4	31	20	59	4
Trial 5	29	20	57	4
Trial 6	20	23	49	3
Trial 7	25	28	76	3

FIGURE 8.16
Luchins's Mental Set

FIGURE 8.17
Overcoming Functional Fixedness
Some people may think of duct tape as something used only for mending ducts. Thinking this way means missing out on the opportunity to use the material more creatively, such as by making an outfit for the prom.

the bulletin board in such a way that the candle can be lit and burn properly. Most people have trouble coming up with an adequate solution (**FIGURE 8.18**).

If people reinterpret the function of the box, however, a solution emerges. The side of the box can be tacked to the bulletin board so that it creates a stand. The candle is then placed on the box and lit. In general, participants have difficulty viewing the box as a possible stand when it is being used as a container for the tacks. When participants are shown representations of this problem with an empty box and the tacks on the table next to it, they solve the problem more easily.

FIGURE 8.18
Duncker's Candle Problem
How would you attach the candle to the bulletin board on the wall so that it can be lit and burns properly? One solution is given on p. 300.

CONSCIOUS STRATEGIES Restructuring mental representations is a valuable way to develop insight into solving a problem. Still, we often find it difficult to enact this strategy consciously when we are stuck. Fortunately, we can always apply other strategies that may help lead to a solution.

One such strategy is using an *algorithm*. An algorithm is a guideline that, if followed correctly, will always yield the correct answer. If you wanted to know the area of a rectangle, for example, you could get the right answer by multiplying its length times its width. This formula is an algorithm because it will always work. Similarly, if you follow a recipe exactly, it should always yield pretty much the same outcome. Suppose, however, you substitute one ingredient for another: You use oil instead of the butter that the recipe calls for. Here, you are using a heuristic that one type of fat is equal to another. Your result will likely be fine, but there is no guarantee.

Another good conscious strategy for overcoming obstacles is *working backward*. When the appropriate steps for solving a problem are not clear, proceeding from the goal state to the initial state can help yield a solution. Consider the water lily problem (Fixx, 1978, p. 50):

> Water lilies double in area every 24 hours. On the first day of summer there is only one water lily on the lake. It takes 60 days for the lake to be completely covered in water lilies. How many days does it take for half of the lake to be covered in water lilies?

One way to solve this problem is to work from the initial state to the goal state: You figure that on day 1 there is one water lily, on day 2 there are two water lilies, on day 3 there are four water lilies, and so on, until you discover how many water lilies there are on day 60 and you see which day had half that many. But if you work backward, from the goal state to the initial state, you realize that if on day 60 the lake is covered in water lilies and that *water lilies double every 24 hours*, then on day 59 half of the lake must have been covered in water lilies.

A third good strategy for overcoming obstacles is *finding an appropriate analogy* (Reeves & Weisberg, 1994). This strategy is also known as analogical problem solving. Say that a surgeon needs to use a laser at high intensity to destroy a patient's tumor, but that laser must be aimed so as to avoid destroying the surrounding healthy tissue. The surgeon remembers reading a story about a general who wanted to capture a fortress. The general needed to move a large number of soldiers up to the fortress, but all the roads to the fortress were planted with mines. A large group of soldiers would have set off the mines, but a small group could travel safely. So the general divided the soldiers into small groups and had each group take a different road to the fortress, where the groups converged and attacked together. Because the medical problem has constraints *analogous* to the general's problem, the surgeon gets the idea to aim several lasers at the tumor from different angles. By itself, each laser will

"Never, ever, think outside the box."

Solution to Figure 8.15
One solution is truly to think outside the box: to see that keeping the lines within the box is not a requirement. Another solution is to use one *very* fat line that covers all nine dots. Solving the problem requires restructuring the representation by eliminating assumed constraints.

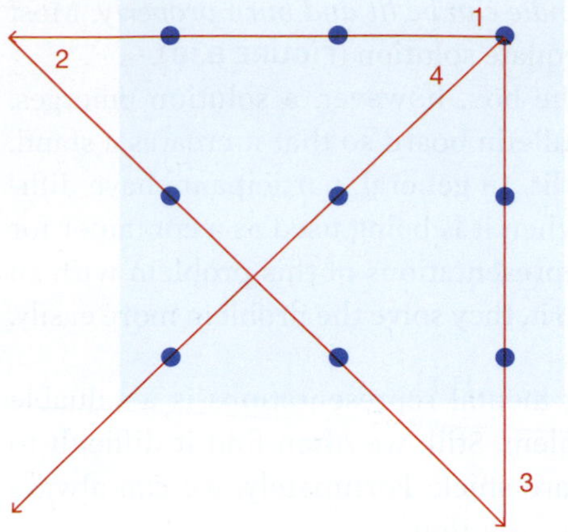

Solution to Figure 8.18
The box for the tacks can be used as a stand for the candle.

be weak enough to avoid destroying the living tissue in its path, but the combined intensity of all the converging lasers will be enough to destroy the tumor.

Transferring a problem-solving strategy means using a strategy that works in one context to solve a problem that is structurally similar. To accomplish this kind of transfer, we must pay attention to the structure of each problem. For this reason, analogous problems may enhance our ability to solve each one. Some researchers have found that participants who solve two or more analogous problems develop a schema that helps them solve similar problems (Gick & Holyoak, 1983). Analogous solutions work, however, only if we recognize the similarities between the problem we face and those we have solved and if the analogy is correct (Keane, 1987; Reeves & Weisberg, 1994).

insight The sudden realization of a solution to a problem.

SUDDEN INSIGHT Often, a problem is not identified as a problem until it seems unsolvable and the problem solver feels stuck. For example, it is only when you spot the keys in the ignition of your locked car that you know you have a problem. Sometimes, as you stand there pondering the problem, a solution will pop into your head—the "Aha" moment. **Insight** is the metaphorical mental lightbulb that goes on in your head when you suddenly realize the solution to a problem.

In 1925, the psychologist Wolfgang Köhler conducted one of psychology's most famous examples of research on insight. Convinced that some nonhuman animals could behave intelligently, Köhler studied whether chimpanzees could solve problems. He would place a banana outside a chimp's cage, just beyond the chimp's reach, and provide several sticks that the chimp could use. Could the chimp figure out how to move the banana within grabbing distance?

FIGURE 8.19
Köhler's Study on Sudden Insight
Chimpanzees try to solve problems, such as reaching bananas that are too high. In one of Köhler's studies, a chimp seemed to suddenly realize a solution. It stacked several boxes on top of each other and stood on them to reach the bananas. This behavior suggested that the chimp solved the problem through insight.

In one situation, neither of two sticks was long enough to reach the banana. One chimpanzee, who sat looking at the sticks for some time, suddenly grabbed the sticks and joined them together by placing one stick inside an opening in the other stick. With this longer stick, the chimp obtained the banana. Köhler argued that, after pondering the problem, the chimp had the insight to join the sticks into a tool long enough to reach the banana. Having solved that problem, the chimp transferred this solution to similar problems and solved them quickly (**FIGURE 8.19**).

In another classic study of insight, Norman Maier (1931) brought participants, one at a time, into a room that had two strings hanging from the ceiling and a table in the corner. On the table were several random objects, including a pair of pliers. Each participant was asked to tie the strings together. However, it was impossible to grab both strings at once: If a participant was holding one string, the other

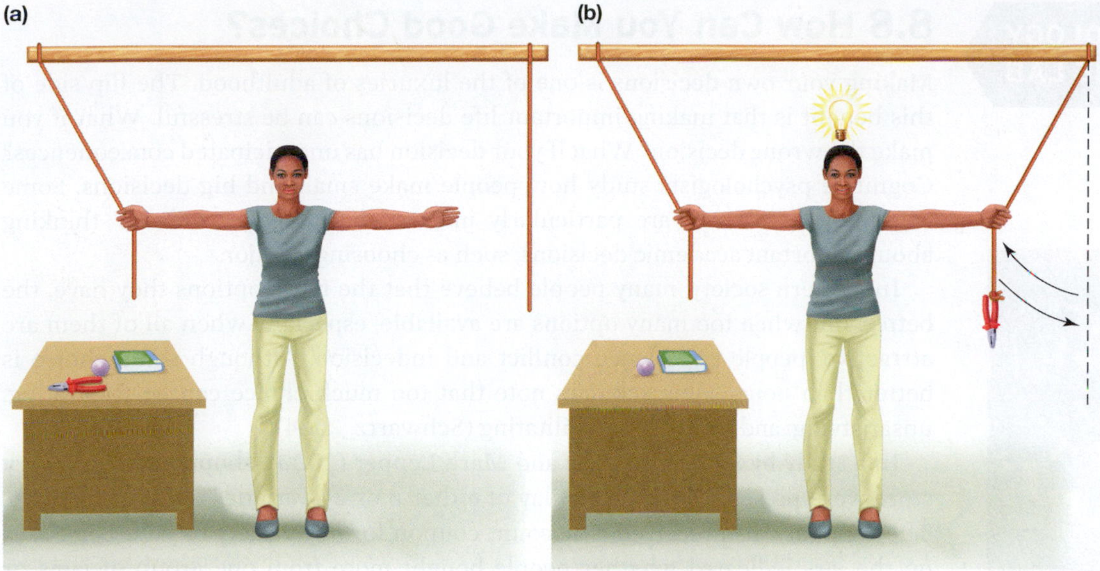

FIGURE 8.20
Maier's Study on Sudden Insight
(a) In this situation, how would you grab both strings so you could tie them together? **(b)** The solution is to weight one string with the pliers, then swing the weighted string as a pendulum that you can grab.

string was too far away to grab (**FIGURE 8.20a**). The solution was to tie the pliers onto one string and use that string as a pendulum. The participant could then hold the other string and grab the pendulum string as it swung by (**FIGURE 8.20b**).

Although a few participants eventually figured out this solution on their own, most people were stumped by the problem. After letting these people ponder the problem for 10 minutes, Maier casually crossed the room and brushed up against the string, causing it to swing back and forth. Once the participants saw the brushed string swinging, most immediately solved the problem, as if they had experienced a new insight. These participants did not report that Maier had given them the solution, however. It is possible that they did not even notice Maier's actions consciously. They all believed they had come up with the solution independently.

Maier's study also provides an example of how insight can be achieved when a problem initially seems unsolvable. In this case, most people were suffering from functional fixedness and failed to see the pliers as a pendulum weight. To solve the problem, these people needed to reconsider the possible functions of the pliers and string. As mentioned earlier, how we view or represent a problem can significantly affect how easily we solve it. Sometimes insight provides these new solutions for overcoming functional fixedness.

Learning Tip

Functional fixedness and mental sets are two problem-solving obstacles related to not thinking flexibly about objects or mental representations, respectively. To remember the difference, think of objects as having functions and of your mind as being set.

Q **Your aunt is outside in the wind and wants to fix her hair, but she does not have a mirror to help her see what she is doing. You suggest using her phone's camera. Why did she fail to think of this?**

ANSWER: Because of functional fixedness, she thinks of using her phone only for texts, calls, and taking pictures.

PSYCHOLOGY OUTSIDE THE LAB

8.8 How Can You Make Good Choices?

Making your own decisions is one of the luxuries of adulthood. The flip side of this benefit is that making important life decisions can be stressful. What if you make the wrong decision? What if your decision has unanticipated consequences? Cognitive psychologists study how people make small and big decisions. Some cognitive researchers are particularly interested in college students' thinking about important academic decisions, such as choosing a major.

In modern society, many people believe that the more options they have, the better. But when too many options are available, especially when all of them are attractive, people experience conflict and indecision. Although some choice is better than none, some scholars note that too much choice can be frustrating, unsatisfying, and ultimately debilitating (Schwartz, 2004).

In a study by Sheena Iyengar and Mark Lepper (2000), shoppers at a grocery store were presented with a display of either 6 or 24 varieties of jam to sample. The shoppers also received a discount coupon for any variety of jam. Bar codes on the jars indicated whether people bought more from one group of jams or the other. The greater variety attracted more shoppers, but it failed to produce more sales: 30 percent of those with the limited choice bought jam, whereas only 3 percent with the greater variety did so (**FIGURE 8.21**). In a second study, the investigators found that people choosing among a small number of chocolates were more satisfied with the ones they selected than were people who chose from a wider variety.

(a)
(b)

FIGURE 8.21
Too Much Choice
As part of Iyengar and Lepper's study, displays presented **(a)** 6 jams and **(b)** 24 jams. The results indicated that having many possibilities can make it difficult to choose one item.

Two approaches to decision making are "maximizing" and "satisficing." Maximizers seek to identify the perfect choice among a set of options, whereas satisficers seek to find a "good enough" choice that meets their minimum requirements (Schwartz et al., 2002). In other words, maximizers want the choice that is maximally beneficial, whereas satisficers go with a choice that is satisfactory enough. It turns out that maximizers, compared with satisficers, tend to select the objectively best choice, but those choices bring them less happiness. For example, college graduates who are maximizers land jobs with much higher salaries than their satisficing counterparts, but in the long run they are also less satisfied with their career choices (Iyengar et al., 2006).

Jennifer Kay Leach and Erika A. Patall (2013) wanted to know if these two different approaches to decision making were related to college students' tendency to second-guess their chosen majors as well as their satisfaction with their choices. The researchers surveyed 378 juniors and seniors, all of whom had declared a major. Maximizers reported engaging in more upward counterfactual thinking than satisficers. In this sort of thinking, people consider how things might have turned out better if they had made different decisions. For example, the maximizers in this study more strongly endorsed self-report items such as "I often consider how other majors would have allowed me more career opportunities/options." Such thinking was related to lower satisfaction with the chosen major. Multiple studies point to the same general pattern: Maximizers go to great effort to make good choices, but they are ultimately less satisfied with the choices they make. To find out if you are a maximizer, complete the maximization scale in **FIGURE 8.22**.

If you are a maximizer, are you doomed to always second-guess your decisions? Will you always be dissatisfied? Not necessarily. Ultimately, you get to decide how you will feel about your decision making.

The psychologist Barry Schwartz leads a research team that has conducted many studies on maximizers. In his book *The Paradox of Choice* (2004), Schwartz

1. No matter how satisfied I am with my job, it's only right for me to be on the lookout for better opportunities.
2. When I am in the car listening to the radio, I often check other stations to see if something better is playing, even if I am relatively satisfied with what I'm listening to.
3. When I watch TV, I channel surf, often scanning through the available options even while attempting to watch one program.
4. I treat relationships like clothing: I expect to try a lot on before finding the perfect fit.
5. I often find it difficult to shop for a gift for a friend.
6. Renting videos is really difficult. I'm always struggling to pick the best one.
7. When shopping, I have a hard time finding clothing that I really love.
8. I'm a big fan of lists that attempt to rank things (the best movies, the best singers, the best athletes, the best novels, etc.).
9. I find that writing is very difficult, even if it's just writing a letter to a friend, because it's so hard to word things just right. I often do several drafts of even simple things.
10. I never settle for second best.
11. Whenever I'm faced with a choice, I try to imagine what all the other possibilities are, even ones that aren't present at the moment.
12. I often fantasize about living in ways that are quite different from my actual life.
13. No matter what I do, I have the highest standards for myself.

FIGURE 8.22
Maximization Scale
For each item on this list, award yourself anywhere from 1 point (for "completely disagree") to 7 points (for "completely agree"). Then add up your points. People who get high scores on this scale are considered maximizers.

offers advice we can all use to navigate choices. Here are some of his ideas applied to the decision of which major to select in college:

1. **Approach the decision with the mindset of a satisficer.** Try to articulate your minimum requirements for a good major. You might, for instance, seek a major that would both allow you to learn about people from different cultures and help you develop business skills. You do not need to find the one best major for achieving your goals. You need to choose a major that will set you on the right path.
2. **Promise yourself that you will stick with your decision.** Schwartz calls this promise "irreversibility." We tend to be less satisfied with our decisions if we know we can change them. Know that you picked your major for a good reason and accept that decision. Schwartz notes, "The only way to find happiness and stability in the presence of seemingly attractive and tempting options is to say, 'I'm simply not going there. I've made my decision. . . . I'm not in the market—end of story'" (p. 299).
3. **Have realistic expectations.** Sure, you will probably have to take some classes that you do not enjoy. A couple of your professors might even be boring. Tests and other requirements may challenge your limits. But all majors will have such drawbacks. As with any decision, you will experience dips in satisfaction.
4. **Practice an attitude of gratitude.** Schwartz finds that people who actively reflect on the good that has come from their decisions are more satisfied with those decisions than people who linger on the bad. Each semester, as you get ready to register for the next semester's classes, list 5 to 10 things you are grateful for related to your major: something surprising you learned, an eye-opening experience you had because of a class, a provocative conversation you had with an engaging professor, a new friend you met in class, and so on.

Finally, whether you are choosing a major or making another major decision, keep in mind that multiple perfectly fine options likely exist. Thinking carefully about your choices and making a "good enough" decision might help free your mind and give you time to engage in other, equally worthwhile pursuits. ■

Q When chef Gordon Ramsay tries to save a failing restaurant, he often reduces the number of items on the menu. Why might fewer options be better for maximizing customers?

ANSWER: With too many options, maximizers find it difficult to choose, causing stress and dissatisfaction. Limiting the menu can reduce negative feelings and thoughts during and after the decision-making process.

How Do We Understand Intelligence?

Learning Objectives

- Identify common measures of intelligence and discuss their validity.
- Review theories and research related to general intelligence, fluid intelligence, crystallized intelligence, and multiple intelligences.
- Discuss the relationship between intelligence and cognitive performance.
- Summarize research examining genetic and environmental influences on intelligence.

So far, this chapter has considered how people use knowledge when they think, how they make decisions, and how they solve problems. All of these cognitive processes are thought to contribute to intelligent behavior. Now it is time to consider what it means to think *intelligently*.

Sometimes thought processes lead to great ideas and creative discoveries, but other times they lead to bad decisions and regret. Inevitably, some people seem to be better at using knowledge than others. When people are good at using knowledge, we say they are intelligent. Thus, **intelligence** is the ability to use knowledge to reason, make decisions, make sense of events, solve problems, understand complex ideas, learn quickly, and adapt to environmental challenges.

intelligence The ability to use knowledge to reason, make decisions, make sense of events, solve problems, understand complex ideas, learn quickly, and adapt to environmental challenges.

Think for a minute about that last skill: adapting to environmental challenges. Because environments differ, environmental challenges can differ. Someone considered intelligent in an industrialized nation may struggle to survive in the jungle, where being able to judge weather, identify local hazards, and find and prepare food are better indicators of intelligence. Do these differences mean that intelligence reflects environment? Psychologists have long struggled to define intelligence, and disagreement continues about what it means to be intelligent.

Psychological research generally focuses on two questions: How do knowledge and its applications in everyday life translate into intelligence? And how much is intelligence determined by genes and by environment (Neisser et al., 1996)?

8.9 Intelligence Is Measured with Standardized Tests

The *psychometric* approach to measuring intelligence focuses on how people perform on standardized tests that assess mental abilities. These tests examine what people know and how they solve problems. For much of the past century, the psychometric approach to intelligence has been dominant and influential. This approach has especially affected how we view intelligence in everyday life, at least within industrialized nations.

There are two main types of standardized tests. *Achievement tests* assess people's current levels of skill and of knowledge. *Aptitude tests* seek to predict what tasks, and perhaps even what jobs, people will be good at in the future. For both kinds of tests, the stakes can be high. People's performance on them can hugely affect their lives.

FIGURE 8.23
Alfred Binet
Binet launched the psychometric approach to assessing intelligence.

The psychometric measurement of intelligence began in the early twentieth century. At the encouragement of the French government, the psychologist Alfred Binet developed a method of assessing intelligence (FIGURE 8.23). Binet's goal was to identify children in the French school system who needed extra attention and special instruction. He proposed that intelligence is best understood as a collection of high-level mental processes. Accordingly, with the help of his assistant Théodore Simon, Binet developed a test for measuring each child's vocabulary, memory, skill with numbers, and other mental abilities. The result was the Binet-Simon Intelligence Scale. One assumption underlying the test was that each child might do better on some components by chance, but how the child performed on average across the different components would indicate an overall level of intelligence. Indeed, Binet found that scores on his tests were consistent with teachers' beliefs about a child's abilities *and* with the child's grades.

In 1919, the psychologist Lewis Terman, at Stanford University, modified the Binet-Simon test and established normative scores for American children (average scores for each age). This test—the Stanford Revision of the Binet-Simon Scale, known colloquially as the Stanford-Binet—remains the most widely used test for children in the United States. In 2003, it was revised for the fifth time.

In 1939, the psychologist David Wechsler developed an intelligence test for adults. Not only was the Stanford-Binet unsuitable for adults, but Wechsler was dissatisfied with various features of that scale, including its reliance on verbal information and its assessment of intelligence by a single score. The Wechsler Adult Intelligence Scale (WAIS)—the most current version being the WAIS-IV, released in 2008—has two parts. Each part consists of several tasks that provide separate scores. The verbal part measures aspects such as comprehension ("Why do people buy home insurance?"), vocabulary ("What does *corrupt* mean?"), and general knowledge ("What day of the year is Independence Day in the United States?"). It also includes tests of working memory, such as short-term memory capacity. The performance part involves nonverbal tasks—such as arranging pictures in proper order, assembling parts to make a whole object, and identifying a picture's missing features—and measures of reaction time (**FIGURE 8.24**).

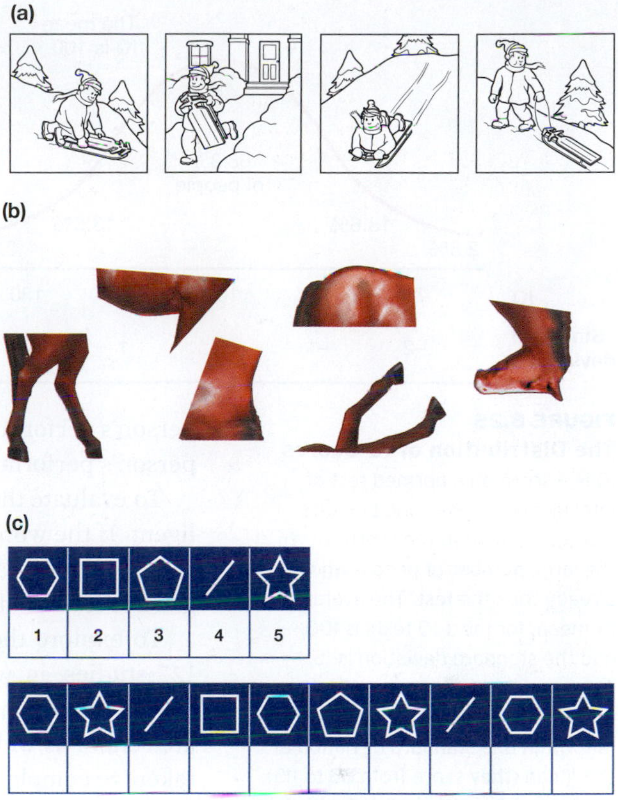

FIGURE 8.24
Test Items Measuring Performance
The performance part of intelligence tests includes nonverbal tasks. Here are some examples similar to items used in the WAIS III. **(a)** Picture arrangement: These pictures tell a story. Put them in the right order to tell the story. **(b)** Object assembly: If these pieces are put together correctly, they make something. Put them together as fast as you can. **(c)** Digit-symbol substitution: Using the code provided, fill in the missing information in the test picture.

INTELLIGENCE QUOTIENT Binet noticed that some children seem to think like children younger or older than themselves. To assess a child's intellectual standing relative to the standing of same-age peers, Binet introduced the important concept of **mental age**. This measure is determined by comparing the child's test score with the average score for children of each chronological age. For instance, a 10-year-old who is able to read novels and do basic algebra might score as well as an average 13-year-old. This 10-year-old would have a mental age of 13.

The **intelligence quotient (IQ)**, developed by the psychologist Wilhelm Stern, is partly based on mental age. IQ is computed by dividing a child's estimated mental age by the child's chronological age and multiplying the result by 100. To calculate the IQ of the 10-year-old with a mental age of 13, we calculate $13/10 \times 100$. The result is 130, a very high score.

The formula breaks down when used with adults, however, so the IQs of adults are measured differently. According to the standard formula, a 60-year-old would need to get twice as many test items correct as a 30-year-old to have the same IQ. Instead, IQ in the adult range is measured in comparison with the average adult and not with adults at different ages. Today, the average IQ is set at 100, with a standard deviation of 15. As discussed in Chapter 2, the statistical concept of standard

mental age An assessment of a child's intellectual standing compared with that of same-age peers; determined by comparing the child's test score with the average score for children of each chronological age.

intelligence quotient (IQ) An index of intelligence computed by dividing a child's estimated mental age by the child's chronological age, then multiplying this number by 100.

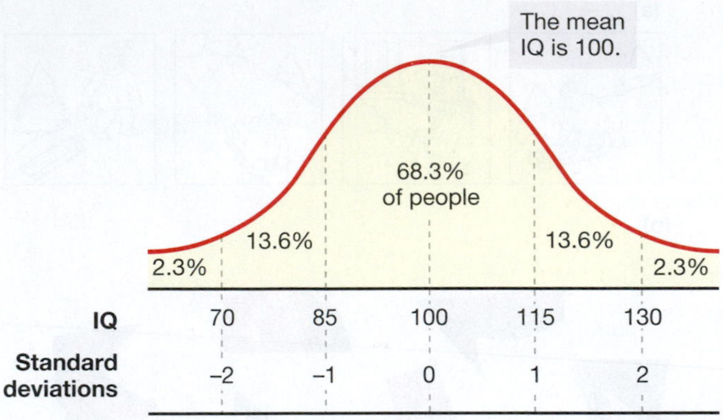

FIGURE 8.25
The Distribution of IQ Scores
IQ is a score on a normed test of intelligence. That is, one person's score is relative to the scores of the large number of people who already took the test. The average, or mean, for most IQ tests is 100, and the standard deviation is 15. As shown in this bell-shaped curve, approximately 68 percent of people fall within one standard deviation of the mean (they score from 85 to 115). Just over 95 percent of people fall within two standard deviations (they score from 70 to 130).

deviation indicates how far people are from an average. Across large groups of people, the distribution of IQ scores forms a bell curve, or *normal distribution*. Most people are close to the average, and fewer and fewer people score at the tails of the distribution. A person's IQ is considered in terms of deviation from the average (**FIGURE 8.25**).

VALIDITY OF TESTING Are intelligence tests reliable and valid? That is, are their results stable over time (demonstrating reliability), and do they really measure what they claim to measure (demonstrating validity)? In terms of reliability, there is considerable evidence that a person's performance on an intelligence test at one time corresponds highly to the person's performance at another time (Matarazzo et al., 1980).

To evaluate the validity of tests, we need to consider what it means to be intelligent. If the word means doing well at school or at a complex career, intelligence tests perform reasonably well: The overall evidence indicates that IQ is a fairly good predictor of such life outcomes (Gottfredson, 2004b).

To explore the validity of intelligence tests, researchers analyzed data from 127 studies, in which more than 20,000 participants took the Miller Analogy Test. This test has been used in the past for admissions decisions into graduate school as well as for hiring decisions in some work settings. It requires test takers to complete analogies such as "Fingers are to hands as toes are to ____." The researchers found that scores on the Miller Analogy Test predicted not only graduate students' academic performance but also individuals' productivity, creativity, and job performance in the workplace (Kuncel et al., 2004).

When considering these findings, note that IQ scores typically predict only about 25 percent of the variation in performance at either school or work, so additional factors contribute as much or more to individuals' success (Neisser et al., 1996). In the late 1800s, the scientist Sir Francis Galton believed that to become eminent in a field—that is, to become an expert—required not only innate ability but also zeal and willingness to work long hours (Ericsson et al., 1993). One study found that children's self-control, assessed through teacher and parent reports as well as laboratory tasks, was much better than IQ in predicting final grades (Duckworth & Seligman, 2005).

Q **Suppose a 4-year-old child performs at the level of an average 5-year-old on the Stanford-Binet. What is the 4-year-old's mental age and IQ score?**

ANSWER: The mental age is 5, and the IQ is 125, because the formula for IQ is mental age (5) divided by chronological age (4) and multiplied by 100.

8.10 General Intelligence Involves Multiple Components

Binet viewed intelligence as a general ability. We all know people, however, who are especially talented in some areas but weak in others. For example, some people write brilliant poems but cannot solve difficult calculus problems—or at least they feel more confident doing one than doing the other. The question, then, is whether intelligence reflects one overall talent or many individual ones. An early line of research examined the correlations among intelligence test items using *factor analysis*. In this statistical technique, items similar to one another are clustered. The clusters are called factors.

Using this type of analysis, Charles Spearman (1904) found that most intelligence test items tended to cluster as one factor. People who scored highly on one type of item also tended to score highly on other types of items. In general, people who are very good at math are also good at writing, problem solving, and other mental challenges. Spearman viewed **general intelligence (*g*)** as a factor that contributes to performance on any intellectual task (**FIGURE 8.26**). In a sense, providing a single IQ score reflects the idea that one general factor underlies intelligence. At the same time, Spearman acknowledged that people could differ in the *specific skills* (*s*) that enabled them to perform better on some tasks than on others.

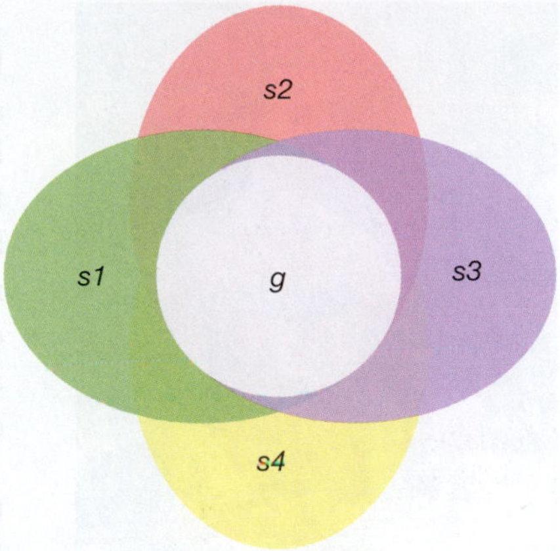

g = general intelligence

s1 = a specific ability (e.g., math)

s2 = a second specific ability (e.g., writing)

s3 = a third specific ability (e.g., problem solving)

s4 = a fourth specific ability (e.g., drawing)

FIGURE 8.26
General Intelligence as a Factor
As depicted in this cluster of overlapping ovals and circle, Spearman viewed *g* as a general factor in intelligence. This underlying factor influences an individual's specific abilities related to intelligence.

FLUID VERSUS CRYSTALLIZED INTELLIGENCE Raymond Cattell (1971) proposed that *g* consists of two types of intelligence. **Fluid intelligence** is the ability to understand abstract relationships and think logically without prior knowledge. It involves information processing, especially in novel or complex circumstances, such as reasoning, drawing analogies, and thinking quickly and flexibly. In contrast, **crystallized intelligence** involves knowledge acquired through experience, such as vocabulary and cultural information, and the ability to use this knowledge to solve problems (Horn, 1968; Horn & McArdle, 2007).

Distinguishing between fluid intelligence and crystallized intelligence is somewhat analogous to distinguishing between working memory (which is more like fluid intelligence) and long-term memory (which is more like crystallized intelligence). As would be expected because both types of intelligence are components of *g*, people who score highly on one factor also tend to score highly on the other. This finding suggests that a strong crystallized intelligence is likely aided by a strong fluid intelligence. As you will see in Chapter 9, crystallized intelligence grows steadily throughout the adult years, while fluid intelligence declines steadily.

Learning Tip

To remember the difference between fluid and crystallized intelligence, think of a crystal as being formed over the years, much as a lifetime of experience builds crystallized intelligence, whereas being fluid is being flexible and fast in your thinking.

THE IMPORTANCE OF *g* Research has shown that *g* is related to important life outcomes, such as by predicting performance in school and at work (Conway et al., 2003; Deary, 2001; Garlick, 2002; Gray & Thompson, 2004; Haier et al., 2005). Low *g* is related to early death from causes including heart disease, diabetes, stroke, Alzheimer's disease, traffic accidents, and drowning (Gottfredson, 2004a; Gottfredson & Deary, 2004). One study followed Scottish people for 55 years, starting when they were schoolchildren, and examined intelligence and a personality variable related to emotional intelligence (described in the next section). Those who scored in the lower half on both measures were more than twice as likely to die over the next half century compared with those who scored in the top half on both measures (Deary et al., 2008).

These patterns might result from the different environmental forces at work on each of us. For example, people who do not perform well in academic settings may end up with different jobs, and people with less dangerous and/or better-paying jobs tend to have better access to health care, and so on. Indeed, it is possible that factors other than intelligence are responsible for early death. A study that followed people from age 10 until age 75 found that the more education people received, the longer they lived, independent of their IQ level (Lager et al., 2009).

general intelligence (*g*) The idea that one general factor underlies intelligence.

fluid intelligence Intelligence that reflects the ability to process information, understand relationships, and think logically, particularly in novel or complex circumstances.

crystallized intelligence Intelligence that reflects both the knowledge acquired through experience and the ability to use that knowledge.

FIGURE 8.27
Brilliant but Clueless
On *The Big Bang Theory*, Sheldon Cooper is undeniably smart, yet he has trouble dealing with people. Perhaps part of Sheldon's problem is a lack of emotional intelligence.

According to Linda Gottfredson (2004a), however, *g* may directly affect health. People who score higher on intelligence tests may generally be more literate about health issues: They may be more motivated to accumulate greater health knowledge, better able to follow medical advice, and better able to understand the link between behavior and health. As medical knowledge rapidly advances and becomes more complex, trying to keep up with and process all this new information is a challenge, and people who are higher in *g* may have an advantage in doing so. This provocative idea warrants further investigation. If it is true, it has a number of important implications for the medical system and the way doctors communicate medical advice.

MULTIPLE INTELLIGENCES Whereas Cattell argued that two types of intelligence contribute to *g*, other researchers have described various types of intelligence. For example, Howard Gardner (1983) proposed that people can be intelligent in any number of ways, such as being musically or athletically talented. According to Gardner, each person has a unique pattern of intelligences, and no one should be viewed as smarter than others—just differently talented. This view strikes some psychologists as a feel-good philosophy with little basis in fact. Yet standard intelligence tests can fail to capture the types of people who are extremely "book smart" but have trouble in the real world because they lack practical sense or social skills. A good example of the brilliant but clueless type is the television character Sheldon Cooper, played by Jim Parsons in the television series *The Big Bang Theory* (**FIGURE 8.27**). Moreover, people can have high IQs but lack curiosity or drive.

Robert Sternberg (1999) proposed the triarchic theory of intelligence, which suggests that there are three types of intelligence: analytical, creative, and practical. *Analytical intelligence* is similar to that measured by psychometric tests—being good at problem solving, completing analogies, figuring out puzzles, and other academic challenges. *Creative intelligence* involves the ability to gain insight and solve novel problems—to think in new and interesting ways. *Practical intelligence* refers to dealing with everyday tasks, such as knowing whether a parking space is large enough for your vehicle, being a good judge of people, being an effective leader, and so on. Although this differentiation makes intuitive sense, some intelligence researchers have been critical, suggesting that the available evidence does not support Sternberg's model (Gottfredson, 2003).

emotional intelligence (EI)
A form of social intelligence that emphasizes managing, recognizing, and understanding emotions and using them to guide appropriate thought and action.

The fictional Sheldon Cooper has great difficulty with social relations and understanding his friends' emotional expressions and gestures. In terms of his social abilities, he would not be considered intelligent. **Emotional intelligence (EI)** consists of four abilities: managing one's emotions, using one's own emotions to guide thoughts and actions, recognizing other people's emotions, and understanding emotional language (Salovey & Grewel, 2005; Salovey & Mayer, 1990). People high in EI recognize emotional experiences in themselves and others and then respond to those emotions productively.

"I don't have to be smart, because someday I'll just hire lots of smart people to work for me."

EI is correlated with the quality of social relationships (Reis et al., 2007). The idea of EI has had a large impact in schools and industry, and programs have been designed to increase students' and workers' EI. These efforts may be valuable, since EI is a good predictor of high school grades (Hogan et al., 2010), and those high in it cope best with the challenges of college exams (Austin et al., 2010). At the same time, some critics have questioned whether EI really is a type of intelligence or whether it stretches the definition of intelligence too far. A recent review found evidence that EI is correlated with more-traditional measures of intelligence as well as academic performance among children and workplace performance among senior executives (Brackett et al., 2011). Whether or not EI is a type of intelligence, it is advantageous for those who have it.

Q **Do trivia questions assess fluid intelligence or crystallized intelligence?**

ANSWER: crystallized intelligence, which involves learned knowledge

8.11 Intelligence Is Related to Cognitive Performance

Francis Galton led one of the earliest efforts to scientifically study intelligence. Galton believed that intelligence was related to the speed of neural responses and the sensitivity of the sensory and perceptual systems. The smartest people, Galton believed, had the quickest responses and the keenest perceptions. Galton also speculated that intelligent people have larger, more efficient brains. Other psychologists believe intelligence is supported by cognitive functions such as mental processing, working memory, and attention. But can we equate these types of cognitive performance with intelligence?

SPEED OF MENTAL PROCESSING People who score higher on intelligence tests respond more quickly and consistently on reaction-time tests than those who score lower on intelligence tests (Deary, 2000). A test of *simple reaction time* might require a person to press a computer key as quickly as possible whenever a stimulus appears on the screen—for example, "Press the X key every time you see an X." A more difficult test might require a person to choose, again as quickly as possible, the right response for the stimulus presented—for example, "Press the X key every time you see an X, press the A key every time you see an A, and so on." Scores on intelligence tests are related even more strongly to this *choice reaction time* (Jensen, 1998).

Further support for the relationship between general intelligence and speed of mental processing comes from *inspection time* tests. If a stimulus is presented and then covered up, how much viewing time does a particular person need to answer a question about the stimulus (FIGURE 8.28)? People who need very little time for this task tend to score higher on psychometric tests of intelligence (Deary, 2001). In addition, by measuring the electrical activity of brains in response to the presentation of stimuli, researchers have found that highly intelligent people's brains work faster than less intelligent people's brains.

The relationship between general intelligence and mental speed appears to be correlated with the greater longevity of people with high IQs. According to a longitudinal study led by Ian Deary, those higher in intelligence and those who had faster reaction times at age 56 were much less likely to die in the next 14 years (Deary & Der, 2005). This outcome was true even after factors such as smoking, social class, and education were controlled for. The relationship between reaction time and longevity was somewhat stronger than the relationship between scores on standardized intelligence tests and longevity. A recent 15-year follow-up study of more than 5,000 Americans found that slower reaction times and more established

The task is to determine whether side A or side B of the stimulus is longer. The stimulus is presented and then quickly followed by a mask.

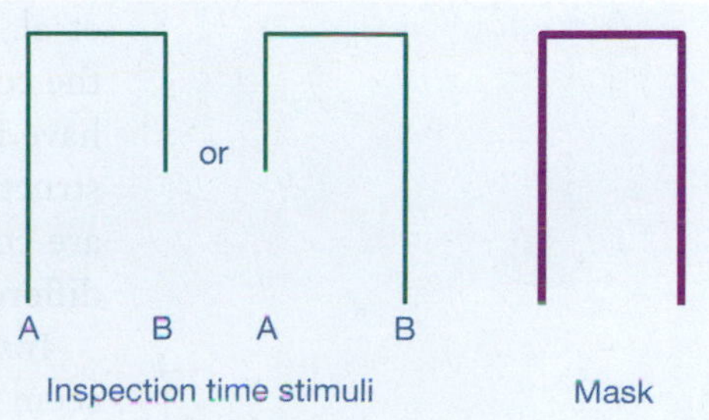

Judging the lengths is easy when you have enough time to view the stimulus but difficult when the mask decreases viewing time severely.

FIGURE 8.28
Inspection Time Tasks

For a simple *word span task,* a participant listens to a short list of words and then repeats the words in order.

For a more difficult *secondary processing task,* a participant has to solve simple mathematical operations at the same time the words are presented. Once again, the person has to repeat the words in the order they are presented (adapted from Conway et al., 2003).

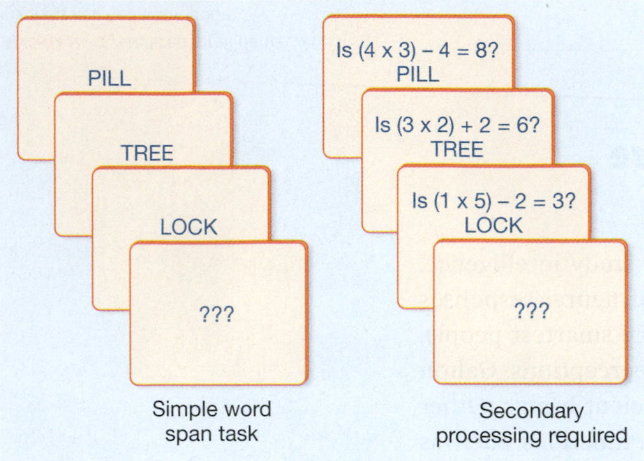

FIGURE 8.29
Memory Span Tasks

health risk factors, such as smoking, have similar relationships to premature death (Hagger-Johnson et al., 2014).

WORKING MEMORY General intelligence scores are closely related to how people process information in working memory (Conway et al., 2003). The two are not identical, however (Ackerman et al., 2005). As discussed in Chapter 7, working memory is the active processing system that holds information for use in activities such as reasoning, comprehension, and problem solving. In that capacity, working memory might be related to intelligence (Kyllonen & Christal, 1990; Süß et al., 2002).

Many studies of the relationship between working memory and intelligence differentiate between simple tests of memory span and memory tests that require some form of secondary processing (**FIGURE 8.29**). Performance on a simple test of memory, such as listening to a list of words and then repeating the list in the same order, is related weakly to general intelligence (Engle et al., 1999). Memory tests that have dual components, however, show a stronger relationship between working memory and general intelligence (Gray & Thompson, 2004; Kane et al., 2005; Oberauer et al., 2005). An example of a memory task with a dual component is the *n*-back task, in which participants might hear a series of letters and have to press a button when a letter was presented two positions back in the list. This requires not only remembering the target item, but also updating the target item on every trial.

The link between working memory and general intelligence may be attention. In particular, being able to pay attention, especially while being bombarded with competing information or other distractions, allows a person to stick to a task until it is successfully completed (Engle & Kane, 2004). The importance of staying focused makes great sense in light of the relationship, discussed earlier in this chapter, between general intelligence and the accomplishment of novel, complex tasks. The question, then, is whether brain regions that support working memory are involved in general intelligence.

INTELLIGENCE AND BRAIN STRUCTURE AND FUNCTION Intelligent people are sometimes called "brainy," but how are the brain and intelligence related? Many studies have documented a relationship between head circumference, which researchers use to estimate brain size, and scores on intelligence tests (Vernon et al., 2000). Head circumference also predicts school performance, although the correlation is quite small (Ivanovic et al., 2004). Studies using brain imaging have found a small but significant correlation between the size of specific brain structures and scores on intelligence tests (Johnson et al., 2008). These findings are correlations, however, so we cannot infer that brain size necessarily causes differences in intelligence.

Instead, the situation is more complicated. Different kinds of intelligence seem to be related to the sizes of certain brain regions (Basten et al., 2015). These regions include ones associated with working memory, planning, reasoning, and problem solving. For example, studies have found that the volume of neuronal cell bodies (gray matter) in the frontal lobes and in other brain regions that support attentional control is related to fluid general intelligence (Frangou et al., 2004; Haier et al., 2005; Kamara et al., 2011; Wilke et al., 2003). Other studies have found no relationship between the volume of frontal gray matter and crystallized intelligence (Gong et al., 2005). These findings are consistent with evidence that injury to the frontal lobes causes impairments in fluid intelligence but not in crystallized intelligence (Duncan et al., 1995). Because different regions of the brain support either fluid or crystallized intelligence, damage or abnormalities in a particular brain region may affect only some aspects of intelligence.

SAVANTS How would you like to be able to read a page of this textbook in 8 to 10 seconds? Perhaps less useful but even more impressive would be the ability to recite all the zip codes and area codes in the United States by the region to which they are assigned, or to name hundreds of classical music pieces just by hearing a few notes of each. These amazing abilities are just a few of the extraordinary memory feats demonstrated by Kim Peek (Treffert & Christensen, 2006). Peek, who died in 2008, was the inspiration for the character played by Dustin Hoffman in the 1988 movie *Rain Man*. He memorized the contents of over 9,000 books, but he could not button his own clothes or manage any of the usual chores of daily living, such as making change. He scored an 87 on an intelligence test, but this number did not adequately describe his intelligence. Peek was born, in 1951, with an enlarged head and many brain anomalies, including a missing corpus callosum, the thick band of nerves that connects the brain's two halves (see Figure 3.17). He also had abnormalities in several other parts of his brain, especially the left hemisphere.

We know very little about *savants* like Peek. Such people have minimal intellectual capacities in most domains, but at a very early age each savant shows an exceptional ability in some "intelligent" process, such as math, music, or art. The combination of prodigious memory and the inability to learn seemingly basic tasks is a great mystery. Nonetheless, this rare combination adds a dimension to our understanding of intelligence.

Oliver Sacks (1995) recounts the story of Stephen Wiltshire, an artistic savant. Wiltshire has autism spectrum disorder (discussed further in Chapter 14, "Psychological Disorders"). In childhood, it took him the utmost effort to acquire language sufficient for simple verbal communication. Years after a single glance at a place, however, Wiltshire can draw a highly accurate picture of it (**FIGURE 8.30**).

FIGURE 8.30
Stephen Wiltshire
Stephen Wiltshire published a book of his remarkably accurate, expressive, memory-based drawings by the time he was a young teenager. Here, in October 2010, he holds his drawing of an architectural site in London, England. Wiltshire observed the site briefly, then completed the picture largely from memory.

Q How do working memory and speed of mental processing relate to intelligence?

ANSWER: Quicker reaction times and working memory capacity, especially for more complex tasks that require secondary processing, correlate to general intelligence.

8.12 Genes and Environment Influence Intelligence

One of the most contentious battles in psychological science has been over the role of genes in determining intelligence. This battle exemplifies the nature/nurture debate. To what degree are individual differences in intelligence due to genes, and to what degree are they due to environment?

Nature and nurture are intertwined in the development of intelligence. For example, the capacity for having a large vocabulary is considerably heritable, but every word in a person's vocabulary is learned in an environment (Neisser et al., 1996). In addition, which words are learned is affected by the culture people are raised in, the amount of schooling they receive, and the general social context.

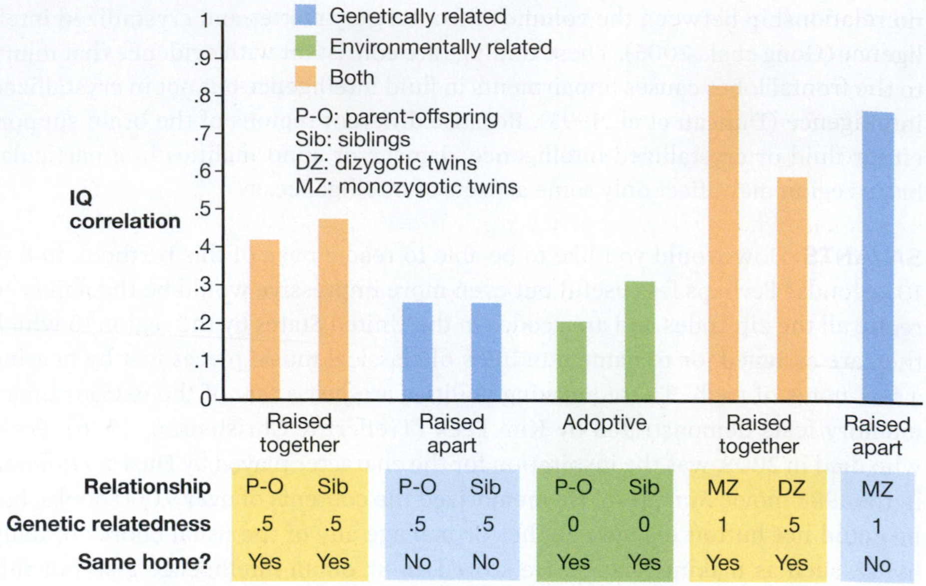

FIGURE 8.31

Genes and Intelligence

This graph represents average IQ correlations from family, adoption, and twin studies. As shown by the parent-offspring relationships (P-O) in the orange and blue bars on the left, a parent and child are more similar in IQ when the parent raises the child than when the child is raised by someone else. As shown by the sibling relationships (Sib) in the orange and blue bars on the left, siblings raised together show more similarity than siblings raised apart. As shown by the orange and blue bars on the right, the highest correlations are found among monozygotic twins, whether they are raised in the same household or not. Overall, the greater the degree of genetic relationship, the greater the correlation in intelligence.

So even if intelligence has a genetic component, the way intelligence becomes expressed is affected by various situational circumstances. Instead of seeking to demonstrate whether nature or nurture is the more important factor, psychologists try to identify how and in what way each of these crucial factors contributes to intelligence.

GENETIC FACTORS As discussed in Chapter 3, behavioral geneticists study the genetic basis of behaviors and traits such as intelligence. They use twin and adoption studies to estimate the extent to which particular traits are heritable. That is, they try to determine the portion of particular traits' variance that can be attributed to genes. Numerous behavioral genetics studies have made clear that genes help determine intelligence (Bouchard, 2014). For example, studies show that twins raised apart are highly similar in intelligence (**FIGURE 8.31**). The "intelligence gene" has eluded researchers, probably because thousands of genes contribute to intelligence and individually each has only a small effect (Plomin & Spinath, 2004). One study that looked at a large number of gene differences across the genome concluded that about 40 percent of the variation in crystallized intelligence and 51 percent of the variation in fluid intelligence are due to genetic influence (Davies et al., 2011).

But are the genes people possess the whole story? Even when raised apart, twins who have inherited an advantage might receive some *social multiplier*, an environmental factor or an entire environment that increases what might have started as a small advantage (Flynn, 2007). Suppose the twins have inherited a higher-than-average verbal ability. Adults who notice this ability might read to them more often and give them more books.

An additional possibility is that the expression of different genes is altered by environmental factors. Epigenetics involves changes to gene expression rather than to DNA. The study of epigenetic processes may help researchers understand how factors such as diet might be related to intelligence through the alteration of gene expression (Haggarty et al., 2010).

ENVIRONMENTAL FACTORS Richard Lewontin (1976) has provided an excellent example of the difficulties inherent in contrasting groups of people who differ in their circumstances. Consider seeds planted in two separate containers. In one container, the soil is poor, and the seeds receive restricted water, few nutrients, and intermittent sunlight. In the other container, the soil is rich, and the seeds receive regular watering, all the necessary nutrients, and abundant sunlight. Within each planter, differences between individual plants' growth can be attributed to the seeds' genetic differences. After all, their environment is identical, so only genes can explain the differences. But the plants in one container will differ from those in the other container because of their different environments. The impoverished environment will stunt growth, whereas the enriched environment will help the seeds reach their potential.

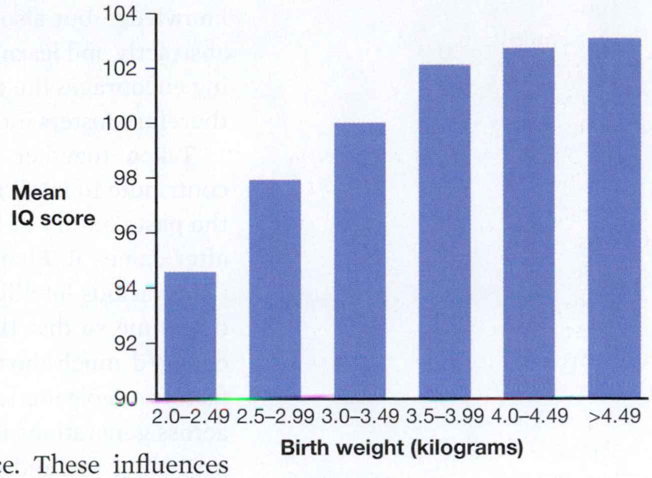

FIGURE 8.32
Birth Weight and Intelligence
Among children of normal birth weight, mean IQ scores increase with weight.

Many environmental influences affect human intelligence. These influences consist of prenatal factors (e.g., parents' nutrition and intake of substances, including drugs) and postnatal factors (e.g., family, social class, education, nutrition, cultural beliefs about the value of education, and the person's intake of substances, including drugs). Each factor is likely to exert an independent influence during development. For instance, breast-feeding during infancy has been shown to be associated with enhanced intellectual development (Mortensen et al., 2002), and children who are breast-fed show higher IQ scores 30 years later (Victora et al., 2015). In an experimental study, more than 17,000 infants from 31 maternity hospitals in Belarus were randomly assigned to either a control group or a condition that encouraged prolonged and exclusive breast-feeding. After 6.5 years, the children in the group receiving the intervention had higher means on standardized measures of intelligence (Kramer et al., 2008). There is also an apparent relationship between birth weight and intelligence later in life (Shenkin et al., 2004; **FIGURE 8.32**).

Another factor that is increasingly recognized as important for intellectual outcomes is family wealth, referred to as *socioeconomic status* (*SES*). According to Richard Nisbett (2009), growing up in a wealthy family significantly increases IQ, by 12 to 18 points, but the mechanism for this finding is not completely clear.

Environmental factors have been shown to influence brain development. As noted in Chapter 3, rats raised in enriched environments show more synaptic connections than those raised in impoverished environments. In one study, genetically identical mice were split into groups. The groups were then exposed to different levels of an enriched environment—given toys, tunnels, and the like. Enrichment was associated with the activation of genes involved in a number of brain functions, including forming new synapses (Rampon et al., 2000). These results suggest that environment can affect properties associated with intelligence by influencing the expression of genes. Research from numerous laboratories has shown that enriched environments enhance cognitive processes as well (Lambert et al., 2005; Tang et al., 2001). The implication is that environment influences how genes involved in brain development are expressed.

Humans as well as mice gain clear advantages from living in stimulating environments, and these environmental effects can be seen in the brain (May, 2011). We know that the intellectual opportunities a child receives affect intelligence. For instance, schooling makes an important contribution to intelligence and is associated with increased synaptic connections among brain regions involved in cognition (Noble et al., 2013). As Stephen Ceci (1999) notes, the longer children remain in school, the higher their IQs will be. In fact, students who start school early because of where their birth dates fall on the calendar have higher test scores than their same-age peers who start school a year later. Schooling not only builds knowledge but also teaches critical thinking skills, such as being able to think abstractly and learn strategies for solving problems (Neisser et al., 1996). Schooling encourages the development of children's brains and cognitive capacities and therefore fosters intelligence.

Taken together, the evidence is considerable that environmental factors contribute to intelligence. For example, IQ scores have risen dramatically during the past century of intelligence testing. This rise has been called the *Flynn effect* after James R. Flynn, the researcher who first described it (Flynn, 1984, 1987). (The various intelligence tests have been restandardized on numerous occasions over time so that the mean IQ score remains 100.) Because genes cannot have changed much during this period, the increase must be due to environmental factors or epigenetic effects. One possible explanation for the increase in IQ scores across generations is that, since every generation needs more education than the preceding one, and since work and leisure activities require more complex cognitive processing than they did in earlier times, cognitive abilities escalate within the span of one generation (Flynn, 2007). Other explanations include better nutrition, better health care, the refinement of education methods, longer school years, prosperity, and smaller families with more intensive parenting, as well as exposure to technology such as computers.

Q **What is the evidence that environment influences how genes involved in cognitive development and IQ are expressed?**

ANSWER: An enriched environment will enhance cognitive performance. Since genes cannot have changed much in modern humans, the increase in cognitive performance and IQ during this period must be due to environmental factors.

How Is Language Learned and Organized?

Learning Objectives

- Discuss the roles of morphemes and phonemes in language.
- Identify the brain areas involved in language.
- Explain how language develops.
- Contrast the phonics and whole language approaches to the teaching of reading.
- Explain dyslexia.

Language may be the most complex wonder of the human brain. It allows humans the unique capacity to express infinite thoughts, creativity, and intelligence. While many species communicate, such as in birds' use of song, language represents a quantum leap beyond other forms of animal communication, and it sets us apart from other species. In over 4,000 languages, humans can speak, write, and read, communicating everything from basic information to complex emotions and the subtle nuances of great literature. Language enables us to live in complex societies, because through language we learn the history, rules, and values of our culture or cultures.

Some aspects of language can be taught formally, such as grammatical rules. Other aspects do not rely on formal teaching, such as when children who are exposed to several languages somehow learn all of them and keep them straight. They know that one set of words is English, one is Spanish, and another is French. Consider, too, that all fluent speakers of a language rely on extensive implicit knowledge of grammar even if they cannot explain the rules. Babies begin speaking without a great deal of formal teaching. What explains the human capacity for language?

8.13 Language Is a System of Communication Using Sounds and Symbols

language A system of communication using sounds and symbols according to grammatical rules.

Language enables us to communicate using sounds and symbols according to grammatical rules. This system can be viewed as a hierarchical structure. That is, sentences can be broken down into smaller units, or *phrases*. Phrases can be broken down into words. Words can be broken down into sounds.

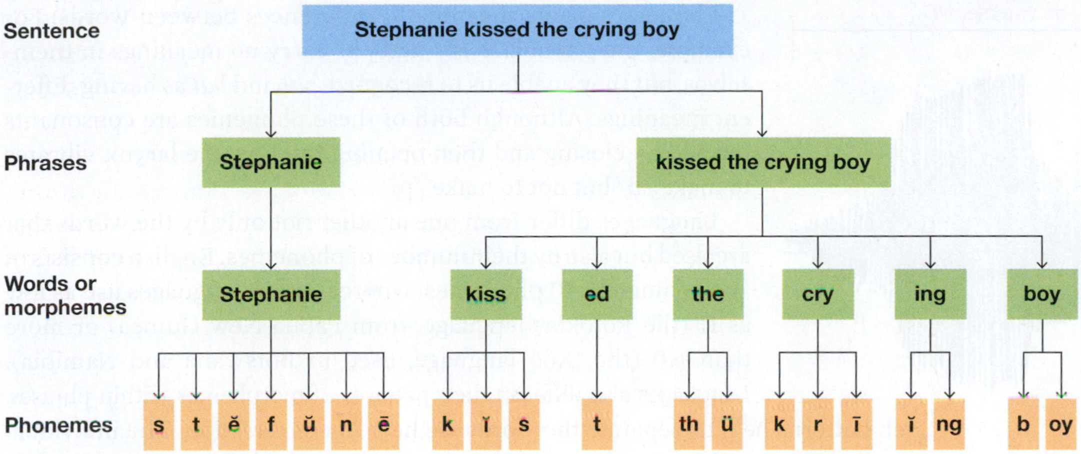

FIGURE 8.33
The Units of Language

Each word consists of one or more **morphemes**. Morphemes are the smallest units of language that have meaning, including suffixes and prefixes. As an example, consider the words *frost*, *defrost*, and *defroster*. The root word, *frost*, is a morpheme. The meaning of this morpheme is changed by adding the prefix *de*, which is also a morpheme. Adding a third morpheme, the suffix *er*, changes the meaning once again (Gazzaniga et al., 2014).

morphemes The smallest language units that have meaning, including suffixes and prefixes.

phonemes The basic sounds of speech, the building blocks of language.

Each morpheme consists of one or more **phonemes**. Phonemes are the basic sounds of speech, the building blocks of language. For example, the word *kissed* has two morphemes ("kiss" and "ed") and four phonemes (the sounds you make when you say the word).

A language's *syntax* is the system of rules that govern how words are combined into phrases and how phrases are combined to make sentences. *Semantics* is the study of the system of meanings that underlie words, phrases, and sentences.

To clarify your understanding of all these terms, consider the sentence *Stephanie kissed the crying boy*. Semantics tells us why that sentence has a different meaning than *Crying, Stephanie kissed the boy*. English-language syntax dictates that the sentence cannot be written as *Kissed the crying boy Stephanie*. As shown in **FIGURE 8.33**, the sentence can be broken down into phrases, the phrases can be broken down into words or morphemes, and the words or morphemes can be broken down into phonemes.

THE SOUNDS OF LANGUAGE Every language is derived from a highly restricted set of phonemes. This fact is intriguing because the human vocal tract has the capacity to make many more sounds than any language uses. People speak by forcing air through the *vocal cords*. The vocal cords are folds of mucous membranes that are part of the larynx, an organ in the neck, often called the voice box (**FIGURE 8.34**). The air passes from the vocal cords to the oral cavity (the part of the mouth behind the teeth and above the tongue). There, jaw, lip, and tongue movements change the shape of the mouth and the flow of the air, altering the sounds produced by the vocal cords. Some of those sounds are phonemes.

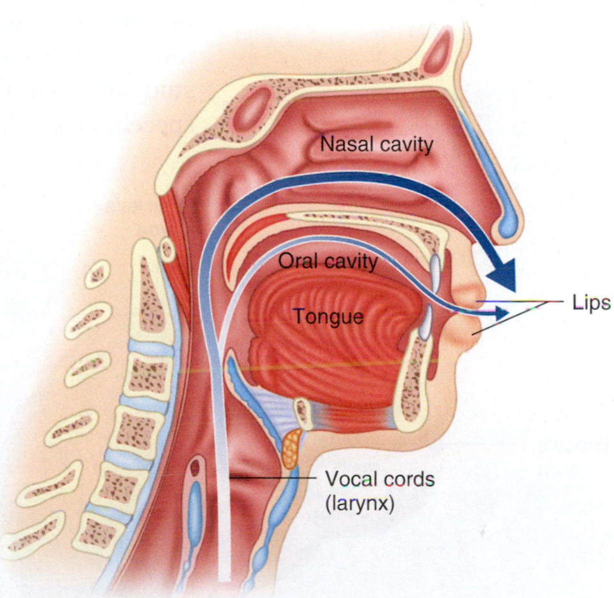

FIGURE 8.34
The Human Vocal Tract
Speech is produced by moving air through the vocal cords, part of the larynx, into the mouth. Lip and tongue movements then control the shape of the oral cavity and the flow of the air, resulting in particular sounds.

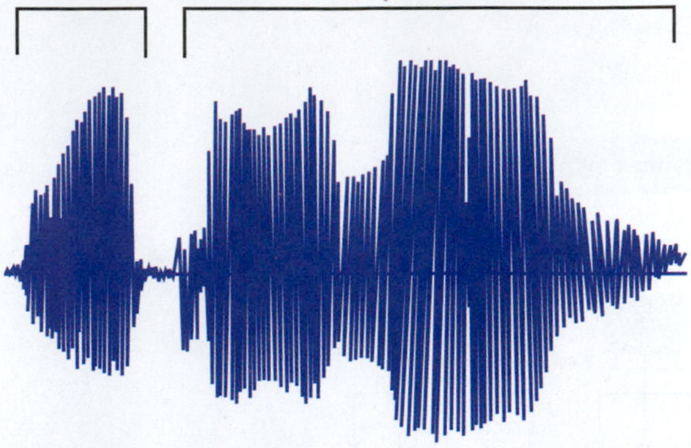

FIGURE 8.35
Speech Waveform
This is the waveform for the question "What do you mean?" There are no spaces between the words, yet the brain normally can segment the waveform so that the words can be understood.

Phonemes signal meaningful differences between words. For example, the phonemes /p/ and /b/ carry no meanings in themselves, but they enable us to recognize *pat* and *bat* as having different meanings. Although both of these phonemes are consonants formed by closing and then opening the lips, the larynx vibrates to make /b/ but not to make /p/.

Languages differ from one another not only by the words that are used but also by their number of phonemes. English consists of approximately 40 phonemes, whereas other languages use as few as 11 (the Rotokias language, from Papua New Guinea) or more than 110 (the !Xóõ language, used in Botswana and Namibia).

Languages also differ in their patterns of morphemes within phrases. Such patterns help us separate the words we hear in conversation. The individual morphemes actually occur in a continuous stream, or waveform (**FIGURE 8.35**). People speak at the rate of about 15 phonemes per second, or about 180 words per minute. As discussed further in the next section, different brain regions work together to separate the relevant sounds into segments that allow for interpretation. Meaning plays an important role in this perception. When you listen to a language you are not fluent in, it can be difficult to separate the stream into segments.

aphasia A language disorder that results in deficits in language comprehension and production.

Wernicke's area An area of the left hemisphere where the temporal and parietal lobes meet, involved in speech comprehension.

LANGUAGE IN THE BRAIN Injuries in certain brain areas can lead to **aphasia**. This language disorder results in deficits in language comprehension and production. About 40 percent of all strokes produce some aphasia, which can be temporary or permanent (Pedersen et al., 1995). Most strokes that cause aphasia occur in the left hemisphere.

Recall from Chapter 3 that the physician and anatomist Paul Broca studied a patient who could say only the word *tan*. In examining the patient's brain, Broca found that this patient had a lesion in the left frontal lobe (see Figure 3.12). After studying other patients, Broca concluded that the area of the brain that produces speech, now called Broca's area, must be located in the left hemisphere. When Broca's area is damaged, patients develop *expressive aphasia* (also called *Broca's aphasia*), which interrupts their ability to speak. These individuals generally understand what is said to them, and they can move their lips and tongues, but they cannot form words or put one word together with another to form a phrase.

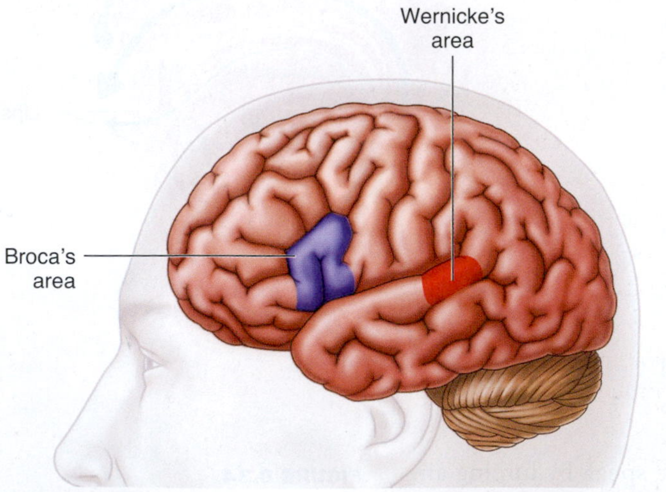

FIGURE 8.36
Left Hemisphere Regions Involved in Speech
Broca's area is important for speech production. Wernicke's area is important for speech comprehension.

In the 1870s, the physician Carl Wernicke identified another brain area involved in language. Wernicke had two patients who, after each had suffered a stroke, had trouble understanding spoken language. These patients could speak fluently, but what they said was nonsensical. After these patients died, Wernicke autopsied them and found damage in a region of the left hemisphere in the temporal lobe. This region is now known as **Wernicke's area** (**FIGURE 8.36**). When Wernicke's area is damaged, patients develop *receptive aphasia* (also called *Wernicke's aphasia*), in which they have trouble understanding the meaning of words. Those with receptive aphasia are often highly verbal, but what they say does not follow the rules of grammar or make sense.

Since the work of Broca and Wernicke, researchers have shown that a network of brain regions work together to facilitate language (Gazzaniga et al., 2014). For about 90 percent of people, the left hemisphere is most important for language. Extensive damage to the left hemisphere can cause *global aphasia*, where the person cannot produce or comprehend language. The right hemisphere also contributes to language in important ways, such as processing the rhythm of speech (Lindell, 2006) and interpreting what is said, especially understanding metaphors (Yang, 2014).

LANGUAGE AND THOUGHT The linguist Benjamin Whorf (1956) hypothesized that language reflects how people think. More specifically, culture determines language, which in turn determines how people form concepts and categorize objects and experiences. Whorf observed that the Inuit people of the Arctic use more words to describe variations in snow than English speakers do. According to Whorf, the greater number of words to describe snow was valuable to the Inuit people because subtleties in snow had practical and important implications for their daily living (**FIGURE 8.37**).

According to Whorf's original version of the **linguistic relativity theory**, language determines thought. That is, Whorf believed, we can think only through language. However, this version of Whorf's hypothesis does not appear to be true (Gelman & Gallistel, 2004; Hunt & Agnoli, 1991). For instance, the theory means that those without language are incapable of thought. Considerable research shows that animals and prelinguistic infants are capable of complex thought (Keil, 2011; Newman et al., 2010; Paulson et al., 2013).

Another version of the theory is that language influences rather than determines thought. This point remains controversial, but some research indicates that language influences thought in a number of domains, such as how people think about time, space, and quantities (Boroditsky et al., 2011; Gordon, 2004; Levinson, 2003). Moreover, the use of sexist language can influence people's thoughts about men and women. Recall from earlier in the chapter that the schema for being a scientist, and words such as *genius* and *smart*, are more often associated with men. Language with a masculine bias might reinforce beliefs about gender roles (Gastil, 1990).

(a)

(b)

FIGURE 8.37
Relative Importance of Snow
According to Whorf, **(a)** the Inuit may have developed many words for snow because different kinds of snow have played such important parts in their daily lives. **(b)** People in warmer climates do not need such an intricate snow-related vocabulary.

linguistic relativity theory
The claim that language determines thought.

Q **What is the difference between Broca's aphasia and Wernicke's aphasia?**

ANSWER: Broca's aphasia is a deficit in language production most often caused by damage to the left frontal lobe, while Wernicke's aphasia is a deficit in language comprehension most often caused by injury to the left temporal lobe.

8.14 Language Develops in an Orderly Way

As the brain develops, so does the ability to speak and form sentences. Thus, as children develop social skills, they also improve their language skills. There is some variation in the rate at which language develops, but overall the stages of language development are remarkably similar across individuals. According to Michael Tomasello (1999), the early social interactions with caregivers are essential to infants' understanding of other people and their ability to communicate through language. Research has demonstrated that infants and caregivers attend to objects in their environment together and that this joint attention promotes learning to speak (Baldwin, 1991; **FIGURE 8.38**). Children understand that speakers are usually thinking about what they are looking at (Bloom, 2002).

LEARNING PHONEMES Newborns are already well on their way to learning how to use language (Kuhl, 2004; Werker et al., 1981). Janet Werker and colleagues found that the language or languages spoken by mothers during pregnancy influences listening preferences in newborns (Byers-Heinlein et al., 2010). Canadian

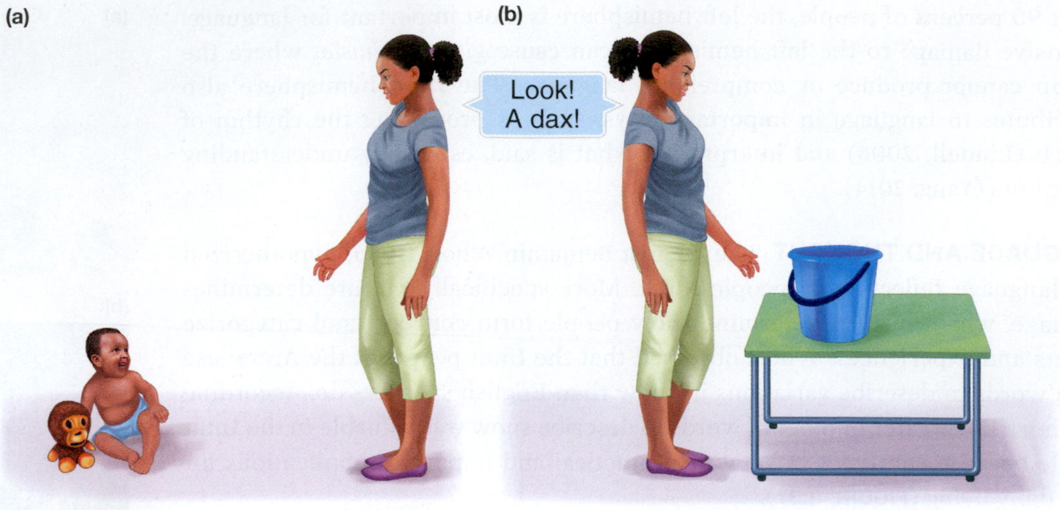

FIGURE 8.38
Joint Attention
Early interactions with caregivers lay the groundwork for children's acquisition of language. **(a)** If the caregiver is looking at the toy when saying a new name, "dax," the child will assign the name "dax" to the toy. **(b)** If the caregiver is looking at something else when saying the new name, the child will not assign the name "dax" to the toy.

newborns whose mothers spoke only English during pregnancy showed a robust preference for sentences in English compared with sentences in Tagalog, a major language of the Philippines. Newborns of mothers who spoke Tagalog and English during pregnancy paid attention to both languages. The latter finding implies that these newborns had sufficient bilingual exposure as fetuses to learn about each language before birth.

Patricia Kuhl and colleagues (Kuhl, 2007; Kuhl et al., 2003; Kuhl et al., 2006) found that up to six months of age, a baby can discriminate all the phonemes that occur in all languages, even if the sounds do not occur in the language spoken in the baby's home. For example, the distinction between the sounds /r/ and /l/ is important in English: *River* means something different from *liver*. The Japanese language does not distinguish those sounds, but it makes other distinctions that English does not make. After several months of exposure to their own language, infants lose the ability to distinguish between sounds that do not matter in their language (Kuhl, 2004). Japanese infants eventually lose the ability to differentiate /r/ from /l/, which makes learning English as a second language challenging for them, as they need to learn to detect the differences in these phonemes (Bradlow et al., 1997).

FROM 0 TO 60,000 From hearing differences between sounds immediately after birth and then learning the sounds of their own languages, young children go on to develop the ability to speak. Humans appear to go from babbling as babies to employing a full vocabulary of about 60,000 words as adults without working very hard at it.

Speech production follows a distinct path. During the first months of life, babies' verbal sounds are limited to cries, gurgles, grunts, and breaths. From three to five months, they begin to coo and laugh. From five to seven months, they begin babbling, using consonants and vowels. From seven to eight months, they babble in syllables (*ba-ba-ba, dee-dee-dee*). By the first year, infants around the world are saying their first words. These first words are typically labels of items in their environment (*kitty, cracker*), simple action words (*go, up, sit*), quantifiers (*all gone!*

more!), qualities or adjectives (*hot*), socially interactive words (*bye, hello, yes, no*), and even internal states (*boo-boo* after being hurt; Pinker, 1984). Thus, even very young children use words to perform a wide range of communicative functions. They name, comment, request, and more.

By about 18 to 24 months, children begin to put words together. Their vocabularies start to grow rapidly. Rudimentary sentences of roughly two words emerge. Though they are missing words and grammatical markings, these mini-sentences have a logic, or syntax. Typically, the words' order indicates what has happened or should happen: For example, *Throw ball. All gone* translates as *I threw the ball, and now it's gone*. The psychologist Roger Brown, often referred to as the father of child language for his pioneering research, called these utterances **telegraphic speech**. The telegraph, discontinued in 2006, was a form of electronic communication that used coded signals. Telegraphic speech involves the use of rudimentary sentences that are missing words and grammatical markers but follow a logical syntax and convey a wealth of meaning. So when these children speak as if sending a telegram, they are putting together bare-bones words according to conventional rules (Brown, 1973).

telegraphic speech The way toddlers speak, using rudimentary sentences that are missing words and grammatical markings but follow a logical syntax and convey a wealth of meaning.

OVERGENERALIZATIONS As children develop more-sophisticated ways of using language, one relatively rare but telling error they make is to overapply new grammar rules they learn. Children may start to make mistakes at ages 3 to 5 with words they used correctly at age 2 or 3. For example, when they learn that adding *-ed* makes a verb past tense, they then add *-ed* to every verb, including irregular verbs that do not follow that rule. Thus they may say "runned" or "holded" even though they may have said "ran" or "held" at a younger age. Similarly, they may overapply the rule to add *-s* to form a plural, saying "mouses" and "mans," even if they said "mice" and "men" at a younger age.

Like many "immature" skills children exhibit as they develop, such overgeneralizations reflect an important aspect of language acquisition. Children are not simply repeating what they have heard others say. After all, they most likely have not heard anyone say "runned." Instead, these errors occur because children are able to use language effectively by perceiving patterns in spoken grammar and then applying rules to new sentences they have never heard before (Marcus, 1996). They make more errors with words used less frequently (such as *drank* and *knew*) because they have heard irregular forms of words less often. Adults tend to do the same thing, making more errors on the past tenses of words they do not use often, such as saying "treaded" for *trod* (Pinker, 1994).

Q How does the ability to differentiate between phonemes change in the first year of life?

ANSWER: When babies are born they can differentiate between phonemes of all human languages, but after 6 months of age this ability becomes limited to the phonemes used in their native language(s).

8.15 There Is an Inborn Capacity for Language

Behaviorists such as B. F. Skinner (1957) proposed that children learn language the same way a rat learns to press a lever to obtain food: through a system of operant reinforcement. According to Skinner, children are reinforced for correctly repeating what their parents say. Speech that is not reinforced by parents is extinguished. Parents use learning principles such as shaping to help children refine their use of language.

But language acquisition does not work this way (Pinker & Bloom, 1990). Studies reveal that parents do not correct children's grammatical errors, nor do they

FIGURE 8.39
Teaching Language
Parents introduce young children to words and help them understand language, but they do not teach language using operant reinforcement.

surface structure In language, the sound and order of words.

deep structure In language, the implicit meanings of sentences.

constantly repeat words and phrases to their children. Parents correct young children if the content of what they say is wrong but not if the grammar is wrong (Brown & Hanlon, 1970; **FIGURE 8.39**). Furthermore, people do not need to see or hear language to learn it. For instance, deaf and blind children can still acquire language. Children also learn language much too quickly for behaviorist theories to make sense.

The linguist Noam Chomsky (1959) transformed the field of linguistics when he hypothesized that language must be governed by *universal grammar*. In other words, according to Chomsky, all languages are based on humans' innate knowledge of a set of universal and specifically linguistic elements and relationships.

Until Chomsky came on the scene, linguists had focused on analyzing language and identifying basic components of grammar. All languages include similar elements, such as nouns and verbs, but how those elements are arranged varies considerably across languages. In his early work, Chomsky argued that how people combine these elements to form sentences and convey meaning is only a language's **surface structure**: the sound and order of words. He introduced the concept of **deep structure**: the implicit meanings of sentences. For instance, *The fat cat chased the rat* implies that there is a cat, it is fat, and it chased the rat. *The rat was chased by the fat cat* implies the same ideas even though on the surface it is a different sentence.

Chomsky believes people automatically and unconsciously transform surface structure to deep structure—the meaning being conveyed. In fact, people remember a sentence's underlying meaning, not its surface structure. For example, you may not remember the exact words of someone who insulted you, but you will certainly recall the deep structure behind that person's meaning. According to Chomsky, humans are born with a *language acquisition device*, which contains universal grammar. This hypothetical neurological structure in the brain enables all humans to come into the world prepared to learn any language. With exposure to a specific cultural context, the synaptic connections in the brain start to narrow toward a deep and rich understanding of that cultural context's dominant language over all other languages (Kuhl, 2000).

ACQUIRING LANGUAGE WITH THE HANDS Suppose that the perception and production of sound are key to language acquisition. In that case, babies exposed to signed languages should acquire these languages differently than babies who acquire spoken languages. Now suppose instead that language, signed or spoken, is a special form of communication because of its highly systematic patterns and the human brain's sensitivity to them. In that case, babies should acquire signed languages and spoken languages in highly similar ways.

FIGURE 8.40
Acquiring Signed Language
Deaf infants have been shown to acquire signed languages at the same rates that hearing infants acquire spoken languages.

To test this second hypothesis, Laura-Ann Petitto and her students videotaped deaf babies of deaf parents in households using two entirely different signed languages: American Sign Language (ASL) and the signed language of Quebec, *langue des signes québécoise* (LSQ). They found that deaf babies exposed to signed languages from birth acquire these languages on an identical maturational timetable as hearing babies acquire spoken languages (Petitto, 2000; **FIGURE 8.40**). For example, deaf babies will "babble" with their hands: Just as hearing infants will repeat sounds such as *da da da*, which are not actually spoken words, deaf infants will repeat imitative hand movements that do not represent actual signs in signed languages.

In demonstrating that speech does not drive all human language acquisition, this research shows that humans must possess a biologically endowed sensitivity to the perception and organization of aspects of language patterns. This sensitivity launches a baby into the course of acquiring language.

SOCIAL AND CULTURAL INFLUENCES Of course, environment greatly influences a child's acquisition of language. Indeed, the fact that you speak English rather than (or in addition to) Swahili is determined entirely by your environment. Interaction across cultures also shapes language. The term *creole* describes a language that evolves over time from the mixing of existing languages (**FIGURE 8.41**). A creole language may develop when a culture colonizes a place, as when the French established themselves in southern Louisiana and had to communicate with people who did not speak French. The creole develops out of rudimentary communications as populations that speak several languages attempt to understand each other. Often, people mix words from each other's languages into a *pidgin*, an informal creole that lacks consistent grammatical rules.

The linguist Derek Bickerton (1998) found that children impose rules on their parents' pidgin, developing it into a creole. Bickerton argued that this is evidence for built-in, universal grammar. In other words, the brain changes a nonconforming language by applying the basic rules of universal grammar to it. Bickerton also found that creoles formed in different parts of the world, with different combinations of languages, are more similar to each other in grammatical structure than to long-lived languages.

FIGURE 8.41
Creole Language
A creole language evolves from a mixing of languages. In Suriname, where this boy is reading a classroom blackboard, over 10 languages are spoken. The official language, Dutch, comes from the nation's colonial background. The other tongues include variants of Chinese, Hindi, Javanese, and half a dozen original creoles, among them Sranan Tongo (literally, "Suriname tongue").

COMMUNICATION IS CRITICAL FOR LEARNING LANGUAGE By studying children who, for different reasons, did not receive typical exposure to language during development, psychologists have determined that two factors are necessary to support normal language learning: Children must have someone to communicate with and must be exposed to language during critical time periods in development.

Evidence that social communication is a critical and a determining factor in language development, even more so than exposure to an existing language, comes from a community of deaf children in Nicaragua (Senghas & Coppola, 2001). These children, who had limited exposure to language, were brought together in a public school that focused on trying to teach them to lip-read spoken Spanish, with limited success. However, the students learned to communicate among themselves. Even though they had never been exposed to sign language or a developed language before, they generated a new sign language. This newly developed sign language had many of the grammatical properties of American Sign Language and spoken languages. The development of this new language indicates that exposure to a developed language is not needed for language acquisition as long as there is a desire and means to communicate with others.

However, in order to learn complex language, communication during critical periods of development is necessary. This was demonstrated in the tragic case of Genie, who suffered horrific abuse as a child and was discovered at the age of 13 having had very little exposure to language. From then on, Genie had extensive exposure to language and training. She was able to learn words to communicate and generate simple sentences, but her ability to acquire grammar was limited (Fromkin et al., 1974). Similar findings were observed with a deaf child, E.M., who was never exposed to sign language (Grimshaw et al., 1998). At the age of 15 he was fitted with hearing aids and began to learn to speak. Like Genie, his ability to learn and use grammar to communicate was impaired, despite extensive training.

ANIMAL LANGUAGE Nonhuman animals have ways of communicating with each other, but no other animal uses language the way humans do (Zuberbühler, 2015). Scientists have tried for years to teach language to chimpanzees, one of the species

FIGURE 8.42
Laura-Ann Petitto with Neam Chimpsky

most closely related to humans. It was long believed that chimps lacked the vocal ability to speak aloud, but recent evidence indicates that some nonhuman primates do have vocal tracts capable of producing speech (Fitch et al., 2016). Researchers have been unsuccessful in coaxing speech out of nonhuman primates, however, so they have used sign language or visual cues to determine whether other primates understand words or concepts such as causation.

Consider the work of the psychologists Herbert Terrace, Laura-Ann Petitto, and Tom Bever. To test Noam Chomsky's assertion that language is a uniquely human trait, these researchers attempted to teach American Sign Language to a chimpanzee. In honor of Chomsky, they named the chimp Neam Chimpsky. His nickname was Nim (**FIGURE 8.42**).

After years of teaching Nim, the team admitted that Chomsky might be right. Like all other language-trained chimps, Nim consistently failed to master key components of human language syntax. While he was adept at communicating with a small set of basic signs ("eat," "play," "more"), he never acquired the ability to generate creative, rule-governed sentences. He was like a broken record, talking about the same thing over and over again in the same old way. As previously discussed, young children can name, comment, request, and more with their first words. Nim and all the ASL-trained chimps used bits and pieces of language almost exclusively to make requests. They wanted things (food, more food) from their caretakers, but otherwise they were not able to express meanings, thoughts, and ideas by generating language (Petitto & Seidenberg, 1979).

Other research projects have found more support for the idea that nonhuman animals can learn and use language. For instance, there is some evidence that some primates, such as orangutans, can imitate humans by controlling their vocal cords (Lameira et al., 2016). Most of the evidence supporting nonhuman language, however, involves the use of symbols to represent information. Kanzi, a bonobo ape, learned to use geometric shapes to represent words. He acquired several hundred words in this way and could use them in many different combinations. His spontaneous use of the symbols generally followed the rules of language. Kanzi was also quite good at following human verbal commands. Researchers gave him 660 commands, including novel ones such as "Hide the toy gorilla" and "Put on the monster mask and scare Linda." Kanzi successfully performed 72 percent of these requests (Savage-Rumbaugh et al., 1998).

In separate research, a parrot named Alex displayed a relatively sophisticated use of human language (Pepperberg, 2010). Alex could use about 150 words, categorize and count objects, and describe the color of objects that were not physically present. He appeared able to express frustration, and he could indicate that he was bored by saying, "Wanna go back." Alex died in 2007, but Irene Pepperberg continues to study language and cognition with other parrots. More recently, she demonstrated that a parrot named Griffin has a sophisticated conceptual understanding of object shape (Pepperberg & Nakayama, 2016).

Many researchers remain enthusiastic about the possibility of using language to communicate with nonhuman animals. Still, learning to use symbols requires intensive training involving social interaction, and nonhuman animals seem unable to develop skills beyond those of human toddlers (Griebel et al., 2016).

Q **In terms of surface structure and deep structure, how do the sentences *James yelled at John* and *John was yelled at by James* compare?**

ANSWER: They differ in surface structure because their sentence structure is different, but they are the same in deep structure because they mean the same thing.

8.16 There Are Different Approaches to Learning to Read

Reading, like speaking, is nearly effortless for most adults. When we look at letters grouped into words, we automatically derive meaning from these groupings, even if they are misspelled. As noted in Chapter 5, Y0U C4N R3AD TH15 PR377Y W3LL even though it is nonsensical.

In the English-speaking world, there are two major schools of thought regarding how to teach reading. Traditional methods use **phonics**, which teaches an association between letters and the phonemes they represent. Children learn to make the appropriate sounds for the letters and then spell out words by how they sound (**FIGURE 8.43**). They learn a small number of simple words that teach the sounds of letters across most words of the English language. Because of the irregularities in English, children first learn the general rules and then learn to recognize exceptions to those rules. This approach emphasizes memorizing the mappings between letters and their sounds rather than building vocabulary or processing words' meanings.

phonics A method of teaching reading in English that focuses on the association between letters and their phonemes.

Because of the complexity of the English language, in which the sounds of letters can vary across words, some educators have advocated *whole language* approaches. These approaches emphasize learning the meanings of words and understanding how words are connected in sentences. Whole language has dominated in most American schools for the past three decades. This popularity may be partly due to the philosophy behind the approach, which emphasizes student interest, enjoyment of reading, creativity, and thought.

The general idea behind whole language instruction is that children should learn to read the way they learn to talk. We do not process speech by breaking the sound stream into phonemes. Instead, we understand speech as a series of connected words that have meaning in the context of the entire sentence. Thus, according to whole language proponents, breaking words into sounds is unnatural, frustrating, and boring. Instead, students should learn to read naturally and unconsciously, by learning individual words and then stringing them together.

Classroom and laboratory research comparing the two approaches to reading instruction has consistently found that phonics is superior to whole language in creating proficient readers (Rayner et al., 2001; Rayner et al., 2012). This result applies especially to children who are at risk of becoming poor readers, such as those whose parents do not read to them on a regular basis. Whole language motivates students to read, but phonics best teaches basic reading skills.

FIGURE 8.43
Using Phonics
In learning to read, these children are combining phonemes into morphemes.

DYSLEXIA Although reading may happen automatically once it's learned, the process of learning to read is challenging for many people. These learners struggle to figure out which symbols are letters, which letters are clumped into words, and which words go together to make meaningful sentences. Sometimes this difficulty is the result of a reading disorder called *dyslexia*. People with dyslexia have trouble reading, spelling, and writing even though they have normal levels of intelligence. A recent meta-analysis of 21 studies found that children who develop dyslexia have more difficulty acquiring language as infants and toddlers, particularly with identifying and using phonemes (Snowling & Melby-Lervåg, 2016). According to the overall evidence, the inability to hear, identify, and use phonemes is a central problem for those with dyslexia (Melby-Lervåg et al., 2012).

Dyslexia may result from impaired sound and image processing, especially for words that rhyme (Temple et al., 2001). Dyslexia appears to run in families, so it may have a strong genetic component (Olson, 2011). However, rates of dyslexia tend to be higher in inner-city samples than in rural samples, so environment appears to be a factor, and factors such as parental education may play a role.

Q **What are the comparative benefits of the whole-language approach versus phonics approach to teaching reading?**

ANSWER: The whole language approach may be better at motivating students to read, but phonics reliably produces better reading skills.

Your Chapter Review

Want to earn a better grade on your test?

It's time to complete your study experience! Go to **INQUIZITIVE** to practice actively with this chapter's concepts and get personalized feedback along the way.

Chapter Summary

What Is Thought?

8.1 Thinking Involves Two Types of Mental Representations Cognition can be broadly defined as the mental activity that includes thinking and the understandings that result from thinking. Knowledge about the world is stored in the brain in representations. Analogical representations are images that contain characteristics of actual objects. Symbolic representations are abstract representations with no relationship to physical qualities of objects in the world. Mental maps rely on both analogical and symbolic representations.

8.2 Concepts Are Symbolic Representations Concepts are mental representations that categorize items around commonalities. According to the prototype model, an individual forms a concept around a category and then chooses a prototype that best represents the concept. According to the exemplar model, an individual's representation of a concept is a combination of all the examples (exemplars) of the category ever encountered by the individual.

8.3 Schemas Organize Useful Information About Environments Schemas are categories used to organize information. Schemas usually work because situations and appropriate behaviors follow consistent rules. Scripts are schemas that guide behavior over time in specific situations, such as going to the movies. A negative consequence of schemas and scripts is that they can reinforce stereotypes and biases. Schemas and scripts are adaptive because they minimize attentional requirements and help people recognize and avoid unusual or dangerous situations.

How Do We Make Decisions and Solve Problems?

8.4 Decision Making Often Involves Heuristics Decision making involves selecting among alternatives. People often use heuristics, or mental shortcuts, to make decisions. Common heuristics include relative comparisons (anchoring and framing), availability, and representativeness.

8.5 Emotions Influence Decision Making Emotions influence many aspects of decision making. A real or anticipated emotional response to a choice option can be integral to determining the value of that choice. Affective forecasting shows that people are typically bad at predicting their feelings further in the future. Incidental affective states, such as mood, that are unrelated to a decision can also bias choices and judgments.

8.6 You Be the Psychologist: Big Data, Mood, and Decisions Massive amounts of data concerning everyday decisions people make are collected by companies, governments, and internet search engines. Psychologists are increasingly turning to big data to understand how emotional factors can influence everyday decisions.

8.7 Problem Solving Achieves Goals Problem solving is the use of available information to achieve a goal. Problem solving can be improved by breaking the problem into subgoals or by restructuring the problem. Mental sets and functional fixedness inhibit problem solving. Two ways of countering these blockages are working backward from the goal and transferring an effective strategy from an analogous situation. Insight is the sudden realization of a solution to a problem and is often achieved by overcoming functional fixedness.

8.8 Psychology Outside the Lab: How Can You Make Good Choices? Even though people prefer having more options, increasing the number of options decreases decision making and decreases satisfaction with decisions. When too many options are available, especially when all of them are attractive, people experience conflict and indecision. Two approaches to decision making are "maximizing" and "satisficing." Maximizers seek to identify the perfect choice among a set of options, whereas satisficers seek to find a "good enough" choice that meets their minimum requirements. Maximizers, compared with satisficers, tend to select the objectively best choice, but those choices bring them less happiness. Several strategies are available for helping people make good decisions that bring them happiness. One such strategy is having realistic expectations.

How Do We Understand Intelligence?

8.9 Intelligence Is Measured with Standardized Tests Intelligence is the ability to use knowledge to reason, make decisions, solve problems, understand complex ideas, learn quickly, and adapt to environmental challenges. The two types of standardized intelligence tests are achievement tests, which measure accumulated skill and knowledge, and aptitude tests, which assess ability and potential. Two commonly used intelligence tests are the Stanford-Binet test for children and the WAIS for adults. Intelligence quotient (IQ) is computed by dividing mental age by chronological age and then multiplying the result by 100. IQ tests have been shown to be valid measures of intelligence. Perseverance, zeal, and willingness to work long hours are also necessary for expertise.

8.10 General Intelligence Involves Multiple Components Some researchers believe that one general factor, called general intelligence (*g*), underlies intelligence. This factor may consist of two components: fluid intelligence (the ability to think logically about abstract concepts without prior knowledge) and crystallized intelligence (accumulated knowledge). Several theories have proposed multiple intelligences, such as emotional intelligence (how well people succeed in social situations). Additional research is needed to verify that multiple intelligences exist.

8.11 Intelligence Is Related to Cognitive Performance High IQ is related to increased speed of mental processing as measured by reaction time and inspection time tasks. Working memory may be related to intelligence for tasks that require attention. People who have higher levels of fluid intelligence have been found to have a greater density of neural cell bodies (gray matter) in the frontal lobes, an area of the brain that regulates working memory. Savants have minimal intellectual capacities in most domains, but at a very early age they show an exceptional ability in some "intelligent" process.

8.12 Genes and Environment Influence Intelligence There is likely a complex genetic component to intelligence, but environment plays a large role in how intelligence is expressed. Epigenetics offers an explanation for how intelligence may develop: Environmental influences such as enrichment and education can alter gene expression to promote synaptic connections and processing efficiency in the brain and thereby increase intelligence.

How Is Language Learned and Organized?

8.13 Language Is a System of Communication Using Sounds and Symbols Morphemes are the smallest units of language that have meaning. Phonemes are the basic sounds of speech, the building blocks of language. A network of left hemisphere brain regions—including Broca's area in the frontal lobe and Wernicke's area at the junction of the temporal and parietal lobes—govern speech production and comprehension. Language may influence thought, but thought does not depend on language.

8.14 Language Develops in an Orderly Way Language production proceeds from babies' cooing to babbling to the use of single words to telegraphic speech to the use of full sentences to the eventual acquisition of some 60,000 words.

8.15 There Is an Inborn Capacity for Language Behaviorists believed that language was learned through operant reinforcement. However, children acquire language even in the absence of reinforcement. Noam Chomsky proposed instead that humans are born with an innate capability for language, called the language acquisition device, which contains universal grammar.

8.16 There Are Different Approaches to Learning to Read For most adults, reading is automatic and effortless, and we derive accurate meaning even from misspelled words. Phonics is a method for teaching reading by associating letters with phonemes. Whole language is a method for teaching reading by emphasizing the meanings of words and how words are connected in sentences. Whole language is a good way to encourage reading. Phonics is the best method for teaching basic reading skills, especially for children unfamiliar with reading. Dyslexia results from a lack of phoneme awareness.

Key Terms

affective forecasting, p. 293
analogical representations, p. 284
anchoring, p. 290
aphasia, p. 316
availability heuristic, p. 291
cognition, p. 284
concept, p. 286
crystallized intelligence, p. 307
decision making, p. 289
deep structure, p. 320
emotional intelligence (EI), p. 308
exemplar model, p. 286
fluid intelligence, p. 307
framing, p. 291
functional fixedness, p. 298
general intelligence (*g*), p. 307
heuristics, p. 290
insight, p. 300
intelligence, p. 304
intelligence quotient (IQ), p. 305
language, p. 314

linguistic relativity theory, p. 317
mental age, p. 305
mental sets, p. 297
morphemes, p. 315
phonemes, p. 315
phonics, p. 323
problem solving, p. 289
prototype model, p. 286
representativeness heuristic, p. 292
restructuring, p. 297
script, p. 287
stereotypes, p. 288
surface structure, p. 320
symbolic representations, p. 284
telegraphic speech, p. 319
thinking, p. 284
Wernicke's area, p. 316

Q Practice Exercises

1. Identify each of the following examples as either an analogical representation, a symbolic representation, or both.
   a. the written word *cat*
   b. a cartoon illustration of a cat
   c. a mental map of the United States
   d. the spoken word *America*

2. Match each of the following decisions with the heuristic used: anchoring, framing, availability heuristic, representativeness heuristic.
   a. Magda chooses not to travel, assuming she is at high risk for contracting the Zika virus, after seeing frequent news reports about it.
   b. Jacob decides to purchase flood insurance, motivated by concern for the potential loss of his valuable property.
   c. Steven's doctor is not concerned by Steven's chest pain because he is thin and young, so does not fit the typical risk profile for heart attack.
   d. Sylvia decides to purchase 10 oranges, rather than her usual 6, because they are being sold "10 for $10."

3. _______ emotions are directly related to a current or anticipated choice, while _______ emotions are present during the appraisal of unrelated choices. _______ can make us more or less likely to choose one option over another.
   a. integral; incidental; both
   b. integral; incidental; neither
   c. incidental; integral; both
   d. incidental; integral; neither

4. Insight can occur when people overcome _______ to see new uses for objects and tools.
   a. stereotype threat
   b. functional fixedness
   c. prototypical models
   d. the use of exemplars

5. Casey is very empathic. He is able to accurately interpret what people are thinking and feeling, if someone is uncomfortable, stressed, or attracted to something. Based on these abilities, which measure of intelligence would Casey score well on?
   a. crystallized intelligence
   b. EI
   c. fluid intelligence
   d. *g*

6. Which of the following characteristics is *not* typically correlated with high scores on intelligence tests?
   a. faster reaction times, particularly in a choice reaction time test
   b. increased likelihood of premature death
   c. increased working memory performance
   d. a stimulating, enriched environment

7. The _______ approach to reading instruction produces better reading skills and focuses on _______.
   a. syntax; matching sounds with letters
   b. whole language; learning complete words and how they relate in sentences
   c. phonics; matching sounds with letters
   d. exemplar; learning complete words and how they relate in sentences

8. Which theory of language development suggests that people are born with a specialized language acquisition device in their brains?
   a. Whorf's language relativity theory
   b. Sternberg's triarchic theory
   c. Skinner's theory of behaviorism
   d. Chomsky's universal grammar theory

9. Which of the following statements about brain regions and language processing is correct?
   a. Broca's area controls speech comprehension.
   b. Wernicke's area controls speech production.
   c. The amygdala controls the acquisition of vocabulary.
   d. The left hemisphere primarily controls speech production and comprehension.

10. A 3-year-old reports that her "foots" are itchy. Which stage of language acquisition does this statement represent?
   a. telegraphic speech
   b. overgeneralization
   c. babbling
   d. joint attention

9 Human Development

Big Questions

THINK BACK TO YOUR CHILDHOOD, or look at an old photo of yourself. Are you the same person now as you were at age 5 or 13? Will you be the same person when you are 50 or 80 or even older? Developmental psychology is concerned with what changes and what remains stable across the life span. As all people do, you have changed in many ways over the years and will continue to do so as you age. By changing, you are continually developing into a new version of yourself. And yet other parts of you are consistent across your life.

Theorists and scientists have long debated the nature and purpose of changes in human psychology across the life span. What are the major social and biological forces that drive the changes people undergo in their lives, and what function do specific developmental changes serve for us? How do earlier life experiences influence how we think, feel, act, and react later in life? This chapter examines the ways biological and social forces combine to shape the path of human development.

Learning Objectives

- Describe how the prenatal environment can affect development.
- Explain how dynamic systems theory illuminates the ways biology and environment work together to shape development.
- Summarize key research findings on infant learning and infant memory.
- Describe the different types of attachment infants have to their caregivers.

What Factors Shape Development?

This chapter is concerned with changes over the human life span in physiology, cognition, emotion, and social behavior. In exploring these changes, the chapter presents the findings of **developmental psychology**. This subfield examines how humans change over the course of their lives and considers which changes are shared across people and which are different. Researchers in developmental psychology seek to understand how people grow and adapt within their cultures to become members of society.

Some parts of human physical development follow a predictable progression. Physically, each human matures at about the same periods in the life span: the prenatal period, which begins with conception and ends with birth; infancy, which begins at birth and lasts 18 to 24 months; childhood, which begins at the end of infancy and lasts until about 10 to 14 years; adolescence, which begins at the end of childhood and lasts until somewhere between 18 and 21 years; and adulthood, which begins at the end of adolescence and lasts until old age and death.

developmental psychology
The study of changes over the life span in physiology, cognition, emotion, and social behavior.

9.1 Human Development Starts in the Womb and Extends into Adulthood

Remarkable developments occur from conception through birth approximately 40 weeks later (**FIGURE 9.1**). The process begins at the moment of conception, when a sperm unites with an egg to create a *zygote*, the first cell of a new life. At about 2 weeks after conception, the zygote is firmly implanted in the uterine wall, and the next stage of development begins. From about 2 weeks to 2 months, the developing human is known as an *embryo*. During this stage, the organs (such as the heart, lungs, liver, kidneys, and sex organs) and internal systems (such as the nervous system) begin to form. During this period, the embryo is especially vulnerable. Exposure to harm—such as toxins, drugs, extreme stress, or poor nutrition—can have lasting effects on developing organ systems.

After 2 months of prenatal development, all the organs are formed, the heart begins to beat, and the growing human is called a *fetus*. The body continues to grow into its infant form. The fetus grows larger and stronger as the body organs mature to a point where survival is possible outside the womb. Many fetuses can now survive outside the womb with current medical technology after as little as 22 weeks of prenatal development (**FIGURE 9.2**). Most healthy full-term pregnancies, however, end with the birth of the baby at between 38 and 42 weeks.

(a)
(b)
(c)

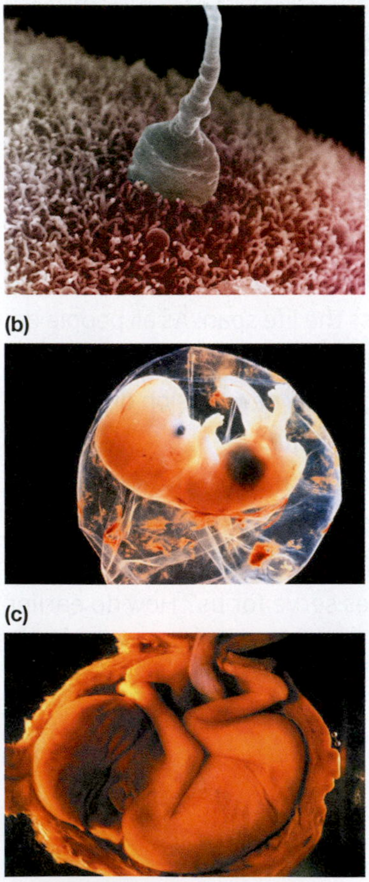

FIGURE 9.1
Development in the Womb
(a) The union of egg and sperm forms a zygote. **(b)** The zygote develops into an embryo. **(c)** The embryo becomes a fetus.

BRAIN DEVELOPMENT Early brain growth has two important aspects. First, specific areas within the brain mature and become functional. Second, regions of the brain learn to communicate with one another through synaptic connections.

One important way that brain circuits mature is through myelination. This process begins on the spinal cord during the first trimester of pregnancy and on the neurons during the second trimester. As discussed in Chapter 3, myelination is the brain's way of insulating its "wires." Nerve fibers are wrapped with a fatty sheath, much like the plastic coating around electrical wire (see Figure 3.3). This wrapping increases the speed with which the fibers are able to transmit signals. The myelinated axons form synapses with other neurons.

Though most neurons are already formed at birth, the brain's physical development continues through the growth of neurons and the new connections they make. By age 4, the human brain has grown to about 80 percent of the adult size. This size increase is due to myelination and to new synaptic connections among neurons, particularly in the frontal lobes (Paredes et al., 2016). Far more of these connections develop than the infant brain will ever use. Genetic instruction leads the brain to grow, but the organ is also highly "plastic." That is, the brain organizes itself in response to its environmental experiences, preserving connections it needs in order to function in a given context and eliminating others. In other words, "use it or lose it." This process of **synaptic pruning** allows every brain to adapt well to any environment in which it may find itself. The brain continues to develop and mature through adolescence and beyond (Matsui et al., 2016).

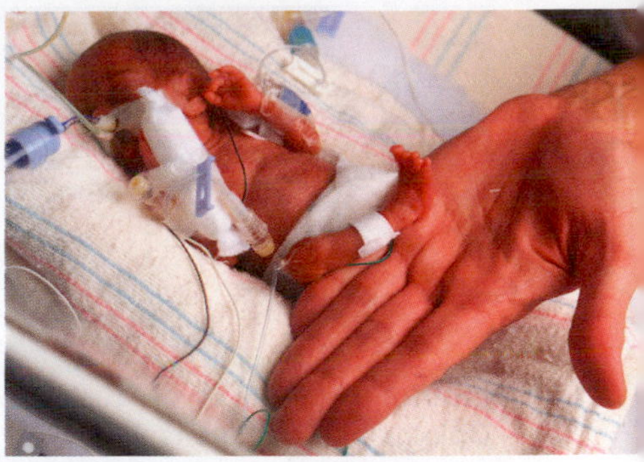

FIGURE 9.2
Extreme Prematurity
Rumaisa Rahman set a record as the smallest surviving baby when she was born in 2004, weighing 8.6 ounces. She was released from the hospital after spending nearly 5 months in the neonatal intensive care unit. Today, she is a healthy teenager.

EARLY EXPERIENCES CAN HAVE LASTING EFFECTS Nutrition affects aspects of brain development, such as myelination, beginning in the womb and extending through childhood. Malnourished children might also lack the energy to interact with objects and people. This lack of stimulation would further undermine brain development. When a child's environment does not stimulate their brain, very few synaptic connections will be made. The brain will be less sophisticated and less able to process complex information, solve problems, or allow the child to develop advanced language skills (Perry, 2002; **FIGURE 9.3**). As discussed in Chapter 3, animals raised in enriched environments show increased generation of new neurons in the hippocampus, which may facilitate learning in complex environments (Garthe et al., 2016).

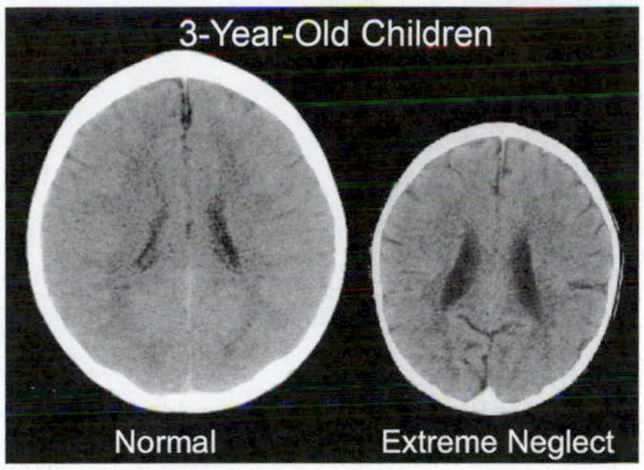

FIGURE 9.3
Environment and Synaptic Connections
These images illustrate the impact of neglect on the developing brain. The CT scan on the left is from a healthy 3-year-old child with an average head size. The CT scan on the right is from a 3-year-old child following severe sensory-deprivation neglect (e.g., minimal exposure to language, touch, and social interaction) during early childhood. This brain is significantly smaller than average, and its cortical, limbic, and midbrain structures are abnormally developed.

Experiences such as stress, neglect, and exposure to violence that often occur in the context of poverty can also influence the development of human brains. The effects begin at a young age—probably before birth—and continue through life (Lawson et al., 2013; Nelson, 2017). One large study of nearly 400 children followed over two years found that living below the U.S. federal poverty level ($26,200 in annual income for a family of four in 2020) was associated with reductions in the size of several brain areas linked to school readiness skills (Hair et al., 2015). These children living in poverty went on to have lower scores on achievement tests. Other research shows that poor brain functioning associated with poverty at age 3 predicts several negative life outcomes 40 years later, including health problems, addiction, and greater criminal activity (Caspi et al., 2016). It is now well established that stressful early life experiences can lead to a wide range of mental and physical health disorders later in life (Taylor, 2010).

However, environmental influences can also foster development and protect children from the harmful effects of stress. Interventions that support families experiencing stressful events and situations such as poverty can improve the environment for infants and children. For instance, a program designed to enhance caregiving support reduced the effects of poverty on brain development (Brody et al., 2017). Similar programs can also help repair the disruptions in the body's stress response system caused by early stress (Roos et al., 2018). Research in the emerging field of *translational neuroscience* seeks to identify the neural systems that are vulnerable to the effects of early life stress and build interventions that protect those systems (Horn et al., 2020).

EXPOSURE TO TERATOGENS DURING PRENATAL DEVELOPMENT Teratogens are agents that harm the embryo or fetus. (The word *teratogens* comes from the Greek for "monster makers.") Specifically, these agents can impair development in the womb, sometimes with terrible consequences. Teratogens include drugs, bacteria, and viruses, as well as chemicals such as caffeine, alcohol, and certain

synaptic pruning The physiological process of preserving synaptic connections that are used, and eliminating those that are not used.

teratogens Agents that harm the embryo or fetus.

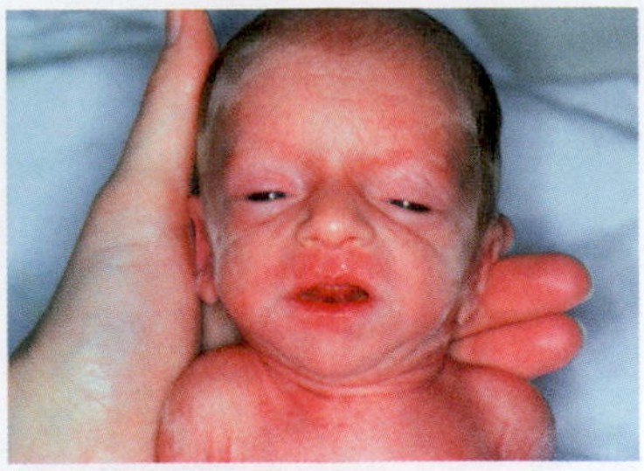

FIGURE 9.4
Opioids as Teratogens
Prenatal exposure to drugs such as opioids can cause infants to experience withdrawal symptoms upon birth.

FIGURE 9.5
Fetal Alcohol Spectrum Disorders
This is a child with one of the FASDs. The three most common features are small eye openings, an absence of the groove that normally appears between the nose and the lips, and a thin upper lip.

prescription drugs. Over the past 20 years, the opioid epidemic ravaging the United States has caused a threefold increase in neonatal opioid withdrawal syndrome (Volkow, 2016). Infants exposed to opioids during pregnancy can be born prematurely and experience excessive crying, tremors, and other symptoms of distress in their first month of life (**FIGURE 9.4**). Some have birth defects and other medical problems and experience slow growth. The physical effects of exposure to teratogens such as opioids may be obvious at birth, but disorders involving language, reasoning, social behavior, or emotional behavior may not become apparent until the child is older (Fill et al., 2018). The extent of the damage depends on when the embryo or fetus is exposed, as well as the length and amount of exposure.

The most common teratogen is alcohol. Drinking alcohol during pregnancy can lead to *fetal alcohol spectrum disorders* (*FASDs*). Among the symptoms of this family of disorders are low birth weight, face and head abnormalities, deficient brain growth, and evidence of impairment such as behavioral or cognitive problems or low IQ (Hoyme et al., 2016; **FIGURE 9.5**). FASDs are most likely to occur among infants of women who drink heavily during pregnancy, especially if they binge-drink. However, no minimal amount of alcohol has been determined to be safe for pregnant women and their developing babies. For this reason, many health workers recommend that women abstain from drinking alcohol when they are pregnant or trying to become pregnant (Mukherjee et al., 2005). In the United States, the prevalence of FASDs is estimated to be between 0.2 and 2.0 cases per 1,000 live births (Centers for Disease Control and Prevention, 2004), though more recent studies have found higher numbers, with an estimated rate closer to 8 out of 1,000 children (May et al., 2014).

An important point to remember is that many people exposed to toxins or stress have normal infants. Conversely, some people with only moderate exposure to teratogens have infants with serious developmental effects. Thus, we cannot say with certainty that any given baby born to a drug user or to a person who works around chemicals will be impaired. Likewise, we cannot be assured that light drinking or minimal teratogen exposure will allow for normal development. All potential caregivers face the responsibility of caring for their own mental and physical health to increase the odds of being able to parent a healthy and robust newborn.

Q **Why is synaptic pruning valuable in the developing brain?**

ANSWER: It eliminates unused synaptic connections, which allows for adaptation to the developmental environment.

9.2 Biology and Environment Influence Motor Development

Although newborn infants cannot survive on their own, they are not completely helpless. Newborns have various motor reflexes that aid survival. Perhaps you have observed the *grasping reflex* when a baby held your finger (**FIGURE 9.6a**). This reflex is a survival mechanism that has persisted from our primate ancestors. Young apes grasp their mothers, and this reflex is adaptive because the offspring need to be carried from place to place. Also appearing at birth is the *rooting reflex*, the turning and sucking that infants automatically engage in when a nipple or similar object touches an area near their mouths (**FIGURE 9.6b**). If they find an object, they will show the *sucking reflex*

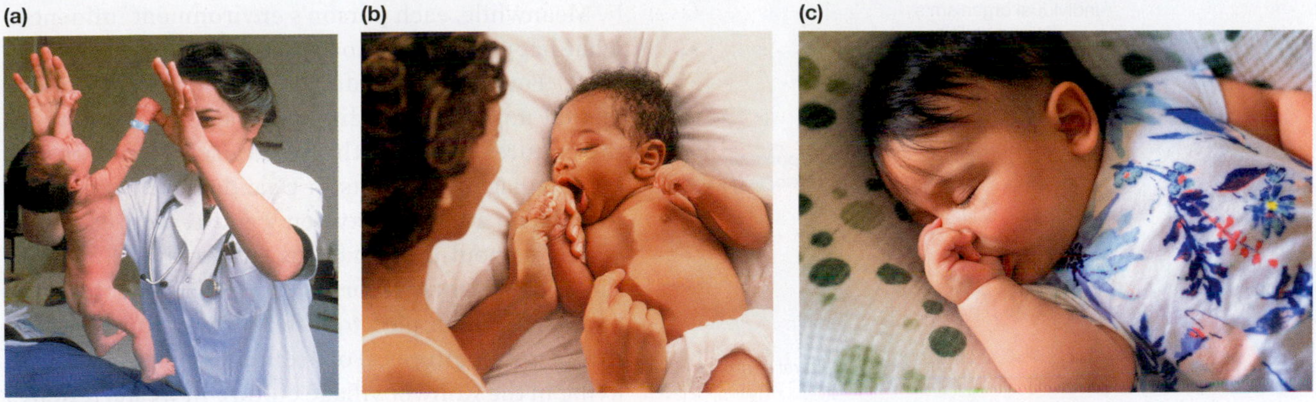

FIGURE 9.6
Infant Reflexes
Infants are born with innate abilities that help them survive, including the **(a)** grasping reflex, **(b)** rooting reflex, and **(c)** sucking reflex.

(FIGURE 9.6c). These reflexes help infants nurse. The brain at birth supports these basic reflexes, which pave the way for learning more complicated behavior patterns as the brain develops.

No newborn talks immediately, nor does any baby walk before it can sit up. But most humans make eye contact quickly after they are born, display a first social smile at around 6 weeks, and learn to roll over, to sit up, to crawl, to stand, to walk, and to talk, in that order (FIGURE 9.7). Occasionally, a child skips one of these steps or reverses a couple of them, but generally each child follows these steps within a predictable range of ages.

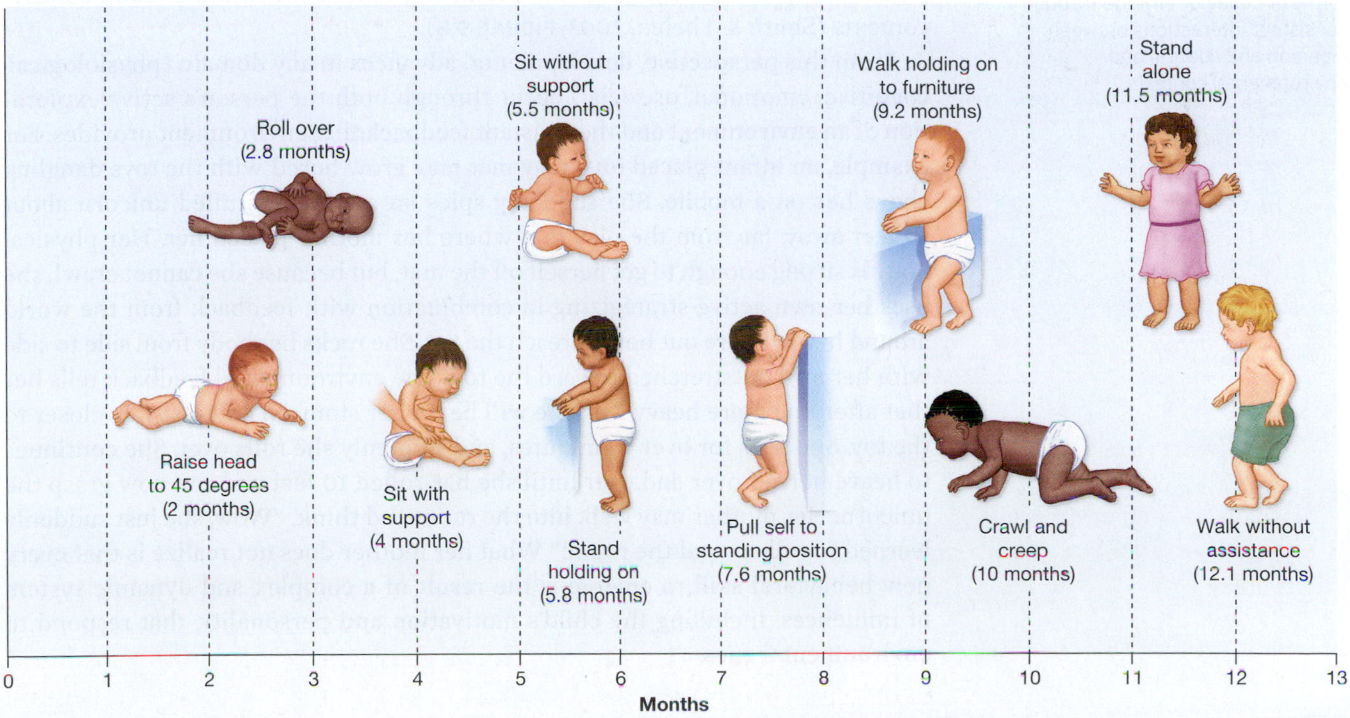

FIGURE 9.7
Learning to Walk
Usually, a human baby learns to walk without formal teaching, in a sequence characteristic of all humans. However, the numbers of months given here are averages. A child might deviate from this sequence or these times but still be developing normally.

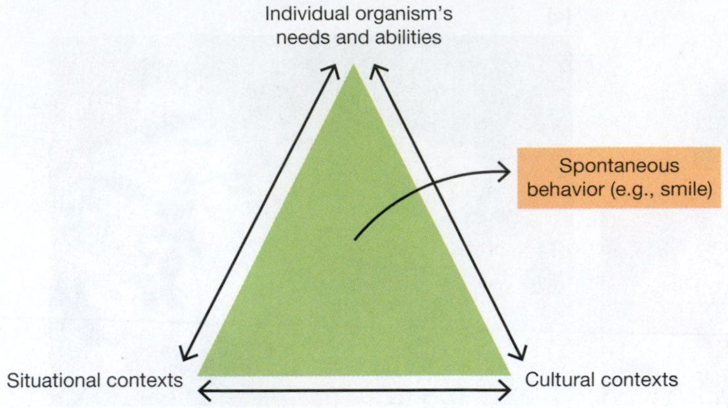

FIGURE 9.8

Dynamic Systems Theory

Throughout life, every new form of behavior emerges through consistent interactions between a biological being and cultural and environmental contexts.

Meanwhile, each person's environment influences what happens throughout that individual's development. For example, infants often achieve developmental milestones at different paces, depending on the cultures in which they are raised. Consider that healthy Baganda infants in Uganda have been found to walk, on average, between 9 and 11 months of age, which is about three months earlier than European American infants (Kilbride et al., 1970). Such differences are due in part to different patterns of infant care across cultures. For example, Kipsigi mothers living in the Kohwet village culture in western Kenya help their children learn to sit upright by placing babies in shallow holes in the ground (Super, 1976). Mothers in that culture help babies learn to walk by marching them around while placing their own arms under their children's underarms. These infants walk about one to two months earlier than American and European infants.

You might be wondering about the relative contributions of genes and environment to development. Does the timing of milestones (such as sitting up and walking) have more to do with nature or with nurture? Contemporary research has moved beyond such questions because we now know that every new development is the result of complex and consistent interplays between biology and environment. Developmental psychologists now consider developmental milestones (such as when an infant is able to walk two weeks after not being able to walk) to be part of a *dynamic system*. **Dynamic systems theory** views development as a self-organizing process in which new forms of behavior emerge from the process of an organism repeatedly engaging and interacting with its environment and cultural contexts (Smith & Thelen, 2003; **FIGURE 9.8**).

dynamic systems theory The view that development is a self-organizing process, in which new forms of behavior emerge through consistent interactions between a person and cultural and environmental contexts.

From this perspective, developmental advances in any domain (physiological, cognitive, emotional, or social) occur through both the person's active exploration of an environment and the constant feedback that environment provides. For example, an infant placed on a play mat may grow bored with the toys dangling above her on a mobile. She suddenly spies an attractive stuffed unicorn about 10 feet away, far from the play mat where her mother placed her. Her physical body is strong enough to get herself off the mat, but because she cannot crawl, she uses her own active strategizing in combination with feedback from the world around her to figure out how to reach the toy. She rocks her body from side to side with her arm outstretched toward the toy. The environmental feedback tells her that after one more heavy roll, she will be on her stomach and possibly closer to the toy. She tries for over 10 minutes, and suddenly she rolls over. She continues to heave herself over and over until she has rolled 10 feet and can now grasp the unicorn. Her mother may walk into the room and think, "Wow, she just suddenly learned to roll around the room!" What her mother does not realize is that every new behavioral skill to emerge is the result of a complex and dynamic system of influences, including the child's motivation and personality, that respond to environmental cues.

Q Why do physical developmental milestones occur in a predictable sequence but sometimes vary in timing between cultures?

ANSWER: Development is part of a dynamic system, guided by biology but influenced by environmental feedback and cultural interactions.

9.3 Infants Are Prepared to Learn

The next time you interact with a newborn, try sticking your tongue out at her. Not always, but often, the baby will react by sticking her tongue right back out at you (FIGURE 9.9). Think about the remarkable activity going on in the baby's young brain. After seeing a face with a tongue sticking out, the baby somehow seems to know that she, too, has a face with a tongue. The brain finds the tongue in its long list of body parts, sends it a command to get a move on, and out it goes. How does the baby know a tongue is a tongue? How does the baby's brain know what brain circuit controls the tongue? How does the baby know how to move the tongue? Why does the baby move her tongue? Obviously, this behavior was not learned by looking in a mirror, nor had it been taught. The ability to imitate must be innate.

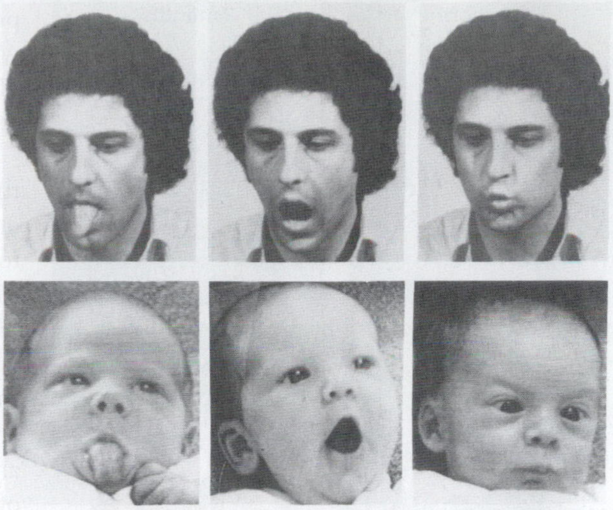

FIGURE 9.9
Infant Learning
Newborns have the ability to imitate adults sticking out their tongues and making other facial expressions (Meltzoff & Moore, 1977).

Babies are discerning about their interaction partners. They show preference for people over things. Babies are born categorizing, and newborns already understand they are in the people category, not the object category. The baby brain already has specific neural circuits for identifying biological motion and inanimate object motion, along with specific circuits to identify faces and facial movement (Lloyd-Fox et al., 2011). Babies are linked to the social world by their interactions with others. Babies do not lie there like lumps of clay but respond in a way that other people can relate to.

PERCEPTION Newborns normally come into the world with basic perceptual skills: smelling, hearing, tasting, and responding to touch. Although some of these skills are not fully developed at birth, the newborn is able to process a considerable range of sensory stimuli. For instance, 2-hour-old infants prefer sweet tastes to all other tastes (Mennella et al., 2016). Young infants also have a reasonably acute sense of smell, at least for smells associated with feeding. In several studies, infants turned their heads toward a pad containing their own mother's milk but not toward pads containing milk from other breast-feeding mothers (e.g., Marin et al., 2015; Winberg & Porter, 1998).

The sense of hearing is also quite good shortly after birth: Infants are startled by loud sounds and often will turn their bodies toward the source of the sounds. When newborns are exposed to the crying of another infant, a distress response is induced, and the newborns will join in the crying. When they hear their own recorded cry played to them, or other random noises, a distress response is not induced, and they do not cry (Dondi et al., 1999). These responses suggest that newborns are able to distinguish between their own cry and other infants' cries and have some innate understanding of the difference between themselves and others (Martin & Clark, 1982). Infants' abilities to recognize sounds and locate those sounds in space improve continuously as the infants gain experience with objects and people and as the auditory cortex develops. By the age of 6 months, babies have a nearly adult level of auditory function (DeCasper & Spence, 1986).

The sense of vision develops more slowly than hearing. The ability to distinguish differences among shapes, patterns, and colors is known as *visual acuity*. Newborns' visual acuity for distant objects is poor, but it increases rapidly over the first 6 months and reaches adult levels when the infant is about a year old

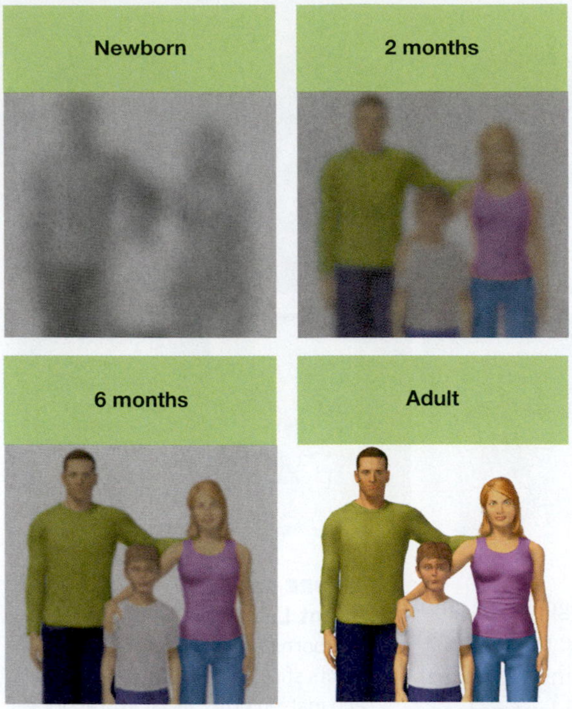

FIGURE 9.10

Infant Vision Improves over Time

Newborns have poor visual acuity and poor ability to see colors. These capacities improve rapidly over the first 6 months of life. By 1 year of age, children can see as well as adults.

(Teller et al., 1974; **FIGURE 9.10**). The increase in visual acuity is probably due to a combination of practice looking at things in the world, the development of the visual cortex, and the development of the cones in the retina (as noted in Chapter 5, the cones are important for perceiving detail).

Infants respond more to objects with high-contrast patterns than to other stimuli. In the early 1960s, Robert Fantz (1963) and other developmental psychologists observed infants' reactions to patterns of black-and-white stripes as well as patches of gray. This type of research makes use of the *preferential-looking technique* (**FIGURE 9.11**). In using this technique, the researchers show an infant two things. If the infant looks longer at one of the things, the researchers know the infant can distinguish between the two and finds one more interesting. In these studies, the mother or another caregiver was asked to hold the infant in front of a display of two images. The experimenter, not knowing which image was on which side, would observe through a peephole to see where the infant preferred to look. This research revealed that infants look at stripes with high contrast more readily than at gray images. The smaller the stripes are—that is, the less contrast between the images—the more difficult it becomes for infants to distinguish them from the gray patches.

Infants are particularly attuned to human faces. Babies prefer to look at faces rather than non-face objects, and they will look longer at familiar faces than unfamiliar ones (Sugden & Marquis, 2017). At around 3 months of age, infants also show a preference for faces of their own race compared with other races (Gaither et al., 2012). One way psychologists study the ability of infants to distinguish between races is with the **habituation technique**. Infants are presented with a series of pictures, such as of faces from their own race, until the time they spend looking at the images decreases. At this point, infants are said to be habituated to the images. (Recall from Chapter 6 that habituation is a decreased response to an unchanging stimulus.) Then infants are shown a new picture that is from the same category as the habituated images or from a different category. In these studies, infants would see a picture of someone from their own race or a different race. Infants will look at the new picture for a longer time if they perceive it as being in a different category from the habituated pictures. Researchers can learn about how infants categorize different stimuli (e.g., same- and other-race faces) by comparing their looking time at the habituated pictures versus the new ones.

habituation technique A way to study how infants categorize a series of objects, such as faces, based on the principle that after looking at objects that are all from the same category, babies will look for a longer time at objects from a new category.

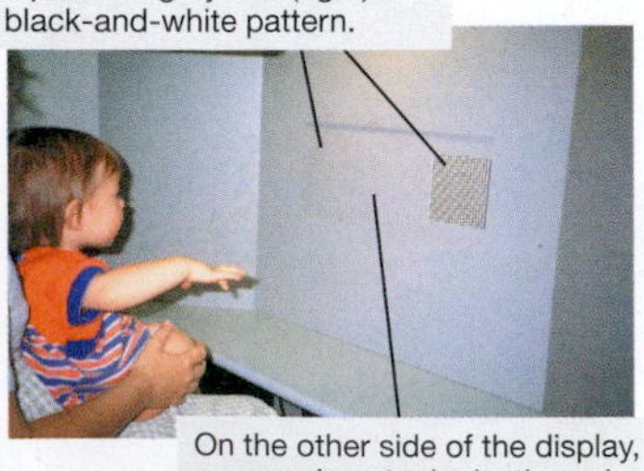

A mother holds her infant in front of a display showing (left) a patch of gray and (right) a black-and-white pattern.
On the other side of the display, an experimenter looks through a peephole and notes whether the infant is looking left or right.

FIGURE 9.11

Preferential-Looking Technique

This research method is used to test visual acuity in infants.

Learning Tip

You might hear your professor refer to the *salient* stimuli in infant research. A "salient" stimulus means something that is visually attention-grabbing (e.g., a shiny toy with flashing lights) or unexpected, or new as opposed to habituated. Humans have an innate tendency to pay more attention to salient stimuli. Psychologists call this the *orienting reflex* (Fantz, 1966). Even from birth, an infant will look away more quickly from something familiar than from something unfamiliar or puzzling.

MEMORY The development of memory helps children learn about the world around them. That is, children use what they already know to process new information. But how do researchers study memory in infants, who cannot speak?

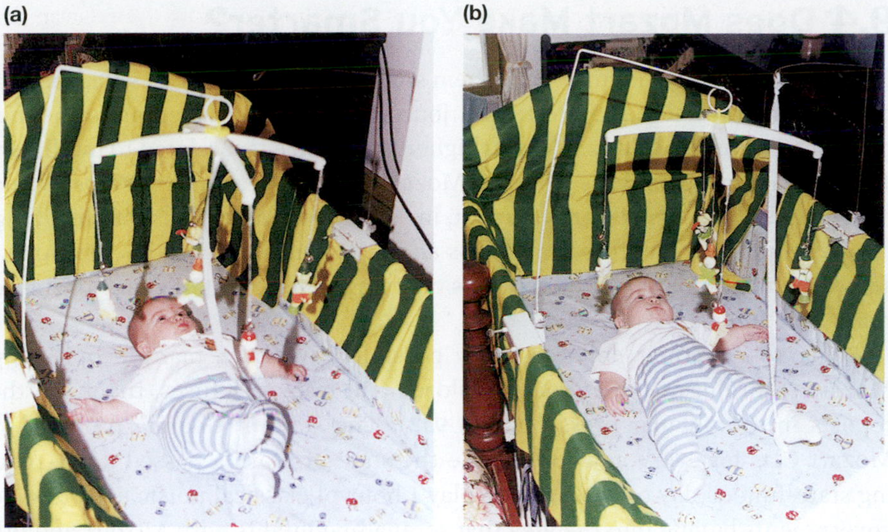

FIGURE 9.12
The Memory-Retention Test
(a) In this test, infants learn that kicking their feet moves a mobile because one foot is attached to the mobile by a ribbon around the ankle. **(b)** After a delay, the infants are placed back under the mobile. If the infants soon kick their feet vigorously to get the mobile to move, they have shown that they remember moving the mobile during the learning phase.

In a clever experiment (Rovee-Collier, 1999), a mobile hanging over a crib was attached to infants' ankles with a ribbon (**FIGURE 9.12**). The infants learned that they could move the mobile by kicking their feet. When each infant was tested later, the ribbon was attached to the ankle but not to the mobile, so the kicks no longer moved the mobile. The rate at which infants kicked when nothing was attached served as the baseline. If the babies recognized the mobile, presumably they would kick faster than the baseline rate to try to make the mobile move. Infants ranging in age from 2 months to 18 months were trained for two days on the mobile task and then tested after different lengths of time. Compared with younger infants, older infants could retain their memories regarding the connection between the ankle kicking and the mobile movement for longer periods of time. By 18 months, the infants could remember the event even if they were tested several weeks after they had learned the initial associations.

The ability to retain explicit memories also develops with age. Most adults remember few events that occurred before they were 3 or 4 years old. Sigmund Freud referred to this inability to remember events from early childhood as **infantile amnesia**. Researchers have offered various explanations for this phenomenon, including immature memory systems in the brain (Madsen & Kim, 2016). Some psychologists believe that children begin to retain explicit memories after developing the ability to create autobiographical memory based on personal experience. Other psychologists suggest that childhood memory develops with language acquisition because the ability to use words and concepts aids in memory retention. Still other psychologists theorize that children younger than 3 or 4 do not perceive contexts well enough to store memories accurately. They argue that improvements in children's abilities to encode new information, retain it for longer periods, and use retrieval-based practice (see Chapter 1) underlie the decrease in infantile amnesia after the first 5 years of life (Hayne, 2004). There are cultural differences in the age at which children retain their earliest memories, however. The native Māori of New Zealand recall memories, on average, from a few months before their third birthdays. Although Māori mothers do not elaborate events in greater detail, it appears they talk about events in a way that enables their children to understand the relative time when events happened (Hayne et al., 2015).

infantile amnesia The inability to remember events from early childhood.

Q Why are many toys for infants black-and-white?

ANSWER: Infants have poor color vision and low visual acuity, so they most easily perceive objects with stark contrasts, such as black against a white background.

YOU BE THE PSYCHOLOGIST

9.4 Does Mozart Make You Smarter?

Can playing music to infants make them smarter? In 1993, Frances Rauscher and colleagues reported in the prestigious journal *Nature* that listening to the music of Wolfgang Amadeus Mozart led to higher scores on a test related to intelligence. The media jumped onto the so-called Mozart effect with abandon. Websites made bold claims about the power of Mozart, including wild assertions that listening to Mozart could cure neurological illness and other maladies. To this day, Amazon sells dozens of Mozart-effect products claiming to boost intelligence or improve brain functioning.

FIGURE 9.13
The Mozart Effect?
In the early 1990s, a study on the cognitive benefits of listening to Mozart inspired people to increase infants' exposure to classical music. However, the research results were misrepresented.

Eager to give their children every possible advantage, many people played Mozart recordings to their young children and even to fetuses, thanks to these reports in the popular press (FIGURE 9.13). The state of Georgia provided free Mozart CDs for every newborn, while the state of Florida passed a law requiring state-funded day care centers to play 1 hour of classical music each day, both governments buying into the idea that serenading infants with Mozart and other composers would produce a smarter populace.

But what was the quality of the evidence behind these claims? What is the true power of Mozart for the developing mind? To see the claims more clearly, we need to step back and critically evaluate the research underlying the Mozart effect. In the study, psychologists played the first 10 minutes of the Mozart Sonata for Two Pianos in D Major (K. 448) to a group of college students (Rauscher et al., 1993). Compared with students who listened to relaxation instructions or who sat in silence, those who heard Mozart performed slightly better on a task that involved folding and cutting paper. This task was part of a larger overall measure of intelligence. The modest increase lasted for about 10–15 minutes.

Take a moment and think like a psychologist. Ask yourself: What do these results really show? Is the manipulation of the independent variable (Mozart versus not Mozart) clean and without confounds? What else might be driving the differences between the two groups? Is the dependent variable a good measure of intelligence? If not, what mental process is actually measured by the dependent variable? Is the sample adequate for drawing conclusions about babies and young children?

After pondering these questions, you might not be surprised to learn that subsequent research largely failed to replicate the original result. Having carefully reviewed the studies testing the Mozart effect, Christopher Chabris (1999) concluded that listening to Mozart is unlikely to increase intelligence among listeners. According to Chabris, listening to Mozart appears to enhance only certain types of motor skills, not abilities more commonly associated with intelligence (such as working memory or verbal ability). A more recent meta-analysis of nearly 40 studies failed to find any specific advantage for Mozart, but it did find a very small influence of music on tasks such as those used in the original study (Pietschnig et al., 2010).

What might have been happening in the original study on the Mozart effect? When thinking about confounds in the manipulation of the independent variable, you might have wondered what emotional reactions participants had to listening to Mozart and whether the emotional reactions of people in the control group were different. A team of researchers has shown that the effect may occur simply because listening to music is more uplifting than sitting in silence or relaxing; that is, the increase in positive mood may be largely responsible for better performance (Schellenberg, 2012; Thompson et al., 2001).

Also note that all the studies to date have been conducted with college students as participants, yet all the publicity focused on infants' intelligence. How well do you think studies of college students can generalize to infants? Most of the claims about music go far beyond the data.

Though the Mozart effect itself is largely debunked, music does relate to intelligence in other ways. Musical training, especially during childhood, is associated with the development of cognitive skills, including spatial reasoning, math, and working memory (Criscuolo et al., 2019). Perhaps less surprisingly, trained musicians also show better auditory perceptual abilities and fine motor control than people without musical training (Habibi et al., 2018). However, none of these studies are true experiments in which researchers randomly assign children to receive musical training or a comparison training over a period of time and then compare the changes in cognition and motor skills between the two groups. Recall from Chapter 2 that it is impossible to make valid causal claims without random assignment. How might children who receive musical training be different from children who do not? Being a psychological scientist means applying your critical thinking skills to all kinds of claims. ■

Q Thinking critically, does the original "Mozart effect" study support the idea that playing classical music to babies will increase their intelligence?

ANSWER: No, for a few reasons. In the original study, "intelligence" was tested in relation to a motor skill; the test results might have been influenced by the temporary mood-enhancing qualities of the music; and the participants were college students, so we cannot generalize the results to infants.

9.5 Infants Develop Attachments

One fundamental need infants have is to bond emotionally with those who care for them. An **attachment** is a strong, intimate, emotional connection between people that persists over time and across circumstances. Such emotional bonds are the building blocks of a successful social life later on. The innate tendency to bond is, in fact, an adaptive trait. Forming bonds with others provides protection for individuals, increases their chances of survival, and thus increases their chances of passing along their genes to future generations (Bowlby, 1982). The importance of attachment is illustrated by what happens when it is missing. Many children raised in Romanian orphanages in the 1980s were deprived of nearly all interpersonal relationships. The psychologist Nathan Fox has documented the devastating effects this deprivation had on the children's cognitive, emotional, behavioral, and even physical development (Fox et al., 2011).

attachment A strong, intimate, emotional connection between people that persists over time and across circumstances.

Human infants need nurturance and care from adults to survive. Unlike horses and deer, which can walk and find food within hours after birth, humans are born profoundly immature. At that early point, human infants cannot even hold up their own heads or roll over. But they are far from passive. Just minutes after birth, infants' cries cause psychological, physiological, and behavioral reactions in caregivers that compel the offering of food and comfort to the newborns. According to John Bowlby (1982), the architect of attachment theory, infants have innate attachment behaviors that motivate adult attention. For instance, they prefer to remain close to caregivers, act distressed when caregivers leave, and rejoice and put out their arms to be lifted when the caregivers return. Between 4 and 6 weeks of age, most infants display a first social smile (FIGURE 9.14). This expression of pleasure typically induces powerful feelings of love in caregivers. Bowlby argued that these behaviors motivate infants and caregivers to stay in proximity.

FIGURE 9.14
Infant Attachment Behaviors
Newborns behave in ways, such as smiling, that make their caregivers want to nurture them.

Because it heightens feelings of security, attachment is adaptive: It is a dynamic relationship that facilitates survival for the infant and parental investment for the caregivers.

Caregivers shape much of an infant's early experience, from what the child eats to where the child sleeps to what social connections the child makes. The essence of attachment theory is that these early interactions with people begin to shape the developing human. They are the first stages in which a person learns how to communicate with others, how to behave appropriately in various situations, and how to establish and maintain relationships. Ultimately, socialization also affects complex human characteristics such as gender roles, a sense of personal identity, and moral reasoning, each of which will be explored in this chapter.

ATTACHMENT IN OTHER SPECIES Attachment is important for survival in many other species as well. For instance, infant birds communicate hunger through crying chirps. In doing so, they prompt caregivers to find food for them. Some bird species seem to have a sensitive period in which fledgling chicks become strongly attached to a nearby adult, even one from another species. This pattern occurs for birds such as chickens, geese, and ducks. Because these birds can walk immediately after hatching, they are at risk of straying from their mothers. Therefore, within about 18 hours after hatching, the birds will attach themselves to an adult (usually to their mothers) and then follow the object of their attachment. The ethologist Konrad Lorenz (1935) called such behavior *imprinting*. He noted that goslings that became imprinted on him did not go back to their biological mothers when later given access to them (**FIGURE 9.15**). Such birds preferentially imprint on a female of their species if one is available, however.

During the late 1950s, the psychologist Harry Harlow began conducting research that later allowed him to discover one of the most striking examples of nonhuman attachment. At that time, psychologists generally believed an infant needed its mother primarily as a food source. But Harlow saw food-based explanations of attachment as inadequate for explaining what he observed in infant monkeys. He recognized that the infants needed comfort and security in addition to food.

In a now-famous series of experiments, Harlow placed infant rhesus monkeys in a cage with two different "mothers" (Harlow & Harlow, 1966). One surrogate mother was made of bare wire and could give milk through an attached bottle. The second surrogate mother was made of soft terry cloth and could not give milk. Which of these two substitute mothers do you think the infant monkeys preferred?

FIGURE 9.15
Imprinting
Here, Konrad Lorenz walks the goslings that had imprinted themselves on him. The little geese followed Lorenz as if he were their mother.

The monkeys' responses were unmistakable: They clung to the cloth mother most of the day. They went to it for comfort in times of threat. The monkeys approached the wire mother only when they were hungry. Harlow tested the monkeys' attachment to these mothers in various ways. For example, he introduced a strange object, such as a menacing metal robot with flashing eyes and large teeth, into the cage. The infants always ran to the mother that provided comfort, never to the mother that fed them. Hence, the mother-as-food theory of mother/child attachment was debunked. Harlow's findings established the importance of contact comfort—the importance of physical touch and reassurance—in aiding social development.

ATTACHMENT STYLE If Bowlby and Harlow were correct in hypothesizing that attachment encourages proximity between infant and caregiver, then we might expect attachment responses to increase when children are able to move themselves away from caregivers. And indeed, just when infants begin to understand the difference between their attachment figures and strangers, at around 8–12 months, they start to move away from strangers by crawling, and they typically display separation anxiety when they cannot see or are separated from their attachment figures. This pattern occurs in all human cultures.

To study attachment behaviors in humans, the developmental psychologist Mary D. Salter Ainsworth created the *strange-situation test* FIGURE 9.16. In a laboratory set up like a playroom, the child, the caregiver, and a friendly but unfamiliar adult engage in a series of eight semi-structured episodes. The crux

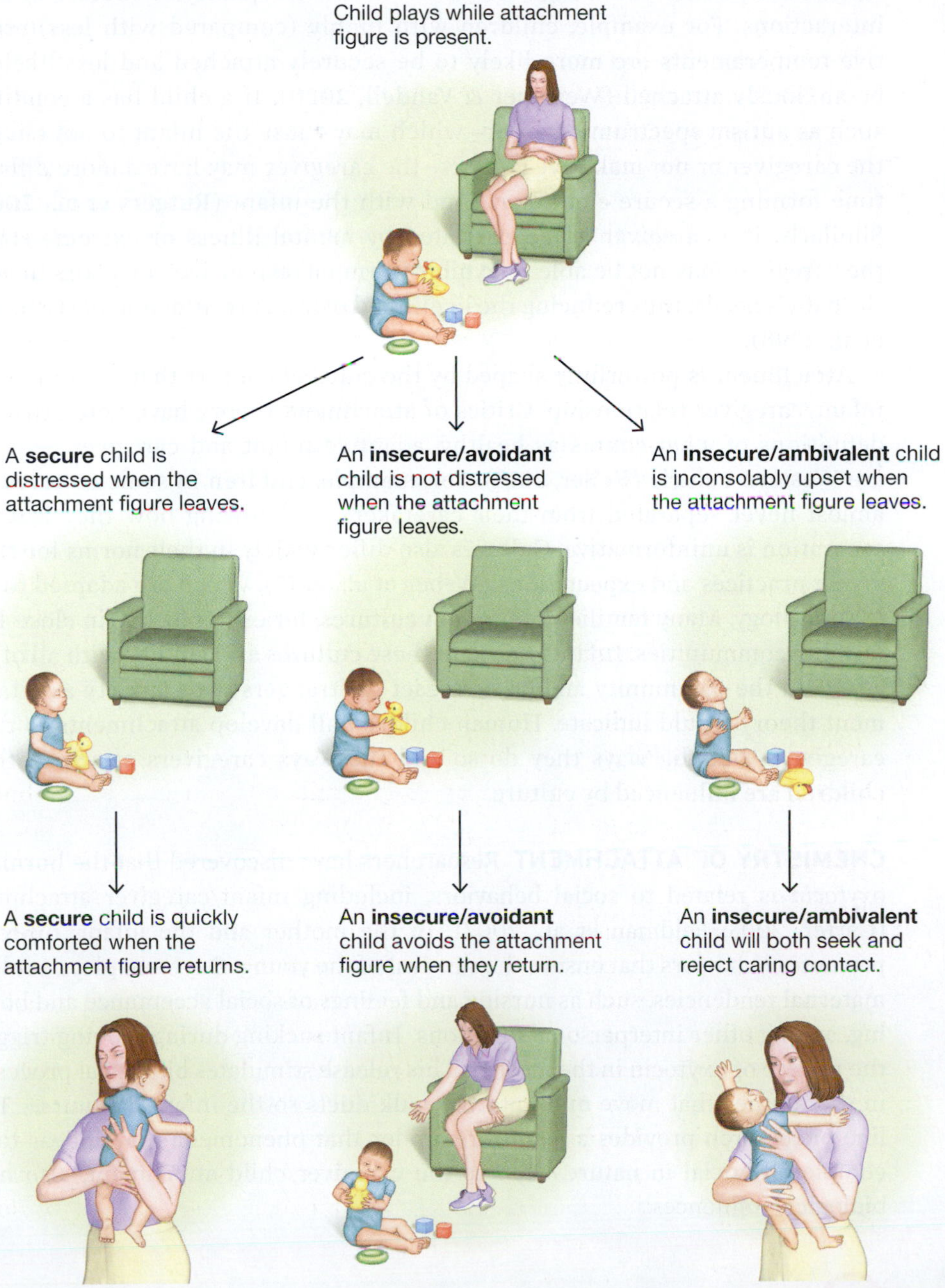

Child plays while attachment figure is present.
A **secure** child is distressed when the attachment figure leaves.
An **insecure/avoidant** child is not distressed when the attachment figure leaves.
An **insecure/ambivalent** child is inconsolably upset when the attachment figure leaves.
A **secure** child is quickly comforted when the attachment figure returns.
An **insecure/avoidant** child avoids the attachment figure when they return.
An **insecure/ambivalent** child will both seek and reject caring contact.

FIGURE 9.16
The Strange-Situation Test

of the procedure is a standard sequence of separations and reunions between the child and each adult. Over the course of the eight episodes, the child experiences increasing distress and a greater need for caregiver proximity. The researchers observe the test through a one-way mirror in the laboratory. The extent to which the child copes with distress and the strategies for doing so indicate the quality of the child's attachment to the caregiver. The researchers record the child's activity level and actions such as crying, playing, and paying attention to the caregiver and the stranger. Using the strange-situation test, Ainsworth classified infant/caregiver pairs as having one of three attachment styles: secure, insecure, or anxious (Ainsworth et al., 1978). Later, other researchers added a fourth attachment style: disoriented-disorganized (Hesse & Main, 2000).

Attachment is a complex developmental phenomenon. As in all relationships, both infants and caregivers contribute to the quality or success of their interactions. For example, children with highly (compared with less) attentive temperaments are more likely to be securely attached and less likely to be anxiously attached (Wegemer & Vandell, 2020). If a child has a condition such as autism spectrum disorder—which may cause the infant to not cling to the caregiver or not make eye contact—the caregiver may have a more difficult time forming a secure emotional bond with the infant (Rutgers et al., 2004). Similarly, if a caregiver is incapacitated by mental illness or extreme stress, the caregiver may not be able to exhibit warm or responsive behaviors to meet the baby's needs, thus reducing the likelihood of a secure attachment (Cicchetti et al., 1998).

Attachment is powerfully shaped by the cultural context that surrounds the infant/caregiver relationship. Critics of attachment theory have noted that the definitions of what counts as healthy, adaptive infant and caregiver behavior are Western-centric (Keller, 2018). For example, children in some cultures are almost never separated from their caretakers, so knowing how they react to separation is uninformative. Cultures also differ widely in their norms for caregiving practices and expectations (Weber et al., 2017), which are adapted to the local ecology. Many families in agrarian cultures, for example, live in close-knit farming communities. Infants raised in these cultures are familiar with all of the adults in the community and do not react to strangers with anxiety as attachment theory would indicate. Human children all develop attachments to their caregivers, but the ways they do so and the ways caregivers attach to their children are influenced by culture.

CHEMISTRY OF ATTACHMENT Researchers have discovered that the hormone *oxytocin* is related to social behaviors, including infant/caregiver attachment (Carter, 2003; Feldman et al., 2007). In the mother and the infant, oxytocin promotes behaviors that ensure the survival of the young. Oxytocin plays a role in maternal tendencies, such as nursing and feelings of social acceptance and bonding, among other interpersonal functions. Infant sucking during nursing triggers the release of oxytocin in the mother. This release stimulates biological processes in the mother that move milk into the milk ducts so the infant can nurse. This line of research provides a helpful reminder that phenomena that appear to be completely social in nature, such as the caregiver/child attachment, also have biological influences.

Q **According to Bowlby's attachment theory, how is attachment adaptive?**

ANSWER: Attachment motivates infants and caregivers to stay near each other, increasing the security that infants need to survive and thrive.

How Do Children Learn About the World?

To learn, children need to obtain information from the world. The development of sensory capacities enables infants to observe and evaluate the objects and events around them. The infants then use the information gained from perception to make sense of how the world works. In other words, children think about things. How does cognition develop in childhood?

Learning Objectives

- List and describe the stages of development proposed by Piaget.
- Discuss challenges to Piaget's theory.
- Define theory of mind and explain its significance for prosocial behavior.
- Compare and contrast theories of moral reasoning and moral emotions.

9.6 Piaget Emphasized Stages of Cognitive Development

Ultimately, how do we account for the differences between children's ways of thinking and adults' ways of thinking? Are children merely inexperienced adults? Do they simply not have the skills and knowledge that adults normally have learned over time? Or do children's minds work in qualitatively different ways from those of adults?

Through careful observations of young children, Jean Piaget (1924) devised an influential theory about the development of thinking (FIGURE 9.17). Piaget viewed children as qualitatively different from adults, not simply as inexperienced adults. He also viewed children as active learners: people trying to understand the world around them by interacting with objects and by observing the consequences of their actions. Some but not all of Piaget's ideas have been supported by subsequent research.

FIGURE 9.17
Jean Piaget
Piaget introduced the idea that cognitive development occurs in stages.

One of Piaget's deepest contributions to developmental psychology was to focus as much on how children make errors as on how they succeed on tasks. Children's mistakes, illogical by adult standards, provide insights into how young minds make sense of the world.

From Piaget's perspective, children think the way they do because their views of how the world works are based on sets of assumptions that are different from those held by adults. Careful study of children's responses to problems, especially their errors, can reveal those assumptions. Developmental psychology researchers now believe that the ways children think serve very important functions for their mental growth (Bjorklund, 2007).

Piaget proposed that children form new schemes as they develop. *Schemes* are ways of thinking based on personal experience. Piaget's idea of schemes is similar to the concept of schemas defined and discussed in Chapter 7. For Piaget, schemes were structured ways of making sense of experience, and they changed as the child acquired new information about objects and events in the world through two learning processes: Through **assimilation**, a new experience is placed into an existing scheme. Through **accommodation** (not to be confused with the process of accommodation in the visual system, in Chapter 5), a new scheme is created or an existing one is dramatically altered to include new information that otherwise would not fit into the scheme.

assimilation The process by which new information is placed into an existing scheme.

accommodation The process by which a new scheme is created or an existing scheme is drastically altered to include new information that otherwise would not fit into the scheme.

For example, a 2-year-old sees a Great Dane and asks, "What's that?" The adult answers that it is a dog. But it does not look anything like the family Chihuahua. The toddler needs to assimilate the Great Dane into the existing dog scheme. The same 2-year-old might see a cow for the first time and shout, "Doggie!" After all, a cow has four legs and fur and is about the same size as a Great Dane. Thus, based on a dog scheme the child has developed, the label "doggie" can be considered logical. But the adult says, "No, honey, that's a cow! See, it doesn't say 'Arf!' It says

FIGURE 9.18
Piaget's Stages of Cognitive Development

STAGE	CHARACTERIZATION	
1 Sensorimotor (birth–2 years)	• Differentiates self from objects • Recognizes self as agent of action and begins to act intentionally; for example, pulls a string to set a mobile in motion or shakes a rattle to make a noise • Achieves object permanence: realizes that things continue to exist even when no longer present to the senses	
2 Preoperational (2–7 years)	• Learns to use language and to represent objects by images and words • Thinking is still egocentric: has difficulty taking the viewpoint of others • Classifies objects by a single feature; for example, groups together all the red blocks regardless of shape or all the square blocks regardless of color	
3 Concrete operational (7–12 years)	• Can think logically about objects and events • Achieves conservation of number (age 7), mass (age 7), and weight (age 9) • Classifies objects by several features and can order them in a series along a single dimension, such as size	
4 Formal operational (12 years and up)	• Can think logically about abstract propositions and test hypotheses systematically • Becomes concerned with the hypothetical, the future, and ideological problems	

'Moo!' And it is much bigger than a dog." Because the child cannot easily fit this new information into the existing dog scheme using the process of assimilation, the child must now create a new scheme, cow, through the process of accommodation.

By systematically analyzing children's thinking, Piaget developed the theory that children go through four *stages of development*, which reflect different ways of thinking about the world. These stages are called *sensorimotor*, *preoperational*, *concrete operational*, and *formal operational* (FIGURE 9.18).

sensorimotor stage The first stage in Piaget's theory of cognitive development; during this stage, infants acquire information about the world through their senses and motor skills. Reflexive responses develop into more deliberate actions through the development and refinement of schemes.

SENSORIMOTOR STAGE (BIRTH TO 2 YEARS) From birth until about age 2, according to Piaget, children are in the **sensorimotor stage**. During this period, children are firmly situated in the present and acquire information primarily through their senses and motor exploration. Thus, very young infants' understanding of objects occurs when they reflexively react to the sensory input from those objects. For example, they learn by sucking on a nipple, grasping a finger, or seeing a face—that is, through perception and observation of the results of their actions. They progress from being reflexive to being reflective. In other words, they become capable of mentally representing their world and experiences with increasingly complex schemes.

As infants begin to control their motor movements, they develop their first schemes. These conceptual models reflect the kinds of actions that can be performed on certain kinds of objects. For instance, the sucking reflex begins as a reaction to the sensory input from the nipple: Infants simply respond reflexively by sucking. Soon they realize they can suck on other things, such as a bottle, a finger, a toy, or a blanket. Piaget described sucking on other objects as an example of assimilation to the scheme of sucking. But sucking on a toy or a blanket does not result in the same experience as the reflexive sucking of a nipple. The difference between these experiences leads children to accommodate their sucking scheme to include new experiences and information. In other words, they must continually adjust their understandings of sucking.

According to Piaget, one important cognitive concept that develops in the sensorimotor stage is **object permanence**. This term refers to the understanding that an object continues to exist even when it is hidden from view. Piaget noted that until 9 months of age, most infants will not search for objects they have seen being hidden under a blanket. At around 9 months, infants will pass the *object permanence test* by looking for the hidden object by picking up the blanket. Still, their search skills have limits. For instance, suppose during several trials an 8-month-old child watches an experimenter hide a toy under a blanket and the child then finds the toy. If the experimenter then hides the toy under a different blanket, in full view of the child, the child will still look for the toy in the first hiding place (the so-called *A-not-B error*). Full comprehension of object permanence was, for Piaget, one key accomplishment of the sensorimotor period.

object permanence The understanding that an object continues to exist even when it cannot be seen.

PREOPERATIONAL STAGE (2 TO 7 YEARS) In the **preoperational stage**, according to Piaget, children can begin to think about objects not in their immediate view. Having formed conceptual models of how the world works, children begin to think symbolically. For example, they can pretend that a stick is a sword or a wand. Piaget believed that what children cannot do at this stage is think "operationally." That is, they cannot imagine the logical outcomes of performing certain actions on certain objects. Instead, they perform intuitive reasoning based on superficial appearances.

preoperational stage The second stage in Piaget's theory of cognitive development; during this stage, children think symbolically about objects, but they reason based on intuition and superficial appearance rather than logic.

For instance, children at this stage have no understanding of the conservation of quantity. This physical principle states that even if a substance's appearance changes, its quantity may remain unchanged. If you pour a short, fat glass of water into a tall, thin glass, you know the amount of water has not changed. However, if you ask children in the preoperational stage which glass contains more, they will pick the tall, thin glass because the water is at a higher level. The children will make this error even when they have seen someone pour the same amount of water into each glass or when they pour the liquid themselves. They are fooled by the appearance of a higher water line. They cannot understand how the thinner diameter of the taller glass compensates for the higher-appearing water level (**FIGURE 9.19**).

FIGURE 9.19
The Preoperational Stage and the Law of Conservation of Quantity
In the preoperational stage, according to Piaget, children cannot yet understand the concept of conservation of quantity. They reason intuitively, not logically.

1 A young child believes that a tall 8 oz. glass contains more juice than a short 8 oz. glass.

2 Here, the child watches the juice being poured from the tall glass into a second short glass.

3 She is surprised to see that the short glass holds the same amount of juice as the tall glass.

FIGURE 9.20
Egocentrism
This little girl is "hiding" behind a tree by covering her own eyes. If she cannot see the searchers, she believes they cannot see her.

Piaget thought that another cognitive limitation characteristic of the preoperational period is *egocentrism*. This term refers to the tendency for preoperational thinkers to view the world through their own experiences. They can understand how others feel, and they have the capacity to care about others. However, they tend to engage in thought processes that revolve around their own perspectives. For example, a 3-year-old may play hide-and-seek by crouching next to a large tree and facing it with her eyes closed (FIGURE 9.20). The child believes that if she cannot see other people, other people cannot see her.

Why might children do this? Modern psychologists adopt a functionalist stance about egocentric thinking. What purpose does it serve for children in this stage to be embedded in a first-person perspective? Perhaps it helps them learn as much as they can about how their own minds and bodies interact with the world. A clear egocentric focus prevents them from trying to expand their schemes too much before they understand all the complex information inside their own experience (Bjorklund, 2018).

concrete operational stage The third stage in Piaget's theory of cognitive development; during this stage, children begin to think about and understand logical operations, and they are no longer fooled by appearances.

formal operational stage The final stage in Piaget's theory of cognitive development; in this stage, people can think abstractly, and they can formulate and test hypotheses through deductive logic.

CONCRETE OPERATIONAL STAGE (7 TO 12 YEARS) At about 7 years of age, according to Piaget, children enter the **concrete operational stage**. They remain in this stage until adolescence. Piaget believed that humans do not develop logic until they begin to perform mental operations, which develop in two steps. The first step is performing mental operations on concrete objects in the world. That is, unlike a preoperational child, a concrete operational child is able to think logically about actual objects. A classic *operation* is an action that can be undone, such as turning a light on and off. According to Piaget, the ability to understand that an action is reversible enables children to begin to understand concepts such as conservation of quantity. Children in this period are not fooled by superficial transformations in the liquid's appearance in conservation tasks. They can reason logically about the problem. And they begin to understand with much more depth how other people view the world and feel about things.

Although this development is the beginning of logical thinking, Piaget believed that children at this stage reason only about concrete things. They have not yet achieved the second step: the ability to reason abstractly, or hypothetically, about what might be possible.

FORMAL OPERATIONAL STAGE (12 YEARS TO ADULTHOOD) Piaget believed that after about age 12, individuals can reason in sophisticated, abstract ways. Thus, the **formal operational stage** is Piaget's final stage of cognitive development. Formal operations involve critical thinking. This kind of thinking is characterized by the ability to form a hypothesis about something and test the hypothesis through deductive logic. It also involves using information to systematically find answers to problems. Critical thinking, a major theme of this book, relies on formal, or abstract, cognitive operations.

Piaget devised a way to study this ability. He gave teenagers and younger children four flasks of colorless liquid and one flask of colored liquid. He then explained that the colored liquid could be obtained by combining two of the colorless liquids. The younger children just randomly combined liquids. Adolescents, he found, can systematically try different combinations to obtain the correct result. In other words, they form hypotheses and test them. They are also able to consider abstract notions and think about many viewpoints at once.

Q **According to Piaget's theory, why would an infant stop reaching for a toy when it is suddenly covered by a towel?**

ANSWER: Because the child does not yet understand object permanence (that the now-hidden toy still exists).

9.7 Piaget Underestimated Children's Cognitive Abilities

Piaget revolutionized the understanding of cognitive development and was right about several things. For example, infants do learn about the world through sensorimotor exploration. Also, people do move from intuitive, illogical thinking to a more logical understanding of the world. Piaget also believed, however, that as children progress through each stage, they all use the same kind of logic to solve problems. His framework thus leaves little room for differing cognitive strategies or skills among individuals—or among cultures.

Work by Piaget's contemporary Lev Vygotsky emphasized social relations over objects in thinking about cognitive development. Vygotsky focused on the role of social and cultural context in the development of cognition and language. He argued that humans are unique because they use symbols and psychological tools—such as speech, writing, maps, art, and so on—through which they create culture. Culture, in turn, dictates what people need to learn and the sorts of skills they need to develop (**FIGURE 9.21**). For example, some cultures value science and rational thinking. Other cultures emphasize supernatural and mystical forces. These cultural values shape how people think about and relate to the world around them. Vygotsky distinguished between elementary mental functions (such as innate sensory experiences) and higher mental functions (such as language, perception, abstraction, and memory). As children develop, their elementary capacities are gradually transformed. Culture exerts the primary influence on these capacities (Vygotsky, 1978).

Central to Vygotsky's theories is the idea that social and cultural context influences language development. In turn, language development influences cognitive development. Children start by directing their speech toward specific communications with others, such as asking for food or for toys. As children develop, they begin directing speech toward themselves, as when they give themselves directions or talk to themselves while playing. Eventually, children internalize their words into inner speech: verbal thoughts that direct both behavior and cognition. From this perspective, your thoughts are based on the language you have acquired through your society and through your culture, and this ongoing inner speech reflects higher-order cognitive processes. In challenging Piaget's framework of universal developmental milestones, Vygotsky proposed the important interaction between self and environment.

Another challenge to Piaget's view is that many children move back and forth between stages if they are working on tasks that require varying skill levels. They may think in concrete operational ways on some tasks but revert to preoperational logic when faced with a novel task. Theorists believe that different areas in the brain are responsible for different skills and that development does not necessarily follow strict and uniform stages (Bidell & Fischer, 1995; Case, 1992; Fischer, 1980; **FIGURE 9.22**).

(a)

(b)

FIGURE 9.21
Culture and Learning
(a) People in technology-driven cultures may learn different information or emphasize different skills than **(b)** people in non-Western, not fully technological cultures.

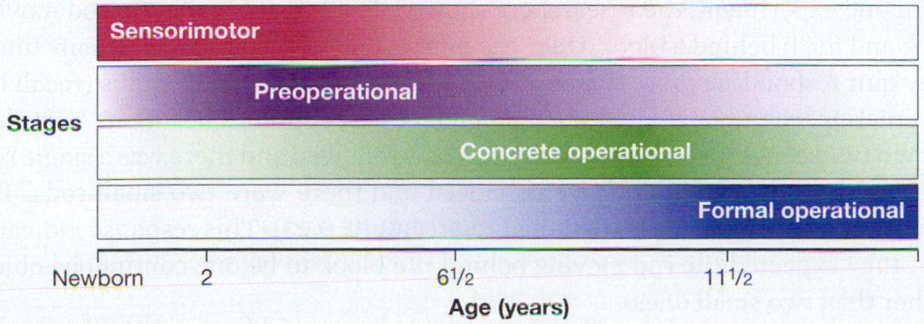

FIGURE 9.22
Trends in Cognitive Development
Modern interpretations view Piaget's theory in terms of trends, not rigid stages. Children shift gradually in their thinking over a wider range of ages than previously thought, and they can demonstrate thinking skills of more than one stage at a time.

In addition, Piaget thought that all adults were formal operational thinkers. But subsequent work has shown that many adults continue to reason in concrete operational ways in the absence of specific training or education in this type of thinking. Formal operational thinking does not just develop—it needs to be taught. Adults might think abstractly regarding topics with which they are familiar but not on new and unfamiliar tasks (De Lisi & Staudt, 1980). A good example of this kind of thinking is the candle-and-tack problem illustrated in Figure 8.18.

Moreover, Piaget underestimated the age at which certain skills develop. For example, contemporary researchers have found that object permanence develops in the first few months of life, instead of at 8 or 9 months of age, as Piaget thought. With new scientific methods that do not require infants to physically search for hidden objects, researchers have found object permanence abilities in infants as early as 3.5 months of age (Baillargeon, 1987).

Consider the apple/carrot test devised by the developmental psychologist Renée Baillargeon (1995). The researcher shows an apple to an infant who is sitting on an adult's lap. The researcher lowers a screen in front of the apple, then raises the screen to show the apple. Then the researcher performs the same actions, but this time raises the screen to show a carrot—a surprising, impossible event. If the infant looks longer at the carrot than at the apple, the researcher can assume that the infant expected to see the apple. By responding differently to such an impossible event than to possible ones, infants demonstrate some understanding that an object continues to exist when it is out of sight. This problem with Piaget's theory amounts to a methodological limitation. The preferential-looking time technique was developed only after Piaget's work, and as a result Piaget might have confused infants' physical capabilities with their cognitive abilities.

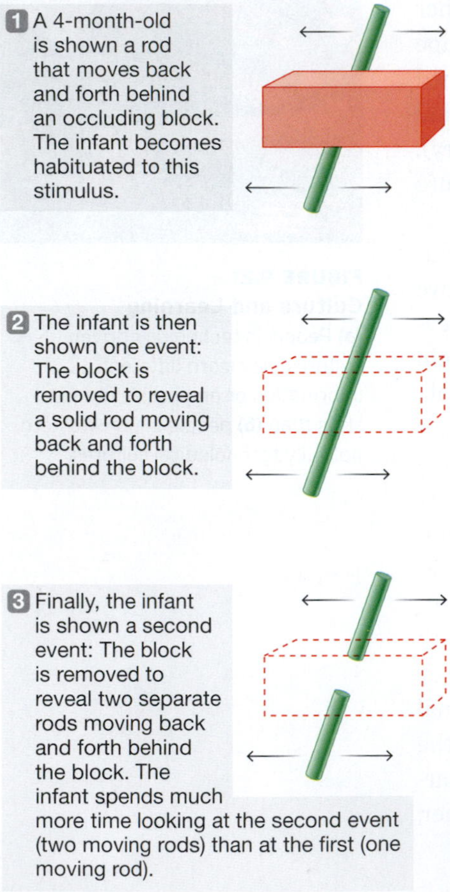

1 A 4-month-old is shown a rod that moves back and forth behind an occluding block. The infant becomes habituated to this stimulus.
2 The infant is then shown one event: The block is removed to reveal a solid rod moving back and forth behind the block.
3 Finally, the infant is shown a second event: The block is removed to reveal two separate rods moving back and forth behind the block. The infant spends much more time looking at the second event (two moving rods) than at the first (one moving rod).

FIGURE 9.23
Perceptual Expectancies in Early Infancy
As shown by this rod-and-block test, infants can perceive that objects moving together are continuous. Understanding the relation between movement and physical properties requires cognitive skills beyond those that Piaget expected 4-month-old infants to have.

UNDERSTANDING THE LAWS OF NATURE: PHYSICS The tasks used by Piaget implied that infants and young children have a relatively poor understanding of physical forces, such as conservation of quantity. Numerous studies conducted by the developmental psychologist Elizabeth Spelke and colleagues have indicated that infants do have a primitive understanding of some of the basic laws of physics (Spelke, 2016). These researchers created cognitive tasks that do not rely on language or physical capabilities. Recall that humans are born with the ability to perceive movement. Newborns will follow a moving stimulus with their eyes and head, and they will also prefer to look at a moving stimulus than to look at a stationary one. Older infants learn to use movement information to determine whether an object is continuous—that is, whether it is all one object—even if the infant cannot see the entire thing because it is partially hidden (Kellman et al., 1986).

In one experiment, the researchers showed 4-month-old infants a rod moving back and forth behind a block. Once the infants had viewed the scene many times, they quit responding to it. That is, they had *habituated* to the stimulus (recall the habituation technique used to study infant face perception). The infants were then shown two scenes. In one scene, the block was removed and there was a single rod. In the other scene, the block was removed and there were two small rods. The infants looked longer at the two small rods (FIGURE 9.23). This response indicated that they expected the rod moving behind the block to be one continuous object rather than two small ones.

UNDERSTANDING THE LAWS OF NATURE: MATHEMATICS Piaget believed that young children do not understand numbers and therefore must learn counting and other number-related skills through memorization. For some of his experiments in this area, he showed two rows of marbles to children 4–5 years old. Both rows had the same number of marbles, but in one row the marbles were spread out. The children usually said the longer row had more marbles (**FIGURE 9.24**). Piaget concluded that children understand quantity—the concepts *more than* and *less than*—in terms of length. He felt that preoperational children do not understand quantity in terms of number.

Challenging Piaget's view, Jacques Mehler and Tom Bever (1967) argued that children younger than 3 years of age can understand *more than* and *less than*. To demonstrate their point, they repeated Piaget's experiment using M&M's candy. They showed the children two rows of four M&M's each and asked if the rows were the same. When the children said yes, the researchers then transformed the rows. For instance, they would add two candies to the second row but compress that row so it was shorter than the row with fewer candies. Then they would ask the children to pick the row they wanted to eat. More than 80 percent picked the row with more M&M's, even though it was the visually shorter row (**FIGURE 9.25**). This research indicated that when children are properly motivated, they understand and can demonstrate their knowledge of *more than* and *less than*.

Piaget made enormous contributions to the understanding of cognitive development. In the years since, developmental psychology researchers have advanced

FIGURE 9.24
Piaget's Marble Test
This test led Piaget to conclude that very young children understand quantity in terms of length rather than number.

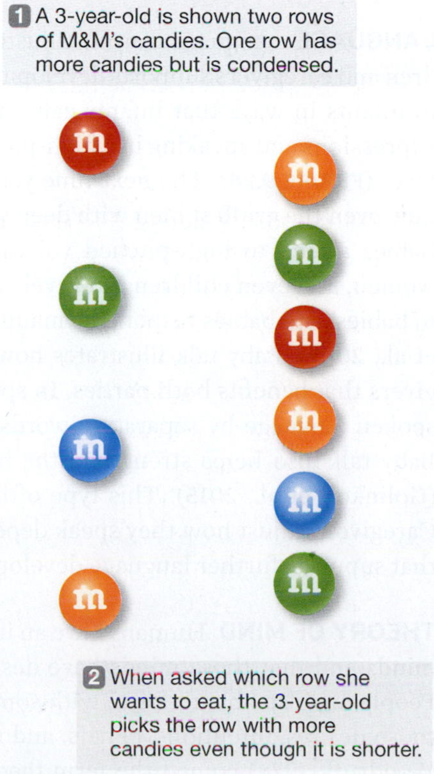

1 A 3-year-old is shown two rows of M&M's candies. One row has more candies but is condensed.
2 When asked which row she wants to eat, the 3-year-old picks the row with more candies even though it is shorter.

FIGURE 9.25
The M&M's Version of Piaget's Marble Test
This test enabled Mehler and Bever to show that very young children can in fact understand quantity in terms of number.

the field by testing the predictions of Piaget's theory. Some of the predictions have been supported by the data and others have not. For instance, despite what Piaget predicted, infants actually possess quite sophisticated thinking about spatial relations, time, and numbers within days after birth (de Hevia et al., 2014). But the purpose of psychological theory is not merely to be correct. Piaget's theory was successful because it spurred researchers to contribute so much knowledge to the field of developmental psychology.

Q In what ways have recent research findings challenged Piaget's theory of cognitive development?

ANSWER: Studies have shown that cognitive abilities related to physics and mathematics develop earlier and developmental stages are not as discrete as Piaget thought.

9.8 Children Learn from Interacting with Others

According to current thinking among developmental psychologists, infants' early social interactions with caregivers are essential for their ability to understand other people and communicate with them through language. In turn, these skills enable individuals to live in society. To interact with other people successfully, individuals need to communicate with others, be aware of others' intentions, behave in ways that generally conform to others' expectations, develop moral codes that guide their actions, learn and follow rules, and so on. Children need to learn that social interaction is bidirectional. Children's actions influence the thoughts and feelings of others, and vice versa.

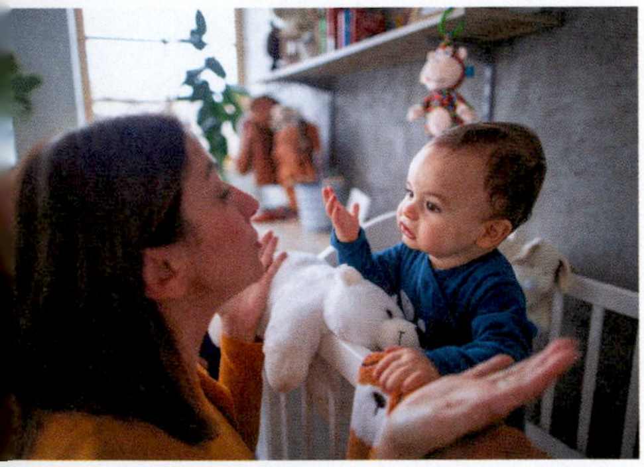

FIGURE 9.26
Parentese
Caregivers speak to infants in a distinctive pattern that helps their children learn the sounds involved in speech and the boundaries between words.

LANGUAGE Language learning illustrates how a dynamic process between children and caregivers supports development. At the beginning of life, adults respond to infants in ways that infants can understand, as in making exaggerated facial expressions and speaking in a high-pitched voice, known as "baby talk" or "parentese" (**FIGURE 9.26**). The next time you observe an adult talking to a baby, notice how even the gruffest men with deep voices change their voices to a higher pitch. Babies attend to high-pitched voices. In virtually every culture studied, men, women, and even children intuitively raise the pitch of their voices when talking to babies, and babies respond by maintaining eye contact (Fernald, 1989; Vallabha et al., 2007). Baby talk illustrates how infants elicit a behavior from their caregivers that benefits both parties. In speaking this way, adults help children learn spoken language by separating words, phrases, and sentences from each other. Baby talk also helps strengthen the bond between caregivers and their infants (Golinkoff et al., 2015). This type of interaction continues into later childhood. Caregivers adjust how they speak depending on their children's abilities in a way that supports further language development.

THEORY OF MIND Humans have an innate ability to understand that others have minds and that those minds have desires, intentions, beliefs, and mental states. People are also able to form, with some degree of accuracy, theories about what those desires, intentions, beliefs, and mental states are. David Premack and Guy Woodruff (1978) coined the term **theory of mind** to describe this ability to infer what another person is feeling or thinking. From that inference, we predict the other person's behavior.

theory of mind The ability to understand that other people have mental states that influence their behavior.

Beginning in infancy, young children come to understand that other people perform actions for reasons (Gergely & Csibra, 2003; Sommerville & Woodward, 2005). The recognition that actions can be intentional reflects a capacity for theory of mind, and it affords people the critical abilities to understand, predict, and attempt to influence others' behavior (Baldwin & Baird, 2001).

In one study, an adult began handing a toy to an infant. On some trials, the adult became unwilling to hand over the toy (e.g., teasing the infant with the toy or playing with it himself). On other trials, the adult became unable to hand it over (e.g., "accidentally" dropping it or being distracted by a ringing telephone). Infants older than 9 months showed greater signs of impatience—for example, reaching for the toy—when the adult was unwilling than when the adult was unable (Behne et al., 2005). This research shows that very young children understand other people's intentions, capabilities, and reasoning behind their actions.

By the end of the second year, perhaps even by 13 to 15 months of age, children become very good at reading intentions (Baillargeon et al., 2009). In other words, even though preschool-age children tend to behave in egocentric ways and view the world through their own perspectives, mounting evidence suggests that they have the cognitive ability to understand others' perspectives (Baillargeon et al., 2016). The understanding of complex mental states, such as that people can have false beliefs, develops later in childhood. A common test of false belief is shown in **FIGURE 9.27**.

Children's development of theory of mind appears to coincide with the maturation of the brain's frontal lobes. The importance of the frontal lobes for theory of mind is also supported by research with adults. In brain imaging studies, prefrontal brain regions become active when both children and adolescents are asked to think about other people's mental states (Mahy et al., 2014). People with damage to this region have difficulty attributing mental states to characters in stories (Stone et al., 1998). Children use these same regions as early as the age of 3 to anticipate what other people might do (Richardson & Saxe, 2020). Brain imaging studies of theory of mind conducted in Canada, the United States, England, France, Germany, Japan, and Sweden have found similar patterns of activity in prefrontal regions (Frank & Temple, 2009).

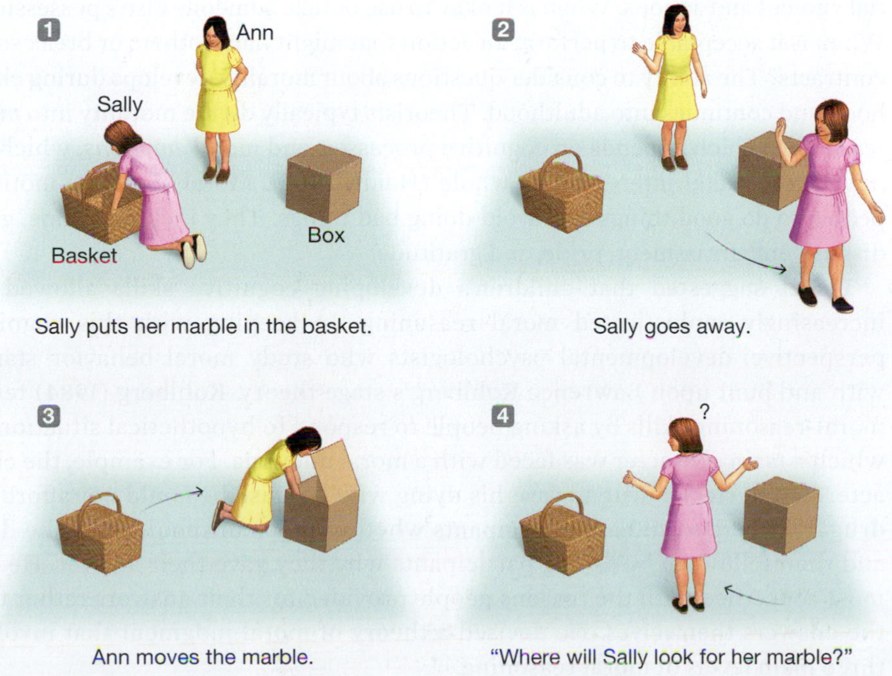
1
Ann
Sally
Basket
Box
Sally puts her marble in the basket.
2
Sally goes away.
3
Ann moves the marble.
4
?
"Where will Sally look for her marble?"

FIGURE 9.27
A Classic Test for a Child's Theory of Mind
When children acquire theory of mind, they are able to understand that different individuals have both different perspectives and knowledge based on their individual experiences.

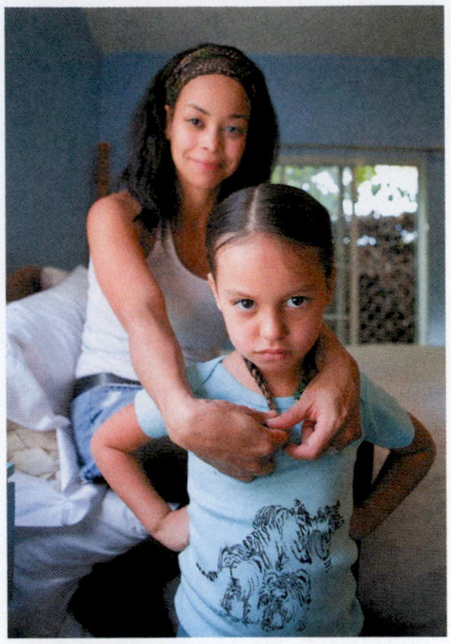

FIGURE 9.28
Caregiving Behavior Affects Children's Behavior
Caregivers who are high in sympathy and who allow their children to express negative emotions without shame or hostility tend to have children who are high in sympathy.

UNDERSTANDING SOCIAL EMOTIONS Having insight into other minds enables us to predict how other people will feel in a given situation. Children learn to predict when their caregivers, siblings, and friends will be angry, sad, embarrassed, and so on. Research on children's social emotions has focused largely on empathy, which involves understanding another's emotional state and relies on theory of mind. For instance, children as young as 4 years old can understand that someone experiencing pain might be in distress and would benefit from a gift or hug (Decety et al., 2018). Seeking to comfort a person who is upset is an example of *prosocial behavior*, which is any voluntary action performed with the specific intent of benefiting another person (Eisenberg et al., 2016). Starting after 1 year of age, children become willing to help others, such as by picking up objects for someone who has dropped them (Warneken, 2015). A recent meta-analysis found that children with higher scores on theory of mind tests are more likely to behave prosocially (Imuta et al., 2016).

Research has established a link between certain caregiving behaviors and children's level of both social emotions and prosocial behavior. When caregivers are high in sympathy, promote an understanding of and focus on others, do not express hostility in the home, allow their children to express negative emotions in ways that do not harm others, and help their children cope with negative emotions, they tend to raise children who are high in sympathy (Eisenberg, 2002; **FIGURE 9.28**). In another example of the bidirectional nature of the caregiver-child relationship, a study of children and their caregivers in eight countries found that children with higher levels of prosocial behavior at age 9 had better relationships with their caregivers two years later (Pastorelli et al., 2016).

Q **What is the relationship between theory of mind and prosocial behavior?**

ANSWER: Those who exhibit greater capacity for theory of mind are more likely to perform prosocial behavior.

9.9 Moral Development Begins in Childhood

Morality plays a central role in human life, influencing both trivial and consequential choices and actions. When is it okay to use or take someone else's possessions? When is it acceptable to perform an action that might harm others or break social contracts? The ability to consider questions about morality develops during childhood and continues into adulthood. Theorists typically divide morality into *moral reasoning*, which depends on cognitive processes, and *moral emotions*, which are linked to societal interests as a whole (Haidt, 2003). Moral emotions motivate people to do good things and avoid doing bad things. They include shame, guilt, disgust, embarrassment, pride, and gratitude.

Piaget suggested that children's developing cognitive skills allowed for increasingly sophisticated moral reasoning. In keeping with this cognitive perspective, developmental psychologists who study moral behavior started with and built upon Lawrence Kohlberg's stage theory. Kohlberg (1984) tested moral-reasoning skills by asking people to respond to hypothetical situations in which a main character was faced with a moral dilemma. For example, the character had to steal a drug to save his dying wife because he could not afford the drug. Kohlberg would ask participants whether the man should steal the drug, and then follow up by asking participants why they gave their answer. He was most concerned with the reasons people provided for their answers rather than the answers themselves. He devised a theory of moral judgment that involved three main levels of moral reasoning.

At the **preconventional level**, people classify answers in terms of self-interest or pleasurable outcomes. For example, a child at this level might say, "He should steal the drug because then he will have it." At the **conventional level**, people's responses conform to rules of law and order or focus on others' disapproval. For example, a person at this level might say, "He shouldn't take the drug. You are not supposed to steal, so everyone will think he is a bad person." At the **postconventional level**, the highest level of moral reasoning, people's responses center around complex reasoning about abstract principles and the value of all life. For example, a person at this level might say, "Sometimes people have to break the law if the law is unjust. In this case, it's wrong to steal, but it's more wrong to charge too much money for a drug that could save a person's life." Thus, Kohlberg considered advanced moral reasoning to include a consideration of the greater good for all people, with less thought given to personal wishes or fear of punishment.

preconventional level Earliest stage of moral development; at this level, self-interest and event outcomes determine what is moral.

conventional level Middle stage of moral development; at this level, strict adherence to societal rules and the approval of others determine what is moral.

postconventional level Highest stage of moral development; at this level, decisions about morality depend on abstract principles and the value of all life.

inequity aversion A preference to avoid unfairness when making decisions about the distribution of resources.

Kohlberg's theory has been criticized because the initial research examined only American males (Gilligan, 1977). At issue is whether the same stage theory applies to females or to those raised in different cultures (Snarey, 1985). Moral-reasoning theories have also been faulted for emphasizing the cognitive aspects of morality to the detriment of emotional issues that influence moral judgments. Of course, cognition and emotions are intertwined. If people lack adequate cognitive abilities, their moral emotions may not translate into moral behaviors (Tangney et al., 2007). Similarly, moral reasoning is enhanced by moral emotions (Moll & de Oliveira-Souza, 2007). As with Piaget's stage theory, some parts of Kohlberg's theory received empirical support and others did not. The theory is now considered as a useful tool for generating new hypotheses rather than the final word on moral development.

INNATE SENSE OF FAIRNESS AS THE BASIS OF MORALITY If you have spent time with toddlers, you know that they are highly attuned to fairness. Try surprising two children with some cookies but giving one child two cookies and the other child only one cookie. After you have quieted the tantrums, ask yourself why the children reacted that way. After all, the child who received one cookie still got a cookie, which is better than zero cookies. Why do children (and adults, for that matter) dislike receiving less than someone else, even if they received more than they expected?

Psychologists call this dislike of unfairness **inequity aversion**. It begins possibly as young as 19 months of age (Sloane et al., 2012) and increases in strength throughout childhood (Fehr et al., 2008). In a classic study, Ernst Fehr (pronounced "fair") and colleagues allowed children to choose how to distribute some candy between themselves and a playmate (**FIGURE 9.29**). Perhaps unsurprisingly, when given the choice between giving themselves one piece of candy and the other person either zero or one piece, most children gave both players one piece of candy. This tendency was especially strong in older children. In another condition, children chose between giving themselves one piece of candy and the other person either one or two pieces of candy. Here, the giver always got the same amount of candy, but the receiver got either the same amount or one additional piece of candy. Again, children chose the equal option of one piece for both partners, indicating a preference for fairness. In a final condition, the giver could keep two pieces of candy or divide the candy evenly. This choice requires the giver to forfeit one piece of candy in order to achieve fairness. The tendency

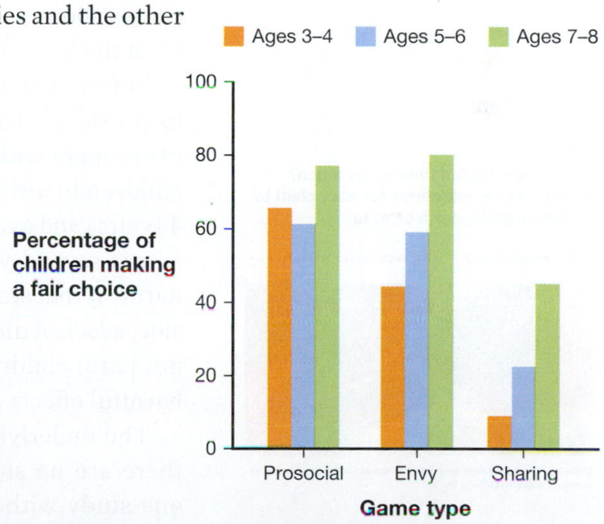

FIGURE 9.29
Children Value Fairness
As children get older, they tend to divide goods such as candy evenly between themselves and companions. They go out of their way to give goods to others ("prosocial game") and take them away ("envy game") to create fairness, and they even give up their own goods to do so ("sharing game").

to select the fair option, even though it was "costly" to the giver, increased across childhood.

A strong sense of inequity aversion in children sets the stage for later moral behavior. Children who demonstrate a dislike of inequality, even if it means losing out on potential personal gains, signal to other people that they are fair (Shaw & Olson, 2012). Learning ways to earn the trust of other people is one of the most important social skills children develop. Throughout adulthood, trustworthiness is one of the first features that we look for in other people (Goodwin, 2015). From this perspective, being fair and demonstrating other moral qualities is important to people because it is a way to interact effectively with others.

Q According to Kohlberg's theory, at which stage of moral development are people focused primarily on the opinions of others?

ANSWER: the conventional stage

YOU BE THE PSYCHOLOGIST

9.10 Is Screen Time Unhealthy for Children?

Anyone growing up in the digital age has heard the warnings about too much screen time. Experts in child development have issued dire warnings about the harms of excessive use of screens, including that it stunts brain growth, harms social development, and causes internet addiction (Cross, 2020; **FIGURE 9.30**). These warnings have been amplified by the American Association of Pediatrics, which recommends specific screen time limits for children of different ages (Pappas, 2020).

Concerns about screen time are understandable. Computers, tablets, and phones are relatively new in human history, and their effects on children are not completely understood. People want their children to thrive and are resistant to taking risks if the potential harms are unknown. Yet a critical thinker will hear claims about the harms of screen time with an open but skeptical mind. What data form the basis of recommendations for screen time limits for children?

Before looking at the results of studies done on the subject, take a moment to consider what good evidence would look like. The gold standard is always an experiment with a large sample. Suppose a preregistered study randomly assigned children to use screens at varying levels per day (for example, 0 hours, 2 hours, or 4 hours) and examined their mental and social functioning at multiple time points across several years of development. A scientist would be convinced of certain harms if that study showed differences in outcomes among the groups. On the flip side, a *lack* of difference among the groups could be taken as a sign that screens do not harm children if the study had enough participants in it to detect even small harmful effects.

The underlying data on the harms of screen time are not compelling because there are no such studies. Instead, correlational studies abound. For example, one study with more than 40,000 children ages 2–17 found that beyond about 2 hours of screen time per day, more screen time was associated with lower well-being, less curiosity, and more caregiver-child conflict (Twenge & Campbell, 2018). However, this study is correlational, which means that the observed relationships are not necessarily causal. Can you think of an alternative reason why hours of screen time might be correlated with caregiver-child conflict instead of the claim that the screen time *causes* the conflict? In fact, another large study showed that the relation between screen time and well-being went to zero after family factors such as household income were accounted for (Przybylski & Weinstein, 2019).

HOME > HEALTH

How much screen time is too much? Follow these guidelines for your child to avoid harmful health effects

Madeline Kennedy Oct 16, 2020, 3:22 PM MEDICALLY REVIEWED

In the US, kids ages 8 to 12 spend an average of 4 to 6 hours per day on screens. Isabel Pavia/Getty Images

- Children younger than 5 years old should have very limited screen time and mainly use screens for educational purposes.

FIGURE 9.30
Expert Warnings About Screen Time
Stories in the media, such as this one, present alarming warnings about the effects of screen time on children. These reports do not always match the data.

Even among the correlational studies that do exist about screen time and child development, not all of them show that more screen time is associated with unwanted outcomes. One study compared the social skills of children ages 6–11 in 1998 (largely before social media and tablets) with those of children of the same ages in 2010 (Downey & Gibbs, 2020). Social skills were rated by both caregivers and teachers of the children. There were no large differences in social skills between the groups. If anything, the interpersonal skills and self-control of the children in the 2010 cohort were rated slightly *higher* than those of the children in the 1998 cohort. Within each group, children who used screens the most had similar social skills to those who used screens the least.

It is easy to get caught up in the media hype about the harms of new technology. People have long worried about the effects of new technology on their children (Mills, 2014). That is one of the reasons critical thinking and amiable skepticism are so important. Claims made in the media often do not live up to the realities of the data. Of course, children need direct interaction with caregivers and peers, physical activity, and time to explore the outside world. Screen time can become harmful if it takes away from those other activities. But there is no strong evidence that screen time itself is harmful. ■

Q What kind of study would be needed to support the claim that excessive screen time causes harm to developing children?

ANSWER: a preregistered study with many participants randomized to experimental and control groups. This type of study has yet to be completed.

What Changes During Adolescence?

Normal human development turns a child into an adolescent. An adolescent then develops into an adult. During these transitions, the person undergoes physical, social, cognitive, and psychological changes. These various forces work together in the creation of a self.

Learning Objectives

- Understand how biology and environment interact to influence puberty.
- Explain key factors that influence sex and gender identity development.
- Describe how peers, parents, and cultural forces shape the sense of self.

9.11 Puberty Causes Physical Changes

Biologically, adolescence begins with **puberty**, the onset of sexual maturity and thus the ability to reproduce. Puberty typically begins around age 8 for females and age 10 for males (Ge et al., 2007). Most girls complete pubertal development by the age of 16, whereas boys end by the age of 18 (Lee, 1980; **FIGURE 9.31**).

During puberty, hormone levels increase throughout the body. The increased hormones stimulate physical changes. For example, the clear dividing line between childhood and the start of puberty is the *adolescent growth spurt*, a rapid, hormonally driven increase in height and weight. Puberty also brings the development of the *primary sex characteristics*, including maturation of the male and female sex organs, the beginning of menstruation (in females), and the beginning of the capacity for ejaculation (in males). Also developing at this time are the *secondary sex characteristics*, including pubic hair, body hair, muscle mass increases for boys, and fat deposits on the hips and breasts for girls. Boys' voices deepen and their jaws become more angular. Girls lose baby fat on their bellies as their waists become more defined (Lee, 1980).

puberty The beginning of adolescence, marked by the onset of sexual maturity and thus the ability to reproduce.

BIOLOGY AND ENVIRONMENT Puberty may appear to be a purely biological phenomenon. Like all aspects of human development, however, it is affected by a complex and dynamic interaction between biological systems and environmental

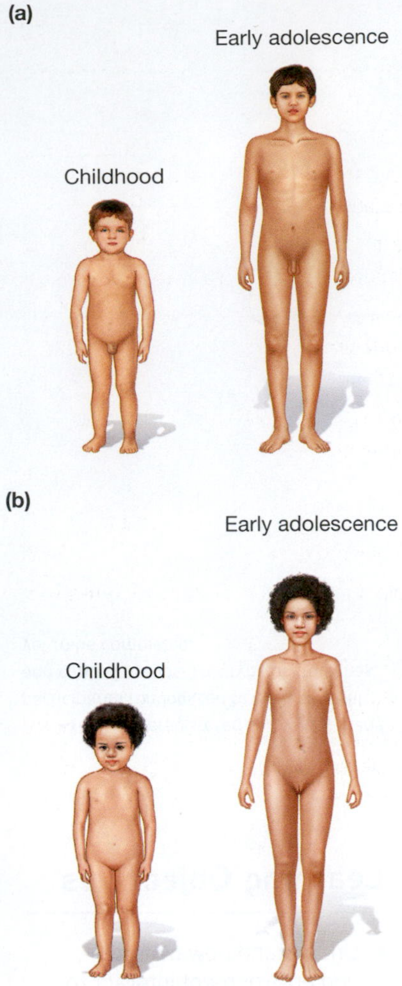

FIGURE 9.31

Physical Development During Adolescence

These images show the major physical changes that occur as girls and boys mature into young adults.

experiences. For example, girls who experience stressful events in early life such as abuse or foster care transitions begin menstruating earlier than girls in peaceful or secure environments (Mendle et al., 2011). Evolutionarily speaking, cues that signal a threatening environment increase a female's need to reproduce sooner to increase her chances of continuing her gene pool. Thus, hormonal changes are triggered by environmental forces, which allow the girl to enter puberty (Belsky et al., 2010).

Despite frequently being characterized as a period of turmoil, adolescence is not necessarily a stressful period of life. For those kids who already have stressful home lives, experience many family changes, or display attachment difficulties, adolescence may be difficult. For most kids, pubertal and brain changes take a bit of adjustment, but they do not necessarily lead to the high rates of depression or anger that many in the general public associate with teenagers (Pfeifer & Allen, 2012). In fact, if adolescents receive warm, supportive caregiving with the proper guidance and discipline, and if they are allowed to express themselves openly, adolescence can be a positive time of growth and change, solidifying the youth's sense of identity (Steinberg & Morris, 2001).

At the same time teenagers are experiencing pubertal changes, their brains are also in an important phase of reorganization; their synaptic connections are refined, and gray matter increases. The frontal cortex of the brain is not fully myelinated until the mid-20s (Mills et al., 2014). It is a common misconception that teenagers are overly emotional and incapable of adult rational thought. However, teenagers' brains can function just as well as those of adults and sometimes even better if the adolescents are properly motivated (Geier et al., 2010; Telzer, 2016). When teenagers behave differently from adults, they do so largely because they have different priorities (Pfeifer & Berkman, 2018).

Q How do scientists know that the timing of physical changes and experience of emotional upheaval during puberty are not completely dependent on biology?

ANSWER: because they vary due to social and environmental experiences, which can alter pubertal timing and influence emotional outcomes during adolescence

9.12 A Sense of Identity Forms

As children develop and learn more about the world, they begin creating a sense of identity. That is, they start to establish who they are. Identity formation is an important part of social development, especially in Western cultures, where individuality is valued.

The psychologist Erik Erikson (1980) proposed a theory of human development that emphasized age-related, culture-neutral psychosocial challenges and their effects on social functioning across the life span. Erikson thought of identity development as composed of eight stages, which ranged from an infant's first year to old age (**TABLE 9.1**). Erikson further conceptualized each stage as having a major developmental "crisis," or development challenge to be confronted. Each of these crises is present throughout life, but each one takes on special importance at a particular stage. According to this theory, while each crisis provides an

Table 9.1 Erikson's Eight Stages of Psychosocial Development

STAGE	AGE	MAJOR PSYCHOSOCIAL CRISIS	SUCCESSFUL RESOLUTION OF CRISIS
1. Infancy	0-1	Trust versus mistrust	Children learn that the world is safe and that people are loving and reliable.
2. Toddler	1-3	Autonomy versus shame and doubt	Encouraged to explore their environment, children gain feelings of independence and positive self-esteem.
3. Preschool	3-6	Initiative versus guilt	Children develop a sense of purpose by taking on responsibilities but also develop the capacity to feel guilty for misdeeds.
4. Childhood	6-12	Industry versus inferiority	By working successfully with others and assessing how others view them, children learn to feel competent.
5. Adolescence	12-18	Identity versus role confusion	By exploring different social roles, adolescents develop a sense of identity.
6. Young adulthood	18-29	Intimacy versus isolation	Young adults gain the ability to commit to long-term relationships.
7. Middle adulthood	30s to 50s	Generativity versus stagnation	Adults gain a sense that they are leaving behind a positive legacy and caring for future generations.
8. Old age	60s and beyond	Integrity versus despair	Older adults feel a sense of satisfaction that they have lived a good life and developed wisdom.

opportunity for psychological development, a lack of progress may impair further psychosocial development (Erikson, 1980). Successful resolution of these challenges depends on the supportive nature of the person's environment as well as the person's active search for information about their own competence.

Erikson's theory has been influential but is lacking empirical support. There is little evidence that there are eight stages of psychosocial development, that psychosocial development is culture neutral, and that human identity develops in this exact sequence. Nonetheless, like the other stage models presented in this chapter, Erikson's stages provided a starting point for psychology researchers and encouraged them to think about the psychosocial challenges that people face at different times in their lives.

According to Erikson's theory, adolescents face perhaps the most fundamental crisis: how to develop an adult identity. Three major changes generally cause adolescents to question who they are: Their physical appearance transforms, leading to shifts in self-image; their cognitive abilities grow more sophisticated, increasing the tendency for introspection; and they receive heightened societal pressure to prepare for the future, prompting exploration of real and hypothetical boundaries. Part of this process of exploring boundaries includes breaking away from childhood beliefs by questioning and challenging parental and societal ideas (Erikson, 1968). Teenagers may investigate alternative social circles, belief systems, and subcultures. They may wonder what they would be like if they were raised in other cultures, by other caregivers, or in other historical times. They may shift between various peer groups and try out different activities, hobbies, and musical styles. As teenagers move away from spending all their time with caregivers and toward a peer-oriented lifestyle, caregivers continue to shape adolescents' development, but peers also play an important role in identity development.

"Do you know its sexual identity?"

SEX AND GENDER IDENTITY Along with the physiological changes that come with puberty, adolescence is a time when many people explore and develop their sexuality and gender identity. Most psychologists use the term *sex* to refer to the genetic status of being either male or female (i.e., having XY versus XX chromosomes), which results in different physical characteristics (see Figure 9.31). Psychologists reserve the term *gender* for the psychological dimensions of masculinity and femininity. **Gender identity** is one's sense of being male, female, or nonbinary. *Gender expression* is the way people outwardly express their gender through their behavior, interests, and appearance. A person's gender expression is separate from who they are romantically and sexually attracted to, or their *sexual orientation*.

The development of sex and gender identity begins very early in prenatal development. It results from a complex cascade of brain chemistry, hormones, changes in brain structure and function, and intrauterine environmental forces (Swaab, 2004). Recall from Chapter 3 that the gonads—testes in males and ovaries in females—influence sexual behavior. They also influence the development of secondary sex characteristics (e.g., breast development in females, growth of facial hair in males). Androgens are more prevalent in males, and estrogens are more prevalent in females.

In addition to biological factors, many of the differences between girls and boys result from socialization, which tends to reinforce culturally defined **gender roles**—norms that differentiate behaviors and attitudes according to maleness and femaleness. In North American culture, for example, most caregivers and teachers discourage girls from playing too roughly and boys from crying. The separation of boys and girls into different play groups is also a powerful socializing force. The distinction between the biological and psychosocial aspects of being female or male is not always easy to make, because they are often so entwined that we cannot separate them (Hyde, 2005). People are treated in certain ways based on how others perceive their gender, and each person's behaviors reflect both biological components and social expectations.

gender identity One's sense of being male, female, or nonbinary.

gender role A behavior that is typically associated with being male or female.

Sex is not binary (Blackless et al., 2000). Some people have physiological aspects of sex that are either ambiguous or inconsistent with each other. This phenomenon is known as *intersexuality*. About 1 or 2 of every 100 people experience some ambiguity in their assigned sex (Intersex Society of North America, 2008). Causes of such ambiguity are atypical patterns in the sex chromosomes or in hormones, both of which can affect how the genitals look (American Psychological Association, 2006). Given intersexuality, many people believe it is more accurate to view sex as not just male or female but as including greater or lesser physical aspects of each sex (**FIGURE 9.32**). In December 2016, New York City issued the first birth certificate in the United States listing "intersex" instead of "male" or "female" in

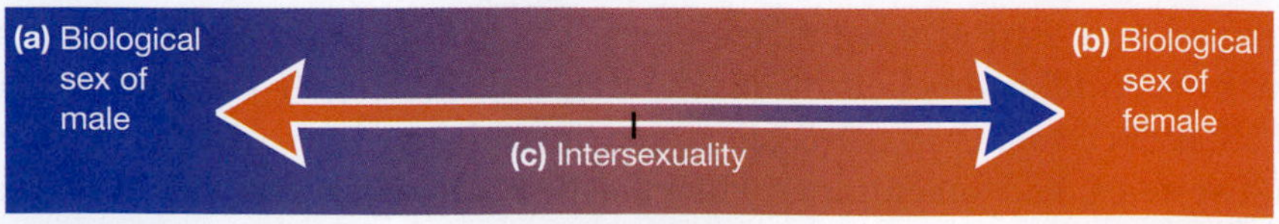

FIGURE 9.32

Biological Sex Can Be Viewed as a Continuum

Some people have biological traits of both sexes, and therefore it might be appropriate to view sex as a continuum of being more or less physically female or male. **(a)** Males have biological traits that are consistently male. **(b)** Females have biological traits that are consistently female. **(c)** People who experience intersexuality have aspects of biological sex that are both male and female.

the sex field. It was issued to 55-year-old Sara Keenan, who was born with male genes, female genitalia, and mixed internal reproductive organs.

Most people have gender identities that conform to their assigned sex at birth and are considered *cisgender* (*cis-* is a Latin pronoun meaning "on this side of"; Diamond & Butterworth, 2008). The term *transgender* refers to people who were assigned one sex at birth but whose gender identity is that of the other sex. These identities are formed early in life: Children as young as 2 years old recognize themselves as being girls or boys. A recent study looked at 32 transgender children 5–12 years old (Olson et al., 2015). The research methods included self-reports and implicit measures of gender identity (see Chapter 12 for more details on implicit measures). The results indicated that the children thought of themselves in terms of their preferred gender identity, not their assigned sex. In addition, the pattern of responses of the transgender children was similar to the pattern of responses from children who accepted their birth-assigned sex as their gender identity.

FIGURE 9.33
Transgender
Attorney Chase Strangio speaks to reporters outside a courthouse after defending his client, who was fired after coming out to their employer as transgender. Strangio is deputy director for transgender justice with the American Civil Liberties Union.

One theory of why gender and sex differ for those who are transgender has to do with the timing of hormonal events during pregnancy. Early in pregnancy, the presence or absence of testosterone leads to the formation of male or female sex organs, respectively. Later in pregnancy, hormones influence the sexual differentiation of the brain (Bao & Swaab, 2011). These developmental processes are independent and may produce different effects for those who are transgender. In keeping with this idea, various brain imaging studies have shown that brains of transgender people are more similar to those who share their gender identity than to those who share their assigned sex (Nawata et al., 2010).

Awareness has been growing about transgender issues over the past several years (**FIGURE 9.33**). For example, federal courts in the United States have interpreted laws against gender discrimination such as the 1964 Civil Rights Act to include protections for people who are transgender and gender nonconforming. Nearly half of U.S. states plus Washington, DC, have laws prohibiting discrimination on the basis of gender identity against people in the workplace (Movement Advancement Project, 2020).

CULTURAL AND ETHNIC IDENTITY In addition to a gender identity, adolescents establish racial, cultural, and ethnic identities, as well as other identities tied to group membership. Children entering middle childhood have acquired an awareness of their cultural and ethnic identities to the extent that they know the labels and attributes that are applied to their groups. All children learn that they are part of many social groups, such as their family and their national, religious, racial, and ethnic groups. The factors that influence processes of group-based identity formation vary widely among individuals and groups. Caregivers, teachers, the media, and spiritual and community leaders among many others play roles in teaching young people the values of their specific cultures in order to help them formulate their social identities.

Because of prejudice and discrimination and the accompanying barriers to economic opportunities, children from underrepresented groups, such as people of color, immigrants, or religious minorities, often face extra challenges with regard to the development of their ethnic identities. Consider children of Mexican immigrants to the United States. These children must balance the cultural expectations of living in both a traditional Mexican household and an American neighborhood and school. They may have to serve as "cultural brokers" for their families, perhaps translating materials sent home from school, calling insurance companies to ask about policies for their older relatives, and handling more adultlike responsibilities than other children the same age. In helping their families adjust to a new life as immigrants in a foreign country, the children may feel additional pressures but may also develop important skills in communication, negotiation, and caregiving (Cooper et al., 1999). Even for people of color born in the United States, it can be quite challenging to persevere in the face of racism and discrimination while also trying to succeed in the mainstream school system and work environments (Spencer et al., 2003). Perhaps due to stress faced by immigrant groups, immigrants in the United States tend to become less healthy with each generation (Alamilla et al., 2020). You will learn more about this "immigrant paradox" in Chapter 11.

ANSWER: from caregivers, teachers, the media, and spiritual and community leaders, among many others

Q How do children learn about their group-based identities such as cultural, religious, or national identities?

9.13 Peers and Caregivers Shape the Adolescent Self

The impact of caregivers versus peers on young people has become a controversial topic in developmental psychology. People often describe individuals as "coming from a good home" or as having "fallen in with the wrong crowd." These clichés reflect the importance of both peers and caregivers in influencing adolescent development.

THE RELATIVE IMPORTANCE OF PEERS AND CAREGIVERS Developmental psychologists increasingly recognize the importance of peers in shaping adolescent identity (**FIGURE 9.34**). Children, regardless of their cultures, tend to spend much of their time interacting with other children, usually playing in various ways. Children in the first year of life interact with peers through imitation, smiling, and vocalizations. But, as captured in attachment theory, young children's primary interaction partners are their caregivers.

During adolescence, children shift from deriving their sense of identity from their family of origin to developing it through their peer group (Nelson et al., 2005). As part of the search for identity, teenagers form friendships with others whose values and worldviews are similar to their own but might differ from those of their caregivers. Adolescents use peer groups to help themselves feel a sense of belonging and acceptance as they venture into the larger world beyond their families. They also draw on peer groups as resources for social support and identity acceptance. Even brain activity changes in adolescence to be more sensitive to the perspectives and values of peers than those of their caregivers (van Hoorn et al., 2018).

FIGURE 9.34
Peers and Identity
Peers play an important role in each adolescent's development of a sense of identity.

This "reorientation" during adolescence can make it a period of increased conflict between caregivers and their teenage children. For most families, however, this conflict leads to minor annoyances and not to feelings of hopelessness or doom. Research shows that such conflict actually helps adolescents develop many important skills, including negotiation, critical thinking, communication, and empathy (Holmbeck, 1996). In fact, even though adolescents and their caregivers may argue and it may seem as though the children are not listening, across cultures caregivers have powerful influence over the development of their children's values and sense of autonomy (Feldman & Rosenthal, 1991).

Caregivers who respond to a difficult child calmly, firmly, patiently, and consistently tend to have the most positive outcomes. They tend not to engage in self-blame for their child's negative behaviors, and they manage to cope with their own frustration with and disappointment in their child. Overprotectiveness can encourage a child's anxiety in response to a new situation, thereby escalating the child's distress. Ultimately, then, the best style of caregiving is dynamic and flexible, and it takes into account the caregivers' personalities, the child's temperament, and the particular situation (Steinberg, 2001).

Other research has shown that caregivers have multiple influences on their children's attitudes, values, and religious beliefs (Bao et al., 1999). Children learn about the world in part from the attitudes expressed by their caregivers, such as the belief in a higher power and even prejudices regarding certain groups of people. Caregivers who demonstrate the most warmth tend to raise children who experience more social emotions, such as appropriate guilt, perhaps because the caregivers encourage an empathic attitude toward others (Eisenberg & Valiente, 2002). Caregivers also help determine the neighborhoods in which their children live, the schools they attend, and the extracurricular activities that provide exercise and stimulation. All of these choices are likely to influence how adolescents develop.

Adolescent identity development is thus shaped by the perceptions of adults, the influences of peers, and the teen's own active exploration of the world. Keep in mind that even though peers become the primary concern for many teenagers, the importance of caregiving support and guidance does not wane with age.

BULLYING Bullying is a complex behavior with many contributing factors. However, experts tend to agree that bullies might not strongly feel the moral emotions of guilt and shame (Hymel et al., 2005). Bullies also often show increased moral disengagement, such as indifference or pride, when explaining their behavior, and positive attitudes about using bullying to respond to difficult social situations. This is especially true of bullies with high self-esteem, who tend to rationalize and justify their mistreatment of others (Menon et al., 2007). The advent of social networking sites produced the phenomenon of cyberbullying. Estimates of the prevalence of cyberbullying vary widely: Across separate studies, anywhere from 3 to 72 percent of adolescents reported being victims (Selkie et al., 2016).

Whether in person or via the web, being bullied can have devastating effects. A study of more than 1,400 participants found that being bullied during childhood is associated with psychological disorders such as anxiety and depression (Copeland et al., 2013). Consider the case of 15-year-old Amanda Todd. In September 2012, Amanda posted a soundless YouTube video displaying a series of handwritten messages that described her years of being bullied (**FIGURE 9.35**). The bullying began in the seventh grade, when Amanda used video chat to meet people over the internet. A man convinced Amanda to pose topless and then threatened to blackmail her unless she posted more-explicit sexual images of herself. Amanda informed her parents, who contacted the police. By this point, Amanda's pictures had been widely circulated over the internet. Her fellow students started verbally abusing her. Amanda went into a tailspin, experiencing feelings of anxiety and depression. About a month after she posted her YouTube video, Amanda died by suicide. This tragic case shows the urgency of preventing bullying and of supporting people who are bullied.

FIGURE 9.35
The Bullying of Amanda Todd
Amanda Todd experienced repeated bullying and cyberbullying so extreme that she suffered from anxiety and depression. Despite attempts to treat Amanda's problems, she ended her life.

Q What positive outcomes have been associated with increased conflict between caregivers and their children during adolescence?

ANSWER: These conflicts may serve as an opportunity for adolescents to develop social skills such as negotiation, critical thinking, communication, and empathy.

What Brings Meaning in Adulthood?

Learning Objectives

- Understand the physical changes that occur as we age.
- Explain key research findings on the benefits of a healthy marriage and how to keep a marriage healthy after the birth of a child.
- Understand why many older adults find life more satisfying than younger adults do.
- Describe the cognitive changes that occur as we age.

For many years, developmental psychologists focused on childhood and adolescence, as if most of the important aspects of development occurred by age 20. In recent decades, researchers working in a wide range of fields have demonstrated that important changes occur physiologically, cognitively, and socioemotionally throughout adulthood and into old age. Contemporary psychology considers development from a life span perspective, trying to understand how mental activity and social relations change over the entire course of life.

9.14 Adults Are Affected by Life Transitions

For many young people, college is a magical time of life. Meeting new friends, learning new ideas, and having a good time occur as adolescents emerge as adults. People in their 20s and 30s undergo significant changes as they pursue career goals, make long-term commitments in relationships, transition to financial independence, and get married and raise children. Each of the major challenges of adulthood reflects the need to find meaning in one's life. Part of that search for meaning includes acknowledging and coping with the physiological, cognitive, and socioemotional changes of adulthood.

PHYSICAL CHANGES FROM EARLY TO MIDDLE ADULTHOOD Evolutionarily speaking, a 40-year-old is quite old. At the beginning of the twentieth century, the average life expectancy in the United States was 47 years! Human bodies remain on that timetable, ready to reproduce when individuals reach their teens and peaking in fitness during their 20s. Since 1900, through modern medicine and improvements in hygiene and food availability, the average life expectancy has increased by about 35 years. Still, between the ages of 20 and 40, people experience a steady decline in muscle mass, bone density, eyesight, and hearing (Shephard, 1997).

These physical changes are not inevitable. Healthy behaviors such as physical activity (Taylor et al., 2019), good diet (Farsijani et al., 2017), and restricted intake of alcohol and tobacco (Peeters et al., 2019) can protect against physical decline. However, people do not always adhere to these recommendations. Health researchers estimate that obesity-related factors will shorten the expected life span by two to five years if the trends in poor health are not reversed (Olshansky et al., 2005). In

the United Kingdom, 8 out of 10 people between 40 and 60 years of age are overweight, drink alcohol excessively, or do not exercise (Public Health England, 2016). Life expectancy in the United States dropped in 2015 for the first time in decades (Xu et al., 2016). One impetus to improving health can be life partners or children. The people we share our lives with sometimes motivate us to take care of ourselves.

MARRIAGE In adulthood, people devote a great deal of effort to achieving and maintaining satisfying relationships. The vast majority of people around the world marry at some point in their lives or form some type of permanent bond with a relationship partner, although people today tend to marry later in life, and the percentage of those who marry is declining slowly in most industrialized countries.

Marriage is generally associated with outcomes that are beneficial to the people involved, particularly men. Overall, married people typically experience greater happiness and joy and are at lower risk for mental illnesses such as depression when compared with unmarried people. Married people also live longer than people who were never married, are divorced, or are widowed (Frisch & Simonsen, 2013). Studies of heterosexual marriages suggest that men may benefit from marriage because their wives make sure they smoke less, eat more healthily, and go to the doctor (Ross et al., 1990). There is also evidence that single men are more likely to die in their 20s and 30s than married men (Gellatly & Störmer, 2017). The benefits of marriage are specific to men, and some studies even find that single women live longer than married women (Schünemann et al., 2020). Men benefit more than women from the unpaid labor of their spouses, particularly in couples with children (Kamp Dush et al., 2018). Married men report higher sexual and relationship satisfaction than cohabiting and single men, while there is no difference across these same groups of women (Hughes & Waite, 2009). Married women report more emotional satisfaction, however, than cohabiting or single women (Christopher & Sprecher, 2000) (**FIGURE 9.36**).

Much of the research on marriage was conducted before same-sex marriage was legalized in many countries around the world, including the United States

FIGURE 9.36
Marriage
Across cultures, marriage remains a building block of society. If the statistics hold true, **(a)** this Indigenous couple in the United States, **(b)** this Nubian couple in Kenya, and **(c)** this Balinese couple in Indonesia will report being happy in their marriages.

in 2015. The few studies conducted so far have found that marriage provides significant physical and mental health benefits for lesbian, gay, and bisexual individuals (Rostosky & Riggle, 2017; Wight et al., 2013). As with heterosexual couples, cohabiting same-sex couples are in better health than people living on their own (Robles & Kiecolt-Glaser, 2003; Williams & Fredriksen-Goldsen, 2014).

All of these findings do not mean that marriage is a cure-all. For example, the benefits of marriage over cohabitation are stronger for European Americans than for African Americans (Liu & Reczek, 2012). In general, people who are in unhappy marriages, are separated, or are divorced have many physical and psychological struggles, from depression to physical illness to violent behavior (Carrère et al., 2000). Note, though, that these studies are largely correlational. It could be that happy, well-adjusted people are more likely to get married and not that marriage causes good outcomes for people. Or perhaps unhappy, negative people have both health problems and strained marriages.

The good news is that according to national surveys, at any given time, the vast majority of married people report satisfaction with their marriages. Those reporting the most satisfaction tend to have sufficient economic resources, share decision making, and together hold the view that marriage should be a lifelong commitment (Amato et al., 2003).

Q Are the benefits of marriage more strongly associated with husbands or wives in heterosexual relationships?

ANSWER: Husbands are more likely to benefit from marriage, in part because wives encourage healthy lifestyles, provide social support, and perform unpaid labor in the household.

PSYCHOLOGY OUTSIDE THE LAB

9.15 Will Parenthood Make You Happy?

For most people, the birth of a first child is a profound event. In fact, this arrival changes their lives in almost every respect. Are these changes generally positive or negative?

Responding to an infant's cries and trying to figure out why the child is distressed often cause anxiety and frustration for first-time parents. Children can strain a marriage, especially when time and money are tight. Research consistently finds that couples with children, especially with adolescent children, report less marital satisfaction than those who are childless (Belsky, 1990; Hansen, 2012).

But new parents also experience great joys. Seeing a baby's first social smile, watching the first few tentative steps, and hearing a child say "Mommy" or "Daddy" provide powerful reinforcement for parents. As a result of such rewards, parents often become immersed in their children's lives. They make sure their children have playmates, expose them to new experiences, and seek ways to make them happy and healthy. Being a parent is central to the self-schemas of many adults. Having children can provide meaning in life and moments of joy (Nelson et al., 2013). In short, parenting is a "mixed bag" experience that illustrates the difference between feeling happy and feeling satisfied with your life (Musick et al., 2016; FIGURE 9.37).

This interpretation applies most strongly in wealthy nations, where people who have children are more likely to be married, richer, better educated, more religious, and healthier (Deaton & Stone, 2014). All of these demographic factors are associated with well-being. In a study of more than 1.8 million Americans, Angus Deaton and Arthur Stone (2014) found that once you take these factors into account, the presence of children has a reliably negative effect on life satisfaction, although the effect is small. Deaton and Stone also examined adults in 161 other

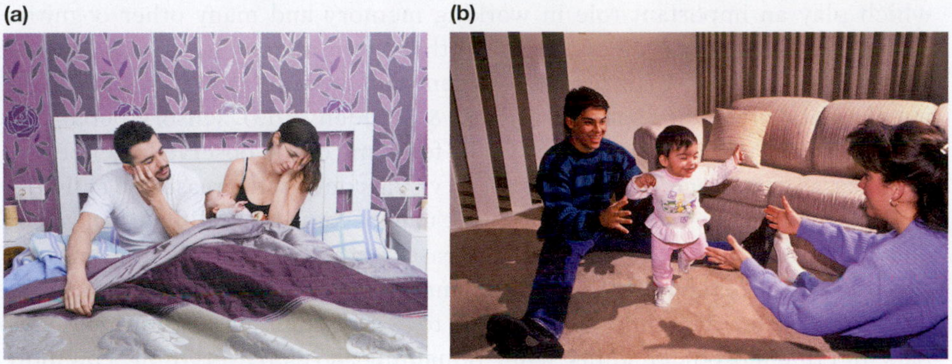

FIGURE 9.37
Having Children
When deciding whether to have children, it is important to consider both **(a)** the minuses, such as the stresses involved, and **(b)** the pluses, such as the rewarding feelings.

nations. They found that having children has a much more negative impact on life satisfaction in less wealthy nations.

The emotional experience of having children is not the same for everyone or at all stages of the child's life. The early years are the hardest, especially for women, who do a disproportionate amount of the hard work of child care. Mothers report being less happy and more stressed than fathers and are more likely to become depressed in the first few years of their children's lives. The social context of parenting has also changed over the past 20 years to favor a style of parenting that is more responsive to children, hands-on, and intensive. Parents in the 2010s were more stressed and less happy than their counterparts were in the 1970s (Nomaguchi & Milkie, 2020). In contrast, having adult children can be a source of well-being for parents, particularly if the children do not live at home with their parents and have strong relationships with them (Tosi & Grundy, 2018).

Over the coming years, you may find yourself considering whether or not you would like to have children. After studying millions of people around the world, Deaton and Stone (2014) concluded, "If parents choose to be parents, and nonparents choose to be nonparents, there is no reason to expect that one group will be better or worse off than the other one" (p. 1328). In other words, if you choose the parenting status that makes sense for you as an individual, the decision to have kids (or not) will not make or break your happiness. Each decision comes with its own tradeoffs for your happiness and well-being. ■

Q Does having a child improve marriage relationships?

ANSWER: The answer differs by person, situation, and developmental period in the child's life. Having a child can increase marital stress if the burdens are not equally shared. However, having a child can increase moments of joy and feelings of purpose, which may benefit a marriage.

9.16 Cognition Changes with Age

In Western societies, people are living much longer, and the number of people over age 85 is growing dramatically. It is becoming commonplace for people to live beyond 100. By 2030, more than 1 in 5 Americans will be over age 65, and these older people will be ethnically diverse, well educated, and physically fit. With this "graying" of the population in Western societies, much greater research attention has been paid to the lives of people over age 60 and the changes that occur later in life.

In addition to physical changes such as graying hair and wrinkling skin, cognitive abilities eventually decline with age. We know that the frontal lobes, which play an important role in working memory and many other cognitive skills, shrink proportionally more than other brain regions (Cabeza & Dennis, 2012). One of the most consistent and identifiable cognitive changes is a slowing of mental processing speed (Salthouse & Madden, 2013). Sensory-perceptual changes occur with age and may account for some of the observed decline. For instance, as people age, their sensitivity to visual contrast decreases, so activities such as climbing stairs or driving at night may become more difficult and more dangerous. Sensitivity to sound also decreases with age, especially the ability to tune out background noise. This change may make older people seem confused or forgetful when they simply are not able to hear adequately. In addition, scientists find that most older adults, while remaining alert, do everything a bit more slowly as they grow older.

MEMORY Older people have difficulty with memory tasks that require juggling multiple pieces of information at the same time. Tasks in which attention is divided, such as driving while listening to the radio, also prove difficult. Some scientists believe these deficits reflect a decreased ability to store multiple pieces of information simultaneously in working memory (Salthouse, 1992).

Generally speaking, long-term memory is less affected by aging than is working memory. However, certain aspects of long-term memory do appear to suffer in advanced age. Older people often need more time to learn new information, though once they learn it they use it as efficiently as younger people do. The elderly also are better at recognition than at retrieval tasks (Craik & McDowd, 1987). For example, if the word *cat* is shown to them, they have no trouble recognizing the word if they are asked, "Did you see the word *cat*?" But if they are simply asked what word they saw or whether they saw an animal name, they do not do as well.

As discussed in Chapter 7, the ability to form associations between items is important for long-term memory. Memories are bundles of images, locations, experiences, and so forth that are bound together into a distinct unit. Recent evidence shows that memory declines in older adults might be due to difficulty forming these associations, or "binding" objects in memory (Naveh-Benjamin & Mayr, 2018). Older adults might have trouble remembering and retrieving events because they have difficulty gluing the pieces together to form a distinct whole.

If memory deficits in older adults follow from difficulties with binding, can strengthening the associations improve memory? Training older adults to encode memories in ways that increase the number and strength of associations improves their memory performance to the point that it is equivalent to that of young adults (Dennis et al., 2019). On the retrieval side, using strategies for recalling information that bring many associations to mind can also help older adults remember details of memories (Aizpurua & Koutstaal, 2015; Cohn et al., 2008).

INTELLIGENCE Research has indicated consistently that intelligence as measured on standard psychometric tests declines with advanced age. As people age, do they really lose IQ points? Or do older people just have a shorter attention span or lack the motivation to complete such tests?

As discussed in Chapter 8, some researchers have distinguished between fluid intelligence and crystallized intelligence (Horn & Hofer, 1992). Fluid intelligence is the ability to process new general information that requires no specific prior knowledge. Many standardized tests measure this kind of intelligence, such as when test takers need to recognize an analogy or arrange blocks to match a picture. Associated with the speed of mental processing, fluid intelligence tends to peak in early adulthood and declines when people are in their 60s or 70s (Schaie, 1990). People who are healthy and active demonstrate less decline in fluid intelligence. Crystallized intelligence is based on specific knowledge—the kind that must be learned or memorized, such as vocabulary, specialized information, or reasoning strategies. This type of intelligence usually increases throughout life. It breaks down only when declines in other cognitive abilities prevent acquiring new information.

DEMENTIA AND ALZHEIMER'S DISEASE Older adults who experience a dramatic loss in mental ability often suffer from *dementia*. This brain condition causes thinking, memory, and behavior to deteriorate progressively. Dementia has many causes, including excessive alcohol intake and HIV, but the major causes are Alzheimer's disease and small strokes that affect the brain's blood supply. The initial symptoms of Alzheimer's are typically minor memory impairments, but as the disease progresses, the person eventually loses all mental capacities, including language. Many people with Alzheimer's experience profound personality changes.

The exact cause of Alzheimer's is not known, but evidence suggests there are genetic influences, including genes involved in cholesterol functioning and in synaptic plasticity and repair (O'Donoghue et al., 2018; Sala Frigerio & De Strooper, 2016). In addition, the memory-related neurotransmitter acetylcholine is very low in people who suffer from Alzheimer's, resulting in abnormal protein accumulation in the brain (Knowles et al., 2014; **FIGURE 9.38**). Examining activity within brain networks can help predict which individuals are likely to progress from mild cognitive impairment to Alzheimer's (Spreng & Turner, 2013).

A genetic predisposition to developing dementia is not a hopeless case, however. Decades of research show that learning new tasks, solving puzzles, reading, and maintaining social bonds reduces the risk of dementia (Fratiglioni et al., 2004; Larson et al., 2006). Physical activity throughout the life span is the strongest protective factor.

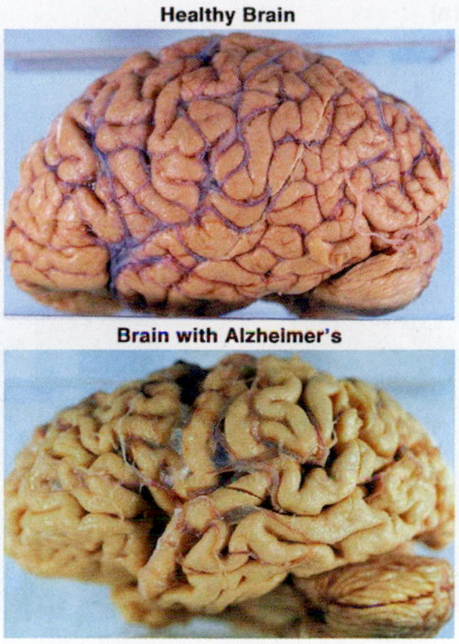

FIGURE 9.38
Damage from Alzheimer's Disease
The brain on the bottom shows the ravages of Alzheimer's disease in comparison to the normal brain on top. The holes (ventricles) in the middle of the brain are extremely large, and every section of gray and white matter has lost density.

Q How do fluid intelligence and crystallized intelligence change with aging?

ANSWER: Fluid intelligence decreases, but crystallized intelligence increases.

9.17 The Transition to Old Age Can Be Satisfying

Although some people experience cognitive and physical decline with age, not all do, and most older adults are relatively healthy and happy. Except for dementia, older adults have fewer mental health problems, including depression, than younger adults (Jorm, 2000). Indeed, many individuals thrive in old age, especially those with adequate financial resources, opportunities for regular exercise, and good health (Hammarberg et al., 2019).

Many positive things happen as people grow older. Today, better health, better nutrition, and medical advances enable people to live longer than in previous generations. Understanding old age is becoming especially important, as most Western cultures are experiencing a boom in the aging population.

Older adults contribute much to modern society. For instance, nearly 40 percent of U.S. federal judges are over 65, and they handle about 20 percent

FIGURE 9.39

Changing Views of the Elderly

(a) Maggie Smith, now in her 80s, enjoys life and remains a cultural force. **(b)** Stevie Wonder, in his 70s, seems as timeless as his music. **(c)** Willie Nelson, now over 85, is still touring the country.

of the caseload (Markon, 2001). Many older adults work productively well past their 70s. Views of the elderly are likely to change a great deal as the baby boom generation ages. Consider music and television stars—such as Maggie Smith, Stevie Wonder, and Willie Nelson—who remain popular and vibrant well into their 70s, 80s, and beyond, certainly in defiance of common stereotypes of old people (**FIGURE 9.39**).

socioemotional selectivity theory A theory proposing that as people grow older, they view time as limited and therefore shift their focus to meaningful events, experiences, and goals.

MEANING People of all ages are concerned with the meaning of life, but meaning often becomes a preoccupation for the elderly. According to Laura Carstensen's **socioemotional selectivity theory**, as people grow older, they view time as limited and therefore shift their focus to emotionally meaningful events, experiences, and goals (Carstensen, 1995; Fung & Carstensen, 2004). Also consistent with socioemotional selectivity theory is the finding that older people show better memory for positive than for negative information (Kennedy et al., 2004). When older adults reminisce about their lives, they report more positive emotions than negative ones (Pasupathi & Carstensen, 2003). They report shorter and fewer negative emotional experiences in their daily lives (Charles et al., 2016). This finding suggests that older people may selectively ignore negative events in order to make their later years feel more positive and meaningful (Mather & Carstensen, 2003).

Older adults are also selective about how they use their time. They tend to spend more time with a smaller group of close friends and family instead of new people (Sims et al., 2015). As with parents caring for children, older adults caring for their grandchildren experience more stress but also greater well-being and meaning in life (Dunifon et al., 2019). In essence, older adults want to savor their final years by putting their time and effort into meaningful and rewarding experiences. Most older adults report being just as satisfied with life as younger adults, if not more so (Mroczek & Kolarz, 1998).

Because life expectancies generally have improved over time, much more research is likely to be devoted to understanding how people can maintain their physical and cognitive capacities to get the most out of their final years. Moreover, research will continue to examine aging through a more nuanced lens. For instance, contemporary work suggests there are strong differences across people both in their genetic susceptibility to cognitive decline in aging (Mortensen & Høgh, 2001) and in how early life factors such as education influence changes in their cognition across age (Seblova et al., 2020).

Thus, this chapter ends where it began, with a reminder that all aspects of human development are caused by a complex cascade of influences. These influences include genes, neurotransmitters, family, social ties, culture, and each individual's motivations and actions (**FIGURE 9.40**). We all play active roles in our own development. We are not passive sponges absorbing our environments, nor are we slaves to our genes. How we experience each phase of the life span depends on our own perceptions, the social support we receive, and the developmental dance that occurs between nature and nurture.

FIGURE 9.40
Maintaining Health and Happiness
By gathering to exercise, these women are taking positive steps to maintain their health and happiness.

Q According to socioemotional selectivity theory, how and why does motivation change in older adulthood?

ANSWER: People start to view their time as limited and therefore prioritize the most important aspects of life.

Your Chapter Review

Want to earn a better grade on your test?

It's time to complete your study experience! Go to **INQUIZITIVE** to practice actively with this chapter's concepts and get personalized feedback along the way.

Chapter Summary

What Factors Shape Development?

9.1 Human Development Starts in the Womb and Extends into Adulthood The prenatal period is from conception (when sperm and egg unite to form a zygote) through birth (which occurs roughly 40 weeks after conception). From 2 weeks to 2 months prenatally, the developing cells are called an embryo and begin to form into organ systems. By 2 months prenatally, organ systems are formed, the heart begins to beat, and the developing human is called a fetus. Brain development begins early in fetal development. Myelination of the spinal cord occurs in the first trimester, and myelination of neurons occurs during the second trimester. Most neurons are formed at birth, but neural development via synaptic connections continues through early adulthood. Synaptic pruning is the reduction of synaptic connections due to nonuse. The embryo and the fetus are vulnerable to teratogens, environmental toxins that include drugs, viruses, and chemicals.

9.2 Biology and Environment Influence Motor Development Genetics and experiences influence motor development. Dynamic systems theory views development as a self-organizing process in which new forms of behavior emerge through the interaction of biology and environment.

9.3 Infants Are Prepared to Learn Infants are capable of learning, although explicit long-term memories do not persist until about the age of 18 months. Virtually all humans experience infantile amnesia, the inability to remember events before the age of 3 or 4. Some psychologists suggest that infantile amnesia disappears with the development of language.

9.4 You Be the Psychologist: Does Mozart Make You Smarter? According to a 1993 study, listening to Mozart can at least briefly enhance cognition. The popular press turned this study's results into the so-called Mozart effect, which inspired caregivers, educators, and politicians to increase infants' exposure to Mozart's music. However, the reporting and subsequent reactions misrepresented the original study, which showed only a motor skill improvement in college-age participants.

9.5 Infants Develop Attachments An attachment is a strong emotional connection that can motivate care, protection, and social support. Research by Harry Harlow demonstrated that attachments form due to receiving comfort and warmth, not food. Most infants display a secure attachment style, expressing confidence in unfamiliar environments as long as the caregiver is present. Other infants display an insecure or anxious attachment style and may avoid contact with the caregiver, or they alternate between seeking and rejecting contact. The hormone oxytocin plays a role in attachment.

How Do Children Learn About the World?

9.6 Piaget Emphasized Stages of Cognitive Development Piaget believed that cognitive development occurs across four stages: sensorimotor (0–2 years), preoperational (2–7 years), concrete operational (7–12 years), and formal operational (12 years–adulthood). During each stage, people develop schemes, cognitive categories used to organize information. Through assimilation and accommodation, individuals revise and adjust schemes so they remain useful throughout their lives.

9.7 Piaget Underestimated Children's Cognitive Abilities While Piaget's theory correctly describes much of how cognitive abilities develop, it may underestimate early knowledge. Theories such as Vygotsky's emphasize that cognitive development is guided by cultural expectations and interactions with others. Young infants can use laws of physics and even demonstrate a basic understanding of addition and subtraction.

9.8 Children Learn from Interacting with Others Theory of mind is the ability to understand that other people have mental states that will influence their behavior. Theory of mind typically develops by 15 months and is related to development of the frontal lobes.

9.9 Moral Development Begins in Childhood According to Kohlberg's stage theory of moral reasoning, moral decisions are based on trying to avoid personal harm, trying to gain approval from others, or having true moral concern for the sanctity of life. Theories of moral reasoning have been criticized for their gender and culture bias and for ignoring emotional aspects of moral decisions.

9.10 You Be the Psychologist: Is Screen Time Unhealthy for Children? Experts have warned about the dangers of screen time for children, but no studies show that screen time is definitively harmful for children. Instead, a number of studies have identified correlations between some kinds of screen time and a limited set of outcomes such as reduced well-being. These studies are inconclusive because they do not experimentally manipulate which children are exposed to high versus low amounts of screen time. These types of studies cannot rule out the possibility that third variables, such as caregiving style, might explain the correlation between screen time and child outcomes.

What Changes During Adolescence?

9.11 Puberty Causes Physical Changes Adolescence begins with puberty, the onset of sexual maturity and thus the ability to reproduce. Biology and environment affect the timing of puberty. During puberty, changing hormone levels stimulate physical changes. Yet adolescence is not characterized by as much emotional turmoil as is commonly believed.

9.12 A Sense of Identity Forms Physical and cognitive changes, along with environmental and societal pressures to prepare for the future, prompt adolescents to establish their identities. Erikson proposed a theory of psychosocial development that describes a series of challenges individuals must overcome from birth through old age, and the challenge during adolescence is to develop an adult identity or risk role confusion. Gender roles are influenced by biology and environment. Cultural and ethnic identities also develop during adolescence.

9.13 Peers and Caregivers Shape the Adolescent Self Adolescents use peer groups to help themselves feel a sense of belonging and acceptance. Adolescents may come into conflict with attachment figures, peers, and community members, but they need support and guidance from people close to them. Caregivers influence peer group identification, values, and religious choices.

What Brings Meaning in Adulthood?

9.14 Adults Are Affected by Life Transitions Adulthood requires people to meet certain challenges, such as physical and cognitive changes, getting married, and raising a family. In general, married people are healthier and happier than those who are single or cohabiting, though this advantage is more pronounced in men.

9.15 Psychology Outside the Lab: Will Parenthood Make You Happy? According to the research, couples with children report less marital satisfaction than couples without children. However, raising children can be richly rewarding. The influence of parenting on well-being relates to the parents' degree of choice in having children.

9.16 Cognition Changes with Age Despite declines in memory and speed of mental processing, people generally maintain their intelligence into very old age. People who engage in social, physical, and mental activities tend to keep mental skills sharp into old age.

9.17 The Transition to Old Age Can Be Satisfying Most older adults remain healthy, alert, and vital. Thoughtful planning and social support can make all phases of adult development rewarding. Older people are often more satisfied with their lives than younger adults are. People increasingly seek meaning in their lives as they age.

Key Terms

accommodation, p. 343
assimilation, p. 343
attachment, p. 339
concrete operational stage, p. 346
conventional level, p. 353
developmental psychology, p. 330
dynamic systems theory, p. 334
formal operational stage, p. 346
gender identity, p. 358
gender role, p. 358
habituation technique, p. 336
inequity aversion, p. 353
infantile amnesia, p. 337
object permanence, p. 345
postconventional level, p. 353
preconventional level, p. 353
preoperational stage, p. 345
puberty, p. 355
sensorimotor stage, p. 344
socioemotional selectivity theory, p. 368
synaptic pruning, p. 331
teratogens, p. 331
theory of mind, p. 350

Practice Exercises

1. One-week-old infants can usually ______. Choose all that apply.
   a. differentiate between sweet and nonsweet tastes
   b. display social smiles
   c. grasp a caregiver's finger
   d. make eye contact
   e. orient toward loud sounds
   f. recognize their names
   g. roll over unassisted
   h. see a caregiver across the room
   i. show preference for the smell of the mother's breast milk
   j. turn toward a nipple near their mouths
2. Piaget's theories of development have been very influential, but recent findings present challenges to some of his ideas. Which statement does *not* describe a recent finding that challenges Piaget's theories?
   a. Children can move back and forth between stages when working on tasks.
   b. Babies can demonstrate object permanence in the first few months of life.
   c. Children younger than 3 can understand the concepts of *more than* and *less than* when using M&M's.
   d. People exclusively use formal operations after adolescence to solve problems.
3. How do the preferential looking technique and habituation technique give insights into the minds of infants?
   a. Infants can innately nod their heads for "yes."
   b. Infants will cry more when shown unfamiliar objects.
   c. Infants will look longer at objects that they perceive to be unfamiliar.
   d. Infants can innately shake their heads for "no."
4. A child watches a conflict between classmates: Aahil calls Emma a mean name and Emma retaliates by biting Aahil. Label each of the child's potential reactions to the situation according to Kohlberg's levels of moral reasoning: preconventional, conventional, postconventional.
   a. "Emma should not bite because Aahil might bite her back."
   b. "Even though Aahil called her a name, Emma should do the right thing and ignore him."
   c. "Emma shouldn't bite because she will get a time-out from the teacher."
5. Which of the following conclusions about the relationship between screen time and child well-being is supported by empirical research? A large amount of screen time ______.
   a. causes harmful effects on a range of child outcomes
   b. is correlated with increased intelligence later in life
   c. causes beneficial effects on some child outcomes
   d. is correlated with reduced well-being
6. When participating in the strange-situation study, a child is not distressed when the caregiver leaves and ignores the caregiver when they return. Which attachment style is exhibited?
   a. secure
   b. insecure/ambivalent
   c. insecure/avoidant
7. Which statement most accurately describes the relationship between a person's sex and their gender identity?
   a. Gender identity begins in adolescence, while sex begins at birth.
   b. Sex and gender identity are not always congruent, so people can be transgender.
   c. Assigned sex is always consistent with gender identity, so everyone is cisgender.
   d. Biology influences a person's sex but not their gender identity.
8. Igor is celebrating his 75th birthday. As he ages into older adulthood, how are his thoughts and behaviors likely to change, according to socioemotional selectivity theory?
   a. He will be motivated to make more money and increase his savings.
   b. He will focus on visiting new places and gaining new experiences.
   c. He will want to spend more time with his best friends and family.
   d. He will feel increasingly regretful and remember the negative parts of his life.

9. Which of the following statements are true regarding the correlations among marriage, children, and well-being? Choose all that apply.
   a. Married people report being happier and healthier than single people.
   b. Having children increases marital satisfaction, especially when children are young and in adolescence.
   c. Marriage is associated with reduced immune functioning and worse physical well-being in men.
   d. Well-being increases in mothers who bear more responsibilities in childcare and housework.
   e. Parents from poorer nations show more benefit from having children than parents from wealthier nations.

10. Which statement most accurately describes the typical trend of well-being older adults?
   a. Older people tend to focus more on negative than positive aspects of their lives.
   b. Older people tend to focus more on positive than negative aspects of their lives.
   c. Older people are more depressed than young people, due to reduced cognitive speed with age.
   d. Older people are often regretful of their life decisions and anxious about their choices.
   e. Older people show dramatic increases in well-being regardless of health, wealth, or social support.

10 Emotion and Motivation

Big Questions

YOU WANT TO DO A REALLY GOOD JOB on your class presentation. You like the course and pride yourself on being a good public speaker. But when your professor starts taking notes during your talk, you become nervous. Your face feels warm, and you begin to sweat. You experience the pressure of living up to your self-image as a confident presenter. You try to picture yourself back in the peaceful room where you practiced so many times, but the silence in the classroom between your sentences terrifies you. You somehow pull yourself together, focus on the material, and do a great job. You walk out of the class feeling like you are floating on air.

Emotions and motivations permeate human life, for better and worse. For thousands of years, people have reflected on why we have emotions and what they do for us. An important and adaptive value of emotions is that they motivate action. We seek out events, activities, and objects that make us feel good, valued, and included. We avoid events, activities, and objects that make us feel bad, incompetent, or rejected. What psychological and neural functions give rise to our feelings? What does it even mean to feel an emotion? And why do those feelings influence our goals in life? This chapter examines how emotions and motivation are tied together.

Learning Objectives

- Distinguish between primary and secondary emotions.
- Discuss the roles that the insula and the amygdala play in emotional experience.
- Compare and contrast the James-Lange, Cannon-Bard, and Schachter-Singer two-factor theories of emotion.
- Define misattribution of arousal and excitation transfer.

What Are Emotions?

People have an intuitive sense of what *emotion* means. Still, the term is difficult to define precisely. The terms *emotion, feeling,* and *mood* are often used interchangeably in everyday language, but psychologists distinguish among them. An **emotion** is an immediate, specific negative or positive response to environmental events or internal thoughts. Emotions typically have some kind of triggering event, interrupt whatever is happening, and prompt changes in thought and behavior. You are sitting at your desk and see a movement out of the corner of your eye and . . . eek, a rat! You are having a negative emotional response. For psychologists, emotion—sometimes called *affect*—has three components: a physiological process (e.g., heart beating fast, sweating), a behavioral response (e.g., eyes and mouth opening wide), and a feeling that is based on cognitive appraisal of the situation and interpretation of bodily states (e.g., I'm scared!). A *feeling* is the subjective experience of the emotion, such as feeling scared, but not the emotion itself.

By contrast, *moods* are diffuse, long-lasting emotional states that do not have an identifiable trigger or a specific behavioral and physiological response. Rather than changing what is happening, they more subtly color thought and behavior. Often people who are in good or bad moods have no idea why they feel the way they do. Thus, moods refer to people's vague senses that they feel certain ways. Think of the difference this way: Getting cut off in traffic can make a person angry (emotion), but for no apparent reason a person can be irritable (mood).

emotion An immediate, specific negative or positive response to environmental events or internal thoughts.

primary emotions Emotions that are innate, evolutionarily adaptive, and universal (shared across cultures).

secondary emotions Blends of primary emotions.

10.1 Emotions Vary in Valence and Arousal

Some theories of emotion distinguish between primary and secondary emotions. **Primary emotions** are innate, evolutionarily adaptive, and universal across cultures. These emotions include anger, fear, sadness, disgust, happiness, surprise, and contempt. **Secondary emotions** are blends of primary emotions, feelings about emotions, or emotions that relate to culturally specific values or concepts. There are numerous secondary emotions, such as remorse, guilt, shame, jealousy, pride, love, and contentment. For example, guilt can feel like a combination of anger at yourself and fear of the potential consequences of your actions. A culturally specific emotion is the feeling of loss of face, a sense of respect, honor, and social regard that is important in many Asian cultures.

Emotions have also been classified along different dimensions. One such system is the *circumplex model.* In this model, emotions are plotted along two continuums: valence, or how negative or positive they are, and arousal, or how activating they are (Kuppens et al., 2013; Russell, 2003; **FIGURE 10.1**). *Arousal* is a generic term used to describe physiological activation (such as increased brain activity) or increased autonomic responses (such as quickened heart rate, increased sweating, or muscle tension).

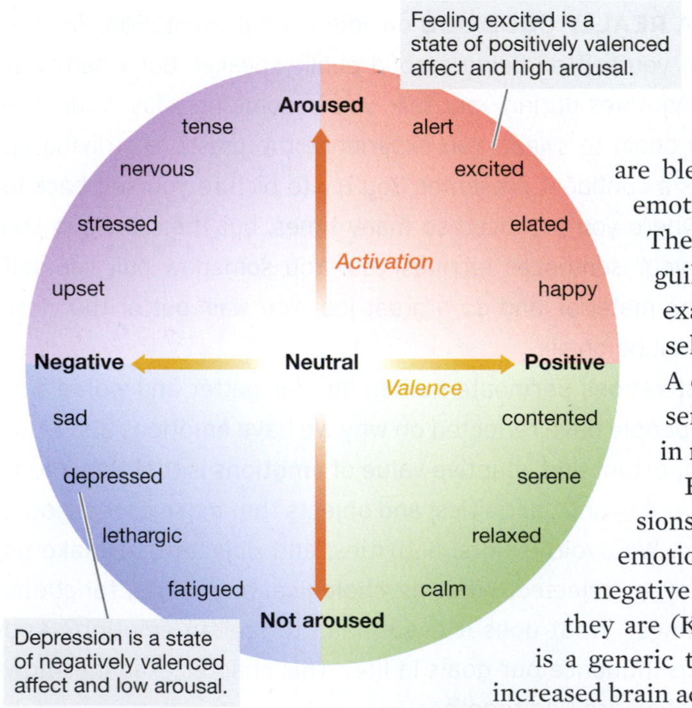

FIGURE 10.1
Circumplex Map of Emotion
Emotions can be categorized by valence (negative to positive) and by level of arousal (low to high).

To understand the difference between valence and arousal, imagine you discover that you have lost the one-dollar bill that was in your pants pocket. This experience will most likely make you unhappy, so you will judge it to have negative valence. It also might make you slightly aroused (increase your autonomic responses somewhat). Now imagine that you find a lottery ticket that turns out to be worth a million dollars. This experience will most likely make you very, very happy, so you will judge it as on the positive side of the valence scale. Your arousal will probably be topping the chart.

Psychologists have debated the names for the emotion dimensions and even the whole idea of dimensions. However, circumplex models have proved useful as a basic classification system for mood states (Barrett et al., 2007).

Some secondary emotions seem to contradict the circumplex approach of viewing emotions on a continuum from negative to positive. Consider the bittersweet feeling of being both happy and sad. For example, you might feel this way when remembering good times you had with someone who has died. People report feeling happy and sad after moving out of their dormitories, after graduating from college, and after playing a risky game where they did not win a monetary reward but did not lose money, either (Norris & Larsen, 2020). Neuroscientists found that a computer using advanced methods could tell the brain responses to positive and negative affect apart from each other, but only when the computer looked at activation in the whole brain (Kragel & LaBar, 2016). This work reveals that any one brain region does not uniquely encode valence or arousal. Instead, those dimensions are represented throughout the brain in both cortical and subcortical areas. Neuroscience research on emotions also supports the idea that the brain is capable of generating mixed emotions that have features of both positive and negative states (Barrett, 2017).

Q According to the circumplex model of emotion, what are the two dimensions on which emotions vary?

ANSWER: valence (positive vs. negative) and arousal (brain and body activation)

10.2 Emotions Have a Physiological Component

While waiting for a job interview, you might find your heart racing. When someone tells you they love you, you might feel warm all over. Even everyday language includes bodily descriptions to describe emotional experiences, such as getting "cold feet" when reconsidering a commitment, being "heartbroken" when extremely distressed, or having "butterflies in your stomach" when anxious. Emotions involve activation of the autonomic nervous system to prepare the body to meet environmental challenges (Levenson, 2003, 2014).

Controversy exists about such physiological responses. Does each emotion have a specific bodily response (Lench et al., 2011)? Or do all emotions share core physical properties related to valence and arousal (Wilson-Mendenhall et al., 2013), making them difficult to distinguish based on bodily response alone? Many of the autonomic responses to emotion overlap. However, the specific patterns across multiple autonomic responses (flushing or blanching, heart rate, sweating, pupil dilation, and goose bumps) suggest some level of specificity for each emotion (Comtesse & Stemmler, 2017; Eisenbarth et al., 2016; Levenson, 2014). There is evidence from fMRI studies that patterns of brain activity differ among emotional experiences (Saarimäki et al., 2016).

To study bodily responses and emotions, Finnish researchers asked people from various cultures to use a computer program to color which areas of the body were involved in feeling various emotions (Nummenmaa et al., 2014). Across five studies, emotions were generated in different ways (e.g., imagining the emotions, reading short stories, or watching movies). The body parts activated by various emotions overlapped somewhat, but most emotions were characterized by

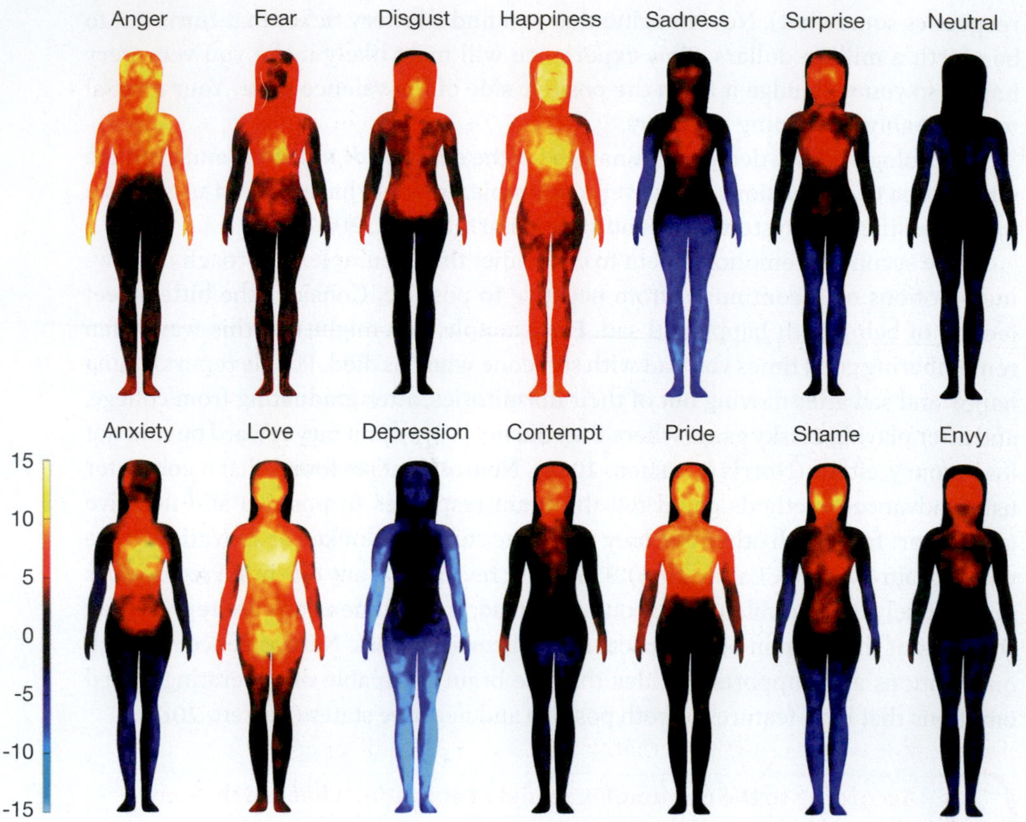

FIGURE 10.2

Body Maps of Emotion

These maps represent areas of the body that are more active (warm colors) or less active (cool colors) when people consider how various emotions make them feel. The color bar reflects the extent of increasing or decreasing activity.

their own specific patterns of activity in the body (**FIGURE 10.2**). According to the researchers, perception of these bodily sensations may play a role in how different emotions are experienced.

LIMBIC SYSTEM In 1937, the neuroanatomist James Papez proposed that many subcortical brain regions are involved in emotion. The physician and neuroscientist Paul MacLean (1952) expanded this list of regions, which border the cerebral cortex, and called it the limbic system. We now know that many brain structures outside the limbic system are involved in emotion and that many limbic structures are not central to emotion per se. For instance, the hippocampus is important for memory, and the hypothalamus is important for motivation. Thus, the term *limbic system* is used mainly in a rough, descriptive way rather than as a means of directly linking brain areas to specific emotional functions. For understanding emotion, the most important limbic system structures are the insula and the amygdala (**FIGURE 10.3**). However, several other areas contribute to emotional processing. In addition, various regions of the prefrontal cortex are important for generating emotions (Satpute & Lindquist, 2019).

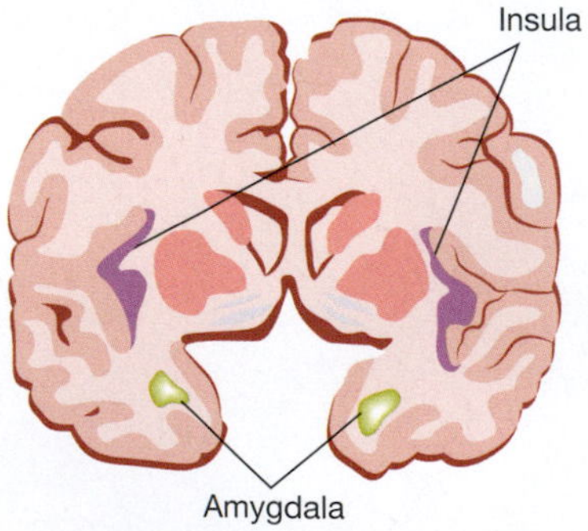

FIGURE 10.3

The Insula and the Amygdala

This figure shows the insula and the amygdala from the front and midway through the brain, indicating their relative locations. Figure 10.4a shows the amygdala from the side.

The insula receives and integrates somatosensory signals from the entire body. It is also involved in the subjective awareness of bodily states, such as sensing your heartbeat, feeling hungry, or needing to urinate. Given that emotions produce bodily responses, it is not surprising that the insula plays an important role in the experience of emotion (Craig, 2009; Zaki et al., 2012). Imaging studies have found that the insula is particularly active when people experience disgust—such as when exposed to bad smells—or observe facial expressions of disgust in other people (Wicker et al., 2003). Damage to the insula interferes with the experience of disgust and also with recognizing disgust expressions in others (Calder et al., 2000). The insula is also activated in a variety of other emotions, including anger, guilt, and anxiety (Chang et al., 2013).

The amygdala processes the emotional significance of stimuli, and it generates immediate emotional and behavioral reactions (Whalen & Phelps, 2009). According to the emotion theorist Joseph LeDoux (2007, 2015a), the processing of emotion in the amygdala involves a circuit that has developed over the course of evolution to protect animals from danger. LeDoux (2014) has established the amygdala as the brain structure most important for emotional learning, as in the development of classically conditioned fear responses (see Chapter 6). People with damage to the amygdala do not develop conditioned fear responses to objects associated with danger. Suppose that study participants receive an electric shock each time they see a picture of a blue square. Normally, such participants will develop a conditioned response—indicated by greater physiological arousal—when they see the blue square. But people with damage to the amygdala do not show classical conditioning of these fear associations (Anderson & Phelps, 2000).

Information reaches the amygdala along two separate pathways. The first path is a "quick and dirty" system that processes sensory information nearly instantaneously. Recall from Chapter 5 that, with the exception of smell, all sensory information travels to the thalamus before going on to other brain structures and the related portions of the cortex (**FIGURE 10.4a**). Along this fast path, sensory information travels quickly through the thalamus directly to the amygdala for priority processing (**FIGURE 10.4b**, green arrow).

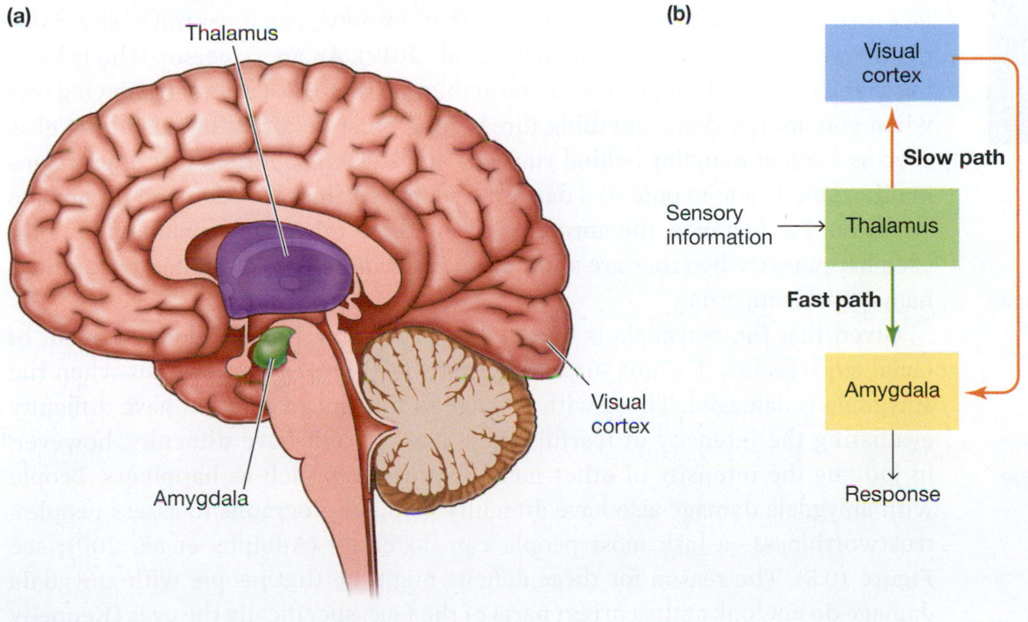

FIGURE 10.4
The Emotional Brain
(a) The amygdala is one of the most important brain structures for processing emotion. Before sensory information reaches the amygdala, it passes through the thalamus. From the thalamus, it may travel through the visual cortex (shown here) or auditory cortex (not shown). **(b)** When sensory information reaches the thalamus, it can take one of two paths: the fast path (from the thalamus to the amygdala) or the slow path (from the thalamus, through the visual cortex or auditory cortex, to the amygdala). The two paths enable people to assess and respond to emotion-producing stimuli in different ways.

(a)

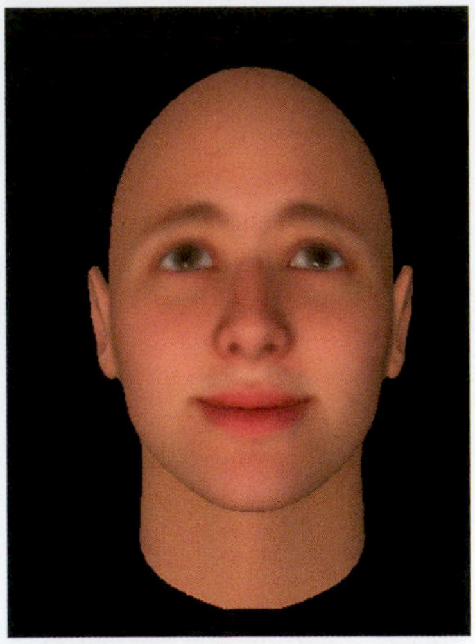

(b)

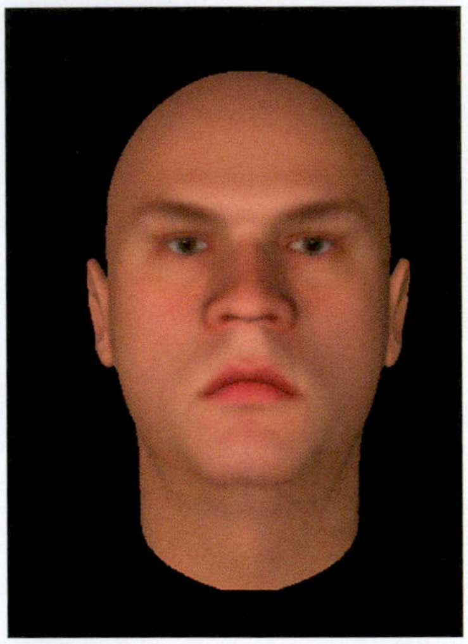

FIGURE 10.5

Evaluating Facial Expressions

Which of these people would you trust? Most people would say that **(a)** this person looks trustworthy and **(b)** this person looks untrustworthy. Viewing the untrustworthy face leads to greater amygdala activity. People with certain brain injuries cannot assess how trustworthy people are from facial expressions such as these.

The second path leads to more deliberate and more thorough evaluations. Along this slow path, sensory material travels from the thalamus to the cortex (the visual cortex or the auditory cortex), where the information is scrutinized in greater depth before it is passed along to the amygdala (see Figure 10.4b, orange arrows). Theorists believe that the fast system prepares animals to respond to a threat in case the slower pathway confirms the threat (LeDoux, 2000). You have experienced the two pathways if, for example, you have shied away from a blurry movement in the grass only to realize it was the wind and not a snake.

AMYGDALA AND COGNITION As noted in Chapter 7, emotional events are especially likely to be stored in memory. The amygdala plays a role in this process. Brain imaging studies have shown that emotional events are likely to increase activity in the amygdala and that increased activity is likely to improve long-term memory for the event (LaBar & Cabeza, 2006; Talmi, 2013). Researchers believe that the amygdala modifies how the hippocampus consolidates memory, especially memory for fearful events (Manns & Bass, 2016; Phelps, 2004, 2006). This adaptive mechanism enables us to remember harmful situations and thus potentially avoid them.

The amygdala is also involved in the perception of social stimuli. It plays a role, for example, when we decipher the emotional meanings of other people's facial expressions, such as their trustworthiness (Freeman et al., 2014; Todorov et al., 2013; **FIGURE 10.5**). Imaging studies demonstrate that the amygdala is especially sensitive to the intensity of fearful faces (Dolan, 2000). This effect occurs even if a face is flashed so quickly on a screen that participants do not know they have seen it (Méndez-Bértolo et al., 2016). Perhaps surprisingly, the amygdala reacts more when a person observes a face displaying fear than when the person observes a face displaying anger. One explanation is that the amygdala is central to situations that involve uncertainty (FeldmanHall et al., 2019). An angry person who is looking at you is probably angry *at* you—no ambiguity there. But a person showing fear when you are not doing anything threatening must be afraid of something else, such as a spider dangling behind you. The amygdala response to fear expressions in others alerts you to potential dangers and other things that demand immediate attention. For instance, the amygdala responds to other emotional expressions, even happiness, when they are particularly relevant to the task at hand (Cunningham & Kirkland, 2014).

Given that the amygdala is involved in processing the emotional content of facial expressions, it is not surprising that social impairments result when the amygdala is damaged. Those with damage to the amygdala often have difficulty evaluating the intensity of fearful faces. They do not have difficulty, however, in judging the intensity of other facial expressions, such as happiness. People with amygdala damage also have difficulty using photographs to assess people's trustworthiness—a task most people can do easily (Adolphs et al., 2001; see Figure 10.5). The reason for these deficits might be that people with amygdala damage do not look at the correct parts of the face, specifically the eyes (Kennedy & Adolphs, 2010).

Q **When wading in the ocean, you sense a dark figure under the water, so you freeze. When you realize it is your own shadow and not a shark, you relax. How did the fast and slow paths for visual information contribute to your emotional response?**

ANSWER: The fast path, from the thalamus directly to the amygdala, signaled potential danger and prompted quick action. Further analysis using the slow path, from the thalamus to the visual cortex and then to the amygdala, prompted you to relax.

10.3 Are Lie Detector Tests Valid?

YOU BE THE PSYCHOLOGIST

One essential characteristic of human nature is that people occasionally lie to one another. As long as there have been lies, people have tried to develop methods for detecting such deception. Potential suspects in criminal investigations and applicants for certain types of jobs, such as those that involve classified documents, are often asked to take a polygraph test, known informally as a lie detector test. A *polygraph* is an electronic instrument that assesses the body's physiological response to questions (**FIGURE 10.6**). It records numerous aspects of arousal, such as breathing rate and heart rate.

The use of polygraphs is highly controversial. In 1988, polygraph results were banned from being used in federal courts as evidence, and they are not allowed to be used as part of hiring in the private sector. Yet they continue to be used by criminal investigators and federal agencies, such as the FBI and CIA.

The goal of a polygraph is to determine a person's level of emotionality, as indicated by autonomic arousal, when confronted with certain information. For instance, criminals might be asked about specific illegal activities, job applicants might be asked about drug use, and potential Secret Service or CIA agents might be asked about sympathies for foreign countries. Lying is stressful for most people, so autonomic arousal should be higher when people are lying than when they are telling the truth.

To assess physiological arousal, polygraphers use a control-question technique in which they ask a variety of questions, some of which are relevant to the critical information and some of which are not. Control questions—such as "Is your hair brown?" and "Have you ever been to Canada?"—are selected on the assumption that they should not produce a strong emotional response. Critical questions, such as "Did you steal the money?" or "Do you use drugs?" are those of specific interest to the investigators. The differences between the physiological

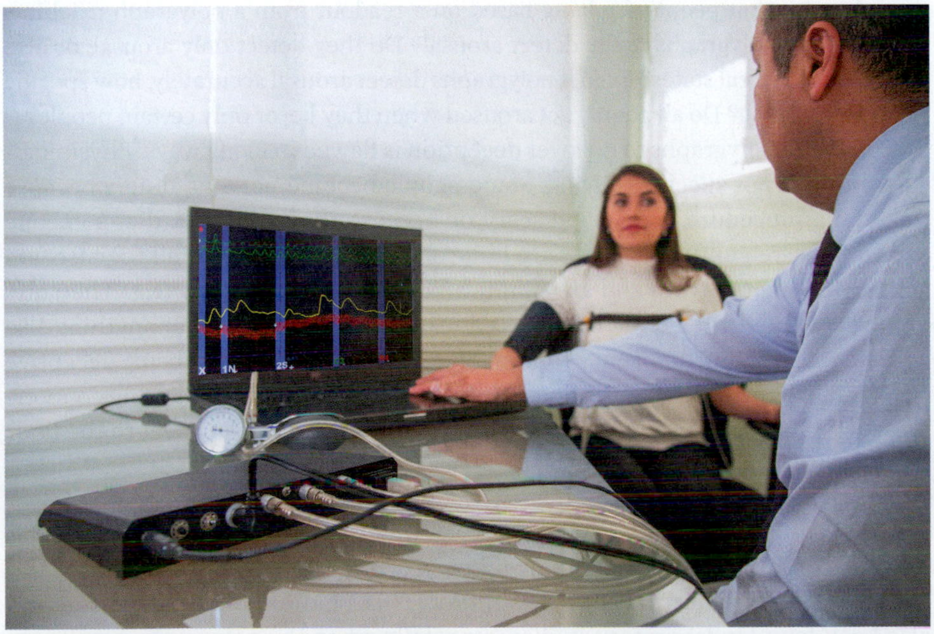

FIGURE 10.6
Polygraph
Here, a person is hooked up to a polygraph apparatus measuring heart rate, respiration, and skin conductance from sweating.

FIGURE 10.7
Lie Detection
A polygraph measures autonomic systems, such as heart rate, respiration, and skin conductance from sweating. Differences in autonomic reactions to critical questions, compared with responses to control questions, indicate arousal. That arousal in turn may indicate nervousness as a result of lying. However, the arousal may instead be due to general nervousness and thus may falsely indicate that the person is lying.

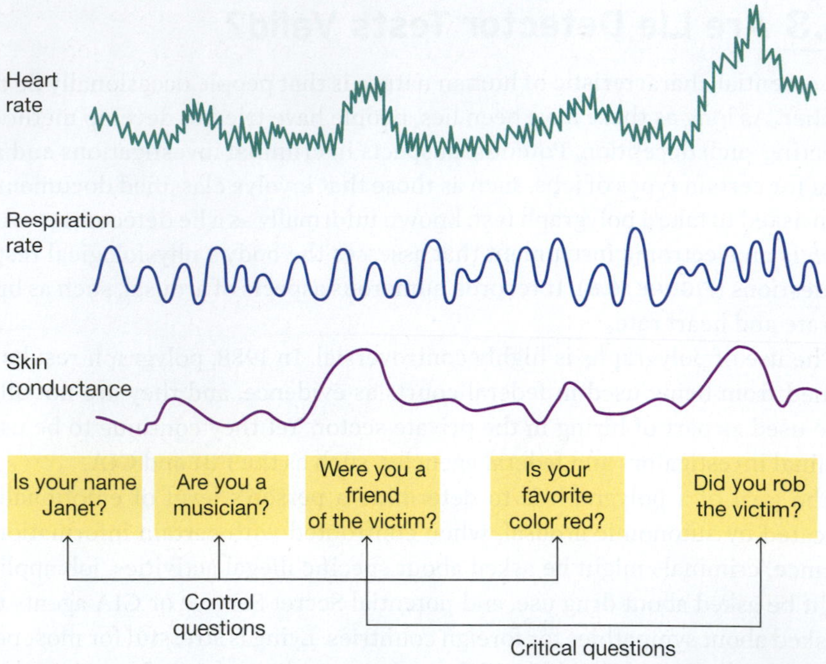

Heart rate
Respiration rate
Skin conductance
Is your name Janet?
Are you a musician?
Were you a friend of the victim?
Is your favorite color red?
Did you rob the victim?
Control questions
Critical questions

responses to the control questions and physiological responses to the critical questions are used to determine whether the person is lying (**FIGURE 10.7**). Sometimes the questions include information that only a guilty party would know, such as how a person was killed or where the body was found. Thus, simply having guilty knowledge should produce arousal and therefore should be detected by the polygraph.

How valid are polygraphs as lie detectors? Engage your critical thinking for a moment. Consider what kinds of evidence you would want to see to conclude that lie detectors are valid. It is important to think through the entire chain of logic to make the inference that people are lying based on a readout from a polygraph machine. How well do polygraphs really detect arousal? Do they detect only arousal, or also other physiological states? Even if polygraphs detect arousal accurately, how specific is arousal to lying? Do all people get aroused when they lie, or only certain people?

The use of polygraphs to uncover deception is flawed in many ways. Physiological arousal is not specific to lying. Some people become nervous simply because the whole procedure is new and scary or because they are upset that someone thinks they are guilty when they are innocent. Most people who fail the tests are actually telling the truth and are simply anxious about taking the test. The polygraph cannot tell whether a response is due to lying, nervousness, or anything else arousing. As a result, innocent people are often falsely classified as being deceptive (Ben-Shakhar et al., 2002). Lie detector tests are also easy to cheat using countermeasures, such as counting backward by sevens or pressing your feet to the floor during critical questions (Honts et al., 1994).

Perhaps the most serious problem with lie detector tests is that the interviewer has to make a subjective judgment as to whether the pattern of arousal indicates deception. This judgment is often influenced by the investigator's preexisting beliefs about whether the person is guilty. This type of confirmation bias has also been found in laboratory studies, especially when the polygraphy results are ambiguous (Elaad et al., 1994). Confirmation bias is a problem throughout forensic assessments, particularly when individuals develop "tunnel vision" and fixate on a particular suspect, ignoring or discounting evidence that is contrary (Kassin et al., 2013).

As you might expect, researchers are seeking new strategies to uncover deception. For instance, numerous studies using EEG and fMRI have detected differences in brain activity between when people are lying and when they are telling the truth (Langleben & Moriarty, 2013). However, the deception tasks in these studies have been relatively trivial, and the participants probably did not feel anxious about being deceptive (after all, the experimenters asked them to lie). Whether the activation of various brain regions indicates genuine deception or simply reflects other cognitive processes is currently unknown. A thoughtful review of this research by a team of neuroscience experts highlighted several methodological problems with fMRI research to detect deception. These experts raised additional ethical issues, such as privacy, that need further consideration before fMRI is ready for the courtroom (Farah et al., 2014). ■

James-Lange theory A theory of emotion stating that people perceive specific patterns of bodily responses and as a result of that perception feel emotion.

Q Can an investigator use a polygraph to differentiate between lying, nervousness, and embarrassment?

ANSWER: A polygraph cannot differentiate the increased physiological arousal associated with these responses.

10.4 There Are Three Major Theories of Emotion

Suppose you are in a rural area. You leave your house and notice your shed door is open. You go to inspect it. Inside, a grizzly bear looks up at you from the bag of dog food it was eating. Thinking like a psychologist, what is your hypothesis about how you would react? You might think that seeing the bear would make you scared. Your heart would start to race, and you would run back into the house. This commonsense hypothesis indicates that experiences, such as seeing a bear, generate emotions, such as fear, which then lead to bodily responses and behavior. But there are other ideas about how emotions are generated. Three major theories have proposed different ways that these processes might work: the James-Lange theory, the Cannon-Bard theory, and the Schachter-Singer two-factor theory.

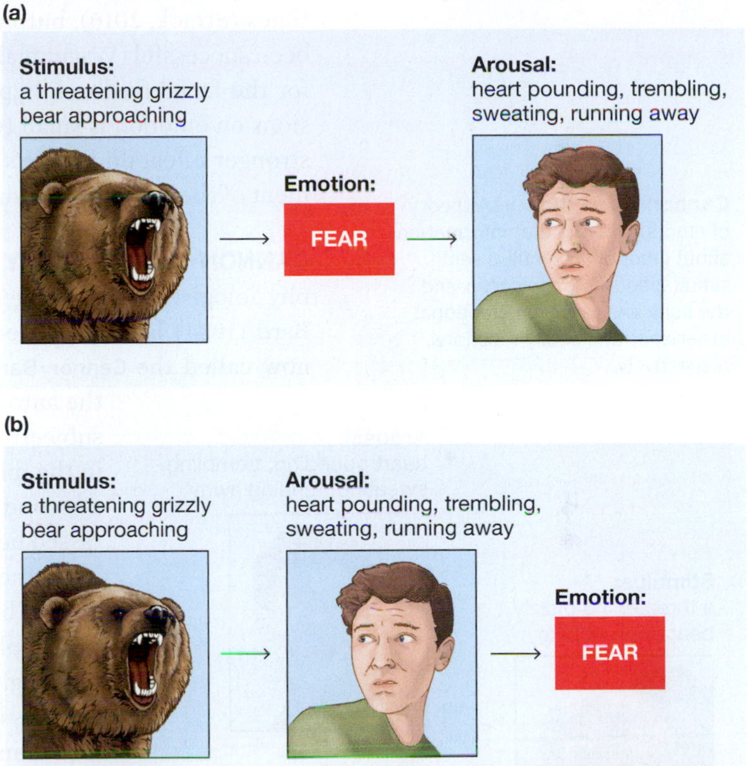

FIGURE 10.8
James-Lange Theory of Emotion
(a) According to the intuitive view of emotion, an experience—such as seeing a grizzly bear—produces an emotion and then a bodily response. **(b)** According to the James-Lange theory, bodily perception comes before the feeling of emotion. For example, when a grizzly bear threatens you, you begin to sweat, experience a pounding heart, and run (if you can). You put together the sight of the bear with these responses to realize that you are feeling fear.

JAMES-LANGE THEORY Although common sense suggests that our bodies respond to emotions, William James (1884) made the counterintuitive argument that the situation is just the opposite. James asserted that a person's interpretation of physiological changes leads that person to feel an emotion. As he put it, "We feel sorry because we cry, angry because we strike, afraid because we tremble[; it is] not that we cry, strike, or tremble because we are sorry, angry, or fearful" (p. 190).

James believed that physical changes occur in distinct patterns that translate directly into specific emotions. Around the same time, a similar theory was independently proposed by the physician and psychologist Carl Lange. According to what is called the **James-Lange theory** of emotion, we perceive specific patterns of bodily responses, and as a result of that perception we feel emotion (FIGURE 10.8).

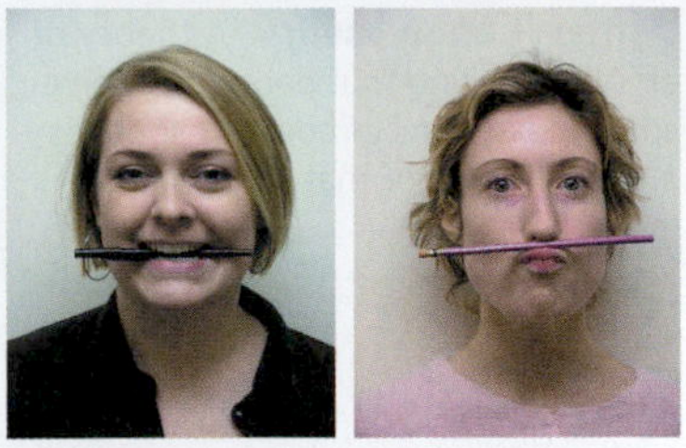

FIGURE 10.9

Facial Feedback Hypothesis

According to this hypothesis, facial expressions trigger the experience of emotion. Even the forced alteration of a person's facial expression can change that person's experience of emotion.

That is, seeing the bear causes your heart to race, and you perceive your racing heart as fear.

Some research supports the James-Lange theory. There is reliable evidence that making specific facial expressions, such as a wide smile, can trigger emotions, such as happiness (Laird & Lacasse, 2014). The opposite also appears to be true: Preventing facial expressions can blunt the experience of emotions. For example, Botox injections reduce wrinkles by paralyzing muscles around the eyes. Patients who received Botox also experienced muted positive emotions when they viewed positive films compared with people who did not receive the injections (Davis et al., 2010).

The idea that you can activate an emotion by molding your facial muscles into the associated expression was described in 1963 by Silvan Tomkins as the *facial feedback hypothesis*. Researchers have tested this idea in many ways—for example, by having people hold a pencil between their teeth or with their mouths in a way that produces a smile or a frown (**FIGURE 10.9**). The general idea that changing one's facial expression changes their emotional state has been demonstrated many times (Strack, 2016), but not every attempt to generate this effect in the lab has been successful (Wagenmakers et al., 2016). A recent meta-analysis found support for the facial feedback hypothesis but noted that the influence of facial expressions on emotion is small (Coles et al., 2019). Facial expressions appear to have a stronger effect on people's experience of their own emotion than on their judgment of the emotion shown in a stimulus.

Cannon-Bard theory A theory of emotion stating that information about emotional stimuli is sent simultaneously to the cortex and the body and results in emotional experience and bodily reactions, respectively.

CANNON-BARD THEORY In 1927, James's former student Walter B. Cannon, a physiologist, offered some objections to James's theory. Cannon's student Philip Bard (1934) later expanded on Cannon's criticisms. Their alternative theory is now called the **Cannon-Bard theory** of emotion. Cannon and Bard thought that the autonomic nervous system was too slow to account for the subjective feelings of emotions. Experience happens quickly in the mind, but bodily events are much slower, taking at least a second or two to develop. For instance, you may feel embarrassed before you blush.

Cannon and Bard also noted that many emotions produce similar bodily responses. The similarities make it too difficult for people to determine quickly which emotion they are experiencing. For instance, anger and excitement produce similar changes in heart rate and blood pressure. Exercise brings about these same changes and may affect your emotional state, but it does not generate a specific emotion.

Cannon and Bard proposed that information about emotional stimuli is sent to the mind and body separately. As a result, mind and body experience emotions independently. According to the Cannon-Bard theory of emotion, the information from an emotion-producing stimulus is processed in subcortical structures. (Cannon originally focused on the thalamus, but it is now known that many brain structures in the limbic system and beyond are involved in emotion.) The subcortical structures then send information separately to the cortex and the body. As a result, people experience two separate things at roughly the same time: the mental idea of an emotion, produced in the cortex, and physical reactions, produced in the body (**FIGURE 10.10**). When you see the bear in the shed, separate signals cause your heart to race and you to feel scared.

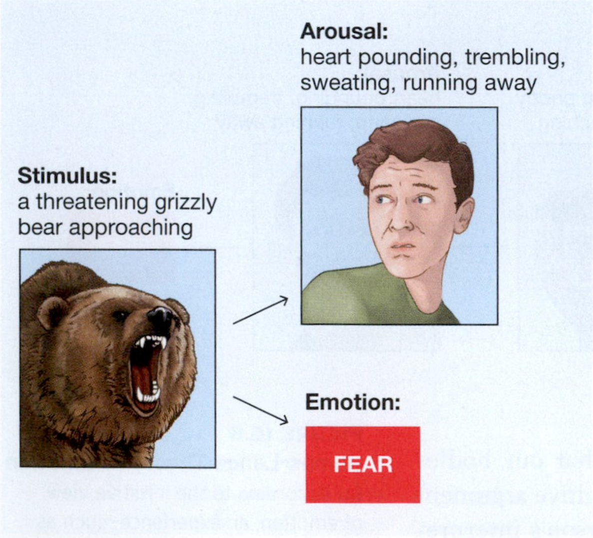

FIGURE 10.10

Cannon-Bard Theory of Emotion

According to this theory, emotion and physical reactions happen independently but at the same time. For example, when a grizzly bear threatens you, you simultaneously feel afraid and begin to sweat, experience a pounding heart, and run (if you can).

Although the terms they use are different, Joseph LeDoux and Daniel Pine (2016) have proposed a similar model that separates behavior and bodily responses. From this perspective, a person can be afraid even in the absence of a genuine threat. The mere awareness of the potential for harm can lead a person to be afraid, such as if a person becomes afraid to go outside because of news reports that bears are raiding local sheds.

SCHACHTER-SINGER TWO-FACTOR THEORY The social psychologists Stanley Schachter and Jerome Singer (1962) saw some merit in both the James-Lange and the Cannon-Bard theories. Schachter and Singer thought that the James-Lange theory was right in equating the perception of the body's reaction with an emotion, but they agreed with Cannon-Bard that too many different emotions existed for there to be a unique autonomic pattern for each. Schachter and Singer proposed a **two-factor theory** of emotion. They thought that the physiological response to all emotional stimuli was essentially the same, which they called undifferentiated physiological arousal. The arousal was just interpreted differently, depending on the situation, and given a *label*.

two-factor theory A theory of emotion stating that the label applied to physiological arousal results in the experience of an emotion.

According to this theory, when people experience arousal, they initiate a search for its source (**FIGURE 10.11**). The search for an explanation, or label, is often quick and straightforward, since a person generally recognizes the event that led to the emotional state. When seeing the bear in the shed, you experience arousal. Your knowledge that bears are dangerous leads you to attribute the arousal to the bear and label the arousal "fear."

But what happens when the situation is more ambiguous? According to the two-factor theory, whatever the person *believes* caused the emotion will determine how the person labels the emotion. A variety of evidence supports this aspect of the two-factor theory. An emotion involves physiological responses in brain and body that are influenced by how the person thinks about the situation (MacCormack & Lindquist, 2017; Satpute et al., 2016). The language people use to describe their feelings has a powerful influence on the emotions they experience (Lindquist & Gendron, 2013).

One interesting implication of the two-factor theory is that physical states caused by a situation can be attributed to the wrong emotion. When people misidentify the source of their arousal, it is called *misattribution of arousal*. In one exploration

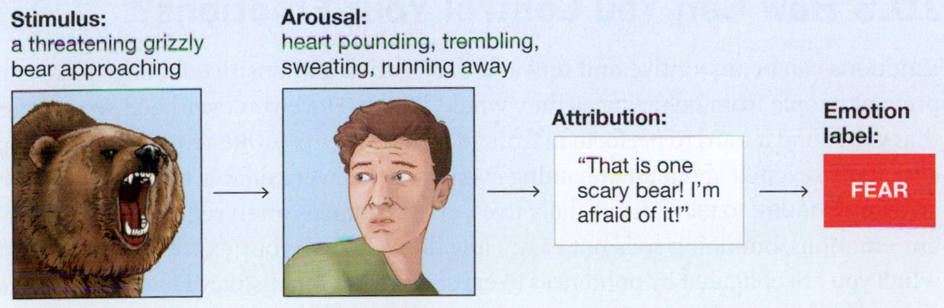

FIGURE 10.11
Schachter-Singer Two-Factor Theory
According to this theory, a person experiences physiological changes and applies a cognitive label to explain those changes. For example, when a grizzly bear threatens you, you begin to sweat, experience a pounding heart, and run (if you can). You then label those bodily actions as responses to the bear. As a result, you know you are experiencing fear.

FIGURE 10.12
Misattribution of Arousal
Men who walked across this narrow and scary bridge over the Capilano River displayed more attraction to the female experimenter on the bridge than did men who walked across a safer bridge.

of this phenomenon, researchers tried to determine whether people could feel romantic attraction through misattribution (Dutton & Aron, 1974). Participants, all of whom were heterosexual males, were approached by a researcher as they crossed one of two bridges over the Capilano River in British Columbia. One was a narrow suspension bridge with a low rail that swayed 230 feet above raging, rocky rapids. The other was a sturdy modern bridge just above the river. At the middle of the bridge, an attractive female research assistant approached each man and interviewed him. She gave him her phone number and offered to explain the results of the study at a later date if he was interested. According to the two-factor theory of emotion, the less stable bridge would produce arousal (sweaty palms, increased heart rate), which could be misattributed as attraction to the interviewer. Indeed, men interviewed on the less stable bridge were more likely to call the interviewer and ask her for a date (**FIGURE 10.12**).

Can you think of any alternative explanations for why men on the less stable bridge were more forward with the interviewer? What about initial differences between the men who chose to cross the less stable bridge and those who chose the safer bridge? Perhaps men who were more likely to take risks were more likely to choose a scary bridge *and* to call for a date. The general idea—that people can misattribute arousal for affection—has been supported in other studies, however (Inzlicht & Al-Khindi, 2012).

Q How does the Schachter-Singer two-factor theory of emotion combine elements of the James-Lange and Cannon-Bard theories?

ANSWER: The two-factor theory includes James-Lange's idea that physiological reactions occur before emotional ones and Cannon-Bard's idea that specific emotional reactions cannot be derived from general physiological reactions alone.

Learning Tip

It is easy to confuse the three theories of emotion described in this learning unit because they all deal with the mental and bodily parts of emotions. (And they all have hyphenated names!) The theories differ in their predictions about how thoughts and bodily sensations come together to give rise to emotions. In James-Lange, the *body* determines the emotion because it comes first and causes the mental label. In Schachter-Singer, the bodily sensation is necessary, but the *label* determines the emotion because the bodily sensation is undifferentiated, and the label is what gives an emotion its specificity.

PSYCHOLOGY OUTSIDE THE LAB

10.5 How Can You Control Your Emotions?

Emotions can be disruptive and unwanted. Negative and positive feelings alike can prevent people from behaving as they would like to. Have you ever been so nervous that you found it hard to perform in front of an audience (**FIGURE 10.13a**)? Or have you ever felt so excited about an upcoming event that you were unable to concentrate on an exam (**FIGURE 10.13b**)? In our daily lives, circumstances often require us to control our emotions, but doing so is not easy. How do you mask your expression of disgust when you are obligated by politeness to eat something you dislike? How do you force yourself to be nice about losing a competition that really matters to you?

The psychologist James Gross (1999, 2013) outlined various strategies people use to regulate their emotions. Some of these strategies help people prevent or prepare for events, and some of them help in dealing with events after they occur. Not all strategies for regulating emotional states are equally successful, however.

What not to do: Two common strategies, suppression and rumination, do not work for most people. With *suppression*, people attempt not to respond at all to the emotional stimulus. This strategy includes suppression of behaviors, such as facial expressions, and of cognitions, such as unpleasant thoughts. Daniel Wegner and colleagues (1990) have demonstrated that trying to suppress thoughts is extremely difficult. In fact, doing so often leads to a *rebound effect*, where people think more about something because they tried to suppress it. For example, people who are dieting and try to not think about how much they want tasty foods end up craving them more than if they had tried to engage in another activity as a way of not thinking about their desire for the food.

Rumination involves thinking about, elaborating on, and becoming stuck in a cycle of undesired thoughts or feelings. This response prolongs the emotion, and it impedes successful emotion regulation strategies, such as distracting oneself or focusing on solutions for the problem (Lyubomirsky & Nolen-Hoeksema, 1995). So what can you do to regulate emotion? Research shows that the following strategies are more successful than thought suppression or rumination.

Change the meaning: You can directly alter emotional reactions to events by *reappraising* those events in more neutral terms. If you get scared while watching a movie, you can remind yourself that the whole spectacle has been staged and no one is actually being hurt. Brain imaging studies have found that engaging in reappraisal changes the activity of brain regions involved in the experience of emotion (Morawetz et al., 2017; Ochsner et al., 2012).

Create mental distance: Taking a different perspective can help temper strong emotions. The University of Michigan psychologist Ethan Kross has discovered that viewing a situation from an outside, "fly-on-the-wall" perspective can reduce emotional responses. This can be accomplished by using language strategically, such as talking to yourself in the second person ("You can handle this and remain calm"). This technique is called *self-distancing* because it works by creating mental distance between yourself and the emotional stimulus (Kross & Ayduk, 2017).

Find humor: Using humor has many benefits for emotional well-being (Braniecka et al., 2019). Most obviously, humor increases positive affect. When you find something humorous, you smile, laugh, and enter a state of pleasurable, relaxed excitation. Research shows that laughter stimulates endocrine secretion; improves the immune system; and stimulates the release of hormones, dopamine, serotonin, and endorphins. When people laugh, they experience rises in circulation, blood pressure, skin temperature, and heart rate, along with a decrease in pain perception (**FIGURE 10.14**). These responses are similar to those resulting from physical exercise, and they are considered beneficial to short-term and long-term health (Tuck et al., 2017).

People sometimes laugh in situations that do not seem very funny, such as at funerals or wakes. According to one theory, laughing in these situations helps people distance themselves from their negative emotions, and it strengthens their connections to other people. In one study on the topic, Dacher Keltner and George Bonanno (1997) interviewed 40 people who had recently lost a spouse. The researchers found that genuine laughter during the interview was associated with positive mental health and fewer negative feelings, such as grief. It was a way of coping with a difficult situation.

Refocus your attention: As you learned in Chapter 4, humans are able to direct their attention to different aspects of an experience. Guiding your attention toward a part of the stimulus that is less emotional can be an effective way to change your emotional experience (Dolcos et al., 2020). If the entire stimulus is emotional, you can instead focus your attention on your own physical sensations. Focused breathing, a technique often taught as part of mindfulness training, helps regulate emotions by orienting attention to breathing and reducing physiological activation (Arch & Craske, 2006).

(a)

(b)

FIGURE 10.13
Disruptive Emotions
Our actions can be disrupted by **(a)** negative feelings, such as nervousness, or **(b)** positive feelings, such as being distracted by looking forward to an exciting upcoming event.

FIGURE 10.14
Physiological Responses to Humor
Laughter brings a variety of physiological changes that, in their strongest forms, can resemble those elicited by exercise.

Distract yourself: Doing something other than the troubling activity or thinking about something other than the troubling thought are especially good strategies for controlling emotion (Webb et al., 2012). For example, if you are afraid of flying, you can distract yourself from your anxiety by helping the family next to you entertain their restless toddler. By absorbing attention, distraction temporarily helps people stop focusing on their problems.

Some distractions backfire, however. People may change their thoughts but end up thinking about other problems. Or they may engage in maladaptive behaviors. To temporarily escape your problems, you might try watching an engaging movie that will not remind you of your troubled situation. Otherwise, you might simply find yourself wallowing in self-pity. (For more suggestions on dealing with your day-to-day problems and stresses, see Chapter 11, "Health and Well-Being.") ■

Q **What are two common, but unhelpful, ways that people try to control their emotions?**

ANSWER: pretending the emotions and related thoughts do not exist (suppression) and repeated elaboration and conscious engagement with the emotion and related thoughts (rumination)

How Are Emotions Adaptive?

Learning Objectives

- Review research on the cross-cultural universality of emotional expressions.
- Define display rules.
- Discuss the interpersonal functions of guilt and embarrassment.

Over the course of human evolution, we have developed ways of responding to environmental challenges. Our emotions have been shaped as our minds solved these adaptive problems. Negative and positive experiences have guided our species to behaviors that increase the probability of our surviving and reproducing. Emotions are adaptive because they prepare and guide successful behaviors, such as running when you are about to be attacked by a dangerous animal.

Emotions provide information about the importance of stimuli to personal goals, and then they prepare us for actions aimed at achieving those goals (Frijda, 1994). Emotions also guide us in learning social rules and are necessary in order to live cooperatively in groups. Indeed, we often regulate the emotional experiences of others (Reeck et al., 2016) by calming them down or cheering them up. Let's look more closely at how emotions have served cognitive and social functions that enable humans to adapt to their physical and social environments.

10.6 Facial Expressions Communicate Emotion

In his 1872 book *The Expression of the Emotions in Man and Animals*, Charles Darwin argued that expressive aspects of emotion are adaptive because they communicate feelings. People interpret facial expressions of emotion to predict other people's behavior. Facial expressions provide many clues about whether our behavior is pleasing to others or whether it is likely to make them reject, attack, or cheat us. Thus, facial expressions, like emotions themselves, provide adaptive information.

Both the eyes and the mouth convey emotional information. The eyes are extremely important in communicating emotion (Todorov et al., 2015). For example, when people are afraid, they open their eyes very wide so that more of their eye whites are showing. If people are presented with pictures of just eyes or just mouths and asked to identify the emotion expressed, they are more accurate when using the eyes (Baron-Cohen et al., 1997). The mouth can also influence perception of emotion. A smile or a frown is so noticeable that it sometimes overrides information provided by the eyes (Kontsevich & Tyler, 2004).

Much of the research on facial expression is conducted by showing people isolated faces. Yet in the real world, faces appear in contexts that provide cues as to what emotion a person is experiencing. In an intriguing study, researchers showed identical facial expressions in different contexts and found that the context profoundly altered how people interpreted the emotion (Aviezer et al., 2008; **FIGURE 10.15**).

FACIAL EXPRESSIONS ACROSS CULTURES Darwin argued that the face innately communicates emotions to others and that these communications are understandable by all people, regardless of culture. His hypothesis was left untested for a century until Paul Ekman set out to disprove it. Ekman believed that facial expression and what it signifies are learned socially and vary from one culture to another. Ekman and his colleagues (1969) tested this hypothesis in Argentina, Brazil, Chile, Japan, and the United States. Ekman found support for Darwin's idea, though researchers have since found considerable evidence for cultural differences in emotions.

In each country, participants viewed photographs of posed emotional expressions and then were asked to identify the emotional responses. In all five countries, the participants recognized the expressions as anger, fear, disgust, happiness, sadness, and surprise. Because people in these countries had extensive exposure to one another's cultures, however, learning and not biology could have been responsible for the cross-cultural agreement. To control for that potential confound, the researchers then traveled to a remote area in New Guinea. The natives there had little exposure to outside cultures and received only minimal formal education. Nonetheless, the study participants were able to select the emotions seen in the photos from a list of emotions, although agreement was not quite as high as in other cultures. Also, their accuracy was found to be far lower when participants had to name the emotion that corresponded with a facial expression rather than selecting it from a list (Crivelli et al., 2017). The researchers also asked participants in New Guinea to display certain facial expressions, and they found that evaluators from other countries identified the expressions at a level better than chance (Ekman & Friesen, 1971).

Subsequent research has found mixed support for cross-cultural agreement in identifying some facial expressions. Support is strongest for happiness and weakest for fear and disgust (Elfenbein & Ambady, 2002). Some scholars believe that the results of these cross-cultural studies may be biased by cultural differences in the use of emotion words and by the way people are asked to identify emotions (Gendron et al., 2014). More recent studies using computational methods reveal differences across cultures in the visual features people use to identify emotions and how those emotions unfold across time (Jack et al., 2012). Overall, the evidence indicates that some basic aspects of facial expressions are shared across cultures, but much of the nuance that characterizes human emotions is culturally determined.

UNIVERSALITY OF EMOTIONS Other evidence beyond facial expressions supports the idea that emotions are similar around the world. Creatively assessing the universality of emotion, researchers devised a computer program in which participants could use slider bars to adjust features of movement or music to indicate a particular emotion (Sievers et al., 2013). For instance, bouncy movement and high notes indicated happiness, whereas fast and erratic movement or music indicated anger. The research team traveled to a rural and isolated village in Cambodia

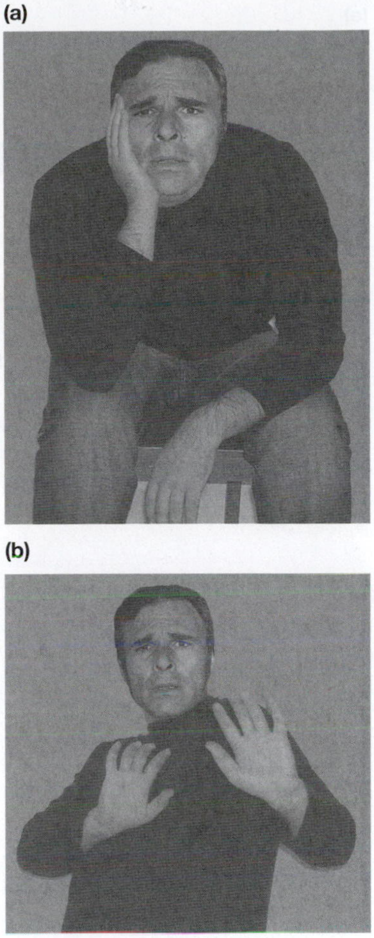

FIGURE 10.15
Contextual Effects on Categorizing Emotional Expression
Research participants were shown images such as these and asked to categorize them as depicting anger, fear, pride, sadness, disgust, surprise, or happiness. **(a)** This photo pairs a sad face with a sad posture. When the face appeared in this context, most participants categorized the expression as sad. **(b)** This photo pairs the same sad face with a fearful posture. When the face appeared in this context, most participants categorized the expression as fearful.

FIGURE 10.16
Assessing the Universality of Emotion
(a) Research participants in the United States and in rural Cambodia manipulated five slider bars corresponding to five dynamic features to create either animations or musical clips that expressed different emotions. **(b)** The Cambodian participants' results and those of American participants agreed considerably.

and taught the villagers to use the computerized slider system (FIGURE 10.16). They found considerable agreement between American and Cambodian participants. For example, the type of movement and music that represented sadness was quite similar between the two groups.

DISPLAY RULES As we have seen, basic emotions, such as pride, seem to be expressed similarly across cultures. The situations in which people display emotions differ substantially, however. **Display rules** govern how and when people exhibit emotions. These rules are learned through socialization, and they dictate which emotions are suitable in given situations. Differences in display rules help explain cultural stereotypes, such as the loud and obnoxious Americans and Australians, the cold and bland English, and the warm and emotional Italians. Display rules also may explain why the identification of facial expressions is much better within cultures than between cultures (Elfenbein & Ambady, 2002).

display rules Rules learned through socialization that dictate which emotions are suitable in given situations.

One reason why different cultures have different display rules is that they value different emotional expressions. The psychologist Jeanne Tsai has studied cultural differences in **ideal affect**, which refers to the types of emotions that cultures value and encourage people to display (Tsai, 2017). Western European and North American cultures prefer high-arousal emotions such as excitement and enthusiasm, whereas Asian cultures value low-arousal emotions such as calmness and tranquility (FIGURE 10.17). Cultural differences in ideal affect indicate the emotions that are expected in a given culture and do not necessarily relate to the emotions people actually feel. For example, sympathy cards written by Germans have more negative and less positive content than sympathy cards written by Americans, even though the groups experience similar affect in response to grief (Koopmann-Holm & Tsai, 2014).

ideal affect Emotional and affective states that people want to feel or that cultures especially value.

FIGURE 10.17
Ideal Affect Varies by Culture
Leaders can signal the kinds of emotions cultures value. Here, U.S. president Joe Biden (left) displays an excited smile, whereas the president of the People's Republic of China, Xi Jinping (right), displays a calm smile.

How much of a given emotional expression is biological and how much is learned? Display rules and ideal affect are just two among the many ways that learning and socialization influence the emotions we display and how intensely we display them. Social influences on emotional expression extend to other social categories beyond national and ethnic groups. For example, display rules for emotions can vary as a function of gender identity, sexuality, and even political affiliation (Tskhay & Rule, 2015). Like many other features of human psychology, emotions are jointly determined by nature and nurture, so it is difficult, if not impossible, to distinguish their effects.

Q **How might display rules contribute to the cultural stereotypes that Italians are very emotional and the English are unemotional?**

ANSWER: Italian culture and English culture may differ in their social expectations regarding appropriate degrees of emotional expression.

10.7 Emotions Strengthen Interpersonal Relations

Humans are fundamentally social animals, so most if not all emotions involve interpersonal dynamics. People feel hurt when teased, angry when insulted, happy when loved, and proud when complimented. During social interactions, emotional expressions are powerful nonverbal signals (FIGURE 10.18). Although the English language alone includes over 550 words that refer to emotions (Averill, 1980), people can communicate their emotions quite well without verbal language. Nonverbal displays of emotions signal inner states, moods, and needs. It can even be argued that the primary purpose of emotional displays is to communicate with other people (Hess & Thibault, 2009). From an evolutionary perspective, facial expressions of emotion exist because they are adaptive. Expressions of sadness can garner empathy, and expressions of fear can trigger vigilance.

For most of the twentieth century, however, psychologists paid little attention to interpersonal emotions. Guilt, embarrassment, and the like were associated with Freudian thinking and therefore were not studied in mainstream psychological science. Theorists have since reconsidered interpersonal emotions in view of humans' evolutionary need to belong to social groups. Given that survival was enhanced for those who lived in groups, those who were expelled would have been less likely to survive and pass along their genes. Thus, social emotions may be important for maintaining social bonds and status within a group.

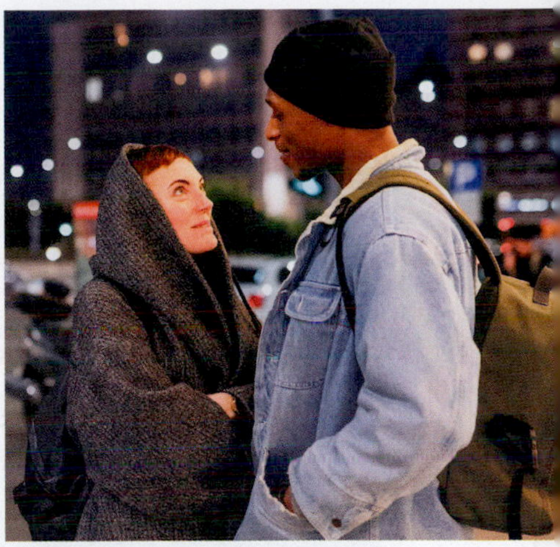

FIGURE 10.18
Emotion as Communication
Nonverbal expressions of emotion, such as these displays of love and joy, can communicate as powerfully as words.

GUILT STRENGTHENS SOCIAL BONDS Guilt is a negative emotional state associated with anxiety, tension, and agitation. The typical guilt experience occurs when someone feels responsible for another person's negative affective state. Thus, when we believe that something we did directly or indirectly harmed another person, we experience feelings of anxiety, tension, and remorse—feelings that can be labeled as guilt. Guilt occasionally can arise even when we are not personally responsible for others' negative situations. Consider, for example, survivor guilt, the guilt felt by people who survive accidents or catastrophes in which others have died.

Though feelings of guilt are unpleasant, guilt can serve important functions for our close relationships. Roy Baumeister and colleagues (1994) contend that guilt protects and strengthens interpersonal relationships in three ways. First, feelings of guilt discourage people from doing things that would harm their relationships, such as cheating on their partners, and encourage behaviors that strengthen relationships, such as phoning their parents regularly. Second, displays of guilt demonstrate that people care about their relationship partners, thereby affirming social bonds. Third, guilt is a tactic that can be used to manipulate others. Guilt is especially effective when used against people who hold power over others. For instance, a person might try to make his boss feel guilty so he does not have to work overtime. Children may use guilt to get adults to buy them presents or grant them privileges.

There is evidence that socialization is more important than biology in determining specifically how children experience guilt (FIGURE 10.19). A longitudinal study involving identical and fraternal twins examined the impact of socialization on the development of various negative emotions (Zahn-Waxler & Robinson, 1995). The study found that all the negative emotions showed considerable genetic influence, but guilt was unique in being highly influenced by social environment. With age, the influence of a shared environment on guilt became stronger, whereas the evidence for genetic influences disappeared. Perhaps surprisingly, parental warmth is associated with greater guilt in children. This finding suggests

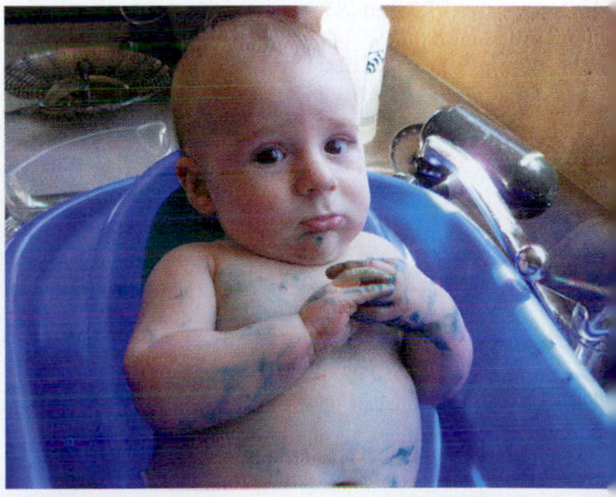

FIGURE 10.19
Guilt in Children
Children's facial expressions of guilt suggest that they recognize when they have transgressed.

that feelings of guilt arise in healthy and happy relationships. As children become citizens in a social world, they develop the capacity to empathize, and they subsequently experience feelings of guilt when they transgress against others.

Head moves down and to the side.
Lips press together, and their corners turn up slightly.

FIGURE 10.20
Embarrassment
In this photo, the psychologist Dacher Keltner is demonstrating the classic facial signals of embarrassment.

EMBARRASSMENT AND BLUSHING ACKNOWLEDGE SOCIAL AWKWARDNESS The writer Mark Twain once said, "Man is the only animal that blushes. Or needs to." Darwin, in his 1872 book, called blushing the "most peculiar and the most human of all expressions," thereby separating it from emotional responses he deemed necessary for survival. Recent theory and research suggest that blushing communicates a realization of interpersonal errors. People tend to feel embarrassed after violating a cultural norm, being clumsy, getting teased, or experiencing a threat to their self-image (Miller, 1996). Some theories of embarrassment suggest that it restores social bonds by signaling to others recognition of the mistake. Embarrassment shows respect for and affiliation with the social group. Research supports these propositions in showing that individuals who look embarrassed after a slip-up elicit more sympathy, more amusement, and more laughter from onlookers (Cupach & Metts, 1990; **FIGURE 10.20**). This nonverbal apology is an appeasement that elicits forgiveness in others, thereby repairing and maintaining relationships (Keltner & Anderson, 2000).

Q **Are variations in the experience of guilt influenced more by socialization or genetics?**

ANSWER: socialization, likely because of guilt's special role in social interaction

What Is Motivation?

Learning Objectives

- Distinguish among a need, a drive, and motivation.
- Describe Maslow's need hierarchy.
- Describe the Yerkes-Dodson law.
- Distinguish between extrinsic motivation and intrinsic motivation.

What inspires you to get up in the morning? Why are you willing to work harder for some rewards than others? What makes some goals harder to achieve than others? Questions such as these are about the forces that motivate people to do what they do. There is a close correspondence between emotion and motivation. In fact, the words *emotion* and *motivation* come from the same Latin word: *movere*, "to move." Whereas emotion concerns how we feel, motivation concerns the forces that guide behavior. When we encounter a snake, we experience alarm or even fear. We are motivated to avoid the potential threat and so we act, such as by stepping back. The feeling and the behavior combine to form an adaptive process that helps the species survive (LeDoux, 2015b).

Motivational states have four essential qualities. First, motivational states are *energizing*, or stimulating. They activate behaviors—that is, they cause animals to do something. For instance, the desire for fitness might motivate you to get up and go for a run on a cold morning. Second, motivational states are *directive*. They guide behaviors toward satisfying specific goals or needs. Hunger motivates you to eat; thirst motivates you to drink; pride (or fear or another feeling) motivates you to study for exams. Third, motivational states help animals *persist* in their behavior until they achieve their goals or satisfy their needs. Hunger gnaws at you until you find something to eat; a desire to perfect your foul shot drives you to practice until you succeed. Fourth, motives differ in *strength*, which depends on psychological factors and external forces. Thus, for psychologists, **motivation** is a process that energizes, guides, and maintains behavior toward a goal.

motivation A process that energizes, guides, and maintains behavior toward a goal.

10.8 Drives Motivate the Satisfaction of Needs

What do we really need to do to stay alive? For one, we have to satisfy our biological needs. We all *need* air, food, and water to survive. But satisfying our basic biological needs is not enough to live a fully satisfying life. We also have social needs, including the needs to be with others and to be respected by them. People *need* other people, although preferences to be solitary or social vary. And we have psychological needs, such as the needs for achievement and consistency. People need to think of themselves as competent agents who make rational decisions that are internally coherent. A **need**, then, is a state of deficiency, which can be biological, social, or psychological. In each case, needs lead to goal-directed behaviors. Failure to satisfy a particular need leads to psychosocial or physical impairment.

need A state of biological, social, or psychological deficiency.

MASLOW'S NEED HIERARCHY In the 1940s, Abraham Maslow proposed an influential "need theory" of motivation. Maslow believed that people are driven by many needs, which he arranged into a **need hierarchy** (**FIGURE 10.21**). He placed survival needs (such as food and water) at the base of the hierarchy, believing they had to be satisfied first. He placed personal growth needs at the top. To experience personal growth, he believed, people must fulfill their biological needs, feel safe and secure, feel loved, and have a good opinion of themselves.

need hierarchy Maslow's arrangement of needs, in which basic survival needs must be met before people can satisfy higher needs.

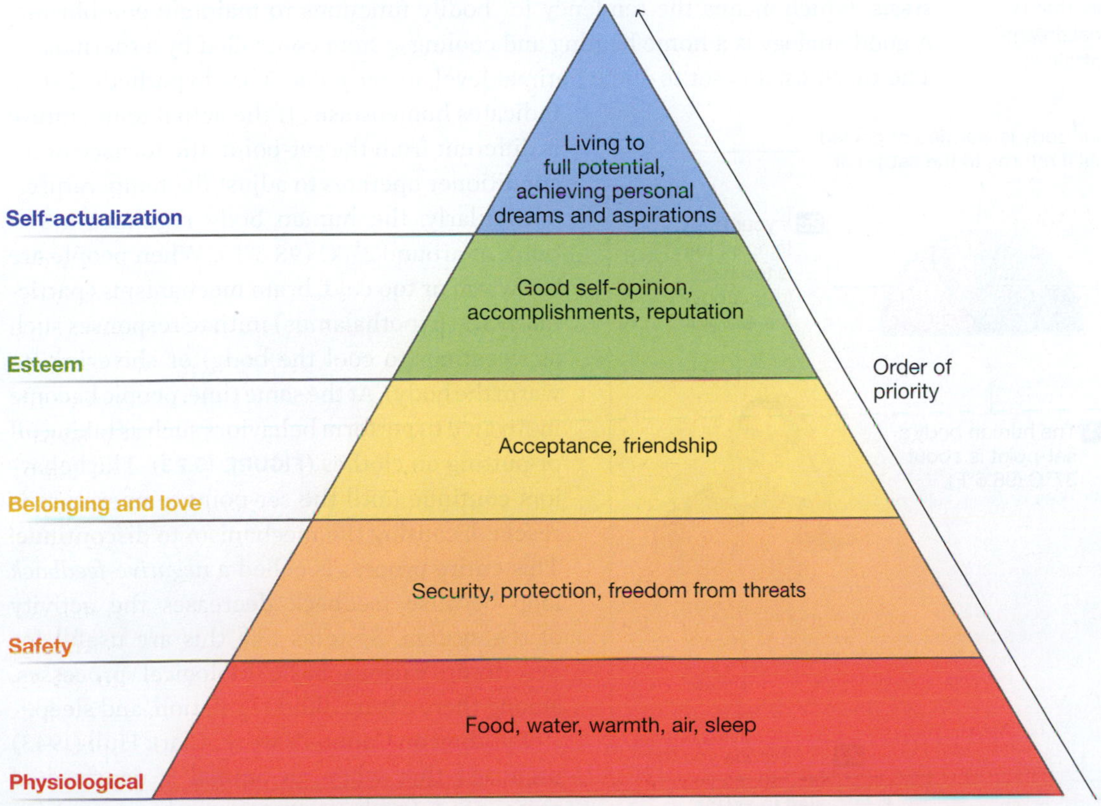

FIGURE 10.21
Need Hierarchy
According to Maslow's classification of needs, basic needs (such as for food and water) must be satisfied before people can address higher needs (such as for achievement).

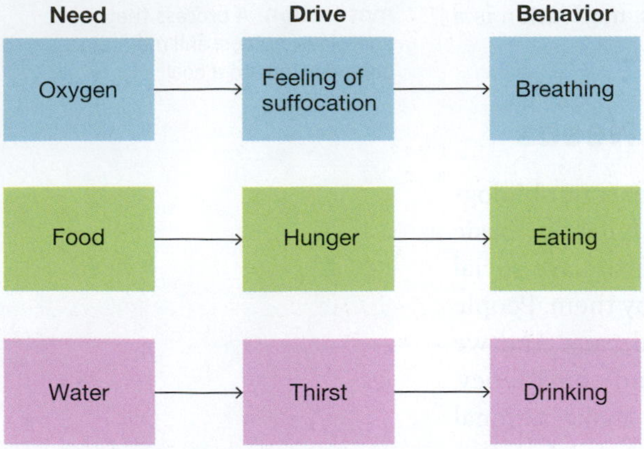
Need
Drive
Behavior
Oxygen
Feeling of suffocation
Breathing
Food
Hunger
Eating
Water
Thirst
Drinking

FIGURE 10.22

Needs, Drives, and Behaviors

A need is a deficiency in some area that creates a drive—an internal psychological state. The drive motivates a person to behave in ways that satisfy the need. For example, if you hold your breath, you will start to feel a strong sense of urgency, even anxiety. This state of arousal is a drive. That drive will force you to breathe, satisfying your need for oxygen.

The pinnacle of Maslow's theory was **self-actualization**. This state occurs when people achieve their own best self. Self-actualized people are living up to their potential and therefore are truly happy. Maslow writes, "A musician must make music, an artist must paint, a poet must write, if he is ultimately to be at peace with himself. What a [hu]man *can* be, he *must* be" (Maslow, 1968, p. 46).

Maslow's need hierarchy has long been embraced in education and business, but it lacks empirical support. Self-actualization might or might not be a requirement for happiness, but the ranking of needs is not as simple or as universal as Maslow suggests. For instance, some people starve themselves in hunger strikes to demonstrate the importance of their personal beliefs. Also, placing individual achievement at the pinnacle of the hierarchy is a distinctly Western concept. Many cultures elevate interpersonal values such as belonging and relatedness above individual goals (Sagiv et al., 2017). Maslow's hierarchy, therefore, is most useful as an example of how some needs can be more important than others. The specific needs people have and their relative priority can vary from person to person and across cultures.

self-actualization A state that is achieved when one's personal dreams and aspirations have been attained.

DRIVE REDUCTION AND HOMEOSTASIS A **drive** is a psychological state that, by creating arousal, motivates an organism to satisfy a need. A particular drive encourages behaviors that will satisfy a particular need (**FIGURE 10.22**).

For biological states such as thirst or hunger, basic drives help animals maintain steadiness, or *equilibrium*. In the 1920s, Walter Cannon coined the term **homeostasis**, which means the tendency for bodily functions to maintain equilibrium. A good analogy is a home heating and cooling system controlled by a thermostat. The thermostat is set to some optimal level, or *set-point*. That hypothetical state indicates homeostasis. If the actual temperature is different from the set-point, the furnace or air conditioner operates to adjust the temperature.

Similarly, the human body regulates a set-point of around 37°C (98.6°F). When people are too warm or too cold, brain mechanisms (particularly the hypothalamus) initiate responses such as sweating (to cool the body) or shivering (to warm the body). At the same time, people become motivated to perform behaviors such as taking off or putting on clothes (**FIGURE 10.23**). The behaviors continue until the set-point temperature is reached, causing the mechanism to discontinue. This entire process is called a *negative-feedback* loop because feedback decreases the activity of the system. Systems like this are useful for describing various basic biological processes, among them eating, fluid regulation, and sleep.

Building on Cannon's work, Clark Hull (1943) proposed that when an animal is deprived of some need (such as water or sleep), a drive increases in proportion to the amount of deprivation. The hungrier you are, the more driven you are to find food. The drive state creates arousal, which encourages you to do something to reduce the drive, such

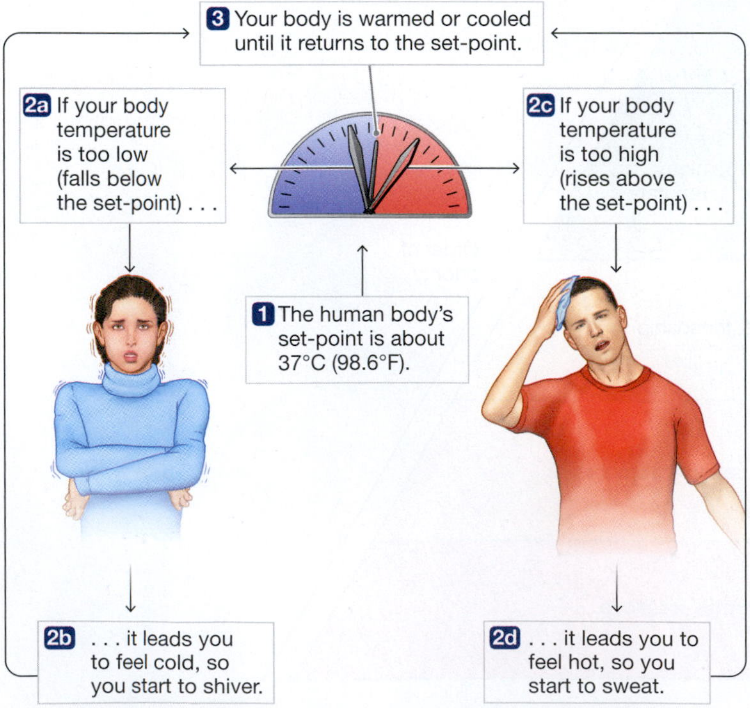
3 Your body is warmed or cooled until it returns to the set-point.
2a If your body temperature is too low (falls below the set-point) . . .
2c If your body temperature is too high (rises above the set-point) . . .
1 The human body's set-point is about 37°C (98.6°F).
2b . . . it leads you to feel cold, so you start to shiver.
2d . . . it leads you to feel hot, so you start to sweat.

FIGURE 10.23

A Negative-Feedback Model of Homeostasis

as having a late-night snack. Although the initial behaviors the animal engages in can be haphazard, any behavior that satisfies a need is reinforced and therefore is more likely to recur in similar conditions. Over time, if a behavior consistently reduces a drive, it becomes a *habit* and therefore the dominant response produced by arousal. The likelihood that a behavior will occur is due to drive and habit.

Suppose you feel the need to forget your troubles. To satisfy that need, you feel driven to distract yourself, so you go to YouTube and watch videos of cute animals. Watching those videos makes you forget your troubles, and that outcome reinforces further video viewing. Over time, you might develop the habit of watching cute animal videos, a behavior that is triggered by stress.

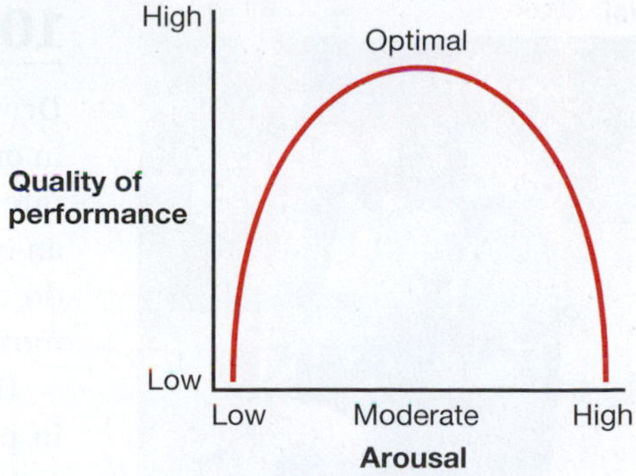

FIGURE 10.24
Graph of the Yerkes-Dodson Law
According to this law, performance on challenging tasks increases with arousal up to a moderate level. After that point, additional arousal interferes with performance.

drive A psychological state that, by creating arousal, motivates an organism to satisfy a need.

homeostasis The tendency for bodily functions to maintain equilibrium.

Yerkes-Dodson law The psychological principle that performance on challenging tasks increases with arousal up to a moderate level. After that, additional arousal impairs performance.

AROUSAL AND DRIVE Because drives motivate behavior by creating arousal, you might think that more arousal will lead to greater drive and thus to better performance. Consider, however, the **Yerkes-Dodson law** (named after the two researchers who formulated it in 1908). This psychological principle dictates that performance on challenging tasks increases with arousal only up to a moderate point. After that, performance is impaired by any additional arousal. A graph of this relationship is shaped like an inverted U (**FIGURE 10.24**). As the Yerkes-Dodson law predicts, students perform best on exams when feeling moderate anxiety. Too little anxiety can make them inattentive or unmotivated, while too much anxiety can interfere with their thinking ability. Likewise, athletes have to pump themselves up for their events, but they can fall apart under too much stress.

All people function better with some arousal. As described earlier, arousal can help activate behavior. People are motivated to seek their optimal level of arousal—the level they most prefer. Too little, and they are bored; too much, and they are overwhelmed. People choose activities that arouse them and absorb their attention (**FIGURE 10.25**), but they differ in how stimulating, exciting, frightening, or pleasurable they want those activities to be (as discussed further in Chapter 13).

Q How can drives lead to habits?

ANSWER: Drives increase behaviors that reduce the drive. If a behavior consistently reduces the drive, the behavior is reinforced and will eventually become a habit.

(a) (b)

FIGURE 10.25
People Differ in Their Optimal Level of Arousal
Each of us has a different level of optimal arousal that motivates us to behave in certain ways. **(a)** Some people have a lower level of optimal arousal. These people tend to prefer calmer activities, such as reading, which keep arousal at an optimal lower level. **(b)** Other people have a higher level of optimal arousal. They tend to prefer exciting activities, such as skydiving, which raise arousal to an optimal higher level.

(a)

(b)

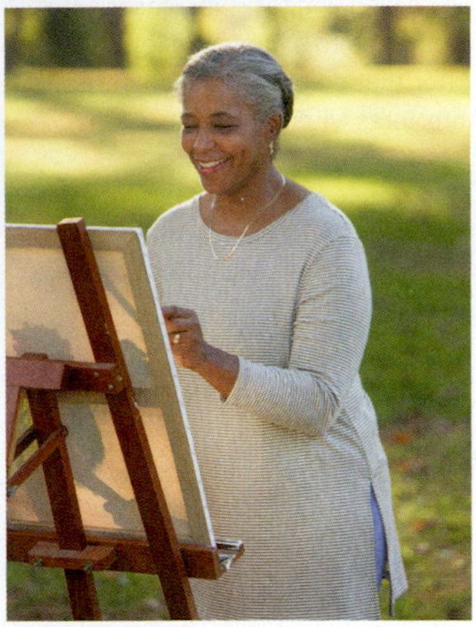

FIGURE 10.26
Extrinsic and Intrinsic Motivation
(a) Money is a familiar example of extrinsic motivation on behavior.
(b) Intrinsic motivation affects behavior simply because the activity itself is enjoyable.

10.9 People Are Motivated by Incentives

Drive states push us to reduce arousal, but we are also pulled toward certain things in our environments. **Incentives** are external objects or external goals, rather than internal drives, that motivate behaviors. For example, getting a good grade on an exam is an incentive for studying hard. According to incentive theory, people do not always wait for needs to drive behavior in daily life. Instead, people are motivated by their desires to achieve external goals.

Even forces outside of conscious awareness can provide incentives to behave in particular ways. For example, smokers sometimes develop cravings for cigarettes after watching people smoke on-screen (Betts et al., 2021). As discussed in Chapter 4, subliminal cues influence behavior even though they appear so quickly that people cannot report what they saw. Researchers from France and England found that study participants worked harder for a larger financial reward—in this case, a subliminally presented pound coin versus a real penny coin—even when they were unable to report how much money was at stake (Pessiglione et al., 2007).

EXTRINSIC AND INTRINSIC MOTIVATION Incentive theories differentiate between two types of incentive motivation (**FIGURE 10.26**). **Extrinsic motivation** is directed toward an external goal, typically a reward. For example, most people work to earn paychecks. Many of the activities people find most satisfying, however—such as reading literature, solving crossword puzzles, or listening to music—seem to fulfill no obvious purpose other than enjoyment. Such activities are directed toward **intrinsic motivation**, value or pleasure associated with an activity, rather than toward any external goal. Intrinsically motivated behaviors are performed for their own sake. Some students study to earn good grades (extrinsic motivation), whereas others study because they are curious and want to learn about the topic (intrinsic motivation). The incentives may differ, but the behaviors they bring about may be the same.

Some intrinsic motives, such as curiosity and creativity, satisfy a need for growth and learning. After playing with a new toy for a long time, children start to lose interest and will seek out something new. Playful exploration is characteristic of all mammals, especially primates. For example, as Harry Harlow and colleagues showed, monkeys have a strong exploratory drive. They will work hard, without the promise of an external reward, to solve relatively complex puzzles (Harlow et al., 1950). One function of play such as this is that it helps people and other animals learn about the objects in an environment. This outcome clearly has survival value, since knowing how things work allows people to use those objects for more serious tasks.

Similarly, many of us are driven toward creative pursuits. Whether we are visiting an art museum or creating artwork ourselves, we may do so simply because we enjoy activities that allow us to express our creativity. Creativity is the tendency to generate ideas or alternatives that may be useful in solving problems, communicating, and entertaining ourselves and others (Franken, 2007). Although many creative pursuits are not adaptive solutions in themselves, creativity is an important factor in solving adaptive problems.

INTRINSIC AND EXTRINSIC MOTIVES HAVE DIFFERENT EFFECTS As discussed in Chapter 6, a basic principle of learning theory is that rewarded behaviors increase in frequency. You might expect that rewarding intrinsically motivated behaviors would reinforce them. Surprisingly, some evidence indicates that extrinsic rewards can undermine intrinsic motivation. In a classic study,

incentives External objects or external goals, rather than internal drives, that motivate behaviors.

extrinsic motivation Motivation to perform an activity because of the external goals toward which that activity is directed.

intrinsic motivation Motivation to perform an activity because of the value or pleasure associated with that activity, rather than for an apparent external goal or purpose.

Mark Lepper and colleagues (1973) allowed children to draw with colored marking pens. Most children find this activity intrinsically motivating. One group of children was extrinsically motivated to draw by being led to expect a "good player award." Another group of children was rewarded unexpectedly following the task. A third group was neither rewarded nor led to expect a reward. During a subsequent free-play period, children who were expecting an extrinsic reward spent much less time playing with the pens than did the children who were never rewarded or the children who received an unexpected reward. The first group of children responded as though it was their job to draw with the colored pens. Why would they play with the pens for free when they were used to being "paid"?

Learning Tip

Look at the word prefixes if you become confused about the distinction between extrinsic and intrinsic motivation. *Extrinsic* shares a prefix with *external*. Extrinsic motivation comes from outside forces, including rules; external incentives, such as money; and social pressure. *Intrinsic* shares a prefix with *internal*. Intrinsic motivation comes from inside forces, such as a desire for achievement, affiliation, or autonomy.

This study was taken to mean that extrinsic rewards can undermine the intrinsic reward inherent to an experience. However, this is not universally true. For example, one study found that only people who had low levels of intrinsic interest in an activity at the beginning of the study lost interest after that activity was extrinsically rewarded (Hagger & Chatzisarantis, 2011). In contrast, people who were more strongly intrinsically motivated did not stop engaging in the task when the reward went away. A meta-analysis of more than 180 studies revealed that the two kinds of motivation are complementary and do not necessarily undercut each other (Cerasoli et al., 2014). Specifically, intrinsic motivation is less important when extrinsic rewards are provided, but it becomes more important in the absence of rewards. Also, intrinsic motivation is more related to the *quality* of the work on the task, whereas extrinsic motivation is more related to the *quantity* of work.

PLEASURE/PAIN AND APPROACH/AVOIDANCE MOTIVATION Sigmund Freud proposed that people act according to the *pleasure principle*, which encourages them to seek pleasure and avoid pain. This idea of seeking pleasure is central to incentive theories of motivation (Schneirla, 1959). Originating with the ancient Greeks, the concept of *hedonism* refers to humans' desire for pleasantness and avoidance of unpleasantness (**FIGURE 10.27**). The idea that pleasure motivates behavior helps us understand a criticism of biological drive theories such as Hull's. If biological drives explain all behaviors, why do animals engage in behaviors that do not necessarily satisfy biological needs? There are ample examples of humans engaging in activities simply because they are pleasurable (Cabanac, 1992). Eating too much of a good meal is a good example of hedonism. People will continue to eat even after they are full simply because it feels good. The incentive to enjoy the taste motivates eating certain foods, regardless of your hunger state.

FIGURE 10.27
Hedonism
The Dutch artist Hieronymus Bosch depicts several forms of hedonism in his painting *The Garden of Earthly Delights*.

From an evolutionary perspective, positive and negative incentives are adaptive. We are motivated to approach certain things and avoid others. People experience *approach motivations* to seek out food, sex, and companionship because they are all typically associated with pleasure. By contrast, *avoidance motivation* encourages people to avoid negative outcomes, such as dangerous animals, because of the association with pain (Corr, 2013). For instance, most animals prefer to eat sweets over neutral or salty foods.

FIGURE 10.28
Early Motivation
As these photos reveal, even newborns prefer sweet tastes to bitter ones.

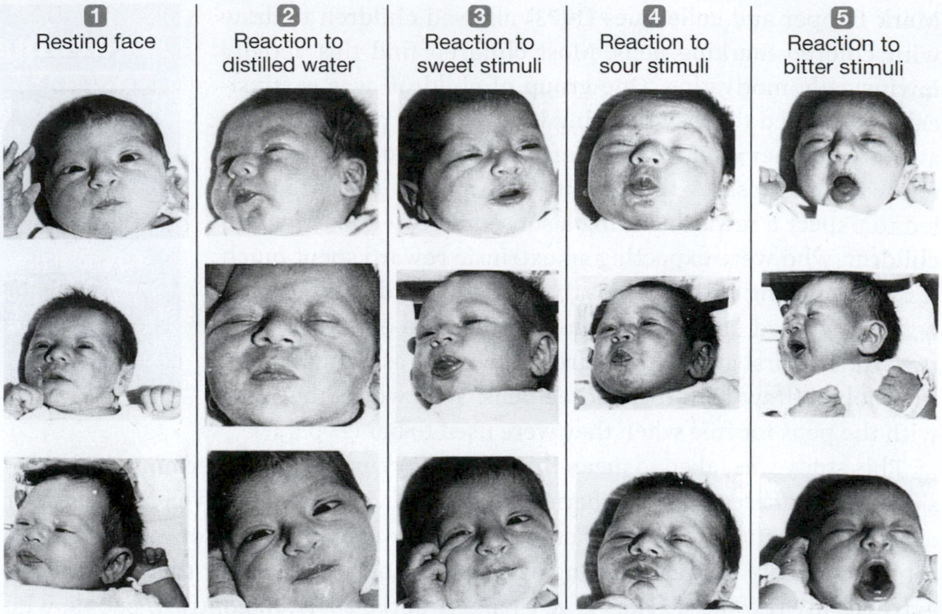

Infants given sweet solutions seem to find them pleasurable, as revealed by their facial expressions (Steiner, 1977; **FIGURE 10.28**). Sweetness usually indicates that food is safe to eat and rich in energy. By contrast, most poisons and toxins taste bitter, so it is not surprising that animals tend to avoid bitter tastes.

The distinction between approach and avoidance behaviors is embedded in the neural systems of humans and other creatures. Invertebrates such as lobsters have individual neurons that can trigger complex approach (swim forward) or avoidance (evasive maneuver) behaviors when activated (Berntson et al., 2012). Approach and avoidance motives are reflected in humans by relative differences in activity between the left and right hemispheres. Greater left than right hemispheric activity is typical of approach motives, whereas greater right than left hemispheric activity is typical of avoidance motives (Kelley et al., 2017). The distinction between approaching and avoiding is so fundamental to survival that it colors many other motives.

Q **How do intrinsic and extrinsic motivation differently influence the quality and quantity of behavior?**

ANSWER: Intrinsic motivation is more likely to increase the quality of the behavior, whereas extrinsic motivation is more likely to increase the quantity of the behavior.

Learning Objectives

- Discuss the relationships among goal achievement, self-efficacy, the achievement motive, grit, and delayed gratification.
- Describe need to belong theory.
- Explain ways people are motivated to be consistent.
- Identify core values and describe how they relate to consistency.

How Does Motivation Give Us Meaning?

People are motivated by more than just pleasure and pain. Humans set long-term goals, some of which can be quite abstract. People want to live a good life, have a satisfying career, and have meaningful relationships. Goals such as these give structure and meaning to our lives. Pursuing long-range goals, sometimes for years or decades and even in the face of obstacles and setbacks, is something that is unique to humans.

Goals are important to us because they are connected to our deeply held core values. Living up to big, abstract ideals such as kindness, achievement, and autonomy is the ultimate kind of goal pursuit because it can take a lifetime. The end point of that kind of goal pursuit is not a time on a marathon clock or a dollar amount in a bank account but a way of being a person in the world. Psychologists have studied the kinds of values people hold and the functions those values and goals serve in our mental life.

10.10 People Set Goals to Achieve

What would you like to be doing 10 years from now? What things about yourself would you change? So far, we have focused on motivation to fulfill short-term goals, such as satisfying hunger or spending a pleasurable afternoon. But people have long-term aspirations as well. How can people be effective in attaining their goals?

Setting effective goals motivates people to work hard and increases their chances of success (Epton et al., 2017). But what is an effective goal? The organizational psychologists Edwin Locke and Gary Latham (1990) developed an influential theory. According to Locke and Latham, challenging and specific goals are the best, if they are not overly difficult. Challenging goals encourage effort, persistence, and concentration. In contrast, goals that are too easy or too hard can undermine motivation and therefore lead to failure. Dividing specific goals into concrete steps also leads to success. If you are interested in running the Boston Marathon, for instance, your first goal might be gaining the stamina to run 1 mile. When you can run a mile, you can set another goal and thus build up to running the 26-mile marathon. Focusing on concrete, short-term goals facilitates achieving long-term goals.

Scholars working in industrial/organizational psychology have refined Locke and Latham's ideas about effective goals. The acronym *SMART* describes goals that are **S**pecific, **M**easurable, **A**chievable, **R**ealistic, and **T**ime bound (Doran, 1981). In addition to being specific and challenging (but achievable), a SMART goal is also clearly defined so the person pursuing the goal knows when it has been achieved. For example, the goal to run 1 mile could be cast to be time bound and measurable. A SMART goal version would be to run a 7-minute mile within the next three months. SMART goals help people divide large projects into smaller chunks and ensure clear feedback on their progress.

SELF-EFFICACY, THE ACHIEVEMENT MOTIVE, AND GRIT Albert Bandura (1977) argued that people's expectations for success play a central role in motivation. For instance, if you believe studying hard will lead to a good grade on an exam, you will be motivated to study. **Self-efficacy** is the expectation that your efforts will lead to success. This expectation helps mobilize your energy. If you have low self-efficacy—that is, if you do not believe your efforts will pay off—you may be too discouraged even to study or may decide that studying is not worth the effort. People with high self-efficacy often set challenging goals that lead to success. Sometimes, however, people whose self-views are inflated set goals they cannot possibly achieve. Again, goals that are challenging but not unrealistic or overwhelming are usually most conducive to success.

self-efficacy The belief that efforts toward a goal will result in success.

"What do you think . . . should we get started on that motivation research or not?"

People differ in how insistently they pursue challenging goals. The *achievement motive* is the desire to do well relative to standards of excellence. Compared with those low in achievement motivation, students high in achievement motivation sit closer to the front of classrooms, score higher on exams, and obtain better grades in courses relevant to their career goals (McClelland, 1987). Students with high achievement motivation are more realistic in their career aspirations than are students low in achievement motivation. Those high in achievement motivation set challenging but attainable personal goals, while those low in achievement motivation set extremely easy or impossibly high goals.

FIGURE 10.29
Grit
Extreme sports such as mountain climbing require a determination to keep making progress despite setbacks.

Another factor that is related to a person's desire to achieve long-term goals is *grit* (**FIGURE 10.29**). People with grit have a deep passion for their goals and a willingness to keep working toward them, even despite hardships and setbacks (Duckworth et al., 2007). By contrast, people who have less grit get discouraged more easily, lose steam in the middle of pursuing their goals, or get sidetracked from their goals by new interests. There is evidence that grit is a better predictor than intelligence for achieving long-term goals in several areas, such as educational attainment, retention in the United States Military Academy at West Point, and ranking in a national spelling bee (Duckworth et al., 2007). In addition, grit has been shown to be a significant predictor for the grades of college students (Duckworth & Quinn, 2009), especially those of African American men (Strayhorn, 2014). Research suggests that perseverance is the most important aspect of grit for predicting student outcomes (Credé et al., 2017; Muenks et al., 2017).

self-regulation The process by which people direct their behavior toward the attainment of goals.

DELAYED GRATIFICATION A key insight is that people are especially motivated to achieve personal goals. **Self-regulation** is the process by which people guide their behavior to attain personal goals. One of the defining features of self-regulation is postponing immediate gratification in the pursuit of long-term goals. For example, students who want to be accepted to graduate school often must stay home and study while their friends are out having fun. Delaying gratification in the service of goals is difficult because of temporal discounting. As described in Chapter 6, people generally value delayed rewards less than immediate ones of equal objective value. How do people overcome this inherent limitation in the way they think about rewards?

In a series of classic studies, the developmental psychologist Walter Mischel gave children the choice of waiting to receive a preferred toy or food item or having a less preferred toy or food item right away (Mischel, 1961). Mischel found that some children had learned to be better at delaying gratification than other children had.

Given the choice between eating one marshmallow right away or two after several minutes, some children engaged in strategies to help them not eat the marshmallow while they waited. One strategy was simply ignoring the tempting item rather than looking at it. Some of the children covered their eyes or looked away. Very young children tended to look directly at the item they were trying to resist, making the delay especially difficult. A related strategy was self-distraction through singing, playing games, or pretending to sleep.

FIGURE 10.30
Delaying Gratification
These three techniques help a person delay gratification.

The most successful strategy involved what Mischel and his colleague Janet Metcalfe (1999) refer to as turning *hot cognitions* into *cold cognitions*. This strategy involves mentally transforming the desired object into something undesired. In one study, children reported imagining a tempting pretzel as a brown log or imagining marshmallows as clouds (**FIGURE 10.30**). Hot cognitions focus on the rewarding, pleasurable aspects of objects. Cold cognitions focus on conceptual or symbolic meanings.

Transforming hot into cold cognitions is similar to cognitive reappraisal, which is described in Section 10.5.

In addition, the ability to delay gratification was predictive of success in life. Children who delayed gratification at age 4 were rated 10 years later as being more socially competent and better able to handle frustration. The ability to delay gratification in childhood has been found to predict higher SAT scores and better school grades (Mischel et al., 1989). A 40-year follow-up study found that the ability to delay gratification remained stable into adulthood (Casey et al., 2011). These researchers also conducted a brain imaging study in which participants had to inhibit responding to a rewarding stimulus. Those low in the ability to delay gratification as children showed greater activity as adults in brain reward regions when they tried not to respond to the rewarding stimulus. These findings indicate that learning to delay gratification and control behavior in childhood can have lifelong implications. Indeed, a study from New Zealand found that self-control in childhood predicted better physical health and personal finances, less substance abuse, and fewer criminal offenses at age 32 (Moffitt et al., 2011).

It is important to think critically about delayed gratification. Mischel's studies have been interpreted to mean that some children are inherently better at delaying gratification than others. However, the tendency to delay gratification can be learned (Mauro & Harris, 2000). Children who delay gratification might do well later in life because they have the kinds of parents who teach them skills for delaying gratification and the importance of achievement. These parents may also impart other useful skills, such as study techniques. In contrast, some children learn that delaying gratification is not worth it. This is especially true for children whose environments are unpredictable or untrustworthy (Michaelson & Munakata, 2016). Why delay the immediate gratification if the larger reward will not show up even if you wait? It is useful to think of delay of gratification as a strategy that children use only if they learn that it can be deployed to get larger rewards.

Q What is an example of a SMART goal for someone who is trying to lose weight?

ANSWER: "I will lose five pounds by the end of a 90-day diet program." This goal is specific, measurable, achievable, realistic, and time bound.

need to belong The need for interpersonal attachments, a fundamental motive that has evolved for adaptive purposes.

10.11 People Have a Need to Belong

Over the course of human evolution, our ancestors who lived with others were more likely to survive and pass along their genes. Children who stayed with adults (and resisted being left alone) were more likely to survive until their reproductive years because the adults would protect and nurture them. Adults capable of developing long-term, committed relationships were more likely to reproduce and to have offspring who survived to reproduce. Effective groups shared food, provided mates, and helped care for offspring, including orphans. Roy Baumeister and Mark Leary (1995) hypothesized that humans have a **need to belong**—a fundamental motive to make and maintain interpersonal attachments that has evolved for adaptive purposes.

The need to belong is the reason that most people care deeply about making friends (**FIGURE 10.31**). Societies differ in their types of groups, but all societies have some form of group membership (Brewer & Caporael, 1990). Not belonging to a group increases a person's risk for various adverse consequences, such as illnesses and premature death (Cacioppo et al., 2006). Such negative effects suggest that the need to belong is a basic motive driving behavior, just as hunger drives people to seek food and avoid dying from starvation.

FIGURE 10.31
Making Friends
College provides many opportunities for making friends. First-year students often make lifelong friendships within days of arriving on campus.

FIGURE 10.32
Desperate for Social Connection
The need to belong can motivate people to restore social connection in any way they can. In the movie *The Martian*, Matt Damon's character uses his journal to connect with people he imagines will hear his messages in the future.

If humans have a fundamental need to belong, they need to have some way of knowing whether they are included in particular groups (MacDonald & Leary, 2005). People need to be sensitive to signs that the group might kick them out, because survival depends on being part of a group. Indeed, evidence indicates that people feel anxious when facing exclusion from their social groups (Heinz et al., 2020). Further, people who are shy and lonely tend to worry most about social evaluation and pay much more attention to social information (Gardner et al., 2005). The take-home message is that just as a lack of food causes hunger, a lack of social contact causes emptiness and despair. In the movie *The Martian*, Matt Damon's character is an astronaut who becomes stranded alone on the surface of Mars for several months (**FIGURE 10.32**). Damon's character staves off the extreme loneliness by writing in his journal, imagining that he is speaking to other people who will read it in the future. In fact, space agencies have studied the increasing feelings of sadness and isolation experienced by astronauts during extended missions (Manzey et al., 1998). And evidence shows that journaling can be an effective way to reduce feelings of sadness, anxiety, and isolation (Smyth et al., 2018).

ANXIETY AND AFFILIATION Do you like to be around other people when you are anxious, or do you prefer to avoid them? In a classic study, the social psychologist Stanley Schachter (1959) manipulated anxiety levels and then measured how much the participants, all female, preferred to be around others. "Dr. Zilstein," a serious and cold-looking man with a vaguely European accent, told participants the study involved measuring "the physiological effects of electric shock." Zilstein would then hook the participants up to some electrical equipment. Those in the low-anxiety condition were told the shocks would be painless—no more than a tickle. Those in the high-anxiety condition were told: "These shocks will hurt; they will be painful. As you can guess, if we're to learn anything that will really help humanity, it is necessary that our shocks be intense. These shocks will be quite painful, but, of course, they will do no permanent damage." As you might imagine, the participants who heard this speech became quite anxious.

There was a 10-minute waiting period before the shocks began. At the beginning of the waiting period, the participants were offered a simple choice: They could spend the waiting time alone or with others. This choice was the critical dependent measure. After the choice was made, the experiment was over. No one received a shock. Schachter found that increased anxiety led to increased affiliative motivations: Those in the high-anxiety condition were much more likely to want to wait with other people.

Thus, misery appears to love company. But does misery love just any company? A further study revealed that high-anxiety participants wanted to wait only with other high-anxiety participants, not with people who supposedly were waiting just to see their research supervisors. So—misery loves miserable company, not just any company.

Why do people in a stressful situation prefer to be around other people in the same situation? One reason is that other people can provide information about a situation and help us tell if we are reacting to it appropriately. According to Leon Festinger's *social comparison theory* (1954), we compare ourselves with those around us to test and validate personal beliefs and emotional responses. This is especially true in situations that are ambiguous and when we have the opportunity to compare ourselves with people who are relatively similar to us.

Q When anxious, what type of social environment do people normally prefer, and why?

ANSWER: the company of similarly anxious people, because they can provide feedback and validation

10.12 People Have a Need for Consistency and Coherence

Being accused of saying one thing while doing another can be devastating. Nobody likes to feel like a hypocrite. It undermines other people's trust in us, which we depend on for our survival as part of a social group. Feeling like a hypocrite also hurts our sense of personal integrity. We have a need to feel internally consistent.

You might have experienced this need for consistency in your personal relationships. Have you ever come to like someone new because they were a friend of your friend? Your friend likes you both, so it makes sense that you might like each other. The psychologist Fritz Heider described this interpersonal phenomenon in his **balance theory**. Balance theory predicts that people have a preference for triads where the relationships are in harmony and an aversion to triads where there is disharmony. Harmonious triads are ones where the relationships are all the same direction (everyone likes or dislikes each other), or when two people like each other but dislike a third (**FIGURE 10.33a**). This second type of triad captures the spirit of the expression "The enemy of my enemy is my friend." Triads have disharmony when two people like each other but disagree about a third person (**FIGURE 10.33b**).

balance theory The idea that people are motivated to achieve harmony in their interpersonal relationships. A triad is balanced when the relationships are all the same direction or if two relationships are negative and one is positive.

According to balance theory, those cases produce a motive to bring the triad into harmony by coming to agreement. Suppose Ibram and Ijeoma are friends, but Ibram likes Layla and Ijeoma does not. This is an unbalanced triad because there is disagreement between Ibram and Ijeoma about Layla even though they are friends. To resolve the disharmony, they can decide either that they both like Layla or that they both dislike Layla. Either outcome will satisfy the motive for balance.

We also strive for consistency in our internal life. We do not like to have conflicting thoughts and actions any more than we like conflict in our friendships. The psychologist Leon Festinger famously invented the theory of **cognitive dissonance** to describe this sense of discomfort with internal conflict and how people respond to it. According to this theory, becoming aware of two conflicting thoughts, or a thought and a behavior, causes an aversive feeling of *dissonance*. People are motivated to reduce the dissonance by changing either a thought or a behavior so the set of thoughts and behaviors is internally consistent (**FIGURE 10.34**).

cognitive dissonance The unpleasant feeling of being aware of holding two conflicting beliefs or a belief that conflicts with a behavior.

FIGURE 10.33
Balance Theory Triads
(a) Balanced triads occur when three people all like or all dislike one another, or when two people like each other but both dislike a third. **(b)** An imbalanced triad occurs when two friends disagree about a third person.

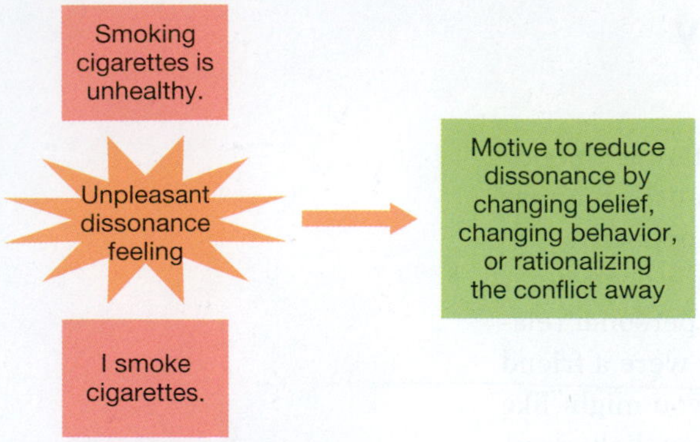

FIGURE 10.34
Cognitive Dissonance
A conflict between two beliefs, or between a belief and a behavior as shown here, leads to an unpleasant tension state called cognitive dissonance. The feeling of dissonance motivates people to change.

When experiencing dissonance, it is almost always easier to change a thought than a behavior. For example, for longtime cigarette smokers, their behavior (smoking) conflicts with the thought that smoking is harmful. Smokers can reduce the dissonance between the behavior and the thought either by quitting smoking, which is difficult, or convincing themselves that smoking is not that harmful, which is relatively easy. Indeed, smokers believe that smoking is less harmful than nonsmokers do (Leavens et al., 2019).

Another way to reduce dissonance is by *rationalizing* away the conflict. Rationalizations are not truths but rather myths that we tell ourselves to reduce dissonance. For example, smokers might believe that smoking is dangerous but rationalize the conflict between the belief and smoking by convincing themselves that the stress of quitting would be worse for their health than smoking is. The ways that cognitive dissonance influences our thoughts and beliefs are discussed further in Chapter 12.

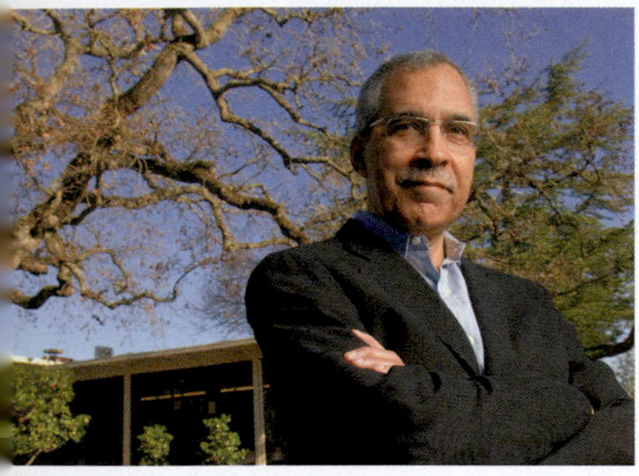

FIGURE 10.35
Claude Steele
The psychologist Claude Steele developed the theory of self-affirmation.

SELF-AFFIRMATION Consistency is an odd motive for people. Humans are complex and encounter a wide variety of situations, so it is understandable that things we think or do in one moment might conflict with something that happened in the past. The philosopher Ralph Waldo Emerson bristled at the attachment to consistency in his essay *Self-Reliance* (1841/1908), where he wrote, "A foolish consistency is the hobgoblin of little minds, adored by little statesmen and philosophers and divines. With consistency a great soul has simply nothing to do" (p. 23).

A fixation on consistency can be limiting. So why do we care about it? The psychologist Claude Steele (**FIGURE 10.35**) argued that people have an intrinsic need to view and present themselves as coherent and stable. He called this a need for **self-affirmation**. Threats to the integrity of a person's self-image, such as a conflict between a thought and a behavior, create a desire to *affirm* the self-image by restoring the sense of self as consistent, coherent, and positive. For example, people feel threatened if they learn they are at increased risk for a health condition such as heart disease. That sense of threat can cause people to reject the important information that their health is at risk. Providing people with a way to affirm their self-image—for example, by taking a moment to consider values that are important to them—can reduce the threat and increase acceptance of the information (Ferrer & Cohen, 2019).

self-affirmation A need for a sense of self that is coherent and stable.

Q **What are ways to reduce the sense of dissonance caused by a conflict between a belief and a behavior?**

ANSWER: change the belief, change the behavior (which is most challenging), or rationalize the inconsistency away

10.13 Core Values Are Motivating

One of the most interesting things about being human is the wide range of rewards that excite us. Hedonic rewards such as food and sex get our attention, as do social ones such as money and status. An even broader range of abstract rewards, such as power, mastery, growth, and connectedness, are also strongly motivating for most people. In the 1930s, the personality psychologist Henry Murray proposed 27 basic *psychosocial needs*, including the needs for power, autonomy, achievement, and play. Several other psychological theories describe these abstract rewards, known as **core values**, and the ways they motivate people.

core values Strongly held beliefs about the enduring principles that are most important and meaningful. Values promote emotions and actions when they are aroused or threatened.

Core values are strongly held beliefs about the enduring principles that are most important and meaningful in life. Values promote emotions and actions when they are aroused or threatened. For example, a person who values connectedness will deeply enjoy positive relationships and will seek to restore social connections following an experience of rejection.

There are some core values that everyone shares. According to *self-determination theory*, people are motivated to satisfy needs for competence, relatedness to others, and autonomy, which is a sense of personal control. Self-determination theory argues that these three basic needs must be satisfied for people to thrive and do their most creative work. People can be motivated for external reasons, but they can maximize their well-being only if they come to see how these external factors are consistent with their core values (Ryan & Deci, 2017).

Studies examining a range of cultures support the idea that satisfying the needs for competency, relatedness, and autonomy is related to better psychological functioning. For example, a large study of people from Belgium, China, the United States, and Peru found that, in all countries, people who felt that they had met these needs in their lives had increased well-being, and people who had not met them had more psychological problems (Chen et al., 2015). Motives to feel competent, autonomous, and connected to others are relevant during life experiences ranging from education to employment to retirement in older adulthood (Koole et al., 2019).

Learning Tip

It is easy to confuse *autonomy* and *competency*. Autonomy is about having a sense of control and self-directedness in life and in specific tasks, regardless of whether you succeed at them. Competency is about being effective and valued, regardless of whether you chose the task at hand.

Everyone wants competency, autonomy, and relatedness, but other values are more personal. The psychologist Shalom Schwartz has spent decades surveying hundreds of thousands of people around the world about their core values. There is quite a bit of variability from person to person and culture to culture (Rudnev et al., 2018). However, nearly everyone can identify at least a few values that they hold strongly from 10 broad categories: power, achievement, hedonism, stimulation, self-direction, universalism, benevolence, tradition, conformity, and security. Specific values can be located within the broad categories (**FIGURE 10.36**). For example, equality and social justice are universalism values, and intelligence and success are achievement values.

Values can be *prioritized*, or ordered by importance, and the ordering is stable for most people. Cultures also vary in how they prioritize values, but the overall structure of the value categories appears to be universal (Schwartz, 2012). Knowing which values are most important to them helps people choose goals and activities that are meaningful. Simply taking a moment to consider your core values and why they are important to you can be self-affirming and energizing (Critcher & Dunning, 2015).

Q Which of Schwartz's 10 core value categories are most analogous to the three needs proposed by self-determination theory?

ANSWER: Self-direction is analogous to autonomy, benevolence is analogous to relatedness, and achievement is analogous to competency.

FIGURE 10.36

Ten Value Domains

Shalom Schwartz identified 10 broad domains of values. Nearly everyone surveyed around the world could identify several core values from this list.

Your Chapter Review

It's time to complete your study experience! Go to **INQUIZITIVE** to practice actively with this chapter's concepts and get personalized feedback along the way.

Chapter Summary

What Are Emotions?

10.1 Emotions Vary in Valence and Arousal Emotions are often classified as primary or secondary. Primary emotions are innate, evolutionarily adaptive, and more consistent across cultures. These emotions include anger, fear, sadness, disgust, happiness, surprise, and contempt. Secondary emotions are blends of primary emotions and are less universal across cultures. They include remorse, guilt, shame, jealousy, pride, love, and contentment. Emotions have a valence (positive or negative) and a level of activation (arousal, from low to high).

10.2 Emotions Have a Physiological Component The insula and amygdala play important roles in the experience of emotion. The insula receives and integrates somatosensory signals, helping us experience emotion, especially disgust, anger, guilt, and anxiety. The amygdala processes the emotional significance of stimuli and generates immediate reactions. It is associated with emotional learning, memory of emotional events, and the interpretation of facial expressions of emotion.

10.3 You Be the Psychologist: Are Lie Detector Tests Valid? Because the use of lie detectors is controversial, most courts will not admit their results as evidence. The goal of polygraphs is to use emotional reactivity to assess whether someone is being deceptive. However, no measure of autonomic arousal can definitively indicate the presence or absence of a lie. Measuring brain activity to detect deception also has methodological and ethical problems.

10.4 There Are Three Major Theories of Emotion Three main theories of emotion differ in their relative emphases on subjective experience, physiological changes, and cognitive interpretation. The James-Lange theory states that specific patterns of physical changes give rise to the perception of associated emotions. The Cannon-Bard theory proposes that two separate pathways, physical changes and subjective experience, are activated at the same time. The Schachter-Singer two-factor theory emphasizes the combination of generalized physiological arousal and cognitive appraisals in determining specific emotions. Consistent with the Schachter-Singer two-factor theory, research has shown that we often misattribute the causes of our emotions, seeking environmental explanations for our feelings.

10.5 Psychology Outside the Lab: How Can You Control Your Emotions? People can use several strategies to regulate their emotions. Some of these strategies help people prevent or prepare for events, and some of them help in dealing with events after they occur. Unsuccessful strategies include suppression and rumination. Successful strategies include changing the meaning of events, mental distancing, finding humor, refocusing attention, and distraction.

How Are Emotions Adaptive?

10.6 Facial Expressions Communicate Emotion Facial expressions of emotion are adaptive because they communicate how we feel. Some expressions of emotion, such as those associated with happiness, sadness, anger, and pride, are recognized moderately well across cultures. Display rules are learned through socialization and dictate which emotions are suitable in given situations. Across cultures, different emotions are valued to different degrees.

10.7 Emotions Strengthen Interpersonal Relations Emotions facilitate the maintenance and repair of social bonds. Interpersonal emotions—for example, guilt and embarrassment—are particularly important for the maintenance and repair of close interpersonal relationships.

What Is Motivation?

10.8 Drives Motivate the Satisfaction of Needs Motivation energizes, directs, and sustains behavior. Needs arise from states of biological or social deficiency. Maslow described a hierarchy of needs. This model is not supported by data but is useful because of the idea that needs are prioritized. Drives are psychological states that create arousal and motivate behaviors to satisfy needs. Drives help us maintain homeostasis—that is, equilibrium of bodily functions. The Yerkes-Dodson law suggests that if people are underaroused or overaroused, their performance will suffer.

10.9 People Are Motivated by Incentives Incentives are external objects or goals. Some incentives are extrinsically motivating (directed toward an external reward). Other incentives are intrinsically motivating (directed toward an internal reward or simply enjoyable). Extrinsic rewards and intrinsic motivation have different effects and can sometimes work together to motivate behavior. People are universally motivated to approach pleasurable stimuli and avoid pain.

How Does Motivation Give Us Meaning?

10.10 People Set Goals to Achieve According to research, the most successful motivation comes from goals that are challenging and specific but not overly difficult. Effective goals are also measurable, realistic, and time bound. People who are high in self-efficacy and have a high achievement motive are more likely to set challenging but attainable goals for themselves. Long-term perseverance, associated with grit, assists goal achievement. People who learn to delay gratification are more likely to report successful outcomes later in life.

10.11 People Have a Need to Belong Need to belong theory suggests that people have a fundamental need for interpersonal attachments. Need to belong explains the ease with which people make friends, their sensitivity to social exclusion, the adverse feelings experienced in the absence of social contact, and efforts to affiliate with others when anxious.

10.12 People Have a Need for Consistency and Coherence People have a drive to maintain a sense of coherence in their interpersonal relations and their inner mental life. Balance theory describes how people strive for coherence in their relationships. Cognitive dissonance is the sense of discomfort people experience when two beliefs or a belief and a behavior conflict. Self-affirmation describes the need to maintain a sense of unified, coherent selfhood. Threats to the integrity of the self prompt a desire to restore self-coherence.

10.13 Core Values Are Motivating Core values are strongly held beliefs about the enduring principles that are most important and meaningful. Self-determination theory describes three universal core values: competence, autonomy, and relatedness. A set of 10 value categories captures most of the values that are important to people around the world. Cultures and individual people prioritize the values that are most important to them.

Key Terms

Practice Exercises

1. Students enrolled in a difficult class are preparing to give end-of-term presentations that will significantly impact final grades. According to the Yerkes-Dodson law, which is likely to perform the best?
   a. Ahn, who is not at all anxious about the presentation and does not give it much thought after his initial preparation.
   b. Sonya, who is moderately anxious about the presentation and continues to review her slides and practice her talk until presentation day.
   c. Marcus, who is extremely anxious about the presentation and spends every waking moment preparing, worrying late into the night and thinking of nothing else.

2. What is *not* one of the motivational human values proposed by self-determination theory?
   a. autonomy
   b. relatedness
   c. benevolence
   d. competency

3. How would the circumplex model of classifying emotions describe anxiety?
   a. positive valence and high arousal
   b. negative valence and low arousal
   c. positive valence and low arousal
   d. negative valence and high arousal

4. Which statement most accurately describes cultural variation in emotions and emotional expressions?
   a. Emotions and emotional expressions hardly vary between cultures.
   b. Emotional expressions vary more than emotional experiences between cultures.
   c. Emotional experiences vary more than emotional expressions between cultures.
   d. Emotions and emotional expressions show almost no similarity between cultures.

5. Identify each of the phenomena as a need or a drive.
   a. food
   b. hunger
   c. thirst
   d. water
   e. oxygen
   f. social connection

6. According to the research, which person is most likely to set challenging but attainable goals for themselves?
   a. a person low in self-efficacy but high in achievement motivation
   b. a person high in self-efficacy but low in achievement motivation
   c. a person low in self-efficacy and low in achievement motivation
   d. a person high in self-efficacy and high in achievement motivation

7. Attending an entertaining concert is an example of ________ motivation. Wearing earplugs to protect your hearing is an example of ______ motivation.
   a. extrinsic; avoidance
   b. avoidance; approach
   c. approach; avoidance
   d. approach; intrinsic

8. Albert dislikes Benicio but likes Carmen. Carmen and Benicio are good friends. According to balance theory, how is Albert most likely to react?
   a. Albert will be unbothered and continue to like Carmen and dislike Benicio.
   b. Albert will switch who he likes: liking Benicio and disliking Carmen.
   c. Albert will either come to like Benicio or convince Carmen that Benicio is unlikable.
   d. Albert will bring a fourth friend into the network for balance.

9. Andrea is a runner who suffered a devastating injury to her knee. She persevered through a long rehabilitation process to return to running and complete an ultramarathon. Which motivational concept best describes her perseverance?
   a. extrinsic motivation
   b. SMART goals
   c. intrinsic motivation
   d. grit

10. Which statement is accurate regarding the amygdala's involvement in emotion?
    a. Information reaches the amygdala along two separate neural pathways.
    b. Increased activity in the amygdala during an emotional event is associated with improved long-term memory for that event.
    c. The amygdala helps process the emotional content of facial expressions.
    d. All of the above are true.

HEY WILLIAMSBURG,
WEAR A MASK!
DOMINO PARK

11 Health and Well-Being

Big Questions

HAVE YOU EVER COME DOWN WITH A COLD around a stressful period in your life, such as after finals week or a big breakup? If that is the case, then you have experienced one kind of effect that your mind can have on your physical health. Stress is caused by a combination of external events and our perceptions of and reactions to them. One of its effects is to reduce the activity of our immune system, which protects our bodies from pathogens such as viruses. People experiencing stress become more vulnerable to a range of illnesses, from the common cold to heart disease and cancer. Stress is only one example of how our mental life can influence our physical health.

This chapter explores how health and well-being are intimately connected to psychological states. First it examines the social, psychological, and biological factors that influence health, and it discusses common behaviors that place health at risk. Then it looks in more detail at the physiological components of stress. Some bodily responses to stress can be beneficial in motivating people to action, but chronic exposure to stress can harm health in numerous ways. So, in addition to considering how people cope with stress and suggesting methods for successful coping, this chapter examines the benefits of a positive attitude to health and well-being.

What Affects Health?

Learning Objectives

- Describe the biopsychosocial model of health.
- Discuss social and cultural effects on health.
- Describe health disparities and their causes.
- Identify several health behaviors and how they relate to health.
- Review the benefits of regular exercise.

People generally think about health and well-being in biological terms. The traditional Western medical model defines health simply as the lack of disease. This medical approach views people as passive recipients of disease and of the medical treatments designed to return them to health after illness. The underlying assumption of the medical model is that people's mental states have little effect on their physical states in times of either health or disease.

Psychologists, physicians, and other health professionals have come to appreciate the importance of lifestyle factors for physical health. The interdisciplinary field of **health psychology** relies on the research methods of psychology to understand the interrelations among thoughts (health-related cognitions), actions, and physical and mental health. These researchers address issues such as ways to help people lead healthier lives. They study how behavior and social systems affect health and how social and cultural differences influence health outcomes. Health psychologists also study the inverse of these relationships: how health-related behaviors and health outcomes affect people's behaviors, thoughts, and emotions.

health psychology A field that involves the application of psychological principles to promote health and well-being.

well-being A positive state that includes striving for optimal health and life satisfaction.

biopsychosocial model An approach to psychological science that integrates biological factors, psychological processes, and social-contextual influences in shaping human mental life and behavior.

11.1 Social Context, Biology, and Behavior Combine to Affect Health

A central lesson in this chapter is that both mental states, such as a person's outlook on life, and behaviors are critical in preventing illness, helping people regain health following illness, and helping achieve well-being. **Well-being** is a positive state that requires health and life satisfaction, not only the absence of disease. People need to actively participate in health-enhancing behaviors to achieve optimal health.

How do people's personalities, thoughts, and behaviors affect their health? To answer this question, you need to understand the **biopsychosocial model**. Recall from Chapter 1 that, according to this model, health and illness result from a combination of factors, particularly biological conditions (e.g., genetic predisposition), behavioral factors (e.g., lifestyle, stress, and beliefs about health), and social contexts (e.g., cultural influences, family relationships, and settings such as work or school). Research that integrates these levels of analysis helps identify strategies that may prevent disease and promote health.

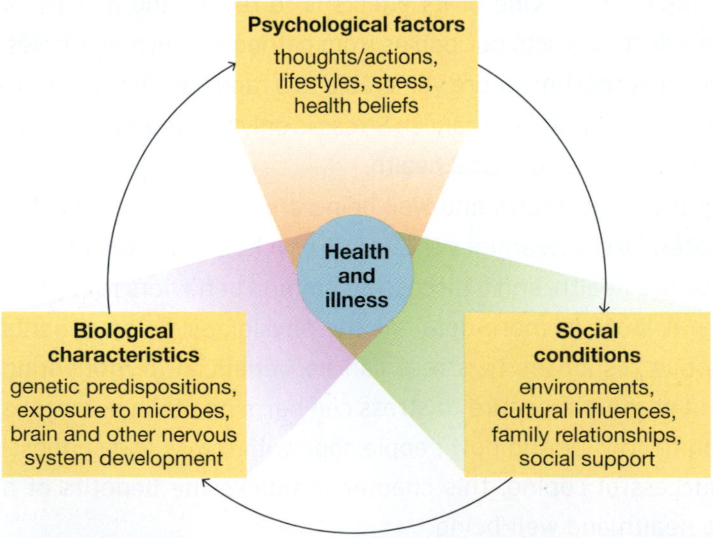

FIGURE 11.1
The Biopsychosocial Model
This model illustrates how health and illness result from a combination of factors.

As shown in **FIGURE 11.1**, thoughts and actions affect people's choices of the environments they interact with. Those environments, in turn, affect the biological underpinnings of thoughts and actions. To understand how this continuous loop operates in real life, consider that some people are genetically predisposed to be anxious. These people may learn that one way to reduce their anxiety is to eat comfort foods such as potato chips, cookies, and ice cream. Consuming these foods in excess causes them to gain weight and eventually become overweight. (In addition, some people have genes that make becoming overweight more likely.) Once they are overweight, they might find that exercise is not very pleasant because of the extra strain on their bodies. If their extra weight makes even moderate exercise difficult, they may decrease their physical activity.

That decrease might slow down their metabolism. The slower metabolism and decreased activity would likely cause them to gain more weight, and thus the cycle repeats. Additional examples of the interplay among biological, social, and psychological factors are presented throughout this chapter.

Our relationships with other people are also critical to health. For instance, many people find it easier to change behaviors linked with health, such as exercising or eating a healthy diet, when their family or romantic partner also changes with them (Pietromonaco & Collins, 2017). The people around us powerfully shape our behavior because we learn from them, care what they think, and desire to live up to their expectations. Chapter 12 further describes how social factors influence our behavior.

The importance of the people around us to our health also extends to our larger social groups. Beliefs and behaviors about health are determined by the norms and conditions of our cultures and communities. A classic example comes from a change in the Netherlands that occurred in the 1970s. Like many countries, the Netherlands saw a swift rise in car ownership through the 1950s and 1960s. With it came an increase of fatalities in car crashes and pedestrian collisions, many of which involved children. Massive nationwide protests against the "kindermoord" (child murder), together with the Middle East oil crisis of 1973, prompted the government to redesign streets to cater to bikes instead of cars (**FIGURE 11.2**). This shift in public policy dramatically increased the number of trips people took by bicycle—and increased the average physical activity of people living in the country, too (Frumkin et al., 2004). A change in behaviors like this can have long-term consequences for people's health and expected life spans (**FIGURE 11.3**).

Societal factors such as how public environments are structured and how much money a country can dedicate to health care can affect health for the better or the worse. Impoverished countries may lack the resources to provide adequate treatments for many health conditions, such as HIV, malaria, and rotavirus, an intestinal virus that kills over half a million children each year. The Bill and Melinda Gates Foundation has provided billions in grant funding to reduce infectious diseases in poor countries. Efforts such as these have lowered deaths from malaria by 42 percent globally and by nearly 50 percent in Africa, where, on average, hundreds of children die each day from the disease (World Health Organization, 2014). Vaccines for rotavirus have led to large reductions in childhood hospitalization and death around the globe, including in North America (Parashar et al., 2013).

(a)

(b)

FIGURE 11.2
Public Infrastructure and Healthy Activities
The Netherlands dramatically increased active transportation, such as biking, by changing how it configured its city streets in the 1970s. Here is Eerste van der Helststraat in 1978 and today.

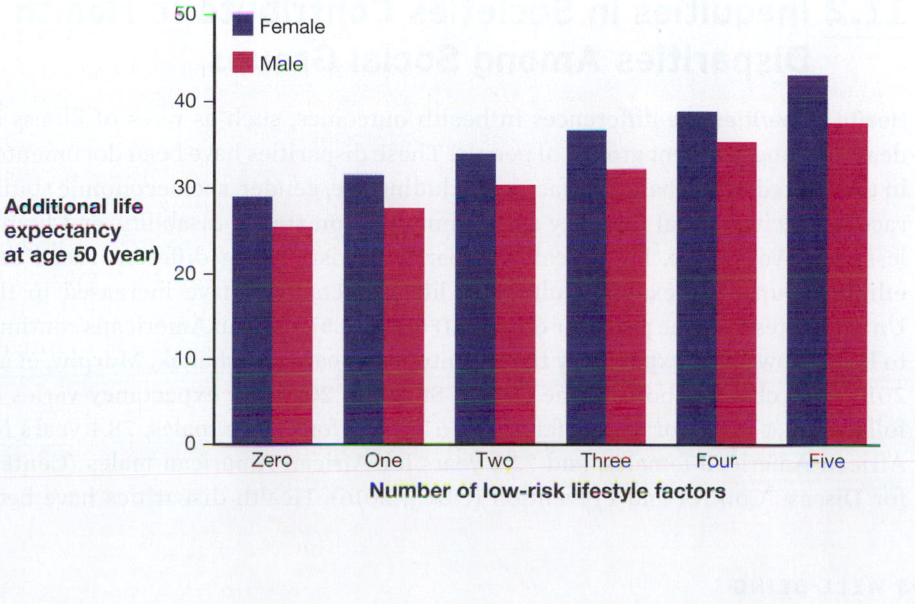

FIGURE 11.3
Life Expectancy Increases with Healthy Activities
How many of the following five healthy activities do you engage in: never smoking, maintaining lean to moderate weight, regularly being physically active, abstaining from alcohol or maintaining no more than moderate intake, and eating a healthy diet? People who exhibit more of these behaviors have longer life expectancies (adapted from Li et al., 2018).

FIGURE 11.4
The Longest-Living People
Japanese people tend to live very long lives. Their longevity is no doubt due to a combination of genetics and behavior. Pictured here are 99-year-old Matsu and 91-year-old Taido, both of Ogimi Village.

Different cultures and lifestyles also contribute to health differences (**FIGURE 11.4**). For example, the adoption of more Westernized behaviors, such as eating junk food and engaging in less physical activity, in countries like India and China has led to increases in diseases related to obesity, such as diabetes (Zabetian et al., 2014). The psychologist Michele Gelfand describes cultures along a "tightness-looseness" spectrum, where tighter cultures place greater value on adherence to social norms than looser cultures do (Gelfand et al., 2011). The relative tightness or looseness of a culture is related to how closely people in that culture follow public health guidelines. This was apparent in the 2020 coronavirus pandemic, where countries with tighter cultures, such as Singapore, saw much higher rates of compliance with mask recommendations than did countries with looser cultures, such as the United States (Leijen & van Herk, 2020; van der Westhuizen, 2020). Thus, researchers seek to understand how culture influences behaviors and how behaviors alter underlying biology. Each level of analysis provides a piece of the intricate puzzle that determines health and well-being.

CAUSES OF MORTALITY Before the twentieth century, most people died from infections and from diseases transmitted person to person. Infections and communicable diseases remain the leading causes of mortality in some developing nations, but in most countries the causes have shifted. For example, in the United States people are now more likely to die from heart disease, cancer, strokes, lung disease, and accidents than from infectious diseases (Heron, 2016). All of these causes of death are at least partially outcomes of lifestyle. Daily habits such as poor nutrition, overeating, smoking, alcohol use, and lack of exercise contribute to nearly every major cause of death in developed nations (Smith et al., 2004). Fewer than 3 percent of Americans are physically active, do not smoke, eat a healthy diet, and maintain the recommended body fat level (Loprinzi et al., 2016). Partially for this reason, life expectancy in the United States dropped in 2015 for the first time in several decades (Xu et al., 2016). A steep rise in unintentional poisonings, mainly opioid overdoses, was the leading cause of higher death rates (the opioid epidemic is discussed in Chapter 4).

Q **What are the three primary factors that interact and contribute to health and well-being according to the model used in health in psychology?**

ANSWER: The biopsychosocial model views well-being as a cyclical interplay among biological, psychological, and social and cultural factors.

11.2 Inequities in Societies Contribute to Health Disparities Among Social Groups

health disparities Differences in health outcomes, such as illness or death rates, between groups of people.

Health disparities are differences in health outcomes, such as rates of illness or death, among different groups of people. These disparities have been documented in the United States based on factors including age, gender, socioeconomic status, race, ethnicity, sexual minority status, immigration status, disability, and homelessness. Worldwide, large health disparities exist among different racial and ethnic groups. For example, although life expectancies have increased in the United States over the past four decades (**FIGURE 11.5**), African Americans continue to have a lower life expectancy than White Americans (Kochanek, Murphy, et al., 2016). For children born in the United States in 2014, life expectancy varies as follows: 81.4 years for White females, 76.7 years for White males, 78.4 years for African American females, and 72.5 years for African American males (Centers for Disease Control and Prevention [CDC], 2016). Health disparities have been

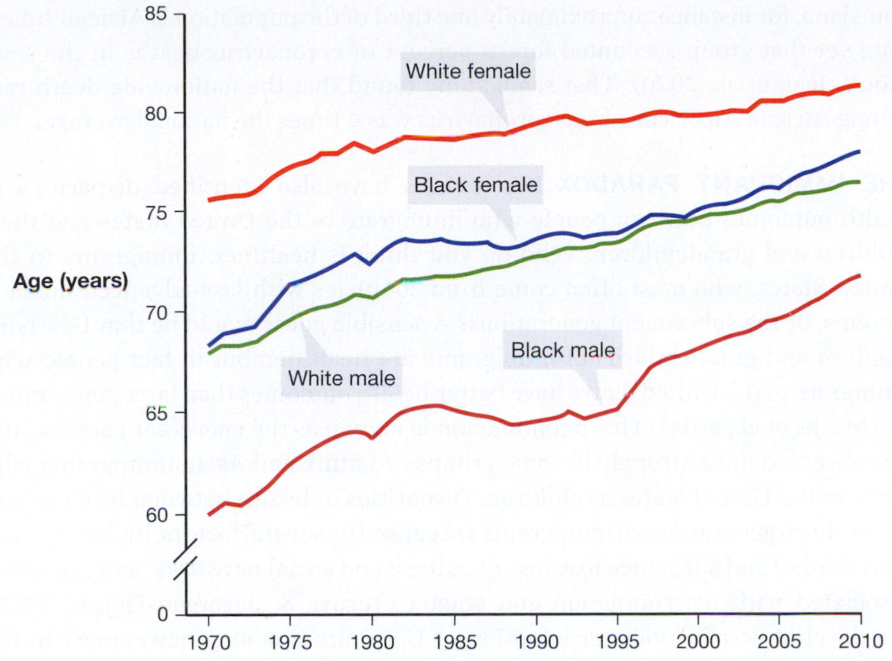

FIGURE 11.5
Life Expectancy by Race and Sex
Although life expectancy has increased in the United States since 1970, African Americans continue to lag behind Whites.
Source: Kochanek, Murphy, et al.

documented between White people and members of other ethnic groups in nearly every chronic disease and major illness (CDC, 2005).

Scientists are still working to understand why health disparities exist. Part of the reason that racial and ethnic groups experience differences in their health include genetic variation in susceptibility to some diseases, access (or lack of access) to affordable health care, and cultural factors such as dietary and exercise habits (Cockerham et al., 2017). For example, African Americans are less likely to have access to cancer screenings. Moreover, they are less likely to receive recommended treatments, and perhaps as a result they have lower survival rates (DeSantis et al., 2013).

A central cause of health disparities is the racial bias inherent in the U.S. medical system (Klonoff, 2014). People from underrepresented racial and ethnic groups in the United States receive lower-quality care, spend less time with medical practitioners, and are offered fewer procedures than White individuals (Williams & Wyatt, 2015). These biases have cumulative effects that can lead to worse health outcomes (**FIGURE 11.6**). African Americans in particular have lower levels of trust in the medical system because of past and ongoing racism and abuse (Williamson et al., 2019). This mistrust plays out at every level of the health care system, from health behavior adherence to preventive tests to recovery from major illness. For instance, African Americans are less likely to follow screening guidelines for colorectal cancer than other groups, even when the groups have equal access to the screening (Adams et al., 2017).

The gap between Black and White Americans has been closing over the past few years, but mainly because White Americans aged 25–54 are dying at higher rates (Kochanek, Arias, et al., 2016). Lifestyle factors, such as alcohol and opioid abuse, have lowered life expectancy more for White, rural Americans than for other racial or ethnic groups (Case & Deaton, 2015; Keyes et al., 2014). Nonetheless, old problems embedded in the health care system re-create disparities even in new diseases. Structural factors, such as low accessibility of good health care in some regions of the country, perpetuate disparities even as other factors mitigate them. Racial disparities during the 2020 coronavirus pandemic illustrate this point. In

FIGURE 11.6
Disparities in Disease Mortality
Racial and ethnic minority group members, particularly African Americans, are more likely to suffer from diseases such as cancer. Actor Chadwick Boseman died from colorectal cancer in 2020.

Louisiana, for instance, approximately one third of the population is African American, yet that group accounted for 70 percent of coronavirus deaths in the state (Louis-Jean et al., 2020). That same study found that the nationwide death rate among African Americans from coronavirus was 4 times the national average.

THE IMMIGRANT PARADOX Researchers have also identified disparities in health outcomes between people who immigrate to the United States and their children and grandchildren. Who do you think is healthier: immigrants to the United States, who most often come from countries with less-advanced medical systems, or the subsequent generations? A sensible guess would be that U.S.-born children and grandchildren of immigrants are healthier, but in fact people who immigrate to the United States have better health outcomes than later generations do (Marks et al., 2014). This phenomenon is known as the **immigrant paradox**, and it is observed most strongly in some groups of Latinx and Asian immigrants who come to the United States as children. Disparities in health between foreign- and native-born generations of immigrants are caused by several factors, including poor diet, alcohol and substance use, loss of culture and social networks, and the stress associated with discrimination and stigma (Teruya & Bazargan-Hejazi, 2013). The level of *acculturation*, or adoption of U.S. culture among newcomers to the country, appears to play a major role. Many aspects of U.S. culture, such as dietary habits, substance use, and level of physical activity, can be harmful to health.

immigrant paradox The pattern among immigrant communities in which foreign-born immigrants to the United States have better health than people in later generations do.

THE SOCIOECONOMIC STATUS HEALTH GRADIENT In addition to health disparities between racial groups and by immigration status, there are also disparities in health between people with greater or fewer resources such as education and wealth (**FIGURE 11.7**). Psychologists consider education, wealth, income, and other resources markers of **socioeconomic status**. Higher socioeconomic status confers a number of material and social advantages in a society. People with lower socioeconomic status have worse health than people with higher socioeconomic status, even when accounting for access to health care (Adler, 2013). For instance, in the United Kingdom, where all residents are provided the same health care through the National Health Service, education and the prestige of a person's job are strongly associated with health outcomes and even mortality rates (Rahman et al., 2016). This kind of disparity is known as the *socioeconomic status health gradient*.

socioeconomic status Relative standing in society as a function of resources such as income, wealth, and education.

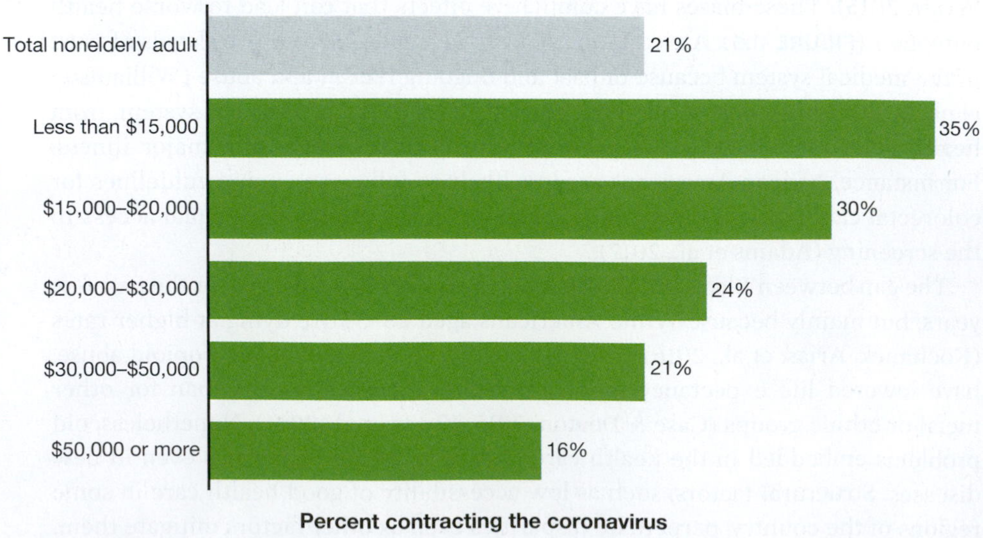

Note: Data includes adults ages 18–64; excludes adults living in nursing homes or other institutional settings.

FIGURE 11.7
Socioeconomic Status and Health
People with fewer resources have worse health outcomes across many diseases. This "health gradient" is caused by multiple factors. During the coronavirus pandemic, people with lower incomes were more likely to contract the disease because many of them were frontline workers, and they had worse health outcomes when they became sick because of restricted access to care and to isolation space.

Source: KFF analysis of 2018 Behavioral Risk Factor Surveillance System. Koma et al., 2020.

Psychological scientists have studied the causes of the socioeconomic status health gradient. Living at the bottom rungs of the social ladder, especially as a child, puts people in the position to experience many conditions that are harmful to long-term health (Cundiff et al., 2020). Lower socioeconomic status is associated with living in environments that are more polluted and more violent, provide less access to healthy foods and safe outdoor spaces, and are more chaotic and unpredictable (Evans & Kim, 2010). Poor sleep, high levels of interpersonal conflict, and frequent major life disruptions are also more likely at lower levels of socioeconomic status. All of these factors add up to the reality that living with low socioeconomic status is highly stressful. As we will see later in this chapter, chronic stress can be damaging to health in many ways.

Q **How does racism and racial bias in the American health care system contribute to health disparities between White and Black Americans?**

ANSWER: Black people may receive less attention from medical providers, receive fewer tests and treatments, and have less access to care, and mistrust medical systems due to past injustices.

11.3 Healthy Eating Is an Important Health Behavior

In the early 1900s, the leading causes of death were infectious diseases such as tuberculosis, smallpox, and malaria. Many people who were otherwise healthy died of these and similar diseases because they can affect anyone and become severe very quickly. As a result, there were few steps people could take to avoid the most common causes of death.

Thanks to advances in medicine such as antibiotics and health practices such as hygiene, the leading causes of sickness and death in the early decades of the 2000s have been quite different. People are much more likely to die of chronic illnesses such as heart disease, cancer, and diabetes. In contrast with infectious diseases, chronic illnesses are slow to develop and strongly influenced by **health behaviors**, which are the actions people can take to promote well-being and to prevent the onset and slow the progression of illness and disease.

health behaviors Actions people can take, such as eating a plant-based diet and being physically active, that promote well-being, prevent the onset of disease, and slow disease progression.

For example, heart disease and cancer account for about half of all U.S. deaths (Hoyert & Xu, 2012). Those who suffer from heart disease or cancer are not always to blame for their conditions, but all of us can change our behaviors in ways that may reduce the likelihood and severity of these illnesses. A report released by the CDC in 2014 indicated that over a quarter of a million early deaths could be prevented each year if people made better health choices (Yoon et al., 2014). Steps we all can take to protect our health include being physically active, eating a diet rich in fruits and vegetables and low in sugar and saturated fats, and avoiding tobacco and alcohol use.

HEALTHY DIET Eating a healthy diet is one of the most effective ways to promote wellness and prevent illness (Jankovic et al., 2014). Different diets come in and out of style, but the basic elements of healthy eating are always the same (**FIGURE 11.8**). The author Michael Pollan, who studied diets around the world and wrote several books about eating, describes a good diet in seven words: "Eat food, not too much, mostly plants" (Pollan, 2013). This simple recipe captures some of the advice scientists give about healthy eating. "Eat food" means to eat natural, less-processed foods instead of artificial, more-processed ones (Elizabeth et al., 2020). An apple is healthier than fruit leather made from apples, sugar, and probably many chemicals. "Not too much" cautions against intake of more calories than

FIGURE 11.8
Healthy Diet
A healthy diet is natural, rich in plants, and light on animal proteins. The so-called Mediterranean diet is characterized by vegetables, legumes, fish, and olive oil.

your body needs (Uauy & Díaz, 2005). And "mostly plants" reflects the fact that diets heavy in fruits and vegetables and light on animal proteins are consistently linked to health and longevity (Satija & Hu, 2018).

In contrast, maladaptive eating habits, such as eating junk food, are linked to a range of illnesses, including heart disease, diabetes, and cancer. People who eat food high in both fat and sugar tend to store more body fat in the abdomen. These individuals are at increased risk for developing *metabolic syndrome*, a constellation of risk factors that includes high blood sugars, insulin resistance (in which the body produces insulin but does not use it efficiently), high blood levels of unhealthy cholesterol, and cardiovascular disease (Ford et al., 2002). Even though unhealthy eating is linked with weight increases, metabolic syndrome is the result of poor nutrition rather than body weight per se (Unger & Scherer, 2010).

An increase in the variety of available food is a major factor that contributes to maladaptive eating. Rats that normally maintain a steady body weight when eating one type of food eat huge amounts and rapidly gain weight when presented with a variety of high-calorie foods, such as chocolate bars, crackers, and potato chips (Sclafani & Springer, 1976; **FIGURE 11.9**). Humans show the same effect, eating much more when various foods are available—as at a buffet—than when only one or two types of food are available (Epstein et al., 2010; Raynor & Epstein, 2001).

People also eat more when portions are larger (Rolls et al., 2007), and portion sizes have increased considerably in many restaurants. In addition, heavier people show more activity in reward regions of the brain when they see tasty-looking foods than do individuals who are not overweight (Rapuano et al., 2017). Together, these findings suggest that in industrialized nations, the increase in weight gain and metabolic syndrome over the past few decades is partly explained by overeating. The overeating stems from three factors: the sheer variety of high-calorie foods, the large portions now served in many restaurants, and individual responses to food cues.

In most industrialized cultures, food is generally abundant. But there is unevenness in the availability of healthy and unhealthy food. In the United States, fresh

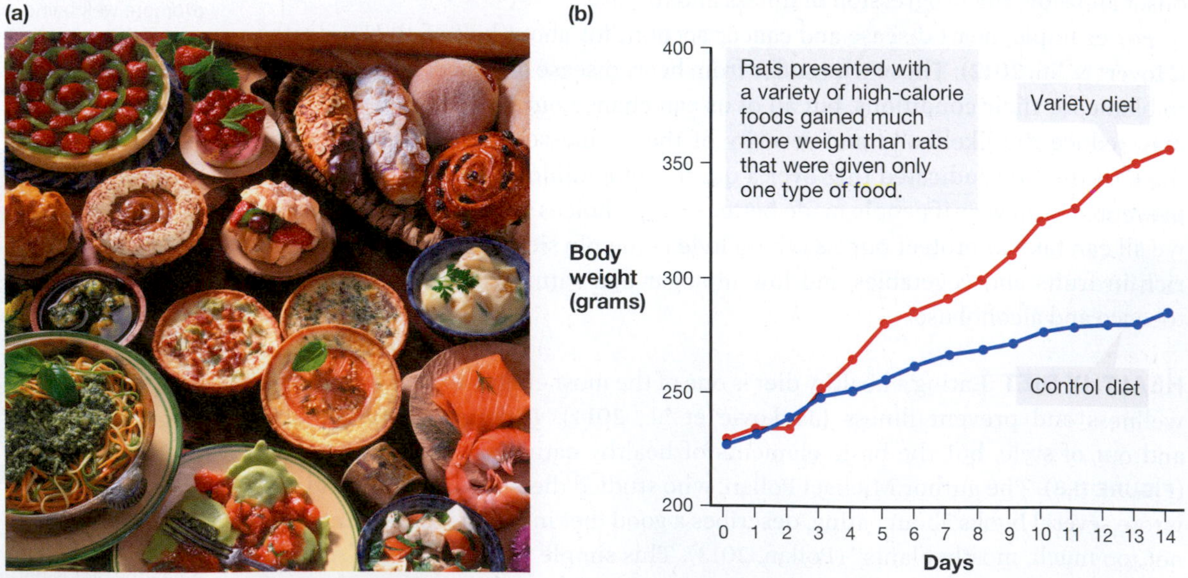

FIGURE 11.9
The Impact of Variety on Eating Behavior
(a) If you were presented with this table full of delicious foods, how many would you eat? Would you be tempted to try them all? **(b)** As shown in this graph, rats will become obese if given ample variety.

and nutritious foods are often more expensive than high-calorie fast food. Therefore, in the industrialized world, being overweight is associated with lower socioeconomic status, especially for women. The relative affordability of fast food may contribute to being overweight among those with limited finances.

Q **The traditional Mediterranean diet consists of moderate intake of vegetables, fruits and nuts, unprocessed grains, and fish, and a low intake of dairy, meat, and poultry. According to research, why is this diet associated with longevity?**

ANSWER: The Mediterranean diet conforms to the basic rules of a healthy diet: eat moderate quantities of natural, mostly plant-based foods.

11.4 Smoking Is a Leading Cause of Death

Despite overwhelming evidence that smoking cigarettes leads to premature death, millions around the globe continue to light up (Fiore et al., 2014). According to the World Health Organization (2020), increasing numbers of people in low-income countries are smoking, and 8 million deaths are caused by tobacco every year. Thirty percent of all smokers worldwide are in China, 10 percent are in India, and an additional 25 percent come from Indonesia, Russia, the United States, Japan, Brazil, Bangladesh, Germany, and Turkey combined (**FIGURE 11.10**). According to a CDC (2019a) report, just under 1 in 7 American adults are current smokers.

Smoking is blamed for more than 480,000 deaths per year in the United States and decreases the typical smoker's life by more than 12 years (Jha et al., 2013). Smoking causes numerous health problems, including heart disease, respiratory ailments, and various cancers. Cigarette smoke also causes health problems for nonsmoking bystanders, a finding that has led to bans on smoking in many public and private places. Besides spending money on cigarettes, smokers pay significantly more for life insurance and health insurance.

Most smokers begin in childhood or early adolescence, largely because of the powerful effect of social influence at that age (Chassin et al., 1990; **FIGURE 11.11**). Adolescents often smoke their first cigarettes in the company of other smokers, or at least with the encouragement of their peers. Children also take up smoking partially to look "tough, cool, and independent of authority" (Leventhal & Cleary, 1980, p. 384). Smoking might be one way for adolescents to enhance their self-images as well as their public images (Chassin et al., 1990). As discussed in Chapter 6, adolescents imitate models through observational learning. Smokers on television and in movies are often portrayed in glamorous ways that appeal to adolescents (**FIGURE 11.12**).

This early start concerns health care providers because of how nicotine may affect the developing brain. Every day, approximately 1,600 Americans ages 11 to 17 smoke their first cigarette (Substance Abuse and Mental Health Services Administration, 2019). About half of young smokers will likely continue smoking into adulthood, and if current smoking rates continue, 5.6 million American children alive today will die prematurely because of smoking (U.S. Department of Health and Human Services [USDHHS], 2014). There has been a dramatic reduction in teenage smoking over the past decades, but the use of e-cigarettes and other forms of smokeless tobacco has increased in that time. More than 1 in 4 high school students report having used e-cigarettes in the past 30 days. In all, nearly 1 in 3 high schoolers use some form of tobacco (CDC, 2019b).

Over time, casual smokers become addicted. It is now widely acknowledged that the drug nicotine is of primary importance in motivating and maintaining smoking behavior (Fagerström & Schneider, 1989; USDHHS, 2004). Once the smoker

(a)

(b)

FIGURE 11.10
Smoking Is a Global Phenomenon
(a) These men are smoking in Tiananmen Square in Beijing, China. **(b)** Smoking among the Mentawi people, a seminomadic hunter-gatherer tribe in Indonesia.

FIGURE 11.11
Social Influence and Smoking
Adolescents are more likely to smoke if their friends or parents smoke.

FIGURE 11.12
Glamorous Portrayals of Smoking
In the AMC series *Preacher*, Dominic Cooper plays the preacher Jesse Custer. Cooper's pose here exemplifies the "cool" factor often seen in depictions of smoking.

becomes "hooked" on nicotine, going without cigarettes will lead to unpleasant withdrawal symptoms, including distress and heightened anxiety (Russell, 1990). Some people appear especially susceptible to nicotine addiction, perhaps because of genetics (Sabol et al., 1999).

Once people are addicted, quitting smoking is very difficult. Numerous behavioral treatments encourage people to quit, teach them effective alternative ways of dealing with stress, and help them try to prevent relapse (Baker et al., 2011). Unfortunately, most people who use these methods do relapse. Only 10–30 percent of people are able to quit smoking over the long term, even in the most effective treatment programs (Schlam & Baker, 2013).

Despite these relatively unimpressive outcomes from treatment studies, millions of people have permanently given up smoking. How did they do it? Around 90 percent of people who successfully quit do so on their own, going "cold turkey" (Smith & Chapman, 2014). Often, some sort of critical event changes the way the smoker thinks about the addiction. The psychologist David Premack provides an example of a man who quit smoking one day because of something that happened when he was picking up his children from the city library: "A thunderstorm greeted him as he arrived there; and at the same time a search of his pockets disclosed a familiar problem: he was out of cigarettes. Glancing back at the library, he caught a glimpse of his children stepping out in the rain, but he continued around the corner, certain that he could find a parking space, rush in, buy the cigarettes and be back before the children got seriously wet" (Premack, 1970, p. 115).

For the smoker, it was a shocking revelation of himself "as a father who would actually leave the kids in the rain while he ran after cigarettes." The man quit smoking on the spot. Researchers have not yet identified the mechanisms that transform critical events into successful smoking cessation (Smith & Chapman, 2014). Because of the difficulty that many people have quitting smoking, much of the current research on smoking examines ways to prevent people from smoking in the first place (USDHHS, 2014).

Q **What chemical makes smoking cigarettes and e-cigarettes addictive and challenging to quit, despite widespread knowledge of the dangers of smoking?**

ANSWER: Addiction to nicotine in both traditional cigarettes and e-cigarettes makes quitting smoking extremely challenging.

11.5 Physical Activity Is a Particularly Beneficial Health Behavior

In general, the more people exercise, the better their physical and mental health. Those with better fitness in middle age are likely to enjoy much longer lives (Ladenvall et al., 2016). They are less likely to have heart problems (Arem et al., 2015) and are at much lower risk for most types of cancer (Moore et al., 2016). Even people who exercise only once or twice a week show reductions in heart disease and cancer (O'Donovan et al., 2017). Scientists do not know exactly how exercise exerts its positive effects.

Unlike societies throughout most of human history, modern society allows and even encourages people to exert little physical energy, so most people need to purposefully exercise during their leisure time. We drive to work, take elevators, spend hours watching remote-controlled television, spend even more hours online, use various labor-saving devices, and complain about not having time to exercise. Once people are out of shape, it is difficult for them to start exercising regularly. Starting an exercise program when you are not used to it can feel unpleasant or even painful.

Research clearly shows that exercise can enhance almost every aspect of our lives, including our memory and cognition (Harburger et al., 2007). Aerobic exercise—the kind that temporarily increases breathing and heart rate—promotes the growth of new neurons (Carmichael, 2007). The additional neurons created through exercise result in a larger brain, and the brain region that experiences the most growth is the hippocampus (Nokia et al., 2016). As discussed in Chapter 3, the hippocampus is important for memory and cognition.

Aerobic exercise is also especially good for cardiovascular health because it lowers blood pressure and strengthens the heart and lungs (Lavie et al., 2015). A meta-analysis found that exercise is as effective as medications for preventing diabetes or heart disease and for promoting recovery following heart attacks (Naci & Ioannidis, 2013). Although the different studies in the meta-analysis varied in terms of the type, frequency, intensity, and duration of physical activity considered, most included aerobic and muscle-strengthening exercises. As little as 10 minutes of exercise can promote feelings of vigor and enhance mood, although at least 30 minutes of daily exercise is associated with the most positive mental state (Hansen et al., 2001). People who are not physically fit are also at greater risk of developing depression (Schuch, Vancampfort, Sui, et al., 2016), and there is compelling evidence that exercise can contribute to positive outcomes for the clinical treatment of depression (Schuch, Vancampfort, Richards, et al., 2016; you will learn more about depression in Chapter 14). It is also beneficial in the treatment of addiction and alcoholism (Read & Brown, 2003).

FIGURE 11.13
Older Adults Exercising
People are never too old to enjoy the benefits of exercise.

Fortunately, it is never too late to start exercising and receiving its benefits (**FIGURE 11.13**). In one study, sedentary adults between the ages of 60 and 79 were randomly assigned to either six months of aerobic training, such as running or fast dancing, or six months of a nonaerobic exercise control group (Colcombe et al., 2006). Participants in aerobic training significantly increased their brain volume, including both white (myelinated) and gray matter. The nonaerobic control group experienced no comparable changes. In another study, older adults were assigned randomly to either three months of aerobic exercise or three months of a nonaerobic control group (Emery et al., 2005). All the participants agreed to have small cuts made on their bodies so the researchers could study whether aerobic exercise hastened the time it took for the wounds to heal. The wounds of the aerobic group took an average of 29.2 days to heal, whereas those of the nonaerobic group took an average of 38.9 days to heal. Besides faster healing time, the aerobic group had better cardiorespiratory (heart and lung) fitness.

In another study, older adults with memory problems were randomly assigned to an exercise group (3 hours a week for two weeks) or to a control group (Lautenschlager et al., 2008). The participants in the exercise group improved in their overall cognition, including memory. The control group showed no changes. The researchers concluded that exercise reduces cognitive decline in older adults with moderate memory problems.

Q **What is the maximum age limit and minimum frequency or duration of physical exercise to gain benefits?**

ANSWER: There are no age, frequency, or duration limits to the benefit from exercise. Even brief, infrequent exercise at any age has some psychological and physiological benefit.

11.6 Why Are People Afraid of Flying but Not of Driving (or Smoking)?

YOU BE THE PSYCHOLOGIST

Are you an anxious flyer? If so, you are not alone. A statistical expert explained the risk of death from flying this way: "It's once every 19,000 years—and that is only provided the person flew on an airplane once a day for 19,000 years!" (SixWise.com,

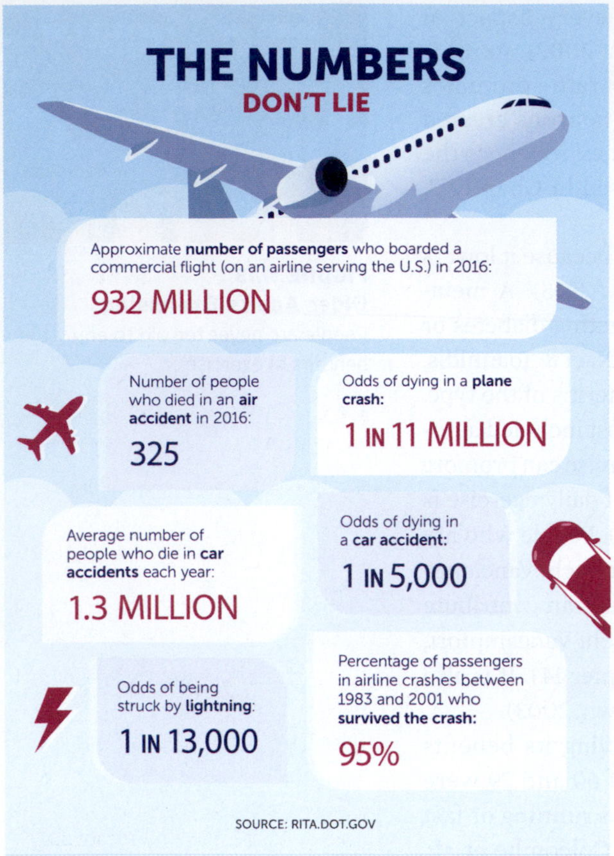

THE NUMBERS
DON'T LIE
Approximate number of passengers who boarded a commercial flight (on an airline serving the U.S.) in 2016:
932 MILLION
Number of people who died in an air accident in 2016:
325
Odds of dying in a plane crash:
1 IN 11 MILLION
Average number of people who die in car accidents each year:
1.3 MILLION
Odds of dying in a car accident:
1 IN 5,000
Odds of being struck by lightning:
1 IN 13,000
Percentage of passengers in airline crashes between 1983 and 2001 who survived the crash:
95%
SOURCE: RITA.DOT.GOV

FIGURE 11.14
Fears Versus Facts
People's fears about flying are disproportionate to the actual risks. The odds of dying in a plane crash are far smaller than the odds of being hit by lightning.

2005). Other researchers have estimated that 1 in 11 million passengers dies in an airplane crash.

In terms of thinking about their health and well-being, people often fear the wrong things. Some people choose to drive instead of fly out of fear of a crash, even though fatal car accidents are hundreds if not thousands of times more likely than airplane crashes (**FIGURE 11.14**). People tend not to be worried at all about the things that are most likely to kill them. Rare causes of death—not just plane crashes, but oddities such as "flesh-eating bacteria" or being murdered while vacationing in a foreign country—are often judged to occur much more frequently than they actually do, while common causes of death are underestimated (Lichtenstein et al., 1978). People are most likely to die from causes that stem from their own health behaviors, which they can learn to modify.

Why do people fear things that are unlikely to harm them but not worry about the things that are truly dangerous? Think about how you consider risk. Do you think about how common car accidents are each time you get behind the wheel? How often do you think about airplane crashes when you fly? What are the thoughts that go through your mind when you answer a question about how often something happens?

Recall from Chapter 8 the availability heuristic, our tendency to believe information that comes most easily to mind. People using this heuristic will judge an event as likely to occur if it is easy to imagine or recall (Slovic et al., 1981). The news media widely and dramatically report plane crashes, as when headlines blazed for weeks after the disappearance of Malaysian Airlines Flight 370 in March 2014. News reports of other crashes often include vivid, memorable pictures or detailed accounts that can easily be imagined. The ease with which people recall this information biases their risk estimates.

By contrast, think about how you go about estimating the risk of eating processed meats or being physically inactive. When you fail to get enough exercise this week or slowly build a habit of drinking too much, are you aware that doing so increases your risk for heart disease and cancer?

These kinds of risk calculations are challenging because the chronic diseases that actually kill most Americans are caused by many factors coming together over time. It would be nearly impossible, for example, to figure out how much a few days of unhealthy eating contributed to your risk of heart disease. Even if you could, you would also have to include in your risk prediction your family history, your other risk behaviors, and other lifestyle factors that might be protective. These computations are difficult mental work! That is why it is hard to feel the same sense of dread about eating unhealthy foods or skipping your gym session that you feel when you board an airplane.

As a student, the riskiest behaviors you can engage in include excessive alcohol intoxication, an overdose of legal or illegal drugs, drinking and driving, and texting while driving. Each year many more college students die from these common behaviors than are killed by rare events such as plane crashes. The irony is that people are willing to take drastic steps—such as never flying—to avoid very unlikely negative events, but they do not take simple steps to avoid life's most common dangers. What do you think could explain this? Optimism bias is one reason young people tend to feel invulnerable to risky behaviors (Radcliffe & Klein, 2002), but there are many others. Consider some of the everyday unhealthy behaviors you or your friends engage in and ponder why they do not scare you nearly as much as other things you might fear: plane crashes, terrorism, rattlesnakes, and so forth. ■

Q **How can vivid media reports affect people's views of health risks and their attempts to reduce those risks?**

ANSWER: News reports of dramatic tragedies create strong memories. Using the availability heuristic, people overestimate the risk for these events and attempt to avoid them.

What Is Stress?

Learning Objectives

- Define stress.
- Describe the hypothalamic-pituitary-adrenal (HPA) axis.
- Describe the general adaptation syndrome.
- Discuss the concept of allostatic load.

Stress is a basic component of our daily lives. However, stress does not exist objectively, out in the world. Instead, it results directly from the ways we think about events in our lives. For example, some students experience final exams as extremely stressful and often get sick at exam time, whereas other students perceive the same finals as mere inconveniences or even as opportunities to demonstrate mastery of the material. When researchers study stress, then, what are they studying?

11.7 Stress Is a Response to Life Events

Stress is a type of response that typically involves an unpleasant state, such as anxiety or tension. A **stressor** is something in the external situation that is perceived as threatening or demanding and therefore produces stress. One person's stressor, such as having to speak in front of a crowd, may be another person's cherished activity. Stress elicits a **coping response**, which is an attempt to avoid, escape from, or minimize the stressor. The coping response is our attempt to reduce the stress and return our bodies and minds back to baseline.

stress A type of response that typically involves an unpleasant state, such as anxiety or tension.

stressor Something in the external situation that is perceived as threatening or demanding and therefore produces stress.

coping response Any attempt made to avoid, escape from, or minimize a stressor.

The key to stress is the gap between the demands of the situation and our resources to cope with them. When we think we can rise to meet the challenge of a situation, there is no gap. But when too much is expected of us or when events are worrisome or scary, we perceive a discrepancy. That discrepancy might be real, or we might be imagining it. In general, positive and negative life changes are stressful. Think about the stresses of going to college, getting a job, marrying, being fired, losing a parent, winning a major award, and so on. The greater the number of changes, the greater the stress, and the more likely the stress will affect physiological states.

Stress is often divided into two types: *Eustress* is the stress of positive events. For example, you might experience eustress when you are admitted to the college you really want to attend or when you are preparing for a party you are looking forward to. *Distress* is the stress of negative events. For example, you might experience distress when you are late for an important meeting and become trapped in traffic or when you are helping a loved one deal with a serious illness.

Most people use the term *stress* only in referring to negative events, but both distress and eustress put strains on the body. The number of stressful events a person experiences, whether negative or positive, predicts health outcomes. Some events are more stressful than others, of course (**FIGURE 11.15**).

FIGURE 11.15
Stress in Everyday Life
How do you cope with the stress in your life? What makes your strategies effective?

One team of researchers assigned point values to 43 different life events. For instance, the death of a spouse was 100 points, pregnancy was 40 points, and a vacation was 13 points (Holmes & Rahe, 1967). A person's stress level could be determined by adding up the points for every event the person had experienced in the previous year. Someone who had gotten married, moved, started a new job, had a child, and had a change in sleeping pattern during the previous year would score very high on this scale and therefore be likely to suffer poor health as a result. A version of the scale for students can be found in **TABLE 11.1**.

Psychologists typically think of stressors as falling into three categories: major life stressors, chronic stress, and daily hassles. *Major life stressors* are changes or disruptions that strain central areas of people's lives (Pillow et al., 1996). Major life stressors include choices made by individuals, not just things that happen to them. For instance, some parents report that having their first child is one of the most joyful—but also one of the most taxing—experiences of their

Table 11.1 Student Stress Scale

To determine the amount of stress in your life, select the events that have happened to you in the past 12 months.

EVENT	LIFE CHANGE UNITS	EVENT	LIFE CHANGE UNITS	EVENT	LIFE CHANGE UNITS
Death of close family member	100	Serious argument with close friend	40	Change in sleeping habits	29
Death of close friend	73	Change in financial status	39	Change in social activities	29
Divorce between parents	65	Change in major	39	Lower grades than expected	29
Jail term	63	Trouble with parents	39	Change in eating habits	28
Major personal injury or illness	63	New girlfriend or boyfriend	38	Chronic car trouble	26
Marriage	58	Increased workload at school	37	Change in number of family get-togethers	26
Being fired from job	50	Outstanding personal achievement	36	Too many missed classes	25
Failing important course	47	First term in college	35	Change of college	24
Change in health of family member	45	Change in living conditions	31	Dropping more than one class	23
Pregnancy	45	Serious argument with instructor	30	Minor traffic violations	20
Sex problems	44				

SCORING

Next to each event is a score that indicates how much a person has to adjust as a result of the change. Both positive events (outstanding personal achievement) and negative events (major personal injury or illness) can be stressful because they require one to make adjustments. Add together the life change unit scores to determine how likely you are to experience illness or mental health problems as a result of the stress of these events.

300 life change units or more: A person has a high risk for a serious health change.

150–299 life change units: About 1 of every 2 people is likely to have a serious health change.

149 life change units or less: About 1 of every 3 people is likely to have a serious health change.

SOURCE: Adapted from Holmes & Rahe (1967).

lives. Nonetheless, research has shown that unpredictable and uncontrollable catastrophic events—such as earthquakes, pandemics, or wars—are especially stressful (Kanno et al., 2013; Tang, 2007). To avoid serious health problems, combat soldiers and others in prolonged stressful situations often must use combinations of strategies to cope with the stress of their situations. Coping strategies are discussed in Section 11.11.

Chronic stress is a set of ongoing challenges often linked to long-term illness, poverty, or caregiving (Cohen et al., 2012). Like major life stressors, chronic stress is most harmful when it is unpredictable and uncontrollable, and it often has grave consequences. Anyone who has a chronic disease such as asthma or Parkinson's, or has cared for someone who does, knows how feelings of anxiety and hopelessness can cloud other aspects of life (**FIGURE 11.16**). Not knowing when an attack might occur and being helpless once it starts means always being on guard. That kind of constant vigilance eventually takes a toll on the body.

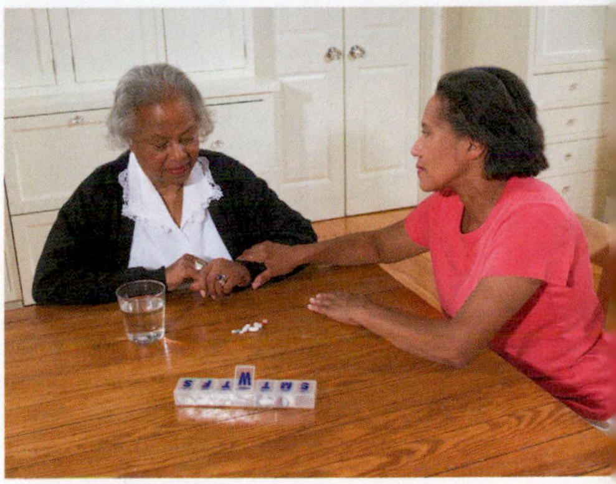

FIGURE 11.16
Chronic Stress
Caretaking can be a chronic stressor because negative events can be unpredictable and uncontrollable and can have dire consequences.

Daily hassles are small, day-to-day irritations and annoyances, such as driving in heavy traffic, dealing with difficult people, or waiting in line. Daily hassles are stressful, and their combined effects can be comparable to the effects of major life changes (DeLongis et al., 1988). Because these low-level irritations are ubiquitous, they pose a threat to coping responses by slowly wearing down personal resources. Studies that ask people to keep diaries of their daily activities find consistently that the more intense and frequent the hassles, the poorer the physical and mental health of the participant (Almeida, 2005). People might habituate to some hassles but not to others. For example, conflicts with other people appear to have a cumulative detrimental effect on health and well-being. Daily hassles can turn into chronic stressors if they happen often enough. Living in poverty or in a crowded, noisy, or polluted place is characterized by daily hassles and chronic stressors that can have cumulative detrimental effects on health and well-being (Santiago et al., 2011).

People who are members of marginalized groups experience *discrimination-related stress* throughout their lives (Goosby et al., 2018). Events ranging from overt racial hostility to microaggressions such as avoiding eye contact all contribute to discrimination-related stress. Like chronic stress, discrimination-related stress can happen anywhere and anytime. Its unpredictable and uncontrollable nature is made worse by the ambiguity of discrimination. Victims of discrimination are often left wondering whether to attribute the stressful experience to their group membership or to something else, which is its own form of daily stress. Discrimination-related stress has been documented in relation to race/ethnicity, gender identity, sexual minority status, disability, and immigration status.

Q **What is the difference between eustress and distress?**

ANSWER: Eustress is associated with positive events whereas distress is associated with negative events. Both types of stress can cause physical and mental strain.

11.8 Stress Has Physiological Components

Researchers have a good understanding of the biological mechanisms that underlie the stress response. A stressor activates two systems, triggering a fast-acting sympathetic nervous system response and a slower-acting response resulting from a complex system of biological events known as the **hypothalamic-pituitary-adrenal (HPA) axis**.

hypothalamic-pituitary-adrenal (HPA) axis A body system involved in stress responses.

Stress begins in the brain with the perception of some stressful event. For our very distant ancestors, the event might have been the sight of a predator

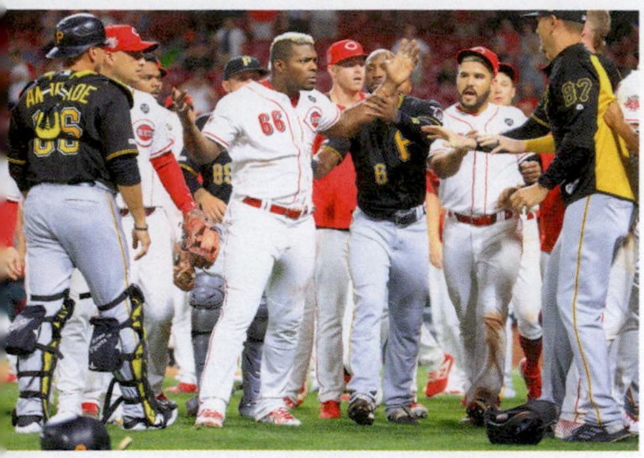

FIGURE 11.17
Fight-or-Flight Response
Players for the Cincinnati Reds and the Pittsburgh Pirates are on the verge of a brawl. If one of the players strikes, players on the other team will need to respond, such as by fighting or fleeing.

approaching rapidly. For us, it is more likely to be an approaching deadline, a stack of unpaid bills, a fight, an illness, and so on. The hypothalamus first activates the sympathetic nervous system, which activates the adrenal glands—located on top of the kidneys—to release epinephrine and norepinephrine. As described in Chapter 3, the resulting physical reaction includes increased heart rate, redistribution of the blood supply from skin and viscera (digestive organs) to muscles and brain, deepening of respiration, dilation of the pupils, inhibition of gastric secretions, and an increase in glucose released from the liver. Within seconds, the sympathetic nervous system's response to a stressor enables the organism to direct all energy to dealing with the threat at hand. Our ancestors needed that energy for either outrunning a charging predator or standing their ground and fighting it. Either response causes further stress. The physiologist Walter Cannon (1932) thus coined the term **fight-or-flight response** to describe the physiological preparation of animals to deal with an attack (**FIGURE 11.17**). From an evolutionary perspective, the ability to deal effectively with stressors is important to survival and reproduction.

fight-or-flight response The physiological preparedness of animals to deal with danger by either fighting or fleeing.

immune system The body's mechanism for dealing with invading microorganisms such as allergens, bacteria, and viruses.

Meanwhile, in the HPA axis (**FIGURE 11.18**), the hypothalamus sends a chemical message to the pituitary gland, a major gland located at the base of the brain. In turn, the pituitary gland sends a hormone that travels through the bloodstream and eventually also reaches the adrenal glands (although a different region of the glands than the faster system). The adrenals then secrete the stress hormone *cortisol*, which circulates throughout the body. In turn, cortisol increases the amount of glucose in the bloodstream and exerts other effects that mobilize fast energy sources and prepare the body for injury. For example, cortisol saves energy by slowing some processes, such as digestion, that consume resources to produce long-term gains. Cortisol also has a variety of effects on the **immune system**, the body's mechanism for dealing with invading microorganisms such as allergens, bacteria, and viruses. The effect of stress on the immune system is described in Section 11.9. All of these actions help the body prepare to respond quickly to the stressor.

FIGURE 11.18
Hypothalamic-Pituitary-Adrenal (HPA) Axis
A stressful event will set off a complex chain of responses in the body.

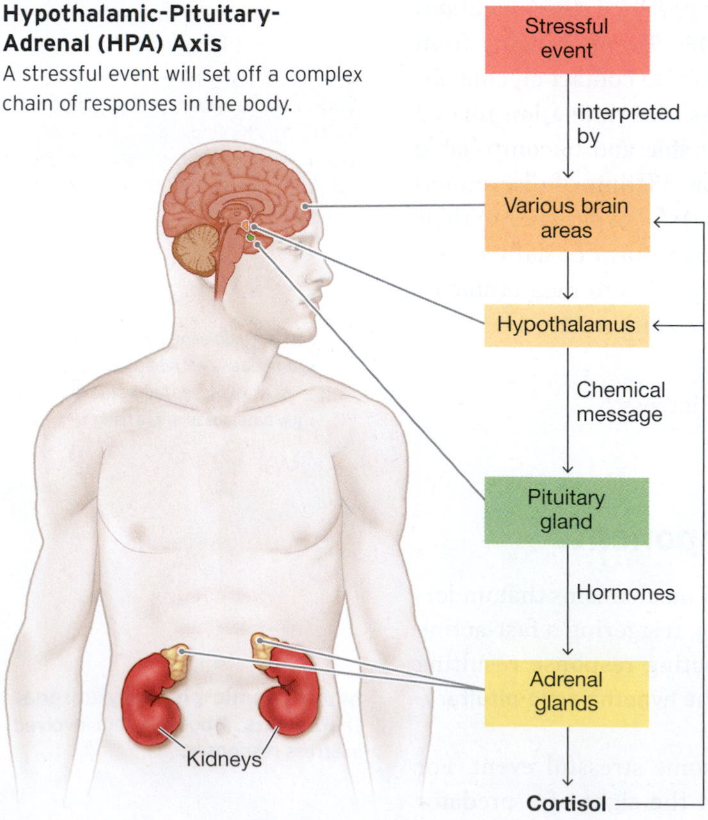

Cortisol circulates throughout the body and to various brain areas, especially the hypothalamus, hippocampus, and amygdala (de Kloet et al., 2005). The hormone has different effects on each of the brain regions. When it reaches the hypothalamus, cortisol triggers a *negative-feedback loop* to turn off the HPA axis. Like a heater shutting off when the thermostat reaches the specified temperature, the hypothalamus reduces the activity of the HPA axis when it detects circulating cortisol. Cortisol signals the hippocampus and amygdala to encode memory and process emotions related to stress.

However, prolonged stress can have paradoxical effects. Brain regions that have receptors for cortisol can become less sensitive to the effects of cortisol over time if they are exposed to it too often, like a thermostat that is activated too much and requires higher temperatures to shut off the heater. This is one way that stress can affect the body even after the stressor has been removed. Studies of stress show that, in human and nonhuman animals, excessive stress disrupts working memory, an effect that is especially noticeable when the demands on working memory are high (Oei et al., 2006; Otto et al., 2013). Chronic stress has also been associated with long-term memory impairments (McEwen, 2016). Excessive cortisol damages neurons in brain areas such as the hippocampus, which is important for storing long-term memories (Sapolsky, 1994). Stress also interferes with the ability to retrieve information from long-term memory (Finsterwald & Alberini, 2014).

GENERAL ADAPTATION SYNDROME In the early 1930s, the endocrinologist Hans Selye began studying the physiological effects of sex hormones by injecting rats with hormones from other animals. The result was damage to a number of bodily systems. Surmising that the foreign hormones must have caused this damage, Selye conducted further tests. He tried different types of chemicals, and he even physically restrained the animals to create stressful situations. Selye found that each manipulation produced roughly the same pattern of physiological changes: enlarged adrenal glands, diminished immune system function, and stomach ulcers. Together, these effects reduced the rats' ability to resist additional stressors. Selye concluded that these responses are the hallmarks of a *nonspecific stress response*. He called this pattern the **general adaptation syndrome** (Selye, 1936).

general adaptation syndrome A consistent pattern of responses to stress that consists of three stages: alarm, resistance, and exhaustion.

The general adaptation syndrome consists of three stages: alarm, resistance, and exhaustion (**FIGURE 11.19**). The *alarm stage* is the same emergency reaction as Cannon's fight-or-flight response. Physiological responses, such as the release of cortisol and epinephrine, are aimed at boosting physical abilities while reducing activities that make the organism vulnerable to infection after injury. There is a brief reduction in immune system activity during this stage, when the body is most likely to be exposed to infection and disease. But then the immune system kicks back in, and the body begins fighting back. During the *resistance stage*, the body prepares for longer, sustained defense from the stressor. Immunity to infection and disease increases somewhat as the body maximizes its defenses. When the body reaches the *exhaustion stage*, various physiological and immune systems fail. Body organs that were already weak before the stress are the first to fail.

ALLOSTATIC LOAD Building on Selye's work, the psychologist Bruce McEwen described how the wear and tear on the body from stress can add up over time with the concept of **allostatic load** (McEwen, 1998). Allostatic load refers to

allostatic load The cumulative "wear and tear" on biological systems, including the stress, digestive, immune, cardiovascular, and hormonal systems, among others, after repeated or chronic stressful events.

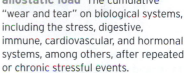

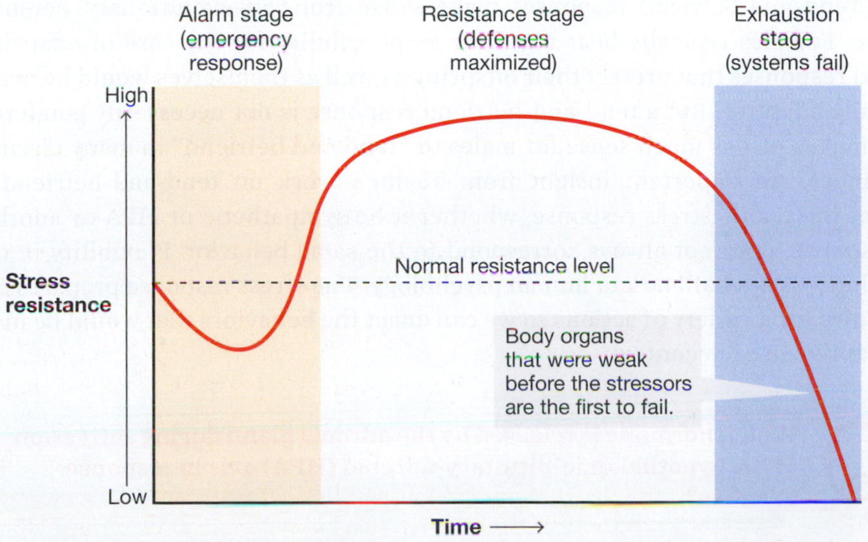

FIGURE 11.19
The General Adaptation Syndrome
Selye described three stages of physiological response to stress. As shown here, the body may progress from alarm to resistance to exhaustion.

the way biological systems, including the stress, digestive, immune, cardiovascular, and hormonal systems, among others, change after repeated or chronic stressful events. Over time, these experiences can cause the systems to become "stuck" in certain states and less responsive to changing conditions in the world. Like the villagers in the parable who learned to ignore the repeated cries for help from the boy who cried wolf—even when he eventually saw a real wolf—our body becomes resistant to the helpful effects of stress if the system cries wolf too often. Allostatic load is one way of understanding why experiencing frequent stress in early life is a risk factor for developing psychological disorders later in life (Heim et al., 2008).

Learning Tip

General adaptation syndrome and allostatic load describe similar processes, so it is easy to get them confused with each other. *General adaptation syndrome* describes the effects of one stress response cycle and how it can cause damage to bodily organs. In contrast, *allostatic load* describes the effects of accumulating stressors over several years and how the stress response system itself can become inflexible.

Emerging research also suggests that stress experienced by mothers may be passed along to their offspring through epigenetics (genetic changes due to environmental factors, which are discussed in Chapter 3). In one study, rats were exposed to unpredictable stress that led to physiological changes in their brains. These rats were mated 14 days later and subsequently had offspring. When those offspring became adults, they showed abnormalities in fear learning and heightened physiological responses to stress (Zaidan et al., 2013). Through epigenetics, the effect of stress on mothers also leads to altered social behaviors in their offspring (Franklin et al., 2011). Thus, highly stressful experiences can affect behavior across generations (Bohacek et al., 2013; Turecki & Meaney, 2016).

DIFFERENT BEHAVIORAL RESPONSES TO DIFFERENT STRESSORS The generalizability of the fight-or-flight response has been questioned by Shelley Taylor and colleagues (Taylor, 2006; Taylor et al., 2002). They argue that because the vast majority of human and nonhuman animal research has been conducted using males (females represent fewer than 1 in 5 of the participants), the results have distorted the scientific understanding of responses to stress. Taylor and colleagues argue that, in very general terms, females respond to stress by protecting and caring for their offspring, as well as by forming alliances with social groups to reduce risks to individuals, including themselves. They coined the phrase **tend-and-befriend response** to describe this pattern (**FIGURE 11.20**). Laboratory research supports the idea that stressed women are more attentive to infant distress than are stressed men (Probst et al., 2017).

FIGURE 11.20
Tend-and-Befriend Response
These students are showing a tend-and-befriend response by holding hands and comforting each other following a classroom shooting in North Carolina.

tend-and-befriend response The tendency to protect and care for offspring and form social alliances rather than fight or flee in response to threat.

Tend-and-befriend responses make sense from an evolutionary perspective. Females typically bear a greater responsibility for the care of offspring, and responses that protect their offspring as well as themselves would be maximally adaptive. But a tend-and-befriend response is not necessarily gendered. It makes just as much sense for males to "tend and befriend" in many circumstances. An important insight from Taylor's work on tend-and-befriend is that the bodily stress response, whether it be sympathetic or HPA or another response, does not always correspond to the same behavior. Flexibility in our behaviors is a hallmark of human psychology. The stress response prepares our bodies for a variety of actions so we can enact the behaviors that would be most adaptive in each context.

Q **Which hormone is released by the adrenal gland during activation of the hypothalamic-pituitary-adrenal (HPA) axis in response to stress?**

ANSWER: Cortisol is released and travels throughout the body, affecting many body systems and structures.

How Does Stress Affect Health?

Learning Objectives

- Describe how stress affects the immune system.
- Describe how stress affects the cardiovascular system.
- Discuss the association between coping differences and health.
- Distinguish between emotion-focused coping and problem-focused coping.

Although stress hormones are essential to normal health, over the long term they negatively affect health. People who have very stressful jobs—such as air traffic controllers, combat soldiers, and firefighters—tend to have many health problems that presumably are due partly to the effects of chronic stress. There is overwhelming evidence that chronic stress is associated with the initiation and progression of a wide variety of diseases, from cancer to AIDS to cardiac disease (Cohen et al., 2007; McEwen & Gianaros, 2011; Thoits, 2010). In addition, many people cope with stress by engaging in damaging behaviors. For instance, the number one reason that problem drinkers give for abusing alcohol is to cope with distress in their lives. When people are stressed, they are more likely to drink, smoke cigarettes, eat junk food, use drugs, and so on (Baumeister et al., 1994). As discussed in Section 11.1, most of the major health problems in industrialized societies are partly attributable to unhealthful behaviors, many of which occur when people feel stressed.

11.9 Stress Disrupts the Immune System

One of Hans Selye's central points was that stress alters the functions of the immune system. Allostatic load goes further to describe how repeated stress can cause permanent disruptions. Normally, when a foreign substance, such as a virus, enters the body, the immune system launches into action to destroy the invaders. As described earlier, stress can turn off the immune system to save energy for other functions that might help us survive a short-term threat. This is adaptive in small doses, but too much stress is harmful. For example, bacteria can cause stomach ulcers when the immune system is less active due to stress (Levenstein et al., 1999). More than 300 studies have demonstrated that short-term stress boosts the immune system, whereas chronic stress weakens it, leaving the body less able to deal with infection (Segerstrom & Miller, 2004).

lymphocytes Specialized white blood cells that make up the immune system; the three types are B cells, T cells, and natural killer cells.

The immune system is made up of three types of specialized white blood cells known as **lymphocytes**: *B cells*, *T cells*, and *natural killer cells* (**FIGURE 11.21**). B cells produce *antibodies*, protein molecules that attach themselves to foreign agents

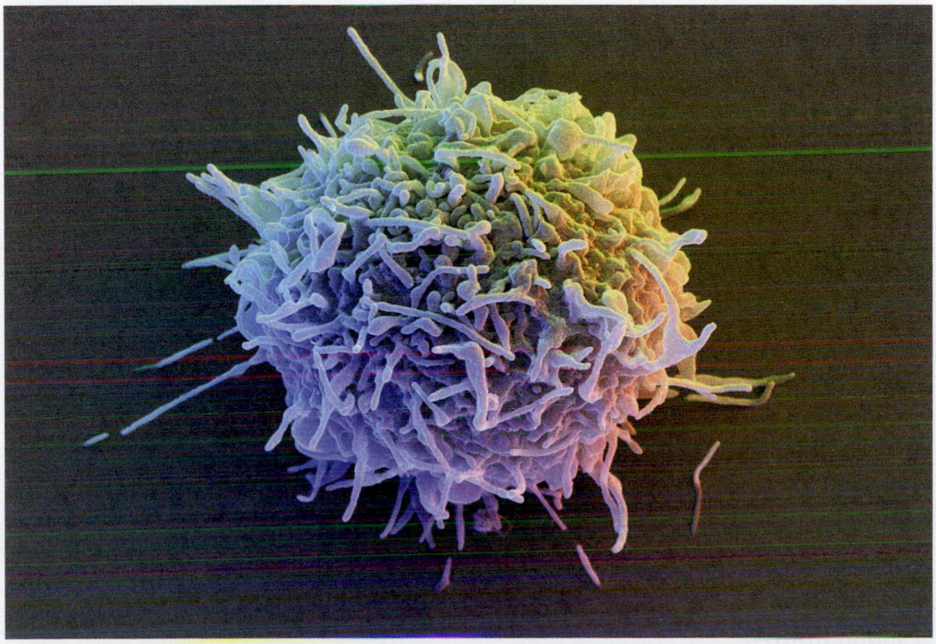

FIGURE 11.21
Lymphocytes
The immune system generates lymphocytes, which are types of white blood cells. Each lymphocyte has a specialized role in protecting against infection and disease.

and mark them for destruction. Some types of B cells remember specific invaders, making for easier identification in the future. For this reason, you have lifelong immunity to some diseases once you have been exposed to them naturally or through inoculation. The T cells assist in attacking the intruders directly and also in increasing the strength of the immune response. Natural killer cells are especially potent in killing viruses and also help attack tumors. Brief stressors, including final exams, temporarily diminish the effectiveness of white blood cells (Kiecolt-Glaser & Glaser, 1991) including natural killer cells (Kang et al., 1997), to fight off infection, in part because of a decrease in their production. The body therefore heals more slowly when people are stressed than when they are not stressed (Robles & Carroll, 2011).

In a particularly clear demonstration that stress affects the immune system, Sheldon Cohen and colleagues (1991) paid healthy volunteers to have cold viruses swabbed into their noses. Those who reported the highest levels of stress before being exposed to the cold viruses developed worse cold symptoms and higher viral counts than those who reported being less stressed. (Surprisingly, behaviors such as smoking, maintaining a poor diet, and not exercising had very small effects on the incidence of colds.) When allostatic load is high because the stress response is activated too often or too intensely, the functioning of the immune system is impaired, and the probability and severity of ill health increase (Herbert & Cohen, 1993; McEwen, 2008).

In a study that looked specifically at the effects of desirable and undesirable events on the immune system, participants kept daily diaries for up to 12 weeks (Stone et al., 1994). In the diaries, they recorded their moods and the events in their lives. They rated the events as desirable or undesirable. Each day, the participants took an antigen, a substance—in this case a protein from a rabbit—that their immune systems recognized as a threat and therefore formed antibodies against. Then the participants provided saliva samples so the researchers could examine their antibody responses. The more desirable events a participant reported, the greater the antibody production. Similarly, the more undesirable events reported, the weaker the antibody production. These and subsequent findings provide substantial evidence that perceived stress influences the immune system. Chronic stress, especially when associated with changes in social roles or identity—such as becoming a refugee, losing a job, or getting divorced—has the greatest impact on the immune system (Segerstrom & Miller, 2004).

Q **How does stress affect the lymphocytes?**

ANSWER: Stress impairs lymphocytes' ability to fight infection, in part by reducing their production.

11.10 Stress Increases the Risk of Heart Disease

Coronary heart disease is the leading cause of death for adults in the industrialized world. According to a World Health Organization (2017a) report, each year more than 17.9 million people die from heart attacks and other cardiovascular diseases (**FIGURE 11.22**). Even though the rate of heart disease is lower in women than in men, heart disease is the number one killer of women. Genetics is among the many factors that determine heart disease, but two extremely important determinants are health behaviors (such as bad eating habits, smoking, and lack of exercise) and a small number of personality traits related to the way people respond to stress.

HOSTILITY, AGGRESSION, AND HEART DISEASE One of the earliest tests of the hypothesis that personality affects coronary heart disease was an eight-and-a-half-year study conducted by the Western Collaborative Group in San Francisco beginning in 1960 (Rosenman et al., 1964). The participants were 3,500 men from Northern California who were free of heart disease at the start of the study. The men were screened annually for established risk factors such as high blood pressure, accelerated heart rate, and high cholesterol. Their overall health practices were assessed. Personal details—such as education level, medical and family history, income, and personality traits—were also assessed.

FIGURE 11.22
Heart Disease Awareness
To increase people's awareness of this growing problem, countries, cities, and local agencies use public service campaigns such as this one.

The results indicated that a set of personality traits predicted heart disease. This set of traits is now known as the **Type A behavior pattern**. Type A describes people who are competitive, achievement oriented, aggressive, hostile, impatient, and time pressed—feeling hurried, restless, and unable to relax (**FIGURE 11.23**). Men who exhibited these traits were much more likely to develop coronary heart disease than were those who exhibited noncompetitive, relaxed, and easygoing behavior. In fact, this study found that a Type A personality was as strong a predictor of heart disease as was high blood pressure, high cholesterol, or smoking (Rosenman et al., 1975). Although the initial work was done only with men, subsequent research demonstrated that these conclusions apply to women as well (Knox et al., 2004; Krantz & McCeney, 2002).

Type A behavior pattern A pattern of behavior characterized by competitiveness, achievement orientation, aggressiveness, hostility, restlessness, impatience with others, and an inability to relax.

More recently, research has shown that only certain components of the Type A behavior pattern are related to heart disease. The most toxic factor on the list is hostility. Hot-tempered people who are frequently angry, cynical, and combative are much more likely to die at an early age from heart disease (Appleton et al., 2016). Indeed, having a high level of hostility while in college predicts greater risk for heart disease later in life (Siegler et al., 2003). There is also considerable evidence that negative emotional states, especially depression, predict heart disease (Carney & Freedland, 2017). Depression is not itself a component of Type A behavior, and it is possible that having a heart condition might *make* people hostile and depressed. Still, having a hostile personality and being depressed each predicted the worsening of heart disease, so causes and effects might be connected in a vicious cycle.

The evidence across multiple studies with different indices of disease and markers for the early development of disease is clear: Hostile, angry people are at greater risk for serious diseases and earlier death than are those with more optimistic and happier personalities. This conclusion appears to extend across cultures. One cross-cultural comparative study of college students replicated the association of anger and impatience with a wide range of health symptoms for students from all ethnic and cultural groups (Nakano & Kitamura, 2001).

FIGURE 11.23
Personality Traits Predict Heart Disease
People with Type A behavior pattern are more likely to experience heart disease.

PHYSIOLOGICAL EFFECTS OF STRESS ON THE HEART Being stressed or feeling negative emotions can cause heart problems in three ways. First, people often cope with these states through behaviors that are bad for health. Second, some personality traits, such as hostility and depression, have negative effects on people's social networks, which exacerbate the effects of stress (Jackson et al., 2007). Third, negative personality traits and stress can produce direct physiological effects on the heart.

The heart pumps nearly 2,000 gallons of blood each day, on average beating more than 100,000 times. A vast network of blood vessels carries oxygen

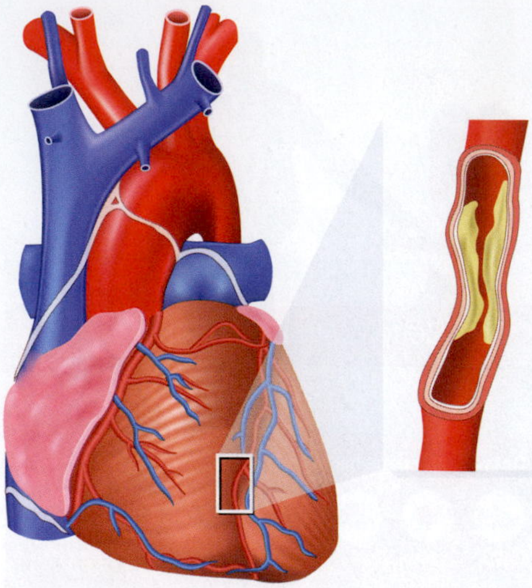

FIGURE 11.24
Heart Disease in Close-Up
Over time, plaque naturally builds up in the blood vessels around the heart, decreasing the heart's ability to function.

and nutrients throughout the body. As people age, the arteries that supply the heart and those leading from the heart become narrow due to the buildup of fatty deposits, known as plaque, and become stiff. This narrowing raises the pressure against which the heart has to pump, making the heart work harder and eventually leading to coronary heart disease (**FIGURE 11.24**).

Like aging, stress decreases blood flow by making blood vessels less able to dilate. Even doing a simple stress test, in which the participants push buttons quickly in response to particular colored lights, reduces by 50 percent the ability of blood vessels to expand, and this effect lasts for 45 minutes (Spieker et al., 2002). Blocking cortisol production prevents this dysfunction, suggesting a mechanism by which stress contributes to coronary heart disease and sudden cardiac death (Russell & Lightman, 2019).

Think about a time when you were very angry with someone. How did it feel to be so angry? Your body responded by increasing your heart rate, shutting down digestion, and moving more blood to your muscles. In short, your body acted as though you were preparing for action and possible injury. You may have seen someone turn red with anger or start to shake. People with hostile personalities frequently experience such physiological responses, and these responses take a toll on the heart. Chronic hostility can lead to the same physical symptoms as chronic stress. Over time, then, being hostile or angry causes wear and tear on the body similar to allostatic load, making the heart more likely to fail.

Q What personality and emotional characteristics increase the risk of developing heart disease?

ANSWER: Frequent negative emotional states, especially hostility, anger, and depression, increase risk of disease.

11.11 Coping Reduces the Negative Health Effects of Stress

We all experience stressful events, and over time we learn various ways to cope. Some people, for instance, use cognitive appraisals that link feelings with thoughts. Richard Lazarus (1993) conceptualized cognitive appraisal as a two-part process: People use **primary appraisals** to decide whether stimuli are stressful, benign, or irrelevant. If the stimuli are determined to be stressful, people use **secondary appraisals** to evaluate ways to respond and choose coping behaviors. Interestingly, appraising stress in this way also affects how people perceive potential stressors and their reactions to stressors in the future. Generating cognitive appraisals can help people prepare for stressful events or downplay them. Coping that occurs before the onset of a future stressor is called *anticipatory coping*. For example, when parents are planning to divorce, they sometimes rehearse how they will tell their children.

primary appraisals Part of the coping process that involves making decisions about whether a stimulus is stressful, benign, or irrelevant.

secondary appraisals Part of the coping process during which people evaluate their response options and choose coping behaviors.

TYPES OF COPING Susan Folkman and Richard Lazarus (1988) have grouped coping strategies into two general categories: emotion-focused coping and problem-focused coping. In **emotion-focused coping**, a person tries to prevent an emotional response to the stressor (**FIGURE 11.25a**). That is, the person adopts strategies to distract from or numb the pain. Such strategies include avoidance,

emotion-focused coping A type of coping in which people try to prevent having an emotional response to a stressor.

minimizing the problem or the feelings, trying to distance oneself from the outcomes of the problem, or engaging in behaviors such as overeating or drinking. Emotion-focused coping can be functional in some circumstances but maladaptive in others. Distracting oneself about the inevitable loss of a loved one, for example, can be an effective (if temporary) way to cope when it is important to continue functioning in other aspects of one's life. In contrast, if you are having difficulty at school, avoiding the problem by skipping class, minimizing the problem by telling yourself school is not all that important, or using alcohol to dull your feelings is unlikely to lead to a successful outcome. Emotion-focused strategies by definition do not solve the problem (if it is even solvable) or prevent it from recurring in the future.

By contrast, **problem-focused coping** involves taking direct steps to solve the problem: generating alternative solutions, weighing their costs and benefits, and choosing between them (**FIGURE 11.25b**). In this case, if you are having academic trouble, you might think about ways to alleviate the problem, such as arranging for a tutor or asking for an extension for a paper. Given these alternatives, you could consider how likely a tutor is to be helpful, discuss the problem with your professors, and so on. People adopt problem-focused behaviors when they perceive stressors as controllable and are experiencing only moderate levels of stress. Problem-focused behaviors can backfire when deployed against uncontrollable stressors by causing frustration and heightening the sense of loss of control.

(a)

(b)

FIGURE 11.25
Emotion-Focused Coping and Problem-Focused Coping
(a) In emotion-focused coping, we avoid the stressor, minimize it, distance ourselves, or try to escape by overeating or drinking. **(b)** In problem-focused coping, we try to address the stressor by solving problems.

problem-focused coping A type of coping in which people take direct steps to confront or minimize a stressor.

The best way to cope with stress depends on personal resources and on the situation. Most people report using both emotion-focused coping and problem-focused coping. Usually, emotion-based strategies are effective only in the short run. For example, if your partner is in a bad mood and is giving you a hard time, just ignoring them until the mood passes can be the best option. In contrast, ignoring your partner's drinking problem will not make it go away, and eventually you will need a better coping strategy. Problem-focused coping strategies work, however, only if the person with the problem can do something about the situation.

POSITIVE REAPPRAISAL Susan Folkman and Judith Moskowitz (2000) have demonstrated that, in addition to problem-focused coping, three strategies can help people use positive thoughts to deal with stress. *Positive reappraisal* is a cognitive process in which a person focuses on possible good things in the current situation. That is, the person looks for the proverbial silver lining. Another strategy is to make a *downward comparison,* comparing oneself to those who are worse off. This kind of comparison has been shown to help people cope with serious illnesses. Finally, *creation of positive events* is a strategy of giving positive meaning to ordinary events.

If you were diagnosed with diabetes, you could use all three strategies. You could focus on how having diabetes will force you to eat a healthy diet and exercise regularly (positive reappraisal). You could recognize that diabetes is not as serious as heart disease (downward comparison). You could take joy in everyday activities (creation of positive events). For example, riding a bike, watching the sunset, or savoring a recent compliment might help you focus on the positive aspects of your life and deal with your negative stress.

Another type of positive reappraisal is to think about the stress itself as adaptive. Instead of thinking of your stress response as your body panicking or "going into fight-or-flight mode," you can tell yourself that stress is your body's natural way of helping you through a difficult situation. In this light, the stress response

is the accumulated wisdom of tens of thousands of years of evolutionary learning expressed in each of our bodies. Reappraising one's own stress response as adaptive reduces the negative effects of stress (Jamieson et al., 2012), in effect making the response more adaptive!

INDIVIDUAL DIFFERENCES IN COPING People differ widely in their perceptions of how stressful life events are. Some people seem *stress resistant* because they are so capable of adapting to life changes by viewing events constructively. Suzanne Kobasa (1979) has named this personality trait *hardiness*. According to Kobasa, hardiness has three components: *commitment*, *challenge*, and *control*.

People high in hardiness are committed to their daily activities, view threats as challenges or as opportunities for growth, and see themselves as being in control of their lives. People low in hardiness typically are alienated, fear or resist change, and view events as being under external control. Numerous studies have found that people high in hardiness report fewer negative responses to stressful events (Maddi, 2013). In a laboratory experiment in which participants were given difficult cognitive tasks, people high in hardiness exhibited physiological changes that indicated active coping (Allred & Smith, 1989). Moreover, a questionnaire completed immediately after the tasks revealed that, in response to the stressors, participants high in hardiness increased the number of positive thoughts they had about themselves.

Generally, some people are more *resilient* than others, better able to cope in the face of adversity (Block & Kremen, 1996). When faced with hardships or difficult circumstances, resilient individuals bend without breaking, which allows them to bounce back quickly when bad things happen. Those who are highest in resilience can use their emotional resources flexibly to meet the demands of stressful situations (Bonanno, 2004).

In a study involving brain imaging, participants received one cue if they were about to see a threatening picture and a different cue if they were about to see a neutral picture (Waugh et al., 2008). Sometimes, however, the threat cue was followed by a neutral picture rather than a threatening picture. In resilient individuals, activity increased in brain regions associated with anxiety only when threatening pictures appeared, regardless of the cue. In individuals low in resilience, heightened brain activity occurred following the cue whether the picture was threatening or not.

Michele Tugade and Barbara Fredrickson (2004) have found that people who are resilient experience positive emotions even when under stress. According to the *broaden-and-build theory*, positive emotions cause people to expand their view of what is possible in a situation (broaden) and develop new ideas and relationships (build). This mental and social expansion helps people generate novel ways to cope with and find solutions to their problems. Thus, resilient people tend to draw on their positive emotions in dealing with setbacks or negative life experiences (Fredrickson, 2001).

Can resilience be taught? Some researchers believe that people can become more resilient by following concrete steps (Algoe & Fredrickson, 2011). The steps in this process include coming to understand when particular emotions are adaptive, learning specific techniques for regulating both positive and negative emotions, and working to build healthy social and emotional relationships with others.

Q **What are the pros and cons of using emotion-focused coping and problem-focused coping?**

ANSWER: Emotion-focused coping can help in the short term and with uncontrollable or unavoidable stressors, but it can backfire for problems that can and should be solved. Problem-focused coping can help solve the problem and avoid future problems, but it can backfire for uncontrollable stressors.

Can a Positive Attitude Keep People Healthy?

Learning Objectives

- Discuss the goals of positive psychology.
- Describe the health benefits of positive affect, social support, and spirituality.

Psychologists from the humanist school of thought focused on what is positive in the human experience. Abraham Maslow, Carl Rogers, and Erik Erikson were among the early pioneers in the field of positive psychology, although it was not known by that title then. These early humanist psychologists enjoyed the greatest success in the decades from 1950 to 1970. Other schools of thought, especially cognitive perspectives, then took the leading roles in psychology. Since the 1990s, positive psychology has enjoyed a tremendous comeback as psychologists have begun to use the methods of science to study the positive aspects of human psychology and their health benefits.

11.12 Being Positive Has Health Benefits

The modern positive psychology movement was launched by the clinical psychologist Martin Seligman. He introduced the theme during his 1998 presidential address to the American Psychological Association. Seligman and others have encouraged scientific study of qualities such as faith, values, creativity, courage, and hope (Seligman & Csikszentmihalyi, 2000). The earliest emphasis in positive psychology was on understanding what makes people authentically happy. According to positive psychologists, happiness has three components: (1) positive emotion and pleasure, (2) engagement in life, and (3) a meaningful life (Seligman et al., 2005). For example, outgoing college students high in authentic happiness might experience pleasure when interacting with other students, might be actively engaged in class discussions and course readings, and might find meaning in how the material influences their lives.

More recently, Seligman has promoted a shift away from focusing on happiness to a greater emphasis on overall well-being. In his book *Flourish* (2011), Seligman argues that a truly successful life involves not only happiness—that is, pleasure, engagement, and meaning—but also good relationships and a history of accomplishment.

The new positive psychology emphasizes the strengths and virtues that help people thrive. Its primary aim is an understanding of psychological well-being. One way to assess well-being is to ask people about various aspects of their lives, such as emotional health, quality of work environment, physical health, health behaviors, and access to food and shelter. Well-being varies across the United States. Ed Diener (2000) has also found that well-being varies across cultures. According to Diener, the wealthiest countries often have the highest levels of satisfaction. This finding fits well with Maslow's proposal that people need to satisfy basic needs such as food, shelter, and safety before they can address self-esteem needs, as discussed in Chapter 10 (**FIGURE 11.26**).

FIGURE 11.26
Well-Being in the United States
These 2018 data are from Gallup's Health and Well-Being Index. Each day, 500 people in the United States were surveyed about their lives, emotional health, work environment, physical health, healthy behaviors, and access to food and shelter. The data reveal a general pattern of people's satisfaction with their lives.

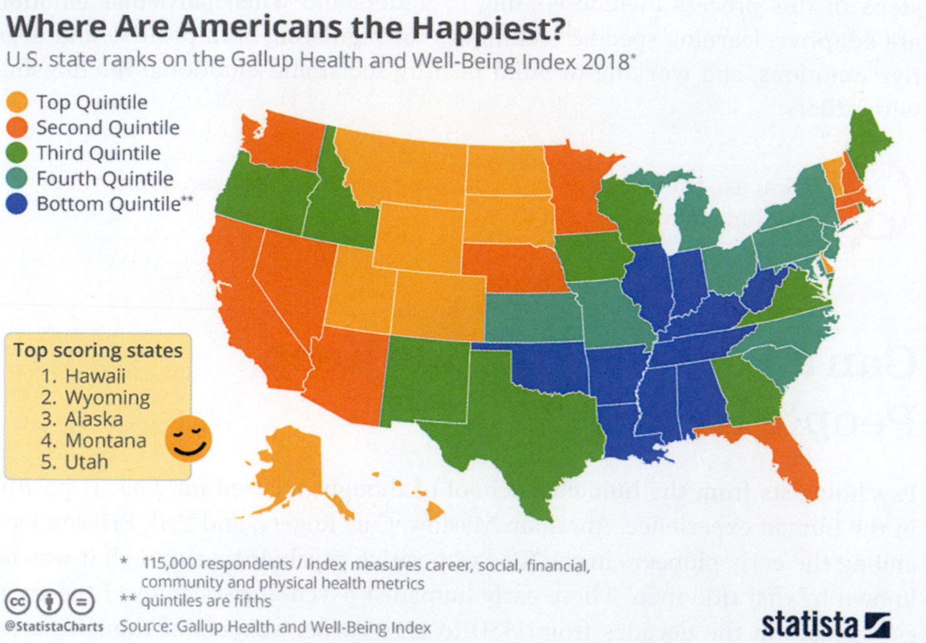

Earlier in this chapter, you read about the health consequences of negative emotions, especially hostility and stress. You may have wondered about the flip side of this relationship: Are positive emotions and well-being associated with good health?

To address this question, researchers asked more than 1,000 patients in a large medical practice to fill out questionnaires about their emotional traits (Richman et al., 2005). The questionnaires included scales that measured positive emotions (hope and curiosity) and negative emotions (anxiety and anger). Two years after receiving the questionnaires, the researchers used the patients' medical files to determine whether there was a relationship between these emotions and three broad types of diseases: high blood pressure, diabetes, and respiratory tract infections. Higher levels of hope were associated with reduced risk of these illnesses, and higher levels of curiosity were associated with reduced risk of hypertension and diabetes. These findings support the suggestion that, in general, positive emotions are related to better health.

A variety of research studies show that having a positive affect, or being generally positive, predicts living longer (Lawrence et al., 2015). For instance, optimistic people tend to be at lower risk for heart disease (Maruta et al., 2002), and happier people are consistently healthier than less-happy people (Steptoe, 2019). It is possible that happy people live longer because they have stronger immune systems (Marsland et al., 2007). People with a positive affect show enhanced immune system functioning and greater longevity than their less-positive peers (Dockray & Steptoe, 2010; Xu & Roberts, 2010). For example, they have fewer illnesses after exposure to cold and flu viruses (Cohen et al., 2006; **FIGURE 11.27**).

FIGURE 11.27
Positivity
Laughing clubs, such as this one in India, believe in laughter as therapy and a way to keep in shape.

Very few studies on positive affect and health are experimental. That means that we do not know for sure whether positive affect *causes* good health, but it may be the case. In a recent study, people who were randomly assigned to receive a treatment to boost well-being used fewer sick days over a three-month period than did people in a control group (Kushlev et al., 2020). But as mentioned earlier, it is also possible that unhappy people, such as those who are stressed, engage in more unhealthy behaviors, such as alcohol or drug use or overeating, than happy people do. Finally, it might be the case that health behaviors, such as eating a healthy diet and being physically active, cause people to be happy and healthy. The only thing we know for sure is that, across multiple studies and types of measures, positive emotions are related to considerable health benefits.

Q What is the current scientific consensus on the relationship between happiness and health?

ANSWER: Positive emotions and good health are related, but directionality and causation have not been fully determined.

11.13 Social Support Is Associated with Good Health

Social interaction is beneficial for physical and mental health. People high in well-being tend to have strong social networks and to be more socially integrated than those lower in well-being (Smith et al., 2005). People who have larger social networks—who regularly interact with more people—are less likely to catch colds (Cohen et al., 1997). Apparently, people who have more friends also live longer than those who have fewer friends.

A study that used a random sample of almost 7,000 adults found that people with smaller social networks were more likely to die during the nine-year period between assessments than were people with more friends (Berkman & Syme, 1979). This effect was strong for everyone but particularly so for women. Women with fewer friends were 2.8 times more likely to die than comparable women with more friends, and men with fewer friends were 2.3 times more likely to die than comparable men with more friends. Social support was independent of other factors, such as stated health at the time of the first contact, obesity, smoking, socioeconomic status, and physical activity. In addition, ill people who are socially isolated are likely to die sooner than ill people who are well connected to others (House et al., 1988).

The health risks of having few social connections might be attributable to chronic loneliness, which is linked with numerous psychological and health problems (Hawkley & Cacioppo, 2010). A recent report from the National Academies of Sciences, Engineering, and Medicine (NASEM, 2020) quantifies the relation between social isolation and loneliness and illness and death among older adults. The magnitude of the impact of isolation was comparable to that of high blood pressure, smoking, and obesity. To make matters worse, loneliness is on the rise in industrialized societies (Cacioppo & Cacioppo, 2018).

Social support helps people cope and maintain good health in several ways. People with social support experience less stress overall. Consider single parents who juggle job and family demands. The lack of a partner places more demands on them, thus increasing their likelihood of feeling stressed. Therefore, social support can take tangible forms, such as providing material help or assisting with daily chores. Social support is most effective, however, when the recipients of the support believe that people care about them, which can lessen the negative effects of stress. The **buffering hypothesis** proposes that when others provide emotional support, the recipient is better able to cope with stressful events (Cohen & Wills, 1985). Examples of emotional support include expressions of caring and a willingness to listen to another person's problems. Finally,

buffering hypothesis The idea that other people can provide direct emotional support in helping individuals cope with stressful events.

FIGURE 11.28
Spirituality and Well-Being
A sense of spirituality can have positive effects on well-being. That sense does not have to be connected with a particular religion.

ANSWER: Social support provides tangible assistance, creates an emotional buffer against stress and loneliness, and increases feelings of gratitude.

receiving social support can prompt feelings of gratitude, which reduces the effects of stress on health (Wood et al., 2008). Gratitude also reduces loneliness by strengthening social bonds (O'Connell & Killeen-Byrt, 2018).

SPIRITUALITY In many studies, people who are religious report greater feelings of well-being than people who are not religious. According to David Myers (2000), religious people are better at coping with crises in their lives. Their religious beliefs serve as a buffer against hard knocks. This effect may occur because people achieve and maintain well-being through the social and physical support provided by faith communities. Many religious and spiritual traditions promote a sense of gratitude, which in turn is linked with better relationships and less overall stress (Kraus et al., 2015). Many religions also support healthy behaviors, such as avoiding alcohol and tobacco.

From their faith, people also derive meaning and purpose in their lives. The positive effects are not associated with any single religion. The benefits come from a sense of spirituality that occurs across religions and the social support that comes from interacting with other people who hold similar beliefs (Nilsson, 2014; **FIGURE 11.28**). As Rabbi Harold Kushner notes, people need to feel they are "something more than just a momentary blip in the universe" (quoted in Myers, 2000, p. 64).

Q What are three ways that social support contributes to health?

PSYCHOLOGY OUTSIDE THE LAB

11.14 Can Psychology Improve Your Health?

Over the past four decades, psychologists have learned much about the complex relationships among stress, behavior, and health. A hundred years ago, people did not know that smoking is so unhealthy, that foods high in both fat and sugar contribute to cardiovascular disease, or that being under prolonged stress can damage the body. We now know that to be healthy, people need to cope with stress, regulate their emotions, and control their daily habits. The following strategies will enhance your health and well-being. Are you willing to adopt them and take control of your life?

HOW DO I KNOW THAT MY EXPERIENCE OF CONSCIOUSNESS IS THE SAME AS OTHER'S EXPERIENCES OF CONSCIOUSNESS?
WHY ARE WE HERE?
WHAT IS MY PURPOSE?
WHAT IS THE MEANING OF LIFE?

COMPLEX CARBOHYDRATES

- **Eat natural foods.** Food fads come and go, but the basic rules never change: Eat a varied diet that emphasizes natural foods (Pollan, 2013). Complex carbohydrates—such as whole grains, fruits, and vegetables—should be part of that diet, but various animal products, such as poultry or other meats, should be kept to a minimum. Avoid processed foods and fast foods, especially those with added sugars. Avoid foods containing trans-fatty acids and other artificial types of fat that prolong shelf life.
- **Eat only when you are hungry.** Eating small snacks between meals may prevent you from becoming too hungry and overeating at your next meal (Berthoud, 2006). Remember that many prepared foods are sold in large portions, which encourages overeating. Over time, the extra calories from large portions may contribute to obesity.
- **Drink alcohol in moderation, if at all.** Some research indicates that one glass of wine per day, or similar quantities of other alcohol-containing drinks, may have cardiovascular benefits

(Klatsky, 2010). But excessive alcohol consumption can cause serious health problems, including alcoholism, liver problems, some cancers, heart disease, and immune system deficiencies.

- **Keep active.** Exercise is an excellent strategy for keeping stress in check. Four times a week or more, engage in at least half an hour of moderate physical activity (Physical Activity Guidelines Advisory Committee, 2018). Moderate activity means you can feel your heart and breathing rates increase but you can still hold a conversation without becoming out of breath. This includes activities such as a brisk walk or riding a bike at three-quarters speed. Ignore the saying *No pain, no gain,* because discomfort may actually deter you from beginning to exercise. Start with moderate exercise that will not leave you breathless, and gradually increase the intensity. Look for other ways to be active, such as taking the stairs or walking to work or school.
- **Do not use tobacco.** This recommendation may seem obvious, yet every year many college students begin using tobacco. Smoking eventually produces undesirable physical effects for all smokers, such as a hacking cough, an unpleasant odor, bad breath, some cancers, and death at a younger age. Many people believe that e-cigarettes are harmless. That is false. They are likely less harmful than traditional cigarettes (though their long-term effects on health are not known), but they contain many toxic substances that can cause a range of lung diseases and cancers (NASEM, 2018).
- **Practice safe sex.** Sexually transmitted diseases (STDs) affect millions of people worldwide—including college students (Smith & Roberts, 2009). Many new HIV cases are occurring among those under age 25, who are infected through sexual activity. Despite the devastating consequences of some STDs, many young adults engage in risky sexual practices, such as not using condoms, and they are especially likely to do so when using alcohol or other drugs. Ways to avoid STDs include condom use and abstinence.
- **Learn to relax or meditate.** Daily hassles and stress can cause many health problems. For example, conditions such as insomnia can interfere with the ability to function. By contrast, relaxation exercises can help soothe the body and mind (Conklin et al., 2019). Seek help from trained counselors who can teach you these methods, such as using biofeedback to measure your physiological activity so you can learn to control it. You might also try a relaxing activity, such as yoga or meditation (for instructions on performing mindfulness meditation, see Chapter 4).
- **Build a strong support network.** Friends and family can help you deal with much of life's stress, from daily frustrations to serious catastrophes. Avoid people who encourage you to act in unhealthy ways or are threatened by your efforts to be healthy. Instead, find people who share your values, who understand what you want from life, and who can listen and provide advice, assistance, or simply encouragement (Hornstein & Eisenberger, 2018).
- **Try some happiness exercises.** Each of the following exercises may enhance your happiness by helping you focus on positive events and more positive explanations of troubling events (Lyubomirsky et al., 2005).

1. In the next week, write a letter of gratitude and deliver it (preferably in person) to someone who has been kind to you but whom you have not fully thanked.
2. Once a week, write down three things that went well that day and explain why they went well.

3. Tell a friend about a time when you did your very best, and then think about the strengths you displayed. Reflect on this story every night for the next week.
4. Imagine yourself 10 years in the future as your best possible self, as having achieved all your most important goals. Describe in writing what your life is like and how you got there.
5. Keep a journal in which you write about the positive aspects of your life. Reflect on your health, freedom, friends, and so on.
6. Act like a happy person. Sometimes just going through the motions of being happy will create happiness.

Activities such as these are called "shotgun interventions" because they are fast acting, cover a broad range of behaviors, have relatively large effects for such a small investment, and pose little risk. However, the long-term effects of the interventions are unknown. ■

Q How might writing a thank-you note improve your health?

ANSWER: It can increase feelings of gratitude and improve social connections, both of which have been linked to positive health outcomes.

Your Chapter Review

Want to earn a better grade on your test?

It's time to complete your study experience! Go to **INQUIZITIVE** to practice actively with this chapter's concepts and get personalized feedback along the way.

Chapter Summary

What Affects Health?

11.1 Social Context, Biology, and Behavior Combine to Affect Health Health is influenced by a mixture of biological, psychological, and social processes. At the psychological level, how we think, feel, and behave can cause or prevent illness. At the social level, our relationships with other people, the communities we live in, and the cultures we participate in all affect health. The leading causes of death in industrialized societies are influenced by lifestyle choices. Overeating, smoking, and lack of exercise contribute to most major causes of death in developed nations.

11.2 Inequities in Societies Contribute to Health Disparities Among Social Groups Health disparities are evident among different racial and ethnic groups. Cultural factors such as preferences for certain foods can contribute to disparities. Systemic racial discrimination embeds disparities in society because of differential access to medicine, healthy food, and clean and safe outdoor spaces. Disparities exist not only among racial groups but also between immigrants and native-born people in the United States and between people with more versus fewer social and economic resources.

11.3 Healthy Eating Is an Important Health Behavior Controllable behaviors contribute to major illnesses such as heart disease and cancer. A healthy diet, consisting of natural, plant-based foods in moderate quantities, can protect health. Processed foods, large portions, and high-sugar foods can harm health. Societal factors, such as the availability of sugar-sweetened beverages, can influence the dietary health of the people in the society.

11.4 Smoking Is a Leading Cause of Death Smoking continues to be a major health concern. Individuals typically begin smoking in adolescence as a consequence of social influences or in an effort to exhibit the positive qualities sometimes associated with smokers, such as toughness and independence. Quitting is difficult because the nicotine in cigarettes is powerfully addictive. Even in the most effective programs, only 10–30 percent of smokers are able to quit over the long term.

11.5 Physical Activity Is a Particularly Beneficial Health Behavior Exercise is one of the best things people can do for their health. Regular physical activity improves memory and cognition, strengthens the heart and lungs, and enhances mental and emotional states. Exercise is healthy in any amount or duration and at any age.

11.6 You Be the Psychologist: Why Are People Afraid of Flying but Not of Driving (or Smoking)? People generally fear the wrong things, such as airplane crashes, being victims of terrorism, and catching rare diseases. The vast majority of deaths worldwide are due to cancer and heart disease, both of which are heavily influenced by lifestyle factors. Because of the availability heuristic, when people think about death, the thoughts that come most easily to mind are those most reported by the media. However, these events tend to be so rare that they do not pose threats to most people.

What Is Stress?

11.7 Stress Is a Response to Life Events Stress is a response that usually involves an unpleasant state. Stressors are situations that are perceived as threatening or demanding beyond a person's available resources or capacity to cope. They include major life changes, chronic stress, and daily hassles. People who are members of underrepresented groups also experience discrimination-related stress.

11.8 Stress Has Physiological Components The hypothalamic-pituitary-adrenal (HPA) axis is a complex series of biological events that responds to stress over longer periods. The sympathetic nervous system responds to stress by releasing epinephrine and norepinephrine into the bloodstream for immediate action. The hypothalamus sends a signal to the pituitary gland, which causes the adrenal gland to release cortisol. The hypothalamus "turns off" the stress response when it detects that cortisol has begun circulating in the body. Hans Selye's general adaptation syndrome identifies three stages of physiological coping: alarm, resistance, and exhaustion. Allostatic load describes how the stress response system can change in harmful ways after repeated stress. Stress does not prompt specific behaviors (such as fight, flight, tend, or befriend) but rather prepares the body for action and repair.

How Does Stress Affect Health?

11.9 Stress Disrupts the Immune System Stress alters the functions of the immune system. Specifically, stress decreases the production of lymphocytes: B cells, T cells, and natural killer cells. Fewer lymphocytes mean the body is less able to fight off infection and illness.

11.10 Stress Increases the Risk of Heart Disease Individuals who are hostile, are depressed, or exhibit a Type A behavior pattern (competitive, achievement oriented, aggressive, and impatient) are more susceptible to heart disease than people who are easygoing and accommodating. Presumably, the hostile and aggressive personality factors increase the frequency of negative physiological responses that adversely affect the heart.

11.11 Coping Reduces the Negative Health Effects of Stress Cognitive appraisals of potential stressors and the coping strategies that are used can alleviate the experience of stress or minimize its harmful effects. Emotion-focused coping strategies are attempts to prevent an emotional response by avoiding the stressor, minimizing the problem, or engaging in behaviors to try to forget, such as overeating or drinking. Problem-focused coping strategies involve taking direct steps to confront or minimize a stressor—for example, establishing alternatives and engaging in behaviors to solve the problem. Reappraisal is a change of thoughts or beliefs about the situation or the stress response itself. Some people are more adept at coping than others, and effective coping strategies can be taught.

Can a Positive Attitude Keep People Healthy?

11.12 Being Positive Has Health Benefits Positive psychology is concerned with the scientific study of the strengths and virtues that contribute to psychological well-being. A number of studies have shown that people who are positive are generally healthier and live longer than their more negative counterparts. The data on the relation between positivity and health are correlational, so it is not known whether positivity *causes* health, health causes positivity, or some other factor, such as healthy behaviors, causes them both.

11.13 Social Support Is Associated with Good Health Social support and being socially integrated in a group are also protective health factors because concerned others provide material and emotional support. Conversely, social isolation and loneliness are particularly harmful to health. Spirituality and gratitude contribute to better health. Well-being is increased for spiritual people, likely because of the support received from faith communities, the health behaviors that are promoted by religions, and the sense of meaning that can be derived from religious beliefs.

11.14 Psychology Outside the Lab: Can Psychology Improve Your Health? People can follow many strategies for living a healthy life, primarily by avoiding things science has shown to be bad for us (e.g., high-sugar foods, excessive alcohol, tobacco use, unsafe sex) and engaging in behaviors known to benefit health (e.g., exercising, relaxing, meditating). Happiness exercises have been shown to help people cope with the stress in their lives.

Key Terms

allostatic load, p. 427
biopsychosocial model, p. 412
buffering hypothesis, p. 437
coping response, p. 423
emotion-focused coping, p. 432
fight-or-flight response, p. 426
general adaptation syndrome, p. 427
health behaviors, p. 417
health disparities, p. 414
health psychology, p. 412
hypothalamic-pituitary-adrenal (HPA) axis, p. 425
immigrant paradox, p. 416
immune system, p. 426
lymphocytes, p. 429
primary appraisals, p. 432
problem-focused coping, p. 433
secondary appraisals, p. 432
socioeconomic status, p. 416
stress, p. 423
stressor, p. 423
tend-and-befriend response, p. 428
Type A behavior pattern, p. 431
well-being, p. 412

Practice Exercises

1. Which model guides health psychologists' current understanding of health and illness?
   a. biomedical
   b. biopsychosocial
   c. moral
   d. self-efficacy
2. Which of the following does *not* contribute to health disparities between White people and members of other racial and ethnic groups?
   a. the tendency of people in marginalized groups to live in communities with more pollutants and toxins
   b. racial discrimination among health care providers
   c. reduced access to high-quality health care and nutritious foods in some areas
   d. discrimination-related stress
   e. the lack of acculturation of first-generation immigrants
3. How do the number of food options and portion size influence the likelihood of overeating?
   a. More options and larger portions increase the likelihood of overeating.
   b. Fewer options and smaller portions increase the likelihood of overeating.
   c. Fewer options and larger portions increase the likelihood of overeating.
   d. More options and smaller portions increase the likelihood of overeating.
4. Which statement is true regarding e-cigarettes and traditional cigarettes?
   a. The negative health outcomes associated with both e-cigarettes and traditional cigarettes are minimal.
   b. Both e-cigarettes and traditional cigarettes are addictive due to the presence of nicotine.
   c. E-cigarettes do not have chemicals while traditional cigarettes do.
   d. People start smoking traditional cigarettes, but not e-cigarettes, for social reasons.
5. Label each of the following statements about stress as true or false.
   a. Stress is always bad.
   b. Stress is always beneficial.
   c. The human stress response is an adaptation to help us deal with challenges in our environment.
   d. Cortisol signals to the hypothalamus to increase the activity of the HPA axis.
   e. Allostatic load increases over time and eventually makes the stress response less flexible.
   f. The stress response can increase some aspects of immune function while decreasing others.
   g. Humans all respond to stress in the same way.
6. True or false: Mothers' highly stressful experiences can affect their offspring's behavior across generations, even if the stress occurs before pregnancy.
7. Chronic stress can have which of the following physiological consequences?
   a. damage to neurons in the hippocampus, leading to memory problems
   b. decreased numbers of lymphocytes, or white blood cells, leading to immune system problems
   c. increased blood pressure and constriction of blood vessels in the heart
   d. all of the above
8. Match each statement with one of the following coping mechanisms: emotion-focused coping, problem-focused coping, positive reappraisal, downward comparison.
   a. "I wish my family wasn't moving, but I'll get a chance to explore a new region of the country."
   b. "My hours at work may have been cut, but at least I didn't lose my job like other people did."
   c. "I'm not getting along with my roommate, so I'll avoid being home much."
   d. "I'd better schedule an appointment with the professor to improve my grades."
9. Identify all of the following that are *not* true regarding well-being and religiousness?
   a. Religiousness is correlated with lower levels of well-being.
   b. The social and community connections from religion benefit well-being.
   c. Higher levels of religiosity in Judaism and Buddhism, but not other religions, correlate to well-being.
   d. The sense of purpose and meaning from religion benefit well-being.
   e. Health behaviors prescribed by religion benefit well-being.
10. Identify the health behaviors that tend to improve health and well-being:
    a. Always eat big meals, even if you don't feel hungry.
    b. Pair sex with alcohol, to avoid social awkwardness.
    c. Write a letter of gratitude to someone you have not properly thanked.
    d. Learn to meditate.
    e. Keep a journal of positive events in your life.
    f. Eat a diet of natural, unprocessed foods.
    g. Smoke e-cigarettes for the social connection.

BLACK LIVES MATTER
Amadou Diallo
Philando Castile
Jordan Davis
Stephon Clark
Angel Unique
Breonna Taylor
Daunte Wright
Tyre King
Dominique Williams
Trayford Pellerin
Deon Kay
Donovan Lynch
Alton Sterling
Sandra Bland
George Floyd
Rayshard Brooks
Jacob Blake
JUSTICE

12 Social Psychology

Big Questions

ONE DAY WHILE WALKING DOWN THE STREET, you notice two people looking up at a window on the eighth floor of a building. Other passersby begin to stop and look, too. Instinctively, you look up. After all, there must be something interesting up there. Why else would people be looking? At this point, many people are stopped on the sidewalk to look at—nothing.

What happened? Why is an entire crowd of people doing something so silly? As a highly social species, humans are readily influenced by the actions of others. The subfield of social psychology is concerned with how real or imagined others influence our thoughts, feelings, and actions. Humans depend on one another for survival, so almost every human activity has a social dimension. Research in social psychology covers expansive and varied territory: how people perceive and understand others, how people function in groups, why people hurt or help others, why people stigmatize and discriminate against certain others, why people fall in love. In this chapter, you will learn the basic principles of how people interact with one another.

Learning Objectives

- Describe the advantages and disadvantages of groups.
- Explain factors that determine ingroup and outgroup formation.
- Describe the effects of group membership on social identity and on brain activity.
- Define group polarization, groupthink, social facilitation, social loafing, and deindividuation.
- Differentiate between conformity and obedience.

How Does Group Membership Affect People?

From our first moments as infants to our development during childhood and adolescence, through our first romantic relationships and the bonds that form our families, to our ability to thrive during old age, humans depend on one another. Each human need that we have, from food and shelter to belonging and meaning, is served by being connected to other people in relationships and as part of a society. For these reasons, social psychologists have labeled humans *the social animal* (Aronson, 1972). We are creatures that evolved to live in groups, so we have adapted in ways that help us get along, fit in, and thrive in group contexts.

We need these adaptations because group membership can be tricky. It is not always obvious, for instance, what our group expects of us in each situation. The *social brain hypothesis* (Dunbar, 1998, 2014) places such challenges in the context of brain size. Humans belong to the order Primates, which includes great apes and monkeys. According to the social brain hypothesis, primates have large brains—in particular, large prefrontal cortices—because they live in complex social groups that change over time (**FIGURE 12.1**). Being a good group member requires the capacity to understand complex and subtle social rules, recognize when actions might offend others, and control desires to engage in behaviors that might violate group norms.

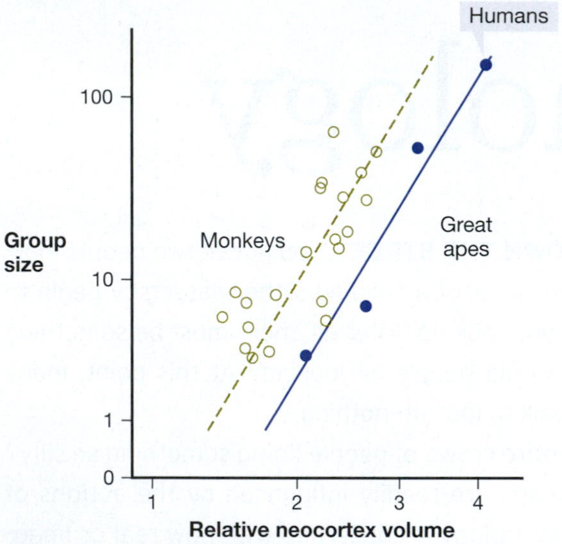

FIGURE 12.1
Social Brain Hypothesis
Most of the cerebral cortex consists of its outer layer, known as the neocortex. According to the social brain hypothesis, the size of a primate species' standard social group is related to the volume of that species' neocortex. Here, each open circle represents a species within the monkey family, and each solid circle represents a species within the great ape family. In terms of neocortex size, great apes may lie on a separate line from monkeys because they need more cognitive resources to support group living. Humans are at the pinnacle of the great apes in terms of neocortex and average group size.

12.1 People Favor Their Own Groups

Social groups, or coalitions, are prevalent in some primate species, such as chimpanzees, and in other social mammals, such as dolphins. Humans automatically and pervasively form groups, and they are powerfully connected to the groups they belong to: sororities and fraternities, sports teams, families, and cultural groups. People cheer on their own groups, fight for them, and sometimes are even willing to die for them (Swann et al., 2014). Those groups to which particular people belong are *ingroups*; those to which they do not belong are *outgroups* (**FIGURE 12.2**). Different groups may compete for the same limited resources. Alternatively, other groups may be able to supply needed resources, as in trade, or to cooperate in attaining the resources.

FORMING INGROUPS AND OUTGROUPS People are especially likely to organize themselves into groups when two conditions are met (Gray et al., 2014). One condition is *reciprocity*, meaning that people treat others as others treat them. In other words, if you scratch my back, I will scratch yours. Another condition is *transitivity*, meaning that people generally share their friends' opinions of other people. Transitivity is exactly the same as the social triangles in Fritz Heider's balance theory (see Chapter 10). If Mac and Dennis are friends, then if Mac likes Charlie and dislikes Dee, Dennis will also tend to like Charlie and dislike Dee.

The social psychologist Kurt Gray and colleagues (2014) developed a computer program—think *SimCity*—where simulated characters interacted in a game that involved simple rules of reciprocity and transitivity. The rules were so simple that the program consisted of only 80 lines of code, whereas most programs include thousands or millions of lines. After 10,000 rounds of interaction, the simulated characters formed into stable groups that showed similar properties to actual

FIGURE 12.2
Ingroups and Outgroups
In this photo from the 2014 World Cup in soccer, it is easy to tell Brazilian supporters (in yellow) from Chilean supporters (in red).

human groups. This research shows that ingroups and outgroups can be formed based on minimal rules of social interaction.

Beginning in infancy, humans readily differentiate between ingroups and outgroups (Quinn et al., 2019). Once people categorize others as ingroup or outgroup members, they treat those others in a predictable set of ways. For instance, people tend to view outgroup members as less varied than ingroup members. This tendency is called the **outgroup homogeneity effect**. People from different racial groups notice more variation among members of their own race and less variation among people of other races (the so-called "they all look alike" effect). The same is true for other types of groups, such as schools (University of Missouri students may think that University of Kansas students are all alike, and vice versa). People also show a positivity bias for ingroup members, such as rating their smiles as indicating greater happiness than similar smiles by outgroup members (Lazerus et al., 2016).

outgroup homogeneity effect The tendency to view outgroup members as less varied than ingroup members.

SOCIAL IDENTITY THEORY Group memberships are an important part of social identities, and they contribute to each group member's overall sense of self-esteem (Hogg, 2012). According to **social identity theory** (Tajfel, 1982; Tajfel & Turner, 1979), people not only identify with certain groups but also value those groups and in doing so experience pride through their group membership. Whether your pride is in your school, your cultural group, your country, or some other social group, defining yourself by that group status is part of your social identity.

social identity theory The idea that ingroups consist of individuals who perceive themselves to be members of the same social category and experience pride through their group membership.

As people define themselves as members of groups, they begin to learn, mimic, and eventually internalize the ways other group members behave toward both ingroup and outgroup members (Hogg, 2016). **Ingroup favoritism** is one of the most consistent features of categorizing people as ingroup or outgroup members. People give preferential treatment to ingroup members—for example, by doing them more favors and being more willing to forgive their mistakes—compared with outgroup members. The simulated individuals in Gray and colleagues' (2014) study, mentioned earlier, showed this kind of behavior. Ingroup favoritism in society at large is one reason that some groups enjoy higher levels of status, power, and resources than others. For instance, there is a substantial wealth gap between White and Black Americans that has not improved over the past 40 years (Kraus et al., 2017).

ingroup favoritism The tendency for people to evaluate favorably and privilege members of the ingroup more than members of the outgroup.

The power of group membership is so strong that people exhibit ingroup favoritism even if the difference between the groups is arbitrary. Henri Tajfel and John Turner (1979) randomly assigned volunteers to two groups using meaningless criteria such as flipping a coin. This procedure is known as the *minimal group paradigm* (**FIGURE 12.3**). Participants were then tasked with dividing up money between the groups. Not surprisingly, they gave more money to their ingroup members. But people also tried to prevent the outgroup members from receiving any money. These effects occurred even when the participants were explicitly reminded that the basis of group membership was arbitrary and that giving money to the outgroup would not affect how much money their own group obtained.

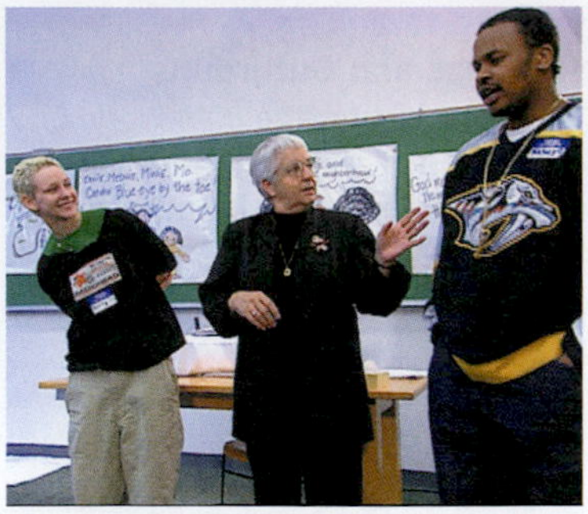

FIGURE 12.3
Minimal Groups
People show ingroup favoritism even when the groups are arbitrary. In 1968, third-grade teacher Jane Elliott divided her class into the blue-eyed and brown-eyed children. She noted that they soon came to demonstrate all the signs of ingroup favoritism.

Why do people favor members of their own groups? One possibility is that people who work together to keep resources within a group and deny resources to outgroup members have a selective advantage over those who are willing to share with the outgroup. Another possibility is that group membership is so important to us that we are willing to hurt people in outgroups as a way of signaling how much we value the people in our ingroup.

BRAIN ACTIVITY ASSOCIATED WITH GROUP MEMBERSHIP Being a good group member requires recognizing and following the group's social rules. When members violate these rules, they risk exclusion from the group. As noted in Chapter 10, group exclusion could be fatal in the ancestral environment. People therefore need to be able to understand what other group members are thinking, especially how others are thinking about them.

The middle region of the prefrontal cortex, called the medial prefrontal cortex, is important for thinking about other people—thinking about them generally or specifically, whether they are in ingroups or outgroups (Lieberman et al., 2019). Activity in this region is also associated with the ingroup bias that emerges after assignment through the minimal group paradigm (Volz et al., 2009). The medial prefrontal cortex is less active when people consider members of outgroups, at least members of extreme outgroups such as people who are homeless or drug addicts (Harris & Fiske, 2006). One explanation for these differences in brain activity is that people see ingroup members as more human than outgroup members (Hackel et al., 2014). The psychologists Phillip Atiba Goff and Jennifer Eberhardt and their colleagues have studied the devastating consequences of *dehumanization* in the criminal justice system of Black Americans, who are more likely to be arrested and tried and to receive harsher punishments than are White Americans (Goff et al., 2008; Hetey & Eberhardt, 2014; **FIGURE 12.4**).

FIGURE 12.4
Phillip Atiba Goff
Phillip Atiba Goff is a professor of African American studies and psychology at Yale whose research focuses on racial disparities in the criminal justice system that stem in part from dehumanization of Black Americans.

Other brain regions are differentially active when we consider ingroup versus outgroup members (Cikara & Van Bavel, 2014). For example, regions linked with pain are more active when we see an ingroup (versus an outgroup) member harmed (Xu et al., 2009). Feeling empathy for outgroup members can reduce this difference (Cikara et al., 2014; Maister et al., 2013).

Q What conditions must be met for humans to form groups and favor ingroups over outgroups?

ANSWER: Even meaningless assignment to groups can produce ingroup favoritism. Ingroup and outgroup differentiation is intensified when reciprocity and transitivity are present.

12.2 Groups Influence Individual Behavior

Given the importance of groups, it is not surprising that people's thoughts, emotions, and actions are strongly influenced by their desire to be good group members. The desire to fit in with the group and avoid being ostracized is so great that under some circumstances people willingly engage in behaviors they otherwise would condemn. As noted throughout this chapter, the power of the social situation is much greater than most people believe—and this truth is perhaps the single most important lesson from social psychology.

GROUP DECISION MAKING Being in a group influences decision making in complex ways. On the one hand, the psychologist James Stoner (1968) noted the *risky-shift effect*: Groups often make riskier decisions than individuals do. It accounts for why corporate boards, for example, might make relatively risky investments that none of the members would have tried alone. On the other hand, groups can sometimes become more cautious. The initial attitudes of group members determine whether the group becomes riskier or more cautious. If most of the group members are somewhat cautious, then the group becomes even more cautious. This tendency is known as **group polarization** (Myers & Lamm, 1976). For example, when a jury discusses a case, the discussion tends to make individual jurors believe more strongly in their initial opinions about a defendant's guilt or innocence. When groups make decisions, they usually choose the course of action that was initially favored by the majority of individuals in the group. Through mutual persuasion, the decision-making individuals come to agreement.

group polarization The process by which initial attitudes of groups become more extreme over time.

Sometimes group members are particularly concerned with preserving the group and maintaining its cohesiveness. Therefore, for the sake of politeness, the group may end up making a bad decision. In 1972, the social psychologist Irving Janis coined the term **groupthink** to describe this extreme form of group polarization. Groupthink typically occurs when a group is under intense pressure, is facing external threats, and is biased in a particular direction to begin with. The group does not carefully process all the information available to it, dissent is discouraged, and group members assure each other they are doing the right thing.

groupthink The tendency of a group to make a bad decision as a result of preserving the group and maintaining its cohesiveness; especially likely when the group is under intense pressure, is facing external threats, and is biased in a particular direction.

Consider some contemporary examples of groupthink: Before the 2016 U.S. presidential election, consensus emerged in the news media, particularly among the left-leaning outlets, that presidential candidate Hillary Clinton was extremely likely to win. For instance, the *Huffington Post* (*Election 2016 Forecast*, 2016) estimated Clinton's chances of winning at 98.2 percent. Journalists became increasingly certain of this result as Election Day drew near. Only after Clinton lost did it become clear that the media had collectively downplayed the role of polling errors, the unusual nature of Clinton's opponent, and foreign interference in the election. Groupthink may also have been evident in many decisions made during the 2020 coronavirus pandemic. For instance, Republican leaders flouted the safety guidelines of their own advisers when they gathered indoors without masks to celebrate the nomination of Judge Amy Coney Barrett to the U.S. Supreme Court. At least a dozen people, including the president, were diagnosed with the coronavirus following the event. University administrators, corporate executives, and even parents made similar risky decisions throughout the world.

To prevent groupthink, leaders must refrain from expressing their opinions too strongly at the beginning of discussions. The group should be encouraged to consider alternative ideas, either by having someone play devil's advocate or by purposefully examining outside opinions. Carefully going through alternatives and weighing the pros and cons of each can help people avoid groupthink. Of course, a group can make a bad decision even without falling victim to groupthink. Other factors, such as political values, can bias a group's decision making. The main point behind the concept of groupthink is that group members sometimes go along with bad decisions to protect group harmony.

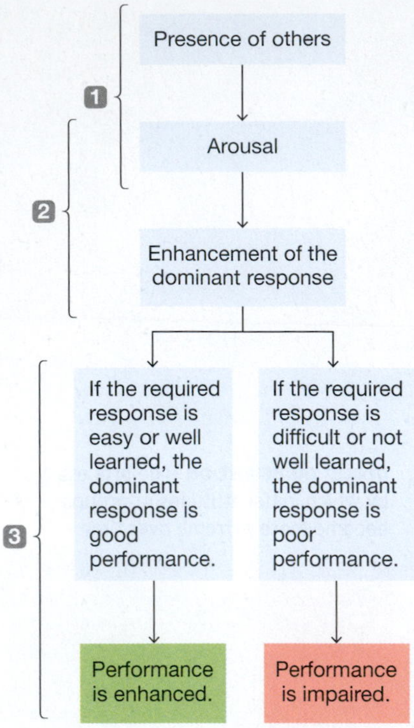

FIGURE 12.5
Zajonc's Model of Social Facilitation
According to this model, the mere presence of others leads to increased arousal. The arousal favors the dominant response (the response most likely to be performed in the situation). If the required response is easy or well learned, performance is enhanced. If the required response is novel or not well learned, performance suffers.

SOCIAL FACILITATION The first social psychology experiment was conducted in 1897. Through that experiment, Norman Triplett showed that bicyclists pedal faster when they ride with other people than when they ride alone. They do so because of **social facilitation**. That is, the presence of others generally enhances performance. Social facilitation also occurs in other animals, including horses, dogs, rats, birds, fish, and even cockroaches.

Robert Zajonc (1965) proposed a model of social facilitation that involves three basic steps (**FIGURE 12.5**). According to Zajonc, all animals are genetically predisposed to become aroused by the presence of others of their own species. Why? Others are associated with most of life's rewards and punishments. Zajonc then invoked Clark Hull's well-known learning principle: Arousal leads animals to exhibit a dominant response—that is, the response most likely to be performed in the situation. In front of food, for example, the dominant response is to eat.

Zajonc's model predicts that social facilitation can either improve or impair performance. The change depends on whether the response that is required in a situation is the individual's dominant response. If the required response is easy or well learned (such as shooting a free throw for a professional basketball player), so that the dominant response is good performance, the presence of others will enhance performance. If the required response is novel or less well learned (such as shooting a half-court shot for a novice), so that the dominant response is poor performance, the presence of others will further impair performance. These effects help explain why crowds of spectators distract professional golfers less than they distract novice golfers. The professionals practice so often that hitting a good shot is their dominant response. Therefore, the professionals may be even more likely to hit well in the presence of spectators. In keeping with this principle, when you need to make a public presentation, try to practice your speech repeatedly so that it becomes easy for you—your dominant response.

SOCIAL LOAFING In some cases, people do not work as hard when in a group as when working alone. This effect is called **social loafing**, and it occurs when people's efforts are pooled so that individuals do not feel personally responsible for the group's output. In a classic study, six blindfolded people wearing headphones were told to shout as loudly as they could. Some were told they were shouting alone. Others were told they were shouting with other people. Participants did not shout as loudly when they believed that others were shouting as well (Latané et al., 1979).

When people know that their individual efforts can be monitored, they do not engage in social loafing. Therefore, if a group is working on a project, each person must feel personally responsible for some component of the project for everyone to exert maximum effort (Williams et al., 1981).

DEINDIVIDUATION People can sometimes lose their individuality when they become part of a group. **Deindividuation** occurs when people are not self-aware and therefore are not paying attention to their personal standards. When self-awareness disappears, so do the usual restraints that guide our behavior. Deindividuated people often do things they would not do if they were alone. People are most often *individuated*, meaning we walk around with a sense of ourselves as individuals who are responsible for our own actions. But there are situations that can cause us to lose that sense of being a moral actor. People are especially likely to become deindividuated when they are aroused and anonymous and when

social facilitation The idea that the presence of others generally enhances performance.

social loafing The tendency for people to work less hard in a group than when working alone.

deindividuation A state of reduced individuality, reduced self-awareness, and reduced attention to personal standards; this phenomenon may occur when people are part of a group.

responsibility is diffused (Diener, 1977). Rioting by fans, looting following disasters, and other mob behaviors are the products of deindividuation.

When our sense of identity is lost, we tend to act according to the expectations of the situation or the people around us. In this way, deindividuation can cause extreme behavior in situations where people believe it is allowed. The sadistic behavior of army guards who tortured Iraqi soldiers at Abu Ghraib prison and police violence against peaceful protesters are examples of how deindividuation can accelerate aggression (**FIGURE 12.6**). The individuals involved make conscious decisions to commit these acts, but they are also caught up in a loss of identity that can influence actions in extreme ways. Deindividuation occurs frequently on the internet. People using anonymous accounts harass others and attack people based on group membership, such as in the racist "Zoom bomb" attacks that occurred during the coronavirus pandemic. Anti-Asian racism, harassment, and discrimination also increased during this period (Misra et al., 2020), fueled in part by hateful messages spread by deindividuated people.

FIGURE 12.6
Deindividuation Can Cause Extreme Behavior
Law enforcement officers committed violence against peaceful protesters at a Black Lives Matter rally. The officers are deindividuated by their uniforms, their numbers, their level of arousal, and reduced expectations of accountability.

Not all deindividuated behavior is so serious, of course. Gamblers cheering each other on in crowded casinos, fans doing the wave, and people dancing the funky chicken while inebriated at a wedding are most likely in deindividuated states. In one study, people who felt deindividuated because they wore a nurse's uniform that hid their identity were more likely to help others than people who were identifiable (Johnson & Downing, 1979).

Q How does social facilitation differ from social loafing?

ANSWER: In social facilitation, the presence of others generally enhances performance. In social loafing, the presence of others detracts from performance.

12.3 People Conform with Others

Another powerful form of social influence is **conformity**. Why do people conform, altering their behaviors or opinions to match those of others or to match what is expected of them? Social psychologists have identified two primary reasons that people conform. **Normative influence** occurs when people go along with the crowd to fit in and to avoid looking foolish. Normative influence can sometimes cause people to conform even when they believe the group is doing the wrong thing. In contrast, **informational influence** occurs when there is uncertainty or ambiguity about what is correct, appropriate, or expected, so people look to other people for cues about how to respond.

conformity The altering of one's behaviors and opinions to match those of other people or to match other people's expectations.

normative influence The tendency for people to conform in order to fit in with the group.

informational influence The tendency for people to conform when they assume that the behavior of others represents the correct way to respond.

Suppose you are traveling in a foreign country where you do not know the customs. You notice that everyone removes their shoes when they enter a restaurant, so you start doing the same. This is an example of informational influence because you learned the custom by watching others and you accepted it. But then you return home and are surprised to find that the latest style for the fall is to wear socks with sandals. You start doing the same, even though you never would have done that before. This is an example of normative influence because you are conforming to fit in with the group.

Normative influence helps societies run smoothly. People need to coordinate their behavior when they live in groups. For example, imagine if you decided to work from 3 AM until 11 AM while the rest of the people in your workplace worked from 9 AM until 5 PM. How would your behavior affect the lives of your coworkers? How would they react to your decision? Expected standards of conduct, such as the times you work or what you do when you enter a restaurant, are called **social norms**. These norms influence behavior in multiple ways. Norms indicate

social norms Expected standards of conduct that influence behavior.

FIGURE 12.7
Social Norms
One social norm in industrialized societies is to stand facing the elevator door and facing away from other passengers. Violating this norm may make the other passengers very uncomfortable.

which behavior is appropriate in a given situation and also how people will respond to those who violate norms. During the coronavirus pandemic, wearing a mask when in public became the social norm in many places, and people who violated that norm were often reprimanded by strangers. Normative influence works because people feel embarrassed when they violate social norms and they worry about what others think of them. The next time you enter an elevator, try standing with your back to the elevator door and facing people. You may find it quite difficult to defy the simple social norm of facing the doors in an elevator (**FIGURE 12.7**).

Muzafer Sherif (1936) became one of the first researchers to demonstrate the power of conformity in social judgment. Sherif's studies relied on the *autokinetic effect*. Through this perceptual phenomenon, a stationary point of light appears to move when viewed in a totally dark environment. This effect occurs because people have no frame of reference and therefore cannot correct for small eye movements. Sherif asked participants who were alone in a room to estimate how far the light moved. People varied in how much they experienced the autokinetic effect: Some saw the light move only an inch or two, whereas others saw it move 8 inches or more.

In the second part of the study, two or more participants sat in the room and called out their estimates. Although there were initial differences, participants quickly revised their estimates until they agreed. They relied on the information provided by others to form a basis for their estimates. People believed the group estimates, too. Sherif had some people participate again, but in a group with new participants. In the new group, repeat participants confidently stated the estimate that their previous group had agreed upon. These participants brought the norm from their previous group to the new one. This result is an example of informational influence. In ambiguous situations, people often compare their reactions with the reactions of others to judge the correct course of action.

Solomon Asch (1955) speculated that Sherif's results probably occurred because the autokinetic effect is a subjective visual illusion. If perceptions were objective, Asch thought, participants would not conform because there would be no uncertainty about the right answer. To test his hypothesis, Asch assembled male participants for a study of visual acuity. In the 18 trials, the participants looked at a reference line and three comparison lines. They decided which of the three comparison lines matched the reference line and said their answers aloud. A key feature of this study is that the task is very easy. When they are alone, people perform nearly flawlessly (**FIGURE 12.8**). But in these studies, Asch included a naive participant with a group of five confederates who were actually working for the experimenter. The real participant always went sixth, giving his answer after the five confederates gave theirs.

FIGURE 12.8
Normative Influence
The stimuli used in Asch's studies on normative influence. Which of the comparison lines is closest in length to the reference line?

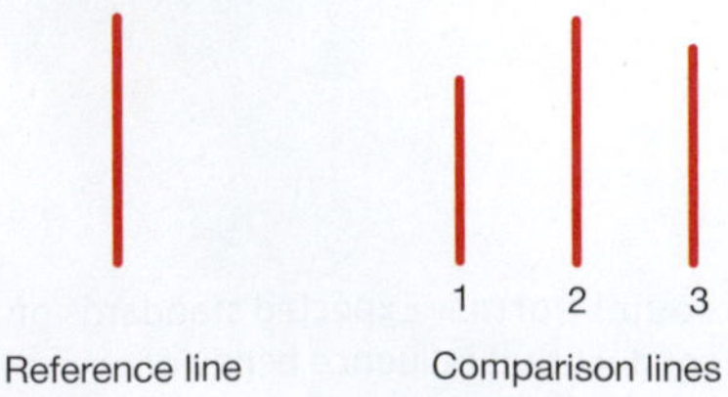

On 12 of the 18 trials, the confederates deliberately gave the same wrong answer. After hearing five wrong answers, the participant then had to state his answer. Asch speculated that the participant would give the correct answer regardless of what the confederates did. After all, the answer was obvious so there was no need to rely on others for information. However, the participant went along with the confederates about one third of the time that confederates gave the wrong answer. Across all the trials, 3 out of 4 people conformed to the incorrect response at least once. Why? It was not because they believed others were providing the right answer. Instead, people conformed because they did not want to look foolish by going against the group. Thus, the findings of the Asch study were attributable to normative influence.

Learning Tip

Groupthink, normative influence, and informational influence are related concepts and often occur together. You can understand groupthink as the result of a group decision process where both normative and informational influence are at play. People in a group learn information from others (informational influence) and alter their behavior to fit in with the group (normative influence). When those two forces are brought to a group that starts with biased, uniform beliefs and forceful leadership, groupthink can occur.

FACTORS AFFECTING CONFORMITY Research has consistently demonstrated that people tend to conform to social norms. This effect can be seen outside the laboratory as well: Adolescents conform to peer pressure to smoke; jury members go along with the group rather than state their own opinions; people stand in line to buy tickets. Social norms set expectations about behavior and the consequences of deviating from those expectations. People who go against the group risk criticism, embarrassment, and ostracism. As the saying goes, the nail that stands out gets hammered down.

But when do people reject social norms? In a series of follow-up studies, Asch (1956) and others identified factors that decrease the chances of conformity. One factor is group size. When there are only one or two confederates, a naive participant usually does not conform. When the confederates number three or more, the participant is more likely to conform. Conformity seems to level off at a certain point, however. Subsequent research has found that even groups as large as 16 do not lead to greater conformity than groups of seven. Asch found that lack of consensus is another factor that diminishes conformity. If even one confederate gives the correct answer, conformity to the group norm decreases a great deal. Any dissent from majority opinion can diminish the influence of social norms. But dissent can be difficult because dissenters are typically not treated well by groups. The social and cultural context also plays a role in conformity (Bond & Smith, 1996). For instance, people tend to conform more in countries that are more collectivistic and conform less in racially diverse groups (Gaither et al., 2018).

In addition, a number of brain imaging studies have examined conformity to group standards. A review of these studies found that activity in the medial prefrontal cortex, the region mentioned earlier in terms of understanding group members, predicted people's conforming behaviors (Wu et al., 2016).

Q **Priya cheers at a sports game because everyone else is cheering and she wants to avoid looking unsupportive. Does this behavior represent normative or informational influence?**

ANSWER: normative influence, because she is adhering to social norms with the intent of avoiding negative social reactions

12.4 Can Social Norms Marketing Reduce Binge Drinking?

YOU BE THE PSYCHOLOGIST

Can the power of social norms be harnessed to modify behavior in positive ways? As noted in Chapter 4, excessive drinking kills more than 1,800 college students each year and can be a factor in other safety problems on campuses. Universities around the world have tried to use social norms marketing to reduce binge

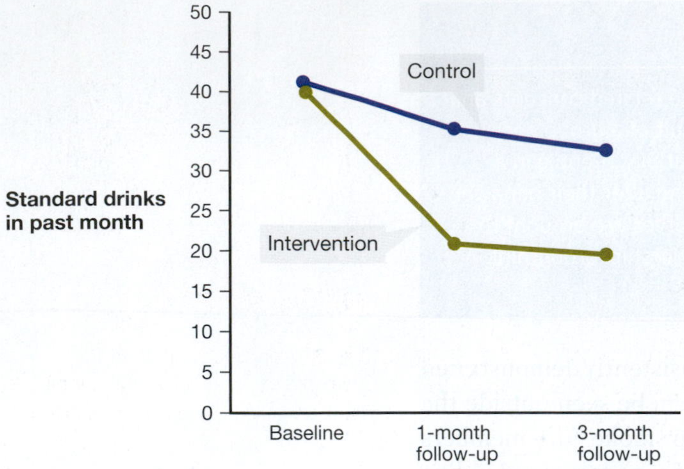

FIGURE 12.9

A Social Norms Study

This graph reports the results of using Facebook for social norms marketing at one college. The group that received the intervention experienced a far greater decrease in drinking than the control group.

drinking on campus. The logic behind such programs is that students often overestimate how often and how much other students drink. Because of normative social influence, students who believe others drink frequently might drink more to fit in with their peer group. Social norms marketing tries to correct these false beliefs by giving factual normative comparisons for average students at a particular college (Miller & Prentice, 2016). Thus, to change norms, colleges put up posters with messages such as "Most students have fewer than four drinks when they party."

Take a moment to think about how effective a social norms approach will be. Start by considering for whom the approach will work best. Who might reduce their drinking the most after learning accurate information about how much college students actually drink? How might psychologists target those individuals?

Some studies have found that social norms marketing reduces the level of binge drinking on college campuses (Mattern & Neighbors, 2004). One recent Australian study used Facebook to provide students with individualized feedback comparing their behavior with the actual behavior of students in their class (Ridout & Campbell, 2014). These students were selected specifically because they reported excessive drinking on an initial survey. They were randomly assigned to the Facebook norms intervention or a control group, and both groups reported their drinking in surveys they completed one and three months later. The researchers found considerable reductions in self-reported alcohol consumption for the intervention group (**FIGURE 12.9**). Because of findings such as these, the use of social norms marketing for students who drink at very high rates has become extremely popular, and most college campuses have adopted some form of it.

Now ask yourself whether there is any chance a social norms program might backfire. Is it possible that some students might conform by drinking *more* than before? If so, who might those students be? Remember, normative influence can push a person to go along with the crowd, even if that person disagrees with what the crowd is doing. How might you alter the message to those students to prevent the unintended side effect of increased drinking?

If you guessed that social norms marketing could backfire for nondrinkers or light drinkers, you are right. Students who usually have only one drink might interpret the posters as suggesting that the norm is to have two or three drinks, and they might adjust their behavior accordingly. Indeed, one large study found that social norms marketing actually increased the drinking behavior the campaign set out to correct (Wechsler et al., 2003). Fortunately, there is a relatively simple solution to this backfire effect. Adding a message to the accurate norms information that the behavior is also undesirable might help prevent social norms marketing from increasing the behavior it is meant to reduce (Schultz et al., 2007). In other words, campuses that want to reduce student drinking need to do more than just publicize drinking norms in terms of average numbers of drinks. Effective marketing also needs to convince students that there are numerous negative consequences associated with excessive drinking. Strategies that both change perceived norms and provide persuasive reasons to avoid binge drinking are most likely to be successful (Miller & Prentice, 2016). ■

Q How can social norms marketing aimed at reducing binge drinking backfire if only the average number of drinks per party is stated?

ANSWER: Light drinkers may drink more to conform to social norms.

12.5 People Obey Authority Figures

One of the most famous and most disturbing psychology experiments was conducted by Stanley Milgram (1963). Milgram wanted to understand why apparently normal German citizens willingly obeyed orders to injure or kill innocent people during World War II (FIGURE 12.10). Milgram was interested in the determinants of **obedience**. That is, he wanted to find out which factors influence people to follow orders given by an authority, such as a boss, parent, or police officer.

FIGURE 12.10
Stanley Milgram
Milgram, pictured here with his infamous shock generator, demonstrated that average people will obey even hideous orders given by an authority figure.

Imagine yourself as a participant in Milgram's experiment. You have agreed to take part in a study on learning. On arriving at the laboratory, you meet your fellow participant, a 60-year-old grandfatherly type. The experimenter describes the study as consisting of a teacher administering electric shocks to a learner engaged in a simple memory task that involves word pairs. Your role as the teacher is determined by an apparently random drawing of your name from a hat. On hearing that he may receive electric shocks, the learner reveals that he has a heart condition and expresses minor reservations. The experimenter says that although the shocks will be painful, they will not cause permanent tissue damage. You help the experimenter take the learner to a small room and hook him up to the electric shock machine (FIGURE 12.11). You then proceed to a nearby room and sit at a table in front of a large shock generator with switches that will deliver from 15 volts to 450 volts. Each voltage level carries a label, and the labels range from "slight" to "danger—severe shock" to, finally, an ominous "XXX."

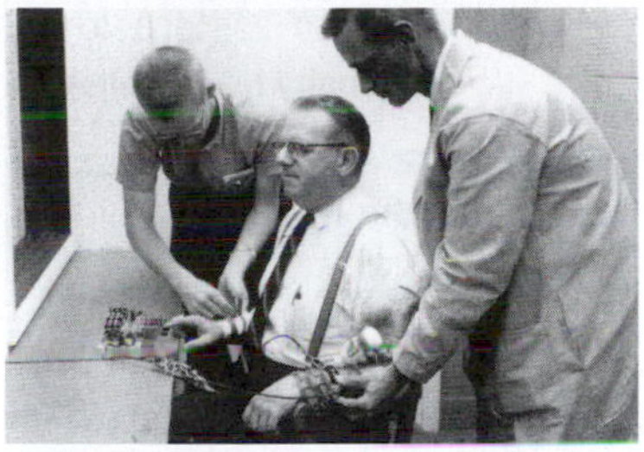

FIGURE 12.11
Obedience in Milgram's Experiment
In this Milgram study, each participant (teacher) was instructed to "shock," from another room, a participant (learner). Here the teacher helps strap the learner to an electric shock machine. The teacher was unaware that the learner was secretly in league with the experimenter.

obedience Following the orders of a person of authority.

Each time the learner makes a mistake, your task as the teacher is to give him a shock. With each subsequent error, you increase the voltage. When you reach 75 volts, over the intercom you hear the man yelp in pain. At 150 volts, he screams, bangs on the wall, and demands that the experiment be stopped. At the experimenter's command, you apply additional, stronger shocks. The learner is clearly in agony. Each time you say you are quitting and try to stop the experiment, the experimenter replies, "The experiment requires that you continue," "It is essential that you go on," "There is no other choice; you must go on!" So you do. At 300 volts, the learner refuses to answer any more questions. After 330 volts, the learner is silent. All along you have wanted to leave, and you severely regret participating in the study. For all you know, you killed him.

Does this scenario sound outlandish to you? If you really were the teacher, at what level would you stop administering the shocks? Would you quit as soon as the learner started to complain? Would you go up to 450 volts? Before conducting the experiment, Milgram asked supposed experts in human behavior and psychology for predictions. These people predicted that most participants would go no higher than 135 volts. They felt that fewer than one in a thousand participants would administer the highest level of shock. But that is not what happened. What did happen changed how people viewed the power of authority.

Almost all the participants tried to quit. Despite some protest, however, nearly two thirds completely obeyed all the experimenter's directives (FIGURE 12.12). The majority were willing to administer 450 volts to an older man who they believed had a heart condition (who was a confederate and did not actually receive shocks). These findings were replicated by Milgram and others around the world. The conclusion of these studies is that ordinary people can be coerced into obedience by insistent authorities. This effect occurs even when the people are coerced into doing something that goes against the way they usually would behave. At the same time, these results do not mean all people are equally obedient. Indeed, some aspects of personality seem related to being obedient, such as the extent to which

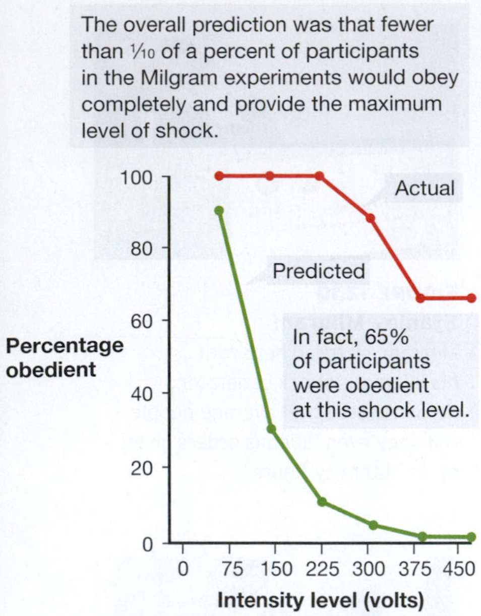
The overall prediction was that fewer than 1⁄10 of a percent of participants in the Milgram experiments would obey completely and provide the maximum level of shock.
100
80
60
40
20
0
Percentage obedient
Actual
Predicted
In fact, 65% of participants were obedient at this shock level.
0 75 150 225 300 375 450
Intensity level (volts)

FIGURE 12.12
Predicting the Results
Psychiatrists, college sophomores, middle-class adults, and both graduate students and professors in the behavioral sciences offered predictions about the results of Milgram's experiments. All their predictions were incorrect.

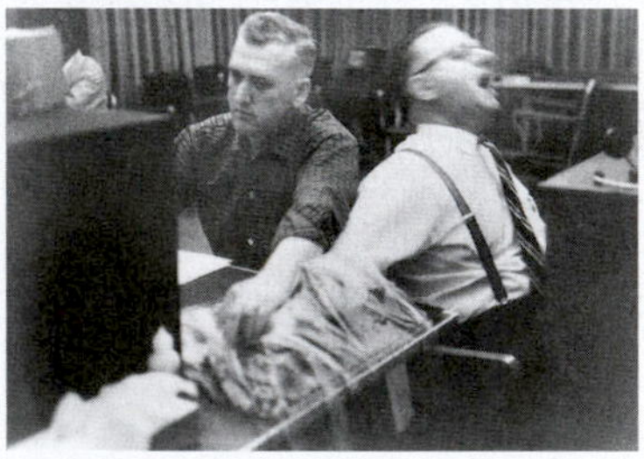

FIGURE 12.13
Personal Closeness Reduced Obedience in Milgram's Experiment
In another condition, teachers were instructed to touch and "shock" a learner sitting next to them. As in the first condition, the shocks were portrayed as increasingly intense and painful. When teachers had to force the learner's hand on the shock plate, only 30 percent completely obeyed the experimenters and administered the maximum voltage.

people are concerned about how others view them (Blass, 1991). As discussed in Chapter 13, both situation and personality influence behavior.

Surprised by the results of his study, Milgram next studied ways to reduce obedience. He found that some situations produced less obedience. For instance, if the teacher could see or had to touch the learner, obedience decreased (**FIGURE 12.13**). When the experimenter gave the orders over the telephone and thus was not physically present and visible, obedience dropped dramatically. By contrast, a number of factors produce maximum obedience. Obedience is heightened when the shock level increases slowly and sequentially, when the victim starts protesting later in the study, when the orders help justify continuing with the study, and when the study is conducted at a high-status school (the original version was conducted at Yale), where the experimenters might be viewed as being more authoritative (Jetten & Mols, 2014).

Criticisms of the Milgram studies have emerged in the decades since they were conducted (Brannigan et al., 2015; Griggs, 2017). For instance, some participants apparently did not fully believe that the victim was receiving a life-threatening shock (Hoffman et al., 2015). Some researchers questioned the motives of participants for obeying (Haslam et al., 2015). Indeed, encouragements to continue for the sake of the experiment have greater impact on participants than telling them that they must obey because they have no choice (Burger et al., 2011).

In some way, these criticisms serve only to underscore an important point of the study: People can justify to themselves almost any kind of behavior. As observers, we think of people who do harmful things as bad or evil. After all, what kind of person wants to intentionally cause pain to others? But the people doing the harm do not think of themselves as evil. Quite the opposite: In their own minds, the participants in Milgram's studies might have been willing to inflict harm because they identified with the goals of science and believed their actions were virtuous (Haslam et al., 2016). Milgram's study is a powerful demonstration not only of what people will do to others but also of how they convince themselves that it is not just acceptable but helpful to inflict significant pain on an innocent victim.

The earliest and most persistent critiques of Milgram's experiments revolved around the ethical treatment of the research participants (Baumrind, 1964). Even though Milgram claimed to be highly concerned with his participants' mental states, not all participants received timely debriefings in which they learned the true nature of the experiments (Nicholson, 2011; Perry, 2013). In an attempt to understand the long-term impact of taking part in the research, Milgram (1974) followed his participants over time and reported that most people were glad they had participated. They felt they had learned something about themselves and about human nature. Nowadays, as discussed in Chapter 2, researchers follow clear guidelines to protect the physical and mental health of research participants.

Despite the studies' flaws, Milgram's results document just how powerful situational influences can be. Milgram's research, and studies that followed up on it, demonstrated that ordinary people may do horrible things when ordered to do so by an authority. Although some people have speculated that these results would not hold true today, a modern replication found that 70 percent of the participants were obedient up to the maximum voltage in the experiment (Burger, 2009).

Q Which variations in Milgram's obedience studies reduced the likelihood that participants obeyed the experimenter's orders?

ANSWER: Obedience declined when participants could see or touch the person they were supposed to shock and when the experimenter was not physically present when giving orders.

When Do People Harm or Help Others?

Though obedience and other forms of social influence can lead people to commit horrible acts, the need to belong to a group can also lead to acts of altruism and of generosity. Around the globe in recent years, we have seen terrorists, special forces, and militias killing civilians. At the same time, we have also seen people being kind, compassionate, and giving in response to natural disasters. For example, members of the group Doctors Without Borders travel to dangerous regions to care for those in need (**FIGURE 12.14**). This tension between our aggressive and altruistic sides is at the core of who we are as a species. Psychologists working at all levels of analysis have provided insight into these fundamental human behaviors.

Learning Objectives

- Identify situational, biological, social, and cultural determinants of aggression.
- Explain how bias against outgroups may be decreased.
- Review evolutionary explanations for altruism.
- Consider four factors that affect the bystander intervention effect.

12.6 Many Factors Can Influence Aggression

Aggression can be expressed through countless behaviors, all of which involve the intention to harm another. Among nonhuman animals, aggression often occurs in the context of fighting over a mate or defending territory from intruders. In some cases, just the threat of aggressive action may be sufficient to dissuade. Among humans, physical aggression is common among young children but relatively rare in adults because of strong social norms discouraging it in most cultures. Adults' aggressive acts more often involve words or other symbols meant to threaten, intimidate, or emotionally harm others.

aggression Any behavior that involves the intention to harm another.

Aggression is associated with several situational factors. Recall from Chapter 6 that people can learn to be aggressive by observational learning and exposure to media violence. Aggression is also likely when people feel socially rejected. Throughout evolutionary history, rejection from the group has been akin to a death warrant, and therefore signs of rejection can activate defensive mechanisms that include lashing out at those who are perceived to be responsible for the rejection (MacDonald & Leary, 2005). Feeling ostracized or rejected and the desire to retaliate have been identified among the factors in school shootings (Fox & DeLateur, 2014).

Another factor that influences aggression is heat (Van Lange et al., 2017). More crime occurs in the summer, and more violence occurs in hotter regions (Anderson, 1989; Anderson & DeLisi, 2011). Major League Baseball pitchers are most likely to hit batters with pitches when the weather is hottest (Reifman et al., 1991), especially when their own teammates have been hit by pitches (Larrick et al., 2011). A common thread through many of the situations that lead to aggression is that they involve negative emotions. Any situation that induces negative emotions—such as being insulted, afraid, frustrated, overly hot, or in pain—can trigger physical aggression (Berkowitz, 1990). This effect may occur because emotional states can disrupt the functioning of brain regions involved in controlling behavior (Tolomeo et al., 2016).

(a)

(b)

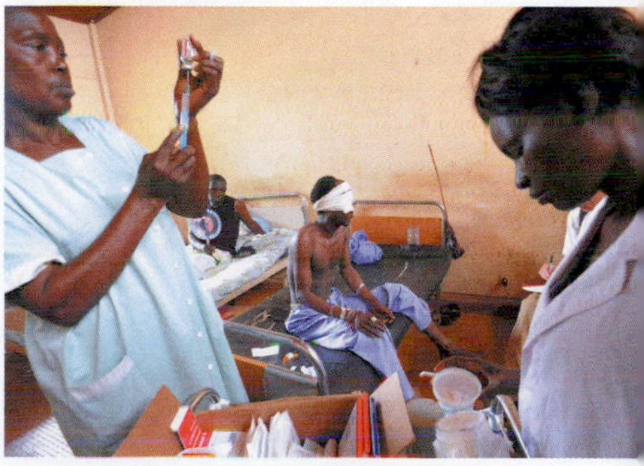

FIGURE 12.14
Harming Versus Helping
(a) Forces from the rebel group Séléka engage in military action in the Central African Republic in 2013. **(b)** Members of Doctors Without Borders treat the wounded during the Central African Republic coup.

BIOLOGICAL FACTORS Like all complex human behaviors, aggression is caused by a blend of social, situational, and biological factors. One biological factor is the hormone testosterone, which has a modest correlation with aggression. Males have more testosterone than females do, and males carry out the vast majority of aggressive and violent acts. Boys play more roughly than girls at an early age. They become especially aggressive during early adolescence, a time when their levels of testosterone rise tenfold (Mazur & Booth, 1998). However, these increases in testosterone in boys coincide with other maturational changes that promote aggression, such as physical growth and changes in social expectations. Exceptionally aggressive men, such as violent criminals, and especially-physical athletes, such as hockey players, have been found to have higher levels of testosterone than other males do (Dabbs & Morris, 1990). This relationship is small, though, and it is unclear how testosterone is linked to greater aggressiveness. Testosterone may increase aggression because it reduces the activity of brain circuits that control impulses (Mehta & Beer, 2010).

In addition, testosterone changes may be the result—rather than the cause—of aggressive behavior. That is, a situation where aggression occurs might change testosterone levels. Several studies have shown that testosterone rises just before athletic competition (Mazur & Booth, 1998). Testosterone remains high for the winners of competitive matches and decreases for the losers (Booth et al., 1989). Even those who simply watch a competition can be affected. Testosterone levels increased in Brazilian television viewers who watched Brazil beat Italy in the 1994 World Cup soccer tournament, but levels decreased in Italian television viewers (Bernhardt et al., 1998). These results suggest that testosterone might not play a direct role in aggression but rather might be related to social dominance, the result of having greater power and status (Mehta et al., 2008).

Several lines of evidence suggest that serotonin is especially important in the regulation of aggressive behavior (Caramaschi et al., 2007). Altered serotonin function has been associated with impulsive aggressiveness in adults and hostility and disruptive behavior in children (Carver & Miller, 2006). Alterations in serotonin activity increase the amygdala response to threat and interfere with the prefrontal cortex's control over aggressive impulses (Buckholtz & Meyer-Lindenberg, 2013). Disrupted serotonin systems may lead people to respond impulsively overall. One form of impulsive response is aggression, particularly when people are provoked (Chester et al., 2015).

Genetic research has implicated the MAOA gene in aggression. The MAOA gene controls the amount of MAO (monoamine oxidase), an enzyme that regulates the activity of neurotransmitters including serotonin and norepinephrine. Numerous studies have shown that the MAOA gene is involved in impulsive behaviors such as aggressive violence (Buckholtz & Meyer-Lindenberg, 2008; Dorfman et al., 2014).

It is important to note that MAOA is not a "violence gene" per se. Genes make proteins, not behaviors. Instead, the long-running effect of having one form of the gene versus another increases a person's susceptibility to environmental risk factors associated with impulsive or antisocial behaviors. For instance, recall the New Zealand study from Chapter 3, which found that people who had one version of the MAOA gene and also suffered childhood maltreatment were more likely to become violent criminals (Caspi et al., 2002).

SOCIAL AND CULTURAL FACTORS Violence varies dramatically across cultures and societies and even within them at different times. For example, over the course of 300 years, Sweden went from being one of the most violent nations on Earth to being one of the most peaceable. The violent crime rate in the United States has dropped by nearly 50 percent in the past 30 years (**FIGURE 12.15**). These societal and cultural changes did not correspond with a change in the gene pool or with other immediately apparent biological changes. Instead, they were caused by a collective shift in expectations and beliefs about aggression and its consequences.

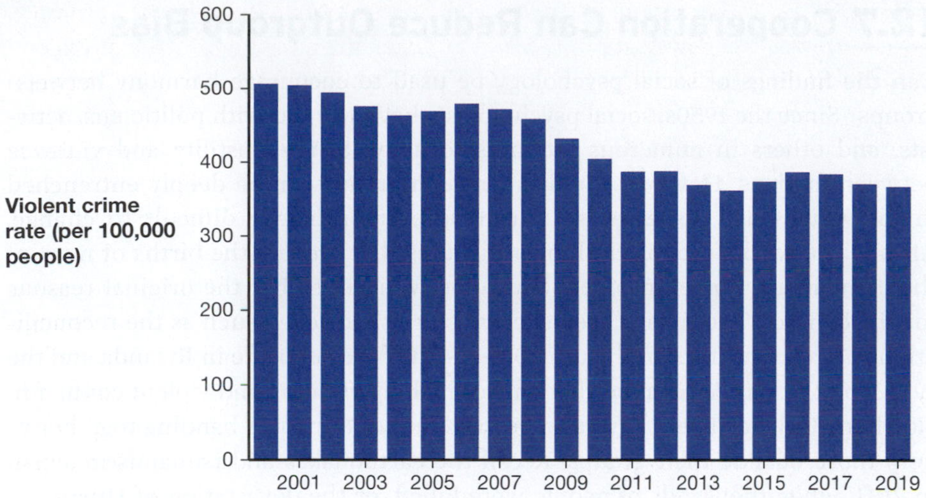

FIGURE 12.15
Violent Crime in the United States
Societal factors can influence aggression. Reports of violent crime in the United States decreased about 50 percent between 1990 and 2019.

Societies also vary quite a bit in the structural factors that influence aggression, such as the odds that criminals will be caught and brought to justice and the prevalence of poverty and inequality. These are among the reasons that murder rates are 10 to 20 times higher in some countries than in others. Aggression may be part of human nature, but society and culture influence people's tendencies to commit violent acts.

Some cultures may be violent because they subscribe to a *culture of honor*. In this belief system, boys and men learn that it is important to protect their reputations through physical aggression (**FIGURE 12.16**). Men in the southern United States, for example, traditionally were (and perhaps still are) raised to be ready to defend their honor and to respond aggressively to personal threats. An analysis of crime statistics in the United States reveals that physical violence is much more prevalent in the South than in the North (United Nations Office on Drugs and Crime, 2013). To determine whether southern males are more likely to be aggressive than northern males, researchers at the University of Michigan conducted a series of studies (Cohen et al., 1996). In each study, a male participant had to walk down a narrow hallway. The participant passed a filing cabinet, where a male confederate was blocking the hallway. As the participant tried to edge past the confederate, the confederate responded angrily and insulted the participant. Compared with participants raised in the North, those raised in the South became more upset and were more likely to feel personally challenged. Perhaps because of a need to express social dominance in this situation, the southern participants were more physiologically aroused (measured by cortisol and testosterone increases), more cognitively primed for aggression, and more likely to act in an aggressive and dominant manner for the rest of the experiment.

FIGURE 12.16
Herding Culture
One hypothesis for different rates in violence across cultures is that herders need to defend their livelihood more aggressively than farmers. Here, a herder attacks a raider.

Q **How is temperature linked to aggression?**

ANSWER: Hotter temperatures can produce more negative emotions, which in turn can increase aggression.

FIGURE 12.17
Global Cooperation
After Hurricane Maria in Puerto Rico and the surrounding islands in 2017, workers from around the world assisted efforts to rebuild the country. Dealing with a natural catastrophe can help people overcome their differences.

12.7 Cooperation Can Reduce Outgroup Bias

Can the findings of social psychology be used to encourage harmony between groups? Since the 1950s, social psychologists have worked with politicians, activists, and others in numerous attempts to alleviate the hostility and violence between factions. However, conflict between groups can be deeply entrenched in individuals and societies, so it can be extraordinarily difficult to change. Around the world, groups clash over disputes that predate the births of most of the combatants. Sometimes people cannot even remember the original reasons for the conflict. There have been success stories, however, such as the reconciliation between the Tutsi and Hutu 20 years after the genocide in Rwanda and the 1998 Good Friday Agreement that ended the long-running and violent conflict in Northern Ireland. There have also been examples of people banding together to help those outside their groups. Recall the earthquakes and tsunamis in Japan in 2011, when thousands of people were killed, or the devastation of Hurricane Maria in Puerto Rico in 2017, when tens of thousands of people lost their homes and nearly 3,000 died (**FIGURE 12.17**). The international responses to these tragedies show that people respond to outgroup members in need. In working together toward a greater purpose, people can overcome intergroup hostilities.

Social psychology may be able to suggest strategies for promoting intergroup harmony and producing greater tolerance for outgroups. The first study to suggest so was conducted in the 1950s by Muzafer Sherif and colleagues (1961). Sherif arranged for 22 well-adjusted and intelligent fifth-grade boys from Oklahoma City to attend a summer camp at a lake. The boys did not know one another. Before arriving at camp, they were divided into two groups that were essentially the same. During the first week, each group lived in a separate camp on a different side of the lake. Neither group knew that the other group existed.

The next week, the groups were introduced, and they competed against each other in a four-day athletic tournament. They played games such as tug-of-war, football, and softball, and the stakes were high. The winning team would receive a trophy, individual medals, and appealing prizes. The losers would receive nothing. The groups named themselves the Rattlers and the Eagles. Group pride was extremely strong, and animosity between the groups quickly escalated. The Eagles burned the Rattlers' flag, and the Rattlers retaliated by trashing the Eagles' cabin. Eventually, confrontations and physical fights had to be broken up by the experimenters. All the typical signs of outgroup bias emerged, including the outgroup homogeneity effect and ingroup favoritism.

Phase 1 of the study was complete. Sherif had shown how easy it was to make people hate each other: Simply divide them into groups and have the groups compete, and conflict and aggression will result (**FIGURE 12.18**). Phase 2 of the study then explored whether the hostility could be undone.

Sherif first tried what psychologists at the time believed would reduce the conflict: simply having the groups come in contact with each other. The researchers quickly found that this approach failed. The hostilities were too strong, and skirmishes continued. Sherif reasoned that if competition led to hostility, then cooperation should reduce hostility. The experimenters created situations in which members of both groups had to cooperate to achieve necessary goals. For instance, the experimenters rigged a truck to break down. Getting the truck moving required all the boys to pull together. In an ironic twist, the boys had to use the same rope they used earlier in the tug-of-war. When they succeeded, a great cheer arose from the boys, with plenty of celebration between the two groups. After a series of tasks that required cooperation, the walls between the two sides broke down, and the

(a)

(b)

FIGURE 12.18
Phase 1 of Sherif's Study of Competition and Cooperation
During Phase 1 of Sherif's study, boys from the two summer camps were pitted against each other and became hostile.

(a) (b)

FIGURE 12.19
Phase 2 of Sherif's Study
During Phase 2, the two groups had to work together to achieve common goals. The shared goals led to cooperation and a reduction of hostility between the groups.

boys formed friendships across the groups (**FIGURE 12.19**). Among strangers, competition and isolation created enemies. Among enemies, cooperation created friends.

A recent investigation into Sherif's studies revealed that he ran several versions of the study, and not all yielded the same result (Perry, 2018). For instance, in one version, the researchers (pretending to be camp counselors) tried to get the two groups to dislike each other, but instead the children bonded together over their distrust of the camp staff. Nonetheless, further research over the past four decades has indicated that only certain types of contact between hostile groups is likely to reduce prejudice and discrimination. Shared *superordinate* goals—goals that require people to cooperate—reduce hostility between groups. People who work together to achieve a common goal often break down subgroup distinctions as they become one larger group (Dovidio et al., 2004).

Q **What is the key to reducing hostility between competitive groups?**

ANSWER: opportunities for cooperation between groups to achieve superordinate goals

12.8 Many Factors Can Influence Helping Behavior

People often act in ways that help others. **Prosocial behaviors** include doing favors, offering assistance, paying compliments, setting aside egocentric desires or needs, or simply being pleasant and cooperative. By providing benefits to others, prosocial behaviors foster positive interpersonal relationships. Engaging in prosocial behaviors such as sharing and cooperating is a central human survival strategy because we live in groups. After all, a group that works well together is a strong group, and belonging to a strong group benefits the individual members.

prosocial behaviors Actions that benefit others, such as doing favors or helping.

Why are humans prosocial? Theoretical explanations range from selflessness to selfishness and from the biological to the philosophical. For instance, Daniel Batson and colleagues (1988, 1995) have argued that prosocial behaviors are motivated by empathy, in which people share other people's emotions. Conversely, Robert Cialdini and colleagues (1987; also Maner et al., 2002) have argued that most prosocial behaviors have selfish motives, such as wanting to manage one's public image or relieve one's negative mood. Other theorists have proposed that people have an inborn tendency to help others. Consider that young infants become distressed when they see other infants crying (Zahn-Waxler & Radke-Yarrow, 1990). This empathic response to other people's suffering suggests that prosocial behavior is hardwired in humans.

Altruism is providing help when it is needed, without any immediate reward for doing so. The fact that people help others, and even risk their own personal safety to do so, might seem contrary to evolutionary principles. After all, those who protect themselves first would appear to have an advantage over those who risk their lives to help others.

altruism Providing help when it is needed, without any apparent reward for doing so.

inclusive fitness An explanation for altruism that focuses on the adaptive benefit of transmitting genes, such as through kin selection, rather than focusing on individual survival.

EVOLUTIONARY EXPLANATIONS Animals increase the chances of passing along their genes to future generations by helping their offspring survive. The geneticist William Hamilton's (1964) concept of **inclusive fitness** describes the adaptive benefits of transmitting genes rather than focusing on individual survival. According to this model, people are altruistic toward those with whom they share genes. When your family members thrive, at least some of your genes survive. This phenomenon is known as *kin selection*. A good example of kin selection occurs among insects such as ants and bees. In these species, workers feed and protect the egg-laying queen, but they never reproduce. By protecting the group's eggs, they maximize the number of their common genes that will survive into future generations (Dugatkin, 2004).

Of course, animals sometimes help nonrelatives. A person who jumps into a lake to save a drowning stranger is probably not acting for the sake of genetic transmission. To help explain altruism toward nonrelatives, Robert Trivers (1971) proposed the idea of reciprocity, introduced earlier, which he called *reciprocal helping*. According to Trivers, one animal helps another because the other may return the favor in the future. Consider grooming, in which primates take turns cleaning each other's fur: "You scratch my back, and I'll scratch yours."

For reciprocal helping to make sense from an evolutionary perspective, its benefits must outweigh its costs. Indeed, people are less likely to help others when the costs of doing so are high (Wagner & Wheeler, 1969). Reciprocal helping is also much more likely to occur in species, such as humans, that live in social groups, because their survival depends on cooperation. Thus, as discussed earlier, people are more likely to help members of their ingroups than to help members of outgroups. Members of ingroups often share genetic material, so helping people in the ingroup is beneficial to the survival of an individual's genes. The altruistic animal may also increase the likelihood that other members of the social group will reciprocate when needed.

bystander intervention effect The failure to offer help by those who observe someone in need when other people are present.

BYSTANDER INTERVENTION In 1964, a young woman named Kitty Genovese was walking home from work in a relatively safe area of New York City. An assailant savagely attacked her for half an hour, eventually killing her. At the time, a newspaper reported that none of the 38 witnesses to the crime tried to help or called the police (**FIGURE 12.20**). As it turns out, the story was not quite correct. Most of the 38 neighbors were not positioned to know what was occurring, and at least two people did call the police (Manning et al., 2007).

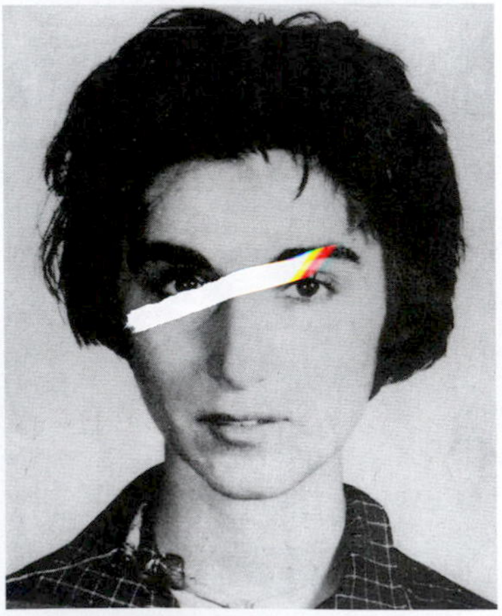

FIGURE 12.20
Kitty Genovese
News reports that 38 witnesses failed to help murder-victim Kitty Genovese caused outrage.

Nonetheless, the idea that people sometimes stand by and fail to help during emergencies resonated. Examples range from indifference to the suffering of unhoused people to failures to report assaults at dorm parties (*Police: Up to 20 People Witnessed Gang Rape*, 2009). The Genovese story and firsthand experiences of this behavior prompted psychologists to undertake research on how people react in emergencies. The social psychologists Bibb Latané and John Darley examined situations that produce the **bystander intervention effect**. This term refers to the failure to offer help by those who observe someone in need, so it might more accurately be thought of as the bystander *non*intervention effect. Common sense might suggest that the more people available to help, the more likely it is that a victim will be helped. Latané and Darley made the paradoxical claim, however, that a person is less likely to offer help if other bystanders are around.

To test their theory, Latané and Darley conducted studies in which people were placed in situations where helping might have been required. In one of the first situations, male college students were in a room filling out questionnaires (Latané & Darley, 1968). Pungent smoke started puffing in through the heating vents. Some participants were alone. Some were with two other naive participants. Some were with two confederates, who noticed the smoke, shrugged, and continued filling out their questionnaires. When participants were on their own, most went for help. When three naive participants were together, however, few initially went for help. With the two calm confederates, only 10 percent of participants went for help in the first 6 minutes (**FIGURE 12.21**). The other 90 percent "coughed, rubbed their eyes, and opened the window—but they did not report the smoke" (p. 218).

In subsequent studies, people were confronted with mock crimes, apparent heart attack victims in subway cars, and people passed out in public places. The experimenters obtained similar results each time. The bystander intervention effect has been shown to occur in a wide variety of contexts. Even divinity students, while rushing to give a lecture on the Good Samaritan—a biblical figure who helps a severely injured traveler—failed to help a person in apparent need of medical attention (Darley & Batson, 1973).

Years of research have indicated four major reasons that bystanders do not consistently intervene in emergencies. First, a *diffusion of responsibility* occurs. In other words, bystanders expect other bystanders to help. Thus, the greater the number of people who witness someone in need of help, the less likely it is that any of them will step forward. Second, people fear making *social blunders* in ambiguous situations. All the laboratory situations had some degree of ambiguity, and people may have worried that they would look foolish if they sought help that was not needed. People can be reluctant to call emergency responders in cases where the situation is unclear, but they feel less constrained if the need for it is apparent (Fischer et al., 2011). Third, people are less likely to help when they are *anonymous* and can remain so. Therefore, if you need help, it is often wise to point to someone and request that person's help by saying something like, "You, in the red shirt, call an ambulance!" Fourth, people weigh two factors: How much harm do they risk to themselves by helping? What benefits might they have to forgo if they help? Imagine you are walking to a potentially dull class on a beautiful day. Right in front of you, someone falls down, twists an ankle, and needs transportation to the nearest clinic. You probably would be willing to help. Now imagine you are running to a final exam that counts for 90 percent of your grade. In this case, you probably would be much less likely to offer assistance.

The factors described above all make people less likely to help in an emergency. What makes people more likely to help? Fortunately, researchers have found that learning about the bystander effect can help people overcome it (**FIGURE 12.22**). Taking an introductory psychology class is one way to learn to avoid the bystander effect.

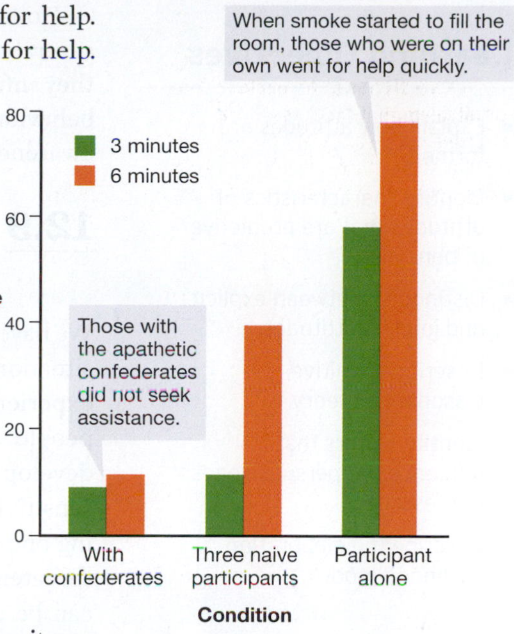

When smoke started to fill the room, those who were on their own went for help quickly.
3 minutes
6 minutes
Percentage going for help
Those with the apathetic confederates did not seek assistance.
80
60
40
20
0
With confederates
Three naive participants
Participant alone
Condition

FIGURE 12.21
The Bystander Intervention Effect
In Latané and Darley's experiments, participants waited with two apathetic confederates, with two other naive participants, or alone. This chart records the participants' reactions to smoke filling the room.

FIGURE 12.22
Learning About the Bystander Effect Can Prevent It
Peter Maduka Jr. was a bystander who rescued an older woman from an overturned car after an accident. He learned of the bystander effect in studying for his medical school exams.

Q **If you are in danger and need assistance in a crowded place, what can you do to improve the likelihood of bystander intervention?**

ANSWER: Communicate that you are in danger to reduce the ambiguity of the situation, and recruit specific individuals to help you to reduce diffusion of responsibility and anonymity.

How Do Attitudes Guide Behavior?

You probably have feelings, opinions, and beliefs about yourself, your friends, your favorite podcast, and so on. These feelings, opinions, and beliefs are called **attitudes**. People's attitudes range from those about trivial matters, such as which laundry detergent works best, to attitudes about grand issues such as morals and religion.

attitudes People's evaluations of other people, objects, events, or ideas.

How attitudes are formed, what they do for us, and how they can be changed are central topics of study in social psychology. Attitudes are shaped by social context, they inform how we evaluate and interact with other people, and they guide our behavior. Some attitudes are held consciously, while others remain below conscious awareness. Attitudes can be changed by other people or even our own actions.

Learning Objectives

- Explain how attitudes are formed.
- Identify characteristics of attitudes that are predictive of behavior.
- Distinguish between explicit and implicit attitudes.
- Describe cognitive dissonance theory.
- Identify factors that influence the persuasiveness of messages.
- Describe the elaboration likelihood model.

12.9 People Form Attitudes Through Experience and Socialization

We have attitudes about all kinds of things, whether they are objects, other people, situations, or abstract concepts. When we hear about something, read about it, or experience it directly, we gain information that shapes our attitudes. Generally, people develop negative attitudes about new things more quickly than they develop positive attitudes about them (Fazio et al., 2004). Throughout evolution, sensitivity to learning about danger would have been particularly adaptive. Missing one opportunity for a reward, such as some tasty berries, is generally not life-threatening. In contrast, missing one threat, such as a tiger lurking in the bushes, can be deadly. In general, bad is always a stronger motivating force than good (Baumeister et al., 2001).

Many factors can cause our initial negative attitudes to become more positive, however. Have you ever disliked a song the first several times you heard it, but after the 50th time your friends played it on TikTok, you decided that the beat was really catchy? Typically, the more people are exposed to something, the more they tend to like it. In a classic set of studies, Robert Zajonc (1968, 2001) exposed people to unfamiliar items a few times or many times. Greater exposure to the item, and therefore greater familiarity with it, caused people to have more-positive attitudes about the item. This process is called the **mere exposure effect**.

mere exposure effect The idea that greater exposure to a stimulus leads to greater liking for it.

In addition, when people are presented with normal photographs of themselves and the same images reversed, they tend to prefer the reversed versions. Why would this be the case? The reversed images correspond to what people see when they look in the mirror. You can try this yourself by taking a selfie and then flipping it. Which image do you prefer? People's friends and family members prefer the true photographs, which correspond to how they view the person. One clever marketing study found that this effect even extended to attitudes about accessories such as glasses or earrings. Shoppers rated the accessories highest when they were shown true photographs of their friends (Cho & Schwarz, 2010). Those same accessories were slightly less preferred on photographs of strangers, and they were rated least favorably on mirror images of their friends (**FIGURE 12.23**).

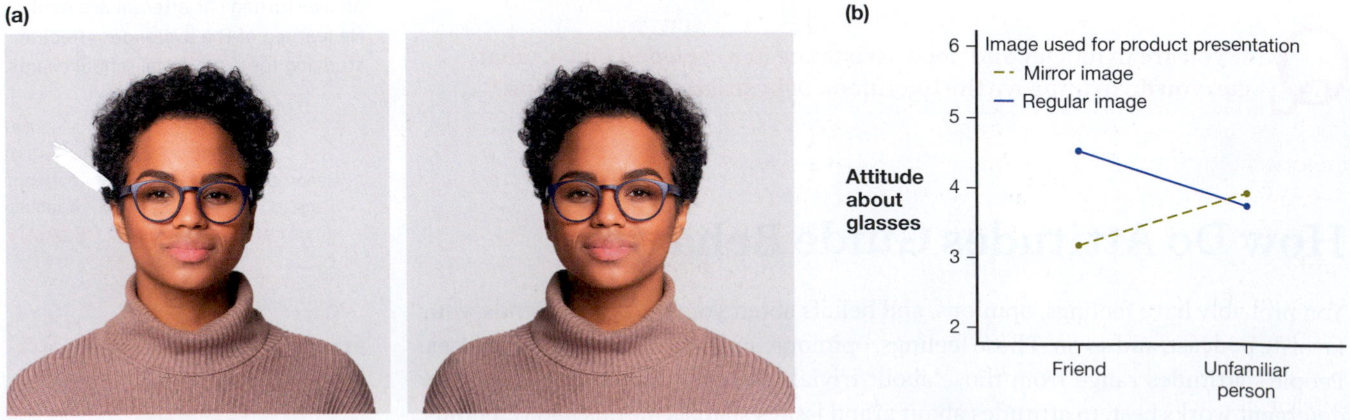

FIGURE 12.23
The Mere Exposure Effect
(a) Shoppers rated glasses displayed on a person's true (left) or mirrored (right) image. **(b)** The shoppers rated the glasses highest when they were displayed on a friend's true image (solid line), and lowest when they were displayed on a friend's mirror image (dashed line).

Attitudes are often shaped through socialization (**FIGURE 12.24**). Caregivers, peers, teachers, religious leaders, politicians, and media figures guide people's attitudes about many things. For example, teenagers' attitudes about clothing styles and music, about behaviors such as smoking and drinking alcohol, and about the latest celebrities are heavily influenced by their peers' beliefs. Society instills many basic attitudes, including attitudes about which things are edible. For instance, many Hindus do not eat beef, whereas many Muslims do not eat pork.

Classical and operant conditioning can also alter attitudes by changing the associations something brings to mind (for a full discussion of conditioning, see Chapter 6). Advertisers often use classical conditioning: When people see a celebrity paired with a product, they tend to develop more-positive attitudes about the product. After conditioning, a formerly neutral stimulus (e.g., a coffee maker) triggers the same attitude response as the paired object (e.g., Chris Pine if he were to endorse the coffee maker). Operant conditioning also shapes attitudes: If you are rewarded with good grades each time you study, you will develop a more positive attitude toward studying.

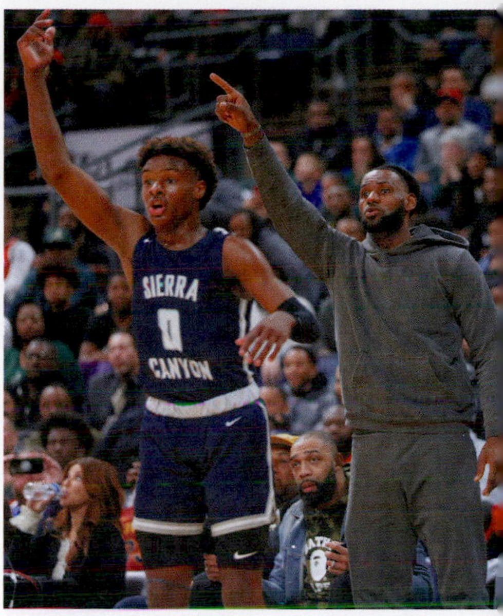

FIGURE 12.24
Socialization Shapes Attitudes
LeBron James's son, Bronny, likely learned many attitudes about basketball from his father.

ATTITUDE-BEHAVIOR CONSISTENCY In general, the stronger and more personally relevant the attitude, the more likely it is to predict behavior and remain stable in the face of challenges. For instance, someone who grew up in a strongly Democratic household, especially one where derogatory comments about Republicans were expressed frequently, is more likely to register as a Democrat and vote Democratic than someone who grew up in a more politically neutral environment.

Moreover, the more specific the attitude, the more predictive it is of behavior. For instance, your attitudes toward recycling are more predictive of whether you take your soda cans to a recycling bin than are your general environmental beliefs. Attitudes formed through direct experience also tend to predict behavior better. Consider your own learning. No matter what you believe before starting college, by the time you have completed your first few years, you will have formed very strong attitudes about effective study skills. These attitudes will predict how you approach studying for the rest of your time in school.

Another factor predicting behavior is how quickly your attitude comes to mind. *Attitude accessibility* refers to the ease or difficulty that a person has in retrieving an attitude from memory. This accessibility predicts behavior consistent with the attitude. Russell Fazio (1995) has shown that attitudes that are easily brought to mind are more stable, predictive of behavior, and resistant to change. Thus, the more quickly you recall that you like your psychology course, the more likely you are to attend lectures and read the textbook.

EXPLICIT AND IMPLICIT ATTITUDES How do you know your attitude about something? Recall from Chapter 4 that our ability to introspect about our own mental processes is limited and that unconscious processes can influence behavior. People's conscious awareness of their attitudes can be limited because of several factors, such as their wish to believe they hold certain attitudes that are socially desirable, but their actions can reveal different attitudes (Nosek et al., 2011).

Over the past 20 years, researchers have demonstrated that attitudes can be explicit or implicit and that these different attitudes have different effects on behavior. **Explicit attitudes** are those you know about and can report to other people. If you say you like bowling, you are stating your explicit attitude toward it. Anthony Greenwald and Mahzarin Banaji (1995) have noted that people's many **implicit attitudes** influence their feelings and behaviors at an unconscious level.

explicit attitudes Attitudes that a person can report.

implicit attitudes Attitudes that influence a person's feelings and behavior at an unconscious level.

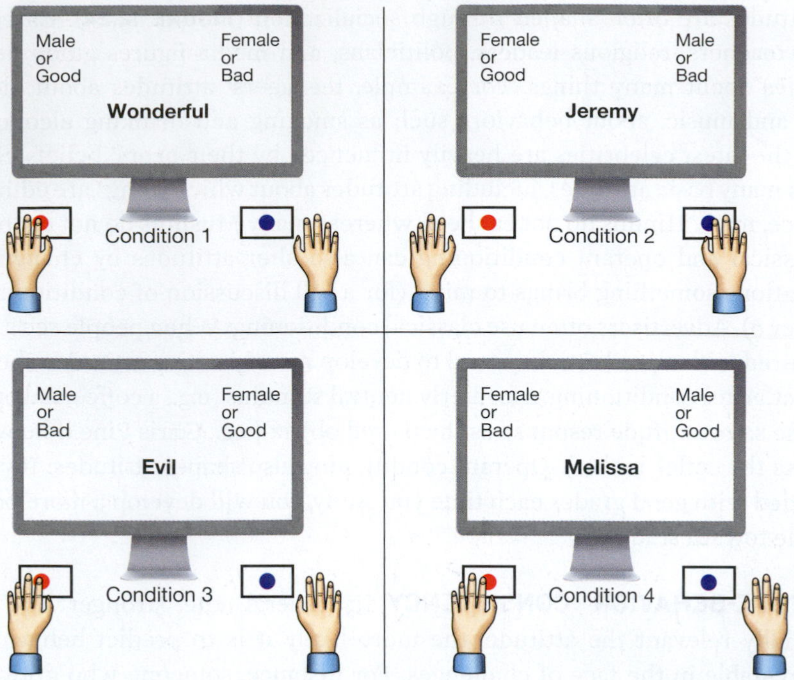

FIGURE 12.25

Implicit Association Test

When a word appears on the screen, a person has to select whether it is bad or good or a male name or a female name. For example, in Condition 1 the person presses the left button to indicate male or good, the right button to indicate female or bad. Which buttons to press changes in different conditions.

People access implicit attitudes from memory quickly, with little conscious effort or control. In this way, implicit attitudes function like implicit memories. As discussed in Chapter 7, implicit memories make it possible for people to perform actions, such as riding a bicycle, without thinking through all the required steps. Similarly, you might purchase a product endorsed by a celebrity even though you have no conscious memory of having seen the celebrity use the product. The product might simply seem appealing or look familiar to you. Some evidence suggests that implicit attitudes involve brain regions associated with implicit rather than explicit memory (Lieberman, 2000).

One method researchers use to assess implicit attitudes is a reaction time task called the Implicit Association Test (IAT; Greenwald et al., 1998). The IAT measures how quickly a person associates concepts or objects with positive or negative words. For example, using the same button to indicate that a name is female or that a word is bad is easier for people who have an implicit association between female and bad (**FIGURE 12.25**). In contrast, people who have an association between female and good will have a more difficult time using the same button to indicate that a name is female or that a word is bad. The logic of the IAT is that the difference in the average speed of responses when a button pairs female and good (Figure 12.25, conditions 2 and 3) versus female and bad (Figure 12.25, conditions 1 and 4) is an index of a person's implicit attitudes about females. People who are relatively faster to pair female with good (versus bad) are thought to have less implicit bias against women.

Use of the IAT has become controversial. There is some question of the reliability and stability of IAT scores. Lack of reliability appears to undermine the ability of the IAT to predict acts of racial and ethnic discrimination (Oswald et al., 2013). However, under the right set of conditions, scores on the IAT can meaningfully relate to measures of discrimination (Kurdi et al., 2019). The emerging consensus in the scientific community is that the IAT provides additional information beyond measures of explicit attitudes. Both types of measures can be useful in predicting behavior, but the IAT is best used as an aggregate measure of bias in a group of people (e.g., within an entire state) rather than as an individual measure of bias for a given person. Because of these nuances in interpreting IAT data, there is growing concern that the public perception of the IAT misrepresents the ability of the IAT to accurately predict racial bias in behavior.

Q According to the mere exposure effect, how would your attitude toward a new food change after repeated trials?

ANSWER: greater exposure across the repeated trials would lead to greater liking

12.10 Discrepancies Lead to Dissonance

Generally, attitudes seem to guide behavior. Citizens vote for candidates they like, and people avoid foods they do not like. What happens when people hold conflicting attitudes? Recall from Chapter 10 Leon Festinger's theory of cognitive dissonance (**FIGURE 12.26**). People have a need for psychological consistency, so when their attitudes conflict, they experience an unpleasant state of dissonance. The feeling of dissonance motivates people to reduce it, which can happen in one of several ways. People generally reduce dissonance by changing their attitudes or behaviors. Another option is to rationalize or trivialize the discrepancies.

FIGURE 12.26
Leon Festinger
Festinger's theory of cognitive dissonance was an important influence on research in experimental social psychology.

INSUFFICIENT JUSTIFICATION In a classic dissonance study, each participant performed an extremely boring task for an hour (Festinger & Carlsmith, 1959). The experimenter then paid the participant either $1 or $20 to lie to the next participant by telling them that the task was very interesting, educational, and worthwhile. Nearly all the participants lied in exchange for the money. Later, in what they thought was a different survey, the same participants were asked how worthwhile and enjoyable the task actually was. Which group of people do you think liked the task more? Participants who had been paid $1 rated the task much more favorably than did those who had been paid $20.

From the perspective of cognitive dissonance theory, this effect occurred because those paid $1 had *insufficient justification* for lying. People generally like to consider themselves to be honest, so the $1 payment simply was not enough for the participants to justify to themselves why they lied to another person. The conflict between the two beliefs, "I lied for (basically) no reason" and "I am an honest person," caused dissonance. Participants reduced this dissonance by changing their attitudes about the dull experimental task ("I did not lie because, in fact, I thought it was interesting"). Those paid $20 had plenty of justification for lying, since $20 was a large amount of money in 1959 (roughly equivalent to $150 today), so they did not experience conflict between their action ("I got paid a lot of money to say that") and their attitude ("I am an honest person") and did not have to change their attitudes about the task (**FIGURE 12.27**). As this research shows, one way to get people to change their attitudes is to change their behaviors first, using as few incentives as possible.

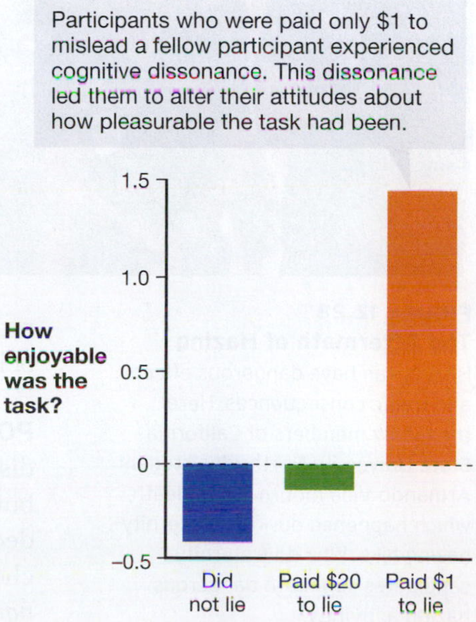

Participants who were paid only $1 to mislead a fellow participant experienced cognitive dissonance. This dissonance led them to alter their attitudes about how pleasurable the task had been.
How enjoyable was the task?
1.5
1.0
0.5
0
−0.5
Did not lie
Paid $20 to lie
Paid $1 to lie

FIGURE 12.27
Cognitive Dissonance
In Festinger and Carlsmith's dissonance study, participants performed an extremely boring task and then reported to other participants how enjoyable it was. Some participants were paid $20 to lie, and some were paid $1.

Learning Tip

The results of the classic Festinger and Carlsmith study are counterintuitive. Students usually expect that people who got paid $20 to lie would have liked the task more, when in fact the people who got paid $1 did. This effect is caused by the dissonance between thinking the task was boring and lying about it, which was insufficiently justified in the $1 condition. Remember that the attitude in question in this study is about the task itself (which was quite boring!), not the whole experiment. People surely liked receiving $20, but people who got that money could separate their attitudes about the money from their attitudes about the boring task.

JUSTIFYING EFFORT So far, the discussion of people's attitudes has focused on changes in individual behavior. What about group-related behavior? Consider the extreme group-related behaviors of initiation rites. On college campuses, administrators impose rules and penalties to discourage hazing, yet some fraternities and sororities continue to do it. The groups require new recruits to undergo embarrassing or difficult rites of passage because these endurance tests make membership in the group seem much more valuable. The rituals also make the group more cohesive.

To test these ideas, Eliot Aronson and Judson Mills (1959) required women to undergo a test to see if they qualified to take part in the second part of the study, a seminar on sexual behavior. Some women had to read a list of obscene words and sexually explicit passages in front of the male experimenter. In the 1950s, this task was very difficult and took considerable effort (and might have even bordered on sexual harassment). A control group read a list of milder words. Participants in both conditions then attended a boring and technical seminar on the sexual behavior of invertebrate animals. Women who had read the embarrassing words reported that the seminar was much more interesting, engaging, and important than did the women who had read the milder words.

FIGURE 12.28
The Aftermath of Hazing
Hazing can have dangerous effects and tragic consequences. Here, the family members of California State University Northridge student Armando Villa mourn Villa's death, which happened during a fraternity-hazing hike. Why do fraternity candidates submit to dangerous hazing activities?

As this research shows, people experience a great deal of dissonance when they put themselves through pain, embarrassment, or discomfort to join a group. The conflict between not liking pain or embarrassment and making the choice to experience it is a powerful source of dissonance. People can resolve the dissonance by inflating the importance of the group and their commitment to it ("The discomfort was worth it because the group is so important"). This justification of effort helps explain why people are willing to subject themselves to humiliating experiences such as hazing (**FIGURE 12.28**). More tragically, it may help explain why some people who give up connections to families and friends to join cults or to follow enigmatic leaders are willing to die rather than leave the groups. If they have sacrificed so much to join a group, people believe the group must be extraordinarily important.

POSTDECISIONAL DISSONANCE According to cognitive dissonance theory, dissonance can arise when a person holds positive attitudes about different options but chooses one of the options anyway. For example, a person might have trouble deciding which of many excellent colleges to attend. The person might narrow the choice to two or three alternatives and then have to choose. *Postdecisional dissonance* then motivates the person to focus on the chosen school's positive aspects and the other schools' negative aspects. This effect occurs automatically, with minimal cognitive processing, and apparently without awareness. Indeed, even patients with long-term memory loss show postdecisional effects for past choices, even if the patients do not consciously recall which items they chose (Lieberman et al., 2001).

Q When Tess started college he was not sure if he wanted to join a fraternity but still decided to pledge. After experiencing harsh hazing, he now feels fraternity membership is one of the best parts of his college experience. How could cognitive dissonance explain his change in attitude?

ANSWER: Tess experienced dissonance during the pain of hazing, so he justified the suffering by changing his attitude toward fraternity membership.

12.11 Attitudes and Behaviors Can Be Changed Through Persuasion

Many forces other than dissonance can change attitudes. People are bombarded by television advertisements; lectures from parents, teachers, and physicians; politicians' appeals for votes; and so on. **Persuasion** is the active and conscious effort to change an attitude or behavior, usually with a message of some kind. In the earliest scientific work on persuasion, Carl Hovland and colleagues (1953) emphasized that persuasion is most likely to occur when people pay attention to a message, understand it, and find it convincing. In addition, the message must be memorable so its impact lasts over time.

persuasion The active and conscious effort to change an attitude through the transmission of a message.

Various factors affect the persuasiveness of a message (Petty & Wegener, 1998). These factors include the *source* (who delivers the message), the *content* (what the message says), and the *receiver* (who processes the message). Sources who are both attractive and credible are the most persuasive. Thus, television ads for medicines and medical services often feature very attractive people playing the roles of physicians. Even better, of course, is when a drug company ad uses a spokesperson who is both attractive *and* an actual doctor. Receivers also find people who are similar to themselves to be more credible and persuasive sources.

Under some circumstances, the arguments in the message are also important for persuasion (Greenwald, 1968). Strong arguments that appeal to emotions are the most persuasive. Advertisers also use the mere exposure effect, repeating the message over and over in the hope that multiple exposures will lead to increased persuasiveness. For this reason, politicians often make the same statements over and over during campaigns. Those who want to persuade (including, of course, politicians) also have to decide whether to deliver one-sided arguments or to consider both sides of particular issues. One-sided arguments work best when the audience is on the speaker's side or is gullible. With a more skeptical crowd, speakers who acknowledge both sides but argue that one is superior tend to be more persuasive than those who completely ignore the opposing view.

According to the **elaboration likelihood model** (Petty & Cacioppo, 1986), persuasive communication leads to attitude change in two ways (**FIGURE 12.29**). When people are motivated and able to process information, persuasion takes the *central route*. That is, people are paying attention to the arguments, considering all the information, and using rational cognitive processes. This route leads to strong attitudes that last over time and that people actively defend. When people are either not motivated to process information or unable to process it, persuasion takes the *peripheral route*. That is, people minimally process the message.

elaboration likelihood model The idea that persuasive messages lead to attitude changes in either of two ways: via the central route or via the peripheral route.

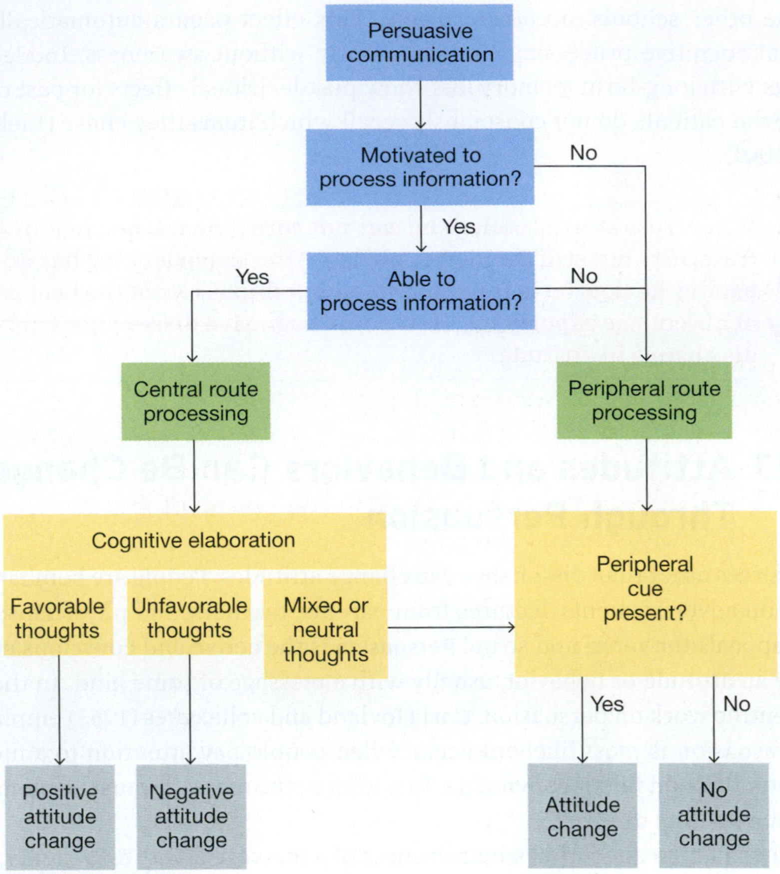

FIGURE 12.29

The Elaboration Likelihood Model

When people are motivated and able to consider information, they process it via the central route. As a result, their attitude changes reflect cognitive elaboration (left). When people are either not motivated or not able to consider information, they process it via the peripheral route. As a result, their attitude changes reflect the presence or absence of shallow peripheral cues. For example, as a result of peripheral processing, people may be persuaded because the person making an argument is attractive or a celebrity (right).

This route leads to more-impulsive action, as when a person decides to purchase a product because a celebrity has endorsed it or because of how an advertisement makes the person feel. Peripheral cues, such as the attractiveness or status of the person making the argument, influence what attitude is adopted. Attitudes developed through the peripheral route are weaker and more likely to change over time.

compliance The tendency to agree to do things requested by others.

COMPLIANCE People often persuade others to change their behavior simply by asking them to do so. If the other people do the requested thing, they are exhibiting **compliance**. A number of factors increase compliance. For instance, Joseph Forgas (1998) has demonstrated that a person in a good mood is especially likely to comply. This tendency may be the basis for "buttering up" others when we want things from them. In addition, Ellen Langer and colleagues (1978) found that people often comply with requests (such as a request to cut in line to use the copier) if a reason—any reason—is given. Because people fail to pay attention and want to avoid conflict, they follow a standard mental shortcut: Comply with a request that is justified by a reason. For example, asking "Can I cut in front of you because I need to make copies?" sounds like a reason but makes little sense (**FIGURE 12.30**). But it is far more effective than asking only "Can I cut in front of you?" Recall from Chapter 1 that heuristic processing is a form of psychological reasoning in which mental shortcuts can yield quick results, but noncritical thinking can also lead to poor conclusions or bad outcomes.

As shown in **TABLE 12.1**, people can use a number of powerful strategies to influence others to comply. Consider the *foot in the door* technique: If people agree to a small request, they become more likely to comply with a large and undesirable request. Jonathan Freedman and Scott Fraser (1966) asked homeowners to allow a large, unattractive "DRIVE CAREFULLY" sign to be placed on their front lawns. As you might imagine, fewer than 1 in 5 people agreed to do so. Other homeowners, however, were first asked to sign a petition that supported legislation intended to reduce traffic accidents. A few weeks later, these same people were approached about having the large sign placed on their lawns, and more than half agreed. Once people *commit* to a course of action, they behave in ways consistent with that commitment. (Recall from Chapter 10 that consistency is an important need.)

The opposite influence technique is the *door in the face*: People are more likely to agree to a small request after they have refused a large request (Cialdini et al., 1975). After all, the second request seems modest in comparison, and people want to seem reasonable. For example, an interviewer might be more successful in asking for five minutes of someone's time after first asking, but being rejected, for two hours. The effectiveness of this strategy relies on reciprocity, in which the compliant person feels compelled to compromise because the requester has compromised. Recall from the beginning of this chapter that reciprocity is one of the basic features of social groups. As you might have encountered, salespeople often use this technique.

Another favorite tactic among salespeople is *low-balling*. Here, a salesperson offers a product—for example, a car—for a very low price. Once the customer agrees, the salesperson may claim that the manager did not approve the price or that there will be additional charges. Someone who has already agreed to buy a product will often agree to pay the increased cost. The big decision was

FIGURE 12.30
Reasons for Compliance
People waiting in line to use the copier were more likely to comply with a request to cut ahead if the person making the request gave a reason, even if it did not make sense: "Can I cut in front of you? I need to make copies."

Table 12.1 The Three Ways of Inducing Compliance

TECHNIQUE	INFLUENCE METHOD	EXAMPLE
Foot in the door	If you agree to a small request, you are more likely to comply with a large request.	You agree to help a friend move a couch. Now you are more likely to comply when she asks you to help her move all of her belongings to her new apartment.
Door in the face	If you refuse a large request, you are more likely to comply with a smaller request.	A marketer calls, and you refuse to answer a product questionnaire that takes 20 minutes. Now you are likely to agree to answer 5 questions about a product.
Low-balling	When you agree to buy a product for a certain price, you are likely to comply with a request to pay more for the product.	You agree to buy a used car for $4,750. When the salesman says he forgot to add some charges, you agree to buy the car for $5,275.

whether to make a purchase at all. Once a person has committed to that option, then deciding to do so by spending a bit more money does not seem like such a big decision.

Q Under what condition is it more persuasive for a source to describe both sides of a position before emphasizing the superiority of one side?

ANSWER: when the receivers are skeptical about the source or the source's position

How Do People Think About Others?

Learning Objectives

- Discuss the roles of appearance and nonverbal behavior in impression formation.
- Define the fundamental attribution error and the actor/observer discrepancy.
- Describe the functions of stereotypes.
- Distinguish between prejudice and discrimination.
- Define modern racism and discuss its impact on prejudice and discrimination.
- Discuss strategies to inhibit stereotypes and reduce prejudice.

Our beliefs about other people are some of the most important attitudes humans hold. Our expectations of what other people will do guide how we think about them and interact with them. Social psychologists have studied the ways we form impressions of others. Sometimes these impressions are accurate, but they can also be mistaken. It is critical to understand how our own perceptual biases inform how we think about others.

12.12 People Make Judgments About Others

When someone walks toward you, you make several quick judgments. For example, do you know the person? Does the person pose a threat? What are this person's intentions?

The first thing people notice about another person is usually their face. When human babies are less than an hour old, they prefer to look at and will track a picture of a human face rather than a blank outline of a head (Morton & Johnson, 1991). After all, the face communicates information such as emotional state, interest, competence, and trustworthiness. In one study, participants were shown pairs of faces of candidates who were competing in U.S. congressional elections. The people selected as the most competent, based solely on facial appearance, won nearly 70 percent of the actual elections (Todorov et al., 2005). Identifying people who are—and are not—trustworthy is key to our survival as social animals. By age 7, children can make judgments about whether a face is trustworthy or not (using descriptors such as *nice* or *mean*) that match adult consensus judgments (Cogsdill et al., 2014). As mentioned in Chapter 10, the amygdala is particularly important for judging trustworthiness.

nonverbal behavior The facial expressions, gestures, mannerisms, and movements by which one communicates with others.

NONVERBAL BEHAVIOR Facial expressions, gestures, mannerisms, and movements are all examples of **nonverbal behavior**, sometimes referred to as *body language* (**FIGURE 12.31a**). How much can be learned from nonverbal behavior? Nalini Ambady and Robert Rosenthal (1993) have found that people can make accurate judgments based on only a few seconds of observation. Ambady and Rosenthal refer to such quick views as *thin slices of behavior*. Thin slices of behavior are powerful cues for impression formation. For instance, videotapes of judges giving instructions to juries reveal that a judge's nonverbal actions can predict whether a jury will find the defendant guilty or not guilty (Hart, 1995). Judges, perhaps unconsciously, may indicate their beliefs about guilt or innocence through facial expressions, tones of voice, and gestures. People show quite a bit of agreement in their ratings of intentions, emotions, and even sexual orientation based on nonverbal behavior (Rule, 2017; Todorov et al., 2015). One research team used what psychologists have learned about the nonverbal cues indicating

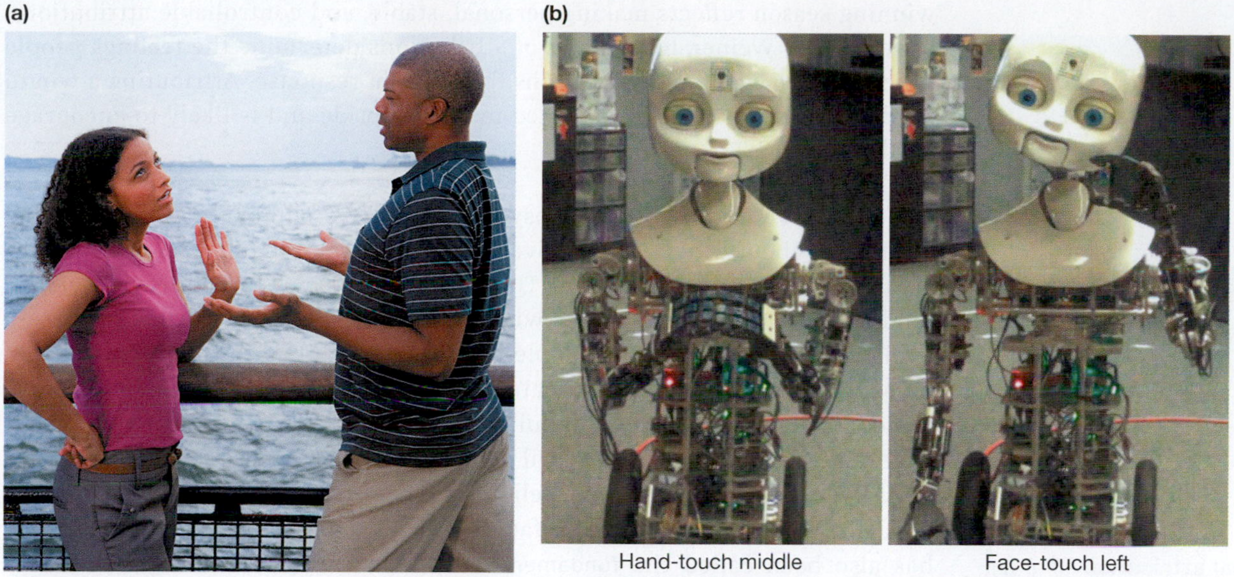

FIGURE 12.31
Reading Nonverbal Behavior
(a) People's body language affects others' impressions of the people and their situations. **(b)** In one study, psychologists programmed a robot, Nexi, to make a range of gestures to identify which cues people use to detect trustworthiness (DeSteno et al., 2012). Which of these gestures seems trustworthy to you?

trustworthiness to build a robot that people found trustworthy (DeSteno et al., 2012; **FIGURE 12.31b**).

ATTRIBUTIONAL DIMENSIONS People continuously try to explain other people's motives, traits, and preferences. **Attributions** are explanations for events or actions, including other people's behavior. Understanding why things happen helps people predict what will happen in the future and provides a sense of order. People prefer to think that things happen for reasons and that therefore they can anticipate future events. For instance, you might expect that if you study for an exam, you will do well on it.

attributions People's explanations for why events or actions occur.

Most events can be explained in several ways. For example, doing well on a test could be due to brilliance, luck, intensive studying, the test being easy, or a combination of factors. Fritz Heider (1944) was among the first psychologists to think systematically about attribution. Heider's foundational theory of attribution drew a distinction between two essential types of attributions. **Personal attributions** place the cause of a behavior on internal factors. These are also known as *dispositional* attributions because they credit behavior to things that are part of the actor, such as abilities, moods, or efforts. If you believe you did well on an exam because you worked hard and are smart, you are making a personal attribution. In contrast, **situational attributions** are external attributions. These explanations place the cause of a behavior on outside events, such as luck, accidents, or the actions of other people. Thus, if you blame poor test performance on the quality of the exam items, you are making a situational attribution.

personal attributions Explanations of people's behavior that refer to their internal characteristics, such as abilities, traits, moods, or efforts.

situational attributions Explanations of people's behavior that refer to external events, such as the weather, luck, accidents, or other people's actions.

Bernard Weiner (1974) noted that attributions can vary on other dimensions. For example, attributions can be stable over time (permanent) or unstable (temporary). They can be controllable or uncontrollable. Blaming your field hockey team's loss on the weather involves making situational, unstable, and uncontrollable attributions. Explaining that hard work produced your team's winning season reflects making personal, stable, and controllable attributions. According to Weiner, these types of attributions determine the feelings people have about an event and the actions they take in response. Attributing a win to hard work, for instance, is expected to lead to pride and is likely to encourage hard work again.

ATTRIBUTIONAL BIAS Social psychologists have compared people making inferences about others to intuitive scientists developing and testing hypotheses about the causes of events. Unlike objective scientists, however, people tend to be systematically biased when they process social information. When explaining others' behavior, people tend to overemphasize the importance of personality traits and underestimate the importance of situations. For example, someone who follows orders to inflict harm on another, as in Milgram's obedience study, is assumed to be an evil person. Edward Jones called this the *correspondence bias*: focusing on the beliefs and dispositions that *correspond* with a behavior while neglecting other factors (Jones & Davis, 1965). This tendency has also been called the **fundamental attribution error** because it involves a mistaken association between a behavior and a fundamental feature about a person (Ross, 1977).

fundamental attribution error In explaining other people's behavior, the tendency to overemphasize personality traits and underestimate situational factors.

These biases are common because the situational and social factors that influence behavior are often invisible. For instance, the social pressure that leads people to obey authority exists inside the heads of the obedient people but is not apparent to outside observers. Consider the phenomenon of actors getting "typecast" for playing a certain kind of role, such as a villain. When actors play these roles, viewers and casting directors alike commit the fundamental attribution error when they believe that the personality of the actor is similar to that of the characters the actor portrays. Some of these actors might be evil people. But when viewers develop this belief based on what they see on-screen, they neglect to consider how much of their belief about the actors' personalities is determined by the characters that writers created (**FIGURE 12.32**).

actor/observer discrepancy The tendency to focus on situations to explain one's own behavior but to focus on dispositions to explain other people's behavior.

FIGURE 12.32
Fundamental Attribution Error
Viewers often believe actors share personality traits with the characters they portray. The actor Tom Felton, who played Draco Malfoy in the Harry Potter series, has been cast as a villain in various roles.

In contrast, when people make attributions about themselves, they tend to take credit for achievements but blame failures on external or situational factors. In conjunction with the fundamental attribution error, this focus on situational explanations for one's own behavior leads to the **actor/observer discrepancy**. This term refers to the combined force of two biases: people's tendency to focus on situations when interpreting their own behavior, and the tendency to focus on dispositions when interpreting other people's behavior. For instance, people tend to attribute their own lateness to external factors, such as traffic or competing demands. They tend to attribute other people's lateness to personal characteristics, such as laziness or lack of organization. According to a meta-analysis of 173 studies, the actor/observer effect is not large and happens mainly for negative events or when people explain the behavior of people they know well (Malle, 2006). The fundamental attribution error and the actor/observer discrepancy tend to cast the person explaining the behavior in a favorable light. This tendency for people to have *self-serving biases* is discussed further in Chapter 13.

Is the fundamental attribution error a global phenomenon or specific to certain cultures? As discussed in Chapter 1, people in Eastern cultures tend to be more holistic in how they perceive the world. They focus on the forest rather than individual trees. On average, people in Eastern cultures use much more information when making attributions than do people in Western cultures. People in Eastern cultures are more likely to take the perspective of other people and understand that their behavior is determined by both personal and situational factors (Chopik et al., 2017). Though Easterners are more likely than Westerners to take situational forces into account, they do still tend to favor personal information over situational information when making attributions about others (Choi et al., 1999). Thus, in interpreting behavior, people from various cultures tend not to differ in whether they emphasize personal factors. Instead, they differ in how much they emphasize the situation.

Q If you are biased by the actor/observer discrepancy, how would you explain your late arrival to class differently from your classmate's late arrival?

ANSWER: You would attribute your lateness to situational factors and your classmate's lateness to personality flaws.

12.13 Stereotypes Can Lead to Prejudice and Discrimination

Do all Italians have fiery tempers? Do all Canadians like hockey? Can women rap? People hold beliefs about groups because such beliefs make it possible to answer these sorts of questions quickly—if not accurately (FIGURE 12.33). As discussed in Chapter 8, such beliefs are stereotypes. That is, they are cognitive schemas in which group membership is used to organize information about people. Stereotypes are mental shortcuts, or heuristics, that allow for easy, fast processing of social information. Stereotyping occurs automatically and, in most cases, outside of awareness (Devine, 1989).

In and of themselves, stereotypes are neutral. They reflect a push for efficiency that is inherent in our mental machinery. They can contain information that is negative or positive. Some stereotypes are based in truth: Older adults tend to be more deliberate in their decisions than younger adults do, whereas younger adults tend to be impulsive. These statements are true on average. However, not all older adults are thoughtful, nor are all younger adults impulsive.

People use stereotypes for one simple reason: to efficiently form impressions of others within the built-in constraints on mental processing (Macrae et al., 1994; Shenhav et al., 2017). Limits on mental resources prevent people from contemplating the unique properties of each person they encounter. Humans are simply not capable of processing that much information, so they simplify the task by categorizing others into groups with known stereotypes. For example, you might

(a) (b)

FIGURE 12.33
Stereotypes
(a) Would this photo of fans at a 2010 Olympic gold medal hockey game between Canada and the United States lead you to think that all Canadians like hockey? **(b)** When you think of a rapper, do you picture a woman? Probably not. But Megan Thee Stallion has won several major music awards since 2016 in a traditionally male-dominated field.

automatically categorize your classmates by their clothing or hairstyles. Once you have placed them into categories, you can apply your existing stereotype beliefs about the categories to each classmate. That is, stereotypes affect the formation of impressions, which can be positive or negative (Kunda & Spencer, 2003).

People maintain stereotypes over time. Stereotypes guide attention toward information that confirms the stereotypes and away from disconfirming evidence. Memories may also become biased to match stereotypes. As a result of directed attention and memory biases, people may see *illusory correlations*. Such correlations are an example of the psychological reasoning error of seeing relationships that do not exist (discussed in Chapter 1 and in Section 6.11, "You Be the Psychologist: Can You Challenge Superstitious Behaviors?"). In this case, people believe false relationships because they notice only information that confirms their stereotypes. For example, one type of behavior might be perceived in different ways so it is consistent with a stereotype. A lawyer described as aggressive and a construction worker described as aggressive conjure up different images.

Moreover, when people encounter someone who does not fit a stereotype, they put that person in a special category rather than alter the stereotype. This latter process is known as *subtyping*. Thus, a racist who believes Latinx people are lazy may categorize highly productive stars such as Selena Gomez or Jennifer Lopez as exceptions to the rule rather than as evidence for the error of the stereotype. Forming subtypes allows people to maintain all kinds of stereotypes, including racist ones such as this.

prejudice Negative feelings, opinions, and beliefs associated with a stereotype.

discrimination The differential treatment of people as a result of prejudice against their group.

PREJUDICE AND DISCRIMINATION Stereotypes can lead to prejudice and discrimination. **Prejudice** involves negative feelings, opinions, and beliefs associated with a stereotype. **Discrimination** is the differential treatment of people based merely on their group membership. Prejudice and discrimination are responsible for much of the conflict and warfare around the world. Groups of people have been discriminated against because of prejudice in nearly all societies in recorded history (Sidanius & Pratto, 2001). Social psychologists have studied the causes and consequences of prejudice, and they have tried to find ways to reduce its destructive effects.

Why do stereotypes so often lead to prejudice and discrimination? One broad explanation, as discussed in Section 12.1, is that evolution has led to two processes that produce prejudice and discrimination: People tend to favor their own groups over other groups, and people tend to stigmatize those who pose threats to their groups. Together, social identity theory and the idea that individuals' survival is dependent on their group obtaining scarce resources lead to the prediction that people might feel threatened by anything that favors the outgroup at the expense of the ingroup. For instance, reminding White Americans of the racial demographic shift toward greater diversity in the United States makes them more likely to favor policies that disadvantage non-White Americans (Craig & Richeson, 2014). People naturally categorize people into groups and identify with and defend their ingroups.

Learning Tip

How do you remember the differences among prejudice, discrimination, and stereotypes? One way is to link them to the ABCs of how social psychology understands human psychology: **A**ffect, **B**ehavior, and **C**ognition. Prejudice is a form of negative affect. Discrimination consists of overtly biased behavior. And stereotypes are thoughts and beliefs (cognition) about other people based on their group membership.

STEREOTYPES AND PERCEPTION As mentioned earlier, stereotypes can affect attention. This influence extends to even basic perceptual processes. In 2017, the Colgate University campus was locked down because of a report of an armed person in the student center. It turned out that a Black student was carrying a glue gun on his way to work on an art project. In a letter to the community, the Colgate president, Brian Casey, suggested that a subtle, *implicit* bias might have played a role in both the reporting of the incident and the response of safety officers, as people assumed the Black person was holding a weapon and was dangerous.

The kind of implicit bias demonstrated by the officers at Colgate is demonstrated in the *shooter bias* effect (Correll et al., 2002). In the standard version of the shooter bias task, participants view pictures of people holding either guns or non-gun objects, such as wallets or cell phones. The participant's job is to respond as quickly as possible by pressing one button to "shoot" if the person in the picture is holding a gun and a different button for "don't shoot" if the person is not holding a gun (**FIGURE 12.34a**). In dozens of versions of this task, the results are the same: On non-gun trials, participants are more likely to mistakenly press "shoot" when the person in the picture is Black, whereas on gun trials, they are more likely to mistakenly press "don't shoot" when the person is White (**FIGURE 12.34b**). These mistakes occur in part because participants are more likely to "see" objects held by Black people as weapons even when they are not. This reaction is likely due to the inclusion of the concepts of "weapon" and "danger" in the stereotype of Black people (Eberhardt et al., 2004).

Fortunately, there is evidence that special training—in which race is unrelated to the presence of a weapon—can help police officers minimize racial bias in deciding when to shoot (Kahn & McMahon, 2015). Research compared police officers who had received this training with community members who had not. In simulated decisions to shoot or not shoot Black and White characters, the police officers were much less likely to shoot unarmed people and were equally likely to shoot armed Black and White people (Correll et al., 2007). The community members were more likely to shoot unarmed Black people. Thus, training seems to partially override the effects of stereotypes.

(a)

(b)

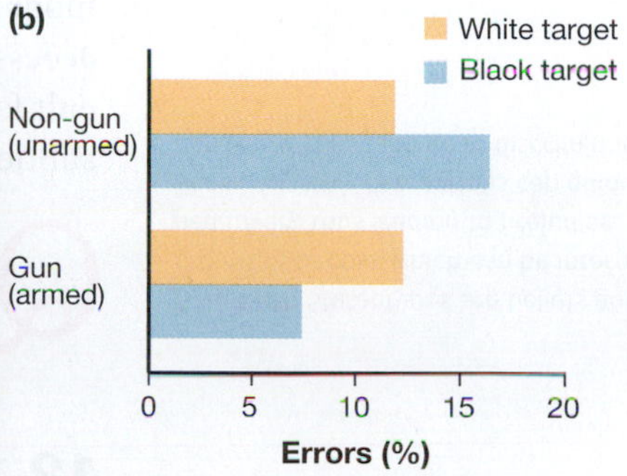

FIGURE 12.34
Stereotypes and Perception
(a) Participants were briefly shown a picture of a Black or White man holding a gun or a non-gun object. **(b)** The participants responded "shoot" if the man had a gun and "don't shoot" if the man had another object. Participants make more "shoot" errors for unarmed Black men and more "don't shoot" errors for armed White men. This study underscores the potentially deadly consequences of the influence of stereotypes on perception.

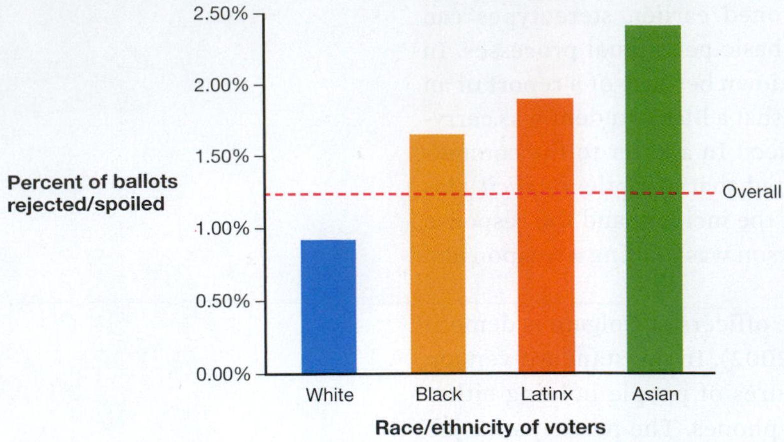

FIGURE 12.35
Modern Prejudice
Voting rights can reveal subtle forms of prejudice. Many supporters of changes to voting procedures do not advocate discrimination against non-White racial groups. But the policies they support have the effect of making it more difficult for those groups to vote. The data here are from the 2020 primary election in Georgia, when the mail-in ballots of Asian, Latinx, and Black voters were about twice as likely to be rejected as the mail-in ballots of White voters.

MODERN PREJUDICE Even people who believe themselves to be egalitarian may hold negative implicit attitudes about certain groups of people. Although nowadays most people do not admit to being racist, and many explicitly reject racist attitudes, there remain more subtle forms of prejudice and discrimination. Social psychologists have introduced the idea of **modern racism**, which refers to subtle forms of prejudice that coexist with the outward rejection of racist beliefs. Modern racism entails believing that discrimination is no longer a serious problem and that minority groups are demanding too much change to "traditional" societal values (Henry & Sears, 2002). Words such as "traditional" and "heritage" are often associated with modern racism because they conjure times in the past when overt prejudice and extreme acts of discrimination were common without explicitly endorsing them.

modern racism Subtle forms of prejudice that coexist with the rejection of racist beliefs.

The essence of modern racism is indirectly endorsing actions or policies that have the same effect as overt discrimination without labeling them as such. Modern racism hides prejudice but still endorses discrimination. For instance, people may condemn racist attitudes toward Latinx people but be unwilling to help a Latinx person in need (Abad-Merino et al., 2013). For this reason, psychologists measure modern racism by asking participants to report their attitudes about policies that would differentially affect racial groups rather than their attitudes about overt prejudice. One study used a questionnaire to assess subtle racism against Asians in Canada (Son Hing et al., 2008). Participants indicated whether they agreed with statements such as "There are too many foreign students of Asian descent being allowed to attend university in Canada," "Discrimination against Asians is no longer a problem in Canada," and "It is too easy for Asians to illegally arrive in Canada and receive refugee status." Those who agreed with the statements were more likely to support policies that discriminated against Asians.

Modern racism arises in part because the equal treatment of minorities can challenge societal structures that benefit the majority. Other prejudices also have modern, subtle forms, such as when people say that everyone should have equal access to voting but support policies that have the effect of making it more difficult for some groups of people to vote than others (**FIGURE 12.35**). The prejudice is subtle, but its effects can be quite harmful.

Q How can stereotypes lead to discrimination?

ANSWER: Stereotypes are beliefs about groups of people, which can be interpreted negatively, thus leading to prejudice. These negative perceptions can guide our behaviors, thus leading to discrimination.

12.14 Prejudice and Its Effects Can Be Reduced

As noted in Section 12.7, people discriminate against people in outgroups less when the groups have common goals. Sharing goals can also reduce prejudice. There are additional ways to reduce prejudice. For example, bilingual instruction in schools reduces ingroup favoritism in elementary school children (Wright & Tropp, 2005). Explicit training about stereotypes can also reduce prejudice. In one study, participants who practiced associating women and counter-stereotypical qualities—for example, strength and dominance—were more likely than participants in a control group to hire women (Kawakami et al., 2005).

Stereotyping and discrimination can have devastating effects on victims, such as violence, stress-induced illness, and premature death. Victims also experience more subtle consequences that can nonetheless have substantial impacts on their well-being. One example is **stereotype threat**. This effect is the concern or fear people experience if they believe that their performance on a task could confirm negative stereotypes about their group (Spencer et al., 2016; Steele and Aronson, 1995; **FIGURE 12.36**). Stereotype threat causes distraction and anxiety, interfering with performance by reducing the capacity of short-term memory and undermining confidence and motivation (Schmader, 2010).

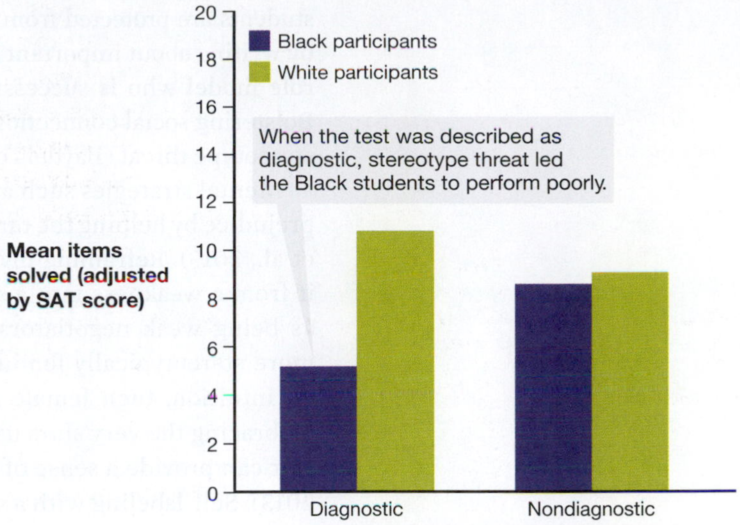

FIGURE 12.36
Stereotype Threat
Stereotype threat can lead Black students to perform poorly on standardized tests that are described as diagnostic of ability in a domain.

Stereotype threat applies to any member of a group who believes that negative stereotypes exist about the group. For example, when women take standardized math tests, those who believe that men do better on such tests tend to do worse than men. Women who do not hold this belief do not achieve measurably different scores than men do (Schmader et al., 2008).

One intriguing study found two examples of stereotype threat among the same people (Shih et al., 1999). Asian American women did well on a math test when the "Asians are good at math" stereotype was primed by having them respond to questions about racial identity. They did poorly when the "women are bad at math" stereotype was primed by having them respond to questions about gender. Notably, in this same study women from Vancouver showed a slightly different pattern. Their scores were reduced when they were primed as women, but their performance was not affected by the Asian prime because the stereotype that Asians score better on math tests is less prevalent in Canada than it is in the United States. These results demonstrate the power of social and cultural stereotypes to create or alleviate the effects of stereotype threat on individual performance.

stereotype threat Fear or concern about confirming negative stereotypes related to one's own group, which in turn impairs performance on a task.

A meta-analysis examined 39 independent laboratory studies on stereotype threat (Walton & Spencer, 2009). Together, these studies included 3,180 participants from five countries (Canada, France, Germany, Sweden, and the United States) and many stereotyped groups (e.g., Blacks, Latinos, Turkish Germans, women). Overall, stereotyped groups performed worse than nonstereotyped groups when a test was presented as evaluative. However, this effect was reversed when the threat was reduced and the exam was presented as nonevaluative, such as by giving questions in the form of games.

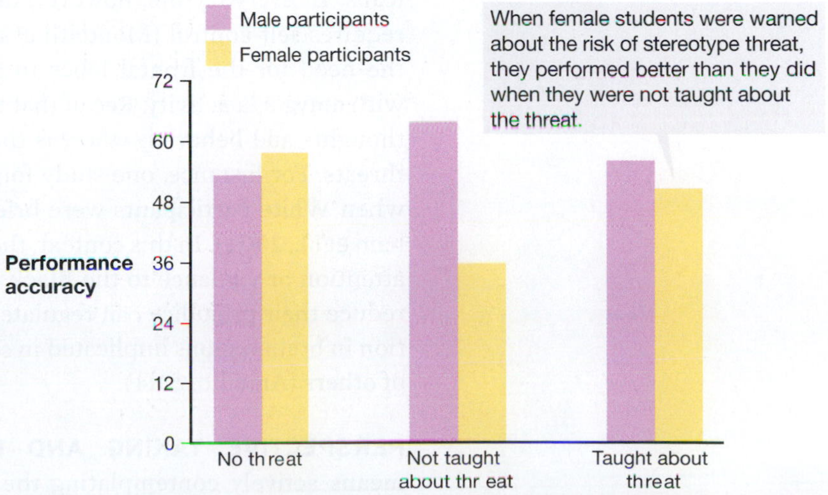

FIGURE 12.37
Stereotype Threat Counteracted
Stereotype threat can be counteracted when people are warned about it.

Interventions to reduce stereotype threat effects are often successful. For instance, informing people about the negative consequences of stereotype threat can shield them from the negative effects (Johns et al., 2005; **FIGURE 12.37**). Black students are protected from stereotype threat when they engage in self-affirmation by writing about important personal values (see Chapter 10) or read about a Black role model who is successful in the stereotyped domain (Shapiro et al., 2013). Bolstering social connections and peer relations more generally can help prevent stereotype threat (Baydala et al., 2009).

Mental strategies such as *reframing* and *self-labeling* can reduce the effects of prejudice by helping the target think about the situation in a different way (Wang et al., 2017). Reframing involves taking a negative stereotype and transforming it from a weakness into a strength. For instance, women are often stereotyped as being weak negotiators. However, if negotiation is reframed as requiring more stereotypically feminine traits, such as being a good listener and relying on intuition, then female negotiators outperform men. Self-labeling involves embracing the very slurs used against you (e.g., *queer*). Taking ownership of the slur can provide a sense of power to those who are stigmatized (Galinsky et al., 2013). Self-labeling with a slur can reduce its negative associations in the minds of observers.

INHIBITING STEREOTYPES Patricia Devine (1989) made the important point that people can override the stereotypes they hold and act in nondiscriminatory ways. For instance, most people in North America know some of the negative stereotypes associated with Muslim Americans. When a non-Muslim North American encounters a Muslim person, the information in the stereotypes often comes to mind. According to Devine, people who are motivated to be low in prejudice can override this automatic activation and act in a nondiscriminatory fashion. Devine has even developed "prejudice habit-breaking" interventions that help people reduce the effects of their biases (Cox & Devine, 2019). Although automatic stereotypes can alter how people perceive and understand the behavior of those they stereotype, simply categorizing people does not necessarily lead to mistreating them.

Evidence shows that people can indeed consciously alter their automatic stereotyping (Kawakami et al., 2000). For instance, Dasgupta and Greenwald (2001) found that presenting positive examples of admired Black individuals (e.g., Denzel Washington) produced more-favorable responses toward African Americans. In everyday life, however, inhibiting stereotyped thinking is difficult and requires self-control (Monteith et al., 2016). The challenge comes, in part, from the need for the frontal lobes to override the emotional responses associated with amygdala activity. Recall that the frontal lobes are important for controlling thoughts and behavior, whereas the amygdala is involved in detecting potential threats. For instance, one study found that activation in the amygdala increased when White participants were briefly shown pictures of Black faces (Cunningham et al., 2004). In this context, the amygdala activity might indicate heightened attention or vigilance to the Black faces. However, people who are motivated to reduce their prejudice can regulate this amygdala activity with increased activation in brain regions implicated in self-control and thinking about the viewpoints of others (Amodio, 2014).

PERSPECTIVE TAKING AND PERSPECTIVE GIVING *Perspective taking* means actively contemplating the psychological experiences of other people. Such contemplation can reduce racial bias and stereotyping and help smooth potentially awkward interracial interactions (Shih et al., 2013). In one study, participants who used perspective taking rated a typical construction worker to be smarter and more invested in their work and a typical doctor to be less intelligent and less invested than did participants in the control condition who did not engage in perspective taking and used their stereotypes to rate a typical construction worker and doctor (Wang et al., 2014). Taking the perspective of a transgender person markedly reduced prejudice in a sample of more than 500 voters in Florida, an effect that persisted three months later (Broockman & Kalla, 2016).

The effectiveness of perspective taking for reducing prejudice might depend on whether the person engaged in the activity is a member of the majority group or the minority group. In a study that included Palestinian and Israeli participants, perspective taking led to the largest positive changes in the Israelis' attitude toward the Palestinians (Bruneau & Saxe, 2012). By contrast, *perspective giving*, in which people share their experiences of being targets of discrimination, led to the largest positive changes in the Palestinians' attitude toward the Israelis. These results illustrate the critical roles in reducing prejudice of *being heard* for people in groups with less political power (e.g., the Palestinians) and *listening* for those in groups with more power (i.e., the Israelis). Bruneau and Saxe (2012) found a similar pattern for Mexican immigrants and White Americans in Arizona (**FIGURE 12.38**). Notably, perspective taking by the Mexican group actually worsened their attitudes about White Americans. Disempowered groups may resent having to consider the perspectives of empowered groups (Bruneau & Saxe, 2010). Indeed, perspective taking can backfire whenever an individual feels threatened by the other group (Sassenrath et al., 2016).

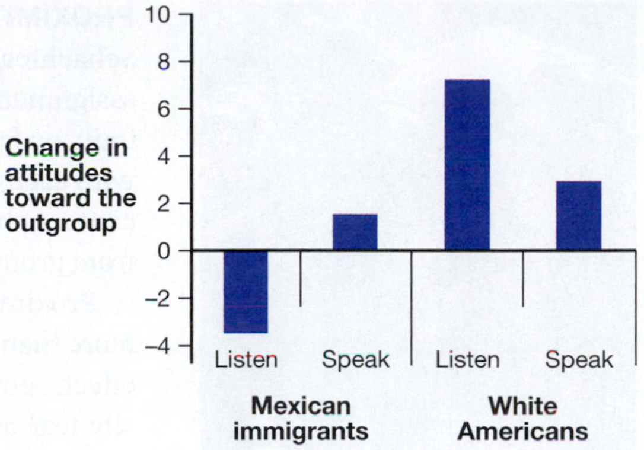

FIGURE 12.38
Power and Perspective
For Mexican immigrants, who have less political power than White Americans, being heard led to more-positive attitudes toward the outgroup. By contrast, perspective taking led to a worsening of attitudes. For White Americans, who have more political power, being heard led to more-positive attitudes toward the outgroup, but listening produced even greater change.

Q **How can stereotype threat undermine the performance of people from a stereotyped group?**

ANSWER: Performance is reduced when stereotyped people become distracted, self-conscious, anxious, and concerned by the threat of confirming the negative stereotype about their group.

What Determines the Quality of Relationships?

Learning Objectives

- Identify factors that influence interpersonal attraction.
- Distinguish between passionate and companionate love.
- Identify attitudes and behaviors that contribute to healthy, satisfying relationships.

A *relationship* is a connection between people, such as friends or romantic partners. Researchers have studied the factors that lead people to form relationships (Berscheid & Regan, 2005). Many of these findings consider the adaptive value of forming lasting affiliative bonds with others. Here, we consider the quality of human relationships: how friendships develop, why people fall in love, why romantic relationships sometimes fail, and how people can work to sustain their romantic relationships.

12.15 Situational and Personal Factors Influence Interpersonal Attraction and Friendships

Psychological research has identified several factors that forecast which people become friends, romantic partners, or even enemies. Some of these are situational, such as the frequency with which people come into contact, whereas others depend on specific personal characteristics, such as whether a person is judged to be trustworthy. For romantic relationships, psychologists have also identified certain physical characteristics that people tend to find attractive in a potential partner.

FIGURE 12.39
Similarity in Attitudes and Attraction
Friends and romantic partners tend to be similar in personal characteristics, attitudes, beliefs, and attractiveness. A good example of this matching is Beyoncé and Jay-Z, both of whom are very attractive, successful musicians and entrepreneurs.

PROXIMITY AND FAMILIARITY In an early study, Leon Festinger, Stanley Schachter, and Kurt Back (1950) examined friends in a college dorm. Because room assignments were random, the researchers were able to examine the effects of proximity on friendship. *Proximity* here simply means how often people come into contact with each other because they are physically nearby. The more often people come into contact, the more likely they are to become friends. Real-life social networks are born from groups of people who are in regular contact (Rivera et al., 2010).

Proximity might have its effects because of familiarity: People like familiar things more than unfamiliar ones. As discussed in Section 12.9, because of the mere exposure effect, people tend to like things they are exposed to repeatedly. In fact, humans generally fear anything novel. This phenomenon is known as *neophobia*. However, there are cases when familiarity can sometimes breed contempt rather than liking. This is particularly the case for things or people we dislike strongly from the very beginning. This dislike can be the result of difference. People tend to prefer similar over dissimilar others. The more we get to know someone, the more aware we become of how different that person is from us, which can lead to disliking (Norton et al., 2007).

BIRDS OF A FEATHER Birds of a feather really do flock together (**FIGURE 12.39**). People similar in attitudes, values, interests, backgrounds, and personalities tend to like each other (Youyou et al., 2017). In high school, people tend to be friends with those of the same sex, race or ethnicity, age, and year in school. The most successful romantic couples also tend to be the most physically similar, a phenomenon called the *matching principle* (Bentler & Newcomb, 1978; Caspi & Herbener, 1990). Of course, people can and do become friends and romantic partners with people who are different from them on some features. Such friendships and relationships tend to be based on other important similarities, such as values, education, and socioeconomic status.

PERSONAL CHARACTERISTICS People tend to especially like those who have admirable personality characteristics and who have physical characteristics considered attractive in their culture. This tendency holds true whether people are choosing friends or romantic partners. In a now-classic study, Norman Anderson (1968) asked college students to rate 555 trait descriptions by how much they would like others who possessed those traits. As you might guess from what you know about the importance of fitting in with the social group, people dislike cheaters and others who drain group resources. Indeed, the least likable characteristics are related to dishonesty, insincerity, and lack of personal warmth. Conversely, people especially like those who are kind, dependable, and trustworthy.

Generally, people like those who have personal characteristics valuable to the group. Those characteristics fall along two fundamental dimensions: warmth and competence (Cuddy et al., 2008). For example, people like those whom they perceive to be competent or reliable much more than they like those they perceive to be incompetent or unreliable. However, making small mistakes on occasion can make a person seem more human and therefore more likable. In one study, a highly competent person who spilled a cup of coffee on himself was rated more favorably than an equally competent person who did not perform this clumsy act (Helmreich et al., 1970). The other critical dimension is warmth. Interpersonal warmth signals acceptance, which in turn builds trust between the partners and fosters lasting relationships (Stinson et al., 2009).

PHYSICAL ATTRACTIVENESS What determines physical attractiveness? Some standards of beauty, such as preferences for particular body types, appear to change over time and across cultures. Nevertheless, there is also some consistency across cultures in how people rate attractiveness (Cunningham et al., 1995). The attractiveness we assign to others can be thought of as a product of their potential value to us in various contexts (Sugiyama, 2015). For example, signals of reproductive fitness, such as facial symmetry, might be attractive in potential mates; signs of trustworthiness might be attractive in trading partners; and culturally determined cues of social status or likability might be attractive in friends.

Signals of high status or dominance can be attractive in friends and romantic partners alike, especially in environments where people compete for resources. As noted earlier in this chapter, the hormone testosterone has been associated with ratings of dominance. One study found that men with the highest levels of testosterone had faces with a higher width-to-height ratio (Lefevre et al., 2013; **FIGURE 12.40**). Do people find potential mates with higher width-to-height ratios more attractive? Researchers tested this idea in a speed dating study, where participants met many potential partners in one session. In contexts such as this, when people have very little information about others except their facial features, width-to-height ratio was associated with men's perceived dominance, physical attractiveness, and likelihood of being chosen for a second date (Valentine et al., 2014).

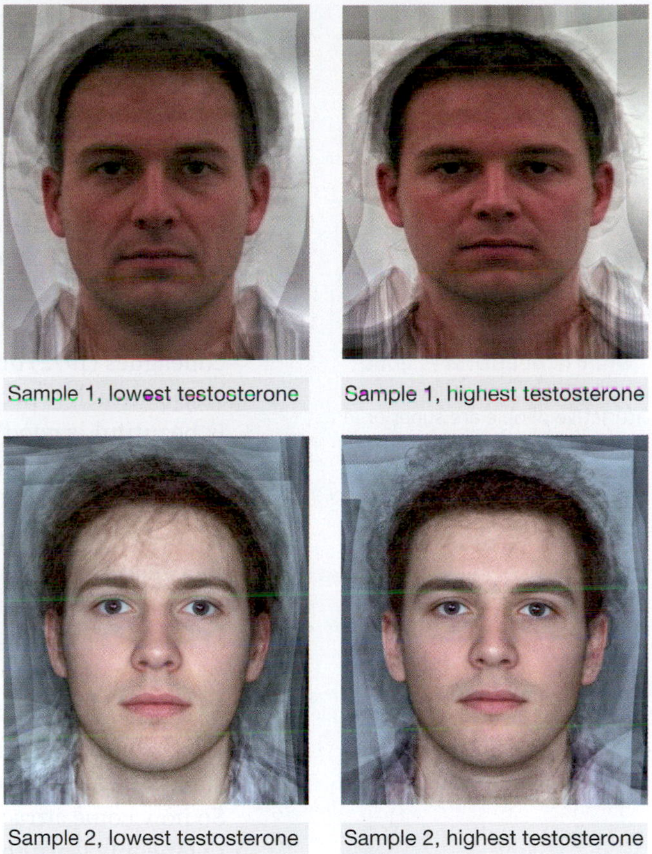

FIGURE 12.40
Testosterone and Facial Width
This figure shows the averaged faces of 20 men with the (left) lowest and (right) highest testosterone levels in two different samples of men. The men with the highest testosterone levels have wider faces.

At a more general level, most people find symmetrical faces more attractive than asymmetrical ones (Perrett et al., 1999). This preference is thought to be adaptive because people use symmetry to evaluate health. For example, one study found evidence that people with more symmetrical faces reported using fewer antibiotics during the preceding three years, indicating they might be more disease resistant (Thornhill & Gangestad, 2006). However, there is not strong evidence that facial symmetry is related to actual physical health (Foo et al., 2017). A preference for facial symmetry might be a heuristic people use to estimate something about others (reproductive fitness) that is difficult to evaluate at a glance. Like all heuristics, the symmetry preference is fast but not always accurate.

In a cleverly designed study of what people find attractive, Langlois and Roggman (1990) used a computer program to combine (or "average") various faces without regard to individual attractiveness. They found that as more faces were combined, participants rated the "averaged" faces as more attractive (**FIGURE 12.41**). People may view averaged faces as attractive because of the mere exposure effect. In other words, averaged faces may be more familiar than unusual faces. It is also possible that averaging faces has the effect of removing asymmetries and distinguishing facial features that are sometimes rated as unattractive, such as blemishes

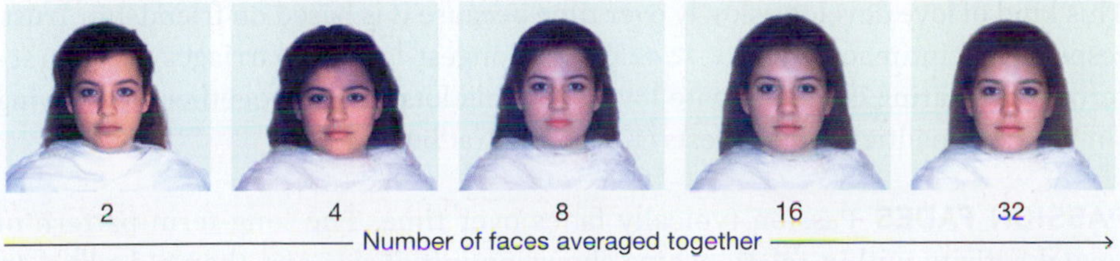

FIGURE 12.41
"Average" Is Attractive
The more faces that are averaged together, the more attractive people find the outcome. The face on the right, a combination of 32 faces, typically is rated most attractive.

and patches of discoloration. People use these features as shortcuts to estimate health, but, as with symmetry, they are not related to objective markers of health such as immune function or illness (Cai et al., 2019).

Being perceived as attractive can bring many important social benefits: Most people are drawn to those they find physically attractive (Langlois et al., 2000). Attractive people are less likely to be perceived as criminals; are given lighter sentences when convicted of crimes; are typically rated as happier, more intelligent, more sociable, more capable, more gifted, more successful, and less socially deviant; are paid more than less attractive people are for doing the same work; and have greater career opportunities. These findings point to what Karen Dion and colleagues (1972) dubbed the **"what is beautiful is good" stereotype**.

"what is beautiful is good" stereotype The belief that attractive people are superior in most ways.

Do attractive people actually possess characteristics consistent with the "what is beautiful is good" stereotype? The evidence on this issue is mixed. Attractive people tend to be more popular, more socially skilled, and healthier, but they are not necessarily smarter or happier (Feingold, 1992). People are warmer and friendlier with attractive others, which in turn elicits certain behaviors from them that help build relationships (Snyder et al., 1977). However, not all studies find attractiveness to be related to good things. In one study of college students, judges objectively rated the attractiveness of the participants, and then researchers tested for associations between those ratings and social outcomes. There was no relationship between appearance and grades, number of personal relationships, financial resources, or just about anything (Diener et al., 1995). Attractive people were similar to less attractive people in intelligence, life satisfaction, and self-esteem. So how come attractiveness does not always lead to good? It might be that attractive people learn to distrust attention from others, especially romantic attention (Reis et al., 1982). They assume that people like them simply for their looks.

Q **According to social psychology research, which adage is more accurate: "Birds of a feather flock together" or "Opposites attract"?**

ANSWER: Birds of a feather flock together, which means that people in relationships often match on important qualities.

12.16 Emotions Play an Important Role in Romantic Relationships

In their pioneering work, Ellen Berscheid and Elaine (Walster) Hatfield (1969) drew an important distinction between passionate love and companionate love. **Passionate love** is a state of intense longing and sexual desire. This kind of love is often portrayed stereotypically in the arts and media. In passionate love, people fall head over heels for each other. They feel an overwhelming urge to be together (**FIGURE 12.42a**). Brain imaging studies show that passionate love is associated with activity in midbrain dopamine systems, the same systems involved in reinforcement learning, reward, and motivation (Cacioppo et al., 2012).

passionate love A state of intense longing and desire.

People experience passionate love early in relationships. In most enduring relationships, passionate love evolves into **companionate love** (Sternberg, 1986), a strong commitment to care for and support a partner (Berscheid & Walster, 1969). This kind of love develops slowly over time because it is based on friendship, trust, respect, and intimacy (**FIGURE 12.42b**). The longest-lasting marriages are characterized by sharing companionate love, spending lots of time together, and having similar personalities and interests (Karney & Bradbury, 2020).

companionate love A strong commitment based on friendship, trust, respect, and intimacy.

PASSION FADES Passion typically fades over time. The long-term pattern of sexual activity within relationships shows an initial rise and then a decline. In the early months or even years of a new relationship, the two people experience frequent, intense desire for each other. Past that peak, however, their interest in physical intimacy with each other decreases. For example, from the first year of marriage to the second, the frequency of sex declines by about half (James, 1983). After that, the frequency continues to decline, but it does so more gradually. In addition, people typically—and normally—experience less passion for their partners over time as they shift from passionate to companionate love. If people do not develop companionate forms of satisfaction in their romantic relationships—such as friendship, social support, and intimacy—the loss of passion leads to dissatisfaction and often to the eventual dissolution of the relationship (Berscheid & Regan, 2005).

Perhaps unsurprisingly, relatively few marriages meet the blissful ideals that newlyweds expect. In the United States, approximately half of all marriages end in divorce or separation. The strongest predictor of divorce is marital stress, often due to external factors such as financial hardship and illness (Neff & Karney, 2017). Given the disparities in income and other socioeconomic resources among racial groups in the United States that can cause considerable stress, it is not surprising that there are considerable racial differences in the probability of divorce. Asian Americans are the most likely to remain married after 20 years and African Americans the least likely (Copen et al., 2012; **FIGURE 12.43**).

ATTACHMENT THEORY One theory of love is based on attachment theory. As discussed in Chapter 9, infants can form different levels of attachment with their parents. According to Cindy Hazan and Phillip Shaver (1987), adult relationships also vary in their attachment styles. Romantic relationships are especially likely to vary in terms of attachment. There is some evidence that one's attachment style in adulthood is related to early childhood experiences, particularly parenting (Cooke et al., 2019; Fraley & Shaver, 2000). People who believe their parents were warm, supportive, and responsive report having secure attachments in their relationships. They find it easy to get close to others and do not fear being abandoned. Just under 60 percent of adults report having this attachment style (Mickelson et al., 1997). The remaining roughly 40 percent have insecure attachments. For example, people who believe their parents were cold and distant report having avoidant attachments. They find it hard to trust or depend on others, and they are wary of those who try to become close to them. Relationship partners make them uncomfortable. About 25 percent of adults report having this attachment style. People whose parents treated them inconsistently—sometimes warm and

(a)

(b)

FIGURE 12.42
Passionate Versus Companionate Love
(a) The arts tend to focus on passionate love. Consider this image from the show *Schitt's Creek*, starring Noah Reid and Dan Levy. **(b)** Some romances, however, depict the development of companionate love, as shown in this image from the 2014 movie *The Fault in Our Stars*, starring Ansel Elgort and Shailene Woodley.

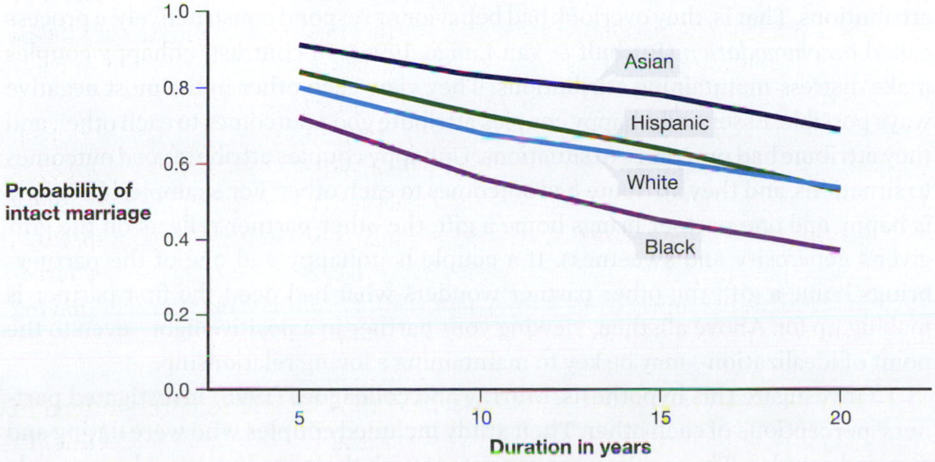

FIGURE 12.43
Success Rates for First Marriages
This graph shows the probability that first marriages in the United States will remain intact, without disruption.

sometimes not—have ambivalent attachments. These people are best described as clingy. They worry that people do not really love them and are bound to leave them. About 11 percent of adults report having this attachment style.

An important caveat is that findings in this research area are based mainly on people's recollections of how their parents treated them. It is possible that people's memories are distorted, or that a third variable, such as genetics or personality, influences people's adult relationships and their recollections of their childhood. Moreover, relationships can change people's attachment styles (Chopik et al., 2019). People are likely to become secure in their attachment style with a patient, understanding, and trustworthy partner. They may become insecure if paired with a "bad" partner.

DEALING WITH CONFLICT Conflict is universal in human relationships. Even the strongest, longest-lasting partnerships have some amount of conflict. The ability to communicate about and resolve conflict is an important aspect of any relationship. The way a couple deals with conflict often determines whether the relationship will last.

John Gottman (1995) describes four interpersonal styles that typically lead couples to discord and dissolution. These maladaptive strategies are *being overly critical, holding the partner in contempt* (i.e., having disdain, lacking respect), *being defensive*, and *mentally withdrawing from the relationship*. Gottman humorously uses the phrase *Four Horsemen of the Apocalypse* (a reference to the biblical Book of Revelation) to reflect the serious threats that these patterns pose to relationships. For example, when one partner voices a complaint, the other partner might respond with further complaints. One partner may raise the stakes by reciting a list of the other person's failings, using sarcasm, or insulting or demeaning the other. Inevitably, any disagreement, no matter how small, escalates into a major fight over the core problems.

When a couple is more satisfied with the relationship, the partners tend to express concern for each other even while they are disagreeing. They manage to stay relatively calm and try to see each other's point of view. They deliver criticism lightly and with compassion when things go wrong, whereas they revel in each other's successes when things go right—a process called *capitalization* (Gable & Reis, 2010). In addition, optimistic people are more likely to use cooperative problem solving; as a result, optimism is linked to having satisfying and happy romantic relationships (Srivastava et al., 2006). For additional suggestions about maintaining strong relationships, see Section 12.17.

ATTRIBUTIONAL STYLE AND ACCOMMODATION Happy couples also differ from unhappy couples in *attributional style*, or how one partner explains the other's behavior (Bradbury & Fincham, 1990). Happy couples make partner-enhancing attributions. That is, they overlook bad behavior or respond constructively, a process called *accommodation* (Rusbult & Van Lange, 1996). In contrast, unhappy couples make distress-maintaining attributions: They view each other in the most negative ways possible. Essentially, happy couples attribute good outcomes to each other, and they attribute bad outcomes to situations. Unhappy couples attribute *good* outcomes to situations, and they attribute *bad* outcomes to each other. For example, if a couple is happy and one partner brings home a gift, the other partner reflects on the gift-giver's generosity and sweetness. If a couple is unhappy and one of the partners brings home a gift, the other partner wonders what bad deed the first partner is making up for. Above all, then, viewing your partner in a positive light—even to the point of idealization—may be key to maintaining a loving relationship.

To investigate this hypothesis, Murray and colleagues (1996) investigated partners' perceptions of each other. Their study included couples who were dating and married couples. The results were consistent with their predictions. Those people who loved their partners the most also idealized their partners the most. That is, they viewed their partners in a more positive light than they viewed other people and even more positively than how their partners viewed themselves. These rosy images of partners are not entirely disconnected from reality. Instead, they are like a filter applied to a social media post that makes a photograph look as good as it possibly can. Those people with the most positively biased views of their partners were more likely to still be in relationships with their partners several months later than were those people with unbiased views of their partners.

Q How does passionate love differ from companionate love?

ANSWER: Passionate love peaks early in relationships and is based on physical desire and sexual attraction. Companionate love develops later in relationships and is based on friendship, trust, and intimacy.

PSYCHOLOGY OUTSIDE THE LAB

12.17 Findings from Psychological Science Can Benefit Your Relationship

Some couples seem loving and supportive. We look at them and think, "That's the kind of relationship I'd like to have someday!" Other couples can be downright harsh to each other. We look at them and think, "That relationship seems toxic! Why are they even together?" What factors help create and maintain these healthy and unhealthy relationships? How can understanding their successes and failures help you create a healthy relationship that will thrive?

Over the past two decades, psychologists such as John Gottman have conducted research on healthy and unhealthy relationships. To understand what predicts marital outcomes, Gottman (1998) has studied thousands of married couples. In *Why Marriages Succeed or Fail . . . and How You Can Make Yours Last* (1995), Gottman outlines numerous differences between couples who are happy and those who are not.

Based on his research, Gottman believes that if a couple has about five positive interactions for every negative one, chances are good that the relationship will be stable. The specific ratio has been disputed, but the basic premise is sound: A healthy relationship needs much more positivity than negativity. If there are as many negatives as positives in a relationship, the chance of success is pretty bleak, so a couple should seek opportunities for positive feelings and interactions within the relationship. According to Gottman and others, the same principles apply to all long-term, committed relationships:

1. **Try to understand your partner's perspective.** Listen carefully when your partner tells you about their experiences. Pay attention when they speak and maintain eye contact. Mutual empathy is strongly related to overall relationship satisfaction (Ulloa et al., 2017). Show you really know what they experienced and can understand why they are feeling the way they are. Such empathy and understanding cannot be faked. To convey that you understand your partner's feelings, indicate with your words and your nonverbal communication that you are listening and taking in what your partner is communicating. Ask follow-up questions to show you are engaged in what your partner is saying.
2. **Be affectionate.** You can show love in very quiet ways, such as simply touching the person once in a while. Reminisce about happy times together. Appreciate the benefits of the relationship and communicate that you do so. Go out of your way to celebrate your partner's successes together (Peters et al., 2018). When partners talk about the joys of their relationship, they tend to be happier with the relationship. Such conversation can include comparing the partnership favorably with the partnerships of other people.
3. **Show you care.** Do spontaneous things such as bringing your partner a special treat from the bakery or texting at an unexpected time just to see how

(a)

(b)

FIGURE 12.44
Principles for a Committed Relationship
Positive interactions help keep a relationship stable. **(a)** A thoughtful gesture is one way to show your partner you care. **(b)** Doing activities you both enjoy is another way to spend quality time together.

things are going (FIGURE 12.44a). Such actions let your partner know that you think about them even when you are not together. When people are dating, they flirt, give each other compliments, and display their best manners. Being in a committed relationship does not mean discarding these things. Be nice to your partner and show that you value your mutual companionship. Praise your partner whenever possible. One study found that newlyweds who were satisfied with their partners' level of warmth, kindness, and responsiveness were more satisfied with their marriage four years later (Valentine et al., 2020).

4. **Spend quality time together.** Partners should pursue independent interests, but having some activities and goals in common helps bring a couple closer. Find time to explore joint interests, such as hobbies or other activities (FIGURE 12.44b). In fact, research shows that when a couple engages in novel and exciting activities, the couple's relationship satisfaction increases (Aron et al., 2000). Having fun together is an important part of any relationship. Share private jokes, engage in playful teasing, be witty, have adventures. Spending too much time in front of separate screens can undermine the positive effects of this shared time (McDaniel et al., 2020).
5. **Maintain trust.** Mutual trust between partners is a critical component of satisfaction in relationships. Anything that threatens that basic sense of trust will harm the relationship. For instance, believing your partner is emotionally or physically involved with another person against your wishes can pose harm to even the healthiest relationship, as can being distrustful or jealous for no reason. When relationship partners dismiss attractive or threatening alternatives, the partners are better able to remain faithful (Rusbult & Buunk, 1993). Having intimate partners outside of a relationship when both partners agree on non-monogamy does not necessarily undermine trust and relationship satisfaction (Conley et al., 2017).
6. **Learn how to handle conflict.** Many people believe that conflict is a sign of a troubled relationship and that couples who never fight must be the happiest. These ideas are not true. Fighting, especially when it allows grievances to come to light, is one of the healthiest things a couple can do for their relationship. Conflict is inevitable in any serious relationship, so partners must learn to resolve conflict positively to maintain the relationship. Do not avoid conflict or pretend you have no serious issues. Rather, try to discuss the conflict in a calm, compassionate, and empathic way. Avoid name-calling, sarcasm, or excessive criticism. If you are unable to do so in the heat of the moment, call for a time-out. Return to the discussion when you both feel ready to engage constructively. Validate your partner's feelings and beliefs even as you express your own feelings and beliefs. Look for areas of compromise.

Much of this advice may seem like common sense. However, it is easy to lose sight of how to express love, commitment, and passion amid the daily routine. When partners get so caught up in everything else in their lives, from work to stress about exams to worries about family, the most visible parts of the relationship become what is wrong about it, and what is right fades into the background. When that happens, the relationship has taken a wrong turn. To make a relationship stronger, partners need to make a deliberate effort to recognize and celebrate all that is good about the relationship. Those affirming experiences help make relationships succeed. ■

Q How can addressing conflict maintain healthy relationships?

ANSWER: Conflict in serious relationships is inevitable, so it must be addressed rather than ignored. Dealing with conflict in a calm, open, and empathic way allows for resolution and improvement.

Your Chapter Review

Want to earn a better grade on your test?

It's time to complete your study experience! Go to **INQUIZITIVE** to practice actively with this chapter's concepts and get personalized feedback along the way.

Chapter Summary

How Does Group Membership Affect People?

12.1 People Favor Their Own Groups Social psychology is the study of how people influence others' thoughts, feelings, and actions. People readily identify ingroups, to which they belong, and outgroups, to which they do not belong. Ingroup and outgroup formation is affected by reciprocity (if you help me, I will help you) and transitivity (friends having the same opinions about other people). The outgroup homogeneity effect is the tendency to perceive outgroup members as stereotypically more similar than ingroup members are. People also tend to dehumanize members of outgroups. According to social identity theory, individual social identity is based on identification with an ingroup. Ingroup favoritism is pervasive and may reflect evolutionary pressure to protect the self and resources. The medial prefrontal cortex appears important for ingroup formation.

12.2 Groups Influence Individual Behavior Group decisions can become extreme (group polarization), and poor decisions may be made to preserve group harmony (groupthink). The presence of others can improve performance (social facilitation). Working in a group can result in decreased effort (social loafing) if group members think their individual efforts cannot be monitored. Loss of individuality and self-awareness (deindividuation) can occur in groups.

12.3 People Conform with Others Conformity occurs when people alter their behaviors or opinions to match the behaviors, opinions, or expectations of others. Conformity results from normative influence (the attempt to fit in with the group and avoid looking foolish) and informational influence (learning the correct way to respond by observing). People may reject social norms and not conform when group size is small or when the group includes at least one other dissenter. Conformity appears in groups of about four or more members and is particularly strong when the group demonstrates unanimity. Conformity likely results from a fear of social rejection.

12.4 You Be the Psychologist: Can Social Norms Marketing Reduce Binge Drinking? Social norms marketing tries to correct false beliefs about drinking behavior by giving factual normative comparisons for average students. Although some programs have been successful, social norms marketing can backfire by increasing consumption of alcohol by light drinkers. The most successful programs include social norms marketing with persuasive arguments about the hazards of excessive alcohol consumption.

12.5 People Obey Authority Figures Obedience occurs when people follow the orders of an authority. As demonstrated by Milgram's famous study, people may inflict harm on others if ordered to do so by an authority. Individuals who are concerned about others' perceptions of them are more likely to be obedient. Obedience decreases with greater distance from the authority.

When Do People Harm or Help Others?

12.6 Many Factors Can Influence Aggression Aggression is influenced by situational, biological, social, and cultural factors. Situational factors that lead to negative emotions—factors including social rejection, fear, heat, and pain—can influence aggression. High levels of the hormone testosterone have been associated with aggressive behavior. However, it is difficult to determine whether high testosterone levels motivate aggression or threatening encounters produce high testosterone levels. It is also possible that testosterone is more important for dominance than for aggression. A mutation in the MAOA gene and serotonin levels have also been linked to aggressive behavior in some individuals. The effects of social and cultural factors on aggression can change over time. In societies that advocate a culture of honor, people are more likely to exhibit violence and aggression.

12.7 Cooperation Can Reduce Outgroup Bias People can respond to outgroup members in need, as demonstrated by global response to natural disasters. Cooperation and working toward superordinate goals can increase harmony across groups.

12.8 Many Factors Can Influence Helping Behavior Prosocial behaviors promote positive interpersonal relationships. Altruism toward kin increases the likelihood of passing on genes shared with relatives. Altruism toward nonrelatives increases the likelihood that others will reciprocate help when we need it. The bystander intervention effect is most likely to occur when people experience diffusion of responsibility, when a situation is unclear and people fear making social blunders, when people are anonymous, and when people perceive greater risk than benefit to helping others.

How Do Attitudes Guide Behavior?

12.9 People Form Attitudes Through Experience and Socialization Attitudes are evaluations of objects, events, or ideas. Attitudes are influenced by familiarity (the mere exposure effect) and are shaped by conditioning and socialization. Attitudes that are strong, personally relevant, specific, formed through personal experience, and easily accessible are most likely to affect behavior. Explicit attitudes are those that people are consciously aware of and can report. Implicit attitudes operate at an unconscious level. Implicit and explicit attitudes can each predict behavior in different contexts.

12.10 Discrepancies Lead to Dissonance A contradiction between attitudes or between an attitude and a behavior produces cognitive dissonance. Dissonance is a tense, unpleasant state that people are motivated to reduce. People reduce dissonance by changing their attitudes or behaviors, trivializing the discrepancies (such as through postdecisional dissonance), or rationalizing the discrepancies (such as through justifying effort).

12.11 Attitudes and Behaviors Can Be Changed Through Persuasion Persuasion involves the use of a message to actively and consciously change an attitude. According to the elaboration likelihood model, persuasion through the central route (which involves careful thought about the message) produces stronger and more persistent attitude change than does persuasion through the peripheral route (which relies on peripheral cues, such as the attractiveness of the person making the argument). Compliance occurs when people agree to the requests of others. Compliance increases when people are in a good mood or are subjected to tactics such as the foot-in-the-door, door-in-the-face, and low-balling techniques.

How Do People Think About Others?

12.12 People Make Judgments About Others People are highly sensitive to nonverbal information (e.g., facial expression, eye contact), and they can develop accurate impressions of others on the basis of very thin slices of behavior. People use personal dispositions and situational factors to explain behavior. The fundamental attribution error occurs when people favor personal attributions over situational attributions in explaining other people's behavior. The actor/observer discrepancy is people's tendency to make personal attributions when explaining other people's behavior and situational attributions when explaining their own behavior.

12.13 Stereotypes Can Lead to Prejudice and Discrimination Stereotypes are cognitive schemas that allow for fast, easy processing of social information. Illusory correlations cause people to see relationships that do not exist, and they result from confirmatory bias toward selecting information that supports stereotypes. Prejudice is negative feelings, opinions, and beliefs associated with a stereotype. Prejudice can lead to discrimination, the differential treatment of others merely on the basis of their group membership. Modern racism is a subtler form of prejudice that has developed as people have learned to inhibit the public expression of their prejudiced beliefs.

12.14 Prejudice and Its Effects Can Be Reduced Working toward shared goals that require cooperation can lead to reduced prejudice and discrimination. Stereotype threat occurs when members of stigmatized groups perform poorly at a task because of anxiety about confirming a negative stereotype about their group. There are several strategies to reduce stereotype threat, such as self-affirmation or viewing a role model. Imagining positive social interactions with outgroup members, inhibiting stereotypes (for instance, by presenting people with positive examples of negatively stereotyped groups), perspective taking (actively contemplating the psychological experiences of other people), and perspective giving (describing personal experiences of discrimination) can also reduce prejudice and discrimination.

What Determines the Quality of Relationships?

12.15 Situational and Personal Factors Influence Interpersonal Attraction and Friendships People are attracted to individuals they are in contact with often, with whom they share similar attributes, and who possess socially desirable characteristics and physical features. People find "averaged" faces and symmetrical faces more attractive, and some people are attracted to others who have traits associated with dominance, such as faces with higher width-to-height ratios. People with physical characteristics deemed desirable in a culture experience many social benefits, but they do not report greater happiness.

12.16 Emotions Play an Important Role in Romantic Relationships Passionate love is characterized by intense longing and physical desire. Companionate love is characterized by commitment and support. In successful romantic relationships, passionate love tends to evolve into companionate love. How a couple deals with conflict influences the stability of the relationship. Couples who attribute positive outcomes to each other and negative outcomes to situational factors and who make partner-enhancing attributions report higher levels of marital happiness.

12.17 Psychology Outside the Lab: Findings from Psychological Science Can Benefit Your Relationship In successful relationships, people listen to and feel empathy for their partners, are affectionate, show they care, spend quality time together, trust each other, and handle conflict appropriately. Putting effort into a relationship and engaging in these actions will increase the likelihood of the relationship enduring over time.

Key Terms

actor/observer discrepancy, p. 474
aggression, p. 457
altruism, p. 461
attitudes, p. 463
attributions, p. 473
bystander intervention effect, p. 462
companionate love, p. 484
compliance, p. 470
conformity, p. 451
deindividuation, p. 450
discrimination, p. 476
elaboration likelihood model, p. 469
explicit attitudes, p. 465
fundamental attribution error, p. 474
group polarization, p. 449
groupthink, p. 449
implicit attitudes, p. 465
inclusive fitness, p. 462
informational influence, p. 451
ingroup favoritism, p. 447
mere exposure effect, p. 464
modern racism, p. 478
nonverbal behavior, p. 472
normative influence, p. 451
obedience, p. 455
outgroup homogeneity effect, p. 447
passionate love, p. 484
personal attributions, p. 473
persuasion, p. 469
prejudice, p. 476
prosocial behaviors, p. 461
situational attributions, p. 473
social facilitation, p. 450
social identity theory, p. 447
social loafing, p. 450
social norms, p. 451
stereotype threat, p. 479
"what is beautiful is good" stereotype, p. 484

Practice Exercises

1. People are most likely to organize into groups when individuals treat each other in similar ways, known as ________, and when individuals share and influence each other's preferences and feelings, known as ________.
   a. reciprocity; transitivity
   b. transitivity; reciprocity
   c. social facilitation; social loafing
   d. social facilitation; social loafing

2. Which situation describes an example of the outgroup homogeneity effect?
   a. Mikel identifies with the University of Texas and believes every student there is superior.
   b. Kayleigh identifies as Black and supports social justice issues involving all racial minorities.
   c. Randy identifies with New York City and believes the people of Boston lack diversity.
   d. Josie practices Judaism and is puzzled by the diversity of the Christian denominations.

3. Which of the following examples of social norms marketing is likely to be the most effective?
   a. "Eighty percent of the residents in your neighborhood recycle."
   b. "Eighty percent of the residents in your neighborhood recycle. Recycling keeps our environment healthy!"
   c. "Recycle!"
   d. "Recycle! It's the right thing to do!"

4. Delta House and Omega House have a long-standing rivalry. Recently, the rivalry has intensified, resulting in destructive acts to property and harassment of outgroup members. Based on social psychology research, which course of action would be most likely to reduce the outgroup bias between the two fraternities?
   a. Planning a series of dinners in which members of the Delta House and Omega House visit and dine with each other.
   b. Delta House members, who are strong math students, offer tutoring to students from Omega House.
   c. The university administration holds a meeting with the house presidents to let them know that funding for fraternity activities will be cut unless the tension subsides.
   d. Organizing a competition where teams of fraternities compete for prizes. Delta House and Omega House form one team to compete against other pairs of fraternities.

5. Match each definition below to the matching term: altruism, inclusive fitness, kin selection, reciprocal helping.
   a. a process in which individuals behave helpfully toward those with whom they share genes
   b. providing help without any apparent or immediate reward for doing so
   c. the tendency for one animal to help another because the other can return the favor in the future
   d. the adaptive benefits of focusing on transmitting genes rather than on individual survival

6. Which of the following conditions are primary reasons of the bystander (non)intervention effect? Choose all that apply.
   a. groupthink
   b. perceived risk is greater than perceived benefit
   c. discrimination against those in need
   d. diffusion of responsibility
   e. apathy
   f. unclear situation and unsureness of the correct response
   g. anonymity
   h. ingroup favoritism
   i. selfishness

7. Adrianna wants to go on a community service trip during her spring break. After struggling for weeks to decide between two good options, she opts to build houses in rural Mexico instead of doing hurricane cleanup in Louisiana. If Adrianna experiences post-decisional dissonance, how will her attitude likely change toward her two options?
   a. She will focus on the positives of the Louisiana trip and the negatives of the Mexico trip.
   b. She will focus on the positives of the Mexico trip and the negatives of the Louisiana trip.
   c. She will focus on the positives of both the Mexico and Louisiana trips.
   d. She will focus on the negatives of both the Mexico and Louisiana trips.

8. Tanya is leading a fundraiser for her organization and needs members to volunteer to make phone calls for 1 hour a night. Which strategy is least likely to increase members' compliance with Tanya's request to volunteer for the 1-hour time slots?
   a. Ask people to sign up for 6-hour time slots. If they say no, ask if they could volunteer for just 1 hour of their time.
   b. Ask people to bring in cookies for a bake sale to support the cause. If they say yes, ask if they could also volunteer for 1 hour of their time to make phone calls.
   c. Ask people to make calls for 15 minutes. If they say yes, ask if they could stay for additional time.
   d. Avoid providing a reason for the volunteer request, so members can use their implicit attitudes instead.

9. Which statement below about Shelly, whom people rate as very physically attractive, is consistent with the "what is beautiful is good" stereotype?
   a. "Shelly is a total ditz!"
   b. "Shelly is easily the happiest person I know!"
   c. "Shelly sure knows how to manipulate other people with her looks!"
   d. "Shelly's has good genes that ought to be transmitted."

10. Which is the most typical relationship between passionate love and companionate love in long-lasting marriages?
   a. An initially high level of passionate love transforms slowly into a high level of companionate love.
   b. A high level of passionate love early in relationships leads to a lower level of companionate love later.
   c. An initially high level of companionate love transforms slowly into passionate love.
   d. A high level of companionate love early in relationships leads to a lower level of passionate love later.

for
Sha Na Na
concert!
A-ha!
Don't
it.

13 Personality

Big Questions

LIKE MANY PEOPLE, YOU SOMETIMES FEEL SHY IN NEW SITUATIONS. Most of the time, though, you are pretty comfortable around other people and outgoing. By contrast, your brother is extremely shy in almost every situation outside the home. He can barely speak or make eye contact with others unless he is at home with just family. How is it that your brother, who grew up in the same house with the same parents and shares half your genes, differs so much from you? Where does personality come from? How much of your personality is a product of your genes, how much is affected by how you were raised, and how much is attributable to some interaction between the two?

Humans are constantly trying to understand one another. So much in our social world revolves around learning why other people behave in certain ways and predicting their behavior. In Chapter 12, you learned about the power of the situation—how invisible social and structural forces can shape human behavior in predictable ways. But people do not all act the same way in a given situation, and each person might act differently across time in the same situation. This chapter explores how people differ. The picture that emerges is a familiar one in psychology: Personality is a combination of people's genetics, forces in their environments, and the life choices they make.

Learning Objectives

- Summarize the results of twin studies and adoption studies pertaining to personality.
- Understand how genes interact with environment to produce personality.
- Identify distinct temperaments.

Where Does Personality Come From?

For psychologists, **personality** consists of people's characteristic thoughts, emotional responses, and behaviors. Some personality psychologists are most interested in understanding *whole persons*. That is, rather than understanding how situations or contexts influence people in general, they ask how much we can understand about one individual person. Other personality psychologists study how particular characteristics, such as self-esteem or shyness, influence behavior. For instance, they want to know how shy people differ from outgoing people. Their interest is in how the characteristic influences behavior. Each characteristic is a **personality trait**: a pattern of thought, emotion, and behavior that is relatively consistent over time and across situations (Funder, 2012).

However, people are more than just the sum of their traits. Gordon Allport (1961), one of the founders of the field, gave a classic scientific definition of personality: "the dynamic organization within the individual of those psychophysical systems that determine [the individual's] characteristic behavior and thought" (p. 28; FIGURE 13.1). This definition includes many of the concepts most important to a contemporary understanding of personality. The notion of *organization* indicates that personality is a coherent whole. This organized whole is *dynamic* in that it is goal seeking, sensitive to particular contexts, adaptive to the person's environment, and fluid over time. By emphasizing *psychophysical systems*, Allport brought together two ideas: He highlighted the mental nature of personality (the *psycho-* part of *psychophysical*), and he recognized that personality arises from both biological processes and external environments (the *-physical* part). In addition, his definition stresses that personality causes people to have *characteristic* behaviors and thoughts (and feelings). In other words, people do and think and feel things relatively consistently over time.

FIGURE 13.1
Gordon Allport
In 1937, Allport published the first major textbook of personality psychology. His book defined the field. He also championed the study of individuals and established traits as a central concept in personality research.

13.1 Genetic Factors Influence the Expression of Personality

Over the past few decades, evidence has emerged that biological factors—such as genes, brain structures, and neurochemistry—play an important role in determining personality. Of course, these factors are all affected by experience. As discussed in Chapter 3, every cell in the body contains the genome, or master recipe, that provides detailed instructions for physical processes. Gene expression—whether a gene is turned off or on—underlies all psychological activity. Ultimately, genes have their effects only if they are expressed. Genetic makeup may predispose certain personality traits or characteristics, but whether these genes are expressed depends on the unique circumstances that each person faces in life. An important theme throughout this book is that nature and nurture work together to produce individuals, and this theme holds particularly true for personality.

There is overwhelming evidence that nearly all personality traits have a genetic component (Plomin et al., 2016; Turkheimer et al., 2014). One of the earliest studies to document the heritability of personality was conducted by James Loehlin and Robert Nichols (1976). The researchers examined similarities in personality in more than 800 pairs of twins. Across a wide variety of traits, identical twins proved much more similar than fraternal twins. This pattern suggests the actions of genes, since identical twins share nearly the same genes, whereas fraternal twins do not (FIGURE 13.2). Results such as these mean that traits run in families, but they do not mean that traits are completely predetermined or cannot change.

personality A person's characteristic thoughts, emotional responses, and behaviors.

personality trait A pattern of thought, emotion, and behavior that is relatively consistent over time and across situations.

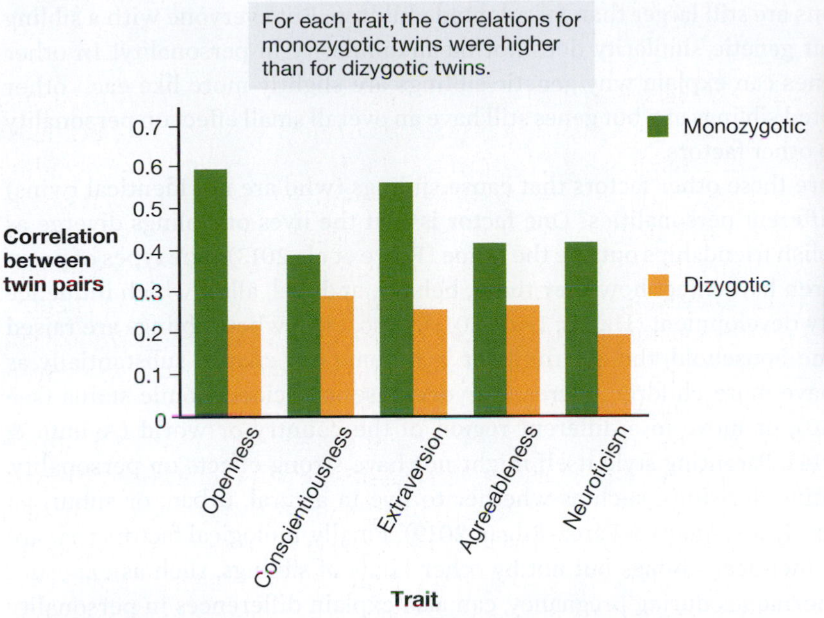

FIGURE 13.2
Correlations in Twins
Researchers examined correlations between 123 pairs of identical (monozygotic) twins and 127 pairs of fraternal (dizygotic) twins in Vancouver, Canada. This chart summarizes some of their findings. (These traits, called the Big Five, are discussed in Section 13.3.)

In general, genetic influence accounts for about half the variability (40–60 percent) between individuals for all personality traits and for attitudes that reflect personality traits, such as how much a person enjoys rollercoaster rides (Olson et al., 2001). Further, the genetic basis of traits has been shown to be the same across cultures (Yamagata et al., 2006). These patterns persist whether the twins rate themselves or whether friends, family, or trained observers rate them.

ADOPTION STUDIES Further evidence for the genetic basis of personality comes from adoption studies. Say that two children who are not biologically related are raised in the same household as adopted siblings. Those two children tend to be no more alike in personality than any two strangers randomly plucked off the street (Plomin & Caspi, 1999). Moreover, the personalities of adopted children bear no significant relationship to those of their adoptive parents. Findings such as these indicate that parenting has much less of an impact on personality than has long been assumed (Turkheimer et al., 2014). However, as noted later in this chapter, parents do influence their children in other important ways.

There is an important caveat to this conclusion. It is not necessarily the case that genes fully determine aspects of psychology, such as personality, that are not accounted for by environmental factors. Recall that many features of humans are determined largely by *interactions* between biological factors and environments—nature and nurture—even if neither one on its own carries much weight. This appears to be the case with personality. For instance, studies typically find only small correlations in personality between biological siblings or between children and their biological parents. It is true that these

"I could cry when I think of the years I wasted accumulating money, only to learn that my cheerful disposition is genetic."

correlations are still larger than for adopted children. But everyone with a sibling knows that genetic similarity does not mean similarity in personality! In other words, genes can explain why genetic siblings are slightly more like each other than adopted siblings are, but genes still have an overall small effect on personality relative to other factors.

What are these other factors that cause siblings (who are not identical twins) to have different personalities? One factor is that the lives of siblings diverge as they establish friendships outside the home (Rowe et al., 2013). The types of peers that children have affect how they think, behave, and feel, all of which influence personality development (Harris, 1995, 2011). Also, even when siblings are raised in the same household, the environment in a home can change substantially as families have more children, increase or decrease in socioeconomic status (see Chapter 10), or move to a different region of the country or world (Avinun & Knafo, 2014). Parenting style itself might not have strong effects on personality, but parenting decisions, such as whether to live in a rural, urban, or suburban area, certainly do (Anaya & Pérez-Edgar, 2019). Finally, biological factors that are shared by identical siblings but not by other kinds of siblings, such as exposure to stress hormones during pregnancy, can also explain differences in personality between siblings (Poole et al., 2020).

ARE THERE SPECIFIC GENES FOR PERSONALITY? Genes code for proteins, not behaviors. Features of human behavior such as personality are so complex that no single gene can account for them. Instead, many genes acting together can make us more or less likely to react in a specific way to certain types of stimuli. These behavioral, mental, or emotional response tendencies are referred to as dispositions. For example, a certain combination of genes paired with a lifetime of experiences might result in a disposition to prefer indoor activities over outdoor pursuits.

Initial research on genetic influences on personality was largely unsuccessful because investigators sought individual genes that had an influence on specific traits (Sanchez-Roige et al., 2018). Some genes can have a strong influence on how available certain neurotransmitters are to neurons. However, even these genes exert only a small effect on traits that are presumably related to the neurotransmitter, such as emotional stability and serotonin (Jang et al., 2001; Munafò, 2012). In fact, any links between specific genes and specific aspects of personality appear to be extraordinarily small (Turkheimer et al., 2014). Instead, thousands of genes contribute to specific traits. These genes combine to influence a person's overall personality (Chabris et al., 2015; Plomin et al., 2016).

Moreover, each person experiences different circumstances that may cause epigenetic changes and the selective expression of certain genes. Recall from Chapter 3 that epigenetic processes describe how environment affects genetic expression. Given the complexity of personality, the complexity of personality's underlying genetic basis is hardly surprising. Even though twin studies provide strong evidence that genes account for about half the variance in personality, it is possible that researchers will never identify the specific genes that produce these effects (Munafò & Flint, 2011). Adding in epigenetic changes that result from interactions with the environment makes it even more difficult to identify the influence of any specific gene (Zhang & Meaney, 2010).

Q **How much variability in personality is attributable to specific genes and how much is attributable to parenting style?**

ANSWER: A great number of genes, rather than any individual genes, influence the likelihood or level of personality traits. Parenting style has very little direct influence on personality.

13.2 Temperaments Are Evident in Infancy

Genes create differences in personality by affecting biological processes. These differences are called **temperaments**: general tendencies to feel or act in certain ways. Temperaments are broader than personality traits. Life experiences may alter personality traits, as will be discussed later in this chapter, but temperaments represent the innate biological structures of personality and are more stable (Rothbart, 2011).

temperaments Biologically based tendencies to feel or act in certain ways.

Arnold Buss and Robert Plomin (1984) have argued that three basic characteristics can be considered temperaments (FIGURE 13.3). *Activity level* is the overall amount of energy and action a person exhibits. For example, some children spent the entire 2020 pandemic racing around the house, others were less vigorous, and still others were content to play in a seated position much of the time. *Emotionality* describes the intensity of emotional reactions. For example, children who cry often or easily become frightened, as well as adults who quickly anger, are likely to be high in emotionality. Finally, *sociability* refers to the general tendency to affiliate with others. People high in sociability prefer to be with others rather than to be alone. Researchers have also identified other temperaments, such as the extent to which children are able to control their behaviors and their emotions (Caspi, 2000).

These temperaments relate to behaviors that can dramatically shape life outcomes, such as where people choose to live. For instance, a study of migration patterns in Finland found that people who scored high on sociability were more likely to migrate to urban areas and to places that were quite distant from their hometowns. Those people who had high activity levels were more likely, in general, to migrate to a new location, regardless of that location (Jokela et al., 2008).

The relation between temperament and life decisions illustrates the *gene-environment correlation* phenomenon in the nature/nurture debate. Genes and environment affect not only behavior but also each other. Even if genes and environments are unrelated to start with, they become complementary over time because of decisions people make. For instance, people who have a highly sociable temperament put themselves in different environments than people who are less sociable. Those environments, interacting with genetic predispositions, then shape behavior in specific ways, which in turn influences the environments, and on and on. In children, genes and environments can become correlated because children with different temperaments, such as highly emotional versus calm, elicit different behaviors from their parents (Ayoub et al., 2019).

LONG-TERM IMPLICATIONS OF TEMPERAMENTS Early-childhood temperaments influence behavior and per-sonality structure throughout a person's development (Caspi, 2000). As discussed in Chapter 3, researchers investigated the health, development, and personalities of more than 1,000 people born during a one-year period (Caspi et al., 2002). These individuals were examined approximately every two years, and 95 percent of the participants remained in the study through their 38th birthdays (Poulton et al., 2015). At 3 years of age, they were classified into temperamental types based on examiners' ratings. Temperament at age 3 predicted personality structure and various behaviors in adulthood (Slutske et al., 2012).

For instance, people's level of social anxiety in adolescence and adulthood has been linked to early differences in temperament. Research has shown that children as young as 6 weeks of age can be identified as likely to be shy (Kagan & Snidman, 1991). Approximately 15–20 percent of newborns react to new

(a)

(b)

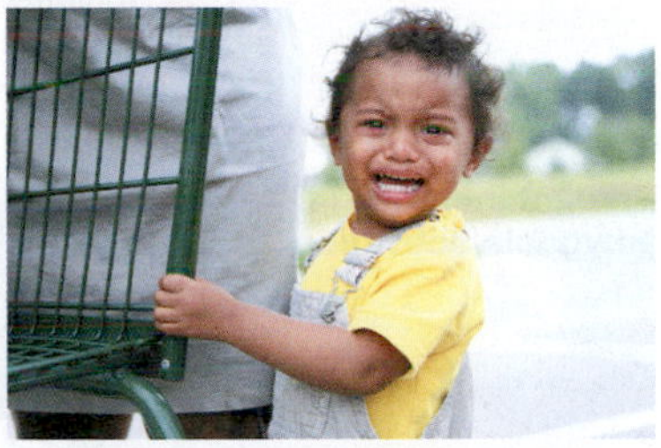

(c)

FIGURE 13.3
Three Types of Temperament
Temperaments are aspects of the personality that are more determined by biology. Temperaments are based on the degree of a child's **(a)** activity level, **(b)** emotionality, and **(c)** sociability.

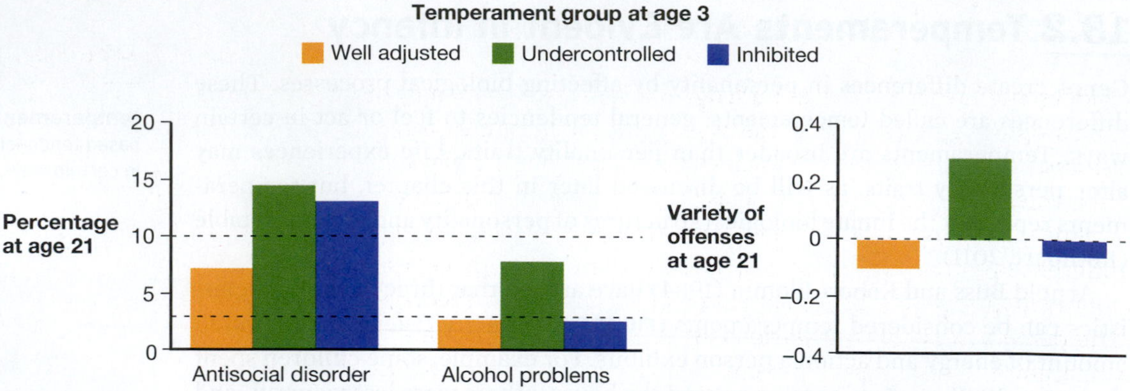

FIGURE 13.4

Predicting Behavior

Researchers investigated the personality development of more than 1,000 people. As shown in these graphs, the individuals judged undercontrolled at age 3 were later more likely to be antisocial, to have alcohol problems, and to be criminals than those judged either well adjusted or inhibited. In each graph, the dotted line indicates the average for the entire sample.

situations or strange objects by becoming startled and distressed, crying, and vigorously moving their arms and legs. The developmental psychologist Jerome Kagan refers to these children as *inhibited*, and he views this characteristic as biologically determined. Showing signs of inhibition at 2 months of age predicts later parental reports that the children are socially anxious at 4 years of age, and such children are likely to be shy well into their teenage years. As discussed further in Chapter 14, socially inhibited children were also much more likely as adults to be anxious, to become depressed, to be unemployed, to have less social support, and to attempt suicide (Caspi, 2000; **FIGURE 13.4**).

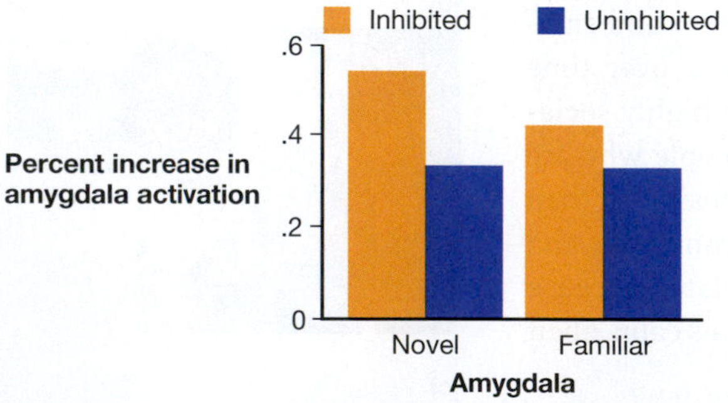

FIGURE 13.5

Inhibition and Social Anxiety

People who were categorized as inhibited before age 2 show greater amygdala activation when viewing novel faces than people who were not inhibited. This suggests people who were inhibited as children might feel greater vigilance or sensitivity to unfamiliar others.

The biological evidence suggests that the amygdala—the brain region involved in emotional responses, especially fear—is involved in social anxiety. In one study, adults received brain scans while viewing pictures of familiar faces and of novel faces (Schwartz et al., 2003). One group of these adults had been categorized as inhibited before age 2. The other group had been categorized as uninhibited before age 2. Compared with the uninhibited group, the inhibited group showed greater activation of the amygdala while viewing the novel faces (**FIGURE 13.5**). That is, after the passage of so many years, the inhibited group still seemed to show a threat response to novel faces. A similar pattern of results was obtained in a study of monkeys, providing a cross-species replication of the relation between inhibition and amygdala function (Shackman et al., 2013).

Although shyness has a biological component, it has a social component as well. Approximately one quarter of behaviorally inhibited children are not shy later in childhood (Kagan, 2011). This development typically occurs when parents create supportive and calm environments in which children can deal with stress and novelty at their own pace. But these parents do not completely shelter their children from stress, so the children gradually learn to deal with their negative feelings in novel situations. This result points to the importance of gene-environment interactions and gene-environment correlations.

Q **How do biologically based temperaments shape our environment?**

ANSWER: Temperament shapes our choices and patterns of behavior, which influence the physical environment and the behaviors of others around us.

What Are the Theories of Personality?

Learning Objectives

- Describe the major approaches to the study of personality.
- Identify theorists associated with the major approaches to the study of personality.

Understanding personality as both dynamic and consistent may be one of humankind's oldest quests. In fact, the word *personality* comes from the Latin word *persona*, meaning "mask." In ancient Greek and Roman plays, actors performed their roles wearing masks. Each mask represented a separate personality.

Since antiquity, many theories have been proposed to explain such basic differences between individuals. During the twentieth century, psychologists approached the study of personality from a number of theoretical perspectives. The perspectives focus on various aspects of personality, each of which tells us something different about a person. Trait approaches characterize people in terms of discrete dimensions of behavior, such as extraversion and open-mindedness, and the biological factors underlying those dimensions. Humanistic approaches describe people in terms of their personal history and the narratives they create to understand themselves. Cognitive approaches distinguish people by how they think about their abilities and the degree of control they feel over their lives. Older theories, such as Sigmund Freud's ideas about unconscious forces determining personality, have been abandoned by modern psychological science because they are difficult to test with data.

13.3 Trait Approaches Describe Behavioral Tendencies

Most contemporary personality psychologists are concerned with describing patterns of behavior in terms of traits. As discussed earlier, traits are patterns of thought, emotion, and behavior that are relatively consistent over time and across situations. For example, in describing a friend, you might say, "Jessica is such an introvert" or "Jorge is a free spirit." Traits exist on a continuum, so most people fall toward the middle and relatively few people fall at the extremes (FIGURE 13.6). Thus, for example, people range from being very introverted to very extraverted, but most are somewhere in the middle. The **trait approach** to personality focuses on how individuals differ in personality dispositions, such as sociability, cheerfulness, and aggressiveness (Funder, 2001).

trait approaches Approaches to studying personality that focus on how individuals differ in personality dispositions.

How many traits are there? Early in his career, Gordon Allport, along with his colleague Henry Odbert, counted the dictionary words that could be used as personality traits (Allport & Odbert, 1936). They found nearly 18,000. Later, the researcher Raymond Cattell (1943) set out to ascertain the basic elements of personality. Cattell believed that statistical procedures would enable him to take the scientific study of personality to a higher level and perhaps uncover

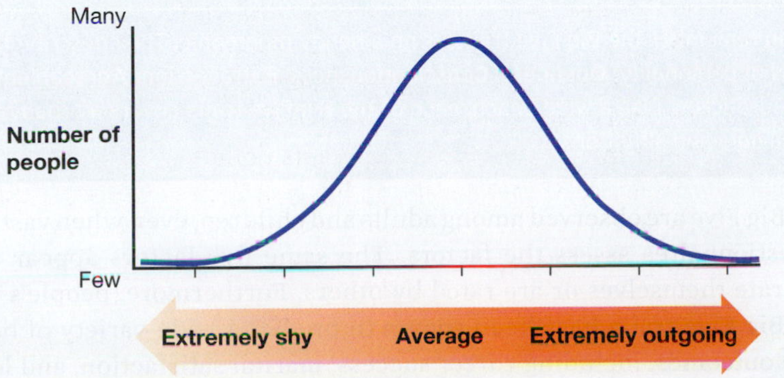

FIGURE 13.6
Personality Traits on a Continuum
Personality traits can be viewed on a continuum. For example, in shyness, people range from extremely shy to extremely outgoing. Most people are in the middle. Relatively few people are at the extremes of any personality trait.

FIGURE 13.7
The Big Five Personality Factors

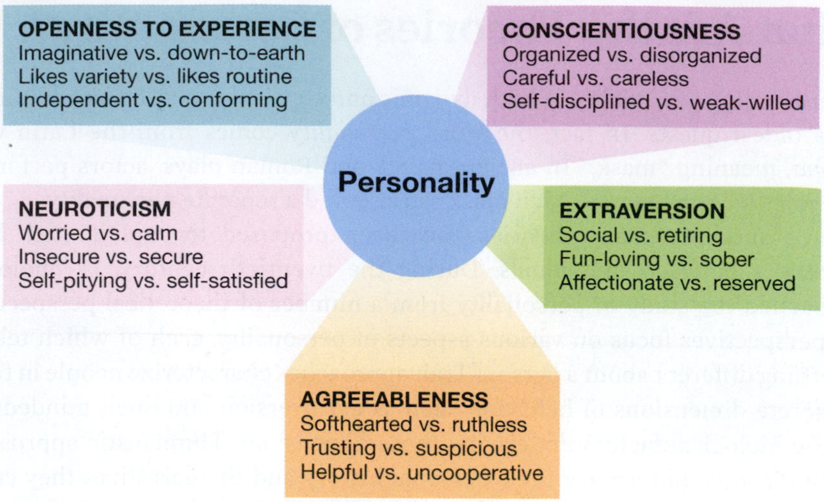

the basic structure of personality. He asked participants to fill out personality questionnaires that presented lists of trait items, which he had reduced from the larger set produced by Allport and Odbert. Cattell then performed *factor analysis*, grouping items according to their similarities. For instance, he grouped all the terms that referred to friendliness: *nice*, *pleasant*, *cooperative*, and so on. Through factor analysis, Cattell (1965) ultimately identified 16 basic dimensions of personality. These dimensions included intelligence, sensitivity, dominance, and self-reliance.

five-factor theory The idea that personality can be described using five factors: openness to experience, conscientiousness, extraversion, agreeableness, and neuroticism.

THE BIG FIVE In the past 30 years or so, many personality psychologists have embraced the **five-factor theory**. This theory identifies five basic personality traits (McCrae & Costa, 1999) that have emerged from factor analyses performed by personality researchers. The so-called *Big Five* are *openness to experience*, *conscientiousness*, *extraversion*, *agreeableness*, and *neuroticism* (**FIGURE 13.7**). For each factor, there is a continuum from low to high. In addition, each factor describes a broad trait that is made up of several related and more-specific traits, or *facets*. For instance, conscientiousness describes how careful, organized, and detail-oriented a person is. A specific facet of conscientiousness is planfulness, which reflects a tendency to make specific and actionable plans (Ludwig et al., 2018). Each of the Big Five traits captures a breadth of different behaviors, whereas the facets within each trait are more specific. Because of this specificity, facets tend to be more predictive of behavior in a given situation than the relevant Big Five trait (Soto & John, 2017).

Learning Tip

You can remember the Big Five traits using a handy mnemonic. They describe the OCEAN of personality: **O**penness, **C**onscientiousness, **E**xtraversion, **A**greeableness, and **N**euroticism. Like a wide beach, each of the Big Five traits covers a broad range of behaviors and situations.

The Big Five are observed among adults and children, even when vastly different questionnaires assess the factors. The same five factors appear whether people rate themselves or are rated by others. Furthermore, people's "scores" on the Big Five traits have been shown to predict a wide variety of behaviors and life outcomes, including career success, marital satisfaction, and longevity

(Paunonen & Ashton, 2001; Roberts et al., 2007). However, some cross-cultural differences emerge in traits related to social interaction. For example, interpersonal relatedness, or harmony, is not an important trait in Western cultures, but personality studies conducted in China have shown that interpersonal relatedness is an important trait there (Cheung et al., 2001, 2008). The Big Five also omits a dimension related to honesty or trustworthiness (Saucier, 2009). The bias toward North American and northern European samples in many personality studies might have led researchers to miss these dimensions, which are central features of personality in most of the world (Saucier et al., 2015).

The five-factor theory of personality remains valuable as an organizational structure for the vast number of traits that describe personality. Moreover, the factors uniquely predict certain outcomes. For instance, conscientiousness predicts grades in college but not scores on standardized tests, whereas openness to experience predicts scores on standardized tests but not grades (Noftle & Robins, 2007). These specific effects may occur because of connections between the traits and the results: Highly conscientious people tend to work very hard, and this characteristic matters for grades. Traits describe stable patterns of behavior, so they can predict future behavior. Beyond that, people's goals are reflected in their behaviors, so traits also capture people's aspirations (McCabe & Fleeson, 2016). For instance, people who are extraverted have goals involving having fun and being the center of attention, whereas those high in conscientiousness have goals involving using time effectively and finishing tasks.

Nonetheless, the five-factor theory is not a complete explanation of personality. After all, the factor terms are descriptive rather than explanatory, and reducing all of human personality to five dimensions ignores individual subtleties. People are more than the sum of their traits. Other approaches to personality provide complementary views about what makes a person unique.

Q How has the statistical procedure of factor analysis been used in the trait approach to personality?

ANSWER: Factor analysis is used to group traits according to their similarity, allowing researchers to organize traits into the Big Five and their specific facets.

13.4 Traits Have a Biological Basis

As with many areas of psychology, neuroscience tools such as brain imaging have provided new insights into the biological basis of personality traits (Abram & DeYoung, 2017; DeYoung et al., 2010). Much like the way multiple genes contribute small effects on personality, multiple brain areas influence how personality develops and is expressed. For example, extraversion is associated with several brain areas involved in reward, whereas neuroticism is associated with brain regions involved in threat and negative affect (DeYoung et al., 2010; Eisenberger et al., 2005). Patterns such as these demonstrate that the Big Five factors can be reliably distinguished based on patterns of brain activity (Dubois & Adolphs, 2016). Two prominent biological theories of personality have guided research within the field.

BIOLOGICAL TRAIT THEORY In the 1960s, the psychologist Hans Eysenck developed the *biological trait theory*. Eysenck (1967) initially proposed that personality traits had two major dimensions: introversion/extraversion and emotional

FIGURE 13.8
Eysenck's Biological Trait Theory of Personality
According to Eysenck, personality is composed of traits that occur in three dimensions: extraversion/introversion, emotionally stable/neurotic, and high constraint/low constraint (originally called psychoticism).

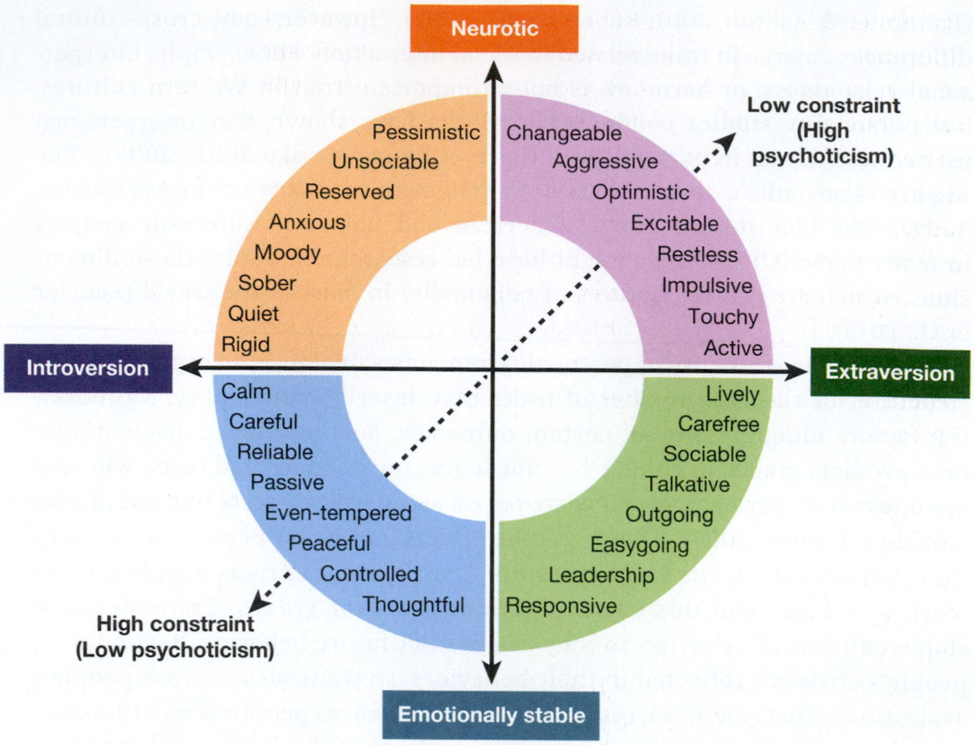

stability (**FIGURE 13.8**). *Introversion* refers to how shy, reserved, and quiet a person is. *Extraversion* refers to how sociable, outgoing, and bold a person is. This dimension is similar to the extraversion trait in the Big Five theory.

Emotional stability refers to consistency in a person's moods and emotions. This dimension is similar to the Big Five trait of neuroticism. A person who is more emotional may be considered *neurotic*. Neurotic people experience frequent and dramatic mood swings, especially toward negative emotions, compared with people who are more emotionally stable. In addition, neurotic people often feel anxious, moody, and depressed and generally hold very low opinions of themselves.

Eysenck later proposed a third dimension of personality traits. *Psychoticism* reflects a mix of aggression, poor impulse control, self-centeredness, and lack of empathy. The term *psychoticism* implies a level of psychological disorder that Eysenck did not intend. As a result, more-recent conceptions of this trait call it *constraint* (see Figure 13.8). According to this view of the trait, people range from generally controlling their impulses to generally not controlling them (Watson & Clark, 1997). This dimension is most similar to the Big Five trait of conscientiousness, or how careful and organized someone is.

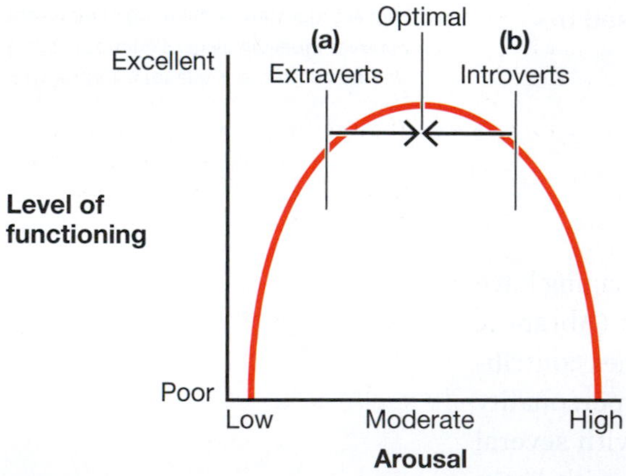

FIGURE 13.9
Optimal Arousal Influences Personality
(a) People who are extraverted have lower baseline levels of arousal. To function optimally, they seek exciting activities. **(b)** By contrast, people who are introverted have higher levels of arousal. To function optimally, they seek calming activities.

Eysenck proposed that personality traits are based on biological processes that produce behaviors, thoughts, and emotions. For instance, Eysenck believed that differences in arousal produce the behavioral differences between extraverts and introverts. As discussed in Chapter 10, each person prefers to operate—and operates best—at some optimal level of arousal. Eysenck proposed that the resting levels of the system that regulates arousal are higher for introverts than for extraverts (**FIGURE 13.9**). Extraverts typically are below their optimal levels or are chronically underaroused. They require greater arousal to operate efficiently, so they seek out new situations and new emotional experiences. In contrast, introverts are typically above their optimal levels of arousal. Because they do not want any additional arousal, they prefer quiet solitude with few stimuli. If you are an introvert, a noisy environment will distract you. If you are an extravert, quiet places will bore you. Consistent with Eysenck's theory, research has demonstrated that extraverts perform better in noisy settings (Dobbs et al., 2011). Introverts appear to be generally more sensitive or reactive to stimuli. For example, they experience pain more intensely than extraverts do (Lynn & Eysenck, 1961).

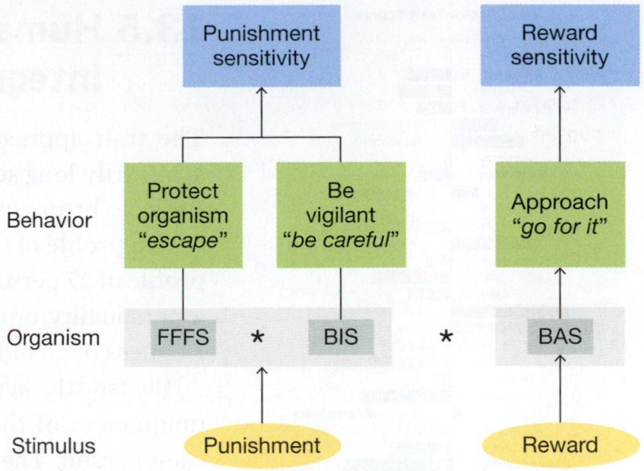

FIGURE 13.10
Behavioral Approach, Behavioral Inhibition, and Fight-Flight-Freeze Systems
BAS reflects reward sensitivity. BIS and FFFS reflect punishment sensitivity and serve separable functions. BIS slows behavior and increases vigilance. FFFS responds to direct threats by engaging in protective behaviors such as flight or freezing.

BEHAVIORAL ACTIVATION AND INHIBITION SYSTEMS Theorists have offered refinements to Eysenck's initial theory that reflect a more current understanding of how the brain functions. The various theories have some common features. For example, each theory differentiates between approach learning and avoidance learning. Jeffrey Gray (1982) incorporated this distinction in his approach/inhibition model of the relationships between learning and personality. Gray proposed that personality is rooted in two motivational functions: to approach rewards and to avoid pain. These functions have evolved to help organisms respond efficiently to reinforcement and punishment. This model has been refined over the years and developed into the revised reinforcement sensitivity theory (rRST) of personality.

In the rRST model, the **behavioral approach system (BAS)** consists of the brain structures that lead organisms to approach stimuli in pursuit of rewards (Smillie, 2008; FIGURE 13.10). This is the "*go*" system. The "*slow down*" system is known as the **behavioral inhibition system (BIS)**. Because it is sensitive to punishment, the BIS cautiously inhibits or slows behavior when there are signs of danger, threats, or pain. The "*stop or escape*" system is known as the **fight-flight-freeze system (FFFS)**. This system promotes behaviors that can protect the organism from harm, such as remaining motionless or escaping. The rRST model has been updated to emphasize that the BIS is related more to anxiety than to fear (Gray & McNaughton, 2000) and to accommodate growing findings in neuroscience (Corr et al., 2013). For instance, neural data revealed a separation between the BIS and FFFS, which had previously been considered parts of the same system (Gable et al., 2018).

behavioral approach system (BAS) The brain system involved in the pursuit of incentives or rewards.

behavioral inhibition system (BIS) The brain system that monitors for threats in the environment and therefore slows or inhibits behavior in order to be vigilant for danger or pain.

fight-flight-freeze system (FFFS) The brain system that responds to punishment by directing an organism to freeze, run away, or engage in defensive fighting.

The BAS is linked to extraversion. Extraverts are more influenced by rewards than by punishments and tend to act impulsively in the face of strong rewards, even following punishment (Patterson & Newman, 1993). The BIS is linked to neuroticism. People high in neuroticism become anxious in social situations in which they anticipate possible negative outcomes. Different brain regions involved in emotion and reward underlie the three rRST systems (DeYoung & Gray, 2009). Gray's model has been particularly useful for understanding personality differences in impulsivity and risk-taking, such as when people drink alcohol or use drugs (Franken et al., 2006).

Q If Eve is highly extraverted, is it more likely that she prefers to study in a noisy café or a quiet library?

ANSWER: a noisy café, because it is a stimulating environment

13.5 Humanistic Approaches Emphasize Integrated Personal Experience

The trait approach describes people in terms of their relative standing on an arbitrarily long series of attributes. Anyone can go to websites such as The SAPA Project (https://www.sapa-project.org), answer several questions, and come out with a profile of their personality (Condon & Revelle, 2015). That website yields a profile of 27 personality dimensions (**FIGURE 13.11**). However, regardless of whether a personality profile has five, 27, or 108 dimensions, none can fully capture the richness of an individual human being.

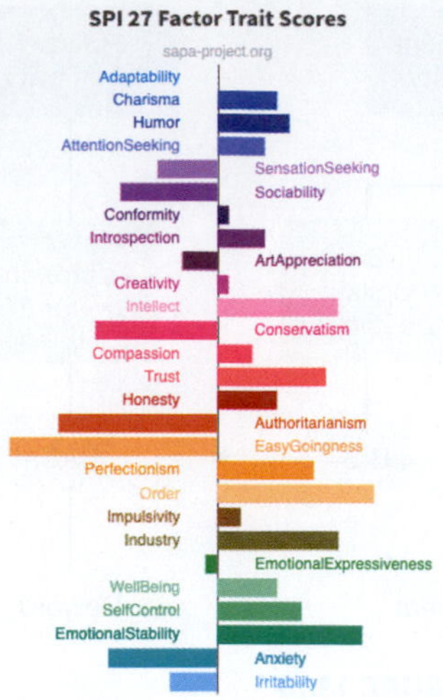

FIGURE 13.11
A Personality Profile
The SAPA (Synthetic Aperture Personality Assessment) Project led by psychologist David Condon generates a profile of personality along 27 dimensions backed by research.

humanistic approaches
Approaches to studying personality that emphasize how people seek to fulfill their potential through greater self-understanding.

Humanistic approaches emphasize personal experience, belief systems, the uniqueness of the narrative of each human life, and the inherent goodness of each person. They propose that people seek to fulfill their potential for personal growth through greater self-understanding. This process is referred to as *self-actualization*. Abraham Maslow's theory of motivation is an example. As discussed in Chapter 10, Maslow believed that the desire to become self-actualized is the ultimate human motive.

The most prominent humanistic psychologist was Carl Rogers, who introduced a *person-centered approach* to understanding personality and human relationships. That is, he emphasized people's subjective understandings of their lives. In the therapeutic technique Rogers advocated, the therapist would create a supportive and accepting environment. The therapist and the client would deal with the client's problems and concerns as the client understood them.

Rogers's theory highlights the importance of how parents show affection for their children and how parental treatment affects personality development (**FIGURE 13.12**). Rogers speculated that most parents provide love and support that

a If parents' affection for a child is conditional on the child acting in an acceptable way, the child's personality develops based solely on the aspects that get approval from others. That is, the child's personality is based on *conditions of worth*.

or

b When parents' affection for a child is unconditional and expressed regardless of how the child acts, the child's personality can develop freely. That is, the child's personality will be based on *unconditional positive regard*.

FIGURE 13.12
Rogers's Person-Centered Approach to Personality
According to Rogers's theory, personality is influenced by how we understand ourselves and how others evaluate us, which leads to conditions of worth or unconditional positive regard.

is conditional: The parents love their children only if the children do what the parents want them to do. Parents who disapprove of their children's behavior might withhold their love. As a result, children quickly abandon their true feelings, dreams, and desires. They accept only those parts of themselves that elicit parental love and support. Thus, people lose touch with their true selves in their pursuit of positive regard from others.

To counteract this effect, Rogers encouraged parents to raise their children with *unconditional positive regard*. That is, parents should accept and prize their children no matter how the children behave. Parents might express disapproval of children's bad behavior, but at the same time they should express their love for the children. According to Rogers, a child raised with unconditional positive regard would develop a healthy sense of self-esteem and would become a *fully functioning person*. Scientists have developed training interventions that can be completed across a few months to help parents express unconditional positive regard and other positive practices, such as warmth and responsivity. These interventions have beneficial effects on children's emotional well-being and cognitive development, on the parent-child relationship, and on parents' stress (Sanders et al., 2014).

The psychologist Dan McAdams has focused on personal narratives as an overlooked humanistic element of personality. According to McAdams, these narratives or "personal myths" are stories that we tell ourselves about where we came from and where we are going as part of understanding our own identity. Research on life narratives has identified consistent themes that help people make sense of their stories (McAdams & McLean, 2013). Common motifs across people's stories include *redemption*, where things start out badly but transform for the better; *contamination*, where things start out well, but then some person or event causes them to turn bad; and *meaning-making*, where an event or episode yields a deep insight about life. People who describe their past and future in terms of narratives that give them agency and connectedness to others have higher overall well-being than people without these narratives (Adler et al., 2016).

Q How would a parent express unconditional positive regard in responding to a child who had broken a vase while running through the house?

ANSWER: "I always love you, but I am upset right now that you acted carelessly and broke the vase."

13.6 Personality Reflects Learning and Cognition

Behavioral psychologists such as B. F. Skinner rejected the idea that personality is the result of internal processes. Instead, behaviorists viewed personality mainly as learned responses to patterns of reinforcement. Over time, however, psychologists became dissatisfied with strict models of learning theory and began to incorporate cognition into the understanding of personality. For instance, Julian Rotter (1954) introduced the idea that behavior is a function of two things: the person's *expectancy* that a reward (reinforcement) will result from the behavior and the *values* the person ascribes to particular rewards. Suppose you are deciding whether to study for an exam or go to a party. You will probably consider the likelihood that studying will lead to a good grade. You will consider how much that grade matters to you. Then you will weigh those two considerations against two others: the likelihood that the party will be fun and the extent to which you value having fun (**FIGURE 13.13**).

FIGURE 13.13
Expectancies and Value
According to Julian Rotter, a student's expectations for the value of events will determine whether he will decide to stay in and study or go out to a party.

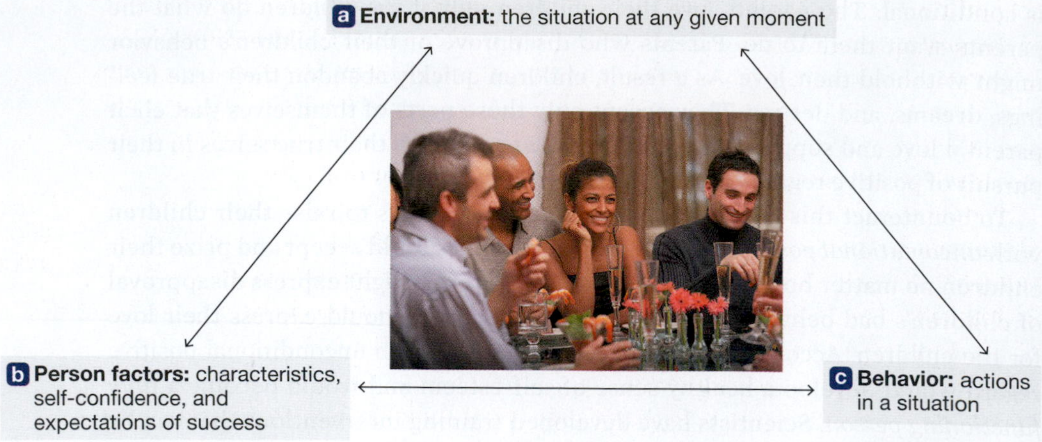

FIGURE 13.14

Bandura's Reciprocal Determinism Theory of Personality

Bandura proposed that three factors interact with one another to influence personality: environment, person factors, and behavior.

locus of control People's personal beliefs about how much control they have over outcomes in their lives.

Rotter also proposed that people differ in how much they believe their efforts will lead to positive outcomes. **Locus of control** refers to how much control people believe they have over what happens in their lives. People with an *internal locus of control* believe they bring about their own rewards. People with an *external locus of control* believe rewards—and therefore their personal fates—result from forces beyond their control. These generalized beliefs affect individuals' behaviors and level of psychological adjustment.

The cognitive theorist George Kelly (1955) emphasized how individuals view and understand their circumstances. He referred to such views and understandings as *personal constructs*: personal theories of how the world works. Kelly believed that people view the world as if they are scientists—constantly testing their theories by observing ongoing events, then revising those theories based on what they observe. According to Kelly, personal constructs develop through experiences and represent individuals' interpretations and explanations for events in their social worlds. Personal constructs are similar to McAdams's idea of personal narratives described in Section 13.5, but personal constructs reflect people's narratives about the world instead of their own life trajectory.

reciprocal determinism The theory that the expression of personality can be explained by the interaction of environment, person factors, and behavior itself.

In another influential social cognitive theory of personality, Albert Bandura (1977a) argued that three factors influence how a person acts. The first factor is the person's environment. The second factor is multiple *person factors*, which include the person's characteristics, self-confidence, and expectations. Bandura's concept of self-efficacy (see Chapter 10) is an example of a person factor. The third factor is behavior itself. In Bandura's view, personality is expressed through behavior, which is influenced by both person factors and environment. Because personality is explained by the interaction of all three factors, the model is called **reciprocal determinism** (**FIGURE 13.14**).

An example can illustrate the reciprocal determinism of personality. Imagine that you are a new transfer student, and you go to a party. According to Bandura's model, the party is the environment. There are many types of parties, and the specifics matter in an environment's effects on behavior. Suppose that most of the people at the party are people you do not know (Figure 13.14a). In addition, you will have your individual person factors. Let's say they are outgoingness and sociability. These characteristics have probably been rewarded by the environment in the past and might stem originally from your temperament (Figure 13.14b). Your behavior in this situation will reflect a combination of the environment and your person factors. At a party with many new faces, you most likely will be friendly and talkative (Figure 13.14c). In turn, your behavior will affect the environment. Because you are outgoing, the party becomes more fun for everyone.

People also differ in terms of how much they enjoy the process of thinking. **Need for cognition** reflects how much a person enjoys and tends to engage in complex thought (Cacioppo & Petty, 1982). People high in need for cognition enjoy puzzles and tasks that require thinking in depth about many sides of a problem. People low in need for cognition find such tasks unpleasant and will avoid them if possible. A person's need for cognition relates to how that person tends to make decisions both big and small. For instance, people high (versus low) in need for cognition are more likely to systematically evaluate and compare information before they vote, make a major purchase such as a house or car, or form an opinion about events in the news (Cacioppo et al., 1996). Need for cognition is a mental tendency that makes someone difficult to persuade without good evidence.

need for cognition The tendency to engage in and enjoy thinking about difficult questions or problems.

Q **Dennis blamed the muggy weather and bugs for the unhappy outcome of his picnic date with Ronald. Does Dennis have an internal or external locus of control?**

ANSWER: He has an external locus of control. He believes that factors beyond his control determined the outcome of the date.

13.7 Personality in the Workplace

PSYCHOLOGY OUTSIDE THE LAB

Have you ever needed to work at a job that you could tell was not the right fit for you? Or have you ever been part of a team where someone else seemed out of sync with the culture of the group? If so, you have experienced firsthand some of the ways personality plays out in the workplace. Scholars in the field of industrial/organizational (I/O) psychology investigate how people's personalities relate to their performance and satisfaction in different roles within organizations, among many other topics. Scientific knowledge of the various traits, skills, and tendencies that are important in a workplace context can make it easier to identify the right people for a job and make sure they can succeed after they are hired.

The lessons that researchers learn about personality are useful throughout organizations and across the human resources cycle. Personality tools and results may be involved in selecting, recruiting, and training employees. I/O psychologists might measure personality traits, such as the Big Five, to optimize the fit between an employee's traits and a particular job requirement. They might observe how employees work in a team and make suggestions to improve productivity or to minimize interpersonal conflicts. NASA, for example, is using research produced by I/O psychologists to study and improve interactions among the team of astronauts traveling together for six months on a scheduled 2030 journey to Mars.

I/O psychology has implications beyond simply identifying fit between people and jobs. Workplaces are often case illustrations of how theories from psychology play out in the real world. Take, for example, the idea from evolutionary psychology that variation on traits exists because the tendencies on both "ends" of the spectrum are adaptive in different contexts. The logic of this prediction is that if it were always better, for example, to be high in conscientiousness, then over the generations everyone would evolve to be high in that trait. It is true that people who are high in conscientiousness are generally desirable in organizations because they are punctual and detail oriented. But one study found that high conscientiousness was also related to low levels of workplace creativity under many conditions (George & Zhou, 2001). Different traits—and even different levels of a given trait—are useful at different times. Just as it is in society at large, it can be beneficial in an organization to have a broad range of personalities working collectively.

Organizations value I/O psychologists because they know how to apply scientific thinking to challenges that arise. For many years, organizations assessed personality with tools that had little validity, such as the Myers-Briggs Type Indicator. Contemporary I/O and personality psychologists using rigorous scientific methods have identified major flaws with this test and the claims that it can predict performance on different job tasks (Pittenger, 2005; Stein & Swan, 2019). A major flaw of personality "type" tests like Myers-Briggs is the underlying assumption that personality traits divide into clear categories. We know from research that traits vary along a continuum. I/O psychologists help ensure that organizations are always working with the best psychological information that is available. I/O psychologists can work in various settings. Some conduct research as university faculty in psychology or business departments. Others are hired by corporations as human resources specialists or as training and development managers, working directly with employees. Finally, I/O psychologists can work as management consultants who are contracted by organizations to help with specific problems.

How do you become an I/O psychologist? The path starts with an undergraduate degree in psychology, perhaps combined with a business minor. It is possible to find employment in this area—for example, as a human resources specialist—with only a baccalaureate degree, but I/O jobs are more plentiful, and provide higher salaries, for those with advanced degrees. Those with master's degrees can find entry-level positions in management or consulting. Those with doctoral degrees have the most opportunities, whether in the academic sector or in the business world. According to the U.S. Bureau of Labor Statistics (2019), the median salary for I/O psychologists is $92,880 per year; those in the top 10 percent can earn nearly $200,000 annually. ■

Q What area of psychology uses personality research to improve businesses' hiring decisions and interpersonal interaction at work?

ANSWER: industrial/organizational (I/O) psychology

Learning Objectives

- Define situationism and interactionism.
- Distinguish between strong situations and weak situations.
- Describe how development and life events alter personality traits.
- Identify cultural influences on personality.

How Stable Is Personality?

If people are shy as adolescents, are they fated to be shy their whole lives? Many people believe that personality is fixed for life and that people are stuck with whatever personality they currently possess. This section considers several issues related to the stability of personality across situations, the situational factors that influence how it is expressed, and how much it changes over time.

13.8 People Sometimes Are Inconsistent

Imagine that you are outgoing. Are you outgoing in all situations? Probably not. Even outgoing people can be uncomfortable in new situations in which they are being evaluated. But they are not usually shy around family and close friends. In 1968, Walter Mischel shook the intellectual pillars of the field of personality by proposing that behaviors are determined more by situations than by personality traits. This idea has come to be called **situationism**. For evidence, Mischel referred to studies in which people who were dishonest in one situation were completely honest in another. Suppose a student is not completely honest with a professor in explaining why a paper is late (**FIGURE 13.15**). That student probably is no more likely to steal or to cheat on taxes than is a student who admits to oversleeping.

Mischel's critique of personality traits caused considerable rifts between social psychologists, who emphasize situational forces, and personality psychologists, who focus on individual dispositions. After all, the most basic definition of personality holds that it is relatively stable across situations. If Mischel was correct and there is relatively little stability, the whole concept of personality seems empty.

As you might expect, there was a vigorous response to Mischel's theory. The discussion has come to be called the *person/situation debate*. After much discussion, psychologists concluded that both sides were right, and both sides were also missing an important piece of the puzzle. On the one hand, social psychologists were right that situational forces do indeed influence behavior. Chapter 12 provides many examples of how forces such as conformity and group influence can shape what people do in a situation. Also, some situations, such as an unexpected noise or the roar of a crowd around a person, elicit very similar behavior from most people. On the other hand, personality psychologists are right that there are stable and predictable person-to-person differences in how people tend to react on average. For instance, shy people may not be shy all the time, but on average they are shy in more situations than people who are not shy. Also, some people are more consistent across situations than others. Consider the trait of *self-monitoring*, which involves being sensitive to cues of situational appropriateness. People high in self-monitoring alter their behavior to match the situation, so they exhibit low levels of consistency. By contrast, people low in self-monitoring are less able to alter their self-presentations to match situational demands, so they tend to be much more consistent across situations.

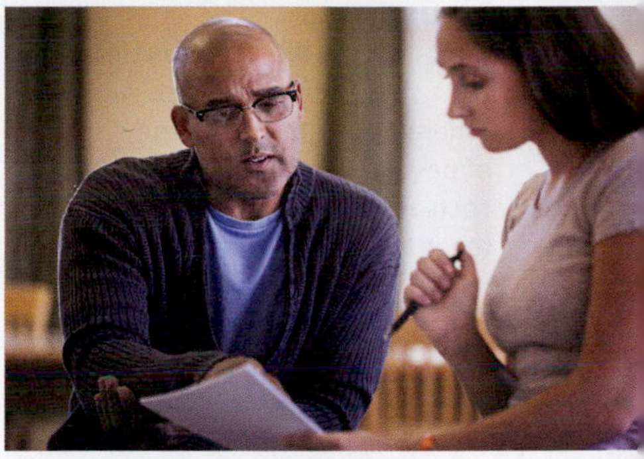

FIGURE 13.15
The Power of Situation
A student who stretches the truth with a professor is not necessarily a dishonest person in all situations.

situationism The theory that behavior is determined more by situations than by personality traits.

PERSON-SITUATION INTERACTION So what is the part that both social and personality psychologists missed? The missing piece is that there is consistency in how a person will react in each situation over time. A shy person might not be shy in every context, but a shy person who tends to avoid large parties will do so consistently. The very same Walter Mischel who launched the person/situation debate in 1968 effectively ended it when he described this idea, which he called the *cognitive affective processing system*, three decades later (Mischel & Shoda, 1995). The core idea of this theory is that people react in predictable ways to specific conditions: If A, then B. If there is a reward, then I am excited to pursue it. If there is an uncertain outcome, then I worry about it.

According to Mischel and Shoda, people will exhibit stable behavior if they find themselves in similar situations over time. Personality in this model is reflected in the fact that people tend to respond in the same way to similar situations. That is where the idea of a person-situation correlation comes in. People do not get randomly assigned to situations. Instead, they place themselves in situations for many reasons, some of which have to do with their own preferences (Sherman et al., 2010). People who tend to enjoy loud places and constant social interactions do not generally become librarians any more than people who prefer quiet solitude become nightclub managers. Personality becomes stable over time in part because people choose the situations into which they place themselves.

Situations also differ in how much they constrain the expression of personality (Kenrick & Funder, 1991). Suppose one person is highly extraverted, aggressive, and boisterous. A second person is shy, thoughtful, and restrained. At a funeral, these

(a) (b)

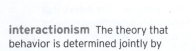

FIGURE 13.16
Strong and Weak Situations
(a) A strong situation, such as a funeral, tends to discourage displays of personality. **(b)** A weak situation, such as hanging out with friends, tends to let people behave more freely.

two people might display similar or even nearly identical behavior. At a party, the same two people would most likely act quite differently. Personality psychologists differentiate between *strong situations* and *weak situations*. Strong situations (e.g., airplanes, religious services, job interviews) tend to mask differences in personality because of the power of the social environment. Weak situations—for example, parks, bars, one's house—tend to reveal differences in personality (**FIGURE 13.16**). Most trait theorists favor **interactionism**. That is, they believe that behavior is determined jointly by situations and underlying dispositions.

interactionism The theory that behavior is determined jointly by situations and underlying dispositions.

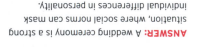

People also affect their social environments. As noted above, people choose their situations, and once they are in those situations their behavior affects those around them. Some extraverts may draw people out and encourage them to have fun, whereas others might act aggressively and turn people off. Some introverts might create an intimate atmosphere that encourages people to open up and reveal personal concerns, whereas others might make people uncomfortable and anxious. A reciprocal interaction occurs between the person and the social environment so that they simultaneously influence each other. The important point is that personality reflects a person's underlying disposition, the activation of the person's goals in a particular situation, and the activation of the person's emotional responses in the pursuit of those goals.

Q **Why might two people who differ substantially in level of extraversion behave similarly at a wedding ceremony?**

ANSWER: A wedding ceremony is a strong situation, where social norms can mask individual differences in personality.

13.9 Development and Life Events Alter Personality Traits

A basic premise of personality psychology is that people's traits, characteristics, and response tendencies are more or less stable across their life span. Some aspects of people, such as their childhood temperaments, do remain stable and predict behaviors throughout their life. But personality psychology also recognizes that people change over time. Scientists in the field study not only what is stable across the life span but also what about people changes, how it changes, and when.

MOST TRAITS ARE STABLE The way we define the essential features of personality has tremendous implications for whether personality is fixed or changeable. Continuity over time and across situations is inherent in the definition of the word *trait*, and most research finds personality traits to be relatively stable over the adult life span (Costa et al., 2019). There are several ways of thinking about stability in a psychological trait, but typically stability in personality refers to a lack of change

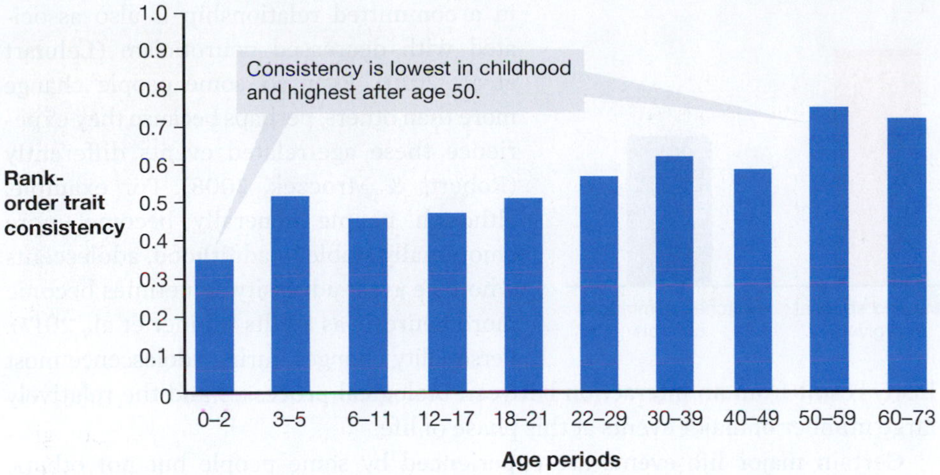

FIGURE 13.17
The Stability of Personality
This graph shows the rank ordering of the study participants' personalities. Participants ranged in age from newborn to 73.

in where a person stands on the trait relative to other people. This is referred to as *rank-order* stability. For instance, over many years the relative rankings of individuals on each of the Big Five personality traits remain stable (McCrae & Costa, 1990). A meta-analysis of 150 studies—through which a total of nearly 50,000 participants had been followed for at least one year—found strong evidence for stability in personality (Roberts & DelVecchio, 2000). The rank orderings of individuals on any personality trait were quite stable over long periods across all age ranges (**FIGURE 13.17**).

AGE-RELATED CHANGE Although traits show relative stability, they also change (Harris et al., 2016). Focusing only on rank-order stability can hide changes in personality that many people experience at the same stages of life, referred to as *mean-level* changes. For example, people in general tend to become more conscientious as they age, even though their rank ordering remains stable (Jackson et al., 2009). A person who is highly conscientious relative to peers at age 18 will remain so at 68, even though most people will be more conscientious than their younger selves.

In addition, people generally develop increased self-control and emotional stability as they age (Caspi et al., 2005). They become less neurotic, less extraverted, and less open to new experiences as they get older (Milojev & Sibley, 2016). They also tend to become more agreeable (Srivastava et al., 2003). Some aspects of personality, such as conscientiousness and emotional stability, change more in young adulthood (ages 20–40) than in any other part of the life course, including adolescence (Roberts et al., 2006).

Life events can produce changes in personality, especially during the transition from adolescence to adulthood. In general, personality changes are observed at times in life when the expectations and experiences associated with age-related roles—such as becoming a spouse, a parent, or an employee—also change (Roberts et al., 2006, 2012). Each of these life events typically leads to an altered lifestyle, in which behaviors, thoughts, and emotions change in predictable ways. For instance, a person's first job brings expectations that the person show up on time, work hard, and interact agreeably with coworkers and respectfully with bosses. Acting in these ways can instill new behaviors and help make the person more conscientious. Moreover, the tangible benefits of working, such as having more money and therefore an improved lifestyle, permit people to regularly engage in enjoyable behaviors. These connections may explain why greater job satisfaction can decrease neuroticism over time (Le et al., 2014). Becoming involved in a committed relationship is also associated with decreased neuroticism (Lehnart et al., 2010). Even so, some people change more than others, perhaps because they experience these age-related events differently (Roberts & Mroczek, 2008). For example, although people generally become more emotionally stable in adulthood, adolescents who face great adversity sometimes become more neurotic as adults (Shiner et al., 2017). Personality changes during adolescence most likely result from an interaction between biological processes and the relatively large number of major events at this phase of life.

Certain major life events are experienced by some people but not others. One study examined personality change among people who were caregivers for a spouse with terminal cancer. They assessed personality before and approximately seven months after the spouse's death. Compared with a control group, the bereaved caregivers became more agreeable, sociable (a component of extraversion), and conscientious (Hoerger et al., 2014; **FIGURE 13.18**). Another study examined college students who traveled abroad compared with a group of control students who did not (Zimmermann & Neyer, 2013). Those who chose to travel were more extraverted and had higher scores on openness to experience at the beginning of the study, as you might imagine. However, one year later they showed reliable increases in openness and agreeableness (**FIGURE 13.19a**), along with a decrease in neuroticism (**FIGURE 13.19b**). These changes typically occur as people

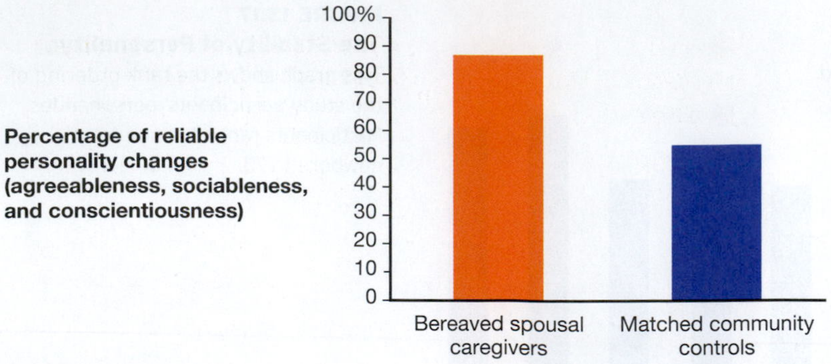

FIGURE 13.18
Bereavement and Personality Change
Bereaved caregivers reliably experienced more positive personality changes than a control group did.

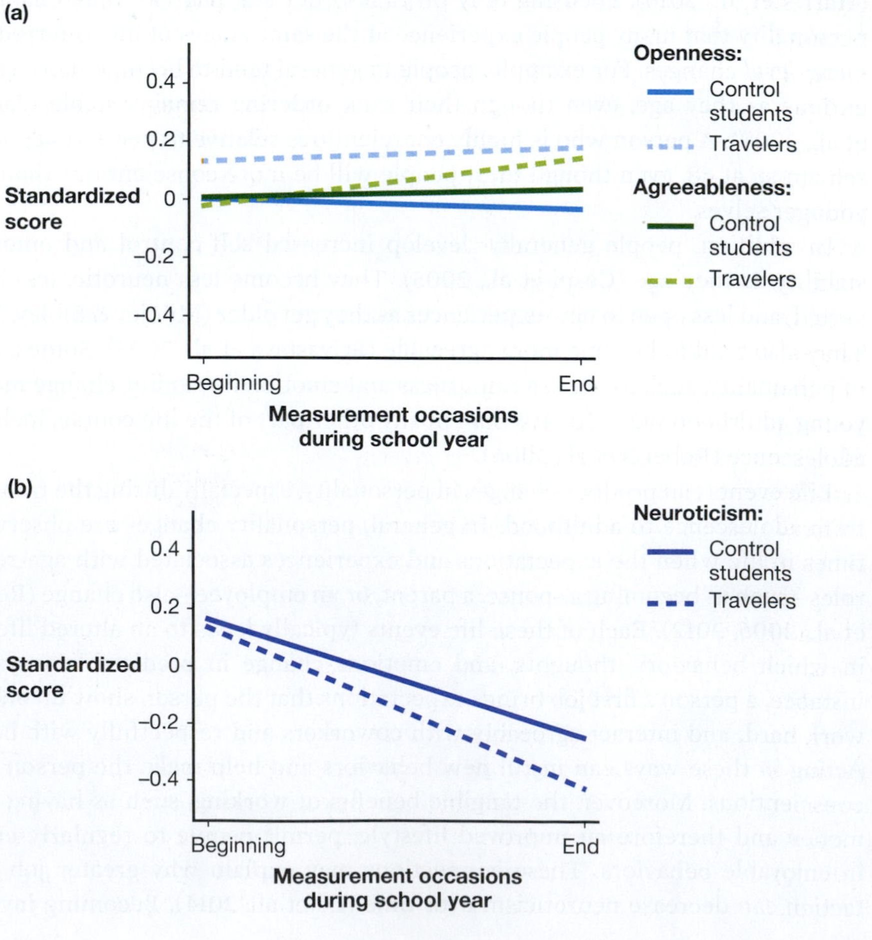

FIGURE 13.19
Travel and Personality Change
College students who traveled abroad **(a)** reliably experienced more positive personality changes and **(b)** became less neurotic compared with a control group.

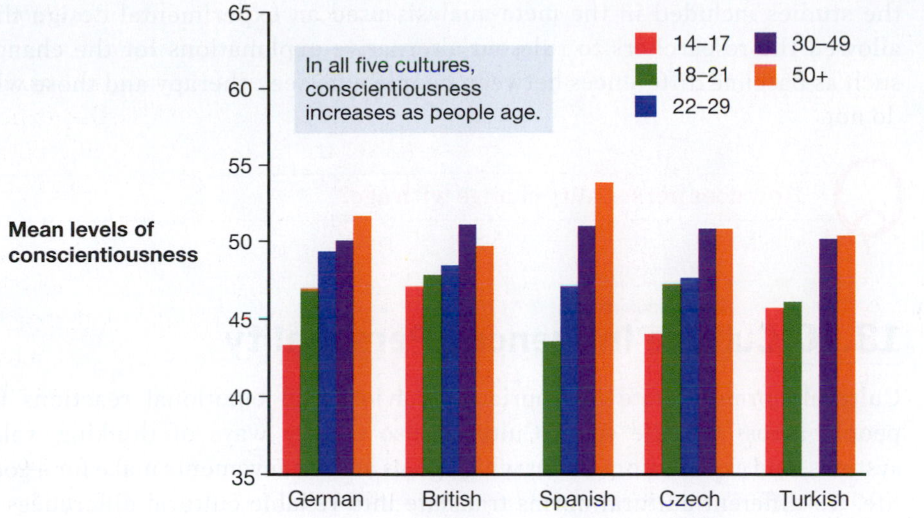

FIGURE 13.20
Conscientiousness at Different Ages in Five Cultures
Note that bars are missing from this graph because data were not available for the 14-17 age group in Spain and the 22-29 age group in Turkey.

get older (Roberts & Wood, 2006), suggesting that international travel is a life event that hastens maturation.

Even apparently trivial life events may have large effects on personality development. Consider that Charles Darwin's uncle generously offered to drive him 30 miles to take a voyage on the *Beagle*. In his autobiography, Darwin described the *Beagle* voyage as the most important event of his life, and it would not have happened except for his uncle's offer (Darwin, 1892). The discoveries he made on the trip not only profoundly shaped modern science but also helped shape him as a person. These twists of fate and apparently arbitrary events might help explain why even those who possess the same genes do not develop identical personalities (Plomin & Daniels, 1987, 2011).

The pattern of personality changes across age holds in different cultures (McCrae et al., 2000; **FIGURE 13.20**). Research findings suggest that age-related changes in personality occur independently of environmental influences that vary considerably by culture. Major life events such as forming a family, having children, and working toward independence occur around the same age in many cultures around the world, so cross-cultural similarity in how personalities change does not necessarily imply that the changes are biological. However, other research finds that the extent of personality change is more similar in monozygotic twins than in dizygotic twins, indicating that personality change is at least partially genetic (McGue et al., 1993).

There is even some evidence that personality can be altered intentionally. In an experimental study, Joshua Jackson and colleagues (2012) had older adults practice cognitive tasks that included a challenging set of sudoku puzzles and training in problem solving. The participants enjoyed the experimental condition, spending an average of 11 hours per week on the puzzles for 16 weeks. Compared with a control group, the experimental group showed an increase in openness to experience (**FIGURE 13.21**). A meta-analysis found substantial and lasting changes in personality as a result of clinical interventions such as psychotherapy (see Chapter 15), particularly in neuroticism and extraversion (Roberts et al., 2017). Many of

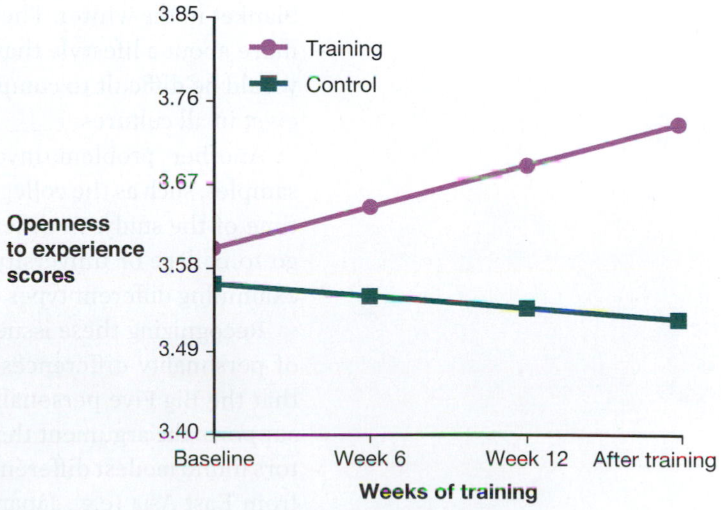

FIGURE 13.21
Experimentally Produced Personality Change
Compared with a control group, the experimental group showed an increase in openness to experience.

the studies included in the meta-analysis used an experimental design that allowed the researchers to rule out alternative explanations for the change, such as baseline differences between people who seek therapy and those who do not.

Q **How does personality change with age?**

ANSWER: People do not change much relative to others, but average levels of personality traits change in the population.

13.10 Culture Influences Personality

Cultural norms dictate appropriate behaviors and emotional reactions for people across the life span. Cultures also convey ways of thinking, value systems, and expectations about which goals and achievements make for a good life. Do different cultural norms translate into reliable cultural differences in personality?

Studying potential personality differences across cultures presents many challenges. As noted in Chapter 2, cross-cultural research can be difficult because people from different cultures might interpret the meaning of questions differently. Recall from Chapter 1 that people from Eastern cultures tend to think in terms of relations with other people, whereas those from Western cultures tend to think in terms of independence. People from Eastern cultures might therefore interpret a question about personality traits as referring to their family or group. People from Western cultures might interpret the same question as referring to them alone.

Making comparisons across cultures requires the use of standardized questionnaires that are reliably translated so that the questions clearly refer to the same personality trait in all cultures and all respondents interpret the questions in the same way. Some traits, particularly ones related to emotion, might be entirely culture specific and have no direct translation in other languages. For example, the Scandinavian concept of *hygge* refers to the pleasure of warmth and contentment associated with small comforts such as cuddling under a heated blanket in the winter. The word *cozy* is the closest English analogue, but hygge is more about a lifestyle than it is about simply being cozy. A trait related to hygge would be difficult to compare across cultures because the concept itself does not exist in all cultures.

Another problem involves sampling: Often researchers use convenience samples, such as the college students who are taking the researchers' classes at the time of the study. In different countries, however, different types of people may go to college or university. Thus, apparent cultural differences may result from examining different types of people in the various cultures.

Recognizing these issues, one research team conducted a careful investigation of personality differences across 56 nations (Schmitt et al., 2007). They found that the Big Five personality traits are valid across all the countries. This finding supports the argument that the Big Five are universal for humans. The investigators found modest differences in those traits across the 56 nations, however. People from East Asia (e.g., Japan, China, Korea) rated themselves comparatively lower than other respondents on extraversion, agreeableness, and conscientiousness, and they rated themselves comparatively higher on neuroticism (**FIGURE 13.22**). By contrast, respondents from countries in Africa rated themselves as more agreeable, more conscientious, and less neurotic than people from most other countries rated themselves. These ratings might have reflected differences, however,

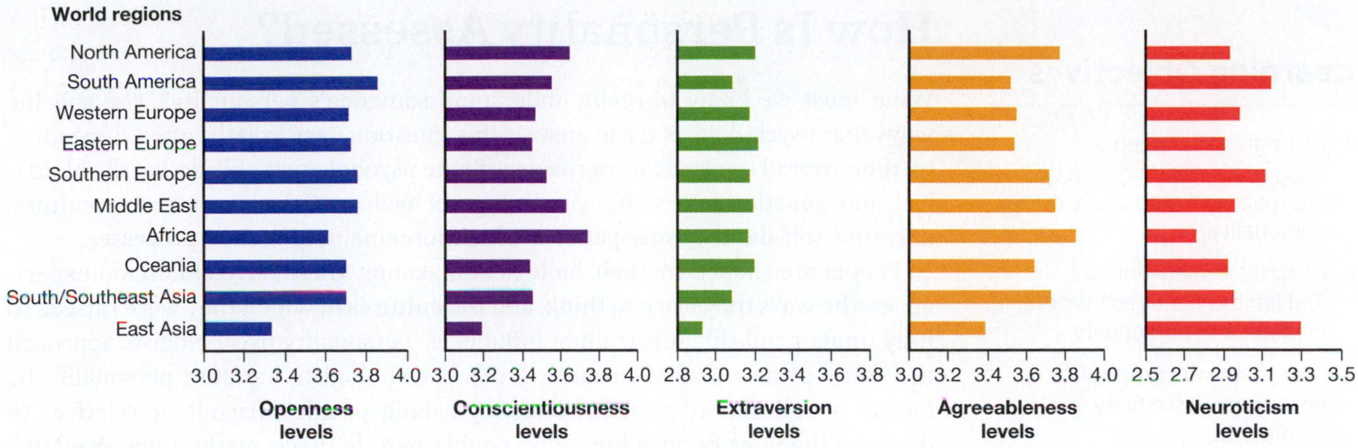

Source: Schmitt et al., 2007.

FIGURE 13.22

Cross-Cultural Research on Personality Traits

A team of more than 120 scientists investigated the Big Five personality traits around the world, from Argentina to Zimbabwe. This chart presents some of their findings.

in cultural norms for saying good and bad things about oneself. People from East Asian countries might simply be the most modest. Indeed, as noted earlier, the Big Five itself was developed in Western cultures, so it is skewed by Western cultural values. It omits dimensions of personality that feature prominently in other cultures, such as modesty and humility, but are less valued in the West (Ion et al., 2017).

The cross-cultural differences in personality that have emerged in the data are not the ones most people expect. One team of researchers examined common beliefs about the personality characteristics of people from 49 cultures (Terracciano et al., 2005). The researchers then compared those beliefs about the 49 cultures with self-reports and observer reports of people from the actual cultures. There was little correspondence. For instance, Canadians were widely believed to be relatively low in neuroticism and high in agreeableness, yet self-reports by Canadians did not support this pattern. Canadians reported themselves to be just as neurotic and disagreeable as people from other cultures. Steven Heine and colleagues (2008) have argued that national reputations may be accurate and that self-reports might be biased by individuals' comparisons of themselves with their national reputations.

To understand this idea, imagine that everyone in Country X works extremely hard and is always on time. People in Country Y work only when the urge strikes them. Therefore, the people in Country X are high in conscientiousness compared with the people in Country Y. Meanwhile, an individual in Country X and an individual in Country Y may be equally conscientious. Compared with their fellow citizens in their respective countries, however, the person in Country X may feel average, whereas the person in Country Y may feel far above average. Thus, people can view the same behavior differently depending on how they compare themselves with others. In other words, maybe Canadians really are especially agreeable, and it is simply hard to notice one person's agreeableness around all those other agreeable Canadians.

Q **Do different levels of self-reported personality traits across cultures necessarily reflect genuine personality differences in those cultures?**

ANSWER: No. Cultural expectations for how to think and talk about oneself can influence the way people respond to personality questions.

How Is Personality Assessed?

Learning Objectives

- Distinguish between idiographic and nomothetic approaches to the study of personality.
- Describe the advantages and limitations of self-report measures of personality.
- Discuss the accuracy of observers' personality judgments.

What must we know to really understand someone's personality? The specific ways that psychologists try to answer this question vary greatly, often depending on their overall theoretical approaches. Some psychologists emphasize the biological and genetic factors that predispose behaviors. Others emphasize culture, narrative self-descriptions, patterns of reinforcement, or mental processes.

People are shaped by their biological makeups, their early-childhood experiences, the ways they learn to think, and the cultures in which they were raised. To fully understand this spectrum of influences, personality psychologists approach the study of personality on many levels. Psychologists measure personality by having people report on themselves, by asking people's friends or relatives to describe them, or by watching how people behave. Each method has strengths and limitations.

13.11 Researchers Use Multiple Methods to Assess Personality

Personality assessment methods include life history data; behavioral data; self-reports; and descriptions from people's friends, relatives, or both. The assessment of personality follows two approaches: idiographic and nomothetic. **Idiographic approaches** are person-centered. They focus on individual lives and how various characteristics are integrated into unique persons. **Nomothetic approaches** focus on characteristics that are common among all people but that vary from person to person. In other words, idiographic approaches use a different metric for each person, such as the way they tell the story of their life. Nomothetic approaches use the same metric to compare all people, such as their relative standing on extraversion.

idiographic approaches Person-centered approaches to assessing personality that focus on individual lives and how various characteristics are integrated into unique persons.

nomothetic approaches Approaches to assessing personality that focus on the variation in common characteristics from person to person.

Idiographic approaches center on the uniqueness of each individual. Suppose your psychology instructor asked people in your class to identify 10 personality traits that describe themselves. If your instructor then compiled a list of everyone's traits, some of the traits would overlap. Other traits would probably apply to just one person in the class. After all, people like to be unique, so they tend to choose traits that distinguish themselves from other people. These *central traits* are especially important for how individuals define themselves. In contrast, people consider *secondary traits* less personally descriptive or not applicable. As you can imagine, certain traits are central for some people and secondary for others. You might define yourself in terms of how bold you are, but someone else might not consider boldness to be particularly important to their self-definition. In general, central traits are more predictive of behavior than secondary traits are.

Nomothetic approaches focus on common traits rather than individual uniqueness. Researchers in this tradition compare people by measuring traits such as agreeableness or extraversion. For example, they might give participants a questionnaire that lists 100 personality traits and have the participants rate themselves on each trait, using a scale of 1 to 10. From the nomothetic perspective, individuals are unique because of their unique combinations of common traits. Figure 13.11 illustrates how a pattern of responses across many traits can convey the uniqueness of an individual. Assessment methods based on the five-factor theory, discussed earlier, are examples of nomothetic approaches.

PROJECTIVE MEASURES Theories dating back to Freud's and extending to Mischel's cognitive affective processing system view personality as the sum total of the ways people tend to respond to stimuli in the world. **Projective measures** map

projective measures Personality tests that examine tendencies to respond in a particular way by having people interpret ambiguous stimuli.

out some of these response patterns by having people describe or tell stories about ambiguous stimulus items. The general idea is that people will fill in the gaps in ambiguous items, and the information they provide to complete a narrative or describe a scene can provide rich information. Procedures such as this are too imprecise for diagnostic purposes but when combined with other measures can help researchers and clinical psychologists get a fuller sense of a person.

One of the best-known projective measures is the Rorschach inkblot test. In this procedure, a person looks at an apparently meaningless inkblot and describes what it appears to be. There is no evidence to support the claims that responses to this test can reveal unconscious conflicts and other problems. The test is also unreliable because raters often disagree with one another in how to interpret people's descriptions. The Rorschach is particularly unsuited for diagnosing specific psychological disorders, and it finds many normal adults and children to be psychologically disturbed (Wood et al., 2002). For this reason, the Rorschach has largely been abandoned by psychologists.

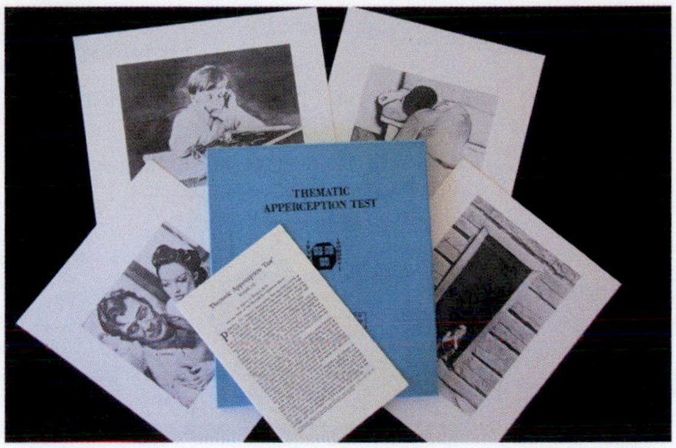

FIGURE 13.23
Projective Measures of Personality
Projective measures are meant to provide insight into a particular person's personality by allowing the person to project unconscious thoughts onto ambiguous images. Shown here is a Thematic Apperception Test (TAT).

A classic projective measure that is still in use today is the Thematic Apperception Test (TAT). In the 1930s, Henry Murray and Christiana Morgan developed the TAT to study various types of motivation. In this test, a person is shown an ambiguous picture and is asked to tell a story about it (**FIGURE 13.23**). Scoring of the story is based on the motivational schemes that emerge, because the schemes are assumed to reflect the storyteller's personal motives. The TAT has been useful for measuring motivational traits—especially those related to achievement, power, and affiliation—and has been validated using modern methods (Tuerlinckx et al., 2002). The TAT has been taken by so many people that psychologists have been able to catalog typical and atypical responses to each picture (Stein et al., 2014). A person's unusual responses can contribute to an idiographic profile of that individual.

SELF-REPORTS Many assessments of personality involve self-report questionnaires. A questionnaire might target a specific trait, such as how much excitement a person seeks out of life. More often, questionnaires will include a large inventory of traits. For example, the NEO Personality Inventory consists of 240 items, which are designed to assess the Big Five personality factors (Costa & McCrae, 1992).

A widely used questionnaire for personality assessment is the Minnesota Multiphasic Personality Inventory (MMPI). Developed during the 1930s, the MMPI was updated in the 1990s for language changes (Butcher & Williams, 2009). The latest full version (MMPI-2) consists of 567 true/false items that assess emotions, thoughts, and behaviors. The scale was originally designed to assess psychopathology (which you will learn more about in Chapter 14) but has also been widely used to assess personality more generally. The MMPI has 10 scales that measure psychological problems (e.g., paranoia, depression, mania, hysteria). By comparing a person's scores on these scales with the average responses of many other people, the assessor can generate a profile that indicates whether a person is likely to have a psychological disorder.

As discussed in Chapter 2, a common problem among all self-report assessments, including the MMPI, is that respondents sometimes distort the truth or lie outright to make favorable impressions. To avoid detection of psychological disorders, they may be evasive or defensive. People might also try to present themselves too positively by agreeing with a large number of items, such as "I always make my bed" and "I never tell lies." To counter such response biases, the MMPI-2 and

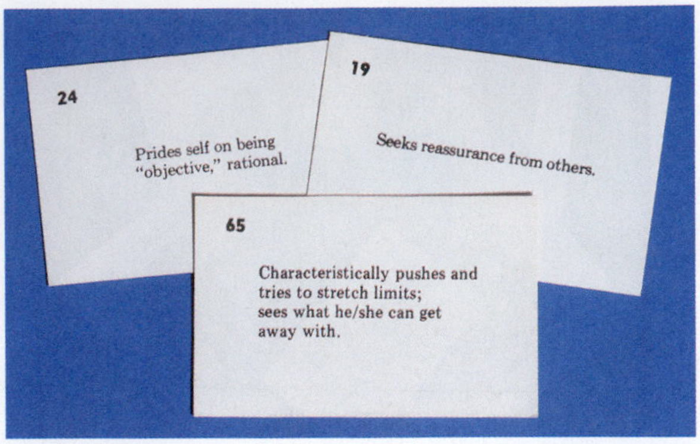

24
Prides self on being "objective," rational.
19
Seeks reassurance from others.
65
Characteristically pushes and tries to stretch limits; sees what he/she can get away with.

FIGURE 13.24
California Q-Sort
These are three of the cards a participant sorts when taking the Q-Sort assessment.

other self-report measures include validity scales among the items. The validity scales measure the probability that respondents are being less than truthful when taking the test.

One technique for assessing traits is the California Q-Sort. In this procedure, each participant is given 100 cards that have statements printed on them. The participant is asked to sort the cards into nine piles according to how accurately the statements describe the person. The piles represent categories that range from "not at all descriptive" to "extremely descriptive" (**FIGURE 13.24**). A participant may place only so many cards in each pile. Fewer cards are allowed at the extreme ends of the scale, giving the Q-Sort a built-in procedure for identifying those traits that people view as most central. The Q-Sort, like most objective measures, can also be used by observers to report about another person. For example, parents, teachers, friends, and romantic partners can sort the cards to describe the person being evaluated.

Do you want to learn about your own personality? There is no shortage of free personality tests that you can take online. Some, such as the SAPA Project, mentioned earlier, are at the cutting edge of modern personality science. Others have adapted scientifically sound measures, such as the Big Five, into fun quizzes, such as "Which *Star Wars* character are you?" (https://www.idrlabs.com/starwars/test.php). Be warned that you might be told you are similar to Darth Vader if you are low on agreeableness. And still others are not backed by science at all or have been debunked, such as the Myers-Briggs, described in Section 13.7. Use your critical thinking skills to evaluate whether the tests you find are valid or unreliable.

LIFE HISTORY DATA Researchers who use idiographic approaches often examine case studies of individuals through interviews or biographical information. The personality psychologist Henry Murray pioneered this approach. Murray was one of many scholars who tried to account for Adolf Hitler's behavior in Nazi Germany by studying Hitler's early-childhood experiences, his physical stature, and his personal motivations. This type of study emphasizes the idea that personality unfolds over the life course as people react to their specific circumstances.

Another idiographic approach considers a human life as a narrative. To study personality, narrative psychologists pay attention to the stories people tell about themselves. As noted above, people weave a *life story*, which integrates self-knowledge into a coherent whole. Whether true or not, these stories help people make sense of the world and find meaning in life. The way life narratives are structured can be measured in a kind of TAT, using key moments from a person's life instead of ambiguous pictures (McAdams, 2018). For instance, a redemption narrative might emerge from a person's description of a challenging social life in adolescence and a thriving one in middle age.

BEHAVIORAL DATA Researchers have also developed objective measures that assess how personality emerges in daily life. For example, Matthias Mehl and James Pennebaker (Mehl et al., 2001) created the Electronically Activated Recorder (EAR). This device unobtrusively tracks a person's real-world moment-to-moment interactions. As the wearer goes about daily life, the EAR picks up snippets of conversations and other auditory information. People quickly get used to wearing the EAR and have no idea when it is recording.

The EAR has revealed that self-reports on the Big Five traits predict real-world behavior (Mehl et al., 2006). According to this study, extraverts talk more and spend less time alone; agreeable people swear less often; conscientious people attend class more often; neurotic people spend more time arguing; and people

(a) (b)

FIGURE 13.25
Behavior and Personality
How a person maintains a home or office is just one area in which personality is on display.

open to experience spend more time in restaurants, bars, and coffee shops. Smartphones and wearable devices such as Fitbits are allowing researchers to learn even more about behavior in the real world and how it relates to other measures of personality (Lind et al., 2018).

Other aspects of your environment can also be used to predict personality. Consider whether you keep your bedroom tidy or messy, warm or cold. In his book *Snoop*, Sam Gosling (2008) notes that each person's personality "leaks out" in many situations, such as through a social media profile (Back et al., 2010) or even the condition of a bedroom or office (Gosling et al., 2002; **FIGURE 13.25**). In each case, study participants who viewed public information about other people were able to form reasonably accurate impressions of how those people rated themselves on the Big Five personality traits.

Q Why do researchers often gather several measures of personality in a study?

ANSWER: A complete picture of a person requires multiple types of information, including trait (nomothetic) and narrative (idiographic) data.

13.12 Observers Show Accuracy About Other People's Traits

People might be able to judge other people's personalities by looking at their bedrooms and Twitter feeds, but how well do the observers really know the other people? Imagine that you often feel shy in new situations, as many people do. Would others know that shyness is part of your personality? Some shy people force themselves to be outgoing to mask their feelings, so their friends might have no idea that they feel shy. Other people react to their own fear of social situations by remaining quiet and aloof, so observers might view them as cold and unfriendly. Right or wrong, these beliefs about the personalities of others will guide our interactions with them (Funder, 2012). An important question, then, is: How accurate are observers' judgments about the personalities of other people?

A foundational study by David Funder (1995) showed that a person's close acquaintances are surprisingly accurate in their trait judgments, at least in some circumstances. In some studies, friends' ratings of personality predicted assertiveness and other behaviors even better than the person's own ratings did (Kolar et al., 1996; Vazire & Mehl, 2008). This effect may occur because our friends are frequent observers of how we behave in situations. As individuals, we might be

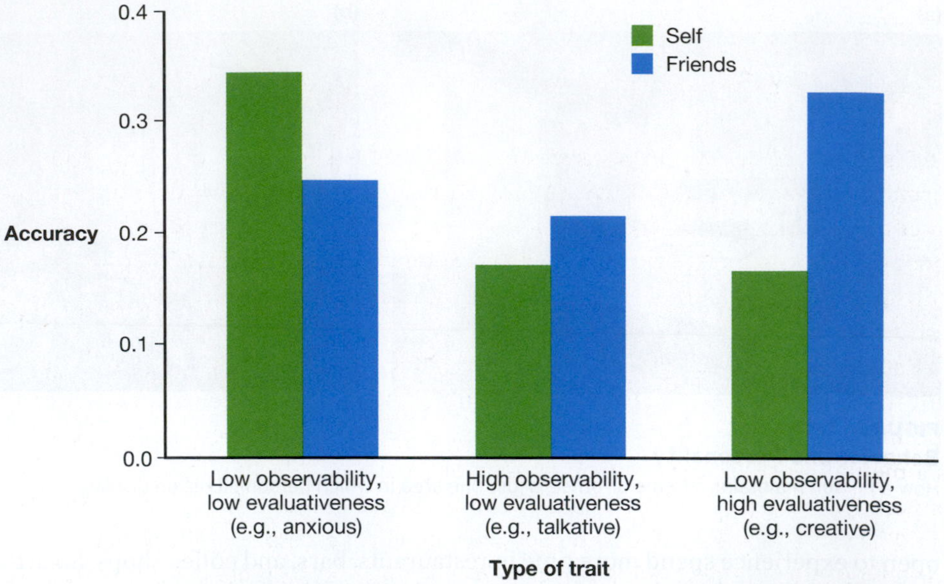

FIGURE 13.26

Self-Rating and Friends' Rating for Different Traits

In judgments of personality traits, how accurate are people's self-ratings versus their friends' ratings? This chart, based on the data from the Vazire (2010) study, shows the average accuracy scores for three types of traits. As shown on the left, self-ratings tend to be more accurate than friends' ratings for traits that are low in both observability and evaluativeness. As shown in the middle, friends' ratings tend to be more accurate than self-ratings for traits that are high in observability and low in evaluativeness. As shown on the right, friends' ratings tend to be especially accurate for traits that are low in observability and high in evaluativeness.

preoccupied with evaluating other people when we are in those situations and therefore fail to notice how we ourselves behave. Not surprisingly, we are more accurate in predicting a close friend's behavior than in predicting the behavior of a mere acquaintance (Biesanz et al., 2007). Another possibility is that our subjective perceptions of our own actions may diverge from our objective behaviors. This explanation is similar to the actor/observer discrepancy described in Chapter 12. Our explanations for our own behavior are different from our explanations of the behavior of others because we tend to explain our behaviors (bad ones in particular) in terms of situational factors and overlook personal factors. In either case, studies on observer ratings of personality imply that there is a gap between how people view themselves and how they behave.

Simine Vazire (2010; Vazire & Carlson, 2011) has compared the accuracy of people's self-judgments with the accuracy of how their friends describe them. In these studies, "accuracy" refers to how well a person's own or their friends' ratings of their personality predict the person's behavior. The comparative accuracy depends on whether the traits are observable and whether the people being rated are motivated to view themselves positively in terms of the traits. Vazire argues that people have blind spots about aspects of their personalities because they want to feel good about themselves. This tendency is particularly true for traits that are highly valued in society, such as creativity. In personality research, these traits are referred to as *evaluative*.

People are biased when judging themselves on highly evaluative traits (biases in self-perception are discussed later in this chapter). In contrast, people are more accurate in rating themselves for traits that are hard to observe (e.g., traits related to internal emotional states such as neuroticism) and for those that are less prone to bias because they are neutral (e.g., openness). For instance, people might be accurate in knowing whether they are anxious or optimistic, because those traits are associated with feelings that can be difficult for others to observe. Friends might be more accurate in knowing whether the person is talkative or charming, because the behaviors associated with those traits are easy to observe. Vazire's key insight is that a trait that is hard to observe but also highly meaningful to people, such as creativity, is more likely to be judged accurately by friends than by the person with the trait (**FIGURE 13.26**).

Q **Why might Amara's good friend Jackson provide a more accurate rating of Amara's level of extraversion than Amara herself?**

ANSWER: Amara may be biased in her self-assessment, and Jackson has observed Amara's social behaviors in various settings.

How Do We Know Our Own Personalities?

Learning Objectives

- Differentiate among self-concept, self-schema, working self-concept, and self-esteem.
- Review theories of self-esteem.
- Discuss research findings regarding the association between self-esteem and life outcomes.
- Identify strategies people use to maintain positive self-views.
- Discuss cultural differences in the self-concept and the prevalence of self-serving biases.

The subject of the previous sections was people's personalities in general terms. The central question was: What must we know to know a person well? In considering our own personalities, we can rephrase that question as: What must we know to know ourselves well? This section examines how we represent information about ourselves and how that knowledge representation shapes our personalities.

Each of us has a notion of something we call the "self." Still, the self is difficult to define. We can say that each person's sense of self involves a set of beliefs and information related to the person's characteristics and experiences. The self is a mental representation including memories and beliefs about oneself as well as perceptions of what is happening at any given moment during the person's life. The self also encompasses the person's thought processes, physical body, and conscious awareness of being separate from others and unique. We experience ourselves as continuous over time and space. We wake up in the morning believing we are the same people we were the night before. (Recall from Chapter 10 that people have a need for consistency and coherence within the self over time.) For example, when you wake up in the morning, you do not have to figure out who you are (even if you sometimes have to figure out where you are, such as when you are on vacation).

13.13 Our Self-Concepts Consist of Self-Knowledge

self-schema A knowledge structure that contains memories, beliefs, and generalizations about the self and that helps people efficiently perceive, organize, interpret, and use information related to themselves.

Beginning with the stem "I am . . . ," write down 10 answers to the question "Who am I?" The information in your answers is part of your *self-concept*, which is a web of information that you know and believe about yourself. For example, answers commonly given by college students include gender, age, student status, interpersonal style (e.g., shy, friendly), personal characteristics (e.g., moody, optimistic), and important social roles. But how would thinking of yourself as shy or optimistic or a good sibling affect how you feel and function from day to day? What you believe about yourself guides your behavior in a given context. If you think of yourself as shy, you might avoid a raucous party. If you believe yourself to be optimistic, you might easily bounce back from a poor grade in organic chemistry. Look back at the 10 answers you provided earlier. Then think of some concrete examples of how those ideas about yourself have influenced your thoughts or behaviors.

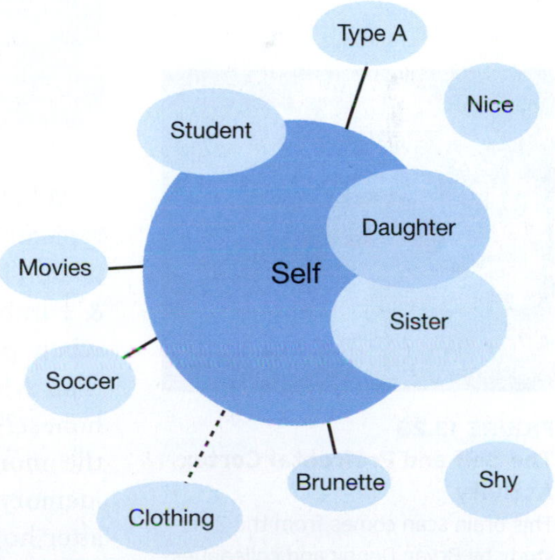

FIGURE 13.27
Self-Schema
Concepts that overlap with the self are most strongly related to the self. Concepts connected to the self with a solid line are not quite as strongly related to self-knowledge. Clothing, connected with a dotted line, is related more weakly. Concepts with no connecting lines are not related to the self.

SELF-SCHEMA An important component of the self-concept is the self-schema. According to Hazel Markus (1977), the **self-schema** consists of an integrated set of memories, beliefs, and generalizations about the self that helps us efficiently perceive, organize, interpret, and use information related to ourselves (**FIGURE 13.27**). It also helps each of us filter information so that we are likely to notice things that are self-relevant, such as our own names or other information that is central to our sense of self. For example, picture yourself at a loud, crowded party. You can barely hear yourself speak. When someone across the room mentions your name, however, you hear it clearly above the noise. As discussed in

Chapter 4, this phenomenon occurs because you process information about yourself deeply, thoroughly, and automatically. In addition, examples of our behavior and aspects of our personalities that are important to us become prominent in our self-schemas. Thus, when asked if you are ambitious, you can answer without pausing to mentally sort through occasions in which you did or did not act ambitiously. If your self-concept contains the idea of yourself as ambitious, your self-schema makes experiences relevant to ambition easy for you to access.

One of the functions of the self-schema is to help you remember information that is relevant to yourself. Tim Rogers and colleagues (1977) showed that when a person thinks about trait adjectives in a self-referential way, the person is likely to recall the words better than comparable words processed only for their general meanings. Suppose you are asked, "What does the word *honest* mean?" If you are later asked to recall the word you were asked about, you might or might not recall *honest*. Now suppose the initial question is, "Does the word *honest* describe you?" When asked later, you will be more likely to remember the word. Increased memory for ideas that reference or are relevant to the self has been found in many studies across many different populations (Klein, 2012; Symons & Johnson, 1997).

Learning Tip

Self-concept and *self-schema* are confusing because they are closely related concepts. Self-concept is the larger idea, encompassing all the information and beliefs we hold about who we are, what made us that way, and what motivates us in life. A person's self-concept is sometimes referred to as their *identity*. The self-schema is an organizational structure within the self-concept that contains specific information (memories, traits) and helps us process incoming information. Think of the self-concept as a large building with all kinds of different architectural features and interesting artifacts inside. The self-schema is the steel backbone that supports the self-concept.

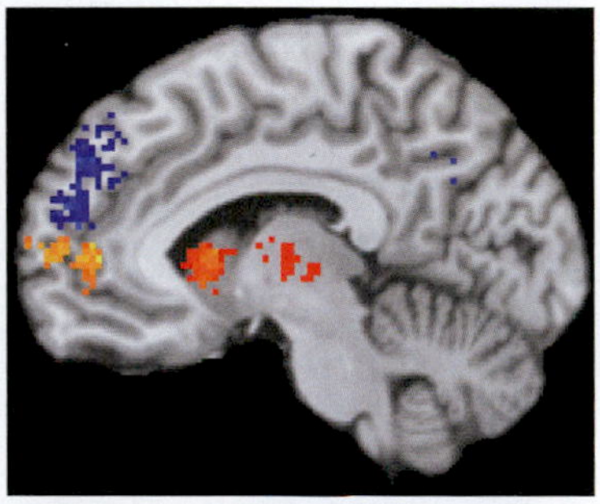

FIGURE 13.28
The Self and Prefrontal Cortex Activity
This brain scan comes from the 2012 study by Bryan Denny and colleagues that compared activation in the brain when people think about themselves versus when they think about other people. The orange area, the medial prefrontal cortex, is more active when people make trait judgments about themselves. The blue area, the dorsomedial prefrontal cortex, is more active when people make trait judgments about others.

What brain regions are active when thinking about the self? Researchers typically find that when people process information about themselves, there is activity in the middle of the prefrontal cortex (Denny et al., 2012; Gillihan & Farah, 2005; FIGURE 13.28). For example, this brain region is more active when people answer questions about themselves (e.g., "Are you honest?") than when they answer questions about other people (e.g., "Is your mother honest?"). The greater the activation of this area during the self-referencing, the more likely a person is to remember the item later during a surprise memory task (Sui & Humphreys, 2015). Damage to the frontal lobes tends to alter how people see themselves. Thus, activation of the middle region of the prefrontal cortex clearly seems to be important for processing information about the self.

WORKING SELF-CONCEPT People can hold only a certain amount of information in mind at a time. Because the self encompasses a vast array of self-knowledge, only a limited amount of personal knowledge can be active in the mind at once. The psychologist Hazel Markus called the part of the self-concept that is available during immediate experience the *working self-concept* (Markus & Kunda, 1986). The working self-concept shifts slightly from situation to situation as

Who am I?
I am a man.
Who am I?
I am Black.

FIGURE 13.29
Working Self-Concept
When considering themselves or their personalities, people are especially likely to mention characteristics that distinguish them from other people. For example, when working with a group of women, a Black man might be most aware of his maleness. When working with a group of White people, he might be most aware of being Black.

different aspects of the self become more or less relevant. Suppose your self-concept includes the traits *fun-loving* and *intelligent*. At a party, you might think of yourself primarily as fun-loving while the "intelligent you" slips into the background. In a study group, the reverse might be true. Your self-descriptions depend on what memories you retrieve, what situation you are in, what people you are with, and what your role is in that situation.

When people consider who they are or think about different features of their personalities, they often emphasize characteristics that make them distinct from others. Think back to your 10 responses to the question "Who am I?" Which answers stressed your similarity to other people or membership in a group? Which ones stressed your differences from other people, or at least from the people immediately around you? A respondent is especially likely to mention features such as ethnicity, gender, or age if the person differs in these respects from others around them at the moment (Sim et al., 2014; **FIGURE 13.29**). For example, Canadians are more likely to note their nationality if they are in Boston than if they are in Toronto. Because the working self-concept guides behavior, this tendency implies that Canadians are also more likely to feel and act like "Canadians" when in Boston than when in Toronto.

Q How is the self-schema useful?

ANSWER: It helps people quickly perceive, organize, interpret, and use information about the self.

13.14 Perceived Social Regard Influences Self-Esteem

self-esteem The evaluative aspect of the self-concept in which people feel worthy or unworthy.

North American culture has been obsessed with self-esteem since at least the 1980s. At a basic level, **self-esteem** indicates a person's emotional response to contemplating personal characteristics: "Am I worthy or unworthy?" and "Am I good or bad?" Although self-esteem is related to self-concept, people can objectively believe positive things about themselves without liking themselves very much. Conversely, people can like themselves very much, and therefore have high self-esteem, even when objective indicators do not support such positive self-views.

Some theories suggest that people's self-esteem is derived from their beliefs about how others perceive them. The process of learning about oneself through the eyes of others is known as *reflected appraisal*. People *internalize* the values and beliefs expressed by important others in their lives, meaning that they adopt those attitudes (and related behaviors) as their own. This can happen with all kinds of attitudes, including those about oneself. Thus, when a person is rejected, ignored, demeaned, or devalued by another person they respect, the person is likely to experience low self-esteem.

Children tend to have high self-esteem relative to adolescents. People tend to have relatively low self-esteem as they enter adulthood around ages 18–22 (Robins et al., 2002; **FIGURE 13.30**). From there, self-esteem increases during adulthood, particularly from ages 50 to 60, and tailing off toward the end of life (Orth & Robins, 2014). Cultures around the world show similar patterns (Bleidorn et al., 2016). Older studies found that men have higher self-esteem than women, particularly during adolescence. However, the gender gap in self-esteem appears to be decreasing (Zuckerman et al., 2016).

SOCIOMETER THEORY Mark Leary and colleagues (1995) proposed that self-esteem is a mechanism for monitoring the likelihood of social exclusion. This theory proposes that humans have a fundamental need to belong, as discussed in Chapter 10. For most of human evolution, those who belonged to social groups have been more likely to survive and reproduce than those who were excluded and left to survive on their own. Because social belonging is so important to survival, humans evolved an internal monitor of their level of social acceptance or rejection. The theory suggests that self-esteem serves as a **sociometer**

sociometer An internal monitor of social acceptance or rejection.

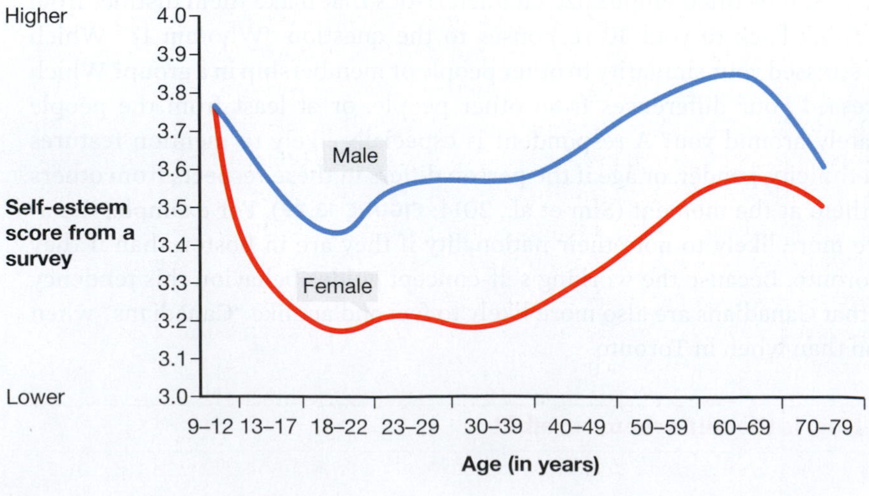

FIGURE 13.30
Self-Esteem Across the Life Span
Self-esteem varies across people's lives. Children tend to have very high self-esteem. After childhood, self-esteem generally follows an inverted-U pattern with low points in adolescence and older adulthood.

that tracks how well a person is fitting in with groups and other people (FIGURE 13.31).

SELF-ESTEEM AND LIFE OUTCOMES With such emphasis placed on self-esteem within Western culture, you might expect that having high self-esteem is the key to life success. However, evidence from psychological science indicates that self-esteem is less important than commonly believed. After reviewing several hundred studies, Roy Baumeister and colleagues (2003, 2005) found that although people with high self-esteem report being much happier, self-esteem is weakly related to objective life outcomes. People with high self-esteem who consider themselves smart, attractive, and well liked do not actually perform better on intelligence or likability measures. That is, self-esteem has little to do with objective facts or opinions.

Many people with high self-esteem are successful in their careers, but so are many people with low self-esteem. A small relationship does exist between self-esteem and some outcomes, such as academic success, but it is possible that success causes high self-esteem. People might have higher self-esteem because they have done well in school.

In fact, there are some downsides to having very high self-esteem. The explanation for this is that people with high self-esteem might feel that they have something to lose if their self-esteem is threatened. Indeed, some people become violent when they feel that others are not treating them with an appropriate level of respect (Baumeister et al., 1996). When people with high self-esteem believe their abilities have been challenged, they take steps to restore their positive self-image, sometimes in ways that cause other people to dislike them (Heatherton & Vohs, 2000; Vohs & Heatherton, 2004). For example, the need to protect their self-worth can lead people to become antagonistic or boastful. Ultimately, having high self-esteem seems to make people happier, but it does not necessarily lead to successful social relationships or life success.

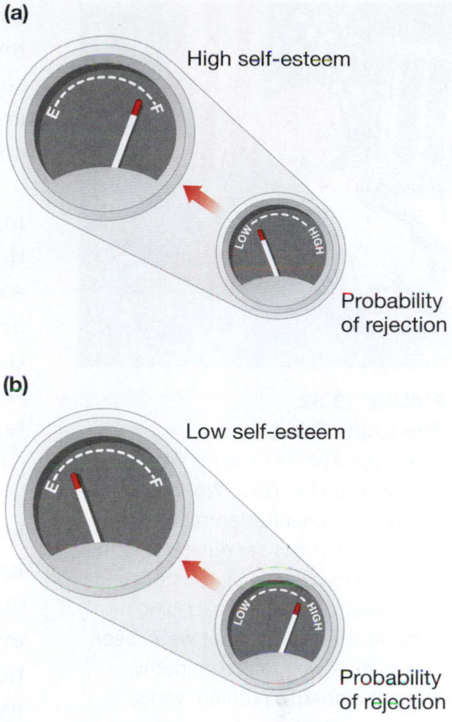

FIGURE 13.31
Sociometers
According to sociometer theory, self-esteem is the gauge that measures the extent to which people believe they are being included in or excluded from a social group. **(a)** If the probability of rejection seems low, a person's self-esteem will tend to be high. **(b)** If the probability of rejection seems high, a person's self-esteem will tend to be low.

NARCISSISM, THE DARK TRIAD, AND THE LIGHT TRIAD One personality trait associated with inflated self-esteem is *narcissism*. The term comes from Greek mythology, in which Narcissus rejected the love of others and fell in love with his own reflection in a pond. In the psychological sense of narcissism, self-centered people view themselves in grandiose terms, feel superior to others and entitled to special treatment, and are manipulative (Bosson et al., 2008). Because narcissists' greatest love is for the self, they tend to have poor relations with others (Campbell et al., 2005). They become angry when challenged, and they abuse people who do not share their lofty opinions of themselves (Bushman & Baumeister, 1998; Rhodewalt & Morf, 1998; Twenge & Campbell, 2003).

Personality psychologists have noticed that high levels of narcissism often come along with two other personality traits that collectively make up a *dark triad*: narcissism, *psychopathy*, and *Machiavellianism* (Paulhus & Williams, 2002). Psychopathy revolves around a general lack of caring for the welfare of others. Those high in psychopathy are callous toward others and cunning in pursuing their personal goals. These individuals also tend to be impulsive and reckless, and they have low levels of fear. Machiavellianism is named after the Italian philosopher Niccolò Machiavelli, who in the 1500s cynically encouraged antisocial behaviors, such as lying and cheating, as effective tools in politics. The personality trait named after him describes people who are especially manipulative of others for their own gain and lack concern with moral norms against harming others.

FIGURE 13.32
The Light Triad
Chef José Andrés used his wealth and celebrity to create World Central Kitchen, a humanitarian-relief nonprofit that has served more than 15 million free meals in disaster zones in the past decade. In describing his work, Andrés says, "What we've been able to do is weaponize empathy. Without empathy, nothing works" (Gregory, 2020).

Uniting the dark triad are a lack of empathy, willingness to be dishonest, and a low level of the trait agreeableness (Furnham et al., 2013). It should be noted that some people's levels of either narcissism or psychopathy are so high that they are considered to have personality disorders. You will learn more about these conditions in Chapter 14.

Possession of the dark triad of traits is associated with career success, such as making more money, being in leadership positions, and winning political elections (Spain et al., 2014; Spurk et al., 2016). Moreover, there is evidence that people sometimes initially view others who possess dark triad traits positively, perhaps because such people display confidence, dominance, and at least superficial charm (Carter et al., 2014). Thus, although the dark triad traits are viewed negatively by society, they may provide benefits to those who possess them, at least in the short term (Paulhus, 2014).

Most personality traits exist on a spectrum with people on both sides, so for every extreme narcissist there is an "everyday saint" at the other end who selflessly loves and cares for others. Psychologists have identified a cluster of traits known as the *light triad*: *humanism*, *faith in humanity*, and *Kantianism* (Kaufman et al., 2019; FIGURE 13.32). Humanism refers to valuing the worth and dignity of every person as an individual. People with high levels of this trait feel admiration for others and enjoy interacting with a variety of people. Faith in humanity is about believing in the inherent goodness of humans. High levels of faith in humanity are defined by trusting others and seeing the best in them. Kantianism is named for the philosopher Immanuel Kant, whose categorical imperative of moral action requires that we never use other people only as means but always as ends unto themselves. People high in Kantianism are honest with others and feel uncomfortable manipulating them to get what they want. A recent study found that people on the dating site Tinder with higher scores on the light triad are more likely than those with lower scores to seek long-term partners on the site (Sevi & Doğruyol, 2020). Once in a relationship, higher scores on the light triad relate to stronger commitment to fidelity in the relationship (Sevi et al., 2020).

Q **It has been said that we love people who love themselves. Are people with high self-esteem generally viewed as more likable?**

ANSWER: High self-esteem is not related to likability in most situations. Sometimes people with high self-esteem may be disliked for their negative reactions to situations that threaten their positive self-image.

13.15 People Use Mental Strategies to Maintain a Positive Sense of Self

A consistent theme that emerges from research is that people show favoritism to anything associated with themselves. For example, people consistently overvalue things they own, even if they were assigned to receive those things at random (Morewedge & Giblin, 2015). People even prefer the letters of their own names, especially their initials, to other letters (Koole et al., 2001; FIGURE 13.33).

Sometimes these positive views of the self are inflated compared with objective standards. For instance, 90 percent of adults claim they are better-than-average drivers (that is, in the top 50 percent of drivers), even if they have been hospitalized for injuries caused by car accidents in which they were one of the drivers involved (Guerin, 1994; Svenson, 1981). Similarly, when the College Entrance Examination Board surveyed more than 800,000 college-bound seniors, not a single senior rated themselves as below average, whereas a whopping 25 percent rated themselves in the top 1 percent (Gilovich, 1991). Most people describe themselves as above

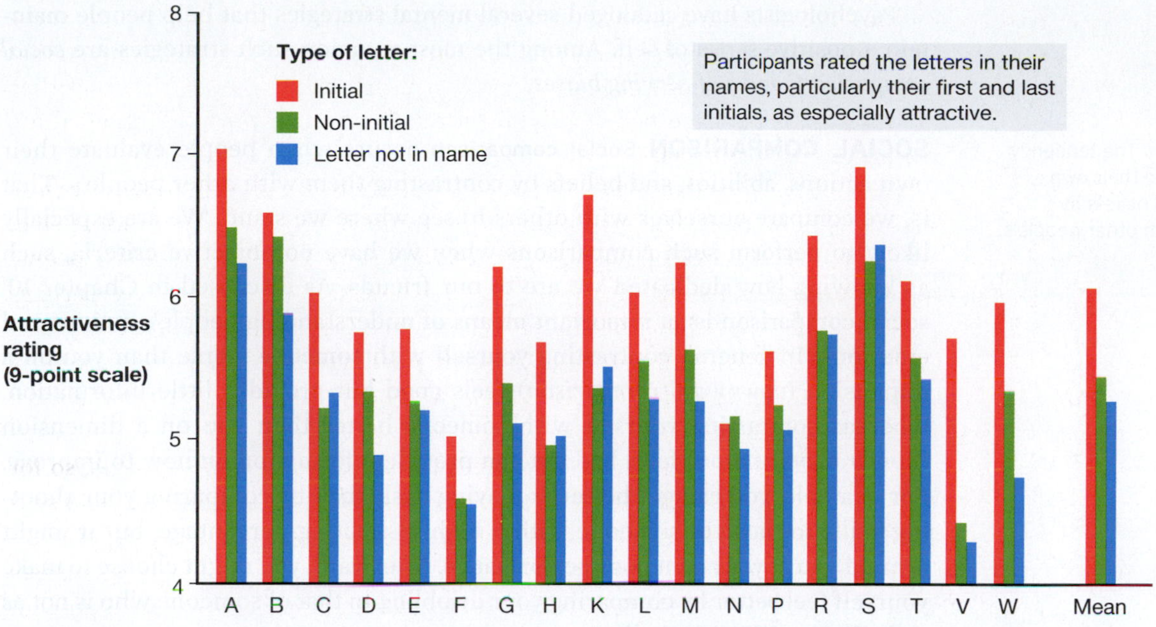

FIGURE 13.33
Favoritism
This graph shows the study participants' ratings of letters of the alphabet.

average in nearly every way; psychologists refer to this phenomenon as the *better-than-average effect* (Zell et al., 2020). People with high self-esteem are especially likely to exhibit this effect, but even those with low self-esteem rate themselves as above average on many dimensions (Suls et al., 2002).

According to Shelley Taylor and Jonathon Brown (1988), most people hold *positive illusions*—overly favorable and unrealistic beliefs—about themselves in at least three domains. First, most people continually experience the better-than-average effect. Second, they unrealistically perceive their personal control over events. That is, they tend to have a strong internal locus of control, especially for positive outcomes. For example, some fans believe they help their favorite sports teams win if they attend games or wear their lucky jerseys. Third, most people are unrealistically optimistic about their personal future. They believe they will probably be successful, marry happily, and live long lives even when they are presented with objective information to the contrary.

It is generally adaptive to hold accurate beliefs about the world, so inflated beliefs about the self seem to be an exception. Why do we allow ourselves to hold these inaccurate views? Taylor identified ways that positive illusions can be adaptive when they promote optimism in meeting life's challenges. She showed how positive self-regard, optimism about one's future, and a sense of control together serve as a kind of *psychological resource* that can help protect people from the harmful effects of stress or threat (Taylor et al., 2000). People who have greater optimism about their future and believe they have control over conditions such as cardiovascular disease, arthritis, and cancer—even if this is unrealistic—tend to show reduced illness and greater likelihood of recovery (Kiecolt-Glaser et al., 2002). Taylor argued that the survival benefit of positive illusions outweighs the potential costs of their inaccuracy. Of course, positive illusions cannot be entirely untethered from reality. They are more like biases than outright fabrications. Excessive positive illusions can lead to trouble when people overestimate their skills and underestimate their vulnerabilities. Recall from Chapter 1 that people often fail to recognize areas where they are unskilled.

Psychologists have cataloged several mental strategies that help people maintain a positive sense of self. Among the most common such strategies are *social comparisons* and *self-serving biases*.

social comparison The tendency for people to evaluate their own actions, abilities, and beliefs by contrasting them with other people's.

SOCIAL COMPARISON **Social comparison** occurs when people evaluate their own actions, abilities, and beliefs by contrasting them with other people's. That is, we compare ourselves with others to see where we stand. We are especially likely to perform such comparisons when we have no objective criteria, such as knowing how dedicated we are to our friends. As discussed in Chapter 10, social comparison is an important means of understanding people's actions and emotions. In general, contrasting yourself with someone worse than you on a dimension (*downward comparison*) feels good but provides little information, whereas contrasting yourself with someone better than you on a dimension (*upward comparison*) feels bad but can provide information on how to improve. For example, you can get better at playing basketball by comparing your shooting skills to those of someone with a higher shooting percentage, but it might remind you of your own poor performance. Afterward, you might choose to make yourself feel better by comparing your dribbling to that of someone who is not as skilled at handling the ball.

Social comparison can lead to biased self-views when it is used selectively. People generally prefer downward social comparison because it feels good and engage in upward social comparison only when they need to learn (Mussweiler, 2003). Over time, people remember and recall more examples of times when they were better than others at some task than when they were worse. People also use a form of downward comparison when they recall their own pasts: They often view their current selves as better than their former selves (Wilson & Ross, 2001; **FIGURE 13.34**). Viewing ourselves as better than we used to be also makes us feel good about ourselves.

self-serving bias The tendency for people to take personal credit for success but blame failure on external factors.

SELF-SERVING BIASES People with high self-esteem tend to take credit for success but blame failure on external factors. Psychologists refer to this tendency as the **self-serving bias**. For instance, students who do extremely well on exams often explain their performance by referring to their skills or hard

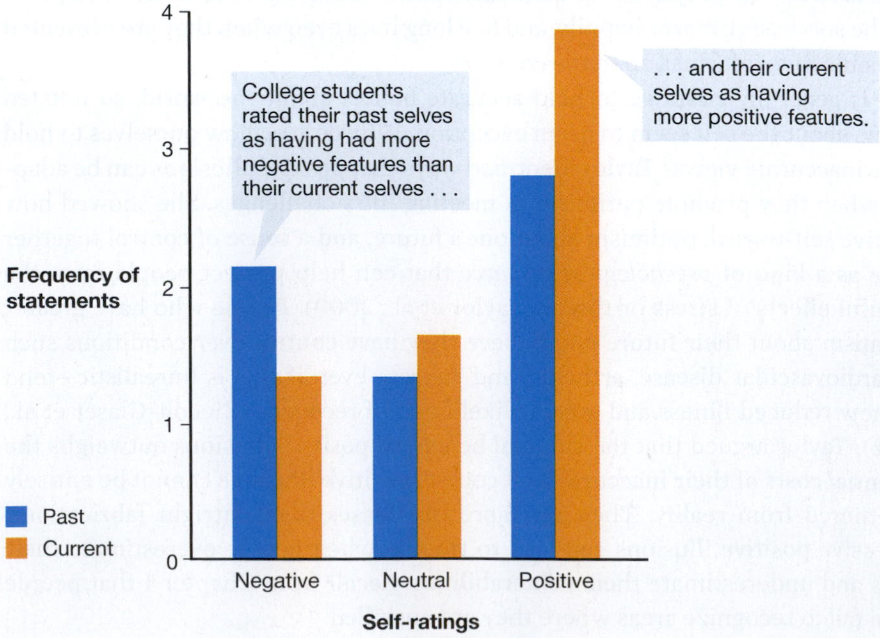

College students rated their past selves as having had more negative features than their current selves . . .
. . . and their current selves as having more positive features.
Frequency of statements
4
3
2
1
0
Past
Current
Negative
Neutral
Positive
Self-ratings

FIGURE 13.34
Rating the Self Across Time
This graph shows the results of Anne Wilson and Michael Ross's 2001 study.

work. Those who do poorly might describe the test as an arbitrary examination of trivial details. People with high self-esteem also assume that criticism is motivated by envy or prejudice. Decisions about where to place blame and apportion credit are called *attributions*. Psychologists have documented in people around the world that attributions of success, failure, and other outcomes influence not only self-esteem but also emotions such as anger, guilt, shame, and pride (Yao & Siegel, 2021).

Over the past 40 years, psychologists have documented many ways that people show bias in thinking about themselves compared with how they think about others (Campbell & Sedikides, 1999). In thinking about our failures, for example, we compare ourselves with others who did worse, we diminish the importance of the challenge, we think about the things we are really good at, and we bask in the reflected glory of both family and friends. The overall picture suggests we are extremely well equipped to protect our positive beliefs about ourselves. The psychologist Dan Gilbert refers to the collection of mechanisms people have to protect their emotional well-being as the *psychological immune system* (Gilbert et al., 1998). Like the physiological immune system, the psychological immune system is constantly monitoring for threats and can mount a variety of defenses against them.

Q What are the different benefits of making upward versus downward comparisons?

ANSWER: Upward comparisons make us feel bad but provide information. Downward comparisons make us feel good but do not provide a learning opportunity.

13.16 Are There Cultural Differences in the Self-Serving Bias?

YOU BE THE PSYCHOLOGIST

Psychologists at first assumed the self-serving bias to be a universal human trait (Sedikides & Gregg, 2008). Some people, such as those with depression, show the effect to a smaller degree. But the adaptive value of positive illusions and the self-serving bias would indicate that most healthy, functioning individuals show robust self-enhancement. Steven Heine and colleagues (1999) have argued, however, that the self-serving bias may be more common in Western cultures than in Eastern cultures (**FIGURE 13.35**). Let us apply a critical thinking lens to some of the evidence.

An important way that self-concept differs is in how much overlap people view between themselves and others. As noted in Chapter 1, people in collectivist cultures (e.g., in Japan, Pakistan, China, and some regions of Africa) tend

(a) (b)

FIGURE 13.35
Individualist Versus Collectivist Cultures
(a) Western cultures tend to value individual success. **(b)** Eastern cultures tend to value harmony and coherence within the group.

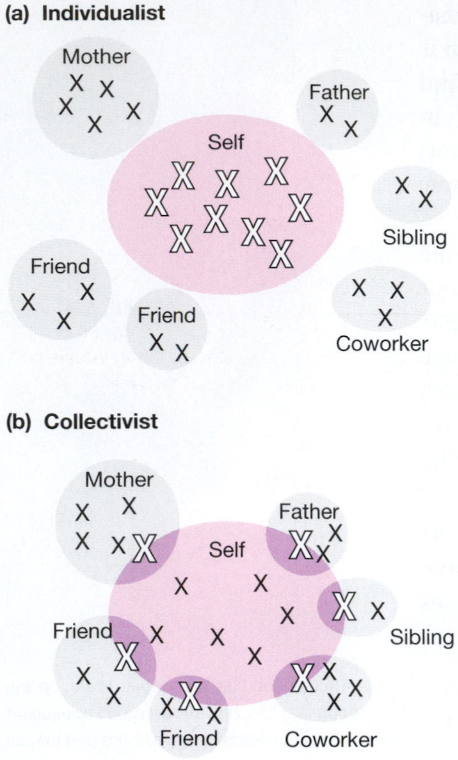

FIGURE 13.36
Cultural Differences in Self-Construal
Self-construal differs across cultures. **(a)** In individualist cultures, self-construal focuses on elements within the person. **(b)** In collectivist cultures, self-construal centers around areas where the person's sense of self is connected with others.

to think of themselves as *interdependent* with others. In other words, their self-concepts are determined to a large extent by their social roles and personal relationships (**FIGURE 13.36**). Their interdependent self-construal is informed by cultural values related to harmony and cohesion in relationships and within social groups (Markus & Kitayama, 1991; Triandis, 1989). By contrast, people in individualist cultures (e.g., in northern and western Europe, Australia, Canada, New Zealand, and the United States) tend to think of themselves as *independent* from others. This type of self-construal is also derived from cultural values, which in Western countries tend to focus on individual achievements and freedoms. Note, however, that as with all cultural factors, there is wide variability in the extent to which specific people hold a given cultural value. Some people in individualist cultures think of themselves in interdependent terms, and some people in collectivist cultures think of themselves as independent from others.

Do you think self-serving biases and positive illusions are more common in Western than Eastern cultures? On the one hand, an evolutionary perspective claims that self-serving bias should be universal because it is adaptive. On the other hand, interdependent norms against self-enhancement in Eastern cultures might reduce the tendency for self-serving attributions. Take a moment to consider the options. What kinds of evidence would provide support for cultural differences in self-serving bias, and what kinds of evidence would indicate there are no differences in self-serving bias? Might there be cultural differences in the tendency to hold self-serving views in some traits but not others? If so, which traits? Is it possible that people in interdependent cultures might *report* less self-serving bias because they are aware of the cultural norms but truly believe something else?

What is the evidence? In one study (Endo & Meijer, 2004), American and Japanese students were asked to list as many of their own successes and failures as they could. The Americans showed a bias for listing successes. The Japanese students listed failures and successes equally. In addition, the Americans used outside forces to explain failure, but the Japanese students used outside forces to explain success. Two meta-analyses both found that people in Western cultures showed a much larger self-serving bias than those in Eastern cultures (Mezulis et al., 2004; Zell et al., 2020). The more recent of the two examined the self-serving bias as a function of trait type and found that the differences in the bias between people from Eastern and Western cultures were particularly large for individualistic traits (Sedikides et al., 2005).

Might these differences reflect cultural rules about publicly admitting positive self-views? Perhaps people in the East engage in strategic self-enhancement, but they are just more modest in public. In studies using anonymous reporting, however—where presumably there is less call for modesty—Easterners continue to show a low level of self-serving bias (Heine, 2003). But when self-enhancement is assessed with an implicit measure, people from China and Japan show a similar bias to that of Americans (Yamaguchi et al., 2007). As discussed in Chapter 12, implicit attitude assessment is useful for situations in which people are hesitant to make explicit reports. In this case, the research finding suggests that Easterners' implicit self-views are just as self-enhancing as those of Westerners, but their implicit self-enhancement does not translate to explicit self-reports.

The debate goes on, but why? The universality issue matters, in part, because it relates to how culture shapes the sense of self (Heine, 2005; Sedikides et al., 2003). Perhaps what is universal is the desire to feel good about one's own behavior with respect to local norms. For instance, might people in Eastern cultures feel better about themselves when they demonstrate that they are modest and self-effacing, whereas Westerners feel better when they can show they are successful? If so, all people might be self-serving. It just takes a different form depending on the culture. ■

Q Why might self-serving biases in people from Eastern cultures be hidden by typical explicit attitude assessments?

ANSWER: Because of cultural norms, people from Eastern cultures may be less likely to report self-enhancing views, even if they have them.

Your Chapter Review

Want to earn a better grade on your test?

It's time to complete your study experience! Go to **INQUIZITIVE** to practice actively with this chapter's concepts and get personalized feedback along the way.

Chapter Summary

Where Does Personality Come From?

13.1 Genetic Factors Influence the Expression of Personality The results of twin studies and adoption studies suggest that 40–60 percent of personality variation is the product of genetic variation. Parents play an important role in selecting the environments that shape their children's personalities. Personality characteristics are influenced by multiple genes, which interact with the environment to produce general dispositions. It is difficult to identify the influence of specific genes on personality because complex human features such as personality are determined by many forces, and individual genes contribute only a tiny amount to a given feature.

13.2 Temperaments Are Evident in Infancy Temperaments are biologically based personality tendencies. They are evident in early childhood and have long-term implications for adult behavior. Researchers have identified activity level, emotionality, and sociability as temperaments. Genes and environments can become correlated as they shape temperament because both contribute to behavior, which in turn influences environment. Childhood temperaments can predict adult personality. Shyness can be predicted as early as 2 months of age and involves the amygdala. Parental support and calm environments can help children overcome shyness.

What Are the Theories of Personality?

13.3 Trait Approaches Describe Behavioral Tendencies Trait theorists assume that personality is a collection of traits or behavioral dispositions. Five-factor theory maintains that there are five higher-order personality traits: openness to experience, conscientiousness, extraversion, agreeableness, and neuroticism. Research supports five-factor theory in a number of ways.

13.4 Traits Have a Biological Basis Brain imaging research has distinguished activity in different brain regions based on traits. According to Eysenck's model of personality, there are three biologically based higher-order dimensions of personality traits: introversion/extraversion, emotional stability, and psychoticism or constraint. Gray's reinforcement sensitivity theory and its revised version describe how the behavioral approach system, the behavioral inhibition system, and the fight-flight-freeze system interact to direct behavior and influence personality.

13.5 Humanistic Approaches Emphasize Integrated Personal Experience Humanistic approaches emphasize experiences, beliefs, the uniqueness of the human condition, and inherent goodness. According to these approaches, people strive to realize their full potential. According to Rogers's person-centered approach, unconditional positive regard in childhood enables people to become fully functioning. McAdams's humanistic theory of personality focuses on the importance of "personal myths" and other narratives we tell ourselves about our past and future.

13.6 Personality Reflects Learning and Cognition According to learning theories, people learn patterns of responding that are guided by their expectancies, values, and personal constructs. Locus of control, the extent to which people feel they have control over outcomes in their lives, is an important determinant of behavior. Reciprocal determinism indicates that the expression of personality can be explained by the interaction of environment, person factors, and behavior itself. Need for cognition is a trait that reflects how much people enjoy and tend to engage in complex thought.

13.7 Psychology Outside the Lab: Personality in the Workplace Researchers in industrial/organizational (I/O) psychology study how personality influences life in the workplace. They have discovered that personality measures can be useful in hiring, recruiting, and training employees. Researchers in the field have made discoveries about different contexts where various personality traits are more or less helpful. I/O psychologists are additionally valuable because they bring the latest scientific knowledge about personality into organizations.

How Stable Is Personality?

13.8 People Sometimes Are Inconsistent According to Mischel's notion of situationism, situations are more important than traits in predicting behavior. The person/situation debate revolves around whether personality traits or situations are more important in predicting behavior. Research suggests that when evaluated over time, personality traits do predict behavior. According to interactionism, behavior is determined by both situations and dispositions. One resolution to the person/situation debate is that personality can be viewed as a tendency to respond in a particular way in a given situation. Strong situations mask differences in personality, whereas weak situations reveal differences in personality. Most trait theorists favor interactionism.

13.9 Development and Life Events Alter Personality Traits A variety of research shows personality traits to be stable over the life span. Although traits are stable in a rank-order way, they undergo developmental change across a person's life span. Developmental changes in personality traits are caused by changes in self-perception generated by life experiences. Mean-level changes seen across time in many people in the Big Five personality factors include decreased neuroticism, extraversion, and openness and increased agreeableness and conscientiousness. Most changes to personality occur between the ages of 20 and 40, likely due to the large number of important life experiences that tend to occur during this period.

13.10 Culture Influences Personality Cross-cultural research suggests that the Big Five personality factors are universal among humans. However, there are linguistic and conceptual challenges to comparing measures of personality across cultures. The Big Five is biased toward Western samples and omits measures of honesty and humility, which are valued in many cultures. Differences in personality are consistent with common stereotypes, although cultural influences may explain these differences. For example, individualistic societies may highlight individual differences, while collectivist societies may minimize them.

How Is Personality Assessed?

13.11 Researchers Use Multiple Methods to Assess Personality Idiographic approaches to the assessment of personality are person-centered. They focus on individual lives and each person's unique characteristics. Nomothetic approaches assess individual variation in characteristics that are common among all people. Personality can be assessed via several measures. Projective measures, such as the Thematic Apperception Test, assess response tendencies by having people interpret ambiguous stimuli. Self-report measures, such as the MMPI and the California Q-Sort, are relatively direct measures of personality, typically involving the use of questionnaires. Life history data and behavioral data can also reveal personality traits.

13.12 Observers Show Accuracy About Other People's Traits Personality traits can be accurately judged by others. Close acquaintances may better predict a person's behavior than the person can. This effect may be due to failure to pay attention to one's own behavior or due to biases in self-perception. Acquaintances are particularly accurate when judging traits that are readily observable.

How Do We Know Our Own Personalities?

13.13 Our Self-Concepts Consist of Self-Knowledge The self-concept consists of everything people know or believe about themselves. The self-schema is the integrated set of memories, beliefs, and generalizations that help organize information about the self. The self-schema allows the individual to remember self-referential information better, and it appears to rely on activation of the middle part of the frontal lobes. The working self-concept is the immediate experience of the self at any given time. The working self-concept does not include the entire vast array of self-knowledge and therefore focuses on traits relevant only to the current situation.

13.14 Perceived Social Regard Influences Self-Esteem Self-esteem is the evaluative aspect of the self-concept. Self-esteem follows an inverted-U pattern with low points in adolescence and one's early 20s and again later in life. Self-esteem peaks in early childhood and then increases again in one's 50s. According to sociometer theory, the need to belong influences self-esteem. Self-esteem is associated with happiness but is only weakly correlated with objective life outcomes. The trait narcissism and the dark triad are associated with excessive self-esteem and focus on the self and a lack of empathy. In contrast, the light triad is associated with concern for others and positive beliefs about humanity.

13.15 People Use Mental Strategies to Maintain a Positive Sense of Self Positive illusions of self are common. Positive illusions are adaptive because they serve as a psychological resource to buffer people against the effects of stress and threat. Positive self-regard and a sense of control and optimism in one's life are related to better health outcomes for several diseases. People use numerous unconscious strategies to maintain positive views of themselves, including downward social comparisons and self-serving biases. These biases are part of a psychological immune system that protects the integrity of the self.

13.16 You Be the Psychologist: Are There Cultural Differences in the Self-Serving Bias? People from collectivist cultures (e.g., Eastern cultures, such as Asian and African countries) tend to have interdependent self-concepts. People from individualist cultures (e.g., Western cultures, such as Australia, Canada, New Zealand, and the United States) tend to have independent self-concepts. Those from Western cultures are more likely to show self-serving biases, particularly in traits related to independence, perhaps in part because people from Eastern cultures are more modest in their self-reports. It is also possible that people in Eastern cultures enhance themselves only in traits related to interdependence.

Key Terms

behavioral approach system (BAS), p. 505
behavioral inhibition system (BIS), p. 505
fight-flight-freeze system (FFFS), p. 505
five-factor theory, p. 502
humanistic approaches, p. 506
idiographic approaches, p. 518
interactionism, p. 512
locus of control, p. 508
need for cognition, p. 509
nomothetic approaches, p. 518
personality, p. 496
personality trait, p. 496
projective measures, p. 518
reciprocal determinism, p. 508
self-esteem, p. 526
self-schema, p. 523
self-serving bias, p. 530
situationism, p. 511
social comparison, p. 530
sociometer, p. 526
temperaments, p. 499
trait approaches, p. 501

Practice Exercises

1. Which statement most accurately summarizes research on the genetic basis of personality?
   a. Specific genes control specific personality traits like conscientiousness.
   b. Only some traits, such as temperament, have a specific genetic basis.
   c. Many genes interact to influence personality, and their expression is affected by epigenetic mechanisms.
   d. Personality has no genetic basis and depends almost entirely on environment.
2. Which statement best describes the distinctions between traits and temperaments?
   a. Temperaments, which include activity level, emotionality, and sociability, are broader and more biologically based than traits.
   b. Temperaments, which include conscientiousness, neuroticism, and introversion, are narrower and more environmentally based than traits.
   c. Traits, which includes activity level, emotionality, and sociability, are narrower and more biologically based than temperament.
   d. Traits, which include conscientiousness, neuroticism, and introversion, are broader and more biologically based than temperament.
3. Match these different perspectives on personality to the statements that follow: trait, humanistic, learning/cognition.
   a. "To know me, you should ask me questions about my character and disposition."
   b. "To know me, you should study my past behavior and what I think about the world."
   c. "To know me, you should learn about my life story, hopes, and aspirations."
4. According to the revised reinforcement sensitivity theory (rRST), which of the following behavioral motivations are associated with the behavioral approach system (BAS), which are associated with the behavioral inhibition system (BIS), and which are associated with the fight-flight-freeze system (FFFS)?
   a. going
   b. avoiding punishments
   c. pursuing rewards
   d. slowing down
   e. displaying vigilance
   f. stopping
   g. escaping

5. Following decades of person/situation debate, most psychologists today favor the ________ perspective, which views personality as ________.
   a. interactionism; determined by both situation and disposition
   b. situationism; determined by the social and environmental context
   c. person factors; determined by stable traits and temperaments
   d. reinforcement; determined completely by learning over time

6. Which statement most accurately summarizes the research on how culture influences personality?
   a. The Big Five personality traits are valid only in Western cultures, so gender differences cannot be studied cross-culturally.
   b. Cross-culturally, there is very little overlap in the structure of personality.
   c. Cultural norms influence how people report on their own personalities.
   d. People in Canada are more agreeable than people in most other countries.

7. June asks people to watch a 5-minute recording of a play in which two characters find themselves in a dangerous situation. Then she asks her research participants to write an ending to the story, which she codes to reveal features of each participant's personality. This proposed measure of personality can best be described as ________ and ________.
   a. idiographic; projective
   b. nomothetic; projective
   c. idiographic; objective
   d. nomothetic; objective

8. Which statement does *not* accurately explain why our close acquaintances can sometimes predict our behaviors better than us?
   a. Predictions of our own behaviors may be biased in favor of our subjective perceptions (how we *think* we act) rather than our objective behaviors (how we *do* act).
   b. Our self-narratives are unimportant in determining our identity, but our friends' stories about us have great influence.
   c. We tend to pay more attention to others than to ourselves in social situations, so sometimes fail to notice our own behavior.

9. According to sociometer theory, self-esteem is ________.
   a. based on self-actualization of goals and desires
   b. highest when perceived risk of social exclusion is high
   c. lowest when perceived risk of social exclusion is low
   d. based on the perceived probability of social rejection

10. After losing an election, a politician makes the following comments during an interview. Which statement does *not* reflect a potential positive illusion of self?
   a. "I didn't win but my platform was superior, and the people know that"
   b. "If I had worn my lucky tie during the debate, the results would have been different."
   c. "I am not the best candidate for the position, and the voters knew that."
   d. "This election was rigged. I will run again and win by a landslide."

THE NORTH FACE
IT'S OK NOT TO BE OK!

14 Psychological Disorders

Big Questions

SOMETIMES YOU FEEL HAPPY, AND SOMETIMES YOU FEEL SAD. Like everyone, you experience life's ups and downs. For some people, however, mood and energy swings are much more intense, quickly changing from episodes of extreme fatigue and sadness, sometimes being stuck in bed for days, to excited states of extraordinary joyfulness and weeklong sprints of energy. This condition is known as bipolar disorder. People you might have heard of who have had a diagnosis of bipolar disorder include Ernest Hemingway, Demi Lovato, and Russell Brand.

Many of us have friends or relatives who have been diagnosed with a psychological disorder or have diagnoses ourselves. These disorders are extremely common. A key question considered throughout this chapter is where societies decide to draw the line between a psychological state and a disorder. When does being frequently sad turn from a temporary state or personality trait into the psychological disorder depression? Or into some other disorder or condition? Cultures have different answers to this question, and their answers change over time. This chapter describes the psychological disorders that are frequently diagnosed right now and examines ideas about what causes them, how they might be diagnosed, and how they affect people's lives.

Learning Objectives

- Understand what is meant by the terms psychopathology and psychological disorder.
- Explain how psychological disorders are classified.
- Identify assessment methods for psychological disorders.
- Describe the diathesis-stress model.
- Identify biological, situational, and cognitive-behavioral causes of psychological disorders.
- Discuss cultural differences in psychological disorders.

How Are Psychological Disorders Conceptualized and Classified?

Those who have psychological disorders display symptoms of **psychopathology**. This term means illness or disorder of the mind. From the writings of Aristotle through those of Sigmund Freud and into the present day, countless descriptions exist of people experiencing from what we now consider to be psychopathology. Though considerable progress has been made over the past century, we are still struggling to determine the causes of psychopathology. To understand any disorder, psychologists investigate its **etiology**: the factors that contribute to its development. For example, they investigate commonalities among people such as Britney Spears and Demi Lovato to identify factors that might explain why they (and others) developed bipolar disorders.

psychopathology Sickness or disorder of the mind; psychological disorder.

etiology Factors that contribute to the development of a disorder.

14.1 Views on Psychopathology Have Changed over Time

The earliest views of psychopathology explained apparent "madness" as resulting from possession by demons or evil spirits (**FIGURE 14.1**). The ancient Babylonians believed a demon called Idta caused madness. Similar examples of demonology can be found among the ancient Chinese, Egyptians, and Greeks. This view of psychopathology continued into the Middle Ages. At that time, there was greater emphasis on possession as having resulted from the wrath of God for some sinful moral transgression. During any of these periods, people we now know to have bipolar disorder might have been persecuted and subjected to an array of methods to cast out their demons. Such "treatments" included exorcism, bloodletting, and the forced ingestion of magical potions. In the Middle Ages, through the Renaissance, and into the nineteenth century, people with psychopathology were imprisoned in institutions called asylums.

FIGURE 14.1
Historical View of Psychological Disorders
Throughout history, people believed that the gods, witches, or evil spirits caused psychological disorders.

In 1793, Philippe Pinel became the head physician at Bicêtre Hospital in Paris. Pinel believed that medical treatments should be based on empirical observations. At that time, among the hospital's 4,000 patients were about 200 with psychopathology who were being cared for by a former patient, Jean-Baptiste Pussin. Pussin treated his patients with kindness and care rather than violence. Impressed by the positive therapeutic results, Pinel removed patients from their chains and banished physical punishment. He instituted what came to be known as *moral treatment*, a therapy that involved close contact with and careful observation of patients. Pinel's benevolent treatment gained a foothold in Europe, and later—through the efforts of a Massachusetts schoolteacher, Dorothea Dix—in America (**FIGURE 14.2**).

As far back as ancient Greece, some people believed that there was a physical basis to psychopathology. Hippocrates (c. 460–377 BCE), often credited as the founder of modern medicine, classified psychopathologies into *mania*, *melancholia*, and *phrenitis*, the latter characterized by mental confusion. Hippocrates believed that such disorders resulted from the relative amount of "humors," or bodily fluids, a person possessed (Maher & Maher, 1994). For instance, having too much black bile led to melancholia, or extreme sadness and depression. Though the idea that bodily fluids cause mental illness was abandoned long ago, the view of psychopathology as a medical condition has endured. During the past 200 years, recognition has grown that psychopathology in part reflects dysfunction of the body, particularly of the brain.

As with many topics in psychology, the modern view is that environment and biology interact to produce psychological disorders. Both factors affect all psychological disorders to some extent. However, disorders vary in how strongly they are influenced by biological or environmental factors. For instance, biology plays an especially large role in schizophrenia.

FIGURE 14.2
Dorothea Dix
Dix spent decades advocating for better treatment for people with psychopathology. Her work resulted in the establishment of state mental hospitals across the United States.

PSYCHOLOGICAL DISORDERS ARE MALADAPTIVE How does a society decide whether someone has a psychological disorder? After all, almost any kind of behavior might be appropriate in the right situation. A person running through the streets screaming, sobbing, and hugging people might have some form of psychological disorder—or might have just won the lottery. Many behaviors considered normal in one setting may be considered deviant in other settings.

In determining whether behavior represents psychopathology, certain criteria should be considered: (1) Does the person act in a way that deviates from cultural norms for acceptable behavior? (2) Is the behavior *maladaptive*? That is, does the behavior interfere with the person's ability to respond appropriately in some situations? For example, a person who is afraid to leave the house may avoid feeling anxious by staying inside, and that behavior might prevent the person from working, having a social life, or both. (3) Is the behavior self-destructive, does it cause the individual personal distress, or does it threaten other people in the community? (4) Does the behavior cause discomfort and concern to others, thus impairing a person's social relationships?

The way societies define psychopathology changes over time. For example, being gay or lesbian was listed as a diagnosis in the United States until 1973 (Drescher, 2015). We now understand that variation in sexual orientation among people and within a person over time is simply part of the human condition. An important recent trend is to define psychopathology in terms of maladaptiveness rather than low numerical frequency. For example, people concerned about germs may wash their hands more than average and therefore be different from others, but that behavior may be beneficial in many ways and therefore adaptive—after all, it is the best way of avoiding contagious disease. The same behavior, however, can be maladaptive when people cannot stop until they have washed their hands raw. Indeed, the current diagnostic criteria for all the major disorder categories state that the symptoms of the disorder must interfere with at least one aspect of the person's life, such as work, social relations, or self-care. This component is critical in determining whether given thoughts, emotions, or behaviors represent psychopathology or are simply unusual.

PSYCHOPATHOLOGY IS COMMON IN CONTEMPORARY SOCIETY Psychological disorders are common around the globe, in all countries and all societies (Patel et al., 2016). These disorders account for the greatest proportion of disability in developed countries, surpassing even cancer and heart disease (Centers for Disease Control and Prevention [CDC], 2011a; World Health Organization, 2017c). Indeed, about 1 in 4 Americans over age 18 has a diagnosable psychological disorder in a given year (Kessler et al., 2005a). About 1 in 5 American adults receives treatment over any two-year period (Kessler et al., 2005b). Nearly half of Americans will have some form of psychological disorder at some point in life, most commonly a depressive disorder, an attention-deficit/hyperactivity disorder, an anxiety disorder, or a substance-related and addictive disorder (Kessler & Wang, 2008). Of course, disorders range in severity, and most people who experience psychopathology do not have the most debilitating disorders.

As you read this chapter, you may realize that you have experienced some of the symptoms of many psychological disorders. Even if particular symptoms seem to describe you (or someone you know) perfectly, resist the urge to make a diagnosis. Just like medical students who worry they have every disease they learn about, you need to guard against pathologizing yourself and others. At the same time, what you learn in this chapter and the next one may help you understand the mental health problems you or others might experience.

Q Why is the maladaptiveness of a condition considered more important than its atypicality in deciding whether a person has a psychopathology?

ANSWER: Maladaptiveness is considered most important in defining psychopathology because it is hard to distinguish between psychopathological behavior and merely unusual behavior.

14.2 Psychological Disorders Are Classified into Categories

FIGURE 14.3
Emil Kraepelin
Kraepelin was one of the first researchers to propose a classification system for psychological disorders.

In the late 1800s, the psychiatrist Emil Kraepelin recognized that not all patients with psychological disorders have the same one (FIGURE 14.3). Kraepelin separated disorders into categories based on what he could observe: groups of symptoms that occur together. For instance, he separated disorders of mood (emotions) from disorders of cognition. He called the latter disorder *dementia praecox*. It is now better known as *schizophrenia* and is discussed in this chapter and Chapter 15. The practice of *diagnosis* by putting a label on a loose cluster of symptoms remains essentially unchanged today.

The idea of categorizing psychological disorders systematically was not officially adopted until 1952, when the American Psychiatric Association published the first edition of the *Diagnostic and Statistical Manual of Mental Disorders* (*DSM*). It remains the standard in psychology and psychiatry, and it is under continuous refinement. The *DSM* has undergone several major revisions since the 1950s, reflecting developments in research and shifting views on mental illness in society. The main purpose of the *DSM* is description. It groups disorders based on similarity in symptoms, thereby providing a shared language and classification scheme for scientists and practitioners to communicate what they have learned about psychopathology. Another purpose of the *DSM* is to allow care providers to bill health insurance companies for treatment. Most insurance companies require a *DSM* diagnosis before they pay providers for care.

The current edition, *DSM-5* (released in 2013), consists of three sections: (1) an introduction with instructions for using the manual; (2) diagnostic criteria for all of the disorders, which are grouped so that similar categories of disorders are located near each other (TABLE 14.1); and (3) a guide for future psychopathology research, which also includes conditions not yet officially recognized as disorders, such as excessive internet gaming and misuse of caffeine. In the second section of the *DSM-5*, disorders are described in terms of measurable symptoms. A client must meet specific criteria to receive a particular diagnosis. In the coming years, updated versions of the *DSM* will be released, with further changes to the description and classification of many disorders.

DIMENSIONAL NATURE OF PSYCHOPATHOLOGY One problem with the *DSM* is that it takes a *categorical approach*, which implies that a person either has a psychological disorder or does not (Bernstein, 2011). This approach fails to capture differences in the severity of a disorder. Moreover, it misleadingly implies

Table 14.1 *DSM-5* Disorders

CATEGORY	EXAMPLE
Neurodevelopmental disorders	Autism spectrum disorder
Schizophrenia spectrum and other psychotic disorders	Schizophrenia
Bipolar and related disorders	Bipolar I disorder
Depressive disorders	Major depressive disorder
Anxiety disorders	Panic disorder
Obsessive-compulsive and related disorders	Body dysmorphic disorder
Trauma- and stressor-related disorders	Posttraumatic stress disorder
Dissociative disorders	Dissociative amnesia
Somatic symptom and related disorders	Illness anxiety disorder
Feeding and eating disorders	Anorexia nervosa
Elimination disorders	Enuresis (bed-wetting)
Sleep-wake disorders	Narcolepsy
Sexual dysfunctions	Erectile disorder
Gender dysphoria	Gender dysphoria
Disruptive, impulse control, and conduct disorders	Pyromania
Substance-related and addictive disorders	Alcohol use disorder
Neurocognitive disorders	Delirium
Personality disorders	Narcissistic personality disorder
Paraphilic disorders	Exhibitionistic disorder

SOURCE: Based on American Psychiatric Association (2013).

that there is a distinct cutoff between the absence and presence of psychopathology. What "counts" as psychopathology is not an objective fact that can be determined with a diagnostic test, like a test for a bacterial infection. Instead, psychopathology reflects a social consensus about what to call a cluster of symptoms or behaviors.

An alternative type of evaluation that addresses this issue is called a *dimensional approach,* which considers psychological disorders along a continuum on which people vary in degree rather than in kind (**FIGURE 14.4**). A dimensional approach recognizes that many psychological disorders are extreme versions of normal feelings. We are all a little sad at times, and sometimes we feel more sad than usual. But no specific amount of sadness passes a threshold for depressive disorders. In a dimensional approach, diagnosis is relatively easy at the extremes but more ambiguous in between. As an analogy, consider how we label someone as a social media influencer. Someone with 40 followers is not an influencer and someone with 40 million is. But there is no

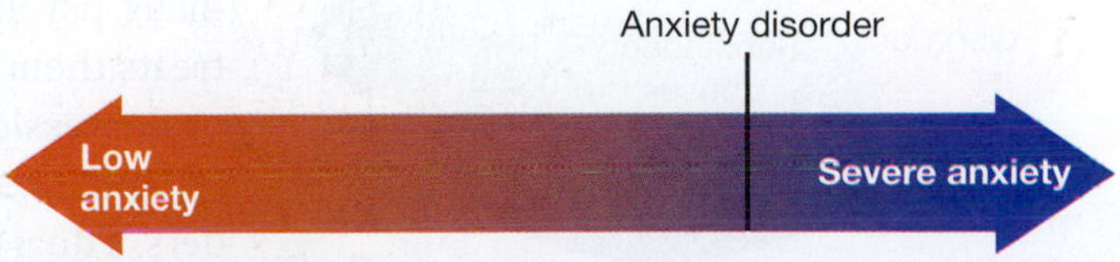

FIGURE 14.4
Dimensional Nature of Psychopathology
Symptoms of psychological disorders occur along continuums. They are not absolute states. People who fall below the cutoff level may not meet the diagnostic criteria but may still experience symptoms that interfere with their lives and will therefore benefit from treatment.

Table 14.2 NIMH Research Domain Criteria (RDoC)

DOMAINS OF HUMAN BEHAVIOR AND FUNCTIONING				
Negative valence systems (i.e., fear, anxiety, threat, loss)	**Positive valence systems** (i.e., decision making, reward, habit, prediction error)	**Cognitive systems** (i.e., attention, memory, perception, cognitive control)	**Social processes** (i.e., social communication, self-knowledge, theory of mind)	**Arousal and regulatory systems** (i.e., arousal, sleep, circadian rhythms)
UNITS OF ANALYSIS				
Genes Molecules Cells Circuits Physiology Behaviors Self-Reports Paradigms				

SOURCE: National Institute of Mental Health, n.d.

Research Domain Criteria (RDoC) A method that defines basic aspects of functioning and considers them across multiple levels of analysis, from genes to brain systems to behavior.

objective threshold between being an influencer and not, and the classification depends on human judgment and societal standards that shift over time.

The U.S. National Institute of Mental Health (NIMH) has proposed an entirely new way of classifying and understanding psychological disorders that is based on a dimensional approach (Insel et al., 2010). Whereas the *DSM* approach classifies disorders by observable symptoms, the **Research Domain Criteria (RDoC)** method defines basic *domains* of functioning (such as attention, social communication, anxiety) and considers them across multiple levels of analysis, from genes to brain systems to behavior (**TABLE 14.2**). For example, researchers might study attention problems for people with anxiety disorders, depression, schizophrenia, and post-traumatic stress disorder.

The RDoC initiative is meant to guide research rather than classify disorders for treatment. In the United States especially, because NIMH funds the majority of research, RDoC will be a driving force for research on psychopathology. The goal of the initiative is to understand the processes that give rise to disordered thoughts, emotions, and behaviors. Many researchers are optimistic that the RDoC approach will bring new insights into how to classify psychological disorders (Lilienfeld & Treadway, 2016), and identifying their causes ultimately may provide insight into treating them.

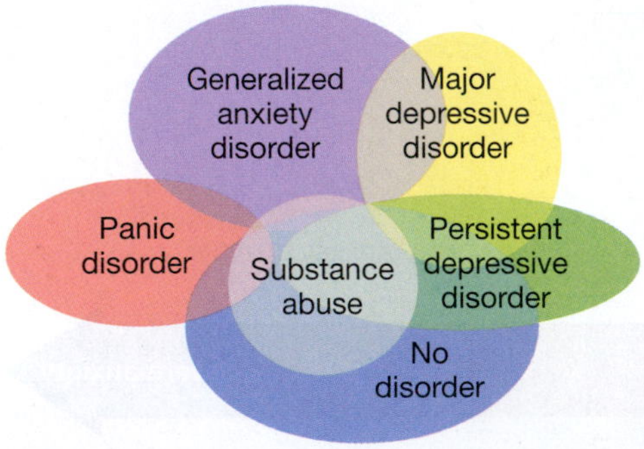

FIGURE 14.5
Comorbidity
Psychological disorders commonly overlap. For instance, substance abuse is common across psychological disorders, and people with major depression (or a milder form known as persistent depressive disorder) often also have anxiety disorders (such as panic disorder or generalized anxiety disorder).

COMORBIDITY Another problem with the *DSM* approach is that people seldom fit neatly into the precise categories provided. Indeed, many psychological disorders occur together even though the *DSM-5* treats them as separate disorders—for example, depression and anxiety, or depression and substance abuse. This state is known as *comorbidity* (**FIGURE 14.5**). Though people may be diagnosed with two or more disorders, a dual diagnosis offers no advantages in terms of treatment because the diagnoses are each merely descriptive and therefore do not indicate whether the disorders are best treated separately or together.

Psychological disorders may be comorbid because of common underlying factors. It has recently been proposed that psychopathology reflects a common general factor, analogous to general intelligence (or *g*, discussed in Chapter 8). Avshalom Caspi and colleagues (2014) examined symptoms of psychopathology in a large sample of individuals who were studied for more than 30 years, from childhood to middle adulthood. The researchers found that one underlying factor, which they called the *p factor*, was involved in all types of psychological disorders. Higher scores on the *p* factor were associated with more life impairment, such as suicide attempts, psychiatric hospitalizations, and criminal behaviors. High *p* scores also predicted a worsening of impairments over time. Just as the *g* dimension of intelligence reflects low to high cognitive abilities, the *p* dimension reflects low to high psychopathology severity. Low or high, an individual's *p* score is likely to remain stable over time (Snyder et al., 2016).

FIGURE 14.6
Assessment
There are many types of assessment for diagnosing psychological disorders. Here, a researcher observes a child at play to assess her mental function.

ASSESSMENT Examining a person's mental functions and psychological condition to diagnose a psychological disorder is known as **assessment**. This process often includes self-reports by the person seeking treatment, psychological testing, observations, and interviews with others who know the person well. It may also involve neuropsychological testing.

In the neuropsychological method, the client performs actions such as copying a picture; drawing a design from memory; sorting cards that show various stimuli into categories based on size, shape, or color; placing blocks into slots on a board while blindfolded; or tapping fingers rapidly (**FIGURE 14.6**). Each task requires an ability such as planning, coordinating, or remembering. By highlighting actions that the client performs poorly, the assessment might indicate problems with a particular brain region. Often a medical evaluation is indicated. For instance, the symptoms of depression or anxiety disorder can be similar to those of hypothyroidism, an endocrine disorder that should be ruled out before the psychological disorder is treated (Ayhan et al., 2014).

The primary goal of assessment is to make a diagnosis so that appropriate treatment can be provided. The course and probable outcome, or *prognosis*, will depend on the psychological disorder that is diagnosed. Therefore, a correct diagnosis will help the client and perhaps their family understand what the future might bring. Assessment does not stop with diagnosis, however. Ongoing assessment helps mental health workers understand whether specific situations might cause a worsening of the disorder, whether progress is being made in treatment, and other factors that might help in understanding unique aspects of a given case (**FIGURE 14.7**).

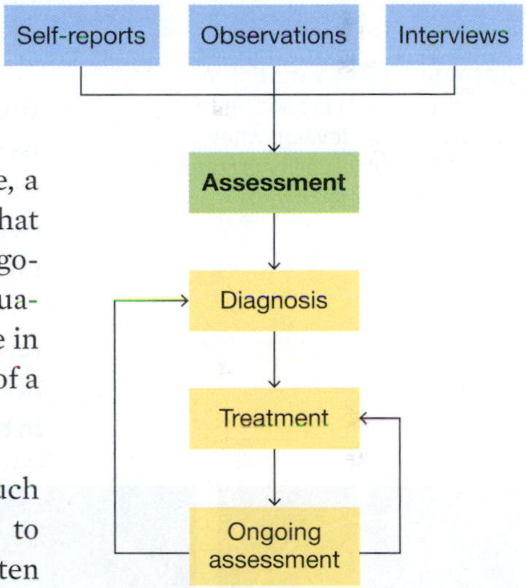

FIGURE 14.7
Assessing a Client
Clinical psychologists examine a person's mental functions and psychological health to diagnose a psychological disorder and determine an appropriate treatment. This flowchart shows the factors that lead to treatment.

EVIDENCE-BASED ASSESSMENT Some popular methods of assessment, such as projective measures (discussed in Chapter 13), do not necessarily lead to reliable diagnosis and treatment plans. Moreover, individual clinicians often choose assessment procedures based on their subjective beliefs and training rather than on scientific studies. For instance, when making diagnoses, some clinicians use their clinical judgment rather than a formal method, such as a structured interview that consists of standardized questions derived from *DSM* criteria in the same order each time.

Evidence-based assessment is an approach to clinical evaluation in which research guides the evaluation of psychopathology, the selection of appropriate psychological tests and neuropsychological methods, and the use of critical thinking in making a diagnosis (Hunsley & Mash, 2007; Joiner et al., 2005). As noted earlier, research shows that many disorders are comorbid. Research also indicates that people who are depressed often have substance use disorders. Therefore, an evidence-based assessment approach would indicate that people found to be depressed should also be assessed for comorbid conditions, such as substance abuse.

assessment In psychology, examination of a person's cognitive, behavioral, or emotional functioning to diagnose possible psychological disorders.

Q What is the dimensional approach to understanding psychological disorders?

ANSWER: The dimensional approach views psychological disorders as existing along a continuum on which people vary.

14.3 Psychological Disorders Have Many Causes

Psychologists do not completely agree about the causes of most psychopathology. Still, some factors are believed to play important roles in the development of psychological disorders. As we have seen throughout this book, environment and the individual person both matter, though perhaps neither matters as much as their interaction. The **diathesis-stress model** (presented as a flowchart in **FIGURE 14.8**) provides one way of thinking about the interaction between environment and person in the onset of psychopathology (Riboni & Belzung, 2017; Walder et al., 2014).

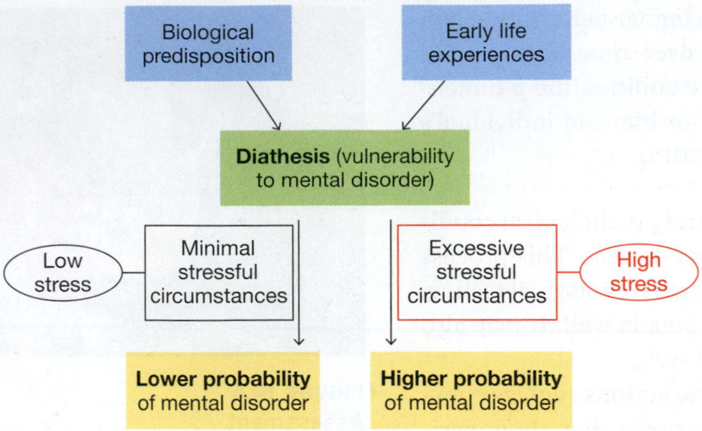

FIGURE 14.8
Diathesis-Stress Model
The onset of psychological disorders can be seen as resulting from the interactions of a diathesis and stress. The diathesis may be biological (e.g., genetic predisposition), environmental (e.g., childhood trauma), or both.

diathesis-stress model A diagnostic model proposing that a disorder may develop when an underlying vulnerability is coupled with a precipitating event.

In this model, an individual can have an underlying vulnerability (known as *diathesis*) to a psychological disorder. This diathesis can be biological, such as a genetic predisposition to a specific disorder, or it can be environmental, such as childhood adversity. The vulnerability may not be sufficient to trigger a disorder, but the addition of stressful circumstances can tip the scales. If the stress level exceeds the individual's ability to cope, the symptoms of psychological disorder will occur. In this view, a family history of psychopathology suggests vulnerability rather than destiny.

BIOLOGICAL FACTORS The biological perspective focuses on how physiological factors, such as genetics, contribute to psychological disorders (Gatt et al., 2015). Comparing the rates of psychological disorders between identical and fraternal twins and studying individuals who have been adopted have revealed the importance of genetic factors (Kendler et al., 2003; Krueger, 1999).

Genetic factors can affect the production and levels of neurotransmitters and their receptor sites. They can also affect the size and shape of brain structures and their level of connectivity. Structural imaging and postmortem studies have revealed differences in brain anatomy between those with psychological disorders and those without. Functional neuroimaging is currently at the forefront of research into the neurological components of mental disorders: PET and fMRI have revealed brain regions that may function differently in individuals with mental disorders (**FIGURE 14.9**). There is growing evidence that neuroimaging might be able to identify biological indicators of psychopathology that predict treatment outcomes (Gabrieli et al., 2015).

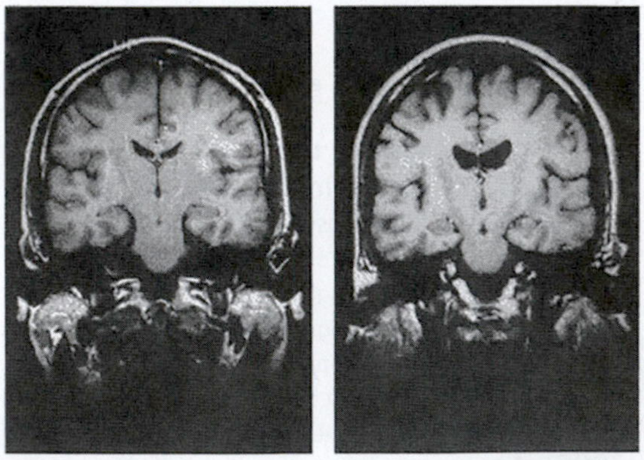

FIGURE 14.9
Biological Factors in Psychopathology
These brain MRIs are from twins. The twin on the right has schizophrenia, and the one on the left does not. In the MRI of the twin with schizophrenia, note the larger ventricles (these fluid-filled cavities appear dark in the image).

Environmental effects on the body also influence the development and course of psychological disorders. The fetus is particularly vulnerable to biological factors—including malnutrition, exposure to toxins (such as drugs and alcohol), and maternal illness—that may affect the central nervous system in ways that contribute to psychological disorders (Salum et al., 2010). Similarly, during childhood and adolescence, environmental toxins, severe stress, and malnutrition can put an individual at risk for psychological disorders. Epigenetic processes (discussed in Chapter 3) might also contribute to brain abnormalities. Environmental stress can change how genes are expressed, in turn causing lasting brain changes that increase the chance of developing psychological disorders (Nestler et al., 2016). Again, biological factors often reflect people's individual vulnerabilities, but as the diathesis-stress model reminds us, single explanations (nature *or* nurture, environment *or* person) are seldom sufficient for understanding psychological disorders (Halldorsdottir & Binder, 2017).

SITUATIONAL FACTORS Thoughts and emotions shaped by a particular environment can profoundly influence behavior, including disordered behavior. Not only traumatic events but also less extreme circumstances, such as constantly being belittled by a parent, can have long-lasting effects. The **family systems model** proposes that an individual's behavior must be considered within a social context, particularly within the family (Kazak et al., 2002). According to this model, problems that arise within an individual are manifestations of problems within the family (Goodman & Gotlib, 1999). Thus, developing a profile of an individual's family interactions can be important for understanding the factors that may be contributing to the disorder. A profile can also be important for determining the course of treatment and whether the family is likely to be helpful or counterproductive to the client's progress in therapy.

Similarly, the **sociocultural model** views psychopathology as the result of the interaction between individuals and their cultures. Some disorders, such as schizophrenia, appear to be more common among those lower in socioeconomic status (Luo et al., 2019). From the sociocultural perspective, these differences in occurrence are due to differences in expectations, norms, and opportunities among classes. There are also biases in people's willingness to ascribe disorders to different social classes. Eccentric behavior among the wealthy elite might be tolerated or viewed as amusing (**FIGURE 14.10**), whereas the same behaviors observed among those living in poverty might be taken as evidence of psychopathology. Moreover, people who develop schizophrenia may have trouble keeping a job, and having less money may in turn make it harder for them to find effective treatment. In this way, lower socioeconomic status and psychopathology may be mutually reinforcing.

FIGURE 14.10
Sociocultural Model of Psychopathology
According to the sociocultural model, psychopathology results from the interaction between individuals and their cultures. In naming their child X Æ A-Xii, Grimes and Elon Musk might signal that they have a psychological disorder. However, eccentric behavior by the wealthy is tolerated in many cultures.

family systems model A diagnostic model that considers problems within an individual as indicating problems within the family.

sociocultural model A diagnostic model that views psychopathology as the result of the interaction between individuals and their cultures.

cognitive-behavioral approach A diagnostic model that views psychopathology as the result of learned, maladaptive thoughts and beliefs.

COGNITIVE-BEHAVIORAL FACTORS The central principle of the **cognitive-behavioral approach** is that many types of abnormal behavior are learned (Butler et al., 2006). As discussed in Chapter 6, through classical conditioning, an initially neutral stimulus paired with an unconditioned stimulus can eventually by itself produce a similar response. As was the case with Little Albert, if a child is playing with a fluffy white rat and is frightened by a loud noise, the white rat alone can later cause fear in the child.

The premise of the cognitive-behavioral perspective is that thoughts can become distorted and produce maladaptive behaviors and emotions. Because these thoughts and beliefs are learned, they can be unlearned through treatment. Cognitive-behavioral psychologists believe that thought processes are available to the conscious mind and can therefore be discussed directly during therapy. Individuals are aware of, or can easily be made aware of, the thought processes that give rise to maladaptive emotions and behaviors. Once they have identified these patterns, people can then learn or condition new responses to the thoughts or stimuli that had been problematic in their daily lives.

Q **Enrique was exposed to toxins prenatally and later experienced depression when his home burned in a fire. How would the diathesis-stress model explain Enrique's depression?**

ANSWER: Exposure to prenatal toxins created a diathesis and the fire caused stress beyond what Enrique could cope with, triggering the onset of the depression.

14.4 Psychological Disorders Vary as a Function of Cultural Context

As described earlier, the boundaries among psychological disorders and between pathological and nonpathological states are fuzzy. One way to avoid the false precision implied with specific diagnostic labels is to divide disorders into groups, or clusters. Psychologists have identified two major types of psychopathology: internalizing

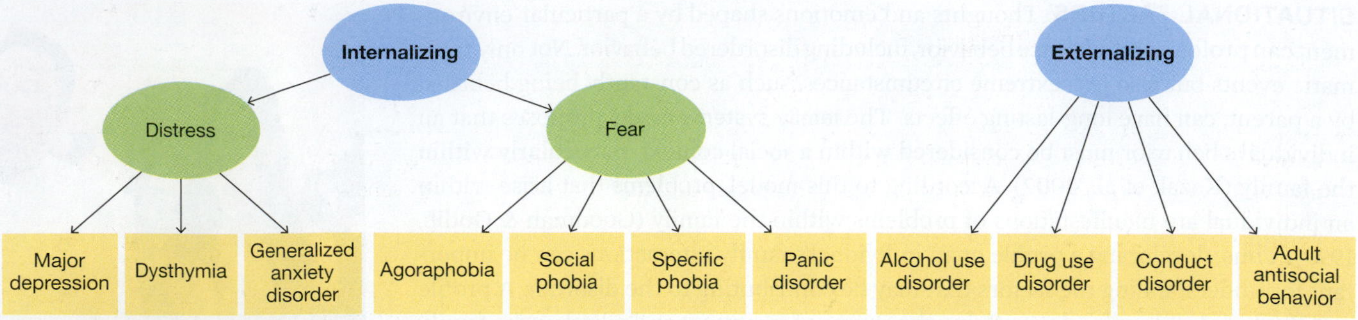

Source: Krueger & Markon, 2006.

FIGURE 14.11
Internalizing and Externalizing Model of Psychological Disorders
This diagram divides disorders into two basic categories, internalizing and externalizing. It also divides internalizing disorders into those related to fear and those related to distress.

and externalizing disorders. *Internalizing disorders* are characterized by negative emotions, and they can be divided into broad categories that reflect the emotions of distress and fear. Examples of internalizing disorders include major depressive disorder, generalized anxiety disorder, and panic disorder. *Externalizing disorders* are characterized by impulsive or out-of-control behavior. These disorders include alcoholism, conduct disorders, and antisocial personality disorder (**FIGURE 14.11**).

In general, the disorders associated with internalizing are more prevalent in people who identify as women, and those associated with externalizing are more prevalent in people who identify as men (Krueger & Markon, 2006). One explanation for gender differences in the presentation of disorders is that psychopathology can take different forms depending on cultural norms and expectations (Hartung & Lefler, 2019). For instance, there is a sexist cliché in Western cultures that men will drown their sorrows in alcohol. Expectations of how women react to emotional distress are different. Indeed, dependence on alcohol is much more likely in men, whereas anorexia nervosa is much more likely in women (**FIGURE 14.12**). However, culture cannot explain all gender-based differences in

FIGURE 14.12
Gender Differences in Psychological Disorders
The bars in this graph represent the prevalence of particular psychological disorders for men and for women.

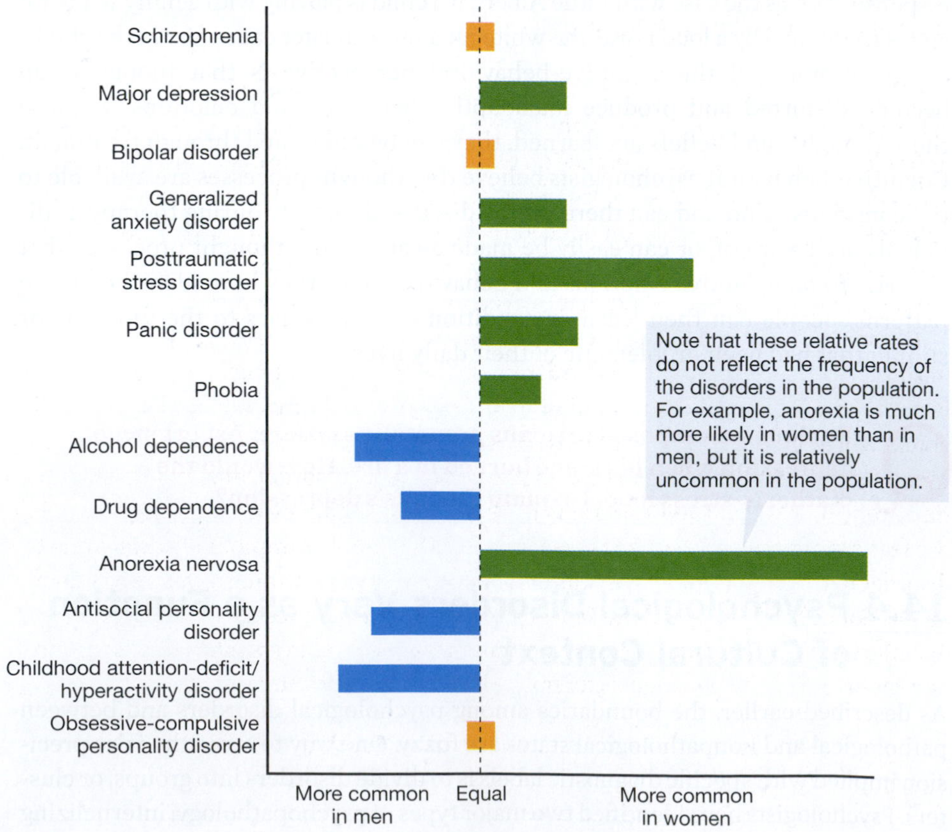

Table 14.3 Cultural Syndromes

NAME	DEFINITION AND LOCATION
Ataque de nervios	Uncontrollable shouting and/or crying; verbal and physical aggression; heat in chest rising to head; feeling of losing control; occasional amnesia for experience (Caribbean and South American Latinos)
Dhat syndrome	Anxiety, fatigue, weakness, weight loss, and other bodily complaints; typically observed in young males who believe their symptoms are due to loss of semen (South Asia)
Khyâl cap	Belief that a "windlike" substance may rise in the body and cause serious effects; acute panic, autonomic arousal, anxiety; catastrophic cognitions (Cambodians in the United States and Cambodia)
Kufungisisa	Belief that thinking too much can damage the mind and body; an explanation for anxiety, depression, and somatic problems indicating distress (Zimbabwe)
Maladi moun	A cultural explanation that sickness has been sent by people to harm their enemies; visible success makes one vulnerable to attack; causes various illnesses, including psychosis, depression, and social failure (Haiti)
Nervios	A phrase used to refer to a general state of vulnerability to stressful life experience; common symptoms include headaches and "brain aches" as well as irritability and nervousness (Latinos in the United States and Latin America)
Shenjing shuairuo	A weakness in the nervous system; mental fatigue, negative emotions, excitement, nervous pain, and sleep disturbances; caused by stress, embarrassment, or acute sense of failure (China)
Susto	An illness attributed to a frightening event that causes the soul to leave the body; sadness, somatic complaints, lack of motivation, and difficulty functioning in daily living (Latinos in the United States and Latin America)
Taijin kyofusho	Intense fear of interpersonal relations; belief that parts of the body give off offensive odors or displease others (Japan)

SOURCE: Based on American Psychiatric Association (2013).

psychopathology, and some disorders, such as schizophrenia and bipolar disorder, are equally likely in all genders.

CULTURAL SYNDROMES Most psychological disorders show both universal and culture-specific symptoms. As is the case with personality traits, cultural expectations likely have a stronger influence on the expression of some disorders than others. A disorder with a strong biological component will tend to be more similar across cultures. A disorder heavily influenced by learning, context, or both is more likely to differ across cultures. For example, depression is a major mental health problem around the world, but the ways that depression manifests can vary by culture.

Clinicians and researchers need to be sensitive to cultural issues to avoid making mistakes in their diagnoses and treatments (Marsella & Yamada, 2007). Cultural factors can be critical in determining how a disorder is expressed and how an individual will respond to different types of therapies. The *DSM-5* incorporates a greater consideration of cultural factors for each psychological disorder, and it updates criteria to reflect cross-cultural variations in how people exhibit symptoms. For example, the fear of "offending others" has been added as a possible symptom of social anxiety disorder to reflect the collectivist cultural concept that not harming others is as important as not harming the self. The *DSM-5* also provides examples of *cultural syndromes*, disorders that include a cluster of symptoms that are found in specific cultural groups or regions. (**TABLE 14.3** presents examples of common cultural syndromes.)

Q **What is the difference between internalizing disorders and externalizing disorders?**

ANSWER: Internalizing disorders, more prevalent in women, involve negative emotions. Externalizing disorders, more prevalent in men, involve disinhibition.

Learning Objectives

- Distinguish among the various anxiety disorders.
- Discuss cultural and gender differences in depressive disorders.
- Distinguish between bipolar I and bipolar II disorder.

Which Disorders Involve Disturbances in Emotions?

Strong emotions such as anxiety and sorrow can be useful. They can prepare people for dealing with future events and motivate them to learn new ways of coping with challenges. Being anxious about tests reminds people to keep up with their homework and study. However, intense or prolonged feelings such as sadness or anxiety can become debilitating and interfere with every aspect of life. Indeed, people diagnosed with anxiety or depressive disorders die about eight years earlier than those without the disorders (Pratt et al., 2016).

Mental health problems associated with anxiety and depression are highly prevalent on college campuses. The recent American College Health Association (2019) National College Health Assessment II survey of more than 54,000 students found that 48.7 percent of female and 37.4 percent of male participants reported that they "felt so depressed it was difficult to function" at some time within the last 12 months. About two thirds of the respondents reported overwhelming anxiety within the last 12 months. According to one study, 40.7 percent of college students had received treatment for depression in the last 12 months (Lipson et al., 2019).

When emotions or moods go from being a normal part of daily living to being extreme enough to disrupt people's ability to work, learn, and play, these states are considered symptoms of psychological disorders. Most forms of psychopathology influence how people think as well as how they feel. However, emotional experiences are more central to some disorders, and thought disturbances are more central to others. In this section, we consider the most common disorders involving emotional states.

14.5 Anxiety Disorders Are Characterized by Fear and Tension

Imagine that you are about to make your first parachute jump out of an airplane. If you are like most people, your heart will be racing, and you will be sweating. You might feel queasy. Under these circumstances, you may find such sensations thrilling, but people who have an anxiety disorder experience these feelings often and are unhappy about them.

anxiety disorders Psychological disorders characterized by excessive fear and anxiety in the absence of true danger.

Anxiety disorders are characterized by excessive fear and anxiety in the absence of true danger. Those with anxiety disorders feel tense and apprehensive. They are often irritable because they cannot see any solution to their anxiety. Constant worry can make falling asleep and staying asleep difficult, and attention span and concentration can be impaired. By continually arousing the autonomic nervous system, chronic anxiety also causes bodily symptoms such as sweating, dry mouth, rapid pulse, shallow breathing, increased blood pressure, and increased muscular tension. Chronic arousal can also result in hypertension, headaches, and other health problems. More than 1 in 4 Americans will have some type of anxiety disorder during their lifetime (Kessler & Wang, 2008).

Because of their high levels of autonomic arousal, people who have anxiety disorders also exhibit restless and pointless motor behaviors. Exaggerated startle response is typical, and behaviors such as toe tapping and excessive fidgeting are common. Cognitive functioning may be affected as well. Chronic stress can produce atrophy in the hippocampus, a brain structure involved in learning and memory (McEwen, 2008). As noted in Chapter 11, chronic stress causes allostatic

Table 14.4 Five Types of Anxiety Disorders

CATEGORY	DESCRIPTION	EXAMPLE
Specific phobia	Fear of something that is disproportionate to the threat	Rachel is so afraid of snakes that if she sees even a picture of a snake, her heart begins to pound and she feels the need to run away.
Social anxiety disorder	Fear of being negatively evaluated by others in a social setting	Linda worries intensely that she will say or do the wrong thing around other people and they will think badly of her. She prefers to be by herself and avoids being around large groups of people.
Generalized anxiety disorder	Nearly constant anxiety not associated with a specific thing	Reginald is feeling very worried and has been for months, but he cannot figure out why. It seems as though he is anxious about everything.
Panic disorder	Sudden attacks of overwhelming terror	Jennifer has had several panic attacks and worries she will have another one. This worry brings on more panic attacks, where she feels extreme fear and her heart pounds in her chest.
Agoraphobia	Fear of being in a situation from which one cannot escape	Rashad works for a company located in a skyscraper, but he is so terrified of not being able to get out of the building that he has begun to have panic attacks at work.

SOURCE: Based on American Psychiatric Association (2013).

load, which can damage the body, including the brain, so it is very important to identify and effectively treat disorders that involve chronic anxiety. The various anxiety disorders share some emotional, cognitive, somatic, and motor symptoms, even though the behavioral manifestations of these disorders are quite different (Barlow, 2002; Brown & Barlow, 2009). These disorders include generalized anxiety disorder, social anxiety disorder, specific phobias, and agoraphobia (TABLE 14.4).

GENERALIZED ANXIETY DISORDER People with **generalized anxiety disorder (GAD)** are constantly anxious and worry incessantly about even minor matters (Newman et al., 2013). They even worry about being worried! Because the anxiety is not focused, it can occur in response to almost anything, so the person is constantly on the alert for problems. This hypervigilance results in distractibility, fatigue, irritability, and sleep problems, as well as headaches, restlessness, light-headedness, and muscle pain. Just under 6 percent of the U.S. population is affected by this disorder at some point in their lives, though women are diagnosed more often than men (Kessler et al., 1994; Kessler & Wang, 2008).

generalized anxiety disorder (GAD) A diffuse state of constant anxiety not associated with any specific object or event.

SOCIAL ANXIETY DISORDER *Social anxiety disorder*, formerly sometimes called *social phobia*, is a fear of being negatively evaluated by others. It includes fears of public speaking, speaking up in class, meeting new people, and eating in front of others. About 1 in 8 people will experience social anxiety disorder at some point in their lifetime, and around 7 percent are experiencing social anxiety disorder at any given time (Ruscio et al., 2008). It is one of the earliest forms of anxiety disorder to develop, often beginning at around age 13. The more social fears a person has, the more likely they are to develop other disorders, particularly depression and substance abuse problems. Indeed, assessment must consider the overlap between social anxiety disorder and related disorders to make an informed diagnosis (Stein & Stein, 2008; **FIGURE 14.13**).

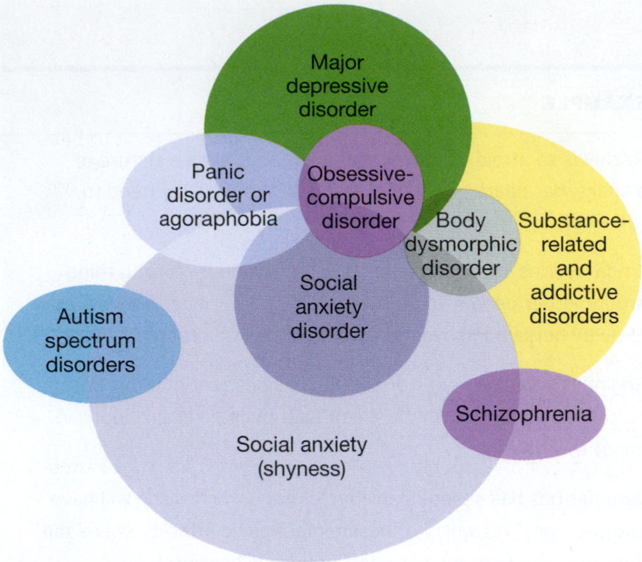

FIGURE 14.13
Comorbidity of Social Anxiety Disorder
As this diagram illustrates, social anxiety disorder is comorbid with many other psychological disorders. If a client has social anxiety disorder, all of these disorders need to be considered to make an accurate and complete diagnosis.

agoraphobia An anxiety disorder marked by fear of being in situations in which escape may be difficult or impossible.

SPECIFIC PHOBIA AND AGORAPHOBIA As discussed in Chapter 6, a phobia is a fear of a specific object or situation. Of course, some fear can be a good thing. As an adaptive force, fear can help people avoid potential dangers, such as venomous snakes and rickety bridges. In phobias, however, the fear is exaggerated and out of proportion to the actual danger.

In *DSM-5*, people are diagnosed with *specific phobia* based on the object of the fear. Specific phobias, which affect about 1 in 8 people around the globe (Wardenaar et al., 2017), involve particular objects and situations. Common specific phobias include fear of snakes (ophidiophobia), fear of enclosed spaces (claustrophobia), and fear of heights (acrophobia). (**TABLE 14.5** lists some unusual specific phobias.) Another common specific phobia is fear of flying. Even though the odds of dying in a plane crash, compared with a car crash, are extraordinarily small, some people find flying terrifying (see Section 11.6, "You Be the Psychologist: Why Are People Afraid of Flying but Not of Driving [or Smoking]?"). For those who need to travel frequently for their jobs, a fear of flying can cause significant impairment in daily living.

A disorder related to specific phobias is **agoraphobia**. People with this disorder are afraid of being in situations in which escape is difficult or impossible. For example, they may fear being in a crowded shopping mall or using public transportation. Their fear is so strong that being in such situations causes *panic attacks*. These are sudden, overwhelming attacks of terror and worry and often involve fears of having additional panic attacks. The attacks seemingly come out of nowhere, or they are cued by external stimuli or internal thought processes. Panic attacks typically last for several minutes, during which the person may begin to sweat and tremble; has a racing heart; feels short of breath; feels chest pain; and may feel dizzy and light-headed, with

Table 14.5 Some Unusual Specific Phobias

- **Arachibutyrophobia:** fear of peanut butter sticking to the roof of one's mouth
- **Automatonophobia:** fear of ventriloquists' dummies
- **Barophobia:** fear of gravity
- **Dextrophobia:** fear of objects at the right side of the body
- **Geliophobia:** fear of laughter
- **Gnomophobia:** fear of garden gnomes
- **Hippopotomonstrosesquipedaliophobia:** fear of long words
- **Ochophobia:** fear of being in a moving automobile
- **Panophobia:** fear of everything
- **Pentheraphobia:** fear of mothers-in-law
- **Triskaidekaphobia:** fear of the number 13

numbness and tingling in the hands and feet. As a result, people who have agoraphobia avoid going into open spaces or to places where there might be crowds. In extreme cases, they may feel unable to leave their homes.

DEVELOPMENT OF ANXIETY DISORDERS The behavioral manifestations of anxiety disorders can vary widely, but all share some causal factors (Barlow, 2002). The first factor is biased thinking. When presented with ambiguous or neutral situations, anxious individuals tend to perceive them as threatening, whereas nonanxious individuals assume they are nonthreatening (Mathews, 2012; Mogg & Bradley, 2016; **FIGURE 14.14**). Anxious individuals also focus excessively on perceived threats (Klein et al., 2017; MacLeod & Mathews, 2012). They thus recall threatening events more easily than nonthreatening ones, exaggerating the events' perceived magnitude and frequency.

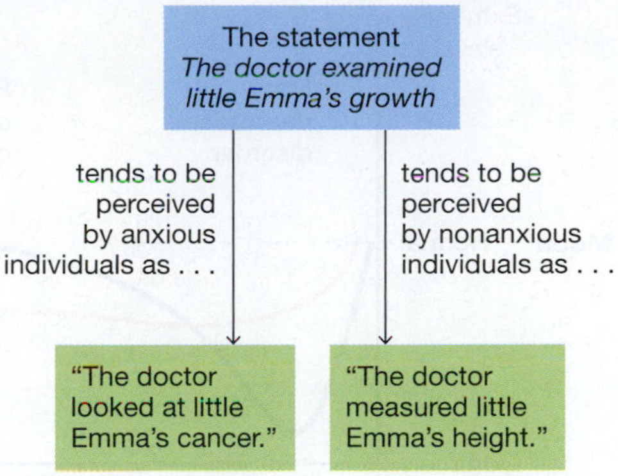

FIGURE 14.14
Anxiety Disorders
As this example illustrates, anxious individuals tend to perceive ambiguous situations as threatening.

A second factor is learning (Lissek et al., 2014). For example, monkeys can develop a fear of snakes if they observe other monkeys responding to snakes fearfully. Similarly, a person could develop a fear of flying by observing another person's fearful reaction to the closing of cabin doors.

Anxiety disorders also may have a biological basis. As noted in Chapter 13, children who have an inhibited temperamental style are usually shy and tend to avoid unfamiliar people and novel objects. These inhibited children are more likely to develop anxiety disorders later in life (Buss & McDoniel, 2016). They are especially at risk for developing social anxiety disorder (Chronis-Tuscano et al., 2009).

Q **How does the cause of anxiety differ in specific phobias and in generalized anxiety disorder?**

ANSWER: With specific phobias, a particular object or situation is associated with fear. Generalized anxiety disorder is diffuse tension and worry, with no specific threat.

14.6 Depressive Disorders Are Characterized by Sad, Empty, or Irritable Moods

When we feel down or sad about something, we often say we are depressed. For some people, however, the negative feelings persist, impair daily life, and turn into a psychological disorder. The *DSM-5* categorizes several disorders as *depressive disorders*. The common feature of all depressive disorders is the presence of sad, empty, or irritable mood along with bodily symptoms and cognitive problems that interfere with daily life.

MAJOR DEPRESSIVE DISORDER The classic disorder in this category is major depressive disorder. According to *DSM-5* criteria, to be diagnosed with **major depressive disorder**, a person must experience a *major depressive episode*, which includes experiencing depressed mood or a loss of interest in pleasurable activities every day for at least two weeks. In addition, the person must have other symptoms, such as appetite and weight changes; sleep disturbances; loss of energy; difficulty concentrating; feelings of self-reproach or guilt; and frequent thoughts of death, perhaps by suicide. The following excerpt is from a case study of a 56-year-old woman diagnosed with depression:

major depressive disorder A disorder characterized by severe negative moods or a lack of interest in normally pleasurable activities.

> She described herself as overwhelmed with feelings of guilt, worthlessness, and hopelessness. She twisted her hands almost continuously and played nervously with her hair. She stated that her family would be better off without her and that she had considered taking her life. . . . She felt that after death she would go to hell, where she would experience eternal torment, but that this would be a just punishment. (Andreasen, 1984, p. 39)

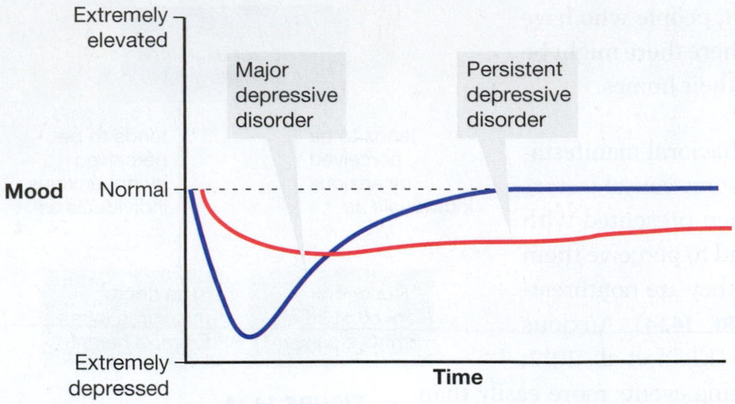

FIGURE 14.15
Depressed Mood in Depressive Disorders
This graphic provides a general way to understand the two main types of depressive disorders in relation to "normal mood." People with major depressive disorder tend to experience extremely depressed moods but for short periods. By contrast, people with persistent depressive disorder experience mildly or moderately depressed moods but for longer periods.

Depression is different from everyday sadness. Only long-lasting episodes that impair a person's life are diagnosed as depressive disorders. Major depression affects about 7–8 percent of Americans at any one time (Pratt & Brody, 2014), whereas approximately 13 percent of Americans will experience major depression at some point in their lives (Lim et al., 2018). Although major depressive disorder varies in severity, those who receive a diagnosis are highly impaired by the condition, and it tends to persist over several months, often lasting for years (Otte et al., 2016).

Depression is the leading risk factor for suicide, which claims approximately 788,000 lives annually around the world (World Health Organization, 2017b) and is among the top three causes of death for people between ages 15 and 35 (Insel & Charney, 2003). You will learn more about suicide, specifically about interventions to help prevent it, in Section 14.8.

PERSISTENT DEPRESSIVE DISORDER Unlike major depressive disorder, **persistent depressive disorder**, sometimes called *dysthymia*, is of mild to moderate severity (FIGURE 14.15). Most individuals with this disorder describe their mood as "down" or "low." People with persistent depressive disorder have many of the same symptoms as people with major depressive disorder, but those symptoms are less intense. People diagnosed with this disorder—approximately 2–3 percent of the population—must have a depressed mood most of the day, more days than not, for at least 2 years. Periods of depressed mood last 2–20 or more years, although the typical duration is about 5–10 years. Because the depressed mood is so long-lasting, some psychologists consider it a personality disorder rather than a mood disorder.

persistent depressive disorder
A form of depression that is not severe enough to be diagnosed as major depressive disorder but lasts longer.

There are no clear distinctions between having a depressive personality, persistent depressive disorder, and major depressive disorder. In keeping with a dimensional view of psychological disorders, these states may be points along a continuum rather than distinct disorders (Lewinsohn et al., 1991, 1999).

THE ROLES OF CULTURE AND GENDER IN DEPRESSIVE DISORDERS
Depression is so prevalent that it is sometimes called the common cold of psychological disorders. In its most severe form, depression is the leading cause of disability worldwide (World Health Organization, 2017c). Major depressive disorder affects about 41 million people in India and 49 million people in China (Baxter et al., 2016). Unfortunately, both countries have large gaps between the prevalence of mental health disorders and available resources to treat those disorders (Patel et al., 2017). The stigma associated with depressive disorder has especially dire consequences in developing countries, where treatment can be difficult to access and people do not want to engage in treatment to avoid admitting to being depressed (Andrade et al., 2014).

Depression also remains stigmatized in some American cultural groups. People with mental illness experience stigma and shame in Asian American, Latinx, LGBTQIA+, and some religious communities (Roeloffs et al., 2003). The increased levels of stigma in these groups and social pressures to hide psychological struggles might contribute to the elevated levels of depression observed in people in those groups, particularly those with intersectional identities in multiple groups (Turan et al., 2019).

Education about the high incidence rates of psychological disorders and the existence of effective treatments can reduce stigma (**FIGURE 14.16**). Promising efforts to reduce the stigma of mental health disorders are underway around the globe, but progress has been slow in developing nations (Thornicroft et al., 2016) and within some communities in the United States (Wong et al., 2021).

FIGURE 14.16
Informing the Public
Public-service ads may help "normalize" the treatment of psychological disorders. The more people hear about talking to doctors about problems, the more inclined they may be to visit doctors when problems arise.

Gender also plays a role in the incidence of depression. Across multiple countries and contexts, about twice as many women as men experience depressive disorders (Kessler et al., 2003; Pratt & Brody, 2014). One possibility is that men experience greater stigma surrounding depression because of social expectations that men remain unemotional, even when they are suffering (Mackenzie et al., 2019). Researchers have also theorized that women's multiple roles in most societies—as wage earners and family caregivers—cause stress that results in increased incidence of depression. Having multiple identities, such as wife, mother, and employee, can have health benefits if the person feels she can fulfill each role (Barnett & Hyde, 2001). So it is not multiple roles per se but more likely overwork, unrealistic societal expectations, and lack of structural and financial support that contribute to the high rate of depression in women.

CAUSES OF DEPRESSION Studies of twins, families, and adoptions support the notion that depression has a genetic component. Although there is some variability among studies, concordance rates—that is, the percentage who share the same disorder—for identical twins are generally around 2–3 times higher than rates for fraternal twins (Levinson, 2006). The genetic contribution to depression is somewhat weaker than the genetic contribution to schizophrenia or to bipolar disorder (Belmaker & Agam, 2008).

The existence of a genetic component implies that biological factors are involved in depression. In fact, there is evidence that major depressive disorder may involve one or more monoamines, neurotransmitters that regulate emotion and arousal and motivate behavior. For instance, medications that increase the availability of norepinephrine, a monoamine, may help alleviate depression. Medications that decrease levels of this neurotransmitter can cause symptoms of depression. Medications such as Prozac are known as *selective serotonin reuptake inhibitors (SSRIs)*. SSRIs selectively increase another monoamine, serotonin, and are often used to treat depression (Barton et al., 2008; SSRIs and other medications are discussed in Chapter 15). Yet depression is not simply due to a lack of norepinephrine or serotonin. Research has found that medications that reduce serotonin can also alleviate depression (Nickel et al., 2003). There is not yet a clear understanding of the role of neurotransmitters in the development of depressive disorders.

Consistent with the diathesis-stress model, studies have implicated situational factors such as life stressors in many cases of depression (Hammen, 2005). Particularly relevant for depression is interpersonal loss, such as the death of a loved one or a divorce (Paykel, 2003). Depression is especially likely in the face of multiple negative events (Brown & Harris, 1978), and patients with depression have often experienced negative life events during the year before the onset of their depression (Dohrenwend et al., 1986).

How an individual reacts to stress, however, can be influenced by interpersonal relationships, which play an extremely important role in depression. For instance, rates of depression across the United States were elevated during the COVID-19

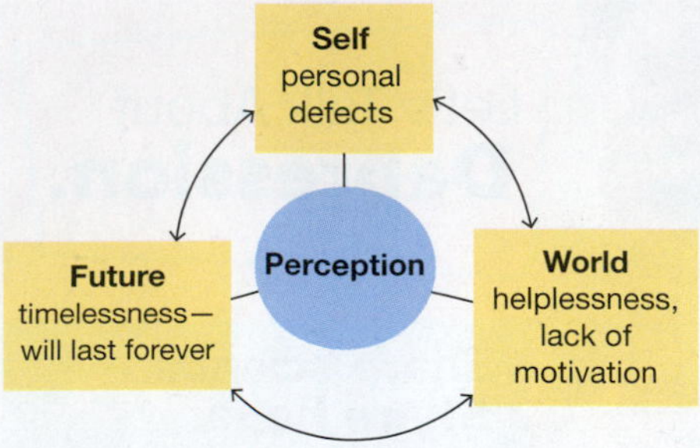

FIGURE 14.17

Cognitive Triad

According to Aaron Beck, people suffering from depression perceive themselves, their situations, and the future negatively. These perceptions influence one another and contribute to the disorder.

quarantine, but people who felt supported in their social relationships were less likely to become depressed (Grey et al., 2020). Feeling strong connections to friends, family, and romantic partners reduces the likelihood of experiencing a depressive episode, particularly among people with high levels of early life stress (Brinker & Cheruvu, 2017). The protection that social relationships offer against depression depends on the quality, not the quantity, of social relationships. However, there is also evidence that having depression can have harmful effects on people's social relationships (Gariepy et al., 2016). Over time, people may avoid interactions with those experiencing depression, thus initiating a downward spiral by making a person even more depressed.

Finally, cognitive processes play a role in depressive disorders. The psychologist Aaron Beck famously described the causes of depression as negative thoughts and beliefs about oneself ("I am worthless"; "I am a failure"; "I am ugly"), the world around one ("Everybody hates me"; "The world is unfair"), and the future ("Things are hopeless"; "I can't change"). Beck refers to these negative thoughts about self, world, and future as the *cognitive triad* (Beck, 1967, 1976; Beck et al., 1979, 1987; **FIGURE 14.17**).

People with depression attribute misfortunes to personal defects while seeing positive occurrences as the result of luck. In other words, they do not show the positive self-illusions that are typical in most people (as discussed in Chapter 13). Beck also notes that people with depression make errors in logic. For example, they overgeneralize based on single events, magnify the seriousness of bad events, think in extremes (such as believing they should either be perfect or not try), and take responsibility for bad events that actually have little to do with them.

learned helplessness A cognitive model of depression in which people feel unable to control events in their lives.

A second cognitive model of depression is based on **learned helplessness** (Seligman, 1974, 1975). This term means that people come to see themselves as unable to have any effect on events in their lives. The psychologist Martin Seligman based this model on years of animal research. When animals are placed in aversive situations that they cannot escape (such as receiving unescapable shock), the animals eventually become passive and unresponsive. They end up lacking the motivation to try new methods of escape when given the opportunity. Similarly, people who experience learned helplessness come to expect that bad things will happen to them and believe they are powerless to avoid negative events. They have an external locus of control (see Chapter 13) and attribute negative events to personal factors that are stable and global, rather than to situational factors that are temporary and specific. These cognitive patterns are detectable before the onset of depression, indicating they might be a cause (instead of a consequence) of depression (Gotlib & Joormann, 2010).

Q **How does depression differ from nondisordered sadness?**

ANSWER: Depression differs from everyday sadness in duration (depression lasts much longer) and intensity (depression impairs functioning).

14.7 Bipolar Disorders Involve Depression and Mania

Most people's day-to-day fluctuations in mood are tiny compared with the extremes experienced by people with *bipolar disorders*. *Mania* refers to an elevated mood that feels like being "on the top of the world." This positive mood can vary in degree and is accompanied by major increases in energy level and physical activity

(**FIGURE 14.18**). For some people, mania involves a sense of agitation and restlessness rather than positivity (Garriga et al., 2016).

True *manic episodes* last at least one week and are characterized by abnormally and persistently elevated mood, increased activity, diminished need for sleep, grandiose ideas, racing thoughts, and extreme distractibility. During episodes of mania, heightened levels of activity and extreme happiness often lead to excessive involvement in activities that feel good at the time but can be harmful in the long run. People may engage in sexual indiscretions, buying sprees, risky business ventures, and similar "out of character" behaviors that they regret once the mania has subsided. They might also have severe thought disturbances and hallucinations. This form of the condition is known as **bipolar I disorder**. Bipolar I disorder is characterized more by manic episodes than by depression. Although those with bipolar I disorder often have depressive episodes, these episodes are not necessary for a *DSM-5* diagnosis. The manic episodes in bipolar I disorder cause significant impairment in daily living and can often result in hospitalization.

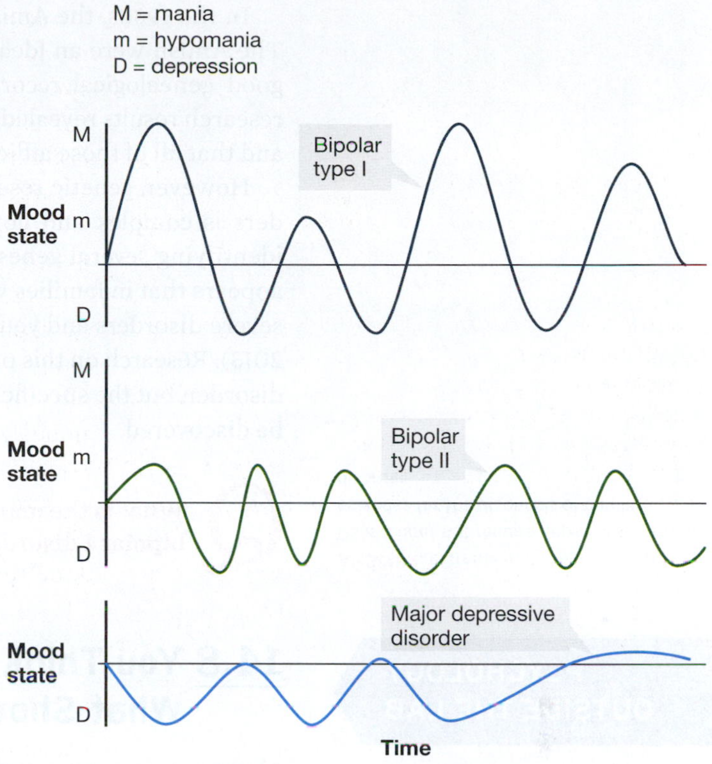

FIGURE 14.18
Bipolar I, Bipolar II, and Major Depressive Disorders
These graphs compare the mood changes over time for three disorders that involve mood states.

bipolar I disorder A disorder characterized by extremely elevated moods during manic episodes and, frequently, depressive episodes as well.

bipolar II disorder A disorder characterized by alternating periods of extremely depressed and mildly elevated moods.

In contrast to the full manic episodes experienced by people with bipolar I disorder, those with **bipolar II disorder** experience less extreme mood elevations, called *hypomania* (Phillips & Kupfer, 2013). These episodes are often characterized by heightened creativity and productivity, and they can be pleasurable and rewarding. Although these less extreme positive moods may be somewhat disruptive to a person's life, they do not necessarily cause significant impairment in daily living or require hospitalization. The bipolar II diagnosis requires at least one major depressive episode.

Bipolar disorders are much less common than depression. The lifetime prevalence for any type is estimated at around 4 percent (Merikangas et al., 2011). In addition, whereas depression is more common in women, bipolar disorders are equally prevalent in women and men. Bipolar disorders usually emerge during late adolescence or early adulthood, although bipolar I disorder is typically first diagnosed at a younger age than bipolar II disorder.

Learning Tip

The main differences between bipolar I and II are the presence of manic episodes and the presence and severity of depression. A major depressive episode is not a requirement for a bipolar I diagnosis, but it is for a bipolar II diagnosis. The impairments to daily living for bipolar I disorder are from the manic episodes, whereas the impairments for bipolar II disorder are the major depressive episodes.

ORIGINS OF BIPOLAR DISORDERS A family history of a bipolar disorder is the strongest and most consistent risk factor for bipolar disorders (Craddock & Sklar, 2013). The concordance rate for bipolar disorders in identical twins is more than 70 percent, versus only 20 percent for fraternal, or dizygotic, twins (Nurnberger et al., 1994).

In the 1980s, the Amish community was involved in a genetic research study. The Amish were an ideal population for this sort of research because they keep good genealogical records and few outsiders marry into the community. The research results revealed that bipolar disorders ran in a limited number of families and that all of those afflicted had a similar genetic anomaly (Egeland et al., 1987).

However, genetic research reveals that the hereditary nature of bipolar disorders is complex and not linked to just one gene. Current research focuses on identifying several genes that may be involved (Wray et al., 2014). In addition, it appears that in families with bipolar disorders, successive generations have more severe disorders and younger ages of onset (Petronis & Kennedy, 1995; Post et al., 2013). Research on this pattern of transmission may help reveal the genetics of the disorder, but the specific nature of the heritability of bipolar disorders remains to be discovered.

Q What is the main cause of impairment for people with bipolar I disorder?

ANSWER: extreme manic episodes—the *DSM-5* does not require depressive episodes for the diagnosis of bipolar I disorder

PSYCHOLOGY OUTSIDE THE LAB

14.8 You Think Your Friend Might Be Suicidal. What Should You Do?

Many people contemplate suicide at some point in their lives. Tragically, in 2018 suicide was the second leading cause of death among Americans ages 15 to 24 (CDC, 2020c). Suicide continues to be prevalent throughout adulthood. It is very common for students to be affected by suicide at some point during college. Perhaps you had a family member who died by suicide. Maybe a friend of yours told you about wanting to die. Or maybe you have considered taking your own life.

Understanding the risk factors associated with suicide is an important step toward preventing suicide. A key distinction in understanding suicide is separating suicide ideation—that is, thinking about suicide—from suicide attempts (Klonsky et al., 2016). In his book *Why People Die by Suicide* (2005), the clinical psychologist Thomas Joiner considers two key questions about suicide: Who *wants* to attempt suicide? And who *can* commit suicide? In answering the first question, Joiner argues that "people desire death when two fundamental needs are frustrated to the point of extinction" (p. 47). The first of these fundamental needs is the need to belong, to feel connected with others (discussed in Chapter 10). That need is thwarted if we do not believe we have enough positive interactions with others who care about us. The second of these fundamental needs is the need for competence. This need is thwarted if we do not feel like capable agents in the world. Joiner's hypothesis is that we desire death when both the need to belong and the need for competence are frustrated.

But as Joiner points out, just because a person wants to attempt suicide does not mean that person will be able to do so. Evolution has hardwired us with a tremendously strong self-preservation instinct. Some form of repeated self-preparation is typically needed for people to overcome the pain or fear of death. Joiner writes that people at high risk for suicide reach that point "through a process of exposure to self-injury and other provocative experiences" (pp. 85–86) and "when people get used to dangerous behavior . . . the groundwork for catastrophe is laid" (p. 48). For example, a person who drives recklessly, engages in self-cutting, and/or experiments with drugs is more practiced at self-harm than someone who does not engage in any of these behaviors and is thus more likely to be able to carry out lethal self-injury.

In **FIGURE 14.19**, the larger oval represents the people in the world who desire suicide. These individuals perceive themselves to be burdens on others and do not perceive themselves as having frequent and positive interactions with others who care about them. In other words, these are the people who may want to attempt suicide. The smaller oval represents the people who, over time, have developed the ability to lethally injure themselves. The overlap between the ovals represents the fraction of people who want to commit suicide and have the ability do so.

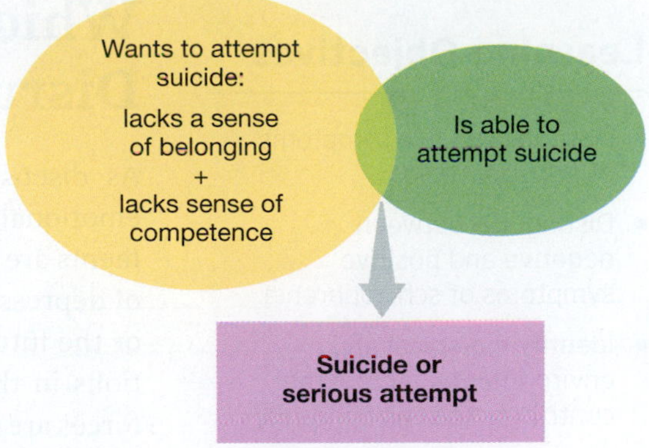

FIGURE 14.19
The Risk of Suicide: Desire + Capability = Attempt?
According to Thomas Joiner, the individuals who are *most* at risk of dying by suicide both want to do so and are able to do so.

Like so many other topics you have learned about in this book, suicide is a very complex psychological phenomenon. People show a variety of emotional responses before attempting suicide, so no single emotional state is a consistent warning sign (Bagge et al., 2017). Perhaps you have heard that suicide tends to run in families or that everyone who dies by suicide has a psychological disorder. Indeed, the data support a genetic risk factor for suicide (Roy, 1992), and the majority of people who die by suicide seem to experience psychological disorders (Cavanagh et al., 2003). But as you are learning in this chapter, psychopathology is quite common. And as you have learned throughout this book, human behavior is complex and determined by a combination of biological influences, situational factors, and their interactions. Many factors might lead someone to want to attempt suicide, and many factors might prompt a person to learn to endure self-harm.

With such risk factors in mind, we can now turn to the important question of what to do if you think a friend might be suicidal. First and foremost, take suicidal threats seriously. If you are concerned that a friend might be suicidal, do not be afraid to ask directly. Bringing up the topic will not put the thought in your friend's head. If you believe a friend is in immediate danger of attempting suicide, call 911. Second, get help. Someone who is considering suicide should be screened as soon as possible, and trained professionals assess for suicide risk frequently. Contact a counselor at your school, ask a religious leader for help, or speak to someone at the National Suicide Prevention Lifeline: 1-800-273-TALK (8255). These individuals are well equipped to help your friend get needed support. Third, let your friend know you care.

Remember that suicide risk is particularly high when people do not feel a sense of connection with others and when they feel a lack of competence. You can remind the suicidal person that you value your relationship, that you care about their well-being, that you would be devastated if they were no longer in your life. These forms of support can challenge the suicidal person's sense of not belonging. To challenge the person's feelings of incompetence, you can remind your friend about the reasons you admire them, or you can ask for help on a project or issue you are genuinely struggling with.

The problems that prompt a person to feel suicidal are often temporary. If you ever find yourself or a friend feeling that suicide offers the best way out of a seemingly overwhelming or hopeless situation, try to focus on the knowledge that other options exist. You or your friend might not be able to see those options right away. Reach out to someone who can help you or your friend find the ways out of current problems and into the future. ■

Q What characteristic usually differentiates people who do and do not act on suicidal ideation?

ANSWER: an acquired capacity or willingness to harm the self

Which Disorders Involve Disruptions in Thought?

Learning Objectives

- Describe the five symptoms of schizophrenia.
- Distinguish between negative and positive symptoms of schizophrenia.
- Identify biological and environmental factors that contribute to schizophrenia.

As discussed in the previous section, many psychological disorders include emotional impairments that influence how people think, even if thought impairments are not the main feature of the disorder. For example, sadness is a hallmark of depression, but the disorder can also include distorted thoughts about oneself or the future. By contrast, other disorders are primarily characterized by disruptions in thought, such as losing one's sense of identity or feeling that external forces are controlling one's thoughts. Many disorders of thought involve *psychosis*, which is a break from reality in which the person has difficulty distinguishing real perceptions from imaginary ones. People experiencing this disorder have extreme difficulty functioning in everyday life.

14.9 Schizophrenia Involves a Disconnection from Reality

schizophrenia A psychological disorder characterized by alterations in thoughts, in perceptions, or in consciousness, resulting in psychosis.

The term *schizophrenia* literally means "splitting of the mind." In popular culture, schizophrenia is often confused with dissociative identity disorder, formerly known as multiple personality disorder, but the two disorders are unrelated. **Schizophrenia** is characterized by alterations in thought, in perceptions, or in consciousness. The essence of schizophrenia is a split or disconnection from reality, known as psychosis.

According to published estimates, around 1 of every 200 people has schizophrenia (Simeone et al., 2015). A meta-analysis of 188 studies from 46 countries found similar rates for men and women, roughly 4–7 per 1,000 people (Saha et al., 2006). These researchers also found that the rate of schizophrenia was slightly lower in developing nations. In addition, the prognosis is better in developing than in developed cultures (Kulhara & Chakrabarti, 2001). Perhaps in developing countries there is more tolerance for symptoms or greater sympathy for unusual or different people (Waxler, 1979).

Schizophrenia is arguably the most devastating disorder for the people who have it and the relatives and friends who support them. It is characterized by a combination of motor, cognitive, behavioral, and perceptual abnormalities. These abnormalities result in impaired social, personal, or vocational functioning. A person must experience continuous signs of disturbances for at least six months to be diagnosed with schizophrenia according to *DSM-5*. Also, a person must show two or more of the five major *DSM-5* symptoms for schizophrenia, including at least delusions, hallucinations, or disorganized speech (**TABLE 14.6**). The symptoms of schizophrenia can be grouped into two categories: positive and negative. *Positive symptoms* are features that are present in schizophrenia but not in typical behavior. The first four *DSM-5* criteria in Table 14.6 are considered positive symptoms. In contrast, *negative symptoms* are characteristics missing in schizophrenia that are typically part of daily functioning. Negative symptoms can include apathy, lack of emotion, and slowed speech and movement.

delusions False beliefs based on incorrect inferences about reality.

DELUSIONS Among the positive (i.e., additional) symptoms most commonly associated with schizophrenia are **delusions**. Delusions are false beliefs based on incorrect inferences about reality. (Common types of delusions are listed in **TABLE 14.7**.) Delusional people persist in their beliefs despite evidence that contradicts those beliefs. Researchers have noted the overwhelmingly social nature of delusions in

Table 14.6 *DSM-5* Diagnostic Criteria for Schizophrenia

A. Two (or more) of the following, present for a significant portion of time during a 1-month period. At least one of these must be (1), (2), or (3).
   1. Delusions
   2. Hallucinations
   3. Disorganized speech (e.g., frequent incoherence)
   4. Grossly disorganized or catatonic behavior
   5. Negative symptoms (i.e., diminished emotional response or lack of motivation)

B. For a significant portion of time since the onset of the disturbance, level of functioning in one or more major areas, such as work, interpersonal relations, or self-care, is markedly below the level achieved prior to the onset.

C. Continuous signs of the disturbance persist for at least 6 months. This 6-month period must include at least 1 month of symptoms that meet criteria A (i.e., active phase symptoms) and may include periods where the symptoms are less extreme.

D. Other disorders and conditions have been ruled out (e.g., bipolar disorder, reactions to drugs, or other medical condition).

SOURCE: Based on American Psychiatric Association (2013).

Table 14.7 Delusions and Associated Beliefs

Persecutory	Belief that others are persecuting, spying on, or trying to harm one
Referential	Belief that objects, events, or other people have particular significance to one
Grandiose	Belief that one has great power, knowledge, or talent
Identity	Belief that one is someone else, such as Jesus Christ or the president of the United States
Guilt	Belief that one has committed a terrible sin
Control	Belief that one's thoughts and behaviors are being controlled by external forces

schizophrenia, such as perceptions of persecution by others or of elevated social standing. Some psychologists have suggested that delusions can be understood as alterations of social processing, affiliation, and group perception (Bell et al., 2021).

Delusions are characteristic of schizophrenia regardless of the culture, but the content of delusion can be influenced by cultural factors (Tateyama et al., 1993). When the delusions of German and Japanese patients with schizophrenia were compared, the two groups had similar rates of grandiose delusions, believing themselves much more powerful and important than they really were. The two groups differed significantly, however, in terms of other types of delusions. The German patients had delusions that involved guilt and sin, particularly as these concepts related to religion. By contrast, the Japanese patients had delusions of harassment, such as the belief that they were being slandered by others. The types of delusions that people with schizophrenia have can also be affected by current events.

HALLUCINATIONS Hallucinations are another positive symptom commonly associated with schizophrenia. Hallucinations are false sensory perceptions that are

hallucinations False sensory perceptions that are experienced without an external source.

experienced without an external source. They are vivid and clear, and they seem real to the person experiencing them. Frequently auditory, they can also be visual, olfactory, or somatosensory.

Auditory hallucinations are often accusatory voices. These voices may tell a person with schizophrenia that they are evil or inept, or they may command the person to do dangerous things. Sometimes the person hears a cacophony of sounds with voices intermingled.

The cause of hallucinations remains unclear. Neuroimaging studies suggest that hallucinations are associated with activation in areas of the cortex that process external sensory stimuli. For example, auditory hallucinations accompany increased activation in brain areas that are normally activated when people engage in inner speech (Kühn & Gallinat, 2012). This finding has led to speculation that auditory hallucinations might be caused by a difficulty in distinguishing normal inner speech (the type we all engage in) from external sounds. Recent research indicates that those with schizophrenia may be likely to have structural abnormalities in the auditory cortex (Mørch-Johnsen et al., 2017).

disorganized speech Incoherent speech patterns that involve frequently changing topics and saying strange or inappropriate things.

disorganized behavior Acting in strange or unusual ways, including strange movement of limbs, bizarre speech, and inappropriate self-care, such as failing to dress properly or bathe.

DISORGANIZED SPEECH Another key positive symptom of schizophrenia is **disorganized speech**. It is disorganized in the sense that it is incoherent, failing to follow a normal conversational or even grammatical structure. A person with schizophrenia may respond to questions with tangential or irrelevant information. It is very difficult to follow what those with schizophrenia are talking about because they demonstrate a *loosening of associations* and frequently change topics. These shifts make it difficult or impossible for a listener to follow the speaker's train of thought, as in this excerpt:

> They're destroying too many cattle and oil just to make soap. If we need soap when you can jump into a pool of water, and then when you go to buy your gasoline, my folks always thought they could get pop, but the best thing to get is motor oil, and money. May as well go there and trade in some pop caps and, uh, tires, and tractors to car garages, so they can pull cars away from wrecks, is what I believed in. (Andreasen, 1984, p. 115)

In more extreme cases, speech is so disorganized that it is totally incomprehensible, which is described by clinicians as *word salad*. Those with schizophrenia might also display strange and inappropriate emotions while talking. Such strange speaking patterns make it very difficult for people with schizophrenia to communicate (Docherty, 2005).

FIGURE 14.20
Disorganized Behavior
The artist Bryan Charnley was diagnosed with schizophrenia. He painted a series of self-portraits as he went off his antipsychotic medication as a way of capturing the experience of schizophrenia. He described himself as "a schizophrene—someone who lived outside of the normal world, separated from a shared reality."

DISORGANIZED BEHAVIOR Another common symptom of schizophrenia is **disorganized behavior**. People with schizophrenia often act strangely, such as displaying unpredictable agitation or childish silliness. People exhibiting this symptom might wear multiple layers of clothing even on hot summer days, walk along muttering to themselves, alternate between anger and laughter, or pace and wring their hands as if extremely worried. They also have poor hygiene, failing to bathe or change clothes regularly. They have problems performing many activities that are necessary for daily living. Disorganized behavior can be isolating and distressing for people with schizophrenia (**FIGURE 14.20**).

Sometimes those with schizophrenia display *catatonic behavior*, where they show a decrease in responsiveness to the environment. For example, they might remain immobilized in one position for hours. Catatonic features can also include a rigid, masklike facial expression with eyes staring into the distance. In addition, people exhibiting catatonic behavior might mindlessly repeat words they hear, which is called *echolalia*.

NEGATIVE SYMPTOMS A number of behavioral deficits or reductions in some feelings or behaviors, called **negative symptoms**, associated with schizophrenia result in patients' becoming isolated and withdrawn (Fusar-Poli et al., 2015). Those with negative symptoms often avoid eye contact and seem apathetic. People with this symptom do not express emotion even when discussing emotional subjects (Üçok & Ergül, 2014). Their speech is slowed, they say less than normal, and they use a monotonous tone of voice. Their speech may be characterized by long pauses before answering, failure to respond to a question, or inability to complete an utterance after initiating it. There is often a similar reduction in motor behavior: Patients' movements may be slowed and their overall amount of movement reduced, with little initiation of behavior and no interest in social participation. Negative symptoms are more common in men than in women (Mendrek & Mancini-Marïe, 2016). These symptoms, though less dramatic than delusions and hallucinations, can be equally serious and are associated with a poorer prognosis.

negative symptoms Symptoms of schizophrenia that are marked by deficits in functioning, such as apathy, lack of emotion, and slowed speech and movement.

Although the positive symptoms of schizophrenia (delusions, hallucinations, and disorganized speech and behavior) can be dramatically reduced or eliminated with antipsychotic medications, the negative symptoms often persist. Because negative symptoms are more resistant to medications, researchers have speculated that positive and negative symptoms have different biological causes. These apparent differences lead some researchers to believe that schizophrenia with negative symptoms is in fact a separate disorder from schizophrenia with positive symptoms (Mucci et al., 2017).

Q **Is disorganized behavior a positive or negative symptom of schizophrenia?**

ANSWER: It is a positive symptom because it involves the presence of dysfunctional features rather than the absence of functional features.

14.10 The Cause of Schizophrenia Involves Biological and Environmental Factors

The causes of schizophrenia are complex and not well understood. However, schizophrenia runs in families and it is clear that genetics plays a role in the development of the disorder (**FIGURE 14.21**). If one twin develops schizophrenia, the likelihood of the other twin's developing it is almost 50 percent if the twins

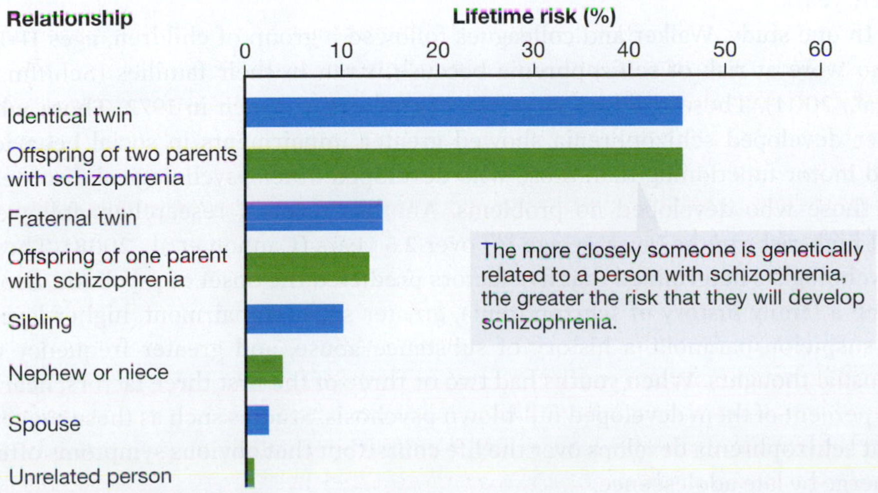

FIGURE 14.21
Genetics and Schizophrenia

are identical but only 7–14 percent if the twins are fraternal. If one parent has schizophrenia, the risk of a child's developing the disease is 13 percent. However, if both parents have schizophrenia, the risk jumps to 40–50 percent (Wray & Gottesman, 2012).

People with schizophrenia have rare mutations of their DNA about 3–4 times more often than healthy individuals do, especially in genes related to brain development and to neurological function (Fromer et al., 2014). No single gene causes schizophrenia. Instead, it is likely that multiple genes or gene mutations contribute in subtle ways to the expression of the disorder (Purcell et al., 2014). More than 100 candidate genes might modestly influence the development of schizophrenia (Schizophrenia Working Group of the Psychiatric Genomics Consortium, 2014).

BRAIN DISORDER Schizophrenia is primarily a brain disorder (Walker et al., 2004). As seen in imaging that shows the structure of the brain, the ventricles are enlarged in people with schizophrenia, and the brain tissue is reduced (see Figure 14.9). Moreover, greater reductions in brain tissue are associated with more-negative outcomes (Mitelman et al., 2005). Longitudinal studies show continued reductions over time (van Haren et al., 2011) that might become progressively worse after middle age (Cropley et al., 2017). This reduction of tissue occurs in many regions of the brain, especially the frontal lobes and medial temporal lobes. Brain activity is also reduced in the frontal and temporal regions in people with schizophrenia (Barch et al., 2003). In addition, people with schizophrenia display altered or reduced connection among brain regions (Sheffield & Barch, 2016).

One possibility is that schizophrenia results from abnormality in neurotransmitters. Since the 1950s, scientists have believed that dopamine may play an important role. Drugs that block dopamine activity decrease symptoms, whereas drugs that increase the activity of dopamine neurons increase symptoms. There is now also evidence that a number of other neurotransmitter systems are involved.

Because schizophrenia is most often diagnosed when people are in their 20s or 30s, it is hard to assess whether these brain abnormalities emerge earlier in life. There is evidence that some neurological signs of schizophrenia can be observed long before the disorder is diagnosed. Elaine Walker and colleagues (2004) have analyzed home movies taken by parents whose children later developed schizophrenia. Compared with their siblings, those who developed the disorder displayed unusual social behaviors, more-severe negative emotions, and motor disturbances. All of these differences often went unnoticed during the children's early years.

In one study, Walker and colleagues followed a group of children, ages 11–13, who were at risk of schizophrenia because it ran in their families (Schiffman et al., 2004). These children were videotaped eating lunch in 1972. Those who later developed schizophrenia showed greater impairments in social behavior and motor functioning than those who developed other psychological disorders or those who developed no problems. Another team of researchers followed 291 high-risk youths (average age 16) over 2.5 years (Cannon et al., 2008). These psychologists determined that five factors predicted the onset of psychotic disorders: a family history of schizophrenia, greater social impairment, higher levels of suspicion/paranoia, a history of substance abuse, and greater frequency of unusual thoughts. When youths had two or three of the first three factors, nearly 80 percent of them developed full-blown psychosis. Studies such as these suggest that schizophrenia develops over the life course but that obvious symptoms often emerge by late adolescence.

ENVIRONMENTAL FACTORS Although schizophrenia has a strong genetic component, genes do not account fully for the onset and severity of the disorder. Environmental stress and gene–environment interactions are also at work. One study looked at adopted children whose biological mothers were diagnosed with schizophrenia (Tienari et al., 1990, 1994). None of the children from adoptive families without dysfunction became psychotic. However, among dysfunctional adoptive families, 11 percent of the children became psychotic and 41 percent had severe psychological disorders. More generally, growing up in a dysfunctional family may increase the risk of developing schizophrenia for those who are genetically at risk (Tienari et al., 2004; Walder et al., 2014; **FIGURE 14.22**).

For those with genetic vulnerability, many factors have been identified that might increase the likelihood of developing schizophrenia (Davis et al., 2016). For instance, there is a wide variety of evidence that heavy cannabis use during adolescence produces a greater risk of developing psychosis (Manrique-Garcia et al., 2012). Some researchers have theorized that the increased stress of urban environments can trigger the onset of the disorder, since being born or raised in an urban area approximately doubles the risk of developing schizophrenia later in life (Torrey, 1999). Others have speculated that some kind of *schizovirus* exists. If so, the close quarters of a big city increase the likelihood of the virus spreading. In support of the virus hypothesis, some researchers have reported finding antibodies in the blood of people with schizophrenia that are not found in those without the disorder (Waltrip et al., 1997). Indeed, there is now strong evidence that maternal inflammation, such as from a virus, plays a significant role in schizophrenia (Brown & Derkits, 2009; Canetta et al., 2014). During the second

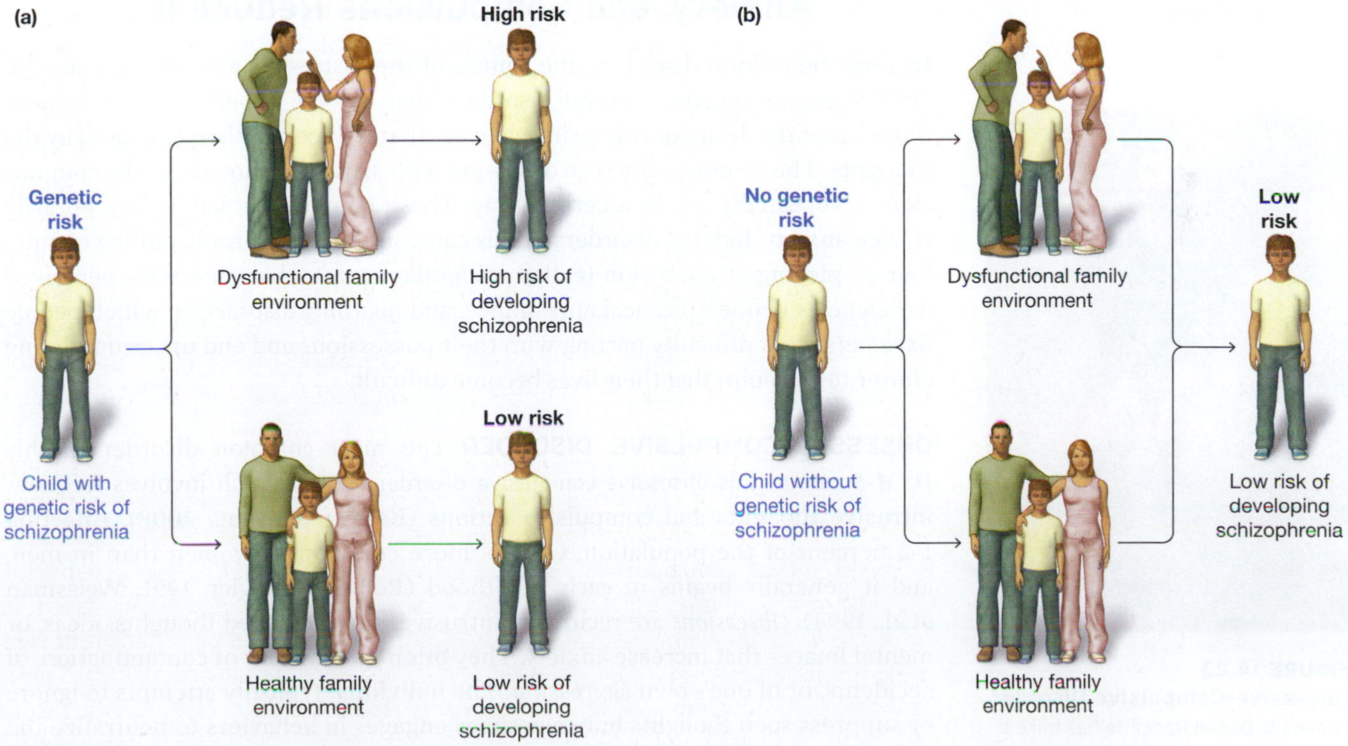

FIGURE 14.22

Effects of Biology and Environment on Schizophrenia

(a) A child who has a genetic risk for schizophrenia and is raised in a dysfunctional family environment will have a high risk of developing schizophrenia. **(b)** By contrast, a child who has no genetic risk for schizophrenia will have a low risk of developing the disorder whether raised in a dysfunctional family environment or a healthy family environment.

trimester of pregnancy, when a great deal of fetal brain development occurs, trauma or pathogens, such as a viral infection, can interfere with the developing organization of brain regions.

Q How does schizophrenia fit the diathesis-stress model of psychopathology?

ANSWER: People who both have a diathesis and who experience environmental stress are most likely to develop schizophrenia.

Which Disorders Involve Maladaptive Behavior?

Learning Objectives

- Understand the various causes of obsessive-compulsive disorder.
- Discuss common eating disorders and their causes.
- Identify physiological and psychological factors associated with addiction.

In many disorders, the main features that cause impairments in daily functioning are patterns of behavior. The behavior can range from repetitive behaviors to excessive intake of food to exposure to dangerous substances. In these disorders, maladaptive behaviors become stuck in a reward learning cycle. People with these disorders have discovered that certain behavior can reduce emotional distress. Through reinforcement learning, the behaviors come to be triggered by emotional distress because they successfully reduce it. These disorders can be difficult to treat because behaviors serve a purpose for the individual, even if they might be maladaptive in other ways.

14.11 Unwanted and Intrusive Thoughts Cause Anxiety, and Compulsions Reduce It

In some behavioral disorders, the source of the distress is a recurring thought. *DSM-5* groups together several disorders that involve experiencing unwanted thoughts or the desire to engage in behaviors that reduce the distress caused by the thoughts. The commonality is an obsession with an idea or thought or the compulsion to repeatedly act in a certain way. These compulsive actions temporarily reduce anxiety. Related disorders in this category include chronic pulling at one's hair or picking at one's skin (called *trichotillomania*), obsession with perceived deficiencies in one's physical appearance, and *hoarding disorder*, in which people have persistent difficulty parting with their possessions and end up accumulating clutter to the point that their lives become difficult.

obsessive-compulsive disorder (OCD) A disorder characterized by frequent intrusive thoughts and compulsive actions.

OBSESSIVE-COMPULSIVE DISORDER The most common disorder in this *DSM-5* category is **obsessive-compulsive disorder (OCD)**, which involves frequent intrusive thoughts and compulsive actions (Kessler & Wang, 2008). Affecting 1–2 percent of the population, OCD is more common in women than in men, and it generally begins in early adulthood (Robins & Regier, 1991; Weissman et al., 1994). *Obsessions* are recurrent, intrusive, and unwanted thoughts, ideas, or mental images that increase anxiety. They often include fear of contamination, of accidents, or of one's own aggression. The individual typically attempts to ignore or suppress such thoughts but sometimes engages in behaviors to neutralize the obsessions and reduce the emotional distress they cause (**FIGURE 14.23**).

FIGURE 14.23
Obsessive-Compulsive Disorder
The actor Daniel Radcliffe has talked openly about his experience with OCD as a child. His symptoms diminished after he was diagnosed and referred to a therapist, and in public statements he has encouraged people with OCD or other mental disorders to seek therapy.

Compulsions are particular acts that people with OCD feel driven to perform over and over to reduce anxiety. The most common compulsive behaviors are cleaning, checking, and counting. For instance, a person might continually check to make sure a door is locked because of an obsession that their home might be invaded, or a person might engage in superstitious counting to protect against accidents, such as counting the number of telephone poles while driving. The compulsive behavior or mental act, such as counting, is aimed at preventing or reducing anxiety or preventing something dreadful from happening.

Not all people with OCD engage in compulsive behaviors. One form of OCD is called *pure obsession* because the obsessive thoughts are not accompanied by an associated behavior. However, the reward cycle that maintains OCD exists even in pure obsession. Typically a second thought or mental ritual, such as mental arithmetic, is used to reduce the anxiety or distress caused by the obsession.

Those with OCD anticipate catastrophe and loss of control. However, as opposed to those with anxiety disorders—who fear what might happen to them—those with OCD fear what they might do or might have done. Checking is one way to calm the anxiety.

"Is the Itsy Bitsy Spider obsessive-compulsive?"

CAUSES OF OBSESSIVE-COMPULSIVE DISORDER A paradoxical aspect of OCD is that people are aware that their obsessions and compulsions are irrational, yet they are unable to stop them. One explanation is that the disorder results from conditioning. In the person with OCD, anxiety is somehow paired with a specific event, probably through classical conditioning. As a result, the person engages in behavior that reduces anxiety and therefore is reinforced through operant conditioning (**FIGURE 14.24**). This reduction of anxiety is reinforcing and increases the person's chance of engaging in that behavior again.

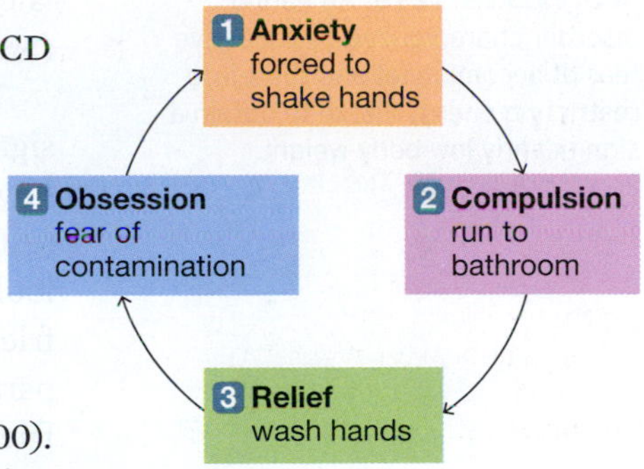

FIGURE 14.24
OCD Cycle
This flowchart illustrates the operations of conditioning for the example given in the text. Classical conditioning (step 1) and operant conditioning (steps 2 and 3) reinforce behavior. Continued reinforcement may contribute to a person's developing OCD (step 4).

There is also good evidence that the etiology of OCD is in part genetic (Crowe, 2000). Indeed, various behavioral genetics methods, such as twin studies, have shown that OCD runs in families. The specific mechanism has not been identified, but the OCD-related genes appear to control the neurotransmitter glutamate (Rajendram et al., 2017), which is the major excitatory transmitter in the brain, causing increased neural firing.

There is also growing evidence that OCD can be triggered by environmental factors. In particular, a streptococcal infection apparently can cause a severe form of OCD in some young children. Originally identified in 1998 by Susan Swedo and her colleagues at the National Institute of Mental Health, this syndrome strikes virtually overnight. The affected children suddenly display odd symptoms of OCD, such as engaging in repetitive behaviors, developing irrational fears and obsessions, and having facial tics. Researchers have speculated that the symptoms of this form of OCD are caused by an autoimmune response that damages an area of the brain involved in reward learning (Snider & Swedo, 2004). Treatments that enhance the immune system have been found to diminish the symptoms of this form of OCD in children. Why some children are susceptible to this autoimmune response is unknown.

Q How do obsessions and compulsions relate to anxiety for people with OCD?

ANSWER: Obsessions increase anxiety and trigger compulsive responses that temporarily reduce anxiety.

14.12 Thoughts and Feelings About Food and Body Image Are Disrupted in Eating Disorders

Many people diet because of the strong stigma against heavier bodies in most countries around the world (Tomiyama et al., 2018). Ironically, attempts to lose weight cause stress, triggering a series of physiological changes that can increase

FIGURE 14.25
Eating Disorders
The photographer Lene Marie Fossen had anorexia nervosa beginning at age 10. Her self-portraits, such as this one, depicted her experience of the disorder.

weight further (Tomiyama, 2019). Over time, chronic dieters tend to feel helpless and depressed. Some eventually engage in more extreme maladaptive behaviors to lose weight, such as taking drugs, fasting, exercising excessively, or purging. For a vulnerable individual, chronic dieting may promote the development of a clinical eating disorder. Eating disorders affect all types of people, though they are diagnosed more frequently in women. It is likely that eating disorders are underestimated among men (Raevuori et al., 2014). The three most common eating disorders are anorexia nervosa, bulimia nervosa, and binge-eating disorder.

anorexia nervosa An eating disorder characterized by excessive fear of becoming fat and therefore restricting energy intake to obtain a significantly low body weight.

ANOREXIA NERVOSA Individuals with **anorexia nervosa** have an excessive fear of becoming fat and severely restrict how much they eat (**FIGURE 14.25**). This reduction in energy intake leads to an unhealthy body weight. Anorexia most often begins in early adolescence. Although many adolescents strive to be thin, fewer than 1 in 100 meet the clinical criteria of anorexia nervosa as described by the *DSM-5*. These criteria include both objective measures of thinness and psychological characteristics that indicate an abnormal obsession with body weight. There is evidence that adolescent boys and girls are equally likely to develop anorexia (Swanson et al., 2011).

Those who have anorexia nervosa fear becoming fat even though they are at a significantly low weight. Issues of food and weight pervade their lives, controlling how they view themselves and how they view the world. Initially, the results of self-imposed starvation may draw favorable comments from others, such as "You look so thin you could be a fashion model." These comments might come from friends who are also influenced by social messages that being thin is an important part of being attractive. But as people with anorexia become emaciated, family and friends usually become concerned. In many cases, medical attention is required to prevent death from starvation. This dangerous disorder causes many serious health problems, in particular a loss of bone density, and about 15–20 percent of those with anorexia eventually die from the disorder—they literally starve themselves to death (American Psychiatric Association, 2000b).

bulimia nervosa An eating disorder characterized by the alternation of dieting, binge eating, and purging (self-induced vomiting).

BULIMIA NERVOSA Individuals with **bulimia nervosa** alternate between dieting, binge eating, and purging (self-induced vomiting) or other harmful compensatory behaviors, such as abusing laxatives or exercising compulsively. Bulimia often develops during late adolescence. Approximately 1–2 percent of women in high school and college meet the criteria for bulimia nervosa. Bulimia is much more frequently diagnosed in women than in men (Klump et al., 2017).

People with bulimia are caught in a vicious cycle: In an effort to cope with negative emotions or other stressors, they eat large quantities of food in a short amount of time. This eating leads them to feel concerned that they may gain weight, and they then engage in one or more compensatory purging behaviors. This behavior tends to occur secretly, so even close friends and family members of people with bulimia are often unaware of their actions. Bulimia is associated with serious health problems, including dental and cardiac disorders (Keel & Mitchell, 1997).

binge-eating disorder An eating disorder characterized by binge eating that causes significant distress.

BINGE-EATING DISORDER A disorder similar to bulimia is **binge-eating disorder**. According to *DSM-5*, people with the disorder engage in binge eating at least once a week, but they do not purge. These individuals often eat very quickly, even when they are not hungry. Those with binge-eating disorder often experience feelings of guilt and embarrassment, and they may binge-eat alone to hide the behavior. Some but not all people with binge-eating disorder are overweight or obese. Although bulimia and binge-eating disorder share many common features—differing most notably in that only people with bulimia purge—they are classified in *DSM-5* as distinct disorders.

Eating disorders tend to run in families. Like other forms of psychopathology, these disorders are due partly to genetics. The incidence of eating disorders in the United States increased up to the 1980s (Keel et al., 2007). This increase suggests that when people have genetic predispositions for eating disorders, they will tend to develop the disorders if they live in societies with an abundance of food. There are large cultural variations in the incidence of bulimia, indicating that this disorder might be determined to a great degree by cultural factors. Anorexia nervosa is prevalent in all societies that have abundant food.

There are many effective treatments for eating disorders. Indeed, the majority of people with eating disorders are symptom-free five years after diagnosis (Keel & Brown, 2010). Most college campuses have counseling centers with expertise in helping people with these disorders.

Q **What is purging and of which eating disorder is it most characteristic?**

ANSWER: Purging is self-induced vomiting used to offset the effects of binge eating. It is characteristic of bulimia nervosa.

14.13 Addiction Has Physical and Psychological Aspects

People use drugs for various medical and recreational purposes, such as alleviating pain or exploring different mental states. However, drug use can sometimes be maladaptive. **Addiction** is defined as drug use that persists despite its negative consequences. Addiction itself is not a *DSM*-5 disorder. Instead, psychologists currently categorize addiction across several substance use disorders, including *alcohol use disorder*, *cannabis use disorder*, *opioid use disorder*, and so forth. The criteria for a person to be diagnosed with a substance use disorder vary slightly depending on the drug. However, most substance use disorders involve taking the substance longer than intended, being unable to stop using it despite attempts to quit, craving the substance, and experiencing impairments in daily life because of the substance.

addiction A behavioral disorder where use of a substance continues despite negative consequences and a desire to quit.

Two prominent negative consequences of addiction are tolerance and withdrawal. Physical dependence on a drug is a physiological state associated with *tolerance*, in which a person needs to consume more of a particular substance to achieve the same subjective effect. Failing to ingest the substance leads to symptoms of *withdrawal*, a physiological and psychological state characterized by feelings of anxiety, tension, and cravings for the addictive substance. The physical symptoms of withdrawal vary widely from drug to drug and from individual to individual, but they often include nausea, chills, body aches, and tremors. A person can be psychologically dependent on a drug, however, without showing tolerance or withdrawal. This section focuses on addiction to substances that alter consciousness, but people can also become psychologically dependent on behaviors, such as shopping or gambling.

CAUSES OF ADDICTION About 8–10 percent of people age 12 or older are addicted to alcohol or other drugs (Volkow et al., 2016). Dopamine activity in the limbic system, particularly the nucleus accumbens (discussed in Chapter 3), appears to be a factor in addiction because this activity underlies the *wanting* properties of taking drugs (Baumgartner et al., 2020). Other brain regions that are

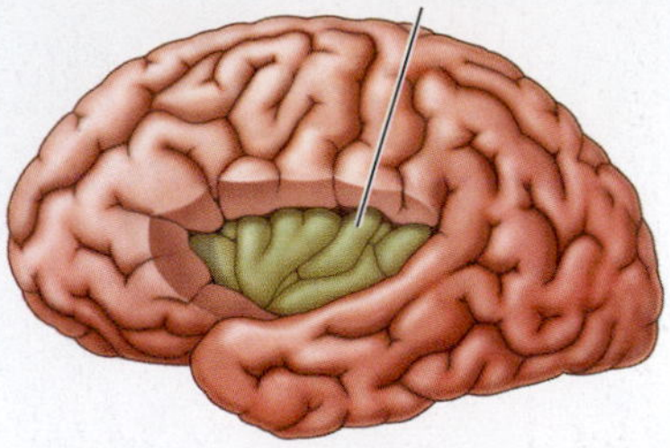

FIGURE 14.26
Insula
The insula in the brain appears to play a role in craving, or an urge to use a substance.

important for addiction include the prefrontal cortex, amygdala, thalamus, and hippocampus (Koob & Volkow, 2010).

A brain region called the insula also seems to be important for the craving component of addiction (Goldstein et al., 2009; **FIGURE 14.26**). Patients with insula damage report that immediately after being injured, they quit smoking easily. In fact, they no longer experience conscious urges to smoke. One patient who had a stroke to his left insula commented that he quit smoking because his "body forgot the urge to smoke" (Naqvi et al., 2007, p. 534).

Addiction appears to develop in stages, and this progression is due to changes in the brain that accompany drug use (Volkow et al., 2016). For most people, initial drug use is associated with euphoria that the person looks forward to enjoying on some occasions. However, tolerance leads people to need to use more and more of the drug, and for some people, the drug starts to lose its ability to provide pleasure. Simultaneously, the person starts desiring the drug more and more often to escape the negative feelings of withdrawal, which can be excruciating. The desire to obtain the drug and avoid withdrawal becomes all-encompassing.

The loss of euphoria that comes from addiction occurs because the brain reward system becomes less sensitive, both to drug-related and non-drug-related rewards (Hyatt et al., 2012). As a consequence, people who are addicted to drugs find them less pleasurable, and they fail to enjoy other activities they used to enjoy, such as spending time with others or working (Koob & Mason, 2016). Thus, people with addictions may neglect their friends and family members in their pursuit of satisfying their obsession with the drug to which they are addicted. People who use substances often cannot understand why they continue to take the drug even though it causes them problems and is no longer as pleasurable as when they started (Volkow et al., 2016). Feeling bad about this situation, unfortunately, further compels them to use drugs. Although the drugs are not as enjoyable as before, at least they provide fleeting pleasure and escape from withdrawal and the feelings of shame and guilt often associated with addiction.

ADDICTION VULNERABILITY Some adolescents are especially likely to experiment with illegal drugs and to abuse alcohol. Adolescents high in sensation seeking (a personality trait that involves attraction to novelty and risk-taking) are more likely to associate with deviant peer groups and to use alcohol, tobacco, and drugs (Patrick & Schulenberg, 2014; Wills et al., 1995). These adolescents tend to have poor relationships with their parents, which in turn promote the adolescents' association with deviant peer groups.

Only about 5–10 percent of those who use drugs become addicted. Indeed, more than 90 million Americans have experimented with illicit drugs, yet most of them use drugs only occasionally or try them for a while and then give them up. The fact that the same level of use leads to addiction for some people and not others points to genetic components of addiction, especially for alcoholism, but little direct evidence points to a *single* "alcoholism" or "addiction" gene. Rather, what people inherit is a cluster of characteristics (Volkow & Muenke, 2012). These inherited risk factors might include personality traits such as risk-taking and impulsivity, a reduced concern about personal harm, a nervous system chronically low in arousal, or a predisposition to finding chemical substances pleasurable. Such factors may make some people more likely to explore drugs and enjoy them.

Social learning theorists have sought to account for the initiation of drug or alcohol use among children or adolescents. They emphasize the roles of parents, the mass media, and peers, including self-identification with high-risk groups (e.g., "stoners" or "druggies"). As discussed in Chapter 9, adolescence is a time of social reorientation away from family and toward friends. It is important and adaptive for teenagers to learn to fit in and earn acceptance in peer groups, even those that society perceives as deviant. Children also imitate the behavior of role models, especially those they admire or with whom they identify. For example, children whose parents smoke tend to have positive attitudes about smoking and begin smoking early (Rowe et al., 1996).

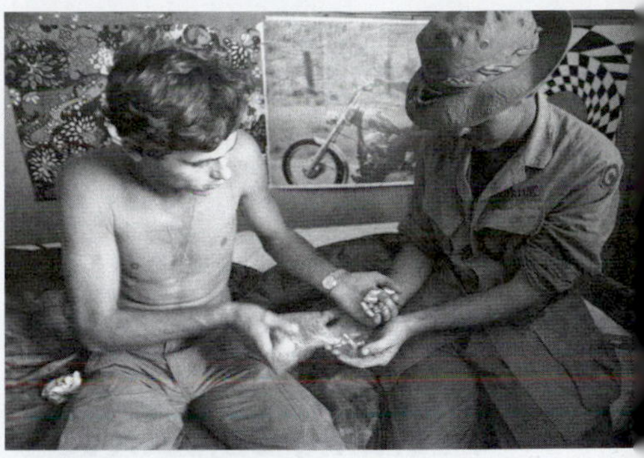

FIGURE 14.27
Drug Use in Context
Many U.S. soldiers who abused drugs while abroad during the Vietnam War were able to quit when returning home. Here, two soldiers exchange vials of heroin in Quang Tri Province, South Vietnam, July 1971.

ADDICTION IN CONTEXT Context is important for understanding addiction. For example, in the late 1960s, drug abuse among U.S. soldiers, including the use of narcotics such as heroin and opium, appeared to be epidemic. The widespread drug use was not surprising. It was a time of youthful drug experimentation, soldiers in Vietnam had easy access to various drugs, and drugs helped the soldiers cope temporarily with fear, depression, homesickness, boredom, and the repressiveness of army regulations (**FIGURE 14.27**). The military commanders mostly ignored drug use among soldiers in an attempt to bolster morale during a period of prolonged conflict.

Beginning in 1971, the military began mandatory drug testing of soldiers to identify and detoxify drug users before they returned to the United States. Amid speculation that a flood of soldiers returning from Vietnam with addictions would swamp treatment facilities back home, the White House asked a team of behavioral scientists to study a group of returning soldiers and assess the extent of the addiction problem. Led by the behavioral epidemiologist Lee Robins, the research team examined a random sample of 898 soldiers who were leaving Vietnam in September 1971.

Robins and her colleagues found extremely high levels of drug use among the soldiers (Robins et al., 1975). More than 90 percent reported drinking alcohol, nearly three quarters smoked marijuana, and nearly half used narcotics such as heroin, morphine, and opium. About half of the soldiers who used narcotics either had symptoms of addiction or reported believing they would be unable to give up their drug habits. The team's findings suggested that approximately 1 soldier in 5 returning from Vietnam was addicted to one or more substances. Given the prevailing view that addiction was a biological disorder with a low rate of recovery, these results indicated that tens of thousands of heroin users would soon be inundating the United States. But that did not happen.

Robins and her colleagues examined drug use among the soldiers after they returned to the United States. Of those who were apparently addicted to narcotics in Vietnam, only half sought out drugs when they returned to the States, and fewer still maintained their narcotic addictions. Approximately 95 percent of the soldiers who used heroin no longer used drugs within months of their return—an astonishing quit rate considering that the success rate of the best treatments is typically only 20–30 percent. A long-term follow-up study conducted in the early 1990s confirmed that only a handful of those who were addicted to substances in Vietnam remained so.

Why did coming home help the soldiers recover? In the United States, they likely did not have the same motivations or opportunities for taking the drugs as they did in Vietnam. The cues that triggered drug craving were removed. It is worth noting that the opioids used by soldiers in Vietnam were also far less potent than the synthetic drugs that are causing the current opioid epidemic. Still, an important lesson from this case study is that addiction is created and maintained within a specific environment. Knowing drugs' physical actions in the brain may give us insights into addiction's biology, but that information fails to account for how these biological impulses can be overcome by other motivations.

Q **What is the current understanding of the influence of genes on alcohol addiction?**

ANSWER: No single gene is responsible for alcohol addiction, but certain inherited characteristics, such as sensitivity to reward and impulsivity, can increase vulnerability to addiction.

Which Disorders Are Linked to Trauma?

Learning Objectives

- Understand the development of posttraumatic stress disorders.
- Describe dissociative amnesia and dissociative fugue.
- Discuss the controversy regarding dissociative identity disorder.
- Identify the symptoms and possible causes of borderline personality disorder.

Experiences in both childhood and adulthood can have lasting effects throughout life in many ways. Events that are particularly distressing, severe, or unexpected can alter how people view the world and relate to others. This section describes several disorders that *DSM-5* recognizes as being connected to traumatic events.

14.14 Trauma Is a Prolonged Response to an Emotional Event

trauma A prolonged psychological and physiological response to a distressing event, often one that profoundly violates the person's beliefs about the world.

Humans have evolved the capacity to deal with many kinds of stress. However, some stressors can overwhelm our ability to respond. In such cases, the physical and mental responses that are usually adaptive, such as a strong fear response and alterations to memory, endure well past the point that those responses are helpful. **Trauma** is a prolonged psychological and physiological response to a distressing event, often one that profoundly violates the person's beliefs about the world. Events such as the threat of death or serious injury, the loss of a loved one, or profound harm or betrayal by a trusted person or institution can be traumatic events.

There is considerable variability in how people experience distressing events. Not every encounter with danger, separation, or even death is traumatic. Trauma is defined by the subjective response to an event and not the event itself. There are times when a person can experience an event that seems severe, such as a car crash involving a fatality, and not experience trauma. Other times, a person might have a traumatic response to an event that does not seem as severe to observers, such as being passed over for a promotion because of discrimination.

Distressing events during childhood such as abuse and neglect are particularly likely to lead to trauma and other long-term effects (McLaughlin & Lambert, 2017). Children who are exposed to repeated stressors are more likely to develop psychopathology as adults and have altered stress responses (Essex et al., 2011). However, as with adults, not all stressful experiences will produce the lingering effects associated with trauma. Several *protective factors* can buffer children from the harmful effects of early life stress, including warm, nurturing parenting and positive memories of other childhood experiences (Narayan et al., 2019).

POSTTRAUMATIC STRESS DISORDER Trauma differs from other stress responses in the way the events are remembered and relived. People with trauma often experience unwanted and intrusive thoughts about the events. The *DSM-5* category *trauma- and stressor-related disorders* (see Table 14.1) describes disorders in which a person has trouble overcoming exposure to a highly stressful event. For example, a person who cries continually, has difficulty studying, and avoids social settings six months after a romantic breakup may have an *adjustment disorder*. This person is having difficulty adjusting to the stressor.

When people suffer severe stress or emotional trauma—such as having a serious accident, experiencing sexual assault, fighting in active combat, or surviving a natural disaster—they often have negative reactions long after the danger has passed. In severe cases, people develop **posttraumatic stress disorder (PTSD)**, a psychological disorder that involves frequent and recurring unwanted thoughts related to the trauma, including nightmares, intrusive memories, and flashbacks. People with PTSD often try to avoid situations or stimuli that remind them of their trauma. The lifetime prevalence of PTSD is around 7 percent, though women are more likely to develop the disorder (Kessler et al., 2005b).

posttraumatic stress disorder (PTSD) A disorder that involves frequent nightmares, intrusive thoughts, and flashbacks related to an earlier trauma.

An opportunity to study susceptibility to PTSD came about because of a tragedy at Northern Illinois University in 2008. On the campus, in front of many observers, a lone gunman murdered 5 people and wounded 21. Among a sample of female students, those with certain genetic markers related to serotonin functioning were much more likely to show PTSD symptoms in the weeks after the shooting (Mercer et al., 2011). This finding suggests that some individuals may be more at risk than others for developing PTSD after exposure to a stressful event.

Those with PTSD often have chronic tension, anxiety, and health problems, and they may experience memory and attention problems in their daily lives. PTSD involves an unusual problem in memory: the inability to forget. PTSD is associated with an attentional bias, such that people with PTSD are hypervigilant to stimuli associated with their traumatic events. For instance, soldiers with combat-induced PTSD show increased physiological responsiveness to pictures of troops, sounds of gunfire, and even words associated with combat. Exposure to stimuli associated with past trauma leads to activation of the amygdala (Shin et al., 2006). It is as if the severe emotional event is "overconsolidated," or burned into memory (see Chapter 7 for a discussion of consolidation of memory). PTSD results in abnormalities in the various brain processes that normally lead to extinction in fear learning (Marin et al., 2016).

Q How can the same event become traumatic for some people but not others?

ANSWER: People differ in their subjective experience of stress, which partially depends on their interpretation of an event, their level of diathesis (vulnerability), and the presence of protective factors.

14.15 Dissociative Disorders Are Disruptions in Memory, Awareness, and Identity

As noted in Chapter 5, we sometimes get lost in our thoughts or daydreams, even to the point of losing track of what is going on around us. Many of us have had the experience of forgetting what we are doing while in the middle of an action ("Why was I headed to the kitchen?"). When we wake up in an unfamiliar location, we may momentarily be disoriented and not know where we are. In other words, our thoughts and experiences can become dissociated, or split, from the external world.

Dissociative disorders are extreme versions of this phenomenon. These disorders involve disruptions of identity, memory, or conscious awareness (Spiegel et al., 2013). Dissociative disorders are thought to be a functional response to an extremely distressing or traumatic event. That is, the dissociative disorder serves a self-protective purpose by splitting the event off from the rest of the person's life and identity. There is some evidence that people with dissociative disorders are also prone to PTSD (Cardeña & Carlson, 2011).

dissociative disorders Disorders that involve disruptions of identity, of memory, or of conscious awareness.

FIGURE 14.28
Dissociative Fugue
Jeff Ingram, pictured here, experienced an episode of dissociative fugue. Though he did not remember his three-year relationship with his fiancée (here, seated next to him), the two eventually married.

DISSOCIATIVE AMNESIA In *dissociative amnesia,* a person forgets that an event happened or loses awareness of a substantial block of time. A person with this disorder may suddenly lose memory for personal facts, including their identity and place of residence. These memory failures cannot be accounted for by ordinary forgetting (such as momentarily forgetting where you parked your car) or by the effects of drugs or alcohol.

Consider the case of Dorothy Joudrie, from Calgary, Canada. In 1995, after suffering years of physical abuse from her husband, Joudrie shot him six times. Her husband survived, and he described her behavior during the shooting as very calm, as if she were detached from what she was doing. When the police arrived, however, Joudrie was extremely distraught. She had no memory of the shooting and told the police that she simply found her husband shot and lying on the garage floor, at which time she called for help. Joudrie was found not criminally responsible for her actions because of her dissociative state (Butcher et al., 2007).

DISSOCIATIVE FUGUE The rarest and most extreme form of dissociative amnesia is *dissociative fugue.* The disorder involves a loss of identity. In addition, it involves travel to another location (the French word *fugue* means "flight") and sometimes the assumption of a new identity. The fugue state often ends suddenly, with the person unsure how they ended up in unfamiliar surroundings. Typically, the person does not remember events that occurred during the fugue state.

Consider the case of Jeff Ingram, who developed retrograde amnesia, a form of dissociative amnesia, after leaving his home in Washington State. He arrived in Denver, Colorado, four days later with no memory of his previous life. He was recognized two months later, when he appeared on the news pleading for help from anyone who knew who he was, and his fiancée brought him home to Washington State (**FIGURE 14.28**). Ingram did not recognize his fiancée's face, but she felt familiar to him, as did his home.

THE CONTROVERSY OVER DISSOCIATIVE IDENTITY DISORDER The *DSM-5* currently contains a disorder known as *dissociative identity disorder* (DID). This disorder used to be known as *multiple personality disorder* and is described as the occurrence of two or more distinct identities in the same individual, along with memory gaps in which the person does not recall everyday events. Many cases of DID can be considered a specific kind of dissociative fugue where a person acts differently enough in the fugue state to seem to be a different person. In extreme cases, individual people can manifest dozens of different personas, each with different memories, preferences, and personalities.

Most people diagnosed with DID report being severely abused as children. According to the most common theory of DID, children cope with abuse by entering a trancelike state in which they dissociate their mental states from their physical bodies. With repeated abuse, this dissociated state takes on its own identity. Different identities develop to deal with different traumas. Often the identities have periods of amnesia, and sometimes only one identity is aware of the others. Indeed, diagnosis often occurs only when a person has difficulty accounting for large chunks of the day. The separate identities can differ substantially, such as in gender identity, sexual orientation, age, language spoken, interests, physiological profiles, and patterns of brain activation (Reinders et al., 2003).

Despite this evidence, many researchers remain skeptical about whether DID is a distinct psychological disorder (Kihlstrom, 2005). The symptoms and treatments of DID are similar to those of other trauma disorders, but a diagnosis of DID can be very stigmatizing. Being labeled as having DID can create professional and personal barriers that a diagnosis of PTSD with some dissociation does not. Moreover, some people may have ulterior motives for claiming DID, such as denying responsibility for their behavior after being accused of a crime.

Ultimately, how can we know whether a diagnosis of DID is valid? As mentioned earlier, there is rarely an objective test for diagnosing a psychological disorder. Likewise, there is no definitive boundary between related disorders. It can be difficult to tell if a person is faking, has come to believe what a therapist said, or has DID versus dissociative fugue. Individuals who fake DID tend to report well-publicized symptoms of the disorder but neglect to mention the more subtle symptoms that are extremely common, such as major depressive episodes or PTSD (American Psychiatric Association, 2013; Boysen & VanBergen, 2014).

Q What is the difference between dissociative amnesia and dissociative fugue?

ANSWER: Dissociative amnesia is the loss of memory for a specific event or for a period of time. Dissociative fugue involves a complete loss of identity and travel to a new location.

14.16 Borderline Personality Disorder Is Marked by Instability in Self-Image and Relationships

Though formally categorized with personality disorders (see the next section), **borderline personality disorder** is often associated with interpersonal trauma in childhood. Some researchers have argued that the disorder is best considered a form of complex PTSD rather than a personality disorder (Jowett et al., 2020). The diagnosis and definition of borderline personality disorder are likely to shift in forthcoming editions of the *DSM* for this reason. As presented in **TABLE 14.8**, the wide variety of clinical features of this disorder reflects its complexity. Approximately 1–2 percent of adults meet the criteria for borderline personality disorder, and the disorder is more than twice as common in women as in men (Lenzenweger et al., 2007).

borderline personality disorder
A personality disorder characterized by disturbances in identity, in affect, and in impulse control.

Table 14.8 *DSM-5* **Diagnostic Criteria of Borderline Personality Disorder**

A pervasive pattern of instability of interpersonal relations, self-image, and affects, along with marked impulsivity, beginning by early adulthood and present in a variety of contexts, as indicated by five (or more) of the following:

1. Frantic efforts to avoid real or imagined abandonment
2. A pattern of unstable and intense interpersonal relationships
3. Identity disturbance: markedly and persistently unstable self-image or sense of self
4. Impulsiveness in at least two areas that are potentially self-damaging (e.g., spending, sex, substance abuse, reckless driving, binge eating)
5. Recurrent suicidal behavior, gestures, or threats, or self-mutilating behavior
6. Affective instability due to a marked reactivity of mood, with periods of extreme depression, irritability, or anxiety usually lasting a few hours and only rarely more than a few days
7. Chronic feelings of emptiness
8. Inappropriate intense anger or difficulty controlling anger (e.g., displays of temper, constant anger, recurrent physical fights)
9. Transient, stress-related paranoid thoughts or severe dissociative symptoms

SOURCE: Based on American Psychiatric Association (2013).

Borderline personality disorder is characterized primarily by instability in several domains: sense of self, interpersonal relationships, goals, emotions, and behaviors. People with borderline personality disorder seem to lack a strong sense of self. They cannot tolerate being alone and have an intense fear of abandonment. People with borderline personality disorder are vigilant for signals of rejection by romantic partners, friends, and therapists, and they often react impulsively when they perceive a rupture in a relationship. Threatened or actual self-harm and suicidal behavior are common in borderline personality disorder.

In addition to problems with identity and relationships, people with borderline personality are emotionally unstable (Hazlett, 2016). Episodes of depression, anxiety, anger, irritability, or some combination of these states can last from a few hours to a few days. Shifts from one mood to another usually occur with no obvious precipitating cause. Consider the therapist Molly Layton's description of her patient Vicki:

> She had chronic and debilitating feelings of emptiness and paralyzing numbness, during which she could only crawl under the covers of her bed and hide. On these days, she was sometimes driven to mutilate her thighs with scissors. Although highly accomplished as a medical student and researcher, who had garnered many grants and fellowships, she would sometimes panic and shut down in the middle of a project, creating unbearable pressures on herself to finish the work. While she longed for intimacy and friendship, she was disablingly shy around men. (Layton, 1995, p. 36)

The third hallmark of borderline personality disorder is impulsivity. This characteristic can include sexual promiscuity, physical fighting, and binge eating and purging. As was the case with Vicki, however, self-mutilation is also commonly associated with this disorder. Cutting and burning of the skin are typical, as is a high risk for suicide. Some evidence indicates that those with borderline personality disorder have diminished capacity in the frontal lobes, which normally help control behavior (Salvador et al., 2016).

Evidence for a strong relationship between borderline personality disorder and trauma comes from studies showing that 70–80 percent of those with borderline personality disorder have experienced physical or sexual abuse or witnessed extreme violence (Lieb et al., 2004; Porter et al., 2020). Other theories suggest that people with borderline personality disorder may have had caretakers early in life who did not accept them or who were unreliable or unavailable. This constant rejection and criticism made it difficult for the individuals to learn to regulate emotions and understand emotional reactions to events (Cavicchioli & Maffei, 2020). An alternative hypothesis is that caregivers encouraged dependence, preventing the children in their care from adequately developing a sense of self that is separate from the evaluations of others. As a result, the individuals became overly sensitive to others' reactions, as if their own self-worth depended entirely on others.

Q **In what aspects of life do people with borderline personality disorder experience instability?**

ANSWER: identity, relationships, emotions, and behaviors

What Are Personality Disorders?

As discussed in Chapter 13, personality reflects individuals' unique responses to their environment. Although individuals change somewhat over time, the ways they interact with the world and cope with events are fairly stable by the end of adolescence. Most often, people interact with their environment in ways that express their values and promote their well-being. However, at times people interact with the world in ways that are maladaptive and unresponsive to feedback. When this style of interaction is long-lasting and causes distress and problems in work and in social situations, it becomes a *personality disorder*.

14.17 Personality Disorders Are Maladaptive Ways of Relating to the World

Learning Objectives

- Distinguish between the clusters of personality disorders.
- Understand controversies related to defining personality disorders.
- Identify the symptoms and possible causes of antisocial personality disorder.

DSM-5 divides personality disorders into three clusters, as listed in **TABLE 14.9**. Disorders in the Cluster A group are characterized by odd or eccentric behavior. *Paranoid, schizoid,* and *schizotypal* personality disorders make up this group. People with these disorders are often reclusive and suspicious, and they have difficulty forming personal relationships because of their strange behavior and aloofness. As you might expect, people with personality disorders in this category show some similarities to people with schizophrenia, but their symptoms are less severe.

Table 14.9 Personality Disorders and Associated Characteristics

CLUSTER A: ODD OR ECCENTRIC BEHAVIOR	
Paranoid	Tense, guarded, suspicious; holds grudges
Schizoid	Socially isolated, with restricted emotional expression
Schizotypal	Peculiarities of thought, appearance, and behavior that are disconcerting to others; emotionally detached and isolated
CLUSTER B: DRAMATIC, EMOTIONAL, OR ERRATIC BEHAVIOR	
Histrionic	Seductive behavior; needs immediate gratification and constant reassurance; rapidly changing moods; shallow emotions
Narcissistic	Self-absorbed; expects special treatment and adulation; envious of attention to others
Borderline	Cannot stand to be alone; intense, unstable moods and personal relationships; chronic anger; drug and alcohol abuse
Antisocial	Manipulative, exploitative; dishonest; disloyal; lacking in guilt; habitually breaks social rules; childhood history of such behavior; often in trouble with the law
CLUSTER C: ANXIOUS OR FEARFUL BEHAVIOR	
Avoidant	Easily hurt and embarrassed; few close friends; sticks to routines to avoid new and possibly stressful experiences
Dependent	Wants others to make decisions; needs constant advice and reassurance; fears being abandoned
Obsessive-compulsive	Perfectionistic; overconscientious; indecisive; preoccupied with details; stiff; unable to express affection

SOURCE: Adapted from American Psychiatric Association (2013).

Disorders in the Cluster B group are characterized by dramatic, emotional, or erratic behaviors. *Histrionic*, *narcissistic*, *borderline*, and *antisocial* personality disorders make up this group. Researchers have focused mostly on borderline personality disorder, which was discussed in the previous section, and antisocial personality disorder, which is considered in more detail in a following section.

Disorders in the Cluster C group are characterized by anxious or fearful behavior. *Avoidant*, *dependent*, and *obsessive-compulsive* personality disorders make up this group. These disorders share some characteristics of anxiety disorders such as social anxiety disorder or generalized anxiety disorder. However, the personality disorders in this group are different from anxiety disorders in that they refer more to general ways of interacting with others and responding to events. For instance, a person with an obsessive-compulsive personality disorder may be excessively neat and orderly. The person might always eat the same food at precisely the same time or perhaps read a newspaper in a particular order each time. This pattern becomes problematic only when it interferes with the person's life, as in making it impossible to travel or to maintain relationships.

Learning Tip

OCD is often confused with obsessive-compulsive personality disorder. However, OCD is primarily a self-reinforcing cycle of compulsive behaviors that reduce the anxiety associated with a distressing obsession. Obsessive-compulsive personality disorder is a far broader pattern of behaviors and is characterized more by an all-encompassing rigidity, orderliness, and perfectionism than by a set of conditioned behaviors attached to specific compulsive thoughts.

In modern clinical practice, defining personality disorders in terms of psychopathology is controversial for several reasons. First, personality disorders appear to be extreme versions of normal personality traits, demonstrating the continuum between what is considered normal and what is considered psychopathological (Clark & Ro, 2014; Widiger, 2011). For example, indecisiveness is characteristic of obsessive-compulsive personality disorder, but the *DSM* does not define the degree to which someone must be indecisive to be diagnosed as obsessive-compulsive. Second, there is overlap among the traits listed as characteristic of different personality disorders and between personality disorders and trauma-related disorders, so the majority of people diagnosed with one personality disorder also meet the criteria for another (Clark, 2007). As noted earlier, borderline personality disorder overlaps considerably with complex PTSD. This overlap suggests that the categories may not be mutually exclusive and that there may be fewer distinct personality disorders than are listed in the *DSM*. Finally, diagnoses of personality disorders are highly stigmatizing and have harmful effects on people's personal and professional lives even after people no longer meet the diagnostic criteria for the disorder.

Acknowledging these objections, but wanting to preserve continuity in current clinical practice, *DSM-5* describes an alternative model for personality disorders that aims to address many of the shortcomings of the traditional *DSM* approach. In this alternative model, personality disorders are viewed as impairments in specific areas of personality, such as self-image or interpersonal or emotional functioning. People with personality disorders also may exhibit pathological personality traits, such as manipulativeness, hostility, and impulsivity. In the alternative model, an individual can be diagnosed with *personality disorder—trait specified* if that person is impaired in some area of function and displays pathological levels of one or more traits, even if the person does not meet the criteria for any other specific personality disorder.

Personality disorders may not seem to affect daily life as much as some of the other disorders discussed in this chapter do, such as schizophrenia or bipolar disorders. Although people with personality disorders might not hallucinate or experience radical mood swings, their ways of interacting with the world can have serious consequences. The following in-depth consideration of antisocial personality disorder illustrates the devastating effect of these disorders on the individual, family and friends, and society.

Q How are personality disorders related to personality traits?

ANSWER: Personality disorders are characterized by extreme levels of certain typical personality traits.

14.18 Antisocial Personality Disorder Is Associated with a Lack of Empathy

In the 1800s, the term *psychopath* was coined to describe people who seem willing to hurt and take advantage of others without any evidence of concern or remorse (Koch, 1891). As discussed in Chapter 13, psychopathy is a personality trait that is part of the dark triad, which describes people who are callous toward others and willing to take advantage of them for personal gain. Psychopathy is a good example of the dimensional nature of personality disorders, in which people vary from having low levels of a particular trait to extreme and maladaptive levels.

In his classic book *The Mask of Sanity* (1941), the psychiatrist Hervey Cleckley described characteristics of psychopaths from his clinical experience. For example, although such individuals could be superficially charming and rational, they were insincere, unsocial, shameless, and incapable of love, and they lacked insight. In 1980 the *DSM* dropped the label *psychopath*, which was seen as pejorative, and adopted the term **antisocial personality disorder**. Antisocial personality disorder is the broad diagnosis for individuals who behave with lack of concern for other people—for example, by disregarding rules and laws, being deceitful and irresponsible, and showing little or no remorse for their behavior. People with this disorder tend to be hedonistic, seeking immediate gratification of their wants and needs.

antisocial personality disorder A personality disorder in which people engage in socially undesirable behavior, are hedonistic and impulsive, and lack empathy.

ANTISOCIAL PERSONALITY DISORDER AND EXTREME PSYCHOPATHY The *DSM*'s change in terminology has led to confusion because *psychopath* is still widely used to refer to a related but not identical type of personality disorder as defined by *DSM-5*. According to this new definition, the term *psychopathy* refers to people with antisocial personality disorder who also are extremely uncaring, are willing to hurt others for personal gain, and display behaviors that are more extreme than those associated with antisocial personality disorder (Coid & Ullrich, 2010). People with psychopathy are also more extreme than others with only antisocial personality disorder in terms of traits such as glibness, a grandiose sense of self-worth, shallow affect, and manipulativeness (Tyrer et al., 2019). People with antisocial personality disorder and high levels of psychopathy are commonly referred to as psychopaths (or sometimes sociopaths). Antisocial personality disorder and psychopathy are believed to be part of the same continuum.

Compared with the vast majority of people with elevated levels of dark triad personality traits, true psychopaths have very high levels of callousness and are particularly dangerous. For instance, one study of murderers found that those with psychopathic tendencies nearly always kill intentionally, typically for a

FIGURE 14.29
Gary Gilmore After His Arrest
Under *DSM-5*, Gilmore would have been given a diagnosis of antisocial personality disorder. He also showed extreme psychopathic traits.

purpose such as attaining money, sex, or drugs. When people without psychopathic tendencies commit murder, they are much more likely to do so impulsively, when provoked or angry (Woodworth & Porter, 2002). Psychopaths fit the stereotype of cold-blooded killers. Infamous examples include Dennis Rader—the BTK strangler, who bound, tortured, and killed 10 victims—and Gary Gilmore (**FIGURE 14.29**). In 1977, Gilmore was executed for the murder he describes here:

> I went in and told the guy to give me the money. I told him to lay on the floor and then I shot him. I then walked out and was carrying the cash drawer with me. I took the money and threw the cash drawer in a bush and I tried to push the gun in the bush, too. But as I was pushing it in the bush, it went off and that's how come I was shot in the arm. It seems like things have always gone bad for me. It seems like I've always done dumb things that just caused trouble for me. (Spitzer et al., 1983, pp. 66–68)

ASSESSMENT AND CONSEQUENCES It is estimated that 1–4 percent of the population has antisocial personality disorder (Compton et al., 2005). People with this condition who also show more-extreme psychopathic traits are less common (Lenzenweger et al., 2007). Both antisocial personality disorder and psychopathy are much more common in men than in women (Goldstein et al., 2017).

Much of what psychologists know about the traits associated with antisocial personality disorder was discovered by the psychologist Robert Hare (1993). Hare also developed many of the assessment tools to identify people with psychopathic tendencies. He and his colleagues have shown that the disorder is most apparent in late adolescence and early adulthood, and it generally improves around age 40 (Hare et al., 1988), at least for those without psychopathic traits. According to the *DSM-5* diagnostic criteria, antisocial personality disorder cannot be diagnosed before age 18, but the person must have displayed antisocial conduct before age 15. This stipulation ensures that only those with a lifetime history of antisocial behaviors can be diagnosed with antisocial personality disorder. They also must meet other criteria, such as repeatedly performing illegal acts, repeatedly lying or using aliases, and showing reckless disregard for their own safety or the safety of others. Because many individuals with antisocial personality disorder are quite bright and highly verbal, they can talk their way out of bad situations. In any event, punishment seems to have very little effect on them (Lykken, 1957, 1995), and they often repeat the problem behaviors a short time later.

THE ETIOLOGY OF ANTISOCIAL PERSONALITY DISORDER Various physiological abnormalities may play a role in antisocial personality disorder. In 1957, David Lykken reported that psychopaths do not become anxious when they are subjected to aversive stimuli. He and other investigators have continued this line of work, showing that such individuals do not seem to feel fear or anxiety (Lykken, 1995).

Electroencephalogram examinations have demonstrated that criminals who meet the criteria for antisocial personality disorder have slower alpha-wave activity (Raine, 1989). This finding indicates a lower overall level of arousal. It is possible that low arousal prompts people with antisocial personality disorder to engage in sensation-seeking behavior. In addition, because of low arousal, these individuals do not learn from punishment because they do not experience punishment as particularly aversive. Adolescents who are at risk for developing psychopathy, having high levels of callous/unemotional traits (such as limited empathy, a lack of guilt, and superficial emotions), also show this pattern of reduced physiological response in the face of punishment (Fung et al., 2005).

People with antisocial personality disorder have atypical patterns of brain activity and connectivity among brain regions when they attempt to empathize with others (Decety et al., 2013). There is also evidence that those with antisocial tendencies may have smaller amygdalas that are less responsive to negative stimuli (Blair, 2003; Marsh et al., 2011). Adolescents who are at risk for antisocial personality disorder show reduced brain responses when viewing pictures of other people in pain (Marsh et al., 2013) and show reduced activity in the amygdala when observing facial expressions of fear (Marsh et al., 2008).

Although brain dysfunction may be at the root of antisocial behaviors and psychopathy, factors such as low socioeconomic status, dysfunctional families, and childhood abuse may also be important. Indeed, malnutrition at age 3 has been found to predict antisocial behavior at age 17 (Liu et al., 2004). An enrichment program for children that included a structured nutrition component was associated with less criminal and antisocial behavior 20 years later (Raine et al., 2003). This finding raises the possibility that malnutrition or similar environmental factors might contribute to the development of antisocial personality disorder. Moreover, it demonstrates that aspects of children's environment might prove protective for those at risk of developing antisocial personality disorder. For instance, the amount of positive reinforcement provided by adoptive mothers helped reduce callous/unemotional behaviors in children (Hyde et al., 2016).

Q According to the *DSM-5*, what is the relationship of antisocial personality disorder and psychopathy?

ANSWER: Psychopathy is an extreme version of antisocial personality disorder that includes a willingness to hurt others for personal gain.

Which Psychological Disorders Are Typically Diagnosed in Childhood?

Learning Objectives

- Understand the childhood context of neurodevelopmental disorders.
- Identify the symptoms and possible causes of autism spectrum disorder.
- Identify the symptoms and possible causes of attention-deficit/hyperactivity disorder.

In his classic text on the classification of psychological disorders, published in 1883, Emil Kraepelin did not mention childhood disorders. The first edition of the *DSM*, published 70 years later, essentially considered children small versions of adults. Consequently, the manual did not consider childhood disorders separately from adulthood disorders. The current version of the manual includes a wide range of childhood disorders (**TABLE 14.10**). Some of these conditions—such as specific learning disorders—affect only limited and particular areas of a child's functioning. Other conditions—such as autism spectrum disorder, attention-deficit/hyperactivity disorder, and others listed in Table 14.10—affect every aspect of a child's life and often continue into adulthood. Some of these disorders, such as autism spectrum disorder, usually do not get better over time. Others, such as attention-deficit/hyperactivity disorder, usually do improve over time.

All of the disorders in this category should be considered within the context of typical childhood development. Some symptoms of childhood psychological disorders are extreme manifestations of normal behavior or are typical behaviors for children at an earlier developmental stage. For example, bed-wetting is expected for 2-year-olds but not for 10-year-olds. Other behaviors, however, deviate significantly from the usual patterns of development. Two disorders of childhood, autism spectrum disorder and attention-deficit/hyperactivity, are explored here as illustrations.

Table 14.10 *DSM-5* **Neurodevelopmental Disorders**

DISORDER	DESCRIPTION
Intellectual disabilities	Deficits in general mental abilities (e.g., reasoning, problem solving, planning, academic learning, learning from experience) and in adaptive functioning (e.g., independent living, working, social participation); begins during childhood or adolescence
Communication disorders	Deficits in language, speech, or communications, such as difficulty learning a language, stuttering, or failure to follow social rules for communication; begins in childhood
Autism spectrum disorder	Persistent impairment in social interaction characterized by unresponsiveness; impaired language, social, and cognitive development; and restricted and repetitive behavior; begins during early childhood
Attention-deficit/ hyperactivity disorder	A pattern of hyperactive, inattentive, and impulsive behavior that causes social or academic impairment; begins before age 12
Specific learning disorders	Difficulty learning and using academic skills; much lower performance in reading, mathematics, or written expression with regard to what is expected for age, amount of education, and intelligence; begins during school-age years
Motor disorders	Recurrent motor and vocal tics that cause marked distress or deficits in developing or being able to show coordinated motor skills; begins in childhood

SOURCE: Based on American Psychiatric Association (2013).

14.19 Autism Spectrum Disorder Involves Social Deficits and Restricted Interests

Before *DSM-5*, a number of similar disorders were considered variants of *autistic disorder*, commonly known as *autism*, which is characterized by impaired communication, restricted interests, and deficits in social interaction (Volkmar et al., 2005). The disorder was first described in 1943 by the psychiatrist and physician Leo Kanner. Struck by the profound isolation of some children, Kanner coined the term *early infantile autism*. Researchers and clinicians recognized that autism varied considerably in severity, from mild social impairments to severe social and intellectual impairments. For example, children with deficits in social interaction but less severe impairments in other domains were considered to have *Asperger's syndrome*, named after the pediatrician who first described it. The social deficits observed in autism and related disorders reflect an underdeveloped theory of mind. As discussed in Chapter 9, theory of mind is both the understanding that other people have mental states and the ability to predict their behavior accordingly.

autism spectrum disorder
A developmental disorder characterized by impaired communication, restricted interests, and deficits in social interaction.

In keeping with the dimensional approach to psychopathology, psychologists now recognize that autism exists along a continuum from mild to severe impairment rather than in discrete diagnostic categories. **Autism spectrum disorder** is the *DSM-5* disorder that groups together all the variants in symptoms of autism, including Asperger's syndrome. Approximately 1–2 percent of children have a disorder along the autism spectrum, though boys are about 5 times more likely to be diagnosed than girls (Blumberg et al., 2013; Christensen et al., 2016). In *DSM-5*, the two essential features of autism spectrum disorder are impairments in social interactions and restrictive or repetitive behaviors, interests, or activities. These symptoms are present in early childhood and limit or impair everyday functioning. Most of the discussion in the following sections focuses on the classic severe end of the autism spectrum, which definitively meets the *DSM-5* criteria.

Autism spectrum disorder is usually diagnosed during childhood, but it is a lifelong disorder. Most of the symptoms of this disorder remains consistent from childhood into adulthood. There are treatments for both children and adults with autism spectrum disorder, though improvement in symptoms is more likely if treatment begins early (Lin et al., 2019).

CORE SYMPTOMS OF AUTISM SPECTRUM DISORDER Children on the more extreme end of the autism spectrum are seemingly unaware of other people. As babies, they do not smile at their caregivers, do not respond to vocalizations, and may actively reject physical contact with others. Children with autism do not establish eye contact and do not use their gazes to gain or direct the attention of those around them (Moriuchi et al., 2016). Although they show attention to the eyes before 2 months of age, they stop making eye contact by 6 months of age (Jones & Klin, 2013). One group of researchers had participants view video footage of the first birthdays of children with autistic disorder to see if characteristics of autism could be detected before the children were diagnosed (Osterling & Dawson, 1994). Participants could classify children as having or not having autism 77 percent of the time by considering only the number of times a child looked at another person's face (**FIGURE 14.30**).

Children with autism show severe impairments in verbal and nonverbal communication. Even if they vocalize, it is often not with any intent to communicate. Communication deficits are apparent by 14 months of age among children who are subsequently diagnosed with autism (Landa et al., 2007). Children with autism who develop language usually exhibit odd speech patterns, such as echolalia (repetition of words or phrases that someone else has spoken, which is also observed in those with schizophrenia). The child may imitate the other speaker's intonation or may use a high-pitched monotone. Those who develop functional language also often interpret words literally, use common phrases or clichés out of context, and lack verbal spontaneity.

(a) (b)

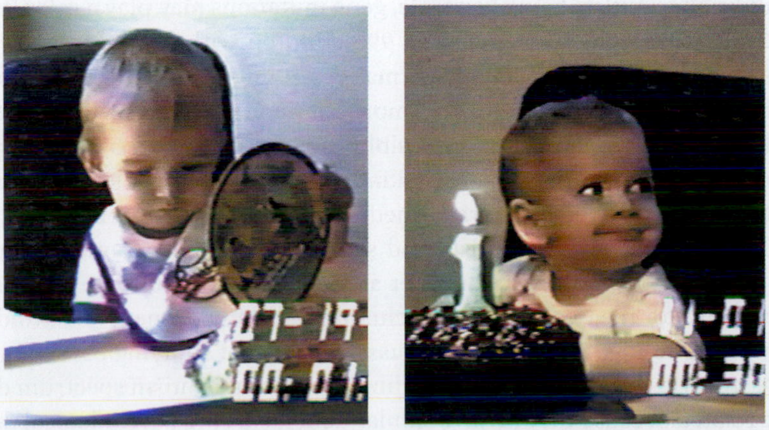

FIGURE 14.30
Scenes from Videotapes of Children's Birthday Parties
(a) This child, who focused more on objects than on people, was later diagnosed with autism. **(b)** This child, who focused on objects and people, developed typically.

FIGURE 14.31
Gaze Pattern of a Toddler with Autism Spectrum Disorder
As shown in these combined video images from a 1994 study of autism, a 2-year-old with autism will focus on the unimportant details in the scene rather than on the social interaction.

Another common feature of autism spectrum disorder is restricted activities and interests. Children with autism spectrum disorder appear oblivious to people around them, but they are acutely aware of their surroundings. Although most children automatically pay attention to the social aspects of a situation, those with autism may focus on seemingly inconsequential details (Klin et al., 2003; FIGURE 14.31). Scientists have detected early signs of autism spectrum disorder by identifying unusual patterns of visual attention in children (de Belen et al., 2020).

Any changes in daily routine or in the placement of furniture or of toys can be very upsetting for children with autism. Once they are upset, the children can become extremely agitated or throw tantrums. In addition, the play of children with autism tends to be repetitive and obsessive, with a focus on objects' sensory aspects. They may smell and taste objects, or they may spin and flick them for visual stimulation. Similarly, their own behavior tends to be repetitive, with hand movements and body rocking. Self-injury is common, and some children must be restrained to prevent accidental harm.

BIOLOGICAL BASIS OF AUTISM SPECTRUM DISORDER Some early scientists believed autism was caused by cold and unresponsive parenting, but this view is no longer endorsed by experts. It is now well established that autism spectrum disorder is the result of biological factors. There is evidence for a strong genetic component to autism. Studies have found concordance rates to be as high as 70–90 percent for identical twins (Holmboe et al., 2013; Ronald & Hoekstra, 2011).

In addition to autism being heritable, gene mutations may play a role (Ronemus et al., 2014). One study that compared 996 children with autism to 1,287 control children found several rare gene abnormalities (Pinto et al., 2010), and a separate study found that these mutations were more common in children with autism spectrum disorder than in their unaffected siblings (Levy et al., 2011). These rare mutations involve cells having an abnormal number of copies of DNA segments and may affect the way neural networks are formed during childhood development (Gilman et al., 2011). It is likely that autism and schizophrenia share several gene mutations (Fromer et al., 2014; McCarthy et al., 2014). There are some similarities in the symptoms for the two disorders, including social impairment and avoidance of eye contact. The RDoC approach (discussed earlier) of studying psychopathology across categories would suggest that schizophrenia and autism spectrum disorder may be related because they involve similar deficits in core psychological domains.

Research into the causes of autism also points to prenatal and/or early-childhood events that may disrupt brain function. The brains of children with autism grow unusually large during the first months of life, and then growth slows until age 5 (Courchesne et al., 2007). Rapid brain growth at 6–12 months of age predicts the likelihood of a diagnosis of autism spectrum disorder at age 2 in children with a genetic risk for the disorder (Hazlett et al., 2017). The brains of children with autism also do not develop normally during adolescence (Uddin, 2020). Adolescents with autism spectrum disorder show atypical connections among brain regions that underlie the ability to adapt flexibly to the environment.

Another possible biological cause of autism is exposure to pathogens in the womb that affect brain development. For example, scientists found abnormal antibodies in the blood of the mothers of 11 percent of children with autism but not in a large sample of mothers with healthy children or mothers of children with other developmental disorders (Braunschweig et al., 2008). Research in humans and animals has confirmed that the presence of infections and certain immune cells in the womb can increase the likelihood of the development of autism spectrum disorder (Brown & Meyer, 2018). The possible role of exposure to pathogens during fetal brain development is another similarity between autism spectrum disorder and schizophrenia.

Q **What are the atypical characteristics of brain development in autism spectrum disorder?**

ANSWER: unusually rapid brain growth in the first year of life and abnormal connections between brain regions in adolescence

14.20 Why Do People Believe Vaccinations Cause Autism?

YOU BE THE PSYCHOLOGIST

What if you heard about a study in which researchers found that moving to Florida or Arizona is a leading cause of death? Or that wearing dentures is another leading cause of death, along with retiring, wearing bifocals, or moving to a nursing home? As a critical thinker, you know that correlation does not equal causation. When someone claims one variable causes another, you are vigilant for lurking third variables that might explain the apparent connection. In these cases, you might have noticed that the variables were all related to aging. It is getting older, rather than moving to Florida or buying bifocals, that is associated with dying.

Recognizing the third variable problem is especially important when trying to understand claims about causes of psychological disorders. In 1998, the British physician Andrew Wakefield published a study in the prestigious journal *Lancet* claiming to find a connection, in only 12 children, between receiving vaccinations to prevent measles, mumps, and rubella (MMR) and developing autism (Wakefield et al., 1998). This finding was widely reported in the media even though most scientists were skeptical and urged people to be patient until the result could be replicated with larger samples. But many people panicked. In 2007, the celebrity Jenny McCarthy publicly blamed the MMR vaccine for her son's autism. She became a prominent spokesperson for the anti-vaccine movement, appearing on television shows such as *Oprah* to warn people about "the autism shot." More recently, Robert F. Kennedy Jr., nephew of John F. Kennedy, was banned from Instagram after years of making claims about the harmful effects of vaccines (FIGURE 14.32).

FIGURE 14.32
Anti-Vaccination Statements
Robert F. Kennedy Jr. was banned from the social media platform Instagram in 2021 for repeatedly making false claims about vaccines and the coronavirus.

Take a moment to think like a psychologist. You have just been presented with a claim that being vaccinated causes autism. What kinds of data would you want to see to support that claim? How should a study be designed to validly test that claim, and what would a decent sample size be? Does the evidence presented live up to that standard? What exactly is the source of the evidence?

It turns out that the Wakefield study was fraudulent. Wakefield altered medical records and lied about several aspects of his study, including a financial conflict of interest (Godlee et al., 2011). His coauthors had earlier retracted the paper when they developed doubts about the data and conclusions (Murch et al., 2004). Wakefield has subsequently been shunned by the British medical community, he was forced to resign his academic positions, and his license to practice medicine has been taken away.

Nonetheless, the claims persisted. In response to the original *Lancet* report, scientists conducted several large international studies to examine the possibility of a link between autism spectrum disorder and the MMR vaccine. A thorough review of these studies by the Institute of Medicine found no evidence of any link between MMR vaccinations and autism (Immunization Safety Review Committee, 2004). Recent studies have continued to find no evidence of any link between childhood vaccinations and autism spectrum disorder (Jain et al., 2015). For example, a study of more than half a million children born in Denmark during a 10-year period found that the rate of autism spectrum disorder among unvaccinated children was 1 percent, identical to the rate among vaccinated children (e.g., Hviid et al., 2019). The results of dozens upon dozens of carefully designed studies have provided a firm conclusion: Vaccines do not cause autism spectrum disorder.

But the fear of autism spectrum disorder led many parents around the globe to forgo vaccinating their children. As one researcher noted, "Unfortunately, the media has given celebrities who comment on an autism-MMR link far more attention than they deserve, and the public, unfamiliar with the background science, has confused celebrity status with authority" (Poland, 2011, p. 870). Even today, with overwhelming scientific evidence that vaccines do not cause autism spectrum disorder, many parents refuse to vaccinate their children because of worries that they might (Goin-Kochel et al., 2020).

Why might parents still believe there is a link between vaccinations and autism? Use your critical thinking skills and see if you can identify a third variable that is related to both vaccination and the diagnosis of autism. What do those two things have in common?

Wakefield originally conducted his study because the parents of the 12 children with autism told him that they remembered the autism symptoms starting right after their children were immunized. Jenny McCarthy told Oprah Winfrey that she noticed a change in her son immediately after he received the vaccine. Many have disputed her account, but the bottom line is that vaccines are given to children at about the same developmental period that symptoms of autism spectrum disorder become apparent. Think about the other characteristics that emerge at the same time in development. For example, lower molars emerge in children's mouths during early childhood. However, few people would suggest that being vaccinated causes molars to grow. Children start speaking at about this age, but no one thinks vaccines cause this ability. People see an apparent connection between vaccines and autism spectrum disorder, but the lurking third variable is age.

Because of the decline in childhood immunizations, there has been an increase in outbreaks of diseases that had become quite rare because of successful vaccine programs. In the first four months of 2013, rubella cases in Japan jumped from a few a year to more than 5,000. In 2015, an unvaccinated child caused an outbreak of measles at Disneyland that infected 125 other children (CDC, 2015). About half of the infected were unvaccinated. Meanwhile, researchers at the CDC estimate that for children born between 1994 and 2013, vaccinations prevented an estimated 322 million illnesses, 21 million hospitalizations, and 732,000 deaths (Whitney et al., 2014).

The failure to engage in critical thinking continues to affect public health. In addition to resisting childhood vaccines, many people are hesitant to be vaccinated against the coronavirus (Chou & Budenz, 2020). One study found that lower levels of cognitive reflection, a close cousin of critical thinking, were linked with increased resistance to taking the coronavirus vaccine (Murphy et al., 2021). Be sure to think like a psychologist the next time you hear a claim about the harmful effects of a vaccine. It just might protect your health and that of your community. ■

Q Is there any evidence that vaccinating children is linked to the development of autism?

ANSWER: No. Dozens of carefully constructed studies have failed to find any evidence of a link.

14.21 Attention-Deficit/Hyperactivity Disorder Is a Disruptive Impulse Control Disorder

Because of its high prevalence rate, it is likely that you or someone you know has been diagnosed with **attention-deficit/hyperactivity disorder (ADHD)**. Common symptoms include hyperactivity, of course, as well as restlessness, inattentiveness, and impulsiveness. Children with ADHD have difficulty with tasks such as keeping clean or remembering rules. At school, children with ADHD often need to ask for help immediately after the teacher has presented detailed instructions to the entire class, and they need to have directions repeated and rules explained over and over. Children with ADHD sometimes make unexpected sounds that inadvertently disturb anyone nearby. Although these children are often friendly and talkative, they can have trouble making and keeping friends because they miss subtle social cues and make unintentional social mistakes. A proneness to accidents is another feature of ADHD.

attention-deficit/hyperactivity disorder (ADHD) A disorder characterized by restlessness, inattentiveness, and impulsivity.

The *DSM-5* requires at least six or more symptoms of inattention (e.g., making careless mistakes, not listening, losing things, being easily distracted) and six or more symptoms of hyperactivity or impulsiveness (e.g., fidgeting, running about when inappropriate, talking excessively, having difficulty waiting) that last for at least six months and interfere with functioning or development. For a diagnosis of ADHD, several of these symptoms must be present before age 12 and occur in multiple settings. Estimates of the prevalence of ADHD vary widely. The best available evidence for children in the United States is that 8 percent of children have the disorder, and it is more common in boys than in girls (Danielson et al., 2018).

Although ADHD traditionally has been most common among White boys, recently girls and people of color have shown increases in the disorder (Collins & Cleary, 2016; Siegel et al., 2015). In addition, ADHD was once associated with being thin or normal weight, but children with ADHD are now more likely to be obese (Cortese et al., 2016). One possible explanation for these differences is that practitioners may be more willing to look beyond stereotypes of who has the disorder (FIGURE 14.33).

FIGURE 14.33
ADHD in Girls
The stereotype of ADHD is a thin and overactive white male. However, ADHD is increasingly diagnosed in girls and people of color, possibly because practitioners are looking beyond stereotypical characteristics in their assessment of disordered behaviors.

THE ETIOLOGY OF ADHD The causes of ADHD are unknown. One difficulty in pinpointing the etiology is that it is most likely a heterogeneous disorder. In other words, the behavioral profiles of children with ADHD vary, so the causes of the disorder most likely vary as well. Children with ADHD may be more likely than

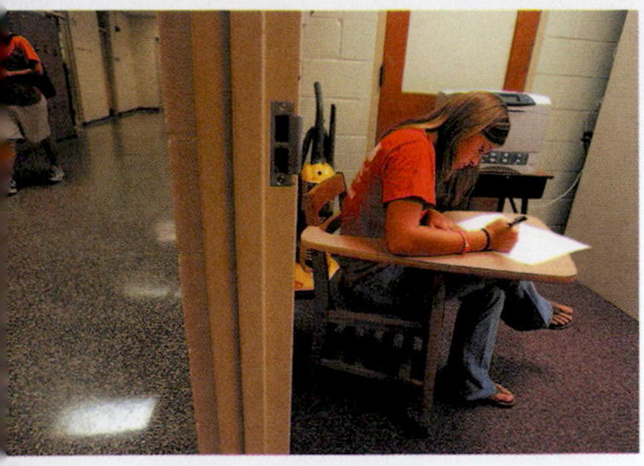

FIGURE 14.34

Living with ADHD

Paula Luper, of North Carolina, was diagnosed with ADHD in elementary school. Here, as a senior in high school, she is taking a quiz in the teachers' lounge to avoid distraction.

other children to come from chaotic households. Factors such as disorganized or inconsistent parenting and social disadvantage may contribute to the onset of symptoms, as is true for all psychological disorders. Still, ADHD clearly has a genetic component: Concordance is about twice as high in identical twins as in dizygotic twins (Larsson et al., 2014).

In an early imaging study, Alan Zametkin and colleagues (1990) found that adults who had been diagnosed with ADHD in childhood had reduced metabolism in brain regions involved in the self-regulation of motor functions and of attentional systems. Studies have also found reduced volume in many regions of the brains in those with ADHD, particularly in regions involving attention, cognitive and motor control, emotional regulation, and motivation (Gallo & Posner, 2016). The brain region most consistently shown to be involved in ADHD is the basal ganglia (see Figure 3.26), and researchers have demonstrated volume reductions in this area as well (Hoogman et al., 2017). Because this structure is involved in regulating motor behavior and impulse control, dysfunction in the basal ganglia could explain the hyperactivity symptoms of ADHD. The pattern of reduced volume in certain brain regions leads to the hypothesis that ADHD is caused by a delay in the maturation of those brain regions (Friedman & Rapoport, 2015; Shaw et al., 2012). In support of this *delayed maturation hypothesis* is evidence that the reduced volume in some brain areas seen in children with ADHD improves with age, along with some of the symptoms of the disorder, but neither fully matches that of adults who were never diagnosed with ADHD (Hoogman et al., 2017; Rubia et al., 2014).

ADHD ACROSS THE LIFE SPAN Children generally are not given diagnoses of ADHD until they enter structured settings in which they must conform to rules, get along with peers, and sit in their seats for long periods. In the past, these things happened when children entered school, between ages 5 and 7. Now, with the increasing prevalence of structured day care settings, the demands on children to conform occur much earlier. However, diagnoses for boys occur at younger ages than for girls, which may reflect a tendency for disruptive behavior in boys to be more readily identified as disordered (Davies, 2014).

The manifestation of ADHD in specific symptoms changes with age as people move through different developmental stages. During adolescence, for example, ADHD is characterized less by hyperactivity and more by impairment in academic performance and peer relationships (Sibley et al., 2012; **FIGURE 14.34**). According to longitudinal studies, people diagnosed with ADHD as children continue to experience symptom reductions over time but do not fully outgrow ADHD even in adulthood (Agnew-Blais et al., 2016; McGough & Barkley, 2004). Adults with ADHD symptoms, about 4 percent of the population (Kessler et al., 2006), may struggle academically and vocationally. Studies conducted up to 30 years after diagnosis show that adults who were diagnosed with ADHD as children generally reach a lower-than-expected socioeconomic level, change jobs more often than other adults, have substance abuse problems, and are more likely to get divorced if they marry (Klein et al., 2012). At the same time, many adults with ADHD learn to adapt to their condition, such as by reducing distractions while they work.

Q **At what point in development are the symptoms of ADHD most often identified and diagnosed?**

ANSWER: when children enter a structured social setting that requires conformity, most often day care or school

Your Chapter Review

Want to earn a better grade on your test?

It's time to complete your study experience! Go to **INQUIZITIVE** to practice actively with this chapter's concepts and get personalized feedback along the way.

Chapter Summary

How Are Psychological Disorders Conceptualized and Classified?

14.1 Views on Psychopathology Have Changed over Time Individuals with psychological disorders behave in ways that deviate from cultural norms and that are maladaptive within their context. Psychological disorders are common in all societies.

14.2 Psychological Disorders Are Classified into Categories The *Diagnostic and Statistical Manual of Mental Disorders* (*DSM*) is a system for diagnosing psychological disorders. The *DSM* is regularly updated to reflect new research and shifting views on mental illness in society. The current version is the *DSM-5*. Psychopathology exists on a continuum ranging from thoughts, feelings, and behaviors that society considers "normal" to symptoms that cause mild impairment to severe disturbances. Psychological disorders are often comorbid—that is, they occur together. Assessment is the process of examining a person's mental functions and psychological condition to make a diagnosis. Assessment is accomplished through self-reports, psychological testing, observations, interviews, and neuropsychological testing.

14.3 Psychological Disorders Have Many Causes According to the diathesis-stress model, mental health problems arise from a vulnerability coupled with stressful circumstances. Psychological disorders may arise from biological factors, situational factors, or cognitive-behavioral factors, and they often result from an interaction between biological and situational factors.

14.4 Psychological Disorders Vary as a Function of Cultural Context Social and cultural expectations can shift how a disorder is expressed in terms of behavior and emotion. Women are more likely to experience distress in the form of internalizing disorders (such as major depressive disorder and generalized anxiety disorder). Men are more likely to experience distress in the form of externalizing disorders (such as alcohol use disorder and conduct disorders). Most psychological disorders show some universal symptoms, but the *DSM* recognizes several cultural syndromes related to mental health problems.

Which Disorders Involve Disturbances in Emotions?

14.5 Anxiety Disorders Are Characterized by Fear and Tension Anxiety disorders are a family of psychopathology related to excessive fear and worry. Generalized anxiety disorder is diffuse and omnipresent. Social anxiety disorder is a fear of being negatively evaluated by others. Specific phobias are exaggerated fears of particular stimuli. Agoraphobia, a fear of being in certain situations, is marked by panic attacks or sudden overwhelming terror. Cognitive, learning, and biological factors contribute to the onset of anxiety disorders.

14.6 Depressive Disorders Are Characterized by Sad, Empty, or Irritable Moods Major depressive disorder is characterized by a number of symptoms, including depressed mood and a loss of interest in pleasurable activities. Persistent depressive disorder is less severe, characterized by sadness most of the day on more days than not for at least two years. Depressive disorders have biological components, including a genetic risk and possible dysfunction of the monoamine neurotransmitters norepinephrine and serotonin. Situational factors (such as poor relationships and stress) and cognitive factors (such as the cognitive triad and learned helplessness) also contribute to the occurrence of depression.

14.7 Bipolar Disorders Involve Depression and Mania Bipolar disorder is characterized by manic episodes—that is, episodes of increased activity and euphoria—and depression. The impairment in bipolar I disorder is due to manic episodes, whereas the impairment in bipolar II disorder is due to depressive episodes. Genes may play a role in bipolar disorders.

14.8 Psychology Outside the Lab: You Think Your Friend Might Be Suicidal. What Should You Do? Suicide is the second leading cause of death for young adults. According to Joiner's model, suicide risk involves a sense of lack of social belonging and feeling like a social burden coupled with an acquired capacity for self-harm. You should take a friend's suicide threats seriously and try to get that person professional help. Remind the suicidal person that you value the relationship.

Which Disorders Involve Disruptions in Thought?

14.9 Schizophrenia Involves a Disconnection from Reality Schizophrenia is characterized by alterations in thought, in perceptions, or in consciousness. The positive symptoms associated with schizophrenia reflect excesses and include delusions, hallucinations, disorganized speech, and disorganized or catatonic behavior. The negative symptoms of schizophrenia reflect deficits and include apathy, lack of emotion, and slowed speech and movement.

14.10 The Cause of Schizophrenia Involves Biological and Environmental Factors Schizophrenia has a strong genetic component, and there is evidence that gene mutations may lead to abnormal brain development. Research suggests that schizophrenia is largely a brain disorder, involving alteration in brain structure and brain chemistry. Environmental factors also play a role in the development of schizophrenia, including dysfunctional family dynamics, urban stress, and exposure to pathogens during fetal development.

Which Disorders Involve Maladaptive Behavior?

14.11 Unwanted and Intrusive Thoughts Cause Anxiety, and Compulsions Reduce It Obsessive-compulsive disorder involves frequent intrusive thoughts, which cause anxiety, and compulsive actions, which reduce the anxiety. OCD grows out of a conditioning process and may also have genetic and environmental causes.

14.12 Thoughts and Feelings About Food and Body Image Are Disrupted in Eating Disorders Excessive focus on eating and weight causes stress. Eating disorders are maladaptive patterns of behavior related to food and eating. Anorexia nervosa involves restricting caloric intake as a way of managing the anxiety and distress associated with food and body image. Bulimia nervosa is a cyclic pattern of binge eating and purging. Binge-eating disorder involves regularly eating an excessive amount of food.

14.13 Addiction Has Physical and Psychological Aspects Addiction is the persistent use of a substance despite negative consequences and attempts to quit. Tolerance occurs when the body or mind requires an increasing amount of the substance to achieve the same effect. Withdrawal is a set of unpleasant thoughts and feelings caused by the lack of a substance. Various brain regions are involved in addiction, particularly the nucleus accumbens. Addiction is influenced by personality factors such as sensation seeking and also by the environment or context where the substance use occurs.

Which Disorders Are Linked to Trauma?

14.14 Trauma Is a Prolonged Response to an Emotional Event *Trauma* refers to the lingering psychological and physiological responses that people can have to an upsetting or disorienting event. Exposure to distressing events, especially during childhood, can cause trauma that endures throughout life. Posttraumatic stress disorder involves frequent and recurring nightmares, intrusive thoughts, and flashbacks related to an earlier trauma. PTSD occurs in approximately 7 percent of the population and affects women more than men.

14.15 Dissociative Disorders Are Disruptions in Memory, Awareness, and Identity Dissociation can help people cope with trauma by splitting off traumatic experiences and their associated distress from the rest of the self. Dissociative amnesia involves forgetting that an event happened or losing awareness of a substantial block of time. Dissociative fugue involves a loss of identity and travel to another location. Other disorders linked with trauma, such as dissociative identity disorder, are controversial because they are not clearly separate from other diagnoses and can be highly stigmatizing.

14.16 Borderline Personality Disorder Is Marked by Instability in Self-Image and Relationships Borderline personality disorder involves instability in identity, emotion, and relationships. People with borderline personality disorder lead tumultuous lives because they have poor impulse control, intense and conflictual relationships, and an unstable sense of self. Borderline personality disorder is associated with reduced frontal lobe capacity and a history of trauma and abuse.

What Are Personality Disorders?

14.17 Personality Disorders Are Maladaptive Ways of Relating to the World The *DSM* identifies 10 personality disorders clustered into three groups. Paranoid, schizoid, and schizotypal make up the odd or eccentric cluster. Histrionic, narcissistic, borderline, and antisocial make up the dramatic, emotional, or erratic cluster. Avoidant, dependent, and obsessive-compulsive make up the anxious or fearful cluster. Obsessive-compulsive personality disorder is distinct from obsessive-compulsive disorder.

14.18 Antisocial Personality Disorder Is Associated with a Lack of Empathy Antisocial personality disorder is characterized by socially undesirable behavior, being deceitful and irresponsible, a lack of remorse, and hedonism. The disorder exists on a continuum with the personality trait of psychopathy. Antisocial personality disorder is associated with low levels of arousal, deficits in frontal lobe functioning, and a relatively small amygdala. Environment seems to contribute to the development of antisocial personality disorder.

Which Psychological Disorders Are Typically Diagnosed in Childhood?

14.19 Autism Spectrum Disorder Involves Social Deficits and Restricted Interests Autism spectrum disorder is marked by impaired social interaction, impaired communication, and restricted interests. The symptoms emerge in infancy. Autism is heritable and may result from genetic mutations. Autism has been linked to abnormal brain growth, exposure to antibodies in the womb, faulty brain wiring, and impairment in brain areas involved in mental flexibility and understanding the intentions of others.

14.20 You Be the Psychologist: Why Do People Believe Vaccinations Cause Autism? A fraudulent report led some people to believe that the measles, mumps, and rubella vaccine causes autism. This conclusion results from a lack of critical thinking and is based on seeing relations that do not exist. The age at which children are vaccinated happens to be at about the same time symptoms of autism appear. Overwhelming research documents the lack of any true association between vaccines and the risk of developing autism.

14.21 Attention-Deficit/Hyperactivity Disorder Is a Disruptive Impulse Control Disorder Children with ADHD are restless, inattentive, and impulsive. The causes of ADHD may include environmental factors such as poor parenting and social disadvantages; genetic factors; and brain abnormalities, particularly with respect to activation of the brain regions involving attention, cognitive and motor control, emotional regulation, and motivation. ADHD continues into adulthood, presenting challenges to academic work and to career pursuits.

Key Terms

addiction, p. 569
agoraphobia, p. 552
anorexia nervosa, p. 568
antisocial personality disorder, p. 579
anxiety disorders, p. 550
assessment, p. 545
attention-deficit/hyperactivity disorder (ADHD), p. 587
autism spectrum disorder, p. 582
binge-eating disorder, p. 568
bipolar I disorder, p. 557
bipolar II disorder, p. 557
borderline personality disorder, p. 575
bulimia nervosa, p. 568
cognitive-behavioral approach, p. 547
delusions, p. 560
diathesis-stress model, p. 546
disorganized behavior, p. 562
disorganized speech, p. 562
dissociative disorders, p. 573
etiology, p. 540
family systems model, p. 547
generalized anxiety disorder (GAD), p. 551
hallucinations, p. 561
learned helplessness, p. 556
major depressive disorder, p. 553
negative symptoms, p. 563
obsessive-compulsive disorder (OCD), p. 566
persistent depressive disorder, p. 554
posttraumatic stress disorder (PTSD), p. 573
psychopathology, p. 540
Research Domain Criteria (RDoC), p. 544
schizophrenia, p. 560
sociocultural model, p. 547
trauma, p. 572

Practice Exercises

1. Which question is *not* necessary to answer when a clinician is determining if a person's behavior represents psychopathology? Select all that apply.
   a. Does the behavior deviate from cultural norms?
   b. Is the behavior causing the individual personal distress?
   c. Is the behavior maladaptive?
   d. Is the behavior immoral?
   e. In what context is the behavior occurring?

2. Research Domain Criteria (RDoC) have been established by the National Institute of Mental Health (NIMH) to reframe how mental disorders are conceptualized and studied. Which of the following statements is *not* accurate about RDoC?
   a. Due to NIMH's funding power, RDoC will likely shape how future research is conducted.
   b. RDoC will completely replace the *DSM-5* and the established classification of psychopathology.
   c. RDoC is based on a dimensional understanding of psychopathology.
   d. RDoC focuses on functional domains that may be similarly disrupted across disorder types.

3. Which statement about neuropsychological assessment is true?
   a. Neuropsychological testing aims at identifying emotional disturbance by exploring memories from childhood.
   b. Neuropsychological testing relies on interviews with the person's family to determine levels of social anxiety.
   c. Neuropsychological testing is a medical procedure that depends on blood test results.
   d. Neuropsychological testing uses tasks that require planning, coordinating, and memory to identify potential dysfunction in certain brain regions.

4. Two students, Sam and Kerry, visit the campus health center. Sam describes feeling constantly fearful and anxious. Kerry describes feeling persistently agitated and often exhibiting violent outbursts. Sam's symptoms are characteristic of an ________ disorder, which is more common in ________; Kerry's symptoms are characteristic of an ________ disorder, which is more common in ________.
   a. externalizing, women; internalizing, men
   b. externalizing, men; internalizing, women
   c. internalizing, women; externalizing, men
   d. internalizing, men; externalizing, women

5. Match each of these anxiety disorders (specific phobia, generalized anxiety disorder, and social anxiety disorder) with the following descriptions:
   a. Harlow is hypervigilant, constantly on the lookout for problems. He often has trouble sleeping and experiences constant fatigue.
   b. While hiking, Susan comes across a snake sunning itself. She becomes intensely frightened and must quit her hike early.
   c. Juan experiences extreme mental tension when in social situations and especially dreads social performances, so much so that his grades and well-being suffer.

6. Match each of these emotional disorders (major depressive disorder, bipolar I disorder, bipolar II disorder) with the following descriptions:
   a. Claudia frequently has high feelings but they rarely last. More often she experiences long periods of extreme sadness that disrupt her relationships.
   b. Since Lorenzo's mother died about a year ago, he has not found any satisfaction in his hobbies or relationships, spends most nights lying awake in bed, and has lost nearly 10 pounds.
   c. Breyaundra experiences manic highs where she barely sleeps for many days, makes risky investments with her life savings, and is so confident in her physical abilities she puts herself in danger.

7. Which statement accurately describes the current understanding of schizophrenia?
   a. Schizophrenia is primarily an emotional disorder with environmental causes.
   b. Schizophrenia is primarily a thought disorder with brain-related causes.
   c. Schizophrenia is primarily an eating disorder with trauma-related causes.
   d. Schizophrenia is primarily a personality disorder with genetic causes.

8. Which statement about trauma is accurate?
   a. Highly distressing events, such as witnessing severe violence, always cause trauma.
   b. Events can be objectively classified as traumatic or not, based on their intensity.
   c. The presence of protective factors, such as positive relationships, can prevent trauma.
   d. Only memories that become dissociated and forgotten can cause trauma.

9. Which of the following statements describe current objections to defining personality disorders as psychopathological in diagnostic systems such as the *DSM-5*? Select all that apply.
   a. Environmental factors are too influential on personality to consider personality traits as disordered.
   b. Overlap in the characteristics between disorders suggests that the categories may not be conceptually clear cut.
   c. Personality is best described categorically so cannot fit into a dimensional treatment approach.
   d. The features of personality disorders are on the continuum of normal personality traits.
   e. Once diagnosed with a personality disorder, people carry the stigma of that disorder with them even after their symptoms improve.

10. Royce is 5 years old and taking swimming lessons at the community pool. He is usually unprepared on arrival, forgetting his towel, a change of clothes, or goggles. During instruction, he often blows bubbles at the water's surface and makes excessive noise. Although Royce tries to listen to what his teacher says, he immediately needs directions repeated to follow them. Which diagnosis aligns closest with Royce's behaviors?
    a. agoraphobia
    b. attention-deficit/hyperactivity disorder
    c. autism spectrum disorder
    d. obsessive-compulsive personality disorder

15 Treatment of Psychological Disorders

Big Questions

MICHAEL PHELPS IS THE MOST ACCOMPLISHED OLYMPIAN of all time, with 28 olympic medals, 23 of them gold. In 2004 he won eight medals, followed by another eight in 2008, and then six each in 2012 and 2016. In every Olympics he competed in, his success was unparalleled. And after each of them was over, he experienced depression. His worst depression episode was after the 2012 Olympic Games, during which time he rarely left his bedroom for days, did not eat, had trouble sleeping, and contemplated suicide. Despite his struggles, he did not seek treatment until 2014. Like many people with depression, for a long time he believed he should be able to deal with his problems on his own. He credits the mental health treatment he got at that time, and since then, with saving his life. Since he retired from competitive swimming, Michael Phelps has taken on a new challenge: to reduce the stigma of mental illness and promote mental health treatment. Today, he reports that he still experiences anxiety and depression at times, but through the tools he has learned in therapy he is able to effectively handle these challenges. He wants others who are suffering to know that they, too, can get help and improve their lives.

This chapter explores the basic principles of therapy and describes how those principles are adapted in the treatment of specific disorders. An important lesson in this coverage is that even though biological factors are present in most psychological disorders, the most effective treatments usually involve changing behavior or cognition. Questions clinical psychologists ask about mental health treatment include: How do you treat psychological disorders, and which treatments are most effective for different disorders? How do you decide whether a treatment is effective? Are some disorders harder to treat than others? How should childhood disorders be treated?

Learning Objectives

- Distinguish among the various forms of psychotherapy.
- Describe the major categories of psychotropic medications.
- Identify alternative biological treatments for psychological disorders.
- Understand the role of empirical studies in determining treatment effectiveness.
- Distinguish among the types of specialized providers of psychological treatment.

How Are Psychological Disorders Treated?

The treatment of psychological disorders has a long history. Evidence of efforts to treat mental health symptoms dates back to prehistoric times (see Section 15.6), and in the late 1800s Sigmund Freud popularized the idea that psychological treatments can help alleviate mental health symptoms. However, the idea that scientific approaches should inform mental health treatments only emerged when the scientific method was applied to psychological questions more broadly (see Chapter 1). Since then, medical and psychological science has transformed the treatment of psychological disorders, and rapid progress continues.

At this time, there are no instant cures for psychological disorders. Disorders need to be managed over time through treatment that helps alleviate symptoms so people can function in their daily lives until treatment is no longer necessary. The choice of treatment depends on the type and severity of symptoms, the diagnosis, and the motivational state of the person needing treatment. Most disorders can be treated in more than one way. However, some disorders are most successfully treated using a particular method or combination of methods.

15.1 Various Methods Have Been Used to Treat Psychopathology

Psychologists use two basic categories of techniques to treat psychological disorders: psychological and biological. Either type of treatment may be used alone, or they may be used in combination. The generic name given to formal psychological treatment is **psychotherapy**. The particular techniques used may depend on the practitioner's training, but all forms of psychotherapy involve interactions between practitioner and client. These interactions are aimed at helping the person understand the symptoms and problems and providing solutions for them. One limitation of any form of psychotherapy is that some psychological disorders are characterized by apathy or indifference, and individuals may not be interested in being treated.

psychotherapy The generic name given to formal psychological treatment.

Biological therapies reflect medical approaches to disease (what is wrong with the body) and to illness (what a person feels as a result). In other words, these therapies are based on the notion that psychological disorders—often referred to as mental disorders in medical settings—result from abnormalities in neural and bodily processes. For example, the client—often referred to as the patient in medical settings—might be experiencing an imbalance in a specific neurotransmitter or a malfunction in a particular brain region.

biological therapies Treatments of psychological disorders based on medical approaches to disease (what is wrong with the body) and to illness (what a person feels as a result).

Biological treatments range from drugs to electrical stimulation of brain regions to surgical intervention. *Psychopharmacology* is the use of medications that affect the brain or body functions to treat psychological disorders. These forms of treatment can be particularly effective for some disorders, at least on a short-term basis. One limitation of biological therapies, however, is that long-term success may require the person to continue treatment, sometimes indefinitely. Moreover, nonbiological treatments may prove more effective for some disorders over the long term. For many disorders, the recent focus has been on combining biological therapies with other approaches to find the best treatment for each client.

RELATION OF THEORY TO TREATMENT As outlined in Chapter 14, psychologists have proposed a number of theories to account for psychopathology. Some of these theories are about general issues, such as the role of learning or cognition in many psychological disorders. Other theories are specific to a particular disorder, such as the theory that certain types of thought patterns underlie depression. Each theory includes treatment strategies that are based on the theory's assumptions about the causes of psychological disorders.

Although researchers are continually gaining better understandings of the causes of particular disorders, these understandings do not always lead to further insights into how best to treat the disorders. For example, autism spectrum disorder is clearly caused by biological factors, but this knowledge has not led to any significant advances in therapies for the disorder. In fact, the best available treatment for autism spectrum disorder is based on behavioral, not biological, principles. Likewise, in a situation where a person's loss of a parent has led to clinical depression, drugs might be useful for treatment, at least in the short term. The therapist might favor biological treatment for this particular person even though the depression was caused by the client's situation.

Regardless of the treatment provider's theoretical perspective, psychotherapy is generally aimed at changing patterns of thought, emotion, or behavior. The ways in which such changes are brought about can differ dramatically, however. It has been estimated that there are more than 400 approaches to treatment (Kazdin, 1994). Many therapists follow an *eclectic* approach, using various techniques that seem appropriate for a given client. The following discussion highlights the major components of the most common approaches, and it describes how therapists use these methods to treat specific psychological disorders.

Q **Why is psychotherapy limited in treating psychopathology that is characterized by apathy and indifference?**

ANSWER: The success of psychotherapy depends on changing patterns of thought, emotion, and behavior, so engagement of the client is necessary for improvement.

15.2 Psychodynamic Therapy Seeks to Reduce Unconscious Conflicts

One of the first people to develop psychological treatments for psychological disorders was Sigmund Freud. Freud believed that such disorders were caused by prior experiences, particularly early traumatic experiences. Along with Josef Breuer, he pioneered the method of psychoanalysis.

In early forms of psychoanalysis, the client would lie on a couch while the therapist sat out of view. This method was meant to reduce the client's inhibitions and allow freer access to unconscious thought processes. Treatment involved uncovering unconscious feelings and drives that Freud believed gave rise to maladaptive thoughts and behaviors (**FIGURE 15.1**). Techniques included *free association* and *dream analysis*. In free association, the client would say whatever came to mind and the therapist would look for signs of unconscious conflicts, especially where the client appeared resistant to discussing certain topics. In dream analysis, the therapist would interpret the hidden meaning of the client's dreams (see the discussion in Chapter 4, "Consciousness").

FIGURE 15.1
Psychoanalysis in Freud's Office
As part of the treatment process, Freud sat behind his desk (partly visible in the lower left corner). His clients reclined on the couch, facing away from him.

The general goal of psychoanalysis is to increase clients' awareness of their own unconscious psychological processes and how these processes affect their daily functioning. By gaining *insight* of this kind, the clients are freed from these unconscious influences. According to psychoanalysis, the clients' symptoms diminish as a result of reducing unconscious conflicts. Traditional psychoanalytic therapy is expensive and time consuming, sometimes continuing for many years. Minimal empirical evidence exists for much of Freudian theorizing, however, and therefore it is not surprising that treatments for psychological disorders based on those theories are largely ineffective.

Psychotherapists later reformulated some of Freud's ideas, and these adaptations are known collectively as **psychodynamic therapy**. In using this approach, a therapist aims to help clients examine their needs, defenses, and motives as a way of understanding why they are distressed. Most proponents of the psychodynamic perspective today continue to embrace Freud's "talking therapy." They have replaced the couch with a chair, however, and the talking tends to be more conversational.

psychodynamic therapy A form of therapy based on Freudian theory; it aims to help clients examine their needs, defenses, and motives as a way of understanding distress.

Some features of contemporary psychodynamic therapy include exploring the client's avoidance of distressing thoughts; looking for recurring themes and patterns in thoughts and feelings; discussing early traumatic experiences; focusing on interpersonal relations and childhood attachments; emphasizing the relationship with the therapist; and exploring fantasies, dreams, and daydreams (Shedler, 2010). Some of these features, such as focusing on patterns in thoughts and feelings and addressing interpersonal relationships, are common to most forms of psychotherapy, and thus they do not distinguish psychodynamic therapy from other types of treatment (Tryon & Tryon, 2011).

During the past few decades, the use of traditional psychoanalytic therapy has become increasingly controversial. A new approach to psychodynamic therapy consists of offering fewer sessions and focusing more on current relationships than on early-childhood experiences. Therapists who use this approach do not necessarily accept all of Freud's ideas, but they do believe that people have underlying conflicts that need to be resolved, such as their relations with other people. Proponents argue that this short-term psychodynamic therapy has been shown in research to be potentially useful for treating certain disorders, including depression, eating disorders, and substance abuse (Leichsenring et al., 2004). Other brief forms of psychodynamic therapy, such as those focusing on emotional conflicts that result from defense mechanisms, have also been found to be more effective than no treatment at all (Lilliengren et al., 2016). However, it is not clear whether the psychodynamic aspects are superior to other brief forms of therapy, such as simply talking about personal problems to a caring therapist. The opportunity to talk about one's problems to someone who will listen plays a role in all therapeutic relationships.

Q **What is the role of insight in psychodynamic therapy?**

ANSWER: Insight provides awareness of unconscious conflicts so they can be resolved.

15.3 Behavioral and Cognitive Treatments Aim to Change Behavior, Emotion, or Thought Directly

Many of the most successful therapies involve trying to change people's behavior, emotion, or thought directly. These therapies are behavioral, cognitive, or a combination of the two. Whereas insight-based therapies consider maladaptive behavior the result of an underlying problem, behavioral and cognitive therapies treat the behavior, emotion, and thought as the problem. For example, the therapist will not be particularly interested in why a person has come to fear elevators, such as whether childhood traumas produced the fear. Instead, the therapist is interested in helping the client overcome the fear.

BEHAVIOR THERAPY The premise of **behavior therapy** is that behavior is learned and therefore can be unlearned through the use of classical and operant conditioning. As discussed in Chapter 6, behavior modification is based on operant conditioning. It is a method of helping people learn desired behaviors and unlearn unwanted behaviors. Desired behaviors are rewarded (rewards might include small treats or praise). Unwanted behaviors are ignored or punished (punishments might include time-outs or additional chores). Many treatment centers use token economies, in which people earn tokens for good behavior and can trade the tokens for rewards or privileges.

For a desired behavior to be rewarded, however, the client first must exhibit the behavior. A therapist can use *social skills training* to elicit desired behavior. A client with a particular interpersonal difficulty, such as initiating a conversation, learns appropriate ways to act in specific social situations. The first step is often *modeling*, in which the therapist acts out an appropriate behavior. Recall from Chapter 6 that people learn many behaviors by observing others perform them. In modeling, the client is encouraged to imitate the displayed behavior, rehearse it in therapy, and later apply the learned behavior to real-world situations. The successful use of newly acquired social skills is itself rewarding and encourages the continued use of those skills.

Many behavioral therapies for psychological disorders include an **exposure** component. Through this technique, the person is exposed repeatedly to the anxiety-producing stimulus or situation (FIGURE 15.2). The principle behind exposure is based on classical conditioning. By confronting feared stimuli in the absence of negative consequences, the person learns new, nonthreatening associations. Exposure therapy is the most effective treatment for any psychological disorder that involves anxiety or fear, including obsessive-compulsive disorder (OCD; Abramowitz, 2013; Foa & McLean, 2016). An intensive form of exposure therapy, called *prolonged exposure*, is effective for posttraumatic stress disorder (PTSD; Cusack et al., 2016; McLean & Foa, 2014). This treatment involves those with PTSD repeatedly revisiting and recounting their traumatic experience and gradually approaching situations that they have been avoiding because of reminders of their traumatic experience.

COGNITIVE THERAPY **Cognitive therapy** is based on the theory that distorted thoughts can produce maladaptive behaviors and emotions. Treatment strategies that modify these thought patterns should thus eliminate the maladaptive behaviors and emotions. A number of approaches to cognitive therapy have been proposed.

1 The little girl has a phobia of dogs.
2 She is encouraged to approach a dog that scares her.
3 From this mild form of exposure she learns that the dog is not dangerous, and she overcomes her fear.

FIGURE 15.2
Exposure
Exposure is a common feature of many cognitive-behavioral therapies. In this sequence, a little girl gradually overcomes her fear of dogs by slowly increasing her level of exposure to a dog.

behavior therapy Treatment based on the premise that behavior is learned and therefore can be unlearned through the use of classical and operant conditioning.

exposure A behavioral therapy technique that involves repeated exposure to an anxiety-producing stimulus or situation.

cognitive therapy Treatment based on the idea that distorted thoughts produce maladaptive behaviors and emotions; treatment strategies attempt to modify these thought patterns.

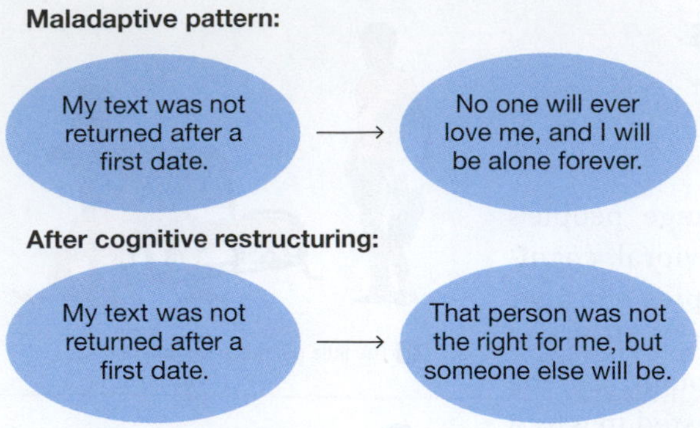

Maladaptive pattern:
My text was not returned after a first date.
No one will ever love me, and I will be alone forever.
After cognitive restructuring:
My text was not returned after a first date.
That person was not the right for me, but someone else will be.

FIGURE 15.3
Cognitive Restructuring
Through this technique, a therapist helps a client learn to replace maladaptive thought patterns, such as those associated with depression, with more-realistic, positive ones.

cognitive restructuring A therapy that strives to help clients recognize maladaptive thought patterns and replace them with ways of viewing the world that are more in tune with reality.

cognitive-behavioral therapy (CBT) A therapy that incorporates techniques from cognitive therapy and behavior therapy to correct faulty thinking and change maladaptive behaviors.

For example, Aaron T. Beck (1964) has advocated **cognitive restructuring**. Through this approach, a clinician seeks to help a person recognize maladaptive thought patterns and replace them with ways of viewing the world that are more in tune with reality (**FIGURE 15.3**). Albert Ellis (1962), another major thinker in this area, introduced *rational-emotive therapy*. Through this approach, the therapist acts as a teacher, explaining the client's errors in thinking and demonstrating adaptive ways to think and behave.

In cognitive therapy and rational-emotive therapy, maladaptive behavior is assumed to result from individual belief systems and ways of thinking rather than from objective conditions. By contrast, *interpersonal therapy* focuses on circumstances—namely, relationships the client attempts to avoid. This approach integrates cognitive therapy with psychodynamic insight therapy (Markowitz & Weissman, 1995). Interpersonal therapy developed out of psychodynamic ideas on how people relate to one another, but it uses cognitive techniques that help people gain more-accurate insight into their social relationships. Because interpersonal functioning is seen as critical to psychological adjustment, treatment focuses on helping clients explore their interpersonal experiences and express their emotions (Blagys & Hilsenroth, 2000).

To help prevent relapse of psychological disorders following treatment, John Teasdale and colleagues (2000) developed *mindfulness-based cognitive therapy*. The principle behind this method is that people who recover from depression continue to be vulnerable to faulty thinking when they experience negative moods. For instance, they may be prone to negative, ruminative thinking. Mindfulness-based cognitive theory is based on principles derived from mindfulness meditation, which originated from Eastern meditation and yoga practices. This therapy has two goals: to help clients become more aware of their negative thoughts and feelings at times when they are vulnerable and to help them learn to disengage from ruminative thinking through meditation. A recent review of studies using this method to prevent recurrence of major depression found that it is quite effective (Kuyken et al., 2016).

Cognitive-behavioral therapy (CBT) incorporates techniques from cognitive therapy and behavior therapy. The goal of CBT is to correct the client's faulty cognitions and to train the client to engage in new behaviors. For example, for clients who have social anxiety disorder—a fear of being viewed negatively by others—the therapist will encourage the clients to examine their thoughts about other people's reactions to them. The aim is to help the clients understand how their appraisals of other people's reactions might be inaccurate. At the same time, the therapist might model social skills and gradually expose clients to social situations. CBT is perhaps the most widely used version of psychotherapy, and it is one of the most effective forms of psychotherapy for many types of psychological disorders, especially anxiety disorders and depressive disorders (Deacon & Abramowitz, 2004; Hollon et al., 2002). Because anxiety disorders and depressive disorders are often comorbid, CBT that addresses symptoms of both disorders at the same time is especially effective (Newby et al., 2015).

Q What kind of disorder is exposure therapy most effective for, and why?

ANSWER: It is most effective for anxiety disorders because the person learns to associate new, nonthreatening reactions with the feared stimulus.

15.4 The Context of Therapy Matters

Some people seek treatment because symptoms, possibly of a psychological disorder, are interfering with their lives. For example, some people would like to overcome feelings of social anxiety that keep them trapped in lonely isolation. By contrast, some people are sent to treatment because they behave in ways that cause others significant distress, such as those with addictions whose behavior causes conflict for their families. The unique circumstances of people's lives affect their symptoms, psychological disorders, and treatments. Accordingly, treatments differ depending on family involvement, client resources, and the culture in which the person needing treatment lives.

One factor that affects the outcome of all therapy is the relationship between the therapist and the client. This connection is important partly because a good relationship can foster an expectation of receiving help (Miller, 2000; Talley et al., 1990). Most people in the mental health field use the curative power of client expectation to help their clients achieve success in therapy. This approach is not limited to psychological disorders, however. A good relationship with a service provider is important for any aspect of physical or mental health.

As noted in Chapter 13, the humanistic approach to personality emphasizes personal experience and the individual's belief systems. The goal of humanistic therapy is to treat the person as a whole, not as a collection of behaviors or as a repository of repressed thoughts. One of the best-known humanistic therapies is **client-centered therapy**. Developed by the psychologist Carl Rogers (1951), this approach encourages people to fulfill their individual potentials for personal growth through greater self-understanding. A key ingredient of client-centered therapy is the creation of a safe and comforting setting for clients to access their true feelings (**FIGURE 15.4**). Therapists strive to be genuine and empathic, to take their clients' perspective, and to accept their clients through unconditional positive regard (see Chapter 13). Instead of directing clients' behavior or passing judgment on their actions or thoughts, the therapist helps clients focus on their subjective experience. Often, a client-centered therapist will use *reflective listening*, in which the therapist repeats clients' concerns to help them clarify their feelings. Although relatively few practitioners follow the tenets of humanistic theory strictly, many techniques advocated by Rogers are used currently to establish a good therapeutic relationship between practitioner and client.

client-centered therapy An empathic approach to therapy; it encourages people to fulfill their individual potentials for personal growth through greater self-understanding.

One modern form of humanistic treatment, motivational interviewing, uses a client-centered approach over a very short period (such as one or two interviews). This treatment addresses the client's ambivalence about problematic behaviors, as when a person with a drug addiction wants to use drugs but recognizes the problems created by drug use. The treatment helps clients identify discrepancies between their current state and "where they would like to be" in their lives. By doing so, the therapist can spark the client's motivation for change. Motivational interviewing has proved to be a useful treatment for many people seeking help with drug and alcohol abuse as well as for people wanting to improve their eating and exercise habits (Burke et al., 2003). William Miller (2000), the psychologist who developed the technique, attributes the outstanding success of this brief form of empathic therapy to the warmth expressed by the therapist toward the client.

FIGURE 15.4
Humanistic Therapy
Carl Rogers founded the form of humanistic therapy called client-centered therapy. Here, Rogers (far right, facing camera) leads a group therapy session, demonstrating the importance of a safe and comforting environment in the pursuit of greater self-understanding.

FAMILY THERAPY FOCUSES ON THE FAMILY CONTEXT The therapy a person receives is, of course, an important element in treating a psychological disorder. The person's family often plays an almost equally important role.

FIGURE 15.5
Family Therapy
The actions, reactions, and interactions of family members can become important topics during therapy.

According to a *systems approach*, an individual is part of a larger context. Any change in individual behavior will affect the whole system. This effect is often most apparent within the family. Each person in a family plays a particular role and interacts with the other members in specific ways. Over the course of therapy, how the individual thinks, behaves, and interacts with others may change. Such changes can profoundly affect the family dynamics. For instance, an alcoholic who gives up drinking may start to criticize other members of the family when they drink. In turn, the family members might provide less support for the person's continuing abstinence. After all, if the family members do not have drinking problems, they might resent the comments. If they do have drinking problems, they might resist the comments because they do not want to give up drinking.

Family attitudes are often critical to long-term prognoses. This is especially true for therapy involving children. For this reason, some therapists insist that family members be involved in therapy when practical, except when including them is impossible or would be counterproductive. All the family members involved in therapy are together considered the client. For instance, suppose a child's defiant behavior has led to conflict between the parents, who disagree about how to respond to the child (**FIGURE 15.5**). In this case, the treatment will involve not only working on the child's behavior but also helping the parents learn to resolve their parenting disagreements.

There is also evidence that helping families provide appropriate social support leads to better therapy outcomes and reduces relapses for individuals in treatment. The key is the type of family involvement. For instance, studies have documented the importance of attitudes expressed by family members toward people with schizophrenia. In this context, *expressed emotion* is a pattern of negative actions by a client's family members. The pattern includes making critical comments about the person, being hostile toward the person, and being emotionally overinvolved (e.g., being overprotective or pitying, or having an exaggerated response to the person's disorder). The level of expressed emotion from family members corresponds to the relapse rate for those with schizophrenia (Hooley, 2007; Hooley & Gotlib, 2000), and relapse rates are highest if the person has a great deal of contact with a family that responds this way.

FIGURE 15.6
Cultural Effects on Therapy
Zou Ran does painting therapy with a relative of a patient at Hunan Cancer Hospital in Changsha, the capital of central China's Hunan Province. She is a member of the psychology-caring group, which has provided free psychotherapy, music therapy, and painting therapy for cancer patients at the hospital since its establishment in 2007.

CULTURAL BELIEFS AFFECT TREATMENT Societal definitions of both psychological health and psychological disorders are central to the treatments used in psychotherapy. Culture influences how psychological disorders are expressed, which people with psychological disorders are likely to recover, and how willing people are to seek help.

Psychotherapy is accepted to different extents in different countries. Some countries, such as China and India, have relatively few psychotherapists. Many of these countries are seeing a growing need, as the past two decades or so of economic expansion have brought increasingly stressful lifestyles and an awareness of the mental health problems that come with them. However, the people in some of these countries are resistant to even discussing psychological problems, much less treating them. Because of traditional cultural beliefs, many Chinese distrust emotional expression and avoid seeking help for depression, anger, or grief (Magnier, 2008). Likewise, in India, because of the stigma of psychological disorders, terms such as *mental illness*, *depression*, and *anxiety* are avoided; instead, terms such as *tension* and *strain* are used to communicate psychological health problems (Kohn, 2008). Thus, providers need to be sensitive both to the cultural meanings of disorders and to how psychological treatments are regarded within those cultures (**FIGURE 15.6**).

GROUP THERAPY BUILDS SOCIAL SUPPORT Group therapy rose in popularity after World War II. Because of the many stresses related to the war, more people needed therapy than there were therapists available to treat them. Therapists came to realize that in some instances group therapy offers advantages over individual therapy. The most obvious benefit is cost: Group therapy is often significantly less expensive than individual treatment. Especially when financial resources are limited, group therapy can be an effective way for people to experience the benefits of treatment. In addition, the group setting provides an opportunity for members to improve their social skills and learn from one another's experiences.

Group therapies vary widely in the types of people enrolled, the duration of treatment, the theoretical perspective of the therapist running the group, and the group size—although some practitioners believe that about eight people is the ideal number. Many groups are organized around a particular type of problem (e.g., a history of sexual abuse) or around a particular type of person (e.g., those who are transgender). Many groups continue over long periods, with some members leaving and others joining the group at various intervals. Depending on the approach favored by the therapist, the group may be highly structured, or it may be a more loosely organized forum for discussion. Behavioral and cognitive-behavioral groups are usually highly structured, with specific goals and techniques designed to modify the thought and behavior patterns of group members. This type of group has been effective for disorders such as bulimia and OCD.

In contrast, less structured groups usually focus on increasing insight and providing social support. One famous example is Alcoholics Anonymous, in which people trying to stay sober support one another in this goal. In fact, the social support that group members can provide one another is one of the most beneficial aspects of this type of therapy. Those who are experiencing similar issues in their lives might more easily empathize with the experiences of other group members (Heck, 2016). As a result, group therapy is often used to augment individual psychotherapy.

Q What is reflective listening?

ANSWER: a part of humanistic approaches to treatment, in which the therapist listens and then repeats the client's concerns to help the person clarify their feelings

15.5 Medication Is Effective for Certain Disorders

Drugs have proved effective for treating some psychological disorders. Their use is based on the assumption that psychological disorders result from deficits or excesses in specific neurotransmitters or from dysfunction in the receptors for those neurotransmitters. Although this assumption is not always supported by evidence, the use of drugs may provide relief from symptoms of psychological disorders. Drugs that affect mental processes, called **psychotropic medications**, act by changing brain neurochemistry. For example, they alter synaptic transmission to increase or decrease the action of particular neurotransmitters (see Chapter 3, "Biology and Behavior").

psychotropic medications Drugs that affect mental processes.

Most psychotropic medications fall into one of three categories: antianxiety drugs, antidepressants, and antipsychotics. Note, however, that sometimes drugs from one category are used to treat a disorder from another category, such as using an antianxiety drug to treat depression. One reason for this is comorbidity. For example, as discussed in Chapter 14, a substantial number of people with depression also meet diagnostic criteria for an anxiety disorder. Another reason is that in most cases there is insufficient evidence about why a particular drug is effective in reducing symptoms of a psychological disorder. That is, many questions remain about how brain chemistry is related to psychological disorders, and many drug treatments have been based on trial-and-error clinical studies in which researchers use different drugs to see if they reduce symptoms.

Other drugs used to treat psychological disorders do not fall into traditional categories. Many of them are used as mood stabilizers. *Lithium* was long considered the most effective treatment for bipolar disorder, although the neural mechanisms of how it works are unknown. Drugs that prevent seizures, called *anticonvulsants*, can also stabilize moods in bipolar disorder. As discussed in Section 15.15, antipsychotic medications are also effective for treatment of bipolar disorder.

antianxiety drugs A class of psychotropic medications used for the treatment of anxiety.

ANTIANXIETY DRUGS **Antianxiety drugs**, also called *anxiolytics*, are used for the short-term treatment of anxiety. One class of antianxiety drugs is the benzodiazepines (such as Xanax and Ativan). These drugs increase the activity of GABA, the most pervasive inhibitory neurotransmitter. Although benzodiazepines reduce anxiety and promote relaxation, they also induce drowsiness and are highly addictive. They should therefore be used sparingly. Sleeping pills (including Ambien and Lunesta) also produce their effects through GABA receptors, although they are not classic benzodiazepines. They bind mainly with receptors that induce sleep rather than relaxation.

antidepressants A class of psychotropic medications used for the treatment of depression.

ANTIDEPRESSANTS The second class of psychotropic medications is the **antidepressants**. These drugs are primarily used to treat depression. However, they are often used for other disorders, particularly anxiety disorders. *Monoamine oxidase (MAO) inhibitors* were the first antidepressants to be discovered. Monoamine oxidase is an enzyme that breaks down serotonin, norepinephrine, and dopamine in the synapse. MAO inhibitors therefore stop this process and result in more of those neurotransmitters being available in the synapse. A second category of antidepressant medications is the *tricyclic antidepressants*, named after their core molecular structure of three rings. These drugs inhibit the reuptake of mainly serotonin and norepinephrine, resulting in more of each neurotransmitter being available in the synapse. More recently, *selective serotonin reuptake inhibitors (SSRIs)* have been introduced; the best-known is Prozac. These drugs inhibit the reuptake of serotonin, but they act on other neurotransmitters to a significantly lesser extent. (**FIGURE 15.7** depicts the way SSRIs work.)

Some critics have charged that SSRIs are too often used to treat people who are sad and have low self-esteem but who are not clinically depressed. Such widespread prescribing of SSRIs is a problem because, like all drugs, SSRIs have side effects, including sexual dysfunction. At the same time, SSRIs have been valuable for various disorders. Therefore, when the use of SSRIs is being considered, the potential side effects should be weighed against the potential benefits.

Learning Tip

The most widely used class of antidepressant drugs is called SSRIs, which are serotonin agonists. To remember how they work, you simply need to remember what the acronym *SSRI* stands for: selective serotonin reuptake inhibitors. As this name indicates, SSRIs block the reuptake of serotonin, which extends the time the neurotransmitter serotonin is available in the synapse.

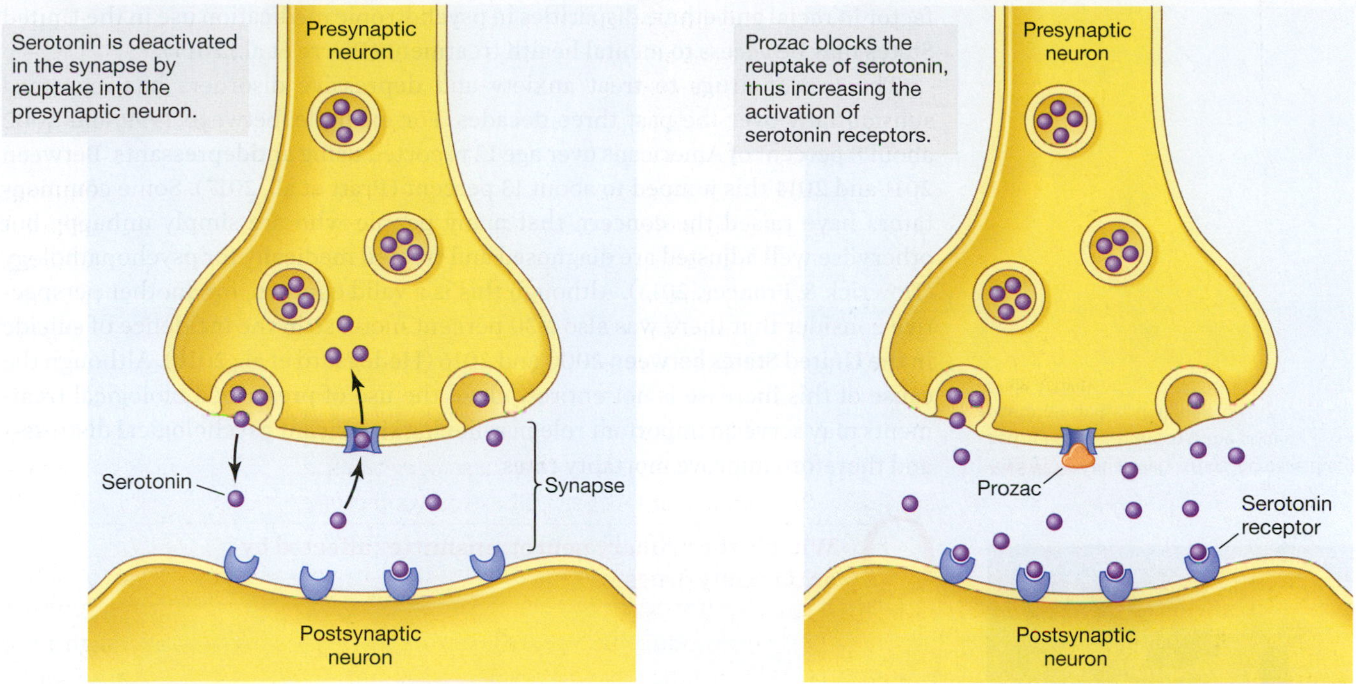
Serotonin is deactivated in the synapse by reuptake into the presynaptic neuron.
Presynaptic neuron
Serotonin
Synapse
Postsynaptic neuron
Prozac blocks the reuptake of serotonin, thus increasing the activation of serotonin receptors.
Presynaptic neuron
Prozac
Serotonin receptor
Postsynaptic neuron

FIGURE 15.7
Selective Serotonin Reuptake Inhibitors
SSRIs, such as Prozac, block reuptake of serotonin into the presynaptic neuron. In this way, they allow serotonin to remain in the synapse, where its effects on postsynaptic receptors are prolonged. The greater amount of serotonin in the synapse is presumed to alleviate depression.

ANTIPSYCHOTICS The third class of psychotropic medications is **antipsychotics**, sometimes called *neuroleptics*. Antipsychotics are used to treat schizophrenia and other disorders that involve psychosis. These drugs reduce symptoms such as delusions and hallucinations. Traditional antipsychotics are dopamine antagonists that bind to dopamine receptors, thus blocking the effects of dopamine. Antipsychotics are not always effective, however, and they have significant side effects that can be irreversible. One such side effect of long-term use is *tardive dyskinesia*, the involuntary twitching of muscles, especially in the neck and face. Moreover, these drugs are not useful for treating the negative symptoms of schizophrenia, such as apathy and social withdrawal (see Chapter 14).

antipsychotics A class of psychotropic medications used for the treatment of schizophrenia and other disorders that involve psychosis.

USE OF PSYCHOTROPIC MEDICATIONS Psychotropic medications are very commonly prescribed in the United States. According to the Centers for Disease Control and Prevention, in 2019 about 1 in 6 U.S. adults took medication for mental health treatment. Women were about twice as likely as men to use psychotropic medication or receive any mental health treatment. Non-Hispanic White Americans were also about twice as likely to take psychotropic medication or receive any mental health treatment compared with Hispanic or Black Americans (Terlizzi & Zablotsky, 2020). Asian Americans are also less likely to use psychotropic medication than White Americans (Pierre et al., 2014).

There are several possible reasons for the discrepancy in the use of psychotropic medication among racial and ethnic groups, including cultural attitudes toward mental health treatment. A study examining racial and ethnic differences in psychotropic medication use in adult American men found that discrepancies in use are drastically reduced if the influence of socioeconomic, health status, and demographic differences is eliminated. These findings suggest that a primary factor in racial and ethnic disparities in psychotropic medication use in the United States may be access to mental health treatment (Pierre et al., 2014).

The use of drugs to treat anxiety and depressive disorders has increased substantially over the past three decades. For example, between 1999 and 2002 about 8 percent of Americans over age 12 reported using antidepressants. Between 2011 and 2014 this jumped to about 13 percent (Pratt et al., 2017). Some commentators have raised the concern that many people who are simply unhappy but otherwise well adjusted are diagnosed and treated medically for psychopathology (Dowrick & Frances, 2013). Although this is a valid concern, for another perspective consider that there was also a 30 percent increase in the incidence of suicide in the United States between 2000 and 2016 (Hedegaard et al., 2018). Although the cause of this increase is not entirely clear, the use of prescribed biological treatments may serve an important role in relieving significant psychological distress—and therefore improve mortality rates.

Q **What is the primary neurotransmitter affected by antianxiety drugs?**

ANSWER: Antianxiety drugs increase the activity of GABA, which is the primary neurotransmitter that inhibits brain activity.

15.6 Alternative Biological Treatments Can Be Effective

Not all people are treated successfully with psychotherapy or medication or both combined. These people are considered *treatment resistant*. To alleviate disorders, treatment providers may attempt alternative biological methods. Such alternatives include brain surgery and brain stimulation techniques, which are used to alter brain function. These treatments are often used as last resorts because they may be more likely than psychotherapy or medication to have serious side effects. Many early efforts reflected crude attempts to control disruptive behavior. More-recent approaches reflect a growing understanding of the brain mechanisms that underlie various psychological disorders.

FIGURE 15.8
Prehistoric Skull with Holes
A skull at the Archaeological Museum in Cusco, Peru, bears the marks of a cranial surgical operation performed by the Incas.

For many centuries, people have recognized that the brain is involved with the mind, including the mind's abnormalities. From locations as varied as France and Peru, scientists have found numerous prehistoric skulls in which holes were made (**FIGURE 15.8**). Many of the holes were healed over to some extent, indicating that the recipients survived for years after their procedures. Such surgery, called *trepanning*, may have been used to let out evil spirits believed to be causing unusual behavior. In parts of Africa and the Pacific, various groups still practice trepanning as a treatment for epilepsy, headaches, and symptoms of mental disturbance.

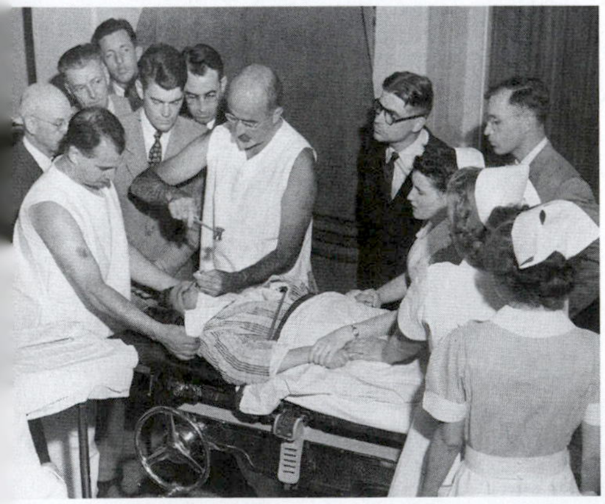

FIGURE 15.9
Lobotomy
This photo shows Dr. Walter Freeman performing a lobotomy in 1949. Freeman is inserting an ice pick–like instrument under the eyelid of his patient to cut the nerve connections in the front part of the brain.

Early in the twentieth century, medical researchers went beyond cutting holes in the skull to manipulating the brain. One of the earliest formal procedures used on people with severe disorders was *psychosurgery*, in which areas of the brain were selectively damaged. Although some brain surgeries were performed as early as the 1880s, António Egas Moniz is credited with bringing the practice to the attention of the medical world. In the late 1930s he developed the lobotomy, later known as prefrontal lobotomy, which involved severing nerve-fiber pathways in the prefrontal cortex (see **FIGURE 15.9**). These prefrontal lobotomies were used to treat severe disorders, including schizophrenia, major depression, and anxiety disorders. To understand such drastic measures, it is important to appreciate that in the early twentieth century there was a significant increase in the number of patients living in mental institutions. Treatment for psychological disorders made almost no progress before the 1950s. Patients with disorders were simply restrained and warehoused in institutions for their entire lives. In this climate of medical desperation, various risky procedures were explored.

After patients received prefrontal lobotomies, they were often listless and had flat affect, and they were therefore much easier to manage. The surgery also impaired other mental functions, such as abstract thought, planning, motivation, and social interaction. Most prefrontal lobotomies were performed in the late 1940s and early 1950s. In 1949, Egas Moniz received the Nobel Prize in Medicine for developing the procedure. With the development of effective pharmacological treatments for severe psychological disorders in the 1950s, the use of lobotomy was discontinued. Nowadays some brain surgery is used for disorders, but it involves small regions of the brain and is typically performed only as a last resort.

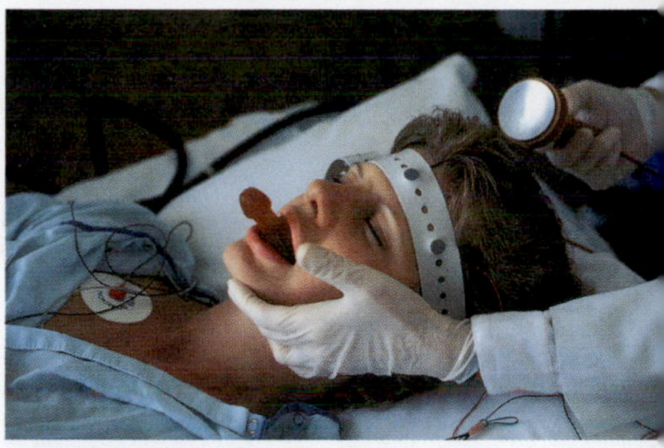

FIGURE 15.10
Electroconvulsive Therapy
A woman being prepared for ECT has a soft object placed between her teeth to prevent her from hurting her tongue. ECT is most commonly used to treat severe depression that has not been responsive to medication or psychotherapy.

ELECTROCONVULSIVE THERAPY **Electroconvulsive therapy (ECT)** involves placing electrodes on a person's head and administering an electrical current strong enough to produce a seizure (**FIGURE 15.10**). This procedure was developed in Europe in the 1930s and tried on the first human in 1938. In the 1950s and 1960s, it was commonly used to treat some psychological disorders, including schizophrenia and depression.

electroconvulsive therapy (ECT) A procedure that involves administering a strong electrical current to the brain to produce a seizure; it is effective for some cases of severe depression.

The general public has a very negative view of ECT. Ken Kesey's 1962 novel *One Flew over the Cuckoo's Nest*, and the award-winning 1975 film version, did a great deal to expose the abuses in mental health care and graphically depicted ECT as well as the tragic effects of lobotomy. Although care for the disordered is still far from perfect, many reforms have been implemented. ECT now generally occurs under anesthesia, with powerful muscle relaxants to eliminate motor convulsions, and the treatment is confined to one hemisphere of the brain. As discussed later in this chapter, ECT is particularly effective for some cases of severe depression, but there are risks to its use.

TRANSCRANIAL MAGNETIC STIMULATION During transcranial magnetic stimulation (TMS), as discussed in Chapter 3, a powerful electrical current runs through a wire coil, producing a magnetic field that is about 40,000 times the strength of Earth's magnetic field. When rapidly switched on and off, this magnetic field induces an electrical current in the brain region directly below the coil, thereby interrupting neural function in that region (**FIGURE 15.11**).

In *single-pulse TMS*, the disruption of brain activity occurs only during the brief period of stimulation. For instance, a pulse given over a motor region might interfere with a person's ability to reach smoothly toward a target object. A pulse given over the speech region may disrupt speaking momentarily. If multiple pulses of TMS occur over an extended time, the procedure is known as *repeated TMS*. Here, the disruption can last beyond the period of direct stimulation. Researchers are investigating the therapeutic potential of this procedure in treating various disorders, and some evidence suggests TMS may be useful for treating depression (Brunoni et al., 2017; Padberg & George, 2009).

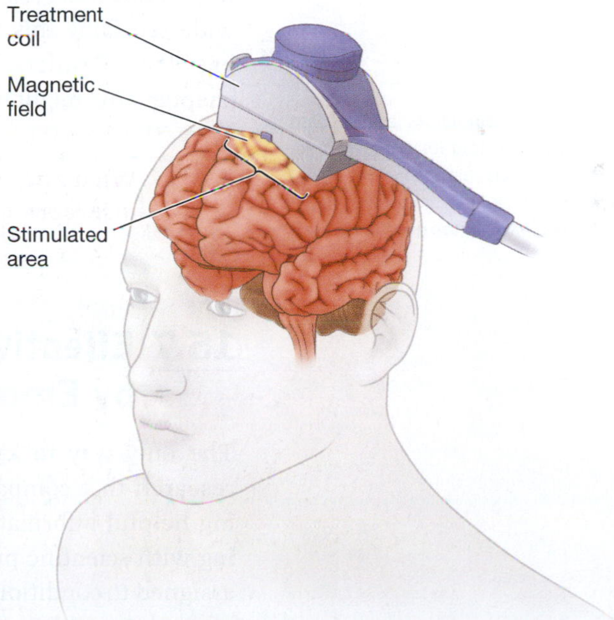

FIGURE 15.11
Transcranial Magnetic Stimulation
In TMS, current flows through a wire coil placed over the scalp where a brain area is to be stimulated. The stimulation interrupts neural function in that region. TMS is used mainly to treat severe depression.

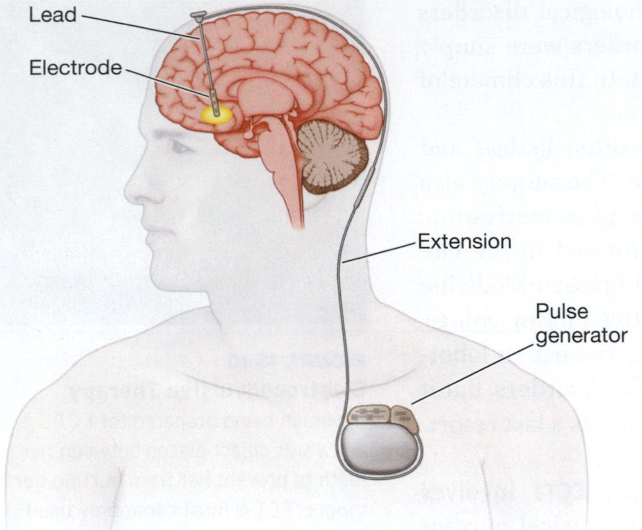

FIGURE 15.12
Deep Brain Stimulation
In DBS, an electrical generator placed just under the skin below the collarbone sends out continuous stimulation to the implanted electrodes. DBS is used for various medical conditions (such as Parkinson's disease), OCD, and major depression.

DEEP BRAIN STIMULATION One of the most dramatic new techniques for treating severe disorders is *deep brain stimulation* (*DBS*). This technique involves surgically implanting electrodes deep within the brain. The location of the electrodes depends on which disorder is being treated. Mild electricity is then used to stimulate the brain at an optimal frequency and intensity, much the way a pacemaker stimulates the heart (**FIGURE 15.12**).

This procedure was first widely used to treat the symptoms of Parkinson's disease. As discussed in Chapter 3, Parkinson's is a disorder of the dopamine system and causes problems with movement. Electrodes implanted into motor regions of the brains of Parkinson's patients reverse many of the movement problems associated with the disease (DeLong & Wichmann, 2008). The success of DBS for Parkinson's is so great that it is now the treatment of choice for many patients. This is true, in part, because the drugs used to treat Parkinson's often cause undesirable side effects, such as increased involuntary movements. By contrast, DBS has few side effects and a low complication rate, as is typical of any minor surgical procedure. Given DBS's tremendous success in treating Parkinson's—with more than 75,000 people worldwide receiving this treatment (Shah et al., 2010)—DBS is being tested for treating other disorders, including psychological disorders. As discussed later in this chapter, DBS might be especially valuable for treating severe OCD and depression.

Q **What alternative biological treatments are used for psychological disorders, and what do they have in common?**

ANSWER: Electroconvulsive therapy (ECT), transcranial magnetic simulation (TMS), and deep brain stimulation (DBS) all attempt to alter brain activity related to psychological symptoms.

15.7 Effectiveness of Treatment Is Determined by Empirical Evidence

The only way to know whether a treatment is valid is to conduct empirical research that compares the treatment with a control condition, such as receiving helpful information or having supportive listeners (Kazdin, 2008). In keeping with scientific principles, client-participants in research should be randomly assigned to conditions. The use of *randomized clinical trials* is one of the hallmarks of good research to establish whether a particular treatment is effective.

PLACEBO EFFECT A placebo is an inert substance. That is, it does not contain any active ingredients. Scientists often study a drug or treatment technique by comparing it with a control condition that consists of a placebo. Research participants are typically assigned at random to either an experimental group or a control group. Randomization helps ensure that groups are comparable and also controls for many potential confounds. In studies of treatments for psychological disorders, the experimental group receives the drug or form of psychotherapy, and the control group receives a comparable placebo treatment. Ideally, everything about the two groups is as similar as possible. If the treatment consists of a large blue pill or weekly meetings with a therapist, the placebo group would take a large blue pill or meet weekly with a therapist. For the placebo group, however, the pill is inert (e.g., a "sugar pill"), or the therapist simply talks with the client rather than teaches them specific cognitive or behavioral techniques being examined in the experimental condition. Any improvement in mental health attributed to the inert drug or minimal contact is called the **placebo effect**.

placebo effect An improvement in physical or mental health following treatment with a placebo—that is, with a drug or treatment that has no active component for the disorder being treated.

For a placebo to reduce symptoms of psychopathology, the participant must believe it will. The person who receives the placebo must not know that, for example, the pills are chemically inert. Indeed, placebos that also produce minor physical reactions that people associate with drug effects—such as having a dry mouth—produce the strongest placebo effects. The placebo effect is "all in the head," but the effect is real—all of our thoughts and feelings are in our heads. Brain imaging shows that when patients have positive expectations about a placebo, the neural processes involved in responding can be similar to the ones activated in response to a biologically active treatment (Benedetti et al., 2005). Consider drugs that interfere with the body's natural method of reducing pain. These drugs also make pain relievers or placebos equally ineffective (Amanzio & Benedetti, 1999). This result indicates that the body has responded in the same way to the pain relievers and to the placebos. Thus, for studies to show that a particular treatment is effective, the results of those studies must illustrate that the treatment's effects are stronger than placebo effects.

The use of placebos for psychotherapy is more complicated than it is for drug research (Herbert & Gaudiano, 2005). Part of the complication is that the therapists likely know whether they are providing the treatment or the control procedure. Moreover, what if just meeting and talking to a therapist is sufficient to treat psychological disorders? One of the long-standing debates in clinical research is whether all therapies are pretty much equally effective because of *common factors* involved in all therapist-client interactions or whether *specific factors* make some treatments better than others (Baskin et al., 2003; Bjornsson, 2011). Although the opportunity to talk about one's problems to someone who is caring and empathic is important in all therapies, compelling evidence indicates that particular treatments are most effective for some disorders and are less effective for others (Barlow et al., 2013).

PSYCHOLOGICAL TREATMENTS David Barlow (2004), a leading researcher on anxiety disorders, points out that findings from medical studies often lead to dramatic changes in treatment practice. For example, within a year after evidence emerged that arthroscopic knee surgery did not produce better outcomes than sham surgery (in which there was no actual procedure), use of the knee surgery declined dramatically. Such developments reflect the increasing importance of *evidence-based treatments* in medicine. Barlow argues that psychological disorders should always be treated in ways that scientific research has shown to be effective. He prefers the term *psychological treatments* to distinguish evidence-based treatment from the more generic term *psychotherapy*, which refers to any form of therapy.

Three features characterize psychological treatments. First, treatments vary according to the particular psychological disorder and the person's specific psychological symptoms. Just as treatment for asthma differs from that for psoriasis, treatments for panic disorder are likely to differ from those for bulimia nervosa. Second, the techniques used in these treatments have been developed and refined using psychological research. Third, no overall grand theory guides all treatment. Instead, treatment is based on evidence of its effectiveness.

There is some debate regarding the most appropriate methods and criteria used to assess clinical research (e.g., Benjamin, 2005; Westen et al., 2004). Jonathan Shedler (2015) has pointed out that evidence-based treatments can be statistically significant without providing any practical improvement in symptoms. That is, even though the treatment group may improve more than the nontreatment group on some measures, the treatment might not provide sufficient relief that people are able to function effectively in their daily lives.

FIGURE 15.13
John Lennon, Yoko Ono, and Primal Scream Therapy
The late Beatle John Lennon and his wife, the artist Yoko Ono, undertook scream therapy for about four months in 1970. After ending the treatment early, Lennon said that he found it helpful but unnecessary. There is no scientific evidence that scream therapy has any beneficial effect.

DANGEROUS TREATMENTS Just as we need to use critical thinking to recognize and avoid flawed science, we also need to recognize and avoid therapies with no scientific basis to confirm their effectiveness. Unfortunately, many available therapies have no scientific basis. Such therapies include ones in which people reenact their own births, scream, or have their body parts manipulated (**FIGURE 15.13**).

Some treatments widely believed to be effective are actually counterproductive. These programs include encouraging people to describe their experiences following major trauma, such as an earthquake; scaring adolescents away from committing crimes by exposing them to prisoners or tough treatments; having police officers run drug education programs such as DARE; and using hypnosis to recover painful memories. These methods not only lack adequate evidence but also may produce results opposite to those intended (Hines, 2003; Lilienfeld, 2007). That is, people debriefed after natural disasters are slightly more likely to develop PTSD than those who are not debriefed, teens in "scared straight" programs show an increase in conduct problems, children in DARE programs are more likely to drink alcohol and smoke cigarettes than children who do not attend such programs, and hypnosis can produce false memories (as discussed in Chapter 7).

In addition, many self-help books make questionable claims. Consider *Make Anyone Fall in Love with You in 5 Minutes* or *Three Easy Steps for Having High Self-Esteem*. It is important to recognize the difference between evidence-based psychotherapies and "alternative" or "fringe" therapies because the latter can prevent people from getting effective treatment and may even be dangerous. In one tragic case, a 10-year-old girl died from suffocation after being wrapped in a blanket for 70 minutes during a supposed therapy session to simulate her own birth, an untested and unscientific method being used to correct the child's unruly behavior (Lowe, 2001). The people conducting the session were unlicensed: They had not passed the tests that certify knowledge about psychotherapy.

Q **Are placebo effects real?**

ANSWER: Yes. Research shows that successful action of placebos is related to changes in brain activity that may be similar to that produced by other treatments.

15.8 Various Providers Can Assist in Treatment for Psychological Disorders

As noted in Chapter 14, nearly half of all Americans meet *DSM* criteria for a psychological disorder at some point in their lives, and 25 percent of the population meets criteria within any given year (Kessler & Wang, 2008). The array of providers offering treatment ranges from those with limited training (e.g., individuals who have recovered from addiction and now provide peer counseling) to those with advanced degrees in psychopathology and its treatment

Table 15.1 Providers of Psychological Treatment

SPECIALTY	TRAINING	DEGREE	TYPICAL EMPLOYMENT
Clinical psychologists	5–7 years of graduate school conducting research on psychological disorders and treatment, including 1 year of clinical internship	PhD	Academic settings, private practice, hospitals, mental health centers, substance abuse programs
	4–6 years of graduate school developing clinical skills to treat people with psychological disorders, followed by 1 year of internship	PsyD	Private practice, medical settings, mental health centers, substance abuse programs
Psychiatrists	4 years of medical school with 3–5 years of additional specialization in residency programs to treat people with psychological disorders	MD	Hospitals, private practice, mental health centers, academic settings, substance abuse programs
Counseling psychologists	4–6 years of graduate school developing clinical skills to treat clients' adjustment and life-stress problems (academic, relationship, work) but not psychological disorders	PhD, EdD	University student health clinics, mental health centers, private practice, schools, wellness programs, rehabilitation facilities, business and organizational settings
Psychiatric social workers	2–3 years of graduate training on directing clients to appropriate social and community agency resources, plus specialized training in mental health care	MSW	Mental health centers, private practice, hospitals, community and social service agencies, substance abuse programs
Psychiatric nurses	2 years for an associate's degree (ASN, RN), 4 years for a bachelor's degree (BSN), or 2–3 additional years of graduate training (MSN), but all focus on nursing plus special training in the care of clients with psychological disorders	ASN, RN, BSN, MSN	Hospitals, mental health centers, residential treatment programs
Paraprofessionals	Work under supervision to assist those with mental health problems in the challenges of daily living	Limited advanced training, no advanced degree	Community outreach programs, crisis centers, substance abuse centers, pastoral counseling, mental health hotlines

Note. PhD = Doctor of Philosophy in Psychology; PsyD = Doctor of Psychology; MD = Doctor of Medicine; EdD = Doctor of Education; MSW = Master of Social Work; ASN = Associate of Science in Nursing; RN = Registered Nurse; BSN = Bachelor of Science in Nursing; MSN = Master of Science in Nursing

(TABLE 15.1). In addition to mental health specialists, regular health care providers (e.g., internists, pediatricians), human-services workers (e.g., school counselors), and volunteers (e.g., self-help groups) also assist people with psychological disorders. No matter who administers the therapy, however, many of the techniques used have emerged from psychological laboratories.

One major difference between psychiatrists and clinical psychologists is the ability to prescribe medications. Clinical psychologists typically are not able to prescribe medications, although efforts are underway to give them such privileges. As of 2021, five U.S. states (Louisiana, New Mexico, Illinois, Iowa, Idaho) allow clinical psychologists with specialized training in psychoactive drugs to prescribe medications. Similar legislation is being proposed elsewhere in the United States and in Europe. However, in most places—including Canada, Australia, and the United Kingdom—only psychiatrists can legally prescribe medications.

TECHNOLOGY AND TREATMENT One of the central problems with treating psychological disorders is that there simply are not enough trained people available to provide traditional one-on-one psychotherapy to all who need it. After all, there is only around one mental health provider for every 504 Americans (Mental Health America, 2020). If one quarter of the U.S. population has a disorder in a given year, then approximately 82 million people could benefit from treatment. Accordingly, a number of programs have been developed to broaden the reach of treatment (Kazdin & Blase, 2011). Through telephone hotlines, for instance, trained volunteers can help people in crisis deal with psychological issues.

Advances in technology have produced other methods for providing treatment without person-to-person contact. *Technology-based treatments* use minimal contact with therapists and rely on smartphones, computer programs, or the internet to offer some form of psychological treatment. For instance, smartphone applications can enable people to keep track of their moods and mental states. The applications can then recommend specific exercises to help people deal with what they are feeling and thinking.

Internet-based treatments have been shown to be successful for a wide range of psychological disorders (Andersson, 2016; Newman et al., 2011; Schmidt & Keough, 2010). For example, the website ModeratedDrinking.com assists people who are dealing with alcohol problems. A study that randomly assigned problem drinkers to a control group or a web-based treatment at ModeratedDrinking.com found that the program led to improved long-term outcomes in terms of days abstaining from alcohol, although it was mainly effective for those who were not heavy drinkers (Hester et al., 2011). A recent meta-analysis of internet-based cognitive-behavioral therapy (iCBT) found that iCBT was effective at treating depression. For patients with moderate to severe depression, therapist-guided iCBT was more effective, whereas patients with milder depression benefited just as much from unguided iCBT (Karyotaki et al., 2021). Because of social-distancing concerns, the pandemic of 2020 accelerated the use and development of online therapies (e.g., Weiner et al., 2020), so it is likely that more internet-based therapies will become available over the next few years.

Q **Can all providers prescribe psychotropic medications?**

ANSWER: No. In most places, only psychiatrists can prescribe medications.

PSYCHOLOGY OUTSIDE THE LAB

15.9 How Do You Find a Therapist Who Can Help You?

FIGURE 15.14
Meeting with a Therapist
Building trust is an important component of a productive relationship between a therapist and a client.

College students are sometimes apprehensive about seeking therapeutic support for dealing with life stressors or psychological problems. That apprehension is understandable. After all, stepping into a stranger's office and disclosing your personal thoughts and feelings is not easy (**FIGURE 15.14**). Nor is it easy to admit—to yourself or others—that you need extra support. If you decide the time has come, knowing how to find a therapist can quell some of the apprehension you might be feeling. The following questions and answers address issues commonly on the minds of therapy-seeking college students.

How do I know if I need therapy? Many times, family members, friends, professors, or physicians encourage college students to seek help for psychological problems. For example, if a student complains about feeling tired all the time, a doctor might ask if the student has been under stress or feeling sad. These conditions might indicate that the person has depression and could be helped by a therapist. Of course, sometimes people know they have psychological problems and do not need encouragement to seek out a therapist. For example, a student who struggles night after night to fall asleep because of constant worry about academic performance might seek help for dealing with anxiety.

You do not have to be 100 percent certain that you need therapy before seeking it out. You can think of the first couple of sessions as a trial period to help you figure out whether therapy might be a valuable tool in your situation.

What kinds of issues can therapists help with? Therapists can help you deal with various issues, ranging from acute stressors (e.g., preparing to move across the country for graduate school) to chronic concerns (e.g., managing generalized anxiety disorder). They can help you make lifestyle or behavioral changes or provide treatments if you have a psychological disorder.

How do I find a therapist who is a good fit with me and my needs? Most college campuses have counselors who can direct students to appropriate treatment providers. In addition, you can ask friends, teachers, and clergy members if they can recommend someone in your area. And organizations such as the American Psychological Association host referral services, many of which are free and web based.

But just because you have the name and phone number of a therapist does not mean that person will be a good fit for you. To make that determination, you will want to do some information gathering up front. First, what are your preferences? Do you think you would be more comfortable working with someone who is the same gender as you? Or with someone from a similar cultural background? Second, it is a good idea to ask therapists about their level of experience helping people with your particular problem (e.g., depression, procrastination, coming out to your parents). Third, pay attention to your comfort level as you interact with a therapist during the first session or two. It is critical that you find a therapist who is trustworthy and caring. The initial consultation should make you feel at ease and hopeful that your issue can be resolved.

If you do not feel a connection with one therapist, seek another. In other words, it might take more than one try for you to find someone you want to work with. This effort will be well spent. Ultimately, the rapport you feel with your therapist will be a key indicator of therapeutic success. Choosing the right therapist can be difficult, but it is extremely important for ensuring successful treatment.

Will my therapist prescribe medication? Typically, only psychiatrists (medical doctors with special training in treating psychological disorders; see Section 15.8) are legally permitted to prescribe medication, though the laws vary by state. That said, almost all therapists have arrangements with physicians who can prescribe medications, including psychotropic drugs, if necessary. The question of the ability to prescribe medication should play only a minor role in the choice of therapist. It is more important to find someone who strikes you as empathic and who is experienced in the effective treatments for your problem.

Remember, therapy involves a kind of relationship. Just as you would not expect every first date to be a love connection, do not expect every therapist to be a good fit for you. As in dating, you might have to shop around to find someone you connect with. ■

Q Do you have to be completely certain you have a psychological disorder to seek help?

ANSWER: No. If you have a condition that is causing you distress or interfering with your ability to function, you should consider seeking the help of a therapist.

Learning Objectives

- Understand why cognitive and behavioral treatments are preferred to drug treatments for anxiety disorders.
- Describe how obsessive-compulsive disorder and addictions are treated.
- Explain why combined or alternative therapies can be effective to treat depressive disorders.
- Understand why lithium and atypical antipsychotics are used to treat bipolar disorder.
- Describe the advantages of atypical antipsychotics in the treatment of schizophrenia.

What Are the Most Effective Treatments?

Research over the past three decades has shown that certain types of treatments are particularly effective for specific types of psychological disorders (Barlow et al., 2013). Other treatments do not have empirical support. Moreover, the scientific study of treatment indicates that although some psychological disorders are quite easily treated, others are not. For instance, highly effective treatments exist for anxiety disorders, depressive disorders, and sexual dysfunction, but few treatments for alcoholism are superior to the natural course of recovery that many people undergo without psychological treatment (Seligman et al., 2001). People who experience depression following the death of a loved one usually feel better with the passage of time. That is, people often resolve personal problems on their own without psychological treatment. Because people tend to enter therapy when they experience crises, they often show improvements no matter what therapy they receive. The following sections examine the evidence used to find the treatments of choice for some of the most common psychological disorders.

15.10 Treatments That Focus on Behavior and Cognition Are Superior for Anxiety Disorders

According to the accumulated evidence, CBT works best to treat most adult anxiety disorders (Hofmann & Smits, 2008). A key ingredient, as mentioned in Section 15.3, is the use of exposure to the threatening stimuli (Foa & McLean, 2016). Exposure to the feared object in a safe environment eventually produces extinction.

Anxiety-reducing drugs are also beneficial in some cases. With drugs, however, there are risks of side effects and, after drug treatment is terminated, the risk of relapse. For instance, anxiolytics work in the short term for generalized anxiety disorder, but they do little to alleviate the source of anxiety and are addictive. Therefore, they are not used much today. Antidepressant drugs that block the reuptake of both serotonin and norepinephrine have been effective for treating generalized anxiety disorder (Hartford et al., 2007; Nicolini et al., 2008). As with all drugs, the effects may be limited to the period during which the drug is taken. By contrast, the effects of CBT persist long after treatment (Hollon et al., 2006).

SPECIFIC PHOBIAS As discussed in Chapter 14, specific phobias are characterized by the fear and avoidance of particular stimuli, such as heights, blood, and spiders. Learning theory suggests these fears are acquired either through experiencing a trauma or by observing similar fear in others. Most phobias, however, apparently develop in the absence of any particular precipitating event. Although learning theory cannot completely explain the development of phobias, behavioral techniques are the treatment of choice.

One of the classic methods used to treat phobias is a form of exposure therapy known as *systematic desensitization*. The client first makes a *fear hierarchy*: a list of situations in which fear is aroused, in ascending order. The example in TABLE 15.2 is from a client who sought therapy to conquer a fear of heights in order to go mountain climbing. The next step is *exposure*, in which the client is asked to imagine or enact scenarios that become progressively more upsetting. The theory

Table 15.2 Anxiety Hierarchy

DEGREE OF FEAR	SITUATION
5	I'm standing on the balcony of the top floor of an apartment tower.
10	I'm standing on a stepladder in the kitchen to change a lightbulb.
15	I'm walking on a ridge. The edge is hidden by shrubs and treetops.
20	I'm sitting on the slope of a mountain, looking out over the horizon.
25	I'm crossing a bridge 6 feet above a creek. The bridge consists of an 18-inch-wide board with a handrail on one side.
30	I'm riding a ski lift 8 feet above the ground.
35	I'm crossing a shallow, wide creek on an 18-inch-wide board, 3 feet above water level.
40	I'm climbing a ladder outside the house to reach a second-story window.
45	I'm pulling myself up a 30-degree wet, slippery slope on a steel cable.
50	I'm scrambling up a rock 8 feet high.
55	I'm walking 10 feet on a resilient, 18-inch-wide board, which spans an 8-foot-deep gulch.
60	I'm walking on a wide plateau 2 feet from the edge of a cliff.
65	I'm skiing an intermediate hill. The snow is packed.
70	I'm walking over a railway trestle.
75	I'm walking on the side of an embankment. The path slopes to the outside.
80	I'm riding a chair lift 15 feet above the ground.
85	I'm walking up a long, steep slope.
90	I'm walking up (or down) a 15-degree slope on a 3-foot-wide trail. On one side of the trail the terrain drops down sharply; on the other side is a steep upward slope.
95	I'm walking on a 3-foot-wide ridge. The trail slopes on one side are more than 25 degrees steep.
100	I'm walking on a 2-foot-wide ridge. The trail slopes on either side are more than 25 degrees.

behind this technique is that exposure to the threatening stimulus will extinguish the fear as the client learns new, nonthreatening associations.

To expose clients without putting them in danger, practitioners may use *virtual environments*, sometimes called *virtual reality*. Computers can simulate the environments and the feared objects (FIGURE 15.15). There is substantial evidence that exposure to these virtual environments can reduce fear responses (Freeman et al., 2017).

Brain imaging data indicate that successful treatment with CBT alters the way the brain processes the fear stimulus. In one study, research participants with severe spider phobia received brain scans while looking at pictures of

FIGURE 15.15
Using Virtual Environments to Conquer Fear
Computer-generated images can simulate feared environments or social interactions. For example, the client can virtually stand on the edge of a very tall building or virtually fly in an aircraft. The client can conquer the virtual environment before taking on the feared situation in real life.

spiders (Straube et al., 2006). The participants whose treatment had been successful showed decreased activation in regions of the brain related to processing and responding to threats. Although it should not be surprising that changes in behavior are reflected in brain activity, these findings suggest that psychotherapy, as well as medication, affects the underlying biology of psychological disorders.

FIGURE 15.16
Panic Attacks
The stress of being in a crowd can bring on a panic attack, especially in someone who has an anxiety disorder.

PANIC DISORDER Many people experience symptoms of a panic attack at some point (**FIGURE 15.16**). They react to these symptoms in different ways. Some shrug off the symptoms. People with panic disorders may interpret heart palpitations as the beginnings of a heart attack or interpret hyperventilation as a sign of suffocation. Panic disorder has multiple components, and each symptom may require a different treatment. This clinical observation is supported by the finding that imipramine, a tricyclic antidepressant, prevents panic attacks but does not reduce the anticipatory anxiety that occurs when people fear they might have an attack.

To break the learned association between the physical symptoms and the feeling of impending doom, CBT can be effective. When people feel anxious, they tend to overestimate the probability of danger. Thus, they potentially contribute to their rising feelings of panic. Cognitive restructuring addresses ways of reacting to the symptoms of a panic attack. First, clients identify their specific fears, such as having a heart attack or fainting. The clients then estimate how many panic attacks they have experienced. The therapist helps clients assign percentages to specific fears and then compare these numbers with the actual number of times the fears have been realized. For example, a client might estimate that they fear having a heart attack during 90 percent of panic attacks and fainting during 85 percent of attacks. The therapist can then point out that the actual rate of occurrence was zero. In fact, people do not faint during panic attacks. The physical symptoms of a panic attack, such as having a racing heart, are the opposite of fainting.

Even if people recognize the irrationality of their fears, they often still have panic attacks. From a cognitive-behavioral perspective, the attacks continue because of a conditioned response to the trigger (e.g., shortness of breath). The goal of therapy is to break the connection between the trigger symptom and the resulting panic. This break can be made by exposure treatment. For example, the therapist might induce feelings of panic—perhaps by having the client breathe in and out through a straw to bring about hyperventilation or by spinning the client rapidly in a chair. Whatever the method, it is done repeatedly to induce habituation and then extinction.

In the treatment of panic attacks, CBT appears to be as effective as or more effective than medication (Schmidt & Keough, 2010). For example, David Barlow and colleagues (2000) found that in the short term, CBT alone and an antidepressant alone were more effective than a placebo for treating panic disorder. Moreover, CBT and the antidepressant did not differ in their results. Six months after treatment had ended, however, those who received CBT were less likely to relapse than those who had taken medication. These results support the conclusion that CBT is the treatment of choice for panic disorder, as it is for the other anxiety disorders.

Q **Why is CBT typically favored over anxiolytics for the treatment of anxiety disorders?**

ANSWER: The results of CBT are as effective as medication treatments for anxiety and the benefits are longer lasting, while the side effects of anxiolytics, such as addiction and greater likelihood of relapse, are avoided.

15.11 Both Antidepressants and CBT Are Effective for Obsessive-Compulsive Disorder

As discussed in Chapter 14, OCD is a combination of recurrent intrusive thoughts (obsessions) and behaviors that an individual feels compelled to perform over and over (compulsions). Because these obsessions make people anxious, many practitioners believed that people with OCD would respond to drug treatment. Traditional antianxiety drugs are completely ineffective for OCD, however. This ineffectiveness is one of the reasons that *DSM-5* separates OCD from anxiety disorders.

When SSRIs were introduced to treat depression, they were particularly effective in reducing the obsessive components of some depressive disorders. For example, they helped reduce the constant feelings of worthlessness experienced by people with depression. We do not know the reasons for these effects. As a result of this initial success in treating the obsessive components of depression, SSRIs were tried in people with OCD and were found to be effective (Rapoport, 1989, 1991). The drug of choice for OCD is clomipramine, a potent serotonin reuptake inhibitor. It is not a true SSRI, since it blocks reuptake of other neurotransmitters as well, but its strong enhancement of the effects of serotonin appears to make it effective for OCD.

CBT is also effective for OCD (Franklin & Foa, 2011). The two most important components of behavioral therapy for OCD are exposure and *response prevention* (Knopp et al., 2013). The person is directly exposed to the stimuli that trigger compulsive behavior but is prevented from engaging in the behavior. This treatment derives from the theory that a particular stimulus triggers anxiety and that performing the compulsive behavior reduces the anxiety. For example, a person might compulsively wash their hands after touching a doorknob or shaking hands with someone. In exposure and response-prevention therapy, the person would be required to touch a doorknob and then would be instructed not to wash their hands afterward. The goal is to break the conditioned link between a particular stimulus and a compulsive behavior (**FIGURE 15.17**). Some cognitive therapies are also useful for OCD, such as helping the client recognize that most people occasionally experience unwanted thoughts and compulsions. In fact, unwanted thoughts and compulsions are a normal part of human experience.

How does drug treatment compare with CBT for OCD? In one study, the use of exposure and response prevention proved superior to the use of clomipramine, although both were better than a placebo (Foa et al., 2005; **FIGURE 15.18**). CBT may thus be a more effective way of treating OCD than medication, especially over the long term (Foa et al., 2005). There is evidence that, at a minimum, adding CBT to SSRI treatment may improve outcomes (Simpson et al., 2008). Therefore, many practitioners recommend the combination of these treatments (Franklin & Foa, 2011).

DEEP BRAIN STIMULATION One exciting possibility is that DBS may be an effective treatment for those with OCD who have not found relief from CBT or medications. Early studies used psychosurgery to remove brain regions thought to contribute to OCD. There were promising outcomes, and these surgical interventions involved much less damage than earlier methods, such as lobotomy. Still, brain surgery is inherently a risky therapy because it is irreversible. DBS offers new hope.

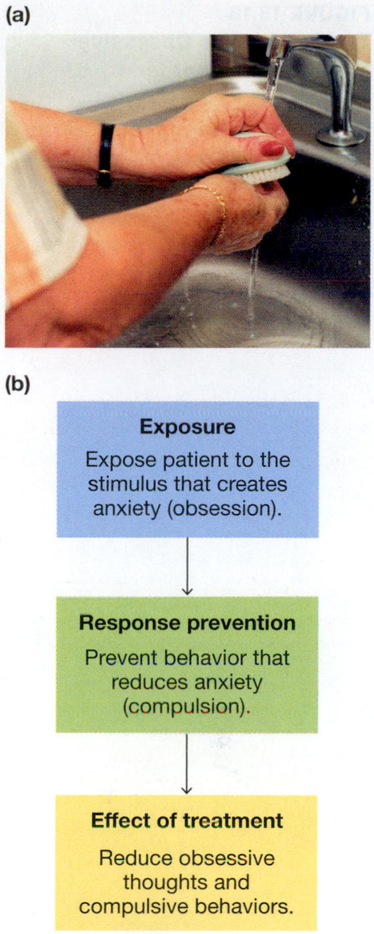

(a)
(b)
Exposure
Expose patient to the stimulus that creates anxiety (obsession).
Response prevention
Prevent behavior that reduces anxiety (compulsion).
Effect of treatment
Reduce obsessive thoughts and compulsive behaviors.

FIGURE 15.17
Using Exposure and Response Prevention to Treat Obsessive-Compulsive Disorder
(a) Someone who obsesses about germs might engage in a compulsive behavior, such as excessive handwashing. **(b)** In exposure and response therapy, the person would be asked to touch something dirty, then would be prevented from handwashing. The effect should be to break the link between the obsession and the compulsion, reducing both.

FIGURE 15.18

Treatments for Obsessive-Compulsive Disorder

Treatments for OCD include the drug clomipramine, exposure and response prevention, or a combination of the two. This graph shows how, in a 2005 study by Edna Foa and colleagues, the numbers of symptoms changed over a period of 12 weeks with each type of treatment.

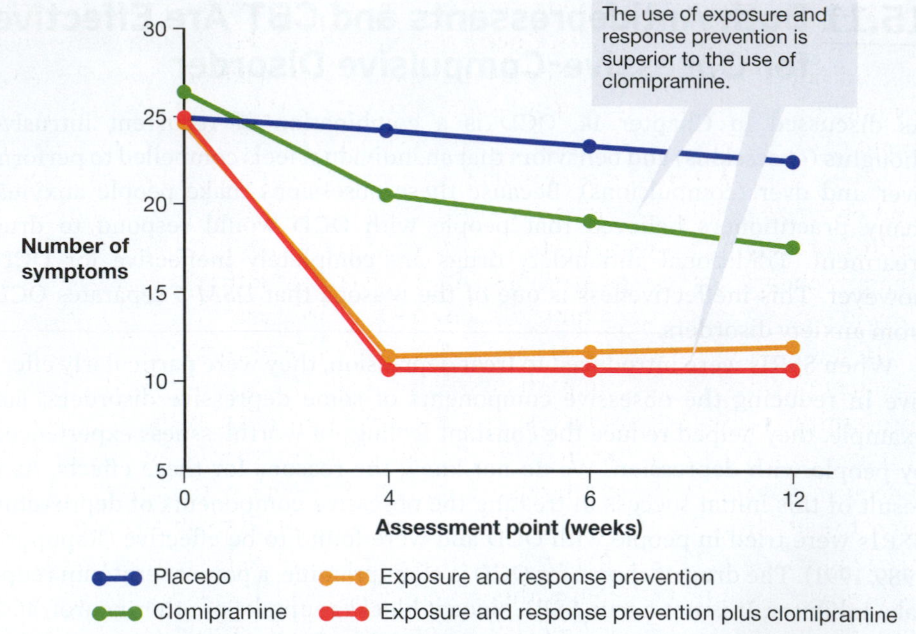

Consider the case of Mr. A., a 56-year-old man with a severely debilitating case of OCD that had lasted for more than four decades. Mr. A. had a number of obsessions about body parts and about gastrointestinal functioning. His compulsions included repetitive movements and dietary restrictions. Researchers implanted DBS electrodes into the caudate, an area of the brain that shows different responses among people with OCD. DBS was very effective for Mr. A., whose symptoms showed significant improvement after six months of treatment. After more than two years, Mr. A. continued to have stunning improvements in psychological functioning and the quality of his daily living (Aouizerate et al., 2004).

DBS leads to a clinically significant reduction of symptoms and increased daily functioning in about two thirds of those with OCD who receive treatment (Greenberg et al., 2008). Although this method remains exploratory, it holds great promise for improving quality of life for those who have not benefited from other forms of treatment (Ooms et al., 2014; Raymaekers et al., 2017).

Q **How do exposure and response prevention reduce obsessions and compulsions?**

ANSWER: Exposure to the feared stimulus in a nonthreatening context, followed by response prevention, extinguishes the conditioned links between the stimulus and anxiety response and the compulsive behavior aimed at reducing the anxiety.

15.12 Cognitive and Behavioral Therapies, Social Support, and Medication Help Treat Addictions

Addictions are chronic disorders, and those who experience them are prone to relapse even after successful treatment. Addiction treatment must help the patient do three things: (1) stop using drugs; (2) stay drug free; and (3) be productive in family life, work, and society. In order to achieve these goals, a combination of treatment approaches is most likely to be effective.

The first step in addiction treatment is for the addicted person to agree to treatment and cease drug use. For many people with addictions, acknowledging that drug use is a problem that needs treatment happens only when there are serious personal or legal consequences. Once a person with an addiction seeks treatment and initially stop using drugs, they may experience significant physical withdrawal symptoms, which can be alleviated with medications. After initial withdrawal, a number of therapies may be used to help the person stay drug free. Cognitive and behavior therapies can assist in modifying attitudes and beliefs toward drug use and enhance healthy life skills. Exposure therapy can be effective in helping to reduce cravings in response to cues and contexts associated with drug use. Family therapy and groups such as Alcoholics Anonymous and Narcotics Anonymous can provide social support structures that help reduce drug use.

In addition to psychological treatments, there is a growing recognition that medication may play an important role in maintaining drug abstinence and preventing relapse. For instance, smokers who want to quit may find that nicotine patches help reduce the craving to smoke. By replacing some of the physiological effects of smoking with a patch, some find it easier to cope with the psychological urge to smoke. For opioid use disorder, medication-assisted treatment has become the gold standard. For example, methadone is an agonist that has many of the same effects as opioids on the brain without producing the high associated with opioid use. By mimicking the effect of opioids on the brain, methadone reduces drug cravings and helps people with addictions stay in treatment longer. Although it may seem counterintuitive to treat an opioid use disorder with an opioid receptor agonist, there is strong evidence that medication-assisted treatment leads to better outcomes than abstinence and psychotherapy alone (Connery, 2015).

One challenge in treating addiction is that many people with addictions also have other psychological disorders. Some people may initially take drugs in an effort to cope with mental health symptoms and become addicted. It is difficult to treat these other disorders when the person is using drugs, but once drug use has stopped, properly diagnosing and treating comorbid psychological disorders is an important component of preventing relapse.

Q How does medication-assisted treatment help prevent relapse in people with opioid use disorder?

ANSWER: Medication can help reduce drug cravings.

15.13 Many Effective Treatments Are Available for Depressive Disorders

As discussed in Chapter 14, depressive disorders are characterized by low mood or loss of interest in pleasurable activities. This condition is one of the most widespread psychological disorders, and it has become more common over the past few decades (Hollon et al., 2002). Fortunately, scientific research has validated a number of effective treatments. There is no "best" way to treat depressive disorders. Many approaches are available, and ongoing research is determining which type of therapy works best for which types of individuals.

ANTIDEPRESSANT TREATMENT In the 1950s, tuberculosis was a major health problem in the United States, particularly in urban areas. A common treatment was iproniazid. This drug reduced bacteria associated with tuberculosis in patients' saliva. It also stimulated patients' appetites, increased their energy levels, and gave them an overall sense of well-being. In 1957, researchers who had noted iproniazid's effect on mood reported preliminary success in using it to treat depression.

In the following year, nearly half a million people experiencing depression were given the drug.

Iproniazid is an MAO inhibitor. MAO inhibitors can be toxic because of their effects on various physiological systems. Patients taking these drugs must avoid ingesting any substances containing tyramine, an amino acid found in various foods, including red wine, cured meats, and aged cheeses. The interaction of an MAO inhibitor and tyramine can result in severe, sometimes lethal elevations in blood pressure. In addition, the interaction of an MAO inhibitor with particular prescription and over-the-counter medications can be fatal. As a result of these complications, MAO inhibitors are generally reserved for people who do not respond to other antidepressants.

Tricyclics, another type of antidepressant, were also identified in the 1950s. One of these—imipramine, developed as an antihistamine—was found effective in relieving clinical depression. This drug and others like it act on neurotransmitters as well as on the histamine system. Tricyclics are extremely effective antidepressants. Because of their broad-based action, however, they have a number of unpleasant side effects. For example, their use can result in drowsiness, weight gain, sweating, constipation, heart palpitations, dry mouth, or any combination of such problems.

The discovery of these early antidepressants was largely serendipitous. Subsequently, researchers began to search for antidepressants that did not affect multiple physiological and neurological systems and so would not have such troublesome side effects. In the 1980s, researchers developed Prozac. This SSRI does not affect histamine or neurotransmitters other than serotonin. Therefore, it has none of the side effects associated with the tricyclic antidepressants, although it occasionally causes insomnia, headache, weight loss, and sexual dysfunction. Because they have fewer serious side effects than MAO inhibitors, Prozac and other SSRIs began to be prescribed more frequently. A number of other drug treatments for depressive disorders have also been validated. For example, bupropion (brand name Wellbutrin) affects many neurotransmitter systems, but it has fewer side effects for most people than other drugs. Unlike most antidepressants, bupropion does not cause sexual dysfunction. Unlike SSRIs, bupropion is not an effective treatment for panic disorder or OCD.

Researchers have attempted to determine how particular types of people will respond to antidepressants. Still, physicians often must resort to a trial-and-error approach in treating people who are experiencing depression. No single drug stands out as being most effective. There is some evidence that tricyclics might be beneficial for the most serious depressive disorders, especially for hospitalized patients (Anderson, 2000). SSRIs and bupropion are generally considered first-line medications because they have the fewest serious side effects (Olfson et al., 2002). They are therefore often used for persistent depressive disorder, which is less severe than major depressive disorder (Craighead & Dunlop, 2014). Often the decision of which drug to use depends on the person's overall medical health and the possible side effects of each medication.

The use of antidepressants is based on the belief that depression (like other psychological disorders) is caused by deficits or excesses in neurotransmitters or problems with neural receptors. Recently, a number of critics have challenged this view, arguing that there is no evidence to suggest that people with depression had abnormal brain functioning before drug treatment (Angell, 2011). Indeed, faulty logical reasoning may be at play.

The success of drugs such as SSRIs in alleviating symptoms of depression has been viewed as evidence that depression is caused by an abnormality in serotonin function. As a critical thinker, you probably recognize that this connection is not good proof. After all, when you have a cold, you might take a medication that treats your runny nose. Doing so does not prove that your cold was caused by your runny nose. Thus, antidepressants may help treat the symptoms of depression without having any influence on the underlying cause. Moreover, as discussed in Section 15.14, some of the success of SSRIs might be due to placebo effects.

COGNITIVE-BEHAVIORAL TREATMENT Not all depressed people benefit from antidepressant medications. In addition, some people cannot or will not tolerate the side effects. Fortunately, CBT is just as effective as antidepressants in treating depressive disorders (Hollon et al., 2002). From a cognitive perspective, people who become depressed do so because of automatic, irrational thoughts. According to the cognitive distortion model developed by Aaron Beck, depression is the result of a cognitive triad of negative thoughts about oneself, the situation, and the future (see Figure 14.17). The thought patterns of people with depressive disorders differ from the thought patterns of people with anxiety disorders. That is, people with anxiety disorders worry about the future. People with depressive disorders think about how they have failed in the past, how poorly they are dealing with the present situation, and how terrible the future will be.

The goal of the cognitive-behavioral treatment of depression is to help the person think more adaptively and thus improve mood and behavior. The specific treatment is adapted to the individual, but some general principles apply to this type of therapy. People may be asked to recognize and record their negative thoughts (**FIGURE 15.19**). Thinking about situations in a negative way can become automatic, and recognizing these thought patterns can be difficult. Once the patterns are identified and monitored, the clinician can help the client recognize other ways of viewing the same situation that are not so dysfunctional.

CBT can be effective on its own, but combining it with antidepressant medication can be more effective than either one of these approaches alone (Cuijpers et al., 2014). In addition, the response rates of the combined-treatment approach are extremely good (Keller et al., 2000; Kocsis et al., 2003). The issue is not drugs versus psychotherapy. The issue is which treatment provides—or which treatments provide—relief for each individual. For instance, drug treatment may be the most effective option for those who are suicidal, in acute distress, or unable to

Date	Event	Feeling	Thought	Change(s)
April 4	Friend forgot my birthday	Sad, anxious, worried	*Oh, what have I done now? Maybe she no longer wants to be my friend.*	Explore alternative interpretations. • *Is it likely she was just busy or distracted?* Don't think of a situation as a catastrophe. • *We are likely still friends and can get together later and have some fun.*
April 5	Failed a test	Sad	*Maybe I am not very intelligent.*	Check to see if thinking is influenced by negative views. • *Actually I am doing well in most of my courses. Next time I will study more for this course.*
April 7	Manager came to check on a report that is overdue	Anxious	*The report is late and it is not going well. I will get fired.*	Make the best of a bad situation. • *The report is late, but I will put in extra time and get it done as I always do.*
April 9	Thought about asking a classmate to go for coffee	Sad, defeated	*She won't want to go with me.*	Question whether there is evidence to support this idea. • *Actually, I don't know if she wants to go. She is friendly in class.*
April 10	Neighbors brought over some cookies	A little happy, mostly sad	*They probably think that I can't cook. I look like such a mess all the time. And my house was a disaster when they came in.*	Stop a cascade of negative thoughts and replace them with positive ones. • *The neighbors just want to help me.*

FIGURE 15.19
Cognitive-Behavioral Therapy
Clients in CBT may be asked to keep a record of events and their reactions to those events, including their automatic thoughts. Such a log can help identify patterns in thought and behavior, and the therapist can then help the client reframe the situations in more productive ways.

commit to regular sessions with a therapist. For most people, especially those who have physical problems such as liver impairment or cardiac problems, psychotherapy may be the treatment of choice because it is long-lasting and does not have the side effects associated with medications (Hollon et al., 2006). Treatment selection also depends on the severity of the depressive disorder. In general, people who have chronic major depressive disorder receive the most benefit from combined drug treatments and psychotherapies (Craighead & Dunlop, 2014).

As with other psychological disorders, treatment of depression with psychotherapy leads to changes in brain activation that overlap with those observed with drug treatments (Brody et al., 2001). One study found that although psychotherapy and drugs involved the same brain regions, activity in those regions was quite different during the two treatments (Goldapple et al., 2004). This finding suggests that psychotherapy and drugs operate through different mechanisms. Indeed, a meta-analysis of combined studies found that the effects of the drugs and psychotherapy are largely independent of each other, supporting other evidence that the combination of the two provides greater effectiveness than either one alone (Cuijpers et al., 2014).

ALTERNATIVE TREATMENTS In people with seasonal affective disorder (SAD), episodes of depression are most likely to occur during winter. A milder form of SAD has been called the winter blues. The rate of these disorders increases with latitude (**FIGURE 15.20**). Although it's not clear why winter months and less daily light are related to depression in some people, many people experiencing SAD respond favorably to *phototherapy*, which involves exposure to a high-intensity light source for part of each day. Studies comparing phototherapy and CBT for treating SAD find that although both therapies can be effective, phototherapy may work faster than CBT in alleviating symptoms (Meyerhoff et al., 2018), whereas CBT may be more effective at reducing depressive symptoms in subsequent winters (Rohan et al., 2020). Interestingly, even though phototherapy is primarily used to treat SAD, there is emerging evidence that it may also be an effective treatment for mild depression that is unrelated to seasonal variation (Tao et al., 2020).

For some people with depressive disorders, regular aerobic exercise can reduce the symptoms and prevent recurrence (Pollock, 2004). Aerobic exercise

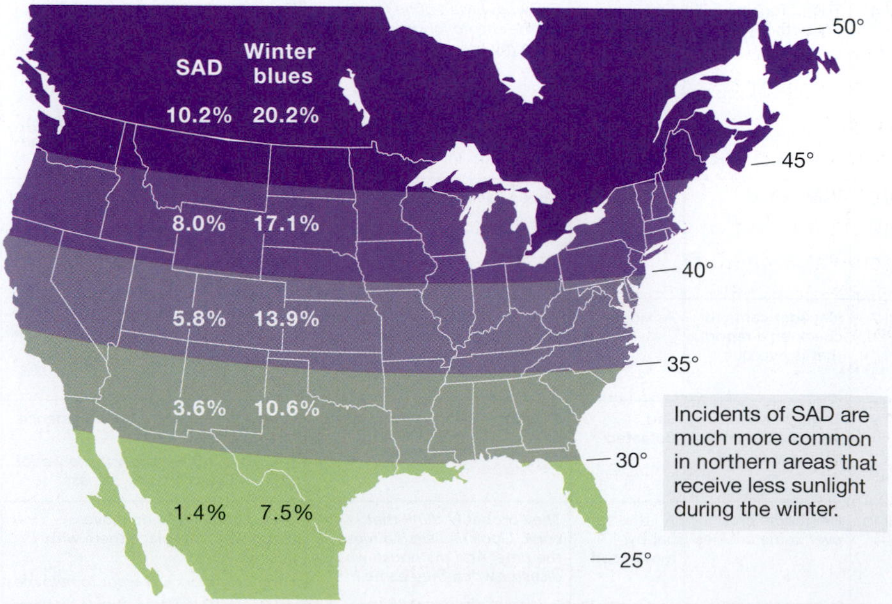

FIGURE 15.20
Incidence of Seasonal Affective Disorder
As shown by this map, the incidence of SAD varies by latitude.

may reduce depression because it releases endorphins, which can cause an overall feeling of well-being (a feeling runners sometimes experience as "runner's high"). Aerobic exercise may also regularize bodily rhythms, improve self-esteem, and provide social support if people exercise with others. However, people with depression may have difficulty finding the energy and motivation to begin an exercise regimen.

ECT is a very effective treatment for those who are severely depressed and do not respond to conventional treatments (Weiner & Reti, 2017). For a number of reasons, ECT might be preferable to other treatments for depression. Antidepressants can take weeks to be effective, whereas ECT works quickly. For a suicidal person, waiting several weeks for relief can literally be deadly. In addition, ECT may be the treatment of choice for depression in pregnant women, since there is no evidence that the seizures harm the developing fetus. In contrast, many psychotropic medications can cause birth defects. Most important, ECT has proved effective in people for whom other treatments have failed.

ECT does, however, have some limitations, including a high relapse rate—often necessitating repeated treatments—and memory impairments (Fink, 2001). In most cases, memory loss is limited to the day of ECT treatment, but some people experience longer-term memory loss (Donahue, 2000). Because of these concerns, most centers today perform unilateral ECT over only the hemisphere not dominant for language, a treatment that seems to reduce memory disruption (Papadimitriou et al., 2001).

According to a series of studies, TMS over the left frontal regions results in a significant reduction in depression (Chistyakov et al., 2005; George et al., 1995, 1999; Pascual-Leone et al., 1996). Because TMS does not involve anesthesia or have any major side effects, it can be administered outside hospital settings. It is not likely, however, that TMS will ever completely replace ECT. The two methods may act via different mechanisms and may therefore be appropriate for different types of patients. The long-term value of TMS is that it is effective even for those who have not responded to treatment with antidepressants (Fitzgerald et al., 2003). In October 2008, TMS was approved by the FDA for the treatment of major depressive disorder in people who are not helped by traditional therapies.

DEEP BRAIN STIMULATION As with obsessive-compulsive disorder, DBS might be valuable for treating severe depressive disorders when all other treatments have failed. In 2003, Helen Mayberg and colleagues became the first to try out this novel treatment. Mayberg's earlier research had pointed to an area of the prefrontal cortex as abnormal in depression. Following the logic of using DBS for Parkinson's, neurosurgeons inserted electrodes into this brain region in six patients with severe depression (Mayberg et al., 2005; McNeely et al., 2008). The results were stunning for four of the patients. In fact, some of them felt relief as soon as the switch was turned on. For all four, it was as if a horrible noise had stopped and a weight had been lifted, as if they had emerged into a more beautiful world (Dobbs, 2006; Ressler & Mayberg, 2007).

Several studies have been conducted examining DBS for treatment-resistant depression, and different brain regions have been targeted with varying success (Drobisz & Damborská, 2019). In studies examining the prefrontal cortex region, at least half of the participants benefited from this treatment (Bewernick et al., 2010; Malone et al., 2009; **FIGURE 15.21**). One study followed 20 patients for three to six years and found that about two thirds showed long-lasting benefits from DBS (Kennedy et al., 2011). These studies demonstrate that DBS is useful for helping people lead more productive lives. For instance, in Kennedy and colleagues'

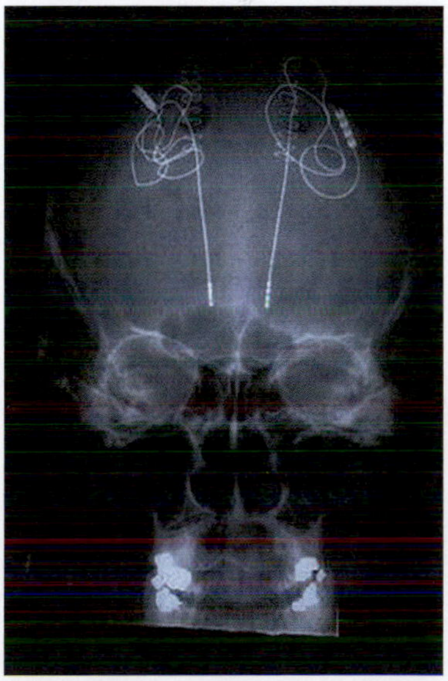

FIGURE 15.21
DBS and Depression
Electrodes have been implanted in a region of the prefrontal cortex that has been targeted for DBS treatment of depression.

(2011) study, only 10 percent of the people were able to work or engage in meaningful activities outside the house (e.g., volunteering) before DBS, whereas two thirds were able to do so after DBS.

DBS differs from other treatments in that researchers can easily alter the electrical current without the person knowing to demonstrate that the DBS is responsible for improvements in psychological functioning. Research using DBS to treat severe depressive disorders is now underway at a number of sites around the globe (Ryder & Holtzheimer, 2016).

GENDER ISSUES IN TREATING DEPRESSIVE DISORDERS As noted in Chapter 14, women are twice as likely as men are to be diagnosed with depressive disorders. Some portion of this difference relates to high rates of domestic and other violence against women, reduced economic resources, and inequities at work (American Psychological Association, 2007). Women are also the primary consumers of psychotherapy. The American Psychological Association therefore has published *Guidelines for Psychological Practice with Girls and Women* (2007). These guidelines remind therapists to be aware of gender-specific stressors, such as the way work and family interact to place additional burdens on women and the biological realities of reproduction and menopause. The guidelines also point out that women of color, lesbians, and women with disabilities are often stereotyped in ways that signal disregard for the challenges they face. All of these factors can interfere with the therapeutic process.

Problems also exist in the treatment of depression in men. Gender stereotypes may contribute to a reluctance among men to admit to depression and even greater reluctance to seek appropriate therapy. This has been described as "a conspiracy of silence that has long surrounded depression in men" (Brody, 1997). As described in the opening vignette of this chapter, stigma about mental health can prevent men from seeking help, and this may be especially true for men. For this reason, public statements from well-respected men, like Michael Phelps, can help break the silence surrounding depression and increase the number of men who seek psychotherapy. One goal is to help men stop masking their depression with alcohol, isolation, and irritability. Any of these retreats from the social world may be a symptom of unacknowledged depression.

YOU BE THE PSYCHOLOGIST

Q **What factors contribute to the less frequent diagnosis and treatment of depression in men?**

ANSWER: Gender stereotypes may make men more reluctant to admit to symptoms of depression, and therefore they avoid treatment. They may be more likely to mask their symptoms with alcohol, isolation, and irritability.

15.14 How Effective Are Antidepressants?

The arrival of Prozac on the market in 1987 led to a dramatic shift in the treatment of depression. Today, most people who experience depression are first treated by a medical doctor. The doctor is likely to prescribe an antidepressant rather than refer the person to a psychotherapist. In the majority of cases, the doctor prescribing the antidepressant is a general practitioner with no specific training in diagnosing or treating psychological disorders (Smith, 2012). Since Prozac was introduced, the use of antidepressants has quadrupled in the United States, and it is estimated that more than 1 in 10 Americans over age 6 takes antidepressant medication (Angell, 2011; Moore & Mattison, 2017; Smith, 2012).

The rapid increase in antidepressant use resulted in concerns that marketing by drug companies influenced doctors to overprescribe them. These concerns prompted some psychologists to ask whether antidepressants are really as effective as drug companies advertise and whether they are more effective for some people than for others.

One problem in determining the answer to these questions is that there are biases in the literature on the effectiveness of drug therapy (Turner et al., 2008). In science, it is much easier to publish positive results—those that indicate treatment success—than negative results. Moreover, drug companies are much more likely to publicize studies that show their drugs are effective than those that do not. They might even attempt to suppress publication of research that questions their drugs' effectiveness. If they paid for the study, part of the agreement may give the drug company control over which aspects of the study can be published. How can researchers tell whether published studies present a different story than unpublished studies? The psychologist Irving Kirsch found a way to answer that question.

In approving a new drug, the U.S. Food and Drug Administration (FDA) requires drug companies to submit all clinical studies they have conducted regardless of whether those findings were ever published. Kirsch and colleagues (2008) used a Freedom of Information Act request to obtain all placebo-controlled studies of the most widely used antidepressants. Of the 42 studies they obtained, most had negative, or null, results, and some had positive results. Overall, placebos were 80 percent as effective as antidepressants, and the change in self-reported depressive symptoms showed that improvement on drugs compared with placebos was modest at best. To be clear: People felt less depressed after taking antidepressants, but they also felt better after taking placebos, and thus it is possible that placebo effects play a prominent role in the success of antidepressant drug treatments.

By looking at all the data, Kirsch found that antidepressants work better than placebos only some of the time. But what led to the variability in the results in the different studies? Why did some studies show antidepressants worked, while others found they were no better than placebos? Were there uncontrolled variables that led to different findings? To explore this question, researchers looked across studies to see whether severity of initial depression was related to whether or not antidepressant treatment was more effective than a placebo at alleviating symptoms. They found that the relative effectiveness of treatment with antidepressants increased with the severity of depression. For those who were severely depressed, antidepressant treatment was more effective than a placebo, but those with mild depression showed no benefit (Fournier et al., 2010). In other words, antidepressant treatment does seem to work for some people. Based on these results, Steven Hollon, a psychology professor at Vanderbilt University, estimates that "at least half the folks who are being treated with antidepressants aren't benefiting from the active pharmacological effects of the drugs themselves but from a placebo effect" (as quoted in Smith, 2012, p. 36).

Because of the widespread use of antidepressants and further investigation into their efficacy, it is now standard practice to look at all the data, not just the positive results, when evaluating the effects of psychotropic drugs (Smith, 2012). By digging deeper into the data, psychologists discovered that antidepressants do work better than placebos, but not for everybody. But how might a therapist decide if an SSRI would be effective for a specific patient? Although these studies show that, on average, antidepressant treatment may be more effective for those with more severe depression, this does not mean that antidepressants will not work for someone with mild or moderate depression, or that they always work for someone with severe depression. The data only indicate who is likely to respond more to antidepressant treatment than to a placebo. What kind of data would be needed to know whether a specific individual will benefit from an antidepressant drug? Psychologists and psychiatrists are currently looking for a diagnostic test or symptom that will signal if an antidepressant will be effective for a specific patient before trying it, but they have yet to discover one. If you are on such a medication and have any concerns, you should discuss your situation with your physician. ■

Q **If a study finds that patients are less depressed after taking an antidepressant, does this mean the drug worked?**

ANSWER: No. The group taking the antidepressant needs to show more symptom relief than the placebo group, since taking a placebo can also lead to improvement.

15.15 Lithium and Atypical Antipsychotics Are Most Effective for Bipolar Disorder

In *DSM-5*, a new category "Bipolar and Related Disorders" has been placed between disorders related to schizophrenia and those related to depression. In bipolar disorder, as discussed in Chapter 14, moods cycle between manic (or less intense hypomanic) episodes and depressive episodes. The manic phase includes alterations in thought that link it to the psychotic states found in schizophrenia. The negative moods associated with the depressive episodes link bipolar disorder to depression. This distinction will be useful as you learn about the treatment options for this disorder. It is one of the few psychological disorders for which there is a clear optimal treatment (**FIGURE 15.22**): psychotropic medications, especially the mood stabilizer lithium (Geddes et al., 2004; Geddes & Miklowitz, 2013).

As with the uses of other psychotropic drugs, the discovery of lithium for the treatment of bipolar disorder was serendipitous. In 1949, the researcher John Cade found that the urine of manic patients was toxic to guinea pigs. He believed that a toxin—specifically, uric acid—might be causing the symptoms of mania. If so, once the uric acid was removed from the body through the urine, the symptoms would diminish (a solution that would explain why the patients were not always manic). When he gave lithium urate, a salt in uric acid, to the guinea pigs, however, it proved nontoxic. To his surprise, it protected them against the toxic effects of the manic patients' urine and also sedated them. He next tried lithium salts on himself. When he was assured of their safety, he gave the salts to 10 hospitalized manic patients. All the patients recovered rapidly.

The mechanisms by which lithium stabilizes mood are not well understood, but the drug seems to modulate neurotransmitter levels, balancing excitatory and inhibitory activities (Jope, 1999). Lithium has unpleasant side effects, however, including thirst, hand tremors, excessive urination, and memory problems. The side effects often diminish after several weeks on the drug. Anticonvulsive medications, more commonly used to reduce seizures, can also stabilize mood and may be effective for intense bipolar episodes.

FIGURE 15.22
Bipolar Disorders Can Be Successfully Treated
The actor Catherine Zeta-Jones has been diagnosed with bipolar II disorder. Zeta-Jones manages her symptoms through psychotropic medications and periodic residential treatment.

More recently, antipsychotic medications have been found to be effective in stabilizing moods and reducing episodes of mania. A class of drugs (commonly used in the treatment of schizophrenia) collectively called second-generation antipsychotics are also known as *atypical antipsychotics* because they differ from traditional antipsychotics in numerous ways. The drug quetiapine—better known as Seroquel—is an atypical antipsychotic that has grown in popularity and is now the most commonly prescribed drug for bipolar disorders (Hooshmand et al., 2014). Some evidence indicates that combining mood stabilizers, such as lithium, with atypical antipsychotics improves treatment outcomes (Buoli et al., 2014; Vieta et al., 2012).

The important lesson here is that there is not a one-to-one mapping of drug treatment to psychological disorder. As discussed in Chapter 14, traditional *DSM* diagnoses might mask similarities between disorders. For instance, within families there is considerable overlap in susceptibility to bipolar disorder and to schizophrenia (Craddock & Sklar, 2013). Family members of those with either of these disorders are at greater risk of developing either bipolar disorder or schizophrenia. Likewise, similar gene mutations are observed for both disorders (Malhotra et al., 2011). Recall that the Research Domain Criteria (RDoC) system classifies disorders according to similar genetic and neurophysiological findings. From the RDoC perspective, the use of drugs from one category to treat symptoms of another category may reflect similar underlying disturbances across diagnostic categories. That is, bipolar disorder and schizophrenia may be variants of the same disorder. Drugs treat symptoms, not disorders. In practice, the use of antipsychotics may be valuable for any disorder that involves impaired thought, regardless of *DSM* diagnosis.

Because lithium and atypical antipsychotics work better on mania than on depression, people are sometimes given an antidepressant as well. The risk of triggering a manic episode makes the use of antidepressants controversial, and they are generally not recommended (Pacchiarotti et al., 2013). When necessary, SSRIs are preferable to other antidepressants because they are less likely to trigger episodes of mania (Gijsman et al., 2004). However, the available evidence suggests that antidepressants may have limited usefulness in treatment of bipolar disorder (Nivoli et al., 2011).

As with all psychological disorders, compliance with drug therapy can be a problem for various reasons. For example, people may skip doses or stop taking the medications completely in an effort to reduce the side effects. In these situations, CBT can help increase compliance with medication regimens (Miller et al., 1989). Those with bipolar disorder also may stop taking their medications because they miss the "highs" of their hypomanic and manic phases. Psychotherapy can help these individuals accept their need for medication and understand the impact their disorder has on them and on those around them.

Q Which medications are most typically prescribed for bipolar disorder, and which symptoms are they best at controlling?

ANSWER: Mood stabilizers, especially lithium, and atypical antipsychotics are the most effective treatments for bipolar disorder. They control manic symptoms better than depression.

15.16 Antipsychotics Are Superior for Schizophrenia

In the early 1900s, Freud's psychoanalytic theory and treatments based on it were widely touted as the answer to many psychological disorders. Freud, however, admitted that his techniques were effective only for what he termed "neuroses" and were unlikely to benefit patients with more-severe "psychotic" disorders, such as schizophrenia. Because psychotic patients can be difficult to handle and even more difficult to treat, they were generally institutionalized in large mental hospitals. By 1934, according to estimates, the physician-to-patient ratio in such institutions in New York State was less than 1 to 200.

In this undesirable situation, the staff and administrators of mental hospitals were willing to try any inexpensive treatment that had a chance of decreasing the patient population or that at least might make the inmates more manageable. Brain surgery, such as prefrontal lobotomy, was considered a viable option for patients with severe disorders. Egas Moniz initially reported that the operation was frequently successful (see Section 15.6). It soon became evident to him that patients with anxiety or depression benefited most from the surgery. Patients with schizophrenia did not seem to improve following the operation. Fortunately, as noted earlier, the introduction of psychotropic medications in the 1950s eliminated the use of lobotomy.

PHARMACOLOGICAL TREATMENTS Since the sixteenth century, extracts from dogbane, a toxic herb, had been used to calm highly agitated people. The critical ingredient was isolated in the 1950s and named reserpine. When given to those with schizophrenia, reserpine not only had a sedative effect but also was effective in reducing the positive symptoms of schizophrenia, such as delusions and hallucinations. Shortly afterward, a synthetic version of reserpine was created that had fewer side effects. This drug, chlorpromazine, acts as a major tranquilizer. It reduces anxiety, sedates without inducing sleep, and decreases the severity and frequency of the positive symptoms of schizophrenia. Later, another antipsychotic, haloperidol, was developed that was chemically different and had less of a sedating effect than chlorpromazine.

Traditional antipsychotics such as haloperidol and chlorpromazine revolutionized the treatment of schizophrenia and became the most frequently used treatment for this disorder. People with schizophrenia who had been hospitalized for years were able to walk out of mental institutions and live independently. These antipsychotic drugs have drawbacks, however. For example, they have little or no impact on the negative symptoms of schizophrenia. In addition, they have significant side effects. Chlorpromazine sedates people, can cause constipation and weight gain, and causes cardiovascular damage. Haloperidol does not cause these symptoms, but both drugs have significant motor side effects that resemble symptoms of Parkinson's disease: immobility of facial muscles, trembling of extremities, muscle spasms, uncontrollable salivation, and a shuffling walk. Tardive dyskinesia—as discussed in Section 15.5, involuntary movements of the lips, tongue, face, legs, or other parts of the body—is another devastating side effect of these medications and is often permanent once it appears, although it can be treated. Despite these side effects, haloperidol and chlorpromazine were the only available options for many years.

The late 1980s saw the introduction of atypical antipsychotics to treat schizophrenia. The initial drug of this type to be used in treatment, clozapine, has two important advantages over traditional antipsychotics. First, it is beneficial in treating the negative as well as the positive symptoms of schizophrenia (**FIGURE 15.23**).

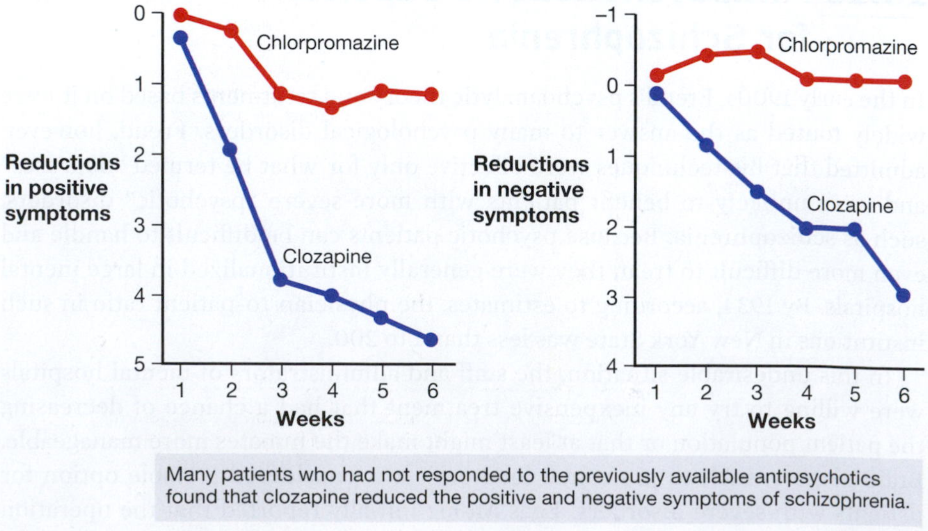

FIGURE 15.23
The Effectiveness of Clozapine
These graphs compare the effects, in representative cases, of using either clozapine or chlorpromazine to treat people with schizophrenia.

Many people with schizophrenia who had not responded to the previously available antipsychotics improved on clozapine. Second, no symptoms of Parkinson's or of tardive dyskinesia appeared in any of the people taking the drug. Clozapine has fewer side effects than chlorpromazine or haloperidol, but its side effects are serious: seizures, heart arrhythmias, and substantial weight gain. Of even greater concern is that clozapine can cause a fatal reduction in white blood cells. Although the risk of this problem is low, those taking the drug must have frequent blood tests. The cost of the blood tests, in addition to the high cost of the medication, has made this drug treatment prohibitively expensive for many who might benefit from it.

Other atypical medications similar to clozapine in structure, pharmacology, and effectiveness have been introduced that do not reduce white blood cell counts. These are Risperdal and Zyprexa, which like clozapine are atypical antipsychotics. Like clozapine, they have about one fifth the risk of producing tardive dyskinesia as compared with the earlier drugs (Correll et al., 2004). These drugs are now the first line of defense in the treatment of schizophrenia (Walker et al., 2004), and clozapine is typically reserved for severe cases because of its more serious side effects. However, other atypical antipsychotics may not be as successful as clozapine at treating negative symptoms (Leucht et al., 2009).

PSYCHOSOCIAL TREATMENTS Medication is essential in the treatment of schizophrenia. Without it, people may deteriorate, experiencing more frequent and severe psychotic episodes. When antipsychotic drugs became available, other types of therapies for schizophrenia were virtually dismissed. It became clear over time, however, that although medication effectively reduces delusions and hallucinations, it does not substantially affect the person's social functioning. Thus, antipsychotic drugs fall short of being a cure. The drugs must be combined with other treatments to help people lead productive lives.

Social skills training is one effective way to address some deficits in those with schizophrenia (**FIGURE 15.24**), who can benefit from intensive training in regulating affect, recognizing social cues, and predicting the effects of their behavior in social situations. With intensive long-term training, people with schizophrenia can generalize the skills learned in therapy to other social environments. Also, when self-care skills are deficient, behavioral interventions can focus on areas such as grooming and bathing, management of medications, and financial planning. Training in specific cognitive skills, such as in modifying thinking patterns and coping with auditory hallucinations, has been less effective.

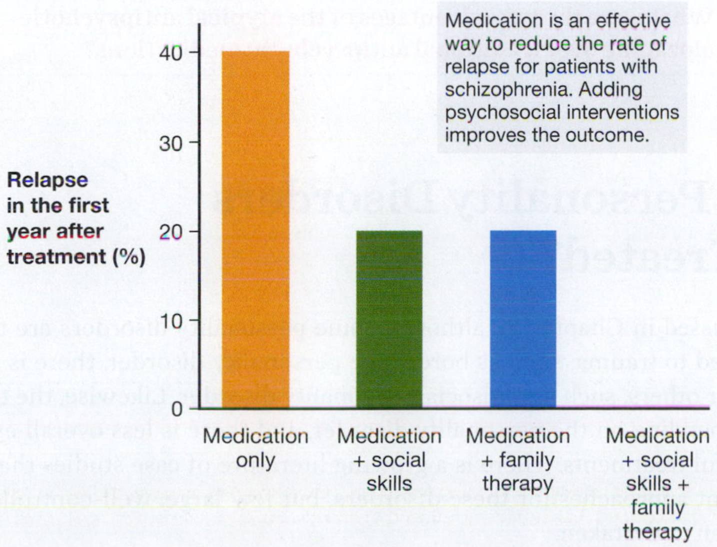

FIGURE 15.24

The Effectiveness of Antipsychotic Medications, Social Skills Training, and Family Therapy

This graph shows the relapse rate, after a year, of using various methods alone or in combination for treatment-compliant patients with schizophrenia. Among patients who received all three treatments, none relapsed within one year (Hogarty et al., 1986).

PROGNOSIS IN SCHIZOPHRENIA Some people with schizophrenia have positive outcomes, eventually overcoming disruptive symptoms and able to function in daily life. However, estimating how frequently this happens is hard because of uncertainty in defining recovery. For instance, how long does a person have to go without symptoms before being considered recovered? One recent analysis looked at outcomes across 50 long-term studies. The researchers assessed the proportion of people who had good outcomes in terms of both reduction in symptoms and good social function for at least two years (Jääskeläinen et al., 2013). They found that only about 1 in 7 individuals achieved recovery by these standards.

One troubling aspect of this literature is the implication that despite major advances in diagnoses and treatment, the prognosis for those with schizophrenia has not improved in recent years (Jääskeläinen et al., 2013; Millan et al., 2016). The available studies have not examined prognosis based on treatments received, however, so it is not possible to know which treatments produce the best chances of recovery. What seems clear is that the longer a person with psychotic symptoms does not receive treatment, the worse the prognosis (Penttilä et al., 2014).

As noted, the cornerstone treatment for people diagnosed with schizophrenia is antipsychotic medications, such as clozapine. The evidence confirms that antipsychotic medications are extremely valuable in the short term for people experiencing psychotic symptoms (Goff et al., 2017; Harrow & Jobe, 2013). At issue is how long the person should remain on the medication. Some studies suggest that long-term use of these drugs may be associated with worse outcomes, possibly because of the effects of the drugs on dopamine receptors (Harrow et al., 2014). That is, long-term use changes dopamine receptors so that antipsychotic medication becomes less effective.

The prognosis for people with schizophrenia also depends on factors that include age of onset and culture. People who experience their first symptoms later in life have a more favorable prognosis than people who start to show symptoms during childhood or adolescence (McGlashan, 1988), possibly because schizophrenia affects brain development, much of which occurs during childhood and adolescence (Millan et al., 2016). Culture also plays a role in prognosis. In some countries, schizophrenia does not appear to be as severe as it is in other countries (Leff et al., 1992), and the chances of recovery also seem to be better (Jääskeläinen et al., 2013). These differences may arise because of cultural differences in how symptoms of schizophrenia are viewed or because of more-extensive family networks in some countries that provide support for people with schizophrenia.

Q **What were the two advantages of the atypical antipsychotic clozapine over traditional antipsychotic medications?**

ANSWER: (1) an improvement in negative symptoms and (2) no side effects of tardive dyskinesia

Can Personality Disorders Be Treated?

Learning Objectives

- Discuss therapeutic approaches for borderline personality disorder and antisocial personality disorder.

As discussed in Chapter 14, although some personality disorders are thought to be related to trauma, such as borderline personality disorder, there is no known cause for others, such as antisocial personality disorder. Likewise, the treatments vary depending on the personality disorder, and there is less overall evidence of successful treatments. There is a growing literature of case studies that describe treatment approaches for these disorders, but few large, well-controlled studies have been undertaken.

The one thing about personality disorders that most therapists agree on is that they are difficult to treat. Individuals with personality disorders who are in therapy are usually also being treated for another disorder, such as OCD or depression. The other disorder is typically the problem for which the patient sought therapy in the first place. People rarely seek therapy for personality disorders because one hallmark of these disorders is that patients see the environment rather than their own behavior as the cause of their problems. This outlook often makes individuals with personality disorders very difficult to engage in therapy.

FIGURE 15.25
Marsha Linehan
The psychologist Marsha Linehan pioneered the therapeutic technique dialectical behavior therapy. Linehan experienced the kind of psychological disorder this technique is used to treat.

15.17 Dialectical Behavior Therapy Is Most Successful for Borderline Personality Disorder

The impulsivity, emotional disturbances, and identity disturbances characteristic of borderline personality disorder make it very challenging to provide therapy for the people affected. Traditional psychotherapy approaches have been largely unsuccessful, so therapists have attempted to develop approaches specific to borderline personality disorder.

dialectical behavior therapy (DBT) A form of therapy used to treat borderline personality disorder that combines elements of the behavioral and cognitive treatments with a mindfulness approach based on Eastern meditative practices.

The most successful treatment approach to date for borderline personality disorder was developed by the psychologist Marsha Linehan in the 1980s (**FIGURE 15.25**). Two decades earlier, as a young woman, Linehan had experienced extreme social withdrawal, physical self-destructiveness, and recurrent suicidality (Carey, 2011). Institutionalized and diagnosed with schizophrenia, she was locked in a seclusion room, treated with various medications, given Freudian analysis, and treated with electroshock therapy.

Eventually, after being released from the hospital with little hope of surviving, Linehan learned to accept herself rather than striving for some impossible ideal. This "radical acceptance," as she puts it, enabled her to function. She earned her PhD in psychology with the goal of helping people who are chronically self-destructive or even suicidal. Linehan's **dialectical behavior therapy** combines elements of the behavioral and cognitive treatments with a mindfulness approach based on Eastern meditative practices (Lieb et al., 2004). All patients are seen in both group and individual sessions, and the responsibilities of the client and the therapist are made explicit.

Therapy proceeds in three stages (**FIGURE 15.26**). In the first stage, the therapist targets the person's most extreme and dysfunctional behaviors. Such behaviors often include self-cutting and threats of suicide or suicide attempts. The focus is on replacing these behaviors with more-appropriate ones. The person learns problem-solving techniques and more-effective ways of coping with their emotions. In this stage, the person is taught to control attention to focus on the present. Strategies for controlling attention are based on mindfulness meditation. In the second stage, the therapist helps the person explore past traumatic experiences that may be at the root of emotional problems. In the third stage, the therapist helps the person develop self-respect and independent problem solving. This stage is crucial because those with borderline personality disorder depend heavily on others for support and validation. These individuals must be able to generate the appropriate attitudes and necessary skills themselves, or they are likely to revert to their previous behavior patterns.

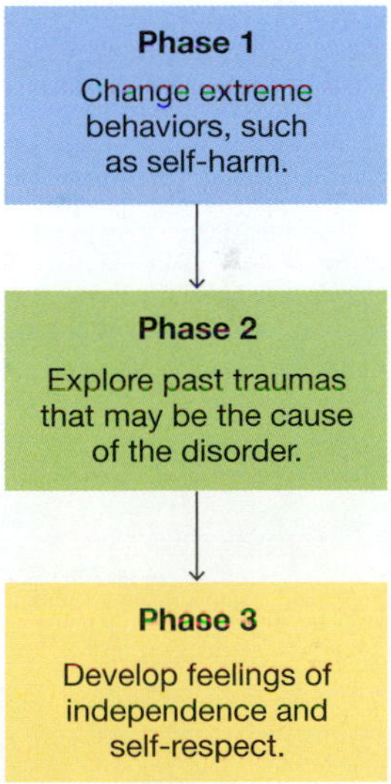

Phase 1
Change extreme behaviors, such as self-harm.
Phase 2
Explore past traumas that may be the cause of the disorder.
Phase 3
Develop feelings of independence and self-respect.

FIGURE 15.26
Dialectical Behavior Therapy Is Used to Treat Borderline Personality Disorder
In phase 1 of DBT, a client will learn to change extreme behaviors through problem solving, coping, and focusing on the present. In phase 2, the therapist helps the client explore past traumas underlying their emotional problems. In phase 3, the client works to increase self-esteem and stop depending on others for validation.

The symptoms experienced by individuals with borderline personality disorder can resemble either psychosis or depression. As a result, researchers previously believed these patients would develop a disorder such as schizophrenia or depression. Studies that have followed individuals with borderline personality disorder over time, however, have demonstrated that their symptoms remain relatively unchanged (Plakun et al., 1985).

Therapeutic approaches targeted at borderline personality disorder, such as dialectical behavior therapy, improve the prognosis for those with the disorder. Studies have demonstrated that people with borderline personality disorder undergoing this treatment are more likely to remain in treatment and less likely to be suicidal than are those in other types of therapy (Linehan et al., 1991, 1993). SSRIs are often prescribed along with dialectical behavior therapy to treat feelings of depression.

Q **What role does mindfulness meditation play in dialectical behavior therapy for borderline personality disorder?**

ANSWER: It is used in the first stage of dialectical behavior therapy to help the person control attention and focus on the present.

15.18 Antisocial Personality Disorder Is Extremely Difficult to Treat

Treating people with antisocial personality disorder is often impossible. These individuals lie without thinking twice about it, care little for other people's feelings, and live for the present without consideration of the future. In addition, they are narcissistic and like themselves the way they are. All these factors make development of a therapeutic relationship and motivation for change remote possibilities at best. Individuals with this disorder are often more interested in manipulating their therapists than in changing their own behavior. Therapists working with these people must be constantly on guard.

THERAPEUTIC APPROACHES FOR ANTISOCIAL PERSONALITY DISORDER

Numerous treatment approaches have been tried for antisocial personality disorder (and the related but not identical disorder commonly called psychopathy; see Section 14.18). Because individuals with antisocial personality disorder apparently have diminished cortical arousal, stimulants have been prescribed to normalize arousal levels. There is evidence that these drugs are beneficial in the short term but not the long term. Antianxiety drugs may lower hostility levels somewhat, and lithium has shown promise in treating the aggressive, impulsive behavior of violent criminals who are psychopathic. Overall, however, psychotropic medications have not been effective in treating this disorder.

Similarly, traditional psychotherapeutic approaches seem of little use in treating antisocial personality disorder. Behavioral and cognitive approaches have had somewhat more success. Behavioral approaches reinforce appropriate behavior. They ignore inappropriate behavior in an attempt to replace maladaptive behavior patterns with behavior patterns that are more socially appropriate. This approach seems to work best when the therapist controls reinforcement, the person cannot leave treatment, and group therapy is used. Individual therapy sessions rarely produce any change in antisocial behavior. Clearly, the behavioral approach cannot be implemented on an outpatient basis, since the person will receive reinforcement for antisocial behavior outside of therapy and can leave treatment at any time. For these reasons, therapy for this disorder is most effective in a residential treatment center or a correctional facility.

Cognitive approaches have been tried for antisocial personality disorder. Therapists try to demonstrate that clients with the disorder can meet their goals more easily by following the rules of society rather than by trying to get around them, as in the following example:

> Therapist: How well has the "beat-the-system" approach actually worked out for you over time?
> Brett: It works great . . . until someone catches on or starts to catch on. Then you have to scrap that plan and come up with a new one.
> Therapist: How difficult was it, you know, to cover up one scheme and come up with a new one?
> Brett: Sometimes it was really easy. There are some real pigeons out there.
> Therapist: Was it always easy?
> Brett: Well, no. . . . Seems like I'm always needing a good plan to beat the system.
> Therapist: Do you think it's ever easier to go with the system instead of trying to beat it in some way?
> Brett: Well, after all that I have been through, I would have to say yes, there have been times that going with the system would have been easier in the long run. . . . But . . . it's such a challenge to beat the system. It feels exciting when I come up with a new plan and think I can make it work. (Beck et al., 1990)

This dialogue illustrates both the cognitive approach and why such clients are so difficult to work with. Even if they know what they are doing is wrong, they do not care. They live for the thrill of getting away with something.

PROGNOSIS FOR ANTISOCIAL PERSONALITY DISORDER The prognosis that people with antisocial personality disorder will change their behaviors as a result of therapy is poor. This conclusion is especially true for those with psychopathic traits. Some of the more recently developed cognitive techniques show promise, but there is no good evidence that they produce long-lasting or even real changes. Fortunately for society, individuals with antisocial personality disorder but without psychopathy typically improve after age 40 (FIGURE 15.27).

The reasons for this improvement are unknown, but it may be due to a reduction in biological drives. Alternative theories suggest that those with this disorder may gain insight into their self-defeating behaviors or may just get worn out and be unable to continue their manipulative ways. The improvement, however, is mainly in the realm of antisocial behavior. The underlying egocentricity, callousness, and manipulativeness can remain unchanged (Harpur & Hare, 1994), especially for those who are psychopathic. In fact, although criminal acts decrease among those with antisocial personality disorder after age 40, more than half of the individuals with psychopathic traits continue to be arrested after age 40 (Hare et al., 1988). Thus, although some aspects of their behavior mellow with age, psychopaths remain largely indifferent to traditional societal norms.

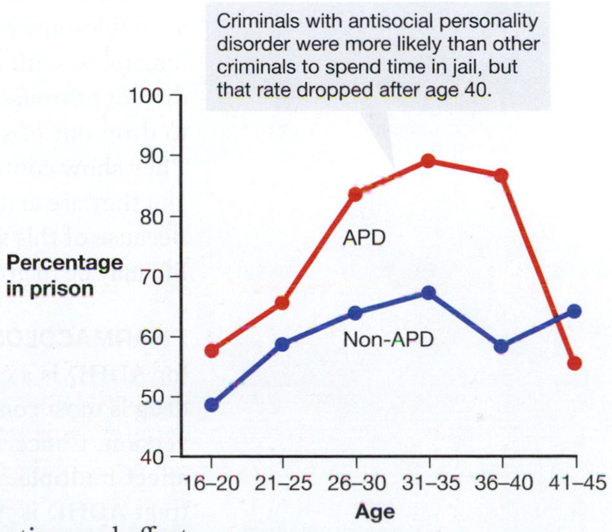

FIGURE 15.27
Antisocial Personality Disorder
For this longitudinal study, the percentage of participants in prison during each five-year period is shown.

Because of the limited effectiveness of therapy for this disorder, time and effort may be better spent in prevention. *Conduct disorder* is a childhood condition known to be a precursor to antisocial personality disorder. It involves a persistent pattern of inappropriate behavior, such as bullying, cruelty to animals, theft, lying, and violating rules and social norms. Some of the environmental and developmental risk factors for conduct disorder have been identified. Focusing on these factors may reduce the likelihood that a child with conduct disorder will grow up to have antisocial personality disorder.

Q What is the general prognosis for those with antisocial personality disorder?

ANSWER: Few therapies work for them, but most people with antisocial personality disorder show a reduction in antisocial behavior after about age 40.

How Should Childhood Disorders Be Treated?

Learning Objectives

- Identify drugs and behavioral treatments for ADHD.
- Describe applied behavioral analysis.
- Discuss the use of oxytocin in the treatment of autism spectrum disorder.

It is estimated that in the United States at least 12–20 percent of children and adolescents experience psychological disorders (Leckman et al., 1995; Merikangas et al., 2010). The experiences and development during early life are critically important to a person's lifelong mental health. Problems not addressed during childhood or adolescence may persist into adulthood. Most theories of human development regard children and adolescents as more malleable than adults and therefore more amenable to treatment.

Medication is often used to treat emotional and behavioral problems in children. According to the Centers for Disease Control and Prevention, in 2019 about 8.5 percent of children ages 5–17 took prescribed medication to treat mental health symptoms (Zablotsky & Terlizzi, 2020). Boys were more likely to receive medications than girls, and children from racial and ethnic minority groups were less likely to receive medications than non-Hispanic White children. To illustrate the issues involved in treating disorders of early life, this section considers treatment approaches for attention-deficit/hyperactivity disorder (ADHD) and autism.

15.19 Children with ADHD Can Benefit from Various Approaches

There is some dispute about whether ADHD is a psychological disorder or simply a troublesome behavioral pattern that children eventually outgrow. Some people diagnosed with ADHD as children grow out of it. Many more, however, have the disorder throughout adolescence and adulthood. These individuals are more likely to drop out of school and to reach a lower socioeconomic level than expected. They show continued patterns of inattention, of impulsivity, and of hyperactivity, and they are at increased risk for other psychiatric disorders (Wilens et al., 2004). Because of this somewhat bleak long-term prognosis, effective treatment early in life may be of great importance.

PHARMACOLOGICAL TREATMENT OF ADHD The most common treatment for ADHD is a central nervous system stimulant, such as methylphenidate. This drug is most commonly known by the brand name Ritalin or, for the time-release version, Concerta. Ritalin's actions are not fully understood, but the drug may affect multiple neurotransmitters, particularly dopamine. Another drug used to treat ADHD is Adderall, which combines two other stimulants. The behavior of children with ADHD might suggest that their brains are overactive, and it may seem surprising that a stimulant would improve their symptoms. In fact, these drugs appear to selectively stimulate activity in frontal lobe regions that support both cognition and behavioral control (Spencer et al., 2015). They act as cognitive enhancers by increasing attention and the ability to concentrate.

When children take these drugs as prescribed, they experience an increase in positive behaviors and a decrease in negative behaviors (**FIGURE 15.28**). They are able to work more effectively on a task without interruption and are less impulsive. It is likely that these improvements in behavior have contributed to the large number of children who take this medication. Parents often feel pressured by school systems to medicate children who have ongoing behavior problems, and parents often pressure physicians to prescribe Ritalin because its effects can make home life much more manageable. Studies have shown that children taking Ritalin are happier, more adept socially, and somewhat more successful academically, although the effects on academic performance are modest (Chronis et al., 2006; Van der Oord et al., 2008). These children also interact more positively with their parents, perhaps because they are more likely to comply with requests.

One classic study measured Ritalin's effects on the behavior of children playing baseball (Pelham et al., 1990). Children with ADHD who were taking the medication would assume the ready position in the outfield and could keep track of the game. Children with ADHD who were not taking the drug would often throw or kick their mitts even while the pitch was in progress.

The medication has its drawbacks, however. Side effects include sleep problems, reduced appetite, body twitches, and the temporary suppression of growth

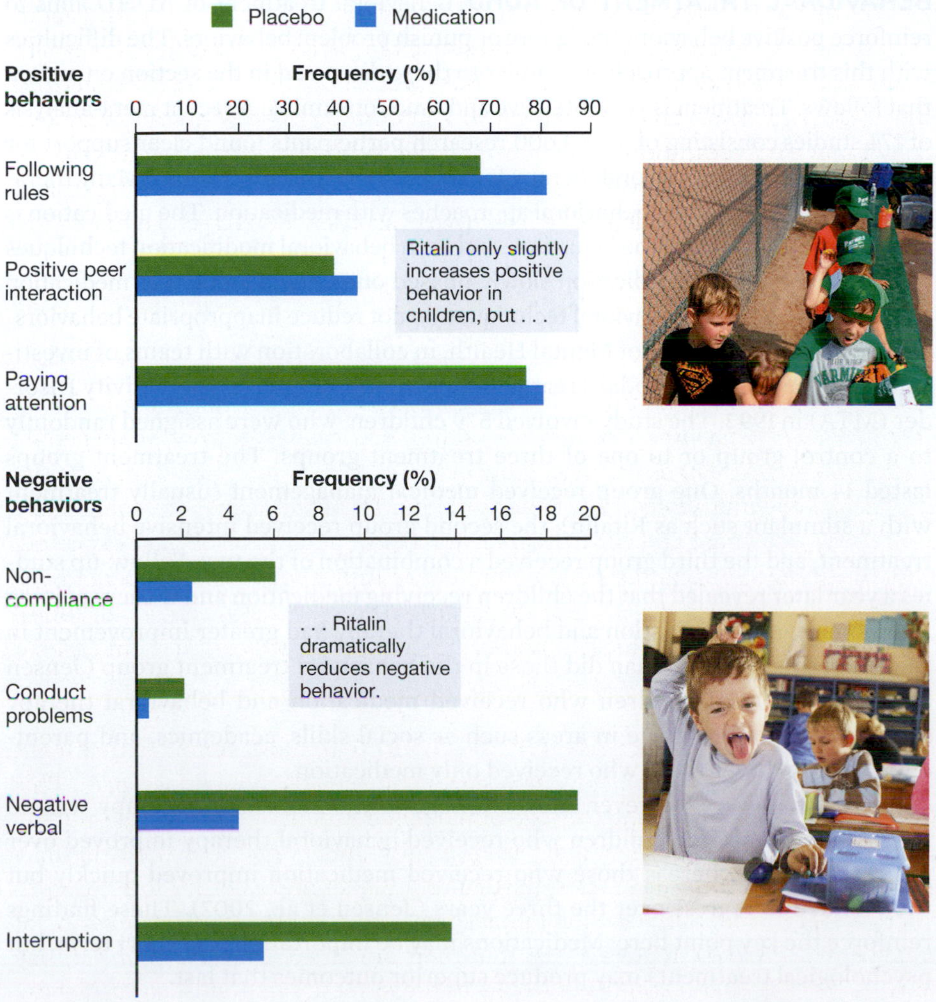

FIGURE 15.28
The Effects of Ritalin
These graphs compare the effects of Ritalin on the positive and negative symptoms of ADHD.

(Rapport & Moffitt, 2002; Schachter et al., 2001). There is evidence that the short-term benefits of stimulants may not be maintained over the long term. In addition, because stimulants affect everyone who takes them, there is a very real risk of abuse, and numerous cases of children and adolescents buying and selling drugs such as Ritalin and Adderall have been documented. One study found that nearly 8 percent of college students had taken a nonprescribed stimulant in the past 30 days and that 60 percent reported knowing students who misused stimulants (Weyandt et al., 2009). Indeed, a controversial issue is whether using stimulants to treat children with ADHD may increase the risk that they will develop substance abuse problems as adults. Two recent studies have demonstrated that substance abuse problems are common among those who had ADHD in childhood, but having taken Ritalin does not seem to have increased or decreased adult rates of substance abuse (Biederman et al., 2008; Mannuzza et al., 2008).

Perhaps most important, some children on medication may see their problems as beyond their control. They may not feel responsible for their behaviors and may not learn the coping strategies they will need if they discontinue their medication or if it ceases to be effective. Most therapists believe medication should be supplemented by psychological therapies, such as behavior modification. Some therapists even urge that medication be replaced by other treatment approaches when possible.

BEHAVIORAL TREATMENT OF ADHD Behavioral treatment of ADHD aims to reinforce positive behaviors and ignore or punish problem behaviors. The difficulties with this treatment approach are similar to those discussed in the section on autism that follows. Treatment is very intensive and time consuming. A recent meta-analysis of 174 studies consisting of over 2,000 research participants found clear support for the effectiveness of behavioral therapy for ADHD (Fabiano et al., 2009). Many therapists advocate combining behavioral approaches with medication. The medication is used to gain control over the behaviors, and then behavioral modification techniques can be taught and the medication slowly phased out. Others argue that medication should be used only if behavioral techniques do not reduce inappropriate behaviors.

The National Institute of Mental Health, in collaboration with teams of investigators, began the Multimodal Treatment of Attention Deficit Hyperactivity Disorder (MTA) in 1992. The study involved 579 children, who were assigned randomly to a control group or to one of three treatment groups. The treatment groups lasted 14 months. One group received medical management (usually treatment with a stimulant such as Ritalin), the second group received intensive behavioral treatment, and the third group received a combination of the two. Follow-up studies a year later revealed that the children receiving medication and those receiving a combination of medication and behavioral therapy had greater improvement in their ADHD symptoms than did those in the behavioral treatment group (Jensen et al., 2001, 2005). Children who received medication and behavioral therapy showed a slight advantage in areas such as social skills, academics, and parent-child relations over those who received only medication.

After three years, however, the advantage of the medication therapy was no longer significant. The children who received behavioral therapy improved over the three years, whereas those who received medication improved quickly but then tended to regress over the three years (Jensen et al., 2007). These findings reinforce the key point here: Medications may be important in the short term, but psychological treatments may produce superior outcomes that last.

Q **What is a possible reason that stimulants can help reduce ADHD?**

ANSWER: These drugs stimulate brain regions involved in behavioral and attentional control.

15.20 Children with Autism Spectrum Disorder Benefit from Structured Behavioral Treatment

The treatment of children with autism spectrum disorder presents unique challenges to mental health professionals. The core symptoms—impaired communication, restricted interests, and deficits in social interaction—make these children particularly difficult to work with. They often exhibit extreme behaviors as well as forms of self-stimulation, such as hand waving, rocking, humming, and jumping up and down. Although these behaviors must be reduced or eliminated before progress can occur in other areas, doing so is difficult because effective reinforcers are hard to find. Most children respond positively to social praise and small prizes, but children with autism spectrum disorder are often oblivious to these rewards. In some cases, food is the only effective reinforcement in the initial stages of treatment.

Another characteristic of children with autism spectrum disorder is an overselectivity of attention. This tendency to focus on specific details while ignoring others interferes with generalizing learned behavior to other stimuli and situations. For example, a child who learns to set the table with plates may not know what to do when presented with bowls instead. Generalization of skills must be explicitly taught. For this reason, structured therapies are more effective for these children than are unstructured interventions, such as play therapy (in which the therapist tries to engage the child in conversation while the child plays with toys).

BEHAVIORAL TREATMENT FOR AUTISM SPECTRUM DISORDER As noted earlier, autism spectrum disorder clearly is caused by biological factors, but this knowledge has not led to any significant advances in therapies for the disorder. One of the best-known and perhaps most effective treatments for children with autism was developed by Ivar Lovaas and his colleagues. The program, **applied behavioral analysis (ABA)**, is based on principles of operant conditioning: Behaviors that are reinforced should increase in frequency, and behaviors that are not reinforced should diminish (**FIGURE 15.29**). There is evidence that this method can be used successfully to treat autism (Warren et al., 2011), particularly if treatment is started early in life (Vismara & Rogers, 2010).

applied behavioral analysis (ABA) An intensive treatment for autism based on operant conditioning.

This very intensive approach requires a minimum of 40 hours of treatment per week. In Lovaas's study, preschool-age children with autism were treated by teachers and by their parents, who received specific training. After more than two years of ABA treatment, the children had gained about 20 IQ points on average and most of them were able to enter a normal kindergarten program (Lovaas, 1987). In contrast, IQ did not change in a comparable control group of children who did not receive any treatment. A group of children who received 10 hours of treatment per week fared no better than the control group. Initiating treatment at a younger age also yielded better results, as did involving the parents and having at least a portion of the therapy take place in the home. Children with better language skills before entering treatment had better outcomes than those who were mute or echolalic (repeating whatever they heard).

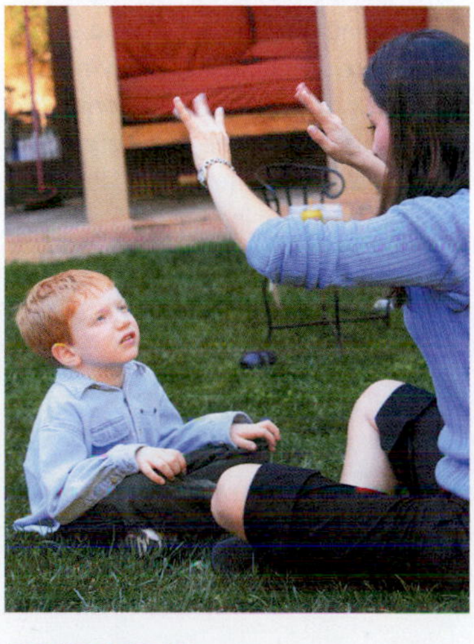

FIGURE 15.29
Applied Behavioral Analysis
This form of treatment involves intensive interaction between children with autism and their teachers and parents.

More recent approaches have shown that other tasks can improve ABA treatment. One study found that teaching children to engage in joint attention during ABA treatment, such as by having the parent or teacher imitate the child's actions and work to maintain eye contact, improved language skills significantly over ABA treatment alone (Kasari et al., 2008). In another condition, children received instruction in symbolic play. Examples of symbolic play include imagining

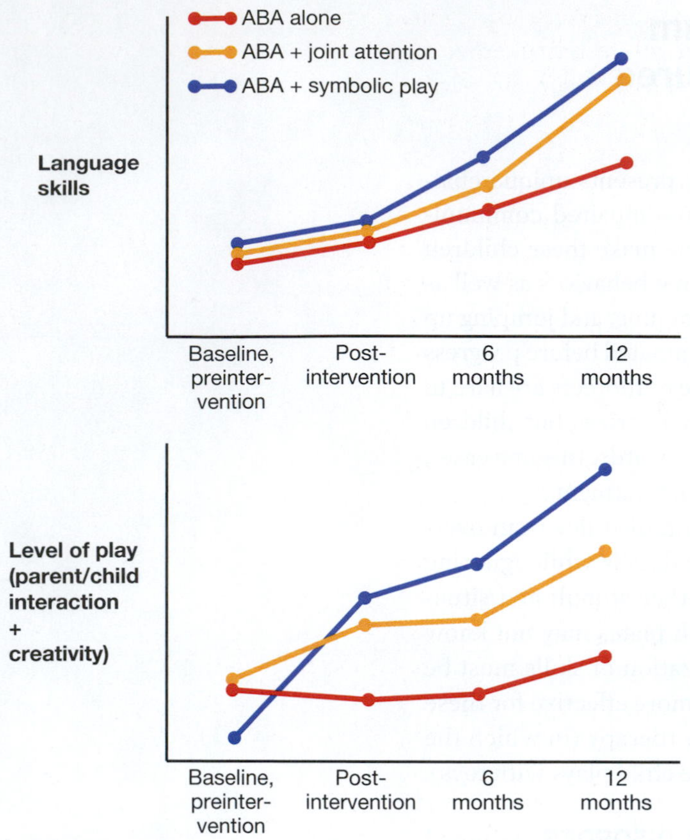

FIGURE 15.30
ABA Treatment, Joint Attention, and Symbolic Play
At the start of this study, the children were 3 or 4 years old. All the children received ABA treatment. Children receiving only ABA treatment were the control condition. In addition, some children received training in maintaining joint attention, and some children received training in symbolic play. Both of these combinations led to better language skills, greater parent-child play interaction, and greater creativity in play than did ABA alone.

something, such as a doll driving a car, or pretending that one object represents another. Instruction in symbolic play also led to increased language use, greater parent-child play, and greater creativity in play (FIGURE 15.30). Other approaches incorporate ABA principles into behaviors tailored toward the child's everyday activities and interests. A recent meta-analysis showed that these ABA-based approaches lead to greater improvement for young children relative to other, less-intensive treatments (Sandbank et al., 2020).

Lovaas's ABA program has some drawbacks. The most obvious is the time commitment, because the therapy is very intensive and lasts for years. Parents essentially become full-time teachers for their children with autism spectrum disorder. The financial and emotional drains on the family can be substantial.

BIOLOGICAL TREATMENT FOR AUTISM SPECTRUM DISORDER There is good evidence that autism spectrum disorder is caused by brain dysfunction. Many attempts have been made to use this knowledge to treat the disorder. It is easy to find compelling case studies of children who have benefited from alternative treatment approaches. When the treatments are assessed in controlled studies, however, there is little or no evidence that most are effective.

For instance, SSRIs have been tried as a treatment for autism spectrum disorder because they reduce compulsions in patients with obsessive-compulsive disorder, and autism involves compulsive and repetitive behavior. There is also some evidence that children with autism spectrum disorder have abnormal serotonin functioning. Despite these connections, a review of pharmacological studies found that SSRIs are not helpful for treating the symptoms of autism spectrum disorder and actually may increase agitation (McPheeters et al., 2011). However, the review also found that antipsychotics, such as Risperdal, appear to reduce repetitive behaviors associated with self-stimulation. Unfortunately, antipsychotics have side effects, such as weight gain.

Given the important role of oxytocin in social relations and affiliation, some researchers have speculated that oxytocin plays a role in autism spectrum disorder. A finding supporting this hypothesis showed that a deficit in oxytocin may be related to some of the behavioral manifestations of autism. Mice lacking oxytocin behave normally except for the fact that they cannot recognize other mice or their mother's scent; a single dose of oxytocin reverses this effect until it wears off (Ferguson et al., 2000). In human studies, researchers have found that administering a nasal spray containing oxytocin leads people to make more eye contact, feel increased trust in others, and better infer emotions from other people's facial expressions (Ross & Young, 2009).

The question is whether oxytocin can improve social functioning in people with autism spectrum disorder. In one study, adults with autism spectrum disorder who received injections of oxytocin showed a dramatic improvement in their symptoms (Novotny et al., 2000). In another study, high-functioning adults with autism spectrum disorder were injected with oxytocin or a placebo. Then they performed a social cognition task in which they listened to spoken sentences (e.g., "The boy went to the store") and had to identify the speaker's emotional tone. The participants who received oxytocin were better able to tell whether the sentence was read in an angry, sad, happy, or indifferent tone than were the participants who received the placebo (Hollander et al., 2007). Oxytocin injections seem particularly useful for reducing repetitive behaviors (e.g., repeating the same phrase), questioning, inappropriate touching, and self-injury (Green & Hollander, 2010; Hollander et al., 2003). These findings are promising, but researchers need to do much more work before we can conclude that oxytocin is an empirically validated treatment for autism (Guastella & Hickie, 2016).

At this point, the neurobiology of autism spectrum disorder is not well understood. Attempts to use psychopharmacology to treat the disorder have led to some improvements in behavior, but much remains to be learned.

PROGNOSIS FOR CHILDREN WITH AUTISM SPECTRUM DISORDER Despite a few reports of remarkable recovery from autism spectrum disorder, the long-term prognosis remains poor. A follow-up study of men in their early 20s revealed that they continued to show the ritualistic self-stimulating behavior typical of autism spectrum disorder. In addition, nearly three quarters had severe social difficulties and were unable to live and work independently (Howlin et al., 2000). Several factors affect the prognosis. Although therapists once believed the prognosis was particularly poor for children whose symptoms were apparent before age 2 (Hoshino et al., 1980), possibly only the most severe cases of autism spectrum disorder were diagnosed that early before public recognition of the disorder increased.

Early diagnosis clearly allows for more effective treatments (National Research Council, 2001). Still, severe cases—especially those involving notable cognitive deficiencies—are less likely to improve with treatment. Early language ability is associated with better outcomes (Howlin et al., 2000), as is higher IQ. Children with autism spectrum disorder have difficulty generalizing from the therapeutic setting to the real world, and this limitation severely restricts their social functioning (Handleman et al., 1988). A higher IQ may mean a better ability to generalize learning and therefore a better overall prognosis.

Q What is the most successful treatment for autism spectrum disorder, and what is the major drawback of that treatment?

ANSWER: Applied behavioral analysis is the most successful treatment, especially when combined with symbolic play or joint attention, but it is limited by the necessary time and energy commitment from families.

Your Chapter Review

Want to earn a better grade on your test?

It's time to complete your study experience! Go to **INQUIZITIVE** to practice actively with this chapter's concepts and get personalized feedback along the way.

Chapter Summary

How Are Psychological Disorders Treated?

15.1 Various Methods Have Been Used to Treat Psychopathology Psychotherapy is the generic name for formal psychological treatment. Biological treatments range from drugs to electrical stimulation of brain regions to surgical intervention. Each theory of psychopathology includes treatment strategies that are based on the theory's assumptions about the causes of psychological disorders. Many therapists follow an eclectic approach.

15.2 Psychodynamic Therapy Seeks to Reduce Unconscious Conflicts Originally developed by Sigmund Freud, psychodynamic therapy aims to identify and resolve unconscious conflicts and help clients develop insight into their problems. Contemporary approaches to psychodynamic therapy focus on interpersonal relations and emotional conflicts. Although there is some supportive evidence, it is unclear whether psychodynamic approaches offer any specific advantages over other forms of psychotherapy.

15.3 Behavioral and Cognitive Treatments Aim to Change Behavior, Emotion, or Thought Directly Behavioral approaches focus on modifying maladaptive behaviors. The premise is that behavior is learned and therefore can be unlearned. Cognitive approaches restructure thinking. Cognitive-behavioral therapy (CBT) combines aspects of cognitive and behavioral therapies. It is the most widely used and perhaps most effective treatment for many psychological disorders.

15.4 The Context of Therapy Matters As emphasized by the humanistic approach, an important factor in the effectiveness of therapy is the relationship between the therapist and the client. Family therapy adopts a systems approach, seeing the individual as part of a larger context. Culture influences the expression of psychological disorders, recovery from psychological disorders, and willingness to seek psychotherapy. Group therapy is cost-effective, improves social skills, and provides social support.

15.5 Medication Is Effective for Certain Disorders Psychotropic medications change neurochemistry. Antianxiety drugs increase GABA activity. Antidepressants affect serotonin availability or levels of norepinephrine and dopamine. Antipsychotics reduce symptoms such as delusions and hallucinations by blocking the effects of dopamine.

15.6 Alternative Biological Treatments Can Be Effective When traditional treatments are not successful, alternative treatments are used. These treatments include psychosurgery, electroconvulsive therapy, transcranial magnetic stimulation, and deep brain stimulation.

15.7 Effectiveness of Treatment Is Determined by Empirical Evidence Randomized clinical trials should be used to assess the effectiveness of treatments for psychological disorders. Psychological treatments vary according to the particular disorder being addressed and the person's specific psychological symptoms. They are based on techniques developed in the lab by psychologists, and they are not guided by a single, overall grand theory. Some treatment approaches that have no scientific basis to support their use have proved detrimental, and they may prevent or delay a patient from receiving effective, evidence-based therapy.

15.8 Various Providers Can Assist in Treatment for Psychological Disorders A variety of providers of psychological treatment exist. The providers differ in their training and work in diverse settings. These specialists include clinical psychologists, psychiatrists, counseling psychologists, psychiatric social workers, and psychiatric nurses.

15.9 Psychology Outside the Lab: How Do You Find a Therapist Who Can Help You? Many college students experience life stressors or psychological problems. The good news is that many resources are available to assist students with psychological issues. Those seeking help should try to identify a therapist who is a good fit, which means someone with whom they feel at ease.

What Are the Most Effective Treatments?

15.10 Treatments That Focus on Behavior and Cognition Are Superior for Anxiety Disorders Behavioral techniques—in particular, systematic desensitization and exposure—alleviate specific phobias. Cognitive restructuring, coupled with exposure, is effective in treating panic disorder.

15.11 Both Antidepressants and CBT Are Effective for Obsessive-Compulsive Disorder Obsessive-compulsive disorder (OCD) responds to medications that block serotonin reuptake and to CBT that includes exposure and response prevention. Deep brain stimulation holds promise for the treatment of severe cases of OCD.

15.12 Cognitive and Behavioral Therapies, Social Support, and Medication Help Treat Addictions Initiating treatment can be challenging for people with addictions since many patients do not acknowledge that taking drugs is a problem. Withdrawal symptoms can be alleviated with medication. CBT and social support groups can help prevent relapse. In some cases, medication can help reduce cravings, thus preventing relapse and increasing the efficacy of treatment.

15.13 Many Effective Treatments Are Available for Depressive Disorders Pharmacological treatments include MAO inhibitors, tricyclics, and SSRIs. Cognitive-behavioral treatments target cognitive distortion—in particular, the cognitive triad. Alternative therapies include phototherapy, aerobic exercise, electroconvulsive therapy, transcranial magnetic stimulation, and deep brain stimulation. Gender issues in treating depressive disorders have resulted in the development of specific guidelines for treatment.

15.14 You Be the Psychologist: How Effective Are Antidepressants? One in 10 Americans over age 6 is prescribed antidepressants, leading some psychologists to ask whether the drugs are as effective as advertised by pharmaceutical companies. By looking at all the data, not just successful studies, psychologists found only a modest benefit to antidepressants over placebos. Further investigation found they are most effective for those with severe depression, but for some the benefit of antidepressants may be due to a placebo effect.

15.15 Lithium and Atypical Antipsychotics Are Most Effective for Bipolar Disorder Lithium has been found to be most effective in stabilizing mood among bipolar patients. This drug has considerable side effects, however. The drug quetiapine (better known as Seroquel) is an atypical antipsychotic that is currently the most commonly prescribed drug for bipolar disorders. Mood stabilizers such as lithium prescribed with atypical antipsychotics may improve treatment outcomes. Psychotherapy can help support compliance with drug treatment.

15.16 Antipsychotics Are Superior for Schizophrenia Earlier antipsychotic medications are most effective for reducing the positive symptoms of schizophrenia. Tardive dyskinesia and other side effects are common with these older antipsychotic drugs. Clozapine reduces positive and negative symptoms, with fewer side effects. Drug therapy is most effective when combined with psychosocial treatment. The prognosis for patients depends on factors such as age of onset and culture.

Can Personality Disorders Be Treated?

15.17 Dialectical Behavior Therapy Is Most Successful for Borderline Personality Disorder Dialectical behavior therapy combines elements of behavioral, cognitive, and mindfulness approaches. It proceeds in three stages. First, the most extreme and dysfunctional behaviors are targeted and replaced with more-appropriate behaviors. Next, the therapist helps the person explore past traumatic events. Finally, the therapist helps the person develop self-respect and independent problem solving.

15.18 Antisocial Personality Disorder Is Extremely Difficult to Treat Traditional psychotherapeutic approaches have not proved effective for treating antisocial personality disorder. Behavioral and cognitive approaches have been more effective, primarily in a controlled residential treatment environment. Generally, the prognosis is poor. Focusing on prevention by addressing conduct disorder in childhood may be the best strategy.

How Should Childhood Disorders Be Treated?

15.19 Children with ADHD Can Benefit from Various Approaches Ritalin, despite its side effects, is an effective pharmacological treatment for ADHD. Research has provided support for the effectiveness of behavioral therapy in the treatment of ADHD, and behavioral therapy results in better long-term outcomes than medication therapy does.

15.20 Children with Autism Spectrum Disorder Benefit from Structured Behavioral Treatment Structured behavioral treatment has proved effective in improving the symptoms of autism. Applied behavioral analysis—an intensive treatment based on the principles of operant conditioning—has been used successfully in the treatment of autism. A biological treatment for autism has not been identified, but treatment with oxytocin holds promise.

Key Terms

antianxiety drugs, p. 604
antidepressants, p. 604
antipsychotics, p. 605
applied behavioral analysis (ABA), p. 637
behavior therapy, p. 599
biological therapies, p. 596
client-centered therapy, p. 601
cognitive-behavioral therapy (CBT), p. 600
cognitive restructuring, p. 600
cognitive therapy, p. 599
dialectical behavior therapy (DBT), p. 631
electroconvulsive therapy (ECT), p. 607
exposure, p. 599
placebo effect, p. 609
psychodynamic therapy, p. 598
psychotherapy, p. 596
psychotropic medications, p. 603

Practice Exercises

1. Categorize each of the following treatments as a psychotherapy, biological treatment, or alternative biological treatment.
   a. Ritalin
   b. electroconvulsive therapy (ECT)
   c. deep brain stimulation (DBS)
   d. selective serotonin reuptake inhibitor (SSRI)
   e. psychodynamic therapy
   f. cognitive-behavioral therapy (CBT)
   g. Lithium
   h. atypical antipsychotic
   i. transcranial magnetic stimulation (TMS)
   j. applied behavior analysis
2. Which of the following statements are true regarding how culture can affect the therapeutic process? Select all that apply.
   a. Culture can influence people's willingness to seek help.
   b. Culture can influence the expression and prognosis of psychological disorders.
   c. Definitions of mental health and disorder are consistent across cultures.
   d. Psychotherapy is accepted universally across cultures as the best treatment course.
   e. Cultures vary in their stigmatization of mental disorders.
3. According to psychologist David Barlow, which of the following characteristics differentiate psychological treatments from general talk therapy? Select all that apply.
   a. Psychological treatments are based on evidence of their effectiveness.
   b. Psychological treatments are specified and appropriate for the particular disorders.
   c. Specific psychological treatments are applied effectively to multiple disorders.
   d. Psychological treatments are united and guided by grand theories.
4. Selective serotonin reuptake inhibitors (SSRIs) are most useful in the treatments of which pair of psychological disorders?
   a. depression and bipolar disorder
   b. antisocial personality disorder and depression
   c. obsessive-compulsive disorder and schizophrenia
   d. depression and schizophrenia
   e. obsessive-compulsive disorder and depression
5. Which statement is *not* true regarding the treatment of addiction?
   a. Cognitive and behavioral techniques can aid in the treatment of addiction.
   b. Medication can help reduce craving and increase the effectiveness of treatment.
   c. Comorbid psychological disorders should be treated before initiating addiction treatment.
   d. Social support groups can aid addiction treatment.
6. Which statements is *not* true about electroconvulsive therapy (ECT)?
   a. ECT is an effective way of treating severe depression that has not improved with other therapy types.
   b. Contemporary use of ECT applies magnetic force to either side of the head to induce muscle convulsions.
   c. ECT is viewed warily by the public due to historical misuse and negative media representation.
   d. ECT can work quickly to reduce the risk of suicide for severely depressed patients.
7. Dialectical behavior therapy takes place in three stages. Place the descriptions of the three stages below in the correct order.
   a. The therapist helps the client explore past traumatic experiences that may be at the root of emotional problems.
   b. The therapist helps the patient develop self-respect and independent problem solving.

c. The therapist works with the client to replace the most dysfunctional behaviors with more-appropriate behaviors.

8. Match each of the following treatments—dialectical behavior therapy, cognitive-behavioral therapy, and pharmacological therapy—with the disorder that it is best suited to treat.
   a. bipolar disorder
   b. anxiety disorders
   c. borderline personality disorder

9. During his early adult years, Joshua was diagnosed with antisocial personality disorder. Joshua is now 40 years old. Over the coming years, his friends and family will likely see a decrease in which of following behaviors?
   a. Joshua's lack of remorse for hurting others' feelings
   b. Joshua's tendency to feel entitled to special treatment
   c. Joshua's tendency to get into fistfights
   d. Joshua's sense of superiority to others

10. Three-year-old Marley recently received a diagnosis of autism. If provided with the most effective treatment, which statement is accurate?
   a. Many individuals will be involved in Marley's treatment, including parents, teachers, and mental health practitioners.
   b. Marley's treatment will focus largely on motivational interviewing to reinforce desired behavior.
   c. Marley's treatment will be mostly unstructured and vary between environments.
   d. Marley's treatment will be high intensity over a short time period.

Q Answer Key for Practice Exercises

Chapter 1

1. c. "You may be surprised by the range of questions psychologists ask about the mind, the brain, and behavior, and the scientific methods they use to answer those questions."
2. a. electroencephalography; b. epigenetics; c. immunology
3. a. social; b. biological; c. cultural; d. individual
4. a. retrieval-based learning; b. elaborative interrogation; c. distributed practice
5. d. stream of consciousness; dualism
6. c. "That's great! Psychologists do research to figure out which interventions are most helpful for people with different concerns."
7. All except h are correct.
8. a. cognitive; b. personality; c. developmental; d. industrial/organizational
9. b. "I played as well as the person who got the spot, and so I should have gotten it."
10. b. "Does the article say how the researchers measured intelligence?"; d. "How did the researchers design the study? Were they doing good science?"; e. "Who sponsored the study? Was it paid for and conducted by researchers at the world's largest ice cream company?"

Chapter 2

1. c. replication.
2. b, because it offers a specific, directional prediction.
3. a, because it is the most random option of the three.
4. c, because it includes both an experimental and a control group.
5. a, because it uses random assignment.
6. b, because it describes how the dependent variable will be measured.
7. natural setting, because you want to know what people do in their daily lives.
8. prespecified categories of behavior, because you want to know whether a specific behavior, discussing politics, occurs; a simple tally of "yes" or "no" would answer this question.
9. No, because they might act differently than they would if they were unaware of your observation.
10. a. validity; b. reliability; c. accuracy

Chapter 3

1. b. sensory neuron
2. c. dopamine
3. a. agonist; b. agonist; c. antagonist; d. antagonist
4. a. Heritability refers to traits passed from parent to offspring.
5. d. It contains ion channels that regulate electrical potential and firing.
6. d. transcranial magnetic stimulation (TMS)
7. c. The left hemisphere can verbally report its perception. The right hemisphere cannot articulate what it saw but can act on its perception.
8. c. The inside is more negatively charged than the outside.
9. d. paralysis of the right side of the body
10. a. underlying and observed

Chapter 4

1. b. The person in the unresponsive wakefulness state is less likely to regain full consciousness at some point in the future.
2. b. Participants in Condition A will drink more water than participants in Condition B, especially if they are thirsty.
3. a. automatic processing; b. shadowing; c. change blindness; d. controlled processing
4. a. narcolepsy; b. somnambulism; c. insomnia; d. apnea
5. b. Some animals, such as some frogs, do not sleep.
6. b. "Lying on your back, rest your hands gently on your abdomen. As you breathe in and out, focus attention on your breath. Notice the rhythmic rise and fall of your abdomen and the slow, deep movement of your chest."
7. b. cocaine
8. c. You attend to an unexpected, sudden loud noise.
9. a. stimulants; b. marijuana; c. alcohol; d. MDMA; e. opiates
10. b. You are more likely to sleepwalk during REM sleep.

Chapter 5

1. d. specialized receptors, thalamus, cortex
2. a. top-down processing; b. sensation; c. perception; d. bottom-up processing
3. e. skin, due to the large surface area
4. b. amplitude, frequency
5. a. shape constancy; b. color constancy; c. size constancy; d. shape constancy; e. lightness constancy
6. c. activated by chemical changes in tissue, slow fibers, nonmyelinated axons
7. a. The call reached the bird-watcher's left ear before the right ear; the call was less intense in the bird-watcher's right ear than the left ear.
8. a. temporal; b. parietal; c. occipital
9. Choices a, c, and d are true.
10. the dorsal ("where") pathway will be activated by a and e; the ventral ("what") pathway will be activated by b, c, and d

Chapter 6

1. The US is heat, the UR is sweating, the CS is the history room, and the CR is sweating.
2. c. It is a form of new learning that replaces the associative bond between the CS and US but does not eliminate it.
3. b. habituation, sensitization
4. b. The door reliably opens shortly before the food is delivered.
5. a. positive reinforcement; b. positive punishment; c. negative reinforcement; d. negative punishment
6. a. fixed interval; b. variable interval; c. fixed ratio; d. variable ratio
7. a. associative; b. nonassociative; c. social
8. Only d. It is true that a conditioned taste aversion can be learned in a single trial.
9. Exposure helps extinguish conditioned responses to the cues, preventing those cues from triggering conditioned craving.
10. b. Dopamine activity in the brain is increased when a behavior leads to an unexpected reward.

Chapter 7

1. d. encoding > storage (consolidation) > retrieval.
2. Choices a, c, d, and e can all lead to forgetting.
3. false
4. d. choices a and b
5. c. chunking
6. a. Alvarado, because of the primacy effect
7. b. Six 1-hour study sessions are more effective than one 6-hour study session.
8. c. false memories
9. a. absentmindedness; b. source misattribution
10. retrograde; anterograde

Chapter 8

1. a. symbolic; b. analogical; c. both; d. symbolic
2. a. availability heuristic; b. framing; c. representative heuristic; d. anchoring
3. a. integral; incidental; both
4. b. functional fixedness
5. b. EI
6. b. increased likelihood of premature death
7. c. phonics, matching sounds with letters
8. d. Chomsky's universal grammar theory
9. d. The left hemisphere primarily controls languages production and comprehension.
10. b. overgeneralization

Chapter 9

1. a. differentiate between sweet and nonsweet tastes; c. grasp a caregiver's finger; d. make eye contact; e. orient toward loud sounds; i. show preference for the smell of the mother's breast milk; j. turn toward a nipple near their mouths
2. d. People exclusively use formal operations after adolescence to solve problems.
3. c. Infants will look longer at objects that they perceive to be unfamiliar.
4. a. preconventional; b. postconventional; c. conventional
5. d. is correlated with reduced well-being
6. c. insecure/avoidant
7. Sex and gender identity are not always congruent, so people can be transgender.
8. c. He will want to spend more time with his best friends and family.
9. a. Married people report being happier and healthier than single people. e. Parents from poorer nations show more benefit from having children than parents from wealthier nations.
10. b. Older people tend to focus more on positive than negative aspects of their lives.

Chapter 10

1. b. Sonya, who is moderately anxious about the presentation and continues to review her slides and practice her talk until presentation day.
2. c. benevolence
3. d. negative valence and high arousal
4. b. Emotional expressions vary more than emotional experiences between cultures.
5. a. need; b. drive; c. drive; d. need; e. need; f. need
6. d. a person high in self-efficacy and high in achievement motivation
7. c. approach; avoidance
8. c. Albert will either come to like Benicio or convince Carmen that Benicio is unlikable.
9. d. grit
10. d. All of the above are true.

Chapter 11

1. b. biopsychosocial
2. e. the lack of acculturation of first-generation immigrants
3. a. More options and larger portions increase the likelihood of overeating.
4. b. Both e-cigarettes and traditional cigarettes are addictive due to the presence of nicotine.
5. a. false; b. false; c. true; d. false; e. true; f. true; g. false
6. True. When female rats were exposed to stress two weeks before pregnancy, their offspring exhibited abnormalities in fear learning and heightened physiological responses to stress as adults.
7. d. all of the above
8. a. positive reappraisal; b. downward comparison; c. emotion-focused coping; d. problem-focused coping
9. a. Religiousness is correlated with lower levels of well-being.; c. Higher levels of religiosity in Judaism and Buddhism, but not other religions, correlate with well-being.
10. c. Write a letter of gratitude to someone you have not properly thanked.; d. Learn to meditate.; e. Keep a journal of positive events in your life.; f. Eat a diet of natural, unprocessed foods.

Chapter 12

1. a. reciprocity; transitivity
2. c. Randy identifies with New York City and believes the people of Boston lack diversity.
3. b. "Eighty percent of the residents in your neighborhood recycle. Recycling keeps our environment healthy!"
4. d. Organizing a competition where teams of fraternities compete for prizes. Delta House and Omega House form one team to compete against other pairs of fraternities.
5. a. kin selection; b. altruism; c. reciprocal helping; d. inclusive fitness
6. b. perceived risk is greater than perceived benefit; d. diffusion of responsibility; f. unclear situation and unsureness of the correct response; g. anonymity
7. b. She will focus on the positives of the Mexico trip and the negatives of the Louisiana trip.
8. d. Avoid providing a reason for the volunteer request, so members can use their implicit attitudes instead.
9. b. "Shelly is easily the happiest person I know!"
10. a. An initially high level of passionate love transforms slowly into a high level of companionate love.

Chapter 13

1. c. Many genes interact to influence personality, and their expression is affected by epigenetic mechanisms.
2. a. Temperaments, which include activity level, emotionality, and sociability, are broader and more biologically based than traits.
3. a. trait; b. learning/cognition; c.humanistic
4. a. BAS; b. BIS and FFFS; c. BAS; d. BIS; e. BIS; f. FFFS; g. FFFS
5. a. interactionism; determined by both situation and disposition
6. c. Cultural norms influence how people report on their own personalities.
7. a. idiographic; projective
8. b. Our self-narratives are unimportant in determining our identity, but our friends' stories about us have great influence.
9. d. based on the perceived probability of social rejection
10. c. "I am not the best candidate for the position, and the voters knew that."

Chapter 14

1. d. Is the behavior immoral?
2. b. RDoC will completely replace the *DSM-5* and the established classification of psychopathology.
3. d. Neuropsychological testing uses tasks that require planning, coordination, and memory to identify potential dysfunction in certain brain regions.
4. c. internalizing, women; externalizing, men
5. a. generalized anxiety disorder; b. specific phobia; c. social anxiety disorder
6. bipolar II disorder; major depressive disorder; bipolar I disorder
7. b. Schizophrenia is primarily a thought disorder with brain-related causes.
8. c. The presence of protective factors, such as positive relationships, can prevent trauma.
9. Choices b, d, and e apply.
10. b. attention-deficit/hyperactivity disorder

Chapter 15

1. a. biological; b. alternative biological; c. alternative biological; d. biological; e. psychotherapy; f. psychotherapy; g. biological; h. biological; i. alternative biological; j. psychotherapy
2. Choices a, b, and e apply.
3. Choices a and b apply.
4. e. obsessive-compulsive disorder and depression
5. c. Comorbid psychological disorders should be treated before initiating addiction treatment.
6. b. Contemporary use of ECT applies magnetic force to either side of the head to induce muscle convulsions.
7. The correct order is c, a, b.
8. a. pharmacological therapy; b. cognitive-behavioral therapy; c. dialectical behavioral therapy
9. c. Joshua's tendency to get into fistfights
10. a. Many individuals will be involved in Marley's treatment, including parents, teachers, and mental health practitioners.

Glossary

absentmindedness The inattentive or shallow encoding of events.

absolute refractory period The brief period of time following an action potential when the ion channel is unable to respond again.

absolute threshold The minimum intensity of stimulation necessary to detect a sensation half the time.

accommodation The process by which a new scheme is created or an existing scheme is drastically altered to include new information that otherwise would not fit into the scheme.

accuracy The degree to which an experimental measure is free from error.

acquisition The gradual formation of an association between the conditioned and unconditioned stimuli.

action potential The electrical signal that passes along the axon and subsequently causes the release of chemicals from the terminal buttons.

activation-synthesis hypothesis A hypothesis of dreaming proposing that the brain tries to make sense of random brain activity that occurs during sleep by synthesizing the activity with stored memories.

actor/observer discrepancy The tendency to focus on situations to explain one's own behavior but to focus on dispositions to explain other people's behavior.

addiction A behavioral disorder where use of a substance continues despite negative consequences and a desire to quit.

affective forecasting The tendency for people to overestimate how events will make them feel in the future.

aggression Any behavior that involves the intention to harm another.

agoraphobia An anxiety disorder marked by fear of being in situations in which escape may be difficult or impossible.

all-or-none principle The principle that when a neuron fires, it fires with the same potency each time; a neuron either fires or not, although the frequency of firing can vary.

allostatic load The cumulative "wear and tear" on biological systems, including the stress, digestive, immune, cardiovascular, and hormonal systems, among others, after repeated or chronic stressful events.

altruism Providing help when it is needed, without any apparent reward for doing so.

amnesia A deficit in long-term memory—resulting from disease, brain injury, or psychological trauma—in which the individual loses the ability to retrieve vast quantities of information.

amygdala A brain structure that serves a vital role in learning to associate things with emotional responses and in processing emotional information.

analogical representations Mental representations that have some of what they represent.

anchoring The tendency, in making judgments, to rely on the first piece of information encountered or information that comes most quickly to mind.

anorexia nervosa An eating disorder characterized by excessive fear of becoming fat and therefore restricting energy intake to obtain a significantly low body weight.

anterograde amnesia A condition in which people lose the ability to form new memories.

antianxiety drugs A class of psychotropic medications used for the treatment of anxiety.

antidepressants A class of psychotropic medications used for the treatment of depression.

antipsychotics A class of psychotropic medications used for the treatment of schizophrenia and other disorders that involve psychosis.

antisocial personality disorder A personality disorder in which people engage in socially undesirable behavior, are hedonistic and impulsive, and lack empathy.

anxiety disorders Psychological disorders characterized by excessive fear and anxiety in the absence of true danger.

aphasia A language disorder that results in deficits in language comprehension and production.

applied behavioral analysis (ABA) An intensive treatment for autism based on operant conditioning.

assessment In psychology, examination of a person's cognitive, behavioral, or emotional functioning to diagnose possible psychological disorders.

assimilation The process by which new information is placed into an existing scheme.

associative learning Linking two stimuli or events that occur together.

attachment A strong, intimate, emotional connection between people that persists over time and across circumstances.

attention-deficit/hyperactivity disorder (ADHD) A disorder characterized by restlessness, inattentiveness, and impulsivity.

attitudes People's evaluations of other people, objects, events, or ideas.

attributions People's explanations for why events or actions occur.

audition Hearing; the sense of sound perception.

autism spectrum disorder A developmental disorder characterized by impaired communication, restricted interests, and deficits in social interaction.

autonomic nervous system (ANS) A component of the peripheral nervous system; it transmits sensory signals and motor signals between the central nervous system and the body's glands and internal organs.

availability heuristic Making a decision based on the answer that most easily comes to mind.

axon A long, narrow outgrowth of a neuron by which information is conducted from the cell body to the terminal buttons.

balance theory The idea that people are motivated to achieve harmony in their interpersonal relationships. A triad is balanced when the relationships are all the same direction or if two relationships are negative and one is positive.

basal ganglia A system of subcortical structures that are important for the planning and production of movement.

Bayesian statistics A class of statistics that combines existing beliefs ("priors") with new data to update the estimated likelihood that a belief is true ("posterior").

behavior therapy Treatment based on the premise that behavior is learned and therefore can be unlearned through the use of classical and operant conditioning.

behavioral approach system (BAS) The brain system involved in the pursuit of incentives or rewards.

behavioral inhibition system (BIS) The brain system that monitors for threats in the environment and therefore slows or inhibits behavior in order to be vigilant for danger or pain.

behaviorism A psychological approach that emphasizes environmental influences on observable behaviors.

big data Science that uses very large data sets and advanced computational methods to discover patterns that would be difficult to detect with smaller data sets.

binge-eating disorder An eating disorder characterized by binge eating that causes significant distress.

binocular depth cues Cues of depth perception that arise from the fact that people have two eyes.

binocular disparity A depth cue; because of the distance between the two eyes, each eye receives a slightly different retinal image.

biological therapies Treatments of psychological disorders based on medical approaches to disease (what is wrong with the body) and to illness (what a person feels as a result).

biopsychosocial model An approach to psychological science that integrates biological factors, psychological processes, and social-contextual influences in shaping human mental life and behavior.

bipolar I disorder A disorder characterized by extremely elevated moods during manic episodes and, frequently, depressive episodes as well.

bipolar II disorder A disorder characterized by alternating periods of extremely depressed and mildly elevated moods.

blocking The temporary inability to remember something.

borderline personality disorder A personality disorder characterized by disturbances in identity, in affect, and in impulse control.

bottom-up processing Perception based on the physical features of the stimulus.

brain stem An extension of the spinal cord; it houses structures that control functions associated with survival, such as heart rate, breathing, swallowing, vomiting, urination, and orgasm.

Broca's area A small portion of the left frontal region of the brain, crucial for the production of language.

buffering hypothesis The idea that other people can provide direct emotional support in helping individuals cope with stressful events.

bulimia nervosa An eating disorder characterized by the alternation of dieting, binge eating, and purging (self-induced vomiting).

bystander intervention effect The failure to offer help by those who observe someone in need when other people are present.

Cannon-Bard theory A theory of emotion stating that information about emotional stimuli is sent simultaneously to the cortex and the body and results in emotional experience and bodily reactions, respectively.

case study A descriptive research method that involves the intensive examination of an atypical person or organization.

cell body The site in the neuron where information from thousands of other neurons is collected and integrated.

central nervous system (CNS) The brain and the spinal cord.

central tendency A measure that represents the typical response or the behavior of a group as a whole.

cerebellum A large, convoluted protuberance at the back of the brain stem; it is essential for coordinated movement and balance.

cerebral cortex The outer layer of brain tissue, which forms the convoluted surface of the brain; the site of all thoughts, perceptions, and complex behaviors.

change blindness A failure to notice large changes in one's environment.

chromosomes Structures within the cell body that are made up of DNA, segments of which comprise individual genes.

chunking Organizing information into meaningful units to make it easier to remember.

circadian rhythms Biological patterns that occur at regular intervals as a function of time of day.

classical conditioning (Pavlovian conditioning) A type of associative learning in which a neutral stimulus comes to elicit a response when it is associated with a stimulus that already produces that response.

client-centered therapy An empathic approach to therapy; it encourages people to fulfill their individual potentials for personal growth through greater self-understanding.

cognition The mental activity that includes thinking and the understandings that result from thinking.

cognitive dissonance The unpleasant feeling of being aware of holding two conflicting beliefs or a belief that conflicts with a behavior.

cognitive restructuring A therapy that strives to help clients recognize maladaptive thought patterns and replace them with ways of viewing the world that are more in tune with reality.

cognitive therapy Treatment based on the idea that distorted thoughts produce maladaptive behaviors and emotions; treatment strategies attempt to modify these thought patterns.

cognitive-behavioral approach A diagnostic model that views psychopathology as the result of learned, maladaptive thoughts and beliefs.

cognitive-behavioral therapy (CBT) A therapy that incorporates techniques from cognitive therapy and behavior therapy to correct faulty thinking and change maladaptive behaviors.

companionate love A strong commitment based on friendship, trust, respect, and intimacy.

compliance The tendency to agree to do things requested by others.

concept A category, or class, of related items consisting of mental representations of those items.

concrete operational stage The third stage in Piaget's theory of cognitive development; during this stage, children begin to think about and understand logical operations, and they are no longer fooled by appearances.

conditioned response (CR) A response to a conditioned stimulus; a response that has been learned.

conditioned stimulus (CS) A stimulus that elicits a response only after learning has taken place.

cones Retinal cells that respond to higher levels of light and result in color perception.

conformity The altering of one's behaviors and opinions to match those of other people or to match other people's expectations.

confound Anything that affects a dependent variable and that may unintentionally vary between the experimental conditions of a study.

consciousness One's moment-to-moment subjective experience of the world.

consolidation The gradual process of memory storage in the brain.

construct validity The extent to which variables measure what they are supposed to measure.

continuous reinforcement A type of learning in which behavior is reinforced each time it occurs.

control group The participants in an experiment who receive no intervention or who receive an intervention that is unrelated to the independent variable being investigated.

conventional level Middle stage of moral development; at this level, strict adherence to societal rules and the approval of others determine what is moral.

convergence A cue of binocular depth perception; when a person views a nearby object, the eye muscles turn the eyes inward.

coping response Any attempt made to avoid, escape from, or minimize a stressor.

core values Strongly held beliefs about the enduring principles that are most important and meaningful. Values promote emotions and actions when they are aroused or threatened.

corpus callosum A massive bridge of millions of axons that connects the hemispheres of the brain and allows information to flow between them.

correlation coefficient A descriptive statistic that indicates the strength and direction of the relationship between two variables.

correlational studies A research method that describes and predicts how variables are naturally related in the real world, without any attempt by the researcher to alter them or assign causation between them.

critical thinking Systematically questioning and evaluating information using well-supported evidence.

cryptomnesia A type of misattribution that occurs when people think they have come up with a new idea yet have retrieved a stored idea and failed to attribute the idea to its proper source.

crystallized intelligence Intelligence that reflects both the knowledge acquired through experience and the ability to use that knowledge.

culturally sensitive research Studies that take into account the role that culture plays in determining thoughts, feelings, and actions.

culture The beliefs, values, rules, norms, and customs that exist within a group of people who share a common language and environment.

data Measurements gathered during the research process.

data ethics The branch of philosophy that addresses ethical issues in data sciences, including data accessibility, identifiability, and autonomy.

decision making A cognitive process that results in the selection of a course of action or belief from several options.

deep structure In language, the implicit meanings of sentences.

deindividuation A state of reduced individuality, reduced self-awareness, and reduced attention to personal standards; this phenomenon may occur when people are part of a group.

delusions False beliefs based on incorrect inferences about reality.

dendrites Branchlike extensions of the neuron that detect information from other neurons.

dependent variable The variable that is measured in a research study.

descriptive research Research methods that involve observing behavior to describe that behavior objectively and systematically.

descriptive statistics Statistics that summarize the data collected in a study.

developmental psychology The study of changes over the life span in physiology, cognition, emotion, and social behavior.

dialectical behavior therapy (DBT) A form of therapy used to treat borderline personality disorder that combines elements of the behavioral and cognitive treatments with a mindfulness approach based on Eastern meditative practices.

diathesis-stress model A diagnostic model proposing that a disorder may develop when an underlying vulnerability is coupled with a precipitating event.

difference threshold The minimum amount of change required to detect a difference between two stimuli.

directionality problem A problem encountered in correlational studies; the researchers find a relationship between two variables, but they cannot determine which variable may have caused changes in the other variable.

discrimination The differential treatment of people as a result of prejudice against their group.

disorganized behavior Acting in strange or unusual ways, including strange movement of limbs, bizarre speech, and inappropriate self-care, such as failing to dress properly or bathe.

disorganized speech Incoherent speech patterns that involve frequently changing topics and saying strange or inappropriate things.

display rules Rules learned through socialization that dictate which emotions are suitable in given situations.

dissociative disorders Disorders that involve disruptions of identity, of memory, or of conscious awareness.

distributed practice Learning material in several bursts over a prolonged time frame.

diversity and inclusion The value and practice of ensuring that psychological science represents the experiences of all humans.

dizygotic twins Also called *fraternal twins*; twin siblings that result from two separately fertilized eggs and therefore are no more similar genetically than nontwin siblings.

dominant gene A gene that is expressed in the offspring whenever it is present.

dreams Products of an altered state of consciousness in which images and fantasies are confused with reality.

drive A psychological state that, by creating arousal, motivates an organism to satisfy a need.

dynamic systems theory The view that development is a self-organizing process, in which new forms of behavior emerge through consistent interactions between a person and cultural and environmental contexts.

eardrum A thin membrane that marks the beginning of the middle ear; sound waves cause it to vibrate.

elaboration likelihood model The idea that persuasive messages lead to attitude changes in either of two ways: via the central route or via the peripheral route.

elaborative interrogation Learning by asking yourself why a fact is true or a process operates the way it does.

electroconvulsive therapy (ECT) A procedure that involves administering a strong electrical current to the brain to produce a seizure; it is effective for some cases of severe depression.

electroencephalography (EEG) A technique for measuring electrical activity in the brain.

emotion An immediate, specific negative or positive response to environmental events or internal thoughts.

emotion-focused coping A type of coping in which people try to prevent having an emotional response to a stressor.

emotional intelligence (EI) A form of social intelligence that emphasizes managing, recognizing, and understanding emotions and using them to guide appropriate thought and action.

encoding specificity principle The idea that any stimulus that is encoded along with an experience can later trigger a memory of the experience.

encoding The process by which the perception of a stimulus or event gets transformed into a memory.

endocrine system A communication system that uses hormones to influence thoughts, behaviors, and actions.

endogenous attention Attention that is directed voluntarily.

epigenetics The study of biological or environmental influences on gene expression that are not part of inherited genes.

episodic memory Memory for one's past experiences that are identified by a time and place.

equipotentiality The principle that any conditioned stimulus paired with any unconditioned stimulus should result in learning.

etiology Factors that contribute to the development of a disorder.

exemplar model A way of thinking about concepts: All members of a category are examples (exemplars); together they form the concept and determine category membership.

exogenous attention Attention that is directed involuntarily by a stimulus.

experiment A research method that tests causal hypotheses by manipulating and measuring variables.

experimental group The participants in an experiment who receive the treatment.

experimentation aversion A tendency for people to prefer to receive an untested treatment than to participate in a randomized study to evaluate the effectiveness of the treatment.

explicit attitudes Attitudes that a person can report.

explicit memory Memory that is consciously retrieved.

exposure A behavioral therapy technique that involves repeated exposure to an anxiety-producing stimulus or situation.

external validity The degree to which the findings of a study can be generalized to other people, settings, or situations.

extinction A process in which the conditioned response is weakened when the conditioned stimulus is repeated without the unconditioned stimulus.

extrinsic motivation Motivation to perform an activity because of the external goals toward which that activity is directed.

false positive A result that occurs when there is no real effect but a study produces a statistically significant result by chance.

family systems model A diagnostic model that considers problems within an individual as indicating problems within the family.

fear conditioning A type of classical conditioning that turns neutral stimuli into threatening stimuli.

fight-flight-freeze system (FFFS) The brain system that responds to punishment by directing an organism to freeze, run away, or engage in defensive fighting.

fight-or-flight response The physiological preparedness of animals to deal with danger by either fighting or fleeing.

five-factor theory The idea that personality can be described using five factors: openness to experience, conscientiousness, extraversion, agreeableness, and neuroticism.

flashbulb memories Vivid episodic memories for the circumstances in which people first learned of a surprising and consequential or emotionally arousing event.

fluid intelligence Intelligence that reflects the ability to process information, understand relationships, and think logically, particularly in novel or complex circumstances.

formal operational stage The final stage in Piaget's theory of cognitive development; in this stage, people can think abstractly, and they can formulate and test hypotheses through deductive logic.

fovea The center of the retina, where cones are densely packed.

framing In decision making, an emphasis on the potential losses or potential gains from at least one alternative.

frontal lobes Regions of the cerebral cortex—at the front of the brain—important for movement and higher-level psychological processes associated with the prefrontal cortex.

functional fixedness In problem solving, having fixed ideas about the typical functions of objects.

functional magnetic resonance imaging (fMRI) An imaging technique used to examine changes in the activity of the working human brain by measuring changes in the blood's oxygen levels.

functionalism An approach to psychology concerned with the adaptive purpose, or function, of mind and behavior.

fundamental attribution error In explaining other people's behavior, the tendency to overemphasize personality traits and underestimate situational factors.

gender identity One's sense of being male, female, or nonbinary.

gender role A behavior that is typically associated with being male or female.

gene expression Whether a particular gene is turned on or off.

general adaptation syndrome A consistent pattern of responses to stress that consists of three stages: alarm, resistance, and exhaustion.

general intelligence (*g*) The idea that one general factor underlies intelligence.

generalized anxiety disorder (GAD) A diffuse state of constant anxiety not associated with any specific object or event.

genes The units of heredity that help determine an organism's characteristics.

genotype The genetic constitution of an organism, determined at the moment of conception.

group polarization The process by which initial attitudes of groups become more extreme over time.

groupthink The tendency of a group to make a bad decision as a result of preserving the group and maintaining its cohesiveness; especially likely when the group is under intense pressure, is facing external threats, and is biased in a particular direction.

gustation The sense of taste.

habituation A decrease in behavioral response after repeated exposure to a stimulus.

habituation technique A way to study how infants categorize a series of objects, such as faces, based on the principle that after looking at objects that are all from the same category, babies will look for a longer time at objects from a new category.

hallucinations False sensory perceptions that are experienced without an external source.

haptic sense The sense of touch.

HARKing "Hypothesizing after the results are known" instead of generating a theory before running the study and analyzing the results.

health behaviors Actions people can take, such as eating a plant-based diet and being physically active, that promote well-being, prevent the onset of disease, and slow disease progression.

health disparities Differences in health outcomes, such as illness or death rates, between groups of people.

health psychology A field that involves the application of psychological principles to promote health and well-being.

heredity Transmission of characteristics from parents to offspring through genes.

heritability A statistical estimate of the extent to which variation in a trait within a population is due to genetics.

heuristics Shortcuts (rules of thumb or informal guidelines) used to reduce the amount of thinking that is needed to make decisions.

hippocampus A brain structure that is associated with the formation of memories.

homeostasis The tendency for bodily functions to maintain equilibrium.

hormones Chemical substances, released from endocrine glands, that travel through the bloodstream to targeted tissues; the tissues are subsequently influenced by the hormones.

humanistic approaches Approaches to studying personality that emphasize how people seek to fulfill their potential through greater self-understanding.

hypnosis A social interaction during which a person, responding to suggestions, experiences changes in memory, perception, and/or voluntary action.

hypothalamic-pituitary-adrenal (HPA) axis A body system involved in stress responses.

hypothalamus A brain structure that is involved in the regulation of bodily functions, including body temperature, body rhythms, blood pressure, and blood glucose levels; it also influences our basic motivated behaviors.

hypothesis A specific, testable prediction, narrower than the theory it is based on.

ideal affect Emotional and affective states that people want to feel or that cultures especially value.

idiographic approaches Person-centered approaches to assessing personality that focus on individual lives and how various characteristics are integrated into unique persons.

immigrant paradox The pattern among immigrant communities in which foreign-born immigrants to the United States have better health than people in later generations do.

immune system The body's mechanism for dealing with invading microorganisms such as allergens, bacteria, and viruses.

implicit attitudes Attitudes that influence a person's feelings and behavior at an unconscious level.

implicit memory Memory that is expressed through responses, actions, or reactions.

incentives External objects or external goals, rather than internal drives, that motivate behaviors.

inclusive fitness An explanation for altruism that focuses on the adaptive benefit of transmitting genes, such as through kin selection, rather than focusing on individual survival.

independent variable The variable that is manipulated in a research study.

inequity aversion A preference to avoid unfairness when making decisions about the distribution of resources.

infantile amnesia The inability to remember events from early childhood.

inferential statistics A set of procedures that enable researchers to decide whether differences between two or more groups are probably just chance variations or whether they reflect true differences in the populations being compared.

informational influence The tendency for people to conform when they assume that the behavior of others represents the correct way to respond.

ingroup favoritism The tendency for people to evaluate favorably and privilege members of the ingroup more than members of the outgroup.

insight The sudden realization of a solution to a problem.

insomnia A disorder characterized by an inability to sleep that causes significant problems in daily living.

institutional review boards (IRBs) Groups of people responsible for reviewing proposed research to ensure that it meets the accepted standards of science and provides for the physical and emotional well-being of research participants.

instructed learning Learning associations and behaviors through verbal communication.

insula The part of the cerebral cortex lying inside the lateral fissure; important for taste, pain, perception of bodily states, and empathy.

intelligence The ability to use knowledge to reason, make decisions, make sense of events, solve problems, understand complex ideas, learn quickly, and adapt to environmental challenges.

intelligence quotient (IQ) An index of intelligence computed by dividing a child's estimated mental age by the child's chronological age, then multiplying this number by 100.

interactionism The theory that behavior is determined jointly by situations and underlying dispositions.

interleaved practice Switching between topics during studying.

internal validity The degree to which the effects observed in an experiment are due to the independent variable and not to confounds.

intrinsic motivation Motivation to perform an activity because of the value or pleasure associated with that activity, rather than for an apparent external goal or purpose.

James-Lange theory A theory of emotion stating that people perceive specific patterns of bodily responses and as a result of that perception feel emotion.

language A system of communication using sounds and symbols according to grammatical rules.

law of effect Thorndike's general theory of learning: Any behavior that leads to a "satisfying state of affairs" is likely to occur again, and any behavior that leads to an "annoying state of affairs" is less likely to occur again. Or, the likelihood of the occurrence of a behavior is influenced by its consequences.

learned helplessness A cognitive model of depression in which people feel unable to control events in their lives.

learning A relatively enduring change in behavior resulting from experience.

linguistic relativity theory The claim that language determines thought.

locus of control People's personal beliefs about how much control they have over outcomes in their lives.

long-term memory The storage of information that lasts from minutes to forever.

long-term potentiation (LTP) Strengthening of a synaptic connection, making the postsynaptic neurons more easily activated by presynaptic neurons.

lymphocytes Specialized white blood cells that make up the immune system; the three types are B cells, T cells, and natural killer cells.

magnetic resonance imaging (MRI) A method of brain imaging that uses a powerful magnetic field to produce high-quality images of the brain.

major depressive disorder A disorder characterized by severe negative moods or a lack of interest in normally pleasurable activities.

mean A measure of central tendency that is the arithmetic average of a set of numbers.

median A measure of central tendency that is the value in a set of numbers that falls exactly halfway between the lowest and highest values.

meditation A mental procedure that focuses attention on an external object an internal event, or a sense of awareness.

memory The ability to store and retrieve information.

memory bias The changing of memories over time so that they become consistent with current beliefs or attitudes.

mental age An assessment of a child's intellectual standing compared with that of same-age peers; determined by comparing the child's test score with the average score for children of each chronological age.

mental sets Problem-solving strategies that have worked in the past.

mere exposure effect The idea that greater exposure to a stimulus leads to greater liking for it.

meta-analysis A "study of studies" that combines the findings of multiple studies to arrive at a conclusion.

mind/body problem A fundamental psychological issue: Are mind and body separate and distinct, or is the mind simply the physical brain's subjective experience?

mnemonics Learning aids or strategies that improve recall through the use of retrieval cues.

mode A measure of central tendency that is the most frequent score or value in a set of numbers.

modeling The imitation of observed behavior.

modern racism Subtle forms of prejudice that coexist with the rejection of racist beliefs.

monocular depth cues Cues of depth perception that are available to each eye alone.

monozygotic twins Also called *identical twins*; twin siblings that result from one zygote splitting in two and that therefore share the same genes.

morphemes The smallest language units that have meaning, including suffixes and prefixes.

motion parallax A monocular depth cue observed when moving relative to objects, in which the objects that are closer appear to move faster than the objects that are farther away.

motivation A process that energizes, guides, and maintains behavior toward a goal.

myelin sheath A fatty material, made up of glial cells, that insulates some axons to allow for faster movement of electrical impulses along the axon.

narcolepsy A sleep disorder in which people experience excessive sleepiness during normal waking hours, sometimes going limp and collapsing.

natural selection In evolutionary theory, the idea that those who inherit characteristics that help them adapt to their particular environments have a selective advantage over those who do not.

naturalistic observation A type of descriptive study in which the researcher is a passive observer, separated from the situation and making no attempt to change or alter ongoing behavior.

nature/nurture debate The arguments concerning whether psychological characteristics are biologically innate or acquired through education, experience, and culture.

need A state of biological, social, or psychological deficiency.

need for cognition The tendency to engage in and enjoy thinking about difficult questions or problems.

need hierarchy Maslow's arrangement of needs, in which basic survival needs must be met before people can satisfy higher needs.

need to belong The need for interpersonal attachments, a fundamental motive that has evolved for adaptive purposes.

negative punishment The removal of a stimulus to decrease the probability of a behavior's recurrence.

negative reinforcement The removal of an unpleasant stimulus to increase the probability of a behavior's recurrence.

negative symptoms Symptoms of schizophrenia that are marked by deficits in functioning, such as apathy, lack of emotion, and slowed speech and movement.

neurons The basic units of the nervous system; cells that receive, integrate, and transmit information. They operate through electrical impulses, communicate with other neurons through chemical signals, and form neural networks.

neurotransmitters Chemical substances that transmit signals from one neuron to another.

nodes of Ranvier Small gaps of exposed axon between the segments of myelin sheath, where action potentials take place.

nomothetic approaches Approaches to assessing personality that focus on the variation in common characteristics from person to person.

nonassociative learning Responding after repeated exposure to a single stimulus or event.

nonverbal behavior The facial expressions, gestures, mannerisms, and movements by which one communicates with others.

normative influence The tendency for people to conform in order to fit in with the group.

obedience Following the orders of a person of authority.

object constancy Correctly perceiving objects as constant in their shape, size, color, and lightness, despite raw sensory data that could mislead perception.

object permanence The understanding that an object continues to exist even when it cannot be seen.

obsessive-compulsive disorder (OCD) A disorder characterized by frequent intrusive thoughts and compulsive actions.

obstructive sleep apnea A disorder in which people, while asleep, stop breathing because their throat closes; the condition results in frequent awakenings during the night.

occipital lobes Regions of the cerebral cortex—at the back of the brain—important for vision.

olfaction The sense of smell.

olfactory bulb The brain center for smell, located below the frontal lobes.

olfactory epithelium A thin layer of tissue within the nasal cavity that contains the receptors for smell.

open science movement A social movement among scientists to improve methods, increase research transparency, and promote data sharing.

operant conditioning (instrumental conditioning) A learning process in which the consequences of an action determine the likelihood that it will be performed in the future.

operational definition A definition that *qualifies* (describes) and *quantifies* (measures) a variable so the variable can be understood objectively.

outgroup homogeneity effect The tendency to view outgroup members as less varied than ingroup members.

p-hacking Testing the same hypothesis using statistical tests in different variations until one produces a statistically significant result.

parasympathetic division A division of the autonomic nervous system; it returns the body to its resting state.

parietal lobes Regions of the cerebral cortex—in front of the occipital lobes and behind the frontal lobes—important for the sense of touch and for attention to the environment.

partial reinforcement A type of learning in which behavior is reinforced intermittently.

partial-reinforcement extinction effect The greater persistence of behavior under partial reinforcement than under continuous reinforcement.

participant observation A type of descriptive study in which the researcher is involved in the situation.

passionate love A state of intense longing and desire.

perception The processing, organization, and interpretation of sensory signals in the brain.

peripheral nervous system (PNS) All nerve cells in the body that are not part of the central nervous system. The peripheral nervous system includes the somatic and autonomic nervous systems.

persistence The continual recurrence of unwanted memories.

persistent depressive disorder A form of depression that is not severe enough to be diagnosed as major depressive disorder but lasts longer.

personal attributions Explanations of people's behavior that refer to their internal characteristics, such as abilities, traits, moods, or efforts.

personality A person's characteristic thoughts, emotional responses, and behaviors.

personality trait A pattern of thought, emotion, and behavior that is relatively consistent over time and across situations.

persuasion The active and conscious effort to change an attitude through the transmission of a message.

phenotype Observable physical characteristics, which result from both genetic and environmental influences.

phobia An acquired fear that is out of proportion to the real threat of an object or a situation.

phonemes The basic sounds of speech, the building blocks of language.

phonics A method of teaching reading in English that focuses on the association between letters and their phonemes.

pituitary gland A gland located at the base of the hypothalamus; it sends hormonal signals to other endocrine glands, controlling their release of hormones.

place coding A mechanism for encoding the frequency of auditory stimuli in which the frequency of the sound wave is encoded by the location of the hair cells along the basilar membrane.

placebo effect An improvement in physical or mental health following treatment with a placebo—that is, with a drug or treatment that has no active component for the disorder being treated.

plasticity A property of the brain that allows it to change as a result of experience or injury.

population Everyone in the group the experimenter is interested in.

positive punishment The administration of a stimulus to decrease the probability of a behavior's recurrence.

positive reinforcement The administration of a stimulus to increase the probability of a behavior's recurrence.

positron emission tomography (PET) A method of brain imaging that assesses metabolic activity by using a radioactive substance injected into the bloodstream.

postconventional level Highest stage of moral development; at this level, decisions about morality depend on abstract principles and the value of all life.

posttraumatic stress disorder (PTSD) A disorder that involves frequent nightmares, intrusive thoughts, and flashbacks related to an earlier trauma.

preconventional level Earliest stage of moral development; at this level, self-interest and event outcomes determine what is moral.

prefrontal cortex The frontmost portion of the frontal lobes, especially prominent in humans; important for attention, working memory, decision making, appropriate social behavior, and personality.

prejudice Negative feelings, opinions, and beliefs associated with a stereotype.

preoperational stage The second stage in Piaget's theory of cognitive development; during this stage, children think symbolically about objects, but they reason based on intuition and superficial appearance rather than logic.

preregistration Documenting a study's hypotheses, methods, and analysis plan ahead of time and publishing it on a time-stamped website.

primary appraisals Part of the coping process that involves making decisions about whether a stimulus is stressful, benign, or irrelevant.

primary emotions Emotions that are innate, evolutionarily adaptive, and universal (shared across cultures).

priming A facilitation in the response to a stimulus due to recent experience with that stimulus or a related stimulus.

proactive interference Interference that occurs when prior information inhibits the ability to remember new information.

problem-focused coping A type of coping in which people take direct steps to confront or minimize a stressor.

problem solving Finding a way around an obstacle to reach a goal.

procedural memory A type of implicit memory that involves skills and habits.

projective measures Personality tests that examine tendencies to respond in a particular way by having people interpret ambiguous stimuli.

prosocial behaviors Actions that benefit others, such as doing favors or helping.

prospective memory Remembering to do something at some future time.

prototype model A way of thinking about concepts: Within each category, there is a best example—a prototype—for that category.

psychodynamic therapy A form of therapy based on Freudian theory; it aims to help clients examine their needs, defenses, and motives as a way of understanding distress.

psychological science The study, through research, of mind, brain, and behavior.

psychopathology Sickness or disorder of the mind; psychological disorder.

psychotherapy The generic name given to formal psychological treatment.

psychotropic medications Drugs that affect mental processes.

puberty The beginning of adolescence, marked by the onset of sexual maturity and thus the ability to reproduce.

punishment A stimulus that follows a behavior and decreases the likelihood that the behavior will be repeated.

questionable research practices Practices that unintentionally make the research less replicable.

random assignment Placing research participants into the conditions of an experiment in such a way that each participant has an equal chance of being assigned to any level of the independent variable.

receptors In neurons, specialized protein molecules on the postsynaptic membrane; neurotransmitters bind to these molecules after passing across the synapse.

recessive gene A gene that is expressed only when it is matched with a similar gene from the other parent.

reciprocal determinism The theory that the expression of personality can be explained by the interaction of environment, person factors, and behavior itself.

reconsolidation The re-storage of memory after retrieval.

reinforcer A stimulus that follows a response and increases the likelihood that the response will be repeated.

relative refractory period The brief period of time following action potential when a neuron's membrane potential is more negative, or hyperpolarized, making it harder to fire again.

reliability The degree to which a measure is stable and consistent over time.

REM sleep The stage of sleep marked by rapid eye movements, paralysis of motor systems, and dreaming.

replicability The likelihood that the results of a study would be very similar if it were run again.

replication Repetition of a research study to confirm or contradict the results.

representativeness heuristic Placing a person or an object in a category if that person or object is similar to one's prototype for that category.

Rescorla-Wagner model A cognitive model of classical conditioning; it holds that learning is determined by the extent to which an unconditioned stimulus is unexpected or surprising.

research A scientific process that involves the careful collection, analysis, and interpretation of data.

Research Domain Criteria (RDoC) A method that defines basic aspects of functioning and considers them across multiple levels of analysis, from genes to brain systems to behavior.

resting membrane potential The electrical charge of a neuron when it is not active.

restructuring A new way of thinking about a problem that aids its solution.

retina The thin inner surface of the back of the eyeball, which contains the sensory receptors that transduce light into neural signals.

retrieval-based learning Learning new information by repeatedly recalling it from long-term memory.

retrieval cue Any stimulus that promotes memory recall.

retrieval-induced forgetting Impairment of the ability to recall an item in the future after retrieving a related item from long-term memory.

retroactive interference Interference that occurs when new information inhibits the ability to remember old information.

retrograde amnesia A condition in which people lose past memories, such as memories for events, facts, people, or even personal information.

reuptake The process whereby a neurotransmitter is taken back into the presynaptic terminal buttons, thereby stopping its activity.

rods Retinal cells that respond to low levels of light and result in black-and-white perception.

sample A subset of a population.

scatterplot A graphical depiction of the relationship between two variables.

schemas Cognitive structures in long-term memory that help us perceive, organize, and understand information.

schizophrenia A psychological disorder characterized by alterations in thoughts, in perceptions, or in consciousness, resulting in psychosis.

scientific method A systematic and dynamic procedure of observing and measuring phenomena, used to achieve the goals of description, prediction, control, and explanation; it involves an interaction among research, theories, and hypotheses.

script A schema that directs behavior over time within a situation.

secondary appraisals Part of the coping process during which people evaluate their response options and choose coping behaviors.

secondary emotions Blends of primary emotions.

self-actualization A state that is achieved when one's personal dreams and aspirations have been attained.

self-affirmation A need for a sense of self that is coherent and stable.

self-efficacy The belief that efforts toward a goal will result in success.

self-esteem The evaluative aspect of the self-concept in which people feel worthy or unworthy.

self-explanation Reflecting on your learning process and trying to make sense of new material in your own words.

self-regulation The process by which people direct their behavior toward the attainment of goals.

self-report methods Methods of data collection in which people are asked to provide information about themselves, such as in surveys or questionnaires.

self-schema A knowledge structure that contains memories, beliefs, and generalizations about the self and that helps people efficiently perceive, organize, interpret, and use information related to themselves.

self-serving bias The tendency for people to take personal credit for success but blame failure on external factors.

semantic memory Memory for facts independent of personal experience.

sensation The detection of physical stimuli and the transmission of this information to the brain.

sensitization An increase in behavioral response after exposure to a stimulus.

sensorimotor stage The first stage in Piaget's theory of cognitive development; during this stage, infants acquire information about the world through their senses and motor skills. Reflexive responses develop into more deliberate actions through the development and refinement of schemes.

sensory adaptation A decrease in sensitivity to a constant level of stimulation.

sensory memory A memory system that very briefly stores sensory information in close to its original sensory form.

serial position effect The finding that the ability to recall items from a list depends on the order of presentation, such that items presented early or late in the list are remembered better than those in the middle.

shaping A process of operant conditioning; it involves reinforcing behaviors that are increasingly similar to the desired behavior.

signal detection theory (SDT) A theory of perception based on the idea that the detection of a stimulus requires a judgment—it is not an all-or-nothing process.

situational attributions Explanations of people's behavior that refer to external events, such as the weather, luck, accidents, or other people's actions.

situationism The theory that behavior is determined more by situations than by personality traits.

social comparison The tendency for people to evaluate their own actions, abilities, and beliefs by contrasting them with other people's.

social facilitation The idea that the presence of others generally enhances performance.

social identity theory The idea that ingroups consist of individuals who perceive themselves to be members of the same social category and experience pride through their group membership.

social learning Acquiring or changing a behavior after verbal instruction or exposure to another individual performing that behavior.

social loafing The tendency for people to work less hard in a group than when working alone.

social norms Expected standards of conduct that influence behavior.

sociocultural model A diagnostic model that views psychopathology as the result of the interaction between individuals and their cultures.

socioeconomic status Relative standing in society as a function of resources such as income, wealth, and education.

socioemotional selectivity theory A theory proposing that as people grow older, they view time as limited and therefore shift their focus to meaningful events, experiences, and goals.

sociometer An internal monitor of social acceptance or rejection.

somatic nervous system (SNS) A component of the peripheral nervous system; it transmits sensory signals and motor signals between the central nervous system and the skin, muscles, and joints.

sound wave A pattern of changes in air pressure during a period of time; it produces the perception of a sound.

source amnesia A type of misattribution that occurs when people have a memory for an event but cannot remember where they encountered the information.

source misattribution Memory distortion that occurs when people misremember the time, place, person, or circumstances involved with a memory.

split brain A condition that occurs when the corpus callosum is surgically cut and the two hemispheres of the brain do not receive information directly from each other.

spontaneous recovery When a previously extinguished conditioned response reemerges after the presentation of the conditioned stimulus.

standard deviation A statistical measure of how far away each value is, on average, from the mean.

stereotype threat Fear or concern about confirming negative stereotypes related to one's own group, which in turn impairs performance on a task.

stereotypes Cognitive schemas that allow for easy, fast processing of information about people based on their membership in certain groups.

stimulus discrimination A differentiation between two similar stimuli when only one of them is consistently associated with the unconditioned stimulus.

stimulus generalization Learning that occurs when stimuli that are similar but not identical to the conditioned stimulus produce the conditioned response.

stream of consciousness A phrase coined by William James to describe each person's continuous series of ever-changing thoughts.

stress A type of response that typically involves an unpleasant state, such as anxiety or tension.

stressor Something in the external situation that is perceived as threatening or demanding and therefore produces stress.

subliminal perception The processing of information by sensory systems without conscious awareness.

suggestibility The development of biased memories from misleading information.

surface structure In language, the sound and order of words.

symbolic representations Abstract mental representations that do not correspond to the physical features of objects or ideas.

sympathetic division A division of the autonomic nervous system; it prepares the body for action.

synapse The gap between the terminal buttons of a "sending" neuron and the dendrites of a "receiving" neuron, where chemical communication occurs between the neurons.

synaptic pruning The physiological process of preserving synaptic connections that are used and eliminating those that are not used.

taste buds Sensory organs in the mouth that contain the receptors for taste.

telegraphic speech The way toddlers speak, using rudimentary sentences that are missing words and grammatical markings but follow a logical syntax and convey a wealth of meaning.

temperaments Biologically based tendencies to feel or act in certain ways.

temporal coding A mechanism for encoding low-frequency auditory stimuli in which the firing rates of cochlear hair cells match the frequency of the sound wave.

temporal discounting The tendency to discount the subjective value of a reward when it is given after a delay.

temporal lobes Regions of the cerebral cortex—below the parietal lobes and in front of the occipital lobes—important for processing auditory information, for memory, and for object and face perception.

tend-and-befriend response The tendency to protect and care for offspring and form social alliances rather than fight or flee in response to threat.

teratogens Agents that harm the embryo or fetus.

terminal buttons At the ends of axons, small nodules that release chemical signals from the neuron into the synapse.

thalamus The gateway to the brain; it receives almost all incoming sensory information before that information reaches the cortex.

theory A model of interconnected ideas or concepts that explains what is observed and makes predictions about future events. Theories are based on empirical evidence.

theory of mind The ability to understand that other people have mental states that influence their behavior.

thinking The mental manipulation of representations of knowledge about the world.

third variable problem A problem that occurs when the researcher cannot directly manipulate variables; as a result, the researcher cannot be confident that another, unmeasured variable is not the actual cause of differences in the variables of interest.

top-down processing The interpretation of sensory information based on knowledge, expectations, and past experiences.

trait approaches Approaches to studying personality that focus on how individuals differ in personality dispositions.

transcranial magnetic stimulation (TMS) The use of strong magnets to briefly interrupt normal brain activity as a way to study brain regions.

transduction The process by which sensory stimuli are converted to neural signals the brain can interpret.

trauma A prolonged psychological and physiological response to a distressing event, often one that profoundly violates the person's beliefs about the world.

traumatic brain injury (TBI) Impairments in mental functioning caused by a blow to or very sharp movement of the head.

two-factor theory A theory of emotion stating that the label applied to physiological arousal results in the experience of an emotion.

Type A behavior pattern A pattern of behavior characterized by competitiveness, achievement orientation, aggressiveness, hostility, restlessness, impatience with others, and an inability to relax.

unconditioned response (UR) A response that does not have to be learned, such as a reflex.

unconditioned stimulus (US) A stimulus that elicits a response, such as a reflex, without any prior learning.

variability In a set of numbers, how widely dispersed the values are from each other and from the mean.

variable Something in the world that can vary and that a researcher can manipulate (change), measure (evaluate), or both.

vestibular sense Perception of balance determined by receptors in the inner ear.

vicarious learning Learning the consequences of an action by watching others being rewarded or punished for performing the action.

well-being A positive state that includes striving for optimal health and life satisfaction.

Wernicke's area An area of the left hemisphere where the temporal and parietal lobes meet, involved in speech comprehension.

"what is beautiful is good" stereotype The belief that attractive people are superior in most ways.

working memory A limited-capacity cognitive system that temporarily stores and manipulates information for current use.

Yerkes-Dodson law The psychological principle that performance on challenging tasks increases with arousal up to a moderate level. After that, additional arousal impairs performance.

References

Abad-Merino, S., Newheiser, A.-K., Dovidio, J. F., Tabernero, C., & González, I. (2013). The dynamics of intergroup helping: The case of subtle bias against Latinos. *Cultural Diversity and Ethnic Minority Psychology, 19*(4), 445–452. https://doi.org/10.1037/a0032658

Abram, S. V., & DeYoung, C. G. (2017). Using personality neuroscience to study personality disorder. *Personality Disorders: Theory, Research, and Treatment, 8*(1), 2–13. https://doi.org/10.1037/per0000195

Abramowitz, J. S. (2013). The practice of exposure therapy: Relevance of cognitive-behavioral theory and extinction theory. *Behavior Therapy, 44*(4), 548–558. https://doi.org/10.1016/j.beth.2013.03.003

Ackerman, P. L., Beier, M. E., & Boyle, M. O. (2005). Working memory and intelligence: The same or different constructs? *Psychological Bulletin, 131*(1), 30–60. https://doi.org/10.1037/0033-2909.131.1.30

Adair, J. G., & Kagitcibasi, C. (1995). Development of psychology in developing countries: Factors facilitating and impeding its progress. *International Journal of Psychology, 30*(6), 633–641. https://doi.org/10.1080/00207599508246591

Adams, L. B., Richmond, J., Corbie-Smith, G., & Powell, W. (2017). Medical mistrust and colorectal cancer screening among African Americans. *Journal of Community Health, 42*(5), 1044–1061. https://doi.org/10.1007/s10900-017-0339-2

Adler, J. M., Lodi-Smith, J., Philippe, F. L., & Houle, I. (2016). The incremental validity of narrative identity in predicting well-being: A review of the field and recommendations for the future. *Personality and Social Psychology Review, 20*(2), 142–175. https://doi.org/10.1177/1088868315585068

Adler, N. E. (2013). Health disparities: Taking on the challenge. *Perspectives on Psychological Science, 8*(6), 679–681. https://doi.org/10.1177/1745691613506909

Adolphs, R., Gosselin, F., Buchanan, T. W., Tranel, D., Schyns, P., & Damasio, A. R. (2005). A mechanism for impaired fear recognition after amygdala damage. *Nature, 433*(7021), 68–72. https://doi.org/10.1038/nature03086

Adolphs, R., Sears, L., & Piven, J. (2001). Abnormal processing of social information from faces in autism. *Journal of Cognitive Neuroscience, 13*(2), 232–240. https://doi.org/10.1162/089892901564289

Agawu, K. (1995). *African rhythm: A Northern Ewe perspective.* Cambridge University Press.

Agnew-Blais, J. C., Polanczyk, G. V., Danese, A., Wertz, J., Moffitt, T. E., & Arseneault, L. (2016). Evaluation of the persistence, remission, and emergence of attention-deficit/hyperactivity disorder in young adulthood. *JAMA Psychiatry, 73*(7), 713–720. https://doi.org/10.1001/jamapsychiatry.2016.0465

Ainsworth, M. D. S., Blehar, M. C., Waters, E., & Wall, S. (1978). *Patterns of attachment: A psychological study of the strange situation.* Erlbaum.

Aizpurua, A., & Koutstaal, W. (2015). A matter of focus: Detailed memory in the intentional autobiographical recall of older and younger adults. *Consciousness and Cognition, 33*, 145–155. https://doi.org/10.1016/j.concog.2014.12.006

Al-Khatib, T. (2013, October 30). *Baseball superstitions not a game to players.* Seeker. https://www.seeker.com/baseball-superstitions-not-a-game-to-players-1768011796.html

Alamilla, S. G., Barney, B. J., Small, R., Wang, S. C., Schwartz, S. J., Donovan, R. A., & Lewis, C. (2020). Explaining the immigrant paradox: The influence of acculturation, enculturation, and acculturative stress on problematic alcohol consumption. *Behavioral Medicine, 46*(1), 21–33. https://doi.org/10.1080/08964289.2018.1539945

Alberini, C. M., & LeDoux, J. E. (2013). Memory reconsolidation. *Current Biology, 23*(17), R746–R750. https://doi.org/10.1016/j.cub.2013.06.046

Alferink, L. A., & Farmer-Dougan, V. (2010). Brain-(not) based education: Dangers of misunderstanding and misapplication of neuroscience research. *Exceptionality, 18*(1), 42–52. https://doi.org/10.1080/09362830903462573

Alfven, G., Grillner, S., & Andersson, E. (2019). Review of childhood pain highlights the role of negative stress. *Acta Paediatrica, 108*(12), 2148–2156. https://doi.org/10.1111/apa.14884

Algoe, S. B., & Fredrickson, B. L. (2011). Emotional fitness and the movement of affective science from lab to field. *American Psychologist, 66*(1), 35–42. https://doi.org/10.1037/a0021720

Allport, G. W. (1961). *Pattern and growth in personality.* Holt, Rinehart & Winston.

Allport, G. W., & Odbert, H. S. (1936). Trait-names: A psycho-lexical study. *Psychological Monographs, 47*(1), i–171. https://doi.org/10.1037/h0093360

Allred, K. D., & Smith, T. W. (1989). The hardy personality: Cognitive and physiological responses to evaluative threat. *Journal of Personality and Social Psychology, 56*(2), 257–266. https://doi.org/10.1037/0022-3514.56.2.257

Almeida, D. M. (2005). Resilience and vulnerability to daily stressors assessed via diary methods. *Current Directions in Psychological Science, 14*(2), 64–68. https://doi.org/10.1111/j.0963-7214.2005.00336.x

Amanzio, M., & Benedetti, F. (1999). Neuropharmacological dissection of placebo analgesia: Expectation-activated opioid systems versus conditioning-activated specific subsystems. *Journal of Neuroscience, 19*(1), 484–494. https://doi.org/10.1523/JNEUROSCI.19-01-00484.1999

Amato, P. R., Johnson, D. R., Booth, A., & Rogers, S. J. (2003). Continuity and change in marital quality between 1980 and 2000. *Journal of Marriage and Family, 65*(1), 1–22. https://doi.org/10.1111/j.1741-3737.2003.00001.x

Ambady, N., & Rosenthal, R. (1993). Half a minute: Predicting teacher evaluations from thin slices of nonverbal behavior and physical attractiveness. *Journal of Personality and Social Psychology, 64*(3), 431–441. https://doi.org/10.1037/0022-3514.64.3.431

American Academy of Neurology. (2013). *Recognizing sports concussions in athletes* [Fact sheet]. https://www.aan.com/Guidelines/home/GetGuidelineContent/913

American College Health Association. (2019). *American College Health Association–National College Health Assessment II: Undergraduate student executive summary spring 2019.* https://www.acha.org/documents/ncha/NCHA-II_SPRING_2019_UNDERGRADUATE_REFERENCE%20_GROUP_EXECUTIVE_SUMMARY.pdf

American Psychiatric Association. (2000). Practice guideline for the treatment of patients with eating disorders (revision). *American Journal of Psychiatry, 157*(1 Suppl), 1–39.

American Psychiatric Association. (2013). *Diagnostic and statistical manual of mental disorders* (5th ed.). American Psychiatric Association.

American Psychological Association. (2006). *Answers to your questions about individuals with intersex conditions.* http://www.apa.org/topics/lgbt/intersex.aspx

American Psychological Association. (2007, February). *Guidelines for psychological practice with girls and women.* http://www.apa.org/practice/guidelines/girls-and-women.pdf

American Psychological Association. (2018). *Careers in psychology* [Interactive data tool]. https://www.apa.org/workforce/data-tools/careers-psychology

American Psychological Association. (2020). *Stress in America: Stress in the time of COVID-19* (Vol. 1) [Press release]. https://www.apa.org/news/press/releases/stress/2020/stress-in-america-covid.pdf

Amodio, D. M. (2014). The neuroscience of prejudice and stereotyping. *Nature Reviews Neuroscience, 15*(10), 670–682. https://doi.org/10.1038/nrn3800

Anaya, B., & Pérez-Edgar, K. (2019). Personality development in the context of individual traits and parenting dynamics. *New Ideas in Psychology, 53*, 37–46. https://doi.org/10.1016/j.newideapsych.2018.03.002

Anderson, A. K., & Phelps, E. A. (2000). Expression without recognition: Contributions of the human amygdala to emotional communication. *Psychological Science, 11*(2), 106–111. https://doi.org/10.1111/1467-9280.00224

Anderson, A. K., Christoff, K., Stappen, I., Panitz, D., Ghahremani, D. G., Glover, G., Gabrieli, J. D. E., & Sobel, N. (2003). Dissociated neural representations of intensity and valence in human olfaction. *Nature Neuroscience, 6*(2), 196–202. https://doi.org/10.1038/nn1001

Anderson, C. A. (1989). Temperature and aggression: Ubiquitous effects of heat on occurrence of human violence. *Psychological Bulletin, 106*(1), 74–96. https://doi.org/10.1037/0033-2909.106.1.74

Anderson, C. A., & DeLisi, M. (2011). Implications of global climate change for violence in developed and developing countries. In J. Forgas, A. Kruglanski, & K. Williams (Eds.), *The psychology of social conflict and aggression* (pp. 249–265). Psychology Press.

Anderson, I. M. (2000). Selective serotonin reuptake inhibitors versus tricyclic antidepressants: A meta-analysis of efficacy and tolerability. *Journal of Affective Disorders, 58*(1), 19–36. https://doi.org/10.1016/S0165-0327(99)00092-0

Anderson, M. C., Bjork, E. L., & Bjork, R. A. (2000). Retrieval-induced forgetting: Evidence for a recall-specific mechanism. *Psychonomic Bulletin & Review, 7*(3), 522–530. https://doi.org/10.3758/BF03214366

Anderson, N. H. (1968). Likableness ratings of 555 personality-trait words. *Journal of Personality and Social Psychology, 9*(3), 272–279. https://doi.org/10.1037/h0025907

Andersson, G. (2016). Internet-delivered psychological treatments. *Annual Review of Clinical Psychology, 12*, 157–179. https://doi.org/10.1146/annurev-clinpsy-021815-093006

Andrade, L. H., Alonso, J., Mneimneh, Z., Wells, J. E., Al-Hamzawi, A., Borges, G., Bromet, E., Bruffaerts, R., de Girolamo, G., de Graaf, R., Florescu, S., Gureje, O., Hinkov, H. R., Hu, C., Huang, Y., Hwang, I., Jin, R., Karam, E. G., Kovess-Masfety, V., . . . Kessler, R. C. (2014). Barriers to mental health treatment: Results from the WHO World Mental Health (WMH) surveys. *Psychological Medicine, 44*(6), 1303–1317. https://doi.org/10.1017/S0033291713001943

Andreasen, N. C. (1984). *The broken brain: The biological revolution in psychiatry.* Harper & Row.

Angell, M. (2011, June 23). The epidemic of mental illness: Why? *The New York Review of Books.* https://www.nybooks.com/articles/2011/06/23/epidemic-mental-illness-why/

Aouizerate, B., Cuny, E., Martin-Guehl, C., Guehl, D., Amieva, H., Benazzouz, A., Fabrigoule, C., Allard, M., Rougier, A., Bioulac, B., Tignol, J., & Burbaud, P. (2004). Deep brain stimulation of the ventral caudate nucleus in the treatment of obsessive-compulsive disorder and major depression: Case report. *Journal of Neurosurgery, 101*(4), 682–686. https://doi.org/10.3171/jns.2004.101.4.0682

Appleton, K. M., Woodside, J. V., Arveiler, D., Haas, B., Amouyel, P., Montaye, M., Ferrieres, J., Ruidavets, J. B., Yarnell, J. W. G., Kee, F., Evans, A., Bingham, A., Ducimetiere, P., & Patterson, C. C. (2016). A role for behavior in the relationships between depression and hostility and cardiovascular disease incidence, mortality, and all-cause mortality: The Prime Study. *Annals of Behavioral Medicine, 50*(4), 582–591. https://doi.org/10.1007/s12160-016-9784-x

Arch, J. J., & Craske, M. G. (2006). Mechanisms of mindfulness: Emotion regulation following a focused breathing induction. *Behaviour Research and Therapy, 44*(12), 1849–1858. https://doi.org/10.1016/j.brat.2005.12.007

Arem, H., Moore, S. C., Patel, A., Hartge, P., de Gonzalez, A. B., Visvanathan, K., Campbell, P. T., Freedman, M., Weiderpass, E., Adami, H. O., Linet, M. S., Lee, I.-M., & Matthews, C. E. (2015). Leisure time physical activity and mortality: A detailed pooled analysis of the dose-response relationship. *JAMA Internal Medicine, 175*(6), 959–967. https://doi.org/10.1001/jamainternmed.2015.0533

Aron, A., Norman, C. C., Aron, E. N., McKenna, C., & Heyman, R. E. (2000). Couples' shared participation in novel and arousing activities and experienced relationship quality. *Journal of Personality and Social Psychology, 78*(2), 273–284. https://doi.org/10.1037/0022-3514.78.2.273

Aronson, E. (1972). *The social animal.* Freeman.

Aronson, E., & Mills, J. (1959). The effects of severity of initiation on liking for a group. *Journal of Abnormal and Social Psychology, 59*(2), 177–181. https://doi.org/10.1037/h0047195

Asch, S. E. (1946). Forming impressions of personality. *Journal of Abnormal and Social Psychology, 41*(3), 258–290. https://doi.org/10.1037/h0055756

Asch, S. E. (1955). Opinions and social pressure. *Scientific American, 193*(5), 31–35. https://doi.org/10.1038/scientificamerican1155-31

Asch, S. E. (1956). Studies of independence and conformity: A minority of one against a unanimous majority. *Psychological Monographs: General and Applied, 70*(9), 1–70. https://doi.org/10.1037/h0093718

Atkinson, R. C., & Shiffrin, R. M. (1968). Human memory: A proposed system and its control processes. *The Psychology of Learning and Motivation, 2*, 89–195. https://doi.org/10.1016/s0079-7421(08)60422-3

Austin, E. J., Saklofske, D. H., & Mastoras, S. M. (2010). Emotional intelligence, coping and exam-related stress in Canadian undergraduate students. *Australian Journal of Psychology, 62*(1), 42–50. https://doi.org/10.1080/00049530903312899

Averill, J. R. (1980). A constructivist view of emotion. In R. Plutchik & H. Kellerman (Eds.), *Theories of emotion* (pp. 305–339). Academic Press.

Aviezer, H., Hassin, R. R., Ryan, J., Grady, C., Susskind, J., Anderson, A., Moscovitch, M., & Bentin, S. (2008). Angry, disgusted, or afraid? Studies on the malleability of emotion perception. *Psychological Science, 19*(7), 724–732. https://doi.org/10.1111/j.1467-9280.2008.02148.x

Avinun, R., & Knafo, A. (2014). Parenting as a reaction evoked by children's genotype: A meta-analysis of children-as-twins studies. *Personality and Social Psychology Review, 18*(1), 87–102. https://doi.org/10.1177/1088868313498308

Ayhan, M. G., Uguz, F., Askin, R., & Gonen, M. S. (2014). The prevalence of depression and anxiety disorders in patients with euthyroid Hashimoto's thyroiditis: A comparative study. *General Hospital Psychiatry, 36*, 95–98. https://doi.org/10.1016/j.genhosppsych.2013.10.002

Ayoub, M., Briley, D. A., Grotzinger, A., Patterson, M. W., Engelhardt, L. E., Tackett, J. L., Harden, K. P., & Tucker-Drob, E. M. (2019). Genetic and environmental associations between child personality and parenting. *Social Psychological and Personality Science, 10*(6), 711–721. https://doi.org/10.1177/1948550618784890

Back, M. D., Stopfer, J. M., Vazire, S., Gaddis, S., Schmukle, S. C., Egloff, B., & Gosling, S. D. (2010). Facebook profiles reflect actual personality not self-idealization. *Psychological Science, 21*(3), 372–374. https://doi.org/10.1177/0956797609360756

Baddeley, A. D. (2002). Is working memory still working? *European Psychologist, 7*(2), 85–97. https://doi.org/10.1027//1016-9040.7.2.85

Baddeley, A. D., & Hitch, G. (1974). Working memory. In G. H. Bower (Ed.), *The psychology of learning and motivation: Advances in-research and theory* (Vol. 8, pp. 47–89). Academic Press.

Bagge, C. L., Littlefield, A. K., & Glenn, C. R. (2017). Trajectories of affective response as warning signs for suicide attempts: An examination of the 48 hours prior to a recent suicide attempt. *Clinical Psychological Science, 5*(2), 259–271. https://doi.org/10.1177/2167702616681628

Bahrick, H. P. (1984). Semantic memory content in permastore: Fifty years of memory for Spanish learned in school. *Journal of Experimental Psychology: General, 113*(1), 1–29. https://doi.org/10.1037/0096-3445.113.1.1

Bailes, J. E., Petraglia, A. L., Omalu, B. I., Nauman, E., & Talavage, T. (2013). Role of subconcussion in repetitive mild traumatic brain injury: A review. *Journal of Neurosurgery*, 119(5), 1235–1245. https://doi.org/10.3171/2013.7.jns121822

Baillargeon, R. (1987). Object permanence in 31/2- and 41/2-month-old infants. *Developmental Psychology, 23*(5), 655–664. https://doi.org/10.1037/0012-1649.23.5.655

Baillargeon, R. (1995). Physical reasoning in infancy. In M. S. Gazzaniga (Ed.), *The cognitive neurosciences* (pp. 181–204). MIT Press.

Baillargeon, R., Li, J., Ng, W., & Yuan, S. (2009). A new account of infants' physical reasoning. In A. Woodward & A. Needham (Eds.), *Learning and the infant mind* (pp. 66–116). Oxford University Press.

Baillargeon, R., Scott, R. M., & Bian, L. (2016). Psychological reasoning in infancy. *Annual Review of Psychology, 67*, 159–186. https://doi.org/10.1146/annurev-psych-010213-115033

Baker, T. B., Mermelstein, R., Collins, L. M., Piper, M. E., Jorenby, D. E., Smith, S. S., Christiansen, B. A., Schlam, T. R., Cook, J. W., & Fiore, M. C. (2011). New methods for tobacco dependence treatment research. *Annals of Behavioral Medicine, 41*(2), 192–207. https://doi.org/10.1007/s12160-010-9252-y

Bakker, M., Hartgerink, C. H. J., Wicherts, J. M., & van der Maas, H. L. J. (2016). Researchers' intuitions about power in psychological research. *Psychological Science, 27*(8), 1069–1077. https://doi.org/10.1177/0956797616647519

Baldwin, D. A. (1991). Infants' contribution to the achievement of joint reference. *Child Development, 62*(5), 875–890. https://doi.org/10.2307/1131140

Baldwin, D. A., & Baird, J. A. (2001). Discerning intentions in dynamic human action. *Trends*

in Cognitive Sciences, 5(4), 171–178. https://doi.org/10.1016/s1364-6613(00)01615-6
Baldwin, G. T., Breiding, M. J., & Sleet, D. (2016). Using the public health model to address unintentional injuries and TBI: A perspective from the Centers for Disease Control and Prevention (CDC). *NeuroRehabilitation, 39*(3), 345–349. https://doi.org/10.3233/NRE-161366
Balthazard, C. G., & Woody, E. Z. (1992). The spectral analysis of hypnotic performance with respect to "absorption." *International Journal of Clinical and Experimental Hypnosis, 40*(1), 21–43. https://doi.org/10.1080/00207149208409644
Baltimore, D. (2001). Our genome unveiled. *Nature, 409*(6822), 814–816. https://doi.org/10.1038/35057267
Bandura, A. (1965). Influence of models' reinforcement contingencies on the acquisition of imitative responses. *Journal of Personality and Social Psychology, 1*(6), 589–595. https://doi.org/10.1037/h0022070
Bandura, A. (1977). Self-efficacy: Toward a unifying theory of behavioral change. *Psychological Review, 84*(2), 191–215. https://doi.org/10.1037/0033-295X.84.2.191
Bandura, A., Ross, D., & Ross, S. A. (1961). Transmission of aggression through imitation of aggressive models. *Journal of Abnormal and Social Psychology, 63*(3), 575–582. https://doi.org/10.1037/h0045925
Bao, A.-M., & Swaab, D. F. (2011). Sexual differentiation of the human brain: Relation to gender identity, sexual orientation and neuropsychiatric disorders. *Frontiers in Neuroendocrinology, 32*(2), 214–226. https://doi.org/10.1016/j.yfrne.2011.02.007
Bao, W.-N., Whitbeck, L. B., Hoyt, D. R., & Conger, R. D. (1999). Perceived parental acceptance as a moderator of religious transmission among adolescent boys and girls. *Journal of Marriage and Family, 61*(2), 362–374. https://doi.org/10.2307/353754
Barch, D. M., Sheline, Y. I., Csernansky, J. G., & Snyder, A. Z. (2003). Working memory and prefrontal cortex dysfunction: Specificity to schizophrenia compared with major depression. *Biological Psychiatry, 53*(5), 376–384. https://doi.org/10.1016/S0006-3223(02)01674-8
Bard, P. (1934). On emotional expression after decortication with some remarks on certain theoretical views: Part I. *Psychological Review, 41*(4), 309–329. https://doi.org/10.1037/h0070765
Barlow, D. H. (2002). *Anxiety and its disorders: The nature and treatment of anxiety and panic* (2nd ed.). Guilford Press.
Barlow, D. H. (2004). Psychological treatments. *American Psychologist, 59*(9), 869–878. https://doi.org/10.1037/0003-066X.59.9.869
Barlow, D. H., Bullis, J. R., Comer, J. S., & Ametaj, A. A. (2013). Evidence-based psychological treatments: An update and a way forward. *Annual Review of Clinical Psychology, 9*, 1–27. https://doi.org/10.1146/annurev-clinpsy-050212-185629
Barlow, D. H., Gorman, J. M., Shear, M. K., & Woods, S. W. (2000). Cognitive-behavioral therapy, imipramine, or their combination for panic disorder: A randomized controlled trial. *Journal of the American Medical Association, 283*(19), 2529–2536. https://doi.org/10.1001/jama.283.19.2529
Barnes, J., Dong, C. Y., McRobbie, H., Walker, N., Mehta, M., & Stead, L. F. (2010). Hypnotherapy for smoking cessation. *Cochrane Database of Systematic Reviews, 10*, Article CD001008. https://doi.org/10.1002/14651858.CD001008.pub2
Barnett, R. C., & Hyde, J. S. (2001). Women, men, work, and family: An expansionist theory. *American Psychologist, 56*(10), 781–796. https://doi.org/10.1037/0003-066X.56.10.781
Baron-Cohen, S., Wheelwright, S., & Jolliffe, T. (1997). Is there a "language of the eyes"? Evidence from normal adults and adults with autism or Asperger syndrome. *Visual Cognition, 4*(3), 311–331. https://doi.org/10.1080/713756761
Barrett, L. F. (2017). The theory of constructed emotion: An active inference account of interoception and categorization. *Social Cognitive and Affective Neuroscience, 12*(1), 1–23. https://doi.org/10.1093/scan/nsw154
Barrett, L. F., Mesquita, B., Ochsner, K. N., & Gross, J. J. (2007). The experience of emotion. *Annual Review of Psychology, 58*(1), 373–403. https://doi.org/10.1146/annurev.psych.58.110405.085709
Barretto, R. P. J., Gillis-Smith, S., Chandrashekar, J., Yarmolinsky, D. A., Schnitzer, M. J., Ryba, N. J., & Zuker, C. S. (2015). The neural representation of taste quality at the periphery. *Nature, 517*(7534), 373–376. https://doi.org/10.1038/nature13873
Barrington-Trimis, J. L., Berhane, K., Unger, J. B., Cruz, T. B., Huh, J., Leventhal, A. M., Urman, R., Wang, K., Howland, S., Gilreath, T. D., Chou, C.-P., Pentz, M. A., & McConnell, R. (2015). Psychosocial factors associated with adolescent electronic cigarette and cigarette use. *Pediatrics, 136*(2), 308–317. https://doi.org/10.1542/peds.2015-0639
Barton, D. A., Esler, M. D., Dawood, T., Lambert, E. A., Haikerwal, D., Brenchley, C., Socratous, F., Hastings, J., Guo, L., Wiesner, G., Kaye, D. M., Bayles, R., Schlaich, M. P., & Lambert, G. W. (2008). Elevated brain serotonin turnover in patients with depression: Effect of genotype and therapy. *Archives of General Psychiatry, 65*(1), 38–46. https://doi.org/10.1001/archgenpsychiatry.2007.11
Bartoshuk, L. M. (2000). Comparing sensory experiences across individuals: Recent psychophysical advances illuminate genetic variation in taste perception. *Chemical Senses, 25*(4), 447–460. https://doi.org/10.1093/chemse/25.4.447
Bartoshuk, L. M., Duffy, V. B., & Miller, I. J. (1994). PTS/PROP tasting: Anatomy, psychophysics, and sex effects. *Physiology & Behavior, 56*(6), 1165–1171. https://doi.org/10.1016/0031-9384(94)90361-1
Baskin, T. W., Tierney, S. C., Minami, T., & Wampold, B. E. (2003). Establishing specificity in psychotherapy: A meta-analysis of structural equivalence of placebo controls. *Journal of Consulting and Clinical Psychology, 71*(6), 973–979. https://doi.org/10.1037/0022-006X.71.6.973
Basten, U., Hilger, K., & Fiebach, C. J. (2015). Where smart brains are different: A quantitative meta-analysis of functional and structural brain imaging studies on intelligence. *Intelligence, 51*, 10–27. https://doi.org/10.1016/j.intell.2015.04.009
Batson, C. D., Dyck, J. L., Brandt, J. R., Batson, J. G., Powell, A. L., McMaster, M. R., & Griffit, C. (1988). Five studies testing two new egoistic alternatives to the empathy-altruism hypothesis. *Journal of Personality and Social Psychology, 55*(1), 52–77. https://doi.org/10.1037/0022-3514.55.1.52
Batson, C. D., Turk, C. L., Shaw, L. L., & Klein, T. R. (1995). Information function of empathic emotion: Learning that we value the other's welfare. *Journal of Personality and Social Psychology, 68*(2), 300–313. https://doi.org/10.1037/0022-3514.68.2.300
Baugh, C. M., Stamm, J. M., Riley, D. O., Gavett, B. E., Shenton, M. E., Lin, A., Nowinski, C. J., Cantu, R. C., McKee, A. C., & Stern, R. A. (2012). Chronic traumatic encephalopathy: Neurodegeneration following repetitive concussive and subconcussive brain trauma. *Brain Imaging and Behavior, 6*(2), 244–254. https://doi.org/10.1007/s11682-012-9164-5
Baumeister, R. F. (1991). *Escaping the self: Alcoholism, spirituality, masochism, and other flights from the burden of selfhood.* Basic Books.
Baumeister, R. F., & Leary, M. R. (1995). The need to belong: Desire for interpersonal attachments as a fundamental human motivation. *Psychological Bulletin, 117*(3), 497–529. https://doi.org/10.1037/0033-2909.117.3.497
Baumeister, R. F., Bratslavsky, E., Finkenauer, C., & Vohs, K. D. (2001). Bad is stronger than good. *Review of General Psychology, 5*(4), 323–370. https://doi.org/10.1037/1089-2680.5.4.323
Baumeister, R. F., Campbell, J. D., Krueger, J. I., & Vohs, K. D. (2003). Does high self-esteem cause better performance, interpersonal success, happiness, or healthier lifestyles? *Psychological Science in the Public Interest, 4*(1), 1–44. https://doi.org/10.1111/1529-1006.01431
Baumeister, R. F., Campbell, J. D., Krueger, J. I., & Vohs, K. D. (2005). Exploding the self-esteem myth. *Scientific American, 292*(1), 70–77. https://www.scientificamerican.com/article/exploding-the-self-esteem-2005-12/
Baumeister, R. F., Heatherton, T. F., & Tice, D. (1994). *Losing control: How and why people fail at self-regulation.* Academic Press.
Baumeister, R. F., Smart, L., & Boden, J. M. (1996). Relation of threatened egotism to violence and aggression: The dark side of high self-esteem. *Psychological Review, 103*(1), 5–33. https://doi.org/10.1037/0033-295X.103.1.5
Baumgartner, H. M., Cole, S. L., Olney, J. J., & Berridge, K. C. (2020). Desire or dread from nucleus accumbens inhibitions: Reversed by same-site optogenetic excitations. *Journal of Neuroscience, 40*(13), 2737–2752. https://doi.org/10.1523/JNEUROSCI.2902-19.2020
Baumrind, D. (1964). Some thoughts on ethics of research: After reading Milgram's "Behavioral Study of Obedience." *American Psychologist, 19*(6), 421–423. https://doi.org/10.1037/h0040128
Baxter, A. J., Charlson, F. J., Cheng, H. G., Shidhaye, R., Ferrari, A. J., & Whiteford, H. A. (2016). Prevalence of mental, neurological, and substance use disorders in China and India: A systematic analysis. *The Lancet Psychiatry, 3*(9), 832–841. https://doi.org/10.1016/S2215-0366(16)30139-0
Baydala, L. T., Sewlal, B., Rasmussen, C., Alexis, K., Fletcher, F., Letendre, L., Odishaw, J., Kennedy, M., & Kootenay, B. (2009). A culturally adapted drug and alcohol abuse

prevention program for Aboriginal children and youth. *Progress in Community Health Partnerships, 3*(1), 37–46. https://doi.org/10.1353/cpr.0.0054

Bechtold, J., Hipwell, A., Lewis, D. A., Loeber, R., & Pardini, D. (2016). Concurrent and sustained cumulative effects of adolescent marijuana use on subclinical psychotic symptoms. *American Journal of Psychiatry, 173*(8), 781–789. https://doi.org/10.1176/appi.ajp.2016.15070878

Beck, A. T. (1964). Thinking and depression: II. Theory and therapy. *Archives of General Psychiatry, 10*(6), 561–571. https://doi.org/10.1001/archpsyc.1964.01720240015003

Beck, A. T. (1967). *Depression: Clinical, experimental and theoretical aspects.* Harper & Row.

Beck, A. T. (1976). *Cognitive therapy and the emotional disorders.* International Universities Press.

Beck, A. T., Brown, G., Seer, R. A., Eidelson, J. L., & Riskind, J. H. (1987). Differentiating anxiety and depression: A test of the cognitive content-specificity hypothesis. *Journal of Abnormal Psychology, 96*(3), 179–183. https://doi.org/10.1037/0021-843X.96.3.179

Beck, A. T., Freeman, A., & Associates. (1990). *Cognitive therapy of personality disorders.* Guilford Press.

Beck, A. T., Rush, A. J., Shaw, B., & Emery, G. (1979). *Cognitive therapy of depression.* Guilford Press.

Behne, T., Carpenter, M., Call, J., & Tomasello, M. (2005). Unwilling versus unable: Infants' understanding of intentional action. *Developmental Psychology, 41*(2), 328–337. https://doi.org/10.1037/0012-1649.41.2.328

Behrmann, M., & Avidan, G. (2005). Congenital prosopagnosia: Face-blind from birth. *Trends in Cognitive Sciences, 9*(4), 180–187. https://doi.org/10.1016/j.tics.2005.02.011

Békésy, G. von. (1957). The ear. *Scientific American, 197*(2), 66–79.

Bell, V., Raihani, N., & Wilkinson, S. (2021). Derationalizing delusions. *Clinical Psychological Science, 9*(1), 24–37. https://doi.org/10.1177/2167702620951553

Belmaker, R. H., & Agam, G. (2008). Major depressive disorder. *New England Journal of Medicine, 358*, 55–68. https://doi.org/10.1056/NEJMra073096

Belsky, J. (1990). Children and marriage. In F. D. Fincham & T. N. Bradbury (Eds.), *The psychology of marriage: Basic issues and applications* (pp. 172–200). Guilford Press.

Belsky, J., Houts, R. M., & Fearon, R. M. P. (2010). Infant attachment security and the timing of puberty: Testing an evolutionary hypothesis. *Psychological Science, 21*(9), 1195–1201. https://doi.org/10.1177/0956797610379867

Bem, D. J. (2011). Feeling the future: Experimental evidence for anomalous retroactive influences on cognition and affect. *Journal of Personality and Social Psychology, 100*(3), 407–425. https://doi.org/10.1037/a0021524

Ben-Shakhar, G., Bar-Hillel, M., & Kremnitzer, M. (2002). Trial by polygraph: Reconsidering the use of the guilty knowledge technique in court. *Law and Human Behavior, 26*(5), 527–541. https://doi.org/10.1023/A:1020204005730

Benedetti, F., Mayberg, H. S., Wager, T. D., Stohler, C. S., & Zubieta, J.-K. (2005). Neurobiological mechanisms of the placebo effect. *Journal of Neuroscience, 25*(45), 10390–10402. https://doi.org/10.1523/JNEUROSCI.3458-05.2005

Benjamin, A. S., & Tullis, J. (2010). What makes distributed practice effective? *Cognitive Psychology, 61*(3), 228–247. https://doi.org/10.1016/j.cogpsych.2010.05.004

Benjamin, L. T., Jr. (2005). A history of clinical psychology as a profession in America (and a glimpse at its future). *Annual Review of Clinical Psychology, 1*, 1–30. https://doi.org/10.1146/annurev.clinpsy.1.102803.143758

Bentler, P. M., & Newcomb, M. D. (1978). Longitudinal study of marital success and failure. *Journal of Consulting and Clinical Psychology, 46*(5), 1053–1070. https://doi.org/10.1037/0022-006X.46.5.1053

Berger, S. L., Kouzarides, T., Shiekhattar, R., & Shilatifard, A. (2009). An operational definition of epigenetics. *Genes & Development, 23*(7), 781–783. https://doi.org/10.1101/gad.1787609

Berkman, L. F., & Syme, S. L. (1979). Social networks, host resistance, and mortality: A nine-year follow-up study of Alameda County residents. *American Journal of Epidemiology, 109*(2), 186–204. https://doi.org/10.1093/oxfordjournals.aje.a112674

Berkowitz, L. (1990). On the formation and regulation of anger and aggression: A cognitive-neoassociationistic analysis. *American Psychologist, 45*(4), 494–503. https://doi.org/10.1037/0003-066X.45.4.494

Berndt, A., Lee, S. Y., Ramakrishnan, C., & Deisseroth, K. (2014). Structure-guided transformation of channelrhodopsin into a light-activated chloride channel. *Science, 344*(6182), 420–424. https://doi.org/10.1126/science.1252367

Bernhardt, P. C., Dabbs, J. M., Fielden, J. A., & Lutter, C. D. (1998). Testosterone changes during vicarious experiences of winning and losing among fans at sporting events. *Physiology & Behavior, 65*(1), 59–62. https://doi.org/10.1016/S0031-9384(98)00147-4

Bernstein, C. A. (2011). Meta-structure in DSM-5 process. *Psychiatric News, 46*, 7. https://doi.org/10.1176/pn.46.5.psychnews_46_5_7

Berntson, G. G., Norman, G. J., Hawkley, L. C., & Cacioppo, J. T. (2012). Evolution of neuroarchitecture, multi-level analyses and calibrative reductionism. *Interface Focus, 2*(1), 65–73. https://doi.org/10.1098/rsfs.2011.0063

Berridge, K. C. (2012). From prediction error to incentive salience: Mesolimbic computation of reward motivation. *European Journal of Neuroscience, 35*(7), 1124–1143. https://doi.org/10.1111/j.1460-9568.2012.07990.x

Berridge, K. C., & Kringelbach, M. L. (2013). Neuroscience of affect: Brain mechanisms of pleasure and displeasure. *Current Opinion in Neurobiology, 23*(3), 294–303. https://doi.org/10.1016/j.conb.2013.01.017

Berridge, K. C., Ho, C.-Y., Richard, J. M., & DiFeliceantonio, A. G. (2010). The tempted brain eats: Pleasure and desire circuits in obesity and eating disorders. *Brain Research, 1350*, 43–64. https://doi.org/10.1016/j.brainres.2010.04.003

Berscheid, E., & Regan, P. (2005). *The psychology of interpersonal relationships.* Prentice-Hall.

Berscheid, E., & Walster, E. H. (1969). *Interpersonal attraction.* Addison-Wesley.

Berthoud, H.-R. (2006). Homeostatic and non-homeostatic pathways involved in the control of food intake and energy balance. *Obesity, 14*(S8), 197S–200S. https://doi.org/10.1038/oby.2006.308

Betancourt, H., & López, S. R. (1993). The study of culture, ethnicity, and race in American psychology. *American Psychologist, 48*(6), 629–637. https://doi.org/10.1037/0003-066X.48.6.629

Betts, J. M., Dowd, A. N., Forney, M., Hetelekides, E., & Tiffany, S. T. (2021). A meta-analysis of cue reactivity in tobacco cigarette smokers. *Nicotine & Tobacco Research, 23*(2), 249–258. https://doi.org/10.1093/ntr/ntaa147

Bewernick, B. H., Hurlemann, R., Matusch, A., Kayser, S., Grubert, C., Hadrysiewicz, B., Axmacher, N., Lemke, M., Cooper-Mahkorn, D., Cohen, M. X., Brockmann, H., Lenartz, D., Sturm, V., & Schlaepfer, T. E. (2010). Nucleus accumbens deep brain stimulation decreases ratings of depression and anxiety in treatment-resistant depression. *Biological Psychiatry, 67*(2), 110–116. https://doi.org/10.1016/j.biopsych.2009.09.013

Bian, L., Leslie, S.-J., & Cimpian, A. (2017). Gender stereotypes about intellectual ability emerge early and influence children's interests. *Science, 355*(6323), 389–391. https://doi.org/10.1126/science.aah6524

Bickerton, D. (1998). The creation and re-creation of language. In C. B. Crawford & D. L. Krebs (Eds.), *Handbook of evolutionary psychology: Ideas, issues, and applications* (pp. 613–634). Erlbaum.

Bidell, T. R., & Fischer, K. W. (1995). Between nature and nurture: The role of agency in the epigenesis of intelligence. In R. Sternberg & E. Grigorenko (Eds.), *Intelligence: Heredity and environment* (pp. 193–242). Cambridge University Press.

Biederman, J., Monuteaux, M. C., Spencer, T., Wilens, T. E., Macpherson, H. A., & Faraone, S. V. (2008). Stimulant therapy and risk for subsequent substance use disorders in male adults with ADHD: A naturalistic controlled 10-year follow-up study. *American Journal of Psychiatry, 165*(5), 597–603. https://doi.org/10.1176/appi.ajp.2007.07091486

Biesanz, J., West, S. G., & Millevoi, A. (2007). What do you learn about someone over time? The relationship between length of acquaintance and consensus and self-other agreement in judgments of personality. *Journal of Personality and Social Psychology, 92*(1), 119–135. https://doi.org/10.1037/0022-3514.92.1.119

Bjorklund, D. F. (2007). *Why youth is not wasted on the young: Immaturity in human development.* Blackwell.

Bjorklund, D. F. (2018). A metatheory for cognitive development (or "Piaget is dead" revisited). *Child Development, 89*(6), 2288–2302. https://doi.org/10.1111/cdev.13019

Bjornsson, A. S. (2011). Beyond the "psychological placebo": Specifying the nonspecific in psychotherapy. *Clinical Psychology: Science and Practice, 18*(2), 113–118. https://doi.org/10.1111/j.1468-2850.2011.01242.x

Blackless, M., Charuvastra, A., Derryck, A., Fausto-Sterling, A., Lauzanne, K., & Lee, E. (2000). How sexually dimorphic are we? Review and synthesis. *American Journal of Human Biology, 12*(2), 151–166. https://doi.org/10.1002/(SICI)1520-6300(200003/04)12:2<3.0.CO;2-F

Blagys, M. D., & Hilsenroth, M. J. (2000). Distinctive feature of short-term psychodynamic-interpersonal psychotherapy: A review of the comparative psychotherapy process literature. *Clinical Psychology: Science and Practice*, *7*(2), 167–188. https://doi.org/10.1093/clipsy.7.2.167

Blair, I. V., Judd, C. M., & Chapleau, K. M. (2004). The influence of Afrocentric facial features in criminal sentencing. *Psychological Science*, *15*(10), 674–679. https://doi.org/10.1111/j.0956-7976.2004.00739.x

Blair, R. J. (2003). Neurobiological basis of psychopathy. *British Journal of Psychiatry*, *182*(1), 5–7. https://doi.org/10.1192/bjp.182.1.5

Blakemore, S.-J., Wolpert, D. M., & Frith, C. D. (1998). Central cancellation of self-produced tickle sensation. *Nature Neuroscience*, *1*(7), 635–640. https://doi.org/10.1038/2870

Blasiman, R. N., Dunlosky, J., & Rawson, K. A. (2017). The what, how much, and when of study strategies: Comparing intended versus actual study behaviour. *Memory*, *25*(6), 784–792. https://doi.org/10.1080/09658211.2016.1221974

Blass, T. (1991). Understanding behavior in the Milgram obedience experiment: The role of personality, situations, and their interactions. *Journal of Personality and Social Psychology*, *60*(3), 398–413. https://doi.org/10.1037/0022-3514.60.3.398

Bleidorn, W., Arslan, R. C., Denissen, J. J. A., Rentfrow, P. J., Gebauer, J. E., Potter, J., & Gosling, S. D. (2016). Age and gender differences in self-esteem—A cross-cultural window. *Journal of Personality and Social Psychology*, *111*(3), 396–410. https://doi.org/10.1037/pspp0000078

Bliss, T. V. P., & Lømo, T. (1973). Long-lasting potentiation of synaptic transmission in the dentate area of the anaesthetized rabbit following stimulation of the perforant path. *Journal of Physiology*, *232*(2), 331–356. https://doi.org/10.1113/jphysiol.1973.sp010273

Block, J., & Kremen, A. M. (1996). IQ and ego-resiliency: Conceptual and empirical connections and separateness. *Journal of Personality and Social Psychology*, *70*(2), 349–361. https://doi.org/10.1037/0022-3514.70.2.349

Bloom, P. (2002). Mindreading, communication and the learning of names for things. *Mind & Language*, *17*(1–2), 37–54. https://doi.org/10.1111/1468-0017.00188

Blumberg, S. J., Bramlett, M. D., Kogan, M. D., Schieve, L. A., Jones, J. R., & Lu, M. C. (2013). Changes in prevalence of parent-reported autism spectrum disorder in school-aged U.S. children: 2007 to 2011–2012. *National Health Statistics Reports*, *65*, 1–11. https://pubmed.ncbi.nlm.nih.gov/24988818/

Bogen, J. E., & Gazzaniga, M. S. (1965). Cerebral commissurotomy in man: Minor hemisphere dominance for certain visuospatial functions. *Journal of Neurosurgery*, *23*(4), 394–399. https://doi.org/10.3171/jns.1965.23.4.0394

Bohacek, J., Gapp, K., Saab, B. J., & Mansuy, I. M. (2013). Transgenerational epigenetic effects on brain functions. *Biological Psychiatry*, *73*(4), 313–320. https://doi.org/10.1016/j.biopsych.2012.08.019

Bolles, R. C. (1970). Species-specific defense reactions and avoidance learning. *Psychological Review*, *77*(1), 32–48. https://doi.org/10.1037/h0028589

Bonanno, G. A. (2004). Loss, trauma, and human resilience: Have we underestimated the human capacity to thrive after extremely aversive events? *American Psychologist*, *59*(1), 20–28. https://doi.org/10.1037/0003-066x.59.1.20

Bond, R., & Smith, P. B. (1996). Culture and conformity: A meta-analysis of studies using Asch's (1952b, 1956) line judgment task. *Psychological Bulletin*, *119*(1), 111–137. https://doi.org/10.1037/0033-2909.119.1.111

Booth, A., Shelley, G., Mazur, A., Tharp, G., & Kittok, R. (1989). Testosterone, and winning and losing in human competition. *Hormones and Behavior*, *23*(4), 556–571. https://doi.org/10.1016/0018-506X(89)90042-1

Bootzin, R. R., & Epstein, D. R. (2011). Understanding and treating insomnia. *Annual Review of Clinical Psychology*, *7*(1), 435–458. https://doi.org/10.1146/annurev.clinpsy.3.022806.091516

Boroditsky, L., Fuhrman, O., & McCormick, K. (2011). Do English and Mandarin speakers think about time differently? *Cognition*, *118*(1), 123–129. https://doi.org/10.1016/j.cognition.2010.09.010

Bosson, J. K., Lakey, C. E., Campbell, W. K., Zeigler-Hill, V., Jordan, C. H., & Kernis, M. H. (2008). Untangling the links between narcissism and self-esteem: A theoretical and empirical review. *Social and Personality Psychology Compass*, *2*(3), 1415–1439. https://doi.org/10.1111/j.1751-9004.2008.00089.x

Bouchard, T. J, Lykken, D. T., McGue, M., Segal, N. L., & Tellegen, A. (1990). Sources of human psychological differences: The Minnesota study of twins reared apart. *Science*, *250*(4978), 223–228. https://doi.org/10.1126/science.2218526

Bouchard, T. J., Jr. (2014). Genes, evolution and intelligence. *Behavior Genetics*, *44*(6), 549–577. https://doi.org/10.1007/s10519-014-9646-x

Bouton, M. E. (1994). Context, ambiguity, and classical conditioning. *Current Directions in Psychological Science*, *3*(2). 49–53. https://doi.org/10.1111/1467-8721.ep10769943

Bouton, M. E., Trask, S., & Carranza-Jasso, R. (2016). Learning to inhibit the response during instrumental (operant) extinction. *Journal of Experimental Psychology: Animal Learning and Cognition*, *42*(3), 246–258. https://doi.org/10.1037/xan0000102

Bowlby, J. (1982). Attachment and loss: Retrospect and prospect. *American Journal of Orthopsychiatry*, *52*(4), 664–678. https://doi.org/10.1111/j.1939-0025.1982.tb01456.x

Boyden, E. S., Zhang, F., Bamberg, E., Nagel, G., & Deisseroth, K. (2005). Millisecond-timescale, genetically targeted optical control of neural activity. *Nature Neuroscience*, *8*(9), 1263–1268. https://doi.org/10.1038/nn1525

Boysen, G. A., & VanBergen, A. (2014). Simulation of multiple personalities: A review of research comparing diagnosed and simulated dissociative identity disorder. *Clinical Psychology Review*, *34*(1), 14–28. https://doi.org/10.1016/j.cpr.2013.10.008

Brackett, M. A., Rivers, S. E., & Salovey, P. (2011). Emotional intelligence: Implications for personal, social, academic, and workplace settings. *Social and Personality Psychology Compass*, *5*(1), 88–103. https://doi.org/10.1111/j.1751-9004.2010.00334.x

Bradbury, T. N., & Fincham, F. D. (1990). Attributions in marriage: Review and critique. *Psychological Bulletin*, *107*(1), 3–33. https://doi.org/10.1037/0033-2909.107.1.3

Bradlow, A. R., Pisoni, D. B., Akahane-Yamada, R., & Tohkura, Y. (1997). Training Japanese listeners to identify English /r/ and /l/: IV. Some effects of perceptual learning on speech production. *Journal of the Acoustical Society of America*, *101*(4), 2299–2310. https://doi.org/10.1121/1.418276

Brakefield, P. M., & French, V. (1999). Butterfly wings: The evolution of development of colour patterns. *BioEssays*, *21*(5), 391–401. https://doi.org/10.1002/(SICI)1521-1878(199905)21:5<391::AID-BIES6>3.0.CO;2-Q

Braniecka, A., Hanć, M., Wołkowicz, I., Chrzczonowicz-Stępień, A., Mikołajonek, A., & Lipiec, M. (2019). Is it worth turning a trigger into a joke? Humor as an emotion regulation strategy in remitted depression. *Brain and Behavior*, *9*(2), Article e01213. https://doi.org/10.1002/brb3.1213

Brannigan, A., Nicholson, I., & Cherry, F. (2015). Introduction to the special issue: Unplugging the Milgram machine. *Theory & Psychology*, *25*(5), 551–563. https://doi.org/10.1177/0959354315604408

Bransford, J. D., & Johnson, M. K. (1972). Contextual prerequisites for understanding: Some investigations of comprehension and recall. *Journal of Verbal Learning and Verbal Behavior*, *11*(6), 717–726. https://doi.org/10.1016/S0022-5371(72)80006-9

Braunschweig, D., Ashwood, P., Krakowiak, P., Hertz-Picciotto, I., Hansen, R., Croen, L. A., Pessah, I. N., & Van de Water, J. (2008). Autism: Maternally derived antibodies specific for fetal brain proteins. *NeuroToxicology*, *29*(2), 226–231. https://doi.org/10.1016/j.neuro.2007.10.010

Breland, K., & Breland, M. (1961). The misbehavior of organisms. *American Psychologist*, *16*(11), 681–684. https://doi.org/10.1037/h0040090

Brewer, M. B., & Caporael, L. R. (1990). Selfish genes vs. selfish people: Sociobiology as origin myth. *Motivation and Emotion*, *14*(4), 237–243. https://doi.org/10.1007/BF00996182

Brickman, P., Coates, D., & Janoff-Bulman, R. (1978). Lottery winners and accident victims: Is happiness relative? *Journal of Personality and Social Psychology*, *36*(8), 917–927. https://doi.org/10.1037/0022-3514.36.8.917

Brinker, J., & Cheruvu, V. K. (2017). Social and emotional support as a protective factor against current depression among individuals with adverse childhood experiences. *Preventive Medicine Reports*, *5*, 127–133. https://doi.org/10.1016/j.pmedr.2016.11.018

Broadbent, D. E. (1958). *Perception and communication*. Oxford University Press.

Brody, A. L., Saxena, S., Stoessel, P., Gillies, L. A., Fairbanks, L. A., Alborzian, S., Phelps, M. E., Huang, S.-C., Wu, H.-M., Ho, M. L., Ho, M. K., Au, S. C., Maidment, K., & Baxter, L. R., Jr. (2001). Regional brain metabolic changes in patients with major depression treated with either paroxetine or interpersonal therapy: Preliminary findings. *Archives of General Psychiatry*, *58*(7), 631–640. https://doi.org/10.1001/archpsyc.58.7.631

Brody, G. H., Gray, J. C., Yu, T., Barton, A. W., Beach, S. R. H., Galván, A., MacKillop, J., Windle, M., Chen, E., Miller, G. E., & Sweet,

L. H. (2017). Protective prevention effects on the association of poverty with brain development. *JAMA Pediatrics, 171*(1), 46–52. https://doi.org/10.1001/jamapediatrics.2016.2988
Brody, J. E. (1997, December 30). Personal health: Despite the despair of depression, few men seek treatment. *New York Times.* https://www.nytimes.com/1997/12/30/science/personal-health-despite-the-despair-of-depression-few-men-seek-treatment.html
Bromley, S. M., & Doty, R. L. (1995). Odor recognition memory is better under bilateral than unilateral test conditions. *Cortex, 31*(1), 25–40. https://doi.org/10.1016/S0010-9452(13)80103-7
Broockman, D., & Kalla, J. (2016). Durably reducing transphobia: A field experiment on door-to-door canvassing. *Science, 352*(6282), 220–224. https://doi.org/10.1126/science.aad9713
Brown, A. S. (1991). A review of the tip-of-the-tongue phenomenon. *Psychological Bulletin, 109*(2), 204–223. https://doi.org/10.1037/0033-2909.109.2.204
Brown, A. S., & Derkits, E. J. (2009). Prenatal infection and schizophrenia: A review of epidemiologic and translational studies. *American Journal of Psychiatry, 167*(3), 261–280. https://doi.org/10.1176/appi.ajp.2009.09030361
Brown, A. S., & Meyer, U. (2018). Maternal immune activation and neuropsychiatric illness: A translational research perspective. *American Journal of Psychiatry, 175*(11), 1073–1083. https://doi.org/10.1176/appi.ajp.2018.17121311
Brown, G. W., & Harris, T. O. (1978). *Social origins of depression: A study of psychiatric disorders in women.* Free Press.
Brown, J. (1958). Some tests of the decay theory of immediate memory. *Quarterly Journal of Experimental Psychology, 10*(1), 12–21. https://doi.org/10.1080/17470215808416249
Brown, R. (1973). Development of the first language in the human species. *American Psychologist, 28*(2), 97–106. https://doi.org/10.1037/h0034209
Brown, R., & Hanlon, C. (1970). Derivational complexity and order of acquisition in child speech. In J. R. Hayes (Ed.), *Cognition and the development of language* (pp. 155–207). Wiley.
Brown, R., & Kulik, J. (1977). Flashbulb memories. *Cognition, 5*(1), 73–99. https://doi.org/10.1016/0010-0277(77)90018-X
Brown, R., & McNeill, D. (1966). The "tip-of-the-tongue" phenomenon. *Journal of Verbal Learning and Verbal Behavior, 5*(4), 325–337. https://doi.org/10.1016/S0022-5371(66)80040-3
Brown, T. A., & Barlow, D. H. (2009). A proposal for a dimensional classification system based on the shared features of the DSM-IV anxiety and mood disorders: Implications for assessment and treatment. *Psychological Assessment, 21*(3), 256–271. https://doi.org/10.1037/a0016608
Bruce, V., & Young, A. (1986). Understanding face recognition. *British Journal of Psychology, 77*(3), 305–327. https://doi.org/10.1111/j.2044-8295.1986.tb02199.x
Bruder, C. E. G., Piotrowski, A., Gijsbers, A. A. C. J., Andersson, R., Erickson, S., de Ståhl, T. D., Menzel, U., Sandgren, J., von Tell, D., Poplawski, A., Crowley, M., Crasto, C., Partridge, E. C., Tiwari, H., Allison, D. B., Komorowski, J., van Ommen, G.-J. B., Boomsma, D. I., Pedersen, N. L., . . . Dumanski, J. P. (2008). Phenotypically concordant and discordant monozygotic twins display different DNA copy-number-variation profiles. *American Journal of Human Genetics, 82*(3), 763–771. https://doi.org/10.1016/j.ajhg.2007.12.01
Bruneau, E. G., & Saxe, R. (2010). Attitudes towards the outgroup are predicted by activity in the precuneus in Arabs and Israelis. *NeuroImage, 52*(4), 1704–1711. https://doi.org/10.1016/j.neuroimage.2010.05.057
Bruneau, E. G., & Saxe, R. (2012). The power of being heard: The benefits of "perspective-giving" in the context of intergroup conflict. *Journal of Experimental Social Psychology, 48*(4), 855–866. https://doi.org/10.1016/j.jesp.2012.02.017
Brunoni, A. R., Chaimani, A., Moffa, A. H., Razza, L. B., Gattaz, W. F., Daskalakis, Z. J., & Carvalho, A. F. (2017). Repetitive transcranial magnetic stimulation for the acute treatment of major depressive episodes: A systematic review with network meta-analysis. *JAMA Psychiatry, 74*(2), 143–152. https://doi.org/10.1001/jamapsychiatry.2016.3644
Buckholtz, J. W., & Meyer-Lindenberg, A. (2008). MAOA and the neurogenetic architecture of human aggression. *Trends in Neurosciences, 31*(3), 120–129. https://doi.org/10.1016/j.tins.2007.12.006
Buckholtz, J. W., & Meyer-Lindenberg, A. (2013). Genetic perspectives on the neurochemistry of human violence and aggression. In T. Canli (Ed.), *The Oxford handbook of molecular psychology.* Oxford University Press.
Buoli, M., Serati, M., & Altamura, A. C. (2014). Is the combination of a mood stabilizer plus an antipsychotic more effective than monotherapies in long-term treatment of bipolar disorder? A systematic review. *Journal of Affective Disorders, 152–154*, 12–18. https://doi.org/10.1016/j.jad.2013.08.024
Burger, J. M. (2009). Replicating Milgram: Would people still obey today? *American Psychologist, 64*(1), 1–11. https://doi.org/10.1037/a0010932
Burger, J. M., Girgis, Z. M., & Manning, C. C. (2011). In their own words: Explaining obedience to authority through an examination of participants' comments. *Social Psychological and Personality Science, 2*(5), 460–466. https://doi.org/10.1177/1948550610397632
Burke, B. L., Arkowitz, H., & Menchola, M. (2003). The efficacy of motivational interviewing: A meta-analysis of controlled clinical trials. *Journal of Consulting and Clinical Psychology, 71*(5), 843–861. https://doi.org/10.1037/0022-006X.71.5.843
Bush, E. C., & Allman, J. M. (2004). The scaling of frontal cortex in primates and carnivores. *Proceedings of the National Academy of Sciences, 101*(11), 3962–3966. https://doi.org/10.1073/pnas.0305760101
Bushman, B. J., & Anderson, C. A. (2015). Understanding causality in the effects of media violence. *American Behavioral Scientist, 59*(14), 1807–1821. https://doi.org/10.1177/0002764215596554
Bushman, B. J., & Baumeister, R. F. (1998). Threatened egotism, narcissism, self-esteem, and direct and displaced aggression: Does self-love or self-hate lead to violence? *Journal of Personality and Social Psychology, 75*(1), 219–229. https://doi.org/10.1037/0022-3514.75.1.219
Buss, A. H., & Plomin, R. (1984). *Temperament: Early developing personality traits.* Erlbaum.
Buss, K. A., & McDoniel, M. E. (2016). Improving the prediction of risk for anxiety development in temperamentally fearful children. *Current Directions in Psychological Science, 25*(1), 14–20. https://doi.org/10.1177/0963721415611601
Butcher, J. N., & Williams, C. L. (2009). Personality assessment with the MMPI-2: Historical roots, international adaptations, and current challenges. *Applied Psychology: Health and Well-Being, 1*(1), 105–135. https://doi.org/10.1111/j.1758-0854.2008.01007.x
Butcher, J. N., Mineka, S., & Hooley, J. M. (2007). *Abnormal psychology* (13th ed.). Allyn & Bacon.
Butler, A. C., Chapman, J. E., Forman, E. M., & Beck, A. T. (2006). The empirical status of cognitive-behavioral therapy: A review of meta-analyses. *Clinical Psychology Review, 26*(1), 17–31. https://doi.org/10.1016/j.cpr.2005.07.003
Byers-Heinlein, K., Burns, T. C., & Werker, J. F. (2010). The roots of bilingualism in newborns. *Psychological Science, 21*(3), 343–348. https://doi.org/10.1177/0956797609360758
Cabanac, M. (1992). Pleasure: The common currency. *Journal of Theoretical Biology, 155*(2), 173–200. https://doi.org/10.1016/S0022-5193(05)80594-6
Cabeza, R., & Dennis, N. A. (2012). Frontal lobes and aging. In D. T. Stuss & R. T. Knight (Eds.), *Principles of frontal lobes function* (pp. 628–652). Oxford University Press.
Cabeza, R., & Moscovitch, M. (2013). Memory systems, processing modes, and components functional neuroimaging evidence. *Perspectives on Psychological Science, 8*(1), 49–55. https://doi.org/10.1177/1745691612469033
Cacioppo, J. T., & Cacioppo, S. (2018). The growing problem of loneliness. *The Lancet, 391*(10119), 426. https://doi.org/10.1016/S0140-6736(18)30142-9
Cacioppo, J. T., & Petty, R. E. (1982). The need for cognition. *Journal of Personality and Social Psychology, 42*(1), 116–131. https://doi.org/10.1037/0022-3514.42.1.116
Cacioppo, J. T., Hughes, M. E., Waite, L. J., Hawkley, L. C., & Thisted, R. A. (2006). Loneliness as a specific risk factor for depressive symptoms: Cross-sectional and longitudinal analyses. *Psychology and Aging, 21*(1), 140–151. https://doi.org/10.1037/0882-7974.21.1.140
Cacioppo, J. T., Petty, R. E., Feinstein, J. A., & Jarvis, W. B. G. (1996). Dispositional differences in cognitive motivation: The life and times of individuals varying in need for cognition. *Psychological Bulletin, 119*(2), 197–253. https://doi.org/10.1037/0033-2909.119.2.197
Cacioppo, S., Bianchi-Demicheli, F., Hatfield, E., & Rapson, R. L. (2012). Social neuroscience of love. *Clinical Neuropsychiatry: Journal of Treatment Evaluation, 9*(1), 3–13.
Cahn, B. R., & Polich, J. (2006). Meditation states and traits: EEG, ERP, and neuroimaging studies. *Psychological Bulletin, 132*(2), 180–211. https://doi.org/10.1037/0033-2909.132.2.180
Cai, H., Wu, L., Shi, Y., Gu, R., & Sedikides, C. (2016). Self-enhancement among Westerners and Easterners: A cultural neuroscience approach. *Social Cognitive and Affective*

Neuroscience, 11(10), 1569–1578. https://doi.org/10.1093/scan/nsw072

Cai, Z., Hahn, A. C., Zhang, W., Holzleitner, I. J., Lee, A. J., DeBruine, L. M., & Jones, B. C. (2019). No evidence that facial attractiveness, femininity, averageness, or coloration are cues to susceptibility to infectious illnesses in a university sample of young adult women. *Evolution and Human Behavior, 40*(2), 156–159. https://doi.org/10.1016/j.evolhumbehav.2018.10.002

Calder, A. J., Keane, J., Manes, F., Antoun, N., & Young, A. W. (2000). Impaired recognition and experience of disgust following brain injury. *Nature Neuroscience, 3*(11), 1077–1078. https://doi.org/10.1038/80586

Camp, G., Wesstein, H., & de Bruin, A. B. H. (2012). Can questioning induce forgetting? Retrieval-induced forgetting of eyewitness information. *Applied Cognitive Psychology, 26*(3), 431–435. https://doi.org/10.1002/acp.2815

Campbell, W. K., & Sedikides, C. (1999). Self-threat magnifies the self-serving bias: A meta-analytic integration. *Review of General Psychology, 3*(1), 23–43. https://doi.org/10.1037/1089-2680.3.1.23

Campbell, W. K., Bush, C. P., Brunell, A. B., & Shelton, J. (2005). Understanding the social costs of narcissism: The case of tragedy of the commons. *Personality and Social Psychology, 31*(10), 1358–1368. https://doi.org/10.1177/0146167205274855

Canetta, S., Sourander, A., Surcel, H. M., Hinkka-Yli-Salomäki, S., Leiviskä, J., Kellendonk, C., McKeague, I. W., & Brown, A. S. (2014). Elevated maternal C-reactive protein and increased risk of schizophrenia in a national birth cohort. *American Journal of Psychiatry, 171*(9), 960–968. https://doi.org/10.1176/appi.ajp.2014.13121579

Cannon, T. D., Cadenhead, K., Cornblatt, B., Woods, S. W., Addington, J., Walker, E., Seidman, L. J., Perkins, D., Tsuang, M., McGlashan, T., & Heinssen, R. (2008). Prediction of psychosis in youth at high clinical risk: A multisite longitudinal study in North America. *Archives of General Psychiatry, 65*(1), 28–37. https://doi.org/10.1001/archgenpsychiatry.2007.3

Cannon, W. B. (1927). The James-Lange theory of emotion: A critical examination and an alternative theory. *American Journal of Psychology, 39*, 106–124. https://doi.org/10.2307/1415404

Cannon, W. B. (1932). *The wisdom of the body.* Norton.

Caramaschi, D., de Boer, S. F., & Koolhaus, J. M. (2007). Differential role of the 5-HT1A receptor in aggressive and non-aggressive mice: An across-strain comparison. *Physiology & Behavior, 90*(4), 590–601. https://doi.org/10.1016/j.physbeh.2006.11.010

Cardeña, E., & Carlson, E. (2011). Acute stress disorder revisited. *Annual Review of Clinical Psychology, 7*(1), 245–267. https://doi.org/10.1146/annurev-clinpsy-032210-104502

Carew, T. J., Pinsker, H. M., & Kandel, E. R. (1972). Long-term habituation of a defensive withdrawal reflex in aplysia. *Science, 175*(4020), https://doi.org/10.1126/science.175.4020.451.

Carey, B. (2011, June 23). Expert on mental illness reveals her own fight. *New York Times*. https://www.nytimes.com/2011/06/23/health/23lives.html

Carmichael, M. (2007, March 26). Stronger, faster, smarter. *Newsweek, 149*(13), 38–46.

Carney, R. M., & Freedland, K. E. (2017). Depression and coronary heart disease. *Nature Reviews Cardiology, 14*(3), 145–155. https://doi.org/10.1038/nrcardio.2016.181

Carrère, S., Buehlman, K. T., Gottman, J. M., Coan, J. A., & Ruckstuhl, L. (2000). Predicting marital stability and divorce in newlywed couples. *Journal of Family Psychology, 14*(1), 42–58. https://doi.org/10.1037/0893-3200.14.1.42

Carstensen, L. L. (1995). Evidence for a life-span theory of socioemotional selectivity. *Current Directions in Psychological Science, 4*(5), 151–156. https://doi.org/10.1111/1467-8721.ep11512261

Carter, C. S. (2003). Developmental consequences of oxytocin. *Physiology & Behavior, 79*(3), 383–397. https://doi.org/10.1016/S0031-9384(03)00151-3

Carter, G. L., Campbell, A. C., & Muncer, S. (2014). The dark triad personality: Attractiveness to women. *Personality and Individual Differences, 56*, 57–61. https://doi.org/10.1016/j.paid.2013.08.021

Carver, C. S., & Miller, C. J. (2006). Relations of serotonin function to personality: Current views and a key methodological issue. *Psychiatry Research, 144*(1), 1–15. https://doi.org/10.1016/j.psychres.2006.03.013

Case, A., & Deaton, A. (2015). Rising morbidity and mortality in midlife among white non-Hispanic Americans in the 21st century. *Proceedings of the National Academy of Sciences, 112*(49), 15078–15083. https://doi.org/10.1073/pnas.1518393112

Case, R. (1992). The role of the frontal lobes in the regulation of cognitive development. *Brain and Cognition, 20*(1), 51–73. https://doi.org/10.1016/0278-2626(92)90061-P

Casey, B. J., Somerville, L. H., Gotlib, I. H., Ayduk, O., Franklin, N. T., Askren, M. K., Jonides, J., Berman, M. G., Wilson, N. L., Teslovich, T., Glover, G., Zayas, V., Mischel, W., & Shoda, Y. (2011). Behavioral and neural correlates of delay of gratification 40 years later. *Proceedings of the National Academy of Sciences, 108*(36), 14998–15003. https://doi.org/10.1073/pnas.1108561108

Caspi, A. (2000). The child is father of the man: Personality continuities from childhood to adulthood. *Journal of Personality and Social Psychology, 78*(1), 158–172. https://doi.org/10.1037/0022-3514.78.1.158

Caspi, A., & Herbener, E. S. (1990). Continuity and change: Assortative marriage and the consistency of personality in adulthood. *Journal of Personality and Social Psychology, 58*(2), 250–258. https://doi.org/10.1037/0022-3514.58.2.250

Caspi, A., Houts, R. M., Belsky, D. W., Goldman-Mellor, S. J., Harrington, H., Israel, S., Meier, M. H., Ramrakha, S., Shalev, I., Poulton, R., & Moffitt, T. E. (2014). The p factor: One general psychopathology factor in the structure of psychiatric disorders? *Clinical Psychological Science, 2*(2), 119–137. https://doi.org/10.1177/2167702613497473

Caspi, A., Houts, R. M., Belsky, D. W., Harrington, H., Hogan, S., Ramrakha, S., Poulton, R., & Moffitt, T. E. (2016). Childhood forecasting of a small segment of the population with large economic burden. *Nature Human Behaviour, 1*, Article 0005. https://doi.org/10.1038/s41562-016-0005

Caspi, A., McClay, J., Moffitt, T. E., Mill, J., Martin, J., Craig, I. W., Taylor, A., & Poulton, R. (2002). Role of genotype in the cycle of violence in maltreated children. *Science, 297*(5582), 851–854. https://doi.org/10.1126/science.1072290

Caspi, A., Roberts, B. W., & Shiner, R. L. (2005). Personality development: Stability and change. *Annual Review of Psychology, 56*(1), 453–484. https://doi.org/10.1146/annurev.psych.55.090902.141913

Cattell, R. B. (1943). The description of personality: Basic traits resolved into clusters. *Journal of Abnormal and Social Psychology, 38*(4), 476–506. https://doi.org/10.1037/h0054116

Cattell, R. B. (1965). *The scientific analysis of personality.* Penguin.

Cattell, R. B. (1971). *Abilities: Their structure, growth, and action.* Houghton Mifflin.

Cavanagh, J. T. O., Carson, A. J., Sharpe, M. M., & Lawrie, S. M. (2003). Psychological autopsy studies of suicide: A systematic review. *Psychological Medicine, 33*(3), 395–405. https://doi.org/10.1017/S0033291702006943

Cavicchioli, M., & Maffei, C. (2020). Rejection sensitivity in borderline personality disorder and the cognitive-affective personality system: A meta-analytic review. *Personality Disorders: Theory, Research, and Treatment, 11*(1), 1–12. https://doi.org/10.1037/per0000359

Ceci, S. J. (1999). Schooling and intelligence. In S. J. Ceci & W. M. Williams (Eds.), *The nature-nurture debate: The essential readings* (pp. 168–175). Blackwell.

Centers for Disease Control and Prevention. (2004, July). *Fetal alcohol syndrome: Guidelines for referral and diagnosis.* http://www.cdc.gov/ncbddd/fasd/documents/fas_guidelines_accessible.pdf

Centers for Disease Control and Prevention. (2005). Health disparities experienced by black or African Americans—United States. *MMWR: Morbidity and Mortality Weekly Report, 54*(1), 1–3. https://pubmed.ncbi.nlm.nih.gov/15647722/

Centers for Disease Control and Prevention. (2011a). Mental illness surveillance among adults in the United States. *Morbidity and Mortality Weekly Report, 60*, 1–32. https://www.cdc.gov/mmwr/preview/mmwrhtml/su6003a1.htm

Centers for Disease Control and Prevention. (2011b). Sickle cell disease. http://www.cdc.gov/ncbddd/sicklecell/data.html

Centers for Disease Control and Prevention. (2015). Measles outbreak—California, December 2014–February 2015. *Morbidity and Mortality Weekly Report, 64*(6), 153–154. https://www.cdc.gov/mmwr/preview/mmwrhtml/mm6406a5.htm

Centers for Disease Control and Prevention. (2016). *Health, United States, 2015: With special feature on racial and ethnic health disparities.* https://www.cdc.gov/nchs/data/hus/hus15.pdf

Centers for Disease Control and Prevention. (2019a). *Current cigarette smoking among adults in the United States.* https://www.cdc.gov/tobacco/data_statistics/fact_sheets/adult_data/cig_smoking/index.htm

Centers for Disease Control and Prevention. (2019b). *Youth and tobacco use.* https://www.cdc.gov/tobacco/data_statistics/fact_sheets/youth_data/tobacco_use/index.htm

Centers for Disease Control and Prevention. (2020a). *Excessive alcohol use*. https://www.cdc.gov/chronicdisease/resources/publications/factsheets/alcohol.htm

Centers for Disease Control and Prevention. (2020b). *October is National Protect Your Hearing Month!* https://www.cdc.gov/nceh/hearing_loss/

Centers for Disease Control and Prevention. (2020c). *Underlying cause of death 1999–2019*. CDC WONDER Online Database. http://wonder.cdc.gov/ucd-icd10.html

Cerasoli, C. P., Nicklin, J. M., & Ford, M. T. (2014). Intrinsic motivation and extrinsic incentives jointly predict performance: A 40-year meta-analysis. *Psychological Bulletin, 140*(4), 980–1008. https://doi.org/10.1037/a0035661

Chabas, D., Taheri, S., Renier, C., & Mignot, E. (2003). The genetics of narcolepsy. *Annual Review of Genomics & Human Genetics, 4*, 459–483. https://doi.org/10.1146/annurev.genom.4.070802.110432

Chabris, C. F., (1999). Prelude or requiem for the "Mozart effect"? *Nature, 400*, 826–827. https://doi.org/10.1038/23608

Chabris, C. F., Lee, J. J., Cesarini, D., Benjamin, D. J., & Laibson, D. I. (2015). The fourth law of behavior genetics. *Current Directions in Psychological Science, 24*(4), 304–312. https://doi.org/10.1177/0963721415580430

Chadwick, M. J., Anjum, R. S., Kumaran, D., Schacter, D. L., Spiers, H. J., & Hassabis, D. (2016). Semantic representations in the temporal pole predict false memories. *Proceedings of the National Academy of Sciences, 113*(36), 10180–10185. https://doi.org/10.1073/pnas.1610686113

Chambers, C. (2017). *The seven deadly sins of psychology: A manifesto for reforming the culture of scientific practice*. Princeton University Press.

Chambers, D. W. (1983). Stereotypic images of the scientist: The draw-a-scientist test. *Science Education, 67*(2), 255–265. https://doi.org/10.1002/sce.3730670213

Chang, L. J., Yarkoni, T., Khaw, M. W., & Sanfey, A. G. (2013). Decoding the role of the insula in human cognition: Functional parcellation and large-scale reverse inference. *Cerebral Cortex, 23*(3), 739–749. https://doi.org/10.1093/cercor/bhs065

Charles, S. T., Mogle, J., Urban, E. J., & Almeida, D. M. (2016). Daily events are important for age differences in mean and duration for negative affect but not positive affect. *Psychology and Aging, 31*(7), 661–671. https://doi.org/10.1037/pag0000118

Chase, V. D. (2006). *Shattered nerves: How science is solving modern medicine's most perplexing problem*. Johns Hopkins University Press.

Chase, W. G., & Simon, H. A. (1973). Perception in chess. *Cognitive Psychology, 4*(1), 55–81. https://doi.org/10.1016/0010-0285(73)90004-2

Chassin, L., Presson, C. C., & Sherman, S. J. (1990). Social psychological contributions to the understanding and prevention of adolescent cigarette smoking. *Personality and Social Psychology Bulletin, 16*(1), 133–151. https://doi.org/10.1177/0146167290161010

Chavez, R. S., Heatherton, T. F., & Wagner, D. D. (2017). Neural population decoding reveals the intrinsic positivity of the self. *Cerebral Cortex, 27*(11), 5222–5229. https://doi.org/10.1093/cercor/bhw302

Chen, B., Vansteenkiste, M., Beyers, W., Boone, L., Deci, E. L., Van der Kaap-Deeder, J., Duriez, B., Lens, W., Matos, L., Mouratidis, A., Ryan, R. M., Sheldon, K. M., Soenens, B., Van Petegem, S., & Verstuyf, J. (2015). Basic psychological need satisfaction, need frustration, and need strength across four cultures. *Motivation and Emotion, 39*(2), 216–236. https://doi.org/10.1007/s11031-014-9450-1

Cherry, E. C. (1953). Some experiments on the recognition of speech, with one and two ears. *Journal of the Acoustical Society of America, 25*, 975–979. https://doi.org/10.1121/1.1907229

Chester, D. S., DeWall, C. N., Derefinko, K. J., Estus, S., Peters, J. R., Lynam, D. R., & Jiang, Y. (2015). Monoamine oxidase A (MAOA) genotype predicts greater aggression through impulsive reactivity to negative affect. *Behavioural Brain Research, 283*, 97–101. https://doi.org/10.1016/j.bbr.2015.01.034

Cheung, F. M., Cheung, S. F., & Leung, F. (2008). Clinical utility of the cross-cultural (Chinese) personality assessment inventory (CPAI-2) in the assessment of substance use disorders among Chinese men. *Psychological Assessment, 20*(2), 103–113. https://doi.org/10.1037/1040-3590.20.2.103

Cheung, F. M., Leung, K., Zhang, J.-X., Sun, H.-F., Gan, Y.-Q., Song, W.-Z., & Xie, D. (2001). Indigenous Chinese personality constructs: Is the five-factor model complete? *Journal of Cross-Cultural Psychology, 32*(4), 407–433. https://doi.org/10.1177/0022022101032004003

Chistyakov, A. V., Kaplan, B., Rubichek, O., Kreinin, I., Koren, D., Feinsod, M., & Klein, E. (2005). Antidepressant effects of different schedules of repetitive transcranial magnetic stimulation vs. clomipramine in patients with major depression: Relationship to changes in cortical excitability. *International Journal of Neuropsychopharmacology, 8*(2), 223–233. https://doi.org/10.1017/S1461145704004912

Cho, H., & Schwarz, N. (2010). I like those glasses on you, but not in the mirror: Fluency, preference, and virtual mirrors. *Journal of Consumer Psychology, 20*(4), 471–475. https://doi.org/10.1016/j.jcps.2010.07.004

Choi, I., Nisbett, R. E., & Norenzayan, A. (1999). Causal attribution across cultures: Variation and universality. *Psychological Bulletin, 125*(1), 47–63. https://doi.org/10.1037/0033-2909.125.1.47

Choleris, E., Gustafsson, J. Å., Korach, K. S., Muglia, L. J., Pfaff, D. W., & Ogawa, S. (2003). An estrogen-dependent four-gene micronet regulating social recognition: A study with oxytocin and estrogen receptor-alpha and -beta knockout mice. *Proceedings of the National Academy of Sciences, 100*(10), 6192–6197. https://doi.org/10.1073/pnas.0631699100

Chomsky, N. (1959). A review of B. F. Skinner's *Verbal Behavior*. *Language, 35*(1), 26–58.

Chopik, W. J., Edelstein, R. S., & Grimm, K. J. (2019). Longitudinal changes in attachment orientation over a 59-year period. *Journal of Personality and Social Psychology, 116*(4), 598–611. https://doi.org/10.1037/pspp0000167

Chopik, W. J., O'Brien, E., & Konrath, S. H. (2017). Differences in empathic concern and perspective taking across 63 countries. *Journal of Cross-Cultural Psychology, 48*(1), 23–38. https://doi.org/10.1177/0022022116673910

Chou, W. Y. S., & Budenz, A. (2020). Considering emotion in COVID-19 vaccine communication: Addressing vaccine hesitancy and fostering vaccine confidence. *Health Communication, 35*(14), 1718–1722. https://doi.org/10.1080/10410236.2020.1838096

Christensen, D. L., Baio, J., Braun, K. V. N., Bilder, D., Charles, J., Constantino, J. N., Daniels, J., Durkin, M. S., Fitzgerald, R. T., Kurzius-Spencer, M., Lee, L.-C., Pettygrove, S., Robinson, C., Schulz, E., Wells, C., Wingate, M. S., Zahorodny, W., & Yeargin-Allsopp, M. (2016). Prevalence and characteristics of autism spectrum disorder among children aged 8 years — Autism and Developmental Disabilities Monitoring Network, 11 Sites, United States, 2012. *MMWR. Surveillance Summaries, 65*(3), 1–23. https://doi.org/10.15585/mmwr.ss6503a1

Christian, K. M., Song, H., & Ming, G. L. (2014). Functions and dysfunctions of adult hippocampal neurogenesis. *Annual Review of Neuroscience, 37*, 243–262. https://doi.org/10.1146/annurev-neuro-071013-014134

Christopher, F. S., & Sprecher, S. (2000). Sexuality in marriage, dating, and other relationships: A decade review. *Journal of Marriage and Family, 62*(4), 999–1017. https://doi.org/10.1111/j.1741-3737.2000.00999.x

Chronis-Tuscano, A., Degnan, K. A., Pine, D. S., Perez-Edgar, K., Henderson, H. A., Diaz, Y., Raggi, V. L., & Fox, N. A. (2009). Stable early maternal report of behavioral inhibition predicts lifetime social anxiety disorder in adolescence. *Journal of the American Academy of Child & Adolescent Psychiatry, 48*(9), 928–935. https://doi.org/10.1097/CHI.0b013e3181ae09df

Chronis, A. M., Jones, H. A., & Raggi, V. L. (2006). Evidence-based psychosocial treatments for children and adolescents with attention-deficit/hyperactivity disorder. *Clinical Psychology Review, 26*(4), 486–502. https://doi.org/10.1016/j.cpr.2006.01.002

Cialdini, R. B., Schaller, M., Houlihan, D., Arps, K., Fultz, J., & Beaman, A. L. (1987). Empathy-based helping: Is it selflessly or selfishly motivated? *Journal of Personality and Social Psychology, 52*(4), 749–758. https://doi.org/10.1037/0022-3514.52.4.749

Cialdini, R. B., Vincent, J. E., Lewis, S. K., Catalan, J., Wheeler, D., & Darby, B. L. (1975). Reciprocal concessions procedure for inducing compliance: The door-in-the-face technique. *Journal of Personality and Social Psychology, 31*(2), 206–215. https://doi.org/10.1037/h0076284

Cicchetti, D., Rogosh, F. A., & Toth, S. L. (1998). Maternal depressive disorder and contextual risk: Contributions to the development of attachment insecurity and behavior problems in toddlerhood. *Development and Psychopathology, 10*(2), 283–300. https://doi.org/10.1017/S0954579498001618

Cikara, M., & Van Bavel, J. J. (2014). The neuroscience of intergroup relations: An integrative review. *Perspectives on Psychological Science, 9*(3), 245–274. https://doi.org/10.1177/1745691614527464

Cikara, M., Bruneau, E., Van Bavel, J. J., & Saxe, R. (2014). Their pain gives us pleasure: How intergroup dynamics shape empathic failures and counter-empathic responses. *Journal of Experimental Social Psychology, 55*, 110–125. https://doi.org/10.1016/j.jesp.2014.06.007

Clark, L. A. (2007). Assessment and diagnosis of personality disorder: Perennial issues and an emerging reconceptualization. *Annual Review of Psychology, 58*, 227–257. https://doi.org/10.1146/annurev.psych.57.102904.190200
Clark, L. A., & Ro, E. (2014). Three-pronged assessment and diagnosis of personality disorder and its consequences: Personality functioning, pathological traits, and psychosocial disability. *Personality Disorders: Theory, Research, and Treatment, 5*(1), 55–69. https://doi.org/10.1037/per0000063
Clark, S. E., & Wells, G. L. (2008). On the diagnosticity of multiple-witness identifications. *Law and Human Behavior, 32*(5), 406–422. https://doi.org/10.1007/s10979-007-9115-7
Cleckley, H. M. (1941). *The mask of sanity: An attempt to reinterpret the so-called psychopathic personality.* Mosby.
Cockerham, W. C., Bauldry, S., Hamby, B. W., Shikany, J. M., & Bae, S. (2017). A comparison of Black and White racial differences in health lifestyles and cardiovascular disease. *American Journal of Preventive Medicine, 52*(1), S56–S62. https://doi.org/10.1016/j.amepre.2016.09.019
Cogsdill, E. J., Todorov, A. T., Spelke, E. S., & Banaji, M. R. (2014). Inferring character from faces: A developmental study. *Psychological Science, 25*(5), 1132–1139. https://doi.org/10.1177/0956797614523297
Cohen, D., Nisbett, R. E., Bowdle, B. F., & Schwarz, N. (1996). Insult, aggression, and the Southern culture of honor: An "experimental ethnography." *Journal of Personality and Social Psychology, 70*(5), 945–960. https://doi.org/10.1037/0022-3514.70.5.945
Cohen, S., & Wills, T. A. (1985). Stress, social support, and the buffering hypothesis. *Psychological Bulletin, 98*(2), 310–357. https://doi.org/10.1037/0033-2909.98.2.310
Cohen, S., Alper, C. M., Doyle, W. J., Treanor, J. J., & Turner, R. B. (2006). Positive emotional style predicts resistance to illness after experimental exposure to rhinovirus or influenza A virus. *Psychomatic Medicine, 68*(6), 809–815. https://doi.org/10.1097/01.psy.0000245867.92364.3c
Cohen, S., Doyle, W. J., Skoner, D. P., Rabin, B. S., & Gwaltney, J. M., Jr. (1997). Social ties and susceptibility to the common cold. *Journal of the American Medical Association, 277*(24), 1940–1944. https://doi.org/10.1001/jama.1997.03540480040036
Cohen, S., Janicki-Deverts, D., & Miller, G. E. (2007). Psychological stress and disease. *Journal of the American Medical Association, 298*(14), 1685–1687. https://doi.org/10.1001/jama.298.14.1685
Cohen, S., Janicki-Deverts, D., Doyle, W. J., Miller, G. E., Frank, E., Rabin, B. S., & Turner, R. B. (2012). Chronic stress, glucocorticoid receptor resistance, inflammation, and disease risk. *Proceedings of the National Academy of Sciences, 109*(16), 5995–5999. https://doi.org/10.1073/pnas.1118355109
Cohen, S., Tyrrell, D. A. J., & Smith, A. P. (1991). Psychological stress and susceptibility to the common cold. *New England Journal of Medicine, 325*(9), 606–612. https://doi.org/10.1056/nejm199108293250903
Cohn, M., Emrich, S. M., & Moscovitch, M. (2008). Age-related deficits in associative memory: The influence of impaired strategic retrieval. *Psychology and Aging, 23*(1), 93–103. https://doi.org/10.1037/0882-7974.23.1.93
Coid, J., & Ullrich, S. (2010). Antisocial personality disorder is on a continuum with psychopathy. *Comprehensive Psychiatry, 51*(4), 426–433. https://doi.org/10.1016/j.comppsych.2009.09.006
Colcombe, S. J., Erickson, K. I., Scalf, P. E., Kim, J. S., Prakash, R., McAuley, E., Elavsky, S., Marquez, D. X., Hu, L., & Kramer, A. F. (2006). Aerobic exercise training increases brain volume in aging humans. *Journal of Gerontology: Medical Sciences, 61*(11), 1166–1170. https://doi.org/10.1093/gerona/61.11.1166
Coles, N. A., Larsen, J. T., & Lench, H. C. (2019). A meta-analysis of the facial feedback literature: Effects of facial feedback on emotional experience are small and variable. *Psychological Bulletin, 145*(6), 610–651. https://doi.org/10.1037/bul0000194
Collins, K. P., & Cleary, S. D. (2016). Racial and ethnic disparities in parent-reported diagnosis of ADHD: National Survey of Children's Health (2003, 2007, and 2011). *Journal of Clinical Psychiatry, 77*(1), 52–59. https://doi.org/10.4088/JCP.14m09364
Collins, T., Tillmann, B., Barrett, F. S., Delbé, C., & Janata, P. (2014). A combined model of sensory and cognitive representations underlying tonal expectations in music: From audio signals to behavior. *Psychological Review, 121*(1), 33–65. https://doi.org/10.1037/a0034695
Compton, W. M., Conway, K. P., Stinson, F. S., Colliver, J. D., & Grant, B. F. (2005). Prevalence, correlates, and comorbidity of DSM-IV antisocial personality syndromes and alcohol and specific drug use disorders in the United States: Results from the national epidemiologic survey on alcohol and related conditions. *Journal of Clinical Psychiatry, 66*(6), 677–685. https://doi.org/10.4088/jcp.v66n0602
Compton, W. M., Han, B., Jones, C. M., Blanco, C., & Hughes, A. (2016). Marijuana use and use disorders in adults in the USA, 2002–14: Analysis of annual cross-sectional surveys. *The Lancet Psychiatry, 3*(10), 954–964. https://doi.org/10.1016/S2215-0366(16)30208-5
Comtesse, H., & Stemmler, G. (2017). Fear and disgust in women: Differentiation of cardiovascular regulation patterns. *Biological Psychology, 123*, 166–176. https://doi.org/10.1016/j.biopsycho.2016.12.002
Condon, D. M., & Revelle, W. (2015). Selected personality data from the SAPA-Project: On the structure of phrased self-report items. *Journal of Open Psychology Data, 3*(1), Article e6. https://doi.org/10.5334/jopd.al
Conklin, Q. A., Crosswell, A. D., Saron, C. D., & Epel, E. S. (2019). Meditation, stress processes, and telomere biology. *Current Opinion in Psychology, 28*, 92–101. https://doi.org/10.1016/j.copsyc.2018.11.009
Conley, T. D., Matsick, J. L., Moors, A. C., & Ziegler, A. (2017). Investigation of consensually nonmonogamous relationships: Theories, methods, and new directions. *Perspectives on Psychological Science, 12*(2), 205–232. https://doi.org/10.1177/1745691616667925
Connery, H. S. (2015). Medication-assisted treatment of opioid use disorder: Review of the evidence and future directions. *Harvard Review of Psychiatry, 23*(2), 63–75. https://doi.org/10.1097/HRP.0000000000000075
Connolly, A. C., Sha, L., Guntupalli, J. S., Oosterhof, N., Halchenko, Y. O., Nastase, S. A., Visconti di Oleggio Castello, M., Abdi, H., Jobst, B. C., Gobbini, M. I., & Haxby, J. V. (2016). How the human brain represents perceived dangerousness or "predacity" of animals. *Journal of Neuroscience, 36*(19), 5373–5384. https://doi.org/10.1523/JNEUROSCI.3395-15.2016
Conway, A. R. A., Kane, M. J., & Engle, R. W. (2003). Working memory capacity and its relation to general intelligence. *Trends in Cognitive Sciences, 7*(12), 547–552. https://doi.org/10.1016/j.tics.2003.10.005
Conway, A. R. A., Kane, M. J., Bunting, M. F., Hambrick, D. Z., Wilhelm, O., & Engle, R. W. (2005). Working memory span tasks: A methodological review and user's guide. *Psychonomic Bulletin & Review, 12*, 769–786. https://doi.org/10.3758/BF03196772
Conway, M., & Ross, M. (1984). Getting what you want by revising what you had. *Journal of Personality and Social Psychology, 47*(4), 738–748. https://doi.org/10.1037/0022-3514.47.4.738
Cook, G. I., Marsh, R. L., Clark-Foos, A., & Meeks, J. T. (2007). Learning is impaired by activated intentions. *Psychonomic Bulletin & Review, 14*(1), 101–106. https://doi.org/10.3758/BF03194035
Cook, M., & Mineka, S. (1989). Observational conditioning of fear to fear-relevant versus fear-irrelevant stimuli in rhesus monkeys. *Journal of Abnormal Psychology, 98*(4), 448–459. https://doi.org/10.1037/0021-843X.98.4.448
Cook, M., & Mineka, S. (1990). Selective associations in the observational conditioning of fear in rhesus monkeys. *Journal of Experimental Psychology: Animal Behavior Processes, 16*(4), 372–389. https://doi.org/10.1037/0097-7403.16.4.372
Cooke, J. E., Racine, N., Plamondon, A., Tough, S., & Madigan, S. (2019). Maternal adverse childhood experiences, attachment style, and mental health: Pathways of transmission to child behavior problems. *Child Abuse & Neglect, 93*, 27–37. https://doi.org/10.1016/j.chiabu.2019.04.011
Cooper, C. R., Denner, J., & Lopez, E. M. (1999). Cultural brokers: Helping Latino children on pathways toward success. *The Future of Children, 9*(2), 51–57. https://doi.org/10.2307/1602705
Copeland, W. E., Wolke, D., Angold, A., & Costello, E. J. (2013). Adult psychiatric outcomes of bullying and being bullied by peers in childhood and adolescence. *Journal of the American Medical Association Psychiatry, 70*(4), 419–426. https://doi.org/10.1001/jamapsychiatry.2013.504
Copen, C. E., Daniels, K., Vespa, J., & Mosher, W. D. (2012, March 22). *First marriages in the United States: Data from the 2006–2010 National Survey of Family Growth* (National Health Statistics Reports, No. 49). Centers for Disease Control and Prevention. https://www.cdc.gov/nchs/data/nhsr/nhsr049.pdf
Coren, S. (1996). Daylight savings time and traffic accidents. *New England Journal of Medicine, 334*(14), 924–925. https://doi.org/10.1056/NEJM199604043341416

Corr, P. J. (2013). Approach and avoidance behaviour: Multiple systems and their interactions. *Emotion Review, 5*(3), 285–290. https://doi.org/10.1177/1754073913477507
Corr, P. J., DeYoung, C. G., & McNaughton, N. (2013). Motivation and personality: A neuropsychological perspective. *Social and Personality Psychology Compass, 7*(3), 158–175. https://doi.org/10.1111/spc3.12016
Correll, C. U., Leucht, S., & Kane, J. M. (2004). Lower risk for tardive dyskinesia associated with second-generation antipsychotics: A systematic review of 1-year studies. *American Journal of Psychiatry, 161*, 414–425. https://doi.org/10.1176/appi.ajp.161.3.414
Correll, J., Park, B., Judd, C. M., & Wittenbrink, B. (2002). The police officer's dilemma: Using ethnicity to disambiguate potentially threatening individuals. *Journal of Personality and Social Psychology, 83*(6), 1314–1329. https://doi.org/10.1037/0022-3514.83.6.1314
Correll, J., Park, B., Judd, C. M., Wittenbrink, B., Sadler, M. S., & Keesee, T. (2007). Across the thin blue line: Police officers and racial bias in the decision to shoot. *Journal of Personality and Social Psychology, 92*(6), 1006–1023. https://doi.org/10.1037/0022-3514.92.6.1006
Cortese, S., Moreira-Maia, C. R., St. Fleur, D., Morcillo-Peñalver, C., Rohde, L. A., & Faraone, S. V. (2016). Association between ADHD and obesity: A systematic review and meta-analysis. *American Journal of Psychiatry, 173*(1), 34–43. https://doi.org/10.1176/appi.ajp.2015.15020266
Costa, P. T., & McCrae, R. R. (1992). *Revised NEO Personality Inventory (NEO-PI-R) and NEO Five-Factor Inventory (NEO-FFI) professional manual.* Psychological Assessment Resources.
Costa, P. T., Jr., McCrae, R. R., & Löckenhoff, C. E. (2019). Personality across the life span. *Annual Review of Psychology, 70*, 423–448. https://doi.org/10.1146/annurev-psych-010418-103244
Courchesne, E., Pierce, K., Schumann, C. M., Redcay, E., Buckwalter, J. A., Kennedy, D. P., & Morgan, J. (2007). Mapping early brain development in autism. *Neuron, 56*(2), 399–413. https://doi.org/10.1016/j.neuron.2007.10.016
Cox, W. T. L., & Devine, P. G. (2019). The prejudice habit-breaking intervention: An empowerment-based confrontation approach. In R. K. Mallett & M. J. Monteith (Eds.), *Confronting prejudice and discrimination: The science of changing minds and behaviors* (pp. 249–274). Academic Press. https://doi.org/10.1016/B978-0-12-814715-3.00015-1
Craddock, N., & Sklar, P. (2013). Genetics of bipolar disorder. *The Lancet, 381*(9878), 1654–1662. https://doi.org/10.1016/S0140-6736(13)60855-7
Craig, A. D. (2009). How do you feel—now? The anterior insula and human awareness. *Nature Reviews Neuroscience, 10*, 59–70. https://doi.org/10.1038/nrn2555
Craig, M. A., & Richeson, J. A. (2014). On the precipice of a "majority-minority" America: Perceived status threat from the racial demographic shift affects White Americans' political ideology. *Psychological Science, 25*(6), 1189–1197. https://doi.org/10.1177/0956797614527113
Craighead, W. E., & Dunlop, B. W. (2014). Combination psychotherapy and antidepressant medication treatment for depression: For whom, when, and how. *Annual Review of Psychology, 65*(1), 267–300. https://doi.org/10.1146/annurev.psych.121208.131653
Craik, F. I. M., & Lockhart, R. S. (1972). Levels of processing: A framework for memory research. *Journal of Verbal Learning and Verbal Behavior, 11*(6), 671–684. https://doi.org/10.1016/s0022-5371(72)80001-x
Craik, F. I. M., & McDowd, J. M. (1987). Age differences in recall and recognition. *Journal of Experimental Psychology: Learning, Memory, and Cognition, 13*(3), 474–479. https://doi.org/10.1037/0278-7393.13.3.474
Craik, F. I. M., & Tulving, E. (1975). Depth of processing and the retention of words in episodic memory. *Journal of Experimental Psychology: General, 104*(3), 268–294. https://doi.org/10.1037/0096-3445.104.3.268
Craik, F. I. M., Govoni, R., Naveh-Benjamin, M., & Anderson, N. D. (1996). The effects of divided attention on encoding and retrieval processes in human memory. *Journal of Experimental Psychology: General, 125*(2), 159–180. https://doi.org/10.1037/0096-3445.125.2.159
Crawford, H. J., Corby, J. C., & Kopell, B. S. (1996). Auditory event-related potentials while ignoring tone stimuli: Attentional differences reflected in stimulus intensity and latency responses in low and highly hypnotizable persons. *International Journal of Neuroscience, 85*(1–2), 57–69. https://doi.org/10.3109/00207459608986351
Credé, M., Tynan, M. C., & Harms, P. D. (2017). Much ado about grit: A meta-analytic synthesis of the grit literature. *Journal of Personality and Social Psychology, 113*(3), 492–511. https://doi.org/10.1037/pspp0000102
Criscuolo, A., Bonetti, L., Särkämö, T., Kliuchko, M., & Brattico, E. (2019). On the association between musical training, intelligence and executive functions in adulthood. *Frontiers in Psychology, 10*, 1704. https://doi.org/10.3389/fpsyg.2019.01704
Critcher, C. R., & Dunning, D. (2015). Self-affirmations provide a broader perspective on self-threat. *Personality and Social Psychology Bulletin, 41*(1), 3–18. https://doi.org/10.1177/0146167214554956
Critchley, H. D., Wiens, S., Rotshtein, P., Öhman, A., & Dolan, R. J. (2004). Neural systems supporting interoceptive awareness. *Nature Neuroscience, 7*(2), 189–195. https://doi.org/10.1038/nn1176
Crivelli, C., Russell, J. A., Jarillo, S., & Fernández-Dols, J.-M. (2017). Recognizing spontaneous facial expressions of emotion in a small-scale society of Papua New Guinea. *Emotion, 17*(2), 337–347. https://doi.org/10.1037/emo0000236
Cropley, V. L., Klauser, P., Lenroot, R. K., Bruggemann, J., Sundram, S., Bousman, C., Pereira, A., Di Biase, M. A., Weickert, T. W., Weickert, C. S., Pantelis, C., & Zalesky, A. (2017). Accelerated gray and white matter deterioration with age in schizophrenia. *American Journal of Psychiatry, 174*(3), 286–295. https://doi.org/10.1176/appi.ajp.2016.16050610
Cross, J. F. (2020). What does too much screen time do to children's brains? *Health Matters* [Newsletter]. https://healthmatters.nyp.org/what-does-too-much-screen-time-do-to-childrens-brains/
Crowe, R. R. (2000). Molecular genetics of anxiety disorders. In D. S. Charney, E. J. Nestler, & B. S. Bunney (Eds.), *Neurobiology of mental illness* (pp. 451–462). Oxford University Press.
Crowley, S. J., & Eastman, C. I. (2015). Phase advancing human circadian rhythms with morning bright light, afternoon melatonin, and gradually shifted sleep: Can we reduce morning bright-light duration? *Sleep Medicine, 16*(2), 288–297. https://doi.org/10.1016/j.sleep.2014.12.004
Csikszentmihalyi, M. (1990). *Flow: The psychology of optimal experience.* Harper & Row.
Csikszentmihalyi, M. (1999). If we are so rich, why aren't we happy? *American Psychologist, 54*(10), 821–827. https://doi.org/10.1037/0003-066X.54.10.821
Cuc, A., Koppel, J., & Hirst, W. (2007). Silence is not golden: A case for socially shared retrieval-induced forgetting. *Psychological Science, 18*(8), 727–733. https://doi.org/10.1111/j.1467-9280.2007.01967.x
Cuddy, A. J. C., Fiske, S. T., & Glick, P. (2008). Warmth and competence as universal dimensions of social perception: The stereotype content model and the BIAS map. *Advances in Experimental Social Psychology, 40*, 61–149. https://doi.org/10.1016/S0065-2601(07)00002-0
Cuijpers, P., Sijbrandij, M., Koole, S. L., Andersson, G., Beekman, A. T., & Reynolds, C. F., III. (2014). Adding psychotherapy to antidepressant medication in depression and anxiety disorders: A meta-analysis. *World Psychiatry, 13*(1), 56–67. https://doi.org/10.1002/wps.20089
Cullen, K. A., Gentzke, A. S., Sawdey, M. D., Chang, J. T., Anic, G. M., Wang, T. W., Creamer, M. R., Jamal, A., Ambrose, B. K., & King, B. A. (2019). e-Cigarette use among youth in the United States, 2019. *Journal of the American Medical Association, 322*(21), 2095–2103. https://doi.org/10.1001/jama.2019.18387
Culler, E., Coakley, J. D., Lowy, K., & Gross, N. (1943). A revised frequency-map of the guinea-pig cochlea. *The American Journal of Psychology, 56*(4), 475–500. https://doi.org/10.2307/1417351
Cundiff, J. M., Boylan, J. M., & Muscatell, K. A. (2020). The pathway from social status to physical health: Taking a closer look at stress as a mediator. *Current Directions in Psychological Science, 29*(2), 147–153. https://doi.org/10.1177/0963721420901596
Cunningham, M. R., Roberts, A. R., Barbee, A. P., Druen, P. B., & Wu, C. (1995). "Their ideas of beauty are, on the whole, the same as ours": Consistency and variability in the cross-cultural perception of female physical attractiveness. *Journal of Personality and Social Psychology, 68*(2), 261–279. https://doi.org/10.1037/0022-3514.68.2.261
Cunningham, W. A., & Kirkland, T. (2014). The joyful, yet balanced, amygdala: Moderated responses to positive but not negative stimuli in trait happiness. *Social Cognitive and Affective Neuroscience, 9*(6), 760–766. https://doi.org/10.1093/scan/nst045
Cunningham, W. A., Johnson, M. K., Raye, C. L., Gatenby, J. C., Gore, J. C., & Banaji, M. R. (2004). Separable neural components in the processing of Black and White faces. *Psychological Science, 15*(12), 806–813. https://doi.org/10.1111/j.0956-7976.2004.00760.x

Cupach, W. R., & Metts, S. (1990). Remedial processes in embarrassing predicaments. In J. Anderson (Ed.), *Communication yearbook* (pp. 323–352). Sage.

Cusack, K., Jonas, D. E., Forneris, C. A., Wines, C., Sonis, J., Middleton, J. C., Feltner, C., Brownley, K. A., Olmsted, K. R., Greenblatt, A., Weil, A., & Gaynes, B. N. (2016). Psychological treatments for adults with posttraumatic stress disorder: A systematic review and meta-analysis. *Clinical Psychology Review, 43*, 128–141. https://doi.org/10.1016/j.cpr.2015.10.003

Cvetkovic-Lopes, V., Bayer, L., Dorsaz, S., Maret, S., Pradervand, S., Dauvilliers, Y., Lecendreux, M., Lammers, G.-J., Donjacour, C. E. H. M., Du Pasquier, R. A., Pfister, C., Petit, B., Hor, H., Mühlethaler, M., & Tafti, M. (2010). Elevated Tribbles homolog 2-specific antibody levels in narcolepsy patients. *Journal of Clinical Investigation, 120*(3), 713–719. https://doi.org/10.1172/JCI41366

Dabbs, J. M., & Morris, R. (1990). Testosterone, social class, and antisocial behavior in a sample of 4,462 men. *Psychological Science, 1*(3), 209–211. https://doi.org/10.1111/j.1467-9280.1990.tb00200.x

Dahl, C. D., Logothetis, N. K., Bülthoff, H. H., & Wallraven, C. (2010). The Thatcher illusion in humans and monkeys. *Proceedings of the Royal Society B: Biological Sciences, 277*(1696), 2973–2981. https://doi.org/10.1098/rspb.2010.0438

Damasio, H., Grabowski, T., Frank, R., Galaburda, A. M., & Damasio, A. R. (1994). The return of Phineas Gage: Clues about the brain from the skull of a famous patient. *Science, 264*(5162), 1102–1105. https://doi.org/10.1126/science.8178168

Danielson, M. L., Bitsko, R. H., Ghandour, R. M., Holbrook, J. R., Kogan, M. D., & Blumberg, S. J. (2018). Prevalence of parent-reported ADHD diagnosis and associated treatment among U.S. children and adolescents, 2016. *Journal of Clinical Child & Adolescent Psychology, 47*(2), 199–212. https://doi.org/10.1080/15374416.2017.1417860

Darley, J. M., & Batson, C. D. (1973). "From Jerusalem to Jericho": A study of situational and dispositional variables in helping behavior. *Journal of Personality and Social Psychology, 27*(1), 100–108. https://doi.org/10.1037/h0034449

Darwin, C. (1872). *The expression of the emotions in man and animals*. John Murray.

Darwin, C. (1892). *The autobiography of Charles Darwin and selected letters* (F. Darwin, Ed.). Dover.

Dasgupta, N., & Greenwald, A. G. (2001) On the malleability of automatic attitudes: Combating automatic prejudice with images of admired and disliked individuals. *Journal of Personality and Social Psychology, 81*(5), 800–814. https://doi.org/10.1037/0022-3514.81.5.800

Davidai, S., Gilovich, T., & Ross, L. D. (2012). The meaning of default options for potential organ donors. *Proceedings of the National Academy of Sciences, 109*(38), 15201–15205. https://doi.org/10.1073/pnas.1211695109

Davidson, R. J., Kabat-Zinn, J., Schumacher, J., Rosenkranz, M., Muller, D., Santorelli, S. F., Urbanowski, F., Harrington, A., Bonus, K., & Sheridan, J. F. (2003). Alterations in brain and immune function produced by mindfulness meditation. *Psychosomatic Medicine, 65*(4), 564–570. https://doi.org/10.1097/01.PSY.0000077505.67574.E3

Davies, G., Tenesa, A., Payton, A., Yang, J., Harris, S. E., Liewald, D., Ke, X., Hellard, S. L., Christoforou, A., Luciano, M., McGhee, K., Lopez, L., Gow, A. J., Corley, J., Redmond, P., Fox, H. C., Haggarty, P., Whalley, L. J., McNeill, G., . . . Deary, I. J. (2011). Genome-wide association studies establish that human intelligence is highly heritable and polygenic. *Molecular Psychiatry, 16*, 996–1005.

Davies, W. (2014). Sex differences in attention deficit hyperactivity disorder: Candidate genetic and endocrine mechanisms. *Frontiers in Neuroendocrinology, 35*(3), 331–346. https://doi.org/10.1016/j.yfrne.2014.03.003

Davis, J. I., Senghas, A., Brandt, F., & Ochsner, K. N. (2010). The effects of BOTOX injections on emotional experience. *Emotion, 10*(3), 433–440. https://doi.org/10.1037/a0018690

Davis, J., Eyre, H., Jacka, F. N., Dodd, S., Dean, O., McEwen, S., Debnath, M., McGrath, J., Maes, M., Amminger, P., McGorry, P. D., Pantelis, C., & Berk, M. (2016). A review of vulnerability and risks for schizophrenia: Beyond the two hit hypothesis. *Neuroscience & Biobehavioral Reviews, 65*, 185–194. https://doi.org/10.1016/j.neubiorev.2016.03.017

Daxinger, L., & Whitelaw, E. (2012). Understanding transgenerational epigenetic inheritance via the gametes in mammals. *Nature Reviews Genetics, 13*(3), 153–162. https://doi.org/10.1038/nrg3188

de Belen, R. A. J., Bednarz, T., Sowmya, A., & Del Favero, D. (2020). Computer vision in autism spectrum disorder research: A systematic review of published studies from 2009 to 2019. *Translational Psychiatry, 10*, Article 333. https://doi.org/10.1038/s41398-020-01015-w

de Hevia, M. D., Izard, V., Coubart, A., Spelke, E. S., & Streri, A. (2014). Representations of space, time, and number in neonates. *Proceedings of the National Academy of Sciences, 111*(13), 4809–4813. https://doi.org/10.1073/pnas.1323628111

de Kloet, E. R., Joëls, M., & Holsboer, F. (2005). Stress and the brain: From adaptation to disease. *Nature Reviews Neuroscience, 6*, 463–475. https://doi.org/10.1038/nrn1683

De Lisi, R., & Staudt, J. (1980). Individual differences in college students' performance on formal operations tasks. *Journal of Applied Developmental Psychology, 1*(3), 201–208. https://doi.org/10.1016/0193-3973(80)90009-X

de Wijk, R. A., Schab, F. R., & Cain, W. S. (1995). Odor identification. In F. R. Schab (Ed.), *Memory for odors* (pp. 21–37). Erlbaum.

Deacon, B. J., & Abramowitz, J. S. (2004). Cognitive and behavioral treatments for anxiety disorders: A review of meta-analytic findings. *Journal of Clinical Psychology, 60*(4), 429–441. https://doi.org/10.1002/jclp.10255

Deal, A. L., Erickson, K. J., Shiers, S. I., & Burman, M. A. (2016). Limbic system development underlies the emergence of classical fear conditioning during the third and fourth weeks of life in the rat. *Behavioral Neuroscience, 130*(2), 212–230. https://doi.org/10.1037/bne0000130

Deary, I. J. (2000). *Looking down on human intelligence*. Oxford University Press.

Deary, I. J. (2001). *Intelligence: A very short introduction*. Oxford University Press.

Deary, I. J., & Der, G. (2005). Reaction time explains IQ's association with death. *Psychological Science, 16*(1), 64–69. https://doi.org/10.1111/j.0956-7976.2005.00781.x

Deary, I. J., Batty, G. D., Pattie, A., & Gale, C. R. (2008). More intelligent, more dependable children live longer: A 55-year longitudinal study of a representative sample of the Scottish nation. *Psychological Science, 19*(9), 874–880. https://doi.org/10.1111/j.1467-9280.2008.02171.x

Deaton, A., & Stone, A. A. (2014). Evaluative and hedonic wellbeing among those with and without children at home. *Proceedings of the National Academy of Science, 111*(4), 1328–1333. https://doi.org/10.1073/pnas.1311600111

DeCasper, A. J., & Spence, M. J. (1986). Prenatal maternal speech influences newborns' perception of speech sounds. *Infant Behavior and Development, 9*(2), 133–150. https://doi.org/10.1016/0163-6383(86)90025-1

Decety, J., Chen, C., Harenski, C., & Kiehl, K. A. (2013). An fMRI study of affective perspective taking in individuals with psychopathy: Imagining another in pain does not evoke empathy. *Frontiers in Human Neuroscience, 7*, Article 489. https://doi.org/10.3389/fnhum.2013.00489

Decety, J., Meidenbauer, K. L., & Cowell, J. M. (2018). The development of cognitive empathy and concern in preschool children: A behavioral neuroscience investigation. *Developmental Science, 21*(3), Article e12570. https://doi.org/10.1111/desc.12570

deCharms, R. C., Maeda, F., Glover, G. H, Ludlow, D., Pauly, J. M., Soneji, D., & Mackey, S. C. (2005). Control over brain activation and pain learned by using real-time functional MRI. *Proceedings of the National Academy of Sciences, 102*(51), 18626–18631. https://doi.org/10.1073/pnas.0505210102

Dekker, S., Lee, N. C., Howard-Jones, P., & Jolles, J. (2012). Neuromyths in education: Prevalence and predictors of misconceptions among teachers. *Frontiers in Neuroscience, 3*, Article 429. https://doi.org/10.3389/fpsyg.2012.00429

Delgado, M. R., Frank, R. H., & Phelps, E. A. (2005). Perceptions of moral character modulate the neural systems of reward during the trust game. *Nature Neuroscience, 8*(11), 1611–1618. https://doi.org/10.1038/nn1575

DeLong, M. R., & Wichmann, T. (2008). *The expanding potential of deep brain stimulation: The 2008 progress report on brain research*. Dana Foundation.

DeLongis, A., Folkman, S., & Lazarus, R. S. (1988). The impact of daily stress on health and mood: Psychological and social resources as mediators. *Journal of Personality and Social Psychology, 54*(3), 486–495. https://doi.org/10.1037/0022-3514.54.3.486

Demerouti, E. (2006). Job characteristics, flow, and performance: The moderating role of conscientiousness. *Journal of Occupational Health Psychology, 11*(3), 266–280. https://doi.org/10.1037/1076-8998.11.3.266

Dempster, F. N. (1988). The spacing effect: A case study in the failure to apply the results of psychological research. *American Psychologist, 43*(8), 627–634. https://doi.org/10.1037/0003-066X.43.8.627

Dennis, N. A., Overman, A. A., Gerver, C. R., McGraw, K. E., Rowley, M. A., & Salerno, J. M. (2019). Different types of associative encoding evoke differential processing in both younger and older adults: Evidence from univariate and multivariate analyses. *Neuropsychologia, 135*, Article 107240. https://doi.org/10.1016/j.neuropsychologia.2019.107240

Denny, B. T., Kober, H., Wager, T. D., & Ochsner, K. N. (2012). A meta-analysis of functional neuroimaging studies of self- and other judgments reveals a spatial gradient for mentalizing in medial prefrontal cortex. *Journal of Cognitive Neuroscience, 24*(8), 1742–1752. https://doi.org/10.1162/jocn_a_00233

DeRoos, L. J., Marrero, W. J., Tapper, E. B., onnenday, C. J., Lavieri, M. S., Hutton, D. W., & Parikh, N. D. (2019). Estimated association between organ availability and presumed consent in solid organ transplant. *JAMA Network Open, 2*(10), Article e1912431. https://doi.org/10.1001/jamanetworkopen.2019.12431

DeSantis, C., Naishadham, D., & Jemal, A. (2013). Cancer statistics for African Americans, 2013. *CA: A Cancer Journal for Clinicians, 63*(3), 151–166. https://doi.org/10.3322/caac.21173

DeSteno, D., Breazeal, C., Frank, R. H., Pizarro, D., Baumann, J., Dickens, L., & Lee, J. J. (2012). Detecting the trustworthiness of novel partners in economic exchange. *Psychological Science, 23*(12), 1549–1556. https://doi.org/10.1177/0956797612448793

Devine, P. G. (1989). Stereotypes and prejudice: Their automatic and controlled components. *Journal of Personality and Social Psychology, 56*(1), 5–18. https://doi.org/10.1037/0022-3514.56.1.5

DeYoung, C. G., & Gray, J. R. (2009). Personality neuroscience: Explaining individual differences in affect, behavior, and cognition. In P. J. Corr & G. Matthews (Eds.), *The Cambridge handbook of personality psychology* (pp. 323–346). Cambridge University Press.

DeYoung, C. G., Hirsh, J. B., Shane, M. S., Papademetris, X., Rajeevan, N., & Gray, J. R. (2010). Testing predictions from personality neuroscience: Brain structure and the Big Five. *Psychological Science, 21*(6), 820–828. https://doi.org/10.1177/0956797610370159

Diamond, L. M., & Butterworth, M. (2008). Questioning gender and sexual identity: Dynamic links over time. *Sex Roles, 59*(5–6), 365–376. https://doi.org/10.1007/s11199-008-9425-3

Dickinson, A., Watt, A., & Griffiths, W. J. H. (1992). Free-operant acquisition with delayed reinforcement. *Quarterly Journal of Experimental Psychology Section B, 45*(3b), 241–258. https://doi.org/10.1080/14640749208401019

Dickson, P. R., & Vaccarino, F. J. (1994). GRF-induced feeding: Evidence for protein selectivity and opiate involvement. *Peptides, 15*(8), 1343–1352. https://doi.org/10.1016/0196-9781(94)90107-4

Diener, E. (1977). Deindividuation: Causes and consequences. *Social Behavior and Personality: An International Journal, 5*(1), 143–155. https://doi.org/10.2224/sbp.1977.5.1.143

Diener, E. (2000). Subjective well-being: The science of happiness and a proposal for a national index. *American Psychologist, 55*(1), 34–43. https://doi.org/10.1037/0003-066X.55.1.34

Diener, E., Wolsic, B., & Fujita, F. (1995). Physical attractiveness and subjective well-being. *Journal of Personality and Social Psychology, 69*(1), 120–129. https://doi.org/10.1037/0022-3514.69.1.120

Dion, K., Berscheid, E., & Walster, E. (1972). What is beautiful is good. *Journal of Personality and Social Psychology, 24*(3), 285–290. https://doi.org/10.1037/h0033731

Dobbs, D. (2006). Turning off depression. *Scientific American Mind*, 26–31. https://www.scientificamerican.com/article/a-pacemaker-for-depressio/

Dobbs, S., Furnham, A., & McClelland, A. (2011). The effect of background music and noise on the cognitive test performance of introverts and extraverts. *Applied Cognitive Psychology, 25*(2), 307–313. https://doi.org/10.1002/acp.1692

Doblin, R., Greer, G., Holland, J., Jerome, L., Mithoefer, M. C., & Sessa, B. (2014). A reconsideration and response to Parrott AC (2013) "Human psychobiology of MDMA or 'Ecstasy': An overview of 25 years of empirical research." *Human Psychopharmacology: Clinical and Experimental, 29*(2), 105–108. https://doi.org/10.1002/hup.2389

Docherty, N. M. (2005). Cognitive impairments and disordered speech in schizophrenia: Thought disorder, disorganization, and communication failure perspectives. *Journal of Abnormal Psychology, 114*(2), 269–278. https://doi.org/10.1037/0021-843X.114.2.269.

Dockray, A., & Steptoe, A. (2010). Positive affect and psychobiological process. *Neuroscience & Biobehavioral Reviews, 35*(1), 69–75. https://doi.org/10.1016/j.neubiorev.2010.01.006

Dohrenwend, B. P., Shrout, P. E., Link, B. G., Skodol, A. E., & Martin, J. L. (1986). Overview and initial results from a risk factor study of depression and schizophrenia. In J. E. Barrett (Ed.), *Mental disorders in the community: Progress and challenge* (pp. 184–215). Guilford Press.

Dolan, P., & Metcalfe, R. (2010). "Oops . . . I did it again": Repeated focusing effects in reports of happiness. *Journal of Economic Psychology, 31*(4), 732–737. https://doi.org/10.1016/j.joep.2010.05.008

Dolan, R. J. (2000). Emotion processing in the human brain revealed through functional neuroimaging. In M. S. Gazzaniga (Ed.), *The new cognitive neurosciences* (pp. 115–131). MIT Press.

Dolcos, F., Bogdan, P. C., O'Brien, M., Iordan, A. D., Madison, A., Buetti, S., Lleras, A., & Dolcos, S. (2020). The impact of focused attention on emotional evaluation: An eye-tracking investigation. *Emotion*. Advance online publication. https://doi.org/10.1037/emo0000895

Domhoff, G. W. (2003). *The scientific study of dreams: Neural networks, cognitive development, and content analysis*. American Psychological Association.

Donahue, A. B. (2000). Electroconvulsive therapy and memory loss: A personal journey. *Journal of ECT, 16*(2), 133–143. https://doi.org/10.1097/00124509-200006000-00005

Donate Life America. (2021). *Organ, eye, and tissue donation statistics*. https://www.donatelife.net/statistics

Dondi, M., Simion, F., & Caltran, G. (1999). Can newborns discriminate between their own cry and the cry of another newborn infant? *Developmental Psychology, 35*(2), 418–426. https://doi.org/10.1037/0012-1649.35.2.418

Doran, G. T. (1981). There's a S.M.A.R.T. way to write management's goals and objectives. *Management Review, 70*(11), 35–36.

Dorfman, H. M., Meyer-Lindenberg, A., & Buckholtz, J. W. (2014). Neurobiological mechanisms for impulsive-aggression: The role of MAOA. In K. Miczek & A. Meyer-Lindenberg (Eds.), *Neuroscience of aggression* (pp. 297–313). Springer. https://doi.org/10.1007/7854_2013_272

Dovidio, J. F., ten Vergert, M., Stewart, T. L., Gaertner, S. L., Johnson, J. D., Esses, V. M., Riek, B. M., & Pearson, A. R. (2004). Perspective and prejudice: Antecedents and mediating mechanisms. *Personality and Social Psychology Bulletin, 30*(12), 1537–1549. https://doi.org/10.1177/0146167204271177

Downey, D. B., & Gibbs, B. G. (2020). Kids these days: Are face-to-face social skills among American children declining? *American Journal of Sociology, 125*(4), 1030–1083. https://doi.org/10.1086/707985

Dowrick, C., & Frances, A. (2013). Medicalising unhappiness: New classification of depression risks more patients being put on drug treatment from which they will not benefit. *BMJ, 347*, Article f7140. https://doi.org/10.1136/bmj.f7140

Drescher, J. (2015). Out of DSM: Depathologizing homosexuality. *Behavioral Sciences, 5*(4), 565–575. https://doi.org/10.3390/bs5040565

Dresler, M., Shirer, W. R., Konrad, B. N., Müller, N. C. J., Wagner, I. C., Fernández, G., Czisch, M., & Greicius, M. D. (2017). Mnemonic training reshapes brain networks to support superior memory. *Neuron, 93*(5), 1227–1235. https://doi.org/10.1016/j.neuron.2017.02.003

Drobisz, D., & Damborská, A. (2019). Deep brain stimulation targets for treating depression. *Behavioural Brain Research, 359*, 266–273. https://doi.org/10.1016/j.bbr.2018.11.004

Dubois, J., & Adolphs, R. (2016). Building a science of individual differences from fMRI. *Trends in Cognitive Sciences, 20*(6), 425–443. https://doi.org/10.1016/j.tics.2016.03.014

Duckworth, A. L., & Quinn, P. D. (2009). Development and validation of the short grit scale (GRIT-S). *Journal of Personality Assessment, 91*(2), 166–174. https://doi.org/10.1080/00223890802634290

Duckworth, A. L., & Seligman, M. E. P. (2005). Self-discipline outdoes IQ in predicting academic performance of adolescents. *Psychological Science, 16*(12), 939–944. https://doi.org/10.1111/j.1467-9280.2005.01641.x

Duckworth, A. L., Peterson, C., Matthews, M. D., & Kelly, D. R. (2007). Grit: Perseverance and passion for long-term goals. *Journal of Personality and Social Psychology, 92*(6), 1087–1101. https://doi.org/10.1037/0022-3514.92.6.1087

Dugatkin, L. A. (2004). *Principles of animal behavior*. Norton.

Dunbar, R. I. M. (1998). The social brain hypothesis. *Evolutionary Anthropology, 6*(5), 178–190. https://doi.org/10.1002/(SICI)1520-6505(1998)6:5<178::AID-EVAN5>3.0.CO;2-8

Dunbar, R. I. M. (2014). The social brain: Psychological underpinnings and implications for the structure of organizations. *Current Directions in Psychological Science, 23*(2), 109–114. https://doi.org/10.1177/0963721413517118

Duncan, J., Burgess, P., & Emslie, H. (1995). Fluid intelligence after frontal lobe lesions. *Neuropsychologia, 33*(3), 261–268. https://doi.org/10.1016/0028-3932(94)00124-8

Duncker, K. (1945). On problem solving. *Psychological Monographs, 58*(5), i–113. https://doi.org/10.1037/h0093599

Dunifon, R. E., Musick, K. A., & Near, C. E. (2019). Time with grandchildren: Subjective well-being among grandparents living with their grandchildren. *Social Indicators Research, 148*, 681–702. https://doi.org/10.1007/s11205-019-02206-9

Dunlosky, J., Rawson, K. A., Marsh, E. J., Nathan, M. J., & Willingham, D. T. (2013). Improving students' learning with effective learning techniques: Promising directions from cognitive and educational psychology. *Psychological Science in the Public Interest, 14*(1), 4–58. https://doi.org/10.1177/1529100612453266

Dunning, D., Johnson, K., Ehrlinger, J., & Kruger, J. (2003). Why people fail to recognize their own incompetence. *Current Directions in Psychological Science, 12*(3), 83–87. https://doi.org/10.1111/1467-8721.01235

Dutton, D. G., & Aron, A. P. (1974). Some evidence for heightened sexual attraction under conditions of high anxiety. *Journal of Personality and Social Psychology, 30*(4), 510–517. https://doi.org/10.1037/h0037031

Eagly, A. H., Karau, S. J., & Makhijani, M. G. (1995). Gender and the effectiveness of leaders: A meta-analysis. *Psychological Bulletin, 117*(1), 125–145. https://doi.org/10.1037/0033-2909.117.1.125

Ebbinghaus, H. (1964). *Memory* (H. A. Ruger & C. E. Bussenius, Trans.). Teachers College. (Original work published as *Das Gedächtnis*, 1885.)

Eberhardt, J. L. (2019). *Biased: Uncovering the hidden prejudice that shapes what we see, think, and do.* Viking.

Eberhardt, J. L., Davies, P. G., Purdie-Vaughns, V. J., & Johnson, S. L. (2006). Looking deathworthy: Perceived stereotypicality of Black defendants predicts capital-sentencing outcomes. *Psychological Science, 17*(5), 383–386. https://doi.org/10.1111/j.1467-9280.2006.01716.x

Eberhardt, J. L., Goff, P. A., Purdie, V. J., & Davies, P. G. (2004). Seeing black: Race, crime, and visual processing. *Journal of Personality and Social Psychology, 87*(6), 876–893. https://doi.org/10.1037/0022-3514.87.6.876

Egeland, J. A., Gerhard, D. S., Pauls, D. L., Sussex, J. N., Kidd, K. K., Allen, C. R., Hostetter, A. M., & Housman, D. E. (1987). Bipolar affective disorders linked to DNA markers on chromosome 11. *Nature, 325*(6107), 783–787. https://doi.org/10.1038/325783a0

Eisenbarth, H., Chang, L. J., & Wager, T. D. (2016). Multivariate brain prediction of heart rate and skin conductance responses to social threat. *Journal of Neuroscience, 36*(47), 11987–11998. https://doi.org/10.1523/JNEUROSCI.3672-15.2016

Eisenberg, N. (2002). Empathy-related emotional responses, altruism, and their socialization. In R. J. Davidson and A. Harrington (Eds.), *Visions of compassion: Western scientists and Tibetan Buddhists examine human nature* (pp. 131–164). Oxford University Press.

Eisenberg, N., & Valiente, C. (2002). Parenting and children's prosocial and moral development. In M. Bornstein (Ed.), *Handbook of parenting* (Vol. 5, pp. 111–142). Erlbaum.

Eisenberg, N., VanSchyndel, S. K., & Spinrad, T. L. (2016). Prosocial motivation: Inferences from an opaque body of work. *Child Development, 87*(6), 1668–1678. https://doi.org/10.1111/cdev.12638

Eisenberger, N. I., Lieberman, M. D., & Satpute, A. B. (2005). Personality from a controlled processing perspective: An fMRI study of neuroticism, extraversion, and self-consciousness. *Cognitive, Affective, & Behavioral Neuroscience, 5*(2), 169–181. https://doi.org/10.3758/cabn.5.2.169

Ekman, P., & Friesen, W. V. (1971). Constants across cultures in the face and emotion. *Journal of Personality and Social Psychology, 17*(2), 124–129. https://doi.org/10.1037/h0030377

Ekman, P., Sorenson, E. R., & Friesen, W. V. (1969). Pan-cultural elements in facial displays of emotions. *Science, 164*(3875), 86–88. https://doi.org/10.1126/science.164.3875.86

Elaad, E., Ginton, A., & Ben-Shakhar, G. (1994). The effects of prior expectations and outcome knowledge on polygraph examiners' decisions. *Journal of Behavioral Decision Making, 7*(4), 279–292. https://doi.org/10.1002/bdm.3960070405

Election 2016 forecast. (2016). HuffPost. https://elections.huffingtonpost.com/2016/forecast/president

Elfenbein, H. A., & Ambady, N. (2002). On the universality of cultural specificity of emotion recognition: A meta-analysis. *Psychological Bulletin, 128*(2), 203–235. https://doi.org/10.1037/0033-2909.128.2.203

Elizabeth, L., Machado, P., Zinöcker, M., Baker, P., & Lawrence, M. (2020). Ultra-processed foods and health outcomes: A narrative review. *Nutrients, 12*(7), Article 1955. https://doi.org/10.3390/nu12071955

Ellis, A. (1962). *Reason and emotion in psychotherapy.* Lyle Stuart.

Emerson, R. W. (1841/1908). *The essay on self-reliance.* The Roycrofters.

Emery, C. F., Kiecolt-Glaser, J. K., Glaser, R., Malarkey, W. B., & Frid, D. J. (2005). Exercise accelerates wound healing among healthy older adults: A preliminary investigation. *Journals of Gerontology, Series A, 60*(11), 1432–1436. https://doi.org/10.1093/gerona/60.11.1432

Endo, Y., & Meijer, Z. (2004). Autobiographical memory of success and failure experiences. In Y. Kashima, Y. Endo, E. S. Kashima, C. Leung, & J. McClure (Eds.), *Progress in Asian social psychology* (Vol. 4, pp. 67–84). Kyoyook-Kwahak-Sa Publishing.

Engle, R. W., & Kane, M. J. (2004). Executive attention, working memory capacity, and a two-factor theory of cognitive control. In B. Ross (Ed.), *The psychology of learning and motivation* (pp. 145–199). Elsevier.

Engle, R. W., Tuholski, S. W., Laughlin, J. E., & Conway, A. R. A. (1999). Working memory, short-term memory, and general fluid intelligence: A latent variable approach. *Journal of Experimental Psychology: General, 128*(3), 309–331. https://doi.org/10.1037/0096-3445.128.3.309

Engwall, M., & Duppils, G. S. (2009). Music as a nursing intervention for postoperative pain: A systematic review. *Journal of PeriAnesthesia Nursing, 24*(6), 370–383. https://doi.org/10.1016/j.jopan.2009.10.013

Enns, J. (2005). *The thinking eye, the seeing brain.* Norton.

Epley, N., & Gilovich, T. (2001). Putting adjustment back in the anchoring and adjustment heuristic: Differential processing of self-generated and experimenter-provided anchors. *Psychological Science, 12*(5), 391–396. https://doi.org/10.1111/1467-9280.00372

Epstein, L. H., Robinson, J. L., Roemmich, J. N., Marusewski, A. L., & Roba, L. G. (2010). What constitutes food variety? Stimulus specificity of food. *Appetite, 54*(1), 23–29. https://doi.org/10.1016/j.appet.2009.09.001

Epton, T., Currie, S., & Armitage, C. J. (2017). Unique effects of setting goals on behavior change: Systematic review and meta-analysis. *Journal of Consulting and Clinical Psychology, 85*(12), 1182–1198. https://doi.org/10.1037/ccp0000260

Ericsson, K. A., Krampe, R. T., & Tesch-Römer, C. (1993). The role of deliberate practice in the acquisition of expert performance. *Psychology Review, 100*(3), 363–406. https://doi.org/10.1037/0033-295X.100.3.363

Erikson, E. H. (1968). *Identity: Youth and crisis.* Norton.

Erikson, E. H. (1980). *Identity and the life cycle.* Norton.

Eriksson, P. S., Perfilieva, E., Bjork-Eriksson, T., Alborn, A.-M., Nordborg, C., Peterson, D. A., & Gage, F. H. (1998). Neurogenesis in the adult human hippocampus. *Nature Medicine, 4*(11), 1313–1317. https://doi.org/10.1038/3305

Eshel, N., Tian, J., & Uchida, N. (2013). Opening the black box: Dopamine, predictions, and learning. *Trends in Cognitive Sciences, 17*(9), 430–431. https://doi.org/10.1016/j.tics.2013.06.010

Espie, C. A. (2002). Insomnia: Conceptual issues in the development, persistence, and treatment of sleep disorders in adults. *Annual Review of Psychology, 53*(1), 215–243. https://doi.org/10.1146/annurev.psych.53.100901.135243

Essex, M. J., Shirtcliff, E. A., Burk, L. R., Ruttle, P. L., Klein, M. H., Slattery, M. J., Kalin, N. H., & Armstrong, J. M. (2011). Influence of early life stress on later hypothalamic–pituitary–adrenal axis functioning and its covariation with mental health symptoms: A study of the allostatic process from childhood into adolescence. *Development and Psychopathology, 23*(4), 1039–1058. https://doi.org/10.1017/S0954579411000484

Evans, G. W., & Kim, P. (2010). Multiple risk exposure as a potential explanatory mechanism for the socioeconomic status–health gradient. *Annals of the New York Academy of Sciences, 1186*(1), 174–189. https://doi.org/10.1111/j.1749-6632.2009.05336.x

Eysenck, H. J. (1967). *The biological basis of personality.* Thomas.

Fabiano, G. A., Pelham, W. E., Coles, E. K., Gnagy, E. M., Chronis-Tuscano, A., & O'Connor, B. C. (2009). A meta-analysis of behavioral treatments for attention-deficit/hyperactivity disorder. *Clinical Psychology Review, 29*(2), 129–140. https://doi.org/10.1016/j.cpr.2008.11.001

Fagerström, K.-O., & Schneider, N. G. (1989). Measuring nicotine dependence: A review of the Fagerström tolerance questionnaire. *Journal of Behavioral Medicine, 12*(2), 159–182. https://doi.org/10.1007/bf00846549

Fantz, R. L. (1963). Pattern vision in newborn infants. *Science, 140*(3564), 296–297. https://doi.org/10.1126/science.140.3564.296

Fantz, R. L. (1966). Pattern discrimination and selective attention as determinants of perceptual development from birth. In A. H. Kidd & L. J. Rivoire (Eds.), *Perceptual development in children* (pp. 143–173). International Universities Press.

Farah, M. J., Hutchinson, J. B., Phelps, E. A., & Wagner, A. D. (2014). Functional MRI-based lie detection: Scientific and societal challenges. *Nature Reviews Neuroscience, 15,* 123–131. https://doi.org/10.1038/nrn3665

Farsijani, S., Payette, H., Morais, J. A., Shatenstein, B., Gaudreau, P., & Chevalier, S. (2017). Even mealtime distribution of protein intake is associated with greater muscle strength, but not with 3-y physical function decline, in free-living older adults: The Quebec longitudinal study on Nutrition as a Determinant of Successful Aging (NuAge study). *The American Journal of Clinical Nutrition, 106*(1), 113–124. https://doi.org/10.3945/ajcn.116.146555

Faul, M., Xu, L., Wald, M. M., & Coronado, V. G. (2010). *Traumatic brain injury in the United States: Emergency department visits, hospitalizations, and deaths.* Centers for Disease Control and Prevention, National Center for Injury Prevention and Control. https://www.cdc.gov/traumaticbraininjury/pdf/blue_book.pdf

Fazio, R. H. (1995). Attitudes as object-evaluation associations: Determinants, consequences, and correlates of attitude accessibility. In R. E. Petty & J. A. Krosnick (Eds.), *Attitude strength: Antecedents and consequences* (pp. 247–282). Erlbaum.

Fazio, R. H., Eisner, J. R., & Shook, N. J. (2004). Attitude formation through exploration: Valence asymmetries. *Journal of Personality and Social Psychology, 87*(3), 293–311. https://doi.org/10.1037/0022-3514.87.3.293

Fehr, E., Bernhard, H., & Rockenbach, B. (2008). Egalitarianism in young children. *Nature, 454*(7208), 1079–1083. https://doi.org/10.1038/nature07155

Feingold, A. (1992). Good-looking people are not what we think. *Psychological Bulletin, 111*(2), 304–341. https://doi.org/10.1037/0033-2909.111.2.304

Feldman, R., Weller, A., Zagoory-Sharon, O., & Levine, A. (2007). Evidence for a neuroendocrinological foundation of human affiliation: Plasma oxytocin levels across pregnancy and the postpartum period predict mother-infant bonding. *Psychological Science, 18*(11), 965–970. https://doi.org/10.1111/j.1467-9280.2007.02010.x

Feldman, S. S., & Rosenthal, D. A. (1991). Age expectations of behavioural autonomy in Hong Kong, Australian and American youth: The influence of family variables and adolescents' values. *International Journal of Psychology, 26*(1), 1–23. https://doi.org/10.1080/00207599108246846

FeldmanHall, O., Glimcher, P., Baker, A. L., NYU PROSPEC Collaboration, & Phelps, E. A. (2019). The functional roles of the amygdala and prefrontal cortex in processing uncertainty. *Journal of Cognitive Neuroscience, 31*(11), 1742–1754. https://doi.org/10.1162/jocn_a_01443

Ferguson, J. N., Young, L. J., Hearn, E. F., Matzuk, M. M., Insel, T. R., & Winslow, J. T. (2000). Social amnesia in mice lacking the oxytocin gene. *Nature Neuroscience, 25,* 284–288. https://doi.org/10.1038/77040

Fernald, A. (1989). Intonation and communicative intent in mothers' speech to infants: Is the melody the message? *Child Development, 60*(6), 1497–1510. https://doi.org/10.2307/1130938

Fernández-Espejo, D., & Owen, A. M. (2013). Detecting awareness after severe brain injury. *Nature Reviews Neuroscience, 14,* 801–809. https://doi.org/10.1038/nrn3608

Ferracioli-Oda, E., Qawasmi, A., & Bloch, M. H. (2013). Meta-analysis: Melatonin for the treatment of primary sleep disorders. *PLoS ONE, 8*(5), Article e63773. https://doi.org/10.1371/journal.pone.0063773

Ferrer, R. A., & Cohen, G. L. (2019). Reconceptualizing self-affirmation with the trigger and channel framework: Lessons from the health domain. *Personality and Social Psychology Review, 23*(3), 285–304. https://doi.org/10.1177/1088868318797036

Ferro, M. J., & Martins, H. F. (2016). Academic plagiarism: Yielding to temptation. *British Journal of Education, Society & Behavioural Science, 13*(1), 1–11. https://doi.org/10.9734/BJESBS/2016/20535

Ferry, G. (Writer/Broadcaster). (2002, 12 & 19 November). *Hearing colours, eating sounds. BBC Radio 4, Science.* http://www.bbc.co.uk/radio4/science/hearingcolours.shtml

Festinger, L. (1954). A theory of social comparison processes. *Human Relations, 7,* 117–140. https://doi.org/10.1177/001872675400700202

Festinger, L. (1987). A personal memory. In N. E. Grunberg, R. E. Nisbett, J. Rodin, & J. E. Singer (Eds.), *A distinctive approach to psychological research: The influence of Stanley Schachter* (pp. 1–9). Erlbaum.

Festinger, L., & Carlsmith, J. M. (1959). Cognitive consequences of forced compliance. *Journal of Abnormal and Social Psychology, 58*(2), 203–210. https://doi.org/10.1037/h0041593

Festinger, L., Schachter, S., & Back, K. W. (1950). *Social pressures in informal groups.* Harper.

Fibiger, H. C. (1993). Mesolimbic dopamine: An analysis of its role in motivated behavior. *Seminars in Neuroscience, 5*(5), 321–327. https://doi.org/10.1016/s1044-5765(05)80039-9

Fill, M.-M. A., Miller, A. M., Wilkinson, R. H., Warren, M. D., Dunn, J. R., Schaffner, W., & Jones, T. F. (2018). Educational disabilities among children born with neonatal abstinence syndrome. *Pediatrics, 142*(3), Article e20180562. https://doi.org/10.1542/peds.2018-0562

Finger, S. (1994). *Origins of neuroscience.* Oxford University Press.

Fink, M. (2001). Convulsive therapy: A review of the first 55 years. *Journal of Affective Disorders, 63*(1–3), 1–15. https://doi.org/10.1016/s0165-0327(00)00367-0

Finsterwald, C., & Alberini, C. M. (2014). Stress and glucocorticoid receptor-dependent mechanisms in long-term memory: From adaptive responses to psychopathologies. *Neurobiology of Learning and Memory, 112,* 17–29. https://doi.org/10.1016/j.nlm.2013.09.017

Fiore, M. C., Schroeder, S. A., & Baker, T. B. (2014). Smoke, the chief killer—Strategies for targeting combustible tobacco use. *New England Journal of Medicine, 370*(4), 297–299. https://doi.org/10.1056/nejmp1314942

Fischer, K. W. (1980). A theory of cognitive development: The control and construction of hierarchies of skills. *Psychological Review, 87*(6), 477–531. https://doi.org/10.1037/0033-295X.87.6.477

Fischer, P., Krueger, J. I., Greitemeyer, T., Vogrincic, C., Kastenmüller, A., Frey, D., Heene, M., Wicher, M., & Kainbacher, M. (2011). The bystander-effect: A meta-analytic review on bystander intervention in dangerous and non-dangerous emergencies. *Psychological Bulletin, 137*(4), 517–537. https://doi.org/10.1037/a0023304

Fitch, W. T., de Boer, B., Mathur, N., & Ghazanfar, A. A. (2016). Monkey vocal tracts are speech-ready. *Science Advances, 2*(12), Article e1600723. https://doi.org/10.1126/sciadv.1600723

Fitzgerald, P. B., Brown, T. L., Marston, N. A. U., Daskalakis, Z. J., De Castella, A., & Kulkarni, J. (2003). Transcranial magnetic stimulation in the treatment of depression: A double-blind, placebo-controlled trial. *Archives of General Psychiatry, 60*(10), 1002–1008. https://doi.org/10.1001/archpsyc.60.9.1002

Fixx, J. F. (1978). *Solve it.* Doubleday.

Flynn, J. R. (1984). The mean IQ of Americans: Massive gains 1932 to 1978. *Psychological Bulletin, 95*(1), 29–51. https://doi.org/10.1037/0033-2909.95.1.29

Flynn, J. R. (1987). Massive IQ gains in 14 nations: What IQ tests really measure. *Psychological Bulletin, 101*(2), 171–191. https://doi.org/10.1037/0033-2909.101.2.171

Flynn, J. R. (2007, October/November). Solving the IQ puzzle. *Scientific American Mind, 18,* 24–31. https://www.scientificamerican.com/article/solving-the-iq-puzzle/

Foa, E. B., & McLean, C. P. (2016). The efficacy of exposure therapy for anxiety-related disorders and its underlying mechanisms: The case of OCD and PTSD. *Annual Review of Clinical Psychology, 12*(1), 1–28. https://doi.org/10.1146/annurev-clinpsy-021815-093533

Foa, E. B., Liebowitz, M. R., Kozak, M. J., Davies, S., Campeas, R., Franklin, M. E., Huppert, J. D., Kjernisted, K., Rowan, V., Schmidt, A. B., Simpson, H. B., & Tu, X. (2005). Randomized, placebo-controlled trial of exposure and ritual prevention, clomipramine, and their combination in the treatment of obsessive-compulsive disorder. *American Journal of Psychiatry, 162*(1), 151–161. https://doi.org/10.1176/appi.ajp.162.1.151

Folkman, S., & Lazarus, R. S. (1988). Coping as a mediator of emotion. *Journal of Personality and Social Psychology, 54*(3), 466–475. https://doi.org/10.1037/0022-3514.54.3.466

Folkman, S., & Moskowitz, J. T. (2000). Positive affect and the other side of coping. *American Psychologist, 55*(6), 647–654. https://doi.org/10.1037/0003-066X.55.6.647

Foo, Y. Z., Simmons, L. W., & Rhodes, G. (2017). Predictors of facial attractiveness and health in humans. *Scientific Reports, 7,* Article 39731. https://doi.org/10.1038/srep39731

Ford, E. S., Giles, W. H., & Dietz, W. H. (2002). Prevalence of the metabolic syndrome among U.S. adults: Findings from the third National Health and Nutrition Examination Survey. *Journal of the American Medical Association, 287*(3), 356–359. https://doi.org/10.1001/jama.287.3.356

Forgas, J. P. (1998). Asking nicely: The effects of mood on responding to more or less polite requests. *Personality and Social Psychology Bulletin, 24*(2), 173–185. https://doi.org/10.1177/0146167298242006

Foster, J. A., Rinaman, L., & Cryan, J. F. (2017). Stress & the gut-brain axis: Regulation by the microbiome. *Neurobiology of Stress, 7*, 124–136. https://doi.org/10.1016/j.ynstr.2017.03.001

Fournier, J. C., DeRubeis, R. J., Hollon, S. D., Dimidjian, S., Amsterdam, J. D., Shelton, R. C., & Fawcett, J. (2010). Antidepressant drug effects and depression severity: A patient-level meta-analysis. *Journal of the American Medical Association, 303*(1), 47–53. https://doi.org/10.1001/jama.2009.1943

Fox, J. A., & DeLateur, M. J. (2014). Mass shootings in America: Moving beyond Newtown. *Homicide Studies, 18*(1), 125–145. https://doi.org/10.1177/1088767913510297

Fox, N. A., Almas, A. N., Degnan, K. A., Nelson, C. A., & Zeanah, C. H. (2011). The effects of severe psychosocial deprivation and foster care intervention on cognitive development at 8 years of age: Findings from the Bucharest Early Intervention Project. *Journal of Child Psychology and Psychiatry, 52*(9), 919–928. https://doi.org/10.1111/j.1469-7610.2010.02355.x

Fraley, R. C., & Shaver, P. R. (2000). Adult romantic attachment: Theoretical developments, emerging controversies, and unanswered questions. *Review of General Psychology, 4*(2), 132–154. https://doi.org/10.1037/1089-2680.4.2.132

Frangou, S., Chitins, X., & Williams, S. C. R. (2004). Mapping IQ and gray matter density in healthy young people. *NeuroImage, 23*(3), 800–805. https://doi.org/10.1016/j.neuroimage.2004.05.027

Frank, C. K., & Temple, E. (2009). Cultural effects on the neural basis of theory of mind. *Progress in Brain Research, 178*, 213–223. https://doi.org/10.1016/S0079-6123(09)17815-9

Franken, I. H. A., Muris, P., & Georgieva, I. (2006). Gray's model of personality and addiction. *Addictive Behaviors, 31*(3), 399–403. https://doi.org/10.1016/j.addbeh.2005.05.022

Franken, R. E. (2007). *Human motivation* (6th ed.). Cengage.

Franklin, M. E., & Foa, E. B. (2011). Treatment of obsessive compulsive disorder. *Annual Review of Clinical Psychology, 7*(1), 229–243. https://doi.org/10.1146/annurev-clinpsy-032210-104533

Franklin, T. B., Linder, N., Russig, H., Thöny, B., & Mansuy, I. M. (2011). Influence of early stress on social abilities and serotonergic functions across generations in mice. *PLoS ONE, 6*(7), Article e21842. https://doi.org/10.1371/journal.pone.0021842

Fratiglioni, L., Paillard-Borg, S., & Winblad, B. (2004). An active and socially integrated lifestyle in late life might protect against dementia. *Lancet Neurology, 3*(6), 343–353. https://doi.org/10.1016/s1474-4422(04)00767-7

Fredrickson, B. L. (2001). The role of positive emotions in positive psychology: The broaden-and-build theory of positive emotions. *American Psychologist, 56*(3), 218–226. https://doi.org/10.1037/0003-066X.56.3.218

Freedman, J. L., & Fraser, S. C. (1966). Compliance without pressure: The foot-in-the-door technique. *Journal of Personality and Social Psychology, 4*(2), 196–202. https://doi.org/10.1037/h0023552

Freeman, D., Reeve, S., Robinson, A., Ehlers, A., Clark, D., Spanlang, B., & Slater, M. (2017). Virtual reality in the assessment, understanding, and treatment of mental health disorders. *Psychological Medicine, 47*(14), 2393–2400. https://doi.org/10.1017/s003329171700040x

Freeman, J. B., & Johnson, K. L. (2016). More than meets the eye: Split-second social perception. *Trends in Cognitive Sciences, 20*(5), 362–374. https://doi.org/10.1016/j.tics.2016.03.003

Freeman, J. B., Stolier, R. M., Ingbretsen, Z. A., & Hehman, E. A. (2014). Amygdala responsivity to high-level social information from unseen faces. *Journal of Neuroscience, 34*(32), 10573–10581. https://doi.org/10.1523/JNEUROSCI.5063-13.2014

Freud, S. (1900). *The interpretation of dreams: The standard edition of the complete psychological works of Sigmund Freud* (vols. 4 and 5). Hogarth Press.

Friedman, L. A., & Rapoport, J. L. (2015). Brain development in ADHD. *Current Opinion in Neurobiology, 30*, 106–111. https://doi.org/10.1016/j.conb.2014.11.007

Frijda, N. H. (1994). Emotions are functional, most of the time. In P. Ekman & R. J. Davidson (Eds.), *The nature of emotion: Fundamental questions, Vol. 4: Series in affective science* (pp. 112–122). Oxford University Press.

Frisch, M., & Simonsen, J. (2013). Marriage, cohabitation and mortality in Denmark: National cohort study of 6.5 million persons followed for up to three decades (1982–2011). *International Journal of Epidemiology, 42*(2), 559–578. https://doi.org/10.1093/ije/dyt024

Fromer, M., Pocklington, A. J., Kavanagh, D. H., Williams, H. J., Dwye, S., Gormley, P., Georgieva, L., Rees, E., Palta, P., Ruderfer, D. M., Carrera, N., Humphreys, I., Johnson, J. S., Roussos, P., Barker, D. D., Banks, E., Milanova, V., Gran, S. G., Hannon, E., . . . O'Donovan, M. C. (2014). De novo mutations in schizophrenia implicate synaptic networks. *Nature, 506*(7487), 179–184. https://doi.org/10.1038/nature12929

Fromkin, V., Krashen, S., Curtiss, S., Rigler, D., & Rigler, M. (1974). The development of language in Genie: A case of language acquisition beyond the "critical period." *Brain and Language, 1*(1), 81–107. https://doi.org/10.1016/0093-934X(74)90027-3

Frumkin, H., Frank, L., & Jackson, R. J. (2004). *Urban sprawl and public health: Designing, planning, and building for healthy communities*. Island Press.

Funayama, E. S., Grillon, C., Davis, M., & Phelps, E. A. (2001). A double dissociation in the affective modulation of startle in humans: Effects of unilateral temporal lobectomy. *Journal of Cognitive Neuroscience, 13*(6), 721–729. https://doi.org/10.1162/08989290152541395

Funder, D. C. (1995). On the accuracy of personality judgment: A realistic approach. *Psychological Review, 102*(4), 652–670. https://doi.org/10.1037/0033-295X.102.4.652

Funder, D. C. (2001). Personality. *Annual Review of Psychology, 52*, 197–221. https://doi.org/10.1146/annurev.psych.52.1.197

Funder, D. C. (2012). Accurate personality judgment. *Current Directions in Psychological Science, 21*(3), 177–182. https://doi.org/10.1177/0963721412445309

Fung, H. H., & Carstensen, L. L. (2004). Motivational changes in response to blocked goals and foreshortened time: Testing alternatives to socioemotional selectivity theory. *Psychology and Aging, 19*(1), 68–78. https://doi.org/10.1037/0882-7974.19.1.68

Fung, M. T., Raine, A., Loeber, R., Lynam, D. R., Steinhauer, S. R., Venables, P. D., & Stouthamer-Loeber, M. (2005). Reduced electrodermal activity in psychopathy-prone adolescents. *Journal of Abnormal Psychology, 114*(2), 187–196. https://doi.org/10.1037/0021-843X.114.2.187

Furnham, A., Richards, S. C., & Paulhus, D. L. (2013). The dark triad of personality: A 10 year review. *Social and Personality Psychology Compass, 7*(3), 199–216. https://doi.org/10.1111/spc3.12018

Fusar-Poli, P., Papanastasiou, E., Stahl, D., Rocchetti, M., Carpenter, W., Shergill, S., & McGuire, P. (2015). Treatments of negative symptoms in schizophrenia: Meta-analysis of 168 randomized placebo-controlled trials. *Schizophrenia Bulletin, 41*(4), 892–899. https://doi.org/10.1093/schbul/sbu170

Gable, P. A., Neal, L. B., & Threadgill, A. H. (2018). Regulatory behavior and frontal activity: Considering the role of revised-BIS in relative right frontal asymmetry. *Psychophysiology, 55*(1), Article e12910. https://doi.org/10.1111/psyp.12910

Gable, S. L., & Reis, H. T. (2010). Good news! Capitalizing on positive events in an interpersonal context. *Advances in Experimental Social Psychology, 42*, 195–257. https://doi.org/10.1016/S0065-2601(10)42004-3

Gabrieli, J. D., Ghosh, S. S., & Whitfield-Gabrieli, S. (2015). Prediction as a humanitarian and pragmatic contribution from human cognitive neuroscience. *Neuron, 85*(1), 11–26. https://doi.org/10.1016/j.neuron.2014.10.047

Gaither, S. E., Apfelbaum, E. P., Birnbaum, H. J., Babbitt, L. G., & Sommers, S. R. (2018). Mere membership in racially diverse groups reduces conformity. *Social Psychological and Personality Science, 9*(4), 402–410. https://doi.org/10.1177/1948550617708013

Gaither, S. E., Pauker, K., & Johnson, S. P. (2012). Biracial and monoracial infant own-race face perception: An eye tracking study. *Developmental Science, 15*(6), 775–782. https://doi.org/10.1111/j.1467-7687.2012.01170.x

Galak, J., LeBoeuf, R. A., Nelson, L. D., & Simmons, J. P. (2012). Correcting the past: Failures to replicate psi. *Journal of Personality and Social Psychology, 103*(6), 933–948. https://doi.org/10.1037/a0029709

Galanter, E. (1962). *Contemporary psychophysics*. Holt, Rinehart, Winston.

Galinsky, A. D., Wang, C. S., Whitson, J. A., Anicich, E. M., Hugenberg, K., & Bodenhausen, G. V. (2013). The reappropriation of stigmatizing labels: The reciprocal relationship between power and self-labeling. *Psychological Science, 24*(10), 2020–2029. https://doi.org/10.1177/0956797613482943

Gallagher, D. T., Hadjiefthyvoulou, F., Fisk, J. E., Montgomery, C., Robinson, S. J., & Judge, J. (2014). Prospective memory deficits in illicit polydrug users are associated with the average long-term typical dose of ecstasy typically consumed in a single session.

Neuropsychology, 28(1), 43–54. https://doi.org/10.1037/neu0000004
Gallo, E. F., & Posner, J. (2016). Moving towards causality in attention-deficit hyperactivity disorder: Overview of neural and genetic mechanisms. *The Lancet Psychiatry, 3*(6), 555–567. https://doi.org/10.1016/s2215-0366(16)00096-1
Galton, F. (1879). Psychometric experiments. *Brain, 2*(2), 149–162. https://doi.org/10.1093/brain/2.2.149
Gandhi, A. V., Mosser, E. A., Oikonomou, G., & Prober, D. A. (2015). Melatonin is required for the circadian regulation of sleep. *Neuron, 85*(6), 1193–1199. https://doi.org/10.1016/j.neuron.2015.02.016
Garcia, J., & Koelling, R. A. (1966). Relation of cue to consequence in avoidance learning. *Psychonomic Science, 4*(3), 123–124. https://doi.org/10.3758/BF03342209
Gardner, H. (1983). *Frames of mind: The theory of multiple intelligences*. Basic Books.
Gardner, W. L., Pickett, C. L., Jefferis, V., & Knowles, M. (2005). On the outside looking in: Loneliness and social monitoring. *Personality and Social Psychology Bulletin, 31*(11), 1549–1560. https://doi.org/10.1177/0146167205277208
Gariépy, G., Honkaniemi, H., & Quesnel-Vallée, A. (2016). Social support and protection from depression: Systematic review of current findings in Western countries. *British Journal of Psychiatry, 209*(4), 284–293. https://doi.org/10.1192/bjp.bp.115.169094
Garlick, D. (2002). Understanding the nature of the general factor of intelligence: The role of individual differences in neural plasticity as an explanatory mechanism. *Psychological Review, 109*(1), 116–136. https://doi.org/10.1037/0033-295X.109.1.116
Garneau, N. L., Nuessle, T. M., Sloan, M. M., Santorico, S. A., Coughlin, B. C., & Hayes, J. E. (2014). Crowdsourcing taste research: Genetic and phenotypic predictors of bitter taste perception as a model. *Frontiers in Integrative Neuroscience, 8*, Article 33. https://doi.org/10.3389/fnint.2014.00033
Garon, N., Bryson, S. E., & Smith, I. M. (2008). Executive function in preschoolers: A review using an integrative framework. *Psychological Bulletin, 134*(1), 31–60. https://doi.org/10.1037/0033-2909.134.1.31
Garriga, M., Pacchiarotti, I., Kasper, S., Zeller, S. L., Allen, M. H., Vázquez, G., Baldaçara, L., San, L., McAllister-Williams, R. H., Fountoulakis, K. N., Courtet, P., Naber, D., Chan, E. W., Fagiolini, A., Möller, H. J., Grunze, H., Llorca, P. M., Jaffe, R. L., Yatham, L. N., ... Vieta, E. (2016). Assessment and management of agitation in psychiatry: Expert consensus. *The World Journal of Biological Psychiatry, 17*(2), 86–128. https://doi.org/10.3109/15622975.2015.1132007.
Garthe, A., Roeder, I., & Kempermann, G. (2016). Mice in an enriched environment learn more flexibly because of adult hippocampal neurogenesis. *Hippocampus, 26*(2), 261–271. https://doi.org/10.1002/hipo.22520
Gastil, J. (1990). Generic pronouns and sexist language: The oxymoronic character of masculine generics. *Sex Roles, 23*, 629–643. https://doi.org/10.1007/BF00289252
Gatt, J. M., Burton, K. L. O., Williams, L. M., & Schofield, P. R. (2015). Specific and common genes implicated across major mental disorders: A review of meta-analysis studies. *Journal of Psychiatric Research, 60*, 1–13. https://doi.org/10.1016/j.jpsychires.2014.09.014
Gauthier, I., Tarr, M. J., Moylan, J., Skudlarski, P., Gore, J. C., & Anderson, A. W. (2000). The fusiform "face area" is part of a network that processes faces at the individual level. *Journal of Cognitive Neuroscience, 12*(3), 495–504. https://doi.org/10.1162/089892900562165
Gazzaniga, M. S. (2000). Cerebral specialization and interhemispheric communication: Does the corpus callosum enable the human condition? *Brain, 123*(7), 1293–1326. https://doi.org/10.1093/brain/123.7.1293
Gazzaniga, M. S. (2015). *Tales from both sides of the brain: A life in neuroscience*. HarperCollins.
Gazzaniga, M. S., & LeDoux, J. E. (1978). *The integrated mind*. Plenum Press.
Gazzaniga, M. S., Ivry, R. B., & Mangun, G. R. (2014). *Cognitive neuroscience: The biology of the mind* (4th ed.). Norton.
Ge, X., Natsuaki, M. N., Neiderhiser, J. M., & Reiss, D. (2007). Genetic and environmental influences on pubertal timing: Results from two national sibling studies. *Journal of Research on Adolescence, 17*(4), 767–788. https://doi.org/10.1111/j.1532-7795.2007.00546.x
Geddes, J. R., & Miklowitz, D. J. (2013). Treatment of bipolar disorder. *The Lancet, 381*(9878), 1672–1682. https://doi.org/10.1016/s0140-6736(13)60857-0
Geddes, J. R., Burgess, S., Hawton, K., Jamison, K., & Goodwin, G. M. (2004). Long-term lithium therapy for bipolar disorder: Systematic review and meta-analysis of randomized controlled trials. *American Journal of Psychiatry, 161*(2), 217–222. https://doi.org/10.1176/appi.ajp.161.2.217
Geier, C. F., Terwilliger, R., Teslovich, T., Velanova, K., & Luna, B. (2010). Immaturities in reward processing and its influence on inhibitory control in adolescence. *Cerebral Cortex, 20*(7), 1613–1629. https://doi.org/10.1093/cercor/bhp225
Gelfand, M. J., Raver, J. L., Nishii, L., Leslie, L. M., Lun, J., Lim, B. C., Duan, L., Almaliach, A., Ang, S., Arnadottir, J., Aycan, Z., Boehnke, K., Boski, P., Cabecinhas, R., Chan, D., Chhokar, J., D'Amato, A., Ferrer, M., Fischlmayr, I. C., ... Yamaguchi, S. (2011). Differences between tight and loose cultures: A 33-nation study. *Science, 332*(6033), 1100–1104. https://doi.org/10.1126/science.1197754
Gellatly, C., & Störmer, C. (2017). How does marriage affect length of life? Analysis of a French historical dataset from an evolutionary perspective. *Evolution and Human Behavior, 38*(4), 536–545. https://doi.org/10.1016/j.evolhumbehav.2017.02.002
Gelman, A., & Loken, E. (2014). The statistical crisis in science. *American Scientist, 102*(6), 460. https://doi.org/10.1511/2014.111.460
Gelman, R., & Gallistel, C. R. (2004). Language and the origin of numerical concepts. *Science, 306*(5695), 441–443. https://doi.org/10.1126/science.1105144
Gendron, M., Roberson, D., van der Vyver, J. M., & Barrett, L. F. (2014). Perceptions of emotion from facial expressions are not culturally universal: Evidence from a remote culture. *Emotion, 14*(2), 251–262. https://doi.org/10.1037/a0036052
Gentile, D. A., Saleem, M., & Anderson, C. A. (2007). Public policy and the effects of media violence on children. *Social Issues and Policy Review, 1*(1), 15–61. https://doi.org/10.1111/j.1751-2409.2007.00003.x
George, J. M., & Zhou, J. (2001). When openness to experience and conscientiousness are related to creative behavior: An interactional approach. *Journal of Applied Psychology, 86*(3), 513–524. https://doi.org/10.1037/0021-9010.86.3.513
George, M. S., Lisanby, S. H., & Sackheim, H. A. (1999). Transcranial magnetic stimulation: Applications in neuropsychiatry. *Archives of General Psychiatry, 56*(4), 300–311. https://doi.org/10.1001/archpsyc.56.4.300
George, M. S., Wassermann, E. M., Williams, W. A., Callahan, A., Ketter, T. A., Basser, P., Hallett, M., & Post, R. M. (1995). Daily repetitive transcxranial magnetic stimulation (rTMS) improves mood in depression. *Neuroreport, 6*(14), 1853–1856. https://doi.org/10.1097/00001756-199510020-00008
Gergely, G., & Csibra, G. (2003). Teleological reasoning in infancy: The naïve theory of rational action. *Trends in Cognitive Sciences, 7*(7), 287–292. https://doi.org/10.1016/S1364-6613(03)00128-1
Gershman, S. J., & Daw, N. D. (2017). Reinforcement learning and episodic memory in humans and animals: An integrative framework. *Annual Review of Psychology, 68*(1), 101–128. https://doi.org/10.1146/annurev-psych-122414-033625
Gershoff, E. T. (2002). Corporal punishment by parents and associated child behaviors and experiences: A meta-analytic and theoretical review. *Psychological Bulletin, 128*(4), 539–579. https://doi.org/10.1037/0033-2909.128.4.539
Gershoff, E. T., & Grogan-Kaylor, A. (2016). Spanking and child outcomes: Old controversies and new meta-analyses. *Journal of Family Psychology, 30*(4), 453–469. https://doi.org/10.1037/fam0000191
Ghio, M., Vaghi, M. M. S., Perani, D., & Tettamanti, M. (2016). Decoding the neural representation of fine-grained conceptual categories. *NeuroImage, 132*, 93–103. https://doi.org/10.1016/j.neuroimage.2016.02.009
Gick, M. L., & Holyoak, K. J. (1983). Schema induction and analogical transfer. *Cognitive Psychology, 15*(1), 1–38. https://doi.org/10.1016/0010-0285(83)90002-6
Gijsman, H. J., Geddes, J. R., Rendell, J. M., Nolen, W. A., & Goodwin, G. M. (2004). Antidepressants for bipolar depression: A systematic review of randomized, controlled trials. *American Journal of Psychiatry, 161*(9), 1537–1547. https://doi.org/10.1176/appi.ajp.161.9.1537
Gilbert, D. T., & Wilson, T. D. (2007). Prospection: Experiencing the future. *Science, 317*(5843), 1351–1354. https://doi.org/10.1126/science.1144161
Gilbert, D. T., Morewedge, C. K., Risen, J. L., & Wilson, T. D. (2004). Looking forward to looking backward: The misprediction of regret. *Psychological Science, 15*(5), 346–350. https://doi.org/10.1111/j.0956-7976.2004.00681.x
Gilbert, D. T., Pinel, E. C., Wilson, T. D., Blumberg, S. J., & Wheatley, T. P. (1998). Immune neglect: A source of durability bias in affective forecasting. *Journal of Personality and Social Psychology, 75*(3), 617–638. https://doi.org/10.1037/0022-3514.75.3.617

Gilligan, C. (1977). In a different voice: Women's conceptions of self and of morality. *Harvard Educational Review, 47*(4), 481–517. https://doi.org/10.17763/haer.47.4.g6167429416hg510

Gillihan, S. J., & Farah, M. J. (2005). Is self special? A critical review of evidence from experimental psychology and cognitive neuroscience. *Psychological Bulletin, 131*(1), 76–97. https://doi.org/10.1037/0033-2909.131.1.76

Gilman, S. R., Iossifov, I., Levy, D., Ronemus, M., Wigler, M., & Vitkup, D. (2011). Rare de novo variants associated with autism implicate a large functional network of genes involved in formation and function of synapses. *Neuron, 70*(5), 898–907. https://doi.org/10.1016/j.neuron.2011.05.021

Gilovich, T. (1991). *How we know what isn't so: The fallibility of human reason in everyday life.* Free Press.

Gingerich, A. C., & Lineweaver, T. T. (2014). OMG! Texting in class = U fail :(Empirical evidence that text messaging during class disrupts comprehension. *Teaching of Psychology, 41*(1), 44–51. https://doi.org/10.1177/0098628313514177

Glimcher, P. W. (2011). Understanding dopamine and reinforcement learning: The dopamine reward prediction error hypothesis. *Proceedings of the National Academy of Sciences, 108*(Supp 3), 15647–15654. https://doi.org/10.1073/pnas.1014269108

Godden, D. R., & Baddeley, A. D. (1975). Context-dependent memory in two natural environments: On land and underwater. *British Journal of Psychology, 66*(3), 325–331. https://doi.org/10.1111/j.2044-8295.1975.tb01468.x

Godlee, F., Smith, J., & Marcovitch, H. (2011). Wakefield's article linking MMR vaccine and autism was fraudulent. *British Medical Journal, 342*, Article c7452. https://doi.org/10.1136/bmj.c7452

Goff, D. C., Falkai, P., Fleischhacker, W. W., Girgis, R. R., Kahn, R. M., Uchida, H., Zhao, J., & Lieberman, J. A. (2017). The long-term effects of antipsychotic medication on clinical course in schizophrenia. *American Journal of Psychiatry, 174*(9), 840–849 https://doi.org/10.1176/appi.ajp.2017.16091016

Goff, P. A., Eberhardt, J. L., Williams, M. J., & Jackson, M. C. (2008). Not yet human: Implicit knowledge, historical dehumanization, and contemporary consequences. *Journal of Personality and Social Psychology, 94*(2), 292–306. https://doi.org/10.1037/0022-3514.94.2.292

Goin-Kochel, R. P., Fombonne, E., Mire, S. S., Minard, C. G., Sahni, L. C., Cunningham, R. M., & Boom, J. A. (2020). Beliefs about causes of autism and vaccine hesitancy among parents of children with autism spectrum disorder. *Vaccine, 38*(40), 6327–6333. https://doi.org/10.1016/j.vaccine.2020.07.034

Goldapple, K., Segal, Z., Garson, C., Lau, M., Bieling, P., Kennedy, S., & Mayberg, H. (2004). Modulation of cortical-limbic pathways in major depression: Treatment-specific effects of cognitive behavior therapy. *Archives of General Psychiatry, 61*(1), 34–41. https://doi.org/10.1001/archpsyc.61.1.34

Goldenberg, M. M. (2012). Multiple sclerosis review. *Pharmacy and Therapeutics, 37*(3), 175–184.

Goldin, C., & Rouse, C. (2000). Orchestrating impartiality: The impact of "blind" auditions on female musicians. *The American Economic Review, 90*, 715–741. https//doi.org/10.1257/aer.90.4.715

Goldstein, R. B., Chou, S. P., Saha, T. D., Smith, S. M., Zhang, H., Pickering, R. P., Ruan, W. J., Huang, B., & Grant, B. F. (2017). The epidemiology of antisocial behavioral syndromes in adulthood: Results from the National Epidemiologic Survey on Alcohol and Related Conditions-III. *Journal of Clinical Psychiatry, 78*(1), 90–98. https://doi.org/10.4088/JCP.15m10358

Goldstein, R. Z., Craig, A. D. B., Bechara, A., Garavan, H., Childress, A. R., Paulus, M. P., & Volkow, N. D. (2009). The neurocircuitry of impaired insight in drug addiction. *Trends in Cognitive Science, 13*(9), 372–380. https://doi.org/10.1016/j.tics.2009.06.004

Golinkoff, R. M., Can, D. D., Soderstrom, M., & Hirsh-Pasek, K. (2015). (Baby) talk to me: The social context of infant-directed speech and its effects on early language acquisition. *Current Directions in Psychological Science, 24*(5), 339–344. https://doi.org/10.1177/0963721415595345

Gong, Q.-Y., Sluming, V., Mayes, A., Keller, S., Barrick, T., Cezayirli, E., & Roberts, N. (2005). Voxel-based morphometry and stereology provide convergent evidence of the importance of medial prefrontal cortex for fluid intelligence in healthy adults. *NeuroImage, 25*(4), 1175–1186. https://doi.org/10.1016/j.neuroimage.2004.12.044

Goodale, M. A., & Milner, A. D. (1992). Separate visual pathways for perception and action. *Trends in Neuroscience, 15*(1), 20–25. https://doi.org/10.1016/0166-2236(92)90344-8

Goodman, S. H., & Gotlib, I. H. (1999). Risk for psychopathology in the children of depressed mothers: A developmental model for understanding mechanisms of transmission. *Psychological Review, 106*(3), 458–490. https://doi.org/10.1037/0033-295X.106.3.458

Goodman, S. N., Fanelli, D., & Ioannidis, J. P. A. (2016). What does research reproducibility mean? *Science Translational Medicine, 8*(341), 341ps12. https://doi.org/10.1126/scitranslmed.aaf5027

Goodwin, D. W., Powell, B., Bremer, D., Hoine, H., & Stern, J. (1969). Alcohol and recall: State-dependent effects in man. *Science, 163*(3873), 1358–1360. https://doi.org/10.1126/science.163.3873.1358

Goodwin, G. P. (2015). Moral character in person perception. *Current Directions in Psychological Science, 24*(1), 38–44. https://doi.org/10.1177/0963721414550709

Goosby, B. J., Cheadle, J. E., & Mitchell, C. (2018). Stress-related biosocial mechanisms of discrimination and African American health inequities. *Annual Review of Sociology, 44*, 319–340. https://doi.org/10.1146/annurev-soc-060116-053403

Gordon, P. (2004). Numerical cognition without words: Evidence from Amazonia. *Science, 306*(5695), 496–499. https://doi.org/10.1126/science.1094492

Gosling, S. D. (2008). *Snoop: What your stuff says about you.* Basic Books.

Gosling, S. D., Ko, S. J., Mannarelli, T., & Morris, M. E. (2002). A room with a cue: Judgments of personality based on offices and bedrooms. *Journal of Personality and Social Psychology, 82*(3), 379–398. https://doi.org/10.1037/0022-3514.82.3.379

Gotlib, I. H., & Joormann, J. (2010). Cognition and depression: Current status and future directions. *Annual Review of Clinical Psychology, 6*, 285–312. https://doi.org/10.1146/annurev.clinpsy.121208.131305

Gottfredson, L. S. (2003). Dissecting practical intelligence theory: Its claims and evidence. *Intelligence, 31*(4), 343–397. https://doi.org/10.1016/S0160-2896(02)00085-5

Gottfredson, L. S. (2004a). Intelligence: Is it the epidemiologists' elusive "fundamental cause" of social class inequalities in health? *Journal of Personality and Social Psychology, 86*(1), 174–199. https://doi.org/10.1037/0022-3514.86.1.174

Gottfredson, L. S. (2004b, Summer). Schools and the *g* factor. *The Wilson Quarterly, 28*, 35–45.

Gottfredson, L. S., & Deary, I. J. (2004). Intelligence predicts health and longevity, but why? *Current Directions in Psychological Science, 13*(1), 1–4. https://doi.org/10.1111/j.0963-7214.2004.01301001.x

Gottman, J. (1995). *Why marriages succeed or fail . . . and how you can make yours last.* Simon & Schuster.

Gottman, J. M. (1998). Psychology and the study of marital processes. *Annual Review of Psychology, 49*, 169–197. https://doi.org/10.1146/annurev.psych.49.1.169

Gould, E., & Tanapat, P. (1999). Stress and hippocampal neurogenesis. *Biological Psychiatry, 46*(11), 1472–1479. https://doi.org/10.1016/S0006-3223(99)00247-4

Graf, P., & Schacter, D. L. (1985). Implicit and explicit memory for new associations in normal and amnesic subjects. *Journal of Experimental Psychology: Learning, Memory and Cognition, 11*(3), 501–518. https://doi.org/10.1037/0278-7393.11.3.501

Graf, P., & Uttl, B. (2001). Prospective memory: A new focus for research. *Consciousness and Cognition, 10*(4), 437–450. https://doi.org/10.1006/ccog.2001.0504

Gray, J. A. (1982). On mapping anxiety. *Behavioral and Brain Sciences, 5*(3), 506–534. https://doi.org/10.1017/S0140525X00013297

Gray, J. A., & McNaughton, N. (2000). *The neuropsychology of anxiety: An enquiry into the functions of the septo-hippocampal system.* Oxford University Press.

Gray, J. R., & Thompson, P. M. (2004). Neurobiology of intelligence: Science and ethics. *Nature Reviews Neuroscience, 5*(6), 471–482. https://doi.org/10.1038/nrn1405

Gray, K., Rand, D. G., Ert, E., Lewis, K., Hershman, S., & Norton, M. I. (2014). The emergence of "us and them" in 80 lines of code: Modeling group genesis in homogeneous populations. *Psychological Science, 25*(4), 982–990. https://doi.org/10.1177/0956797614521816

Green, D. M., & Swets, J. A. (1966). *Signal detection theory and psychophysics.* Wiley.

Green, E. D., Watson, J. D., & Collins, F. S. (2015). Human Genome Project: Twenty-five years of big biology. *Nature, 526*(7571), 29–31. https://doi.org/10.1038/526029a

Green, J. J., & Hollander, E. (2010). Autism and oxytocin: New developments in translational approaches to therapeutics. *Neurotherapeutics, 7*, 250–257. https://doi.org/10.1016/j.nurt.2010.05.006

Greenberg, B. D., Gabriels, L. A., Malone, D. A., Jr., Rezai, A. R., Friehs, G. M., Okun, M. S.,

Shapira, N. A., Foote, K. D., Cosyns, P. R., Kubu, C. S., Malloy, P. F., Salloway, S. P., Giftakis, J. E., Rise, M. T., Machado, A. G., Baker, K. B., Stypulkowski, P. H., Goodman, W. K., Rasmussen, S. A., & Nuttin, B. J. (2008). Deep brain stimulation of the ventral internal capsule/ventral striatum for obsessive-compulsive disorder: Worldwide experience. *Molecular Psychiatry, 15*, 64–79. https://doi.org/10.1038/mp.2008.55

Greenwald, A. G. (1968). Cognitive learning, cognitive response to persuasion, and attitude change. In A. G. Greenwald, T. C. Brock, & T. M. Ostrom (Eds.), *Psychological foundations of attitudes* (pp. 147–170). Academic Press.

Greenwald, A. G. (1992). New Look 3: Reclaiming unconscious cognition. *American Psychologist, 47*(6), 766–779. https://doi.org/10.1037/0003-066X.47.6.766

Greenwald, A. G., & Banaji, M. R. (1995). Implicit social cognition: Attitudes, self-esteem, and stereotypes. *Psychological Review, 102*(1), 4–27. https://doi.org/10.1037/0033-295X.102.1.4

Greenwald, A. G., McGhee, D. E., & Schwartz, J. L. K. (1998). Measuring individual differences in implicit cognition: The implicit association test. *Journal of Personality and Social Psychology, 74*(6), 1464–1480. https://doi.org/10.1037/0022-3514.74.6.1464

Gregory, S. (2020, March 26). 'Without empathy, nothing works': Chef José Andrés wants to feed the world through the pandemic. *Time*. https://time.com/collection/apart-not-alone/5809169/jose-andres-coronavirus-food/

Grey, I., Arora, T., Thomas, J., Saneh, A., Tohme, P., & Abi-Habib, R. (2020). The role of perceived social support on depression and sleep during the COVID-19 pandemic. *Psychiatry Research, 293*, Article 113452. https://doi.org/10.1016/j.psychres.2020.113452

Griebel, U., Pepperberg, I. M., & Oller, D. K. (2016). Developmental plasticity and language: A comparative perspective. *Topics in Cognitive Science, 8*(2), 435–445. https://doi.org/10.1111/tops.12200

Griggs, R. A. (2015). Psychology's lost boy: Will the real Little Albert please stand up? *Teaching of Psychology, 42*(1), 14–18. https://doi.org/10.1177/0098628314562668

Griggs, R. A. (2017). Milgram's obedience study: A contentious classic reinterpreted. *Teaching of Psychology, 44*(1), 32–37. https://doi.org/10.1177/0098628316677644

Grill-Spector, K., Knouf, N., & Kanwisher, N. (2004). The fusiform face area subserves face perception, not generic within-category identification. *Nature Neuroscience, 7*, 555–562. https://doi.org/10.1038/nn1224

Grimshaw, G. M., Adelstein, A., Bryden, M. P., & MacKinnon, G. E. (1998). First-language acquisition in adolescence: Evidence for a critical period for verbal language development. *Brain and Language, 63*(2), 237–255. https://doi.org/10.1006/brln.1997.1943

Gross, J. J. (1999). Emotion and emotion regulation. In L. A. Pervin & O. P. John (Eds.), *Handbook of personality: Theory and research* (2nd ed., pp. 525–552). Guilford Press.

Gross, J. J. (2013). Emotion regulation: Taking stock and moving forward. *Emotion, 13*(3), 359–365. https://doi.org/10.1037/a0032135

Grossniklaus, U., Kelly, W. G., Ferguson-Smith, A. C., Pembrey, M., & Lindquist, S. (2013). Transgenerational epigenetic inheritance: How important is it? *Nature Reviews Genetics, 14*, 228–235. https://doi.org/10.1038/nrg3435

Grüter, T., Grüter, M., & Carbon, C.-C. (2008). Neural and genetic foundations of face recognition and prosopagnosia. *Journal of Neuropsychology, 2*(1), 79–97. https://doi.org/10.1348/174866407X231001

Gruzelier, J. H. (2000). Redefining hypnosis: Theory, methods, and integration. *Contemporary Hypnosis, 17*(2), 51–70. https://doi.org/10.1002/ch.193

Guastella, A. J., & Hickie, I. B. (2016). Oxytocin treatment, circuitry, and autism: A critical review of the literature placing oxytocin into the autism context. *Biological Psychiatry, 79*(3), 234–242. https://doi.org/10.1016/j.biopsych.2015.06.028

Guerin, B. (1994). What do people think about the risks of driving? Implications for traffic safety interventions. *Journal of Applied Social Psychology, 24*(11), 994–1021. https://doi.org/10.1111/j.1559-1816.1994.tb02370.x

Habibi, A., Damasio, A., Ilari, B., Sachs, M. E., & Damasio, H. (2018). Music training and child development: A review of recent findings from a longitudinal study. *Annals of the New York Academy of Sciences, 1423*(1), 73–81. https://doi.org/10.1111/nyas.13606

Hackel, L. M., Looser, C. E., & Van Bavel, J. J. (2014). Group membership alters the threshold for mind perception: The role of social identity, collective identification, and intergroup threat. *Journal of Experimental Social Psychology, 52*, 15–23. https://doi.org/10.1016/j.jesp.2013.12.001

Haggarty, P., Hoad, G., Harris, S. E., Starr, J. M., Fox, H. C., Deary, I. J., & Whalley, L. J. (2010). Human intelligence and polymorphisms in the DNA methyltransferase genes involved in epigenetic marking. *PLoS ONE, 5*(6), Article e11329. https://doi.org/10.1371/journal.pone.0011329

Hagger-Johnson, G., Deary, I. J., Davies, C. A., Weiss, A., & Batty, G. D. (2014). Reaction time and mortality from the major causes of death: The NHANES-III study. *PLoS ONE, 9*(1), Article e82959. https://doi.org/10.1371/journal.pone.0082959

Hagger, M. S., & Chatzisarantis, N. L. D. (2011). Causality orientations moderate the undermining effect of rewards on intrinsic motivation. *Journal of Experimental Social Psychology, 47*(2), 485–489. https://doi.org/10.1016/j.jesp.2010.10.010

Haidt, J. (2003). The moral emotions. In R. J. Davidson, K. R. Scherer, & H. H. Goldsmith (Eds.), *Handbook of affective sciences* (pp. 852–870). Oxford University Press.

Haier, R. J., Jung, R. E., Yeo, R. A., Head, K., & Alkire, M. T. (2005). The neuroanatomy of general intelligence: Sex matters. *NeuroImage, 25*(1), 320–327. https://doi.org/10.1016/j.neuroimage.2004.11.019

Hair, N. L., Hanson, J. L., Wolfe, B. L., & Pollak, S. D. (2015). Association of child poverty, brain development, and academic achievement. *JAMA Pediatrics, 169*(9), 822–829. https://doi.org/10.1001/jamapediatrics.2015.1475

Halász, P. (2016). The K-complex as a special reactive sleep slow wave—A theoretical update. *Sleep Medicine Reviews, 29*, 34–40. https://doi.org/10.1016/j.smrv.2015.09.004

Hallam, S., Cross, I., & Thaut, M. (2016). *Oxford handbook of music psychology* (2nd ed.). Oxford University Press.

Halldorsdottir, T., & Binder, E. B. (2017). Gene × environment interactions: From molecular mechanisms to behavior. *Annual Review of Psychology, 68*(1), 215–241. https://doi.org/10.1146/annurev-psych-010416-044053

Halpin, L. E., Collins, S. A., & Yamamoto, B. K. (2014). Neurotoxicity of methamphetamine and 3, 4-methylenedioxymethamphetamine. *Life Sciences, 97*(1), 37–44. https://doi.org/10.1016/j.lfs.2013.07.014

Hamel, L., Kearney, A., Kirzinger, A., Lopes, L., Muñana, C., & Brodie, M. (2020, May 27). KFF Health Tracking Poll—May 2020. Kaiser Family Foundation. https://www.kff.org/coronavirus-covid-19/report/kff-health-tracking-poll-may-2020/

Hamilton, J. P., Farmer, M., Fogelman, P., & Gotlib, I. H. (2015). Depressive rumination, the default-mode network, and the dark matter of clinical neuroscience. *Biological Psychiatry, 78*(4), 224–230. https://doi.org/10.1016/j.biopsych.2015.02.020

Hamilton, W. D. (1964). The genetical evolution of social behaviour. I. *Journal of Theoretical Biology, 7*(1), 1–16. https://doi.org/10.1016/0022-5193(64)90038-4

Hammarberg, K., Holton, S., Michelmore, J., Fisher, J., & Hickey, M. (2019). Thriving in older age: A national survey of women in Australia. *Maturitas, 122*, 60–65. https://doi.org/10.1016/j.maturitas.2019.01.011

Hammen, C. (2005). Stress and depression. *Annual Review of Clinical Psychology, 1*(1), 293–319. https://doi.org/10.1146/annurev.clinpsy.1.102803.143938

Handleman, J. S., Gill, M. J., & Alessandri, M. (1988). Generalization by severely developmentally disabled children: Issues, advances, and future directions. *Behavior Therapist, 11*, 221–223.

Hansen, C. J., Stevens, L. C., & Coast, J. R. (2001). Exercise duration and mood state: How much is enough to feel better? *Health Psychology, 20*(4), 267–275. https://doi.org/10.1037/0278-6133.20.4.267

Hansen, T. (2012). Parenthood and happiness: A review of folk theories versus empirical evidence. *Social Indicators Research, 108*, 29–64. https://doi.org/10.1007/s11205-011-9865-y

Harburger, L. L., Nzerem, C. K., & Frick, K. M. (2007). Single enrichment variables differentially reduce age-related memory decline in female mice. *Behavioral Neuroscience, 121*(4), 679–688. https://doi.org/10.1037/0735-7044.121.4.679

Hare, R. D. (1993). *Without conscience: The disturbing world of the psychopaths among us*. Pocket Books.

Hare, R. D., McPherson, L. M., & Forth, A. E. (1988). Male psychopaths and their criminal careers. *Journal of Consulting and Clinical Psychology, 56*(5), 710–714. https://doi.org/10.1037/0022-006X.56.5.710

Harlow, H. F., & Harlow, M. K (1966). Learning to love. *American Scientist, 54*(3), 244–272. https://www.ncbi.nlm.nih.gov/pubmed/4958465

Harlow, H. F., Harlow, M. K., & Meyer, D. R. (1950). Learning motivated by a manipulation drive. *Journal of Experimental Psychology, 40*(2), 228–234. https://doi.org/10.1037/h0056906

Harlow, J. M. (1868). Recovery from the passage of an iron bar through the head. *Publications of the Massachusetts Medical Society, 2*, 327–347.
Harmon, K. G., Drezner, J. A., Gammons, M., Guskiewicz, K. M., Halstead, M., Herring, S. A., Kutcher, J. S., Pana, A., Putukian, M., & Roberts, W. O. (2013). American Medical Society for Sports Medicine position statement: Concussion in sport. *British Journal of Sports Medicine, 47*(1), 15–26. https://doi.org/10.1136/bjsports-2012-091941
Harpur, T. J., & Hare, R. D. (1994). Assessment of psychopathy as a function of age. *Journal of Abnormal Psychology, 103*(4), 604–609. https://doi.org/10.1037/0021-843X.103.4.604
Harris, J. R. (1995). Where is the child's environment? A group socialization theory of development. *Psychological Review, 102*(3), 458–489. https://doi.org/10.1037/0033-295X.102.3.458
Harris, J. R. (2011). *The nurture assumption: Why children turn out the way they do.* Simon & Schuster.
Harris, L. T., & Fiske, S. T. (2006). Dehumanizing the lowest of the low: Neuroimaging responses to extreme out-groups. *Psychological Science, 17*(10), 847–853. https://doi.org/10.1111/j.1467-9280.2006.01793.x
Harris, M. A., Brett, C. E., Johnson, W., & Deary, I. J. (2016). Personality stability from age 14 to age 77 years. *Psychology and Aging, 31*(8), 862–874. https://doi.org/10.1037/pag0000133
Harrow, M., & Jobe, T. H. (2013). Does long-term treatment of schizophrenia with antipsychotic medications facilitate recovery? *Schizophrenia Bulletin, 39*(5), 962–965. https://doi.org/10.1093/schbul/sbt034
Harrow, M., Jobe, T. H., & Faull, R. N. (2014). Does treatment of schizophrenia with antipsychotic medications eliminate or reduce psychosis? A 20-year multi-follow-up study. *Psychological Medicine, 44*(14), 3007–3016. https://doi.org/10.1017/S0033291714000610
Hart, A. J. (1995). Naturally occurring expectation effects. *Journal of Personality and Social Psychology, 68*(1), 109–115. https://doi.org/10.1037/0022-3514.68.1.109
Hartford, J., Kornstein, S., Liebowitz, M., Pigott, T., Russell, J., Detke, M., Walker, D., Ball, S., Dunayevich, E., Dinkel, J., & Erickson, J. (2007). Duloxetine as an SNRI treatment for generalized anxiety disorder: Results from a placebo and active-controlled trial. *International Clinical Psychopharmacology, 22*(3), 167–174. https://doi.org/10.1097/YIC.0b013e32807fb1b2
Hartung, C. M., & Lefler, E. K. (2019). Sex and gender in psychopathology: DSM-5 and beyond. Psychological Bulletin, 145(4), 390–409. https://doi.org/10.1037/bul0000183
Haslam, S. A., Reicher, S. D., & Birney, M. E. (2016). Questioning authority: New perspectives on Milgram's "obedience" research and its implications for intergroup relations. *Current Opinion in Psychology, 11*, 6–9. https://doi.org/10.1016/j.copsyc.2016.03.007
Haslam, S. A., Reicher, S. D., Millard, K., & McDonald, R. (2015). "Happy to have been of service": The Yale archive as a window into the engaged followership of participants in Milgram's "obedience" experiments. *British Journal of Social Psychology, 54*(1), 55–83. https://doi.org/10.1111/bjso.12074
Hawkley, L., & Cacioppo, J. T. (2010). Loneliness matters: A theoretical and empirical review of consequences and mechanisms. *Annals of Behavioral Medicine, 40*(2), 218–227. https://doi.org/10.1007/s12160-010-9210-8
Haxby, J. V., Connolly, A. C., & Guntupalli, J. S. (2014). Decoding neural representational spaces using multivariate pattern analysis. *Annual Review of Neuroscience, 37*(1), 435–456. https://doi.org/10.1146/annurev-neuro-062012-170325
Haxby, J. V., Hoffman, E. A., & Gobbini, M. I. (2000). The distributed human neural system for face perception. *Trends in Cognitive Sciences, 4*(6), 223–233. https://doi.org/10.1016/S1364-6613(00)01482-0
Hayakawa, S., Kawai, N., & Masataka, N. (2011). The influence of color on snake detection in visual search in human children. *Scientific Reports, 1*, 1–4. https://doi.org/10.1038/srep00080
Hayne, H. (2004). Infant memory development: Implications for childhood amnesia. *Developmental Review, 24*(1), 33–73. https://doi.org/10.1016/j.dr.2003.09.007
Hayne, H., Imuta, K., & Scarf, D. (2015). Memory development during infancy and early childhood across cultures. In J. D. Wright (Ed.), *International encyclopedia of the social & behavioral sciences* (2nd ed., Vol. 15, pp. 147–154). Elsevier.
Hayward, W. G., Crookes, K., Chu, M. H., Favelle, S. K., & Rhodes, G. (2016). Holistic processing of face configurations and components. *Journal of Experimental Psychology: Human Perception and Performance, 42*(10), 1482–1489. https://doi.org/10.1037/xhp0000246
Hazan, C., & Shaver, P. R. (1987). Romantic love conceptualized as an attachment process. *Journal of Personality and Social Psychology, 52*(3), 511–524. https://doi.org/10.1037/0022-3514.52.3.511
Hazlett, E. A. (2016). Neural substrates of emotion-processing abnormalities in borderline personality disorder. *Biological Psychiatry, 79*(2), 74–75. https://doi.org/10.1016/j.biopsych.2015.10.008
Hazlett, H. C., Gu, H., Munsell, B. C., Kim, S. H., Styner, M., Wolff, J. J., Elison, J. T., Swanson, M. R., Zhu, H., Botteron, K. N., Collins, D. L., Constantino, J. N., Dager, S. R., Estes, A. M., Evans, A. C., Fonov, V. S., Gerig, G., Kostopoulos, P., McKinstry, R. C., . . . Piven, J. (2017). Early brain development in infants at high risk for autism spectrum disorder. *Nature, 542*(7641), 348–351. https://doi.org/10.1038/nature21369
Heatherton, T. F., & Vohs, K. D. (2000). Interpersonal evaluations following threats to self: Role of self-esteem. *Journal of Personality and Social Psychology, 78*(4), 725–736. https://doi.org/10.1037/0022-3514.78.4.725
Hebb, D. O. (1949). *The organization of behavior: A neuropsychological approach.* Wiley.
Heck, N. C. (2016). Group psychotherapy with transgender and gender nonconforming adults: Evidence-based practice applications. *Psychiatric Clinics of North America, 40*(1), 157–175. https://doi.org/10.1016/j.psc.2016.10.010
Hedegaard, H., Curtin, S. C., & Warner, M. (2018). *Suicide rates in the United States continue to increase* (National Center for Health Statistics Data Brief, No 309). Centers for Disease Control and Prevention. https://www.cdc.gov/nchs/data/databriefs/db309.pdf
Heider, F. (1944). Social perception and phenomenal causality. *Psychological Review, 51*(6), 358–374. https://doi.org/10.1037/h0055425
Heim, C., Newport, D. J., Mletzko, T., Miller, A. H., & Nemeroff, C. B. (2008). The link between childhood trauma and depression: Insights from HPA axis studies in humans. *Psychoneuroendocrinology, 33*(6), 693–710. https://doi.org/10.1016/j.psyneuen.2008.03.008
Heine, S. J. (2003). An exploration of cultural variation in self-enhancing and self-improving motivations. In V. Murphy-Berman & J. J. Berman (Eds.), *Nebraska symposium on motivation: Vol. 49. Cross-cultural differences in perspectives on the self* (pp. 101–128). University of Nebraska Press.
Heine, S. J. (2005). Where is the evidence for pancultural self-enhancement? A reply to Sedikides, Gaertner, and Toguchi. *Journal of Personality and Social Psychology, 89*(4), 531–538. https://doi.org/10.1037/0022-3514.89.4.531
Heine, S. J., Buchtel, E. E., & Norenzayan, A. (2008). What do cross-national comparisons of self-reported personality traits tell us? The case of conscientiousness. *Psychological Science, 19*(4), 309–313. https://doi.org/10.1111/j.1467-9280.2008.02085.x
Heine, S. J., Lehman, D. R., Markus, H. R., & Kitayama, S. (1999). Is there a universal need for positive self-regard? *Psychological Review, 106*(4), 766–794. https://doi.org/10.1037/0033-295X.106.4.766
Heinz, A., Zhao, X., & Liu, S. (2020). Implications of the association of social exclusion with mental health. *JAMA Psychiatry, 77*(2), 113–114. https://doi.org/10.1001/jamapsychiatry.2019.3009
Helmreich, R., Aronson, E., & LeFan, J. (1970). To err is humanizing sometimes: Effects of self-esteem, competence, and a pratfall on interpersonal attraction. *Journal of Personality and Social Psychology, 16*(2), 259–264. https://doi.org/10.1037/h0029848
Henrich, J., Heine, S. J., & Norenzayan, A. (2010). The weirdest people in the world? *Behavioral and Brain Sciences, 33*(2–3), 61–83. https://doi.org/10.1017/s0140525x0999152x
Henry, P. J., & Sears, D. O. (2002). The Symbolic Racism (2000) Scale. *Political Psychology, 23*(2), 253–283. https://doi.org/10.1111/0162-895x.00281
Herbert, J. D., & Gaudiano, B. A. (2005). Introduction to the special issue on the placebo concept in psychotherapy. *Journal of Clinical Psychology, 61*(7), 787–790. https://doi.org/10.1002/jclp.20125
Herbert, T. B., & Cohen, S. (1993). Stress and immunity in humans: A meta-analytic review. *Psychosomatic Medicine, 55*(4), 364–379. https://doi.org/10.1097/00006842-199307000-00004
Herdener, M., Esposito, F., di Salle, F., Boller, C., Hilti, C. C., Habermeyer, B., Schleffler, K., Wetzel, S., Seifritz, E., & Cattapan-Ludewig, K. (2010). Musical training induces functional plasticity in human hippocampus. *Journal of Neuroscience, 30*(4), 1377–1384. https://doi.org/10.1523/JNEUROSCI.4513-09.2010

Hering, E. (1964). *Outlines of a theory of the light sense* (L. M. Hurvich & D. Jameson, Trans.). Harvard University Press. (Original work published 1878)

Heron, M. (2016). *Deaths: Leading causes for 2014* (National Vital Statistics Reports Volume 65, No. 5). Centers for Disease Control. https://www.cdc.gov/nchs/data/nvsr/nvsr65/nvsr65_05.pdf

Herring, B. E., & Nicoll, R. A. (2016). Long-term potentiation: From CaMKII to AMPA receptor trafficking. *Annual Review of Physiology, 78*(1), 351–365. https://doi.org/10.1146/annurev-physiol-021014-071753

Hess, U., & Thibault, P. (2009). Darwin and emotion expression. *American Psychologist, 64*(2), 120–128. https://doi.org/10.1037/a0013386

Hesse, E., & Main, M. (2000). Disorganized infant, child, and adult attachment: Collapse in behavioral and attentional strategies. *Journal of the American Psychoanalytic Association, 48*(4), 1097–1127. https://doi.org/10.1177/00030651000480041101

Hester, R. K., Delaney, H. D., & Campbell, W. (2011). ModerateDrinking.com and moderation management: Outcomes of a randomized clinical trial with non-dependent problem drinkers. *Journal of Consulting and Clinical Psychology, 79*(2), 215–224. https://doi.org/10.1037/a0022487

Hetey, R. C., & Eberhardt, J. L. (2014). Cops and criminals: The interplay of mechanistic and animalistic dehumanization in the criminal justice system. In P. G. Bain, J. Vaes, & J.-P. Leyens (Eds.), *Humanness and dehumanization* (pp. 147–166). Psychology Press.

Higgins, L. T., & Zheng, M. (2002). An introduction to Chinese psychology—its historical roots until the present day. *Journal of Psychology, 136*(2), 225–239. https://doi.org/10.1080/00223980209604152

Hilgard, E. R. (1973). A neodissociation interpretation of pain reduction in hypnosis. *Psychological Review, 80*(5), 396–411. https://doi.org/10.1037/h0020073

Hilgard, E. R., & Hilgard, J. R. (1975). *Hypnosis in the relief of pain*. Kaufmann.

Hines, T. (1987). Left brain/right brain mythology and implications for management and training. *Academy of Management Review, 12*(4), 600–606. https://doi.org/10.5465/amr.1987.4306708

Hines, T. (2003). *Pseudoscience and the paranormal*. Prometheus.

Hingson, R. W., Zha, W., & Weitzman, E. R. (2009). Magnitude of and trends in alcohol-related mortality and morbidity among U.S. college students ages 18–24, 1998–2005. *Journal of Studies on Alcohol and Drugs, s16*, 12–20. https://doi.org/10.15288/jsads.2009.s16.12

Hirst, W., & Phelps, E. A. (2016). Flashbulb memories. *Current Directions in Psychological Science, 25*(1), 36–41. https://doi.org/10.1177/0963721415622487

Hirst, W., Phelps, E. A., Buckner, R. L., Budson, A. E., Cuc, A., Gabrieli, J. D. E., Johnson, M. K., Lustig, C., Lyle, K. B., Mather, M., Meksin, R., Mitchell, K. J., Ochsner, K. N., Schacter, D. L., Simons, J. S., & Vaidya, C. J. (2009). Long-term memory for the terrorist attack of September 11: Flashbulb memories, event memories, and the factors that influence their retention. *Journal of Experimental Psychology: General, 138*(2), 161–176. https://doi.org/10.1037/a0015527

Hirst, W., Phelps, E. A., Meksin, R., Vaidya, C. J., Johnson, M. K., Mitchell, K. J., Buckner, R. L., Budson, A. E., Gabrieli, J. D. E., Lustig, C., Mather, M., Ochsner, K. N., Schacter, D., Simons, J. S., Lyle, K. B., Cuc, A. F., & Olsson, A. (2015). A ten-year follow-up of a study of memory for the attack of September 11, 2001: Flashbulb memories and memories for flashbulb events. *Journal of Experimental Psychology: General, 144*(3), 604–623. https://doi.org/10.1037/xge0000055

Hobson, J. A. (1999). *Dreaming as delirium: How the brain goes out of its mind*. MIT Press.

Hobson, J. A. (2009). REM sleep and dreaming: Towards a theory of protoconsciousness. *Nature Reviews Neuroscience, 10*(11), 803–813. https://doi.org/10.1038/nrn2716

Hobson, J. A., & McCarley, R. W. (1977). The brain as a dream state generator: An activation-synthesis hypothesis of the dream process. *American Journal of Psychiatry, 134*(12), 1335–1348. https://doi.org/10.1176/ajp.134.12.1335

Hockley, W. E. (2008). The effect of environmental context on recognition memory and claims of remembering. *Journal of Experimental Psychology: Learning, Memory, and Cognition, 34*(6), 1412–1429. https://doi.org/10.1037/a0013016

Hoerger, M., Chapman, B. P., Prigerson, H. G., Fagerlin, A., Mohile, S. G., Epstein, R. M., Lyness, J. M., & Duberstein, P. R. (2014). Personality change pre- to post-loss in spousal caregivers of patients with terminal lung cancer. *Social Psychological and Personality Science, 5*(6), 722–729. https://doi.org/10.1177/1948550614524448

Hoffman, E., Myerberg, N. R., & Morawski, J. G. (2015). Acting otherwise: Resistance, agency, and subjectivities in Milgram's studies of obedience. *Theory & Psychology, 25*(5), 670–689. https://doi.org/10.1177/0959354315608705

Hofmann, S. G., & Smits, J. A. J. (2008). Cognitive-behavioral therapy for adult anxiety disorders: A meta-analysis of randomized placebo-controlled trials. *Journal of Clinical Psychiatry, 69*(4), 621–632. https://doi.org/10.4088/jcp.v69n0415

Hogan, M. J., Parker, J. D., Wiener, J., Watters, C., Wood, L. M., & Oke, A. (2010). Academic success in adolescence: Relationships among verbal IQ, social support and emotional intelligence. *Australian Journal of Psychology, 62*(1), 30–41. https://doi.org/10.1080/00049530903312881

Hogarty, G. E., Anderson, C. M., Reiss, D. J., Kornblith, S. J., Greenwald, D. P., Javna, C. D., & Madonia, M. J. (1986). Family psychoeducation, social skills training, and maintenance chemotherapy in the aftercare treatment of schizophrenia: I. One-year effects of a controlled study on relapse and expressed emotion. *Archives of General Psychiatry, 43*(7), 633–642. https://doi.org/10.1001/archpsyc.1986.01800070019003

Hogg, M. A. (2012). *Social identity and the psychology of groups*. In M. R. Leary & J. P. Tangney (Eds.), *Handbook of self and identity* (pp. 502–519). Guilford Press.

Hogg, M. A. (2016). Social identity theory. In S. McKeown, R. Haji, & N. Ferguson (Eds)., *Understanding peace and conflict through social identity theory* (pp. 3–17). Springer.

Holland, P. C. (1977). Conditioned stimulus as a determinant of the form of the Pavlovian conditioned response. *Journal of Experimental Psychology: Animal Behavior Processes, 3*(1), 77–104. https://doi.org/10.1037/0097-7403.3.1.77

Hollander, E., Bartz, J., Chaplin, W., Phillips, A., Sumner, J., Soorya, L., Anagnostou, E., & Wasserman, S. (2007). Oxytocin increases retention of social cognition in autism. *Biological Psychiatry, 61*(4), 498–503. https://doi.org/10.1016/j.biopsych.2006.05.030

Hollander, E., Novotny, S., Hanratty, M., Yaffe, R., DeCaria, C. M., Aronowitz, B. R., & Mosovich, S. (2003). Oxytocin infusion reduces repetitive behaviors in adults with autistic and Asperger's disorders. *Neuropsychopharmacology, 28*, 193–198. https://doi.org/10.1038/sj.npp.1300021

Holliday, R. (1987). The inheritance of epigenetic defects. *Science, 238*(4824), 163–170. https://doi.org/10.1126/science.3310230

Hollon, S. D., Stewart, M. O., & Strunk, D. (2006). Enduring effects for cognitive behavior therapy in the treatment of depression and anxiety. *Annual Review of Psychology, 57*(1), 285–315. https://doi.org/10.1146/annurev.psych.57.102904.190044

Hollon, S. D., Thase, M. E., & Markowitz, J. C. (2002). Treatment and prevention of depression. *Psychological Science in the Public Interest, 3*(2), 39–77. https://doi.org/10.1111/1529-1006.00008

Holmbeck, G. N. (1996). A model of family relational transformations during the transition to adolescence: Parent-adolescent conflict and adaptation. In J. A. Graber, J. Brooks-Gunn, & A. C. Petersen (Eds.), *Transitions through adolescence* (pp. 67–200). Erlbaum.

Holmboe, K., Rijsdijk, F. V., Hallett, V., Happé, F., Plomin, R., & Ronald, A. (2013). Strong genetic influences on the stability of autistic traits in childhood. *Journal of the American Academy of Child & Adolescent Psychiatry, 53*(2), 221–230. https://doi.org/10.1016/j.jaac.2013.11.001

Holmes, T. H., & Rahe, R. H. (1967). The Social Readjustment Rating Scale. *Journal of Psychosomatic Research, 11*(2), 213–218. https://doi.org/10.1016/0022-3999(67)90010-4

Holstein, S. B., & Premack, D. (1965). On the different effects of random reinforcement and presolution reversal on human concept identification. *Journal of Experimental Psychology, 70*(3), 335–337. https://doi.org/10.1037/h0022276

Honts, C. R., Raskin, D. C., & Kircher, J. C. (1994). Mental and physical countermeasures reduce the accuracy of polygraph tests. *Journal of Applied Psychology, 79*(2), 252–259. https://doi.org/10.1037/0021-9010.79.2.252

Hoogman, M., Bralten, J., Hibar, D. P., Mennes, M., Zwiers, M. P., Schweren, L. S., van Hulzen, K. J. E., Medland, S. E., Shumskaya, E., Jahanshad, N., Zeeuw, P. de, Szekely, E., Sudre, G., Wolfers, T., Onnink, A. M. H., Dammers, J. T., Mostert, J. C., Vives-Gilabert, Y., Kohls, G., . . . Franke, B. (2017). Subcortical brain volume differences in participants with attention deficit hyperactivity disorder in children and adults: A cross-sectional mega-analysis. *The Lancet Psychiatry, 4*(4), 310–319. https://doi.org/10.1016/S2215-0366(17)30049-4

Hooley, J. M (2007). Expressed emotion and relapse of psychopathology. *Annual Review of Clinical Psychology, 3*, 329–352. https://doi.org/10.1146/annurev.clinpsy.2.022305.095236

Hooley, J. M., & Gotlib, I. H. (2000). A diathesis-stress conceptualization of expressed emotion and clinical outcome. *Applied and Preventive Psychology, 9*(3), 135–151. https://doi.org/10.1016/S0962-1849(05)80001-0

Hooshmand, F., Miller, S., Dore, J., Wang, P. W., Hill, S. J., Portillo, N., & Ketter, T. A. (2014). Trends in pharmacotherapy in patients referred to a bipolar specialty clinic, 2000–2011. *Journal of Affective Disorders, 155*, 283–287. https://doi.org/10.1016/j.jad.2013.10.054

Horikawa, T., Tamaki, M., Miyawaki, Y., & Kamitani, Y. (2013). Neural decoding of visual imagery during sleep. *Science, 340*(6132), 639–642. https://doi.org/10.1126/science.1234330

Horn, J. L. (1968). Organization of abilities and the development of intelligence. *Psychological Review, 75*(3), 242–259. https://doi.org/10.1037/h0025662

Horn, J. L., & Hofer, S. M. (1992). Major abilities and development in the adult period. In R. J. Sternberg & C. A. Berg (Eds.), *Intellectual development* (pp. 44–99). Cambridge University Press.

Horn, J. L., & McArdle, J. J. (2007). Understanding human intelligence since Spearman. In R. Cudeck & R. C. MacCallum (Eds.), *Factor analysis at 100: Historical developments and future directions* (pp. 205–247). Erlbaum.

Horn, S. R., Fisher, P. A., Pfeifer, J. H., Allen, N. B., & Berkman, E. T. (2020). Levers and barriers to success in the use of translational neuroscience for the prevention and treatment of mental health and promotion of well-being across the lifespan. *Journal of Abnormal Psychology, 129*(1), 38–48. https://doi.org/10.1037/abn0000465

Hornstein, E. A., & Eisenberger, N. I. (2018). A social safety net: Developing a model of social-support figures as prepared safety stimuli. *Current Directions in Psychological Science, 27*(1), 25–31. https://doi.org/10.1177/0963721417729036

Hoshino, Y., Kumashiro, H., Yashima, Y., Tachibana, R., Watanabe, M., & Furukawa, H. (1980). Early symptoms of autism in children and their diagnostic significance. *Japanese Journal of Child and Adolescent Psychiatry, 21*, 284–299.

House, J. S., Landis, K. R., & Umberson, D. (1988). Social relationships and health. *Science, 241*(4865), 540–545. https://doi.org/10.1126/science.3399889

Hovland, C. I., Janis, I. L., & Kelley, H. H. (1953). *Communication and persuasion: Psychological studies of opinion change*. Yale University Press.

Howlin, P., Mawhood, L., & Rutter, M. (2000). Autism and developmental receptive language disorder—A follow-up comparison in early adult life. II: Social, behavioural, and psychiatric outcomes. *Journal of Child Psychology and Psychiatry, 41*(5), 561–578. https://doi.org/10.1111/1469-7610.00643

Hoyert, D. L., & Xu, J. (2012, October 10). *Deaths: Preliminary data for 2011 (National Vital Statistics Reports* Volume *61, No. 6)*. Centers for Disease Control and Prevention. https://www.cdc.gov/nchs/data/nvsr/nvsr61/nvsr61_06.pdf

Hoyme, H. E., Kalberg, W. O., Elliott, A. J., Blankenship, J., Buckley, D., Marais, A.-S., Manning, M. A., Robinson, L. K., Adam, M. P., Abdul-Rahman, O., Jewett, T., Coles, C. D., Chambers, C., Jones, K. L., Adnams, C. M., Shah, P. E., Riley, E. P., Charness, M. E., Warren, K. R., & May, P. A. (2016). Updated clinical guidelines for diagnosing fetal alcohol spectrum disorders. *Pediatrics, 138*(2), Article e20154256. https://doi.org/10.1542/peds.2015-4256

Hu, X., Cheng, L. Y., Chiu, M. H., & Paller, K. A. (2020). Promoting memory consolidation during sleep: A meta-analysis of targeted memory reactivation. *Psychological Bulletin, 146*(3), 218–244. https://doi.org/10.1037/bul0000223

Huang, C. Y., & Zane, N. (2016). Cultural influences in mental health treatment. *Current Opinion in Psychology, 8*, 131–136. https://doi.org/10.1016/j.copsyc.2015.10.009

Hughes, M. E., & Waite, L. J. (2009). Marital biography and health at mid-life. *Journal of Health and Social Behavior, 50*(3), 344–358. https://doi.org/10.1177/002214650905000307

Hull, C. L. (1943). *Principles of behavior: An introduction to behavior theory*. Appleton-Century.

Hull, J. G., & Bond, C. F. (1986). Social and behavioral consequences of alcohol consumption and expectancy: A meta-analysis. *Psychological Bulletin, 99*(3), 347–360. https://doi.org/10.1037/0033-2909.99.3.347

Hunsley, J., & Mash, E. J. (2007). Evidence-based assessment. *Annual Review of Clinical Psychology, 3*, 29–51. https://doi.org/10.1146/annurev.clinpsy.3.022806.091419

Hunt, E., & Agnoli, F. (1991). The Whorfian hypothesis: A cognitive psychology perspective. *Psychological Review, 98*(3), 377–389. https://doi.org/10.1037/0033-295X.98.3.377

Hunt, R. R., & Einstein, G. O. (1981). Relational and item-specific information in memory. *Journal of Verbal Learning and Verbal Behavior, 20*(5), 497–514. https://doi.org/10.1016/S0022-5371(81)90138-9

Hviid, A., Hansen, J. V., Frisch, M., & Melbye, M. (2019). Measles, mumps, rubella vaccination and autism: A nationwide cohort study. *Annals of Internal Medicine, 170*(8), 513–520. https://doi.org/10.7326/M18-2101

Hyatt, C. J., Assaf, M., Muska, C. E., Rosen, R. I., Thomas, A. D., Johnson, M. R., Hylton, J. L., Andrews, M. M., Reynolds, B. A., Krystal, J. H., Potenza, M. N., & Pearlson, G. D. (2012). Reward-related dorsal striatal activity differences between former and current cocaine dependent individuals during an interactive competitive game. *PLoS ONE, 7*(5), Article e34917. https://doi.org/10.1371/journal.pone.0034917

Hyde, J. S. (2005). The gender similarities hypothesis. *American Psychologist, 60*(6), 581–592. https://doi.org/10.1037/0003-066X.60.6.581

Hyde, L. W., Waller, R., Trentacosta, C. J., Shaw, D. S., Neiderhiser, J. M., Ganiban, J. M., Reiss, D., & Leve, L. D. (2016). Heritable and nonheritable pathways to early callous-unemotional behaviors. *American Journal of Psychiatry, 173*(9), 903–910. https://doi.org/10.1176/appi.ajp.2016.15111381

Hyman, I. E., Boss, S. M., Wise, B. M., McKenzie, K. E., & Caggiano, J. M. (2010). Did you see the unicycling clown? Inattentional blindness while walking and talking on a cell phone. *Applied Cognitive Psychology, 24*(5), 597–607. https://doi.org/10.1002/acp.1638

Hymel, S., Rocke-Henderson, N., & Bonanno, R. A. (2005). Moral disengagement: A framework for understanding bullying among adolescents. *Journal of Social Sciences, 8*, 1–11.

Ilan, A. B., Smith, M. E., & Gevins, A. (2004). Effects of marijuana on neurophysiological signals of working and episodic memory. *Psychopharmacology, 176*(2), 214–222. https://doi.org/10.1007/s00213-004-1868-9

Immunization Safety Review Committee. (2004). *Immunization safety review: Vaccines and autism*. National Academies Press.

Imuta, K., Henry, J. D., Slaughter, V., Selcuk, B., & Ruffman, T. (2016). Theory of mind and prosocial behavior in childhood: A meta-analytic review. *Developmental Psychology, 52*(8), 1192–1205. https://doi.org/10.1037/dev0000140

Innocence Project. (n.d.). *Eyewitness identification reform*. https://innocenceproject.org/eyewitness-identification-reform/

Insel, T. R., & Charney, D. S. (2003). Research on major depression: Strategies and priorities. *Journal of the American Medical Association, 289*(23), 3167–3168. https://doi.org/10.1001/jama.289.23.3167

Insel, T. R., & Young, L. J. (2001). The neurobiology of attachment. *Nature Reviews Neuroscience, 2*(2), 129–136. https://doi.org/10.1038/35053579

Insel, T. R., Cuthbert, B., Garvey, M., Heinssen, R., Pine, D. S., Quinn, K., Sanislow, C., & Wang, P. (2010). Research domain criteria (RDoC): Toward a new classification framework for research on mental disorders. *American Journal of Psychiatry, 167*(7), 748–751. https://doi.org/10.1176/appi.ajp.2010.09091379

Intersex Society of North America. (2008). *How common is intersex?* http://www.isna.org/faq/frequency

Inzlicht, M., & Al-Khindi, T. (2012). ERN and the placebo: A misattribution approach to studying the arousal properties of the error-related negativity. *Journal of Experimental Psychology: General, 141*(4), 799–807. https://doi.org/10.1037/a0027586

Ioannidis, J. P. A. (2014). How to make more published research true. *PLoS Medicine, 11*(10), Article e1001747. https://doi.org/10.1371/journal.pmed.1001747

Ion, A., Iliescu, D., Aldhafri, S., Rana, N., Ratanadilok, K., Widyanti, A., & Nedelcea, C. (2017). A cross-cultural analysis of personality structure through the lens of the HEXACO model. *Journal of Personality Assessment, 99*(1), 25–34. https://doi.org/10.1080/00223891.2016.1187155

Ivanovic, D. M., Leiva, B. P., Pérez, H. T., Olivares, M. G., Díaz, N. S., Urrutia, M. S. C., Almagià, A. F., Toro, T. D., Miller, P. T., Bosch, E. O., & Larraín, C. G. (2004). Head size and intelligence, learning, nutritional status and brain development: Head, IQ, learning, nutrition and brain. *Neuropsychologia, 42*(8), 1118–1131. https://doi.org/10.1016/j.neuropsychologia.2003.11.022

Iyengar, S. S., & Lepper, M. R. (2000). When choice is demotivating: Can one desire too much of a good thing? *Journal of Personality and Social Psychology, 79*(6), 995–1006. https://doi.org/10.1037/0022-3514.79.6.995

Iyengar, S. S., Wells, R. E., & Schwartz, B. (2006). Doing better but feeling worse: Looking for the best job undermines satisfaction. *Psychological Science, 17*(2), 143–150. https://doi.org/10.1111/j.1467-9280.2006.01677.x

Jääskeläinen, E., Juola, P., Hirvonen, N., McGrath, J. J., Saha, S., Isohanni, M., Veijola, J., & Miettunen, J. (2013). A systematic review and meta-analysis of recovery in schizophrenia. *Schizophrenia Bulletin, 39*(6), 1296–1306. https://doi.org/10.1093/schbul/sbs130

Jack, R. E., Garrod, O. G. B., Yu, H., Caldara, R., & Schyns, P. G. (2012). Facial expressions of emotion are not culturally universal. *Proceedings of the National Academy of Sciences, 109*(19), 7241–7244. https://doi.org/10.1073/pnas.1200155109

Jackson, B., Kubzansky, L. D., Cohen, S., Jacobs, D. R., Jr., & Wright, R. J. (2007). Does harboring hostility hurt? Associations between hostility and pulmonary function in the Coronary Artery Risk Development in (Young) Adults (CARDIA) study. *Health Psychology, 26*(3), 333–340. https://doi.org/10.1037/0278-6133.26.3.333

Jackson, J. J., Bogg, T., Walton, K. E., Wood, D., Harms, P. D., Lodi-Smith, J., Edmonds, G. W., & Roberts, B. W. (2009). Not all conscientiousness scales change alike: A multimethod, multisample study of age differences in the facets of conscientiousness. *Journal of Personality and Social Psychology, 96*(2), 446–459. https://doi.org/10.1037/a0014156

Jackson, J. J., Hill, P. L., Payne, B. R., Roberts, B. W., & Stine-Morrow, E. A. L. (2012). Can an old dog learn (and want to experience) new tricks? Cognitive training increases openness to experience in older adults. *Psychology and Aging, 27*(2), 286–292. https://doi.org/10.1037/a0025918

Jackson, S. A., Thomas, P. R., Marsh, H. W., & Smethurst, C. J. (2001). Relationships between flow, self-concept, psychological skills, and performance. *Journal of Applied Sport Psychology, 13*(2), 129–153. https://doi.org/10.1080/104132001753149865

Jacoby, L. L., Kelley, C., Brown, J., & Jasechko, J. (1989). Becoming famous overnight: Limits on the ability to avoid unconscious influences of the past. *Journal of Personality and Social Psychology, 56*(3), 326–338. https://doi.org/10.1037/0022-3514.56.3.326

Jacowitz, K. E., & Kahneman, D. (1995). Measures of anchoring in estimation tasks. *Personality and Social Psychology Bulletin, 21*(11), 1161–1167. https://doi.org/10.1177/01461672952111004

Jain, A., Marshall, J., Buikema, A., Bancroft, T., Kelly, J. P., & Newschaffer, C. (2015). Autism occurrence by MMR vaccine status among US children with older siblings with and without autism. *Journal of the American Medical Association, 313*(15), 1534–1540. https://doi.org/10.1001/jama.2015.3077

James, W. (1884). What is an emotion? *Mind, 9*, 188–205. https://doi.org/10.1093/mind/os-IX.34.188

James, W. (1890). *The principles of psychology*. Henry Holt.

James, W. H. (1983). Decline in coital rates with spouses' ages and duration of marriage. *Journal of Biosocial Science, 15*(1), 83–87. https://doi.org/10.1017/S0021932083006288

Jamieson, G. A. (2007). *Hypnosis and conscious states: The cognitive neuroscience perspective*. Oxford University Press.

Jamieson, J. P., Nock, M. K., & Mendes, W. B. (2012). Mind over matter: Reappraising arousal improves cardiovascular and cognitive responses to stress. *Journal of Experimental Psychology: General, 141*(3), 417–422. https://doi.org/10.1037/a0025719

Janata, P. (2009). The neural architecture of music-evoked autobiographical memories. *Cerebral Cortex, 19*(11), 2579–2594. https://doi.org/10.1093/cercor/bhp008

Jang, K. L., Hu, S., Livesley, W. J., Angleitner, A., Riemann, R., Ando, J., Ono, Y., & Hamer, D. H. (2001). Covariance structure of neuroticism and agreeableness: A twin and molecular genetic analysis of the role of the serotonin transporter gene. *Journal of Personality and Social Psychology, 81*(2), 295–304. https://doi.org/10.1037/0022-3514.81.2.295

Janis, I. L. (1972). *Victims of groupthink: A psychological study of foreign-policy decisions and fiascoes*. Houghton Mifflin.

Jankovic, N., Geelen, A., Streppel, M. T., de Groot, L. C. P. G. M., Orfanos, P., van den Hooven, E. H., Pikhart, H., Boffetta, P., Trichopoulou, A, Bobak, M., Bueno-de-Mesquita, H. B., Kee, F., Franco, O. H., Park, Y., Hallmans, G., Tjønneland, A., May, A. M., Pajak, A., Malyutina, S., . . . Feskens, E. J. (2014). Adherence to a healthy diet according to the World Health Organization guidelines and all-cause mortality in elderly adults from Europe and the United States. *American Journal of Epidemiology, 180*(10), 978–988. https://doi.org/10.1093/aje/kwu229

Jaschik, S. (2015, February 9). Rate my word choice. *Inside Higher Ed*. https://www.insidehighered.com/news/2015/02/09/new-analysis-rate-my-professors-finds-patterns-words-used-describe-men-and-women

Jensen, A. R. (1998). *The g factor: The science of mental ability*. Praeger.

Jensen, P. S., Arnold, L. E., Swanson, J. M., Vitiello, B., Abikoff, H. B., Greenhill, L. L., Hechtman, L., Hinshaw, S. P., Pelham, W. E., Wells, K. C., Conners, C. K., Elliott, G. R., Epstein, J. N., Hoza, B., March, J. S., Molina, B. S. G., Newcorn, J. H., Severe, J. B., Wigal, T., . . . Hur, K. (2007). 3-year follow-up of the NIMH MTA study. *Journal of the American Academy of Child and Adolescent Psychiatry, 46*(8), 989–1002. https://doi.org/10.1097/CHI.0b013e3180686d48

Jensen, P. S., Garcia, J. A., Glied, S., Crowe, M., Foster, M., Schlander, M., Hinshaw, S., Vitiello, B., Arnold, L. E., Elliott, G., Hechtman, L., Newcorn, J. H., Pelham, W. E., Swanson, J., & Wells, K. (2005). Cost-effectiveness of ADHD treatments: Findings from the multimodal treatment study of children with ADHD. *American Journal of Psychiatry, 162*(9), 1628–1636. https://doi.org/10.1176/appi.ajp.162.9.1628

Jensen, P. S., Hinshaw, S. P., Swanson, J. M., Greenhill, L. L., Conners, C. K., Arnold, L. E., Abikoff, H. B., Elliott, G., Hechtman, L., Hoza, B., March, J. S., Newcorn, J. H., Severe, J. B., Vitiello, B., Wells, K., & Wigal, T. (2001). Findings from the NIMH multimodal treatment study of ADHD (MTA): Implications and applications for primary care providers. *Journal of Developmental and Behavioral Pediatrics, 22*(1), 60–73. https://doi.org/10.1097/00004703-200102000-00008

Jetten, J., & Mols, F. (2014). 50:50 hindsight: Appreciating anew the contributions of Milgram's obedience experiments. *Journal of Social Issues, 70*(3), 587–602. https://doi.org/10.1111/josi.12080

Jha, P., Ramasundarahettige, C., Landsman, V., Rostron, B., Thun, M., Anderson, R. N., McAfee, T., & Peto, R. (2013). 21st-century hazards of smoking and benefits of cessation in the United States. *New England Journal of Medicine, 368*(4), 341–350. https://doi.org/10.1056/NEJMsa1211128

Johns, F., Schmader, T., & Martens, A. (2005). Knowing is half the battle—Teaching stereotype threat as a means of improving women's math performance. *Psychological Science, 16*(3), 175–179. https://doi.org/10.1111/j.0956-7976.2005.00799.x

Johnson, R. D., & Downing, L. L. (1979). Deindividuation and valence of cues: Effects on prosocial and antisocial behavior. *Journal of Personality and Social Psychology, 37*(9), 1532–1538. https://doi.org/10.1037/0022-3514.37.9.1532

Johnson, W., Jung, R. E., Colom, R., & Haier, R. J. (2008). Cognitive abilities independent of IQ correlate with regional brain structure. *Intelligence, 36*(1), 18–28. https://doi.org/10.1016/j.intell.2007.01.005

Joiner, T. E. (2005). *Why people die by suicide*. Harvard University Press.

Joiner, T. E., Walker, R. L., Pettit, J. W., Perez, M., & Cukrowicz, K. C. (2005). Evidence-based assessment of depression in adults. *Psychological Assessment, 17*(3), 267–277. https://doi.org/10.1037/1040-3590.17.3.267

Jokela, M., Elovainio, M., Kivimäki, M., & Keltikangas-Järvinen, L. (2008). Temperament and migration patterns in Finland. *Psychological Science, 19*(9), 831–837. https://doi.org/10.1111/j.1467-9280.2008.02164.x

Jones, E. E., & Davis, K. E. (1965). From acts to dispositions: The attribution process in person perception. *Advances in Experimental Social Psychology, 2*, 219–266. https://doi.org/10.1016/S0065-2601(08)60107-0

Jones, M. C. (1924). A laboratory study of fear: The case of Peter. *The Pedagogical Seminary, 31*, 308–315. https://doi.org/10.1080/08856559.1924.9944851

Jones, W., & Klin, A. (2013). Attention to eyes is present but in decline in 2–6-month-old infants later diagnosed with autism. *Nature, 504*, 427–431. https://doi.org/10.1038/nature12715

Jope, R. S. (1999). Anti-bipolar therapy: Mechanism of action of lithium. *Molecular Psychiatry, 4*(2), 117–128. https://doi.org/10.1038/sj.mp.4000494

Jorm, A. F. (2000). Does old age reduce the risk of anxiety and depression?: A review of epidemiological studies across the adult life span. *Psychological Medicine, 30*(1), 11–22. https://doi.org/10.1017/s0033291799001452

Jowett, S., Karatzias, T., Shevlin, M., & Albert, I. (2020). Differentiating symptom profiles of ICD-11 PTSD, complex PTSD, and borderline personality disorder: A latent class analysis in a multiply traumatized sample. *Personality Disorders: Theory, Research, and Treatment, 11*(1), 36–45. https://doi.org/10.1037/per0000346

Junco, R., & Cotten, S. R. (2012). No A 4 U: The relationship between multitasking and academic performance. *Computers & Education, 59*(2), 505–514. https://doi.org/10.1016/j.compedu.2011.12.023

Kagan, J. (2011). Three lessons learned. *Perspectives in Psychological Science, 6*(2), 107–113. https://doi.org/10.1177/1745691611400205

Kagan, J., & Snidman, N. (1991). Infant predictors of inhibited and uninhibited profiles.

Psychological Science, 2(1), 40–44. https://doi.org/10.1111/j.1467-9280.1991.tb00094.x
Kahn, K. B., & McMahon, J. M. (2015). Shooting deaths of unarmed racial minorities: Understanding the role of racial stereotypes on decisions to shoot. *Translational Issues in Psychological Science, 1*(4), 310–320. https://doi.org/10.1037/tps0000047
Kahneman, D. (2007, July 20–22). *A short course in thinking about thinking: A master class by Danny Kahneman.* [Online video.] http://www.edge.org/3rd_culture/kahneman07/kahneman07_index.html/
Kahneman, D. (2011). *Thinking, fast and slow.* Macmillan.
Kahneman, D., & Tversky, A. (1979). Prospect theory: An analysis of decision under risk. *Econometrica, 47*(2), 263–291. https://doi.org/0012-9682(197903)47:2<263:PTAAOD>2.0.CO;2-3
Kallio, S., & Revonsuo, A. (2003). Hypnotic phenomena and altered states of consciousness: A multilevel framework of description and explanation. *Contemporary Hypnosis, 20*(3), 111–164. https://doi.org/10.1002/ch.273
Kamara, S., Colom, R., Johnson, W., Deary, I. J., Haier, R., Waber, D. P., Lepage, C., Ganjavi, H., Jung, R., Evans, A. C., & the Brain Development Cooperative Groups. (2011). Cortical thickness correlates of specific cognitive performance accounted for by the general factor of intelligence in healthy children aged 6 to 18. *NeuroImage, 55*(4), 1443–1453. https://doi.org/10.1016/j.neuroimage.2011.01.016
Kamin, L. J. (1959). The delay-of-punishment gradient. *Journal of Comparative and Physiological Psychology, 52*(4), 434–437. https://doi.org/10.1037/h0045089
Kamp Dush, C. M., Yavorsky, J. E., & Schoppe-Sullivan, S. J. (2018). What are men doing while women perform extra unpaid labor? Leisure and specialization at the transitions to parenthood. *Sex Roles, 78*, 715–730. https://doi.org/10.1007/s11199-017-0841-0
Kandel, E. R. (2001). The molecular biology of memory storage: A dialogue between genes and synapses. *Science, 294*(5544), 1030–1038. https://doi.org/10.1126/science.1067020
Kandel, E. R., Dudai, Y., & Mayford, M. R. (2014). The molecular and systems biology of memory. *Cell, 157*(1), 163–186. https://doi.org/10.1016/j.cell.2014.03.001
Kane, M. J., Hambrick, D. Z., & Conway, A. R. A. (2005). Working memory capacity and fluid intelligence are strongly related constructs: Comment on Ackerman, Beier, and Boyle (2005). *Psychological Bulletin, 131*(1), 66–71. https://doi.org/10.1037/0033-2909.131.1.66
Kang, D. H., Coe, C. L., McCarthy, D. O., & Ershler, W. B. (1997). Immune responses to final exams in healthy and asthmatic adolescents. *Nursing Research, 46*(1), 12–19. https://doi.org/10.1097/00006199-199701000-00003
Kanno, T., Iijima, K., Abe, Y., Koike, T., Shimada, N., Hoshi, T., Sano, N., Ohyauchi, M., Atsumi, T., Konishi, H., Asonuma, S., & Shimosegawa, T. (2013). Hemorrhagic ulcers after Great East Japan earthquake and tsunami: Features of post-disaster hemorrhagic ulcers. *Digestion, 87*, 40–46. https://doi.org/10.1159/000343937
Kanwisher, N., Tong, F., & Nakayama, K. (1998). The effect of face inversion on the human fusiform face area. *Cognition, 68*(1), B1–B11. https://doi.org/10.1016/S0010-0277(98)00035-3
Kapur, S. E., Craik, F. I. M., Tulving, E., Wilson, A. A., Houle, S., & Brown, G. M. (1994). Neuroanatomical correlates of encoding in episodic memory: Levels of processing effects. *Proceedings of the National Academy of Sciences, 91*(6), 2008–2011. https://doi.org/10.1073/pnas.91.6.2008
Karney, B. R., & Bradbury, T. N. (2020). Research on marital satisfaction and stability in the 2010s: Challenging conventional wisdom. *Journal of Marriage and Family, 82*(1), 100–116. https://doi.org/10.1111/jomf.12635
Karpicke, J. D. (2012). Retrieval-based learning: Active retrieval promotes meaningful learning. *Current Directions in Psychological Science, 21*(3), 157–163. https://doi.org/10.1177/0963721412443552
Karpicke, J. D., & Blunt, J. R. (2011). Retrieval practice produces more learning than elaborative studying with concept mapping. *Science, 331*(6018), 772–775. https://doi.org/10.1126/science.1199327
Karyotaki, E., Efthimiou, O., Miguel, C., Bermpohl, F., Furukawa, T. A., Cuijpers, P., Individual Patient Data Meta-Analyses for Depression (IPDMA-DE) Collaboration, Riper, H., Patel, V., Mira, A., Gemmil, A. W., Yeung, A. S., Lange, A., Williams, A. D., Mackinnon, A., Geraedts, A., van Straten, A., Meyer, B., Björkelund, C., . . . Forsell, Y. (2021). Internet-based cognitive behavioral therapy for depression: A systematic review and individual patient data network meta-analysis. *JAMA Psychiatry, 78*(4), 361–371. https://doi.org/10.1001/jamapsychiatry.2020.4364
Kasari, C., Paparella, T., Freeman, S., & Jahromi, L. B. (2008). Language outcomes in autism: Randomized comparison of joint attention and play interventions. *Journal of Counseling and Clinical Psychology, 76*(1), 125–137. https://doi.org/10.1037/0022-006X.76.1.125
Kassin, S. M., Dror, I. E., & Kukucka, J. (2013). The forensic confirmation bias: Problems, perspectives, and proposed solutions. *Journal of Applied Research in Memory and Cognition, 2*(1), 42–52. https://doi.org/10.1016/j.jarmac.2013.01.001
Kaufman, S. B., Yaden, D. B., Hyde, E., & Tsukayama, E. (2019). The light vs. dark triad of personality: Contrasting two very different profiles of human nature. *Frontiers in Psychology, 10*, Article 467. https://doi.org/10.3389/fpsyg.2019.00467
Kawakami, K., Dovidio, J. F., & van Kamp, S. (2005). Kicking the habit: Effects of nonstereotypic association training and correction processes on hiring decisions. *Journal of Experimental Social Psychology, 41*(1), 68–75. https://doi.org/10.1016/j.jesp.2004.05.004
Kawakami, K., Dovidio, J. F., Moll, J., Hermsen, S., & Russin, A. (2000). Just say no (to stereotyping): Effects of training in the negation of stereotypic associations on stereotype activation. *Journal of Personality and Social Psychology, 78*(5), 871–888. https://doi.org/10.1037/0022-3514.78.5.871
Kazak, A., Simms, S., & Rourke, M. (2002). Family systems practice in pediatric psychology. *Journal of Pediatric Psychology, 27*(2), 133–143. https://doi.org/10.1093/jpepsy/27.2.133
Kazdin, A. E. (1994). Methodology, design, and evaluation in psychotherapy research. In A. E. Bergin & S. L. Garfield (Eds.), *International handbook of behavior modification and behavior change* (4th ed., pp. 19–71). Wiley.
Kazdin, A. E. (2008). Evidence-based treatment and practice: New opportunities to bridge clinical research and practice, enhance the knowledge base, and improve patient care. *American Psychologist, 63*(3), 146–159. https://doi.org/10.1037/0003-066x.63.3.146
Kazdin, A. E., & Benjet, C. (2003). Spanking children: Evidence and issues. *Current Directions in Psychological Science, 12*(3), 99–103. https://doi.org/10.1111/1467-8721.01239
Kazdin, A. E., & Blase, S. L. (2011). Rebooting psychotherapy research and practice to reduce the burden of mental illness. *Perspectives on Psychological Science, 6*(1), 21–37. https://doi.org/10.1177/1745691610393527
Keane, M. (1987). On retrieving analogues when solving problems. *The Quarterly Journal of Experimental Psychology, 39*(1), 29–41. https://doi.org/10.1080/02724988743000015
Keane, M. M., Gabrieli, J. D. E., Mapstone, H. C., Johnson, K. A., & Corkin, S. (1995). Double dissociation of memory capacities after bilateral occipital-lobe or medial temporal-lobe lesions. *Brain, 118*(5), 1129–1148. https://doi.org/10.1093/brain/118.5.1129
Keel, P. K., & Brown, T. A. (2010). Update on course and outcome in eating disorders. *International Journal of Eating Disorders, 43*(3), 195–204. https://doi.org/10.1002/eat.20810
Keel, P. K., & Mitchell, J. E. (1997). Outcome in bulimia nervosa. *American Journal of Psychiatry, 154*(3), 313–321. https://doi.org/10.1176/ajp.154.3.313
Keel, P. K., Baxter, M. G., Heatherton, T. F., & Joiner, T. E., Jr. (2007). A 20-year longitudinal study of body weight, dieting, and eating disorder symptoms. *Journal of Abnormal Psychology, 116*(2), 422–432. https://doi.org/10.1037/0021-843X.116.2.422
Keil, F. C. (2011). Science starts early. *Science, 331*(6020), 1022–1023. https://doi.org/10.1126/science.1195221
Keller, H. (2018). Universality claim of attachment theory: Children's socioemotional development across cultures. *Proceedings of the National Academy of Sciences, 115*(45), 11414–11419. https://doi.org/10.1073/pnas.1720325115
Keller, J., & Bless, H. (2008). Flow and regulatory compatibility: An experimental approach to the flow model of intrinsic motivation. *Personality and Social Psychology Bulletin, 34*(2), 196–209. https://doi.org/10.1177/0146167207310026
Keller, M. B., McCullough, J. P., Klein, D. N., Arnow, B., Dunner, D. L., Gelenberg, A. J., Markowitz, J. C., Nemeroff, C. B., Russell, J. M., Thase, M. E., Trivedi, M. H., Blalock, J. A., Borian, F. E., Jody, D. N, DeBattista, C., Koran, L. M., Schatzberg, A. F., Fawcett, J., Hirschfeld, R. M. A., . . . Zajecka, J. (2000). A comparison of nefazodone, a cognitive behavioral analysis system of psychotherapy, and their combination for the treatment of chronic depression. *New England Journal of Medicine, 342*, 1462–1470. https://doi.org/10.1056/NEJM200005183422001
Kelley, N. J., Hortensius, R., Schutter, D. J. L. G., & Harmon-Jones, E. (2017). The relationship of approach/avoidance motivation and asymmetric frontal cortical activity: A review of studies manipulating frontal asymmetry. *International Journal of Psychophysiology, 119*, 19–30. https://doi.org/10.1016/j.ijpsycho.2017.03.001

Kellman, P. J., Spelke, E. S., & Short, K. R. (1986). Infant perception of object unity from translatory motion in depth and vertical translation. *Child Development, 57*(1), 72–86. https://doi.org/10.2307/1130639

Kelly, G. A. (1955). *The psychology of personal constructs*. Norton.

Keltner, D., & Anderson, C. (2000). Saving face for Darwin: The functions and uses of embarrassment. *Current Directions in Psychological Science, 9*(6), 187–192. https://doi.org/10.1111/1467-8721.00091

Keltner, D., & Bonanno, G. A. (1997). A study of laughter and dissociation: Distinct correlates of laughter and smiling during bereavement. *Journal of Personality and Social Psychology, 73*(4), 687–702. https://doi.org/10.1037/0022-3514.73.4.687

Kendler, K. S., Prescott, C. A., Myers, J., & Neale, M. C. (2003). The structure of genetic and environmental risk factors for common psychiatric and substance use disorders in men and women. *Archives of General Psychiatry, 60*(9), 929–937. https://doi.org/10.1001/archpsyc.60.9.929

Kennedy, D. P., & Adolphs, R. (2010). Impaired fixation to eyes following amygdala damage arises from abnormal bottom-up attention. *Neuropsychologia, 48*(12), 3392–3398. https://doi.org/10.1016/j.neuropsychologia.2010.06.025

Kennedy, D. P., & Adolphs, R. (2010). Impaired fixation to eyes following amygdala damage arises from abnormal bottom-up attention. *Neuropsychologia, 48*(12), 3392–3398. https://doi.org/10.1016/j.neuropsychologia.2010.06.025

Kennedy, Q., Mather, M., & Carstensen, L. L. (2004). The role of motivation in the age-related positivity effect in autobiographical memory. *Psychological Science, 15*(3), 208–214. https://doi.org/10.1111/j.0956-7976.2004.01503011.x

Kennedy, S. (2018). Raising awareness about prescription and stimulant abuse in college students through on-campus community involvement projects. *Journal of Undergraduate Neuroscience Education, 17*(1), A50–A53.

Kennedy, S. H., Giacobbe, P., Rizvi, S., Placenza, F. M., Nishikawa, Y., Mayberg, H. S., & Lozano, A. M. (2011). Deep brain stimulation for treatment-resistant depression: Follow-up after 3 to 6 years. *American Journal of Psychiatry, 168*(5), 502–510. https://doi.org/10.1176/appi.ajp.2010.10081187

Kenrick, D. T., & Funder, D. C. (1991). The person-situation debate: Do personality traits really exist? In V. J. Derlega, B. A. Winstead, & W. H. Jones (Eds.), *Personality: Contemporary theory and research* (pp. 149–174). Nelson Hall.

Kerr, N. L. (1998). HARKing: Hypothesizing after the results are known. *Personality and Social Psychology Review, 2*(3), 196–217. https://doi.org/10.1207/s15327957pspr0203_4

Kessler, R. C., & Wang, P. S. (2008). The descriptive epidemiology of commonly occurring mental disorders in the United States. *Annual Review of Public Health, 29*(1), 115–129. https://doi.org/10.1146/annurev.publhealth.29.020907.090847

Kessler, R. C., Adler, L., Barkley, R., Biederman, J., Conners, C. K., Demler, O., Faraone, S. V., Greenhill, L. L., Howes, M. J., Secnik, K., Spencer, T., Ustun, T. B., Walters, E. E., & Zaslavsky, A. M. (2006). The prevalence and correlates of adult ADHD in the United States: Results from the national comorbidity survey replication. *American Journal of Psychiatry, 163*(4), 716–723. https://doi.org/10.1176/ajp.2006.163.4.716

Kessler, R. C., Berglund, P., Demler, O., Jin, R., Koretz, D., Merikangas, K. R., Rush, A. J., Walters, E. E., & Wang, P. S. (2003). The epidemiology of major depressive disorder: Results from the national comorbidity survey replication (NCS-R). *Journal of the American Medical Association, 289*(23), 3095–3105. https://doi.org/10.1001/jama.289.23.3095

Kessler, R. C., Chiu, W. T., Demler, O., & Walters, E. E. (2005a). Prevalence, severity, and comorbidity of twelve-month DSM-IV disorders in the national comorbidity survey replication (NCS-R). *Archives of General Psychiatry, 62*(6), 617–627. https://doi.org/10.1001/archpsyc.62.6.617

Kessler, R. C., Demler, O., Frank, R. G., Olfson, M., Pincus, H. A., Walters, E. E., Wang, P., Wells, K. B., & Zaslavsky, A. M. (2005b). Prevalence and treatment of mental disorders, 1990 to 2003. *New England Journal of Medicine, 352*, 2515–2523. https://doi.org/10.1056/NEJMsa043266

Kessler, R. C., McGonagle, K. A., Zhao, S., Nelson, C. B., Hughes, M., Eshleman, S., Wittchen, H.-U., & Kendler, K. S. (1994). Lifetime and 12-month prevalence of DSM-III-R psychiatric disorders in the United States: Results from the national comorbidity study. *Archives of General Psychiatry, 51*(1), 8–19. https://doi.org/10.1001/archpsyc.1994.03950010008002

Keyes, K. M., Cerdá, M., Brady, J. E., Havens, J. R., & Galea, S. (2014). Understanding the rural–urban differences in nonmedical prescription opioid use and abuse in the United States. *American Journal of Public Health, 104*(2), e52–e59. https://doi.org/10.2105/AJPH.2013.301709

Kida, T. E. (2006). *Don't believe everything you think: The 6 basic mistakes we make in thinking*. Prometheus Books.

Kiecolt-Glaser, J. K., & Glaser, R. I. (1991). Stress and immune function in humans. In R. Ader, D. Felten, and N. Cohen (Eds.), *Psychoneuroimmunology II* (pp. 849–867). Academic Press.

Kiecolt-Glaser, J. K., McGuire, L., Robles, T. F., & Glaser, R. (2002). Emotions, morbidity, and mortality: New perspectives from psychoneuroimmunology. *Annual Review of Psychology, 53*(1), 83–107. https://doi.org/10.1146/annurev.psych.53.100901.135217

Kihlstrom, J. F. (2005). Dissociative disorder. *Annual Review of Clinical Psychology, 1*(1), 227–253. https://doi.org/10.1146/annurev.clinpsy.1.102803.143925

Kihlstrom, J. F. (2016a). Unconscious mental life. In H. S. Friedman (Ed.), *Encyclopedia of mental health* (2nd ed., pp. 345–349). Academic Press.

Kihlstrom, J. F. (2016b). Hypnosis. In H. S. Friedman (Ed.), *Encyclopedia of mental health* (2nd ed., Vol. 2, pp. 361–365). Academic Press.

Kihlstrom, J. F., & Eich, E. (1994). Altering states of consciousness. In D. Druckman & R. A. Bjork (Eds.), *Learning, remembering, and believing: Enhancing performance* (pp. 207–248). National Academy Press.

Kilbride, J. E., Robbins, M. C., & Kilbride, P. L. (1970). The comparative motor development of Baganda, American white, and American black infants. *American Anthropologist, 72*(6), 1422–1428. https://doi.org/10.1525/aa.1970.72.6.02a00160

Kim, M. J., Solomon, K. M., Neta, M., Davis, F. C., Oler, J. A., Mazzulla, E. C., & Whalen, P. J. (2016). A face versus non-face context influences amygdala responses to masked fearful eye whites. *Social Cognitive and Affective Neuroscience, 11*(12), 1933–1941. https://doi.org/10.1093/scan/nsw110

Kim, S. J., Lyoo, I. K., Hwang, J., Chung, A., Hoon Sung, Y., Kim, J., Kwon, D.-H., Chang, K. H., & Renshaw, P. F. (2006). Prefrontal grey-matter changes in short-term and long-term abstinent methamphetamine abusers. *International Journal of Neuropsychopharmacology, 9*(2), 221–228. https://doi.org/10.1017/S1461145705005699

Kirsch, I., & Lynn, S. J. (1995). The altered state of hypnosis: Changes in the theoretical landscape. *American Psychologist, 50*(10), 846–858. https://doi.org/10.1037/0003-066X.50.10.846

Kirsch, I., Deacon, B. J., Huedo-Medina, T. B., Scoboria, A., Moore, T. J., & Johnson, B. T. (2008). Initial severity and antidepressant benefits: A metaanalysis of data submitted to the Food and Drug Administration. *PLoS Medicine, 5*(2), Article e45. https://doi.org/10.1371/journal.pmed.0050045

Klatsky, A. (2010). Alcohol and cardiovascular health. *Physiology and Behavior, 100*(1), 76–81. https://doi.org/10.1016/j.physbeh.2009.12.019

Klein, A. M., van Niekerk, R., ten Brink, G., Rapee, R. M., Hudson, J. L., Bögels, S. M., Becker, E. S., & Rinck, M. (2017). Biases in attention, interpretation, memory, and associations in children with varying levels of spider fear: Inter-relations and prediction of behavior. *Journal of Behavior Therapy and Experimental Psychiatry, 54*, 285–291. https://doi.org/10.1016/j.jbtep.2016.10.001

Klein, R. A., Ratliff, K. A., Vianello, M., Adams, R. B., Jr., Bahník, Š., Bernstein, M. J., Bocian, K., Brandt, M. J., Brooks, B., Brumbaugh, C. C., Cemalcilar, Z., Chandler, J., Cheong, W., Davis, W. E., Devos, T., Eisner, M., Frankowska, N., Furrow, D., Galliani, E. M., . . . Nosek, B. A. (2014). Investigating variation in replicability: A "many labs" replication project. *Social Psychology, 45*(3), 142–152. https://doi.org/10.1027/1864-9335/a000178

Klein, R. G., Mannuzza, S., Olazagasti, M. A. R., Roizen, E., Hutchison, J. A., Lashua, E. C., & Castellanos, F. X. (2012). Clinical and functional outcome of childhood attention-deficit/hyperactivity disorder 33 years later. *Archives of General Psychiatry, 69*(2), 1295–1303. https://doi.org/10.1001/archgenpsychiatry.2012.271

Klein, S. B. (2012). Self, memory, and the self-reference effect: An examination of conceptual and methodological issues. *Personality and Social Psychology Review, 16*(3), 283–300. https://doi.org/10.1177/1088868311434214

Klin, A., Jones, W., Schultz, R., & Volkmar, F. (2003). The enactive mind, or from actions to cognition: Lessons from autism. *Philosophical Transactions of the Royal Society of London. Series B: Biological Sciences, 358*(1430), 345–360. https://doi.org/10.1098/rstb.2002.1202

Klingberg, T. (2010). Training and plasticity of working memory. *Trends in Cognitive Sciences, 14*(7), 317–324. https://doi.org/10.1016/j.tics.2010.05.002
Klonoff, E. A. (2014). Introduction to the special section on discrimination. *Health Psychology, 33*(1), 1–2. https://doi.org/10.1037/hea0000070
Klonsky, E. D., May, A. M., & Saffer, B. Y. (2016). Suicide, suicide attempts, and suicidal ideation. *Annual Review of Clinical Psychology, 12*, 307–330. https://doi.org/10.1146/annurev-clinpsy-021815-093204
Klump, K. L., Culbert, K. M., & Sisk, C. L. (2017). Sex differences in binge eating: Gonadal hormone effects across development. *Annual Review of Clinical Psychology, 13*, 183–207. https://doi.org/10.1146/annurev-clinpsy-032816-045309
Knopp, J., Knowles, S., Bee, P., Lovell, K., & Bower, P. (2013). A systematic review of predictors and moderators of response to psychological therapies in OCD: Do we have enough empirical evidence to target treatment? *Clinical Psychology Review, 33*(8), 1067–1081. https://doi.org/10.1016/j.cpr.2013.08.008
Knowles, T. P., Vendruscolo, M., & Dobson, C. M. (2014). The amyloid state and its association with protein misfolding diseases. *Nature Reviews: Molecular Cell Biology, 15*, 384–396. https://doi.org/10.1038/nrm3810
Knox, S. S., Weidner, G., Adelman, A., Stoney, C. M., & Ellison, R. C. (2004). Hostility and physiological risk in the National Heart, Lung, and Blood Institute Family Heart Study. *Archives of Internal Medicine, 164*(22), 2442–2447. https://doi.org/10.1001/archinte.164.22.2442
Knutson, B., Fong, G. W., Adams, C. M., Varner, J. L., & Hommer, D. (2001). Dissociation of reward anticipation and outcome with event-related fMRI. *NeuroReport, 12*(17), 3683–3687. https://doi.org/10.1097/00001756-200112040-00016
Kobasa, S. C. (1979). Personality and resistance to illness. *American Journal of Community Psychology, 7*(4), 413–423. https://doi.org/10.1007/BF00894383
Koch, J. L. (1891). *Die psychopathischen minderwertigkeiten*. Maier.
Kochanek, K. D., Arias, E., & Bastian, B. A. (2016, June). *The effect of changes in selected age-specific causes of death on non-Hispanic white life expectancy between 2000 and 2014* (National Center for Health Statistics Data Brief, No. 250). Centers for Disease Control and Prevention. https://www.cdc.gov/nchs/data/databriefs/db250.pdf
Kochanek, K. D., Murphy, S. L., Xu, J., & Tejada-Vera, B. (2016, June 30). *Deaths: Final data for 2014* (National Vital Statistics Reports Volume 65, No. 4). Centers for Disease Control and Prevention. https://www.cdc.gov/nchs/data/nvsr/nvsr65/nvsr65_04.pdf
Kocsis, J. H., Rush, A. J., Markowitz, J. C., Borian, F. E., Dunner, D. L., Koran, L. M., Klein, D. N., Trivedi, M. H., Arnow, B., Keitner, G., Kornstein, S. G., & Keller, M. B. (2003). Continuation treatment of chronic depression: A comparison of nefazodone, cognitive behavioral analysis system of psychotherapy, and their combination. *Psychopharmacology Bulletin, 37*(4), 73–87.
Koh, K., Joiner, W. J., Wu, M. N., Yue, Z., Smith, C. J., & Sehgal, A. (2008). Identification of SLEEPLESS, a sleep-promoting factor. *Science, 321*(5887), 372–376. https://doi.org/10.1126/science.1155942
Kohlberg, L. (1984). *Essays on moral development: Vol. 2. The psychology of moral development*. Harper & Row.
Köhler, W. (1925). *The mentality of apes*. Harcourt Brace.
Kohn, D. (2008, March 11). Cases without borders: Psychotherapy for all. *New York Times*. http://www.nytimes.com/2008/03/11/health/11psych.html
Kolar, D. W., Funder, D. C., & Colvin, C. R. (1996). Comparing the accuracy of personality judgments by the self and knowledgeable others. *Journal of Personality, 64*(2), 311–337. https://doi.org/10.1111/j.1467-6494.1996.tb00513.x
Koma, W., Artiga, S., Neuman, T., Claxton, G., Rae, M., Kates, J., & Michaud, J. (2020). *Low-income and communities of color at higher risk of serious illness if infected with coronavirus*. Kaiser Family Foundation. https://www.kff.org/coronavirus-covid-19/issue-brief/low-income-and-communities-of-color-at-higher-risk-of-serious-illness-if-infected-with-coronavirus/
Kontsevich, L. L., & Tyler, C. W. (2004). What makes Mona Lisa smile? *Vision Research, 44*(13), 1493–1498. https://doi.org/10.1016/j.visres.2003.11.027
Koob, G. F., & Mason, B. J. (2016). Existing and future drugs for the treatment of the dark side of addiction. *Annual Review of Pharmacology and Toxicology, 56*, 299–322. https://doi.org/10.1146/annurev-pharmtox-010715-103143
Koob, G. F., & Volkow, N. D. (2010). *Neurocircuitry of addiction. Neuropharmacology, 35*, 217–238. https://doi.org/10.1038/npp.2009.110
Koole, S. L., Dijksterhuis, A., & van Knippenberg, A. (2001). What's in a name: Implicit self-esteem and the automatic self. *Journal of Personality and Social Psychology, 80*(4), 669–685. https://doi.org/10.1037/0022-3514.80.4.669
Koole, S. L., Schlinkert, C., Maldei, T., & Baumann, N. (2019). Becoming who you are: An integrative review of self-determination theory and personality systems interactions theory. *Journal of Personality, 87*(1), 15–36. https://doi.org/10.1111/jopy.12380
Koopmann-Holm, B., & Tsai, J. L. (2014). Focusing on the negative: Cultural differences in expressions of sympathy. *Journal of Personality and Social Psychology, 107*(6), 1092–1115. https://doi.org/10.1037/a0037684
Kosslyn, S. M., Thompson, W. L., Costantini-Ferrando, M. F., Alpert, N. M., & Spiegel, D. (2000). Hypnotic visual illusion alters color processing in the brain. *American Journal of Psychiatry, 157*(8), 1279–1284. https://doi.org/10.1176/appi.ajp.157.8.1279
Kowalski, P., & Taylor, A. K. (2004). Ability and critical thinking as predictors of change in students' psychological misconceptions. *Journal of Instructional Psychology, 31*(4), 297–303.
Kozorovitskiy, Y., & Gould, E. (2004). Dominance hierarchy influences adult neurogenesis in the dentate gyrus. *Journal of Neuroscience, 24*(30), 6755–6759. https://doi.org/10.1523/JNEUROSCI.0345-04.2004
Kragel, P. A., & LaBar, K. S. (2016). Decoding the nature of emotion in the brain. *Trends in Cognitive Sciences, 20*(6), 444–455. https://doi.org/10.1016/j.tics.2016.03.011
Kramer, A. D. I., Guillory, J. E., & Hancock, J. T. (2014). Experimental evidence of massive-scale emotional contagion through social networks. *Proceedings of the National Academy of Sciences, 111*(24), 8788–8790. https://doi.org/10.1073/pnas.1320040111
Kramer, M. S., Aboud, F., Mironova, E., Vanilovich, I., Platt, R. W., Matush, L., Igumnov, S., Fombonne, E., Bogdanovich, N., Ducruet, T., Collet, J.-P., Chalmers, B., Hodnett, E., Davidovsky, S., Skugarevsky, O., Trofimovich, O., Kozlova, L., Shapiro, S., & Promotion of Breastfeeding Intervention Trial (PROBIT) Study Group. (2008). Breastfeeding and child cognitive development: New evidence from a large randomized trial. *Archives of General Psychiatry, 65*(5), 578–584. https://doi.org/10.1001/archpsyc.65.5.578
Krantz, D. S., & McCeney, M. K. (2002). Effects of psychological and social factors on organic disease: A critical assessment of research on coronary heart disease. *Annual Review of Psychology, 53*(1), 341–369. https://doi.org/10.1146/annurev.psych.53.100901.135208
Kraus, M. W., Rucker, J. M., & Richeson, J. A. (2017). Americans misperceive racial economic equality. *Proceedings of the National Academy of Sciences, 114*(39), 10324–10331. https://doi.org/10.1073/pnas.1707719114
Kraus, R., Desmond, S. A., & Palmer, Z. D. (2015). Being thankful: Examining the relationship between young adult religiosity and gratitude. *Journal of Religion and Health, 54*(4), 1331–1344. https://doi.org/10.1007/s10943-014-9923-2
Kringelbach, M. L., & Berridge, K. C. (2009). Towards a functional neuroanatomy of pleasure and happiness. *Trends in Cognitive Sciences, 13*(11), 479–487. https://doi.org/10.1016/j.tics.2009.08.006
Kroes, M. C. W., Schiller, D., LeDoux, J. E., & Phelps, E. A. (2016). Translational approaches targeting reconsolidation. *Current Topics in Behavioral Neurosciences, 28*, 197–230. https://doi.org/10.1007/7854_2015_5008
Kross, E., & Ayduk, O. (2017). Self-distancing: Theory, research, and current directions. In J. M. Olson (Ed.), *Advances in experimental social psychology* (Vol. 55, pp. 81–136). Academic Press. https://doi.org/10.1016/bs.aesp.2016.10.002
Krueger, R. F. (1999). The structure of common mental disorders. *Archives of General Psychiatry, 56*(10), 921–926. https://doi.org/10.1001/archpsyc.56.10.921
Krueger, R. F., & Markon, K. E. (2006). Understanding psychopathology: Melding behavior genetics, personality, and quantitative psychology to develop an empirically based model. *Current Directions in Psychological Science, 15*(3), 113–117. https://doi.org/10.1111/j.0963-7214.2006.00418.x
Kruger, J., & Dunning, D. (1999). Unskilled and unaware of it: How difficulties in recognizing one's own incompetence lead to inflated self-assessments. *Journal of Personality and Social Psychology, 77*(6), 1121–1134. https://doi.org/10.1037/0022-3514.77.6.1121

Kuchibhotla, K. V., Goldman, S. T., Lattarulo, C. R., Wu, H.-Y., Hyman, B. T., & Bacskai, B. J. (2008). Aß plaques lead to aberrant regulation of calcium homeostasis *in vivo* resulting in structural and functional disruption of neuronal networks. *Neuron, 59*(2), 214–225. https://doi.org/10.1016/j.neuron.2008.06.008

Kuhl, P. K. (2000). A new view of language acquisition. *Proceedings of the National Academy of Sciences, 97*(22), 11850–11857. https://doi.org/10.1073/pnas.97.22.11850

Kuhl, P. K. (2004). Early language acquisition: Cracking the speech code. *Nature Reviews Neuroscience, 5*, 831–843. https://doi.org/10.1038/nrn1533

Kuhl, P. K. (2007). Is speech learning "gated" by the social brain? *Developmental Science, 10*(1), 110–120. https://doi.org/10.1111/j.1467-7687.2007.00572.x

Kuhl, P. K., Stevens, E., Hayashi, A., Deguchi, T., Kiritani, S., & Iverson, P. (2006). Infants show a facilitation effect for native language phonetic perception between 6 and 12 months. *Developmental Science, 9*(2), F13–F21. https://doi.org/10.1111/j.1467-7687.2006.00468.x

Kuhl, P. K., Tsao, F.-M., & Liu, H.-M. (2003). Foreign-language experience in infancy: Effects of short-term exposure and social interaction on phonetic learning. *Proceedings of the National Academy of Sciences, 100*(15), 9096–9101. https://doi.org/10.1073/pnas.1532872100

Kuhn, C., Swartzwelder, S., & Wilson, W. (2003). *Buzzed: The straight facts about the most used and abused drugs from alcohol to ecstasy* (2nd ed.). Norton.

Kühn, S., & Gallinat, J. (2012). Quantitative meta-analysis on state and trait aspects of auditory verbal hallucinations in schizophrenia. *Schizophrenia Bulletin, 38*(4), 779–786. https://doi.org/10.1093/schbul/sbq152

Kulhara, P., & Chakrabarti, S. (2001). Culture and schizophrenia and other psychotic disorders. *Psychiatric Clinics of North America, 24*(3), 449–464. https://doi.org/10.1016/S0193-953X(05)70240-9

Kuncel, N. R., Hezlett, S. A., & Ones, D. S. (2004). Academic performance, career potential, creativity, and job performance: Can one construct predict them all? *Journal of Personality and Social Psychology, 86*(1), 148–161. https://doi.org/10.1037/0022-3514.86.1.148

Kunda, Z., & Spencer, S. J. (2003). When do stereotypes come to mind and when do they color judgment? A goal-based theoretical framework for stereotype activation and application. *Psychological Bulletin, 129*(4), 522–544. https://doi.org/10.1037/0033-2909.129.4.522

Kuppens, P., Tuerlinckx, F., Russell, J. A., & Barrett, L. F. (2013). The relation between valence and arousal in subjective experience. *Psychological Bulletin, 139*(4), 917–940. https://doi.org/10.1037/a0030811

Kurdi, B., Seitchik, A. E., Axt, J. R., Carroll, T. J., Karapetyan, A., Kaushik, N., Tomezsko, D., Greenwald, A. G., & Banaji, M. R. (2019). Relationship between the Implicit Association Test and intergroup behavior: A meta-analysis. *American Psychologist, 74*(5), 569–586. https://doi.org/10.1037/amp0000364

Kushlev, K., Heintzelman, S. J., Lutes, L. D., Wirtz, D., Kanippayoor, J. M., Leitner, D., & Diener, E. (2020). Does happiness improve health? Evidence from a randomized controlled trial. *Psychological Science, 31*(7), 807–821. https://doi.org/10.1177/0956797620919673

Kuyken, W., Warren, F. C., Taylor, R. S., Whalley, B., Crane, C., Bondolfi, G., Hayes, R., Huijbers, M., Ma, H., Schweizer, S., Segal, Z., Speckens, A., Teasdale, J. D., Van Heeringen, K., Williams, M., Byford, S., Byng, R., & Dalgleish, T. (2016). Efficacy of mindfulness-based cognitive therapy in prevention of depressive relapse: An individual patient data meta-analysis from randomized trials. *JAMA Psychiatry, 73*(6), 565–574. https://doi.org/10.1001/jamapsychiatry.2016.0076

Kyllonen, P. C., & Christal, R. E. (1990). Reasoning ability is (little more than) working-memory capacity?! *Intelligence, 14*(4), 389–433. https://doi.org/10.1016/S0160-2896(05)80012-1

LaBar, K. S., & Cabeza, R. (2006). Cognitive neuroscience of emotional memory. *Nature Reviews Neuroscience, 7*, 54–64. https://doi.org/10.1038/nrn1825

LaBar, K. S., LeDoux, J. E., Spencer, D. D., & Phelps, E. A. (1995). Impaired fear conditioning following unilateral temporal lobectomy in humans. *Journal of Neuroscience, 15*(10), 6846–6855. https://doi.org/10.1523/JNEUROSCI.15-10-06846.1995

Ladenvall, P., Persson, C. U., Mandalenakis, Z., Wilhelmsen, L., Grimby, G., Svärdsudd, K., & Hansson, P.-O. (2016). Low aerobic capacity in middle-aged men associated with increased mortality rates during 45 years of follow-up. *European Journal of Preventive Cardiology, 23*(14), 1557–1564. https://doi.org/10.1177/2047487316655466

Lager, A., Bremberg, S., & Vågerö, D. (2009). The association of early IQ and education with mortality: 65 year longitudinal study in Malmö, Sweden. *British Medical Journal, 339*, Article b5282. https://doi.org/10.1136/bmj.b5282

Laird, J. D., & Lacasse, K. (2014). Bodily influences on emotional feelings: Accumulating evidence and extensions of William James's theory of emotion. *Emotion Review, 6*(1), 27–34. https://doi.org/10.1177/1754073913494899

Lambert, T. J., Fernandez, S. M., & Frick, K. M. (2005). Different types of environmental enrichment have discrepant effects on spatial memory and synaptophysin levels in female mice. *Neurobiology of Learning and Memory, 83*(3), 206–216. https://doi.org/10.1016/j.nlm.2004.12.001

Lameira, A. R., Hardus, M. E., Mielke, A., Wich, S. A., & Shumaker, R. W. (2016). Vocal fold control beyond the species-specific repertoire in an orang-utan. *Scientific Reports, 6*, Article 30315. https://doi.org/10.1038/srep30315

LaMotte, S. (2008, October 15.) *Banning spanking and other corporal punishment tied to less youth violence.* CNN. https://edition.cnn.com/2018/10/15/health/spanking-ban-global-youth-violence/index.html

Landa, R., Holman, K., & Garrett-Mayer, E. (2007). Social and communication development in toddlers with early and later diagnosis of autism spectrum disorders. *Archives of General Psychiatry, 64*(7), 853–864. https://doi.org/10.1001/archpsyc.64.7.853

Langer, E. J., Blank, A., & Chanowitz, B. (1978). The mindlessness of ostensibly thoughtful action: The role of "placebic" information in interpersonal interaction. *Journal of Personality and Social Psychology, 36*(6), 635–642. https://doi.org/10.1037/0022-3514.36.6.635

Langleben, D. D., & Moriarty, J. C. (2013). Using brain imaging for lie detection: Where science, law, and policy collide. *Psychology, Public Policy, and Law, 19*(2), 222–234. https://doi.org/10.1037/a0028841

Langlois, J. H., & Roggman, L. A. (1990). Attractive faces are only average. *Psychological Science, 1*(2), 115–121. https://doi.org/10.1111/j.1467-9280.1990.tb00079.x

Langlois, J. H., Kalakanis, L., Rubenstein, A. J., Larson, A., Hallam, M., & Smoot, M. (2000). Maxims or myths of beauty? A meta-analytic and theoretical review. *Psychological Bulletin, 126*(3), 390–423. https://doi.org/10.1037/0033-2909.126.3.390

Larrick, R. P., Timmerman, T. A., Carton, A. M., & Abrevaya, J. (2011). Temper, temperature, and temptation: Heat-related retaliation in baseball. *Psychological Science, 22*(4), 423–428. https://doi.org/10.1177/0956797611399292

Larson, E. B., Wang, L., Bowen, J. D., McCormick, W. C., Teri, L., Crane, P., & Kukull, W. (2006). Exercise is associated with reduced risk for incident dementia among persons 65 years of age and older. *Annals of Internal Medicine, 144*(2), 73–81. https://doi.org/10.7326/0003-4819-144-2-200601170-00004

Larsson, H., Chang, Z., D'Onofrio, B. M., & Lichtenstein, P. (2014). The heritability of clinically diagnosed attention deficit hyperactivity disorder across the lifespan. *Psychological Medicine, 44*(10), 2223–2229. https://doi.org/10.1017/s0033291713002493

Latané, B., & Darley, J. M. (1968). Group inhibition of bystander intervention in emergencies. *Journal of Personality and Social Psychology, 10*(3), 215–221. https://doi.org/10.1037/h0026570

Latané, B., Williams, K., & Harkins, S. G. (1979). Many hands make light the work: The causes and consequences of social loafing. *Journal of Personality and Social Psychology, 37*(6), 822–832. https://doi.org/10.1037/0022-3514.37.6.822

Laureys, S., Celesia, G. G., Cohadon, F., Lavrijsen, J., León-Carrión, J., Sannita, W. G., Sazbon, L., Schmutzhard, E., von Wild, K. R., Zeman, A., & Dolce, G. (2010). Unresponsive wakefulness syndrome: A new name for the vegetative state or apallic syndrome. *BMC Medicine, 8*(1), Article 68. https://doi.org/10.1186/1741-7015-8-68

Lautenschlager, N. T., Cox, K. L., Flicker, L., Foster, J. K., van Bockxmeer, F. M., Xiao, J., Greenop, K. R., & Almeida, O. P. (2008). Effect of physical exercise on cognitive function in older adults at risk for Alzheimer disease. *Journal of the American Medical Association, 300*(9), 1027–1037. https://doi.org/10.1001/jama.300.9.1027

Lavie, C. J., Arena, R., Swift, D. L., Johannsen, N. M., Sui, X., Lee, D. C., Earnest, C. P., Church, T. S., O'Keefe, J. H., Milani, R. V., & Blair, S. N. (2015). Exercise and the cardiovascular system. *Circulation Research, 117*(2), 207–219. https://doi.org/10.1161/CIRCRESAHA.117.305205

Lawrence, E. M., Rogers, R. G., & Wadsworth, T. (2015). Happiness and longevity in the United States. *Social Science & Medicine, 145*, 115–119. https://doi.org/10.1161/circresaha.117.305205

Lawson, G. M., Duda, J. T., Avants, B. B., Wu, J., & Farah, M. J. (2013). Associations between children's socioeconomic status and prefrontal cortical thickness. *Developmental Science, 16*(5), 641–652. https://doi.org/10.1111/desc.12096

Layton, M. (1995, May/June). Emerging from the shadows. *Family Therapy Networker,* 35–41.

Lazarus, R. S. (1993). From psychological stress to the emotions: A history of changing outlooks. *Annual Review of Psychology, 44,* 1–21. https://doi.org/10.1146/annurev.ps.44.020193.000245

Lazerus, T., Ingbretsen, Z. A., Stolier, R. M., Freeman, J. B., & Cikara, M. (2016). Positivity bias in judging in-group members' emotional expressions. *Emotion, 16*(8), 1117–1125. https://doi.org/10.1037/emo0000227

Le, K., Donnellan, M. B., & Conger, R. (2014). Personality development at work: Workplace conditions, personality changes, and the corresponsive principle. *Journal of Personality, 82*(1), 44–56. https://doi.org/10.1111/jopy.12032

Leach, J. K., & Patall, E. A. (2013). Maximizing and counterfactual thinking in academic major decision making. *Journal of Career Assessment, 21*(3), 414–429. https://doi.org/10.1177/1069072712475178

Leary, M. R., Tambor, E. S., Terdal, S. K., & Downs, D. L. (1995). Self-esteem as an interpersonal monitor: The sociometer hypothesis. *Journal of Personality and Social Psychology, 68*(3), 518–530. https://doi.org/10.1037/0022-3514.68.3.518

Leavens, E. L. S., Meier, E., Brett, E. I., Stevens, E. M., Tackett, A. P., Villanti, A. C., & Wagener, T. L. (2019). Polytobacco use and risk perceptions among young adults: The potential role of habituation to risk. *Addictive Behaviors, 90,* 278–284. https://doi.org/10.1016/j.addbeh.2018.11.003

Leckman, J. F., Elliott, G. R., Bromet, E. J., Campbell, M., Cicchetti, D., Cohen, D. J., Conger, J., Coyle, J., Earls, F., Feldman, R., Green, M., Hamburg, B., Kazdin, A., Offord, D., Purpura, D., Sonit, A., & Solomon, F. (1995). Report card on the national plan for research on child and adolescent mental disorders: The midway point. *Archives of General Psychiatry, 52*(9), 715–723. https://doi.org/10.1001/archpsyc.1995.03950210009002

LeDoux, J. (2002). *Synaptic self: How our brains become who we are.* Penguin.

LeDoux, J. E. (2000). Emotion circuits in the brain. *Annual Review of Neuroscience, 23*(1), 155–184. https://doi.org/10.1146/annurev.neuro.23.1.155

LeDoux, J. E. (2007). The amygdala. *Current Biology, 17*(20), R868–R874. https://doi.org/10.1016/j.cub.2007.08.005

LeDoux, J. E. (2014). Coming to terms with fear. *Proceedings of the National Academy of Sciences, 111*(8), 2871–2878. https://doi.org/10.1073/pnas.1400335111

LeDoux, J. E. (2015a). *Anxious: Using the brain to understand and treat fear and anxiety.* Penguin.

LeDoux, J. E. (2015b). Feelings: What are they & how does the brain make them? *Daedalus, 144*(1), 96–111. https://doi.org/10.1162/DAED_a_00319

LeDoux, J. E., & Pine, D. S. (2016). Using neuroscience to help understand fear and anxiety: A two-system framework. *American Journal of Psychiatry, 173*(11), 1083–1093. https://doi.org/10.1176/appi.ajp.2016.16030353

Lee, P. A. (1980). Normal ages of pubertal events among American males and females. *Journal of Adolescent Health Care, 1*(1), 26–29. https://doi.org/10.1016/s0197-0070(80)80005-2

Lefevre, C. E., Lewis, G. J., Perrett, D. I., & Penke, L. (2013). Telling facial metrics: Facial width is associated with testosterone levels in men. *Evolution and Human Behavior, 34*(4), 273–279. https://doi.org/10.1016/j.evolhumbehav.2013.03.005

Leff, J., Sartorius, N., Jablensky, A., Korten, A., & Ernberg, G. (1992). The international pilot study of schizophrenia: Five-year follow-up findings. *Psychological Medicine, 22*(2), 131–145. https://doi.org/10.1017/S0033291700032797

Lehnart, J., Neyer, F. J., & Eccles, J. (2010). Long-term effects of social investment: The case of partnering in young adulthood. *Journal of Personality, 78*(2), 639–670. https://doi.org/10.1111/j.1467-6494.2010.00629.x

Leichsenring, F., Rabung, S., & Leibing, E. (2004). The efficacy of short-term psychodynamic psychotherapy in specific psychiatric disorders: A meta-analysis. *Archives of General Psychiatry, 61*(12), 1208–1216. https://doi.org/10.1001/archpsyc.61.12.1208

Leigh, B. C., & Schafer, J. C. (1993). Heavy drinking occasions and the occurrence of sexual activity. *Psychology of Addictive Behaviors, 7*(3), 197–200. https://doi.org/10.1037/0893-164X.7.3.197

Leigh, B. C., & Stacy, A. W. (2004). Alcohol expectancies and drinking in different age groups. *Addiction, 99*(2), 215–217. https://doi.org/10.1111/j.1360-0443.2003.00641.x

Leijen, I., & van Herk, H. (2020). Health and culture: National and individual drivers of preference for professional medical help. *European Journal of Public Health, 30*(Supplement_5), Article ckaa166.300. https://doi.org/10.1093/eurpub/ckaa166.300

Lench, H. C., Flores, S. A., & Bench, S. W. (2011). Discrete emotions predict changes in cognition, judgment, experience, behavior, and physiology: A meta-analysis of experimental emotion elicitations. *Psychological Bulletin, 137*(5), 834–855. https://doi.org/10.1037/a0024244

Lenzenweger, M. F., Lane, M. C., Loranger, A. W., & Kessler, R. C. (2007). DSM-IV personality disorders in the national comorbidity survey replication. *Biological Psychiatry, 62*(6), 553–564. https://doi.org/10.1016/j.biopsych.2006.09.019

Lepper, M. R., Greene, D., & Nisbett, R. E. (1973). Undermining children's intrinsic interest with extrinsic reward: A test of the "overjustification" hypothesis. *Journal of Personality and Social Psychology, 28*(1), 129–137. https://doi.org/10.1037/h0035519

Lerner, J. S., Li, Y., Valdesolo, P., & Kassam, K. S. (2015). Emotion and decision making. *Annual Review of Psychology, 66*(1), 799–823. https://doi.org/10.1146/annurev-psych-010213-115043

Lerner, J. S., Small, D. A., & Loewenstein, G. (2004). Heart strings and purse strings: Carryover effects of emotions on economic decisions. *Psychological Science, 15*(5), 337–341. https://doi.org/10.1111/j.0956-7976.2004.00679.x

Leucht, S., Corves, C., Arbter, D., Engel, R. R., Li, C., & Davis, J. M. (2009). Second-generation versus first-generation antipsychotic drugs for schizophrenia: A meta-analysis. *The Lancet, 373*(9657), 31–41. https://doi.org/10.1016/s0140-6736(08)61764-x

Levenson, R. W. (2003). Blood, sweat, and fears: The autonomic architecture of emotion. *Annals of the New York Academy of Sciences, 1000,* 348–366. https://doi.org/10.1196/annals.1280.016

Levenson, R. W. (2014). The autonomic nervous system and emotion. *Emotion Review, 6*(2), 100–112. https://doi.org/10.1177/1754073913512003

Levenstein, S., Ackerman, S., Kiecolt-Glaser, J. K., & Dubois, A. (1999). Stress and peptic ulcer disease. *Journal of the American Medical Association, 281*(1), 10–11. https://doi.org/10.1001/jama.281.1.10

Leventhal, H., & Cleary, P. D. (1980). The smoking problem: A review of research and theory in behavioral risk modification. *Psychological Bulletin, 88*(2), 370–405. https://doi.org/10.1037/0033-2909.88.2.370

Levey, S., Levey, T., & Fligor, B. J. (2011). Noise exposure estimates of urban MP3 player users. *Journal of Speech, Language, and Hearing Research, 54*(1), 263–277. https://doi.org/10.1044/1092-4388(2010/09-0283)

Levinson, D. F. (2006). The genetics of depression: A review. *Biological Psychiatry, 60*(2), 84–92. https://doi.org/10.1016/j.biopsych.2005.08.024

Levinson, S. C. (2003). *Space in language and cognition: Explorations in cognitive diversity.* Cambridge University Press.

Levitin, D. J. (2006). *This is your brain on music: The science of a human obsession.* Dutton/Penguin.

Levitin, D. J., & Menon, V. (2003). Musical structure in "language" areas of the brain: A possible role for Brodmann Area 47 in temporal coherence. *NeuroImage, 20*(4), 2142–2152. https://doi.org/10.1016/j.neuroimage.2003.08.016

Levy, D. A., Stark, C. E. L., & Squire, L. R. (2004). Intact conceptual priming in the absence of declarative memory. *Psychological Science, 15*(10), 680–686. https://doi.org/10.1111/j.0956-7976.2004.00740.x

Levy, D., Ronemus, M., Yamrom, B., Lee, Y., Leotta, A., Kendall, J., Marks, S., Lakshmi, B., Pai, D., Ye, K., Buja, A., Krieger, A., Yoon, S., Troge, J., Rodgers, L., Iossifov, I., & Wigler, M. (2011). Rare de novo and transmitted copy-number variation in autistic spectrum disorders. *Neuron, 70*(5), 886–897. https://doi.org/10.1016/j.neuron.2011.05.015

Lewinsohn, P. M., Allen, N. B., Seeley, J. R., & Gotlib, I. H. (1999). First onset versus recurrence of depression: Differential processes of psychosocial risk. *Journal of Abnormal Psychology,108*(3), 483–489. https://doi.org/10.1037/0021-843X.108.3.483

Lewinsohn, P. M., Rodhe, P. D., Seeley, J. R., & Hops, H. (1991). Comorbidity of unipolar depression: I. Major depression with dysthymia. *Journal of Abnormal Psychology, 100*(2), 205–213. https://doi.org/10.1037/0021-843X.100.2.205

Lewontin, R. C. (1976). Race and intelligence. In N. J. Block & G. Dworkin (Eds.), *The IQ controversy.* Pantheon Books.

Li, Y., Pan, A., Wang, D. D., Liu, X., Dhana, K., Franco, O. H., Kaptoge, S., Di Angelantonio, E.,

Stampfer, M., Willett, W. C. & Hu, F. B. (2018). Impact of healthy lifestyle factors on life expectancies in the US population. *Circulation, 138*(4), 345–355. https://doi.org/10.1161/CIRCULATIONAHA.117.032047

Lichtenstein, S., Slovic, P., Fischhoff, B., Layman, M., & Combs, B. (1978). Judged frequency of lethal events. *Journal of Experimental Psychology: Human Learning and Memory, 4*(6), 551–578. https://doi.org/10.1037/0278-7393.4.6.551

Lick, D. J., Cortland, C. I., & Johnson, K. L. (2016). The pupils are the windows to sexuality: Pupil dilation as a visual cue to others' sexual interest. *Evolution and Human Behavior, 37*(2), 117–124. https://doi.org/10.1016/j.evolhumbehav.2015.09.004

Lieb, K., Zanarini, M. C., Schmahl, C., Linehan, M. M., & Bohus, M. (2004). Borderline personality disorder. *The Lancet, 364*(9432), 453–461. https://doi.org/10.1016/s0140-6736(04)16770-6

Lieberman, M. D. (2000). Intuition: A social cognitive neuroscience approach. *Psychological Bulletin, 126*(1), 109–137. https://doi.org/10.1037/0033-2909.126.1.109

Lieberman, M. D., Ochsner, K. N., Gilbert, D. T., & Schacter, D. L. (2001). Do amnesics exhibit cognitive dissonance reduction? The role of explicit memory and attention in attitude change. *Psychological Science, 12*(2), 135–140. https://doi.org/10.1111/1467-9280.00323

Lieberman, M. D., Straccia, M. A., Meyer, M. L., Du, M., & Tan, K. M. (2019). Social, self, (situational), and affective processes in medial prefrontal cortex (MPFC): Causal, multivariate, and reverse inference evidence. *Neuroscience & Biobehavioral Reviews, 99*, 311–328. https://doi.org/10.1016/j.neubiorev.2018.12.021

Lilienfeld, S. O. (2007). Psychological treatments that cause harm. *Perspectives on Psychological Science, 2*(1), 53–70. https://doi.org/10.1111/j.1745-6916.2007.00029.x

Lilienfeld, S. O., & Treadway, M. T. (2016). Clashing diagnostic approaches: DSM-ICD versus RDoC. *Annual Review of Clinical Psychology, 12*, 435–463. https://doi.org/10.1146/annurev-clinpsy-021815-093122

Lilliengren, P., Johansson, R., Lindqvist, K., Mechler, J., & Andersson, G. (2016). Efficacy of experiential dynamic therapy for psychiatric conditions: A meta-analysis of randomized controlled trials. *Psychotherapy, 53*(1), 90–104. https://doi.org/10.1037/pst0000024

Lim, G. Y., Tam, W. W., Lu, Y., Ho, C. S., Zhang, M. W., & Ho, R. C. (2018). Prevalence of depression in the community from 30 countries between 1994 and 2014. *Scientific Reports, 8*(1), Article 2861. https://doi.org/10.1038/s41598-018-21243-x

Lin, H. Y., Perry, A., Cocchi, L., Roberts, J. A., Tseng, W. Y. I., Breakspear, M., & Gau, S. S.-F. (2019). Development of frontoparietal connectivity predicts longitudinal symptom changes in young people with autism spectrum disorder. *Translational Psychiatry, 9*(1), Article 86. https://doi.org/10.1038/s41398-019-0418-5

Lin, J. Y., Arthurs, J., & Reilly, S. (2017). Conditioned taste aversions: From poisons to pain to drugs of abuse. *Psychonomic Bulletin & Review, 24*(2), 335–351. https://doi.org/10.3758/s13423-016-1092-8

Lind, M. N., Byrne, M. L., Wicks, G., Smidt, A. M., & Allen, N. B. (2018). The Effortless Assessment of Risk States (EARS) tool: An interpersonal approach to mobile sensing. *JMIR Mental Health, 5*(3), Article e10334. https://doi.org/10.2196/10334

Lindell, A. K. (2006). In your right mind: Right hemisphere contributions to language processing and production. *Neuropsychology Review, 16*, 131–148. https://doi.org/10.1007/s11065-006-9011-9

Lindemann, B. (2001). Receptors and transduction in taste. *Nature, 413*, 219–225. https://doi.org/10.1038/35093032

Lindquist, K. A., & Gendron, M. (2013). What's in a word? Language constructs emotion perception. *Emotion Review, 5*(1), 66–71. https://doi.org/10.1177/1754073912451351

Linehan, M. M., Armstrong, H. E., Suarez, A., Allmon, D., & Heard, H. L. (1991). Cognitive behavioral treatment of chronically parasuicidal borderline patients. *Archives of General Psychiatry, 48*(12), 1060–1064. https://doi.org/10.1001/archpsyc.1991.01810360024003

Linehan, M. M., Heard, H. L., & Armstrong, H. E. (1993). Naturalistic follow-up of a behavioral treatment for chronically parasuicidal borderline patients. *Archives of General Psychiatry, 50*(12), 971–974. https://doi.org/10.1001/archpsyc.1993.01820240055007

Linnemann, A., Strahler, J., & Nater, U. M. (2016). The stress-reducing effect of music listening varies depending on the social context. *Psychoneuroendocrinology, 72*, 97–105. https://doi.org/10.1016/j.psyneuen.2016.06.003

Lipson, S. K., Lattie, E. G., & Eisenberg, D. (2019). Increased rates of mental health service utilization by U.S. college students: 10-year population-level trends (2007–2017). *Psychiatric Services, 70*(1), 60–63. https://doi.org/10.1176/appi.ps.201800332

Lissek, S., Kaczkurkin, A. N., Rabin, S., Geraci, M., Pine, D. S., & Grillon, C. (2014). Generalized anxiety disorder is associated with overgeneralization of classically conditioned fear. *Biological Psychiatry, 75*(11), 909–915. https://doi.org/10.1016/j.biopsych.2013.07.025

Liu, H., & Reczek, C. (2012). Cohabitation and U.S. adult mortality: An examination by gender and race. *Journal of Marriage and Family, 74*(4), 794–811. https://doi.org/10.1111/j.1741-3737.2012.00983.x

Liu, J., Raine, A., Venables, P. H., & Mednick, S. A. (2004). Malnutrition at age 3 years and externalizing behavior problems at ages 8, 11, and 17 years. *American Journal of Psychiatry, 161*(11), 2005–2013. https://doi.org/10.1176/appi.ajp.161.11.2005

Lledo, P.-M., Gheusi, G., & Vincent, J.-D. (2005). Information processing in the mammalian olfactory system. *Physiological Review, 85*(1), 281–317. https://doi.org/10.1152/physrev.00008.2004

Lloyd-Fox, S., Blasi, A., Everdell, N., Elwell, C. E., & Johnson, M. H. (2011). Selective cortical mapping of biological motion processing in young infants. *Journal of Cognitive Neuroscience, 23*(9), 2521–2532. https://doi.org/10.1162/jocn.2010.21598

Lo, A. W., & Repin, D. V. (2002). The psychophysiology of real-time financial risk processing. *Journal of Cognitive Neuroscience, 14*(3), 323–339. https://doi.org/10.1162/089892902317361877

Locke, E. A., & Latham, G. P. (1990). *A theory of goal setting and task performance*. Prentice-Hall.

Loehlin, J. C., & Nichols, R. C. (1976). *Heredity, environment, and personality: A study of 850 sets of twins*. University of Texas Press.

Loftus, E. F. (1993). The reality of repressed memories. *American Psychologist, 48*(5), 518–537. https://doi.org/10.1037/0003-066X.48.5.518

Loftus, E. F., & Palmer, J. C. (1974). Reconstruction of automobile destruction: An example of the interaction between language and memory. *Journal of Learning and Verbal Behavior, 13*(5), 585–589. https://doi.org/10.1016/S0022-5371(74)80011-3

Loftus, E. F., Miller, D. G., & Burns, H. J. (1978). Semantic integration of verbal information into a visual memory. *Journal of Experimental Psychology: Human Learning and Memory, 4*(1), 19–31. https://doi.org/10.1037/0278-7393.4.1.19

Loggia, M. L., Mogil, J. S., & Bushnell, M. C. (2008). Experimentally induced mood changes preferentially affect pain unpleasantness. *Journal of Pain, 9*(9), 784–791. https://doi.org/10.1016/j.jpain.2008.03.014

Loprinzi, P. D., Branscum, A., Hanks, J., & Smit, E. (2016). Healthy lifestyle characteristics and their joint association with cardiovascular disease biomarkers in US adults. *Mayo Clinic Proceedings, 91*(4), 432–442. https://doi.org/10.1016/j.mayocp.2016.01.009

Lorenz, K. (1935). Der kumpan in der umwelt des vogels. *Journal of Ornithology, 83*, 137–213. https://doi.org/10.1007/BF01905355

Louis-Jean, J., Cenat, K., Njoku, C. V., Angelo, J., & Sanon, D. (2020). Coronavirus (COVID-19) and racial disparities: A perspective analysis. *Journal of Racial and Ethnic Health Disparities, 7*(6), 1039–1045. https://doi.org/10.1007/s40615-020-00879-4

Lovaas, O. I. (1987). Behavioral treatment and normal educational and intellectual functioning in young autistic children. *Journal of Consulting and Clinical Psychology, 55*(1), 3–9. https://doi.org/10.1037/0022-006X.55.1.3

Lowe, P. (2001, October 12). No prison for Candace's adoptive mom. *Denver Rocky Mountain News*, p. 26A.

Luchins, A. S. (1942). Mechanization in problem solving. *Psychological Monographs, 54*(6), i–95. https://doi.org/10.1037/h0093502

Ludwig, R. M., Srivastava, S., & Berkman, E. T. (2018). Planfulness: A process-focused construct of individual differences in goal achievement. *Collabra: Psychology, 4*(1), Article 28. https://doi.org/10.1525/collabra.136

Luo, Y., Zhang, L., He, P., Pang, L., Guo, C., & Zheng, X. (2019). Individual-level and area-level socioeconomic status (SES) and schizophrenia: Cross-sectional analyses using the evidence from 1.9 million Chinese adults. *BMJ Open, 9*(9), Article e026532. https://doi.org/10.1136/bmjopen-2018-026532

Luria, A. R. (1968). *The mind of a mnemonist*. Avon.

Luttrell, A., Petty, R. E., & Xu, M. (2017). Replicating and fixing failed replications: The case of need for cognition and argument quality. *Journal of Experimental Social Psychology, 69*, 178–183. https://doi.org/10.1016/j.jesp.2016.09.006

Luus, C. A. E., & Wells, G. L. (1994). The malleability of eyewitness confidence: Co-witness and perseverance effects. *Journal of Applied*

Psychology, 79(5), 714–723. https://doi.org/10.1037/0021-9010.79.5.714
Lykken, D. T. (1957). A study of anxiety in the sociopathic personality. *Journal of Abnormal Social Psychology, 55*(1), 6–10. https://doi.org/10.1037/h0047232
Lykken, D. T. (1995). *The antisocial personalities.* Erlbaum.
Lynn, R., & Eysenck, H. J. (1961). Tolerance for pain, extraversion and neuroticism. *Perceptual and Motor Skills, 12*(2), 161–162. https://doi.org/10.2466/pms.1961.12.2.161
Lyubomirsky, S., & Nolen-Hoeksema, S. (1995). Effects of self-focused rumination on negative thinking and interpersonal problem solving. *Journal of Personality and Social Psychology, 69*(1), 176–190. https://doi.org/10.1037/0022-3514.69.1.176
Lyubomirsky, S., King, L., & Diener, E. (2005). The benefits of frequent positive affect: Does happiness lead to success? *Psychological Bulletin, 131*(6), 803–855. https://doi.org/10.1037/0033-2909.131.6.803
MacCormack, J. K., & Lindquist, K. A. (2017). Bodily contributions to emotion: Schachter's legacy for a psychological constructionist view on emotion. *Emotion Review, 9*(1), 36–45. https://doi.org/10.1177/1754073916639664
MacDonald, G., & Leary, M. R. (2005). Why does social exclusion hurt? The relationship between social and physical pain. *Psychological Bulletin, 131*(2), 202–223. https://doi.org/10.1037/0033-2909.131.2.202
MacKay, D. G. (1973). Aspects of the theory of comprehension, memory and attention. *Quarterly Journal of Experimental Psychology, 25*(1), 22–40. https://doi.org/10.1080/14640747308400320
Mackenzie, C. S., Visperas, A., Ogrodniczuk, J. S., Oliffe, J. L., & Nurmi, M. A. (2019). Age and sex differences in self-stigma and public stigma concerning depression and suicide in men. *Stigma and Health, 4*(2), 233–241. https://doi.org/10.1037/sah0000138
MacLean, P. D. (1952). Some psychiatric implications of physiological studies on frontotemporal portion of limbic system (visceral brain). *Electroencephalography and Clinical Neurophysiology, 4*, 407–418. https://doi.org/10.1016/0013-4694(52)90073-4
MacLeod, C., & Mathews, A. (2012). Cognitive bias modification approaches to anxiety. *Annual Review of Clinical Psychology, 8*, 189–217. https://doi.org/10.1146/annurev-clinpsy-032511-143052
MacLeod, M. (2002). Retrieval-induced forgetting in eyewitness memory: Forgetting as a consequence of remembering. *Applied Cognitive Psychology, 16*(2), 135–149. https://doi.org/10.1002/acp.782
Macrae, C. N., Bodenhausen, G. V., & Calvini, G. (1999). Contexts of cryptomnesia: May the source be with you. *Social Cognition, 17*(3), 273–297. https://doi.org/10.1521/soco.1999.17.3.273
Macrae, C. N., Milne, A. B., & Bodenhausen, G. V. (1994). Stereotypes as energy-saving devices: A peek inside the cognitive toolbox. *Journal of Personality and Social Psychology, 66*(1), 37–47. https://doi.org/10.1037/0022-3514.66.1.37
Maddi, S. (2013). *Hardiness: Turning stressful circumstances into resilient growth.* Springer Netherlands.
Madsen, H. B., & Kim, J. H. (2016). Ontogeny of memory: An update on 40 years of work on infantile amnesia. *Behavioural Brain Research, 298*(A), 4–14. https://doi.org/10.1016/j.bbr.2015.07.030
Magnier, M. (2008, May 26). Listening to the quake survivors. *Los Angeles Times*, https://www.latimes.com/archives/la-xpm-2008-may-26-fg-stress26-story.html
Maguire, E. A., Spiers, H. J., Good, C. D., Hartley, T., Frackowiak, R. S. J., & Burgess, N. (2003). Navigation expertise and the human hippocampus: A structural brain imaging analysis. *Hippocampus, 13*(2), 250–259. https://doi.org/10.1002/hipo.10087
Maher, B. A., & Maher, W. B. (1994). Personality and psychopathology: A historical perspective. *Journal of Abnormal Psychology, 103*(1), 72–77. https://doi.org/10.1037/0021-843X.103.1.72
Mahlios, J., De la Herrán-Arita, A. K., & Mignot, E. (2013). The autoimmune basis of narcolepsy. *Current Opinion in Neurobiology, 23*(5), 767–773. https://doi.org/10.1016/j.conb.2013.04.013
Mahy, C. E. V., Moses, L. J., & Pfeifer, J. H. (2014). How and where: Theory-of-mind in the brain. *Developmental Cognitive Neuroscience, 9*, 68–81. https://doi.org/10.1016/j.dcn.2014.01.002
Maier, N. R. F. (1931). Reasoning in humans, II: The solution of a problem and its appearance in consciousness. *Journal of Comparative Psychology, 12*(2), 181–194. https://doi.org/10.1037/h0071361
Maister, L., Sebanz, N., Knoblich, G., & Tsakiris, M. (2013). Experiencing ownership over a dark-skinned body reduces implicit racial bias. *Cognition, 128*(2), 170–178. https://doi.org/10.1016/j.cognition.2013.04.002
Malhotra, D., McCarthy, S., Michaelson, J. J., Vacic, V., Burdick, K. E., Yoon, S., Cichon, S., Corvin, A., Gary, S., Gershon, E. S., Gill, M., Karayiorgou, M., Kelsoe, J. R., Kratoshevsky, O., Krause, V., Leibenluft, E., Levy, D. L., Makarov, V., Bhandari, A., . . . Schulze, T. G. (2011). High frequencies of de novo CNVs in bipolar disorder and schizophrenia. *Neuron, 72*(6), 951–963. https://doi.org/10.1016/j.neuron.2011.11.007
Malle, B. F. (2006). The actor-observer asymmetry in causal attribution: A (surprising) meta-analysis. *Psychological Bulletin, 132*(6), 895–919. https://doi.org/10.1037/0033-2909.132.6.895
Malone, D. A., Jr., Dougherty, D. D., Rezai, A. R., Carpenter, L. L., Friehs, G. M., Eskandar, E. N., Rauch, S. L., Rasmussen, S. A., Machado, A. G., Kubu, C. S., Tyrka, A. R., Price, L. H., Stypulkowski, P. H., Giftakis, J. E., Rise, M. T., Malloy, P. F., Salloway, S. P., & Greenberg, B. D. (2009). Deep brain stimulation of the ventral capsule/ventral striatum for treatment-resistant depression. *Biological Psychiatry, 65*(4), 267–275. https://doi.org/10.1016/j.biopsych.2008.08.029
Maner, J. K., Luce, C. L., Neuberg, S. L., Cialdini, R. B., Brown, S., & Sagarin, B. J. (2002). The effects of perspective taking on motivations for helping: Still no evidence for altruism. *Personality and Social Psychology Bulletin, 28*(11), 1601–1610. https://doi.org/10.1177/014616702237586
Manning, R., Levine, M., & Collins, A. (2007). The Kitty Genovese murder and the social psychology of helping: The parable of the 38 witnesses. *American Psychologist, 62*(6), 555–562. https://doi.org/10.1037/0003-066X.62.6.555
Manns, J. R., & Bass, D. I. (2016). The amygdala and prioritization of declarative memories. *Current Directions in Psychological Science, 25*(4), 261–265. https://doi.org/10.1177/0963721416654456
Mannuzza, S., Klein, R. G., Truong, N. L., Moulton, J. L., III, Roizen, E. R., Howell, K. H., Castellanos, F. X. (2008). Age of methylphenidate treatment initiation in children with ADHD and later substance abuse: Prospective follow-up into adulthood. *American Journal of Psychiatry, 165*(5), 604–609. https://doi.org/10.1176/appi.ajp.2008.07091465
Manrique-Garcia, E., Zammit, S., Dalman, C., Hemmingsson, T., Andreasson, S., & Allebeck, P. (2012). Cannabis, schizophrenia and other non-affective psychoses: 35 years of follow-up of a population-based cohort. *Psychological Medicine, 42*(6), 1321–1328. https://doi.org/10.1017/S0033291711002078
Manzey, D., Lorenz, B., & Poljakov, V. (1998). Mental performance in extreme environments: Results from a performance monitoring study during a 438-day spaceflight. *Ergonomics, 41*(4), 537–559. https://doi.org/10.1080/001401398186991
Marcus, G. F. (1996). Why do children say "breaked"? *Current Directions in Psychological Science, 5*(3), 81–85. https://doi.org/10.1111/1467-8721.ep10772799
Marcus, G. F. (2004). *The birth of the mind: How a tiny number of genes creates the complexities of human thought.* Basic Books.
Marin, M. F., Song, H., VanElzakker, M. B., Staples-Bradley, L. K., Linnman, C., Pace-Schott, E. F., Lasko, N. B., Shin, L. M., & Milad, M. R. (2016). Association of resting metabolism in the fear neural network with extinction recall activations and clinical measures in trauma-exposed individuals. *American Journal of Psychiatry, 173*(9), 930–938. https://doi.org/10.1176/appi.ajp.2015.14111460
Marin, M. M., Rapisardi, G., & Tani, F. (2015). Two-day-old newborn infants recognise their mother by her axillary odour. *Acta Paediatrica, 104*(3), 237–240. https://doi.org/10.1111/apa.12905
Markon, J. (2001, October 8). Elderly judges handle 20 percent of U. S. caseload. *The Wall Street Journal*, p. A15.
Markowitz, J. C., & Weissman, M. M. (1995). Interpersonal psychotherapy. In E. E. Beckham & W. R. Leber (Eds.), *Handbook of depression* (2nd ed., pp. 376–390). Guilford Press.
Marks, A. K., Ejesi, K., & Coll, C. G. (2014). Understanding the U.S. immigrant paradox in childhood and adolescence. *Child Development Perspectives, 8*(2), 59–64. https://doi.org/10.1111/cdep.12071
Markus, H. R. (1977). Self-schemata and processing information about the self. *Journal of Personality and Social Psychology, 35*(2), 63–78. https://doi.org/10.1037/0022-3514.35.2.63
Markus, H. R., & Kitayama, S. (1991). Culture and the self: Implications for cognition, emotion, and motivation. *Psychological Review, 98*(2), 224–253. https://doi.org/10.1037/0033-295X.98.2.224
Markus, H., & Kunda, Z. (1986). Stability and malleability of the self-concept. *Journal of Personality and Social Psychology, 51*(4),

858–866. https://doi.org/10.1037/0022-3514.51.4.858
Marlatt, G. A. (1999). Alcohol, the magic elixir? In S. Peele & M. Grant (Eds.), *Alcohol and pleasure: A health perspective* (pp. 233–248). Brunner/Mazel.
Marsella, A. J., & Yamada, A. M. (2007). Culture and psychopathology: Foundations, issues, directions. In S. Kitayama & D. Cohen (Eds.), *Handbook of cultural psychology* (pp. 797–819). Guilford Press.
Marsh, A. A., Finger, E. C., Fowler, K. A., Adalio, C. J., Jurkowitz, I. T., Schechter, J. C., Pine, D. S., Decety, J., & Blair, R. J. R. (2013). Empathic responsiveness in amygdala and anterior cingulate cortex in youths with psychopathic traits. *Journal of Child Psychology and Psychiatry, 54*(8), 900–910. https://doi.org/10.1111/jcpp.12063
Marsh, A. A., Finger, E. C., Mitchell, D. G., Reid, M. E., Sims, C., Kosson, D. S., Towbin, K. E., Leibenluft, E., Pine, D. S., & Blair, R. J. R. (2008). Reduced amygdala response to fearful expressions in children and adolescents with callous-unemotional traits and disruptive behavior disorders. *American Journal of Psychiatry, 165*(6), 712–720. https://doi.org/10.1176/appi.ajp.2007.07071145
Marsh, A. A., Finger, E. C., Schechter, J. C., Jurkowitz, I. T. N., Reid, M. E., & Blair, R. J. R. (2011). Adolescents with psychopathic traits report reductions in physiological responses to fear. *Journal of Child Psychology & Psychiatry, 52*(8), 834–841. https://doi.org/10.1111/j.1469-7610.2010.02353.x
Marsland, A. L., Pressman, S., & Cohen, S. (2007). Positive affect and immune function. In R. Ader (Ed.), *Psychoneuroimmunology* (4th ed., pp. 761–779). Academic Press.
Martin, A. (2007). The representation of object concepts in the brain. *Annual Review of Psychology, 58*, 25–45. https://doi.org/10.1146/annurev.psych.57.102904.190143
Martin, A., Wiggs, C. L., Ungerleider, L. G., & Haxby, J. V. (1996). Neural correlates of category-specific knowledge. *Nature, 379*, 649–652. https://doi.org/10.1038/379649a0
Martin, G. B., & Clark, R. D. (1982). Distress crying in neonates: Species and peer specificity. *Developmental Psychology, 18*(1), 3–9. https://doi.org/10.1037/0012-1649.18.1.3
Maruta, T., Colligan, R. C., Malinchoc, M., & Offord, K. P. (2002). Optimism-pessimism assessed in the 1960s and self-reported health status 30 years later. *Mayo Clinic Proceedings, 77*(8), 748–753. https://doi.org/10.4065/77.8.748
Maslow, A. (1968). *Toward a psychology of being.* Van Nostrand.
Matarazzo, J. D., Carmody, T. P., & Jacobs, L. D. (1980). Test-retest reliability and stability of the WAIS: A literature review with implications for clinical practice. *Journal of Clinical and Experimental Neuropsychology, 2*(2), 89–105. https://doi.org/10.1080/01688638008403784
Mather, M., & Carstensen, L. L. (2003). Aging and attentional biases for emotional faces. *Psychological Science, 14*(5), 409–415. https://doi.org/10.1111/1467-9280.01455
Mathews, A. (2012). Effects of modifying the interpretation of emotional ambiguity. *Journal of Cognitive Psychology, 24*(1), 92–105. https://doi.org/10.1080/20445911.2011.584527
Matsui, M., Tanaka, C., Niu, L., Noguchi, K., Bilker, W. B., Wierzbicki, M., & Gur, R. C. (2016). Age-related volumetric changes of prefrontal gray and white matter from healthy infancy to adulthood. *International Journal of Clinical and Experimental Neurology, 4*(1), 1–8. https://doi.org/10.12691/ijcen-4-1-1
Mattern, J. L., & Neighbors, C. (2004). Social norms campaigns: Examining the relationship between changes in perceived norms and changes in drinking levels. *Journal of Studies on Alcohol and Drugs, 65*(4), 489–493. https://doi.org/10.15288/jsa.2004.65.489
Mauro, C. F., & Harris, Y. R. (2000). The influence of maternal child-rearing attitudes and teaching behaviors on preschoolers' delay of gratification. *Journal of Genetic Psychology, 161*(3), 292–306. https://doi.org/10.1080/00221320009596712
May, A. (2011). Experience-dependent structural plasticity in the adult human brain. *Trends in Cognitive Sciences, 15*(10), 475–482. https://doi.org/10.1016/j.tics.2011.08.002
May, P. A., Baete, A., Russo, J., Elliott, A. J., Blankenship, J., Kalberg, W. O., Buckley, D., Brooks, M., Hasken, J., Abdul-Rahman, O., Adam, M. P., Robinson, L. K., Manning, M., & Hoyme, H. E. (2014). Prevalence and characteristics of fetal alcohol spectrum disorders. *Pediatrics, 134*(5), 855–866. https://doi.org/10.1542/peds.2013-3319
Mayberg, H. S., Lozano, A. M., Voon, V., McNeely, H. E., Seminowicz, D., Hamani, C., Schwalb, J. M., & Kennedy, S. H. (2005). Deep brain stimulation for treatment-resistant depression. *Neuron, 45*(5), 651–660. https://doi.org/10.1016/j.neuron.2005.02.014
Mazur, A., & Booth, A. (1998). Testosterone and dominance in men. *Behavioral and Brain Sciences, 21*(3), 353–397. https://doi.org/10.1017/S0140525X98001228
Mazza, S., Gerbier, E., Gustin, M.-P., Kasikci, Z., Koenig, O., Toppino, T. C., & Magnin, M. (2016). Relearn faster and retain longer: Along with practice, sleep makes perfect. *Psychological Science, 27*(10), 1321–1330. https://doi.org/10.1177/0956797616659930
McAdams, D. P. (2018). Narrative identity: What is it? What does it do? How do you measure it? *Imagination, Cognition and Personality, 37*(3), 359–372. https://doi.org/10.1177/0276236618756704
McAdams, D. P., & McLean, K. C. (2013). Narrative identity. *Current Directions in Psychological Science, 22*(3), 233–238. https://doi.org/10.1177/0963721413475622
McCabe, D. P., Roediger, H. L. III, McDaniel, M. A., Balota, D. A., & Hambrick, D. Z. (2010). The relationship between working memory capacity and executive functioning: Evidence for a common executive attention construct. *Neuropsychology, 24*(2), 222–243. https://doi.org/10.1037/a0017619
McCabe, K. O., & Fleeson, W. (2016). Are traits useful? Explaining trait manifestations as tools in the pursuit of goals. *Journal of Personality and Social Psychology, 110*(2), 287–301. https://doi.org/10.1037/a0039490
McCabe, S. E., West, B. T., Teter, C. J., & Boyd, C. J. (2014). Trends in medical use, diversion, and nonmedical use of prescription medications among college students from 2003 to 2013: Connecting the dots. *Addictive Behaviors, 39*(7), 1176–1182. https://doi.org/10.1016/j.addbeh.2014.03.008
McCann, F. F., & Marek, E. A. (2016). Achieving diversity in STEM: The role of drawing-based instruments. *Creative Education, 7*(15), 2293–2304. https://doi.org/10.4236/ce.2016.715223
McCarthy, G., Puce, A., Gore, J. C., & Allison, T. (1997). Face-specific processing in the human fusiform gyrus. *Journal of Cognitive Neuroscience, 9*(5), 605–610. https://doi.org/10.1162/jocn.1997.9.5.605
McCarthy, S. E., Gillis, J., Kramer, M., Lihm, J., Yoon, S., Berstein, Y., Mistry, M., Pavlidis, P., Solomon, R., Ghiban, E., Antoniou, E., Kelleher, E., O'Brien, C., Donohoe, G., Gill, M., Morris, D. W., McCombie, W. R., Corvin, A. (2014). De novo mutations in schizophrenia implicate chromatin remodeling and support a genetic overlap with autism and intellectual disability. *Molecular Psychiatry, 19*, 652–658. https://doi.org/10.1038/mp.2014.29
McClelland, D. C. (1987). *Human motivation.* Cambridge University Press.
McCrae, R. R., & Costa, P. T., Jr. (1990). *Personality in adulthood.* Guilford Press.
McCrae, R. R., & Costa, P. T., Jr. (1999). A five-factor theory of personality. In L. A. Pervin & O. P. John (Eds.), *Handbook of personality: Theory and research* (2nd ed., pp. 139–153). Guilford Press.
McCrae, R. R., Costa, P. T., Jr., Ostendorf, F., Angleitner, A., Hrebickova, M., Avia, M. D., Sanz, J., Sánchez-Bernardos, M. L., Kusdil, M. E., Woodfield, R., Saunders, P. R., & Smith, P. B. (2000). Nature over nurture: Temperament, personality, and life span development. *Journal of Personality and Social Psychology, 78*(1), 173–186. https://doi.org/10.1037/0022-3514.78.1.173
McDaniel, B. T., Galovan, A. M., & Drouin, M. (2020). Daily technoference, technology use during couple leisure time, and relationship quality. *Media Psychology*, 1–29. https://doi.org/10.1080/15213269.2020.1783561
McEwen, B. S. (1998). Stress, adaptation, and disease: Allostasis and allostatic load. *Annals of the New York Academy of Sciences, 840*(1), 33–44. https://doi.org/10.1111/j.1749-6632.1998.tb09546.x
McEwen, B. S. (2008). Central effects of stress hormones in health and disease: Understanding the protective and damaging effects of stress and stress mediators. *European Journal of Pharmacology, 583*(2–3), 174–185. https://doi.org/10.1016/j.ejphar.2007.11.071
McEwen, B. S. (2016). Stress-induced remodeling of hippocampal CA3 pyramidal neurons. *Brain Research, 1645*, 50–54. https://doi.org/10.1016/j.brainres.2015.12.043
McEwen, B. S., & Gianaros, P. J. (2011). Stress- and allostasis-induced brain plasticity. *Annual Review of Medicine, 62*, 431–445. https://doi.org/10.1146/annurev-med-052209-100430
McGaugh, J. L. (2000). Memory—A century of consolidation. *Science, 287*(5451), 248–251. https://doi.org/10.1126/science.287.5451.248
McGlashan, T. H. (1988). A selective review of recent North American long-term follow-up studies of schizophrenia. *Schizophrenia Bulletin, 14*(4), 515–542. https://doi.org/10.1093/schbul/14.4.515
McGough, J. J., & Barkley, R. A. (2004). Diagnostic controversies in adult attention deficit

hyperactivity disorder. *American Journal of Psychiatry, 161*(11), 1948–1956. https://doi.org/10.1176/appi.ajp.161.11.1948
McGue, M., Bacon, S., & Lykken, D. T. (1993). Personality stability and change in early adulthood: A behavioral genetic analysis. *Developmental Psychology, 29*(1), 96–109. https://doi.org/10.1037/0012-1649.29.1.96
McGurk, H., & MacDonald, J. (1976). Hearing lips and seeing voices. *Nature, 264*(5588), 746–748. https://doi.org/10.1038/264746a0
McLaughlin, K. A., & Lambert, H. K. (2017). Child trauma exposure and psychopathology: Mechanisms of risk and resilience. *Current Opinion in Psychology, 14*, 29–34. https://doi.org/10.1016/j.copsyc.2016.10.004
McLean, C. P., & Foa, E. B. (2014). The use of prolonged exposure therapy to help patients with post-traumatic stress disorder. *Clinical Practice, 11*(2), 233–241. https://doi.org/10.2217/CPR.13.96
McNeely, H. E., Mayberg, H. S., Lozano, A. M., & Kennedy, S. H. (2008). Neuropsychological impact of Cg25 deep brain stimulation for treatment-resistant depression: Preliminary results over 12 months. *Journal of Nervous and Mental Disease, 196*(5), 405–410. https://doi.org/10.1097/nmd.0b013e3181710927
McNeil, D. G., Jr. (2006, November 23). For rare few, taste is in the ear of the beholder. *The New York Times*. http://www.nytimes.com/2006/11/23/science/23taste.html
McPheeters, M. L., Warren, Z., Sathe, N., Bruzek, J. L., Krishnaswami, S., Jerome, R. N., & Veenstra-VanderWeele, J. (2011). A systematic review of medical treatments for children with autism spectrum disorders. *Pediatrics, 127*(5), e1312–e1321. https://doi.org/10.1542/peds.2011-0427
Meddis, R. (1977). *The sleep instinct*. Routledge & Kegan Paul.
Medin, D. L., & Schaffer, M. M. (1978). Context theory of classification learning. *Psychological Review, 85*(3), 207–238. https://doi.org/10.1037/0033-295X.85.3.207
Mehl, M. R., Gosling, S. D., & Pennebaker, J. W. (2006). Personality in its natural habitat: Manifestations and implicit folk theories of personality in daily life. *Journal of Personality and Social Psychology, 90*(5), 862–877. https://doi.org/10.1037/0022-3514.90.5.862
Mehl, M. R., Pennebaker, J. W., Crow, M. D., Dabbs, J., & Price, J. H. (2001). The electronically activated recorder (EAR): A device for sampling naturalistic daily activities and conversations. *Behavior Research Methods, Instruments, and Computers, 33*(4), 517–523. https://doi.org/10.3758/bf03195410
Mehler, J., & Bever, T. G. (1967). Cognitive capacity of very young children. *Science, 158*(3797), 141–142. https://doi.org/10.1126/science.158.3797.141
Mehta, P. H., & Beer, J. (2010). Neural mechanisms of the testosterone-aggression relation: The role of orbitofrontal cortex. *Journal of Cognitive Neuroscience, 22*(10), 2357–2368. https://doi.org/10.1162/jocn.2009.21389
Mehta, P. H., Jones, A. C., & Josephs, R. A. (2008). The social endocrinology of dominance: Basal testosterone predicts cortisol changes and behavior following victory and defeat. *Journal of Personality and Social Psychology, 94*(6), 1078–1093. https://doi.org/10.1037/0022-3514.94.6.1078
Meier, M. H., Caspi, A., Ambler, A., Harrington, H., Houts, R., Keefe, R. S. E., McDonald, K., Ward, A., Poulton, R., & Moffitt, T. E. (2012). Persistent cannabis users show neuropsychological decline from childhood to midlife. *Proceedings of the National Academy of Sciences, 109*(40), E2657–E2664. https://doi.org/10.1073/pnas.1206820109
Melby-Lervåg, M., Lyster, S.-A. H., & Hulme, C. (2012). Phonological skills and their role in learning to read: A meta-analytic review. *Psychological Bulletin, 138*(2), 322–352. https://doi.org/10.1037/a0026744
Meltzoff, A. N., & Moore, M. K. (1977). Imitation of facial and manual gestures by human neonates. *Science, 198*(4312), 75–78. https://doi.org/10.1126/science.198.4312.75
Melzack, R., & Wall, P. D. (1965). Pain mechanisms: A new theory. *Science, 150*(3699), 971–979. https://doi.org/10.1126/science.150.3699.971
Melzack, R., & Wall, P. D. (1982). *The challenge of pain*. Basic Books.
Méndez-Bértolo, C., Moratti, S., Toledano, R., Lopez-Sosa, F., Martínez-Alvarez, R., Mah, Y. H., Vuilleumier, P., Gil-Nagel, A., & Strange, B. A. (2016). A fast pathway for fear in human amygdala. *Nature Neuroscience, 19*(8), 1041–1049. https://doi.org/10.1038/nn.4324
Mendle, J., Leve, L. D., Van Ryzin, M., Natsuaki, M. N., & Ge, X. (2011). Associations between early life stress, child maltreatment, and pubertal development among girls in foster care. *Journal of Research on Adolescence, 21*(4), 871–880. https://doi.org/10.1111/j.1532-7795.2011.00746.x
Mendrek, A., & Mancini-Marïe, A. (2016). Sex/gender differences in the brain and cognition in schizophrenia. *Neuroscience & Biobehavioral Reviews, 67*, 57–78. https://doi.org/10.1016/j.neubiorev.2015.10.013
Mennella, J. A., Bobowski, N. K., & Reed, D. R. (2016). The development of sweet taste: From biology to hedonics. *Reviews in Endocrine and Metabolic Disorders, 17*(2), 171–178. https://doi.org/10.1007/s11154-016-9360-5
Mennella, J. A., Jagnow, C. P., & Beauchamp, G. K. (2001). Prenatal and postnatal flavor learning by human infants. *Pediatrics, 107*(6), Article e88. https://doi.org/10.1542/peds.107.6.e88
Menon, M., Tobin, D. D., Corby, B. C., Menon, M., Hodges, E. V. E., & Perry, D. G. (2007). The developmental costs of high self-esteem for antisocial children. *Child Development, 78*(6), 1627–1639. https://doi.org/10.1111/j.1467-8624.2007.01089.x
Mental Health America. (2020). *The state of mental health in America 2020*. https://mhanational.org/sites/default/files/2021%20State%20of%20Mental%20Health%20in%20America_0.pdf
Mercer, K. B., Orcutt, H. K., Quinn, J. F., Fitzgerald, C. A., Conneely, K. N., Barfield, R. T., Gillespie, C. F., & Ressler, K. J. (2011). Acute and posttraumatic stress symptoms in a prospective gene x environment study of a university campus shooting. *Archives of General Psychiatry, 69*(1), 89–97. https://doi.org/10.1001/archgenpsychiatry.2011.109
Merikangas, K. R., He, J.-P., Burstein, M., Swanson, S. A., Avenevoli, S., Cui, L., Benjet, C., Georgiades, K., & Swendsen, J. (2010). Lifetime prevalence of mental disorders in U.S. adolescents: Results from the National Comorbidity Survey Replication—Adolescent Supplement (NCS-A). *Journal of the American Academy of Child and Adolescent Psychiatry, 49*(10), 980–989. https://doi.org/10.1016/j.jaac.2010.05.017
Merikangas, K. R., Jin, R., He, J. P., Kessler, R. C., Lee, S., Sampson, N. A., Viana, M. C., Andrade, L. H., Hu, C., Karam, E., Ladea, M., Medina-Mora, M. E., Ono, Y., Posada-Villa, J., Sagar, R., Wells, E., & Zarkov, Z. (2011). Prevalence and correlates of bipolar spectrum disorder in the world mental health survey initiative. *Archives of General Psychiatry, 68*(3), 241–251. https://doi.org/10.1001/archgenpsychiatry.2011.12
Metcalfe, J., & Mischel, W. (1999). A hot/cool-system analysis of delay of gratification: Dynamics of willpower. *Psychological Review, 106*(1), 3–19. https://doi.org/10.1037/0033-295X.106.1.3
Meyer, M. N., Heck, P. R., Holtzman, G. S., Anderson, S. M., Cai, W., Watts, D. J., & Chabris, C. F. (2019). Objecting to experiments that compare two unobjectionable policies or treatments. *Proceedings of the National Academy of Sciences, 116*(22), 10723–10728. https://doi.org/10.1073/pnas.1820701116
Meyerhoff, J., Young, M. A., & Rohan, K. J. (2018). Patterns of depressive symptom remission during the treatment of seasonal affective disorder with cognitive-behavioral therapy or light therapy. *Depression and Anxiety, 35*(5), 457–467. https://doi.org/10.1002/da.22739
Mez, J., Daneshvar, D. H., Kiernan, P. T., Abdolmohammadi, B., Alvarez, V. E., Huber, B. R., Alosco, M. L., Solomon, T. M., Nowinski, C. J., McHale, L., Cormier, K. A., Kubilus, C. A., Martin, B. M., Murphy, L., Baugh, C. M., Montenigro, P. H., Chaisson, C. E., Tripodis, Y., Kowall, N. W., . . . McKee, A. C. (2017). Clinicopathological evaluation of chronic traumatic encephalopathy in players of American football. *Journal of the American Medical Association, 318*(4), 360–370. https://doi.org/10.1001/jama.2017.8334
Mezulis, A. H., Abramson, L. Y., Hyde, J. S., & Hankin, B. L. (2004). Is there a universal positivity bias in attributions? A meta-analytic review of individual, developmental, and culture differences in the self-serving attributional bias. *Psychological Bulletin, 130*(5), 711–747. https://doi.org/10.1037/0033-2909.130.5.711
Michaelson, L. E., & Munakata, Y. (2016). Trust matters: Seeing how an adult treats another person influences preschoolers' willingness to delay gratification. *Developmental Science, 19*(6), 1011–1019. https://doi.org/10.1111/desc.12388
Mickelson, K. D., Kessler, R. C., & Shaver, P. R. (1997). Adult attachment in a nationally representative sample. *Journal of Personality and Social Psychology, 73*(5), 1092–1106. https://doi.org/10.1037/0022-3514.73.5.1092
Milgram, S. (1963). Behavioral study of obedience. *Journal of Abnormal and Social Psychology, 67*(4), 371–378. https://doi.org/10.1037/h0040525
Milgram, S. (1974). *Obedience to authority: An experimental view*. Harper & Row.
Mill, J. S. (1843). *A system of logic, ratiocinative and inductive: Being a connected view of the principles of evidence and the methods of scientific investigation*. John W. Parker.

Millan, M. J., Andrieux, A., Bartzokis, G., Cadenhead, K., Dazzan, P., Fusar-Poli, P., Gallinat, J., Giedd, J., Grayson, D. R., Heinrichs, M., Kahn, R., Krebs, M.-O., Leboyer, M., Lewis, D., Marin, O., Marin, P., Meyer-Lindenberg, A., McGorry, P., McGuire, P., . . . Weinberger, D. (2016). Altering the course of schizophrenia: Progress and perspectives. *Nature Reviews Drug Discovery, 15*(7), 485–515. https://doi.org/10.1038/nrd.2016.28

Miller, D. T., & Prentice, D. A. (2016). Changing norms to change behavior. *Annual Review of Psychology, 67,* 339–361. https://doi.org/10.1146/annurev-psych-010814-015013

Miller, G. A. (1956). The magical number seven, plus or minus two: Some limits on our capacity for processing information. *Psychological Review, 63*(2), 81–97. https://doi.org/10.1037/h0043158

Miller, I. W., Norman, W. H., & Keitner, G. I. (1989). Cognitive-behavioral treatment of depressed inpatients: Six- and twelve-month follow-up. *American Journal of Psychiatry, 146*(10), 1274–1279. https://doi.org/10.1176/ajp.146.10.1274

Miller, R. S. (1996). *Embarrassment: Poise and peril in everyday life.* Guilford Press.

Miller, W. R. (2000). Rediscovering fire: Small interventions, large effects. *Psychology of Addictive Behaviors, 14*(1), 6–18. https://doi.org/10.1037/0893-164X.14.1.6

Mills, K. L. (2014). Effects of internet use on the adolescent brain: Despite popular claims, experimental evidence remains scarce. *Trends in Cognitive Sciences, 18*(8), 385–387. https://doi.org/10.1016/j.tics.2014.04.011

Mills, K. L., Lalonde, F., Clasen, L. S., Giedd, J. N., & Blakemore, S.-J. (2014). Developmental changes in the structure of the social brain in late childhood and adolescence. *Social Cognitive and Affective Neuroscience, 9*(1), 123–131. https://doi.org/10.1093/scan/nss113

Milner, B. (1962). Les troubles de la memoire accompagnant des lesions hippocampiques bilaterales. *Physiologie de l'hippocampe, 207,* 257–272.

Milner, B., Corkin, S., & Teuber, H.-L. (1968). Further analysis of the hippocampal amnesic syndrome: 14-year follow-up study of HM. *Neuropsychologia, 6*(3), 215–234. https://doi.org/10.1016/0028-3932(68)90021-3

Milojev, P., & Sibley, C. G. (2016). Normative personality trait development in adulthood: A 6-year cohort-sequential growth model. *Journal of Personality and Social Psychology, 112*(3), 510–526. https://doi.org/10.1037/pspp0000121

Mischel, W. (1961). Delay of gratification, need for achievement, and acquiescence in another culture. *Journal of Abnormal and Social Psychology, 62*(3), 543–552. https://doi.org/10.1037/h0039842

Mischel, W., & Shoda, Y. (1995). A cognitive-affective system theory of personality: Reconceptualizing situations, dispositions, dynamics, and invariance in personality structure. *Psychological Review, 102*(2), 246–268. https://doi.org/10.1037/0033-295x.102.2.246

Mischel, W., Shoda, Y., & Rodriguez, M. L. (1989). Delay of gratification in children. *Science, 244*(4907), 933–938. https://doi.org/10.1126/science.2658056

Misra, S., Le, P. D., Goldmann, E., & Yang, L. H. (2020). Psychological impact of anti-Asian stigma due to the COVID-19 pandemic: A call for research, practice, and policy responses. *Psychological Trauma: Theory, Research, Practice, and Policy, 12*(5), 461–464. https://doi.org/10.1037/tra0000821

Mitelman, S. A., Shihabuddin, L., Brickman, A. M., Hazlett, E. A., & Buchsbaum, M. S. (2005). Volume of the cingulate and outcome in schizophrenia. *Schizophrenia Research, 72*(2–3), 91–108. https://doi.org/10.1016/j.schres.2004.02.011

Mithoefer, M. C., Grob, C. S., & Brewerton, T. D. (2016). Novel psychopharmacological therapies for psychiatric disorders: Psilocybin and MDMA. *The Lancet Psychiatry, 3*(5), 481–488. https://doi.org/10.1016/S2215-0366(15)00576-3

Mithoefer, M. C., Wagner, M. T., Mithoefer, A. T., Jerome, L., Martin, S. F., Yazar-Klosinski, B., Michel, Y., Brewerton, T. D., & Doblin, R. (2013). Durability of improvement in post-traumatic stress disorder symptoms and absence of harmful effects or drug dependency after 3, 4-methylenedioxymethamphetamine-assisted psychotherapy: A prospective long-term follow-up study. *Journal of Psychopharmacology, 27*(1), 28–39. https://doi.org/10.1177/0269881112456611

Mobbs, D., Greicius, M. D., Abdel-Azim, E., Menon, V., & Reiss, A. L. (2003). Humor modulates the mesolimbic reward centers. *Neuron, 40*(5), 1041–1048. https://doi.org/10.1016/S0896-6273(03)00751-7

Moffitt, T. E., Arseneault, L., Belsky, D., Dickson, N., Hancox, R. J., Harrington, H., Houts, R., Poulton, R., Roberts, B. W., Ross, S., Sears, M. R., Thomson, W. M., & Caspi, A. (2011). A gradient of childhood self-control predicts health, wealth, and public safety. *Proceedings of the National Academy of Sciences, 108*(7), 2693–2698. https://doi.org/10.1073/pnas.1010076108

Mogg, K., & Bradley, B. P. (2016). Anxiety and attention to threat: Cognitive mechanisms and treatment with attention bias modification. *Behaviour Research and Therapy, 87,* 76–108. https://doi.org/10.1016/j.brat.2016.08.001

Moll, J., & de Oliveira-Souza, R. (2007). Moral judgments, emotions and the utilitarian brain. *Trends in Cognitive Sciences, 11*(8), 319–321. https://doi.org/10.1016/j.tics.2007.06.001

Monaghan, P., Sio, U. N., Lau, S. W., Woo, H. K., Linkenauger, S. A., & Ormerod, T. C. (2015). Sleep promotes analogical transfer in problem solving. *Cognition, 143,* 25–30. https://doi.org/10.1016/j.cognition.2015.06.005

Monfils, M.-H., Cowansage, K. K., Klann, E., & LeDoux, J. E. (2009). Extinction-reconsolidation boundaries: Key to persistent attenuation of fear memories. *Science, 324*(5929), 951–955. https://doi.org/10.1126/science.1167975

Monteith, M. J., Parker, L. R., & Burns, M. D. (2016). The self-regulation of prejudice. In T. D. Nelson (Ed.), *Handbook of prejudice, stereotyping, and discrimination* (pp. 409–432). Psychology Press.

Montgomery, G. H., DuHamel, K. N., & Redd, W. H. (2000). A meta-analysis of hypnotically induced analgesia: How effective is hypnosis? *International Journal of Clinical and Experimental Hypnosis, 48*(2), 138–153. https://doi.org/10.1080/00207140008410045

Monti, M. M., Vanhaudenhuyse, A., Coleman, M. R., Boly, M., Pickard, J. D., Tshibanda, L., Owen, A. M., & Laureys, S. (2010). Willful modulation of brain activity in disorders of consciousness. *New England Journal of Medicine, 362*(7), 579–589. https://doi.org/10.1056/nejmoa0905370

Moore, S. C., Lee, I. M., Weiderpass, E., Campbell, P. T., Sampson, J. N., Kitahara, C. M., Keadle, S. K., Arem, H., Berrington de Gonzalez, A., Hartge, P., Adami, H.-O., Blair, C. K., Borch, K. B., Boyd, E., Check, D. P., Fournier, A., Freedman, N. D., Gunter, M., Johannson, M., . . . Patel, A. V. (2016). Association of leisure-time physical activity with risk of 26 types of cancer in 1.44 million adults. *JAMA Internal Medicine, 176*(6), 816–825. https://doi.org/10.1001/jamainternmed.2016.1548

Moore, T. J., & Mattison, D. R. (2017). Adult utilization of psychiatric drugs and differences by sex, age, and race. *JAMA Internal Medicine, 177*(2), 274–275. https://doi.org/10.1001/jamainternmed.2016.7507

Morawetz, C., Bode, S., Derntl, B., & Heekeren, H. R. (2017). The effect of strategies, goals and stimulus material on the neural mechanisms of emotion regulation: A meta-analysis of fMRI studies. *Neuroscience & Biobehavioral Reviews, 72,* 111–128. https://doi.org/10.1016/j.neubiorev.2016.11.014

Mørch-Johnsen, L., Nesvåg, R., Jørgensen, K. N., Lange, E. H., Hartberg, C. B., Haukvik, K. V., Kompus, K., Westerhausen, R., Osnes, K., Andreassen, O. A., Melle, I., Hugdahl, K., & Agartz, I. (2017). Auditory cortex characteristics in schizophrenia: Associations with auditory hallucinations. *Schizophrenia Bulletin, 43*(1), 75–83. https://doi.org/10.1093/schbul/sbw130

Morefield, K. M., Keane, M., Felgate, P., White, J. M., & Irvine, R. J. (2011). Pill content, dose and resulting plasma concentrations of 3, 4-methylendioxymethamphetamine (MDMA) in recreational "ecstasy" users. *Addiction, 106*(7), 1293–1300. https://doi.org/10.1111/j.1360-0443.2011.03399.x

Morewedge, C. K., & Giblin, C. E. (2015). Explanations of the endowment effect: An integrative review. *Trends in Cognitive Sciences, 19*(6), 339–348. https://doi.org/10.1016/j.tics.2015.04.004

Morin, C. M., Vallières, A., Guay, B., Ivers, H., Savard, J., Mérette, C., Bastien, C., & Baillargeon, L. (2009). Cognitive behavioral therapy, singly and combined with medication, for persistent insomnia: A randomized controlled trial. *Journal of the American Medical Association, 301*(19), 2005–2015. https://doi.org/10.1001/jama.2009.682

Moriuchi, J. M., Klin, A., & Jones, W. (2016). Mechanisms of diminished attention to eyes in autism. *American Journal of Psychiatry, 174*(1), 26–35. https://doi.org/10.1176/appi.ajp.2016.15091222

Morris, J. S., Öhman, A., & Dolan, R. J. (1998). Conscious and unconscious emotional learning in the human amygdala. *Nature, 393*(6684), 467–470. https://doi.org/10.1038/30976

Morrison, A. B., & Chein, J. M. (2011). Does working memory training work? The promise and challenges of enhancing cognition by training working memory. *Psychonomic Bulletin & Review, 18,* 46–60. https://doi.org/10.3758/s13423-010-0034-0

Mortensen, E. L., & Høgh, P. (2001). A gender difference in the association between APOE genotype and age-related cognitive decline. *Neurology, 57*(1), 89–95. https://doi.org/10.1212/WNL.57.1.89

Mortensen, E. L., Michaelsen, K. F., Sanders, S. A., & Reinisch, J. M. (2002). The association between duration of breastfeeding and adult intelligence. *Journal of the American Medical Association, 287*(18), 2365–2371. https://doi.org/10.1001/jama.287.18.2365

Morton, J., & Johnson, M. H. (1991). CONSPEC and CONLERN: A two-process theory of infant face recognition. *Psychological Review, 98*(2), 164–181. https://doi.org/10.1037/0033-295X.98.2.164

Movement Advancement Project. (2020). *Non-discrimination laws*. http://www.lgbtmap.org/equality-maps/non_discrimination_laws

Mroczek, D. K., & Kolarz, C. M. (1998). The effect of age on positive and negative affect: A developmental perspective on happiness. *Journal of Personality and Social Psychology, 75*(5), 1333–1349. https://doi.org/10.1037/0022-3514.75.5.1333

Mucci, A., Merlotti, E., Üçok, A., Aleman, A., & Galderisi, S. (2017). Primary and persistent negative symptoms: Concepts, assessments and neurobiological bases. *Schizophrenia Research, 186*, 19–28. https://doi.org/10.1016/j.schres.2016.05.014

Mueller, P. A., & Oppenheimer, D. M. (2014). The pen is mightier than the keyboard: Advantages of longhand over laptop note taking. *Psychological Science, 25*(6), 1159–1168. https://doi.org/10.1177/0956797614524581

Muenks, K., Wigfield, A., Yang, J. S., & O'Neal, C. R. (2017). How true is grit? Assessing its relations to high school and college students' personality characteristics, self-regulation, engagement, and achievement. *Journal of Educational Psychology, 109*(5), 599–620. https://doi.org/10.1037/edu0000153

Mukherjee, R. A. S., Hollins, S., Abou-Saleh, M. T., & Turk, J. (2005). Low levels of alcohol consumption and the fetus. *British Medical Journal, 330*(7488), 375–385. https://doi.org/10.1136/bmj.330.7488.375

Munafò, M. R. (2012). The serotonin transporter gene and depression. *Depression and Anxiety, 29*(11), 915–917. https://doi.org/10.1002/da.22009

Munafò, M. R., & Flint, J. (2011). Dissecting the genetic architecture of human personality. *Trends in Cognitive Sciences, 15*(9), 395–400. https://doi.org/10.1016/j.tics.2011.07.007

Murch, S. H., Anthony, A., Casson, D. H., Malik, M., Berelowitz, M., Dhillon, A. P., Thomson, M. A., Valentine, A., Davies, S. E., & Walker-Smith, J. A. (2004). Retraction of an interpretation. *The Lancet, 363*(9411), 750. https://doi.org/10.1016/S0140-6736(04)15715-2

Murphy, J., Vallières, F., Bentall, R. P., Shevlin, M., McBride, O., Hartman, T. K., McKay, R., Bennett, K., Mason, L., Gibson-Miller, J., Levita, L., Martinez, A. P., Stocks, T. V. A., Karatzias, T., & Hyland, P. (2021). Psychological characteristics associated with COVID-19 vaccine hesitancy and resistance in Ireland and the United Kingdom. *Nature Communications, 12*(1), Article 29. https://doi.org/10.1038/s41467-020-20226-9

Murray, S. L., Holmes, J. G., & Griffin, D. W. (1996). The benefits of positive illusions: Idealization and the construction of satisfaction in close relationships. *Journal of Personality and Social Psychology, 70*(1), 79–98. https://doi.org/10.1037/0022-3514.70.1.79

Musick, K., Meier, A., & Flood, S. (2016). How parents fare: Mothers' and fathers' subjective well-being in time with children. *American Sociological Review, 81*(5), 1069–1095. https://doi.org/10.1177/0003122416663917

Mussweiler, T. (2003). Comparison processes in social judgment: Mechanisms and consequences. *Psychological Review, 110*(3), 472–489. https://doi.org/10.1037/0033-295X.110.3.472

Mustroph, M. L., Chen, S., Desai, S. C., Cay, E. B., DeYoung, E. K., & Rhodes, J. S. (2012). Aerobic exercise is the critical variable in an enriched environment that increases hippocampal neurogenesis and water maze learning in male C57BL/6J mice. *Neuroscience, 219*, 62–71. https://doi.org/10.1016/j.neuroscience.2012.06.007

Myers, D. G. (2000). The funds, friends, and faith of happy people. *American Psychologist, 55*(1), 56–67. https://doi.org/10.1037/0003-066X.55.1.56

Myers, D. G., & Lamm, H. (1976). The group polarization phenomenon. *Psychological Bulletin, 83*(4), 602–627. https://doi.org/10.1037/0033-2909.83.4.602

Naci, H., & Ioannidis, J. P. A. (2013). Comparative effectiveness of exercise and drug interventions on mortality outcomes: Metaepidemiological study. *BMJ, 347*, Article f5577. https://doi.org/10.1136/bmj.f5577

Nadel, L., Hoscheidt, S., & Ryan, L. R. (2013). Spatial cognition and the hippocampus: The anterior-posterior axis. *Journal of Cognitive Neuroscience, 25*(1), 22–28. https://doi.org/10.1162/jocn_a_00313

Nakano, K., & Kitamura, T. (2001). The relation of the anger subcomponent of Type A behavior to psychological symptoms in Japanese and foreign students. *Japanese Psychological Research, 43*(1), 50–54. https://doi.org/10.1111/1468-5884.00159

Naqvi, N. H., Rudrauf, D., Damasio, H., & Bechara, A. (2007). Damage to the insula disrupts addiction to cigarette smoking. *Science, 315*(5811), 531–534. https://doi.org/10.1126/science.1135926

Narayan, A. J., Ippen, C. G., Harris, W. W., & Lieberman, A. F. (2019). Protective factors that buffer against the intergenerational transmission of trauma from mothers to young children: A replication study of angels in the nursery. *Development and Psychopathology, 31*(1), 173–187. https://doi.org/10.1017/S0954579418001530

Nash, M., & Barnier, A. (2008). *The Oxford handbook of hypnosis: Theory, research, and practice*. Oxford University Press.

National Academies of Sciences, Engineering, and Medicine. (2018). *Public health consequences of e-cigarettes*. National Academies Press. https://doi.org/10.17226/24952

National Academies of Sciences, Engineering, and Medicine. (2020). *Social isolation and loneliness in older adults: Opportunities for the health care system*. National Academies Press. https://doi.org/10.17226/25663

National Association of Colleges and Employers. (2019). Salary survey. https://www.cpp.edu/career/nace_salary_survey_winter_2019.pdf

National Institute of Mental Health. (n.d.). *RDoC matrix*. https://www.nimh.nih.gov/research/research-funded-by-nimh/rdoc/constructs/rdoc-matrix

National Institute on Drug Abuse. (2020). *National survey on drug use and health*. https://www.drugabuse.gov/drug-topics/trends-statistics/national-drug-early-warning-system-ndews/national-survey-drug-use-health

National Institutes of Health. (2017). *Noise-induced hearing loss*. http://www.nidcd.nih.gov/health/hearing/pages/noise.aspx

National Research Council, Committee on Educational Interventions for Children with Autism. (2001). *Educating young children with autism*. National Academy Press.

Naveh-Benjamin, M., & Mayr, U. (2018). Age-related differences in associative memory: Empirical evidence and theoretical perspectives. *Psychology and Aging, 33*(1), 1–6. https://doi.org/10.1037/pag0000235

Nawata, H., Ogomori, K., Tanaka, M., Nishimura, R., Urashima, H., Yano, R., Takano, K., & Kuwabara, Y. (2010). Regional cerebral blood flow changes in female to male gender identity disorder. *Psychiatry and Clinical Neurosciences, 64*(2), 157–161. https://doi.org/10.1111/j.1440-1819.2009.02059.x

Neff, L. A., & Karney, B. R. (2017). Acknowledging the elephant in the room: How stressful environmental contexts shape relationship dynamics. *Current Opinion in Psychology, 13*, 107–110. https://doi.org/10.1016/j.copsyc.2016.05.013

Neisser, U. (1967). *Cognitive psychology*. Appleton-Century-Crofts.

Neisser, U., Boodoo, G., Bouchard, T. J., Jr., Boykin, A. W., Brody, N., Ceci, S. J., Halpern, D. F., Loehlin, J. C., Perloff, R., Sternberg, R. J., & Urbina, S. (1996). Intelligence: Knowns and unknowns. *American Psychologist, 51*(2), 77–101. https://doi.org/10.1037/0003-066X.51.2.77

Nelson, C. A., III. (2017). Hazards to early development: The biological embedding of early life adversity. *Neuron, 96*(2), 262–266. https://doi.org/10.1016/j.neuron.2017.09.027

Nelson, E. E., Leibenluft, E., McClure, E. B., & Pine, D. S. (2005). The social re-orientation of adolescence: A neuroscience perspective on the process and its relation to psychopathology. *Psychological Medicine, 35*(2), 163–174. https://doi.org/10.1017/S0033291704003915

Nelson, S. K., Kushlev, K., English, T., Dunn, E. W., & Lyubomirsky, S. (2013). In defense of parenthood: Children are associated with more joy than misery. *Psychological Science, 24*(1), 3–10. https://doi.org/10.1177/0956797612447798

Nestler, E. J., Peña, C. J., Kundakovic, M., Mitchell, A., & Akbarian, S. (2016). Epigenetic basis of mental illness. *The Neuroscientist, 22*(5), 447–463. https://doi.org/10.1177/1073858415608147

Newby, J. M., McKinnon, A., Kuyken, W., Gilbody, S., & Dalgleish, T. (2015). Systematic review and meta-analysis of transdiagnostic psychological treatments for anxiety and depressive disorders in adulthood. *Clinical Psychology Review, 40*, 91–110. https://doi.org/10.1016/j.cpr.2015.06.002

Newman, G. E., Keil, F. C., Kuhlmeier, V. A., & Wynn, K. (2010). Early understandings of the link between agents and order. *Proceedings of the National Academy of Sciences, 107*(40), 17140–17145. https://doi.org/10.1073/pnas.0914056107

Newman, M. G., Llera, S. J., Erickson, T. M., Przeworski, A., & Castonguay, L. G. (2013).

Worry and generalized anxiety disorder: A review and theoretical synthesis of evidence on nature, etiology, mechanisms, and treatment. *Annual Review of Clinical Psychology, 9*(1), 275–297. https://doi.org/10.1146/annurev-clinpsy-050212-185544

Newman, M. G., Szkodny, L., Llera, S. J., & Przeworski, A. (2011). A review of technology assisted self-help and minimal contact therapies for drug and alcohol abuse and smoking addiction: Is human contact necessary for therapeutic efficacy? *Clinical Psychology Review, 31*(1), 178–186. https://doi.org/10.1016/j.cpr.2010.10.002

Nicholson, I. (2011). "Torture at Yale": Experimental subjects, laboratory torment and the "rehabilitation" of Milgram's "Obedience to Authority." *Theory & Psychology, 21*(6), 737–761. https://doi.org/10.1177/0959354311420199

Nickel, T., Sonntag, A., Schill, J., Zobel, A. W., Ackl, N., Brunnauer, A., Murck, H., Ising, M., Yassouridis, A., Steiger, A., Zihl, J., & Holsboer, F. (2003). Clinical and neurobiological effects of tianeptine and paroxetine in major depression. *Journal of Clinical Psychopharmacology, 23*(2), 153–168. https://doi.org/10.1097/00004714-200304000-00008

Nicolini, H., Bakish, D., Duenas, H., Spann, M., Erickson, J., Hallberg, C., Ball, S., Sagman, D., & Russell, J. M. (2008). Improvement of psychic and somatic symptoms in adult patients with generalized anxiety disorder: Examination from a duloxetine, venlafaxine extended-release and placebo-controlled trial. *Psychological Medicine, 39*(2), 267–276. https://doi.org/10.1017/S0033291708003401

Nielsen, J. A., Zielinski, B. A., Ferguson, M. A., Lainhart, J. E., & Anderson, J. S. (2013). An evaluation of the left-brain vs. right-brain hypothesis with resting state functional connectivity magnetic resonance imaging. *PLoS ONE, 8*(8), Article e71275. https://doi.org/10.1371/journal.pone.0071275

Nilsson, H. (2014). A four-dimensional model of mindfulness and its implications for health. *Psychology of Religion and Spirituality, 6*(2), 162–174. https://doi.org/10.1037/a0036067

Nir, Y., & Tononi, G. (2010). Dreaming and the brain: From phenomenology to neurophysiology. *Trends in Cognitive Sciences, 14*(2), 88–100. https://doi.org/10.1016/j.tics.2009.12.001

Nisbett, R. E. (2009). *Intelligence and how to get it: Why schools and cultures count*. Norton.

Nisbett, R. E., Peng, K., Choi, I., & Norenzayan, A. (2001). Culture and systems of thought: Holistic versus analytic cognition. *Psychological Review, 108*(2), 291–310. https://doi.org/10.1037/0033-295x.108.2.291

Nishino, S. (2007). Narcolepsy: Pathophysiology and pharmacology. *Journal of Clinical Psychiatry, 68 Suppl 13*, 9–15. https://www.ncbi.nlm.nih.gov/pubmed/18078360

Nivoli, A. M. A., Colom, F., Murru, A., Pacchiarotti, I., Castro-Loli, P., González-Pinto, A., Fountoulakis, K. N., & Vieta, E. (2011). New treatment guidelines for acute bipolar depression: A systematic review. *Journal of Affective Disorders, 129*(1–3), 14–26. https://doi.org/10.1016/j.jad.2010.05.018

Noble, K. G., Korgaonkar, M. S., Grieve, S. M., & Brickman, A. M. (2013). Higher education is an age-independent predictor of white matter integrity and cognitive control in late adolescence. *Developmental Science, 16*(5), 653–664. https://doi.org/10.1111/desc.12077

Noftle, E. E., & Robins, R. W. (2007). Personality predictors of academic outcomes: Big Five correlates of GPA and SAT scores. *Journal of Personality and Social Psychology, 93*(1), 116–130. https://doi.org/10.1037/0022-3514.93.1.116

Noheatstroke.org. (2021). *Heatstroke deaths of children in vehicles*. https://www.noheatstroke.org/index.htm

Nokia, M. S., Lensu, S., Ahtiainen, J. P., Johansson, P. P., Koch, L. G., Britton, S. L., & Kainulainen, H. (2016). Physical exercise increases adult hippocampal neurogenesis in male rats provided it is aerobic and sustained. *Journal of Physiology, 594*(7), 1855–1873. https://doi.org/10.1113/JP271552

Nomaguchi, K., & Milkie, M. A. (2020). Parenthood and well-being: A decade in review. *Journal of Marriage and Family, 82*(1), 198–223. https://doi.org/10.1111/jomf.12646

Norman, K. A., Polyn, S. M., Detre, G. J., & Haxby, J. V. (2006). Beyond mind-reading: Multi-voxel pattern analysis of fMRI data. *Trends in Cognitive Sciences, 10*(9), 424–430. https://doi.org/10.1016/j.tics.2006.07.005

Norris, C. J., & Larsen, J. T. (2020). Feeling good and bad about nothing at all: Evidence that the status quo can elicit mixed feelings. *Emotion, 20*(6), 1104–1108. https://doi.org/10.1037/emo0000595

Norton, M. I., Frost, J. H., & Ariely, D. (2007). Less is more: The lure of ambiguity, or why familiarity breeds contempt. *Journal of Personality and Social Psychology, 92*(1), 97–105. https://doi.org/10.1037/0022-3514.92.1.97

Nosek, B. A., & Bar-Anan, Y. (2012). Scientific utopia: I. Opening scientific communication. *Psychological Inquiry, 23*(3), 217–243. https://doi.org/10.1080/1047840X.2012.692215

Nosek, B. A., & Lindsay, D. S. (2018). Preregistration becoming the norm in psychological science. *APS Observer, 31*(3), 19–22. https://www.psychologicalscience.org/observer/preregistration-becoming-the-norm-in-psychological-science

Nosek, B. A., Hawkins, C. B., & Frazier, R. S. (2011). Implicit social cognition: From measures to mechanisms. *Trends in Cognitive Sciences, 15*(4), 152–159. https://doi.org/10.1016/j.tics.2011.01.005

Novotny, S. L., Hollander, E., Allen, A., Aronowitz, B. R., DeCaria, C., Cartwright, C., & Yaffe, R. (2000). Behavioral response to oxytocin challenge in adult autistic disorders. *Biological Psychiatry, 47*(8), S159. https://doi.org/10.1016/S0006-3223(00)00793-9

Nummenmaa, L., Glerean, E., Hari, R., & Hietanen, J. K. (2014). Bodily maps of emotions. *Proceedings of the National Academy of Sciences, 111*(2), 646–651. https://doi.org/10.1073/pnas.1321664111

Nurnberger, J. J., Goldin, L. R., & Gershon, E. S. (1994). Genetics of psychiatric disorders. In G. Winokur & P. M. Clayton (Eds.), *The medical basis of psychiatry* (pp. 459–492). Saunders.

O'Brien, L. T., Hitti, A., Shaffer, E., Van Camp, A. R., Henry, D., & Gilbert, P. N. (2017). Improving girls' sense of fit in science: Increasing the impact of role models. *Social Psychological and Personality Science, 8*(3), 301–309. https://doi.org/10.1177/1948550616671997

O'Connell, B. H., & Killeen-Byrt, M. (2018). Psychosocial health mediates the gratitude-physical health link. *Psychology, Health & Medicine, 23*(9), 1145–1150. https://doi.org/10.1080/13548506.2018.1469782

O'Donoghue, M. C., Murphy, S. E., Zamboni, G., Nobre, A. C., & Mackay, C. E. (2018). APOE genotype and cognition in healthy individuals at risk of Alzheimer's disease: A review. *Cortex, 104*, 103–123. https://doi.org/10.1016/j.cortex.2018.03.025

O'Donovan, G., Lee, I. M., Hamer, M., & Stamatakis, E. (2017). Association of "weekend warrior" and other leisure-time physical activity patterns with risks for all-cause, cardiovascular disease, and cancer mortality. *JAMA Internal Medicine, 177*(3), 335–342. https://doi.org/10.1001/jamainternmed.2016.8014

O'Neil, S. (1999). Flow theory and the development of musical performance skills. *Bulletin of the Council for Research in Music Education, 141*, 129–134.

O'Toole, A. J., Natu, V., An, X., Rice, A., Ryland, J., & Phillips, P. J. (2014). The neural representation of faces and bodies in motion and at rest. *NeuroImage, 91*, 1–11. https://doi.org/10.1016/j.neuroimage.2014.01.038

Oberauer, K., Schulze, R., Wilhelm, O., & Süß, H. M. (2005). Working memory and intelligence—Their correlation and their relation: Comment on Ackerman, Beier, and Boyle (2005). *Psychological Bulletin, 131*(1), 61–65. https://doi.org/10.1037/0033-2909.131.1.61

Ochsner, K. N., Silvers, J. A., & Buhle, J. T. (2012). Functional imaging studies of emotion regulation: A synthetic review and evolving model of the cognitive control of emotion. *Annals of the New York Academy of Sciences, 1251*(1), E1–E24. https://doi.org/10.1111/j.1749-6632.2012.06751.x

Oei, N. Y. L., Everaerd, W. T. A. M., Elzinga, B. M., van Well, S., & Bermond, B. (2006). Psychosocial stress impairs working memory at high loads: An association with cortisol levels and memory retrieval. *Stress, 9*(3), 133–141. https://doi.org/10.1080/10253890600965773

Ogino, Y., Nemoto, H., Inui, K., Saito, S., Kakigi, R., & Goto, F. (2007). Inner experience of pain: Imagination of pain while viewing images showing painful events forms subjective pain representation in human brain. *Cerebral Cortex, 17*(5), 1139–1146. https://doi.org/10.1093/cercor/bhl023

Ohla, K., & Lundström, J. N. (2013). Sex differences in chemosensation: Sensory or emotional? *Frontiers in Human Neuroscience, 7*, 607. https://doi.org/10.3389/fnhum.2013.00607

Ohloff, G. (1994). *Scent and fragrances: The fascination of odors and their chemical perspectives* (W. Pickenhagen and B. M. Lawrence, Trans.). Springer-Verlag.

Olfson, M., Marcus, S. C., Druss, B., Elinson, L., Tanielian, T., & Pincus, H. A. (2002). National trends in the outpatient treatment of depression. *Journal of the American Medical Association, 287*(2), 203–209. https://doi.org/10.1001/jama.287.2.203

Oliveira-Pinto, A. V., Santos, R. M., Coutinho, R. A., Oliveira, L. M., Santos, G. B., Alho, A. T., Leite, R. E. P., Farfel, J. M., Suemoto, C. K., Grinberg, L. T., Pasqualucci, C. A., Jacob-Filho, W., & Lent, R. (2014). Sexual dimorphism in the human olfactory bulb: Females have more neurons and glial cells than males. *PLoS*

ONE, *9*(11), e111733. https://doi.org/10.1371/journal.pone.0111733
Olshansky, S. J., Passaro, D. J., Hershow, R. C., Layden, J., Carnes, B. A., Brody, J., Hayflick, L., Butler, R. N., Allison, D. B., & Ludwig, D. S. (2005). A potential decline in life expectancy in the United States in the 21st century. *Journal of Obstetrical & Gynecological Survey*, *60*(7), 450–452. https://doi.org/10.1097/01.ogx.0000167407.83915.e7
Olson, J. M., Vernon, P. A., Harris, J. A., & Jang, K. L. (2001). The heritability of attitudes: A study of twins. *Journal of Personality and Social Psychology*, *80*(6), 845–860. https://doi.org/10.1037/0022-3514.80.6.845
Olson, K. R., Key, A. C., & Eaton, N. R. (2015). Gender cognition in transgender children. *Psychological Science*, *26*(4), 467–474. https://doi.org/10.1177/0956797614568156
Olson, R. K. (2011). Genetic and environmental influences on phonological abilities and reading achievement. In S. Brady, D. Braze, & C. Fowler (Eds.), *Explaining individual differences in reading: Theory and evidence* (pp. 197–216). Psychology Press/Taylor-Francis.
Olsson, A., & Phelps, E. A. (2007). Social learning of fear. *Nature Neuroscience*, *10*, 1095–1102. https://doi.org/10.1038/nn1968
Olsson, A., Ebert, J. P., Banaji, M. R., & Phelps, E. A. (2005). The role of social groups in the persistence of learned fear. *Science*, *309*(5735), 785–787. https://doi.org/10.1126/science.1113551
Olsson, A., Nearing, K. I., & Phelps, E. A. (2007). Learning fears by observing others: The neural systems of social fear transmission. *Social Cognitive and Affective Neuroscience*, *2*(1), 3–11. https://doi.org/10.1093/scan/nsm005
Omalu, B. I., DeKosky, S. T., Minster, R. L., Kamboh, M. I., Hamilton, R. L., & Wecht, C. H. (2005). Chronic traumatic encephalopathy in a National Football League player. *Neurosurgery*, *57*(1), 128–134. https://doi.org/10.1227/01.NEU.0000163407.92769.
Ooms, P., Mantione, M., Figee, M., Schuurman, P. R., van den Munckhof, P., & Denys, D. (2014). Deep brain stimulation for obsessive-compulsive disorders: Long-term analysis of quality of life. *Journal of Neurology, Neurosurgery & Psychiatry*, *85*(2), 153–158. https://doi.org/10.1136/jnnp-2012-302550
Open Science Collaboration. (2015). Estimating the reproducibility of psychological science. *Science*, *349*(6251), Article aac4716. https://doi.org/10.1126/science.aac4716
Opendak, M., Briones, B. A., & Gould, E. (2016). Social behavior, hormones and adult neurogenesis. *Frontiers in Neuroendocrinology*, *41*, 71–86. https://doi.org/10.1016/j.yfrne.2016.02.002
Orth, U., & Robins, R. W. (2014). The development of self-esteem. *Current Directions in Psychological Science*, *23*(5), 381–387. https://doi.org/10.1177/0963721414547414
Osterling, J., & Dawson, G. (1994). Early recognition of children with autism: A study of first birthday home videotapes. *Journal of Autism and Developmental Disorders*, *24*(3), 247–257. https://doi.org/10.1007/bf02172225
Oswald, F. L., Mitchell, G., Blanton, H., Jaccard, J., & Tetlock, P. E. (2013). Predicting ethnic and racial discrimination: A meta-analysis of IAT criterion studies. *Journal of Personality and Social Psychology*, *105*(2), 171–192. https://doi.org/10.1037/a0032734
Otte, C., Gold, S. M., Penninx, B. W., Pariante, C. M., Etkin, A., Fava, M., Mohr, D. C., & Schatzberg, A. F. (2016). Major depressive disorder. *Nature Reviews Disease Primers*, *2*(1), Article 16065. https://doi.org/10.1038/nrdp.2016.65
Ottieger, A. E., Tressell, P. A., Inciardi, J. A., & Rosales, T. A. (1992). Cocaine use patterns and overdose. *Journal of Psychoactive Drugs*, *24*(4), 399–410. https://doi.org/10.1080/02791072.1992.10471664
Otto, A. R., Fleming, S. M., & Glimcher, P. W. (2016). Unexpected but incidental positive outcomes predict real-world gambling. *Psychological Science*, *27*(3), 299–311. https://doi.org/10.1177/0956797615618366
Otto, A. R., Raio, C. M., Chiang, A., Phelps, E. A., & Daw, N. D. (2013). Working-memory capacity protects model-based learning from stress. *Proceedings of the National Academy of Sciences*, *110*(52), 20941–20946. https://doi.org/10.1073/pnas.1312011110
Oudiette, D., & Paller, K. A. (2013). Upgrading the sleeping brain with targeted memory reactivation. *Trends in Cognitive Sciences*, *17*(3), 142–149. https://doi.org/10.1016/j.tics.2013.01.006
Owen, A. M., Coleman, M. R., Boly, M., Davis, M. H., Laureys, S., & Pickard, J. D. (2006). Detecting awareness in the vegetative state. *Science*, *313*(5792), 1402. https://doi.org/10.1126/science.1130197
Owens, C. (2020, May 22). *The coronavirus invades Trump country.* Axios. https://www.axios.com/coronavirus-invades-trump-country-8526833c-4c1-4a58-b255-fd79500cad09.html
Pacchiarotti, I., Bond, D. J., Baldessarini, R. J., Nolen, W. A., Grunze, H., Licht, R. W., Post, R. M., Berk, M., Goodwin, G. M., Sachs, G. S., Tondo, L., Findling, R. L., Youngstrom, E. A., Tohen, M., Undurraga, J., González-Pinto, A., Goldberg, J. F., Yildiz, A., Altshuler, L. L., . . . Vieta, E. (2013). The International Society for Bipolar Disorders (ISBD) Task Force Report on antidepressant use in bipolar disorders. *American Journal of Psychiatry*, *170*(11), 1249–1262. https://doi.org/10.1176/appi.ajp.2013.13020185
Pack, A. I., & Pien, G. W. (2011). Update on sleep and its disorders. *Annual Review of Medicine*, *62*, 447–460. https://doi.org/10.1146/annurev-med-050409-104056
Padberg, F., & George, M. S. (2009). Repetitive transcranial magnetic stimulation of the prefrontal cortex in depression. *Experimental Neurology*, *219*(1), 2–13. https://doi.org/10.1016/j.expneurol.2009.04.020
Pagnoni, G., & Cekic, M. (2007). Age effects on gray matter volume and attentional performance in Zen meditation. *Neurobiology of Aging*, *28*(10), 1623–1627. https://doi.org/10.1016/j.neurobiolaging.2007.06.008
Paivio, A., & Csapo, K. (1969). Concrete image and verbal memory codes. *Journal of Experimental Psychology*, *80*(2, Pt. 1), 279–285. https://doi.org/10.1037/h0027273
Paluck, E. L., Shepherd, H., & Aronow, P. M. (2016). Changing climates of conflict: A social network experiment in 56 schools. *Proceedings of the National Academy of Sciences*, *113*(3), 566–571. https://doi.org/10.1073/pnas.1514483113
Papadimitriou, G. N., Zervas, I. M., & Papakostas, Y. G. (2001). Unilateral ECT for prophylaxis in affective illness. *Journal of ECT*, *17*(3), 229–231. https://doi.org/10.1097/00124509-200109000-00024
Papez, J. W. (1937). A proposed mechanism of emotion. *Archives of Neurology & Psychiatry*, *38*, 725–743. https://doi.org/10.1001/archneurpsyc.1937.02260220069003
Pappas, S. (2020, April 1). What do we really know about kids and screens? *Monitor on Psychology*, *51*(3), 42. https://www.apa.org/monitor/2020/04/cover-kids-screens
Parashar, U., Steele, D., Neuzil, K., de Quadros, C., Tharmaphornpilas, P., Serhan, F., Santosham, M., Patel, M., & Glass, R. (2013). Progress with rotavirus vaccines: Summary of the Tenth International Rotavirus Symposium. *Expert Review of Vaccines*, *12*(2), 113–117. https://doi.org/10.1586/erv.12.148
Paredes, M. F., James, D., Gil-Perotin, S., Kim, H., Cotter, J. A., Ng, C., Sandoval, K., Rowitch, D. H., Xu, D., McQuillen, P. S., Garcia-Verdugo, J.-M., Huang, E. J., & Alvarez-Buylla, A. (2016). Extensive migration of young neurons into the infant human frontal lobe. *Science*, *354*(6308), Article aaf7073. https://doi.org/10.1126/science.aaf7073
Parrott, A. C. (2013). MDMA, serotonergic neurotoxicity, and the diverse functional deficits of recreational "Ecstasy" users. *Neuroscience & Biobehavioral Reviews*, *37*(8), 1466–1484. https://doi.org/10.1016/j.neubiorev.2013.04.016
Pascual-Leone, A., Catala, M. D., & Pascual-Leone Pascal, A. (1996). Lateralized effect of rapid-rate transcranial magnetic stimulation of the prefrontal cortex on mood. *Neurology*, *46*(2), 499–502. https://doi.org/10.1212/wnl.46.2.499
Pastorelli, C., Lansford, J. E., Luengo Kanacri, B. P., Malone, P. S., Di Giunta, L., Bacchini, D., Bombi, A. S., Zelli, A., Miranda, M. C., Bornstein, M. H., Tapanya, S., Uribe Tirado, L. M., Alampay, L. P., Al-Hassan, S. M., Chang, L., Deater-Deckard, K., Dodge, K. A., Oburu, P., Skinner, A. T., & Sorbring, E. (2016). Positive parenting and children's prosocial behavior in eight countries. *Journal of Child Psychology and Psychiatry*, *57*(7), 824–834. https://doi.org/10.1111/jcpp.12477
Pasupathi, M., & Carstensen, L. L. (2003). Age and emotional experience during mutual reminiscing. *Psychology and Aging*, *18*(3), 430–442. https://doi.org/10.1037/0882-7974.18.3.430
Patel, V., Chisholm, D., Parikh, R., Charlson, F. J., Degenhardt, L., Dua, T., Ferrari, A. J., Hyman, S., Laxminarayan, R., Levin, C., Lund, C., Medina Mora, M. E., Petersen, I., Scott, J., Shidhaye, R., Vijayakumar, L., Thornicroft, G., & Whiteford, H. (2016). Addressing the burden of mental, neurological, and substance use disorders: Key messages from Disease Control Priorities. *The Lancet*, *387*(10028), 1672–1685. https://doi.org/10.1016/s0140-6736(15)00390-6
Patel, V., Xiao, S., Chen, H., Hanna, F., Jotheeswaran, A. T., Luo, D., Parikh, R., Sharma, E., Usmani, S., Yu, Y., Druss, B. G., & Saxena, S. (2017). The magnitude of and health system responses to the mental health treatment gap in adults in India and China. *The Lancet*, *388*(10063), 3074–3084. https://doi.org/10.1016/s0140-6736(16)00160-4
Patrick, M. E., & Schulenberg, J. E. (2014). Prevalence and predictors of adolescent

alcohol use and binge drinking in the United States. *Alcohol Research: Current Reviews, 35*(2), 193–200.
Patrick, M. E., Schulenberg, J. E., Martz, M. E., Maggs, J. L., O'Malley, P. M., & Johnston, L. D. (2013). Extreme binge drinking among 12th-grade students in the United States: Prevalence and predictors. *JAMA Pediatrics, 167*(11), 1019–1025. https://doi.org/10.1001/jamapediatrics.2013.2392
Patterson, C. M., & Newman, J. P. (1993). Reflectivity and learning from aversive events: Toward a psychological mechanism for the syndromes of disinhibition. *Psychological Review, 100*(4), 716–736. https://doi.org/10.1037/0033-295X.100.4.716
Patterson, D. R., & Jensen, M. P. (2003). Hypnosis and clinical pain. *Psychological Bulletin, 129*(4), 495–521. https://doi.org/10.1037/0033-2909.129.4.495
Paul-Labrador, M., Polk, D., Dwyer, J. H., Velasquez, I., Nidich, S., Rainforth, M., Schneider, R., & Merz, C. N. B. (2006). Effects of a randomized controlled trial of transcendental meditation on components of the metabolic syndrome in subjects with coronary heart disease. *Archives of Internal Medicine, 166*(11), 1218–1224. https://doi.org/10.1001/archinte.166.11.1218
Paulhus, D. L. (2014). Toward a taxonomy of dark personalities. *Current Directions in Psychological Science, 23*(6), 421–426. https://doi.org/10.1177/0963721414547737
Paulhus, D. L., & Williams, K. M. (2002). The dark triad of personality: Narcissism, Machiavellianism, and psychopathy. *Journal of Research in Personality, 36*(6), 556–563. https://doi.org/10.1016/S0092-6566(02)00505-6
Paulson, S., Chalmers, D., Kahneman, D., Santos, L., & Schiff, N. (2013). The thinking ape: The enigma of human consciousness. *Annals of the New York Academy of Sciences, 1303*(1), 4–24. https://doi.org/10.1111/nyas.12165
Paunonen, S. V., & Ashton, M. C. (2001). Big Five factors and facets and the prediction of behavior. *Journal of Personality and Social Psychology, 81*(3), 524–539. https://doi.org/10.1037/0022-3514.81.3.524
Paykel, E. S. (2003). Life events and affective disorders. *Acta Psychiatrica Scandinavica, 108*(s418), 61–66. https://doi.org/10.1034/j.1600-0447.108.s418.13.x
Pedersen, P. M., Stig Jørgensen, H., Nakayama, H., Raaschou, H. O., & Olsen, T. S. (1995). Aphasia in acute stroke: Incidence, determinants, and recovery. *Annals of Neurology, 38*(4), 659–666. https://doi.org/10.1002/ana.410380416
Peeters, G., Beard, J. R., Deeg, D. J. H., Tooth, L. R., Brown, W. J., & Dobson, A. J. (2019). Longitudinal associations between lifestyle, socio-economic position and physical functioning in women at different life stages. *European Journal of Ageing, 16*, 167–179. https://doi.org/10.1007/s10433-018-0484-1
Peirce, J. M., & Alviña, K. (2019). The role of inflammation and the gut microbiome in depression and anxiety. *Journal of Neuroscience Research, 97*(10), 1223–1241. https://doi.org/10.1002/jnr.24476
Pelham, W. E., McBurnett, K., Harper, G. W., Milich, R., Murphy, D. A., Clinton, J., & Thiele, C. (1990). Methylphenidate and baseball playing in ADHD children: Who's on first? *Journal of Consulting and Clinical Psychology, 58*(1), 130–133. https://doi.org/10.1037/0022-006X.58.1.130
Pembrey, M. E., Bygren, L. O., Kaati, G., Edvinsson, S., Northstone, K., Sjöström, M., & Golding, J. (2006). Sex-specific, male-line transgenerational responses in humans. *European Journal of Human Genetics, 14*(2), 159–166. https://doi.org/10.1038/sj.ejhg.5201538
Penttilä, M., Jääskeläinen, E., Hirvonen, N., Isohanni, M., & Miettunen, J. (2014). Duration of untreated psychosis as predictor of long-term outcome in schizophrenia: Systematic review and meta-analysis. *British Journal of Psychiatry, 205*(2), 88–94. https://doi.org/10.1192/bjp.bp.113.127753
Pepperberg, I. M. (2010). Vocal learning in Grey parrots: A brief review of perception, production, and cross-species comparisons. *Brain & Language, 115*(1), 81–91. https://doi.org/10.1016/j.bandl.2009.11.002
Pepperberg, I. M., & Nakayama, K. (2016). Robust representation of shape in a Grey parrot (*Psittacus erithacus*). *Cognition, 153*, 146–160. https://doi.org/10.1016/j.cognition.2016.04.014
Peretz, I., & Zatorre, R. J. (2005). Brain organization for music processing. *Annual Review of Psychology, 56*, 89–114. https://doi.org/10.1146/annurev.psych.56.091103.070225
Perkins, W. J. (2007). How does anesthesia work? *Scientific American Mind, 18*, 84.
Perrett, D. I., Burt, D. M., Penton-Voak, I. S., Lee, K. J., Rowland, D. A., & Edwards, R. (1999). Symmetry and human facial attractiveness. *Evolution and Human Behavior, 20*(5), 295–307. https://doi.org/10.1016/S1090-5138(99)00014-8
Perry, B. D. (2002). Childhood experience and the expression of genetic potential: What childhood neglect tells us about nature and nurture. *Brain and Mind, 3*, 79–100.
Perry, G. (2013). *Behind the shock machine: The untold story of the notorious Milgram psychology experiments*. The New Press.
Perry, G. (2018). *The lost boys: Inside Muzafer Sherif's Robbers Cave experiment*. Scribe Publications.
Pessiglione, M., Schmidt, L., Draganski, B., Kalisch, R., Lau, H., Dolan, R. J., & Frith, C. D. (2007). How the brain translates money into force: A neuroimaging study of subliminal motivation. *Science, 316*(5826), 904–906. https://doi.org/10.1126/science.1140459
Peters, B. J., Reis, H. T., & Gable, S. L. (2018). Making the good even better: A review and theoretical model of interpersonal capitalization. *Social and Personality Psychology Compass, 12*(7), Article e12407. https://doi.org/10.1111/spc3.12407
Peterson, L., & Peterson, M. J. (1959). Short-term retention of individual verbal items. *Journal of Experimental Psychology, 58*(3), 193–198. https://doi.org/10.1037/h0049234
Petitto, L. A. (2000). On the biological foundations of human language. In H. Lane & K. Emmorey (Eds.), *The signs of language revisited* (pp. 447–471). Erlbaum.
Petitto, L. A., & Seidenberg, M. S. (1979). On the evidence for linguistic abilities in signing apes. *Brain and Language, 8*(2), 162–183. https://doi.org/10.1016/0093-934X(79)90047-6
Petronis, A., & Kennedy, J. L. (1995). Unstable genes—Unstable mind? *American Journal of Psychiatry, 152*(2), 164–172. https://doi.org/10.1176/ajp.152.2.164
Petty, R. E., & Cacioppo, J. T. (1986). *Communication and persuasion: Central and peripheral routes to attitude change*. Springer-Verlag.
Petty, R. E., & Wegener, D. T. (1998). Attitude change: Multiple roles for persuasion variables. In D. T. Gilbert, S. T. Fiske, & G. Lindzey (Eds.), *The handbook of social psychology* (4th ed., pp. 323–390). McGraw-Hill.
Pezdek, K., & Hodge, D. (1999). Planting false childhood memories in children: The role of event plausibility. *Child Development, 70*(4), 887–895. https://doi.org/10.1111/1467-8624.00064
Pfeifer, J. H., & Allen, N. B. (2012). Arrested development? Reconsidering dual-systems models of brain function in adolescence and disorders. *Trends in Cognitive Sciences, 16*(6), 322–329. https://doi.org/10.1016/j.tics.2012.04.011
Pfeifer, J. H., & Berkman, E. T. (2018). The development of self and identity in adolescence: Neural evidence and implications for a value-based choice perspective on motivated behavior. *Child Development Perspectives, 12*(3), 158–164. https://doi.org/10.1111/cdep.12279
Phelps, E. A. (2004). Human emotion and memory: Interactions of the amygdala and hippocampal complex. *Current Opinion in Neurobiology, 14*(2), 198–202. https://doi.org/10.1016/j.conb.2004.03.015
Phelps, E. A. (2006). Emotion and cognition: Insights from studies of the human amygdala. *Annual Review of Psychology, 57*(1), 27–53. https://doi.org/10.1146/annurev.psych.56.091103.070234
Phelps, E. A., & Hofmann, S. G. (2019). Memory editing from science fiction to clinical practice. *Nature, 572*(7767), 43–50. https://doi.org/10.1038/s41586-019-1433-7
Phelps, E. A., Lempert, K. M., & Sokol-Hessner, P. (2014). Emotion and decision making: Multiple modulatory neural circuits. *Annual Review of Neuroscience, 37*, 263–287. https://doi.org/10.1146/annurev-neuro-071013-014119
Phelps, E. A., Ling, S., & Carrasco, M. (2006). Emotion facilitates perception and potentiates the perceptual benefits of attention. *Psychological Science, 17*(4), 292–299. https://doi.org/10.1111/j.1467-9280.2006.01701.x
Phelps, E. A., O'Connor, K. J., Gatenby, J. C., Gore, J. C., Grillon, C., & Davis, M. (2001). Activation of the left amygdala to a cognitive representation of fear. *Nature Neuroscience, 4*(4), 437–441. https://doi.org/10.1038/86110
Phillips, M. L., & Kupfer, D. J. (2013). Bipolar disorder diagnosis: Challenges and future directions. *The Lancet, 381*(9878), 1663–1671. https://doi.org/10.1016/S0140-6736(13)60989-7
Physical Activity Guidelines Advisory Committee. (2018). *2018 Physical Activity Guidelines Advisory Committee scientific report*. https://health.gov/our-work/physical-activity/current-guidelines/scientific-report
Piaget, J. (1924). *Judgment and reasoning in the child*. Routledge.
Pierre, G., Thorpe, R. J., Jr., Dinwiddie, G. Y., & Gaskin, D. J. (2014). Are there racial disparities in psychotropic drug use and expenditures in a nationally representative sample of men in the United States? Evidence from the Medical Expenditure Panel Survey. *American*

Journal of Men's Health, 8(1), 82–90. https://doi.org/10.1177/1557988313496564
Pietromonaco, P. R., & Collins, N. L. (2017). Interpersonal mechanisms linking close relationships to health. *American Psychologist, 72*(6), 531–542. https://doi.org/10.1037/amp0000129
Pietschnig, J., Voracek, M., & Formann, A. K. (2010). Mozart effect–Shmozart effect: A meta-analysis. *Intelligence, 38*(3), 314–323. https://doi.org/10.1016/j.intell.2010.03.001
Pillow, D. R., Zautra, A. J., & Sandler, I. (1996). Major life events and minor stressors: Identifying mediational links in the stress process. *Journal of Personality and Social Psychology, 70*(2), 381–394. https://doi.org/10.1037/0022-3514.70.2.381
Pinker, S. (1984). *Language learnability and language development*. Harvard University Press.
Pinker, S. (1994). *The language instinct*. Morrow.
Pinker, S., & Bloom, P. (1990). Natural language and natural selection. *Behavioral and Brain Sciences, 13*(4), 707–784. https://doi.org/10.1017/S0140525X00081061
Pinto, D., Pagnamenta, A. T., Klei, L., Anney, R., Merico, D., Regan, R., Conroy, J., Magalhaes, T. R., Correia, C., Abrahams, B. S., Almeida, J., Bacchelli, E., Bader, G. D., Bailey, A. J, Baird, G., Battaglia, A., Berney, T., Bolshakova, N., Bölte, S., . . . Betancur, C. (2010). Functional impact of global rare copy number variation in autism spectrum disorders. *Nature, 466*, 368–372. https://doi.org/10.1038/nature09146
Pittenger, D. J. (2005). Cautionary comments regarding the Myers-Briggs Type Indicator. *Consulting Psychology Journal: Practice and Research, 57*(3), 210–221. https://doi.org/10.1037/1065-9293.57.3.210
Plakun, E. M., Burkhardt, P. E., & Muller, A. P. (1985). 14-year follow-up of borderline and schizotypal personality disorders. *Comprehensive Psychiatry, 26*(5), 448–455. https://doi.org/10.1016/0010-440X(85)90081-1
Plassmann, H., & Wager, T. D. (2014). How expectancies shape consumption experiences. In S. D. Preston, M. L. Kringelbach, & B. Knutson (Eds.), *The Interdisciplinary science of consumption* (pp. 219–240). MIT Press.
Plomin, R., & Caspi, A. (1999). Behavioral genetics and personality. In L. A. Pervin & O. P. John (Eds.), *Handbook of personality: Theory and research* (2nd ed., pp. 251–276). Guilford Press.
Plomin, R., & Daniels, D. (1987). Why are children in the same family so different from one another? *Behavioral and Brain Sciences, 10*(1), 1–16. https://doi.org/10.1017/S0140525X00055941
Plomin, R., & Daniels, D. (2011). Why are children in the same family so different from one another? *International Journal of Epidemiology, 40*(3), 563–582. https://doi.org/10.1093/ije/dyq148
Plomin, R., & Spinath, F. M. (2004). Intelligence: Genetics, genes, and genomics. *Journal of Personality and Social Psychology, 86*(1), 112–129. https://doi.org/10.1037/0022-3514.86.1.112
Plomin, R., DeFries, J. C., Knopik, V. S., & Neiderhiser, J. M. (2016). Top 10 replicated findings from behavioral genetics. *Perspectives on Psychological Science, 11*(1), 3–23. https://doi.org/10.1177/1745691615617439
Poland, G. A. (2011). MMR vaccine and autism: Vaccine nihilism and postmodern science. *Mayo Clinic Proceedings, 86*(9), 869–871. https://doi.org/10.4065/mcp.2011.0467
Police: Up to 20 people witnessed gang rape. (2009. October 28). CNN. https://www.cnn.com/2009/CRIME/10/27/california.gang.rape.investigation/
Pollan, M. (2013). *Food rules: An eater's manual*. Penguin.
Pollock, K. M. (2004). Exercise in treating depression: Broadening the psychotherapist's role. *Journal of Clinical Psychology, 57*(11), 1289–1300. https://doi.org/10.1002/jclp.1097
Poole, K. L., Saigal, S., Van Lieshout, R. J., & Schmidt, L. A. (2020). Developmental programming of shyness: A longitudinal, prospective study across four decades. *Development and Psychopathology, 32*(2), 455–464. https://doi.org/10.1017/S0954579419000208
Porter, C., Palmier-Claus, J., Branitsky, A., Mansell, W., Warwick, H., & Varese, F. (2020). Childhood adversity and borderline personality disorder: A meta-analysis. *Acta Psychiatrica Scandinavica, 141*(1), 6–20. https://doi.org/10.1111/acps.13118
Post, R. M., Leverich, G. S., Kupka, R., Keck, P., McElroy, S., Altshuler, L., Frye, M. A., Luckenbaugh, D. A., Rowe, M., Grunze, H., Suppes, T., & Nolen, W. A. (2013). Increased parental history of bipolar disorder in the United States: Association with early age of onset. *Acta Psychiatrica Scandinavica, 129*(5), 375–382. https://doi.org/10.1111/acps.12208
Postle, B. R., & Corkin, S. (1998). Impaired word-stem completion priming but intact perceptual identification priming with novel words: Evidence from the amnesic patient H.M. *Neuropsychologia, 36*(5), 421–440. https://doi.org/10.1016/S0028-3932(97)00155-3
Poulton, R., Moffitt, T. E., & Silva, P. A. (2015). The Dunedin Multidisciplinary Health and Development Study: Overview of the first 40 years, with an eye to the future. *Social Psychiatry and Psychiatric Epidemiology, 50*(5), 679–693. https://doi.org/10.1007/s00127-015-1048-8
Powell, R. A., Digdon, N., Harris, B., & Smithson, C. (2014). Correcting the record on Watson, Rayner, and Little Albert: Albert Barger as "psychology's lost boy." *American Psychologist, 69*(6), 600–611. https://doi.org/10.1037/a0036854
Pratkanis, A. R., Eskenazi, J., & Greenwald, A. G. (1994). What you expect is what you believe (but not necessarily what you get): A test of the effectiveness of subliminal self-help audiotapes. *Basic and Applied Social Psychology, 15*(3), 251–276. https://doi.org/10.1207/s15324834basp1503_3
Pratt, L. A., & Brody, D. J. (2014). *Depression in the US household population, 2009–2012* (National Center for Health Statistics Data Brief, No. 172). Centers for Disease Control and Prevention. https://www.cdc.gov/nchs/products/databriefs/db172.htm
Pratt, L. A., Brody, D. J., & Gu, Q. (2017). *Antidepressant use among persons aged 12 and over: United States, 2011–2014* (National Center for Health Statistics Data Brief, No. 283). Centers for Disease Control and Prevention. https://www.cdc.gov/nchs/data/databriefs/db283.pdf
Pratt, L. A., Druss, B. G., Manderscheid, R. W., & Walker, E. R. (2016). Excess mortality due to depression and anxiety in the United States: Results from a nationally representative survey. *General Hospital Psychiatry, 39*, 39–45. https://doi.org/10.1016/j.genhosppsych.2015.12.003
Premack, D. (1959). Toward empirical behavior laws: 1. Positive reinforcement. *Psychological Review, 66*(4), 219–233. https://doi.org/10.1037/h0040891
Premack, D. (1970). Mechanisms of self-control. In W. A. Hunt (Ed.), *Learning mechanisms in smoking* (pp. 107–123). Aldine.
Premack, D., & Woodruff, G. (1978). Does the chimpanzee have a theory of mind? *Behavioral and Brain Sciences, 1*(4), 515–526. https://doi.org/10.1017/S0140525X00076512
Price, D. D., Harkins, S. W., & Baker, C. (1987). Sensory-affective relationships among different types of clinical and experimental pain. *Pain, 28*(3), 297–307. https://doi.org/10.1016/0304-3959(87)90065-0
Pritchard, T. C., Macaluso, D. A., & Eslinger, P. J. (1999). Taste perception in patients with insular cortex lesions. *Behavioral Neuroscience, 113*(4), 663–671. https://doi.org/10.1037/0735-7044.113.4.663
Probst, F., Meng-Hentschel, J., Golle, J., Stucki, S., Akyildiz-Kunz, C., & Lobmaier, J. S. (2017). Do women tend while men fight or flee? Differential emotive reactions of stressed men and women while viewing newborn infants. *Psychoneuroendocrinology, 75*, 213–221. https://doi.org/10.1016/j.psyneuen.2016.11.005
Przybylski, A. K., & Weinstein, N. (2019). Digital screen time limits and young children's psychological well-being: Evidence from a population-based study. *Child Development, 90*(1), e56–e65. https://doi.org/10.1111/cdev.13007
Public Health England. (2016). *Modern life responsible for "worrying" health in middle aged*. Department of Health. https://www.gov.uk/government/news/modern-life-responsible-for-worrying-health-in-middle-aged
Purcell, S. M., Moran, J. L., Fromer, M., Ruderfer, D., Solovieff, N., Roussos, P., O'Dushlaine, C., Chambert, K., Bergen, S. E., Kähler, A., Duncan, L., Stahl, E., Genovese, G., Fernández, E., Collins, M. O., Komiyama, N. H., Choudhary, J. S., Magnusson, P. K. E., Banks, E, . . . Sklar, P. (2014). A polygenic burden of rare disruptive mutations in schizophrenia. *Nature, 506*, 185–190. https://doi.org/10.1038/nature12975
Putnam, A. L., Sungkhasettee, V. W., & Roediger, H. L. (2016). Optimizing learning in college: Tips from cognitive psychology. *Perspectives on Psychological Science, 11*(5), 652–660. https://doi.org/10.1177/1745691616645770
Quinn, P. C., Lee, K., & Pascalis, O. (2019). Face processing in infancy and beyond: The case of social categories. *Annual Review of Psychology, 70*, 165–189. https://doi.org/10.1146/annurev-psych-010418-102753
Radcliffe, N. M., & Klein, W. M. P. (2002). Dispositional, unrealistic, and comparative optimism: Differential relations with the knowledge and processing of risk information and beliefs about personal risk. *Personality and Social Psychology*

Bulletin, 28(6), 836–846. https://doi.org/10.1177/0146167202289012

Raevuori, A., Keski-Rahkonen, A., & Hoek, H. W. (2014). A review of eating disorders in males. *Current Opinion in Psychiatry, 27*(6), 426–430. https://doi.org/10.1097/YCO.0000000000000113

Rahman, M. M., Khan, H. T. A., & Hafford-Letchfield, T. (2016). Correlates of socioeconomic status and the health of older people in the United Kingdom: A review. *Illness, Crisis & Loss, 24*(4), 195–216. https://doi.org/10.1177/1054137315608347

Raine, A. (1989). Evoked potentials and psychopathy. *International Journal of Psychophysiology, 8*(1), 1–16. https://doi.org/10.1016/0167-8760(89)90013-5

Raine, A., Mellingen, K., Liu, J., Venables, P., & Mednick, S. A. (2003). Effects of environmental enrichment at ages 3–5 years on schizotypal personality and antisocial behavior at ages 17 and 23 years. *American Journal of Psychiatry, 160*(9), 1627–1635. https://doi.org/10.1176/appi.ajp.160.9.1627

Rainville, P., Duncan, G. H., Price, D. D., Carrier, B., & Bushnell, M. C. (1997). Pain affect encoded in human anterior cingulate but not somatosensory cortex. *Science, 277*(5328), 968–971. https://doi.org/10.1126/science.277.5328.968

Rainville, P., Hofbauer, R. K., Bushnell, M. C., Duncan, G. H., & Price, D. D. (2002). Hypnosis modulates activity in brain structures involved in the regulation of consciousness. *Journal of Cognitive Neuroscience, 14*(6), 887–901. https://doi.org/10.1162/089892902760191117

Rajendram, R., Kronenberg, S., Burton, C. L., & Arnold, P. D. (2017). Glutamate genetics in obsessive-compulsive disorder: A review. *Journal of the Canadian Academy of Child and Adolescent Psychiatry, 26*(3), 205–213. https://www.ncbi.nlm.nih.gov/pmc/articles/PMC5642460/

Ram, S., Seirawan, H., Kumar, S. K. S., & Clark, G. T. (2010). Prevalence and impact of sleep disorders and sleep habits in the United States. *Sleep and Breathing, 14*(1), 63–70. https://doi.org/10.1007/s11325-009-0281-3

Ramachandran, V. S., & Hirstein, W. (1998). The perception of phantom limbs: The D. O. Hebb lecture. *Brain, 121*(9), 1603–1630. https://doi.org/10.1093/brain/121.9.1603

Ramachandran, V. S., & Hubbard, E. M. (2001). Psychophysical investigations into the neural basis of synaesthesia. *Proceedings of the Royal Society B: Biological Sciences, 268*(1470), 979–983. https://doi.org/10.1098/rspb.2000.1576

Rampon, C., Jiang, C. H., Dong, H., Tang, Y.-P., Lockhart, D. J., Schultz, P. G., Tsien, J. Z., & Hu, Y. (2000). Effects of environmental enrichment on gene expression in the brain. *Proceedings of the National Academy of Sciences, 97*(23), 12880–12884. https://doi.org/10.1073/pnas.97.23.12880

Rapoport, J. L. (1989). The biology of obsessions and compulsions. *Scientific American, 260*, 83–89. https://www.scientificamerican.com/article/the-biology-of-obsessions-and-compu/

Rapoport, J. L. (1991). Recent advances in obsessive-compulsive disorder. *Neuropsychopharmacology, 5*(1), 1–10.

Rapport, M. D., & Moffitt, C. (2002). Attention-deficit/hyperactivity disorder and methylphenidate: A review of the height/weight, cardiovascular, and somatic complaint side effects. *Clinical Psychology Review, 22*(8), 1107–1131. https://doi.org/10.1016/s0272-7358(02)00129-0

Rapuano, K. M., Zieselman, A. L., Kelley, W. M., Sargent, J. D., Heatherton, T. F., & Gilbert-Diamond, D. (2017). Genetic risk for obesity predicts nucleus accumbens size and responsivity to real-world food cues. *Proceedings of the National Academy of Sciences, 114*(1), 160–165. https://doi.org/10.1073/pnas.1605548113

Rauscher, F. H., Shaw, G. L., & Ky, C. N. (1993). Music and spatial task performance. *Nature, 365*(6447), 611. https://doi.org/10.1038/365611a0

Raymaekers, S., Vansteelandt, K., Luyten, L., Bervoets, C., Demyttenaere, K., Gabriëls, L., & Nuttin, B. (2017). Long-term electrical stimulation of bed nucleus of stria terminalis for obsessive-compulsive disorder. *Molecular Psychiatry, 22*, 931–934. https://doi.org/10.1038/mp.2016.124

Rayner, K., Foorman, B. R., Perfetti, C. A., Pesetsky, D., & Seidenberg, M. S. (2001). How psychological science informs the teaching of reading. *Psychological Science in the Public Interest, 2*(2), 31–74. https://doi.org/10.1111/1529-1006.00004

Rayner, K., Pollatsek, A., Ashby, J., & Clifton Jr., C. (2012). *Psychology of reading.* Psychology Press.

Rayner, R. M. C., Sahinkaya, M. N., & Hicks, B. (2017). Improving the design of high speed mechanisms through multi-level kinematic synthesis, dynamic optimization and velocity profiling. *Mechanism and Machine Theory, 118*, 100–114. https://doi.org/10.1016/j.mechmachtheory.2017.07.022

Raynor, H. A., & Epstein, L. H. (2001). Dietary variety, energy regulation, and obesity. *Psychological Bulletin, 127*(3), 325–341. https://doi.org/10.1037/0033-2909.127.3.325

Read, J. P., & Brown, R. A. (2003). The role of exercise in alcoholism treatment and recovery. *Professional Psychology: Research and Practice, 34*(1), 49–56. https://doi.org/10.1037/0735-7028.34.1.49

Redick, T. S., Shipstead, Z., Harrison, T. L., Hicks, K. L., Fried, D. E., Hambrick, D. Z., Kane, M. J., & Engle, R. W. (2013). No evidence of intelligence improvement after working memory training: A randomized, placebo-controlled study. *Journal of Experimental Psychology: General, 142*(2), 359–379. https://doi.org/10.1037/a0029082

Reeck, C., Ames, D. R., & Ochsner, K. N. (2016). The social regulation of emotion: An integrative, cross-disciplinary model. *Trends in Cognitive Sciences, 20*(1), 47–63. https://doi.org/10.1016/j.tics.2015.09.003

Reeves, L. M., & Weisberg, R. W. (1994). The role of content and abstract information in analogical transfer. *Psychological Bulletin, 115*(3), 381–400. https://doi.org/10.1037/0033-2909.115.3.381

Reifman, A. S., Larrick, R. P., & Fein, S. (1991). Temper and temperature on the diamond: The heat-aggression relationship in Major League Baseball. *Personality and Social Psychology Bulletin, 17*(5), 580–585. https://doi.org/10.1177/0146167291175013

Reinders, A. A. T. S., Nijenhuis, E. R. S., Paans, A. M. J., Korf, J., Willemsen, A. T. M., & den Boer, J. A. (2003). One brain, two selves. *NeuroImage, 20*(4), 2119–2125. https://doi.org/10.1016/j.neuroimage.2003.08.021

Reis, D. L., Brackett, M. A., Shamosh, N. A., Kiehl, K. A., Salovey, P., & Gray, J. R. (2007). Emotional intelligence predicts individual differences in social exchange reasoning. *NeuroImage, 35*(3), 1385–1391. https://doi.org/10.1016/j.neuroimage.2006.12.045

Reis, H. T., Wheeler, L., Spiegel, N., Kernis, M. H., Nezlek, J., & Perri, M. (1982). Physical attractiveness in social interaction: II. Why does appearance affect social experience? *Journal of Personality and Social Psychology, 43*(5), 979–996. https://doi.org/10.1037/0022-3514.43.5.979

Rescorla, R. A. (1966). Predictability and number of pairings in Pavlovian fear conditioning. *Psychonomic Science, 4*(11), 383–384. https://doi.org/10.3758/bf03342350

Rescorla, R. A., & Wagner, A. R. (1972). A theory of Pavlovian conditioning: Variations in the effectiveness of reinforcement and non-reinforcement. In A. H. Black & W. F. Prokosy (Eds.), *Classical conditioning II: Current research and theory* (pp. 64–99). Appleton-Century-Crofts.

Ressler, K. J., & Mayberg, H. S. (2007). Targeting abnormal neural circuits in mood and anxiety disorders: From the laboratory to the clinic. *Nature Neuroscience, 10*(9), 1116–1124. https://doi.org/10.1038/nn1944

Reyna, C., Brandt, M., & Viki, G. T. (2009). Blame it on hip-hop: Anti-rap attitudes as a proxy for prejudice. *Group Process and Intergroup Relations, 12*(3), 361–380. https://doi.org/10.1177/1368430209102848

Rhodewalt, F., & Morf, C. C. (1998). On self-aggrandizement and anger: A temporal analysis of narcissism and affective reactions to success and failure. *Journal of Personality and Social Psychology, 74*(3), 672–685. https://doi.org/10.1037/0022-3514.74.3.672

Riboni, F. V., & Belzung, C. (2017). Stress and psychiatric disorders: From categorical to dimensional approaches. *Current Opinion in Behavioral Sciences, 14*, 72–77. https://doi.org/10.1016/j.cobeha.2016.12.011

Richardson, H., & Saxe, R. (2020). Development of predictive responses in theory of mind brain regions. *Developmental Science, 23*(1), Article e12863. https://doi.org/10.1111/desc.12863

Richman, L. S., Kubzansky, L., Maselko, J., Kawachi, I., Choo, P., & Bauer, M. (2005). Positive emotion and health: Going beyond the negative. *Health Psychology, 24*(4), 422–429. https://doi.org/10.1037/0278-6133.24.4.422

Ridley, M. (2003). *Nature via nurture: Genes, experience, and what makes us human.* HarperCollins.

Ridout, B., & Campbell, A. (2014). Using Facebook to deliver a social norm intervention to reduce problem drinking at university. *Drug and Alcohol Review, 33*(6), 667–673. https://doi.org/10.1111/dar.12141

Rimmele, U., Davachi, L., & Phelps, E. A. (2012). Memory for time and place contributes to enhanced confidence in memories for emotional events. *Emotion, 12*(4), 834–846. https://doi.org/10.1037/a0028003

Rivera, M. T., Soderstrom, S. B., & Uzzi, B. (2010). Dynamics of dyads in social networks: Assortative, relational, and proximity mechanisms. *Annual Review of Sociology,*

36, 91–115. https://doi.org/10.1146/annurev.soc.34.040507.134743

Roberts, B. W., & DelVecchio, W. F. (2000). The rank-order consistency of personality traits from childhood to old age: A quantitative review of longitudinal studies. *Psychological Bulletin, 126*(1), 3–25. https://doi.org/10.1037/0033-2909.126.1.3

Roberts, B. W., & Mroczek, D. (2008). Personality trait change in adulthood. *Current Directions in Psychological Science, 17*(1), 31–35. https://doi.org/10.1111/j.1467-8721.2008.00543.x

Roberts, B. W., & Wood, D. (2006). Personality development in the context of the neo-socioanalytic model of personality. In D. Mroczek & T. Little (Eds.), *Handbook of personality development* (pp. 11–39). Erlbaum.

Roberts, B. W., Donnellan, M. B., & Hill, P. L. (2012). Personality trait development in adulthood: Findings and implications. In H. Tennen & J. Suls (Eds.), *Handbook of psychology* (2nd ed., pp. 183–196). Wiley.

Roberts, B. W., Kuncel, N. R., Shiner, R., Caspi, A., & Goldberg, L. R. (2007). The power of personality: The comparative validity of personality traits, socioeconomic status, and cognitive ability for predicting important life outcomes. *Perspectives on Psychological Science, 2*(4), 313–345. https://doi.org/10.1111/j.1745-6916.2007.00047.x

Roberts, B. W., Luo, J., Briley, D. A., Chow, P. I., Su, R., & Hill, P. L. (2017). A systematic review of personality trait change through intervention. *Psychological Bulletin, 143*(2), 117–141. https://doi.org/10.1037/bul0000088

Roberts, B. W., Walton, K. E., & Viechtbauer, W. (2006). Patterns of mean-level change in personality traits across the life course: A meta-analysis of longitudinal studies. *Psychological Bulletin, 132*(1), 1–25. https://doi.org/10.1037/0033-2909.132.1.1

Robins, L. N., & Regier, D. A. (1991). *Psychiatric disorders in America: The epidemiological catchment areas study.* Free Press.

Robins, L. N., Helzer, J. E., & Davis, D. H. (1975). Narcotic use in Southeast Asia and afterward: An interview study of 898 Vietnam returnees. *Archives of General Psychiatry, 32*(8), 955–961. https://doi.org/10.1001/archpsyc.1975.01760260019001

Robins, R. W., Trzesniewski, K. H., Tracy, J. L., Gosling, S. D., & Potter, J. (2002). Global self-esteem across the life span. *Psychology and Aging, 17*(3), 423–434. https://doi.org/10.1037/0882-7974.17.3.423

Robinson, T. E., & Berridge, K. C. (1993). The neural basis of drug craving: An incentive-sensitization theory of addiction. *Brain Research Reviews, 18*(3), 247–291. https://doi.org/10.1016/0165-0173(93)90013-P

Robles, T. F., & Carroll, J. E. (2011). Restorative biological processes and health. *Social and Personality Psychology Compass, 5*(8), 518–537. https://doi.org/10.1111/j.1751-9004.2011.00368.x

Robles, T. F., & Kiecolt-Glaser, J. K. (2003). The physiology of marriage: Pathways to health. *Physiology & Behavior, 79*(3), 409–416. https://doi.org/10.1016/s0031-9384(03)00160-4

Rock, I. (1984). *Perception.* Scientific American Books.

Roediger, H. L. (2013). Applying cognitive psychology to education: Translational educational science. *Psychological Science in the Public Interest, 14*(1), 1–3. https://doi.org/10.1177/1529100612454415

Roediger, H. L., III, & Karpicke, J. D. (2006). The power of testing memory: Basic research and implications for educational practice. *Psychological Science, 1*(3), 181–210. https://doi.org/10.1111/j.1745-6916.2006.00012.x

Roediger, H. L., III, & McDermott, K. B. (1995). Creating false memories: Remembering words not presented in lists. *Journal of Experimental Psychology: Learning, Memory, and Cognition, 21*(4), 803–814. https://doi.org/10.1037/0278-7393.21.4.803

Roediger, H. L., Weldon, M. S., Stadler, M. L., & Riegler, G. L. (1992). Direct comparison of two implicit memory tests: Word fragment and word stem completion. *Journal of Experimental Psychology: Learning, Memory, and Cognition, 18*(6), 1251–1269. https://doi.org/10.1037/0278-7393.18.6.1251

Roeloffs, C., Sherbourne, C., Unützer, J., Fink, A., Tang, L., & Wells, K. B. (2003). Stigma and depression among primary care patients. *General Hospital Psychiatry, 25*(5), 311–315. https://doi.org/10.1016/S0163-8343(03)00066-5

Rogeberg, O. (2013). Correlations between cannabis use and IQ change in the Dunedin cohort are consistent with confounding from socioeconomic status. *Proceedings of the National Academy of Sciences, 110*(11), 4251–4254. https://doi.org/10.1073/pnas.1215678110

Rogers, C. R. (1951). *Client-centered therapy: Its current practice, implications and theory.* Houghton Mifflin.

Rogers, T. B., Kuiper, N. A., & Kirker, W. S. (1977). Self-reference and the encoding of personal information. *Journal of Personality and Social Psychology, 35*(9), 677–688. https://doi.org/10.1037/0022-3514.35.9.677

Rohan, K. J., Camuso, J., Perez, J., Iyiewuare, P., Meyerhoff, J., DeSarno, M. J., & Vacek, P. M. (2020). Detecting critical decision points during cognitive-behavioral therapy and light therapy for winter depression nonremission and recurrence. *Journal of Behavioral and Cognitive Therapy, 30*(4), 241–252. https://doi.org/10.1016/j.jbct.2020.10.002

Rolls, B. J., Roe, L. S., & Meengs, J. S. (2007). The effect of large portion sizes on energy intake is sustained for 11 days. *Obesity, 15*(6), 1535–1543. https://doi.org/10.1038/oby.2007.182

Rolls, E. T., Burton, M. J., & Mora, F. (1980). Neurophysiological analysis of brain-stimulation reward in the monkey. *Brain Research, 194*(2), 339–357. https://doi.org/10.1016/0006-8993(80)91216-0

Ronald, A., & Hoekstra, R. A. (2011). Autism spectrum disorders and autistic traits: A decade of new twin studies. *American Journal of Medical Genetics Part B: Neuropsychiatric Genetics, 156*(3), 255–274. https://doi.org/10.1002/ajmg.b.31159

Ronemus, M., Iossifov, I., Levy, D., & Wigler, M. (2014). The role of de novo mutations in the genetics of autism spectrum disorders. *Nature Reviews Genetics, 15*, 133–141. https://doi.org/10.1038/nrg3585

Roos, L. E., Horn, S., Berkman, E. T., Pears, K., & Fisher, P. A. (2018). Leveraging translational neuroscience to inform early intervention and addiction prevention for children exposed to early life stress. *Neurobiology of Stress, 9*, 231–240. https://doi.org/10.1016/j.ynstr.2018.10.004

Rosch, E. (1975). Cognitive representations of semantic categories. *Journal of Experimental Psychology: General, 104*, 192–233.

Rosenman, R. H., Brand, R. J., Jenkins, C. D., Friedman, M., Straus, R., & Wurm, M. (1975). Coronary heart disease in the Western Collaborative Group Study: Final follow-up experience of 81/2 years. *Journal of the American Medical Association, 233*(8), 872–877. https://doi.org/10.1001/jama.1975.03260080034016

Rosenman, R. H., Friedman, M., Straus, R., Wurm, M., Kositchek, R., Hahn, W., & Werthessen, N. T. (1964). A predictive study of heart disease. *Journal of the American Medical Association, 189*(1), 15–22. https://doi.org/10.1001/jama.1964.03070010021004

Rosenzweig, M. R., Bennett, E. L., & Diamond, M. C. (1972). Brain changes in response to experience. *Scientific American, 226*(2), 22–29. https://doi.org/10.1038/scientificamerican0272-22

Rosnow, R. L., & Rosenthal, R. (1989). Statistical procedures and the justification of knowledge in psychological science. *American Psychologist, 44*(10), 1276–1284. https://doi.org/10.1037/0003-066X.44.10.1276

Ross, C. E., Mirowsky, J., & Goldsteen, K. (1990). The impact of the family on health: The decade in review. *Journal of Marriage and the Family, 52*(4), 1059–1078. https://doi.org/10.2307/353319

Ross, H. E., & Young, L. J. (2009). Oxytocin and the neural mechanisms regulating social cognition and affiliative behavior. *Frontiers in Neuroendocrinology, 30*(4), 534–547. https://doi.org/10.1016/j.yfrne.2009.05.004

Ross, L. (1977). The intuitive psychologist and his shortcomings: Distortions in the attribution process. *Advances in Experimental Social Psychology, 10*, 173–220. https://doi.org/10.1016/S0065-2601(08)60357-3

Rostosky, S. S., & Riggle, E. D. B. (2017). Same-sex couple relationship strengths: A review and synthesis of the empirical literature (2000–2016). *Psychology of Sexual Orientation and Gender Diversity, 4*(1), 1–13. https://doi.org/10.1037/sgd0000216

Rothbart, M. K. (2011). *Becoming who we are: Temperament and personality in development.* Guilford Press.

Rotter, J. B. (1954). *Social learning and clinical psychology.* Prentice-Hall.

Rovee-Collier, C. (1999). The development of infant memory. *Current Directions in Psychological Science, 8*(3), 80–85. https://doi.org/10.1111/1467-8721.00019

Rowe, D. C., Chassin, L., Presson, C., & Sherman, S. J. (1996). Parental smoking and the "epidemic" spread of cigarette smoking. *Journal of Applied Social Psychology, 26*(5), 437–445. https://doi.org/10.1111/j.1559-1816.1996.tb01858.x

Rowe, D. C., Woulbroun, E. J., & Gulley, B. L. (2013). Peers and friends as nonshared environmental influences. In E. Hetherington, D. Reiss, & R. Plomin (Eds.), *Separate social worlds of siblings: The impact of nonshared environment on development* (pp. 159–174). Erlbaum.

Roy, A. (1992). Are there genetic factors in suicide? *International Review of Psychiatry, 4*(2), 169–175. https://doi.org/10.3109/09540269209066314

Rubia, K., Alegria, A., & Brinson, H. (2014). Imaging the ADHD brain: Disorder-specificity, medication effects and clinical translation. *Expert Review of Neurotherapeutics, 14*(5), 519–538. https://doi.org/10.1586/14737175.2014.907526
Rudnev, M., Magun, V., & Schwartz, S. (2018). Relations among higher order values around the world. *Journal of Cross-Cultural Psychology, 49*(8), 1165–1182. https://doi.org/10.1177/0022022118782644
Rule, N. O. (2017). Perceptions of sexual orientation from minimal cues. *Archives of Sexual Behavior, 46*(1), 129–139. https://doi.org/10.1007/s10508-016-0779-2
Rusbult, C. E., & Buunk, B. P. (1993). Commitment processes in close relationships: An interdependence analysis. *Journal of Social and Personal Relationships, 10*(2), 175–204. https://doi.org/10.1177/026540759301000202
Rusbult, C. E., & Van Lange, P. A. M. (1996). Interdependence processes. In E. T. Higgins & A. Kruglanski (Eds.), *Social psychology: Handbook of basic principles* (pp. 564–596). Guilford Press.
Ruscio, A. M., Brown, T. A., Chiu, W. T., Sareen, J., Stein, M. B., & Kessler, R. C. (2008). Social fears and social phobia in the USA: Results from the national comorbidity survey replication. *Psychological Medicine, 38*(1), 15–28. https://doi.org/10.1017/s0033291707001699
Russell, G., & Lightman, S. (2019). The human stress response. *Nature Reviews Endocrinology, 15*(9), 525–534. https://doi.org/10.1038/s41574-019-0228-0
Russell, J. A. (2003). Core affect and the psychological construction of emotion. *Psychological Review, 110*(1), 145–172. https://doi.org/10.1037/0033-295X.110.1.145
Russell, M. A. H. (1990). The nicotine trap: A 40-year sentence for four cigarettes. *British Journal of Addiction, 85*(2), 293–300. https://doi.org/10.1111/j.1360-0443.1990.tb03085.x
Rutgers, A. H., Bakermans-Kranenburg, M. J., van Ijzendoorn, M. H., & van Berckelaer-Onnes, I. A. (2004). Autism and attachment: A meta-analytic review. *Journal of Child Psychology and Psychiatry, 45*(6), 1123–1134. https://doi.org/10.1111/j.1469-7610.2004.t01-1-00305.x
Rutledge, R. B., Skandali, N., Dayan, P., & Dolan, R. J. (2014). A computational and neural model of momentary subjective well-being. *Proceedings of the National Academy of Sciences, 111*(33), 12252–12257. https://doi.org/10.1073/pnas.1407535111
Ryan, R. M., & Deci, E. L. (2017). *Self-determination theory: Basic psychological needs in motivation, development, and wellness.* Guilford Press.
Ryan, S. A., Ammerman, S. D., & AAP Committee on Substance Use and Prevention (2017). Counseling parents and teens about marijuana use in the era of legalization of marijuana. *Pediatrics, 139*(3), Article e20164069. https://doi.org/10.1542/peds.2016-4069
Ryder, J. G., & Holtzheimer, P. E. (2016). Deep brain stimulation for depression: An update. *Current Behavioral Neuroscience Reports, 3*(2), 102–108. https://doi.org/10.1007/s40473-016-0073-6
Saarimäki, H., Gotsopoulos, A., Jääskeläinen, I. P., Lampinen, J., Vuilleumier, P., Hari, R., Sams, M., & Nummenmaa, L. (2016). Discrete neural signatures of basic emotions. *Cerebral Cortex, 26*(6), 2563–2573. https://doi.org/10.1093/cercor/bhv086
Sabol, S. Z., Nelson, M. L., Fisher, C., Gunzerath, L., Brody, C. L., Hu, S., Sirota, L. A., Marcus, S. E., Greenberg, B. D., Lucas, F. R., Benjamin, J., Murphy, D. L., & Hamer, D. H. (1999). A genetic association for cigarette smoking behavior. *Health Psychology, 18*(1), 7–13. https://doi.org/10.1037/0278-6133.18.1.7
Sacks, O. (1995). *An anthropologist on Mars: Seven paradoxical tales.* Knopf.
Sagiv, L., Roccas, S., Cieciuch, J., & Schwartz, S. H. (2017). Personal values in human life. *Nature Human Behaviour, 1*(9), 630–639. https://doi.org/10.1038/s41562-017-0185-3
Saha, S., Chant, D. C., Welham, J. L., & McGrath, J. J. (2006). The incidence and prevalence of schizophrenia varies with latitude. *Acta Psychiatrica Scandinavica, 114*(1), 36–39. https://doi.org/10.1111/j.1600-0447.2005.00742.x
Sala Frigerio, C., & De Strooper, B. (2016). Alzheimer's disease mechanisms and emerging roads to novel therapeutics. *Annual Review of Neuroscience, 39*(1), 57–79. https://doi.org/10.1146/annurev-neuro-070815-014015
Salimpoor, V. N., Benovoy, M., Larcher, K., Dagher, A., & Zatorre, R. J. (2011). Anatomically distinct dopamine release during anticipation and experience of peak emotion to music. *Nature Neuroscience, 14*, 257–262. https://doi.org/10.1038/nn.2726
Salovey, P., & Grewal, D. (2005). The science of emotional intelligence. *Current Directions in Psychological Science, 14*(6), 281–285. https://doi.org/10.1111/j.0963-7214.2005.00381.x
Salovey, P., & Mayer, J. D. (1990). Emotional intelligence. *Imagination, Cognition, and Personality, 9*(3), 185–211. https://doi.org/10.2190/dugg-p24e-52wk-6cdg
Salthouse, T. (1992). The information-processing perspective on cognitive aging. In R. Sternberg & C. Berg (Eds.), *Intellectual development* (pp. 261–277). Cambridge University Press.
Salthouse, T. A., & Madden, D. J. (2013). Information processing speed and aging. In J. DeLuca & J. H. Kalmar (Eds.), *Information processing speed in clinical populations* (pp. 221–241). Taylor & Francis.
Salum, G. A., Polanczyk, G. V., Miguel, E. C., & Rohde, L. A. P. (2010). Effects of childhood development on late-life mental disorders. *Current Opinion in Psychiatry, 23*(6), 498–503. https://doi.org/10.1097/YCO.0b013e32833ead33
Salvador, R., Vega, D., Pascual, J. C., Marco, J., Canales-Rodríguez, E. J., Aguilar, S., Anguera, M., Soto, A., Ribas, J., Soler, J., Maristany, T., Rodríguez-Fornells, A., & Pomarol-Clotet, E. (2016). Converging medial frontal resting state and diffusion-based abnormalities in borderline personality disorder. *Biological Psychiatry, 79*(2), 107–116. https://doi.org/10.1016/j.biopsych.2014.08.026
Sana, F., Weston, T., & Cepeda, N. J. (2013). Laptop multitasking hinders classroom learning for both users and nearby peers. *Computers & Education, 62*, 24–31. https://doi.org/10.1016/j.compedu.2012.10.003
Sanchez-Roige, S., Gray, J. C., MacKillop, J., Chen, C.-H., & Palmer, A. A. (2018). The genetics of human personality. *Genes, Brain and Behavior, 17*(3), Article e12439. https://doi.org/10.1111/gbb.12439
Sandbank, M., Bottema-Beutel, K., Crowley, S., Cassidy, M., Dunham, K., Feldman, J. I., Crank, J., Albarran, S. A., Raj, S., Mahbub, P., & Woynaroski, T. G. (2020). Project AIM: Autism intervention meta-analysis for studies of young children. *Psychological Bulletin, 146*(1), 1–29. https://doi.org/10.1037/bul0000215
Sanders, M. R., Kirby, J. N., Tellegen, C. L., & Day, J. J. (2014). The Triple P-Positive Parenting Program: A systematic review and meta-analysis of a multi-level system of parenting support. *Clinical Psychology Review, 34*(4), 337–357. https://doi.org/10.1016/j.cpr.2014.04.003
Santiago, C. D., Wadsworth, M. E., & Stump, J. (2011). Socioeconomic status, neighborhood disadvantage, and poverty-related stress: Prospective effects on psychological syndromes among diverse low-income families. *Journal of Economic Psychology, 32*(2), 218–230. https://doi.org/10.1016/j.joep.2009.10.008
Sapolsky, R. M. (1994). *Why zebras don't get ulcers.* Freeman.
Sargent, J. D., & Heatherton, T. F. (2009). Comparison of trends for adolescent smoking and smoking in movies, 1990–2007. *Journal of the American Medical Association, 301*(21), 2211–2213. https://doi.org/10.1001/jama.2009.745
Sargent, J. D., Beach, M. L., Adachi-Mejia, A. M., Gibson, J. J., Titus-Ernstoff, L. T., Carusi, C. P., Swain, S. D., Heatherton, T. F., & Dalton, M. A. (2005). Exposure to movie smoking: Its relation to smoking initiation among US adolescents. *Pediatrics, 116*(5), 1183–1191. https://doi.org/10.1542/peds.2005-0714
Sassenrath, C., Hodges, S. D., & Pfattheicher, S. (2016). It's all about the self: When perspective taking backfires. *Current Directions in Psychological Science, 25*(6), 405–410. https://doi.org/10.1177/0963721416659253
Satija, A., & Hu, F. B. (2018). Plant-based diets and cardiovascular health. *Trends in Cardiovascular Medicine, 28*(7), 437–441. https://doi.org/10.1016/j.tcm.2018.02.004
Satpute, A. B., & Lindquist, K. A. (2019). The default mode network's role in discrete emotion. *Trends in Cognitive Sciences, 23*(10), 851–864. https://doi.org/10.1016/j.tics.2019.07.003
Satpute, A. B., Nook, E. C., Narayanan, S., Shu, J., Weber, J., & Ochsner, K. N. (2016). Emotions in "black and white" or shades of gray? How we think about emotion shapes our perception and neural representation of emotion. *Psychological Science, 27*(11), 1428–1442. https://doi.org/10.1177/0956797616661555
Saucier, G. (2009). Recurrent personality dimensions in inclusive lexical studies: Indications for a Big Six structure. *Journal of Personality, 77*(5), 1577–1614. https://doi.org/10.1111/j.1467-6494.2009.00593.x
Saucier, G., Kenner, J., Iurino, K., Bou Malham, P., Chen, Z., Thalmayer, A. G., Kemmelmeier, M., Tov, W., Boutti, R., Metaferia, H., Çankaya, B., Mastor, K. A., Hsu, K.-Y., Wu, R., Maniruzzaman, M., Rugira, J., Tsaousis, I., Sosnyuk, O., Adhikary, J. R., . . . Altschul, C. (2015). Cross-cultural differences in a global "survey of world views." *Journal of Cross-Cultural Psychology, 46*(1), 53–70. https://doi.org/10.1177/0022022114551791

Savage-Rumbaugh, S., Shanker, S. G., & Taylor, T. J. (1998). *Apes, language, and the human mind*. Oxford University Press.
Sayette, M. A. (1993). An appraisal-disruption model of alcohol's effects on stress responses in social drinkers. *Psychological Bulletin, 114*(3), 459–476. https://doi.org/10.1037/0033-2909.114.3.459
Schachter, H. M., Pham, B., King, J., Langford, S., & Moher, D. (2001). How efficacious and safe is short-acting methylphenidate for the treatment of attention-deficit hyperactivity disorder in children and adolescents? A meta-analysis. *Canadian Medical Association Journal, 165*(11), 1475–1488. https://www.ncbi.nlm.nih.gov/pmc/articles/PMC81663/
Schachter, S. (1959). *The psychology of affiliation*. Stanford University Press.
Schachter, S., & Singer, J. (1962). Cognitive, social, and physiological determinants of emotional state. *Psychological Review, 69*(5), 379–399. https://doi.org/10.1037/h0046234
Schacter, D. L. (1996). *Searching for memory: The brain, the mind, and the past*. Basic Books.
Schaie, K. W. (1990). Intellectual development in adulthood. In J. E. Birren & K. W. Schaie (Eds.), *Handbook of the psychology of aging* (3rd ed., pp. 291–319). Van Nostrand Reinhold.
Schank, R. C., & Abelson, R. P. (1977). *Scripts, plans, goals, and understanding*. Erlbaum.
Scheerer, M. (1963). Problem-solving. *Scientific American, 208*(4), 118–128. https://doi.org/10.1038/scientificamerican0463-118
Schellenberg, E. G. (2012). Cognitive performance after listening to music: A review of the Mozart effect. In R. A. Macdonald, G. Kreutz, & L. Mitchell (Eds.), *Music, health, and well-being* (pp. 324–338). Oxford University Press.
Schiffman, J., Walker, E., Ekstrom, M., Schulsinger, F., Sorensen, H., & Mednick, S. (2004). Childhood videotaped social and neuro-motor precursors of schizophrenia: A prospective investigation. *American Journal of Psychiatry, 161*(11), 2021–2027.
Schizophrenia Working Group of the Psychiatric Genomics Consortium. (2014). Biological insights from 108 schizophrenia-associated genetic loci. *Nature, 511*, 421–427. https://doi.org/10.1038/nature13595
Schlam, T. R., & Baker, T. B. (2013). Interventions for tobacco smoking. *Annual Review of Clinical Psychology, 9*, 675–702. https://doi.org/10.1146/annurev-clinpsy-050212-185602
Schlitz, M., Bem, D., Cardeña, E., Lyke, J., Grover, R., Blackmore, S., Tressoldi, P., Roney-Dougal, S., Bierman, D., Jolij, J., Lobach, E., Marcusson-Clavertz, D., Hartelius, G., & Delorme, A. (2018). Experimenter effect and replication in psi research II: A global initiative. *Journal of Parapsychology, 82*(2), 115.
Schmader, T. (2010). Stereotype threat deconstructed. *Current Directions in Psychological Science, 19*(1), 14–18. https://doi.org/10.1177/0963721409359292
Schmader, T., Johns, M., & Forbes, C. (2008). An integrated process model of stereotype threat effects on performance. *Psychological Review, 115*(2), 336–356. https://doi.org/10.1037/0033-295X.115.2.336
Schmidt, N. B., & Keough, M. E. (2010). Treatment of panic. *Annual Review of Clinical Psychology, 6*(1), 241–256. https://doi.org/10.1146/annurev.clinpsy.121208.131317
Schmitt, D. P., Allik, J., McCrae, R. R., & Benet-Martínez, V. (2007). The geographic distribution of Big Five personality traits: Patterns and profiles of human self-description across 56 nations. *Journal of Cross-Cultural Psychology, 38*(2), 173–212. https://doi.org/10.1177/0022022106297299
Schmitt, G. R., Reedt, L., & Blackwell, K. (2017). *Demographic differences in sentencing*. https://www.ussc.gov/research/research-reports/demographic-differences-sentencing
Schmitz, T. W., De Rosa, E., & Anderson, A. K. (2009). Opposing influences of affective state valence on visual cortical encoding. *Journal of Neuroscience, 29*(22), 7199–7207. https://doi.org/10.1523/JNEUROSCI.5387-08.2009
Schneirla, T. C. (1959). An evolutionary and developmental theory of biphasic processes underlying approach and withdrawal. In M. R. Jones (Ed.), *Nebraska symposium on motivation, 1959* (pp. 1–42). University of Nebraska Press.
Schoenbaum, G., Esber, G. R., & Iordanova, M. D. (2013). Dopamine signals mimic reward prediction errors. *Nature Neuroscience, 16*, 777–779. https://doi.org/10.1038/nn.3448
Schoenemann, P. T., Sheehan, M. J., & Glotzer, L. D. (2005). Prefrontal white matter volume is disproportionately larger in humans than in other primates. *Nature Neuroscience, 8*(2), 242–252. https://doi.org/10.1038/nn1394
Schuch, F. B., Vancampfort, D., Richards, J., Rosenbaum, S., Ward, P., & Stubbs, B. (2016). Exercise as a treatment for depression: A meta-analysis adjusting for publication bias. *Journal of Psychiatric Research, 77*, 42–51. https://doi.org/10.1016/j.jpsychires.2016.02.023
Schuch, F. B., Vancampfort, D., Sui, X., Rosenbaum, S., Firth, J., Richards, J., Ward, P. B., & Stubbs, B. (2016). Are lower levels of cardiorespiratory fitness associated with incident depression? A systematic review of prospective cohort studies. *Preventive Medicine, 93*, 159–165. https://doi.org/10.1016/j.ypmed.2016.10.011
Schultz, P. W., Nolan, J. M., Cialdini, R. B., Goldstein, N. J., & Griskevicius, V. (2007). The constructive, destructive, and reconstructive power of social norms. *Psychological Science, 18*(5), 429–434. https://doi.org/10.1111/j.1467-9280.2007.01917.x
Schultz, W. (1998). Predictive reward signal of dopamine neurons. *Journal of Neurophysiology, 80*(1), 1–27. https://doi.org/10.1152/jn.1998.80.1.1
Schultz, W. (2016). Dopamine reward prediction-error signalling: A two-component response. *Nature Reviews Neuroscience, 17*(3), 183–195. https://doi.org/10.1038/nrn.2015.26
Schultz, W., Dayan, P., & Montague, P. R. (1997). A neural substrate of prediction and reward. *Science, 275*(5306), 1593–1599. https://doi.org/10.1126/science.275.5306.1593
Schünemann, J., Strulik, H., & Trimborn, T. (2020). The marriage gap: Optimal aging and death in partnerships. *Review of Economic Dynamics, 36*, 158–176. https://doi.org/10.1016/j.red.2019.09.004
Schwartz, B. (2004). *The paradox of choice: Why more is less*. Ecco.
Schwartz, B., Ward, A., Monterosso, J., Lyubomirsky, S., White, K., & Lehman, D. R. (2002). Maximizing versus satisficing: Happiness is a matter of choice. *Journal of Personality and Social Psychology, 83*(5), 1178–1197. https://doi.org/10.1037/0022-3514.83.5.1178
Schwartz, C. E., Wright, C. I., Shin, L. M., Kagan, J., & Rauch, S. L. (2003). Inhibited and uninhibited infants "grown up": Adult amygdalar response to novelty. *Science, 300*(5627), 1952–1953. https://doi.org/10.1126/science.1083703
Schwartz, S. H. (2012). An overview of the Schwartz theory of basic values. *Online Readings in Psychology and Culture, 2*(1). https://doi.org/10.9707/2307-0919.1116
Schwartz, S., & Maquet, P. (2002). Sleep imaging and the neuropsychological assessment of dreams. *Trends in Cognitive Sciences, 6*(1), 23–30. https://doi.org/10.1016/s1364-6613(00)01818-0
Schwarz, N., & Clore, G. L. (1983). Mood, misattribution, and judgments of well-being: Informative and directive functions of affective states. *Journal of Personality and Social Psychology, 45*(3), 513–523. https://doi.org/10.1037/0022-3514.45.3.513
Sclafani, A., & Springer, D. (1976). Dietary obesity in adult rats: Similarities to hypothalamic and human obesity syndromes. *Physiology and Behavior, 17*(3), 461–471. https://doi.org/10.1016/0031-9384(76)90109-8
Seblova, D., Berggren, R., & Lövdén, M. (2020). Education and age-related decline in cognitive performance: Systematic review and meta-analysis of longitudinal cohort studies. *Ageing Research Reviews, 58*, Article 101005. https://doi.org/10.1016/j.arr.2019.101005
Sedikides, C., & Gregg, A. P. (2008). Self-enhancement: Food for thought. *Perspectives on Psychological Science, 3*(2), 102–116. https://doi.org/10.1111/j.1745-6916.2008.00068.x
Sedikides, C., Gaertner, L., & Toguchi, Y. (2003). Pancultural self-enhancement. *Journal of Personality and Social Psychology, 84*(1), 60–79. https://doi.org/10.1037/0022-3514.84.1.60
Sedikides, C., Gaertner, L., & Vevea, J. L. (2005). Pancultural self-enhancement reloaded: A meta-analytic reply to Heine (2005). *Journal of Personality and Social Psychology, 89*, 539–551. https://doi.org/10.1037/0022-3514.89.4.539
Segerstrom, S. C., & Miller, G. E. (2004). Psychological stress and the human immune system: A meta-analytic study of 30 years of inquiry. *Psychological Bulletin, 130*(4), 601–630. https://doi.org/10.1037/0033-2909.130.4.601
Seligman, M. E. (1970). On the generality of the laws of learning. *Psychological Review, 77*(5), 406–418. https://doi.org/10.1037/h0029790
Seligman, M. E. P. (1974). Depression and learned helplessness. In R. J. Friedman & M. M. Katz (Eds.), *The psychology of depression: Contemporary theory and research* (pp. 83–113). V. H. Winston.
Seligman, M. E. P. (1975). *Helplessness: On depression, development, and death*. Freeman.
Seligman, M. E. P. (2011). *Flourish*. Simon & Schuster.
Seligman, M. E. P., & Csikszentmihalyi, M. (2000). Positive psychology: An introduction. *American Psychologist, 55*(1), 5–14. https://doi.org/10.1037/0003-066X.55.1.5
Seligman, M. E. P., Steen, T. A., Park, N., & Peterson, C. (2005). Positive psychology progress: Empirical validation of interventions.

American Psychologist, 60(5), 410–421. https://doi.org/10.1037/0003-066X.60.5.410
Seligman, M. E. P., Walker, E. F., & Rosenhan, D. L. (2001). *Abnormal psychology* (4th ed.). Norton.
Selkie, E. M., Fales, J. L., & Moreno, M. A. (2016). Cyberbullying prevalence among US middle and high school–aged adolescents: A systematic review and quality assessment. *Journal of Adolescent Health, 58*(2), 125–133. https://doi.org/10.1016/j.jadohealth.2015.09.026
Selye, H. (1936). A syndrome produced by diverse nocuous agents. *Nature, 138*, 32. https://doi.org/10.1038/138032a0
Senghas, A., & Coppola, M. (2001). Children creating language: How Nicaraguan sign language acquired a spatial grammar. *Psychological Science, 12*(4), 323–328. https://doi.org/10.1111/1467-9280.00359
Sentencing Project. (2018). *Report to the United Nations on racial disparities in the U.S. criminal justice system*. https://www.sentencingproject.org/publications/un-report-on-racial-disparities/
Sevi, B., & Doğruyol, B. (2020). Looking from the bright side: The Light Triad predicts Tinder use for love. *Journal of Social and Personal Relationships, 37*(7), 2136–2144. https://doi.org/10.1177/0265407520918942
Sevi, B., Urganci, B. & Sakman, E. (2020). Who cheats? An examination of light and dark personality traits as predictors of infidelity. *Personality and Individual Differences, 164*, Article 110126. https://doi.org/10.1016/j.paid.2020.110126
Shackman, A. J., Fox, A. S., Oler, J. A., Shelton, S. E., Davidson, R. J., & Kalin, N. H. (2013). Neural mechanisms underlying heterogeneity in the presentation of anxious temperament. *Proceedings of the National Academy of Sciences, 110*(15), 6145–6150. https://doi.org/10.1073/pnas.1214364110
Shah, R. S., Chang, S., Min, H., Cho, Z., Blaha, C., & Lee, K. H. (2010). Deep brain stimulation: Technology at the cutting edge. *Journal of Clinical Neurology, 6*(4), 167–182. https://doi.org/10.3988/jcn.2010.6.4.167
Shallice, T., & Warrington, E. K. (1970). Independent functioning of verbal memory stores: A neuropsychological study. *Quarterly Journal of Experimental Psychology, 22*(2), 261–273. https://doi.org/10.1080/00335557043000203
Shapiro, J. R., Williams, A. M., & Hambarchyan, M. (2013). Are all interventions created equal? A multi-threat approach to tailoring stereotype threat interventions. *Journal of Personality and Social Psychology, 104*(2), 277–288. https://doi.org/10.1037/a0030461
Shaw, A., & Olson, K. R. (2012). Children discard a resource to avoid inequity. *Journal of Experimental Psychology: General, 141*(2), 382–395. https://doi.org/10.1037/a0025907
Shaw, J. S., Bjork, R. A., & Handal, A. (1995). Retrieval-induced forgetting in an eyewitness-memory paradigm. *Psychonomic Bulletin & Review, 2*, 249–253. https://doi.org/10.3758/BF03210965
Shaw, P., Malek, M., Watson, B., Sharp, W., Evans, A., & Greenstein, D. (2012). Development of cortical surface area and gyrification in attention-deficit/hyperactivity disorder. *Biological Psychiatry, 72*(3), 191–197. https://doi.org/10.1016/j.biopsych.2012.01.031
Shedler, J. (2010). The efficacy of psychodynamic psychotherapy. *American Psychologist, 65*(2), 98–109. https://doi.org/10.1037/a0018378
Shedler, J. (2015). Where is the evidence for "evidence-based" therapy? *Journal of Psychological Therapies in Primary Care, 4*, 47–59.
Sheffield, J. M., & Barch, D. M. (2016). Cognition and resting-state functional connectivity in schizophrenia. *Neuroscience & Biobehavioral Reviews, 61*, 108–120. https://doi.org/10.1016/j.neubiorev.2015.12.007
Shenhav, A., Musslick, S., Lieder, F., Kool, W., Griffiths, T. L., Cohen, J. D., & Botvinick, M. M. (2017). Toward a rational and mechanistic account of mental effort. *Annual Review of Neuroscience, 40*, 99–124. https://doi.org/10.1146/annurev-neuro-072116-031526
Shenkin, S. D., Starr, J. M., & Deary, I. J. (2004). Birth weight and cognitive ability in childhood: A systematic review. *Psychological Bulletin, 130*(6), 989–1013. https://doi.org/10.1037/0033-2909.130.6.989
Shephard, R. J. (1997). *Aging, physical activity, and health*. Human Kinetics Publishers.
Sherif, M. (1936). *The psychology of social norms*. Harper.
Sherif, M., Harvey, O. J., White, B. J., Hood, W. R., & Sherif, C. W. (1961). *Intergroup cooperation and competition: The Robbers Cave experiment*. University Book Exchange.
Sherman, R. A., Nave, C. S., & Funder, D. C. (2010). Situational similarity and personality predict behavioral consistency. *Journal of Personality and Social Psychology, 99*(2), 330–343. https://doi.org/10.1037/a0019796
Shih, M. J., Stotzer, R., & Gutiérrez, A. S. (2013). Perspective-taking and empathy: Generalizing the reduction of group bias towards Asian Americans to general outgroups. *Asian American Journal of Psychology, 4*(2), 79–83. https://doi.org/10.1037/a0029790
Shih, M., Pittinsky, T. L., & Ambady, N. (1999). Stereotype susceptibility: Identity salience and shifts in quantitative performance. *Psychological Science, 10*(1), 80–83. https://doi.org/10.1111/1467-9280.00111
Shin, L. M., Rauch, S. L., & Pitman, R. K. (2006). Amygdala, medial prefrontal cortex, and hippocampal function in PTSD. *Annals of the New York Academy of Sciences, 1071*(1), 67–79. https://doi.org/10.1196/annals.1364.007
Shiner, R. L., Allen, T. A., & Masten, A. S. (2017). Adversity in adolescence predicts personality trait change from childhood to adulthood. *Journal of Research in Personality, 67*, 171–182. https://doi.org/10.1016/j.jrp.2016.10.002
Shipstead, Z., Redick, T. S., & Engle, R. W. (2012). Is working memory training effective? *Psychological Bulletin, 138*(4), 628–654. https://doi.org/10.1037/a0027473
Sibley, M. H., Pelham, W. E., Jr., Molina, B. S. G., Gnagy, E. M., Waschbusch, D. A., Garefino, A. C., Kuriyan, A. B., Babinski, D. E., & Karch, K. M. (2012). Diagnosing ADHD in adolescence. *Journal of Consulting and Clinical Psychology, 80*(1), 139–150. https://doi.org/10.1037/a0026577
Sidanius, J., & Pratto, F. (2001). *Social dominance: An intergroup theory of social hierarchy and oppression*. Cambridge University Press.
Siegel, C. E., Laska, E. M., Wanderling, J. A., Hernandez, J. C., & Levenson, R. B. (2015). Prevalence and diagnosis rates of childhood ADHD among racial-ethnic groups in a public mental health system. *Psychiatric Services, 67*(2), 199–205. https://doi.org/10.1176/appi.ps.201400364
Siegel, J. M. (2008). Do all animals sleep? *Trends in Neuroscience, 31*(4), 208–213. https://doi.org/10.1016/j.tins.2008.02.001
Siegel, S. (1984). Pavlovian conditioning and heroin overdose: Reports by overdose victims. *Bulletin of the Psychonomic Society, 22*(5), 428–430. https://doi.org/10.3758/BF03333867
Siegel, S. (2005). Drug tolerance, drug addiction, and drug anticipation. *Current Directions in Psychological Science, 14*(6), 296–300. https://doi.org/10.1111/j.0963-7214.2005.00384.x
Siegel, S. (2016). The heroin overdose mystery. *Current Directions in Psychological Science, 25*(6), 375–379. https://doi.org/10.1177/0963721416664404
Siegel, S., Baptista, M. A. S., Kim, J. A., McDonald, R. V., & Weise-Kelly, L. (2000). Pavlovian psychopharmacology: The associative basis of tolerance. *Experimental and Clinical Psychopharmacology, 8*(3), 276–293. https://doi.org/10.1037/1064-1297.8.3.276
Siegel, S., Hinson, R. E., Krank, M. D., & McCully, J. (1982). Heroin "overdose" death: Contribution of drug-associated environmental cues. *Science, 216*(4544), 436–437. https://doi.org/10.1126/science.7200260
Siegler, I. C., Costa, P. T., Brummett, B. H., Helms, M. J., Barefoot, J. C., Williams, R., Dahlstrom, W. G., Kaplan, B. H., Vitaliano, P. P., Nichaman, M. Z., Day, R. S., & Rimer, B. K. (2003). Patterns of change in hostility from college to midlife in the UNC alumni heart study predict high-risk status. *Psychosomatic Medicine, 65*(5), 738–745. https://doi.org/10.1097/01.PSY.0000088583.25140.9C
Sievers, B., Polansky, L., Casey, M., & Wheatley, T. (2013). Music and movement share a dynamic structure that supports universal expressions of emotion. *Proceedings of the National Academy of Sciences, 110*(1), 70–75. https://doi.org/10.1073/pnas.1209023110
Silber, M. H., Ancoli-Israel, S., Bonnet, M. H., Chokroverty, S., Grigg-Damberger, M. M., Hirshkowitz, M., Kapen, S., Keenan, S. A., Kryger, M. H., Penzel, T., Pressman, M. R., & Iber, C. (2007). The visual scoring of sleep in adults. *Journal of Clinical Sleep Medicine, 3*(2), 121–131. https://doi.org/10.5664/jcsm.26814
Silva, C. E., & Kirsch, I. (1992). Interpretive sets, expectancy, fantasy proneness, and dissociation as predictors of hypnotic response. *Journal of Personality and Social Psychology, 63*(5), 847–856. https://doi.org/10.1037/0022-3514.63.5.847
Silvers, J. A., Insel, C., Powers, A., Franz, P., Helion, C., Martin, R., Weber, J., Mischel, W., Casey, B. J., & Ochsner, K. N. (2017). The transition from childhood to adolescence is marked by a general decrease in amygdala reactivity and an affect-specific ventral-to-dorsal shift in medial prefrontal recruitment. *Developmental Cognitive Neuroscience, 25*, 128–137. https://doi.org/10.1016/j.dcn.2016.06.005
Sim, J. J., Goyle, A., McKedy, W., Eidelman, S., & Correll, J. (2014). How social identity shapes the working self-concept. *Journal of Experimental Social Psychology, 55*, 271–277. https://doi.org/10.1016/j.jesp.2014.07.015

Simeone, J. C., Ward, A. J., Rotella, P., Collins, J., & Windisch, R. (2015). An evaluation of variation in published estimates of schizophrenia prevalence from 1990–2013: A systematic literature review. *BMC Psychiatry, 15*(1), Article 193. https://doi.org/10.1186/s12888-015-0578-7

Simmons, J. P., Nelson, L. D., & Simonsohn, U. (2011). False-positive psychology: Undisclosed flexibility in data collection and analysis allows presenting anything as significant. *Psychological Science, 22*(11), 1359–1366. https://doi.org/10.1177/0956797611417632

Simner, J., Mulvenna, C., Sagiv, N., Tsakanikos, E., Witherby, S. A., Fraser, C., Scott, K., & Ward, J. (2006). Synaesthesia: The prevalence of atypical cross-modal experiences. *Perception, 35*(8), 1024–1033. https://doi.org/10.1068/p5469

Simons, D. J., & Levin, D. T. (1998). Failure to detect changes to people during a real-world interaction. *Psychonomic Bulletin & Review, 5*(4), 644–649. https://doi.org/10.3758/BF03208840

Simons, D. J., Boot, W. R., Charness, N., Gathercole, S. E., Chabris, C. F., Hambrick, D. Z., & Stine-Morrow, E. A. (2016). Do "brain-training" programs work? *Psychological Science in the Public Interest, 17*(3), 103–186. https://doi.org/10.1177/1529100616661983

Simpson, H. B., Foa, E. B., Liebowitz, M. R., Ledley, D. R., Huppert, J. D., Cahill, S., Vermes, D., Schmidt, A. B., Hembree, E., Franklin, M., Campeas, R., Hahn, C.-G., & Petkova, E. (2008). A randomized, controlled trial of cognitive-behavioral therapy for augmenting pharmacotherapy in obsessive-compulsive disorder. *American Journal of Psychiatry, 165*(5), 621–630. https://doi.org/10.1176/appi.ajp.2007.07091440

Simpson, J., & Kelly, J. P. (2011). The impact of environmental enrichment in laboratory rats—behavioural and neurochemical aspects. *Behavioural Brain Research, 222*(1), 246–264. https://doi.org/10.1016/j.bbr.2011.04.002

Sims, T., Hogan, C. L., & Carstensen, L. L. (2015). Selectivity as an emotion regulation strategy: Lessons from older adults. *Current Opinion in Psychology, 3*, 80–84. https://doi.org/10.1016/j.copsyc.2015.02.012

Sinclair, A. H., & Barense, M. D. (2019). Prediction error and memory reactivation: How incomplete reminders drive reconsolidation. *Trends in Neurosciences, 42*(10), 727–739. https://doi.org/10.1016/j.tins.2019.08.007

Singer, T. (2006). The neuronal basis and ontogeny of empathy and mind reading: Review of literature and implications for future research. *Neuroscience & Biobehavioral Reviews, 30*(6), 855–863. https://doi.org/10.1016/j.neubiorev.2006.06.011

SixWise.com (2005, July 13). *Six most feared but least likely causes of death*. http://www.sixwise.com/newsletters/05/07/13/the_six_most_feared_but_least_likely_causes_of_death.htm

Skinner, B. F. (1948a). "Superstition" in the pigeon. *Journal of Experimental Psychology, 38*(2), 168–172. https://doi.org/10.1037/h0055873

Skinner, B. F. (1948b). *Walden two*. Hackett.

Skinner, B. F. (1957). *Verbal behavior*. Appleton-Century-Crofts.

Skinner, B. F. (1974). *About behaviorism*. Knopf.

Sloane, S., Baillargeon, R., & Premack, D. (2012). Do infants have a sense of fairness? *Psychological Science, 23*(2), 196–204. https://doi.org/10.1177/0956797611422072

Slovic, P., Fischhoff, B., Lichtenstein, S. (1981). Perceived risk: Psychological factors and social implications. *Proceedings of the Royal Society A: Mathematical and Physical Sciences, 376*(1764), 17–34. https://doi.org/10.1098/rspa.1981.0073

Slutske, W. S., Moffitt, T. E., Poulton, R., & Caspi, A. (2012). Undercontrolled temperament at age 3 predicts disordered gambling at age 32: A longitudinal study of a complete birth cohort. *Psychological Science, 23*(5), 510–516. https://doi.org/10.1177/0956797611429708

Small, G. W., Kepe, V., Siddarth, P., Ercoli, L. M., Merrill, D. A., Donoghue, N., Bookheimer, S. Y., Martinez, J., Omalu, B., Mailes, J., & Barrio, J. R. (2013). PET scanning of brain tau in retired National Football League players: Preliminary findings. *American Journal of Geriatric Psychiatry, 21*(2), 138–144. https://doi.org/10.1016/j.jagp.2012.11.019

Smillie, L. D. (2008). What is reinforcement sensitivity? Neuroscience paradigms for approach-avoidance process theories of personality. *European Journal of Personality, 22*(5), 359–384. https://doi.org/10.1002/per.674

Smith, A. L., & Chapman, S. (2014). Quitting smoking unassisted: The 50-year research neglect of a major public health phenomenon. *Journal of the American Medical Association, 311*(2), 137–138. https://doi.org/10.1001/jama.2013.282618

Smith, A. M., Floerke, V. A., & Thomas, A. K. (2016). Retrieval practice protects memory against acute stress. *Science, 354*(6315), 1046–1048. https://doi.org/10.1126/science.aah5067

Smith, B. L. (2012). Inappropriate prescribing. *Monitor on Psychology, 43*(6), 36. http://www.apa.org/monitor/2012/06/prescribing

Smith, C., & Lapp, L. (1991). Increases in number of REMs and REM density in humans following an intensive learning period. *Sleep, 14*(4), 325–330. https://doi.org/10.1093/sleep/14.4.325

Smith, D. M., Langa, K. M., Kabeto, M. U., & Ubel, P. A. (2005). Health, wealth, and happiness: Financial resources buffer subjective well-being after the onset of a disability. *Psychological Science, 16*(9), 663–666. https://doi.org/10.1111/j.1467-9280.2005.01592.x

Smith, K. S., Berridge, K. C., & Aldridge, J. W. (2011). Disentangling pleasure from incentive salience and learning signals in brain reward circuitry. *Proceedings of the National Academy of Sciences, 108*(27), E255–E264. https://doi.org/10.1073/pnas.1101920108

Smith, L. B., & Thelen, E. (2003). Development as a dynamic system. *Trends in Cognitive Sciences, 7*(8), 343–348. https://doi.org/10.1016/S1364-6613(03)00156-6

Smith, P. D., & Roberts, C. M. (2009). American College Health Association annual Pap test and sexually transmitted infection survey: 2006. *Journal of American College Health, 57*(4), 389–394. https://doi.org/10.3200/JACH.57.4.389-394

Smith, S. M., Glenberg, A. M., & Bjork, R. A. (1978). Environmental context and human memory. *Memory and Cognition, 6*(4), 342–353. https://doi.org/10.3758/BF03197465

Smith, T. W., Orleans, C. T., & Jenkins, C. D. (2004). Prevention and health promotion: Decades of progress, new challenges, and an emerging agenda. *Health Psychology, 23*(2), 126–131. https://doi.org/10.1037/0278-6133.23.2.126

Smyth, J. M., Johnson, J. A., Auer, B. J., Lehman, E., Talamo, G., & Sciamanna, C. N. (2018). Online positive affect journaling in the improvement of mental distress and well-being in general medical patients with elevated anxiety symptoms: A preliminary randomized controlled trial. *JMIR Mental Health, 5*(4), Article e11290. https://doi.org/10.2196/11290

Snarey, J. R. (1985). Cross-cultural universality of social-moral development: A critical review of Kohlbergian research. *Psychological Bulletin, 97*(2), 202–232. https://doi.org/10.1037/0033-2909.97.2.202

Snider, L. A., & Swedo, S. E. (2004). PANDAS: Current status and directions for research. *Molecular Psychiatry, 9*, 900–907. https://doi.org/10.1038/sj.mp.4001542

Snowling, M. J., & Melby-Lervåg, M. (2016). Oral language deficits in familial dyslexia: A meta-analysis and review. *Psychological Bulletin, 142*(5), 498–545. https://doi.org/10.1037/bul0000037

Snyder, H. R., Young, J. F., & Hankin, B. L. (2016). Strong homotypic continuity in common psychopathology-, internalizing-, and externalizing-specific factors over time in adolescents. *Clinical Psychological Science, 5*(1), 98–110. https://doi.org/10.1177/2167702616651076

Snyder, M., Tanke, E. D., & Berscheid, E. (1977). Social perception and interpersonal behavior: On the self-fulfilling nature of social stereotypes. *Journal of Personality and Social Psychology, 35*(9), 656–666. https://doi.org/10.1037/0022-3514.35.9.656

Sokol-Hessner, P., Hsu, M., Curley, N. G., Delgado, M. R., Camerer, C. F., & Phelps, E. A. (2009). Thinking like a trader selectively reduces individuals' loss aversion. *Proceedings of the National Academy of Sciences, 106*(13), 5035–5040. https://doi.org/10.1073/pnas.0806761106

Sokol-Hessner, P., Lackovic, S. F., Tobe, R. H., Camerer, C. F., Leventhal, B. L., & Phelps, E. A. (2015). Determinants of propranolol's selective effect on loss aversion. *Psychological Science, 26*(7), 1123–1130. https://doi.org/10.1177/0956797615582026

Solms, M. (2000). Dreaming and REM sleep are controlled by different brain mechanisms. *Behavioral and Brain Sciences, 23*(6), 843–850. https://doi.org/10.1017/s0140525x00003988

Sommerville, J. A., & Woodward, A. L. (2005). Pulling out the intentional structure of action: The relation between action processing and action production in infancy. *Cognition, 95*(1), 1–30. https://doi.org/10.1016/j.cognition.2003.12.004

Son Hing, L. S., Chung-Yan, G. A., Hamilton, L. K., & Zanna, M. P. (2008). A two-dimensional model that employs explicit and implicit attitudes to characterize prejudice. *Journal of Personality and Social Psychology, 94*(6), 971–987. https://doi.org/10.1037/0022-3514.94.6.971

Soto, C. J., & John, O. P. (2017). The next Big Five Inventory (BFI-2): Developing and assessing a hierarchical model with 15 facets to enhance bandwidth, fidelity, and predictive power. *Journal of Personality and Social Psychology, 113*(1), 117–143. https://doi.org/10.1037/pspp0000096

Spain, S. M., Harms, P., & LeBreton, J. M. (2014). The dark side of personality at work. *Journal of Organizational Behavior, 35*(Suppl 1), S41–S60. https://doi.org/10.1002/job.1894

Spanos, N. P., & Coe, W. C. (1992). A social-psychological approach to hypnosis. In E. Fromm & M. Nash (Eds.), *Contemporary hypnosis research* (pp. 102–130). Guilford Press.

Spearman, C. (1904). "General intelligence," objectively determined and measured. *American Journal of Psychology, 15*(2), 201–293. https://doi.org/10.2307/1412107

Spelke, E. S. (2016). Cognitive abilities of infants. In R. J. Sternberg, S. T. Fiske, & D. J. Foss (Eds.), *Scientists making a difference: One hundred eminent behavioral and brain scientists talk about their most important contributions* (pp. 22–234). Cambridge University Press.

Spencer, M. B., Fegley, S. G., & Harpalani, V. (2003). A theoretical and empirical examination of identity as coping: Linking coping resources to the self processes of African American youth. *Applied Developmental Science, 7*(3), 181–188. https://doi.org/10.1207/S1532480XADS0703_9

Spencer, R. C., Devilbiss, D. M., & Berridge, C. W. (2015). The cognition-enhancing effects of psychostimulants involve direct action in the prefrontal cortex. *Biological Psychiatry, 77*(11), 940–950. https://doi.org/10.1016/j.biopsych.2014.09.013

Spencer, S. J., Logel, C., & Davies, P. G. (2016). Stereotype threat. *Annual Review of Psychology, 67*(1), 415–437. https://doi.org/10.1146/annurev-psych-073115-103235

Sperling, G. (1960). The information available in brief visual presentations. *Psychological Monographs: General and Applied, 74*(11), 1–29. https://doi.org/10.1037/h0093759

Spiegel, D., Lewis-Fernández, R., Lanius, R., Vermetten, E., Simeon, D., & Friedman, M. (2013). Dissociative disorders in DSM-5. *Annual Review of Clinical Psychology, 9*, 299–326. https://doi.org/10.1146/annurev-clinpsy-050212-185531

Spieker, L. E., Hürlimann, D., Ruschitzka, F., Corti, R., Enseleit, F., Shaw, S., Hayoz, D., Deanfield, J. E., Lüscher, T. F., & Noll, G. (2002). Mental stress induces prolonged endothelial dysfunction via endothelin-A receptors. *Circulation, 105*, 2817–2820. https://doi.org/10.1161/01.CIR.0000021598.15895.34

Spitzer, R. L., Skodol, A. E., Gibbon, M., & Williams, J. B. W. (1983). *Psychopathology: A case book.* McGraw-Hill.

Spreng, R. N., & Turner, G. R. (2013). Structural covariance of the default network in healthy and pathological aging. *Journal of Neuroscience, 33*(38), 15226–15234. https://doi.org/10.1523/JNEUROSCI.2261-13.2013

Spurk, D., Keller, A. C., & Hirschi, A. (2016). Do bad guys get ahead or fall behind? Relationships of the dark triad of personality with objective and subjective career success. *Social Psychological and Personality Science, 7*(2), 113–121. https://doi.org/10.1177/1948550615609735

Spurr, K. F., Graven, M. A., & Gilbert, R. W. (2008). Prevalence of unspecified sleep apnea and the use of continuous positive airway pressure in hospitalized patients, 2004 national hospital discharge survey. *Sleep and Breathing, 12*(3), 229–234. https://doi.org/10.1007/s11325-007-0166-2

Squire, L. R. (1987). *Memory and brain.* Oxford University Press.

Squire, L. R., Stark, C. E. L., & Clark, R. E. (2004). The medial temporal lobe. *Annual Review of Neuroscience, 27*(1), 279–306. https://doi.org/10.1146/annurev.neuro.27.070203.144130

Srivastava, S., John, O. P., Gosling, S. D., & Potter, J. (2003). Development of personality in early and middle adulthood: Set like plaster or persistent change? *Journal of Personality and Social Psychology, 84*(5), 1041–1053. https://doi.org/10.1037/0022-3514.84.5.1041

Srivastava, S., McGonigal, K. M., Richards, J. M., Butler, E. A., & Gross, J. J. (2006). Optimism in close relationships: How seeing things in a positive light makes them so. *Journal of Personality and Social Psychology, 91*(1), 143–153. https://doi.org/10.1037/0022-3514.91.1.143

Stanovich, K. E. (2013). *How to think straight about psychology* (10th ed.). Pearson.

Steele, C. M., & Aronson, J. (1995). Stereotype threat and the intellectual test performance of African-Americans. *Journal of Personality and Social Psychology, 69*(5), 797–811. https://doi.org/10.1037/0022-3514.69.5.797

Steeves, J. K. E., Culham, J. C., Duchaine, B. C., Pratesi, C. C., Valyear, K. F., Schindler, I., Humphrey, G. K., Milner, A. D., & Goodale, M. A. (2006). The fusiform face area is not sufficient for face recognition: Evidence from a patient with dense prosopagnosia and no occipital face area. *Neuropsychologia, 44*(4), 594–609. https://doi.org/10.1016/j.neuropsychologia.2005.06.013

Stefanik, M. T., Moussawi, K., Kupchik, Y. M., Smith, K. C., Miller, R. L., Huff, M. L., Deisseroth, K., Kalivas, P. W., & LaLumiere, R. T. (2013). Optogenetic inhibition of cocaine seeking in rats. *Addiction Biology, 18*(1), 50–53. https://doi.org/10.1111/j.1369-1600.2012.00479.x

Stein, M. B., & Stein, D. J. (2008). Social anxiety disorder. *The Lancet, 371*(9618), 1115–1125. https://doi.org/10.1016/s0140-6736(08)60488-2

Stein, M. B., Slavin-Mulford, J., Siefert, C. J., Sinclair, S. J., Renna, M., Malone, J., Bello, I., & Blais, M. A. (2014). SCORS-G stimulus characteristics of select Thematic Apperception Test cards. *Journal of Personality Assessment, 96*(3), 339–349. https://doi.org/10.1080/00223891.2013.823440

Stein, R., & Swan, A. B. (2019). Evaluating the validity of Myers-Briggs Type Indicator theory: A teaching tool and window into intuitive psychology. *Social and Personality Psychology Compass, 13*(2), Article e12434. https://doi.org/10.1111/spc3.12434

Steinberg, L. (2001). We know some things: Parent–adolescent relationships in retrospect and prospect. *Journal of Research on Adolescence, 11*(1), 1–19. https://doi.org/10.1111/1532-7795.00001

Steinberg, L., & Morris, A. S. (2001). Adolescent development. *Journal of Cognitive Education and Psychology, 2*(1), 55–87. https://doi.org/10.1891/194589501787383444

Steiner, J. E. (1977). Facial expressions of the neonate infant indicating the hedonics of food-related chemical stimuli. In J. M. Weiffenbach (Ed.), *Taste and development* (pp. 173–189). National Institutes of Health.

Stender, J., Mortensen, K. N., Thibaut, A., Darkner, S., Laureys, S., Gjedde, A., & Kupers, R. (2016). The minimal energetic requirement of sustained awareness after brain injury. *Current Biology, 26*(11), 1494–1499. https://doi.org/10.1016/j.cub.2016.04.024

Steptoe, A. (2019). Happiness and health. *Annual Review of Public Health, 40*, 339–359. https://doi.org/10.1146/annurev-publhealth-040218-044150

Sternberg, R. J. (1986). A triangular theory of love. *Psychological Review, 93*(2), 119–135. https://doi.org/10.1037/0033-295X.93.2.119

Sternberg, R. J. (1999). The theory of successful intelligence. *Review of General Psychology, 3*(4), 292–316. https://doi.org/10.1037/1089-2680.3.4.292

Stickgold, R., Whidbee, D., Schirmer, B., Patel, V., & Hobson, J. A. (2000). Visual discrimination task improvement: A multi-step process occurring during sleep. *Journal of Cognitive Neuroscience, 12*(2), 246–254. https://doi.org/10.1162/089892900562075

Stinson, D. A., Cameron, J. J., Wood, J. V., Gaucher, D., & Holmes, J. G. (2009). Deconstructing the "reign of error": Interpersonal warmth explains the self-fulfilling prophecy of anticipated acceptance. *Personality and Social Psychology Bulletin, 35*(9), 1165–1178. https://doi.org/10.1177/0146167209338629

Stockwell, T., Zhao, J., Panwar, S., Roemer, A., Naimi, T., & Chikritzhs, T. (2016). Do "moderate" drinkers have reduced mortality risk? A systematic review and meta-analysis of alcohol consumption and all-cause mortality. *Journal of Studies on Alcohol and Drugs, 77*(2), 185–198. https://doi.org/10.15288/jsad.2016.77.185

Stone, A. A., Neale, J. M., Cox, D. S., Napoli, A., Valdimarsdottir, H., & Kennedy-Moore, E. (1994). Daily events are associated with a secretory immune response to an oral antigen in men. *Health Psychology, 13*(5), 440–446. https://doi.org/10.1037/0278-6133.13.5.440

Stone, V. E., Baron-Cohen, S., & Knight, R. T. (1998). Frontal lobe contributions to theory of mind. *Journal of Cognitive Neuroscience, 10*(5), 640–656. https://doi.org/10.1162/089892998562942

Stoner, J. A. (1968). Risky and cautious shifts in group decisions: The influence of widely held values. *Journal of Experimental Social Psychology, 4*(4), 442–459. https://doi.org/10.1016/0022-1031(68)90069-3

Strack, F. (2016). Reflection on the smiling registered replication report. *Perspectives on Psychological Science, 11*(6), 929–930. https://doi.org/10.1177/1745691616674460

Strahan, E. J., Spencer, S. J., & Zanna, M. P. (2002). Subliminal priming and persuasion: Striking while the iron is hot. *Journal of Experimental Social Psychology, 38*(6), 556–568. https://doi.org/10.1016/S0022-1031(02)00502-4

Straube, T., Glauer, M., Dilger, S., Mentzel, H.-J., & Miltner, W. H. R. (2006). Effects of cognitive-behavioral therapy on brain activation in specific phobia. *NeuroImage, 29*(1), 125–135. https://doi.org/10.1016/j.neuroimage.2005.07.007

Strayhorn, T. L. (2014). What role does grit play in the academic success of black male

collegians at predominantly white institutions? *Journal of African American Studies, 18*(1), 1–10. https://doi.org/10.1007/s12111-012-9243-0
Stroop, J. R. (1935). Studies of interference in serial verbal reactions. *Journal of Experimental Psychology, 18*(6), 643–662. https://doi.org/10.1037/h0054651
Substance Abuse and Mental Health Services Administration. (2019). *2018 national survey on drug use and health: Detailed tables.* https://www.samhsa.gov/data/report/2018-nsduh-detailed-tables
Sugden, N. A., & Marquis, A. R. (2017). Meta-analytic review of the development of face discrimination in infancy: Face race, face gender, infant age, and methodology moderate face discrimination. *Psychological Bulletin, 143*(11), 1201–1244. https://doi.org/10.1037/bul0000116
Sugiyama, L. S. (2015). Physical attractiveness in adaptationist perspective. In D. M. Buss (Ed.), *The handbook of evolutionary psychology* (pp. 292–343). Wiley. https://doi.org/10.1002/9780470939376.ch10
Sui, J., & Humphreys, G. W. (2015). The integrative self: How self-reference integrates perception and memory. *Trends in Cognitive Sciences, 19*(12), 719–728. https://doi.org/10.1016/j.tics.2015.08.015
Suls, J., Lemos, K., & Stewart, H. L. (2002). Self-esteem, construal, and comparisons with the self, friends, and peers. *Journal of Personality and Social Psychology, 82*(2), 252–261. https://doi.org/10.1037/0022-3514.82.2.252
Super, C. M. (1976). Environmental effects on motor development: The case of African infant precocity. *Developmental Medicine and Child Neurology, 18*(5), 561–567. https://doi.org/10.1111/j.1469-8749.1976.tb04202.x
Susilo, T., & Duchaine, B. (2013). Advances in developmental prosopagnosia research. *Current Opinion in Neurobiology, 23*(3), 423–429. https://doi.org/10.1016/j.conb.2012.12.011
Süß, H. M., Oberauer, K., Wittman, W. W., Wilhelm, O., & Schulze, R. (2002). Working-memory capacity explains reasoning ability—and a little bit more. *Intelligence, 30*(3), 261–288. https://doi.org/10.1016/S0160-2896(01)00100-3
Svenson, O. (1981). Are we all less risky and more skillful than our fellow drivers? *Acta Psychologica, 47*(2), 143–148. https://doi.org/10.1016/0001-6918(81)90005-6
Swaab, D. F. (2004). Sexual differentiation of the human brain: Relevance for gender identity, transsexualism and sexual orientation. *Gynecological Endocrinology, 19*(6), 301–312. https://doi.org/10.1080/09513590400018231
Swann, W. B., Jr., Buhrmester, M. D., Gómez, A., Jetten, J., Bastian, B., Vázquez, A., Ariyanto, A., Besta, T., Christ, O., Cui, L., Finchilescu, G., González, R., Goto, N., Hornsey, M., Sharma, S., Susianto, H., & Zhang, A. (2014). What makes a group worth dying for? Identity fusion fosters perception of familial ties, promoting self-sacrifice. *Journal of Personality and Social Psychology, 106*(6), 912–926. https://doi.org/10.1037/a0036089
Swanson, S. A., Crow, S. J., Le Grange, D., Swendsen, J., & Merikangas, K. R. (2011). Prevalence and correlates of eating disorders in adolescents: Results from the national comorbidity survey replication adolescent supplement. *Archives of General Psychiatry, 68*(7), 714–723. https://doi.org/10.1001/archgenpsychiatry.2011.22
Swendsen, J., Burstein, M., Case, B., Conway, K. P., Dierker, L., He, J., & Merikangas, K. R. (2012). Use and abuse of alcohol and illicit drugs in U.S. adolescents: Results of the National Comorbidity Survey—Adolescent supplement. *Archives of General Psychiatry, 69*(4), 390–398. https://doi.org/10.1001/archgenpsychiatry.2011.1503
Symons, C. S., & Johnson, B. T. (1997). The self-reference effect in memory: A meta-analysis. *Psychological Bulletin, 121*(3), 371–394. https://doi.org/10.1037/0033-2909.121.3.371
Tajfel, H. (1982). Social psychology of intergroup relations. *Annual Review of Psychology, 33*, 1–39. https://doi.org/10.1146/annurev.ps.33.020182.000245
Tajfel, H., & Turner, J. C. (1979). An integrative theory of intergroup conflict. In W. G. Austin & S. Worchel (Eds.), *The social psychology of intergroup relations* (pp. 33–47). Brooks/Cole.
Talarico, J. M., & Rubin, D. C. (2003). Confidence, not consistency, characterizes flashbulb memories. *Psychological Science, 14*(5), 455–461. https://doi.org/10.1111/1467-9280.02453
Talley, P. R., Strupp, H. H., & Morey, L. C. (1990). Matchmaking in psychotherapy: Patient-therapist dimensions and their impact on outcome. *Journal of Consulting and Clinical Psychology, 58*(2), 182–188. https://doi.org/10.1037/0022-006X.58.2.182
Talmi, D. (2013). Enhanced emotional memory: Cognitive and neural mechanisms. *Current Directions in Psychological Science, 22*(6), 430–436. https://doi.org/10.1177/0963721413498893
Tang, C. S. K. (2007). Trajectory of traumatic stress symptoms in the aftermath of extreme natural disaster: A study of adult Thai survivors of the 2004 Southeast Asian earthquake and tsunami. *Journal of Nervous and Mental Disease, 195*(1), 54–59. https://doi.org/10.1097/01.nmd.0000242971.84798.bc
Tang, Y. Y., Ma, Y. H., Wang, J. H., Fan, Y. X., Feng, S. G., Lu, Q. L., Yu, Q., Sui, D., Rothbart, M. K., Fan, M., & Posner, M. I. (2007). Short-term meditation training improves attention and self-regulation. *Proceedings of the National Academy of Sciences, 104*(43), 17152–17156. https://doi.org/10.1073/pnas.0707678104
Tang, Y.-P., Wang, H., Feng, R., Kyin, M., Tsien, J. Z. (2001). Differential effects of enrichment on learning and memory function in NR2B transgenic mice. *Neuropharmacology, 41*(6), 779–790. https://doi.org/10.1016/S0028-3908(01)00122-8
Tangney, J. P., Stuewig, J., & Mashek, D. J. (2007). Moral emotions and moral behavior. *Annual Review of Psychology, 58*(1), 345–372. https://doi.org/10.1146/annurev.psych.56.091103.070145
Tao, L., Jiang, R., Zhang, K., Qian, Z., Chen, P., Lv, Y., & Yao, Y. (2020). Light therapy in non-seasonal depression: An update meta-analysis. *Psychiatry Research, 291*, Article 113247. https://doi.org/10.1016/j.psychres.2020.113247
Tateyama, M., Asai, M., Kamisada, M., Hashimoto, M., Bartels, M., & Heimann, H. (1993). Comparison of schizophrenic delusions between Japan and Germany. *Psychopathology, 26*(3–4), 151–158. https://doi.org/10.1159/000284815
Taylor, A., & Kowalski, P. (2012). Students' misconceptions in psychology: How you ask matters . . . sometimes. *Journal of the Scholarship of Teaching and Learning, 12*(3), 62–72.
Taylor, M. E., Boripuntakul, S., Toson, B., Close, J. C. T., Lord, S. R., Kochan, N. A., Sachdev, P. S., Brodaty, H., & Delbaere, K. (2019). The role of cognitive function and physical activity in physical decline in older adults across the cognitive spectrum. *Aging & Mental Health, 23*(7), 863–871. https://doi.org/10.1080/13607863.2018.1474446
Taylor, S. E. (2006). Tend and befriend: Biobehavioral bases of affiliation under stress. *Current Directions in Psychological Science, 15*(6), 273–277. https://doi.org/10.1111/j.1467-8721.2006.00451.x
Taylor, S. E. (2010). Mechanisms linking early life stress to adult health outcomes. *Proceedings of the National Academy of Sciences, 107*(19), 8507–8512. https://doi.org/10.1073/pnas.1003890107
Taylor, S. E., & Brown, J. D. (1988). Illusion and well-being: A social psychological perspective on mental health. *Psychological Bulletin, 103*(2), 193–210. https://doi.org/10.1037/0033-2909.103.2.19
Taylor, S. E., Kemeny, M. E., Reed, G. M., Bower, J. E., & Gruenewald, T. L. (2000). Psychological resources, positive illusions, and health. *American Psychologist, 55*(1), 99–109. https://doi.org/10.1037/0003-066X.55.1.99
Taylor, S. E., Lewis, B. P., Gruenewald, T. L., Gurung, R. A. R., Updegraff, J. A., & Klein, L. C. (2002). Sex differences in biobehavioral responses to threat: Reply to Geary and Flinn (2002). *Psychological Review, 109*(4), 751–753. https://doi.org/10.1037/0033-295X.109.4.751
Teasdale, J. D., Segal, Z. V., Williams, J. M. G., Ridgeway, V. A., Soulsby, J. M., & Lau, M. A. (2000). Prevention of relapse/recurrence in major depression by mindfulness-based cognitive therapy. *Journal of Consulting and Clinical Psychology, 68*(4), 615–623. https://doi.org/10.1037/0022-006X.68.4.615
Teller, D. Y., Morse, R., Borton, R., & Regal, D. (1974). Visual acuity for vertical and diagonal gratings in human infants. *Vision Research, 14*(12), 1433–1439. https://doi.org/10.1016/0042-6989(74)90018-2
Telzer, E. H. (2016). Dopaminergic reward sensitivity can promote adolescent health: A new perspective on the mechanism of ventral striatum activation. *Developmental Cognitive Neuroscience, 17*, 57–67. https://doi.org/10.1016/j.dcn.2015.10.010
Temple, E., Poldrack, R. A., Salidis, J., Deutsch, G. K., Tallal, P., Merzenich, M. M., & Gabrieli, J. D. E. (2001). Disrupted neural responses to phonological and orthographic processing in dyslexic children: An fMRI study. *NeuroReport, 12*(2), 299–307. https://doi.org/10.1097/00001756-200102120-00024
Terlizzi, E. P., & Zablotsky, B. (2020). *Mental health treatment among adults: United States, 2019* (National Center for Health Statistics Data Brief, No. 380). Centers for Disease Control and Prevention. https://www.cdc.gov/nchs/data/databriefs/db380-H.pdf
Terracciano, A., Abdel-Khalek, A. M., Ádám, N., Adamovová, L., Ahn, C.-K., Ahn, H.-N., Alansari, B. M., Alcalay, L., Allik, J., Angleitner, A.,

Avia, M. D., Ayearst, L. E., Barbaranelli, C., Beer, A., Borg-Cunen, M. A., Bratko, D., Brunner-Sciarra, M., Budzinski, L., Camart, N., . . . McCrae, R. R. (2005). National character does not reflect mean personality trait levels in 49 cultures. *Science, 310*(5745), 96–100. https://doi.org/10.1126/science.1117199

Teruya, S. A., & Bazargan-Hejazi, S. (2013). The immigrant and Hispanic paradoxes: A systematic review of their predictions and effects. *Hispanic Journal of Behavioral Sciences, 35*(4), 486–509. https://doi.org/10.1177/0739986313499004

Thoits, P. A. (2010) Stress and health: Major findings and policy implications. *Journal of Health and Social Behavior, 51*(1_suppl), S41–S53. https://doi.org/10.1177/0022146510383499

Thompson, K. M., & Huynh, C. (2017). Alone and at risk: A statistical profile of alcohol-related college student deaths. *Journal of Substance Use, 22*(5), 549–554. https://doi.org/10.1080/14659891.2016.1271032

Thompson, P. (1980). Margaret Thatcher: A new illusion. *Perception, 9*(4), 483–484. https://doi.org/10.1068/p090483

Thompson, P. M., Hayashi, K. M., Simon, S. L., Geaga, J. A., Hong, M. S., Sui, Y., Lee, J. Y., Toga, A. W., Ling, W., & London, E. D. (2004). Structural abnormalities in the brains of human subjects who use methamphetamine. *Journal of Neuroscience, 24*(26), 6028–6036. https://doi.org/10.1523/JNEUROSCI.0713-04.2004

Thompson, W. F., Schellenberg, E. G., & Husain, G. (2001). Arousal, mood, and the Mozart effect. *Psychological Science, 12*(3), 248–251. https://doi.org/10.1111/1467-9280.00345

Thorndike, E. L. (1927). The law of effect. *American Journal of Psychology, 39*, 212–222. https://doi.org/10.2307/1415413

Thornhill, R., & Gangestad, S. W. (2006). Facial sexual dimorphism, developmental stability, and susceptibility to disease in men and women. *Evolution and Human Behavior, 27*(2), 131–144. https://doi.org/10.1016/j.evolhumbehav.2005.06.001

Thornicroft, G., Mehta, N., Clement, S., Evans-Lacko, S., Doherty, M., Rose, D., Koschorke, M., Shidhaye, R., O'Reilly, C., & Henderson, C. (2016). Evidence for effective interventions to reduce mental-health-related stigma and discrimination. *The Lancet, 387*(10023), 1123–1132. https://doi.org/10.1016/S0140-6736(15)00298-6

Tickle, J. J., Sargent, J. D., Dalton, M. A., Beach, M. L., & Heatherton, T. F. (2001). Favorite movie stars, their tobacco use in contemporary movies and its association with adolescent smoking. *Tobacco Control, 10*(1), 16–22. https://doi.org/10.1136/tc.10.1.16

Tienari, P., Lahti, I., Sorri, A., Naarala, M., Moring, J., Kaleva, M., Wahlberg, K.-E., & Wynne, L. C. (1990). Adopted-away offspring of schizophrenics and controls: The Finnish adoptive family study of schizophrenia. In L. Robins & M. Rutter (Eds.), *Straight and devious pathways from childhood to adulthood* (pp. 365–379). Cambridge University Press.

Tienari, P., Wynne, L. C., Moring, J., Lahti, I., Naarala, M., Sorri, A., Wahlberg, K. E., Saarento, O., Seitamaa, M., & Kaleva, M. (1994). The Finnish adoptive family study of schizophrenia: Implications for family research. *British Journal of Psychiatry, 23*, 20–26. https://www.ncbi.nlm.nih.gov/pubmed/8037897

Tienari, P., Wynne, L. C., Sorri, A., Lahti, I., Läksy, K., Moring, J., Naarala, M., Nieminen, P., & Wahlberg, K.-E. (2004). Genotype-environment interaction in schizophrenia spectrum disorder. *British Journal of Psychiatry, 184*(3), 216–222. https://doi.org/10.1192/bjp.184.3.216

Tipper, C. M., Handy, T. C., Giesbrecht, B., & Kingstone, A. (2008). Brain responses to biological relevance. *Journal of Cognitive Neuroscience, 20*(5), 879–891. https://doi.org/10.1162/jocn.2008.20510

Todorov, A., Mandisodza, A. N., Goren, A., & Hall, C. C. (2005). Inferences of competence from faces predict election outcomes. *Science, 308*(5728), 1623–1626. https://doi.org/10.1126/science.1110589

Todorov, A., Mende-Siedlecki, P., & Dotsch, R. (2013). Social judgments from faces. *Current Opinion in Neurobiology, 23*(3), 373–380. https://doi.org/10.1016/j.conb.2012.12.010

Todorov, A., Olivola, C. Y., Dotsch, R., & Mende-Siedlecki, P. (2015). Social attributions from faces: Determinants, consequences, accuracy, and functional significance. *Annual Review of Psychology, 66*, 519–545. https://doi.org/10.1146/annurev-psych-113011-143831

Tolomeo, S., Christmas, D., Jentzsch, I., Johnston, B., Sprengelmeyer, R., Matthews, K., & Steele, J. D. (2016). A causal role for the anterior mid-cingulate cortex in negative affect and cognitive control. *Brain, 139*(6), 1844–1854. https://doi.org/10.1093/brain/aww069

Tomasello, M. (1999). *The cultural origins of human cognition.* Harvard University Press.

Tomasello, M., Kruger, A. C., & Ratner, H. H. (1993). Cultural learning. *Behavioral and Brain Sciences, 16*(3), 495–511. https://doi.org/10.1017/S0140525X0003123X

Tomiyama, A. J. (2019). Stress and obesity. *Annual Review of Psychology, 70*, 703–718. https://doi.org/10.1146/annurev-psych-010418-102936

Tomiyama, A. J., Carr, D., Granberg, E. M., Major, B., Robinson, E., Sutin, A. R., & Brewis, A. (2018). How and why weight stigma drives the obesity "epidemic" and harms health. *BMC Medicine, 16*, Article 123. https://doi.org/10.1186/s12916-018-1116-5

Tomkins, S. S. (1963). *Affect imagery consciousness: Vol. 2. The negative affects.* Tavistock/Routledge.

Tonegawa, S., Liu, X., Ramirez, S., & Redondo, R. (2015). Memory engram cells have come of age. *Neuron, 87*(5), 918–931. https://doi.org/10.1016/j.neuron.2015.08.002

Tong, F., Nakayama, K., Vaughan, J. T., & Kanwisher, N. (1998). Binocular rivalry and visual awareness in human extrastriate cortex. *Neuron, 21*(4), 753–759. https://doi.org/10.1016/s0896-6273(00)80592-9

Torrey, E. F. (1999). Epidemiological comparison of schizophrenia and bipolar disorder. *Schizophrenia Research, 39*(2), 101–106. https://doi.org/10.1016/S0920-9964(99)00107-3

Tosi, M., & Grundy, E. (2018). Returns home by children and changes in parents' well-being in Europe. *Social Science & Medicine, 200*, 99–106. https://doi.org/10.1016/j.socscimed.2018.01.016

Tovote, P., Esposito, M. S., Botta, P., Chaudun, F., Fadok, J. P., Markovic, M., Wolff, S. B. E., Ramakrishnan, C., Fenno, L., Deisseroth, K., Herry, C., Arber, S., & Lüthi, A. (2016). Midbrain circuits for defensive behaviour. *Nature, 534*, 206–212. https://doi.org/10.1038/nature17996

Treffert, D. A., & Christensen, D. D. (2006, June/July). Inside the mind of a savant. *Scientific American Mind, 17*, 50–55. https://www.scientificamerican.com/article/inside-the-mind-of-a-sava/

Triandis, H. C. (1989). The self and social behavior in differing cultural contexts. *Psychological Review, 96*(3), 506–520. https://doi.org/10.1037/0033-295X.96.3.506

Trivers, R. L. (1971). The evolution of reciprocal altruism. *Quarterly Review of Biology, 46*(1), 35–57. https://doi.org/10.1086/406755

Tryon, W. W., & Tryon, G. S. (2011). No ownership of common factors. *American Psychologist, 66*(2), 151–152. https://doi.org/10.1037/a0021056

Tsai, J. L. (2017). Ideal affect in daily life: Implications for affective experience, health, and social behavior. *Current Opinion in Psychology, 17*, 118–128. https://doi.org/10.1016/j.copsyc.2017.07.004

Tsien, J. Z. (2000). Building a brainier mouse. *Scientific American, 282*(4), 62–68.

Tskhay, K. O., & Rule, N. O. (2015). Emotions facilitate the communication of ambiguous group memberships. *Emotion, 15*(6), 812–826. https://doi.org/10.1037/emo0000077

Tuck, N. L., Adams, K. S., Pressman, S. D., & Consedine, N. S. (2017). Greater ability to express positive emotion is associated with lower projected cardiovascular disease risk. *Journal of Behavioral Medicine, 40*(6), 855–863. https://doi.org/10.1007/s10865-017-9852-0

Tuerlinckx, F., De Boeck, P., & Lens, W. (2002). Measuring needs with the Thematic Apperception Test: A psychometric study. *Journal of Personality and Social Psychology, 82*(3), 448–461. https://doi.org/10.1037/0022-3514.82.3.448

Tugade, M. M., & Fredrickson, B. L. (2004). Resilient individuals use positive emotions to bounce back from negative emotional experiences. *Journal of Personality and Social Psychology, 86*(2), 320–333. https://doi.org/10.1037/0022-3514.86.2.320

Tulving, E. (1972). Episodic and semantic memory. In E. Tulving & W. Donaldson (Eds.), *Organization of memory* (pp. 381–403). Academic Press.

Tulving, E., & Thomson, D. M. (1973). Encoding specificity and retrieval processes in episodic memory. *Psychological Review, 80*(5), 352–373. https://doi.org/10.1037/h0020071

Turan, J. M., Elafros, M. A., Logie, C. H., Banik, S., Turan, B., Crockett, K. B., Pescosolido, B., & Murray, S. M. (2019). Challenges and opportunities in examining and addressing intersectional stigma and health. *BMC Medicine, 17*, Article 7. https://doi.org/10.1186/s12916-018-1246-9

Turecki, G., & Meaney, M. J. (2016). Effects of the social environment and stress on glucocorticoid receptor gene methylation: A systematic review. *Biological Psychiatry, 79*(2), 87–96. https://doi.org/10.1016/j.biopsych.2014.11.022

Turkheimer, E., Pettersson, E., & Horn, E. E. (2014). A phenotypic null hypothesis for the genetics of personality. *Annual Review of Psychology, 65*, 515–540. https://doi.org/10.1146/annurev-psych-113011-143752

Turner, E. H., Matthews, A. M., Linardatos, B. S., Tell, R. A., & Rosenthal, R. (2008). Selective publication of antidepressant trials and its influence on apparent efficacy. *New England Journal of Medicine, 358*, 252–260. https://doi.org/10.1056/NEJMsa065779

Twenge, J. M., & Campbell, W. K. (2003). "Isn't it fun to get the respect that we're going to deserve?" Narcissism, social rejection, and aggression. *Personality and Social Psychology Bulletin, 29*(2), 261–272. https://doi.org/10.1177/0146167202239051

Twenge, J. M., & Campbell, W. K. (2018). Associations between screen time and lower psychological well-being among children and adolescents: Evidence from a population-based study. *Preventive Medicine Reports, 12*, 271–283. https://doi.org/10.1016/j.pmedr.2018.10.003

Tye, K. M., Prakash, R., Kim, S.-Y., Fenno, L. E., Grosenick, L., Zarabi, H., Thompson, K. R., Gradinaru, V., Ramakrishnan, C., & Deisseroth, K. (2011). Amygdala circuitry mediating reversible and bidirectional control of anxiety. *Nature, 471*(7338), 358–362. https://doi.org/10.1038/nature09820

Tyrer, P., Mulder, R., Kim, Y.-R., & Crawford, M. J. (2019). The development of the ICD-11 classification of personality disorders: An amalgam of science, pragmatism, and politics. *Annual Review of Clinical Psychology, 15*, 481–502. https://doi.org/10.1146/annurev-clinpsy-050718-095736

U.S. Bureau of Labor Statistics, U.S. Department of Labor. (2015). *Occupational outlook handbook, 2014–2015 edition*. https://www.bls.gov/ooh

U.S. Bureau of Labor Statistics. (2019, May). *Occupational employment statistics. Occupational employment and wages. Industrial organizational psychologists*. U.S. Department of Labor. https://www.bls.gov/oes/current/oes193032.htm

U.S. Census Bureau. (2014, July 10). *Where do college graduates work? A special focus on science, technology, engineering and math*. http://www.census.gov/dataviz/visualizations/stem/stem-html/

U.S. Department of Health and Human Services. (2004, May 27). *The health consequences of smoking: A report of the Surgeon General*. https://www.cdc.gov/tobacco/data_statistics/sgr/2004/index.htm

U.S. Department of Health and Human Services. (2014). *The health consequences of smoking—50 years of progress: A report of the Surgeon General*. https://www.cdc.gov/tobacco/data_statistics/sgr/50th-anniversary/index.htm

Uauy, R., & Díaz, E. (2005). Consequences of food energy excess and positive energy balance. *Public Health Nutrition, 8*(7a), 1077–1099. https://doi.org/10.1079/PHN2005797

Üçok, A., & Ergül, C. (2014). Persistent negative symptoms after first episode schizophrenia: A 2-year follow-up study. *Schizophrenia Research, 158*(1–3), 241–246. https://doi.org/10.1016/j.schres.2014.07.021

Uddin, L. Q. (2020). Brain mechanisms supporting flexible cognition and behavior in adolescents with autism spectrum disorder. *Biological Psychiatry, 89*(2), 172–183. https://doi.org/10.1016/j.biopsych.2020.05.010

Ulloa, E. C., Hammett, J. F., Meda, N. A., & Rubalcaba, S. J. (2017). Empathy and romantic relationship quality among cohabitating couples: An actor–partner interdependence model. *The Family Journal, 25*(3), 208–214. https://doi.org/10.1177/1066480717710644

Unger, R. H., & Scherer, P. E. (2010). Gluttony, sloth and the metabolic syndrome: A roadmap to lipotoxicity. *Trends in Endocrinology & Metabolism, 21*(6), 345–352. https://doi.org/10.1016/j.tem.2010.01.009

Ungerleider, L. G., & Mishkin, M. (1982). Two cortical visual systems. In D. J. Ingle, R. J. W. Mansfield, & M. S. Goodale (Eds.), *The analysis of visual behavior* (pp. 549–586). MIT Press.

United Nations Office on Drugs and Crime. (2013). *Global study on homicide 2013: Trends, contexts, data*. https://www.unodc.org/documents/gsh/pdfs/2014_GLOBAL_HOMICIDE_BOOK_web.pdf

United States Department of Transportation. (2020). *Drunk driving*. National Highway Traffic Safety Administration. https://www.nhtsa.gov/risky-driving/drunk-driving

University of Pittsburgh Medical Center Sports Medicine Concussion Program. (2020). *Concussions statistics and facts*. https://www.upmc.com/services/sports-medicine/services/concussion/facts-statistics

Valentine, K. A., Li, N. P., Meltzer, A. L., & Tsai, M.-H. (2020). Mate preferences for warmth-trustworthiness predict romantic attraction in the early stages of mate selection and satisfaction in ongoing relationships. *Personality and Social Psychology Bulletin, 46*(2), 298–311. https://doi.org/10.1177/0146167219855048

Valentine, K. A., Li, N. P., Penke, L., & Perrett, D. I. (2014). Judging a man by the width of his face: The role of facial ratios and dominance in mate choice at speed-dating events. *Psychological Science, 25*(3), 806–811. https://doi.org/10.1177/0956797613511823

Vallabha, G. K., McClelland, J. L., Pons, F., Werker, J. F., & Amano, S. (2007). Unsupervised learning of vowel categories from infant-directed speech. *Proceedings of the National Academy of Sciences, 104*(33), 13273–13278. https://doi.org/10.1073/pnas.0705369104

Van Bavel, J. J., Mende-Siedlecki, P., Brady, W. J., & Reinero, D. A. (2016). Contextual sensitivity in scientific reproducibility. *Proceedings of the National Academy of Sciences, 113*, 6454–6459. https://doi.org/10.1073/pnas.1521897113

Van der Oord, S., Prins, P. J. M., Oosterlaan, J., & Emmelkamp, P. M. G. (2008). Efficacy of methylphenidate, psychosocial treatments and their combination in school-aged children with ADHD: A meta-analysis. *Clinical Psychology Review, 28*(5), 783–800. https://doi.org/10.1016/j.cpr.2007.10.007

van der Westhuizen, H.-M., Kotze, K., Tonkin-Crine, S., Gobat, N., & Greenhalgh, T. (2020). Face coverings for COVID-19: From medical intervention to social practice. *BMJ, 370*, Article M3021. https://doi.org/10.1136/bmj.m3021

van Haren, N. E., Schnack, H. G., Cahn, W., van den Heuvel, M. P., Lepage, C., Collins, L., Evans, A. C., Hulshoff, H. E., & Kahn, R. S. (2011). Changes in cortical thickness during the course of illness in schizophrenia. *Archives of General Psychiatry, 68*(9), 871–880. https://doi.org/10.1001/archgenpsychiatry.2011.88

van Hoorn, J., McCormick, E. M., Rogers, C. R., Ivory, S. L., & Telzer, E. H. (2018). Differential effects of parent and peer presence on neural correlates of risk taking in adolescence. *Social Cognitive and Affective Neuroscience, 13*(9), 945–955. https://doi.org/10.1093/scan/nsy071

Van Lange, P. A. M., Rinderu, M. I., & Bushman, B. J. (2017). Aggression and violence around the world: A model of CLimate, Aggression, and Self-control in Humans (CLASH). *Behavioral and Brain Sciences, 40*, Article e75. https://doi.org/10.1017/S0140525X16000406

Vargha-Khadem, F., Gadian, D. G., Watkins, K. E., Connelly, A., Van Paesschen, W., & Mishkin, M. (1997). Differential effects of early hippocampal pathology on episodic and semantic memory. *Science, 277*(5324), 376–380. https://doi.org/10.1126/science.277.5324.376

Vazire, S. (2010). Who knows what about a person? The self–other knowledge asymmetry (SOKA) model. *Journal of Personality and Social Psychology, 98*(2), 281–300. https://doi.org/10.1037/a0017908

Vazire, S. (2018). Implications of the credibility revolution for productivity, creativity, and progress. *Perspectives on Psychological Science, 13*(4), 411–417. https://doi.org/10.1177/1745691617751884

Vazire, S., & Carlson, E. N. (2011). Others sometimes know us better than we know ourselves. *Current Directions in Psychological Science, 20*(2), 104–108. https://doi.org/10.1177/0963721411402478

Vazire, S., & Mehl, M. R. (2008). Knowing me, knowing you: The accuracy and unique predictive validity of self and other ratings of daily behavior. *Journal of Personality and Social Psychology, 95*(5), 1202–1216. https://doi.org/10.1037/a0013314

Verma, I. M. (2014). Editorial expression of concern: Experimental evidence of massive-scale emotional contagion through social networks. *Proceedings of the National Academy of Sciences, 111*(29), 10779. https://doi.org/10.1073/pnas.1412469111

Vernon, P. A., Wickett, J. C., Bazana, P. G., Stelmack, R. M., & Sternberg, R. J. (2000). The neuropsychology and psychophysiology of human intelligence. In R. J. Sternberg (Ed.), *Handbook of intelligence* (pp. 245–264). Cambridge University Press.

Victora, C. G., Horta, B. L., de Mola, C. L., Quevedo, L., Pinheiro, R. T., Gigante, D. P., Gonçalves, H., & Barros, F. C. (2015). Association between breastfeeding and intelligence, educational attainment, and income at 30 years of age: A prospective birth cohort study from Brazil. *The Lancet Global Health, 3*(4), e199–e205. https://doi.org/10.1016/S2214-109X(15)70002-1

Vieta, E., Suppes, T., Ekholm, B., Udd, M., & Gustafsson, U. (2012). Long-term efficacy of quetiapine in combination with lithium or divalproex on mixed symptoms in bipolar I disorder. *Journal of Affective Disorders, 142*(1–3), 36–44. https://doi.org/10.1016/j.jad.2012.04.014

Vismara, L. A., & Rogers, S. J. (2010). Behavioral treatments in autism spectrum disorders: What do we know? *Annual Review of Clinical Psychology, 6*(1), 447–468. https://doi.org/10.1146/annurev.clinpsy.121208.131151

Vohs, K. D., & Heatherton, T. F. (2004). Ego threat elicits different social comparison processes among high and low self-esteem people: Implications for interpersonal perceptions. *Social Cognition, 22*(1), 168–191. https://doi.org/10.1521/soco.22.1.168.30983

Volkmar, F., Chawarska, K., & Klin, A. (2005). Autism in infancy and early childhood. *Annual Review of Psychology, 56*(1), 315–336. https://doi.org/10.1146/annurev.psych.56.091103.070159

Volkow, N. D. (2016). Opioids in pregnancy. *British Medical Journal, 352,* Article i19. https://doi.org/10.1136/bmj.i19

Volkow, N. D., & Muenke, M. (2012). The genetics of addiction. *Human Genetics, 131,* 773–777. https://doi.org/10.1007/s00439-012-1173-3

Volkow, N. D., Koob, G. F., & McLellan, A. T. (2016). Neurobiologic advances from the brain disease model of addiction. *New England Journal of Medicine, 374*(4), 363–371. https://doi.org/10.1056/NEJMra1511480

Volkow, N. D., Wang, G.-J., & Baler, R. D. (2011). Reward, dopamine, and the control of food intake: Implications for obesity. *Trends in Cognitive Science, 15*(1), 37–46. https://doi.org/10.1016/j.tics.2010.11.001

Volz, K. G., Kessler, T., & von Cramon, D. Y. (2009). In-group as part of the self: In-group favoritism is mediated by medial prefrontal cortex activation. *Social Neuroscience, 4*(3), 244–260. https://doi.org/10.1080/17470910802553565

Vygotsky, L. S. (1962). *Thought and language.* MIT Press.

Vygotsky, L. S. (1978). *Mind in society.* Harvard University Press.

Wadden, T. A., & Anderton, C. H. (1982). The clinical use of hypnosis. *Psychological Bulletin, 91*(2), 215–243. https://doi.org/10.1037/0033-2909.91.2.215

Wagenmakers, E. J., Beek, T., Dijkhoff, L., Gronau, Q. F., Acosta, A., Adams, R. B., Jr., Albohn, D. N., Allard, E. S., Benning, S. D., Blouin-Hudon, E.-M., Bulnes, L. C., Caldwell, T. L., Calin-Jageman, R. J., Capaldi, C. A., Carfagno, N. S., Chasten, K. T., Cleeremans, A., Connell, L., DeCicco, J. M., . . . Zwaan, R. A. (2016). Registered replication report: Strack, Martin, & Stepper (1988). *Perspectives on Psychological Science, 11*(6), 917–928. https://doi.org/10.1177/1745691616674458

Wagenmakers, E.-J., Wetzels, R., Borsboom, D., & van der Maas, H. L. J. (2011). Why psychologists must change the way they analyze their data: The case of psi: Comment on Bem (2011). *Journal of Personality and Social Psychology, 100*(3), 426–432. https://doi.org/10.1037/a0022790

Wagner, C., & Wheeler, L. (1969). Model, need, and cost effects in helping behavior. *Journal of Personality and Social Psychology, 12*(2), 111–116. https://doi.org/10.1037/h0027569

Wakefield, A. J., Murch, S. H., Anthony, A., Linnell, J., Casson, D. M., Malik, M., Berelowitz, M, Dhillon, A. P., Thomson, M. A., Harvey, P., Valentine, A., Davies, S. E., Walker-Smith, J. A. (1998). RETRACTED: Ileal-lymphoid-nodular hyperplasia, non-specific colitis, and pervasive developmental disorder in children. *The Lancet, 351*(9103), 637–641. https://doi.org/10.1016/S0140-6736(97)11096-0

Walder, D. J., Faraone, S. V., Glatt, S. J., Tsuang, M. T., & Seidman, L. J. (2014). Genetic liability, prenatal health, stress and family environment: Risk factors in the Harvard Adolescent Family High Risk for Schizophrenia Study. *Schizophrenia Research, 157*(1–3), 142–148. https://doi.org/10.1016/j.schres.2014.04.015

Walker, E., Kestler, L., Bollini, A., & Hochman, K. M. (2004). Schizophrenia: Etiology and course. *Annual Review of Psychology, 55,* 401–430. https://doi.org/10.1146/annurev.psych.55.090902.141950

Walton, G. M., & Spencer, S. J. (2009). Latent ability: Grades and test scores systematically underestimate the intellectual ability of negatively stereotyped students. *Psychological Science, 20*(9), 1132–1139. https://doi.org/10.1111/j.1467-9280.2009.02417.x

Waltrip, R. W., II, Buchanan, R. W., Carpenter, W. T., Jr., Kirkpatrick, B., Summerfelt, A., Breier, A., Rubin, S. A., & Carbone, K. M. (1997). Borna disease virus antibodies and the deficit syndrome of schizophrenia. *Schizophrenia Research, 23*(3), 253–257. https://doi.org/10.1016/S0920-9964(96)00114-4

Wamsley, E. J., Tucker, M., Payne, J. D., Benavides, J. A., & Stickgold, R. (2010). Dreaming of a learning task is associated with enhanced sleep-dependent memory consolidation. *Current Biology, 20*(9), 850–855. https://doi.org/10.1016/j.cub.2010.03.027

Wang, C. S., Ku, G., Tai, K., & Galinsky, A. D. (2014). Stupid doctors and smart construction workers: Perspective-taking reduces stereotyping of both negative and positive targets. *Social Psychological and Personality Science, 5*(4), 430–436. https://doi.org/10.1177/1948550613504968

Wang, C. S., Whitson, J. A., Anicich, E. M., Kray, L. J., & Galinsky, A. D. (2017). Challenge your stigma: How to reframe and revalue negative stereotypes and slurs. *Current Directions in Psychological Science, 26*(1), 75–80. https://doi.org/10.1177/0963721416676578

Wardenaar, K. J., Lim, C. C. W., Al-Hamzawi, A. O., Alonso, J., Andrade, L. H., Benjet, C., Bunting, B., de Girolamo, G., Demyttenaere, K., Florescu, S. E., Gureje, O., Hisateru, T., Hu, C., Huang, Y., Karam, E., Kiejna, A., Lepine, J. P., Navarro-Mateu, F., Oakley Browne, M., . . . de Jonge, P. (2017). The cross-national epidemiology of specific phobia in the World Mental Health Surveys. *Psychological Medicine, 47*(10), 1744–1760. https://doi.org/10.1017/S0033291717000174

Warneken, F. (2015). Precocious prosociality: Why do young children help? *Child Development Perspectives, 9*(1), 1–6. https://doi.org/10.1111/cdep.12101

Warren, Z., McPheeters, M. L., Sathe, N., Foss-Feig, J. H., Glasser, A., & Veenstra-VanderWeele, J. (2011). A systematic review of early intensive intervention for autism spectrum disorders. *Pediatrics, 127*(5), e1303–e1311. https://doi.org/10.1542/peds.2011-0426

Watson, D., & Clark, L. A. (1997). Extraversion and its positive emotional core. In R. Hogan, J. Johnson, & S. Briggs (Eds.), *Handbook of personality psychology* (pp. 767–793). Academic Press.

Watson, J. B. (1924). *Behaviorism.* Norton.

Watson, J. B., & Rayner, R. (1920). Conditioned emotional reactions. *Journal of Experimental Psychology, 3*(1), 1–14. https://doi.org/10.1037/h0069608

Waugh, C. E., Wager, T. D., Fredrickson, B. L., Noll, D. C., & Taylor, S. F. (2008). The neural correlates of trait resilience when anticipating and recovering from threat. *Social Cognitive and Affective Neuroscience, 3*(4), 322–332. https://doi.org/10.1093/scan/nsn024

Waxler, N. E. (1979). Is outcome for schizophrenia better in nonindustrial societies? The case of Sri Lanka. *Journal of Nervous and Mental Disease, 167*(3), 144–158. https://doi.org/10.1097/00005053-197903000-00002

Webb, T. L., Miles, E., & Sheeran, P. (2012). Dealing with feeling: A meta-analysis of the effectiveness of strategies derived from the process model of emotion regulation. *Psychological Bulletin, 138*(4), 775–808. https://doi.org/10.1037/a0027600

Weber, A., Fernald, A., & Diop, Y. (2017). When cultural norms discourage talking to babies: Effectiveness of a parenting program in rural Senegal. *Child Development, 88*(5), 1513–1526. https://doi.org/10.1111/cdev.12882

Wechsler, H., Nelson, T. E., Lee, J. E., Seibring, M., Lewis, C., & Keeling, R. P. (2003). Perception and reality: A national evaluation of social norms marketing interventions to reduce college students' heavy alcohol use. *Journal of Studies on Alcohol and Drugs, 64*(4), 484–494. https://doi.org/10.15288/jsa.2003.64.484

Wegemer, C. M., & Vandell, D. L. (2020). Parenting, temperament, and attachment security as antecedents of political orientation: Longitudinal evidence from early childhood to age 26. *Developmental Psychology, 56*(7), 1360–1371. https://doi.org/10.1037/dev0000965

Wegner, D. M., Shortt, J. W., Blake, A. W., & Page, M. S. (1990). The suppression of exciting thoughts. *Journal of Personality and Social Psychology, 58*(3), 409–418. https://doi.org/10.1037/0022-3514.58.3.409

Weiner, B. (1974). *Achievement motivation and attribution theory.* General Learning Press.

Weiner, L., Berna, F., Nourry, N., Severac, F., Vidailhet, P., & Mengin, A. C. (2020). Efficacy of an online cognitive behavioral therapy program developed for healthcare workers during the COVID-19 pandemic: The REduction of STress (REST) study protocol for a randomized controlled trial. *Trials, 21*(1), —Article 870. https://doi.org/10.1186/s13063-020-04772-7

Weiner, R. D., & Reti, I. M. (2017). Key updates in the clinical application of electroconvulsive therapy. *International Review of Psychiatry, 29*(2), 54–62. https://doi.org/10.1080/09540261.2017.1309362

Weissman, M. M., Bland, R. C., Canino, G. J., Greenwald, S., Hwu, H. G., Lee, C. K., Newman, S. C., Oakley-Browne, M. A., Rubio-Stipec, M., & Wickramaratne, P. J. (1994). The cross national epidemiology of obsessive compulsive disorder: The cross national collaborative group. *Journal of Clinical Psychiatry, 55 Suppl,* 5–10. https://www.ncbi.nlm.nih.gov/pubmed/8077177

Wells, G. L. (2008). Field experiments on eyewitness identification: Towards a better understanding of pitfalls and prospects. *Law*

and Human Behavior, 32(1), 6–10. https://doi.org/10.1007/s10979-007-9098-4
Wells, G. L., & Seelau, E. P. (1995). Eyewitness identification: Psychological research and legal policy on lineups. *Psychology, Public Policy, and Law, 1*(4), 765–791. https://doi.org/10.1037/1076-8971.1.4.765
Werker, J. F., Gilbert, J. H., Humphrey, K., & Tees, R. C. (1981). Developmental aspects of cross-language speech perception. *Child Development, 52*(1), 349–355. https://doi.org/10.2307/1129249
Wertz, A. E., & Wynn, K. (2014). Selective social learning of plant edibility in 6- and 18-month-old infants. *Psychological Science, 25*(4), 874–882. https://doi.org/10.1177/0956797613516145
Westen, D., Novotny, C. M., & Thompson-Brenner, H. (2004). The empirical status of empirically supported psychotherapies: Assumptions, findings, and reporting in controlled clinical trials. *Psychological Bulletin, 130*(4), 631–663. https://doi.org/10.1037/0033-2909.130.4.631
Weyandt, L. L., Janusis, G., Wilson, K. G., Verdi, G., Paquin, G., Lopes, J., Varejao, M., & Dussault, C. (2009). Nonmedical prescription stimulant use among a sample of college students: Relationships with psychological variables. *Journal of Attention Disorders, 13*(3), 284–296. https://doi.org/10.1177/1087054709342212
Whalen, P. J., & Phelps, E. A. (2009). *The human amygdala*. Guilford Press.
Whalen, P. J., Raila, H., Bennett, R., Mattek, A., Brown, A., Taylor, J., van Tieghem, M., Tanner, A., Miner, M., & Palmer, A. (2013). Neuroscience and facial expressions of emotion: The role of amygdala–prefrontal interactions. *Emotion Review, 5*(1), 78–83. https://doi.org/10.1177/1754073912457231
Wheatley, T., & Haidt, J. (2005). Hypnotic disgust makes moral judgments more severe. *Psychological Science, 16*(10), 780–784. https://doi.org/10.1111/j.1467-9280.2005.01614.x
White, A., & Hingson, R. (2014). The burden of alcohol use: Excessive alcohol consumption and related consequences among college students. *Alcohol Research: Current Reviews, 35*(2), 201–218.
White, C. M. (2014). 3, 4-Methylenedioxymethamphetamine's (MDMA's) impact on posttraumatic stress disorder. *Annals of Pharmacotherapy, 48*(7), 908–915. https://doi.org/10.1177/1060028014532236
Whitney, C. G., Zhou, F., Singleton, J., & Schuchat, A. (2014). Benefits from immunization during the Vaccines for Children program era—United States, 1994–2013. *Morbidity and Mortality Weekly Report, 63*(16), 352–355. https://www.cdc.gov/mmwr/preview/mmwrhtml/mm6316a4.htm
Whorf, B. L. (1956). *Language, thought, and reality*. MIT Press.
Wicker, B., Keysers, C., Plailly, J., Royet, J.-P., Gallese, V., & Rizzolatti, G. (2003). Both of us disgusted in *my* insula: The common neural basis of seeing and feeling disgust. *Neuron, 40*(3), 655–664. https://doi.org/10.1016/S0896-6273(03)00679-2
Widiger, T. A. (2011). Personality and psychopathology. *World Psychiatry, 10*(2), 103–106. https://doi.org/10.1002/j.2051-5545.2011.tb00024.x
Wiesel, T. N., & Hubel, D. H. (1963). Single-cell responses in striate cortex of kittens deprived of vision in one eye. *Journal of Neurophysiology, 26*, 1003–1017. https://doi.org/10.1152/jn.1963.26.6.1003
Wight, R. G., LeBlanc, A. J., & Lee Badgett, M. V. (2013). Same-sex legal marriage and psychological well-being: Findings from the California Health Interview Survey. *American Journal of Public Health, 103*(2), 339–346. https://doi.org/10.2105/ajph.2012.301113
Wilens, T. E., Faraone, S. V., & Biederman, J. (2004). Attention-deficit/hyperactivity disorder in adults. *Journal of the American Medical Association, 292*(5), 619–623. https://doi.org/10.1001/jama.292.5.619
Wilke, M., Sohn, J.-H., Byars, A. W., & Holland, S. K. (2003). Bright spots: Correlations of gray matter volume with IQ in a normal pediatric population. *NeuroImage, 20*(1), 202–215. https://doi.org/10.1016/S1053-8119(03)00199-X
Williams, D. R., & Wyatt, R. (2015). Racial bias in health care and health: Challenges and opportunities. *Journal of the American Medical Association, 314*(6), 555–556. https://doi.org/10.1001/jama.2015.9260
Williams, K., Harkins, S. G., & Latané, B. (1981). Identifiability as a deterrent to social loafing: Two cheering experiments. *Journal of Personality and Social Psychology, 40*(2), 303–311. https://doi.org/10.1037/0022-3514.40.2.303
Williams, M. E., & Fredriksen-Goldsen, K. I. (2014). Same-sex partnerships and the health of older adults. *Journal of Community Psychology, 42*(5), 558–570. https://doi.org/10.1002/jcop.21637
Williams, S. C. P., & Deisseroth, K. (2013). Optogenetics. *Proceedings of the National Academy of Sciences, 110*(41), Article 16287. https://doi.org/10.1073/pnas.1317033110
Williamson, L. D., Smith, M. A., & Bigman, C. A. (2019). Does discrimination breed mistrust? Examining the role of mediated and non-mediated discrimination experiences in medical mistrust. *Journal of Health Communication, 24*(10), 791–799. https://doi.org/10.1080/10810730.2019.1669742
Wills, T. A., DuHamel, K., & Vaccaro, D. (1995). Activity and mood temperament as predictors of adolescent substance use: Test of a self-regulation mediational model. *Journal of Personality and Social Psychology, 68*(5), 901–916. https://doi.org/10.1037/0022-3514.68.5.901
Wilson-Mendenhall, C. D., Barrett, L. F., & Barsalou, L. W. (2013). Neural evidence that human emotions share core affective properties. *Psychological Science, 24*(6), 947–956. https://doi.org/10.1177/0956797612464242
Wilson, A. E., & Ross, M. (2001). From chump to champ: People's appraisals of their earlier and present selves. *Journal of Personality and Social Psychology, 80*(4), 572–584. https://doi.org/10.1037/0022-3514.80.4.572
Wilson, M. A., & McNaughton, B. L. (1994). Reactivation of hippocampal ensemble memories during sleep. *Science, 265*(5172), 676–679. https://doi.org/10.1126/science.8036517
Wilson, T. D., & Gilbert, D. T. (2003). Affective forecasting. In M. Zanna (Ed.), *Advances in experimental social psychology* (Vol. 35, pp. 345–411). Elsevier.
Winberg, J., & Porter, R. H. (1998). Olfaction and human neonatal behaviour: Clinical implications. *Acta Paediatrica, 87*(1), 6–10. https://doi.org/10.1080/08035259850157787
Wolf, E., Kuhn, M., Normann, C., Mainberger, F., Maier, J. G., Maywald, S., Bredl, A., Klöppel, S., Biber, K., van Calker, D., Riemann, D., Sterr, A., & Nissen, C. (2016). Synaptic plasticity model of therapeutic sleep deprivation in major depression. *Sleep Medicine Reviews, 30*, 53–62. https://doi.org/10.1016/j.smrv.2015.11.003
Wong, E. C., Collins, R. L., McBain, R. K., Breslau, J., Burnam, M. A., Cefalu, M. S., & Roth, E. (2021). Racial-ethnic differences in mental health stigma and changes over the course of a statewide campaign. *Psychiatric Services, 72*(5), 514–520. https://doi.org/10.1176/appi.ps.201900630
Wood, A. M., Maltby, J., Gillett, R., Linley, P. A., & Joseph, S. (2008). The role of gratitude in the development of social support, stress, and depression: Two longitudinal studies. *Journal of Research in Personality, 42*(4), 854–871. https://doi.org/10.1016/j.jrp.2007.11.003
Wood, D. M., Stribley, V., Dargan, P. I., Davies, S., Holt, D. W., & Ramsey, J. (2011). Variability in the 3, 4-methylenedioxymethamphetamine content of "ecstasy" tablets in the UK. *Emergency Medicine Journal, 28*(9), 764–765. https://doi.org/10.1136/emj.2010.092270
Wood, J. M., Garb, H. N., Lilienfeld, S. O., & Nezworski, M. T. (2002). Clinical assessment. *Annual Review of Psychology, 53*(1), 519–543. https://doi.org/10.1146/annurev.psych.53.100901.135136
Woodworth, M., & Porter, S. (2002). In cold blood: Characteristics of criminal homicides as a function of psychopathy. *Journal of Abnormal Psychology, 111*(3), 436–445. https://doi.org/10.1037/0021-843X.111.3.436
World Health Organization. (2014). *Malaria* [Fact sheet]. http://www.who.int/mediacentre/factsheets/fs094/en/
World Health Organization. (2017a). *Cardiovascular diseases (CVDs)* [Fact sheet]. https://www.who.int/news-room/fact-sheets/detail/cardiovascular-diseases-(cvds)
World Health Organization. (2017b). *Depression*. http://www.who.int/mediacentre/factsheets/fs369/en/
World Health Organization. (2017c). *Depression and other common mental disorders: Global health estimates*. https://apps.who.int/iris/bitstream/handle/10665/254610/WHO-MSD-MER-2017.2-eng.pdf
World Health Organization. (2020). *Tobacco*. https://www.who.int/health-topics/tobacco#tab=tab_1
Wray, N. R., & Gottesman, I. I. (2012). Using summary data from the Danish national registers to estimate heritabilities for schizophrenia, bipolar disorder, and major depressive disorder. *Frontiers in Genetics, 3*, Article 118. https://doi.org/10.3389/fgene.2012.00118
Wray, N. R., Byrne, E. M., Stringer, S., & Mowry, B. J. (2014). Future directions in genetics of psychiatric disorders. In S. H. Rhee & A. Ronald (Eds.), *Behavior genetics of psychopathology* (pp. 311–337). Springer.
Wright, S. C., & Tropp, L. R. (2005). Language and intergroup contact: Investigating the impact of bilingual instruction on children's intergroup attitudes. *Group Processes and Intergroup Relations, 8*(3), 309–328. https://doi.org/10.1177/1368430205053945

Wu, H., Luo, Y., & Feng, C. (2016). Neural signatures of social conformity: A coordinate-based activation likelihood estimation meta-analysis of functional brain imaging studies. *Neuroscience & Biobehavioral Reviews, 71*, 101–111. https://doi.org/10.1016/j.neubiorev.2016.08.038

Wuttke-Linnemann, A., Nater, U. M., Ehlert, U., & Ditzen, B. (2019). Sex-specific effects of music listening on couples' stress in everyday life. *Scientific Reports, 9*(1), 1–10. https://doi.org/10.1038/s41598-019-40056-0

Xie, L., Kang, H., Xu, Q., Chen, M. J., Liao, Y., Thiyagarajan, M., O'Donnell, J., Christensen, D. J., Nicholson, C., Iliff, J. J., Takano, T., Deane, R., & Nedergaard, M. (2013). Sleep drives metabolite clearance from the adult brain. *Science, 342*(6156), 373–377. https://doi.org/10.1126/science.1241224

Xu, J., & Roberts, R. E. (2010). The power of positive emotions: It's a matter of life or death—subjective well-being and longevity in a general population. *Health Psychology, 29*(1), 9–19. https://doi.org/10.1037/a0016767

Xu, J., Murphy, S. L., Kochanek, K. D., & Arias, E. (2016). *Mortality in the United States, 2015* (National Center for Health Statistics Data Brief, No. 267). Centers for Disease Control and Prevention. https://www.ncbi.nlm.nih.gov/pubmed/27930283

Xu, X., Zuo, X., Wang, X., & Han, S. (2009). Do you feel my pain? Racial group membership modulates empathic neural responses. *Journal of Neuroscience, 29*(26), 8525–8529. https://doi.org/10.1523/JNEUROSCI.2418-09.2009

Yamagata, S., Suzuki, A., Ando, J., Ono, Y., Kijima, N., Yoshimura, K., Ostendorf, F., Angleitner, A., Riemann, R., Spinath, F. M., Livesley, W. J., & Jang, K. L. (2006). Is the genetic structure of human personality universal? A cross-cultural twin study from North America, Europe, and Asia. *Journal of Personality and Social Psychology, 90*(6), 987–998. https://doi.org/10.1037/0022-3514.90.6.987

Yamaguchi, S., Greenwald, A. G., Banaji, M. R., Murakami, F., Chen, D., Shiomura, K., Kobayashi, C., Cai, H., & Krendl, A. (2007). Apparent universality of positive implicit self-esteem. *Psychological Science, 18*(6), 498–500. https://doi.org/10.1111/j.1467-9280.2007.01928.x

Yang, J. (2014). The role of the right hemisphere in metaphor comprehension: A meta-analysis of functional magnetic resonance imaging studies. *Human Brain Mapping, 35*, 107–122. https://doi.org/10.1002/hbm.22160

Yao, E., & Siegel, J. T. (2021). Examining the role of interpersonal relationship on attribution, emotion, and depression support provision: Experimental evidence from the People's Republic of China. *Motivation Science, 7*(1), 46–55. https://doi.org/10.1037/mot0000180

Yerkes, R. M., & Dodson, J. D. (1908). The relation of strength of stimulus to rapidity of habit formation. *Journal of Comparative Neurology & Psychology, 18*(5), 459–482. https://doi.org/10.1002/cne.920180503

Yeshurun, Y., & Sobel, N. (2010). An odor is not worth a thousand words: From multidimensional odors to unidimensional odor objects. *Annual Review of Psychology, 61*(1), 219–241. https://doi.org/10.1146/annurev.psych.60.110707.163639

Yoo, S.-S., Hu, P. T., Gujar, N., Jolesz, F. A., & Walker, M. P. (2007). A deficit in the ability to form new human memories without sleep. *Nature Neuroscience, 10*(3), 385–392. https://doi.org/10.1038/nn1851

Yoon, P. W., Bastian, B., Anderson, R. N., Collins, J. L., & Jaffe, H. W. (2014, May 2). Potentially preventable deaths from the five leading causes of death—United States, 2008–2010. *Morbidity and Mortality Weekly Report, 63*(17), 368–374. https://www.cdc.gov/mmwr/preview/mmwrhtml/mm6317a1.htm

Youyou, W., Stillwell, D., Schwartz, H. A., & Kosinski, M. (2017). Birds of a feather do flock together: Behavior-based personality-assessment method reveals personality similarity among couples and friends. *Psychological Science, 28*(3), 276–284. https://doi.org/10.1177/0956797616678187

Yücel, M., Solowij, N., Respondek, C., Whittle, S., Fornito, A., Pantelis, C., & Lubman, D. I. (2008). Regional brain abnormalities associated with long-term heavy cannabis use. *Archives of General Psychiatry, 65*(6), 694–701. https://doi.org/10.1001/archpsyc.65.6.694

Yuille, J. C., & Cutshall, J. L. (1986). A case study of eyewitness memory of a crime. *Journal of Applied Psychology, 71*(2), 291–301. https://doi.org/10.1037/0021-9010.71.2.291

Zabetian, A., Sanchez, I. M., Narayan, K. M. V., Hwang, C. K., & Ali, M. K. (2014). Global rural diabetes prevalence: A systematic review and meta-analysis covering 1990–2012. *Diabetes Research and Clinical Practice, 104*(2), 206–213. https://doi.org/10.1016/j.diabres.2014.01.005

Zablotsky, B., & Terlizzi, E. P. (2020). *Mental health treatment among children aged 5–17 years: United States, 2019* (National Center for Health Statistics Data Brief, No. 381). Centers for Disease Control and Prevention. https://www.cdc.gov/nchs/products/databriefs/db381.htm

Zahn-Waxler, C., & Radke-Yarrow, M. (1990). The origins of empathic concern. *Motivation and Emotion, 14*(2), 107–130. https://doi.org/10.1007/BF00991639

Zahn-Waxler, C., & Robinson, J. (1995). Empathy and guilt: Early origins of feelings of responsibility. In J. P. Tangney & K. W. Fischer (Eds.), *Self-conscious emotions: The psychology of shame, guilt, embarrassment, and pride* (pp. 143–173). Guilford Press.

Zaidan, H., Leshem, M., & Gaisler-Salomon, I. (2013). Prereproductive stress to female rats alters corticotropin releasing factor type 1 expression in ova and behavior and brain corticotropin releasing factor type 1 expression in offspring. *Biological Psychiatry, 74*(9), 680–687. https://doi.org/10.1016/j.biopsych.2013.04.014

Zajonc, R. B. (1965). Social facilitation. *Science, 149*(Whole No. 3681), 269–274. https://doi.org/10.1126/science.149.3681.269

Zajonc, R. B. (1968). Attitudinal effects of mere exposure. *Journal of Personality and Social Psychology, 9*(2, Pt.2), 1–27. https://doi.org/10.1037/h0025848

Zajonc, R. B. (2001). Mere exposure: A gateway to the subliminal. *Current Directions in Psychological Science, 10*(6), 224–228. https://doi.org/10.1111/1467-8721.00154

Zaki, J., Davis, J. I., & Ochsner, K. N. (2012). Overlapping activity in anterior insula during interoception and emotional experience. *NeuroImage, 62*(1), 493–499. https://doi.org/10.1016/j.neuroimage.2012.05.012

Zametkin, A. J., Nordahl, T. E., Gross, M., King, A. C., Stemple, W. E., Rumsey, J., Hamburger, S., & Cohen, R. M. (1990). Cerebral glucose metabolism in adults with hyperactivity of childhood onset. *New England Journal of Medicine, 323*(20), 1361–1366. https://doi.org/10.1056/nejm199011153232001

Zebian, S., Alamuddin, R., Maalouf, M., & Chatila, Y. (2007). Developing an appropriate psychology through culturally sensitive research practices in the Arabic-speaking world: A content analysis of psychological research published between 1950 and 2004. *Journal of Cross-Cultural Psychology, 38*(2), 91–122. https://doi.org/10.1177/0022022106295442

Zell, E., Strickhouser, J. E., Sedikides, C., & Alicke, M. D. (2020). The better-than-average effect in comparative self-evaluation: A comprehensive review and meta-analysis. *Psychological Bulletin, 146*(2), 118–149. https://doi.org/10.1037/bul0000218

Zetterberg, H., Smith, D. H., & Blennow, K. (2013). Biomarkers of mild traumatic brain injury in cerebrospinal fluid and blood. *Nature Reviews Neurology, 9*(4), 201–210. https://doi.org/10.1038/nrneurol.2013.9

Zhang, T.-Y., & Meaney, M. J. (2010). Epigenetics and the environmental regulation of the genome and its function. *Annual Review of Psychology, 61*, 439–466. https://doi.org/10.1146/annurev.psych.60.110707.163625

Zihl, J., von Cramon, D., & Mai, N. (1983). Selective disturbance of movement vision after bilateral brain damage. *Brain, 106*(2), 313–340. https://doi.org/10.1093/brain/106.2.313

Zimmermann, J., & Neyer, F. J. (2013). Do we become a different person when hitting the road? Personality development of sojourners. *Journal of Personality and Social Psychology, 105*(3), 515–530. https://doi.org/10.1037/a0033019

Ziv, N., & Goshen, M. (2006). The effect of "sad" and "happy" background music on the interpretation of a story in 5- to 6-year-old children. *British Journal of Music Education, 23*(3), 303–314. https://doi.org/10.1017/S0265051706007078

Zuberbühler, K. (2015). Linguistic capacity of non-human animals. *WIREs Cognitive Science, 6*(3), 313–321. https://doi.org/10.1002/wcs.1338

Zucchi, F. C. R., Yao, Y., Ward, I. D., Ilnytskyy, Y., Olson, D. M., Benzies, K., Kovalchuk, I., Kovalchuk, O., & Metz, G. A. S. (2013). Maternal stress induces epigenetic signatures of psychiatric and neurological diseases in the offspring. *PLoS ONE, 8*(2), Article e56967. https://doi.org/10.1371/journal.pone.0056967

Zuckerman, M., Li, C., & Hall, J. A. (2016). When men and women differ in self-esteem and when they don't: A meta-analysis. *Journal of Research in Personality, 64*, 34–51. https://doi.org/10.1016/j.jrp.2016.07.007

Permissions Acknowledgments

Front Matter

p. ii Suranto Riadi / EyeEm / Getty Images **xxiii top** SDI Productions / Getty Images **bottom** Katleho Seisa / Getty Images **xxiv** FOTOGRAFIA INC. / E+ / Getty Images **xxv top** Suranto Riadi / EyeEm / Getty Images **bottom** Tom Wang / Shutterstock **xxvi** Alessandra Sarti / imageBROKER / Alamy Stock Photo **xxvii** Photo courtesy of Dr. Cathy Chen **xxviii top** FILMCRAFT / WONDERFUL FILMS / NETFLIX / Album / Alamy Stock Photo **bottom** Willie B. Thomas / Getty Images **xix top** Tim Robberts / Getty Images **bottom** Roy Rochlin / Getty Images **xxx** Johnny Silvercloud / Shutterstock **xxxi top** ©RADiUS-TWC / Courtesy Everett Collection **bottom** Dermot Blackburn / Alamy Stock Photo **xxxii** Jamel Toppin / The Forbes Collection / Contour by Getty Images

Author Photos

Michael S. Gazzaniga courtesy of Michael Gazzaniga

Elizabeth A. Phelps Kathryn Huang

Elliot T. Berkman courtesy of Elliot Berkman

Chapter 1

p. 2 SDI Productions / Getty Images **4** Sam Gross / www.CartoonStock.com **5 bottom** Courtesy Dr. Elliot T. Berkman **6** Ramin Talaie / Getty Images **7** Red Huber / Orlando Sentinel / TNS / Alamy Live News **8** John Lamparski / WireImage / Getty Images **9** Keren Su / China Span / Alamy Stock Photo **10** Sarin Images / Granger NYC. All rights reserved **11 top and bottom** The Drs. Nicholas and Dorothy Cummings Center for the History of Psychology The University of Akron **15 top** materials are reprinted with permission of the University of Oregon **bottom** © John D. and Catherine T. MacArthur Foundation- used with permission. Creative Commons Attribution 4.0 International License https://creativecommons.org/licenses/by/4.0/ **17 top** Courtesy of George Miller Princeton University © 2001 Pryde Brown Photographs Princeton NJ **bottom** yaruna / Shutterstock **19 top** Monkey Business Images / Shutterstock **bottom** davidf / Getty Images **20 top** Petr Janata / UC Davis Image **top center** Stockbyte / Alamy **bottom center** Aleksandr Davydov / Alamy Stock Photo **bottom** Carl De Souza / AFP / Getty Images **21** Janata, P (2009). The neural architecture of music-evoked autobiographical memories. *Cerebral Cortex*, 01 Nov 2009, Vol. 19, Issue 11, pages 2579–2594 **22** Ammentorp Photography / Alamy Stock Photo **24 top** Monkey Business Images / Shutterstock **bottom** Neustockimages / Getty Images

Chapter 2

p. 28 Katleho Seisa / Getty Images **29** Zefrog / Alamy Stock Photo **30** E Cigarettes and Kids published August 31 2018 by Jimmy Margulies politicalcartoons.com **34** Courtesy of Wesleyan University **35** Sidney Harris / www.CartoonStock.com **38** Corbis / SuperStock **39** Courtesy of Mr. Brian Nosek **40** Squire et al. (1989) Description of Brain Injury in the Amnesic Patient N.S. Based on Magnetic Resonance Imaging. *Experimental Neurology* 105 23–35 (July 1989). ©1989 Elsevier **41 top** David Paul Morris / Bloomberg via Getty Images **bottom** Karl Ammann / Nature Picture Library **43** xkcd.com **45** Michael J. LeBrecht II / Sports Illustrated / Getty Images **49 left** ibnjaafar / Getty Images **right** galit seligmann / Alamy Stock Photo **50** United States. National Commission for the Protection of Human Subjects of Biomedical and Behavioral Research. The Belmont Report: Ethical Principles and Guidelines for the Protection of Human Subjects of Research: Appendix Volume 1 report 1978 [Bethesda Maryland]. (https://digital.library.unt.edu/ark:/67531/metadc1213677/m1/1/: accessed December 4 2020) University of North Texas Libraries UNT Digital Library https://digital.library.unt.edu crediting UNT Libraries Government Documents Department **51 bottom** AP Photo / Doug Mills **52** Facebook **53** © Sidney Harris sciencecartoonsplus.com **54** Aleksei Gorodenkov / Alamy Stock Photo **57** © Sidney Harris sciencecartoonsplus.com **59** Photo courtesy of Matt Buck **60** © Columbia Pictures / courtesy Everett Collection

Chapter 3

p. 66 FOTOGRAFIA INC. / E+ / Getty Images **69** James Cavallini / Science Source **77** AP Photo / Morry Gash **78** ImageZoo / Alamy **79 top** Rorden 2004 Using human brain lesions to infer function. *Nature Reviews Neuroscience* 5 812–819. © 2004 Rights Managed by Nature Publishing Group **bottom left** AJ Photo / Science Source **bottom right** James Cavallini / Science Source **80 left** Mark Harmel / Alamy **right** Courtesy of Psych Central **81 left** Marcello Massimini / University of Wisconsin-Madison **right** Dr K Singh dLiverpool University / Dr S Hamdy & Dr Q Aziz Manchester University **83 left and right** From Penfield Wilder (1958)The excitable cortex in conscious man. Liverpool University Press **84** Ramachandran V. S. and Blakeslee S. Fig. 6.1 Drawing made by a neglect patient from Phantoms in the brain. Copyright © 1998 by V. S. Ramachandran and Sandra Blakeslee. Reprinted by permission of HarperCollins Publishers Inc. **85 left** Collection of Jack and Beverly Wilgus / Wikimedia Commons Attribution License **center** Center for the History of Medicine Countway Library Harvard Medical School **right** Damasio et al. (1994) The Return of Phineas Gage. Science. Copyright © 1994 AAAS **90** The Photo Works / Alamy Stock Photo **95** LightField Studios / Shutterstock **99** Stringer / Photoshot / Newscom **100 top and bottom** Provided by The Mack Family **102 left** Shutterstock **center** Dennis Kunkel Microscopy / Science Source **right** CNRI / Science Source **103 top** Courtesy Fred Nijhout **bottom** AP Photo / Ron Edmonds **104 top** Dave J Williams / Alamy **bottom** James Jenkins / Natural History Photography / Alamy **106 top** Michael Willmer Forbes Tweedie / Science Source **bottom** Oliver Meckes / Eye of Science / Science Source **108 top** Big Cheese Photo LLC / Alamy Stock Photo **bottom** Flashpop / Getty Images RAW / Album / Alamy Stock Photo **109** RAW / Album / Alamy Stock Photo **111** Maggie Bartlett, NHGRI **112** Popular Science via Getty Images

Chapter 4

p. 118 Suranto Riadi / EyeEm / Getty Images **121** Simons D. J. & Levin D. T. (1998). Failure to detect changes to people during a real-world interaction. *Psychonomic Bulletin and Review* 5 644–649. from Simon & Levin Study (1998.) © 1998 Psychonomic Society Inc. Figure Courtesy Daniel J. Simons **123** Tetra Images / Alamy **124** Sidney Harris / www.CartoonStock.com **126** Conrado Dela Cruz / EyeEm / Alamy Stock Photo **128** JGI / Jamie Grill / Tetra Images LLC / Alamy Stock Photo **130 top** CountrySideCollection Homer Sykes / Alamy **bottom** Gerber86 / Getty Images **131** Carlos Osorio / Toronto Star via Getty Images **132** Courtesy Steve G. Jones Ed.D. Clinical Hypnotherapist **140** Illustration courtesy Frontiers for Young Minds https://kids.frontiersin.org/article/10.3389/frym.2020.00051 based on Ontogenetic Development of the Human Sleep-Dream Cycle By Howard P. Roffwarg Joseph N. Muzio William C. Dement Science 29 Apr 1966: Vol. 152 Issue 3722 pp. 604–619 DOI: 10.1126 / science.152.3722.604 **141** JPC-PROD / Shutterstock **143 top** PonyWang / Getty Images **bottom** Sergio Victor Vega / Addictive Creative / Shutterstock **144** Columbia / REX / Shutterstock **145 top** Mark Reinstein / Alamy Stock Photo **bottom** Owen et al. (2006) Detecting Awareness in the Vegetative State Science. Copyright © 2006 American Association for the Advancement of Science **147** John Powell Photographer / Alamy Stock Photo **148** Wikimedia Commons **149 top** Brookhave National Laboratory / Science Photo Library / Science Source **bottom** Wikimedia Common **150** Matthew Staver / New York Times / Redux

151 Camera Press / Tina Paul / Redux **152** Image Source / Getty Images

Chapter 5

p. 158 Tom Wang / Shutterstock **160** ©Cecilia Bleasdale **161** Figure 3 from Selfridge, O. G., "Pattern Recognition and Modern Computers." *AFIPS '55 (Western) Proceedings of the March 1-3, 1955, western joint computer conference.* Copyright © 1955 by the Association for Computing Machinery, Inc. doi:10.1145/1455292.1455310. Reprinted by permission. **164 top** Radius Images / Getty Images **bottom** Fred Guerdin / Reporters / Science Source **169** Michael Jung / Shutterstock **172** Figure: "Color contrast and color appearance: brightness constancy and color" from *Vision and Visual Perception*, by C.H. Graham, editor, with Neil R. Bartlett, John Lott Brown, Yun Hsia, Conrad G. Mueller, Lorrin A. Riggs (New York: Wiley,1965). Reprinted with permission. **173 top** Martin Janecek / Shutterstock **bottom** American Journal of Psychology © 1974 by the Board of Trustees of the University of Illinois. Used with permission of the University of Illinois Press **174** Figure by Jerome Kuhl, from Kanizsa, G. "Subjective Contours." *Scientific American* 234 (1976). Reprinted by permission of Jerome Kuhl. **175** © 2004 W.W. Norton **176 top** Figure: "Turning Tables" from the book *Mind Sights: Original Visual Illusions, Ambiguities and Other Anomalies, With a Commentary on the Play of Mind in Perception and Art* by Roger N. Shepard. Copyright © 1990 by Roger N. Shepard. Reprinted by permission of Henry Holt and Company. All rights reserved. **bottom** Keren Su / China Span / Alamy Stock Photo **177 left and right** Steve Granitz / Getty Images **180** Kumar Sriskandan / Alamy **181** © Exploratorium www.exploratorium.edu **185** andresr / Getty Images **186 top** James King-Holmes / Science Source **bottom** © The New Yorker Collection Pat Byrnes from Cartoonbank.com. All Rights Reserved **188 top** Stephen Dalton / Science Source **bottom** Peter Bernik / Shutterstock **191 top** John-Francis Bourke / Getty Images **bottom** Marcy Maloy / Getty Images **192 left** Steven Errico / Digital Vision / Getty Images **right** Jose Luis Pelaez Inc / Blend Images / Getty Images **193** Anna Bizon / 123RF **195** AP Photo / John Bazemore

Chapter 6

p. 202 Alessandra Sarti / imageBROKER / Alamy Stock Photo **204** Hurst Photo / Shutterstock **206** FLPA / Steve Trewhella / Shutterstock **207** Bettmann / Getty Images **208** Courtesy of Everett Collection **212** PEANUTS © 1989 Peanuts Worldwide LLC. Dist. By ANDREWS MCMEEL SYNDICATION. Reprinted with permission. All rights reserved **213 top** Scott Camazine / Alamy **center** Wildlife GmbH / Alamy **bottom** Kathy Clark / Shutterstock **215 top** Nina Leen / The LIFE Picture Collection / Shutterstock **bottom** Robert Mearns Yerkes papers 1822–1985 (inclusive). Manuscripts & Archives Yale University **219** Gina Ferazzi / Los Angeles Times via Getty Images **220 top** Pegaz / Alamy **bottom** Jonathan Storey / Getty Images **226** Rolf Nussbaumer Photography / Alamy Stock Photo **227 part a clockwise from top left** Hong Xia / Shutterstock Nirut Jindawong / Shutterstock Shutterstock Fedor Selivanov / Shutterstock Shutterstock Sabza / Shutterstock Design Pics Inc. / AgeFotostock GmbH / Shutterstock Shutterstock **part b clockwise from top left** Corbis / AgeFotostock Guenter Fischer / Image / AgeFotostock Frank L. Junior / Shutterstock Design Pics Inc. / AgeFotostock Lydie Gigerichova / Ima / AgeFotostock Gerald A. DeBoer / Shutterstock Matt Jeppson / Shutterstock Hans Lang / Imagebroker / AgeFotostock Jack Goldfarb / AgeFotostock **228 top** Fuse / Getty Images **bottom** Christopher Bernard / Getty Images **230 left** The Drs. Nicholas and Dorothy Cummings Center for the History of Psychology The University of Akron **right** Benjamin Harris University of New Hampshire **231 top** Courtesy of Dorothy Parthree **bottom** Chris Bernard / Getty Images **233** Albert Bandura Dept. of Psychology Stanford University **234** Andrew D. Bernstein / NBAE via Getty Images **235** kali9 / Getty Images **236** Olsson & Phelps (2007). Social Learning of Fear. *Nature Neuroscience* 10 1095–1102) **237** LiPo Ching

Chapter 7

p. 242 Photo courtesy of Dr. Cathy Chen **244** Henry Molaison aged 60 at MIT in 1986. Photograph and copyright: Jenni Ogden. First published in Ogden: "Trouble In Mind: Stories from a Neuropsychologist's Casebook" OUP New York 2012 **248** Tracy Fowler / MBI / Alamy Stock Photo **249 top left** David Turnley / Getty Images **top right** Scott Wintrow / Getty Images **bottom** Wheeler et al. (2000). Memory's echo: vivid remembering reactivates sensory specific cortex. Proceedings of the National Academy of Sciences 97 11125–11129 **252 top** Richard Levine / Alamy **bottom** shoults / Alamy Stock Photo **254 top** Nelson Dellis **bottom** © WMC 2020 **256** Keith R. Allen / Getty Images / Flickr RF **260** Princeton University / KRT / Newscom **262 top** Shafkat Anowar / AP Photo **bottom** Spencer Platt / Getty Images **265 left** Bjorn Svensson / Alamy **right** Chris A Crumley / Alamy **266** Shutterstock **271** AP Photo / Robert E. Klein **274** Loftus Miller and Burns 1978. Courtesy Elizabeth Loftus **276 top** AP Photo / Peter DaSilva **bottom** AP Photo / Paul Sakuma **277** Chuck Burton / AP Photo

Chapter 8

p. 282 FILMCRAFT / WONDERFUL FILMS / NETFLIX / Album / Alamy Stock Photo **286** Geza Farkas / 123RF **287 top** Nicolas McComber / Getty Images **center** Klaus Vedfelt / Getty Images **bottom** Pitinan Piyavatin / Alamy Stock Photo **288 top** Drawings courtesy L. Kraatz / Virginia Institute of Marine Science **center** akg-images **bottom** Hiroyuki Ito / Getty Images **289 Eiffel Tower** TonyV3112 / Shutterstock **plane** Mayskyphoto / Shutterstock **Cancun** Helen Filatova / Shuttterstock **money** Vadim Georgiev / Shutterstock **294** AP Photo / Ivan Sekretarev **295 top** Janine Wiedel Photolibrary / Alamy **bottom** Peter Bischoff / Getty Images **296 top** Reuters / Shannon Stapleton / Newscom **bottom** Kathy Willens / AP Photo **298** Courtesy Lydia Jordan Smith **299** Leo Cullum / www.CartoonStock.com **300** Wolfgang Kohler The Mentality of Apes. Routledge & Kegan Paul Ltd. London 1927. Reproduced by permission of Taylor & Francis Books UK **302** Courtesy Sheena Iyengar **304** Rue des Archives / Granger NYC. All rights reserved **308 top** CBS / Photofest **bottom** © The New Yorker Collection 2001 David Sipress. New Yorker cartoonbank.com. All Rights Reserved **311** Dan Kitwood / Getty Images **313** Figure from Shenkin, Susan D.; Starr, John M.; Deary, Ian J., "Birth weight and cognitive ability in childhood: A systematic review," *Psychological Bulletin*, Vol 130 (6), Nov 2004, 989-1013. Copyright © 2004 by the American Psychological Association. Adapted with permission. **317 top** ton koene / Alamy Stock Photo **bottom** Steve Rabin / Getty Images **320 top** Asia Images Group / Getty Images **bottom** Christina Kennedy / Alamy **321** Tomas Munita / The New York Times / Redux **322** Courtesy of Laura Ann Petitto **323** Lawrence Migdale / Science Source

Chapter 9

p. 328 Willie B. Thomas / Getty Images **330 top** David M. Phillips / Science Source **center** Science Source **bottom** Biophoto Associates / Science Source **331 top** Photo by Loyola Univ. Medical Center via Getty Images **bottom** From studies conducted by researchers from The Child Trauma Academy (www.ChildTrauma.org) led by Bruce D. Perry M.D. Ph.D. **332 top** Stevie Grand / Science Source **bottom** Andy Levin / Science Source **333 left** Petit Format / Science Source **center** Francisco Cruz / Purestock / Alamy Stock Photo **right** Layland Masuda / Getty Images **335** Fig. 1 from Imitation of facial and manual gestures by human neonates AN Meltzoff MK Moore Science 07 Oct 1977: Vol. 198 Issue 4312 pp. 74–78 DOI: 10.1126 / science.897687 **336** Courtesy Velma Dobson University of Arizona **337** Dr. Carolyn Rovee-Collier Director Rutgers Early Learning Project **338** btree / Alamy Stock Photo **339** Ashley Gill / Getty Images **340** Nina Leen / The LIFE Picture Collection / Shutterstock **343** Bettmann / Getty Images **344 top** Sally and Richard Greenhill / Alamy **center top** Tetra Images LLC / Alamy Stock Photo **center bottom** Ian Shaw / Alamy **bottom** Jon Feingersh / Getty Images **345 left center right** Maya Barnes Johansen / TopFoto **346** Radius Images / Alamy **347 top** Moment / Getty Images **bottom** David H. Wells / Danita Delimont Photography / Newscom **350** miodrag ignjatovic / Getty Images **352** Alamy **354** Isabel Pavia / Getty Images **358** © The New Yorker Collection 2001 Edward Koren from cartoonbank.com **359** Jeff Malet Photography / Newscom **360** Janine Wiedel Photolibrary / Alamy Stock Photo **361** Courtesy of Carol Todd **362** Sidney Harris / www.CartoonStock.com **363 left** Angel Wynn / Danita Delimont Photography / Newscom **center** Thomas Mukoya (KENYA SOCIETY) / Reuters / Alamy Stock Photo **right** Anne-Marie Palmer / Alamy Stock Photo **365 left** FotoAndalucia / Shutterstock **right** Ted Foxx / Alamy **367** Science Source **368 left** Richard Gillard / Camera Press / Redux **center** Erika Goldring / Getty Images **right**

James Jeffrey Taylor / Alamy Stock Photo **369** Peter Cade / Getty Images

Chapter 10

p. 374 Tim Robberts / Getty Images **380** Oosterhof N.N. & Todorov A. (2008). The functional basis of face evaluation. Proceedings of the National Academy of Sciences 105(32) 11087–11092 **381** clicksdemexico / Shutterstock **384** Courtesy of W. W. Norton & Co. Inc. **386** Alison Wright / robertharding / Alamy Stock Photo **387 top** Jim Weber / The Commercial Appeal / ZUMA Press Inc. / Alamy Stock Photo **center** Rayman / Getty Images **bottom** Kevin Kozicki / Cultura Creative RF / Alamy Stock Photo **389 top and bottom** Paul Ekman, Ph.D. / Paul Ekman Group, LLC. **390 top left** Figure 1 from Beau Sievers, et. al., "Music and movement share a dynamic structure that supports universal expressions of emotion," *Proceedings of the National Academy of Sciences*, 110(1): 70-75. Reprinted by permission of PNAS. **top right** Sievers B. Polansky L Casey M. & Wheatley T. (2013). Music and movement share a dynamic structure that supports universal expressions of emotion. Proceedings of the National Academy of Sciences 110(1) 70–75 **bottom** Ren Chenming / Color China Photo / AP Images **391 top** Westend61 GmbH / Alamy Stock Photo **bottom** Cynthia Larkins / Shutterstock **392** Courtesy of Dacher Keltner **395 left** Radius Images / Alamy **right** 2happy / Alamy **396 top** RossHelen editorial / Alamy Stock Photo **bottom** Tetra Images LLC / Alamy Stock Photo **397** Fine Art Images / Heritage Image Partnership Ltd / Alamy Stock Photo **398** Jacob E. Steiner PhD Laboratory of Oral Physiology The Hebrew University **399** © The New Yorker Collection 2005 Bob Zahn from cartoonbank.com. All rights reserved **400** Andrey Bandurenko / Alamy Stock Photo **401** Peopleimages / Getty Images **402** Moviestore Collection Ltd / Alamy Stock Photo **404** Linda A. Cicero / Stanford News Service

Chapter 11

p. 410 Roy Rochlin / Getty Images **413 top** Archives of the Spatial Planning Department / Amsterdam City Archives **bottom** © Thomas Schlijper **414** Ana Nance / Redux **415** Jay L. Clendenin / Los Angeles Times / Contour RA / Getty Images **416** Fig 2 from Wyatt Koma Samantha Artiga Tricia Neuman Gary Claxton Matthew Rae Jennifer Kates and Josh Michaud Low-Income and Communities of Color at Higher Risk of Serious Illness if Infected with Coronavirus (KFF May 07 2020) https://www.kff.org/coronavirus **417** Anna Ivanova / Alamy Stock Photo **418** Tim Hill / Alamy Stock Photo **419 top** Teh Eng Koon / AFP / Getty Images **center** Brian Garrett / LatitudeStock / Alamy Stock Photo **bottom** Image Source / Getty Images **420** AMC / Photofest **421** Ariel Skelley / Getty Images **422** Fix.com **423** M. Arkhipov / Shutterstock **425** D. Anshutz / Getty Images **426** Andy Lyons / Getty Images **428** David T. Foster III / Charlotte Observer / TNS / Alamy Live News **429** David Scharf / Science Source **431 top** American Heart Association **bottom** Digital Vision / Getty Images **433 top** Lev Dolgachov / Alamy Stock Photo **bottom** MBI / Alamy Stock Photo **434** PEANUTS © 1961 Peanuts Worldwide LLC. Dist. By ANDREWS MCMEEL SYNDICATION. Reprinted with permission. All rights reserved **436 top** Statista https://creativecommons.org/licenses/by-nd/4.0/ **bottom** AFP / Getty Images **438 top** Directphoto Collection / Alamy **bottom** © Gemma Correll www.gemmacorrell.com

Chapter 12

p. 444 Johnny Silvercloud / Shutterstock **446** Figure 1 from R.I.M. Dunbar, "The social brain: Psychological underpinnings and implications for the structure of organizations," *Current Directions in Psychological Science* 23(2). Copyright © 2014 by Association for Psychological Science. Reprinted by permission of SAGE Publications. **447** AP Photo / Hassan Ammar **448 top** Copyright Elliott & Elliott Eyes Inc. **bottom** Arpi Pap **451** Stephanie Kenner / Shutterstock **452** Thinkstock / Getty Images. **454** Figure 1 from Brad Ridout and Andrew Campbell, "Using Facebook to deliver a social norm intervention to reduce problem drinking at university," *Drug and Alcohol Review*, November 2014, 33(6). Copyright © 2014 Australasian Professional Society on Alcohol and other Drugs. Used by permission of John Wiley & Sons, Inc. **455 top and bottom** Courtesy Alexandra Milgram **456** Courtesy Alexandra Milgram **457 top** AFP / Getty Images **bottom** Sia Kambou / AFP / Getty Images **459** Harvard Art Museums / Fogg Museum Acquisition Fund for Prints Photo © President and Fellows of Harvard College **460 top** Federico Parra / AFP via Getty Images **center and bottom** The Drs. Nicholas and Dorothy Cummings Center for the History of Psychology The University of Akron **461 left and right** The Drs. Nicholas and Dorothy Cummings Center for the History of Psychology The University of Akron **462** The New York Times Photo Archive / Redux **463** Samm Smith **464 left** fizkes / Shutterstock **right** Figure 1b from Hyejeung Cho, Norbert Schwarz, "I like those glasses on you, but not in the mirror: Fluency, preference, and virtual mirrors," *Journal of Consumer Psychology*, 2010, 20(4). Copyright © 2010 Society for Consumer Psychology. Used by permission of John Wiley & Sons, Inc. **465** AP Photo / Jay LaPrete **467** ©1982 Karen Zebuion Courtesy New School Public Relations Dept. **468** AP Photo / Damian Dovarganes **471** LightField Studios / Shutterstock **473 left** Image Source Pink / Alamy **right** Used with permission of David DeSteno MIT Media Lab and Jin Joo Lee **474** Reuters / Lucas Jackson / Alamy Stock Photo **475 left** AP Photo / The Canadian Press Ryan Remiorz **right** Alberto E. Rodriguez / Getty Images for dick clark productions **477** Joshua Correll **482** AP Photo / Ramon Espinosa **483 top** Lefevre et al. (2013). Telling facial metrics: facial width is associated with testosterone levels in men. Evolution and Human Behavior 34(4) Copyright © 2013 Elsevier **bottom** Langlois J.H. & Ruggerman L. A. (1990) Attractive faces are only average. Psychological Science Copyright © 1990 Association for Psychological Science. Photographs courtesy Judith Hall Langlois UT Austin **485 top** CBC / ITV / Kobal / Shutterstock **bottom** James Bridges / Temple Hill / Kobal / REX / Shutterstock **488 top** Andersen Ross / Getty Images **bottom** mixetto / Getty Images

Chapter 13

p. 494 ©RADiUS-TWC / Courtesy Everett Collection **496** Bettmann / Getty Images **497 top** Camera Press Ltd / Alamy Stock Photo **center** Brand New Images / Getty Images **bottom** J.B. Handelsma / www.CartoonStock.com **499 top** Photodisc / Getty Images **center** Agnieszka Kirinicjanow / Getty Images **bottom** Randy Faris / Corbis **506 top** © Developed by David M. Condon as part of the Personality Project. Condon D.M. and Revelle W. 2015. Selected personality data from the SAPA-Project: On the structure of phrased self-report items. Journal of Open Psychology Data 3(1) p.e6. DOI: http://doi.org/10.5334/jopd.al **bottom** Jessica Peterson / Tetra Images / Corbis **507** Prostock-studio / Alamy Stock Photo **508** Masterfile **511** Hill Street Studios / Getty Images **512 left** Sally and Richard Greenhill / Alamy **right** Martin Thomas Photography / Alamy **520** Courtesy David Funder University of California Riverside. **521 left** David Papazian / Getty Images **right** parkerphotography / Alamy Stock Photo **524** Figure 3 (top left slice x=-7mm) from "Meta-analysis of Functional Neuroimaging Studies of Self and Other Judgments Reveals a Spatial Gradient for Mentalizing in Medial Prefrontal Cortex" © 2012 Massachusetts Institute of Technology *Journal of Cognitive Neuroscience* 24:8 pp. 1747–1752 **528** Jemal Countess / UPI / Newscom **531 left** Gennaro Leonardi / Alamy Live News **right** Kyodo via AP Images

Chapter 14

p. 538 Dermot Blackburn / Alamy Stock Photo **540** Museo Lazaro Galdiano Madrid Spain / Giraudon / The Bridgeman Art Library **541** Historic Images / Alamy Stock Photo **542** Science History Images / Alamy Stock Photo **545** Howard Lipin / San Diego Union-Tribune via ZUMA Wire / Alamy Stock Photo **546** William T. Carpenter Jr. and Robert W. Buchanan N Engl J Med 1994 330:681–690 **547** Charles Sykes / Invision / AP Photo **555** National Institute of Mental Health **inset** Ridofranz / Getty Images **562** James Charnley **566** Corey Nickols / Contour by Getty Images **567** © The New Yorker Collection 2003 Michael Shaw from cartoonbank.com All Rights Reserved. **568** Self-portrait by Lene Marie Fossen Untitled Chios 2016 Courtesy WILLAS contemporary. **571** Bettmann / Getty Images **574** AP Photo **580** Peter Aprahamian / Getty Images **583 left and right** Photographs courtesy Geraldine Dawson. Osterlin J. & Dawson G. (1994). Early recognition of children with autism. A study of first birthday home videotapes. *Journal of Autism and Developmental Disorders* 24 247–257 **584** Courtesy of Dr. Ami Klin (2003) The enactive mind from actions to cognition: Lessons from autism. Philosophical Transactions of the Royal Society **585** AP Photo / Hans Pennink **587** Anna Bizoń / Alamy Stock Photo **588** Juli Leonard / Raleigh News & Observer / MCT via Getty Images

Chapter 15

p. 594 Jamel Toppin / The Forbes Collection / Contour by Getty Images **597** © The New Yorker Collection 1989 Danny Shanahan from cartoonbank.com. All Rights Reserved **598** Chris Miller / Camera Press / Redux **601** Michael Rougier / The LIFE Picture Collection / Shutterstock **602 top** David Grossman / Alamy **bottom** Xue Yuge / Xinhua News Agency / Newscom **606 top** Daniele Pellegrini / Science Source **bottom** Bettmann / Getty Images **607** Will McIntyre / Science Source **610** George Konig / REX / Shutterstock **612** KlingSup / Shutterstock **615** Alain Jocard / AFP / Getty Images **616** Israel images / Alamy **617** Stockbyte Photography / Veer **623** Courtesy of Helen Mayberg M.D. **626** Eamonn McCormack / Getty Images **631** Peter Yates / The New York Times / Redux **635 top** imac / Alamy **bottom** Lemoine / AgeFotostock **637** The Lovaas Institute For Early Intervention

Name Index

Page numbers in *italics* refer to figures and tables.

Subject Index

Page numbers in *italics* refer to figures and tables.